Social Psychology in the Seventies

Social Psychology in the Seventies

LAWRENCE S. WRIGHTSMAN

George Peabody College for Teachers

In Collaboration with Stuart Oskamp, Keith E. Davis, Norma J. Baker, Anne Smead, John O'Connor, Carol K. Sigelman, Carl E. Young, and Gilbert R. Kaats

Brooks/Cole Publishing Company
Monterey, California
A Division of Wadsworth Publishing Company, Inc.
Belmont, California

L.C. Cat. Card No.: 70–187968
ISBN 0–8185–0036–0
Printed in the United States of America

1 2 3 4 5 6 7 8 9 10—76 75 74 73 72

This book was edited by Linda Harris, with production supervision by Micky Stay. It was designed by Linda Marcetti. Technical illustrations were drawn by Reese Thornton. The book was typeset by Holmes Typography, Inc., San Jose, California, and printed and bound by Kingsport Press, Kingsport, Tennessee.

To Stanley Schachter, Stuart W. Cook, and the memory of Fillmore H. Sanford – three quite different social psychologists, each of whom has influenced this book immeasurably.

Foreword

Because book publishers are generous with "examination copies," I own about two dozen recent social psychology textbooks. Most of these books are "up to date" —that is, they attempt to summarize the current state of knowledge in social psychology. Many of them are also "relevant": they discuss the social issues that emerge just prior to their press deadlines. *Social Psychology in the Seventies* is also "up to date" and "relevant." But it is even more ambitious than that, since Larry Wrightsman has required himself and his collaborators to anticipate social issues that are going to emerge *after* the press deadline—a task I had previously supposed to be the province of psychics rather than psychologists. In the absence of genuine clairvoyance, how does one accomplish this feat? From reading this book, I think I can discern a number of useful tactics.

First, one assumes that the basic principles and processes of human behavior have not changed just because the decade has. A corollary assumption is that social issues of the future will have parallels to current issues because they have the same components. One then organizes the book according to the basic principles and discusses each social issue whenever one of its component parts becomes pertinent. In this way the book is prepared to serve as a useful tool for analyzing issues that have not yet emerged and for predicting the probable course of issues just beginning to unfold. For example, in predicting the outcome of the debate over marijuana legalization, it is not irrelevant to recall that the United States has tried the Prohibition trip before and that social psychologists have learned a few principles about legislation, social mores, and attitude change. The organizing structure of this book enables the authors to obtain maximum mileage from parallels like these, while at the same time permitting the reader to see where the components of two separate issues do not match. (For example, the different physiological and psychological effects of marijuana versus alcohol *do* make a social psychological difference in how the issue is viewed by proponents and opponents and in who lines up on which side of the debate.)

A second tactic for ensuring that one has anticipated as many issues as possible is to write a big book. And this is a big book. More important than its size, however, is its broad scope. From its early discussion of philosophies of man to its thoughtful consideration of methods of social change, this book has a much bolder sweep than most texts in the area. Moreover, this daring transforms the more traditional topics as well. For instance, I have always considered the topic of leadership to be about the dullest in social psychology, but in this book the subject takes on exciting new life because of the broad sociological framework in which it is discussed.

And, finally, one guesses. One guesses which issues current at press time will die next week and which issues will grow well beyond their early beginnings. For example, marijuana may be legal by the time you read this, and everyone will be wondering what all the fuss was about. But I suspect that the issues surrounding the new feminist movement will have coalesced into a genuine revolution—a basic reshaping of many of our societal institutions. When the United States stops referring to the issue as "women's liberation" and, like Sweden, begins to see it as a basic "sex-role question," we will know that its profound impact is becoming more fully appreciated. (Perhaps the author of this book will have to change his name to Wrightsperson.) This text is one of the first in social psychology to explore some of the implications of the new feminist movement. If the authors of this book have exercised equal foresight on the other issues they discuss here—and I believe they have—then this book will truly be the handbook for social psychology in the seventies.

Daryl J. Bem
Stanford University

Contents

Preface

Times change. It now appears that the 1970s are destined to be as different from the 1960s as that decade was from the 1950s. What does this observation mean for us? Compilations of knowledge must reflect these changes. Perhaps of all the scientific disciplines and specialties, social psychology should be most sensitive to changes in the times. Hence there is a need to continually develop new social psychology textbooks that superimpose the old *and* new constructs of the field on always-changing contemporary social phenomena. But social psychology has been reluctant to do this; contemporary issues such as drug usage, violence in the streets, sexual freedom, and invasion of privacy often do not get the attention they deserve. A textbook appropriate for the 1970s, as this one aspires to be, must interrelate theory-derived knowledge with real-world applications in a mix that enhances both.

ASSUMPTIONS AND OBJECTIVES

The author of any textbook develops and utilizes basic assumptions about what the book should be. The proliferation of texts on the same subject reflects the divergence in assumptions. Perhaps it will be helpful to you if we make explicit at this point the assumptions and objectives we followed in preparing this text.

1. We have sought to develop a comprehensive text. Social psychology deals with such diverse topics as language development in lower-class children, the future of nonaggressive societies, and college students' reactions to false feedback about their emotional states. It investigates abilities, motives, and personality traits, as well as social behavior. It gathers its data from settings as different as perception laboratories and public restrooms. This textbook seeks to be comprehensive in introducing the reader to the wide variety of topics within the domain of our field. Such a goal results in a long book—one that may be too long to be covered in one academic term. Chapters may have to be omitted. Yet we would rather have the breadth of material here, so that instructors and students have an opportunity to select what is most important to them for study.

2. We have sought to develop a book that extends the field. Certainly there should be solid coverage of the traditional topics of social psychology—prejudice, attitude change, conformity, leadership, group dynamics, and others. But we have tried also to extend the coverage to topics about which solid theory-based knowledge is less but interest is great. This text concerns itself with topics that are usually slighted or ignored in many other texts. We have chosen to include sections on love, student activism, and utopias and communes, as well as entire chapters on sexual behavior, racial differences, moral development, drug usage, social change, and community problems. Although the difficulties in defining, measuring, or understanding many of these phenomena are immense, we believe that the topics cannot be overlooked by any contemporary text.

3. *This book reflects a belief that theories are the foundation of our field.* This assumption seemingly contradicts the one before it, and we recognize that it has, in places, been violated in order to bring under consideration important topics that have been studied from a nontheory-based perspective. But our goal has been to show how different theoretical orientations explain the same social behavior. For example, in Chapter 1 we consider a fascinating interpersonal relationship—the influence that the "mad monk" Rasputin had over Nicholas and Alexandra, Tsar and Tsarina of Russia—and then explore how each basic theory of social psychology would conceptualize and explain this relationship. We do this because we believe that theories serve as a way of organizing information and seeing how facts and findings do or do not hang together. Wherever possible throughout the book—and especially with topics of moral development, cooperation, attitude change, and interpersonal attraction—we have indicated how different theories would explain the process under study. In each case our goal has been to contrast different approaches and to make the reader aware that no one theory is adequate in explaining every interpersonal behavior. Such a lack of closure may leave readers dissatisfied, but it is an honest representation of the present state of theory development in social psychology.

4. *This textbook looks to the future as well as reviews the past.* Traditionally, textbooks have been seen as repositories of our past knowledge about a topic. But the times demand materials that provide extrapolations into the future. Although we realize the dangers in trying to predict the future course of such phenomena as authoritarian governmental actions, reductions in censorship, or methods of conflict resolution, we have nevertheless attempted to do so. We have sought to answer such questions as: Will drug usage rates increase? Will "Standard English" continue to be taught in black schools? Will the Women's Liberation movement go through the same stages as the Black Power movement? By advancing expectations about the future (or expectations about which factors will determine the future), we hope to produce a book that reflects the *utilization* of knowledge, rather than the mere accumulation of it. We may often be wrong, but we know that instructors and students are there to correct us—and we are somewhat happy about that.

5. *We have sought to develop a book that will facilitate teaching and learning.* This book reflects our conviction that the most important benefit of a textbook is that it facilitates the learning process. We believe we have written in a clear, understandable style. Each chapter begins with a numbered outline of its contents, and the topics within each chapter are also outlined in detail. At the end of each chapter a number of brief statements summarize the important points within it. A list of suggested readings is available for each major topic. Terms are defined in a glossary at the end of the book. The list of references includes 1500 entries—more than any other

recent social psychology text. Topics are cross-referenced throughout the text (to facilitate understanding when chapters are read in a different sequence from their order in the book). A separate Instructor's Manual provides multiple-choice and discussion questions for each chapter and further consideration of each major topic.

6. *This textbook is organized around two central themes.* The field of psychology does not naturally organize itself around one common theme; hence the usual outcome in textbooks is a series of chapters appearing to be unrelated essays on independent topics. To a large degree, this book shares that problem. However, we have capitalized on two themes to give some continuity to seemingly diverse chapters.

The theme of *assumptions about human nature* serves, in Chapter 3, as an introduction to a basic orientation of the book. This concept is subsequently related to moral development (Chapter 4), cooperation and competition (Chapter 5), aggression (Chapter 6), prejudice (Chapter 9), attitude change (Chapter 10), social change (Chapter 12), leadership styles (Chapter 17), and sexual behavior (Chapter 19).

A second major theme is the *complexity of human social behavior.* Simple one-factor explanations of social behavior are insufficient; several alternative or even contradictory explanations may all be partially correct. The topics of moral development (Chapter 4), aggression (Chapter 6), racial differences in tested IQ (Chapter 7), social-class factors in language development (Chapter 8), attitude change (Chapters 10 and 11), conformity (Chapter 16), leadership (Chapter 17), and drug usage (Chapter 18) all reflect this theme—that no social phenomenon can be explained without reliance on a variety of concepts.

GRATITUDES

It is fitting that the preparation of this social psychology textbook has been a group enterprise from beginning to end. Although we cannot possibly acknowledge all the participants in our endeavor, we nevertheless want to try.

Barbara Hearn read drafts of many of the chapters and later corrected galley proofs; her professional experience as an editor and her good grace in modifying inelegancies have helped. The following doctoral students or graduates of Peabody College or Vanderbilt University read and critiqued one or more chapters: Jack Nottingham, Lois Stack, Bill Wright, Jim Cobb, Lee Stewart, Tom Cash, Thomas Caulkins, Susan Falsey, Warren Fitzgerald, Joseph Gaida, Larry Gates, Virginia George, Mary Hannah, Maureen Holovaty, Sandra Hendrix, Rick Jensen, Ann Neeley, Algene Pearson, Barbara Ramsey, Larry Seeman, Harry Spencer, April Westfall, Les Wuescher, Ron Rogers, Bob Claxton, Bert Hodges, and Sam McFarland. Among colleagues at Peabody College we are especially indebted to Frank C. Noble, J. R. Newbrough, Phil Schoggen, Richard Gorsuch, William Bricker, Paul Dokecki, and Hardy Wilcoxon. Chapter 18 on drug usage benefited from comments by Selden Bacon, Richard Blum, Mary L. Brehm, Don Cahalan, Richard Jessor, George Maddox, Lee Robins, and Stan Sadava. Russell D. Clark III of Florida State University, Kenneth Ring of the University of Connecticut, and Bibb Latané of Ohio State University read and commented on one or more chapters.

The entire manuscript in draft form was read and reviewed by Daryl J. Bem of

Stanford University, John C. Brigham of Florida State University, Chester A. Insko of the University of North Carolina at Chapel Hill, Daniel Perlman of the University of Manitoba, and Harry Triandis of the University of Illinois. Their suggestions were followed in preparing a revised manuscript, and Daryl Bem graciously prepared a Foreword.

A special debt of gratitude goes to the eight other authors who not only prepared their own chapters but read and critiqued the other chapters. One of the many pleasures of this enterprise has been the opportunity to work with each chapter author on a mutually rewarding task. The staff members of Brooks/Cole Publishing Company have been a part of this book from the beginning. Charles T. Hendrix, Jack Thornton, Bonnie Fitzwater, and Micky Stay have offered a gentle nudge or a pellet of reinforcement at the most appropriate times. Mrs. Robert Lovelace, the senior author's secretary, has typed magnificently, edited judiciously, and laughed uproariously over parts of the manuscript. Mrs. Helen King and Miss Carol Bryant assisted in typing and bibliographic work. And, as always, Shirley Wrightsman has made herself available to check references, type drafts, make indexes, prepare test items, and read proofs. All these people share in the causation of whatever desirable qualities this book may possess.

Finally, a word of gratitude for the presence of students and for the opportunity to be with them. Hortense Callisher has written: "The habit of the lectern instills the habit of knowing. The habit of writing instills the habit of finding out." It gives me joy to have become habituated to both.

Lawrence S. Wrightsman

Social Psychology in the Seventies

Part One

Theories, Methods, and Orientation

Chapter One

Theories in Social Psychology

I do not say it is good; I do not say it is bad; I say it is the way it is. *Talleyrand*

There is nothing so practical as a good theory. *Kurt Lewin*

A young co-ed takes one last look in the mirror before leaving her dormitory room to meet a blind date—her first date as a freshman at college. She wonders what he will be like. In another part of the city, a black high school football player waits for the bus that will take his team to the most important game of the season, against an all-white school from the other side of the tracks. He is apprehensive about losing his temper if racial tensions arise. Meanwhile, in Washington, D. C., foreign policy advisors and military officers meet with the President in an emergency session to decide what measures should be taken in response to aggression on the part of a Middle Eastern nation. They debate whether ships should be sent or missiles readied.

All of these situations (whether many persons or only one person is involved) entail social behaviors and, thus, are the concern of social psychology. As a field of study, social psychology investigates the effects of people upon an individual's behavior; or, as Gordon Allport (1968) has defined the field, "With few exceptions, social psychologists regard their discipline as an attempt to understand and explain how *the thought, feeling, or behavior* of individuals are influenced by the *actual, imagined, or implied* presence of others" [p. 3, italics added]. Here, the term *implied presence* refers to the fact that an individual's actions often reflect an awareness of a particular role in a complex social structure or a membership in a specific cultural, occupational, or social group. The ramifications of Allport's definition are far reaching. A man's behavior in an elevator when two women are present—even if the women are strangers—is clearly within the realm of social psychology. Should he remove his hat? Should he wait for them to leave the elevator first? When the same man enters a doctor's office to take an eye examination, his actions may again be affected by the presence of others. The ophthalmologist asks him to look at an eye chart, trying first one lens, then another. The man's task seems to be a straightforward matter of determining and reporting which lens is clearer, but he

Figure 1-1. *Social behavior does not have to involve more than one individual—if that individual's behavior is influenced by the imagined or implied presence of others. A young woman dressing for her first date at college demonstrates social behavior. (Photograph courtesy of Carl Young.)*

may be thinking: "Am I giving the right answer? What if I really can't tell any difference? Could I be wrong?" In short, responses to a medical examination are social behavior, and regardless of the accuracy or inaccuracy of the patient's responses, his behavior reflects some degree of influence from the presence of another person.

Human activity includes behaviors that are not social. If you pick an apple, eat it, immediately get sick, and thereafter avoid eating apples, all behaviors in the sequence may be nonsocial. Reflex actions, such as removing one's hand from a hot stove, are nonsocial, and the immediate physical response is the same regardless of other considerations. A person's verbal response when he touches a hot stove, however, may very well be influenced by the presence of others. An abrupt action such as hitting the brake of a car in an emergency may also be nonsocial in the sense that the driver may be momentarily unaware of the presence of others. But associated acts that come immediately after the act of hitting the brake—such as the driver grabbing for the person sitting next to him—are social behaviors. Certain internal responses—glandular, digestive, excretory—are often beyond the realm of social psychology, but just as often such physical responses will be of concern to the social psychologist. The development of everything from nausea to constipation may result from tensions associated with the actions or presence of other people.

A great deal of any person's behavior can be classified as social behavior because other people account for so much of our environment. As opposed to our great-grandfathers 100 years ago, contemporary man generally does not have to battle the physical environment; modern man is more likely to be involved with other people than with physical objects. Indeed, the degree to which we succeed in life is largely determined by how well we are able to understand and predict other people's behavior. Thus, modern man increasingly spends more hours of his day in behaviors that are the concern of social psychology.

Social psychology may best be considered a branch of general psychology. Allport, for example, feels that social psychology and general psychology overlap but are not identical. According to Allport (1968, p. 4), many problems of human nature—such as psychophysics, sensory processes, emotional functions, memory span, and the nature of personality integrations—need to be solved apart from social considerations. In the present volume, however, a different orientation is preferred. While sensory processes should continue to be a topic of general psychology, they should also be studied from a social psychological orientation. Even though sensory processes—as abstract phenomena—may not be social, certainly their **observation*** and **measurement** are. Thus, while the traditional study of sensation should be continued in the experimental psychology laboratory, a social psychological approach to the study of sensory processes should also be carried out. Such an approach might attempt to answer the following questions:

(a) How much difference, if any, does the manner of the experimenter (friendly versus cold, for example) make upon the responses of the subject?

(b) Does the setting (doctor's office versus psychology laboratory, for example) influence the subject's responses?

(c) If the subject has volunteered, are his responses different from those he would have given as a participant in a required project? Do his attitudes toward the project affect his responses?

We shall see in Chapter 2 how social psychological factors can influence the outcomes of a seemingly nonsocial experiment. As Krech, Crutchfield, and Ballachey (1962) conclude, social psychology can give an added degree of understanding to the results of virtually every phenomenon of general psychology.

I. THEORIES IN SOCIAL PSYCHOLOGY

Social behavior and interpersonal relationships are conceptualized by various theories. In psychology, a theory is a set of conventions, created by the theorist, as a way of representing reality (Hall & Lindzey, 1970). Thus, no theory is given or predetermined; each theory makes a set of assumptions about the nature of the behavior it seeks to describe and explain. In addition to such assumptions, a theory contains a set of empirical definitions and constructs (concepts). While social psychological theories clearly differ from each other with regard to assumptions, constructs, and emphases, all such theories serve common purposes, one of which is to organize and explicate the relationships between diverse bits of knowledge about social phenomena. Each of us has a tremendous accumulation of knowledge about man as a social organism. Some of this knowledge is based on personal experience; some is based on historical events (such as the bombing of Hiroshima or the Woodstock music festival); and some of our knowledge about man is based on fictional materials. How much, for example, has the movie *Easy Rider* influenced our conceptions of the rural Southerner? A theory offers a unified set of constructs and relationships that enables us to handle all these pieces of knowledge. In short, a

*Terms printed in **boldface** are defined in the Glossary.

theory permits us to incorporate known empirical findings within a logically consistent and reasonably simple framework (Hall & Lindzey, 1970, p. 13).

Another function of any theory in social psychology is to indicate gaps in knowledge, so that further research will present a more comprehensive understanding of social phenomena. Research generated by a theory may ultimately mean that the theory itself has to be revised or even rejected. Since theories attempt to arrange all that is known in some meaningful framework, they are constantly in a state of change. Without the use of some theory, however, the task of understanding the myriad varieties of social phenomena would be tremendously difficult. The question is: which theory should be used? No one theory adequately accounts for all social phenomena. At present, social psychology possesses several basic theoretical approaches, each of which contributes in some degree to the understanding of the same phenomenon. Even though two theories may rely upon different constructs and may offer different explanations of a phenomenon, each theory may be partially correct since the data of experience may not be in conflict with the outcomes predicted by the theories. Furthermore, if one theory is generally successful in explaining phenomena and predicting future outcomes, the success of another approach is not necessarily precluded; each theory could use different constructs and be generally accurate at the same time. Social psychologists in the distant future will probably be able to judge that some one theory has proved most accurate or most verifiable, but present theories in social psychology have not been developed or tested extensively enough to allow a consensus on their relative usefulness.

Theories need to be understood because they serve as basic orientations and because they offer hypotheses that spawn understanding and generate further exploration. In addition, the constructs of theories serve as tools for the study of social behavior. For these reasons, then, we shall review here five broad theories of social psychology—each having a different orientation, set of assumptions, and set of constructs. The goal is to understand how each of these theories explains the same social behavior. An actual event from history—the provocative case of Rasputin, the notorious holy man who gained ascendancy over Tsarina Alexandra of Russia—shall serve as our focal point. We want to know how each social psychological approach—stimulus-response theory, Gestalt theory, field theory, psychoanalytic theory, and role theory—can offer an explanation of how Rasputin attained such a powerful position.

II. WHY DID RASPUTIN GAIN CONTROL OVER THE TSARINA OF RUSSIA?

By the year 1905, Tsar Nicholas II had entered into the remaining days of an uncertain rule in Russia. Unbeknownst to the Tsar, the demise of the Russian monarchy was at hand. Great inequities continued to exist in Russia, even though a minor revolution among the masses had forced Nicholas to establish a parliament through which the citizens could voice their grievances. Many peasants were starving, while the Tsar and his court enjoyed the opulent world of glittering palaces, sleek yachts, and massive estates.

Aside from the political turmoils, Tsar Nicholas and Tsarina Alexandra were concerned about the lack of a male heir. In August, 1904, a male was born, but when the young Tsarevich Alexis was only six weeks old, he began hemorrhaging from the navel. It was discovered that the crown prince had hemophilia—the failure of the blood to clot, which results in frequent and profuse bleeding. From that point on, Alexis had to be carefully sheltered; a normal life was impossible. Accidents still occurred, however, and Alexis often suffered a long list of agonizing complaints—high fever, delirium, swollen joints—which resulted in excruciating pain. On many occasions the attacks were so crippling the young prince remained bedridden for several days; yet the physicians could do nothing.

As the full implications of Alexis's illness were realized, Rasputin entered the scene. In 1905 Rasputin was in his early thirties; he was well known throughout Russia for his drunken brawls and for his frequent licentious affairs with both willing and unwilling females. Apparently the essence of vulgarity, Rasputin dressed roughly in loose peasant blouses and baggy trousers tucked into heavy, crudely made leather boots. He was filthy, rising and sleeping and rising again without bothering to wash or change his clothes. His hands were grimy; his beard was tangled and encrusted with debris; his hair was long and greasy, and not surprisingly, he gave off a powerful, acrid odor (Massie, 1967, p. 190). Despite such repugnant aspects, Rasputin's eyes were his most powerful feature. Looking at Rasputin eye to eye was said to render a person extremely responsive to Rasputin's wishes.

A brief review of the background of this charismatic figure tells us that Gregory Efimovitch Rasputin was born in Siberia in 1871 (three years after the birth of of Tsar Nicholas). As the son of a poor peasant, Rasputin received no education and never learned to write properly. He fought, drank, stole horses, and debauched local girls. His usual manner was direct—if talking to the girl did not achieve his goals, attacking her usually did. At least Rasputin was successful enough to earn a reputation as an intemperate satyr. In fact, Rasputin was not his true name, but a nickname meaning dissolute or debauched.

Figure 1-2. *Rasputin. Why was the "mad monk" able to influence the Tsarina of Russia? Various theories of social psychology employ different assumptions and constructs in explaining their relationship. (Photograph courtesy of Culver Pictures, Inc.)*

By 1904 Rasputin claimed to have repented; he took up the vows of the church, became a monk, and began a life in which poverty, solitude, and asceticism were the avowed goals.[1] By the time Rasputin appeared in St. Petersburg in 1905, his reputation as a monk with mystical powers had preceded him. A relative of the royal family, herself caught up in the cult of mysticism, soon brought Rasputin to the royal family's residence in Tsarskoe Selo, a short distance from St. Petersburg.

Rasputin ingratiated himself to the Tsar and Tsarina. He played with the children, telling folktales and anecdotes about village life. More importantly, he appeared to relieve the suffering of young Alexis. Time and again, after the doctors could do nothing for Alexis's pain, Rasputin seemingly brought about an improvement. Rasputin would visit Alexis in the evening, foretelling that the bleeding and pain would subside by the next morning, and often his predictions were correct. Thus, Rasputin assured the Tsar and Tsarina that as long as he remained in the palace no harm would befall Alexis. Was this a case of cause and effect, or was Rasputin simply blessed by coincidence? The Tsarina became convinced that Rasputin was a personal emissary from God. There is no direct evidence of what Rasputin did or whether any action of Rasputin was actually beneficial, but it has been speculated that Rasputin either hypnotized the child, telling him that the bleeding would stop, or simply influenced the prince with personal magnetism and self-confidence. There is some evidence that emotional stress can aggravate or even spontaneously induce bleeding in hemophiliac persons; and, if tension and emotionality can be reduced, the blood flow may also be reduced (Mattson & Gross, 1965a, 1965b; Lucas, Finkelman, & Tocantino, 1962). While hemophilia cannot be completely regulated by voluntary means, Rasputin's charismatic personality could possibly have lessened the child's emotionality.

Regardless of his actual effects, Rasputin assumed a tremendous influence over the Tsarina—not only in matters related to the child, but in the political sphere as well. To a large degree, Rasputin ruled Russia. In 1916, when Russia was involved in World War I, Rasputin instructed the Tsarina as to the timing and direction of military attacks on the German front. The Tsarina in turn directed Rasputin's instructions to the Tsar, who had assumed charge of military operations on the front line. In a word, Rasputin's recommendations were calamitous.[2]

The influential monk also became a favorite in the inner circle of the royal court. To many women in the pleasure-seeking St. Petersburg society, Rasputin was an exotic diversion. For his part, Rasputin appeared to have an insatiable need to seduce women. To every attractive woman, he proposed that salvation was impossible unless one could be redeemed from sin and that true redemption was unattainable unless a sin had been committed. Rasputin reputedly offered his women all three: sin, redemption, and salvation (Massie, 1967).

Not all of Rasputin's ventures were successful; some women were scandalized by his vulgarity and blatant advances. At court banquets, he was unspeakably crude, plunging his filthy hands into bowls of soup or food and scooping up the

[1] Such holy men (or *starets*) were rather numerous in Russia during those times. A few of them, like Rasputin, subscribed to the beliefs of the *Khlysty* sect, a group of mystics who believed that God could be permanently incarnated in the individual (Vernadsky, 1944). The *Khlysty* repudiated marriage, but their secret meetings, in which they tried to call forth the presence of God, often ended in orgies.

[2] Rasputin had advised the Tsar not to plan war, prophesying that it would mean the end of Russia and the monarchy. This advice, however, was not followed, and Rasputin's prophecy proved correct (Lawrence, 1960).

contents. In fact, by 1911 all of St. Petersburg was in an uproar over Rasputin's excesses. The public reacted to him with both fear and contempt. Common people were indignant that such a grotesque person had influence over the royal family. Having been denounced in a Moscow paper as a conspirator against the Holy Church, Rasputin was then investigated by church authorities. The fact that he was a fraudulent monk—that in reality he was married and had three children in Siberia—was revealed and publicized, and Rasputin's ecclesiastical patrons renounced him.

Tsar Nicholas and the Tsarina rejected some and suppressed the rest of this barrage of criticism. One high church official was dismissed, and Nicholas announced a fine for any newspaper that continued to mention Rasputin. The royal couple contented themselves by dismissing the charges as false claims brought by worldly men against holy ones. Rasputin continued in his capacity as court advisor, but rumors about him increased in intensity and frequency. Some speculated that the Tsarina had taken Rasputin as her lover, although this assertion was not verified. Eventually, a plot against Rasputin's life was formulated. Yet even the events associated with Rasputin's assassination convey something about his indefatigable style, his strength, and his zest for life.

A young aristocrat, Prince Felix Yussoupov, determined that Rasputin was destroying the monarchy and that the monk had to be killed (Massie, 1967, p. 373). Yussoupov and his fellow conspirators scheduled the murder for the evening of December 29, 1916. Rasputin was induced to make a midnight visit to Yussoupov's Moika palace, expecting that the prince's attractive young wife would be there to entertain him.[3] Prior to Rasputin's arrival, cyanide of potassium crystals were ground into powder and sprinkled into the little cakes that Rasputin liked so much. According to the physician who poisoned the cakes, the dose was strong enough to kill several men instantly.

Rasputin was escorted to the cellar and offered some of the cakes. He ate two immediately; but, as Yussoupov watched, nothing happened. Rasputin then asked for and drank two glasses of wine, which were also poisoned. Still nothing happened. Rasputin then asked Prince Yussoupov to play his guitar and sing. Completely unnerved, the prince proceeded to entertain Rasputin, while the other conspirators waited nearby, hearing voices but not knowing what to do. After two hours Yussoupov could bear the tension no longer; he dashed upstairs, seized a revolver, and returned to the cellar, where he found Rasputin drinking more poisoned wine and planning to seek out companionship among gypsies. Yussoupov led Rasputin to a crucifix, told him to pray, and shot him in the region of the heart (Yussoupov, 1927, p. 169).

Rasputin fell to the floor, after which the conspirators came down to the cellar. The doctor took Rasputin's pulse and pronounced him dead. The other conspirators took the gun and returned upstairs to prepare for disposing of the body, while Prince Yussoupov remained in the cellar. But Rasputin was not dead; he opened one eye, then the other, leapt to his feet, and began to choke Yussoupov. The Prince hastily retreated with Rasputin following. Incredibly, Rasputin made his way to the front entrance of the palace, attempting to escape through the courtyard. A conspirator fired four shots as the monk was escaping. One shot hit him in the

[3]Prince Yussoupov presented his own account of the assassination in his book *Rasputin: His Malignant Influence and His Assassination* (New York: Cape, 1927). The Prince died in 1970 at the age of 80.

shoulder, another apparently in the head; Rasputin fell to the snow, tried to rise, but could not. The conspirators dashed up, beat the bleeding man with a club, wrapped his bloody, unmoving body in a curtain, and tied it with a rope. The body was carried to the frozen Neva River and shoved in through a hole cut in the ice. When Rasputin's body was later discovered, an autopsy revealed that his lungs were full of water. Despite the poison, the bullets, and the beating, Rasputin had died by drowning! Tsarina Alexandra had Rasputin's body brought to the park at Tsarskoe Selo, where a special chapel was erected and where she went every night to pray over the monk's grave (*Encyclopedia Britannica,* 1957). Within four months of Rasputin's death, revolution broke out, and soon the monarchy was overthrown. The Tsar, Tsarina, and their children were captured and removed to a remote Ural Mountain village, where in the summer of 1918 they were killed.

Some historians (Vernadsky, 1944) claim that Rasputin's death led to a disorganization of the royal household and that the emperor ceased to rule after the assassination. It is, of course, a vast oversimplification to assume that it was only Rasputin's domination of the royal family that led to the downfall of the Romanov dynasty and to the eventual establishment of the Bolshevik government in Russia. Many other factors contributed to the succession of revolutions in 1917. Famine was rampant in the land; and the major part of the Russian resources and two million of its finest young men had been consumed by a war that was lost. Nevertheless, Rasputin's powerful and unwholesome influence was clearly a part of the downfall of the monarchy. In the presence of Rasputin, Nicholas was incapable of heeding sensible advice until it was too late. In reaction to the powerful monk, the masses abandoned their support of the Tsar and even the parliament.

This incredible account of Rasputin is related here because it contains a social psychological question that seeks explanation. Despite everything she knew about Rasputin's behavior in the court, Tsarina Alexandra relied upon Rasputin not only in the treatment of her son but in making decisions of national importance. The question is: why? In the following discussion we shall see how each major theoretical approach to social psychology would handle this question. Although many concepts will be introduced, they need not be fully understood at this point. The major objective for the time being is to portray how each theory offers a general explanation (even though each selects a different emphasis) for the same social phenomenon.[4] Comparisons of the different approaches will be made at the end of the chapter.

III. STIMULUS-RESPONSE AND REINFORCEMENT THEORIES

A. Basic Concepts and Assumptions

Stimulus-response theory (S-R theory) proposes that social behavior can be best understood by studying the associations between stimuli and responses. A **stimulus,** as defined by Kimble (1961), is an external or internal event that brings about

[4]Two excellent sources of information on the basic concepts and assumptions of the social psychological theories reviewed in this chapter are: M. Deutsch and R. M. Krauss, *Theories in Social Psychology* (New York: Basic Books, 1965) and M. E. Shaw and P. R. Costanzo, *Theories in Social Psychology* (New York: McGraw-Hill, 1970).

an alteration in the behavior of the person. This alteration in the person's behavior is called a **response.** The degree of reinforcement associated with the response is important in determining whether the response will be made again. In other words, an S-R association gains strength if the consequences that follow it are reinforcing (Shaw & Costanzo, 1970). Thus a response that is rewarded when made in association with a certain stimulus is more likely to be repeated when that stimulus again appears; responses that are not rewarded (or, to some degree, responses that are punished) are less likely to be repeated. To the S-R theorists, complex behaviors are seen as a chain of simpler S-R associations. Within the stimulus-response framework, several viewpoints emphasize different constructs. Miller and Dollard's emphasis on imitation, social learning theory, Skinner's stress on the principle of reinforcement, and social-exchange theories are varying positions held by S-R theorists.

1. Miller and Dollard on imitation. Stimulus-response theory grew out of research on learning, but its application to social behavior has been rich and varied. Neal Miller and John Dollard (1941) proposed more than 30 years ago that *imitation* could be understood in terms of S-R relationships and reinforcement. Their basic assumptions were that imitation, like most human behavior, is learned and that social behavior and social learning could be understood through the use of general learning principles. Miller and Dollard gave imitation a central place in explaining how a child learns to talk and to behave socially. Furthermore, they proposed that imitation was important in maintaining social conformity and discipline. Suppose, for example, that both a younger brother and an older brother wait for their father to arrive home from work, since it is the father's custom to bring each son a piece of candy. The older brother hears a car pull up in the driveway and starts running toward the garage. Upon imitating his brother's response, the younger brother is rewarded. In similar situations the younger son continues to emulate his brother's behavior; he learns to imitate, and he proceeds to generalize by making this response in other similar situations.

2. Social learning theory. Bandura and Walters (1963; Bandura, Ross, & Ross, 1961, 1963; Bandura, 1965a, 1965b) have shown that if a child witnesses an adult being rewarded for a certain response to frustration, the child is more likely to imitate the adult's response when placed in a similarly frustrating situation. The reinforcement in such instances can be vicarious (Berger, 1962). The child as an observer makes no response, so he cannot be reinforced; yet he learns to make the response, even without a practice trial.

3. Skinner, the principle of reinforcement, and utopian societies. Among contemporary American psychologists, B. F. Skinner has been most influential in applying the principle of **reinforcement** to a variety of situations, ranging from training pigeons to be missile navigators to constructing a utopian community upon S-R and reinforcement procedures. (The latter is described in his novel, *Walden Two.*) Here again the consequences of behavior are hypothesized to be the main determinants of future behaviors. The application of Skinnerian principles to the development of social behaviors and attitudes has been advanced by the provocative work of Daryl Bem (1965, 1970). Social behavior, according to Bem, results from the power of other people to reinforce a person for having performed desired behaviors. Bem's explanation for the development of attitudes will be explored in Chapter 9.

4. Social-exchange theories. Theories of social psychology that emphasize social exchange employ principles similar to those of stimulus-response and reinforcement theories. Although John Thibaut and Harold Kelley (1959) would not classify themselves as S-R theorists, they have developed a theory of group interaction that may be translated into S-R principles. To Thibaut and Kelley the participants in each social interaction are dependent upon each other for attaining positive outcomes or rewards, and hence each interaction carries with it both costs and rewards to each participant. If for each participant the rewards are greater than the costs, interaction continues; if the costs become greater, interaction is terminated. (The decision to continue in the social interaction is also a function of the comparison level for alternatives, or the attractiveness of other possible social interactions.)

B. Contributions to Social Psychology

As Berger and Lambert (1968) indicate, stimulus-response theory deals effectively with many more complex activities than the maze learning of rats or human muscle twitches. The contributions of S-R theory to the understanding of social behavior are vast. In succeeding chapters descriptions will be offered as to how S-R theory helps us understand various social phenomena such as assumptions about people (Chapter 3), aggression (Chapter 6), attitude formation (Chapter 9), attitude change (Chapter 10), and impression formation (Chapter 15).

C. Applications to Rasputin and the Tsarina

Let us turn now to a discussion of how the stimulus-response approach could be used to explain the case of Rasputin and Tsarina Alexandra, a worried mother who also happened to be an empress. S-R theorists, in explaining Rasputin's domination over the Tsarina, would first note that every one of Alexis's hemophiliac attacks was a stimulus to his mother. Certain responses made by the Tsarina were not successful—calling in the physicians, personal prayer, comforting the child. One response—allowing Rasputin to be in the company of the child—was apparently successful. Since the desired outcome was attained, Rasputin was called upon again and again whenever Alexis had another attack. The consequences of calling upon Rasputin were reinforcing, so this particular response was placed at the top of a sort of hierarchy of responses.

The S-R concept of **stimulus generalization** would be used to explain why Rasputin's advice was followed in other matters. After the Tsarina learned that Rasputin could reduce the weight of one problem stimulus (the hemophiliac attacks), it followed that when other problem stimuli occurred, Rasputin would be consulted there again. Unfortunately, the correctness of these decisions could not be evaluated clearly, and hence the reinforcement value of other decisions was ambiguous. Following Rasputin's advice regarding the child could clearly be seen as successful because the child's bleeding and pain decreased. But the wisdom of rejecting a prime minister (as Alexandra did on one occasion) because Rasputin felt the candidate was immoral could not be so easily determined.

The continued interaction between Rasputin and the Tsarina would, according to the social-exchange theory of Thibaut and Kelley, be viewed as a situation in which the rewards for each of the participants were greater than the costs. For Rasputin, the rewards of power and accessibility to women were clearly greater than the costs. For Alexandra, the costs may have been great; but, when placed against the alternatives (the continued suffering of her child), the costs were not sufficient to terminate the relationship.

IV. GESTALT THEORY AND COGNITIVE THEORY

A. Basic Assumptions and Concepts

Gestalt is a German word which is not easily translated into English; generally speaking, it refers to form or pattern. A basic assumption of the Gestalt approach is that *the whole is greater than the sum of the parts*—in other words, when behavior is broken down into specific stimulus-response associations, its essence is lost. To the Gestaltists, behavior is integrated, purposeful, and goal oriented; hence Gestalt psychology may be contrasted with the S-R approach in regard to what is emphasized in the study of social behavior. To Gestaltists, focusing on habits and chains of stimulus-response bonds demeans the nature of man, reducing him to a passive series of reactions. Gestalt theorists feel that the S-R approach fails to recognize that at all times man's responses are interrelated with one another, moving him toward the goals he is striving to achieve. Gestalt theory also assumes that the brain gives a cognitive structure to sensations and perceptions. Gestalt and cognitive theories emphasize central processes in perception of learning. The nervous system and brain are considered *organizers* and *interpreters*. In contrast, stimulus-response theory focuses upon peripheral processes, such as the actions of receptors and muscle responses, while the brain is believed to serve passively as a communication center only. Gestalt and cognitive theories differ from S-R theories in conceptualizing a more active role for the nervous system.

Some Gestalt theorists use the **phenomenological approach,** which hypothesizes that knowing how one perceives the world is useful in understanding that person's behavior. In the words of sociologist W. I. Thomas, "situations defined as real are real in their consequences" [quoted in Hollander, 1971]. Suppose, for example, that a man comes home from work everyday, finding that his dinner has been poorly cooked and that it tastes very bad. The man soon begins to believe that the food has been poisoned and that his wife is trying to kill him. In actuality, the wife is concerned about his health and is trying to help him lose weight. In attempting to understand the man's subsequent behavior, the phenomenological approach would concentrate upon the man's **perceptions** of the wife's intent and of the taste of the food, rather than upon the actual intent and nature of the food.

The work of Solomon Asch exemplifies the Gestalt approach. One topic studied by Asch (1946) was the formation of impressions. Two groups of students were used in the study. To one group, Asch read a list of characteristics of a fictitious person including such words as intelligent, skillful, industrious, warm, determined, practical, and cautious. The same list was read to a second group, with the exception that the word cold was substituted for the word warm. The single variation had rather strong effects upon the impressions that the two groups formed about the imaginary person. Similar results were obtained in a clever study done by Harold

Kelley (1950). A guest lecturer in a college class was described to half of the class by a list of adjectives that included the word cold. The rest of the class was supplied with the same description, with the exception of the substitution of the word warm. Not only were there differences between the ratings that the two groups gave the same instructor, but there were also differences in how many group members were willing to ask the lecturer questions after class. To those students who were supplied with the description including the word warm, the instructor actually appeared to be warmer and friendlier; yet all of the differences in impressions were solely the result of a single variation in the descriptions given to the students.

These findings give some credence to the Gestalt assumption that a list of descriptive characteristics is not simply an array of words to be added or averaged (Zajonc, 1968b, p. 323). To the contrary, certain characteristics are central and have great impact upon either overall impressions or impressions about specific qualities of another person. (See Chapter 15 for a discussion of how a stimulus-response approach can also be used to explain such findings.) The **halo effect,** or the tendency to use one's general impression of another person to shape an opinion about a specific characteristic of that person, also reflects the Gestalt assumption.

Asch (1948, 1952) also demonstrated that when one is given a political slogan, the person's interpretation will be influenced by his evaluation of the apparent author of the statement. In Asch's study, one group was told that the author of the statement, "A little rebellion, now and then, is a good thing," was Thomas Jefferson. A second group was told that the statement came from Lenin, the Russian revolutionary. The study showed that interpretations of the meaning of the statement were dependent upon the purported authorship. (See Figure 1-3.)

A related body of literature on **attribution theory** has also been developed in social psychology (Heider, 1958; Jones & Davis, 1965; Kelley, 1967); in essence, this theory is concerned with the process of interpreting or judging the properties of people and objects in our environment (Kelley, 1967). Attribution theory reflects the Gestalt assumption that stimuli from the outside world cannot be processed apart from other information acquired through the past experience of the perceiver. To say, as Marshall McLuhan (1964) does, that "the medium is the message" is an exaggeration of this viewpoint. Attribution theory does note, however, that the medium (in other words, the speaker, the source, or the communication mode) clearly influences the perception, interpretation, and acceptance of the message.

B. Contributions to Social Psychology

The interests and assumptions of many American social psychologists reflect a basic Gestalt orientation to social behavior, and examples of this orientation will be frequent in forthcoming chapters. Theories of attitude change (Chapter 10) reflect strains toward balanced attitudes (Heider, 1958) or attempts to reduce cognitive dissonance (Festinger, 1957). Asch's work has been influential in the study of conformity (Chapter 16). With strong emphasis on the role of perception in behavior, Gestalt theory has contributed significantly to our understanding of assumptions about other people (Chapter 3), prejudices (Chapter 9), and social perceptions (Chapter 15).

"I hold that a little rebellion, now and then, is a good thing, and as necessary in the political world as storms are in the physical."

Figure 1-3. *Who Said It and What Difference Does It Make? When students read this quotation and were told that Lenin, the leader of the Russian Bolshevik Revolution, had made the statement, they interpreted rebellion to mean revolution and talked about "purging the old order" or "letting loose of pent-up forces." When told that Thomas Jefferson had made the statement, students emphasized "a little rebellion" and spoke of a need for "new ideas in government and politics." The effect of substituting one author for another was "to alter the cognitive content of the statement" [Asch, 1952, p. 422]. The perceiver assimilated the content to his assumptions about the author and the author's intent, demonstrating the Gestalt assumption that the whole is greater than the sum of its parts. The actual author of the statement was Jefferson.*

C. Applications to Rasputin and the Tsarina

Returning now to our example of the enigmatic Rasputin, we should note that one of the perplexing aspects of the Rasputin-Tsarina relationship is Alexandra's continued acceptance of and reliance upon the monk in the face of all the negative information that came from others. The Gestalt theorist would point out, however, that Alexandra's general impression of Rasputin was so favorable that she would readily accept his denials of any wrongdoing. The Tsarina was even able to incorporate rumors about Rasputin's drunkenness and sexuality into her conception of the monk as a religious mystic sent by God to help Alexis. Gestalt principles of *good fit* or *closure* emphasize the human need to make sense out of the world—in other words, we need to fill in the gaps or reinterpret or reject information that cannot be easily integrated with our predominant impression.

Festinger's (1957) theory of **cognitive dissonance** proposes that holding two cognitions or beliefs that are in opposition to each other motivates the person to relieve the dissonance (conflict) between the beliefs. In our example, the Tsarina's knowledge about Rasputin's licentious activities might have been dissonant with her belief that the monk was an agent of God; thus, one means of relieving the dissonance was to reconstrue one of the cognitions. In a message to Nicholas, Alexandra wrote: "They accuse our Friend [(Rasputin)] of kissing women. Read the apostles; they kissed everybody as a form of greeting" [Moorehead, 1965, p. 73].

The Tsarina also discredited some of the rumors about Rasputin because the criticisms came from persons who, she believed, envied Rasputin (Lawrence, 1960). Thus, in terms of balance theory (Heider, 1958) or attribution theory, negative information that comes from negative sources will be rejected by the recipient. In fact, such information might have reinforced the Tsarina's faith in Rasputin—if undesirable people were trying to get rid of the monk, then surely he must be good.

V. FIELD THEORY

A. Basic Assumptions and Theoretical Position

The Gestalt approach and **field theory** are similar, but the differences are great enough to warrant separation. The fundamental contribution of field theory, as developed by Kurt Lewin (1946, 1951), is the proposition that human behavior (B) is a function (f) of the person (P) and the environment (E). Expressed in symbolic terms, $B = f(P, E)$. The first implication of this proposition is that a person's behavior is related both to characteristics within himself (his heredity, abilities, personality, state of health, and so on) and to the social situation in which he presently exists (the presence or absence of others, the extent to which his goals may be blocked, attitudes in the community, and the like). Such a two-factor explanation of behavior is worthy of special notice because other schools of thought in psychology sometimes fail to give weight to both aspects. On the one hand, personality theorists—particularly trait theorists and type theorists—claim that behavior is a result of internal personality determinants, giving little or no recognition to the situation as an influence on behavior. On the other hand, role theorists—intent on showing that a person's behavior is a response to the role he occupies—fail to recognize individual differences in response to a role situation; that is, role theorists ignore the contribution that each subject's idiosyncratic personality makes to his behavior. A second implication of field theory is related to field theory in physics. As used in physics and as used by Lewin in psychology, field theory assumes that "the properties of any event are determined by its relations to the system of events of which it is a component" [Deutsch, 1968, p. 414]. In other words, behavior takes place within a field, which includes other behaviors by the person and other aspects of the environment.

The most basic construct in field theory is the **life space** (Deutsch, 1968). "All psychological events (thinking, acting, dreaming, hoping, etc.) are conceived to be a function of the life space, which consists of the person and the environment viewed as one constellation of interdependent factors" [Deutsch, 1968, p. 417]. For purposes of research and analysis, the person and the environment are separated but are clearly interrelated; it is meaningless to consider the determinants of behavior without reference to both the individual and the environment. Explanations that fail to recognize this interdependence are inadequate. The statement "He became leader of the group because of his aggressiveness" is an unacceptable explanation to field theorists (Deutsch, 1968). Equally simplified and unacceptable is a statement that a "highly cohesive group will be more productive than a less cohesive group."

Another major emphasis of field theory is the here and now. To Lewin, psychological events must be explained by properties of the life space that exist in the present. Historic causation, a frequent device of psychoanalytic theory, is rejected. According to field theorists, if a 29-year-old male is unmarried, shy, and self-deprecatory in his relationships with others, the fact that an auto accident scarred and permanently disfigured his face at age 12 is not relevant as an explanation. The young man's present reluctance to date girls is only a function of contemporary properties of the field, which may include his present feelings toward his appearance or his present memories of humiliating comments about his face. The past can influence present behavior only indirectly—only as representations or alterations of past events are carried into the present. This operating principle may seem obvious, but it is often violated in other theoretical explanations. An adult's sexual aberrations, for example, may often be explained by reference to a past event: say, the person witnessed his parents in the act of intercourse at the age of 3 or the person was raped at the age of 15. In contrast to such explanations, Lewinian field theory would emphasize that the present sexual aberration is a result of contemporary expectations, self-evaluations, memories, and situational components.

The concept of *tension system* is also basic to field theory. Psychological needs that have been aroused but not yet satisfied are unresolved tension systems, which serve to engage a person in actions that will move him toward the goal. According to Lewin, unfinished tasks perpetuate unresolved tension systems; when the task is completed, the associated tension is then dissipated.

B. Influence on Social Psychology

Field theory, as a present-day influence upon social psychology, is very broad but weak. Lewinian theory has stimulated such diverse approaches to the study of social behavior as Roger Barker's ecological psychology (1960, 1963, 1968) and Morton Deutsch's approach to cooperative and competitive goals (1949a, 1949b). Lewin's theoretical constructs are not central to much current research in social psychology, but his impact is reflected in his general orientation to psychology, which has left impressions on his colleagues and students (Deutsch, 1968, p. 478).

C. Applications to Rasputin and the Tsarina

Returning once again to an explanation of the influence Rasputin had over the Tsarina, we would first note, in accordance with the precepts of field theory, that the Tsarina's behavior was a result both of her own personality and of the situation in which she existed. Part of the Tsarina's motivations came from within herself—including her guilt about being the carrier of the hemophilia. In addition, the external situation—the importance of providing a living male heir to the monarchy—contributed to Alexandra's acceptance of Rasputin. (We do not know whether Alexandra could have or desired to have any more children, but we know that she did not.) Field theory would note that had the empress given birth to other male offspring or had her son been other than an heir to the Russian Empire, the Tsarina's reaction to Rasputin might have been quite different. A Lewinian representation of the life space of the Tsarina would include an indication of (a) an unresolved tension system oriented toward her goal of a healthy male heir, (b) the blockage of that goal resulting from Alexis's attacks, and (c) the forces upon Alexandra to move toward her goal. Rasputin would be represented as a factor that facilitated overcoming the blockage of the goal and further movement toward the goal.

In addition to representing all behavior as responses to tension systems that occur within a field of forces, Lewin contributed a number of other useful constructs to the field of social psychology. He conceptualized conflicts as falling into one of three categories: approach-approach, avoidance-avoidance, or approach-avoidance. In the last type of conflict the person is exposed to opposing forces that possess both positive and negative features (Lewin, 1935, Chapter 4; Deutsch, 1968). For example, the person may seek a desirable region (having a healthy son), which is accessible only by passing through an undesirable region (tolerating Rasputin's crudities). When the goal is a highly desired or important one, as in the case of Alexis's health, the forces that devaluate an undesirable region (Rasputin's vulgarity) tend to diminish or weaken rapidly. In other words, the Tsarina was able to tolerate Rasputin because of the importance of reaching the positive goal of saving Alexis.

VI. PSYCHOANALYTIC THEORY

A. Basic Assumptions and Theoretical Constructs

Psychoanalytic theory, as developed by Sigmund Freud and his followers, is essentially a theory of personality, stemming from one approach to psychotherapy but having great applicability to social behavior. Aggression, moral judgment, the authoritarian personality syndrome, leadership, attitude formation, and affiliation are topics that have been studied by psychoanalytically oriented social psychologists. In brief, psychoanalytic theory is concerned with the structure and development of personality. The adult's personality is seen as a result of what happens to him as he progresses through childhood, adolescence, and other various stages of development. During the early formative years (ages 1 through 6), each stage is conceptualized in accordance with the child's preoccupation with one part of the body. The infant, for example, is oriented toward his mouth; in this **oral stage,** the child has oral needs (sucking and biting) that are either sufficiently satisfied or left unsatisfied. If the oral needs are unsatisfied, even though the child grows into adulthood, he may become *fixated* at the oral stage. Part of his **libido,** or psychic energy, is devoted to the satisfaction of these oral needs; as an adult, such a person would reflect manifestations of his oral needs in his choice of occupation, hobby, style, and expression of his everyday behavior. According to psychoanalytic theory, every child moves through the same series of stages as he grows older—from oral to **anal,** to **phallic,** to **genital** stages. In each stage if the relevant needs are not satisfied, some degree of fixation may result, causing some amount of psychic energy to be committed to that need rather than to the next stage of development. Thus, an adult may never reach mature psychological development (the genital stage) if all his psychic energy remains invested in earlier stages.

In conceptualizing the structure of personality, Freud posited three sets of forces that are constantly in conflict over the control of behavior. These forces—the **ego,** the **id,** and the **superego**—are discussed in Chapters 4 and 13. When the ego has greater degrees of control over the other forces in the personality, it is felt that the person has made a rational adjustment to his environment. Even though unconscious forces such as aggressive and sexual urges seek discharge, these will be released in healthy, socially acceptable ways if the ego is in control. (Dreams and slips of the tongue, for example, are seen as means by which unconscious urges express themselves.) In essence, then, the goal of the ego is to steer the individual into activities that permit opportunities for growth. The ego also utilizes a number of devices, called *defense mechanisms,* which, if used wisely, permit the person to regroup his forces in the face of incipient psychological disturbance.

B. Contributions to Social Psychology

The contributions of psychoanalytic theory to social psychology have been pervasive. Hall and Lindzey's (1968) review lists five major contributions of psychoanalytic theory: socialization of the individual, group psychology, notions about the origin of society, ideas on the nature and functions of culture and society, and family structure and dynamics.

1. Socialization of the individual is one precept of psychoanalytic theory, referring to the process of learning expected behaviors and becoming assimilated into society. How does a child learn to be a responsible, moral person? According to Freud, a set of forces in the personality, called the superego, is primarily responsible for socialization. The contents of the superego are derived from the admonitions of parents, teachers, other authorities, and peers. These warnings become internalized as a conscience. Freud's analysis of the stages of personality development provides a map of the pathways toward being an unselfish, loving, responsible adult; and his conceptualizations have been elaborated by others who are specifically concerned with moral development. Peck and Havighurst (1960), for example, have proposed that children move from an amoral stage in infancy, to an expedient stage in early childhood, to either a conforming stage or an irrational-conscientious stage in later childhood, to a rational-altruistic stage in adolescence or adulthood. As in Freud's theory, however, an individual may fixate at any of these stages.

2. A second contribution of psychoanalytic theory is group psychology. To Freud, a group is held together by its system of libidinal ties (Hall & Lindzey, 1968). When each group member has accepted the group leader as his ideal, an identity is formed among all group members. Such an approach might explain relationships within certain groups, but it has had little influence upon the conceptualizations of leadership developed by social psychologists. (The writings of social critic, Eric Hoffer, however, regarding the need of the true believer to affiliate with some movement, regardless of the movement's goals or ideology, may be indirectly influenced by Freud's speculations.)

3. Notions about the origin of society are a third contribution of psychoanalytic theory. In *Totem and Taboo* (1913) and *Moses and Monotheism* (1939), Freud expressed his theory of the origin of society. In the beginnings of human society, people lived in small groups under the control of a strong, autocratic male ruler. When the ruler chose one of his sons to be his successor, the other sons were driven

from the tribe but organized together to seek the destruction of their father. Thus a *social contract* between individuals developed—first, to combine forces to defeat a common enemy who could otherwise not be defeated and, second, to prevent self-destruction resulting from aggression among brothers. Instinctual gratifications (first, aggression, then later, incestual sex) were renounced in order to preserve oneself and one's companions. The notion of a social contract as the means of forming society was, of course, not original with Freud. What he added, however, was an emphasis upon controlling aggressive and other instinctual impulses. Wars with alien tribes served as an acceptable means of draining off instinctual aggression. To Freud, aggression is basic to human nature, and he believed that wars will always be with us.

4. The nature and functions of culture and society is another area to which psychoanalytic theory has made contributions. Freud's theory about the nature and functions of society was related to his conceptions about the origin of society. According to Freud, one function of society is to restrain man from expressing instinctual impulses that are unacceptable in civilized society. Certainly, for Freud, modern man is not free; rather, as society becomes more complex, more prohibitions and more severe punishments for expressions of natural man are established. Hence civilization is inevitably repressive and authoritarian. More recent social analysis such as that done by Herbert Marcuse (1955, 1964) and Charles Reich (1970) has responded to—and often objected to—Freud's pessimistic beliefs about the effects of society upon the individual. (See Chapter 13.)

5. Family structure and dynamics is one final area to which psychoanalytic theory has made contributions. Hall and Lindzey (1968) call Freud's analysis of the structure and dynamics of the family "one of his greatest achievements and his most notable contribution to social psychology" [p. 273]. At each stage of personality development, the orientation of the child toward each parent is central. For the male infant, the mother is the child's first libidinal object, and the father is seen as a rival and interloper. Around age 4 or 5 the child will begin to identify with his father and vicariously satisfy his libidinal needs. The female child, at this stage, shows a similar identification with the mother. According to Freud, then, the foundation for future social behavior is thus firmly laid by the age of 6 or 7.

The impact of childhood orientations upon adult behavior is reflected in the writings of Karen Horney (1937, 1939), who—along with Harry Stack Sullivan, Erich Fromm, and others—is classified as a neo-Freudian. In other words, Horney accepts Freud's basic psychoanalytic approach but includes some qualifications and variations in emphasis. To Horney, a child learns early in life to develop a particular type of response to other people—either moving toward others (affiliation, dependence), moving against others (hostility, rigidity), or moving away from others (isolation, autonomy). The child's characteristic response to his parents, according to such an analysis, serves as a characteristic style of response to others later in life.

C. Applications to Rasputin and the Tsarina

Let us turn now to a consideration of how the psychoanalytic approach can be employed to explain the relationship between Rasputin and Tsarina Alexandra. The psychoanalytic theorist would first seek clues from the Tsarina's childhood.

We know that the Tsarina was born in 1872 to German nobility in the city of Darmstadt, Germany. Despite the fact that Alexandra's mother and governess were English, the German language, the German church (Lutheran), and German customs became her own. As a child, Alexandra (originally, she was named Alix) was described as a sweet, merry little person, who was always laughing. She had the privileges of nobility, but apparently was not overly spoiled. Her governess believed in keeping a strict schedule with fixed hours for every activity—a habit that the child carried to Russia. As the Tsarina, Alexandra made sure that the Russian royal family ate at the stroke of the hour and that the mornings and afternoons were divided into rigid little blocks of time (Massie, 1967).

When Alix was 6 an epidemic of diphtheria swept through the German palace. Her 4-year-old sister was the first victim, and her mother's death followed a week later. The loss of her mother had a shattering effect on Alix. According to the historian Massie (1967), the young girl "began to seal herself off from other people. A hard shell of aloofness formed over her emotions, and her radiant smile appeared less frequently. Although craving intimacy and affection, she held herself back. She grew to dislike unfamiliar places and to avoid unfamiliar people. Only in cozy family gatherings where she could count on warmth and understanding did Alix unwind" [p. 30]. After this the child's grandmother, Queen Victoria of England, took special responsibility for her upbringing and education, though Alix remained in Germany with her father.

Alix first met her future husband on a visit to Russia when she was 12. Nicholas and Alix met again five years later and saw each other frequently during Alix's extended visit with her older sister, who had married a member of the Russian royal family. Clearly, Alix and Nicholas were falling in love. Within a year they became engaged and were married on November 26, 1894, in a ceremony that was severely restrained by the death of Nicholas's father, Tsar Alexander III, three weeks before. Thus, within one month, the 26-year-old Nicholas and the 22-year-old Alexandra became husband and wife as well as the rulers of Imperial Russia.

From reports of witnesses (Mouchanow, 1918; Buxhoeveden, 1930) the marriage was a happy one throughout its existence. Both Nicholas and Alexandra were affectionate and devoted to each other; yet there were difficult adjustments for Alexandra—a new country, a new language, a new religion, a new husband, a new name, and a new position as the empress of Russia! In the spring of the following year, it was learned that Alexandra was carrying a child. Both parents hoped for a much wanted male heir, but it was not to be—not then and not for the next three offspring. Not until 1904, when Alexandra was 32, was the ill-fated male heir born.

In explaining the Tsarina's later actions, the psychoanalytic theorist would also wish to probe Alexandra's relationship with her husband and her children. (Such a retrospective analysis would depend upon letters and diaries, if available, and reminiscences of friends and associates.) Several aspects of Alexandra's past and present would be given special emphasis. For example, the death of her mother might have caused Alexandra a feeling of guilt; as a 6-year-old girl, she was working through the Electra complex—in other words, the child had envied her mother earlier but was later beginning to identify with the mother. There may have been, however, a residue of hostility—secret desires that the mother were dead. The sudden death of the mother might have caused both secret pleasure and guilt—as well as some fixation of libidinal development at the phallic stage.

We may assume that the death of the mother accentuated Alexandra's relationship with her father. An obstacle to the satisfaction of libidinal wishes for an intimate relationship had been removed. The Grand Duke, as a father, was dominant, patriarchal, and strong willed. If Alexandra had fixated at the phallic stage of development, she might seek, as a husband, a man who resembled her father. Nicholas apparently did not fit this mold; he is usually described as a well-meaning but rather weak individual who did not possess the strength of will or conviction of purpose necessary for his position. Possibly Alexandra's needs for a father figure were met in Rasputin, who clearly possessed the self-confidence and charisma that Nicholas lacked.

Alexandra's personality would be another important factor in the psychoanalytic approach to explaining her relationship to Rasputin. It is known that the empress was devoted to her family (Almedingen, 1961); she was religious, even pious, and was attracted to the occult and the spiritual (Wolfe, 1964). She did not get along with her mother-in-law or with her elder sister, who was married to a Russian Grand Duke. With strangers she was shy and aloof; toward her servants she was kind but distant. She was moralistic and prudish; quick to adopt prejudices and slow to shake them. Alexandra saw things in all-or-none terms. People were either entirely good or entirely bad; beyond this, she responded to them emotionally and impulsively, rather than rationally (Buxhoeveden, 1930). Her maid-in-waiting described her as pessimistic, "prone to melancholy," and "never well balanced" [Mouchanow, 1918, pp. 30–31].

The psychoanalyst would describe Alexandra as a person with a weak ego and a strong primitive superego that caused her to see things in moralistic terms. Although she tried to become acquainted with all the court gossip, she expressed her disgust at what she called the loose morals of St. Petersburg society; but such behavior might have been a reflection of a defense mechanism of **projection,** as a way of justifying some of her own sexual impulses that were castigated by the superego and repressed by the ego. To the psychoanalyst, the female suffers from penis envy, but a male offspring is a means of fulfilling this desire for a penis. The fact that her one male offspring was so unsatisfactory—and that she was responsible—may have intensified the development of a neurotic personality.[5]

The Tsarina's moralistic and mystical orientation implies the presence of an *authoritarian personality syndrome.* We previously mentioned the Tsarina's way of disparaging the immoral behavior in the Russian court while demonstrating a strong interest in such activities. Alexandra's superstitious nature would confirm the acceptance of mysticism and supernatural solutions to problems. She never began a task on Friday; she was always careful to look at the new moon from the right side; she never put on a green dress for fear of bad luck; and "the sight of three candles on a table made her frantic" [Mouchanow, 1918, pp. 118–119]. (Further components of the authoritarian personality syndrome are described in Chapter 13.) In summary, the psychoanalytic approach would rely almost entirely upon personality factors rather than situational factors in explaining why the Tsarina was influenced by Rasputin. While credence is given to contemporary factors, it is not an

[5] Alexis's hemophilia was inherited from his mother's side of the family, hemophilia being a sex-linked characteristic which is passed by females to their male offspring. Alexis's mother, Alexandra, was from a German royal family and was the granddaughter of Queen Victoria of Great Britain. Of Queen Victoria's nine children, two daughters (and possibly a third) were carriers, and one son was a victim of hemophilia (McKusick, 1965).

exaggeration to say that of all the theoretical approaches, psychoanalytic theory relies most heavily upon historical causation.

VII. ROLE THEORY

A. Basic Assumptions and Concepts

Role theory, as an explanation of social behavior, possesses two distinctions. First, it is less well organized and less well developed than any other approach and is best considered a loosely linked network of hypotheses or set of rather broad constructs (Shaw & Costanzo, 1970). In essence, role theory is an orientation toward interpersonal behavior, rather than a theory possessing well-developed postulates and testable hypotheses. Second, role theory does not recognize any individualized, within-the-person determinants of interpersonal behavior. An attempt is made to explain behavior solely in terms of roles, role expectations, role skills, and reference groups operating upon the participants in a social interaction. Concepts such as personality, attitudes, and motivation are not employed. Hence the approach of role theory is the most sociological of the five approaches considered here.

The term **role** is usually defined as the set of behaviors or functions appropriate for a person holding a particular position within a particular social context (Biddle & Thomas, 1966; Shaw & Costanzo, 1970). A student, when acting as a student, performs certain behaviors—he attends classes, prepares assignments, makes an application for graduation, and so on. When interacting with this person in his role as student, other people expect him to act in certain ways; these are called *role expectations*. For example, faculty members expect their students to attend class with some regularity and show some concern over grades; some faculty may expect some degree of deference from their students, while others may not. **Norms** are more general expectations, which refer to the behaviors that are deemed appropriate for all persons in a social context, regardless of the position they hold. For example, both students and faculty members are expected to remove their hats in class (a norm), but faculty are expected to call the class to order (a role).

Role conflict results when a person holds several positions that are incompatible with one another (interrole conflict) or when a person in a single position has expectations that are incompatible (intrarole conflict). For example, while studying for an important final exam, a student may receive a call from his mother requiring prolonged discussion about a certain problem at home. Expectations about his role as a student and his role as a family member cannot both be satisfied at the same time, and interrole conflict is produced. An example of intrarole conflict would occur if a student had to choose between studying for a history exam or typing a term paper, when both were due the next day.

B. Applications to Rasputin and the Tsarina

Turning now to our example of Rasputin and Alexandra, we note that the role theorist would conceptualize the relationship in terms of the roles, role obligations, and role expectations of each party. (The role expectations that Rasputin

Figure 1-4. *A Person Holding One Role Can Be Seen From Many Perspectives*

and Alexandra had for each other would also be examined.) Alexandra's role as a mother demanded that she explore all means of improving her child's health. Rasputin was introduced to her as a man of the church, and with the royal family he always maintained the respectful manner of a peasant before his sovereign (Buxhoeveden, 1930). He was always sober when he came to the royal palace; he entertained the children and acted ingratiatingly toward the parents. On the basis of Rasputin's behavior in her presence, Alexandra saw no reason to doubt that the monk possessed the supernatural powers that he was reputed to have. In the opinion of the empress, Rasputin was clearly God's answer to the problems of Imperial Russia. With such expectations, it is no surprise that the Tsarina was so pervasively influenced by Rasputin.

Role theory also notes that when the behavior of one who occupies a certain position is out of line with the behavior that is expected of that position, observers tend to believe they know more about the individual in question (Jones, Davis, & Gergen, 1961). It would be an understatement at this point to describe Rasputin as unconventional for his place and time. But the ways in which the monk deviated from his expected role behaviors may have been part of his attraction. In support of this explanation, Alan Moorehead (1965) writes:

> His [(Rasputin's)] real crime, of course, in the eyes of society was that he broke the conventions, he outraged their way of life. He had a sadistic glee in showing up the pretentiousness, the pomposity and the silliness of his wealthy patrons. Petrograd (St. Petersburg) society was very corrupt and Rasputin knew it. He could degrade and humiliate the sycophants around the Tsar precisely because they were sycophants, and therefore venal as well as frightened. . . . He was, moreover, very shrewd. His casual observations about people . . . were extremely revealing, and he could handle backstairs politics rather more ably than most of the bureaucrats in Petrograd. Finally, he was a superb actor; he played his role as though he believed in it absolutely, and perhaps he really did [p.71].

While Moorehead does not clarify Rasputin's conception of his own role, the analysis does indicate the potential uses of role theory in understanding an individual's relationships with a variety of others.

VIII. A COMPARISON OF THEORIES

Even though each approach aims toward comprehensiveness and generality, none of the above theories can provide a full explanation for the significant and prolonged human interaction between Rasputin and Alexandra. Nor can any one theory deal with all the diverse phenomena included within the domain of social psychology. Thus, it is unlikely that any broad or grand theory—in its present form—will be accepted by all social psychologists in the near future. In fact, the movement is now toward the development of minitheories or theories that seek to explain a narrower band of behavior or a more specific phenomenon. The theory of cognitive dissonance is an example of this approach, concerning itself only with limited situations, such as one where a person holds two inconsistent beliefs. As we shall see in Chapter 10, even this situation is of sufficient complexity to cause Festinger (1957) to revise and revise again his initial theoretical statement regarding cognitive dissonance theory. Conceivably, in the distant future a number of minitheories may be joined together into a grand theory, but such a theory will not closely resemble the theories that are available now.

The broad theories presented in this chapter, however, still serve as general orientations toward research problems. As explanations of social behavior, each theory has some successes and some failures. In the case of each theory, there are aspects of the Tsarina-Rasputin relationship, for example, which conflict with theoretical explanations. But instead of making a premature decision about the relative adequacy of theories, we should focus on the differences and the unique strengths of each. The following is a discussion of the basic differences among theories as listed in Table 1-1.

A. Contemporary versus Historical Causes of Interpersonal Behavior

Field theory is the strongest of the five approaches in its emphasis upon the assumption that only present events can explain other present events. In contrast, psychoanalytic theory makes an implicit assumption that present interpersonal

Table 1-1. *A Comparison of Theories in Social Psychology*

Theory	*Causes of behavior: historical or contemporary?*	*Intrapersonal factors versus situational factors*	*Units of analysis*	*Assumptions about the nature of man*
S-R theory	Contemporary though concerned with antecedents of behavior	Largely situational (that is, vary the reward structure) but recognizes that internal factors may determine what is rewarding	Specific responses, habits	Man can be molded into almost any behavior pattern through reinforcement
Gestalt theory	Contemporary in emphasis on phenomenological approach	Recognizes place of both	More molar behavior, though often unspecified	Man is active, purposive, goal-seeking, seeking self-improvement
Field theory	Strongly contemporary	Emphasizes the place of both types of factors	Great variation in units used	Little in the way of substantive assumptions
Psychoanalytic theory	Some emphasis on historical but recognition of contemporary	Emphasizes intrapersonal factors (personality, motives)	Personality traits and general characteristics	Initial asocial infant learns to control his impulses and perhaps becomes an altruistic, loving adult
Role theory	Contemporary	Emphasizes roles and situational influences; ignores internal factors	Responses to various situations	Man acts in response to the role he holds

behavior is strongly influenced by past events. Stimulus-response theory, while assuming that behavior can be changed through the modification of reinforcements, recognizes that antecedents (or the person's reinforcement history) may be important.

B. Internal Factors versus Situational Factors

Psychoanalytic theory gives strongest emphasis to the personality and motives of the participants as determinants of interpersonal behavior. Role theory ignores internal individual differences and sees social behavior as a function of roles, role expectations, and role conflicts. Most comprehensive here is field theory, because of its conviction that every interpersonal action is a result of both the person and the environment.

C. The Unit of Analysis

Stimulus-response theory and Gestalt theory are the most distinctive on the issue of the unit of analysis. S-R theory assumes that social behavior can be adequately described and explained by looking at specific responses. Gestalt theory rejects this assumption, claiming that subdividing behavior into discrete elements destroys its essence.

D. Assumptions about the Nature of Man

Both reinforcement theory and role theory convey an assumption that man lacks much essence; rather he acts in response to stimuli fed into him (S-R theory) or in response to the expectations of the role he is fulfilling (role theory). Gestalt theory and field theory, however, emphasize that man is purposive and goal oriented and that he develops long-term aspirations and acts in accordance with them. Psychoanalytic theory, as explicated by Sigmund Freud, sees man's instinctual nature as selfish and aggressive and held in abeyance by the restrictions of society.

IX. WHAT DO SOCIAL PSYCHOLOGISTS DO?

Our extended analysis of the Rasputin-Tsarina relationship may imply that social psychologists spend most of their time attempting to explain—many years after the fact—great and not-so-great happenings from history. This is not the case. The social psychologist's primary activities are the acquisition and application of knowledge to the problems of our world. The knowledge that is accumulated may be theory oriented or atheoretical. Examples of atheoretical research include public opinion polls, which might ask about a person's preferences for president or reactions to women's liberation. Comparisons of the attributes of different racial groups (such as IQ differences between blacks and whites) or evaluations of the effectiveness of a storefront mental health clinic may also be atheoretical. Theory-based research seeks to test the utility of the theoretical viewpoint. The typical researcher tends to think in the language of one theory and to rely upon it for explanations of findings, rather than mixing concepts from different approaches. Increasingly, theory-oriented social psychologists are seeking minitheories, or theories of limited applicability, as explanations of social behavior.

In attempting to understand social behavior and in testing their theories, social psychologists use a variety of research methods. Observations of people on subways, experiments in psychology laboratories, comparisons of the reactions of persons in different parts of the world, and the ubiquitous questionnaires filled out by college sophomores all reflect social psychological methodology. (These research methods are described in Chapter 2.)

X. SUMMARY

Social psychology is the field of study concerned with interpersonal behavior. It includes in its domain not only actual interpersonal behavior but additionally any behavior in which the presence of others is imagined or anticipated. Thus very little human behavior escapes the concern of social psychology.

Stimulus-response and *reinforcement* theories, in explaining social behavior, study the associations between specific stimuli and responses. These approaches assume that complex social behavior can be understood as a chaining together of simple responses and that the consequences of a social behavior are highly influential in determining whether similar responses will be made in the future.

Gestalt theory emphasizes that social behavior cannot be properly understood if it is analyzed or reduced to specific responses. To the Gestalt psychologist, the essence of social behavior is complex, interrelated, and purposive. *The whole is greater than the sum of its parts* is the credo of Gestalt psychology.

A *phenomenological* approach to the study of behavior assumes that the perceptions of the environment are more important in understanding a person's social behavior than is an objective description of the environment. According to *field* theory, social behavior is always a function of both the person and the environment at a specific point in time.

Psychoanalysis, basically a theory of personality structure and development, explains social behavior in terms of the level of personality development and the forces at work within the personality of each participant. Experiences during childhood are considered to be strong determinants of adult social behavior.

Role theory seeks to explain social behavior through an analysis of roles, role obligations, role expectations, and role conflicts. Roles are behaviors a person performs when holding a particular position within a social context.

No one theory is successful in predicting or explaining all kinds of social behavior. For instance, in the relationship between Rasputin and the Tsarina, each theory highlights different elements, and each fails to explain some aspects. Theories in social psychology differ in regard to historical versus contemporary causation, emphasis upon internal versus situational factors or both, the unit of analysis, and assumptions about the nature of man.

XI. SUGGESTED READINGS

Deutsch, M., & Krauss, R. *Theories in social psychology*. New York: Basic Books, 1965. A clearly written review of theories in social psychology. Stimulus-response theory, Gestalt theory, field theory, psychoanalytic theory, and role theory discussed in separate chapters. The place that each theory occupies in general psychology described before the social psychological ramifications are amplified. Basic constructs and principles of each theory described. Highly recommended.

Lana, R. *Assumptions of social psychology.* New York: Appleton-Century-Crofts, 1968. (Paperback.) A technical analysis of the adequacy of various theories in social psychology.

Lindzey, G., & Aronson, E. *Handbook of social psychology.* (2nd ed.) Reading, Mass.: Addison-Wesley, 1968. Volume I contains extended treatments of each theory reviewed in this chapter, prepared by social psychologists who are experts on the topic. Highly technical.

Massie, R. *Nicholas and Alexandra.* New York: Atheneum, 1967. (Paperback edition available.) Highly readable, well-received account of the demise of the Russian monarchy. Contains much about Rasputin's relationship with Alexandra but no social psychological theories. Also, an extensive bibliography.

Shaw, M. E., & Costanzo, P. R. *Theories in social psychology.* New York: McGraw-Hill, 1970. A comprehensive review of theories. Much more difficult reading than Deutsch and Krauss, but the two books complement each other. Contains concluding chapter that compares social psychological theories in the context of evolving criteria for a grand theory.

Chapter Two

Methods of Studying Human Behavior

by Stuart Oskamp

When you have eliminated the impossible, whatever remains, *however improbable*, must be the truth. *Sherlock Holmes*

If people feel that they are "guinea pigs" being experimented with, or if they feel that they are being "tested" and must make a good impression, or if the method of data collection suggests responses . . . the measuring process may distort the experimental results. *Claire Selltiz, Marie Jahoda, Morton Deutsch, and Stuart W. Cook,* 1959

There are many reasons why social psychologists study human behavior. Some researchers are often motivated by a mixture of personal interest, scientific curiosity, and a desire to help solve some of the problems of society. Perhaps most commonly, however, social psychologists believe in Alexander Pope's famous maxim: "The proper study of mankind is man." Several examples of the kind of research questions studied by social psychologists may be cited. Donley and Winter (1970), for instance, undertook an innovative study that attempted to discover how the personal motives of American presidents related to the actual accomplishments of their respective administrations. During the study, some of the standard ways of measuring personal motivation toward achievement and power were used to analyze the inaugural addresses of presidents from Theodore Roosevelt to Richard Nixon. (See Figure 2-1.)

Attempting to explain such phenomena as why scientific polling methods often fail is a second example of the kinds of problems studied by social psychologists. In the 1970 British elections, the Labour Party under Harold Wilson was heavily favored to win. With one exception, all the major British public opinion polling organizations predicted a Labourite victory of anywhere from 2 percent to 9 percent of the vote. Yet the Conservative Party under Edward Heath scored a smashing upset, winning by nearly 5 percent. How can this failure of scientific polling methods be explained?

Figure 2-1. *Are a President's Motives Revealed Here? Donley and Winter (1970) determined the degree to which achievement and power themes were present in the inaugural addresses of U. S. Presidents in this century. Presidents' motives, as shown in this first official statement, were found to correspond closely to the subsequent accomplishments of their administrations. Perhaps this method may also be used to give us predictions of future presidential accomplishments. (Photographs courtesy of Black Star.)*

A third example of the kinds of issues that stimulate the thoughts of social psychologists is the California F scale—a method devised as part of a far-reaching social psychological research project to measure authoritarian attitudes. The F scale was used in hundreds of subsequent research studies; yet a battle raged for many years as to whether the scale measured authoritarianism at all, or whether it merely measured the respondents' willingness to agree with certain items (a characteristic called *acquiescence response set*).

A fourth example of the kinds of behaviors studied by social psychologists is the well-known case of Kitty Genovese, a victim who was slowly and brutally stabbed to death as she returned home to her New York City apartment. At least 38 of her neighbors saw the attack and heard her screaming for help. Since her attacker was frightened away and then returned to finish her off, the whole incident took over half an hour; yet not once during that period did any of her neighbors assist her or even call the police. The implications of this tragic event shocked much of America, and it stimulated two young psychologists (Darley & Latané, 1968a, 1968b; Latané & Darley, 1968, 1970a, 1970b) to study the conditions under which people are or are not willing to help others in an emergency. In doing so, the researchers again raised one of the existential questions that has troubled mankind since the dawn of recorded history: "Am I my brother's keeper?"

Psychologists are not alone in studying human behavior; all of us in our daily lives try to understand and influence other people. The main difference between the professional psychologist and the average man, however, is the method that is used to seek understanding of other people's behavior. In this chapter, we will describe and evaluate the advantages and limitations of the social psychologist's principal methods. But first, we will need to look carefully at scientific method in general. In the age of science and technology, most people have some understanding of how scientists work, but many misconceptions also exist (Kemeny, 1959; Kuhn, 1962). A closer look at scientific method in general should help us dispel some of those misconceptions and set the stage for the consideration of the particular methods of social psychologists.

I. SCIENTIFIC METHOD

Aside from the social psychologist, the historian and the creative writer, to mention only two examples, also study human behavior. Men like Toynbee or Gibbon, Dostoevski or Shakespeare, possessed very great insight into human behavior, but their study and understanding of behavior did not make them scientists (as they would be the first to agree) because they used different methods than the ones used by the scientific researcher. Here, we shall be concerned with defining the methods of scientists.

First of all, scientific method is cyclical in nature—starting with facts, progressing through theories and predictions, and returning to new facts that form the end of one cycle and the beginning of the next. We may define a **fact** as an observation that has been made (or could be made) repeatedly and consistently by different observers. That is, a fact is determined by the consensus of different observers. A **theory** may be defined, very simplistically, as a system of ideas containing some abstract concepts, some rules about the interconnection of these concepts, and some ways of linking these concepts to observed facts (Deutsch & Krauss, 1965). On the one hand, for example, it is a fact that people who are made to fail on experimental tasks will often express anger and hostility toward the experimenter. On the other hand, it is a theory that frustration always leads to some form of aggression.(This frustration-aggression formula is a famous social psychological theory and will be discussed in detail in Chapter 6.)

In addition to its cyclical nature, the scientific method involves three major steps, as illustrated in Figure 2-2. The first step is **induction,** or the process of starting with observed facts and constructing a theory that is consistent with those facts. Induction is a leap from some particular instances to a more general rule—a highly creative step since it involves dreaming up a set of principles that are adequate to account for the known facts. The second step is **deduction.** Constructing a theory that is consistent with some observed facts is not enough, since clever theory builders

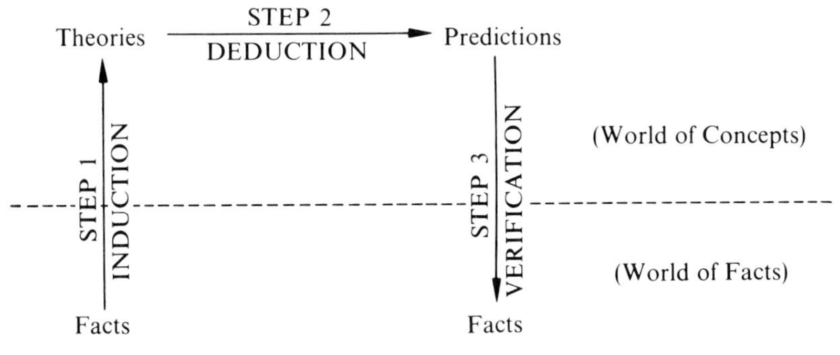

Figure 2-2. *The Three Steps of the Scientific Method. (Adapted from* A Philosopher Looks at Science, *by J. G. Kemeny. Copyright © 1959 by Litton Educational Publishing, Inc. Reprinted by permission of Van Nostrand Reinhold Company.)*

could probably develop several different theories that would all explain the original facts. Thus, the second step in the scientific method is logical deduction of some additional consequences of the theory that was induced in step one. These consequences are stated as predictions of what would happen under certain conditions, still at the abstract or theoretical level. Thus, an adequate theory must not only be verifiable but also falsifiable; we must be able to detect when its predictions are incorrect, too. The third step in the scientific method is **verification.** At this point, the method returns to the level of facts and collects new observations to support or refute the predictions made during the deductive step. If, as often happens, there are some discrepancies between the predictions and the verifying observations, these discrepancies become new facts that form the basis for a modification of the theory and for a new cycle of induction, deduction, and verification.

Let us consider a concrete example of social psychological research that clearly illustrates the three steps of the scientific method. Darley and Latané's study concerning the conditions under which people are willing to help one another will be the case in point. The initial facts that stimulated the study were the following: Kitty Genovese was murdered during one-half hour of screams and cries for help; 38 persons witnessed the event; and no move was made to help her or to call the police. From this situation Darley and Latané (1968a, 1968b) induced several theorctical propositions—the main one dealing with diffusion of responsibility in a social situation. Having induced this principle as a theoretical explanation of the original facts, the researchers deduced other logical consequences from their minitheory and made predictions about what would happen in a laboratory experiment designed to test the theory. Specifically, Darley and Latané deduced that the more people that are present in an emergency situation, the less likely it is that any one of them will make a helpful action. The experiment was controlled to prevent any direct inhibition of rescue efforts resulting from eye contacts between subjects by placing subjects in separate rooms. The subjects participated in a group discussion by means of an intercom system, each speaking in turn about his own problems in adjusting to life at a high-pressure urban university. Some subjects were told there was only one other discussion participant; some were told that two others were participating; and some were told that five others were participating. In each instance, the number of voices heard matched the instructions.

On the first round of discussion, one of the participants mentioned, with obvious embarrassment, that he was susceptible to nervous seizures somewhat like epilepsy. On the second round of discussion, the same participant gradually became disorganized in his speech; he stated that his problem was affecting him right now and asked for help. The participant said something about a seizure, made choking sounds, and finally lapsed into complete silence. During this cry for help, the experimenter waited outside the room of the real subject to see whether or how soon he would emerge to offer help. As mentioned, the authors had predicted that the more people present, the less the likelihood of an individual offering help. The results showed that when only one person was present in addition to the victim, 85 percent of the subjects tested came out to help. When two people were present in addition to the victim, 62 percent of the subjects came out to help; but when five people were present in addition to the victim, only 31 percent of the subjects came out to help. Thus the prediction was very strongly verified, and the authors' minitheory about the diffusion of responsibility received its initial experimental support.

One other point about the scientific method is worth mentioning in order to counteract claims for its complete objectivity. Since the collection of data is guided by theories and predictions, scientific method can never be completely impartial in nature. Similarly, the areas that scientists choose to study and the theories they develop are guided by their own personal beliefs and values and by their judgments about what is most important to study and how best to study the chosen subject. Therefore, even though science aims at being objective and unbiased, it never completely achieves that aim because of the human limitations of scientists.

Scientific method, or the sequence of proceeding from initial facts to new facts by the three steps of induction, deduction, and verification, can occur in any field of study and is not limited to the sciences alone. Historically, scientific method was used earliest and most frequently in the physical sciences such as astronomy and physics. Scientific method can also be employed in the social sciences such as psychology, sociology, economics, and political science and sometimes may be used in the humanities.[1]

Having defined and illustrated scientific method, we can now briefly list its unique features.

1. Scientific method is based on the assumption of **determinism,** a viewpoint holding that nature is orderly and lawful. Accordingly, events are determined by the principles of cause and effect, rather than by chance or accidental factors.

2. Scientific method uses the **empirical approach,** which means an active, planned collection of data. The approach is often contrasted with the armchair or **rational approach** of the philosopher or literary critic.

3. The **operational definition** of concepts is required by scientific method. This means definition through the specification of the operations that will measure the concepts. Authoritarianism, for example, is often operationally defined as an individual's total score on the 28 items of the California F scale. Operational definitions are necessary in order to permit communication between researchers and observable, repeatable methods of measurement.

4. Scientific method differs from the methods of the historian or novelist in its **objectivity**—that is, its susceptibility to consensual agreement. (Induction, or the creative leap, is common to both the artistic and the scientific fields of study.) The historian or writer may often make deductions and attempt verifications, but the scientist's objectivity of deductions and particularly of verifications is what sets him apart from his other intellectual and artistic colleagues.

These features of the scientific method give it both advantages and disadvantages as an intellectual tool. On the one hand, scientific method may limit the concern and focus of our study to concepts that can be measured objectively. On the other hand, when carefully used, scientific method ensures the accuracy of conclusions, as opposed to the speculative nature of conclusions in many nonscientific fields such as history or literary criticism. With these points in mind, let us now consider the narrower topic of studying human behavior scientifically. Basically, there are four main approaches to the study of human behavior: collecting and analyzing

[1]The recent studies investigating the disputed authorship of twelve of *The Federalist Papers* are an example of how scientific method can be employed in the humanities (Mosteller & Wallace, 1964; Rokeach, Homant, & Penner, 1970). By counting the usage of key words and value statements, the investigators were able to provide overwhelming support for the view that the papers in dispute were written by James Madison rather than by Alexander Hamilton.

existing documents, asking people questions, watching people, and experimenting. These approaches are often combined to compound their strengths and compensate for some of their weaknesses.

The first approach—collecting and analyzing existing documents and/or artifacts—is frequently used by historians, archeologists, and biographers but seldom by psychologists (who should, perhaps, use it more often). One fascinating application of this method is Donley and Winter's (1970) analysis of presidential inaugural addresses. The second approach to studying human behavior—asking people questions—is a method that includes the familiar gamut of psychological tests, questionnaires, and interviews. The third approach—watching people—is an observational method that concentrates on overt behavior rather than on what people say about themselves. Often people can accurately discuss their own behavior so that the asking method is sufficient, but watching is necessary when subjects are unable to describe their behavior or when circumstances (embarrassing situations or socially disapproved behavior) might make them unwilling to do so accurately.

Finally, the fourth approach to the study of human behavior—experimenting—means, in a broad sense, that a situation is set up to observe behavior by holding constant (controlling) some aspects of the situation while intentionally varying (manipulating) others. Control and manipulation are the two features of this method that distinguish it from the methods of asking and watching.

II. THE EXPERIMENTAL METHOD

The experimental method may be defined by its three components—manipulation of one or more **independent variables,** control of related variables, and observation of one or more **dependent variables.** Darley and Latané's study will again be used to illustrate how these three components of the experimental method are utilized.

Manipulation of one or more independent variables—the first component of the experimental method—means that at least two levels (or values) of the variable must be used and that these values must be used systematically in a planned design. In Darley and Latané's study there was only one independent variable—the number of other discussion participants in addition to the seizure victim. This variable was given three different values in the experimental design: 1, 2, and 5. Approximately one-third of the subjects took part in each of these three conditions.

Control of related variables—the second component of experimental method—includes (a) holding some aspects of the situation constant for all subjects, (b) eliminating some aspects that might distort the results, and (c) systematically setting up the situation or choosing subjects so that an extraneous variable will have an equal or measurable effect on every experimental condition. One of the main variables controlled in the Darley-Latané study was face-to-face interaction of the subjects—an important variable since such interaction has been shown to inhibit a subject's willingness to help in an emergency. This possibility of inhibiting a subject was controlled by eliminating face-to-face interaction and substituting an intercom system. Another factor needing control was the occupation and status of the subjects, since such characteristics might affect the subjects' willingness to help a seizure victim. This possibility was controlled by holding the factor constant: all the subjects were students. Many other factors also might have affected the subjects' willingness to help. Consider, for example, the subjects' level of anxiety. Though this factor was not mentioned by the experimenters, it was nevertheless controlled by means of **randomization,** or random assignment of subjects to the three experimental conditions. Random assignment ensures, with a small and specifiable margin of error, that each group has an approximately equal quota of high-anxiety subjects and low-anxiety subjects. The same result could be attained by systematically assigning precisely equal numbers of high- and low-anxiety subjects to each condition, but this procedure would require the prior measurement of the subjects' anxiety levels by some sort of questionnaire or test. The same goal can be accomplished more simply by randomization, which can also control other extraneous or contaminating variables, known or unknown. Randomization acts as a safeguard and is unique to the experimental method.

Observation of one or more dependent variables—the third component of the experimental method—implies that there must be at least two clearly distinguishable values or categories in which the dependent variable may fall. Usually, we try to measure or quantify the dependent variable along a continuous numerical scale. In regard to the Darley-Latané study, we will consider just one dependent variable having only two categories: the subject either did or did not come out of his room to report the emergency during the specified six-minute period of time. This two-fold dependent variable was converted to a quantitative scale by taking the percentage of subjects in each experimental condition who came out of their rooms within the specified time.

As we have seen, in this experiment a very large difference was obtained (in the predicted direction) in the dependent variable scores for each of the three independent variable conditions: 85 percent, 62 percent, and 31 percent. One final refinement provided by the authors was subjecting this difference in scores to a **statistical test.** The function of such a test (be it a correlation coefficient, chi-square, analysis of variance, t test, or whatever) is to render a probability statement on the likelihood that a difference of this magnitude could occur by chance (rather than being a real difference in scores). The .05 level of significance is customarily accepted in most social psychological research, which means that a result of such magnitude could occur by chance alone only 5 times out of 100. Since the p value (probability of a chance finding) for the Darley-Latané experiment was .02, we may be confident that the percentages given above represent real (nonchance) differences in the dependent variable. Furthermore, to the extent that other possible contaminating factors have been adequately controlled, we may conclude that these nonchance differences in the dependent variable are due to real and meaningful differences in the independent variable conditions.

The experimental method in psychology is often contrasted with another approach, usually called the *correlational* method. (See, for instance, the comprehensive comparison by Cronbach, 1957.) The term correlational method is somewhat confusing, for it seems to imply that correlation coefficients or other similar statistical techniques must be used. (This is emphatically not the case, and the method might better be named the nonmanipulative method.) The correlational method focuses on the naturally occurring differences between individuals' characteristics or traits (such as hostility, helpfulness, or authoritarianism). At least two such variables must be measured, and a relationship (a concomitant variation) is sought between the magnitude of scores on one variable and the magnitude of scores on the other.

An example of the correlational method may be seen in a study conducted by researchers at the University of Michigan (Kasl & French, 1962), who found that the occupational status of industrial workers is positively related to physical and emotional health. Neither job status nor health was manipulated by the researchers. (Indeed, it would be hard to imagine how these variables could be noticeably influenced by a researcher.) Instead, job status and health were simply measured as objectively as possible; the two sets of scores were then compared and found to be related. The major problem with the correlational method is that it often gives us few clues as to the direction of causality. Which of these characteristics, job status and health, is the independent (antecedent) variable, and which is the dependent (consequent) variable? Which is cause, and which is effect? Perhaps high occupational status is the cause, and good health the effect. Perhaps good physical and emotional health leads to a higher probability of promotion and hence to higher job status. Or perhaps both variables are effects, dependent on some other ultimate causal variable, such as the worker's level of education. Without more information, we cannot choose among these three causal hypotheses.

The correlational method has certain drawbacks, but this does not mean that the experimental method is therefore the sine qua non of precise science. A classic example to the contrary is the field of astronomy, perhaps the first of the physical sciences to emerge into a truly scientific state. Until the post-Sputnik era of man-made satellites, astronomy was forced to rely almost entirely on the correlational method. After all, a scientist cannot manipulate planets or the occurrence of comets in order to test his theories! But even though astronomy was able to advance by way of the correlational method, scientists prefer the experimental method for one important reason: the experimental method more than any other method makes it easier to infer cause and effect. At this point, then, let us digress briefly into a discussion of how causation is determined.

First, a widespread misconception should be dispelled; contrary to common opinion, experiments do not prove cause and effect. Indeed, scientists generally believe that causation can never be proven, since ultimately causation is an inference we make from all the data at our disposal. What then are the factors that help us make causal inferences accurately, and why do experiments make it easier than other methods to infer cause and effect? In answering these questions, Selltiz, Jahoda, Deutsch, and Cook (1959, pp. 80–143) have listed three factors involved in making causal inferences: concomitant variation, time order of the occurrence of variables, and elimination of other possible causal factors.

Concomitant variation means that two variables vary together in a regular and systematic way. Suppose we have two variables, X and Y, that are personal characteristics or traits of an individual. Concomitant variation would be shown by the amount of Y increasing as the amount of X increases (a positive relationship), or by the amount of Y increasing as the amount of X decreases (a negative relationship). If we found a significant degree of concomitant variation, it would suggest the possibility of—but not prove—a causal relationship. It must be remembered that correlation does not prove causation.

In considering the time order of occurrence of variables, we realize that, by definition, a cause must be prior to or simultaneous with an effect; it cannot occur after the effect. For instance, early childhood experiences might be a cause of later behavior, such as criminality, but such behavior could not be a cause of the early life experiences.

Elimination of other possible causal factors is accomplished through the use of controls in an experiment. Competing causal hypotheses are disproved by holding constant or eliminating the variables that are suggested as causal factors. Nonexperimental studies, by their very nature, cannot be so carefully controlled, but some control can still be exercised. Typical methods include careful selection of subjects and detailed specification of observational methods and conditions. If the hypothesis stated, for example, that lack of warmth from the mother was a causal factor in the son's later criminality, the selection of subjects might be controlled by excluding those subjects whose parents had separated or divorced during the child's early years. Thus, a possibly contaminating variable could be eliminated. Similarly, since memory is highly fallible, evidence of a mother's warmth might be obtained from records made during the son's childhood rather than from retrospective interviews made years later.

The most important considerations in making causal inferences from the available data in an experiment are the last two factors—the time order of variables and the elimination of other causal factors. Concomitant variation is used in correlational as well as in experimental studies. An experiment, once again, has great advantages over other means of data collection in that normally much more information about these factors is provided, and thus inferring cause and effect is made easier. Hence, the experimental method is preferred in scientific studies. However, when using independent variables such as a mother's warmth, we should be reminded that such types of variables (ones involving the personal characteristics of individuals) usually cannot be manipulated. Thus we are often forced to use nonexperimental evidence and to exercise all of our ingenuity in developing causal inferences from the data.

III. GOALS OF SCIENTIFIC RESEARCH

Making causal inferences is not the only goal of scientific research; there are, indeed, a number of other goals, some of which are more limited and some, more far reaching. In the following discussion these goals are arranged in a hierarchical order, so they may also be considered as stages or levels in scientific development.

A. Description of Events

A great deal of factual information must be collected before our knowledge is complete, reliable, and precise enough to allow us to approach the far-reaching goals of science. Description is the foundation upon which classification systems (taxonomies) are built, and classification is an important step in discovering the inherent relationships between events.

B. Discovery of Relationships between Events

Much of science is directed toward the goal of discovering relationships. For the social psychologist the events to be studied are social situations and human behavior and characteristics. Relationships between such variables are often studied using the correlational method, and they do not carry any necessary implication of causality. For instance, we know that in recent national elections, blacks have been much more likely to vote for Democratic candidates than for Republican ones, but this does not mean that the people vote Democratic because they are black.

C. Explanation or Understanding of Events

At this stage of science, we begin to make causal inferences, since the terms explanation and understanding generally refer to constructing causal statements about events. An example may be seen in considering the empirical relationship between being black and voting Democratic. Knowledge of this fact does not give us any understanding of why the relationship occurs; for that explanation, a theory is needed. For instance, one might theorize that people generally vote in accordance with their self-interests and that black Americans have generally seen the Democratic party as serving their interests better than the Republican party. Development of such a theory represents the inductive step of scientific method. When the consequences of the theory are deduced and verified, we then have some true causal understanding about the phenomena involved.

D. Prediction of Events

Prediction can be either a more advanced goal than causal understanding or a less advanced goal, depending upon the method used. One method of prediction is strictly empirical, using the discovery of relationships between events as the basis for prediction. Examples of empirical predictions would be: the sun came up today and yesterday, so it will come up tomorrow; or, blacks voted Democratic in the last election, so they will do so again in the next election. Such predictions may be quite accurate, but they are relatively unsophisticated because they are not based on any understanding (that is, causal knowledge) of the events involved.

A more advanced method of prediction is rational—that is, mediated by theory. Rational prediction uses the understanding or explanation of events as a basis for making predictions; thus, the subsequent predictions may be considerably more complicated and contingent than predictions evolved through the empirical method. For instance, we might predict that blacks will continue to vote Democratic in national elections as long as they continue to view the Democratic party as the proponent of their general welfare. This kind of prediction is not necessarily any more accurate than predictions by the empirical method, if the structure of events continues unchanged. Rational prediction clearly has a great advantage, however, whenever new variables enter the picture or relationships between old variables begin to change.

E. Control of Events

Control of or influence on events is often the ultimate goal of science. Successful heart transplants and the landing of astronauts on the moon are examples of areas in which human knowledge has progressed so far that a detailed control of events is possible. However, in the social sciences, events are so complex, and the causes of behaviors so multifaceted, that the likelihood of really substantial control over human behavior is remote. Thus, influence on events rather than control of events may be a more realistic statement of this goal for the social sciences.

Nevertheless, even the remote prospect of scientific control over human behavior excites a great deal of controversy and raises in the minds of many psychologists the fear of a world like the one portrayed in George Orwell's *1984*.

On the reverse side of the coin, however, psychologist B. F. Skinner has pointed out in *Walden Two* that controlling human behavior would enable us to eliminate much human misery stemming from ignorance, prejudice, crime, and mental illness. According to Skinner, much of man's behavior is already controlled by external influences, which are poorly understood and often not beneficial in nature. Modern science, he suggests, offers us the opportunity to substitute control that is publicly understood and to work for beneficial ends rather than depend upon the much less desirable control that exists now. Many social psychologists would agree with this Skinnerian view, while many others support the opposing view of Carl Rogers (Rogers & Skinner, 1956). Rogers' position holds that the goal of social science should be to free men to become what they are uniquely capable of becoming, to allow them to self-actualize their potentialities for creativity and growth.

Regardless of where one stands in this debate about the goals of science, we are clearly a very long way from any possibility of major control over human behavior. A case in point was the great public furor created in the late 1950s over the possibility of using **subliminal perception** in advertising. Nationwide publicity was given to the purported experiment of a commercial firm, which claimed it had succeeded in using subliminal (unseen) messages flashed instantaneously on the movie screen to get moviegoers to buy soft drinks and popcorn. After several years of public debate and scientific experimentation on the topic, a thorough review by McConnell, Cutler, and McNeil (1958) concluded that the effectiveness of subliminal perception had been greatly overrated.

IV. MAJOR METHODS OF SOCIAL PSYCHOLOGICAL RESEARCH

Let us now move from considerations of the general goals of science to a discussion of the methods of social psychological research. Archival research, the survey, the field study, the natural experiment, the field experiment, and the laboratory experiment are the major methods that will be discussed. Brief examples of research work will be given to illustrate the results obtained when using each method. The order in which the methods are presented indicates the use of an increasing degree of control of the research conditions.[2]

[2] For further details on the research methods of social psychology, readers are advised to consult L. Festinger and D. Katz, *Research Methods in the Behavioral Sciences* (New York: Dryden, 1953), pp. 13–172.

A. Archival Research

In 1961, David McClelland launched an ambitious research program to test the hypothesis that a high level of achievement motivation among the citizens of a country is a factor in attaining later economic growth in that country. Since McClelland was not able to give psychological tests to representative citizens from many countries, he relied upon public records as sources for the measurement of both independent and dependent variables. For independent variables, McClelland took second-, third-, and fourth-grade reading textbooks that had been widely used by children in each of 23 major countries around the year 1925. From these texts, 21 stories were chosen at random for each country and were scored according to a previously developed measure of achievement motivation. In this content analysis, each story was scored for achievement-related ideas, such as references to standards of excellence or to striving to do a task well.

For one dependent variable measuring national economic growth, McClelland used the increase in the amount of electricity produced per capita in each country between 1929 and 1950. Despite major problems in obtaining adequate data and the possibility of inaccurate measurement, the results of the study were very impressive. The correlation between national need for achievement in 1925 and a greater-than-expected per capita growth in kilowatt-hours of electricity from 1929 to 1950 was +.53 (significant at the $p = .01$ level). Even more remarkable was another finding, which showed that the relationship between these two variables was not merely artifactual—that is, not merely the spurious result of other causal factors. The same correlation using need-for-achievement data gleaned from primary school readers for 1950 was only +.03 (or, completely nonsignificant). Thus, the achievement goals taught to school children are related to a nation's economic growth when the children have grown up and become the nation's producers a generation later. The past rate of economic growth, however, is not related to the current achievement goals taught to children. One may reasonably conclude that the need for achievement is the causal factor, while the nation's economic growth is the effect—rather than vice versa.

McClelland's study shows many of the characteristics of archival research, which by definition uses the technique of collecting existing materials. Here, the term archival research is used broadly to include analysis of any existing data and not only the records contained in public archives. There is a wide variety in the kinds of data that can be used. Data may be obtained from one individual, or they may be aggregates of information about many individuals; in addition, they may be psychological, economic, literary, or anthropological in nature. Materials for analysis could include letters written by eminent persons, folk stories of a preliterate society, newspaper editorials, wartime propaganda broadcasts, or public statistics such as census data or stock market averages. McClelland's study illustrates the use of both numerical data (production of electricity) and verbal material (stories from grade school readers).

One of the greatest advantages of archival research is that it uses unobtrusive measures that are nonreactive in nature; this means that the act of measuring something for research purposes does not change the phenomenon being measured. (By contrast, asking people's opinions about an issue may often be a reactive method because they may be induced to think about the issue more than usual and, thus, develop or change their opinions.) Another great advantage of archival research is that the examination of trends over time is made possible. Archival research also allows retrospective studies of past events, which could not be investigated in any other way, and it makes possible cross-cultural comparisons, which would not otherwise be feasible. As McClelland's study clearly shows, archival research permits the testing of hypotheses as well as exploratory and descriptive studies. And finally, the method can sometimes provide evidence about the direction of causality in relationships—though this kind of evidence is likely to be equivocal.

Against these advantages, there are also disadvantages to the method of archival research. Often, the necessary materials for analysis are difficult to obtain, for even if the materials exist, the source may be unknown or unavailable. Similarly, the researcher can only study materials that do exist, even though they may not adequately test his hypothesis. Content analysis projects are apt to be lengthy and expensive, but this problem has been greatly alleviated by the recent development of computer programs for the analysis of verbal materials. Finally, careful attention must be given to sampling from available materials, so that the materials studied will be representative of the whole. The sampling process also affects the validity of the results and the ability of the researcher to generalize from his findings.

B. The Survey

Racial attitudes in 15 American cities was the topic of a large-scale survey by Angus Campbell and Howard Schuman (1968). The study was initiated by the National Advisory Commission on Civil Disorders and was conducted by the Survey Research Center at the University of Michigan. The design of the study was to compare cities in border states to cities in northern states; cities that had experienced riots to cities that had not; and cities having black mayors to cities having white mayors. In each city a list of addresses was selected from the total number of addresses in the city; these were chosen so as to provide representative samples of the white and black populations in each city. Interviews were conducted with individuals between the ages of 16 and 69, living at these addresses. About 200 persons from each race were interviewed in each city, making a total of 5759 interviews. Nearly 500 interviewers took part in the data collection over a period of three months, with blacks interviewing black respondents and whites interviewing whites. The questions in the interview had been extensively tested before the actual survey began; the average respondent took slightly over one hour to answer all the questions. After interviewers had written down the respondents' answers verbatim, these verbal statements were classified into numerical categories for computer analysis by 37 coders at the study headquarters. If respondents were not at home, the interviewers made several later calls, ultimately succeeding in interviewing slightly more than 70 percent of the potential sample.

Some scattered results from this massive survey will illustrate the major findings. (Other results are presented in Chapter 9.) Comparison of black and white attitudes about the adequacy of city services showed the blacks were less satisfied on every item and particularly on those items concerning police protection and parks and playgrounds. Only 4 percent of the black respondents had themselves experienced uncalled for roughness from the police, but 35 percent believed such incidents had happened in their neighborhood. Only 10 percent of the white respondents believed that misconduct on the part of the police had occurred in their neighborhood. Most blacks viewed the city riots as spontaneous protests against real grievances. About half of the whites viewed riots in the same way, while most of the rest of the white respondents saw riots as excuses for looting. Strikingly, one-third of the white respondents made no distinction between riots and nonviolent demonstrations. Though most black respondents felt the riots had been justified protests, only 15 percent favored using violence to gain their rights, and only 4 percent of those in major riot cities reported having taken part in the riots.

From this example, many of the characteristics of the survey may be seen. By definition, the survey uses the technique of asking, rather than collecting, watching, or experimenting. The questions may be asked orally, as in an interview or test that is administered individually, or the questions may be asked in writing, as in a questionnaire or written test. The subject matter of the questions may vary widely. Surveys most commonly ask about attitudes and opinions, but they can also include questions on knowledge, behavior, personal experiences, environmental situations, and demographic information such as the age and occupation of the respondent.

All surveys are studies of some **population** of respondents, but the size of the population can vary markedly. In public opinion polls, the population is apt to be very large, such as the total number of adults in the United States. In questionnaire studies, the population is apt to be rather small, such as the total freshman class of a college. Where the population is large, sampling is almost always used—that is, only a subset of the members of the total population is actually given the survey interview or questionnaire. (One of the very few exceptions is the decennial census, which is a survey of the entire population of the United States.) Where the population is small, the investigator may choose to contact every member (a 100 percent sample), or he may decide to contact a smaller group (say, a 10 percent sample of the members of a freshman class). Such decisions by the experimenter are made primarily on the basis of the cost of data collection as weighed against the degree of precision desired in the final data. The degree of precision is positively related to the size of the sample and, therefore, can be estimated in advance by the use of statistical formulas. Wherever sampling is used in a survey, there will be some inaccuracy in the results because of sampling error. Even with very large populations (such as all adults in the United States), however, a properly drawn sample of about 1500 cases is enough to give a precise estimate of the total population's views, with a margin for error of less than 3 percent in either direction.

C. The Field Study

In 1954, Roger Barker and Herbert Wright published a book entitled *Midwest and Its Children,* which describes life in a small town in Kansas, with a population of about 750. The book summarizes research done over a period of many years by the staff of a field station established in the town of Oskaloosa, fictitiously named "Midwest." The staff members and their families, usually 15 to 20 in number, lived in Midwest and tried to participate normally in community activities according to their interests, avoiding the extremes of either nonparticipation or initiating new activities or procedures. The research purposes and methods were frankly and fully explained to Midwest's residents through public meetings, exhibits, and newspaper stories. This procedure was successful in eliciting the understanding and cooperation of the residents, which was a vital factor in carrying out the research.

During the study, many research methods were used. One method was to follow a single child all day from the time he awoke in the morning to the time he fell asleep at night; a crew of seven to nine observers took turns recording a detailed account of the child's conversations, actions, and interactions. Subsequently this specimen record was objectively divided into behavior episodes, which might number more than 1000 in a day. A second method used in the study was to make a complete inventory and classification of the town's behavior settings, defined as places or occasions that evoke their own typical patterns of behavior. Midwest was found to have nearly 600 community behavior settings, examples being Kane's Grocery, the 4-H Club picnic, and Thanksgiving Day. A third method employed in the study was to count, in the specimen records, all of the behavior objects (including people) that a child interacted with during a day; typically, well over 500 behavior objects were found for a single day.

This particular field study was a pioneering venture and, therefore, largely descriptive in nature. The goal was to study the psychological ecology of Midwest's children—that is, their psychological habitats and the nature of their behavior in various habitats. A few findings will illustrate the characteristics of the study. Because of the town's small population and large number of behavior settings, every resident was under pressure to enter many settings, while specialization of activity was rare. The average resident, including children, participated in positions of trust and responsibility in seven different community settings during a year (many more than is typical in larger communities). Children commonly interacted with more than 100 different people in a day. The social interaction episodes of children were harmonious about twice as often as disharmonious, and outright conflict occurred in only 5 percent of the social interaction episodes. In the concluding portions of their report, the authors speculate as to whether these figures would be substantially different had the study been done in Brooklyn or in an English village.

As shown by this example, a field study involves greater depth than a survey but usually less breadth in the sample being studied. Basically, the field study is a watching technique, though it may often use multiple measurement methods, including collecting and asking techniques. Whereas the survey researcher takes great pains to ensure the representativeness of his sample, the field study investigator is much less concerned about this aspect of his group. Instead, the aim of the researcher is to understand fully the structural characteristics of a single community and the dynamic processes that occur there. Since the investigator is often involved with the group for long periods of time, he takes great care to avoid disrupting or modifying the group processes, and he hopes that his presence as an observer will eventually be largely ignored by the group members. In addition to the unstructured participant observation method, field studies can incorporate a variety of structured observations, interviews with knowledgeable informants, and questionnaires. The combination of these methods can give great breadth of coverage and depth of insight into the structure and dynamics of the group under study. Above all, field studies have the advantage of frequently generating hypotheses that apply to real life because the studies were directly derived from a real-life situation. The generalizability of the findings to other real groups is a different question, however, and depends mainly upon the degree to which the group chosen for study is typical.

The field study isn't so good a method for testing hypotheses as the experiment.

The investigator should do pilot work until he has some clear-cut hypotheses to test in the field study; but there is still a great temptation to do post hoc (after-the-fact) theorizing on the basis of the data obtained rather than stick closely to the a priori hypothesis with which the study began. Whether in an experiment or a field study, such post hoc theorizing is usually very speculative and should not be accepted as adequate proof of any proposition. Another problem in the field study is that it is usually difficult to determine the direction of causality because the obtained relationships are correlational in nature rather than the result of manipulating variables, as in an experiment. One last problem is that the observer's presence may alter the behavior he is observing. Recent developments, however, have reduced this possibility. Observations can now be made without the subjects' knowledge.

D. The Natural Experiment

A book entitled *When Prophecy Fails,* by L. Festinger, H. Riecken, and S. Schachter (1956), describes a fascinating study of a doomsday group. The authors conducted the study in order to test theoretical predictions about the outcomes when a group's strongly held beliefs are proven wrong. The researchers were fortunate to discover a cultist group organized around a woman who was prophesying the destruction of much of the United States by a great flood on a specific date. The prophecy, according to Mrs. Keech, the clairvoyant, was received by automatic writing and was sent to her from the planet Clarion by superior beings called the Guardians. Notwithstanding the bizarre nature of these beliefs, a small group of disciples had formed (including several college students), who believed variously in flying saucers and mystic experiences. Members of this group suffered ridicule from friends; yet they showed their commitment to their beliefs in various actions such as quitting their jobs, giving away their property, or, in the case of the student members, dropping out of college.

To study this group, the researchers became **participant observers,** joining the group in the guise of convinced members. They attended lengthy seances in which messages were received from the Guardians, took notes when possible, and dictated their observations onto tapes shortly after each meeting. Their experimental prediction, derived from Festinger's cognitive dissonance theory, was a surprising one. They predicted that when the cataclysm failed to occur, the group would experience an increase in conviction and an upsurge in proselytizing activity. Since Mrs. Keech specified a particular date for the cataclysm, the prophecy could clearly be proven wrong.

In the weeks before the predicted flood the group members had become wary of inquiries about their beliefs. Opportunities for publicizing their beliefs and gaining converts were intentionally shunned, and reporters were invariably turned away. However, after an all-night vigil on the eve of the purported disaster, this group behavior changed dramatically. When spacemen did not appear at midnight to pick up the group of believers in flying saucers, five hours of terrific tension passed. Then a message arrived from the Guardians saying that because this small group of believers had spread so much light God had spared the world and the cataclysm had been averted.

Overjoyed, the group accepted this explanation and immediately felt a great sense of urgency to spread the glad tidings to the world. In contrast to their former secrecy and avoidance of publicity, the group members now contacted all newspapers and national wire services (before 6:00 A.M.) to proclaim their message. For several days the group held open house, explained their beliefs in great detail to all comers, called many press conferences to describe the new prophecies sent to Mrs. Keech, and generally proselytized as vigorously as possible. Though Mrs. Keech's prophecy was proven wrong, the experimental hypothesis of the authors was confirmed!

As seen previously, the hallmark of any experiment is manipulation of one or more variables. What distinguishes the natural experiment from other kinds of experiments is that the manipulation occurs without the intervention of the investigator. Mrs. Keech's catastrophic flood is one example of an event that could not be affected by the investigator. The experimental event may be an act of God, such as a hurricane or earthquake; it may be an action of governmental policy makers, such as the decision to integrate the armed forces in World War II; or it may be a joint action of many people, such as the election of a president or a protest demonstration on the Washington Mall. In any case the event must be dramatic and clear-cut enough to have an impact on the subjects being studied. The researcher has to obtain measures of the subjects' attitudes or other variables of interest both before and after the experimental event occurs, so that the amount of change caused by the event can be determined. However, to be completely sure that this change is a result of the event in question, the investigator also needs to have a control group of comparable subjects who were not exposed to the event. In the study cited here, this requirement was only partially met. Some members of the doomsday group were separated geographically from the majority of the group members on the fateful night. Later, it was found that these members did not proselytize as much as did the members of the intact group.

There are several advantages to using the natural experiment as a research design. Like all experiments, it yields valuable information about the direction of causality; and, like the field study, it involves little or no disruption of the group by the investigator. Perhaps most important, the natural experiment often involves very strong variables that have powerful effects on people's attitudes and behavior and that could not practicably nor ethically be manipulated by an experimenter. To counterbalance these advantages, there is the unfortunate fact that natural experiments usually arrive with little or no warning. This means that the investigator must grab the opportunity when it comes, often without sufficient planning and with inadequate premeasures. It also means that the researcher can only study events that do occur and not other events that might be more illuminating. Many studies, for instance, were carried out to assess the effect of President Kennedy's assassination on the American people (Greenberg & Parker, 1965), but the equally interesting question of how the public would have reacted had the assassination failed will never be answered. A final problem with the natural experiment is that the researcher may find himself participating in the group of subjects (as in the example cited here), thereby risking the introduction of bias.

E. The Field Experiment

The famous Robbers Cave in Oklahoma gave its name to an experiment conducted in a nearby summer camp for boys (Sherif, Harvey, White, Hood, & Sherif, 1961). Though the boys did not know they were in an experiment, the camp was actually set up by the researchers expressly for this purpose. The boys were selected from different schools to eliminate any previous acquaintance and were screened for good health and psychological adjustment. The researchers took the roles of normal camp counselors and sports directors and made their research notes only in private.

During the three weeks of camp, the researchers set up several phases of activities and for each phase manipulated some independent variables of intergroup contact and interaction. By so doing, the researchers tested a number of hypotheses concerning formation, structure, norms, and interactions of groups, focusing particularly on the antecedents of conflict and cooperation. In addition to unstructured observations, a number of questionnaires and objectively scored games were used to collect quantitative data. In several similar experiments conducted by Muzafer Sherif and his colleagues, the course of events typically ran as follows. The first days in camp were spent in campwide activities allowing a free choice of buddies and companions. After this period of spontaneous development of friendships, the 24 boys were housed separately in two cabins. The groups were chosen in such a way that about two-thirds of a boy's best friends were in the other cabin. As predicted, within a few days former friendships changed to a pattern of almost exclusive in-group choices, and shared norms about group activities began to develop.

During the second week a pattern of intergroup conflict was instituted by means of a tournament of competitive sports between the two cabins and prizes for the winners. As predicted, this competitive activity quickly developed into hostility toward the out-group. Out-group members were stereotyped; plans for ambushes and raids were formed; and new leaders who were effective in combat emerged. Interestingly, the conflict between the groups produced increased solidarity within each group.

During the third week the staff attempted to reduce intergroup conflict and replace it with cooperation. Several *superordinate goals* were introduced, which compelled the participation of both groups in solving a common problem. For instance, there was a stoppage in the water supply that had to be found and repaired; a truck broke down and had to be pulled to get it started; and an expensive movie was rented by the pooling of the funds of both groups. These joint efforts did not immediately dispel hostility, but the cumulative impact reduced unfriendly attitudes and stereotypes and allowed the development of new cooperative activities and friendship patterns cutting across groups. At the end of camp, the two groups were largely favorable toward each other, and the researchers undoubtedly heaved a collective sigh of relief.

As the above example illustrates, in the field experiment the experimental conditions are planned and introduced by the experimenter, but the setting is a real-life one for the subjects. The importance of prior planning can hardly be stressed enough. To make such an experiment successful, the investigator must have a great deal of knowledge about the situation and the experimental and control variables, and he needs to have done much pilot work and pretesting of his measuring instruments and manipulations. Furthermore, the investigator must have carefully thought through his experimental hypothesis and must have planned his operations at every step of the experiment so as to provide a stringent test of the hypothesis. Obviously, all this is not an easy task, and there are often other obstacles. Usually the experimenter must get permission (for instance, from a company president or a commanding general) to do the study, but even then he may not be able to control other crucial variables (such as layoffs in the middle of an industrial study or new duty assignments for military subjects).

Other problems can also occur in the field experiment. Often very strong variations in the independent variable may be needed because of relatively insensitive measuring instruments for the dependent variable (for example, industrial production, which can be influenced by many factors in addition to whatever independent variable is being manipulated). Yet at the same time it is frequently impossible to change the independent variable enough to have the necessary impact on the dependent variable (for instance, if the manipulation were an attempt to change the leadership style of foremen from authoritarian to democratic, the investigator would very likely find it impossible, in the time allotted to him, to create changes great enough to have a significant effect on the dependent variable). It is particularly difficult to study conflict areas in organizations because of the sensitive nature of these conflicts, and even in relatively conflict-free areas the necessity for secrecy about the experimental hypotheses may give rise to misunderstandings and suspicion.

If all of these potential obstacles are successfully surmounted, the investigator will have a very powerful research technique that is of practical as well as scientific value. As with the field study, the findings of the field experiment apply to real-life situations, and the problem of generalizability is minimized because the study is usually done in the setting that gave rise to the research question in the first place. Thus the field experiment is particularly good for studying complex processes of social change or social influence or other problems that may be too complex to be studied in a laboratory experiment or that would be changed dynamically if transferred to a laboratory context. Because the field experiment is carried out in a real-life setting, it can discover patterns of variables that covary naturally and that might be artificially separated in a laboratory experiment. Like all experiments, the field experiment gives us a relatively clear idea of causal relationships. In addition, it can sometimes control conditions so as to eliminate the effects of spurious or contaminating variables, but it lacks analytical precision, the one great asset of the laboratory experiment.

F. The Laboratory Experiment

The topic of *social facilitation* of behavior was one of the earliest and most important research areas in the development of social psychology. We have long known that the level of an individual's performance on a standard task will usually be improved by the presence of passive spectators or of other individuals engaged in the same task. However, the opposite effect often seems to occur when subjects are engaged in learning or problem-solving tasks. After the 1930s, interest in social facilitation almost died, and this paradox was left unresolved until an experiment in 1966 by Zajonc and Sales, who proposed an explanation based on established principles of learning theory. The researchers suggested that the presence of other individuals has general arousal properties and, therefore, should have the same effects as an increased generalized drive state. One of the results of increased drive is the enhancement of dominant responses; therefore, if dominant responses of a particular task are largely correct ones (as in performance of well-practiced skills), the presence of other people should result in better performance. However, if dominant responses are largely incorrect (as in the early stages of learning), the presence of others should cause more incorrect responses and thus delay learning.

In the experiment, 30 subjects were individually trained to pronounce ten nonsense words. Two of these words were presented to the subject at each of five different frequencies (1, 2, 4, 8, and 16 times). The ten words were counterbalanced across training frequencies for different subjects, and the 62 presentations were arranged in a random order for each subject. When this training was completed, each subject was given a subliminal perception test in which the words were supposedly flashed on a screen one at a time for 1/100 of a second, while the subject guessed which word was exposed each time. Actually, the test slides had irregular black lines in place of letters, so any correct recognition was impossible.

Half of the subjects were shown these slides while alone in an experimental cubicle (the control condition). The other half of the subjects were told that two other persons would witness the experiment in the cubicle during the recognition test (the facilitated condition). The two spectators were always strangers to the subject and merely watched without speaking or reacting to the subject's responses.

The experimental prediction was that highly trained responses would be increased by the presence of an audience, while poorly trained responses would be decreased. (In both cases the facilitated condition was compared with the control condition as a baseline.) The prediction was verified—the interaction of these two conditions and training frequency being significant at the $p = .05$ level. Thus the results lend support to the authors' theory of social facilitation of dominant responses and social interference with subordinate responses.

Laboratory experiments, it should be emphasized, do not have to be done in a laboratory; occasionally, they can even be conducted in a real-life setting. The essential conditions for a laboratory experiment are a high degree of **control** and **precision.** The experimenter (a) designs the situation specifically for his purposes, (b) manipulates some variables, and (c) controls other variables as carefully as possible. It should also be emphasized that a laboratory experiment is not an attempt to duplicate real-life situations; if such were the purpose, a field study would be in order. Instead, the laboratory experiment is an attempt to isolate factors that may often occur together in real life, to vary some and to control others, so that the operation of each factor will be seen clearly under pure conditions. The analogy of physics experiments done in a vacuum in order to eliminate air resistance may help illustrate this point. With this degree of control and precision, definitive results are often possible, and conflicting theories can frequently be pitted against each other. By the choice of research subjects and events the researcher can even control the past history of the experimental group, a technique that would not be possible in any other setting.

Despite the many advantages of laboratory experiments, there are a number of problems. To an even greater degree than in the field experiment, the researcher using the laboratory experiment must have a great deal of knowledge about the variables involved in the study, and he must have done a great deal of pilot research before the laboratory experiment can be designed effectively. Another persistent problem for laboratory experiments is the effect of the mental set that is brought to the experiment by the subject. The subject's mental set is largely determined by the **demand characteristics** of the situation, a topic that will be discussed in more detail later. Because of the artificiality of the experimental situation, it is often difficult to create strong effects by means of experimental manipulations. For instance, it may be possible to create a mild degree of liking between subjects, but we could not possibly manipulate love experimentally. This problem means that nonsignificant results are inconclusive: results may show that our theory is wrong, or they may merely indicate that the manipulation is too weak to produce effects on the dependent variable. To help the investigator decide between these two alternatives, there should be an independent check on whether the manipulation of the experiment was successful.

An inevitable problem of laboratory experiments is the difficulty in generalizing their results back to real social situations. Because we have artificially isolated the effects of naturally covarying factors, a single experiment will tell us nothing about the real-life interactions of the variables that have been experimentally separated. Thus, the researcher must take the results back to more realistic situations and investigate the interactions of the experimental variable with other related variables. For instance, since experimenters often use groups of subjects that were formed solely for the purposes of the experiment, the researchers need to ask the additional question of whether the results with such groups would hold true for ongoing groups with a unique history, such as athletic teams, fraternity groups, or Young Democrats' clubs. Festinger, a social psychologist who is particularly noted for his laboratory experiments, expresses this last point very well in the following quotation:

> . . . laboratory experimentation, as a technique for the development of an empirical body of knowledge, cannot exist by itself. Experiments in the laboratory must derive their direction from studies of real-life situations, and results must continually be checked by studies of real-life situations. The laboratory experiment is a technique for basic and theoretical research *and is not the goal of an empirical science* [1953b, pp. 169–170, italics added].

V. RESEARCH PROBLEMS WITH POLLS AND INTERVIEWS

The following three sections of this chapter will look in greater detail at the research problems associated with three main data-collection techniques: polls and interviews, questionnaires (both of which are survey methods), and experiments. The present section takes up the problems involved with polls and interviews. As illustrated by the results of the 1970 British election, public opinion polls are sometimes spectacularly wrong. Thus, we must ask the basic question: are polls and interviews valid? The answer to this question depends on a number of dimensions, such as sampling, question wording, memory errors, social desirability needs of respondents, interviewer effects, and other factors. Failure to use proper safeguards on any one of these dimensions may be enough to invalidate the results of an opinion survey, no matter how carefully the other dimensions are handled.

A. Sampling—Choosing the Respondents

Four different types of sampling may be distinguished: haphazard sampling, systematically biased sampling, quota sampling, and probability sampling. The first, **haphazard sampling,** has no scientific value at all; yet it is used distressingly often. As the name implies, haphazard sampling involves a completely unsystematic approach to the choice of respondents; it is the usual method of inquiring reporters, who choose respondents according to a momentary whim. The key to all sampling problems is **representativeness;** in other words, the sample must be representative of some specifiable population in order to have any usefulness. The haphazard sample is not representative of any population and, therefore, has no scientific value.

The second type of sampling, **systematically biased sampling,** is also a procedure to be avoided, which usually results from an unanticipated error in an attempt to achieve representativeness. A monumental example of the errors that can result from biased sampling is a prediction made by the magazine *Literary Digest* in 1936. The magazine attempted to predict the results of the presidential elections and, in doing so, sent out tens of millions of postcard ballots to citizens all around the country. More than two million postcards were returned to the magazine, so any errors could not have been the fault of a small sample! However, there was a serious sampling bias, for the magazine had chosen its respondents from automobile registration listings and telephone books. In 1932 and previously, a similar technique had predicted the election successfully, but by 1936 a polarization had occurred in the country due to the prolonged effects of the Great Depression. The responses to the poll favored the Republican candidate, Alfred Landon, and the magazine predicted his victory. Instead, Franklin Roosevelt won by a smashing landslide, carrying all but two states; confidence in the *Literary Digest* was so badly shaken that the magazine expired two years later.

While the *Literary Digest* was failing so spectacularly, a little-known pollster named George Gallup found himself suddenly propelled to fame and fortune by correctly predicting President Roosevelt's reelection in 1936. Gallup used the quota method of sampling, which is still the basic method used by the major commercial polling organizations, though many refinements and modifications have been added since 1936. **Quota sampling,** the third major method, seeks to attain representativeness by first determining some major characteristics of the population. For instance, the population of all registered voters in the United States might be taken and broken down along several dimensions known to be related to voting patterns in past elections (for example, geographic area of the country, sex, age, rural versus urban location, economic status, race, and so on). Then a quota is established for the number of respondents in each category so that the sample has the same proportion of people in each category as does the population. This procedure avoids the most frequent sources of systematic bias and thus is more likely to yield accurate predictions than haphazard sampling or systematically biased sampling. Unfortunately, however, quota sampling does not avoid the more subtle forms of systematic bias because it still allows the interviewer a free choice of respondents within the limitations of the quota assigned him.

The fourth major type of sampling, **probability sampling,** is carried out in such a way that every member of the population has a known probability (usually an equal probability) of being contacted. The complex procedures that are necessary to ensure the satisfaction of this prerequisite make probability sampling too expensive and too slow for the major commercial pollsters. The greatest advantage to using probability sampling, however, is that the expected amount of sampling error can be stated exactly, based on the size of the sample. This is a possibility that cannot be

Figure 2-3. *A Source of Bias in Quota Sampling. In quota sampling, the interviewer, within the limits of the quotas prescribed, selects his respondents. He may choose to avoid a particular house because of its looks; he may go at only certain times of the day; or he may avoid certain people. Thus, his results can be biased by his selection procedures. (Photograph courtesy of Carl Young.)*

attained with any other sampling method, and therefore commercial polling organizations using quota sampling can only guess at the amount of error in their predictions. In general, however, commercial pollsters have done very well; during the 1950–1960 period, the Gallup Poll erred, on the average, less than 1 percent in predicting six congressional and presidential elections (Perry, 1962). There have also been fiascos, though, such as the pollsters' prediction that Dewey would defeat Truman in 1948. In a really close election, such as the 1960 contest between Kennedy and Nixon, the pollsters are forced to admit that their data are not precise enough to predict a winner.

A probability sample may be obtained in several ways. The simplest ways are **random sampling** (drawing from a container that has been shaken thoroughly or from a table of random numbers) and **systematic sampling** (picking every *n*th name from a list). Both of these methods require a complete listing of all the members of the population. When that is impossible, probability sampling becomes much more difficult and expensive. The method usually used then is *area sampling* (also called *stratified random sampling*), in which the total population is broken down into more homogeneous units such as counties and then broken down again into smaller units such as precincts or census tracts. An enumerator is sent to the randomly chosen tracts to list every dwelling unit in each tract; the sampling personnel then make a random choice of a few dwelling units, and interviewers are sent to those specific units with instructions to interview a specific person in each unit. Though area sampling is expensive and slow, this method is better than any other in ensuring the representativeness of the sample.

B. Question Wording

Planning and constructing a survey interview is a very large and complicated task, which deserves a broader treatment than is given here. Due to the limitations of space, however, only the major problems and considerations in constructing interview schedules can be listed.

1. Establishing rapport between the interviewer and the interviewee is an important aspect. The interview should usually begin with an explanation of its purpose and sponsorship, and then some simple questions should be used to put the respondent at ease.

2. A second consideration in constructing the interview is the format of the questions asked. The questions may be either structured (as in multiple choice) or unstructured. Both kinds of questions have important and legitimate uses, and many interviews use each type.

3. The order of questions is another important aspect of the interview. A frequently used approach is the *funnel sequence* of questions: broad, open-ended questions are asked first; then somewhat more limited questions are asked; and finally the questions focus very specifically on narrow aspects of the topic.

4. The vocabulary used in a question is one other important consideration. In most surveys, many respondents will have little education, limited vocabulary, and poor understanding of colloquial or technical terms. In addition to careful wording of questions, *pretesting* is essential to determine how respondents interpret the question wording.

5. A final major problem in the wording of questions in an interview is clarity. Ambiguity should be avoided by keeping the questions simple and direct. No confusing wording should be allowed, such as double negatives or double-barreled questions—ones that really ask two questions, such as: Do you favor lowering taxes and cutting government services?

Other ways of biasing a question that should be avoided are the use of emotionally charged words or phrases (terms such as communist agitators, police brutality, and the like) and the use of prestige names or symbols. If an idea is credited to a well-known public figure (for example, President Nixon's policy), usually more people will agree with the idea than had the prestige name been omitted from the question.

C. Memory Errors

Human memory is fallible, and hence many studies have been done to investigate the degree of interviewing errors resulting from faulty memory. Results show that a number of procedures can be used to increase the respondent's motivation to remember events accurately. Two such procedures are asking the respondent to consult available records (diaries, income tax forms, birth certificates, and the like) and using questions that require recognition of a response (from a list of possible responses) instead of unaided recall (Cannell & Kahn, 1968, p. 562).

D. Social Desirability Needs of Respondents

The wording of interview questions often implies that the respondent knows something about the topic: for example, "How do you feel about the government's farm policy?" Many respondents want to be obliging but do not want to show their ignorance; thus, they are inclined to fake a knowledge about the topic with replies such as, "I think it's pretty good." Since answers of this sort lead to erroneous or misleading conclusions, it is important to learn the degree of interest a respondent has in a topic before asking detailed questions.

Social desirability bias is extremely pervasive. On any topic where society's norms dictate or even suggest that one answer is more socially desirable than another, we can expect an overreporting of the good behaviors and an underreporting of the bad ones. Examples of social desirability bias are listed in Figure 2-4.

Several techniques can be used to combat social desirability bias in interviews. The interviewer should establish good rapport with the respondent and reassure the respondent by the wording of the questions and the manner of asking that a socially undesirable response is perfectly acceptable in the interviewing situation.

E. Interviewer Effects on Responses

A vast body of scientific literature shows that the interviewer's behavior and personal characteristics can influence the respondent's answers. Some of the most interesting and most pervasive factors of the interviewer's effects are listed briefly.

1. Lack of personal sensitivity and ability to build rapport with respondents is one way an interviewer affects the responses. Such interviewer characteristics lead to invalid responses (in fact, often to no responses at all).

2. Inadequate training is a second factor that affects responses. Interviewing performance can be greatly improved by careful training in field research methods (Richardson, 1954).

3. A third problem for the interviewer is variations in the stating of questions.

The following are some documented ways of the degree to which people misrepresent themselves in interviews.

1. Of 920 Denver adults interviewed in 1949, at least 34 percent who claimed to have made contributions to the Community Chest (United Givers' Fund) had not actually done so according to official records (Parry & Crossley, 1950).

2. Of the same group, 10 percent falsely claimed to have a driver's license, and 2 percent reported they did not when they actually did.

3. In a World War II study, Hyman (1944) found that 17 percent of his respondents falsely denied having cashed in any war bonds, and among upper-income groups, 43 percent refused to admit it.

4. Finally, with the passage of time, there is an increasing tendency for respondents to report that they voted for the winning candidate in past elections, no matter how they actually voted. By 1964, 66 percent of respondents reported having voted for Kennedy in 1960 instead of the 50 percent who actually did so.[a]

---

[a]Personal communication from Angus Campbell, June 29, 1967. Reprinted by permission.

Figure 2-4. *Examples of Social Desirability Bias.*

Even well-trained interviewers have been found to vary in minor—but influential—ways in their reading of questions.

4. Variations in reinforcing a respondent's answers is a fourth factor. For instance, an interviewer's use of the word good can systematically influence the respondent's subsequent answers (Hildum & Brown, 1956).

5. The interviewer's expectations can also affect the respondent's answers. One example is that interviewers expect consistency in responses to related questions and consequently often miss inconsistencies that are present (Smith & Hyman, 1950). Other expectations also undoubtedly decrease validity.

6. The interviewer's attitudes often affect responses. Interviewers tend to get (or hear) an excess of responses that are similar to their own attitudes and opinions, and thus the results obtained by interviewers with opposing opinions are often in strong disagreement (Cannell & Kahn, 1968, p. 549).

7. The interviewer's age is another factor that affects responses. It may have an effect on information obtained, particularly across the generation gap (Erlich & Riesman, 1961).

8. A final factor that can affect responses is the interviewer's race. Many studies agree that black respondents tend to give different answers to white interviewers than to black interviewers. For instance, Hyman, Cobb, Feldman, Hart, and Stember (1954) reported that black interviewers got significantly more indications of resentment over discrimination from black respondents than did white interviewers. Similar kinds of effects have been found for Jewish interviewers asking questions about attitudes toward Jews (Robinson & Rohde, 1946).

The solutions to these problems of interviewer effects are not easy. Sensitive and well-trained interviewers are a first requirement that many polling organizations fail to meet. Training can reduce variability in reading questions, in the use of probing questions, and in the types of verbal reinforcement used; and to some extent training can alert interviewers to expectational halo effects. The interviewer's attitudes, social class, sex, and age can be dealt with by the principle of balanced bias—that is, by trying to get equal numbers of interviewers from each class, age group, sex, and the like. However, this is rarely done, and the great majority of interviewers are middle-aged, middle-class women. The problem of the respondent's race, and often age and social class, can best be met by using interviewers of the same race, age, and/or social class as the respondent. Encouragingly, this is being done increasingly in recent years, especially with race; and the consequence is much more valid survey results than in the past. There is, however, always room for improvement.

F. Other Reasons for Polling Failures

Some additional reasons why polling methods fail are last-minute changes in the respondent's voting intentions, the undecided vote, people who cannot be found at home, the effects of the poll itself, and differential turnouts. Last-minute changes in voting intentions was apparently the major factor causing the wrong predictions in Truman's 1948 defeat of Dewey. Since that fiasco, the major commercial pollsters have extended the time period of their polling as late as possible, and many have adopted a last-minute telegraphic poll taken the weekend before the election. The undecided vote was also a major factor in the 1948 election, for an unusually high 19 percent of the votes were still undecided one month before the election (Campbell, Gurin, & Miller, 1954). Usually, the assumption is made that undecided respondents will split their votes in the same proportion as the respondents who have already decided, but in 1948 most of the undecided votes went for Truman.

Finding no one at home is always a headache for the pollster. Hilgard and Payne (1944) showed that people who could not be found at home until the second, third, or fourth visit had significantly different characteristics than their less peripatetic neighbors. The moral is clear: always call back. The effects of the polls themselves have not been much studied, but it is widely believed that polls affect voter turnout and the undecided vote. In the 1970 British election, a disgruntled Labour party worker concluded: "They should ban the polls. They lost it for us. Our people just stayed at home, resting on the polls' prediction that it was in the bag" (*Newsweek*, 1970c). Another possible poll effect has occurred in the United States in the last few national elections, when national television networks predicted the winning party on the basis of East Coast returns well before the close of voting on the West Coast. (In reviewing this issue, however, Weiss 1969, concludes that studies of the 1964 presidential election show no significant effect on West Coast voting from such telecasts.)

Differential turnout was apparently a major reason for the polling errors in the 1970 British election (*Newsweek*, 1970c). The only polling firm that correctly picked the Conservative party to win did so on the basis of its observation that in 1970 Labourite voters had an even lower degree of enthusiasm for their preferred candidate than usual. As the head of the polling firm put it, "We took the calculated risk—we adjusted more than usual for the turnout factor." Apparently taking risks sometimes helps in the polling business. But, in addition, it should be clear by now that there are many ways of substantially reducing every possible source of invalidity. As in other fields, eternal vigilance is the price of polling validity.

VI. RESEARCH PROBLEMS WITH QUESTIONNAIRES

Let us now turn to a consideration of the problems associated with another survey method and data-collection technique—the questionnaire. The major focus here will be on the extent to which **response sets** invalidate questionnaire answers. Response sets are systematic ways of giving answers that are not directly related to the content of the question but are related to the form or social characteristics of the alternative answers. **Social desirability** is one response set that has already been mentioned in connection with the research problems of interviews. Questionnaire studies are also hampered by social desirability as well as by other kinds of response sets such as carelessness and inconsistency of the response, faking bad, extremity of responses, yea-saying (acquiescence), or nay-saying (opposition).

A. Carelessness and Inconsistency of Response

When respondents are careless or unmotivated, their answers will be inconsistent from moment to moment or from one testing occasion to another. As a result, the questionnaire will have diminished **reliability** (consistency of measurement). Tests or questionnaires that are unreliable cannot be very high in **validity** (accuracy or correctness of measurement) and resemble an elastic tape measure that stretches a different amount each time it is used. The measurements that result from using such a device have no real value.

B. Faking Good, or Social Desirability

The response set to give socially acceptable answers (faking good) operates just as strongly in questionnaires as in interviews. Edwards (1964) has shown that the social desirability scale value of specific items on the Minnesota Multiphasic Personality Inventory (MMPI) is highly correlated with the number of "yes" answers received from people in a different group of respondents who were asked whether those items applied to them personally. Apparently traits that are judged as desirable in a given culture are also apt to be quite common among members of that culture.

Edwards has developed a set of items that indicates the degree to which an individual tends to give socially desirable answers about himself; he has also developed his own personality inventory (Edwards, 1953), which attempts to control for the social desirability of items by a *forced-choice* technique. Two items of equal social desirability, but relating to different social needs, are paired together, and the respondent has to pick the item that is most true of himself. This was a creative proposal for solving the problem of social desirability response sets, but the evidence of its success is disappointing. W. A. Scott (1968, p. 241) points out that the results are conflicting and inconclusive, while Barron (1959, p. 116) concludes that the attempt, although noble, was a failure.

A different approach to the social desirability problem was used on the MMPI (McKinley, Hathaway, & Meehl, 1948). A scale was developed to measure *defensiveness*, and scores on this scale were used as corrections for several other scales where respondents might be reluctant to admit undesirable traits or experiences. A similar, but preferable, approach was used by Gough (1957) in developing the California Psychological Inventory. He constructed a scale to measure a person's attempt to make a good impression but did not use his scale to correct other scale scores, thus allowing the identification of defensive respondents without risking the danger of distorting the respondents' other scores.

C. Faking Bad

The response set to give socially unacceptable answers (faking bad) is the exact opposite of the social desirability response set. In the general population, this tendency is probably a very rare characteristic; but, in mental health clinics, Veterans' Administration hospitals, and other psychiatric settings, it is not uncommon to find malingerers (or goldbrickers, as it is termed in the armed services), who have something to gain by claiming to be ill or upset. Since the MMPI was developed for use in such settings, its authors included a scale that has proved useful in identifying respondents who are faking bad (Hathaway & McKinley, 1951).

D. Extremity of Responses

This response set can only occur on questionnaire items where there are more than two alternative answers. For instance, a Likert-type attitude scale might have the following alternatives: $+3$ = strongly agree; $+2$ = moderately agree; $+1$ = mildly agree; -1 = mildly disagree; -2 = moderately disagree; -3 = strongly disagree. Here an extremity response set would be shown by an unusually strong tendency to pick $+3$ and -3 answers. The effects of the extremity response set on questionnaire validity have been studied very little. These effects can be diminished if equal numbers of items on any given scale are keyed in the positive and negative directions, since the $+3$ scores will then tend to counterbalance the -3 scores. Another remedy for the effects of extremity response is to eliminate the set altogether by using dichotomous items (Yes-No or Agree-Disagree). Most personality inventories usually do not suffer from this source of possible error since the dichotomous format for items is used.

E. Acquiescence, or Yea-Saying

The acquiescence response set (yea-saying) is defined as the tendency to agree with any questionnaire item regardless of its content. This response set has been studied extensively in the California F-scale measure of authoritarianism and in the MMPI, but it is also an issue in many other attitude and personality scales. The purported effects of yea-saying on the California F scale are examined in Chapter 13. Bass (1955), Gage, Leavitt, and Stone (1957), and Christie, Havel, and Seidenberg (1958) have evaluated the issue of the effects on the F scale, while Block (1965), Jackson and Messick (1965), and Rorer and Goldberg (1965) have reviewed the effects of acquiescence on MMPI responses.

F. Opposition, or Nay-Saying

A tendency to disagree with any item regardless of its content is opposition, or nay-saying, the opposite of acquiescence. This response set can be measured by low scores on the Couch and Keniston (1960) agreeing response set scale. Nay-saying is relatively rare and has been little studied; but, when it does occur, the opposition response set seems to be most common among highly educated individuals. (Perhaps it could be an occupational hazard of professors.)

G. Unobtrusive Behavioral Measures as One Solution

Clearly, response sets do affect the answers of some respondents—particularly when the questionnaire items are ambiguous or unimportant to the respondent. As we have seen, there are ways in which each kind of response set can be controlled or overcome. One additional method of circumventing the limitations of questionnaires is suggested in a fascinating paperback book called *Unobtrusive Measures* (Webb, Campbell, Schwartz, & Sechrest, 1966). If questionnaires were supplemented with the regular use of unobtrusive behavioral measures (made without attracting the attention of the persons being studied), the limitations of verbal techniques would be offset and a richer, more valid view of the respondents would be obtained. Some examples of unobtrusive measures include: (a) the amount of wear on floor tiles as an index of the popularity of museum exhibits, (b) the amount of clustering of blacks and whites in lecture halls as an indication of the comparative racial attitudes in two colleges, and (c) the number of whiskey bottles in trashcans as a measure of the level of liquor consumption in a town that was officially dry. Further use of unobtrusive approaches could overcome some of the uncertainties of interpreting interview and questionnaire research methods.

VII. RESEARCH PROBLEMS WITH EXPERIMENTS

The third main data-collection technique is the experiment. As with polls and questionnaires, there are many research problems associated with experiments. Using volunteer subjects, for example, could produce some problems in the development of general scientific principles. Other problems encountered in experimental situations include: the demand characteristics of the experiment, the effects of the experimenter's own characteristics, ethical questions involved in experimenting with human subjects, and the problem of obtaining internal and external validity.

A. Use of Volunteer Subjects

On first thought, one might assume that experimenters always use volunteer subjects because such subjects would be easiest to recruit. However, if people who volunteer for experiments differ systematically from people who do not volunteer, then the research results obtained with volunteer subjects may not apply to the rest of the population. Clearly, this would be a serious problem in the development of general scientific principles. As a matter of fact, studies on the characteristics of volunteer subjects do show that volunteers differ substantially from nonvolunteers (Rosenthal & Rosnow, 1969). Volunteers tend to have a higher educational and occupational status; they are usually more intelligent, have a greater need for approval, and are lower in authoritarianism than nonvolunteers. Since these differences might lead to differences in reactions to experimental situations, it is safest to avoid using volunteer subjects if one wishes to generalize the results to the entire population.

B. Demand Characteristics

Any situation, not only an experiment, has demand characteristics for the people who enter it. For instance, the behavior called forth upon entering a classroom is usually to sit in a row, to watch and listen to the teacher, and perhaps to ask questions, enter a general discussion, or take notes. Such demand characteristics influence our behavior in a situation, and they are defined as the perceptual cues, both explicit and implicit, which communicate what is expected in the situation (Orne, 1969).

One of the main demand characteristics in an experimental situation, according to M. T. Orne, is to be a good subject, to do what the experimenter wants, and perhaps ultimately to provide him with data that fit his hypothesis. Certainly, cooperativeness is fine, but such cooperation becomes a problem when it extends to "psyching out" the experimenter and giving him the "right" data or the "wrong" data—for either extreme is just as damaging to scientific validity. Demand characteristics cannot be eliminated from an experimental situation; however, Orne has suggested several ways in which the researcher can attempt to understand how demand characteristics might affect the data and thus take steps to minimize or counterbalance that effect. Recent research by Cook, Bean, Calder, Frey, Krovotz, and Reisman (1970) has led to the encouraging conclusion that subjects are often conscientious in following the experimental instructions even when they suspect that they have been deceived in the experiment.

C. Experimenter Effects

Experimenter effects are changes or distortions in the results of an experiment produced by the characteristics or behavior of the experimenter. Robert Rosenthal (1964, 1966) and his colleagues have studied these effects very extensively and have classified many different types. Some experimenter effects operate on the data without influencing the subject's behavior. These effects include: observation errors, recording errors, computation errors, errors in interpreting the results, and even occasional data faking. However, most experimenters affect the data by influencing the subject's behavior, in much the same way that interviewers affect the answers of respondents in polls or interviews. For instance, the experimenter's sex, race, class, warmth or hostility, anxiety, approval needs, authoritarianism, status, and research experience have all been shown to affect the behavior of experimental subjects. Evidence shows that the degree of influence and the consistency of the effects of these factors vary from one experiment to another. Two factors with rather clear-cut findings, however, are the experimenter's status and warmth. Rosenthal (1966, p. 86) has found that higher status experimenters tend to obtain more conforming but less pleasant responses from their subjects, while warmer experimenters tend to obtain more competent and more pleasant responses from their subjects.

The experimenter characteristic that has received the most attention is the experimenter's expectancies about the subject's behavior. In investigating this factor, Rosenthal and his colleagues used a large number of experimenters, usually graduates or undergraduates in psychology, some of whom were given instructions establishing one set of expectations about their subject's behavior, while the others were given contradicting expectations. The typical task used in experiments with human subjects was judging photographs of people's faces on a dimension of success or failure, using a scale from -10 to $+10$. One group of experimenters was led to believe that subjects typically rate these particular pictures in the negative part of the scale, with a mean around -5. The other group of experimenters was led to expect a mean around $+5$. The results of several similar experiments were consistent in producing the hypothesized differences between the two groups of experimenters (Rosenthal, 1966). However, the mean scores of their subjects averaged around -0.1 and $+1.1$, showing much less bias than the 5 points the experimenters were led to expect.

It should be emphasized that the experimenters were given procedures and a standard script to follow, so they could not simply tell their subjects what they expected. Instead, the expectancies of the experimenters must have been transmitted by subtle cues of voice tone, facial expression, and gestures. It has been established that auditory cues alone are sufficient to affect a subject's behavior, though a much more pronounced effect is obtained when visual cues are added. Also, the effect is often strongest at the very beginning of data collection, so the experimenter's influence must be established during the brief period when the subjects are greeted and given instructions. Surprisingly, Rosenthal and his colleagues (Rosenthal & Fode, 1963) have even found that experimenters' expectancies affect data obtained in experiments on rats. A number of suggestions for controlling experimenter expectancy effects are shown in Table 2-1 (Rosenthal, 1966, p. 402).

Another very important area of Rosenthal's research has been to investigate expectancies on the part of teachers in the public schools (Rosenthal & Jacobson, 1968). This research report, entitled *Pygmalion in the Classroom,* suggests that teachers' expectations about their pupils are like self-fulfilling prophecies, making the good student a success and the poor student a failure. The design of this research was to randomly pick 20 percent of the children in an elementary school and then point out to their teachers that, according to tests, these pupils were likely to bloom academically during the coming year. At the end of the year the whole student body (grades 1-6) was again given an academic aptitude test. In the first and second grades only, the designated bloomers were found to have gained significantly more in IQ than their classmates. Differences in achievement were also shown in reading grades assigned by the teachers and in the teachers' ratings of the children's personalities and behavior patterns. In a follow-up study at the end of the second year of research, there were still differences favoring the children in the experimental group, but most of the differences had decreased to a nonsignificant size. The mechanism by which these changes in the designated bloomers were induced is not known, since the teachers were not directly observed during the year. Rosenthal and Jacobson suggest, however, that there were probably qualitative differences in the ways teachers interacted with the bloomers as compared to interactions with the other children.

Rosenthal's research has by no means gone unchallenged; indeed, some parts have become highly controversial. Snow (1969), for example, has written a critical review of *Pygmalion in the Classroom*, in which Rosenthal and Jacobson are taken to task for a variety of improper or inappropriate statistical procedures. Along a similar vein, Barber and Silver (1968a, 1968b) have made an exhaustive analysis of 31 published studies on expectancy effects and conclude that the weight of the evidence

Table 2-1. *Suggestions for Controlling Experimenter Expectancy Effects*[a]

1. Increase number of experimenters.
2. Observe behavior of experimenters.
3. Analyze experiment for order effects.
4. Analyze experiment for computational errors.
5. Develop experimenter selection procedures.
6. Develop experimenter training procedures.
7. Maintain blind conditions (where experimenter does not know which group subjects are in).
8. Minimize experimenter-subject contact.
9. Use expectancy control groups.

[a]Adapted from Rosenthal, 1966, p. 402.

is still not sufficient to consider the effects proven. These researchers do not claim, however, that expectancy effects do not or cannot occur.

Overall, Rosenthal's research has made an important contribution to scientific knowledge. Demonstration of error, or even of potential error, is an advance in science for which Rosenthal is certainly responsible. Without question, some of the experimenter errors and influences that Rosenthal has brought attention to do occur and should be avoided wherever possible. The major questions are: How often do these errors occur, and how serious are they? Many of Rosenthal's studies may have exaggerated the generality and practical importance of the effects of experimenter bias, but in the expectancy area there is little doubt about the possibility of self-fulfilling prophecies. Perhaps Rosenthal's own expectancies may have influenced his research results; if so, can one ever avoid being the victim of his own schemes?

D. Ethical Questions

When one becomes an experimenter with human subjects and begins to manipulate and control experimental conditions, ethical questions inevitably arise. Historically, psychologists have long recognized the importance of these ethical issues. In 1953 and again in 1967, the American Psychological Association (APA) published *Ethical Standards of Psychologists*. These manuals are presently being revised in light of increased concerns about the ethicality of research practices on this topic. Only a few of the most important issues in conducting psychological research will be considered here: invasion of privacy, harmful consequences, and deception.

1. Invasion of Privacy. In 1965, both houses of Congress held extensive committee hearings on issues relating to the ethical issues of invasion of privacy. The hearings posed the threat of future government control over the use of tests and other research procedures by psychologists, and parts of the fascinating records of these hearings were reprinted in a special issue of the *American Psychologist* (*APA*, 1965). Many psychologists gave testimony about the safeguards necessary for the proper use of tests in government agencies and in individual clinical work and research.

The principles of confidentiality and anonymity of clinical and research findings have long been realized as essential safeguards of the privacy of research subjects and clients. More recently, the principle of *informed consent* has become an essential ethical requirement in experiments; this means that subjects must be given a choice as to whether they wish to participate in an experiment and that they must be told beforehand about any dangers, unpleasant experiences, or other reasons that might make them wish to withdraw.

2. Harmful Consequences. Another ethical question encountered in research studies is the possibility of harmful consequences to the subjects. In 1966 a major scandal developed over the way some medical research on cancer had been conducted (Lear, 1966). Aged and infirm hospital patients were injected with live cancer cells, having had only a very cursory description of the research and no knowledge that cancer was involved in any way. Partly as a result of the national publicity over this incident, President Johnson appointed a Panel on Privacy and Behavioral Research; the panel's report, which dealt at length with the questions of informed consent and harmful consequences, was published in *Science* in 1967 and has since been implemented by a ruling of the Surgeon General of the United States.

Several important ethical principles are involved in the issue of harmful consequences. First, an experimenter should never subject people or animals to any harmful procedures if it can be avoided. Second, risking harmful effects can only be justified if the experimental goal is of great importance in relation to the degree of risk. Third, if risks are necessary, all possible means should be adopted to minimize them. Fourth, continuing treatment or assistance should be made available to any subjects who have suffered emotionally or physically as the result of an experimental treatment. Finally, no subject should be exposed to any potentially harmful conditions without his informed consent.

These rules apply mainly to medical experiments with potentially dangerous drugs or unproven treatments; but occasionally psychological experiments involve potential dangers such as the use of stimulating drugs, electric shock, or unpleasant emotional experiences. An important example is Stanley Milgram's (1963) research on the topic of obedience, which is described in Chapters 3 and 13.

3. Deception. One other ethical principle involved in conducting research experiments is deception. It is essential that research subjects be unaware of the hypotheses of experiments if the results of the study are to be valid. In fact, the literature on experimenter bias indicates that even the experimenters should not know the hypotheses of the studies! Thus, there is considerable need for secrecy about any experiment. Further, there is need for experimental realism (Aronson & Carlsmith, 1968), so that the events of the experiment will seem convincing and have the maximum possible impact on the subjects.

Because of these needs for secrecy and experimental realism, deception has been commonly used in social psychological experiments. A frequent procedure is to present a cover story, which will mislead subjects about the main purpose of the experiment and prevent them from guessing the hypotheses being tested. Sometimes deception takes more extensive forms, such as presenting false feedback about the subject's success or failure on a task or having confederates of the experimenter make preplanned statements.

Such deception presents serious ethical questions. It is generally agreed that deception should not be used if there are other legitimate ways of achieving the same experimental goal. Also, deception should only be used when the importance of the goal of the experiment warrants the degree of deception involved. But since these principles are essentially subjective judgments, there is still controversy as to how extensive deception should be and how long it should be continued before the truth is revealed. One point on which scholars generally agree is that the subject should be very carefully debriefed at the end of the experiment. This means telling the subject the truth about all deceptions, the reasons that made deceptions necessary, and the purpose and goals of the experiment, and reassuring the subject about any relevant doubts or worries that might remain. If debriefing is done sensitively and thoroughly, most experimenters feel that subjects accept the necessity of deception and do not feel unfairly treated (Aronson & Carlsmith, 1968, p. 32).

E. Internal Validity and External Validity

In a trenchant analysis of research designs, D. T. Campbell and J. Stanley (1966) popularized the terms **internal validity** and **external validity**—two essential aspects of an experiment with any scientific value. The following definitions of the terms are offered by Campbell and Stanley.

> *Internal validity* is the basic minimum without which any experiment is uninterpretable: Did in fact the experimental treatments make a difference in this specific experimental instance? *External validity* asks the question of *generalizability*: To what populations, settings, treatment variables, and measurement variables can this effect be generalized? Both types of criteria are obviously important, even though they are frequently at odds in that features increasing one may jeopardize the other. While *internal validity* is the *sine qua non*, and while the question of *external validity*, like the question of inductive inference, is never completely answerable, the selection of designs strong in both types of validity is obviously our ideal [1966, p. 5].

Lack of internal validity can occur if experimental procedures are not sufficiently careful. For instance, if the control group was not really comparable to the experimental group, as in many of the studies that evaluated effects of the Head Start preschool program, any findings based on comparison of these two groups would be invalid. Lack of external validity or generalizability, on the other hand, can occur even if the experimental procedures are beyond reproach. A common example is experiments in which academically motivated undergraduates learn lists of nonsense syllables. Are their findings applicable to differing students in other situations, such as slow learners in a slum-area elementary school?

F. Applicability to Major Social Problems

By their very nature, most experiments are artificial situations that are not intended to duplicate any situation in the real world. As Festinger (1953b) has stated, "The laboratory experiment is a technique for basic and theoretical research"; and, as such, it is not designed to allow the direct application of its results to real social situations. Even less is the experiment intended to solve major social problems. Yet many psychologists believe that they should make some contribution to the solutions of our social problems, and many also feel that they are doing so.

It is important for one not to become irate at experiments that seem far removed from "where it's at" in the real world. One should remember that the aim of such experiments is to add a small bit to our basic supply of knowledge and not to solve social problems directly. Again, as Festinger (1953b) has stated, "Experiments in the laboratory must derive their direction from studies of real-life situations, and results must continually be checked by studies of real-life situations."

VIII. EXPECTATIONS FOR THE FUTURE

One might expect to see increasing attempts to make experimental studies and other types of research on human behavior relevant to the problems of our society. (This approach is discussed in more detail in Chapters 12, 18, 19, and 20.) However, opposing arguments state that this would be a wasteful way to use our scientific skills. Kuhn (1962, p. 163), for instance, writes:

> . . . the insulation of the scientific community from society permits the individual scientist to concentrate his attention upon problems that he has good reason to believe he will be able

to solve. Unlike the engineer, and many doctors, and most theologians, the scientist need not choose problems because they urgently need solution and without regard for the tools available to solve them.

Despite such arguments, the trend toward greater social relevance of research seems unmistakable. In 1969, for example, a presidential task force was appointed to develop social indicators to measure the state of our morale, health, and well-being in the same way that the economic indicators of gross national product and the stock market have traditionally measured our economic condition (U.S. Department of Health, Education and Welfare, 1969).

Another trend that is just beginning is the search for more unobtrusive measures to replace or to supplement our traditional reliance on interviews and questionnaires. This trend will undoubtedly continue, particularly if the concern about testing and invasion of privacy increases in coming years.

A third pattern that is developing in social psychology is a trend toward greater integration of field studies with laboratory studies (McGuire, 1967a, 1967b). In the past, there has often been little interchange between proponents of the two methods, but now quite a few researchers are making major programmatic efforts to utilize both methods and to check their results back and forth continually between the two settings. (This point will be handled again in the final chapter.)

In addition, there is a continuing thrust for more careful attention to ethical issues in research. Soon after the appearance of the 1967 report of the Presidential Panel on Privacy and Behavioral Research, the American Psychological Association began a new study of ethical questions in research with human subjects, which will add to the official APA ethical code.

A final development that is looming on the horizon is the likelihood of more governmental and legal control over research projects and their methods. The major question at this point is whether Congress and the public will consider the APA ethical code sufficient protection for subjects, or whether restrictive legislation will be necessary.

IX. SUMMARY

Scientific method is a cyclical process of establishing facts about the world. Its main steps are (a) induction of one or more theoretical propositions from observed facts, (b) deduction of some logical consequences of these theoretical propositions, and (c) verification of the predicted consequences by collecting new observations. Other distinguishing features of the scientific method are that it is based on the assumption of determinism, uses the empirical approach, utilizes operational definitions of concepts, and is objective in its deductions and verifications. To the extent that these requirements are met, any field of study can be scientific.

The experimental method consists of (a) manipulation of one or more independent variables, (b) control of related variables, and (c) observation of one or more dependent variables. In contrast, the correlational method is nonmanipulative in nature, for it studies naturally occurring relationships between variables. The correlational method is essential for studying variables such as personality traits, which cannot be manipulated; it is less satisfactory than the experimental method in providing information upon which to base inferences about cause and effect.

This chapter has described and illustrated the six major research methods of the social psychologist: (a) archival research, (b) surveys, (c) field studies, (d) natural experiments, (e) field experiments, and (f) laboratory experiments. The three data-collection techniques discussed in this chapter are (a) polls and interviews, (b) questionnaires, and (c) experiments.

Research problems in using polls and interviews include decisions about sampling and question wording, memory errors and social desirability needs of respondents, interviewer effects on responses, and other situational factors affecting the validity of the data. The major research problem in using questionnaires involves determining the extent to which many kinds of response sets may invalidate questionnaire answers and then finding ways to control or overcome the effects of each kind of response set. Research problems in experiments include the use of volunteers or other atypical subjects, the demand characteristics of the experimental situation, the effects caused by the experimenter himself, and ethical questions about issues such as invasion of privacy, deception, and possible harmful consequences of the experiment. Additional considerations that should be weighed are the experiment's internal and external validity and its applicability to real-life situations.

Trends that seem to be growing in social psychological research include the use of unobtrusive behavioral measures, greater integration of laboratory and field studies, efforts to apply research findings to the problems of society, increasing attention to ethical questions in research, and the possibility of increased governmental and legal restrictions on research methods and topics.

X. SUGGESTED READINGS

Campbell, D. T., & Stanley, J. C. *Experimental and quasi-experimental designs for research.* Chicago: Rand McNally, 1966. (Paperback) A very thorough, detailed description of many different research designs, emphasizing the relative vulnerability of each design to 12 different sources of invalidity.

Festinger, L., & Katz, D. (Eds.) *Research methods in the behavioral sciences.* New York: Dryden, 1953. Very thorough discussions of the survey method, field studies, field experiments, and laboratory experiments (pp. 13–172). Also, a useful discussion of some of the technical aspects of sampling procedures (pp. 173–239).

Kemeny, J. G. *A philosopher looks at science.* Princeton, N. J.: Van Nostrand, 1959. A very readable and lucid presentation of the philosophy of science. Particularly good descriptions of the scientific method contained in Chapter 5 and Chapter 10.

Selltiz, C., Jahoda, M., Deutsch, M., & Cook, S. W. *Research methods in social relations.* (Rev. ed.) New York: Holt, 1959. An excellent discussion of factors involved in making causal inferences from nonexperimental studies (pp. 127–143).

Webb, E. J., Campbell, D. T., Schwartz, R. D., & Sechrest, L. *Unobtrusive measures: Nonreactive research in the social sciences.* Chicago: Rand McNally, 1966. (Paperback) An intriguing account of unusual methods of studying social attitudes and behavior without attracting the attention of the people being studied.

I. *ASSUMPTIONS ABOUT HUMAN NATURE IN OTHER DISCIPLINES*
   A. *Contemporary literature*
   B. *Social and political philosophy*
      1. *Hedonism*
      2. *Egoism (power)*
      3. *Other proposed explanatory concepts*

II. *ASSUMPTIONS ABOUT THE NATURE OF MAN IN PSYCHOLOGY*

III. *EARLY APPROACHES TO HUMAN NATURE*
   A. *Theory X and Theory Y*
   B. *Maslow's hierarchy of motives*

IV. *CONCEPTUALIZING ASSUMPTIONS ABOUT HUMAN NATURE*
   A. *Philosophies of human nature*
      1. *Dimensions of philosophies of human nature*
      2. *Measurement and findings*
   B. *Machiavellianism and Machiavellian assumptions about human nature*
      1. *What is Machiavellianism?*
      2. *Are the attitudes of most individuals highly Machiavellian or un-Machiavellian?*
      3. *The interpersonal behavior of Machiavellian persons*
   C. *Conceptual systems*
      1. *System 1*
      2. *System 2*
      3. *System 3*
      4. *System 4*

V. *ASSUMPTIONS ABOUT PEOPLE IN THE FUTURE*
   A. *Our introspective society*
   B. *Implications for blueprinting a theory of human nature*
   C. *Psychology's role in determining assumptions about human nature*

VI. *SUMMARY*

VII. *SUGGESTED READINGS*

Chapter Three

Our Assumptions about the Nature of Man

The difference between us, Wells, is fundamental. You don't care for humanity but think they are to be improved. I love humanity but know they are not.
Joseph Conrad, writing to H. G. Wells.

For most of us, human nature is a pervasive and useful concept. We rely upon it frequently to justify our own behavior and the behavior of others, saying it is only human nature to do this or that. Our beliefs about human nature may influence everything from the way we bargain with a used-car dealer to our expectations about nuclear war. But if one person's beliefs about human nature differ from the next person's, who is correct? Indeed, one can legitimately ask whether there is such a thing as human nature. Social psychologists recognize that there are some consistent characteristics of human nature regardless of the culture, the times, or the specific environment. Not only are there universalities in physiological responses but also consistencies in psychological characteristics—perception of emotions, linguistic structure, and the like. But social psychologists vigorously reject the idea that there is one basic human nature common to all religious groups, all ages, and all situations. At the same time, it is agreed that our beliefs about human nature can be studied from the viewpoint of social psychology. People's assumptions about the nature of man can be conceptualized and measured, and one can determine if these beliefs influence behavior toward others.

Recent developments in our society and within the field of psychology lead us to expect that beliefs or assumptions about human nature will increase in importance within the domain of social psychology. The purpose of this chapter is to explore these assumptions about people or basic beliefs that people are generally good or bad, trustworthy or untrustworthy, strong or weak, simple or complex, and so on. We will first describe how other disciplines, such as literature and social and political philosophy, generate assumptions about the nature of man; then we will look at three social psychological approaches, which employ the concepts of philosophies of human nature, Machiavellianism and conceptual systems.

Figure 3-1. *Assumptions about Human Nature. A man rings your doorbell late at night when you are alone and asks to use your telephone. He claims his car has broken down, and he needs to call for help. How do you respond? What assumptions do you make about the nature of such requests? About the man? Does it make any difference if the man is unshaven? A policeman? A black? Well-dressed? (Photograph courtesy of Carl Young.)*

I. ASSUMPTIONS ABOUT HUMAN NATURE IN OTHER DISCIPLINES

A. Contemporary Literature

Fictional literature has always served as a vehicle for analyzing man's apparent nature. Since World War II, a succession of novels has excited the interest of college-age youth. The first of these was *Catcher in the Rye,* then *Lord of the Flies,* then *Catch-22,* and more recently *Stranger in a Strange Land.* Doubtless, there are many reasons why one particular book is a success while another is not, but the reason we wish to emphasize is that a popular book deals with salient aspects of the nature of man and thus appeals to those who are trying to resolve or clarify beliefs about their own nature. For example, in *Catcher in the Rye,* Holden Caulfield wants to love and care for other people; the title of the book comes from Caulfield's dream of catching any child who falls while playing in a field of rye grass. Yet Holden sees the adult world as pervasively phony, ugly, and materialistic, and he is unwilling to accept that world as his. In one sense he is a precursor of today's anarchist (Grunwald, 1962).

In *Lord of the Flies,* the nature of the noble savage is clinically examined. The author, William Golding, admits that the violence of World War II caused him to revise completely his youthful conception of man (Baker, 1965) and shift to what might be described as a Calvinistic belief in the evil nature of man bereft of any possibility of redemption. Readers may agree or disagree with Golding's prediction that violence and chaos would result after a group of upper-class English boys descended upon an uninhabited tropic island. Yet there is something about *Lord of the Flies*—perhaps the discovery of evil within the self (Oldsey & Weintraub, 1965)—that has intrigued the younger generation, a feat never accomplished by Robert Ballantyne's *Coral Island,* a seemingly similar book. In *Coral Island,* the same situation holds, but everything comes off auspiciously. The boys master the difficult environment with ingenuity. "The fierce pirates who invade the island are defeated by sheer moral force, and the tribe of cannibalistic savages is easily converted and reformed by the example of Christian conduct afforded them" (Baker, 1965). By comparing *Lord of the Flies* and *Coral Island,* we can hold before us two radically different pictures of human nature and society—two hypotheses about what would happen if the ordinary laws and rules of society were to be removed. The question is: which hypothesis is more accurate?

In *Catch-22,* the basic issue is whether the world is rational, man is irrational, or just which one of the two is crazy. The irrationality of the situation is demonstrated by the meaning of the title *Catch-22.* An airman can escape from the situation if he obtains a medical discharge because of insanity. But to get a medical discharge he must apply for one, and to apply for a medical discharge—to attempt to escape from an irrational situation—is proof of one's sanity. That is the "catch" and the system's way of preventing a rational man from escaping it. The protagonist, Yossarian, is a crew member of an American bomber squadron in Italy during World War II. He awakes from a nightmare that the Germans are trying to kill him. "No one's trying to kill you," his buddy tells him. "Then why are they shooting at me?" Yossarian asks. "They're shooting at everyone," his buddy replies; "They're trying to kill everyone." Although Yossarian's undiscerning buddy is a fictional character, we are reminded of his real-life counterparts by comments such as the one made by a U. S. Army major during the Vietnam war; said the officer: "We had to destroy the village in order to save it."

A more recent book of significance is Robert Heinlein's *Stranger in a Strange Land,* an iconoclastic book that calls into question the basic structure of our society, challenging the system of economics, religion, and marriage, and substituting a simplistic ethic of universal love. The book also recognizes that until the world is converted to this ethic, steps may have to be taken to eliminate or "discorporate" those who oppose this philosophy. Thus, a theme is apparent here, which espouses both a very positive and a very negative view of human nature.

Fiction of all kinds abounds with references about the nature of man. We may quote, for example, from one of America's most widely read contemporary fictional characters: "I have an undying faith in human nature. . . . I believe that people who want to change can do so, and I believe they should be given a chance to do so." That was spoken by Charlie Brown, of Peanuts cartoon fame, on the eve of one of his annual football place-kicking episodes. In the scene, Lucy offers to hold the ball for a place-kick; but from past experience, Charlie distrusts her for a fleeting instant. Then he becomes convinced that Lucy has truly redeemed herself. Only when his foot is in the air does Charlie Brown realize that once again Lucy has, at the last instant, withdrawn the ball. As Charlie Brown tumbles to the ground, not only is his anatomy sorely abused, but so is his "undying faith in human nature."

B. Social and Political Philosophy

Throughout history, social and political philosophers have sought answers to the question: what is the social nature of man? In an attempt to answer this question,

Figure 3-2. *Charlie Brown's Assumptions about Human Nature. (Reprinted with permission; © 1968, United Feature Syndicate, Inc.)*

philosophers constructed theories tied together with conceptions about the nature of the polity and of society. Plato, for example, believing that men formed social groups because they needed to, developed a utilitarian or social contract theory for the affiliative nature of man. Aristotle, however, saw man's gregarious or affiliative nature as something instinctive or constitutional: "Man," wrote the philosopher, "is by nature a political social animal." Contemporary social psychology largely ignored this basic question of why people want to be with others, until Stanley Schachter began his work in the middle 1950s. (This topic is reviewed in Chapter 14.)

Social and political philosophers have also advanced certain concepts, such as **hedonism** and **power,** in an attempt to capsulate the basic nature of man. Moreover, questions about the formation of human nature have persisted. "Are all men basically alike and only superficially different, or are the differences among them basic? How does man become the way he is? Is his basic nature 'built in,' or does he change through experience?" (McGrath, 1964, p. 6).

1. Hedonism. From the concepts that have been used to explain man's basic nature, hedonism must have had the longest hearing. The Greek philosopher Epicurus, who lived in the 3rd century B.C., proposed that pleasure was man's ultimate goal and should be a determinant of behavior (Wilcoxon, 1969). Jeremy Bentham (1749–1832) further advanced the concept of hedonism with the theory that men act to secure pleasure and avoid pain. Some thinkers feel that the principle of hedonism can explain all of human behavior, even behaviors that are deliberately painful. Going to the dentist, for example, can be viewed as hedonism, or the securing of pleasure, as long as greater pain is avoided in the long run. Even such painful and mortal actions as a soldier sacrificing his own life for the rest of his platoon may be seen as a verification of hedonism, if—as the hedonist would have it—we conclude that the soldier's alternative—letting his buddies die—would cause even more pain.

The basic difficulty of hedonism as a concept to explain human behavior, however, is that hedonism is tautological. In other words, there are no definitions of pleasure and pain apart from the actions taken. Pleasure is simply defined in the context of what is chosen.

As a philosophical position, hedonism is more or less a dead issue; but some question remains as to whether the field of psychology encompasses certain hedonistic assumptions that man *does* seek to pursue pleasure and avoid pain. On the one hand, Wilcoxon (1969), in reviewing philosophical antecedents of reinforcement theory, sees hedonism as of little direct relevance to contemporary psychology. Gordon Allport (1968), on the other hand, sees a similarity in the concepts of psychological hedonism and reinforcement. While pleasure is presently not an operational term in psychology, reinforcement is. Dollard and Miller (1950, p. 9), for example, have stated that the principle of reinforcement has been substituted for Freud's pleasure principle, while the concept of pleasure has proved a difficult and slippery notion in the history of psychology. Even though reinforcement refers to past pleasure or satisfaction rather than future pleasure, Allport concludes that the hedonistic flavor is still present in reinforcement theory, which is a dominant theory in contemporary psychology. This hedonistic flavor may be detected in the assumptions of early versions of reinforcement theory—that is, all actions seek tension reduction and man's behavior is always an attempt to avoid pain. As long as a psychological theory assumes that *all* motivation seeks to avoid or reduce tensions or deficits, the conception of man contained therein is a hedonistic one. Such a conception, however, is waning in psychology, and reinforcement theorists like Neal Miller (1959) conclude that the evidence does not verify the universal applicability of a tension-reduction or drive-reduction hypothesis. In fact, Wilcoxon (1969, pp. 41–42) presents a recent review of findings that indicate some behavior seeks increases in stimulation rather than drive reduction.

2. Ego m (power). Thomas Hobbes (1588–1679) theorized that egoistic conflict is so prominent that the state of mankind must be viewed as a "war of all against all." To Hobbes, power was man's foremost preoccupation; and, through it, one gets pleasure and all else. Social contracts arise from the need to curb insatiable power and to obtain protection. Nietzsche also saw power as the dominant motive of man; in *The Will to Power* (1912), he wrote: "What man wills, what every smallest part of a living organism wills, is a plus of power. Both pleasure and unpleasure are consequences of striving for it." Machiavelli, acting as a consultant to an Italian prince, likewise advised that power was the vehicle by which a leader could lead; the prince "should prefer to be feared than to be beloved." In our own times, a contemporary American social psychologist, Richard Christie (1970), has created a scale to measure the degree of one's Machiavellian orientation. (The results of Christie's research program will be described subsequently.)

To these thinkers, then, all social behavior is a direct or disguised reflection of power seeking. Alleged motives of altruism, love, truth, and religion turn out to be, in Allport's words, "hollow shams."

Such stark conceptions of human nature like Hobbes's and Machiavelli's have had only minimal influence in contemporary social psychology, Christie's work notwithstanding. Power is still recognized as a basic motive but has been studied much less than the achievement motive or the affiliative motive. In this sense, the interests of social psychologists have been responsive to the dominant needs of contemporary society. We may speculate that in the future the visibility and strength of the achievement motive in American society (and hence in social psychology) will weaken, as the work week shrinks and technology replaces manpower. The affiliation motive will remain strong, however, and the power motive will gain in influence and study.

3. Other proposed explanatory concepts. Although space does not permit us to describe in appropriate detail other concepts that have been advanced as simple and sovereign explanations of the nature of man, they may be mentioned briefly. Among such concepts are: rationality and irrationality, suggestibility, sympathy, and imitation. The reader may consult Allport (1968) for an extensive review.

II. ASSUMPTIONS ABOUT THE NATURE OF MAN IN PSYCHOLOGY

In the last ten years, social psychologists have abandoned their early reluctance to study assumptions about the nature of man. Growing interest in operational assumptions stems partly from an increasing conviction that emulating the methodology of advanced sciences such as physics has caused, in psychology, a tendency to avoid studying some of the important aspects of human behavior. For example, concern with objectivity and precision in measurement has led to a disproportionate number of studies on attackable, constricted topics. In opposition to traditional views, Nevitt Sanford (1965) has stated that society "ought to encourage psychologists to study problems that people really worry about [rather] than only those problems formulated on the basis of reading the professional journals" (p. 192). Indeed, a growing movement within psychology is approaching the basic concerns of human beings from a combination of both the scientific and humanistic viewpoints.

Hand in hand with this movement toward an increasingly humanistic approach is the belief that assumptions about the nature of man required by a strictly scientific approach communicate an image of man that is mechanistic, passive, and—most important—unreal. Psychologist Frederick Wyatt (1963, p. 575) has stated that "unless psychologists wish to insist on offering the world a distorted and incomplete image of man, they cannot continue to reject contact with the humanities." Unfortunately, however, psychology still offers incomplete images of man. The words of one prominent, contemporary behavior-shaper may be taken as an example: "I would conceive of man clearly in the robot end of the continuum. That is, his behavior can be completely determined by outside stimuli. Even if man's behavior is determined by internal mediating events such as awareness, or thinking, or anxiety, or insight, these events can be manipulated by outside stimuli so that it is these stimuli which basically determine our behavior" (Krasner, 1965, p. 22). In defense of this position, we should note that such an assumption is felt to be necessary to the progress of a scientific study of human behavior. But Isidor Chein (1962), among others, has helped psychologists recognize the inconsistency between man as conceptualized and man as experienced. Chein in particular has noted the discrepancy between our everyday actions as free agents and the psychological espousal of determinism as a scientific principle of our lives. For example, it may be necessary for some psychologists, as scientists, to assume that all man's behaviors have causes that can ultimately be identified. (Within the assumption of determinism, all events must have causes.) But the psychologist, as a living, breathing, choosing person, may assume that he and others possess free will.

Ira Gordon (1966) has shown how warped images of human nature apply to teachers' conceptions of children. According to the Newtonian model of human nature, man was a fixed, closed system, characterized by fixed intelligence, orderly development, and fixed—though indeterminable—potential. In a similar manner of thinking, teachers have assumed that the IQ is a fixed entity in young children. But as Gordon says, this kind of world does not exist. Currently, there is a shift to the "Einsteinian view, in which development is seen as open-ended and intelligence as modifiable" (Gordon, 1966, p. 2).

III. EARLY APPROACHES TO HUMAN NATURE

Psychologists are becoming concerned about the images of man that we promote. However, the subject matter of these images and the consequent beliefs about human nature have received little empirical study until recently. The work of two psychologists, Douglas McGregor and Abraham Maslow, provided theory-based stimulants for recent interest.

A. Theory X and Theory Y

Douglas McGregor (1960) observed and analyzed two theories of motivation prevalent in industry, each reflecting a different set of assumptions about human nature. These two contradictory theories are summarized in Table 3-1. Theory X and Theory Y represent two extreme views of the nature of man. The two theories are provocative, but they fail to provide a middle ground or recognize the individual differences between people. For example, a plant manager might find that Theory Y is appropriate to some workers, while Theory X is necessary for others. A teacher may

Table 3-1. *McGregor's Theory X and Theory Y*

Assumptions in Theory X: The traditional view
1. The average human being has an inherent dislike of work and will avoid it if he can.
2. Because of this human characteristic of disliking work, most people must be coerced, controlled, directed, and threatened with punishment before they will put forth adequate effort toward the achievement of organizational objectives.
3. The average human being prefers to be directed, wishes to avoid responsibility, has relatively little ambition, and wants security above all.
Assumptions in Theory Y: The integrative view
1. The expenditure of physical and mental effort in work is as natural as play or rest.
2. External control and the threat of punishment are not the only means for bringing about movements toward organizational objectives. Man will exercise self-direction and self-control in the services to which he is committed.
3. Commitment to objectives is a function of the rewards associated with achievement of the objectives.
4. The average human being learns, under proper conditions, not only to accept but to seek responsibility.
5. The capacity to exercise a relatively high degree of imagination, ingenuity, and creativity in the solution of organizational problems is widely, not narrowly, distributed in the population.
6. Under the conditions of modern industrial life, the intellectual potentialities of the average human being are only partially utilized.

(*From* The Human Side of Enterprise *by D. McGregor. Copyright 1960 by McGraw-Hill Book Company. Used by permission.*)

find that Johnny studies only in anticipation of an exam, while Sterling studies for the love of acquiring knowledge. McGregor did not develop his theory extensively and proposed no measuring devices, but a team of psychologists (Herzberg, Mausner, & Snyderman, 1959; Herzberg, 1966) has applied the theory to an analysis of job satisfactions and dissatisfactions. Table 3-2 presents some of their findings.

B. Maslow's Hierarchy of Motives

Implicit within the framework of Theory X and Theory Y is the assumption that man can be shifted from traditional ways of behaving (Theory X) to integrative ways of behaving (Theory Y), if environmental controls are loosened. The assumption of a hierarchy of motives within man's nature is more explicit than this in the theory of Abraham Maslow (1954). Maslow's approach to man's nature holds that a set of potent physiological needs exists—such as hunger, thirst, and the like—which must be satisfied before the individual can demonstratè concern for needs that are higher in the hierarchy. As first described by Maslow (1954), this hierarchy is summarized in Table 3-3.

According to Maslow's theory, as long as man must devote his energies to the satisfaction of a lower need, he will not be able to show any or much concern for higher social needs. In order for self-actualizing motives to become activated and to lead to behavior, the individual must be free from deficits—or pressing needs to seek physiological goals, safety goals, or even the social goals of love and belonging-

Table 3-2. *Can a Job Be Satisfying and Unsatisfying at the Same Time?*

McGregor distinguished between two contrasting theories about the nature of the worker. From this approach, Herzberg and his colleagues postulated that the worker possesses two sets of needs: a set of needs to avoid pain and a set to grow psychologically. This conception led to the possibility that factors causing a worker to be dissatisfied with a job might not be the opposite of those factors that made a job satisfying. After interviewing a large number of engineers and accountants, Herzberg, Mausner, and Snyderman (1959) established the following factors as relevant in the worker's evaluation of his job.

Job satisfaction	*Job dissatisfaction*
1. Opportunities for achievement	1. Undesirable company policies and administration
2. Degree of recognition	2. Lack of supervision or poor supervision
3. The nature of the work itself	3. Poor salary
4. Degree of responsibility in the job	4. Bad interpersonal relationships
5. Opportunities for advancement	5. Bad working conditions

Surprisingly, the two sets of factors are largely unrelated. The "job satisfaction" factors all describe the worker's relation to what he does; the "job dissatisfaction" factors deal with the environment or setting in which the worker does his job. The satisfaction factors contribute to what is now called a *motivator* orientation; here, the worker seeks a job with opportunities for professional stimulation and growth in one's own capabilities. In contrast, the worker with a *hygiene* orientation is more interested in finding a job where the job dissatisfaction factors are minimized.

Measures are now available by which the degree of motivator orientation and hygiene orientation can be assessed for individual workers. Knowing the worker's orientation on each issue is important.

The demonstration that factors contributing to job satisfaction are *separate* and *distinct* from factors contributing to job dissatisfaction is relevant to McGregor's original Theory X-Theory Y distinction. The innovative view of Theory Y deals with factors included in the motivator orientation. While we hope that employees will increasingly implement the assumptions of Theory Y, they should not forget that meeting motivator needs or the conditions of Theory Y does not necessarily remove the possibility of job dissatisfaction.

Source: Herzberg, Mausner, & Synderman, 1959; Herzberg, 1966.

Table 3-3. *Maslow's Hierarchy of Needs*

1. *The physiological needs*: hunger, thirst, air, and the like.
2. *The safety needs*: the need for freedom from threat or danger and the need to ally oneself with the familiar and the secure.
3. *The belongingness and love needs*: the need for affiliation, belongingness, and acceptance.
4. *The esteem needs*: the need for achievement, strength, competence, reputation, and status or prestige.
5. *Cognitive needs*: the need to know and understand, the need to satisfy curiosity, the need to understand the mysterious, and the need to tackle the unknown.
6. *Aesthetic needs*: the need for symmetry, order, system, and structure.
7. *The need for self-actualization*: the need for self-fulfillment and the realization of potentialities and the need to become what one is capable of becoming.

ness. Thus, Maslow conceives of the development of needs as **invariant,** in the sense that they must be satisfied in a prescribed order. As will be seen in Chapter 4, theories of the development of morality also rely upon a conception of invariant stages.

IV. CONCEPTUALIZING ASSUMPTIONS ABOUT HUMAN NATURE

If we grant that persons carry around their own somewhat idiosyncratic beliefs about human nature, how do we go about conceptualizing, defining, and measuring these beliefs? Three ways of conceptualizing assumptions about human nature shall be discussed here—possessing a philosophy of human nature, Machiavellian assumptions about human nature, and conceptual systems.

A. Philosophies of Human Nature

The first approach to conceptualizing assumptions about man postulates that everyone possesses a **philosophy of human nature,** or some expectancy that people have certain qualities and will behave in certain ways (Wrightsman, 1964a). Thus, although one person's philosophy of human nature may be quite different from another's, what is common to both of them is the fact that they employ some philosophy or set of beliefs about the nature of man. We must construct philosophies because people account for so much of our environment that we could not tolerate life if others were constantly surprising us. As Herzberg has stated, "No society can exist without an implicit conception of what people are like" (1966, p. 13).

Within this broad concept of philosophies of human nature, there are more specific and significant dimensions. In accordance with Osgood's (Osgood, Suci & Tannenbaum, 1957) finding that an evaluative component accounts for a large part of our attitudes toward any object, one basic evaluative dimension could be postulated—one believes that people are either good or bad. On the one hand, for example, novelist Pearl Buck has written: "My knowledge of people compels me to believe that the normal human heart is born good. . . . If through circumstances it is overcome by evil, it never becomes entirely evil." On the other hand, Sigmund Freud wrote in a letter to Fliess that he believed "with a few exceptions, human nature is basically worthless" (E. Freud, 1960). It is intriguing to compare Freud's statement to a comment by Carl Rogers, the originator of client-centered therapy: "In my experience I have discovered man to have characteristics which seem inherent in his species . . . terms such as positive, forward-moving, constructive, realistic, trustworthy" (1957, p. 200). The differences between the counseling techniques of Freud and Rogers reflect these differences in assumptions about human nature.

1. Dimensions of philosophies of human nature. More specific dimensions than a basic evaluative one appear to be operative in various philosophies of human nature. An analysis of writings by philosophers, theologians, and social scientists has generated the postulation that our beliefs about human nature have six basic dimensions (Wrightsman, 1964a). Each dimension will be described here, along with some examples of different viewpoints on each dimension and examples of social psychological findings relevant to each dimension.

The first dimension of a personal philosophy of human nature is *trustworthiness* versus *untrustworthiness*—or the extent to which one believes that people are basically trustworthy, honest, and responsible as opposed to believing that people are untrustworthy, immoral, and irresponsible. Carl Rogers' vigorous affirmation of man's trustworthiness has already been mentioned. Erik Erikson (1950, 1959, 1964) has postulated that the first conflict in an infant's psychological development is whether he trusts or distrusts his mother. In a similar vein, Edith Weigert (1962), a psychoanalyst, says that man is a creature who must experience trust: "Before the child develops any thinking or verbal expression of his emotions he learns to trust, since he experiences without consciousness that his needs for survival, growth, and development fit into his parents' needs to give gratification and protection in mutually adaptive, tender cooperation" (p. 7).

Contrary to the beliefs of Rogers, Erikson, and Weigert, recent speculations have advanced the notion that man has a basically aggressive, uncooperative instinct. Evidence from recent fossil discoveries (Ardrey, 1961, 1966) and from ethological observations (Lorenz, 1966) has been used to support these notions. (These speculations will be further examined in Chapter 6.) Certain philosophical influences also emphasize the sinful nature of man. Albert Outler, a contemporary theologian, has criticized Carl Rogers for considering only one side of man's nature. Similarly, Calvinist and fundamentalist theology holds that man is born and continues to live in sin—although implicit within this viewpoint is the belief that man should still be trusted.[1]

The second dimension of philosophies of human nature is *altruism* versus *selfishness*—or the extent to which one believes that people are basically unselfish and sincerely interested in others as opposed to believing that they are basically selfish and unconcerned about others. Again, both theories and research on this issue are conflicting. The Golden Rule is a guide for behavior in our society, which no doubt many people adhere to, but perhaps it is a mode of behavior that is honored more in the breach than in the observance and sometimes not advocated at all. George Bernard Shaw, in fact, advised us not to follow it: "Do not do unto others what you would like done unto you—their tastes may be different" (quoted in Erikson, 1964).

[1] Rotter (1971) has developed a similar concept to trustworthiness, which he calls "interpersonal trust." The concept is described as "a person's generalized expectancy that the promises of other individuals or of groups with regard to future behavior can be relied upon" (Hochreich & Rotter, 1970, p. 211). Rotter has found that recent college classes possess lowered degrees of interpersonal trust—a finding that corroborates evidence from another study that freshmen classes between the years 1962 and 1968 became progressively more negative in their philosophies of human nature (Wrightsman & Baker, 1969).

Recent well-publicized incidents where persons seeking help were ignored by many passersby have caused Americans to reevaluate their beliefs about the extent of altruism in human nature. The murder of Kitty Genovese, discussed in Chapter 2, is a case in point. This incident deservedly received much publicity, and it has frequently been interpreted as an indication of the growing apathy and indifference to human distress that results from the impersonal complexities of modern life (Wainwright, 1964). The incident also led to a research program by Darley and Latané (1968a, 1968b, Latané & Darley, 1968, 1970a, 1970b), who found that one reason why each person failed to act was because of an awareness that a large number of other people were also watching. (See Chapter 2 for a discussion of this explanation of *diffusion of responsibility.)*

Subsequent research by Latané and Rodin (1969) has dealt with responses to the victim of a fall. The findings show the impossibility of making a general statement about the degree of altruism present in human nature. For example, if the observers to the accident were strangers to one another, they were less likely to aid the victim than if they had been prior acquaintances. Other situational factors are also important. If a person has just observed another person perform a helpful act, he himself is more likely to act as a good Samaritan (Bryan & Test, 1967; Bryan, 1970). When mixed racial groups observe a victim in difficulty, there is some tendency for observers of the same race as the victim to offer help more often than for observers of another race to do so (Piliavin, Rodin & Piliavin, 1969). Population differences also appear to be important in willingness to help. People in urban areas are less likely to help than those from smaller towns or rural areas (Milgram, 1970; Clark & Word, 1971).

The presence or absence of communication between witnesses may be an important determinant of the degree of help offered. Piliavin, Rodin, and Piliavin used a New York City subway train as the locale in which a victim (actually a confederate) staggered and fell to the floor of the car in motion. (The trains selected were express trains, which do not stop for periods of seven and one-half minutes.) On different trips (all between 11 A.M. and 3 P.M. on weekdays), four different victims were used. All were males between the ages of 26 and 35; three were white, and one was black. All the victims were dressed the same, in Eisenhower jackets, old slacks, and no tie. The mean number of passengers in the critical area of the car where the incident was staged was 8.5. On 38 of the trips, the victim smelled of liquor and carried à liquor bottle wrapped tightly in a brown bag (this was called the "drunk" condition); on the remaining 65 trips, the victim appeared sober and carried a black cane (the "cane" condition). The degree to which observers came to the aid of the victim was impressive. The victim with the cane received spontaneous help in 62 of 65 trips, while the drunk victim received help on 19 of the 38 trips. Helpful responses also occurred more quickly with the seemingly ill victim than with the drunk one.

Figure 3-3 represents the setting for this study. Since on the average there were 8.5 observers in the area of the car where the victim fell and anywhere from 15 to 120 passengers in the whole car, this high incidence of giving aid may at first seem to contradict the principle of diffusion of responsibility, where the larger the group, the less likely it is that an individual will take action (Latané & Darley, 1968). We must remember, however, that the subjects used by Darley and Latané were not in visual or auditory communication, while the subway observers were. The latter group not only felt more cohesive because of their mutual visibility but could also see whether anyone else had yet made a move to help. Nonetheless, there are far too many

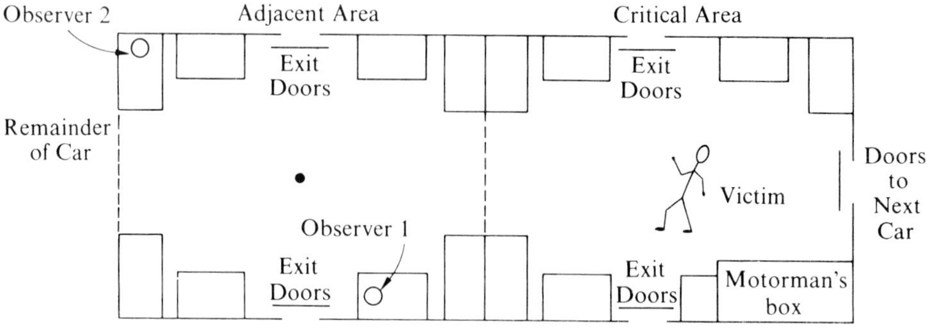

Layout of adjacent and critical areas of subway car

Figure 3-3. *Setting for "The Subway Victim Study." Reprinted from Piliavin, Rodin, & Piliavin, "Good Samaritanism: An Underground Phenomenon?" In* Journal of Personality and Social Psychology, **13**, *1969, 289–299. Copyright 1969 by the American Psychological Association, and reproduced by permission.*

variations among the subjects, tasks, and procedures of the laboratory experiments of Darley and Latané and the field experiment of Piliavin et al. to conclude that inter-subject visibility causes different results.[2]

The third dimension of philosophies of human nature is *independence versus conformity to group pressures*—or the extent to which one believes that a person can maintain his convictions in the face of pressures to conform from a group, society, or some authority figure. Indeed, ours has sometimes been called the age of conformity. In his book, *The Organization Man,* William H. Whyte, Jr., has deplored the emergence of the person whose advancement through the business organization progresses, not because of his creativity or motivation, but because he can roll with the tides of authority. Stanley Milgram's work on obedience (1963, 1965) likewise elicits a pessimistic view of man. In Milgram's study, men from a community were hired to participate in what appeared to be a learning experiment. Each man had to give a series of shocks (which increased in intensity) to another person in an adjoining room. At a certain point, the person receiving these shocks began screaming and pounding the wall. Milgram's basic research question was what percent of the subjects would continue to obey the experimenter despite these reactions of the person receiving the shock—that is, what percentage would keep on administering shocks of ever-increasing intensity even after hearing screams and pounding on the wall. Milgram had asked psychologists and Yale undergraduates to estimate what percent of the subjects would continue administering shocks to the end of the shock series (450 volts); in effect, Milgram asked for a measure of their beliefs about human nature in a specific situation. All respondents predicted that only an insignificant minority of subjects would go to the end of the shock series. The estimates ranged from 0 to 3 percent; in other words, the most pessimistic member of the Yale class predicted that 3 out of 100 persons would proceed to give the most potent shock possible on the shock generator. Yet 26 of Milgram's 40 subjects, or 65 percent, administered shocks

[2] Recent research, exemplified by the work of Clark and Word (1971), has pointed us toward another factor—the ambiguity of the situation—as a determinant of the degree of helping behavior. Clark and Word found that 100 percent of their college student subjects came to the aid of a victim in cases where it was clear to the subject that the victim had been severely hurt. The Piliavin et al. study, in which rates of helping were high, also involved an unambiguous situation.

all the way through to the 450-volt maximum. This obedience to the experimenter was manifested despite great tension and anguish, which appeared in many ways—stuttering, groaning, biting one's lip, nervous laughter, and even one convulsive seizure. Despite the qualms we may have about the ethics or propriety of such experimental manipulations (the subjects were told afterwards that the accomplice did not really get shocked), the outcome of Milgram's study is provocative and disturbing evidence of the dominant need to obey and conform to the demands of an authority figure. All of the world's Adolf Eichmanns and Lieutenant Calleys are not thousands of miles away from our own neighborhoods.

The fourth dimension of philosophies of human nature, *strength of will and rationality versus an external locus of control and irrationality,* is the extent to which one believes that people have control over their own outcomes and understand the motives behind their behavior. The core of the American culture has traditionally been characterized by a belief in the effectiveness of willpower and motivation. The self-help movement, from Mary Baker Eddy to Dale Carnegie to Norman Vincent Peale, has long been a strong force in amateur American philosophy. Yet the opposite view has had its adherents. St. Paul believed that willpower was not enough: "I can will what is right, but I cannot do it." Our contemporary society with its heavy emphasis upon technology also evokes pessimism; with a growing number of skilled jobs and increasing emphasis on aptitude test results for personnel selection and academic admission, there appears to be less and less room for sheer motivation or willpower as a determinant of success.

This fourth dimension of philosophies of the nature of man also includes beliefs about man's rationality and/or irrationality. Rationality here means that one's ego is in control and that cognitions dominate over emotions. Yet there seems to be a growing belief among psychologists (Carl Rogers to the contrary) that people are not basically rational. Leonard Krasner (1965), for instance, views man as "being at the robot end of the continuum"; and even Freud's views have re-emerged in a posthumous publication of a book about Woodrow Wilson (Freud & Bullitt, 1967). In the book, President Wilson's virtues are portrayed as weaknesses and his visions as the fruits of compulsion; his idealization of the League of Nations is interpreted by Freud as evidence of a passive, feminine relationship between Wilson and his father (L. F. Brown, 1967). According to Freud then, subconscious factors are the major influence on decisions even at the highest levels of international affairs. Indeed, freedom may be a vanishing orientation, and the rationalist wonders whether there is no place for the rational decisions of free men. In a fascinating study, Charlotte Doyle (1965, 1966; also see Walker, 1970) has shown that experimental psychologists believe more strongly in determinism than any other academic group, including physical and biological scientists, who tend toward the opposite end of the continuum. Experimental psychologists have also been found to believe that freedom is illusory, whereas physical scientists accept freedom as a reality, rather than as a word relating an absence of the knowledge of causes.

If we turn to the man on the street, however, we find that most people believe that man is rational and that one's outcomes in the world are sensible and orderly. In Melvin Lerner's words, "There is an appropriate fit between what [people] do and what happens to them" (1966, p. 3); people cannot believe they live in a "world governed by a schedule of random reinforcements." Yet this belief in justice—in other words, the belief that people get what they deserve—leads to some perverse findings. Lichtman, as cited by Lerner (1966), exposed ninth-grade students to a tape recording of a number of people talking about a particular boy named Bill Johnson. The students learned that Bill had had an automobile accident resulting from a blowout in a front tire of a used car he had recently bought. Bill was hospitalized and suffered two weeks of intense pain, facing the possibility that he would have a permanent limp. All the subjects were led to believe that Bill had been warned about the tires when he bought the car. One group of subjects was told that Bill bought new tires and that it was one of these that blew out. The other group was told that he had definitely neglected to buy new tires. Couched within this ruse were questions concerning the degree of Bill's responsibility for the accident and Bill's attractiveness to the subjects. Surprisingly, Bill was judged to be less attractive when it was established that he had bought new tires prior to the blowout. To be sure, he was described as less responsible for his suffering, but also—and most important—he was described as a less attractive, desirable person (Lerner, 1966, p. 6).

One might tend to explain this irrationality in the rendering of justice as simply the product of ninth-grade minds; but Lerner has found similar results with college undergraduates (Lerner & Simmons, 1966). Figure 3-4 indicates that a significant minority of American adults use the argument of a "just world" to explain the assassination of a public figure. After a series of intriguing experiments, Lerner concluded that "Anyone [who is] suffering is most likely to arouse people's dislike if he conveys the impression that he was a noble victim. He gets off with somewhat less rejection if he appears to be an innocent victim. And finally the victim who allows people to believe that he brought his suffering upon himself will be the best liked" (Lerner, 1966, p. 9).[3] People generally believe that you deserve what you get; and, if you have a bad experience, you must also be bad. This principle of a just outcome is apparently a strong assumption about human nature.

The conceptualization of philosophies of human nature includes the four substantive dimensions mentioned thus far and two further dimensions that cut across the four substantive dimensions and deal with beliefs about individual differences in human nature. In a sense, these beliefs about individual differences constitute a separate part in one's philosophy of human nature and its effects on behavior. Two college students, for example, may each possess an extremely positive belief about the amount of trustworthiness in man; yet they may have divergent beliefs about the individual differences in human nature. The student who believes that people are trustworthy and that all people are alike may be less likely to seek information about another person before interacting with that person. The student who believes that each person is different, even though all people are basically trustworthy, may behave differently in various interpersonal situations. Therefore, in arriving at a conceptualization of the philosophies of human nature, one must include beliefs about individual differences as well as the substantive dimensions.

The fifth dimension, then, which deals with beliefs about individual differences, is *complexity versus simplicity*—or the extent to which one believes that people are complicated and hard to understand as opposed to believing people are simple and easy to understand. Most psychologists appear to agree that one goal of psychological

[3]A more recent review of Lerner's work may be found in his article appearing in a compilation of studies on altruism and helping behavior (Macauley & Berkowitz, 1970).

Figure 3-4. *Martin Luther King, Victim of Assassination. In April, 1968, right after Dr. King's murder, a representative sample of 1337 American adults were asked: "When you heard the news [of the assassination] which of these things was your strongest reaction: (1) anger, (2) sadness, (3) shame, (4) fear, (5) he brought it on himself?" About one-third (426) of the respondents chose the response "brought it on himself" (Rokeach, 1970). For these respondents, Lerner's "just world" hypothesis applies: since Dr. King was killed he must have deserved to be killed. (Photograph by Charles Moore, Black Star.)*

training is the development of a strong belief in human complexity. Seward Hiltner (1962) writes that there now seems to be "a greater consensus among psychologists about their view of man than in any previous time in our century, and this view includes more factors of greater complexity" (p. 246). Still, there is little theorizing on the subject of complexity, with the exception of George Kelly's role construct theory (G. A. Kelly, 1955, 1963; Bannister, 1970) and O. J. Harvey's work (Harvey, Hunt, & Schroder, 1961) on four levels of conceptual systems. A few rudimentary studies have shown that there are individual differences in beliefs about the complexity of human behavior. Gordon Allport (1958, 1966) conducted a small investigation showing that when asked to list the essential characteristics of some friend, 90 percent of the subjects employed between 3 and 10 trait names, the average being 7.2. The difference between 3 and 10, we may agree, is a large difference in complexity.

The sixth dimension, which deals with beliefs about human differences, is *similarity versus variability*—or the extent to which one believes that people differ in their basic nature. Again, most clinical psychologists, at least, would agree to the desirability of believing that people are different and that each is unique. Yet, with the exception of Gordon Allport's (1961, 1962) consistent advocacy for recognition of man's uniqueness, most personality theorists have taken the easy way out by implying that most people are basically alike.

2. Measurement and findings. Philosophies of human nature have been conceptualized as possessing six dimensions, four of a substantive nature and two reflecting the complexity of human nature. In order to measure these six dimensions, a **Likert-type scale,** referred to hereafter as the *PHN* scale, was constructed, with six subscales of 14 items each (Wrightsman, 1964a). (See Table 3-4 for a summary

Table 3-4. *The Dimensions and Subscales of "Philosophies of Human Nature"*

The Philosophies of Human Nature (PHN) scale measures one's beliefs about human nature. It is a Likert-type scale, with each subscale being composed of 14 statements (items). Subjects indicate their agreement or disagreement with each item by circling a number from +3 to −3.

The six subscales are:	*Range*
1. Trustworthiness versus untrustworthiness + = belief that people are trustworthy, moral, and responsible. − = belief that people are untrustworthy, immoral, and irresponsible.	+42 to −42
2. Strength of will and rationality versus lack of will power and irrationality + = belief that people can control their outcomes and that they understand themselves. − = people lack self-determination and are irrational.	+42 to −42
3. Altruism versus selfishness + = belief that people are altruistic, unselfish, and sincerely interested in others. − = belief that people are selfish and self-centered.	+42 to −42
4. Independence versus conformity to group pressures + = belief that people are able to maintain their beliefs in the face of group pressures to the contrary. − = belief that people give in to pressures of group and society.	+42 to −42
5. Complexity versus simplicity + = belief that people are complex, complicated, and hard to understand. − = belief that people are simple and easy to understand.	+42 to −42
6. Variability versus similarity + = belief that people are different from each other in personality and interests and that a person can change from time to time. − = belief that people are similar in interests and are not changeable over time.	+42 to −42

The first four subscales (T, S, A, and I) can be summed to give a *positive-negative* score (range +168 to −168), indicating one's general positive or negative beliefs about substantive characteristics of human nature. The last two subscales (C and V) can be summed to give a *multiplexity* score (range of +84 to −84), indicating one's beliefs about the extent of individual differences in human nature.

of subscales and dimensions.) Relying upon scale scores as operational definitions of philosophies of human nature, we may now indicate some conclusions regarding beliefs about human nature. Pooling together subjects of different ages, sexes, races, and occupations, we find that the average person believes human nature to be: (a) neither extremely trustworthy nor extremely untrustworthy, (b) neither extremely altruistic nor extremely selfish, (c) somewhat rational and possessing a moderate degree of strength of will, (d) somewhat more likely to conform to group pressures than to remain independent of group pressures, (e) moderately complex and hard to understand, and (f) moderately different from each other—that is, to a moderate degree, people are variable and unique (Wrightsman & Satterfield, 1967).

There are significant—in fact, huge—differences among student bodies at different colleges, particularly in regard to the four substantive dimensions. The student bodies of some institutions have generally positive beliefs about human nature; students in southern schools, for example, more characteristically have trusting beliefs than do students from eastern colleges. Some student bodies have consistently negative beliefs about human nature. The mean scores of these colleges on measures of trustworthiness and altruism are one or more standard deviations below the mean scores of other colleges. One institution with an extremely negative score is a private college in the midwest that attracts bright, religiously sophisticated students who have been brought up in a strict Calvinist tradition. In fact, in a doctrinal statement of faith, the catalog of the college states: "We believe . . . that human beings are born with a sinful nature, and in the case of all those who reach moral responsibility, become sinners in thought, word, and deed." Thus, it is not surprising that these students see human nature (although not necessarily themselves) as selfish, conformist, and untrustworthy.

A person's philosophy of human nature may be changed temporarily by a dramatic piece of information or personal experience. For example, within five days after President Kennedy's assassination, the PHN scale was readministered to 30 undergraduates who had taken the scale 14 months previously. The students were also asked how upset they were about the President's death. Those (approximately half) who were most disturbed by the President's death had become more negative than other students in their substantive beliefs about human nature, while the scores of those who were less concerned did not change significantly. All the subjects were retested again five months later; by that time, those who had become more negative had returned to the beliefs they held prior to the assassination (Wrightsman & Noble, 1965).

New experiences can also affect a positive change in beliefs about human nature. James Young (1970) administered the PHN scale to 90 undergraduates who participated in a weekend sensitivity training program. Compared with their pretraining scores, the scores obtained immediately after the sensitivity training indicated significantly more favorable beliefs about the trustworthiness of human nature. However, when retested a third time two months later, the participants' scores were, on the average, about halfway between their pretraining scores and the scores obtained immediately after sensitivity training.

Both of these studies demonstrate that dramatic occurrences can affect one's beliefs about human nature but that these effects are only temporary. Apparently, one's beliefs about human nature become established rather early in life and are quite resistant to permanent change. Evidence for this claim comes from Baxter's study (1968) of changes in philosophies of human nature in the first one or two years of college. Baxter used students who had taken the PHN scale during freshman orientation week and readminstered the scale after these students had completed their freshman or sophomore year. Although some students' substantive scores became more favorable while others' scores became more unfavorable, there was very little in the way of a consistent direction of change—except that stronger beliefs in the complexity of human nature emerged in all groups. Test-retest correlations over one or two years ranged from +.45 to +.65, indicating a moderate to high degree of consistency between testings. Numerous personality measures were studied to see whether they related to degree or direction of change, but nothing of significance emerged. Contrary to the fact that the first year of college is often seen as a period of dramatic change in one's values, there is little evidence here that predictable changes occur in beliefs about the goodness of man. If we wish to induce favorable beliefs about human nature, we must intervene at an earlier age than late adolescence.

Differences in beliefs about human nature also exist between occupational groups. Of all occupational groups surveyed, high school guidance counselors have the most favorable beliefs about human nature, a finding consistent with the goals of counselor educators. Arbuckle (1965), for example, and Kell (1967) are both prominent counselor-educators who advocate that counselors should be altruistic, acceptant, and positive. In contrast, graduate students in experimental psychology (as opposed to graduate students in clinical psychology) believe human nature to be untrustworthy, conforming, and selfish. Another group, Peace Corps trainees, has been found to possess somewhat favorable beliefs about human nature, confirming the label of realistic idealists.

When students are given the task of evaluating an instructor at the end of a course, the favorableness of their evaluation is related to their philosophies of human nature. In a study by Wrightsman (1964a), groups with favorable and unfavorable beliefs on the PHN scale differed significantly in their evaluations of the instructor; those subjects possessing unfavorable beliefs about human nature gave more negative evaluations of the teacher than students possessing favorable beliefs. Thus, the favorableness of one's beliefs about human nature in general is related to the evaluation one gives a specific individual.

A rather unique situation provided the opportunity to test the effects of beliefs about the complexity and variability of human nature upon student evaluations of teachers (Wrightsman, 1964b). Education majors at Peabody College are required to take concurrently two psychology courses taught by two different instructors. Each course is divided into two sections, one for elementary education majors and one for secondary education majors. At the end of the courses, after each student had been exposed to the two instructors for an entire quarter, the students completed teacher evaluation forms for each instructor and the PHN scale. As expected, female elementary education majors saw human nature as significantly more trustworthy, altruistic, and independent than did female secondary education majors. Both female groups had more favorable views of human nature than did males in education classes, who also saw people as less complex than did females. In all college samples studied, female students believed human nature to be more favorable and more complex than did males.

It was predicted that students who had more multiplex views of human nature (that is, high complexity and high variability scores) would give evaluations that differentiated more between the two instructors than the evaluations of students who were low in multiplexity. This expectation was partially confirmed. The correlations between the extent to which students differentiated their ratings and their beliefs about the degree of complexity of human nature were $+.36$ ($p < .05$), $+.35$ ($p < .05$), and $-.08$ for the three groups of students (males, females in secondary education, and females in elementary education). Two of the three groups showed the expected relationship to a statistically significant degree. Correlations of the extent of differentiation in ratings between instructors and variability scores were $+.12$, $+.20$, and $+.39$ ($p < .05$), only one group producing a significant relationship. There is evidence, then, that both the substantive quality of a person's beliefs about human nature and a person's beliefs about the extent of differences in human nature play some role in a person's evaluations of particular individuals.

In summary, people do possess a rather organized, consistent set of beliefs about the nature of man. The beliefs held by a person are related to his reactions to specific individuals. The nature of one's own beliefs is partially accounted for by one's sex, race, and occupational role in society. Since a person's beliefs are apparently formed at an early age, interventions during adolescence or adulthood for the purpose of changing these beliefs are only temporarily successful.

B. Machiavellianism and Machiavellian Assumptions about Human Nature

Niccolo Machiavelli lived in Italy 400 years ago, but his influence has survived to this day. Not only is his name used to describe the person who manipulates others through guile, deceit, and opportunism (Christie & Geis, 1970), but Machiavelli's ideas have also been adopted—either outwardly or tacitly—by countless politicians, military officers, business executives, and college professors. In fact, any person who must control or influence the actions of others in order to satisfy his own occupational or personal needs can find in Machiavelli's writings suggested behaviors that may enhance success. Machiavelli was the ultimate pragmatist who wrote what he believed would be effective, regardless of how unflattering it might appear.

In *The Prince* and other writings, Machiavelli expressed his assumptions about human nature quite explicitly. His assumptions do not make us prouder of our species; yet they do have the virtues of being clearly expressed and testable—so much so that Richard Christie, a social psychologist at Columbia University, and his colleagues have been able to convert Machiavelli's writings into attitude statements that can be used to determine one's agreement with Machiavelli's philosophy (Christie & Geis, 1970). In this section we will examine the nature of **Machiavellianism,** describe how it is measured, and see how highly Machiavellian character affects everyday interpersonal behavior.

1. What is Machiavellianism? Operationally, a person is Machiavellian to the degree that his answer to items on the *Mach scale* agree with the answers Machiavelli would have given. Statements on the scale were either drawn from Machiavelli's writings ("The best way to handle people is to tell them what they want to hear"), or new statements with a similar orientation were constructed ("Barnum was probably right when he said there's a sucker born every minute"). Agreement with such statements indicates acceptance of Machiavelli's views. Because of *the acquiescent response set* according to which some respondents agree with almost any statement presented on an attitude questionnaire, half of the statements were worded so that agreement indicated rejection of a Machiavellian view. "Most people who get ahead in the world lead clean moral lives" is an example of such a reversed item. As a second way of combating response sets, a forced-choice version of the Mach scale was prepared. Christie classified the statements on the scale into three types, based upon their content; happily, two **factor analyses** (a complex set of statistical procedures that identifies the statements that intercorrelate and cluster together) generally agreed with his judgments (Christie & Geis, 1970, Appendix A). The three types of statements were as follows (Christie, 1970, p. 14):

(a) statements that advocated the use of manipulative interpersonal tactics. (For example, "It is wise to flatter important people.")
(b) statements that expressed an unfavorable view of human nature. (For example, "Generally speaking, men won't work hard unless they're forced to do so.")
(c) a set of statements dealing with abstract or generalized morality. (For example, "People suffering from incurable diseases should have the choice of being put painlessly to death.")

Fewer statements were in this third category, because in following Machiavelli's writings closely, Christie found less concern with abstractions and ethical judgments than with pragmatic advice.

2. *Are the attitudes of most individuals highly Machiavellian or un-Machiavellian?* Christie has reported the mean scores for 1744 college students who took the Mach scale (Christie & Geis, 1970). Both males and females averaged between "slight disagreement" and "neutrality"—females coming closer to "slight disagreement" and males approaching "neutrality." Thus, generally speaking, the attitudes of the average college student are neither strongly Machiavellian nor strongly un-Machiavellian, but rather strike a balance between the two. However, there is enough variation between respondents to characterize some college students as highly Machiavellian, some as moderately Machiavellian, and others as either strongly or moderately un-Machiavellian. Little evidence on systematic group differences in Machiavellian attitudes has been accumulated so far, although Christie reports that medical students have higher Mach scores than college undergraduates but lower scores than graduate psychology students.

Despite this lack of evidence, relationships with other measures of personality and aptitude help us picture what the highly Machiavellian person is and is not. For example, highly Machiavellian college students, as a group, do not score higher or lower on IQ tests than do un-Machiavellian students. Nor are there differences in political preferences, strength of needs for academic achievement, levels of anxiety (when corrected for social desirability), or psychopathology of Machiavellian and un-Machiavellian students. However, the highly Machiavellian student is more willing than the un-Machiavellian to admit hostile feelings within himself, possesses more unfavorable beliefs about human nature on the PHN scale, and tends to rate other students more unfavorably in a standardized situation.

3. *The interpersonal behavior of Machiavellian persons.* After defining one's degree of Machiavellianism by the responses obtained on the attitude scale, do we find that highly Machiavellian subjects behave differently toward their fellow men than less Machiavellian persons? Within limits that will be specified, the answer to this question is clearly yes. The highly Machiavellian subject not only enters into activities with a zest for competition and success in interpersonal tasks but is also skilled in such activities and is likely to be successful. Some specific examples may be cited.

Highly Machiavellian and un-Machiavellian college students participated in an experimental task involving two persons (Exline, Thibaut, Hickey, & Gumpert, 1970). While the experimenter was absent from the room, the other participant (a confederate of the experimenter) induced the subject to cheat on the task. (On the first attempts, highly Machiavellian subjects resisted cheating more strongly than un-Machiavellian subjects.) Later, during the post-experimental interview (ostensibly done to document the subjects' approaches to the task), the experimenter became suspicious and accused each participant of cheating. Highly Machiavellian cheaters looked the interrogator in the eye and denied cheating longer than less Machiavellian felons. Moreover, highly Machiavellian subjects confessed less often and lied more plausibly after the accusation than un-Machiavellian subjects.

Such behavior on the part of the highly Machiavellian subjects may be considered *defensive manipulation,* since the student was caught in a difficult situation and attempted to manipulate the accuser in self-defense against the accusations. But what about a situation where *offensive manipulation*—manipulation chosen by the subject at his own option and for his own reasons—is legitimized? Geis, Christie, and Nelson (1970) placed subjects in the role of test examiner and gave them the task of administering an important embedded-figures test to other subjects. All subject-examiners (some highly Machiavellian, some not) were told they had arbitrary power over the test subject. Specifically, the examiners were told, "Once you've been assigned to the experimental condition you remain in it, so we are asking you to use your power arbitrarily—to confuse or distract the subject who will be taking the test. Now precisely how you go about doing this, and how much of it you do, is up to your imagination—and your conscience. Obviously, we want you to be in the position of having absolute power to use as you choose to use it. Some people will find this very uncongenial . . . and they do very little. Other people find it a great deal of fun. What you do is up to you" (Geis, Christie, & Nelson, 1970, p. 82). Thus, all examiners were given the license to manipulate, distract, or interrupt the test-taker. Observers recorded and categorized verbal and nonverbal behavior on the part of each examiner. Highly Machiavellian subjects performed an average of 15.43 manipulative acts during their test administration, compared to an average of 7.08 manipulative acts by un-Machiavellian subjects (a difference significant at the .005 level). Furthermore, highly Machiavellian subjects were more innovative in the types of manipulations they used, and afterwards they reported more often than un-Machiavellians having enjoyed the experimental manipulation. The imaginative flavor of the manipulations produced by examiners is illustrated in Table 3-5.

In several types of bargaining tasks involving three persons, highly Machiavellian subjects are more successful than un-Machiavellian participants. Machiavellian subjects initiate and control the interaction in the group more often than un-Machiavellians. Overwhelmingly, Machiavellians are the dominant, decisive, sought-after

Table 3-5. *The Strategems of the Highly Machiavellian Examiner*

Given license to distract a subject taking a test, one highly Machiavellian tester went through the following gestures.

[The tester] rubs hands together in the stereotyped gesture of anticipation, bends over double, unties shoe, shakes foot, reties shoe; jingles contents of pocket noisily, pulls out Chapstick and applies it while staring absentmindedly at ceiling; whistles, slaps leg and straightens up noisily and abruptly in chair; taps pencil rhythmically on table; hums, reaches around divider and carefully knocks it over (this produces a loud crash and sends papers on table flying in all directions); after 10-second dead silence apologizes profusely to [test-taker] for distracting him; erases vigorously on blank margin of [test-taker's] score sheet (divider board prevents test-taker from seeing that "examiner" is not erasing actual marks); comments, with serious frown at one-way vision mirror, "I feel like I'm on TV, don't you?" (followed by grin at mirror as soon as test-taker returns his attention to test booklet); holds matchbook in both hands above divider board in full view of [test-taker] (pretending to ignore stopwatch), tears out matches one by one, dropping each into ashtray, tears up empty matchbook cover and drops pieces ostentatiously into ashtray; dismantles a ballpoint pen behind divider board, uses spring to shoot it, parts flying, across the room; jumps from chair, dashes across room to retrieve pen parts saying, "Sorry, I'm a little nervous."

All this occurred in the 15 minutes or so necessary to administer 10 embedded-figures problems! The innocent subject should indeed beware of the Machiavel! (*From Geis, Christie, & Nelson, "In Search of the Machiavel." In R. Christie and F. L. Geis (Eds.),* Studies in Machiavellianism. *Copyright 1970 by Academic Press, Inc. Reprinted by permission.*)

member of the triad (Geis, 1970), and they are particularly successful when the rules and procedures of the game are ambiguous. In contrast to un-Machiavellian participants, Machiavellians appear unresponsive to the personal or ethical concerns of others and tend to approach interpersonal situations in an analytic and impersonal way (Geis, 1970).

To some extent, highly Machiavellian college students get better grades than their IQ scores would predict (Singer, 1964). This is the case with males more than females, since for females, physical attractiveness replaces high Machiavellianism as a determinant of higher grades.

Clearly Machiavellian attitudes play a role in interpersonal behavior, but there are limits to the tasks in which Machiavellianism influences success. For instance, the available evidence indicates that when subjects are not in the physical presence of one another or have no chance to directly communicate with each other, highly Machiavellian participants are no more successful in interpersonal competition than other participants. Similarly, when a subject's behavior is limited to choosing between a predetermined number of alternative responses, Machiavellianism plays no role in success at specific choice points. However, if the task permits *latitude for improvisation,* highly Machiavellian persons capitalize on this freedom and use it to achieve their own goals.

In sum, Machiavellianism may impress the reader as an odious concept. Social psychologists have been only partially successful in reserving their judgment about it and have chosen to study it because of the demonstrated importance of Machiavellianism in determining success in a competitive society. (See Christie and Geis, 1970, p. 9.) Machiavellianism even enters into campaigns for the highest positions in our government, as demonstrated by McGinniss's book, *The Selling of the President, 1968.* McGinniss was granted permission by the Republican Campaign Committee to sit in on the planning and execution of the party's 1968 presidential election campaign. In this successful effort, the candidate was marketed as a product; the audience was told only what it wanted to hear; and the advertising managers expressed a cynical set of beliefs about the intelligence of the voting populace—all examples of the work of a highly Machiavellian staff of image manipulators.[4]

C. Conceptual Systems

The *content* of one's beliefs has been emphasized both in our discussion of the philosophies of human nature and in our examination of Machiavellianism. In contrast, the work of O. J. Harvey and his associates (Harvey, Hunt, & Schroder, 1961; Harvey, 1966; Harvey & Ware, 1967; Kaats, 1969) gives more attention to the *process* of forming judgments about human nature and the *structure* of the resultant judgments and beliefs. In his work on **conceptual systems,** or belief systems, Harvey proposes four different kinds of systems, which differ in both structure and content. Harvey's systems progress from a more concrete to a more abstract nature, as can be seen in the subsequent descriptions.

[4]One should not infer from this that the campaigns of other politicians lack a Machiavellian flavor. In fact, McGinniss was inspired to document his ideas when he heard in mid-1968 that an advertising agency intended "to turn Hubert Humphrey into Abraham Lincoln" by election time; but the agency rejected McGinniss's request to sit in on the transformation.

1. System 1. Harvey's first system is a highly concrete and rigid belief system. Emphasis is placed on conforming to rules and on extrinsic rather than intrinsic rewards for good performance. The result is a relatively undifferentiated and poorly integrated conceptual system, with behavioral manifestations including superstition, extrinsic religiosity, authoritarianism, conventionality, and extremes of evaluation in judging others.

2. System 2. This conceptual system is somewhat more abstract than System 1, but the essential difference is that System 2 possesses a "negative and rebellious orientation toward authority and training agents" (Kaats, 1969, p. 22). The rejection of traditional authority is accompanied by a high degree of anxiety, resulting from the absence of any authoritative guidelines (Felknor & Harvey, 1968). System 2 appears to be similar to a negative set of beliefs on the PHN scale. Beyond this, the structural emphasis of the conceptual systems approach would note that System-2 persons maintain an inflexibility and a lack of differentiation and integration much like System-1 persons.

3. System 3. The third conceptual system is a more abstract system and has more differentiation and integration and more cognitive planning than the first two systems. The *content* of beliefs about people in System-3 persons is positive. People are seen as likeable and attractive. System-3 persons are "thought to manifest both a need to be dependent upon others as well as a need for others to depend upon them" (Kaats, 1969, p. 24). But the respect for other people in System-3 is purposeful—the System-3 person, in his quest for control and interpersonal manipulation, is attracted to others because they can do things for him. Helpfulness on the part of System-3 persons is a guise in order to achieve one's own goals (Felknor & Harvey, 1968). Thus the System-3 approach is reminiscent of the goals, if not the tactics, of the Machiavellian.

4. System 4. This is the most abstract and highly developed system, characterized by the establishment of interdependent relationships with others, self-confidence, a positive self-concept, an openness to change, and an absence of authoritarianism (Kaats, 1969). The System-4 person is highly differentiated and integrated; he can view another person or an issue from a multitude of varying perspectives. His rewards stem from internal considerations, rather than from the opinions of others. System 4 is considered the healthiest of the four systems.

A variety of studies (reviewed by Harvey, 1969, and by Kaats, 1969) indicate that the level of a person's conceptual system is related to important behaviors. For example, persons with more concrete conceptual systems tend to (a) make more extreme, either-or judgments (Ware & Harvey, 1967; D. K. Adams, Harvey & Heslin, 1966); (b) show more prejudiced racial attitudes (Severy & Brigham, 1971); (c) be more likely to vote for Nixon or Wallace rather than for Humphrey in the 1968 presidential election (Severy & Brigham, 1971); (d) rely more upon status and power than upon expertise and information as guidelines for their own judgments (Harvey & Ware, 1967); (e) show less ability to change sets in attacking complex problems that have changing rules (Harvey, 1966); and (f) show more conventional behavior and less creativity (Harvey, 1966). Greater abstractness (in other words, Systems 3 and 4) results in the opposite behavior patterns in these and other behavioral tests. Harvey's theory of conceptual systems offers a promising approach to the study of assumptions about people, but further work is necessary to clarify the differentiation between the systems and to specify how a person moves from one system to another.

V. ASSUMPTIONS ABOUT PEOPLE IN THE FUTURE

A. Our Introspective Society

Despite the fact that there are people in America and every other country who are poorly fed, poorly clothed, and poorly housed, mankind's physical needs are better provided for now than at any time in the past. Applying Maslow's hierarchy of needs, we might say that America—while still concerned with its physiological needs—is beginning to direct more concern to needs of a higher order. That is, even though hunger, shelter, and the cleansing of the air are not completely satisfied needs, our nation has begun to study how well we are achieving our higher-order needs. This introspection about the quality of human life is painful but healthy in the long run.

Because of this orientation, we can expect continued concern about incidents that seemingly reflect upon the social nature of man—whether these incidents be massacres of unarmed civilians in Southeast Asia or failures to aid a victim attacked on a city street. The nature of the human condition will be tested continually.

B. Implications for Blueprinting a Theory of Human Nature

Even though concerns about the essential nature of man will increase, a blueprint of man's basic social traits is impossible. Although there are consistencies across cultures in some social psychological characteristics—for example, some type of family structure exists in every society—it appears impossible to extract a basic nature from these human characteristics. Attempts to measure human nature in a way that will enable us to make statements like "60 percent of American adults are trustworthy and 40 percent are not" are futile. Even if we could agree upon what represents trustworthy and untrustworthy behavior, we would find the behavior under study influenced by the nature of the person involved, the nature of the situation, and the recent reinforcement history of the trustworthy or untrustworthy person being studied.

R. E. Feldman's (1968) study clearly illustrates some of the complexities in seeking an answer to a seemingly simple question: who is more helpful to a stranger—a Frenchman, a Greek, or an American? Feldman employed five behavior settings in Paris, Athens, and Boston, and trained locals and foreigners in the five settings of each city to ask for help. Feldman was interested not only in nationality differences in helping behavior but also whether a foreign stranger was treated differently from a compatriot. But the results are, at first glance, so inconsistent that only a few general conclusions may be drawn.

In the first behavior setting, for example, the purpose was to determine whether people helped individuals who asked them for directions. Main shopping areas were used in Paris, Athens, and Boston, and only males over age 18 were stopped; each person who was stopped was asked for directions to a familiar location.

In this setting, both the Parisians and the Athenians gave help to a fellow citizen more frequently than to a foreigner. For example, 24 percent of the Parisians did not give directions to a compatriot, while 45 percent did not help a foreigner (or gave the foreigner wrong instructions). (Even if the foreigner asked the question in French, he was less likely to receive helpful information than a compatriot.) In the Athenian sample, 36 percent either did not give directions to the foreigner or misdirected him, while 32 percent did not help fellow Greeks. Twenty percent of the Bostonians either did not respond or responded wrongly to foreigners, while 21 percent responded not at all or wrongly to American compatriots.

In another behavior setting, Feldman tested whether cashiers in Paris, Athens, and Boston would keep or return an overpayment of money after a small purchase. Again, both compatriots or foreigners did the purchasing; but, in this case, only the language of the host country was used. Pastry shops were used for the setting, since they are numerous in all parts of all three cities, and frequent purchases for small amounts of money could be made. In Paris, 39 percent of all the pastry shops were used; 31 percent of the shops were used in Athens, and 18 percent in Boston. In making a purchase of around 20 cents, a few pennies, centimes, or drachmas above the actual cost were added to the payment by the purchaser, who then slowly walked out of the store. The amount of overpayment was always one-fourth to one-third of the purchase price.

No important differences occurred between how cashiers treated the foreigner as opposed to the compatriot in any of the three cities. In Paris pastry shops, 54 percent of the cashiers kept the money from both types of purchasers. In Athens, the overpayment was not returned to the foreigner 51 percent of the time and not returned to the compatriot 50 percent of the time. In Boston, the money was kept from the compatriot 38 percent of the time and from the foreigner 27 percent of the time.

A third behavior setting involved the foreigner or compatriot in a taxi ride. Sixty rides were taken in Paris, 42 in Athens, and 44 in Boston; in each city, half the riders were compatriots, and half were foreigners. The foreigner did not simply announce his destination but read the location of the destination from a slip of paper and then handed the paper to the driver. In neither Boston nor Athens was the foreigner overcharged more often than the compatriot; but, in Paris, the American foreigner was overcharged significantly more often than the French compatriot ($p < .02$). Of the 30 pairs of equivalent rides in Paris, the American rider was charged more than the French rider 18 times, the same amount as the French compatriot 7 times, and less than the Frenchman 5 times. The French taxi drivers illustrated a wide variety of techniques for increasing the distance traveled and/or fare charged to the foreigner.

Testings of more than 3000 subjects in these and two other behavior settings produced differences that were not consistent from one culture setting to another. When a difference was observed, though, "the Athenians treated the foreigner better than the compatriot, but Parisians and Bostonians treated compatriots better than foreigners" (Feldman, 1968, p. 212). Even within the limited number of settings in this study, it is impossible to extract consistent human natures across cities or across settings within cities. However, when differences in the five settings are considered, some degree of consistency does emerge. Harry Triandis[5] suggests that in traditional societies, such as Greece, people cooperate with members of their in-groups but not with members of out-groups. Also, the nature of the social setting is crucial. In settings where the relationship is stable (customer-client), there is more consistency in treatment of locals and foreigners than in situations where the relationship is unstable.

[5] Personal communication, May 27, 1971.

C. Psychology's Role in Determining Assumptions about Human Nature

Despite the cautionary tone of the foregoing section, psychology as a scientific discipline can play a role in influencing the popular conception of human nature. George Miller, in his 1969 presidential address to the American Psychological Association, identified two possible sets of beliefs about human nature that could result from the impact of scientific advances in psychology. One set of beliefs emphasizes the control of behavior, the viewpoint that living organisms are nothing but machines, and the impact of external reinforcements. Miller does not question the validity of this conception but rather its effect upon the populace. This image of man, Miller states, "has great appeal to an authoritarian mind, and fits well with our traditional competitive ideology based on coercion, punishment, and retribution" (1969, p. 1069).

Miller's second set of beliefs about human nature closely resembles Douglas McGregor's Theory Y. According to this image, people may be inspired to do well both by the stick and the carrot; they possess degrees of imagination, ingenuity, and creativity that are not well utilized under most working conditions; and they "exercise self-direction and self-control in the service of objectives to which they are committed" (Miller, 1969, p. 1070). For Miller, the challenge to psychology is the fostering of a social climate in which this second conception of man's nature will take root and flourish. Such a conception is slowly gaining ground, but the traditional view of man's nature (that man must be threatened in order to achieve and that he can be successfully controlled) remains pervasive. Perhaps, when recognizing the differences among people, we must conclude that both views of human nature have their place.

VI. SUMMARY

Persons make assumptions about the nature of people in general, and these assumptions about human nature influence our everyday behavior toward others. Throughout history, social and political philosophies have been concerned with human nature, asking such questions as: are men irrational or rational? Are all men basically alike, or are the differences among them basic? Is human nature good or evil?

In recent years, social psychologists have increasingly been concerned with the image of man's nature as promoted by scientific psychology. This image has emphasized a mechanistic, passive view of man. Two social psychologists in the forefront in advancing new conceptions of man's nature are Douglas McGregor and Abraham Maslow. McGregor contrasted Theory X (a traditional view of man's nature) with Theory Y (a view of man as being responsible, internally motivated, and possessing creativity, imagination, and ingenuity).

Maslow posited a hierarchy of needs in man, ranging from lower needs (such as physiological and safety needs) to higher-order needs (such as cognitive and aesthetic needs). As long as man must devote his energies toward satisfying the lower needs, according to Maslow, the higher needs are unlikely to be met.

Philosophies of human nature are expectancies that people in general possess certain qualities and will behave in certain ways. Six dimensions of philosophies of human nature have been identified.

Machiavellianism is an orientation toward manipulating other people in order to achieve one's own goals. A part of Machiavellianism is a cynical view of human nature, including beliefs that people are best manipulated through use of threats, deceit, and flattery. Also included in Machiavellianism is the advocacy of any kind of tactics necessary to achieve one's goals. Under certain conditions highly Machiavellian persons are more successful in reaching their own goals in an interpersonal conflict situation than are un-Machiavellian persons.

Conceptual systems refer to ways of viewing the world. Harvey has proposed that people move through four stages of conceptual systems.

It is expected that in the future society will intensify its quest for the achievement of man's higher-order needs. Social psychology can play a role by creating a climate where more positive conceptions of man's nature can flourish.

VII. SUGGESTED READINGS

Christie, R., & Geis, F. L. (Eds.) *Studies in Machiavellianism.* New York: Academic Press, 1970. An engaging report on the research program on Machiavellian attitudes. The authors trace the project from its beginnings, through attitude scale construction, to creative ways of relating Machiavellian attitudes to interpersonal behavior. Highly recommended.

Doniger, S. (Ed.) *The nature of man.* New York: Harper, 1962. A compilation of theories and speculations about the nature of man, by influential social scientists, theologians, and philosophers. Includes a statement by Carl Rogers.

Fuller, E. *Man in modern fiction.* New York: Random House Vintage Books, 1958 (Paperback.) An example of literary analysis of the nature of man. This particular book criticizes contemporary writers, such as Norman Mailer and Tennessee Williams, who (in Fuller's words) "glorify the depraved and corrupt in man."

Harvey, O. J., Hunt, D. E., & Schroder, H. M. *Conceptual systems and personality organization.* New York: Wiley, 1961. Includes a description of Harvey's four conceptual systems. Rather difficult reading but a useful analysis.

Latané, B., & Darley, J. M. *The unresponsive bystander: Why doesn't he help?* New York: Appleton-Century-Crofts, 1970. (Paperback.) A prize-winning report of studies of helping behavior generated by the Kitty Genovese murder case. An excellent example of the application of social psychological procedures to a problem of great contemporary concern.

Macaulay, J., & Berkowitz, L. (Eds.) *Altruism and helping behavior.* New York: Academic Press, 1970. A representative series of studies on altruism and helping behavior by psychologists whose work is reviewed in this chapter (for example, Lerner, Bryan, and Darley and Latané). Among the topics discussed are justice and reciprocation, the influence of social norms on helping, and the socialization of altruism.

McGregor, D. *The human side of enterprise.* New York: McGraw-Hill, 1960. Two theories of the nature of man are contrasted, and implications for labor-management relations are presented.

Skinner, B. F. *Beyond freedom and dignity.* New York: Knopf, 1971. A highly controversial and important book by the foremost representative of behaviorism. For Skinner, our behavior is already under the control of others. He seeks ways to make this control beneficial.

Part Two

Social Factors in the Development of Personality, Motives, and Abilities

Chapter Four

Moral Development and the Development of Motives

By John O'Connor and Lawrence S. Wrightsman

Three great magicians who have been friends since boyhood have continued to admit to their fellowship a simple fellow who was also a companion of their youth. When the three set out on a journey to demonstrate to a wider world the greatness of their art they reluctantly permit their humble friend to accompany them, and before they have gone very far, they come upon a pile of bones under a tree. Upon this opportunity to practice their art they eagerly seize. "I," says the first, "can cause these dead bones to reassemble themselves into a skeleton." And at his command they do so. "I," says the second, "can clothe that skeleton with flesh." And his miracle, also, is performed. Then, "I," says the third, "can now endow the whole with life."

At this moment the simpleton interposes. "Don't you realize," he asks, "that this is a tiger?" But the wise men are scornful. Their science is "pure"; it has no concern with such vulgar facts. "Well then," says the simpleton, "wait a moment." And he climbs a tree. A few moments later the tiger is indeed brought to life. He devours the three wise men and departs. Thereupon the simpleton comes down from the tree and goes home. *A fable from Sanskrit Panchatantra*

Many people believe that various magicians and magical products of the present time are about to destroy us. The Industrial Revolution, with its emphasis on material production culminating in the Atomic Age, has sent many scrambling for the trees. Conventional values of American society—such as the striving to achieve material success and as many possessions as possible—are being rejected by an increasing number of young people. Even that bellwether of success, the ever-increasing Gross National Product (GNP) is no longer considered desirable by many experts.

Other observers of society reject conventional assumptions that man is rational. These critics offer a new magic in which the only truth is an awareness of an apocalyptic spirit, derived from introspection of their own feelings. The mystics of Eastern religions have, of course, claimed for many years that, "There is no such thing as truth; there is only my Truth!" But this denial of rationalism is reborn in an age of Aquarius, which sees feeling as the ultimate goal and which faults language as a barrier to self-expression and communication.

The fact that there exist diverse assumptions about man's nature is not new to any of us, but in this chapter we shall take a different approach to the subject. We shall ask what man wants from his society and how man learns to participate in society and incorporate its values. An individual's moral and ethical stance and his motivation to achieve reflects in some way his participation as a member of a given society. How much of this stance is emotional, and how much is part of a more generalized cognitive orientation of the individual? These are the questions that will serve as the focus of the present chapter.

I. CONCEPTIONS OF THE DEVELOPMENT OF MORALITY IN WESTERN CULTURE

Throughout the recorded history of Western civilization, man has been preoccupied with the nature of his own morality. The early Greek philosophers considered reason the epitome of the good or virtuous man. Training and education were seen as the pathways to goodness, although the skeptical Socrates admitted that he did not know what virtue really was nor how it could be taught. With the rise of an organized Christian dogma man found a new definition of moral judgment and conduct. According to doctrines advanced by St. Augustine, man is born in sin, is basically evil, and can never hope to achieve virtue by his reason alone. Therefore, man must be educated to the faith. During these early Christian times, the good man was seen as the one who glorified God, and the teachings of the Catholic church pointed toward moral thought and conduct in order to ensure man's eternal salvation. With the Protestant Reformation man turned to reason and science in his search for an answer to the perplexing question of morality. A belief that rational man could come to correct moral decisions led to the conviction that man should be trained in the use of reason. In short, rationality would insure morality.

With the writings and influence of Sigmund Freud in the early 1900s, man's ability to reach moral decisions through reason alone again came into serious question. Civilization was ripe for a more complex, sophisticated analysis of the nature of morality (albeit a more pessimistic one), and had Freud not advanced his theories someone else probably would have. While his concern was with the transformation of the child into a socialized adult, Freud was the first who systematically pointed to irrational psychosexual urges as the primary determinants of behavior and to the apparent necessity for the person to place constraints upon his feelings and behavior.

The early part of the twentieth century saw the beginning of a scientific study of morality, which derived its impetus not only from the clinical insights of Freud, but from academic psychology as well. William McDougall (1908) conceptualized the problem in the following way in the first textbook on social psychology.

> The fundamental problem of social psychology is the moralization of the individual into the society into which he is born as an amoral and egoistic infant. There are successive stages, each of which must be traversed by every individual before he can attain the next higher: (1) the stage in which the operation of the instinctive impulses is modified by the influence

of rewards and punishments, (2) the stage in which conduct is controlled in the main by anticipation of social praise or blame, (3) the highest stage in which conduct is regulated by an ideal that enables a man to act in the way that seems to him right regardless of the praise or blame of his immediate social environment (p. 6).

While Freud and McDougall share some common assumptions (for example, the amorality of infants or the necessity of the child's developing through a lock step set of stages), the great differences in their approaches anticipated the discordant research on morality that was to follow. In more recent times, the differences have been illuminated by researchers who ask whether emotional-motivational or cognitive factors are more important in the development of morality.[1]

The psychoanalytic theory of Freud has utilized emotional and motivational constructs to explain the development of personality and character, while the cognitive approach has concerned itself with a different phenomenon—the development of rules, violation of moral norms, and the learning of universal principles. Cognitive theories hold that these developments serve as coding processes in the child, intervening between stimulus and response (Baldwin, 1969). For example, Piaget and Kohlberg have studied how the individual structures the external moral order and how these structurings change during the process of development.

A third approach to the study of moral development, exemplified by reinforcement theories and social learning theories, has been most interested in other phenomena—how the individual behaves in specific situations, how much of this behavior generalizes to other situations, and how this behavior is learned. Reinforcement theorists and social learning theorists have rejected the necessity of postulating any intervening variables and have studied specific aspects of moral behavior directly. Such investigators as Bandura and Walters (1963) and Aronfreed (1968) have sought to determine what types of environmental variations change behavior. Most of the research in this area may be subsumed under the topic of **resistance to temptation,** which refers to the person's suppression of a behavior that would have a high incidence except for the influence of a prohibition or norm.

Hence, it is necessary to begin our review with the predominant theories of moral development and then use these theories to coordinate the scraps of empirical cloth that come to us in different textures, colors, and shapes. After seeing how each theory approaches moral development, we will be prepared to describe what is known about the topic.

II. A FREUDIAN EXPLANATION OF MORAL DEVELOPMENT

In developing his emotional-motivational approach to personality and morality, Freud postulated that three systems of energies operate within the individual. The

[1] Freud's approach may be contrasted with the emotional-motivational approach of Carl Rogers (1969). Like Freud, Rogers discusses the process of the young child's introjection of the values of society. But while Freud postulates that this is a necessary part of maintaining a complex society, Rogers sees the introjection of values as a potential block to personal development. The basic disagreement between the two thinkers seems to be that Freud considers the child's impulses as potentially destructive, while Rogers sees the impulses as basically constructive. Not only do Freud and Rogers differ in their basic assumptions, but they differ radically in the behavior that they construe as moral (Seeman, 1971).

interaction of these energy systems accounts for the character and morality shown by a person in his dealings with others. Each system—the **id,** the **ego,** and the **superego**—has its own province of the mind, and each functions as a relatively independent system, although continually interacting with the other systems.

A. The Id

The id can roughly be equated with the quantity of biologically determined energy in the organism. The id is below the level of awareness (in other words, is part of the *unconscious*) and is the source of impulse energies, which persistently strive for selfish gratification. Not only does the id contain all the various sexual drives manifested by the child during his or her psychosexual development, but it also contains aggressive impulses that seek expression. The id remains unconscious, even when the ego is so weakened that it can offer little resistance to the selfish demands of the id. One cannot simply equate the id with the unconscious, however, for the latter also contains portions of the ego and the superego as well as defense mechanisms used in protecting the ego from attack.

B. The Ego

While the id is inborn, according to Freudian theory, the ego is developed through learning and through encounters with one's environment. The basic purpose of the ego is to maintain the organism on its path toward realistic goals; and, in doing so, the ego mediates between the "three harsh masters"—the id, the superego, and external reality. As one of its tasks is the minimizing of conflicts between these three entities, the ego serves a synthesizing function as well as an executive one.

The ego is also the principal system by which a person learns about and deals with the reality of the environment. The ego begins to develop at birth, and its development continues throughout the life cycle. According to psychoanalytic theory, the ego emerges as a result of the child's failures to gratify his needs. Fenichel (1945) has written, for example, that if the needs of the infant (mostly the id) were always satisfied immediately, there would be no ego. This is the case because initially the infant does not differentiate between self and not self; he knows only his own states of tension and relaxation. It is only when the child begins to perceive external objects as sources of gratification that the ego emerges. The development of a *body image*, or the sum of the mental impressions of one's own body and its organs, is particularly important in the early development of ego and self.

In some of his formulations, Freud seemed to conclude that the ego possessed no energies of its own—at least none traceable to biological sources. All of the executive powers of the ego were borrowed from the id and the superego, and the ego maintained itself by organizing the dynamic trends of these other two systems. Many psychologists regard this as a rather curious conclusion, since the suggestion is that the major integrative and organizing aspect of personality—the ego—is only a derivative of more basic impulses. The neo-Freudians, who operate within a basic psychoanalytic framework but alter aspects of Freud's views, have elevated the status of the ego. Unlike Freud, most neo-Freudians posit that the ego is innate and has a source of energy all its own.

C. The Superego

The third aspect of Freud's mental triad, the superego, contains the *conscience,* or censorship function of personality. The superego also encompasses the *ego ideal,* or the child's perception of the kind of person he would like to be. In observing his patients (and perhaps himself), Freud was struck by the impression that censoring or inhibiting forces within the personality were often as compelling and irrational as the id impulses themselves—and just as likely to lead to maladjustment. The phenomenon of melancholia or depression, in which the person cruelly punished himself for often trivial shortcomings, especially demanded understanding. The superego was postulated as a mechanism that encompasses such urges.

Parents, teachers, siblings, and others in the environment contribute to the formation of the superego. What the child introjects from these agents is principally prohibitions. Since the young child is seen as amoral, preoccupied with the satisfaction of his own impulses, and lacking in any internalized inhibitions, these prohibitions are considered necessary. Only parents or others who threaten punishment can effectively control the expression of the child's impulses. At the onset, the child conforms to parental dictates only because he fears their punishments. Later, around the age of 6 or 7, if development has been optimal, the child comes to identify with his parents (the powerful aggressors), and their image and standards become introjected—or become the child's own. In one sense the child becomes the parent; he follows his conscience as though its commands were coming directly from the parent. The most important aspect of this notion of identification and introjection is that the standards embraced by the child continue to operate with all the force they possessed at the time of introjection. The period of introjection is usually a time of great anxiety for the child, and hence the conscience can be excessively severe and unyielding. The child can become excessively self-critical and equally critical of others.

In the absence of adequate parental figures, the superego may fail to develop. According to psychoanalytic theory, children raised without adequate identification figures are likely to be deficient in the control of impulses and in concern for others; in extreme cases their adult behavior becomes psychopathic.

D. Freudian Stages of Development

Freud hypothesized that as a child grows older his psychic energy, or **libido,** is directed toward the satisfaction of needs associated with different parts of the body. If a child's needs are not satisfied at a particular stage, a portion of his energy remains oriented toward that need (that is, a part of the child's energy fixates), even though biological development requires the child to pass on to the next stage of development. Coincident with his biological development is the child's discovery that he must adapt his behaviors to become a member of the community. He must learn to control his bladder; he must not play with his genitals, and so on. Thus, each stage demands new requirements. Freud arrived at the following stages, which center on parts of the body and related needs.

The **oral stage** occurs at age 1 and is concerned with sucking and biting needs. The **anal stage** occurs between ages 2 and 3 and is centered on toilet training and the regulation of elimination. The **phallic stage,** which takes place between the ages of 4 and 6, centers on an attraction to the parent of the opposite sex and envy of the parent of the same sex (Oedipus complex). Between the ages of 6 and 14, the child enters into a **latency period,** or period of quiescence; and around the age of 14 and beyond, the individual enters the **genital stage,** which centers on the development of love for others. According to Freud, fixation at a particular stage means two things: (a) in adulthood, the person will not be able to achieve the genital stage (love others and act unselfishly) because most of his psychic energy is devoted to unsatisfied selfish needs; and (b) his adult personality will reflect the presence of these early unsatisfied needs. For example, a person who fixated at the oral stage of development would show his oral needs as an adult by engaging in excessive talking, chewing, or smoking, and by choosing an orally oriented occupation—such as selling, preaching, or teaching.

With this formulation in mind, we can see why psychoanalytic theory proposes that by the age of 6 an individual's major drives and interpersonal relationships have established an organization that remains fundamental throughout his life. However, one of the inadequacies of classical psychoanalytic theory as an explanation of moral development is that, during the latency period, the child's moral development may be accelerating; yet the theory—with its accentuation on psychosexual development—overlooks this. Neo-Freudians, notably Erik Erikson (1950, 1963, 1964) and Harry Stack Sullivan (1953), have given more attention to this period of early adolescence as they moved away from a sexually saturated view of development.

III. ERIK ERIKSON AND NEO-FREUDIAN THEORY

To Freud, identity comes to the young child during the phallic stage, when the child gains vicarious pleasure and power by imagining an association between himself and his parent of the same sex. Erik Erikson has expanded this concept and proposed that the adolescent must also develop an identity and that this identity represents more than a rebirth of the phallic-stage identification with the parent of the same sex. The problem of the adolescent is not only to control and direct sexual drives but also to establish a selfhood in light of the variety of roles available. Adolescent love is viewed by Erikson as an attempt at defining one's identity rather than as a purely sexual matter; the adolescent projects his image onto others and in seeing his image reflected is able to clarify his self-concept.

Like Freud, Erikson postulated a set of stages of development; but, unlike Freud, Erikson built his stages around ego development and concentrated upon adaptive, reality-oriented aspects of personality rather than upon sexual drives. Furthermore, according to Erikson, each person possesses an energy for learning—a curiosity, which is not merely displaced sexual energy. Erikson's eight stages of development, together with the construct that is realized through the successful resolution of each stage, are described in Table 4-1.

The first stage merits special attention, since it is concerned with trust and mistrust. The infant takes in the world through his senses at the same time he takes in food through his mouth. To Erikson, the basic attitude to be learned by the infant is that "you can trust the world in the form of your mother, that she will come back and

Table 4-1. *Erikson's Stages and Conflicts*

Stage of Life (or nuclear conflict)	*Construct ideally realized or achieved*	*Age or equivalent Freudian stage*
1. Acquiring a sense of basic trust versus a sense of mistrust	Hope	Oral-sensory stage
2. Acquiring a sense of autonomy versus a sense of doubt and shame	Will	Anal-muscular
3. Acquiring a sense of initiative versus a sense of guilt	Purpose	Genital-locomotor
4. Acquiring a sense of industry versus a sense of inferiority	Competence	Latency period
5. Acquiring a sense of identity versus a sense of identity diffusion	Fidelity	Puberty and adolescence
6. Acquiring a sense of intimacy and solidarity versus a sense of isolation	Love	Young adulthood
7. Acquiring a sense of generativity versus a sense of self-absorption or stagnation	Care	Adulthood
8. Acquiring a sense of integrity versus a sense of despair and disgust	Wisdom	Maturity

feed you the right thing in the right quantity at the right time" (Erikson, as quoted in R. I. Evans, 1969, p. 15). Basic trust is defined as a correspondence between the infant's needs and his world. Erikson believes this quality is instinctive in animals; but it must be learned by man, and the mother is the person who must teach it. Mothers of different races, social classes, and cultures will teach it in different ways—but always in the manner that fits the group's perception of the nature of the world.

Basic mistrust is equally important. Erikson does not see each stage as a task to be accomplished by the complete domination of some positive quality. In the first stage, Erikson proposes that "a certain ratio of trust and mistrust in our basic social attitude is the critical factor" (Erikson, as quoted in R. I. Evans, 1969, p. 15). When a person enters a new situation, he must be able to determine how much he can trust and how much he can mistrust. Erikson defines mistrust as a sense of readiness for danger and an anticipation of discomfort. Here again, we learn this readiness from our environment, while in animals this ability is instinctively given. Thus, we may say that Erikson is evolving an orientation toward human nature that says: "Trust others when it is appropriate, and distrust them when that is justified." He does not see this first stage—or any stage—as one where a person completely arrives on the desirable side of the conflict at the nucleus of the stage.

Erikson is not explicit about what this "certain ratio of trust to mistrust" should be, but clearly the ratio should be favorable—in other words, there should be more trust than mistrust. Only with such a ratio can the construct or goal of hope be realized. (Table 4-1 shows the constructs achieved through the resolution of the nuclear conflict at each stage.) Erikson does not see hope as merely some hypothetical construct invented by philosophers and theologians; rather, it is a "very basic human strength without which we couldn't stay alive" (Erikson, as quoted in Evans, 1969, p. 17).

Each stage in one's development is structured in the same way. For example, a goal of *will* or self-control is achieved during the second stage, which occurs as the child learns to master his anal and sphincter musculature. Here again, the ideal is the development of both a positive trait (autonomy) and a negative one (shame or doubt), but ideally the ratio favors autonomy. The achievement of willpower is an outgrowth of the development of autonomy.

The failure to handle any one nuclear conflict adequately can result in a permanent impairment relating to the problem involved. Each level of conflict demands progressively more ego strength for its mastery. Thus, mature integrity depends upon the basic development of trust, autonomy, initiative, and other adaptive skills. The stages have a snowballing effect and are not just a sequence; each stage adds something specific to all later stages and creates a new ensemble from earlier ones. The development at each stage must be supported by strong cultural institutions—first as represented by the parents, and later, as represented by all the various aspects of society.

Erikson's position, besides giving us a useful classification scheme for considering development, is especially valuable because it integrates (a) basic Freudian notions of psychosexual development, (b) widely recognized social and cultural influences, and (c) locomotor and muscular aspects of growth. Erikson's theory has been with us for more than twenty years, and his thinking has had a slowly increasing influence upon psychology; but at present we still lack well-developed procedures specially designed to assess the child's resolution of each nuclear conflict. How do we know, for example, whether a 3-year-old child trusts or mistrusts others, or whether a 15-year-old has developed a clearcut identity for himself? Existing concepts and measures could be used for studying some conflicts and stages. Trust versus mistrust, for example, seems similar to concepts of **interpersonal trust** (Rotter, 1971) and the *trustworthiness of human nature* (Wrightsman, 1964a). Constructs at other stages of life might be tapped with a concept of achievement motivation; for example, concerns with "industry *vs.* inferiority" (latency stage) and "generativity *vs.* stagnation" (adulthood stage) seem particularly fruitful for this approach. Later in this chapter, the achievement motive will be considered in detail.

IV. COGNITIVE THEORIES OF MORAL DEVELOPMENT

Jean Piaget, a Swiss, and Lawrence Kohlberg, an American, have done much to elucidate how moral development can be understood through a cognitive approach that concentrates on the learning of rules, laws, and higher principles. In this section the contributions of each of these theorists will be reviewed.

A. Piaget—Two Stages of Moral Development

Piaget and Freud, the two leading theoreticians of moral development, were similar in their methodology. Each observed, asked questions, and talked to people who had been ignored by others. Freud spent hours listening to the dreams and free associations of neurotic Viennese women, while Piaget (1948, 1960) sat on the sidewalks of Geneva playing marbles with children. Both thinkers employed a concept of stages of development, but for Piaget these stages were mental or cognitive in nature.

As Piaget used the term, *cognitive stages* possess the following characteristics:

1. They imply that children of different ages possess *qualitatively* different ways of thinking or solving the same problems.

2. These different ways of thinking may be ordered in an *invariant* sequence; that is, there is a consistent series of steps in the sequence, along which each child must progress.

3. Each successive cognitive stage is a hierarchical integration of what has gone before. Higher stages do not replace lower stages, but rather, reintegrate them. Previous ways of doing things are maintained for the functions they serve, but increasingly a solution at the highest level available to the person is preferred.

In his theory of mental development, Piaget proposed that the child moves through four stages of increasingly abstract reasoning. Progressing to a higher stage of mental development is a necessary, but not a sufficient, condition for shifting to a higher stage of moral development. In regard to the latter, Piaget proposed the presence of only two stages. In the *heteronomous stage,* or the stage of moral realism, the child accepts rules as given from authority. In the second stage, the stage of *autonomous morality* or moral independence, the individual believes in modifying rules to fit the needs of the situation.

1. The development of rules. Piaget observed that when young children (aged 3 years) play marbles together, they have no rules and no cooperative play. Children that young really do not play "together," even if they share the same space at the same time. From ages 3 to 5, some trend toward a group of players emerges, but each child is *egocentric* in the sense that he considers his own point of view the only possible one. At this age, the child is unable to put himself in someone else's place because he is unaware that the other person has a point of view. Around the age of 7 or 8, *incipient cooperation* emerges—the first incidence of concern about mutual benefits and the unification of rules. However, at this stage the ideas about rules in general are still rather vague. It is not until the fourth stage, or the period of *codification of rules* around age 11 or 12, that every detail of the game is fixed and agreed upon.

While the child is progressing in the practice of rules, his attitude toward rules is also changing. (Piaget, 1948, called this "the consciousness of rules.") To the 3-year-old, rules are received almost without thought. During the next few years, rules are held sacred and untouchable; 4- and 5-year-olds see rules as coming from adults and lasting forever, even though children at this age often break rules indiscriminately. During later ages (10 to 11 years old), a rule is looked upon as a law resulting from mutual consent. At this age, rules are seen as modifiable, but the ones actually agreed upon are adhered to scrupulously.

2. Intentions vs. *consequences.* The child's conception of rules is not the only thing that changes between the stage of moral realism and the stage of moral independence. Conceptions of the seriousness of crimes also change. In explicating these changes in conceptions, Piaget chose to deal with natural occurrences common to many children—clumsiness and lying. The young of any species are incredibly clumsy; puppies are forever stumbling and crashing into things, much the same as young children are. A child is constantly dropping, breaking, soiling or otherwise disturbing the tranquility of the adult world, and a parent's reaction to a child's spilling milk or knocking the salt shaker off the table is usually an angry one, however unjustified. Thus, clumsiness plays an important part in the lives of children, and the child inevitably attaches some meaning to adults' reactions to his transgressions.

Piaget asked children to compare and evaluate the seriousness of two kinds of clumsiness—one a well-intentioned act that did considerable damage, the other a disobedient act that had negligible consequences. These were compared by using pairs of stories like those in Figure 4-1.

Piaget found that younger children judged actions according to their *material consequences*; to them, the boy who broke the most cups was the naughtiest. Older children took *intentions* into account and judged the second boy in Figure 4-1 as committing the more serious offense. This finding may provoke the question whether society values intention or consequences when determining punishment for a crime. What if I want to kill you and I deliberately shoot you, but my aim is so bad that I miss you completely? How does the punishment for that act compare with the punish-

A. A little boy who is called John is in his room. He is called to dinner. He goes into the dining room. But behind the door there was a chair, and on the chair there was a tray with fifteen cups on it. John couldn't have known that there was all this behind the door. He goes in; the door knocks against the tray; bang go the fifteen cups, and they all get broken!

B. Once there was a little boy whose name was Henry. One day when his mother was out he tried to get some jam out of the cupboard. He climbed onto a chair and stretched out his arm. But the jam was too high up, and he couldn't reach it and have any. While he was trying to get it, he knocked over a cup. The cup fell down and broke.

Figure 4-1. *Piaget's Moral Decision Stories. (From J. Piaget,* The Moral Judgment of the Child. *Copyright 1935 by Routledge & Kegan Paul, Ltd. Copyright 1965 by The Macmillan Company. Reprinted by permission of the publishers.)*

ment for an action where my intention is the same, but my aim is so good that I kill you? What punishment would result if I were showing friends my new gun and it went off, accidentally killing a bystander?

The nature and consequences of lying also showed changes occurring between the stage of moral realism and the stage of moral independence. To find out how children evaluate lying, Piaget asked each child, "Do you know what a lie is?" The younger children defined a lie simply as "naughty words" or something bad "like words no one is supposed to say." Intent to deceive did not enter into the younger child's definition of a lie. In somewhat older children, lies were described as "things you can't believe; the more unlikely the lie—the farther from reality—the worse it is." Piaget (1948) compared reactions to a story innocently told about a dog as big as a horse with reactions to a story containing a more believable falsehood and the deliberate intent to deceive. Younger children judged the far-fetched lie to be worse, while older children emphasized the intent and motives involved.

3. Two types of punishment: expiatory and reciprocal. Piaget and his associates also studied the types of punishment that younger children (up to age 8) and older children (age 8 and older) advocated for breaking rules. Simple stories of natural transgressions centering on parent-child interactions were used to identify the child's conception of justice. Punishments were divided into two types: **expiatory punishment** and punishment through **reciprocity.** Expiatory punishments demand that the transgressor must suffer; the punishment need not be related to the *content* of the guilty act, but a due proportion should be maintained between the *degree* of suffering inflicted and the gravity of the misdeed. Examples of expiatory punishment abound in our society: spanking, revoking or decreasing the child's allowance, or taking the child's toys (or the family car) off limits for a time.

Reciprocity attempts to relate the punishment to the crime, so that the rule-breaker will be able to understand the implications of his misconduct. One type of reciprocity involves *restitutive* punishment, such as having the person pay for and replace the window that he broke. *Exclusion* is another type of reciprocity, exemplified by statements such as, "I'm not going to play with you anymore because you play too rough with me."

Punishment by reciprocity corresponds with the more advanced stage of moral development—the stage of moral independence. For example, Piaget reports the results of interviewing about 100 children between the ages of 6 and 12. Only 30 percent of the 6- to 7-year-olds, compared to 50 percent of the 8- to 10-year-olds and 80 percent of the 11- to 12-year-olds, prefer the reciprocity type of punishment.

Along with moral realism and the advocacy of expiatory punishment, the younger child believes in **immanent justice**—the concept that justice dwells within the things involved and that misdeeds will be punished by natural acts or occurrences. If a child is running across a bridge when he should be walking, and the bridge happens to collapse at that moment and toss the child into the water, younger children will conclude that the child was punished for "being bad." Piaget finds in older children a very clear decrease in the belief in immanent justice. Almost all young children believe in immanent justice, while less than one-fourth of the 11- to 12-year-olds studied believe in the same.

4. Two kinds of distributive justice: equality and equity. In his analysis of justice, Piaget made a further distinction on *distributive justice*–or beliefs about how punishments and rewards should be distributed to members of a group. Two types of distributive justice were distinguished: equality and equity. Equality has the same meaning in Piaget's system as it does for most of us: everyone should be treated the same. There is here a subtle distinction from *equity*, which allows for consideration of individual circumstances. Piaget measured the children's responses to stories resembling the following.

On Thursday afternoon, a mother asked her little girl and boy to help her about the house because she was tired. The girl was to dry the plates, and the boy was to fetch in some wood. But the little boy (or girl) went and played in the street. So the mother asked the other one to do all the work. What did this other one say?

In response to stories of this kind, younger children felt that the child should obey the mother, while older children (ages 8 to 10) opted for equality. Still older children (11 and older) gave responses that reflected equity: "It wasn't fair, but she did it to help her mother." From these responses, Piaget distinguished three levels in the development of concepts of distributive justice. At the first level, "just" is whatever is commanded by an adult; it's the law. At the second level, equality orientation—or equalitarianism—reigns supreme, even at the expense of obedience and punishment. At the third level, equity dominates—in other words, equality is never defined without taking into account the way that each individual is situated. Thus, in Piaget's observations, there emerges a consistent pattern of movement from one stage to another that is correlated with age.[2]

B. Kohlberg—An Extension of the Stages

Just as Erikson was a revisionist of Freud, so Kohlberg has extended Piaget's basic theory. While Kohlberg uses Piaget's basic approach of confronting a child with stories that pose a moral dilemma, Kohlberg's stories and situations are more complex. (An example is given in Figure 4-2.) In fact, Kohlberg's stories are qualitatively different from Piaget's. The dilemmas posed are challenging to adults as well as children, and they encourage the respondent to answer on the basis of his general theory of morality (R. Brown, 1965). Hence it is not surprising that Kohlberg has found greater complexity and more extended moral development than did Piaget. Kohlberg (1958, 1963, 1968) proposes that there are six possible stages of moral development experienced by the child as he passes into adolescence and adulthood. In conjunction with the six stages of development, the child passes from one level of moral maturity to a second and then to a third level. These three levels and the two stages within each level are as follows.

Kohlberg's moral-judgment stories tend to set up an opposition between a legal rule or social norm and a human need (R. Brown, 1965). Here is a typical example (from Kohlberg, 1963, 1969):

In Europe, a woman was near death from a special kind of cancer. There was one drug that the doctors thought might save her. It was a form of radium that a druggist in the same town had recently discovered. The drug was expensive to make, but the druggist was charging

[2]Piaget and Freud both describe an ongoing process whereby rules and commands are "internalized" or "interiorized." There are differences, however, between Freud's and Piaget's meaning of interiorized. Roger Brown (1965) interprets their concepts as being different in the same way that ingestion is different from digestion. To Brown, Freud's idea of internalization is like ingestion—a swallowing whole of adult laws and ideas, which then become a part of the child without any further process of assimilation. For Piaget, the process resembles digestion—adult ideas are only food for the developing moral system, which assimilates and transforms the food before it becomes a part of the child's own organization. Kohlberg's approach resembles Piaget's in this regard, also.

Figure 4-2. *Kohlberg's Decision Story*

ten times what the drug cost him to make. He paid $200 for the radium and charged $2,000 for a small dose of the drug. The sick woman's husband, Heinz, went to everyone he knew to borrow money, but he could only get together about $1,000, which is half of what it cost. He told the druggist that his wife was dying, and asked him to sell it cheaper or let him pay later. But the druggist said, "No, I discovered the drug and I'm going to make money from it." So Heinz got desperate and broke into the man's store to steal the drug for his wife.

Should Heinz have done that? Was it actually wrong or right? Why?

Is it a husband's duty to steal the drug for his wife, if he can get it no other way? Would a good husband do it?

Did the druggist have the right to charge that much when there was no law actually setting a limit to the price? Why?

If the husband does not feel very close or affectionate to his wife, should he still steal the drug?

Suppose it wasn't Heinz's wife who was dying of cancer, but it was Heinz's best friend. His friend didn't have any money, and there was no one in his family willing to steal the drug. Should Heinz steal the drug for his friend in that case? Why?

Suppose it was a person whom he knew that was dying but who was not a good friend. There was no one else who could get him the drug. Would it be right to steal it for him? Why?

What is there to be said on the side of the law in this case?

Would you steal the drug to save your wife's life? Why?

If you were dying of cancer but were strong enough, would you steal the drug to save your own life?

Heinz broke in the store and stole the drug and gave it to his wife. He was caught and brought before the judge. Should the judge send Heinz to jail for stealing, or should he let him go free? Why?

1. Preconventional level. At this level the child is responsive to cultural rules and labels such as good and bad, or right and wrong; however, the child interprets these labels in light of the physical or the hedonistic consequences of action (punishment, reward, exchange of favors) or in light of the physical power of those who enunciate the rules and labels. This preconventional level is divided into the following two stages.

The first stage is the *punishment and obedience orientation.* To the child at this stage, the *consequences* of action determine the goodness or badness of the action, regardless of the human meaning of these consequences. Avoidance of punishment and unquestioning deference to power are valued in their own right, rather than in accordance with an underlying moral order that employs punishment and authority.

The second stage is the *instrumental relativist orientation,* or *hedonistic orientation.* At this stage, right action consists of that which instrumentally satisfies one's own needs and occasionally the needs of others. Human relations are viewed in the terms of the market place: elements of fairness, reciprocity, and equal sharing are present, but they are always interpreted in a physical, pragmatic way. Reciprocity is a matter of "you scratch my back and I'll scratch yours"—not of loyalty, love, or justice (Kohlberg, 1968).

2. Conventional level. At this level of moral maturity, maintaining the expectations of one's family, group, or nation is perceived as valuable in its own right, regardless of immediate and obvious consequences. The attitude is not only one of **conformity** to personal expectations and social order, but also there is an attitude of loyalty involved. Emphasis is upon actively maintaining, supporting, and justifying the social order and identifying with the persons or group in it. This level encompasses two further stages of moral development.

The *interpersonal concordance* or *good boy-nice girl orientation* is the third stage in Kohlberg's scheme. Good behavior is that which pleases, helps, or is approved by others. There is much conformity in one's assumptions of what is majority or natural behavior. Behavior is frequently judged by intention. The notion that "he means well" becomes important for the first time, and one earns approval by being "nice."

The *law and order orientation* makes up the fourth stage. Here the orientation is toward authority, established rules, and the maintenance of the social order. Right behavior consists of doing one's duty, showing that one respects authority, and maintaining the given social order because it is the given social order (Kohlberg, 1968).

3. Postconventional, autonomous, or principled level. At this level, there is a clear effort to define moral values and principles that have validity and application apart from the authority of the groups or persons advocating these principles and apart from the individual's own identification with these groups. This level again has two stages.

The *social-contract legalistic orientation* falls into this third level of maturity and is the fifth stage in moral development. This stage generally has utilitarian overtones. Right action tends to be defined in relation to general individual rights and with respect to standards that have been critically examined and agreed upon by the whole society. There is a clear awareness of the individual differences in personal values and opinions; hence this fifth stage emphasizes procedural rules for reaching consensus. Aside from what is constitutionally and democratically agreed upon, the social-contract, legalistic orientation sees right and wrong as matters of personal values and opinion. Although the legal point of view is accepted, the possibility of changing the law in light of what seems best for society is emphasized (Kohlberg, 1968). (This approach contrasts with morality as seen at the fourth stage, which accepts law as right and does not seek to change it.) The fifth stage represents the "official" morality of the American government and the United States Constitution.

The *orientation of universal ethical principles* is the sixth stage in Kohlberg's scheme of moral development. At this highest stage, what is morally right is defined not by laws and rules of the social order but by one's own conscience, in accordance with self-determined ethical principles. Rather than being concrete moral rules, these principles are broad and abstract and might include universal principles of justice, principles of the reciprocity and equality of human rights, and respect for the dignity of human beings as individuals.[3]

Examples of how persons at each stage would respond to the dilemma posed in Figure 4-2 are shown in Table 4-2. The responses of a specific person—the Nazi executioner Adolf Eichmann—are shown in Table 4-3, with the appropriate stage assigned to each response.

Like Piaget, Kohlberg conceives that if a person is to achieve the highest stage of moral development, he must pass through the other five stages in a generally invariant manner. In doing so, the individual constantly restructures his experience, and perhaps moves toward a more mature level of moral judgment. At the same time, temporary regression is possible, as when a college student at the sixth stage rejects society's values and returns to the hedonism of stage two. Fixation may occur at any stage and is more likely to occur when no confrontation with higher stages is available.

The notion that an individual must pass through a series of stages in order to achieve moral maturity is quite an assumption, but a comparison of different theorists (presented in Table 4-4) reveals that a variety of viewpoints arrive at the same position—a stage in which principles rather than rules are relied upon, and actions are autonomous. But the assumption that a principle-oriented morality is higher than a law-oriented morality is laden with value judgments, and for this reason Kohlberg has received his share of criticisms. Nonetheless, Kohlberg's approach offers an extremely provocative way of looking at morality, and the validity of his assumptions may, to a large degree, be evaluated by research and empirical work.

V. MORALITY RESEARCH

A. Early Empirical Work—The Search for a General Trait

While Freud, Erikson, Piaget, and Kohlberg have relied almost exclusively upon observation and interviews for sources of their theories, most of the early empirical studies on morality used written tests as measures and an atheoretical approach. The most extensive of these empirical studies was the Character Education Inquiry, begun by Hartshorne, May, and Maller in 1928, which attempted to examine the degree of consistency of moral behavior across situations. They wanted to answer

[3] More recently, Kohlberg (1971) has revised his conception to include a subdivision of the fifth stage called an *individual conscience* orientation. This transition period between stage 5 and stage 6 is reflected in persons who act on the basis of their own consciences but not out of adherence to a universal moral principle. An example might be a college-age draft resister, who says, "My conscience makes me do this, but yours may not."

Table 4-2. *Examples of Answers Reflecting Each Stage of Kohlberg's Moral-Judgment Theory*

Stage 1: *No differentiation between moral value of life and its physical or social status value.*

Tommy, age ten (III, Why should the druggist give the drug to the dying woman when her husband couldn't pay for it?): "If someone important is in a plane and is allergic to heights and the stewardess won't give him medicine because she's only got enough for one and she's got a sick one, a friend, in back, they'd probably put the stewardess in a lady's jail because she didn't help the important one."
(Is it better to save the life of one important person or a lot of unimportant people?): "All the people that aren't important because one man has just one house, maybe a lot of furniture, but a whole bunch of people have an awful lot of furniture and some of these poor people might have a lot of money and it doesn't look it."

Stage 2: *The value of a human life is seen as instrumental to the satisfaction of the needs of its possessor or of other persons. Decision to save life is relative to, or to be made by, its possessor. (Differentiation of physical and interest value of life, differentiation of its value to self and to other.)*

Tommy, age thirteen (IV, Should the doctor "mercy kill" a fatally ill woman requesting death because of her pain?): "Maybe it would be good to put her out of her pain, she'd be better off that way. But the husband wouldn't want it, it's not like an animal. If a pet dies you can get along without it—it isn't something you really need. Well, you can get a new wife, but it's not really the same."
Jim, age thirteen (same question): "If she requests it, it's really up to her. She is in such terrible pain, just the same as people are always putting animals out of their pain."

Stage 3: *The value of a human life is based on the empathy and affection of family members and others toward its possessor. (The value of human life, as based on social sharing, community, and love, is differentiated from the instrumental and hedonistic value of life applicable also to animals.)*

Tommy, age sixteen (same question): "It might be best for her, but not for her husband—and it's a human life—not like an animal. It just doesn't have the same relationship that a human being does to a family. You can become attached to a dog, but nothing like a human you know."

Stage 4: *Life is conceived as sacred in terms of its place in a categorical moral or religious order of rights and duties. (The value of human life, as a categorical member of a moral order, is differentiated from its value to specific other people in the family, etc. Value of life is still partly dependent upon serving the group, the state, and God, however.)*

Jim, age sixteen (same question): "I don't know. In one way, it's murder, it's not a right or privilege of man to decide who shall live and who should die. God put life into everybody on earth and you're taking away something from that person that came directly from God and it's almost destroying a part of God when you kill a person. There's something of God in everyone."

Stage 5: *Life is valued both in terms of its relation to community welfare and in terms of being a universal human right. (Obligation to respect the basic right to life is differentiated from generalized respect for the socio-moral order. The general value of the independent human life is a primary autonomous value not dependent upon other values.)*

Jim, age twenty (same question): "Given the ethics of the doctor who has taken on responsibility to save human life—from that point of view he probably shouldn't but there is another side, there are more and more people in the medical profession who are thinking it is a hardship on everyone, the person, the family, when you know they are going to die. When a person is kept alive by an artificial lung or kidney it's more like being a vegetable than being a human who is alive. If it's her own choice I think there are certain rights and privileges that go along with being a human being. I am a human being and have certain desires for life and I think everyone else does, too, and in that sense we're all equal."

Stage 6: *Belief in the sacredness of human life as representing a universal human value of respect for the individual. (The moral value of a human being, as an object of moral principle, is differentiated from a formal recognition of his rights.)*

Jim, age twenty-four (III, Should the husband steal the drug to save his wife? How about for someone he just knows?) "Yes, A human life takes precedence over any other moral or legal value, whoever it is. A human life has inherent value whether or not it is valued by a particular individual."
(Why is that?): "The inherent worth of the individual human being is the central value in a set of values where the principles of justice and love are normative for all human relationships."

Note: Roman numerals refer to Kohlberg's stories. Material in parentheses reflects questions or interpretations by interviewer.

Table 4-3. *How Statements of Adolf Eichmann Would Be Scored, Using Kohlberg's Moral-Judgment Scale*

Statements	*Stage*
In actual fact, I was merely a little cog in the machinery that carried out the directives of the German Reich.	1
I am neither a murderer nor a mass-murderer. I am a man of average character, with good qualities and many faults.	3
Yet what is there to "admit"? I carried out my orders. It would be as pointless to blame me for the whole final solution of the Jewish problem as to blame the official in charge of the railroads over which the Jewish transports traveled.	1
Where would we have been if everyone had thought things out in those days? You can do that today in the "new" German army. But with us an order was an order.	1
If I had sabotaged the order of the one-time Fuhrer of the German Reich, Adolf Hitler, I would have been not only a scoundrel but a despicable pig like those who broke their military oath to join the ranks of the anti-Hitler criminals in the conspiracy of July 20, 1944.	1
I would like to stress again, however, that my department never gave a single annihilation order. We were responsible only for deportation.	2
My interest was only in the number of transport trains I had to provide. Whether they were bank directors or mental cases, the people who were loaded on these trains meant nothing to me. It was really none of my business.	2
But to sum it all up, I must say that I regret nothing. Adolf Hitler may have been wrong all down the line, but one thing is beyond dispute: the man was able to work his way up from lance corporal in the German army to Fuhrer of a people of almost eighty million.	1
I never met him personally, but his success alone proves to me that I should subordinate myself to this man. He was somehow so supremely capable that the people recognized him. And so with that justification I recognized him joyfully, and I still defend him.	1
I must say truthfully, that if we had killed all the ten million Jews that Himmler's statisticians originally listed in 1933, I would say, "Good, we have destroyed an enemy."	2
But here I do not mean wiping them out entirely. That would not be proper—and we carried on a proper war.	1

questions such as: how general or how situation-specific is moral behavior? Are children who behave morally or ethically in one situation also moral or ethical in another situation? The Hartshorne et al. project covered five years and examined the conduct of high school students in the classroom, on the playing fields, at parties, at church, and at scouting activities. Almost all of the experimental tasks placed the students in different situations that tempted them to act in an immoral way. For example, the students were asked to score their own true-false tests without supervision by the teacher. (The subjects did not know that the researchers had

Table 4-4. *A Comparison of Stages of Moral Judgment and Character Development*

Theorist	*Amoral Type*	*Fearful-Dependent*	*Opportunistic*	*Conforming to Persons*	*Conforming to Rules*	*Operates from Principles; Autonomous*
			Moral Judgment Stages:			
McDougall (1908)	1. Instinctive		2. Reward and punishment	3. Anticipation of praise and blame		4. Regulation by an internal ideal
Piaget (1948)	1. Premoral	2. Heteronomous—obedience to adult authority	3. Autonomous—reciprocity and equality oriented			4. Autonomous—ideal reciprocity and equality
Peck & Havighurst (1960)	1. Amoral		2. Expedient	3. Conforming	4. Irrational-conscientious	5. Rational-altruistic
Kohlberg (1958)		1. Punishment and obedience orientation	2. Instrumental relativist orientation; selfish exchange	3. Interpersonal concordance or "good-boy nice-girl" orientation	4. "Law-and-order" and rule orientation	5. Social contract, legalistic orientation 5B. Individual conscience orientation 6. Orientation of universal ethical principles
Fromm (1955)		1. Receptive	2. Exploitative	3. Marketing	4. Hoarding	5. Productive, autonomous
Riesman (1950)		1. Tradition-directed man		2. Other-directed man	3. Inner-directed man	
Harvey, Hunt, & Schroder (1961)		1. System 1: Absolutistic, evaluative	2. System 2: Negativistic	3. System 3: Conforming, people oriented		4. System 4: Integrated, independent

Note: This table compares the terms used by different theorists concerned with the development of moral judgment or character. By reading across from left to right, the different stages for each theory are presented. By reading down one column, the equivalent stages of different theorists are presented. The similarity is impressive. Figure 4-2, Table 4-2, Table 4-3, and Table 4-4 are adapted from Lawrence Kohlberg, "Stage and Sequence: The Cognitive-Developmental Approach to Socialization," in David A. Goslin (Ed.), *Handbook of Socialization Theory and Research.* © 1969 by Rand McNally & Company, Chicago. Reprinted by permission.

copies of their papers and would know how many changes were made in the process of scoring.)[4]

Hartshorne and May were unable to find many correlations of great magnitude in the reactions to different tasks, which tempted students to lie, cheat, and steal in a variety of situations. The researchers concluded that expressions of morality exhibit no general consistency at all and that the morality or immorality of the subject's behavior is specific to his particular situation at the time. The student who cheated in scoring his test was not the one who stole money from the teacher's desk. When these results were published in the early 1930s, the predominant reaction among psychologists was that research on moral development was rather futile and the search for any organized system of development was fruitless.

Not all psychologists were content to accept the conclusion that moral behavior is entirely situation-specific. Burton (1963) reanalyzed the Hartshorne-May data and found evidence for a small degree of consistency along a dimension of morality in a subject's response from one situation to another. Taking another approach, Gordon Allport (1961) pointed out that a consistency of orientation might even exist when the same student cheats on a test but does not steal money from the teacher's desk; in both of these situations the student's behavior may be guided by a motive to please the teacher. In other words, cheating may be a response to the student's desire to achieve the teacher's goals. The example may be far fetched, but the point is correct enough. Cases of apparently inconsistent behavior may actually reflect consistency at a deeper level.

B. Tests of Psychoanalytic Theory

A massive longitudinal test of the Freudian theory of moral development was carried out by Peck and Havighurst (1960), who tested all the children in a small town, once at age 10 and again six years later. Using a conception of five stages of moral development or character development based on psychoanalytic theory, the researchers found that—as opposed to Freud's postulation—the child's moral growth continues beyond the age of 6. (Peck and Havighurst's stages of development are presented in Table 4-5.) Although different 16-year-olds manifested different stages of development, they tended to maintain the same motives and attitudes they held at age 10.

Many other researchers have examined Freud's hypothesis about the development of a conscience. Sears, Maccoby, and Levin (1957) defined conscience as an internalized control whereby the child rewards or punishes himself as though his parents' standards had become his own. Conscience was assessed through asking the mother questions about the child's behavior in a task that tempted the child to violate a rule or command. Sears et al. concluded that warm, loving parents and stable relations were most predictive of advanced moral development. (One problem with this study, however, was that the mother was the source of measures both of the

[4]It is sadly ironic that many scientists who study moral behavior either induce their subjects to cheat and lie or otherwise deceive their subjects during experiments, even while trying to determine the specificity or generality of morality. Scientists lie in the specific situation of the study, and the reader must assume that the scientists lie only when gathering data and not while analyzing or reporting. Indeed, the generality-specificity argument is rather complex.

Table 4-5. *Character Types and Developmental Periods of Peck and Havighurst*

Character Types	*Developmental Period*
Amoral	Infancy
Expedient	Early Childhood
Conforming	Later Childhood
Irrational–Conscientious	Later Childhood
Rational–Altruistic	Adolescence and Adulthood

child's behavior and of parental attitudes; such a procedure may encourage spuriously high relationships between factors.) More recent studies also indicate that the frequent use of power assertion—in other words, instances where the parent uses his physical power to control the child—leads to the development of a weak conscience (Allinsmith, 1960; Aronfreed, 1961; Hoffman & Saltzstein, 1967; and Holstein, 1969, reviewed by Shoffeitt, 1971).

Other tests for psychoanalytic theory reveal that Freud's suggestion that females do not develop as strong superegos as males cannot be confirmed by available research. Sears et al. (1957) found that 20 percent of the boys who were studied had strong consciences, as compared to 29 percent of the girls. Also Rempel and Signori (1964) report that, compared to males, females rated themselves significantly higher on conscience as a factor in determining their behavior.

When we look for empirical support for the Freudian proposal that the superego controls morality, we find very little or no evidence for this notion. Even recent psychoanalytic theorizing emphasizes ego strength more than the superego. Among the characteristics of the ego that contribute to moral conduct are general intelligence, ability to delay gratification, capacity for focused attention, ability to control socially unacceptable fantasies, and degree of self-esteem (Kohlberg, 1963). Rather than emphasizing an early, fully developed superego evolved from the Oedipal conflict, researchers are currently emphasizing the decision-making capacity of the ego, which gradually develops with age. Thus, widespread dissatisfaction with the Freudian theory of moral development exists, for reasons cited above and because of inconsistent findings from one study to the next.

C. Resistance to Temptation—Social-Learning Theory's Approach to Morality

While the Freudian generally interprets morality as a heavy-handed superego dispensing guilt, the social-learning theorist operationally defines morality as **resistance to temptation,** which is accounted for by an *ethical risk* hypothesis (Rettig & Rawson, 1963). That is, the greater the likelihood of getting caught, the less likely the child is to engage in immoral behaviors. To social-learning theorists, the child responds to each situation in these terms, and hence it is fruitless to expect much generalization in the degree of socialization across tasks or generalized traits of personality over many situations. Even early environmental factors may be irrelevant to the development of resistance to temptation.

The effects of punishment on resistance to temptation have been widely studied. Experiments using animals as subjects have indicated that both the timing of the punishment and the intensity of the punishment contribute to its effectiveness as a suppressor of behavior. Studies have also been conducted to determine whether the timing of the punishment of children influences the degree to which the child internalizes the prohibitions. Aronfreed (1968) confronted children with a discrimination learning task in which each child had to choose between two toys and tell a story about one of the toys. If the child chose the attractive toy, he was sharply told "No! That's for the older boys!" In one condition (pretouching condition), the "No" was uttered just as the child reached for the toy and before he touched it. In a second condition the experimenter said "No" two or three seconds after the child picked up the toy. In a control condition, each boy simply pointed to the toy of his choice, and the experimenter made no comment. The boys who were punished at the initiation of the transgression suppressed their choice of the attractive toy after fewer punishments than did the children who were punished after they picked up the toy. Internalization of the proscription against touching the toy was assessed by using a covert marker that could show whether the child had picked up an attractive toy while the experimenter was out of the room. The boys in the pretouching condition transgressed less than the boys who touched the toy in the second condition. In generalizing to natural settings, Aronfreed (1968) suggests that restricting the opportunity to transgress is insufficient, by itself, to bring about an internalized suppression of the child's temptation. Explicit punishment is also necessary.

Although social-learning theorists rely primarily on such factors as the timing and intensity of reinforcements, they also consider cognitive determinants of resistance to the temptation in their approach to morality. Aronfreed (1968), for example, finds that a child will be more resistant to temptation if he is given a reason for his punishment than if he is given no clue as to why he is being punished. The effects of increased cognitive structure upon resistance to temptation suggest that children acquire complex rules as they increase their ability to consider the multiple consequences of their behavior.

D. Empirical Verifications of Piaget's Stage Approach

During the period between 1946 and 1956, Gesell, Ilg, and Ames (1956) traced the development of children from ages 5 to 16. The researchers found a spiral pattern of development in the morality of an individual from early childhood to age 16—the foundation of the moral development being laid during the first five years of life. Two periods or stages were discovered—one covering ages 5 to 10, the other covering ages 10 to 16. Gesell sees this development as sequential and supports the Piagetian view, stating that there is "an unmistakable trend from the specific to the general and from the concrete to the abstract" (1956, p. 73). Also supportive of Piaget's conception is Gesell's conclusion that this development comes about as the result of a tension between stability and conflict in human experience. All in all, Gesell's observations lend positive support to the hypothesis that morality can be traced through a pattern of development, which exhibits clear-cut stages of growth.

Piaget's conclusions have not always been supported in research, however, and many have criticized the two-stage theory as too simplistic (Lerner, 1937; Isaacs, 1966; Kohlberg, 1969). Other researchers (MacRae, 1954, for example) have questioned the presence of distinct stages. Apparently the time periods Piaget assigned for the emergence of each stage become less applicable the further one is removed from the locale of Piaget's children in Geneva. However, the change to a different type of moral development with increasing age is consistent in every society studied. For example, seeing intention as more important than physical consequences in judging the wrongness of an action is found more often in older children than in younger ones "in every culture, in every social class, in every sex group, and in every subculture studied (Switzerland, United States, Belgium, Chinese, Malaysian-aboriginal, Mexican, Israel, Hopi, Zuni, Sioux, Papago)" (Kohlberg, 1969, p. 374).

E. Kohlberg's Moral-Judgment Stages and Moral Behavior

The dilemmas posed in the stories used by Piaget and by Kohlberg seek to measure **moral judgment**—or the moral attitudes that determine how a person feels one should respond to a certain situation. Some remaining questions are: do moral attitudes lead to moral behaviors? Do subjects at different stages of moral judgment respond to the same stimulus with different behaviors? If not, the application of a conception of stages in moral judgment to everyday behaviors is greatly weakened. Fortunately, a number of researchers have examined behavior in relation to moral-judgment stages. For example, Krebs (1967) observed the extent of cheating among sixth-grade children on four tests. The results, reprinted in Table 4-6, indicate that among the five sixth graders who had achieved a principled moral-judgment level, only one of five cheated, while between 67 and 83 percent of the children at other moral-judgment levels cheated.

Table 4-6. *Percentage of Students Cheating*

N	*Level*	*Percent Cheating*
55	Premoral (Stages 1-2)	83
63	Conventional (Stages 3-4)	67
5	Principled (Stages 5-6)	20

From Krebs, 1967.

The Kohlberg moral-judgment stories were given to college students who had previously participated in Milgram's (1963) obedience study (summarized in Chapter 3). Kohlberg expected that subjects who were more advanced in moral judgment (stages 5 and 6) would be more likely to refuse to continue giving shocks to another participant after the latter had indicated he was in pain. Although the number of subjects was small—only 34—the results were most revealing. Eight of the subjects were at stages 5 or 6 in moral judgment; six, or 75 percent, of these refused to continue giving shocks. Twenty-four subjects were at conventional levels of moral judgment (stages 3 or 4); and only three, or 12.5 percent, of these refused to continue. Principled morality was strongly related to the refusal to collaborate in an act that inflicted pain upon another human being, while levels of conventional morality indicated that those persons were likely to collaborate with the experimenter.

To date, the most comprehensive test of Kohlberg's moral-judgment theory has been presented by Haan, Smith, and Block (1968), who related student's moral-judgment stages to their political behavior, their participation in student protests, their backgrounds, their perceptions of their parents, and their self- and ideal self-descriptions. Students from the University of California at Berkeley, San Francisco State College, and Peace Corps volunteers served as subjects—making a total of 957 respondents. However, only 54 percent of the subjects gave responses which could reliably be classified into one of the six moral-judgment stages. (Such occurrences indicate that either the measuring instrument is not precise enough to classify every subject, or that some subjects do not clearly fall into only one stage at any point in time. Probably both possibilities apply.) As shown in Table 4-7, few respondents were at the preconventional stages; about two-thirds of the men and 80 percent of the women possessed conventional moral judgment (stages 3 and 4); and 28 percent of the males and 18 percent of the females possessed postconventional, or principled morality. (Kohlberg believes that fewer women achieve higher stages of moral development because allegiance to their children precludes the development of abstract moral principles.) For respondents at each moral-judgment level, Haan, et al. found that somewhat different personality and behavior patterns emerged.

1. Preconventional morality (stages 1 and 2). At this level, males were found to be politically radical, active, and protesting, while the women were found to be moderates and inactive, even though joiners. Persons at the preconventional stages do not endorse the obligation to take the role of others and, instead, are more concerned with their personal fulfillment—"the women by a stubborn practicality and the men for personal flair and expressiveness" (Haan, et al., 1968, p. 195).

2. Conventional morality (stages 3 and 4). Respondents at the conventional level of morality were found to have modeled themselves after their parents, having accepted the traditional values of American society. They reported that their parents provided clear rules, punishments, and rewards (a strategy very similar to the one recommended by social-learning theorists for the development of morality). These respondents were found to have harmonious, nonskeptical relationships with institutions and authority figures.

3. Postconventional morality (stages 5 and 6). The young people at this principled level of morality were characterized by a firm sense of autonomy in their life patterns and ideological positions. They were found to be candid about themselves and their families and espoused both new values and new politics. Although they rejected the traditional values implicit in the Protestant ethic, they maintained a concern about their responsibilities to others. Their parents seem to have permitted and perhaps encouraged them to learn from and be challenged by their own life experi-

Table 4-7. *Percent of Subjects at Each of Kohlberg Stages*

Stages	*Males (N = 253)*	*Females (N = 257)*
1 & 2	7 %	3 %
3	22 %	41 %
4	43 %	38 %
5	21 %	14 %
6	7 %	4 %

From Haan, Smith, & Block, 1968.

ences. While males reported that their fathers encouraged them to take chances and try new things, the females reported that their fathers did not give them responsibilities. Respondents at the sixth stage particularly showed self-honesty and self-condemnation consistent with Kohlberg's theory.

Haan, et al. also reported the extent of participation in the 1965 Berkeley Free Speech Movement sit-in, according to moral-judgment levels. The percentages of the moral types arrested at the sit-in are interesting. (See Table 4-8.) Among the men at preconventional stages 1 and 2, 60 percent participated and 40 percent did not. The percentages of stage-5 and stage-6 men who attended the sit-in were also high— 41 percent and 75 percent, respectively. Participation levels by stage-3 and stage-4 men

Table 4-8. *Percentages of Pure Moral Types Arrested in the Free Speech Movement Sit-in*

Stages	*Men (N = 117)*	*Women (N = 97)*
1 & 2	60 %	33 %
3	18 %	9 %
4	6 %	12 %
5	41 %	57 %
6	75 %	86 %

From Haan, Smith, & Block, "Moral Reasoning of Young Adults," *Journal of Personality and Social Psychology*, 1968, **10**, 183–201. Copyright 1968 by the American Psychological Association, and reproduced by permission. Berkeley Strike photograph by Stephen Shames, Black Star.

were much lower—18 percent and 6 percent, respectively. Percentages of participating women were similar to those of the men in that more preconventional and postconventional women were present at the sit-in.

While conventional types generally reject the opportunity to protest, significant percentages of both preconventional and postconventional types participate in protests—but for different reasons. The preconventional stage-2 types see the protest in terms of a power conflict in which they are out to better their own status. The principled protesters (stage 5 and 6) are concerned about basic issues of civil liberties and the role of students as citizens within a university community. These findings are consistent with the subjects' reported activities and substantiate the general relationship between moral judgment and behavior. Interestingly enough, the few stage-3 arrestees stated that they had participated in the sit-in because the University of California administrators had failed as good authorities. Similarly, the few stage-4 arrestees justified their position by claiming that the administration had violated proper legal procedures.

Probably the most important contribution of this study by Haan, et al. is the clear differentiation of various stages in regard to empathy. Both conventional and principled morality are made possible by the capacity to assume the role of another—which means that one must be able to extend one's self and not be fixed. The person at stage 5, with a strong sense of being contractually obligated, is not able to separate himself from the social order, even when he recognizes its injustices. He may try to change the social order but recognizes that an injustice exists because of the will of the majority. The stage-6 orientation in a moral confrontation will involve the expression of universal and logically consistent, ideal principles of justice. The stage-6 person will reject a social contract or law if it violates his individual principles, but this same person also understands the essential contractual nature of the social order and human affairs. The question is: how can a stage-6 person exist in a society that operates on the stage-4 level? The stage-6 response is to accept the penalties for breaking the law. Martin Luther King's letter from a Birmingham jail (Figure 4-3) is cited by Kohlberg (1970) as an example of the kind of civil disobedience that exemplifies stage-6 morality.

Figure 4-3. *Letter from a Birmingham Jail by Martin Luther King*

There is a type of constructive non-violent tension which is necessary for growth. Just as Socrates felt it was necessary to create a tension in the mind so that individuals could rise from the bondage of half-truths, so must we see the need for non-violent gadflies to create the kind of tension in society that will help men rise from the dark depths of prejudice and racism.

One may well ask, "How can you advocate breaking some laws and obeying others?" The answer lies in the fact that there are two types of laws, just and unjust. One has not only a legal but a moral responsibility to obey just laws. One has a moral responsibility to disobey unjust laws. An unjust law is a human law that is not rooted in eternal law and natural law. Any law that uplifts human personality is just, any law that degrades human personality is unjust. An unjust law is a code that a numerical or power majority group compels a minority group to obey but does not make binding on itself. This difference is made legal.

I do not advocate evading or defying the law as would the rabid segregationist. That would lead to anarchy. One who breaks an unjust law must do so openly, lovingly, and with a willingness to accept the penalty. An individual who breaks a law that conscience tells him is unjust, and willingly accepts the penalty of imprisonment in order to arouse the conscience of the community over its injustice, is in reality expressing the highest respect for the law.

The above examples demonstrate a degree of relationship between moral judgment and behavior. In some situations, stage-5 and stage-6 persons demonstrate behaviors different from those who, in Kohlberg's scheme, possess less developed levels of moral judgment. In other situations, the behavior of postconventional persons resembles that of preconventional persons and differs from conventionally moral subjects. In both cases, the differences are predictable and consistent with Kohlberg's theory of moral judgment. In ambiguous situations, one's level of moral judgment defines one's responsibilities, duties, and rights in distinctive ways, which lead to stage-related behavior (Kohlberg, 1969).

Kohlberg's proposition that movement through the stages occurs in an invariant sequence has less solid support than his other proposals. Cross-sectional studies (Kohlberg, 1969) using children of different ages as subjects found that, on the average, older children are at higher stages of moral development than young children. While the average age at which change takes place is not the same in each society, children in the United States, Taiwan, Great Britain, Mexico, and Turkey show the following patterns of development: from age 10 to age 16, the extent of conventional moral thought (stages 3 and 4) increases steadily; however, stage 4 is the dominant stage of most adults.

Longitudinal studies (Kramer, 1968) indicate some degree of movement consistent with Kohlberg's proposed sequence. Fifty young males were interviewed every three years over a 12-year period. At the beginning of the study, the subjects were from ages 10 to 16, and all were in their twenties upon completion of the study. Half the subjects were from middle-class backgrounds, while the others were from lower-class families. Most of the subjects remained at the same stage or increased in stage development with age; however, there was a regression or drop in stage level (usually back to the hedonism of stage 2) in about 20 percent of the middle-class males between the end of high school and the middle of their college years. This regression was temporary, and these young men increased in moral development after college.

Few young adults achieve the highest stages of moral development, and Kohlberg himself recognizes the possibility that stage 5 and stage 6 may not be the end point in moral development. Possibly, stages 4, 5, and 6 are "alternative types of mature response rather than . . . a sequence" (Kohlberg, 1969, p. 385). At any rate, the theory will continue to be revised and tested. While it may be neither possible nor desirable to pigeonhole every person at some specific judgment stage, Kohlberg's analysis is a useful system for elucidating the development of morality.

VI. THE DEVELOPMENT OF THE ACHIEVEMENT MOTIVE

As a child becomes socialized, he is introduced to the basic social motives of his society. In America, Canada, and similar countries these social motives include achievement, affiliation, power, self-actualization, dependence, autonomy, and numerous others. In Chapter 3, Maslow's conception of the process of developing self-actualizing values was reviewed. In this section, a different motive will be considered.

Achievement was perhaps the dominant value in America in the first half of the twentieth century. The **achievement motive** (often called need for achievement, or *nAch*) may be defined as an energizing condition that causes a person to internalize evaluations of his own performance and then seek to meet these standards (Atkinson & Feather, 1966). The person high in the achievement motive seeks goals, whether or not a trophy, popularity, or other external criteria of success are associated with the goals. Achievement of one's internalized goals results in pride; failure results in humiliation (Weinstein, 1969). Since the late 1940s, this condition has been studied intensively—first by a small group of psychologists at Wesleyan University (McClelland, Atkinson, Clark, & Lowell, 1953) and later by other researchers both in America and abroad (Atkinson, 1958; McClelland, 1961, 1971; McClelland & Winter, 1969; Heckhausen, 1967).

A. Measurement of the Achievement Motive

By showing pictures and having a person write stories about the pictures, we may make a quantitative assessment of the strength of the person's achievement motive (McClelland et al., 1953). The four pictures initially used by McClelland and his colleagues were (a) a work situation, showing a man at a machine; (b) an academic situation, showing a boy at a desk; (c) a father-and-son picture; and (d) a boy apparently daydreaming. When shown these or similar pictures, subjects are asked to tell what is happening at the moment, what led to the situation, what is being thought, and what the outcome will be. The person's responses can be scored in accordance with the number of achievement-related ideas or themes that his stories contain.

Abundant evidence indicates that scores on this projective measure do indeed tap an underlying condition—a condition that, when aroused, causes the individual to strive to achieve his standards of successful performance. This projective measure is reminiscent of Freud's conception of unconscious motives, in that it points to an aspect of personal motivation of which the individual may not be aware. When persons are given a questionnaire asking about their desire for achievement, their answers do not agree very closely with the themes that emerge in their stories about the projective-test pictures (deCharms, Morrison, Reitman, & McClelland, 1955; Marlowe, 1959). Apparently, the projective approach is more closely related to actual levels of performance than to what people think of as their levels of achievement. The individual who forthrightly reports his concern with achievement tends to defer to authority and to conform in his stories. In contrast, high achievers, as measured by the projective measure, emphasize matters of effectiveness and striving in their stories. As McClelland says, "When you make up a story to go with an otherwise meaningless picture, you project a lot more of yourself than you realize. You provide an unfiltered specimen of your normal working thoughts" (1971, p. 36). The projective measure of *nAch*, however, has its weaknesses; neither the test-retest reliability nor the internal consistency of the device is high (Weinstein, 1969). Moreover, different projective measures of *nAch* produce inconsistent results (Klinger,

1966). Regrettably rather than resolving these problems, researchers have continued to use the instruments in a quest for the determinants of the achievement motive.

B. Child Rearing and the Strength of the Achievement Motive

Available evidence points to a direct correlation between the learning of the achievement motive and the nature of childhood training. Early research indicated that individuals high in achievement motive were subjected as children to relatively rigorous training in independence. The mothers of 8- to 10-year-old boys who were high in *nAch* reported that their children were expected to have mastered at a relatively early age such independent behaviors as obeying traffic lights, entertaining themselves, earning their own spending money, and choosing their own clothes. The mothers of boys low in *nAch* reported that they expected the same indications of independence but at a significantly later age (Winterbottom, 1953). Apparently, the relatively demanding parent who clearly instigates self-reliance in the child and who then rewards independent behavior is teaching the child a need for achievement. No strong degree of achievement motive is developed in a child who is left to his own devices by a parent or parents. This child is still independent, however, because no one is there to encourage and reinforce his self-reliance. The ghetto child may learn early to dress himself or to fix his own breakfast, but he does not necessarily internalize standards of excellence (B. C. Rosen, 1959).

Similar results have been obtained from studies of achievement motivation in nonindustrialized societies. In these societies where there is early and rigorous independence training of children, the adults are achievement oriented. Where the independence training is late and casual, adult achieving is less emphasized (McClelland & Friedman, 1952; Child, Storm, & Veroff, 1958). Navaho youngsters, for example, are pushed early and vigorously toward high standards of independence, and Navaho adults are strivers (McClelland & Friedman, 1952).

C. The Effect of the Achievement Motive upon the Development of a Society

Research on the achievement motive has gone beyond a concern with the function of this motive in the life of an individual and has begun to explore the achievement motive as it functions in whole societies. The general question in this research venture has been: "what happens in a society if large numbers of individual members are highly motivated to achieve?" Such a question becomes amenable to study when (a) the achievement motive is measurable and (b) techniques are invented for measuring certain social phenomena. Both these criteria seem to have been met in a number of studies on achieving societies.

In one such study, McClelland (1958) related the achievement motivation of the ancient Greeks to the economic activity of their society. Achievement motivation was measured by counting the number of achievement themes occurring in comparable samples of literature from three periods of Greek history: (a) the period of growth, from 900 B.C. to 475 B.C.; (b) the plateau period of high development, from 475 B.C. to 362 B.C.; and (c) the period of decline, from 362 B.C. to 100 B.C. The size of the Greek area of trade was used as an index of economic activity. It was found that achievement themes were significantly more frequent in the period of growth than in either of the other periods and that during the period of growth there was a great interest in trade, which reached its maximum around 450 B.C. By this time, however, achievement themes in Greek literature had fallen off greatly. From 450 B.C. onward, there was a decline both in the trade area and in the frequency of achievement themes in the literature.

Similar studies have related the frequency of achievement themes in English ballads to an index of economic growth across several centuries of English history. Other studies have analyzed the achievement themes appearing in primary school readers of 25 different countries in 1925 and in 1950 and have found that the extent of such themes is related to indices of economic development (McClelland, 1961). Some evidence even suggests (Rudin, 1968) that, in countries with a high index of achievement motivation, the death rates from ulcers and hypertension are relatively high. Undoubtedly, when many individuals in a society are highly motivated to achieve (a condition that results from certain child-rearing practices), then that society will demonstrate relatively vigorous economic growth.

One may reasonably assume that economic development in a society is partly brought about by individual entrepreneurs who are motivated to achieve and who take risks that are most likely to lead to success. The question is, however: how do many individuals simultaneously learn a need to achieve? To answer this question we must return to the evidence on independence training in children. In the period of early development in Greece, for example, there was little in the way of a stable urban society: a relatively nomadic way of life prevailed. Children of nomads were not likely to be long pampered; parents taught their children to fend for themselves, and they thus tended to grow into achieving adults. When Greek society became more stable, more civilized children had things easier. Frequently, these children were reared by slaves who, wanting to keep relatively pleasant household jobs, discouraged childhood independence. The likely result was a population of adults—one generation later—who were characterized by low achievement motivation. Such reasoning is, of course, speculative. We can only say that such a sequence of events is consonant with the data, but does not follow inexorably. Nevertheless, one might speculate further and raise questions about the effect of present child-rearing practices on the achievement motivation of future adults in our own society. What about independence training in our kindergartens and primary grades? Since teachers of young children are, so to speak, professional child rearers, we may wonder whether they encourage independence or, like the Greek slaves, tend to foster dependence.

VII. THE FUTURE OF MORALITY: PROTEAN MAN?

The constructive nonviolent tension described by Martin Luther King in his letter from a Birmingham jail is greatest in times of change—when traditional values no longer seem to serve man. According to Robert Lifton (1968), the *psychohistorical dislocation* and *flooding of imagery* of the present times have created the need for a Protean man. Psychohistorical dislocation is a break occurring in our sense of connection with the important symbols of our cultural tradition—such as family, religion, schools, government, and other social institutions. (Some of the effects of this dislocation will be described in Chapter 12.) The flooding of imagery from the mass media overwhelms the individual with information and superficial messages. Like Proteus of Greek mythology, who could change his shape easily but could not commit himself to a single form, Protean man is characterized by a series of quests, each readily abandoned for new experiences. This on-going quest resembles Erikson's "identity conflict" yet is not limited to the young. In present-day American culture, we are expected to be Protean in that each person is expected to be expert in a number of roles. The problem is we can no longer identify the "real" person. The Protean man, for example, is one who traditionally values science and technology yet is sensitive to their inconsistencies. He knows that science has liberated man from irrationality but also threatens our species with annihilation. Protean man furthermore has a profound inner sense of the absurd and seeks new ways for symbolic immortality through expanding his consciousness or unifying himself with nature. This new individual may not, however, be a product of contemporary times alone. As in the Sanskrit fable, the simpleton of a thousand years ago also had to deal with the purveyors of magic. Perhaps, now there are just more magicians—and fewer trees.

VIII. SUMMARY

In seeking to understand the development of morality, some theorists, such as Freud and Erikson, have emphasized motivational and emotional determinants, while others, like Piaget and Kohlberg, have stressed cognitive factors. Reinforcement theorists and social-learning theorists have avoided introducing any intervening variables—either motivational or cognitive—and have focused on behavior and the changes it undergoes. Resistance to temptation, or the suppression of responses that are prohibited by society, has been studied extensively by these theorists.

Freud proposed that three systems of energy operate within the person and that each system—the *id*, the *ego*, and the *superego*—has its own goals. In addition, Freud posited that a child passes through several stages of personality development—the *oral* stage, the *anal* stage, the *phallic* stage, the *latency* period, and the *genital* stage. Preoccupation with a specific part of the body is central to each stage, and, if the related needs are not satisfied, part of the person's psychic energy remains oriented toward these needs.

In psychoanalytic theory, morality is seen as a result of the child's identification with the parents and as an outcome of the child's introjection of their standards.

As a neo-Freudian, Erik Erikson has extended the period of psychological development beyond childhood into adolescence, young adulthood, and mature ages. Erikson has proposed that each age period has its own *nuclear conflict* to resolve. In contrast to Freud, Erikson and other neo-Freudians recognize the ego as a stable factor in early development.

Piaget's theory is an example of a cognitive approach to moral development, emphasizing the acquisition of rules, laws, and principles. Children pass from an earlier stage of moral realism (accepting rules as given by authority) to moral independence (rules may be altered by consensus to fit the needs of the situation). According to Piaget, as the child moves from one stage to another, he comes to emphasize the intentions rather than the consequences of an act; he gradually favors reciprocity rather than expiatory types of punishment, and he finally discards a belief in immanent justice.

Kohlberg has extended Piaget's conception and proposed three levels of moral development: preconventional, conventional, and postconventional (also called autonomous or principled level). Within these levels, there are six stages of moral development, which (according to Kohlberg) the child must pass through in invariant order.

Insofar as morality research is concerned, empirical tests of Freud's theory of moral development have been inconsistent in the degree to which the theory can be supported. Kohlberg's measurements of moral-judgment levels have been related to moral behavior.

Persons at advanced stages of moral judgment have been found to be less likely to cheat on tests or to obey an experimenter who tells them to hurt a fellow subject.

The *achievement motive* is defined as an energizing condition which causes the person to internalize high standards of performance. Evidence shows that persons high in the achievement motive (*nAch*) are more likely to succeed in appropriate tasks. Relatively early training in independence produces in the adult a high level of achievement motivation.

IX. SUGGESTED READINGS

Berkowitz, L. *The development of motives and values in the child.* New York: Basic Books, 1964. A summary of findings regarding cultural, religious, social-class, and familial influences on the development of morality and achievement motivation.

Erikson, E. H. *Childhood and society.* (2nd ed.) New York: Norton, 1963. (Paperback.) An extended, yet readable, treatment of Erikson's theory of psychological development throughout the life cycle. Also recommended are Erikson's treatments of specific persons in *Gandhi's Truth* and *Young Man Luther.*

Evans, R. I. *Dialogue with Erik Erikson.* New York: Dutton, 1969. (Paperback.) A series of conversations between Erik Erikson and psychologist Richard I. Evans. Evans is a sympathetic questioner, and Erikson's responses are clear, informative, and charming. Highly recommended as a way of learning more about Erikson, the man, and Erikson, the theorist.

Heckhausen, H. *The anatomy of achievement motivation.* New York: Academic Press, 1967. A review of work on achievement motivation. Includes an extensive set of references.

Kohlberg, L. Development of moral character and moral ideology. In M. L. Hoffman and L. W. Hoffman (Eds.), *Review of child development research.* Vol. I. New York: Russell Sage Foundation, 1964. Pp. 383–431. Reviews Kohlberg's theory of moral development through six stages. Relevant research is described.

Piaget, J. *The moral judgment of the child.* New York: Free Press, 1965. (Paperback.) Piaget's account of how children grow in morality, as derived from his observations of countless marbles games and extended conversations with children.

I. *EFFECTS OF REWARD STRUCTURES ON COHESIVENESS AND PRODUCTIVITY*
   A. *Group atmosphere and cohesiveness*
   B. *Groups possessing intragroup cooperation and intergroup competition: team-competitive structure*
   C. *Children's preferences*
   D. *The effects of failure*
   E. *Competition, cooperation, and learning in the classroom*

II. *COOPERATIVE AND COMPETITIVE REWARD STRUCTURES IN OTHER REAL-LIFE SETTINGS*
   A. *The ecological approach: A ballet company*
   B. *A systems approach: A complex business organization*
   C. *Reward structures in a dyad: Marriage*

III. *THE DEVELOPMENT OF COOPERATIVE AND COMPETITIVE MOTIVES*
   A. *Development of awareness of others*
   B. *Subcultural differences in the development of motives*
   C. *Orientation of the family and the development of motives*

IV. *THE INTERACTION OF REWARD STRUCTURES AND MOTIVES*
   A. *The Prisoner's Dilemma*
   B. *Factors influencing degree of cooperation*
      1. *The reward structure*
      2. *The value of pay-offs*
      3. *The strategy of the other participant*
      4. *Opportunities for communication*
      5. *Effects of personality and attitudes*
   C. *Generalizing from laboratory game situations to the real world*

V. *COOPERATION AND COMPETITION IN THE FUTURE*

VI. *SUMMARY*

VII. *SUGGESTED READINGS*

Chapter Five

Cooperation and Competition

by Anne Smead

> The law of life should not be the competition of acquisitiveness, but cooperation, the good of each contributing to the good of all. *Jawaharlal Nehru*
>
> While the law of competition may be sometimes hard for the individual, it is best for the race, because it insures the survival of the fittest in every department. *Andrew Carnegie*

Many of the situations of our everyday life entail cooperation and/or competition. A few examples may briefly demonstrate how our environmental situation elicits either cooperative or competitive behavior. Carol Brochmeister, for example, had enjoyed making dolls for the orphanage last year. She and others in her high school social club had a huge assembly line where each girl was responsible for a certain task. Carol's job had been to cut out the arms from a pattern another girl had drawn on the cloth. Last year, the goal was to make a doll for every orphan; and, after the completion of the project, the cafeteria served steaks to the entire group. This year, however, things are different; the project has been set up as a contest to see which girl can produce the most dolls, and no one is willing to help anyone else.

A second example involves a car salesman, Harold Davis. Harold has been talking to his fellow salesman, Jim Roberts, about the financial troubles he is in after having his child hospitalized. "I sure would like to win the bonus this month," said Harold, referring to the 300 dollars that would be awarded to the salesman who sells the most cars. Jim Roberts is sympathetic, but Harold knows Jim will be working just as hard to win the bonus for himself. In fact, Harold observes Jim edging toward the front door as a couple of potential buyers enter.

Ed Hargis finds himself in still another kind of situation. Ed has planned to spend the evening studying for his German exam, scheduled for 8 o'clock the next morning. It is his last final exam of the fall semester. As he sits down to study, Steve Lewis, a classmate, comes into his room. Steve needs help; he has missed the last three weeks of his math course, and he wants somebody to review the material with him before tomorrow morning. Ed took the math exam this morning: would he spend a couple of hours now helping Steve?

Each of these situations deals with cooperation and competition. Cooperation is demonstrated through acts of working together for mutual benefit and is often accompanied by a shared or common goal. Competition is reflected in acts of striving to excel, often in order to obtain an exclusive goal. Cooperation involves sharing, helping, and often coordinating efforts between two or more people, while competition includes a reluctance to help or give information, or even a withdrawal of support.

There are a multitude of reasons why a person cooperates or competes. Cooperation and competition may be brought about through certain types of incentives or goals or through other aspects of the environmental situation. Certain cultures may encourage either cooperation or competition to the extent that the persons involved customarily behave in accepted ways. But while many situations have a potential for eliciting competition—for example, shopping at a market in Egypt or waiting in several lines of traffic for the light to turn green—not all persons in such situations show competitive behavior. An understanding of cooperation and competition requires an awareness of both situational and intrapersonal determinants.

Cooperation and competition can be confused because they both refer to personal motives, behaviors, or aspects of the situation such as instructions, incentives, or reward structures. To compound the confusion, there is a third type of behavior, *individualism*, which must be considered along with cooperation and competition. Here, the meanings of each of these types of behavior—cooperation, competition, and individualism—will be spelled out as a motive and as a reward structure. A real-life situation can be used to illustrate.

Suppose it is the first day of class, and the professor is describing his grading procedures. "I grade on the curve: 15 percent of the class will get A's; 25 percent, B's; 35 percent, C's; 15 percent, D's; and 10 percent, F's. There may be a little variation from this, but these percentages are about it." This situation represents competitive reward structure, where competition is defined as a condition in which the achievement of a goal by one participant prevents attainment of the goal by any other participant. If, in a class of 100, 15 students have higher scores than yours, you cannot achieve your goal of earning an A, regardless of the absolute value of your test score. Likewise, in a competitive reward structure, if someone succeeds, someone else must inevitably fail. Morton Deutsch (1949a) described this reward structure as **contrient interdependence**; the interdependence of participants is mutually exclusive.

In another class, a different professor may tell his students that he intends to conduct a different type of course: "I want us all to work together. Meeting the goals of the course is a group task. If the class clearly meets the goals, everyone gets an A; if it doesn't, then no one will get an A. It is possible for everyone to get an A, or for everyone to get a B or an F." Here is a cooperative reward structure; if one person achieves or moves toward his goal it helps others in achieving their goals. In this situation, goal achievement is an all-or-nothing proposition. Deutsch (1949a) refers to this reward structure as **promotive interdependence,** where the interdependence of participants is mutually beneficial.

We may consider one more professor who tells his class that his grading system is flexible. "Your grade is based upon the number of assignments you carry out successfully. It is possible for each and every student to receive an A; however, it could be that no one will receive an A. The same is true with any other letter grade. The grade you get has no influence upon what grades the other students achieve." Grading that converts absolute percentages to letter grades is an example of **individualistic reward structure,** where goal achievement by one participant has no effect upon the goal achievement of others. In contrast to the two previous situations, goal attainment by one participant is not interdependent upon another. Thus, the reward structure for any task involving more than one person could be competitive, cooperative, or individualistic.

Part of the confusion about cooperation and competition is that in addition to reward structures, they can also involve the motives of the individuals in a group. A *cooperative motive* is a mutual or shared one; the person who possesses a cooperative motive seeks the outcome that is most beneficial to all participants. In contrast, a *competitive motive* seeks an outcome that is most beneficial to oneself and most detrimental to the other participants. In other words, a competitive motive seeks not only to achieve personal success but also to cause other participants to fail. A person with the third type of motivation, an *individualistic motive,* seeks an outcome that is the best for himself, regardless of whether others achieve their goals.

Thus, in situations such as the college classroom, the reward structure may be cooperative, competitive, or individualistic; and the motive of each student may also

Figure 5-1. *A College Class—What Is the Reward Structure and What Are the Students' Motives? A class may have a cooperative, competitive, or individualistic reward structure. A student's primary motive may be cooperative, competitive, or individualistic. What might result if the reward structure is competitive and a student's motive is cooperative? (Photograph by Joe Zinn.)*

be cooperative, competitive, or individualistic. Most real-life situations and motives are not pure types, but the preceding analysis permits further understanding of more complex phenomena.

I. EFFECTS OF REWARD STRUCTURES ON COHESIVENESS AND PRODUCTIVITY

Let us now turn to a consideration of how cooperative, competitive and individualistic reward structures affect group relationships in school and employment settings. In subsequent sections, these factors will be considered in other real-life settings.

A. Group Atmosphere and Cohesiveness

Cohesiveness refers to the degree of liking each member has for the group. The questions to be asked here are: how do cooperative or competitive reward structures affect the cohesiveness of a group? Which reward structure produces more cohesiveness and a better group atmosphere? Which is accompanied by an increase in anxiety? The evidence clearly shows that, in comparison to competitive structures, cooperative reward structures are consistently associated with increased communication, greater cohesiveness, and greater congeniality (Grossack, 1954; Raven & Eachus, 1963; Crombag, 1966). For example, in a study comparing methods of conducting discussion sections in an introductory psychology course, Haines and McKeachie (1967) varied the reward structures by grading individual versus group projects. In competitive classes, a higher level of tension resulted, often leading to a disruption of the student's performance. The study also showed that students preferred being in a cooperative class.

Blau (1954) obtained similar results when comparing the reward structures in a public employment agency. The supervisors of two sections of the agency used different reward structures in evaluating the work of the employment interviewers. The supervisor in Section A stressed individual productivity; the job security of each interviewer was dependent upon his filling more job openings and serving more clients than any other interviewer—clearly, a competitive reward structure. The supervisor of Section B discouraged individual productivity as a goal and encouraged the section as a whole to place as many applicants as possible. In addition, members of Section B had an opportunity to develop a common professional orientation. The differences in group atmospheres were striking. The interviewers in Section A were preoccupied with productivity and were unable to spend time or energy cultivating friendships or developing any sense of common purpose. Section A interviewers did not communicate with one another, and they concealed job opportunities from each other, thereby preventing clients of the other interviewers from learning about appropriate jobs. In contrast, the members of the cooperatively oriented section took coffee breaks together, maintained friendly relationships, and assisted one another in placing job applicants. As a group, Section B placed more applicants in jobs than did Section A.

B. Groups Possessing Intragroup Cooperation and Intergroup Competition: Team-Competitive Structure

Certain situations demand that people cooperate with each other in a group, while the group as a whole competes with another group. Athletic teams are a clear-cut example of such a situation. The type of reward structure involved here can be described as intergroup competition-intragroup cooperation. We prefer to call it a team-competitive structure. Studies on the adjustment of group members (Fiedler, 1967b) indicate that intergroup competition assists group members in attaining personal adjustment and in eliminating the demoralizing effects of failure. The men involved in intergroup competition became more cohesive than men in other groups and viewed each other as interdependent. To the contrary, intragroup competition divided the members of the group and engendered resentment. Thus, intergroup competition—in contrast to intragroup competition—is associated with group cohesion. A group with a cooperative reward structure may increase its cohesiveness by instigating intergroup competition.

This point was demonstrated in the Robber's Cave experiment of Sherif, Harvey, White, Hood, and Sherif (1961). When Sherif encouraged intergroup competition between two cabins of boys, close friendships developed within each cabin—among boys who previously had not been particularly friendly with one another. In fact, the cohesiveness within each cabin group became so strong—and the hostility toward the other group so institutionalized—it was difficult for Sherif to bring the two groups back together. Reintegrating the groups was achieved only through activities that required both groups to work together to bring about the goals sought by each individual boy.

Dunn and Goldman (1966) have conducted a study that compared all these types of reward structures. Sixty recruits from an introductory psychology class served as subjects; they were divided into groups and met one hour a week to discuss human relations problems. Each group had a different reward structure—either individualistic, cooperative, competitive, or team competitive. Group and individual performances were evaluated by questionnaires, by sociometric choices, and by written reports. The students in the team-competitive groups had the highest percentage of mature, goal-directed comments (65 percent), followed by the cooperative groups (50 percent), the competitive groups (10 percent), and individualistic groups (0 percent). The two types of cooperatively oriented groups (team-competitive and cooperative reward structures) differed significantly in performance from the competitive and individualistic groups. In other words, the study demonstrates that team competition resembles cooperation more closely than competition. However, another measure of the group members' reactions indicated that cooperative group members accepted other students in their group more readily than team-competitive group members; perhaps, students in team-competitive groups were critical of their own group members because of competition with other groups.

C. Children's Preferences

Children seem to enjoy competitive reward structures as long as they are winning and as long as they can exhibit some mastery of the task (Greenberg, 1932). When given a choice, children prefer to work competitively with problems rather than individualistically. However, when playing marbles, filling pails with sand, or picking up pegs, children frequently refuse to work under a competitive reward structure. Perhaps the nature of such tasks—and the opportunities these tasks provide for self-evaluation—contributes to the inconsistencies of the findings.

D. The Effects of Failure

Whenever groups or individuals compete against one another, someone loses. The very nature of the competitive reward structure demands that someone will fail. Myers (1962) and Fiedler (1967b) found that association with a group cushioned the normal effects of failure on adult males. However, when children are involved, association with a group may not provide enough compensation. Hurlock (1927), in an experiment with children, found that members of a section that was defeated on the first of four days of competition never overcame their initial failure and attained inferior scores for the entire duration of the experiment. This resulted even though the groups had been matched on the basis of ability.

Not surprisingly, as rewards increase in value, so do tension and the frustration of failure (Tseng, 1969). But less apparent and more important is the fact that subsequent performances of children are affected by previous failures in competitive situations.

E. Competition, Cooperation, and Learning in the Classroom

Classroom learning involves a complex interaction that may include all types of reward structures. Learning groups in public school classrooms may consist of a large or small number of children, ranging from high to low ability, and coming from different socioeconomic levels. Such groups may be highly cohesive but usually are not. The degree of cohesiveness influences reactions to the reward structure of the task. For example, individuals in highly cohesive groups are motivated under competition, while pupils in less cohesive groups are motivated under cooperation (B. N. Phillips, 1954).

Classroom learning is influenced not only by variations in the cohesiveness of groups but also by differences in the tasks to be performed. Some tasks involve speed; others reward accuracy. Although most work is done individually, occasionally a small group will work on a project together. Thus, the problem is to find the method that will most effectively accomplish the goal of the task.

Memorization is often required in classroom learning. Research on this topic has compared group memory (the recall of persons in groups) to individual memory. In most cases group memory was found superior to individual memory, with cooperative foursomes superior to competitive ones (Yuker, 1955). When groups discussed a subject, individuals recalled more of the statements they themselves had made than would have been expected by chance (Smith, Madden, & Sobol, 1957).

In a study contrasting cooperative and competitive rewards (Fay, 1970), fifth- and sixth-grade girls learned a great deal more when they were members of cooperative groups than when they belonged to competitive groups. Learning in this study was dependent on the willingness of the children to participate in task-relevant discussions in groups of four persons. Girls operating under a competitive reward structure were unwilling to give their information to others, apparently because their own chances of winning might be harmed. Thus, a cooperative reward structure was found to foster increased learning in situations where persons must learn from one another.

The inhibition of communication in groups with competitive reward structures has also been demonstrated in college students (Grossack, 1954). Female students were to solve a problem by communicating via written messages. When the reward structure was cooperative, subjects more frequently sent communications containing relevant information and showed less tension than subjects in a competitive condition.

An impressive demonstration of how a cooperative reward structure affects performance in a college classroom was carried out by Deutsch (1949b). Ten groups of five students each were taking an introductory psychology course at M.I.T. Some groups participated under a team-competitive grading system, while other students took part in a competitive situation where only one person could achieve a high grade. Problems involving puzzles and problems in human relations were discussed by all groups. The results of the study showed that participants in the team-competitive system consistently solved more puzzle problems and did them more quickly than competitive group members. Under the team-competitive system, participants handled a greater number of human relations problems than participants in other groups, producing more fruitful ideas and showing more understanding of the nature of the problems. The morale of the students in the team-competitive groups was also higher than in other groups.

So far both cooperative and team-competitive systems have been found superior to the competitive system in the area of learning; but this conclusion does not always apply. When sheer quantity of work is desired on a project that requires little help from another person, competition seems to be more effective than cooperation or team competition (L. K. Miller & Hamblin, 1963). For example, one can pick up pegs or carry marbles without assistance, and children do such tasks more efficiently when the rewards are competitive (Sorokin, Tranquist, Parten, & Zimmerman, 1930). The same conclusion can be applied to situations with similar tasks, such as addition problems (Maller, 1929; B. N. Phillips, 1954; Julian & Perry, 1967). However, a cooperative reward structure is more suited to tasks where the individual needs assistance from another person (Miller & Hamblin, 1963). Putting together a jigsaw puzzle or making paper dolls are examples of tasks that can be accomplished more rapidly through some division of labor. A cooperative reward system facilitates quantity and quality of production on such tasks (Blau, 1954; Raven & Eachus, 1963; Crombag, 1966).

II. COOPERATIVE AND COMPETITIVE REWARD STRUCTURES IN OTHER REAL-LIFE SETTINGS

A. The Ecological Approach: A Ballet Company

As reward structures, cooperation and competition may exist within the same system. The New York Yankees not only seek the American League pennant as a cooperative goal, but each player seeks to better those who aspire to his position. Even if his team finishes last, the player who bats an average of .350 or hits 50 home runs will receive competitive rewards. Unfortunately there has been little ecological observation of how these motives interact in a field situation. One excellent exception is a project by Forsyth and Kolenda (1966), who studied the social system of a ballet company. The researchers wanted to discover how a ballet troupe reconciles cooperation and competition.

Since this type of system offers both types of rewards, how is one reward prevented from destroying the other? Through careful observation, Forsyth and Kolenda discovered that individual goals (which were more important in stimulating competition) were counteracted by group goals and norms that prevented the expression of resentment and jealousy or the outbreak of conflict. These group goals contributed to the development of group solidarity and integration.

A dancer was motivated to compete and to improve through various means, including the critical acclaim given the première ballerinas. Group norms discouraged friendships among the company members, but a number of factors seemed to prevent competition from being disruptive. First, all members were oriented toward one goal—that the performances of the company be excellent. Second, the competition was fair, and each person's talents could be observed continuously in classes, rehearsals, and performances. The standards for judging were shared by the teachers and the dancers. Each performer had only a few rivals; their respective abilities were usually apparent; and the judgments and awards were made by a noncompeting expert. In addition, the scarcity of praise from the teacher may have prevented the arousal of envy, and the teacher's negative comments certainly aroused feelings of sympathy. Other restraining factors were norms against gossip, the expression of antagonism, and other divisive tendencies.

The company performed publicly, and maintaining a good reputation was important to every member, since the company would fold without rather frequent successful performances. Hence the fate of each member was bound to that of the others, and each individual's self-interest was promoted by the success of the company. This payoff was maximized by the norms operating upon the company.

B. A Systems Approach: A Complex Business Organization

Cooperation and competition are both found in business organizations. Each employee of a company contributes in some way to the manufacture of a product or development of a service that consumers compare with other products and services. Thus, competition among producers may be viewed as a way of cooperating with the consumer in that higher quality or lower prices may result. In their study on competition and cooperation, May and Doob (1937) write: "When the beer with the vitamins competes against the beer with the reputation, both manufacturers, unless they cooperate by fixing prices, are benefiting the beer-drinker by forcing one another to offer their respective products more cheaply. Every businessman, therefore, whether he realizes it or not, is in business to satisfy as economically as possible the demands of the consumers. Through such verbal manipulation, it is possible to dub the competitive system an exceedingly subtle cooperative device" (p. 4). Price-fixing practices indicate, however, that the intent is not always one of cooperation with the consumer.

A systems approach emphasizes that cooperation and competition operate at all levels *within* a business organization as well as outside the organization. At the departmental level, the common goal of manufacturing a desirable product at the lowest possible cost must be shared, while interdepartmentally, competition exists in relation to budgets, allocations of space, and similar issues. Furthermore, within each department a similar combination of cooperation and competition exists.

C. Reward Structures in a Dyad: Marriage

In times past, marriage clearly fitted a cooperative reward structure. While the men of the family brought in the harvest, the women canned it and otherwise provided for food needs. The children milked the cows or gathered the eggs. A promotively interdependent goal was possessed by all, and the family unit was a necessity for survival (Lederer & Jackson, 1968).

More recently, there has been a shift from rural to urban living. Household conveniences are readily available, and men and women have assumed different roles. One significant purveyor of change was the total manpower (and womanpower) required by the production demands of World War II. Women discovered that they too could handle jobs in factories and offices. Now, in many families, girls are expected to choose and pursue a career, and a young woman is no longer indoctrinated with the belief that baking and sewing skills are essential to marriage. Men, too, need not rely on a woman to get to the office with a full stomach and a clean suit. In short, both male and female roles in today's families reflect less promotive interdependence in regard to physical and economic needs. This does not mean, however, that psychological or social needs are similarly affected by the changes in roles.

When marriage as a cooperative reward system loses reinforcement through economic necessity and dependence on the roles of others, additional supports must be used to maintain a cooperative framework. Each person involved in a marriage possesses goals that influence the marriage (Barry, 1970). A cooperative relationship in marriage can be strengthened by clearly compatible goals and complementary behaviors that will lead to the understood goals (Lederer & Jackson, 1968). One theory (Winch, 1952) has been advanced that extends the role of complementary behaviors to a system of mutual needs.[1] The basis for the theory is that a cooperative reward structure can be established when the needs of both persons are effectively communicated and when each person can gain from the other those capabilities that he cannot supply for himself. A competitive reward structure is more likely to evolve when the needs of each partner are not understood and when the abilities of each are interchangeable. In other words, if Jim knows that Sue needs to feel protected and he can help her feel protected, Sue will need him. If Sue feels protected anyway (because the landlord has installed a superior burglar alarm), she may need Jim less; and to a small extent the possibilities for a cooperative situation are weakened. The more needs Sue has, which can be supplied by Jim alone, the more rewarding it will be for her to interact with him; and such behavior would reinforce the marital bond.

[1] Winch theorizes that the *complementarity* of a man's and a woman's needs serves to attract the man and woman to one another. An example of such a situation is when one partner is dominant and the other is submissive. Other theorists, using a value-consensus theory (Tharp, 1963), emphasize that in mate selection, one chooses a partner like oneself. See Chapter 14 for further discussion of this topic.

But, we may wonder about competition in marriage. Doubtless, in the long run, a marriage cannot maintain itself if the reward structure permits only one partner to satisfy his or her needs. Possible solutions to this situation exist, however. First, couples need to view marriage as a cooperative reward structure, where the happiness of one partner is achieved only when the happiness of the other person is also attained. Another approach is to conceptualize marriage as a series of competitive reward settings. That is, in marriage there are a multitude of occasions where only one partner can achieve his goal and where that achievement prevents the attainment of the other partner's goal. The wife, for example, might want to live close to her parents, while the husband wants to live thousands of miles away on the ocean. This dilemma presents a competitive reward structure, if the couple is unable to conceptualize more promotively interdependent goals. An alternation can be set up so that each partner achieves his goals in some of the competitive situations. If the couple move close to the wife's family, then the husband will determine the kind of house they buy or how frequently they go visiting. Alternation of success in a series of conflicts with competitive reward structures may permit a couple to maintain a marriage. A spirit of mutual trust can be developed, if communication and understanding are maintained through applying ground rules that say, in effect—"I'll let you have your way this time, and you'll let me have my way next time." This may lead eventually to a broader sharing of goals and to an essentially cooperative reward structure rather than an alternating competitive reward structure.

III. THE DEVELOPMENT OF COOPERATIVE AND COMPETITIVE MOTIVES

Cooperation and competition derive both from the situation and from the participants. In any situation where a variety of behaviors is acceptable, some people will choose to cooperate, and some will choose to compete. For example, observe two people with grocery carts headed for the same checkout counter at the same instant. Does one defer, while the other pushes ahead? In this section, the motives behind cooperative and competitive behaviors shall be explored. We recognize that motives are not observable and must often be inferred from behavior. Often, especially with children, inferring a motive from the observed behavior is tenuous. Yet the rudiments of behavior develop from motives that are learned in childhood. As a child becomes socialized, he develops characteristic motives. Here, we will be interested in how these characteristic motives develop.

A. Development of Awareness of Others

Apparently, in order for competition or cooperation to take place, one must be aware of the existence of other persons. Maudry and Nekula (1939) observed that 6- to 8-month-old children were often more interested in the general environment than they were in another baby. Even children of 25 months were more attracted to a toy than to another child, but after this age the infants adjusted their behavior to the existence or activity of another playmate. Thus, the beginnings of social behavior appear.

Two- to 3-year-old children characteristically do not compete with others (Greenberg, 1932); but, as they become older (3 to 4 years), they manifest the rudiments of competitive thought by talking about what other children are doing.

Greater competition is displayed by 4- to 6-year-olds. By this time, most children have developed the ability to use building blocks and similar toys, and they are interested in improving their ability to work with the toys. Among 4- and 5-year-old children, at least half exhibit competitive behaviors. A definite relationship exists between the child's mastery of the task and the degree of competition he displays. As he develops his skill, the child is more interested in using that skill in competition with others. Cooperative play likewise increases with age (Graves, 1937).

Children can be taught to cooperate by rewarding them for each cooperative response. Azrin and Lindsley (1956) taught pairs of children between the ages of 7 and 12 to cooperate in the first ten minutes of play. For a cooperative response by the pair, one piece of candy was awarded to each child. By manipulating the nature and distribution of the rewards, Azrin and Lindsley were able to establish, eliminate, and then reestablish cooperation.

Competitiveness, however, is more predominant in our society than cooperation. With increasing age, children begin to understand the meaning of winning and losing; competition increases (Baldwin, 1955); and different strategies are developed in coping with competitive situations. In comparison with 14- to 16-year-olds, children from ages 7 to 8 bargain less actively, establish unnecessary alliances more frequently, and make more cooperative efforts to achieve mutual satisfaction. Similar behaviors are more characteristic of girls than of boys in bargaining tasks (Vinacke & Gullickson, 1964). In addition, older males tend to be more exploitative than younger ones.

B. Subcultural Differences in the Development of Motives

In a provocative study, Madsen (1967) has shown that the subculture in which a child grows up may help determine which motive predominates. Three groups of Mexican children were engaged in various tasks to study the effect of cooperative and competitive reward structures. The rural children had been reared in environments where the whole family worked together for material benefits; cooperation was expected and competitive, aggressive actions were discouraged. In contrast, the middle-class, urban children were brought up in environments where the father was generally involved in competitive work situations and where both parents provided models for such behavior, though not actually rewarding competitive actions. Poor urban children—the third type—were reared in families that were most concerned with obtaining food. Children of these families were reprimanded for competing for more than their share.

One of the tasks assigned each group of children required a great deal of cooperation in order for any child to obtain a reward. At first, each child was rewarded only when all four members of the group had completed a certain part of the task in a specified order (cooperative reward structure). All children performed the task well. Then the experimenter stated that order was unimportant and that each child would be rewarded for doing a certain part of the task, regardless of the work done by others (an individualistic structure). The task still required the same degree of cooperation, and each child would have received the maximum reward, if the group members had cooperated as much as before. However, the stronger competitive motive of the middle-class children interfered with performing a task in which cooperation was the most beneficial strategy. Under an individualistic reward structure the poor urban children and particularly the rural children maintained a cooperative response.

When the task was again changed so that competitive behavior led to the reward, the poor urban children and the rural children continued to behave cooperatively and gave significantly fewer competitive responses than the middle-class urban children.

In a more recent study, Madsen and Shapira (1970) used the same approach to look at the performance of 7- to 9-year-old children from varying racial and ethnic groups in the United States. Groups of Chicanos, blacks, and white children performed more competitively than did children from Mexican villages, even in tasks where competition was detrimental.

The powerful influence of culturally instilled ways of behaving is also demonstrated by the problems white teachers faced in using traditional teaching methods with Sioux Indian children. In middle-class America, one can easily get two boys to race each other across a field. But in some Indian tribes, children hesitate at the start of a race, knowing that the winner will be ridiculed by the other children (Erikson, 1963). In the Sioux culture, generosity and cooperativeness are valued. To demonstrate superiority or to excel is to lose face among one's friends. Thus, a reward structure effective in one culture may lose its effectiveness when superimposed on a culture that esteems different basic motives.

C. Orientation of the Family and the Development of Motives

The amount of cooperation or competition shown by children may be related to their family's orientation to life. In one study (Berkowitz & Friedman, 1967), teenage boys were divided into three groups: entrepreneurial, bureaucratic, or working class. The boys were classified as members of an entrepreneurial family if their fathers were professionals, salesmen, or owners of businesses. If their fathers worked for someone else or were members of a multilevel organization, the boys were listed as members of the bureaucratic group. Sons of blue-collar workers were listed as working-class members. Berkowitz and Friedman found that entrepreneurial boys helped others according to the degree of help they had received previously. They were particularly inclined to reciprocate little help when the recipient was from a lower class. Boys with bureaucratic fathers were more likely to help another person, even when they possessed an unfavorable attitude toward that person.

One might now ask how differences in family backgrounds explain differences in the competitive behaviors of children. Some theorists postulate that child-rearing practices tend to reflect and perpetuate the way of life of the family (D. R. Miller & Swanson, 1958). The entrepreneurial family stresses independence, makes use of opportunity, and is manipulative. The child must face the world on his own and get what he wants by himself. Bureaucratic parents are organization oriented; they encourage the belief that one should cooperate with and emulate superiors. Their children are expected to be warm, friendly, and accommodative.

In summary, then, the development of competition and cooperation in children includes the following.

(a) Desires to compete and to cooperate increase with age.

(b) Cooperation and competition may be fostered through reinforcement, modeling, and comparison with peers.
(c) In some societies, the nature of reliance on others facilitates the development of cooperative motives.
(d) The career orientation and life style of the parents influence the development of motives in children.

IV. THE INTERACTION OF REWARD STRUCTURES AND MOTIVES

We have recognized that behavior is a function of the individual's motives as well as of the reward structure and other aspects of the situation. Can we say which factor is most influential? How do they interact? These problems can be studied by looking at tasks that pose choices between conflicting motives. The Prisoner's Dilemma is the most frequently studied of these mixed-motive tasks.

A. The Prisoner's Dilemma

The situation of the Prisoner's Dilemma takes its name from the following predicament described by Luce and Raiffa (1957).

> Two subjects are taken into custody and separated. The district attorney is certain they are guilty of a specific crime, but he does not have adequate evidence to convict them at a trial. He points out to each prisoner that each has two alternatives: to confess to the crime the police are sure they have done or not to confess. If they both do not confess then the district attorney will book them on some very minor trumped-up charge . . . ; if they both confess, they will be prosecuted, [and] he will recommend [a rather severe] sentence; but if one confesses and the other does not, then the confessor will receive rather lenient treatment for turning state's evidence whereas the latter will get the "book" slapped at him (p. 95).

Notice the dilemma between motives in the above situation. If each prisoner chooses what is best for him individually—without consideration of what the other will choose—he would decide not to confess. But if the first prisoner decides not to confess and the other prisoner chooses to confess, the first prisoner will then get the "book" thrown at him. The outcome for each prisoner is determined by the combination of the choices made by him and the other prisoner. As shown in Figure 5-2 matrices can be developed that represent the choices available to the prisoners. The matrix highlights the fact that the outcome for each person depends upon the responses of the other participant. Using the matrix, we can easily quantify the choices by substituting some hypothetical numerical values (days in jail) for the descriptive punishments. (See, for example, the second matrix in Figure 5-2.)

Fortunately for college students involved in experimental Prisoner's Dilemma situations, social psychological studies have generally utilized less severe pay-offs than jail sentences. In fact, rewards have been used instead of punishments, usually in the form of money or points added to the student's final exam score. In varying studies, the amounts of money have ranged from mere pennies per trial to as much as 60 dollars for an experiment of ten trials. If a study were to use somewhere between 30

		2nd Prisoner	
		Not confess	Confess
1st Prisoner	Not confess	Minor charge for 1st, minor charge for 2nd	"Book" slapped at 1st, leniency for 2nd
	Confess	Leniency for 1st, "book" slapped at 2nd	Severe sentence for 1st, severe sentence for 2nd

		2nd Prisoner	
		Not confess	Confess
1st Prisoner	Not confess	3 days, 3 days	60 days, 1 day
	Confess	1 day, 60 days	20 days, 20 days

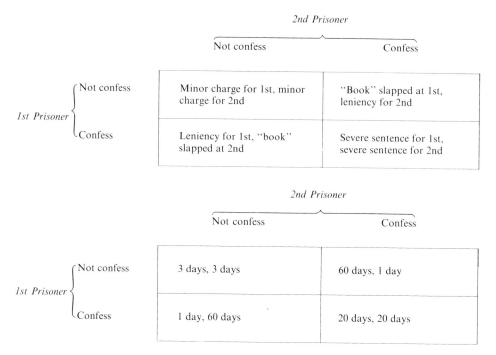

Figure 5-2. *Matrices Showing Choices Available to Participants in a Prisoner's Dilemma*

and 60 trials, its matrix for each trial might look like the first matrix in Figure 5-3. In the situation represented by this matrix, each person must choose between blue and red. The first figure in each box indicates the pay-off going to the first person; the second figure is the pay-off going to the second person. Notice the possibilities. If the first person picks blue, the second person can pick either blue or red. If both participants pick blue, they each receive 3 cents for that trial. But if the second person picks red and the first selects blue, the second person gets 5 cents and the first gets nothing. If the first person picks red and the second person picks blue, the pay-offs are 5 cents and nothing, respectively; in seeking a mutually cooperative choice, the second person allows the other participant to exploit him. If both participants choose red, then each gains a small pay-off (1 cent).

These examples imply that the second person chooses after the first person and knows what the first has chosen. This procedure, known as *successive responding*, gives a great deal of control to the second person but violates the strict application of the dilemma, which assumes that each prisoner acts without knowledge of the other's choice. More frequently, the rules of the task use *simultaneous responding*, where each person chooses without knowledge of the other's choice. (Subjects are usually informed of the outcome and the other participant's choice after both have chosen on each trial.) Some studies have used only one trial (with much greater pay-offs than those shown here), while other studies utilize as many as 300 trials.

The essential nature of the Prisoner's Dilemma situation is consistent: a choice that seems to lead to the greatest individual gain is, in the long run, self-defeating. If each participant opts for the greatest individual gain, a red-red combination would result, with a pay-off of 1 cent each. The most beneficial combination of choices—if one can assume that the other will cooperate—is blue-blue, paying each 3 cents per trial.

B. Factors Influencing Degree of Cooperation

When college students participate in the Prisoner's Dilemma task, by no means do they always learn to establish a cooperative relationship, whereby each chooses blue on each trial. The degree of cooperation (measured by the percentage of blue responses) is, on the average, around 50 percent (Gallo & McClintock, 1965). To establish any one percentage as the typical rate of responding is misleading, however, for several reasons. First of all, the instructions, the number of trials, the sex of the subjects, and many other variables influence the degree of cooperation observed. Second, over a series of trials in a free-play situation, a lock-in effect almost always occurs—in other words, the subjects' responses evolve into a string of either blue-blue or red-red choices. A long series of blue-blue choices is 100 percent cooperation, while a series of red-red choices represents no cooperation. The basic finding of note is that neither type of lock-in is a general outcome—some dyads end up consistently competitive; others, consistently cooperative.

		2nd person chooses between: Blue	Red
1st person chooses between	Blue	3¢, 3¢	0¢, 5¢
	Red	5¢, 0¢	1¢, 1¢

		2nd person chooses between: Blue	Red
1st person chooses between	Blue	4¢, 4¢	1¢, 3¢
	Red	3¢, 1¢	0¢, 0¢

		2nd person chooses between: Blue	Red
1st person chooses between	Blue	3¢, 3¢	1¢, 5¢
	Red	5¢, 1¢	−5¢, −5¢

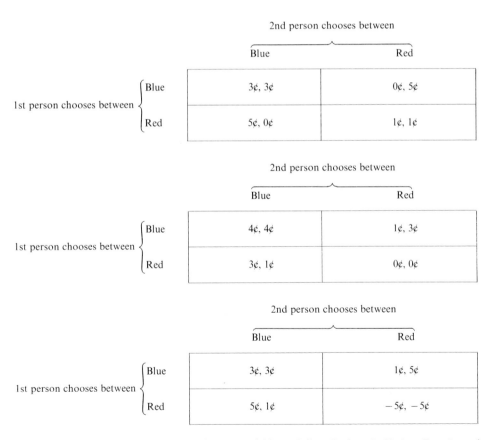

Figure 5-3. *Matrices Representing Choices Available to College Students in Various Experimental Games.*

When a phenomenon has such a degree of individual variation, we seek factors that might explain these variations. First, situational factors are distinguished from intrapersonal factors. Situational factors include the effects of (a) the reward structure of the situation, (b) the value of the pay-offs, (c) the strategy of the other participant, and (d) the opportunities for communication between participants. Included in the category of intrapersonal determinants are the effects of personality, motivational, and attitudinal characteristics.

1. The reward structure. The reward structure of the Prisoner's Dilemma creates a conflict between cooperative and competitive choices. (This reward structure may be contrasted with other pay-off matrices in which the structure is entirely cooperative or entirely competitive. See Figure 5-4.) Consider, for example, the second matrix in Figure 5-3. It would appear that this is a cooperative reward structure, in that a blue-blue choice is the best individual outcome and the best group outcome. Choosing red pays oneself less than choosing blue. One might expect pairs of participants with this matrix to choose blue 100 percent of the time. But Scodel (1962) found that 47 percent of his female subjects with this matrix chose red. Possibly, in these subjects an orientation that maximizes differences is in operation, rather than a cooperative one—in other words, the subject's goal is not to win the most in absolute value but to win relatively more than the other subject. Subsequent studies by Scodel showed that the desire to maximize pay-off differences between oneself and the other participant was strong in many subjects.

The reward structure of a matrix can be altered in other ways. The pay-off for a mutual defection (the red-red choices) can be made worse for each individual than the outcome of a red-blue combination. Consider, for example, the third matrix in Figure 5-3. Note that a mutual defection here causes each person to lose money—a worse eventuality than the small amount gained if one person's cooperative choice is met with exploitation by the other participant. A matrix with extremely undesirable pay-offs for double defection is called a Chicken Matrix, suggesting the catastrophe of a head-on collision. Sermat (1967) has shown that the rate of cooperation is higher here than in the traditional Prisoner's Dilemma matrix.

2. The value of pay-offs. Perhaps the low rates of cooperation in the Prisoner's

	Prisoner's Dilemma	*Chicken*	*Asymmetrical Prisoner's Dilemma*	*Maximizing Difference*
	Player 2 Blue Red	Player 2 Blue Red	Player 2 Blue Red	Player 2 Blue Red
Player 1 Blue Red	 3,3 0,5 5,0 1,1	 3,3 1,5 5,1 0,0	 6,3 0,5 10,0 2,1	 6,6 0,5 5,0 0,0

The first number in each pair of numbers is Player 1's pay-off, and the second number is Player 2's pay-off. Notice the variations in games. For example, in the chicken game, the worst individual outcome *and* the worst group outcome is a red-red combination of choices. That is not the case, however, in the prisoner's dilemma game. Notice in the asymmetrical game the pay-offs for one player are not the reverse of the other's pay-offs. In the maximizing difference game, if a subject chooses red, his apparent intent is to win more than the other player, rather than to win the greatest amount possible, as would be accomplished through choosing blue. (Adapted from Oskamp, "Effects of Programmed Strategies on Cooperation in the Prisoner's Dilemma and other Mixed-Motive Games." In *Journal of Conflict Resolution*, 1972. Reprinted with permission of the publisher.)

Figure 5-4. *Examples of Different Reward Structures in Different Types of Mixed-Motive Games*

Dilemma are the result of miniscule payments per trial (Gallo & McClintock, 1965). In the usual experiment, the pay-off per trial for cooperating is small (approximately 3 cents), and the difference between pay-offs for cooperative as opposed to competitive behavior is even less (usually 2 cents). When the amounts of payoffs are increased, however, there is often no increase in the degree of cooperation (Oskamp & Kleinke, 1970). For example, Knox and Douglas (1968) had subjects play ten trials with the possibility of winning 60 cents. Other subjects, playing the same number of trials, could make as much as 60 dollars. There was no difference in the degree of cooperation induced by these two pay-offs.

One is mistaken to assume, however, that monetary pay-offs are the only factors operating on participants in the Prisoner's Dilemma or, for that matter, in any mixed-motive situation. Clearly, other matters are at stake, such as achievement needs, self-esteem, or one's public image. Gallo (1968) has called these factors *symbolic rewards*, in contrast to the *tangible rewards* of pay-off money. Symbolic rewards suggest the possibility of extending mixed-motive game findings to the real world. In international relations, losses of troops or missile bases may be a transitory setback in comparison to the loss of prestige in the eyes of other nations. Further understanding of symbolic rewards in game play is still needed. We need to know how symbolic rewards can be classified and measured, and how they interact with tangible rewards. Money, as a reward, has the virtue of being quantifiable, and its meaning is easily communicated. Again, however, it would be wrong to assume that a monetary manipulation covers all the rewards involved in game play.

Bert R. Brown (1968, 1971) has shown that the opportunity to save face is a powerful symbolic reward in mixed-motive game play. In his study, subjects were placed in a two-person bargaining game, during which they were consistently exploited by the other player. Each subject was told that other people had observed the game play. Brown manipulated the observers' reaction to the subject's choices. Half of the subjects were complimented for playing fairly and looking good in the face of an exploitative opponent, while the other half of the subjects were chastised and humiliated for letting the other player take advantage of them. Each subject then played a second game under observation. In the second game opportunity to save face was operationally defined as choosing to retaliate against the other player at cost to oneself, rather than choosing to maximize one's own financial outcome. Subjects who were humiliated in the first game retaliated more often and with greater severity than subjects who (though similarly exploited) had received favorable feedback. Humiliated subjects retaliated despite the loss of tangible rewards.

3. The strategy of the other participant. As mentioned previously, when two persons are allowed to respond to each other in a free-play situation, the average rate of cooperation is approximately 50 percent. It is possible to intervene in the situation by programming the responses of the second participant so as to make the choices of that participant always seem cooperative. (See Figure 5-5 for examples of programmed strategies.) Since the two participants ordinarily do not see or hear each other in the Prisoner's Dilemma, the experimenter may intervene without creating undue suspicion in the first participant. If the second participant continues to choose the blue, or cooperative, response regardless of what the first participant chooses, he is using a *unilaterally cooperative strategy*. Note that this strategy gives the first participant two choices: he can either reciprocate the cooperation extended by the other by choosing blue and giving the dyad a mutually beneficial payoff, or he can exploit the

The experimenter, in studying whether the other player's choices influence the subject's degree of cooperation, may choose to vary the strategy of the other player. This is done by preprogramming the choices of an apparent other player. Several possible strategies may be used, including the following:

1. *Unilaterally cooperative.* The other player chooses the blue, or cooperative, response on every trial regardless of the subject's choice.
2. *Unilaterally competitive.* The other player chooses the red, or competitive, response on every trial regardless of the subject's choice.
3. *Matching* (also called tit-for-tat or accommodative). The other player chooses the same response as the subject. If, on each trial, both the subject and the other player respond at the same time, the matching strategy would dictate that on the next trial the other player would give the same choice as the subject on the preceding trial.
4. *Shifting.* The other player may choose cooperatively for the first series of trials, then shift to a unilaterally competitive strategy.

Figure 5-5. *Examples of Other Participant's Strategies Programmed by the Experimenter*

other subject by choosing red and taking the maximum gain for himself, while punishing the other. Apparently, however, the unilaterally cooperative strategy does not especially facilitate cooperation, as it leads to cooperation in some subjects but encourages exploitation in others. When the responses of all subjects in a unilaterally cooperative system are averaged, only about 50 percent of the responses are cooperative.

In the Prisoner's Dilemma, a matching or tit-for-tat strategy appears to be most effective in facilitating cooperation (Oskamp, 1972). According to this strategy, the second participant responds on each trial with the same choice as that of the first participant. The first participant quickly learns that if he picks red, the other player will also pick red, and each will lose or get only a minimal payment. If the first participant picks blue, he finds the other player will likewise pick blue, resulting in a solid payment for each player. When the second participant adheres to the tit-for-tat strategy, in general, the first participant will eventually start making a cooperative response in almost every trial. Rates of cooperation reach 85 to 90 percent with such an intervention (Whitworth & Lucker, 1969, 1970; Wrightsman, Davis, Lucker, Bruininks, Evans, Wilde, Paulson, & Clark, 1967; Wrightsman, Bruininks, Lucker, & Anderson, 1967). Reinforcement theory serves as an explanation for such a phenomenon; the participant learns that he is punished when he picks red and he is rewarded when he picks blue.

4. Opportunities for communication. The standard Prisoner's Dilemma game task does not permit any type of communication between the two participants. They know nothing about each other, although they doubtless make certain assumptions (for example, that the other participant is a student at the same college or that he is from the same psychology class). The scant evidence available indicates that the lack of communication and/or the lack of knowledge about the other player inhibits the possibilities for cooperation.

Durkin (1967) employed a moment-of-truth visual communication between subjects in a free-play Prisoner's Dilemma. The usual procedures of screening subjects from one another's view were used—with the exception that, immediately before responding, some subjects had a momentary glimpse of the other subject. This brief exposure (one-half second) led to an increased rate of mutually cooperative responses (41 percent, as compared to a 12 percent response rate in subjects who participated in a standard procedure).

An equally impressive demonstration of how communication affects cooperation was carried out in a study by Wichman (1970), who varied the type of communication possible. In one condition, isolated subjects could neither see nor hear each other; in a second condition they could hear each other; in a third condition they could see each other; and in a fourth condition they could both see and hear each other. As Figure 5-6 indicates, the more extensive the communication, the higher the rate of cooperation in a free-play situation.

Neither Durkin's study nor Wichman's is very helpful in explaining what makes opportunities for communication increase the rate of cooperation. For example, if the second subject gazes toward the first subject during a game, the first subject's rate of cooperation is unaffected (Kleinke & Pohlen, 1971). Apparently, a prolonged gaze does not have the same effects that Durkin's brief visual encountering has.

Opportunities for communication can lead to either conciliatory gestures or belligerent ones on the part of the communicator. For example, when one participant has the opportunity to threaten the second, and the second has no means to retaliate, the degree of cooperation is less than if no communication were possible at all (Deutsch & Krauss, 1960, 1962).

5. *Effects of personality and attitudes.* A field-theory conception of cooperation would emphasize that intrapersonal factors as well as situational factors or environmental states contribute to the degree of cooperation shown in a Prisoner's Dilemma. Studies have shown that, in one-trial Prisoner's Dilemma games, the subjects' attitudes, personality characteristics, and motives seem to be reflected in their choices (Terhune, 1968, 1970; Wrightsman, 1966). For example, some subjects superimpose their own motives upon the game structure. Even though the task is described as a

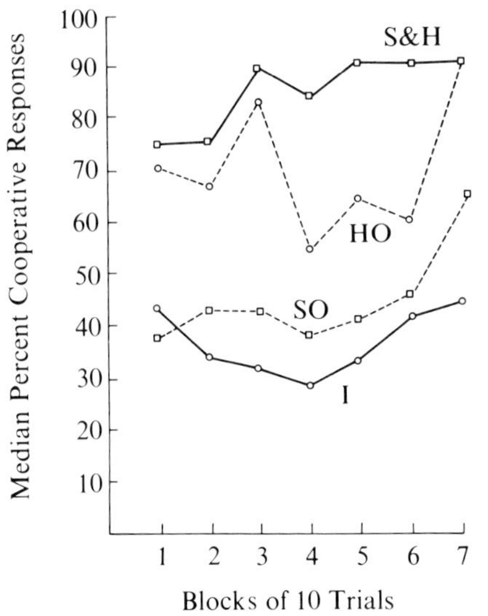

Figure 5-6. *Median Levels of Cooperation Under Four Types of Communication in Wichman's Study.* I = *isolated;* SO = *see only;* HO = *hear only; and* S&H = *see and hear. From Wichman, "Effects of Isolation and Communication in a Two-Person Game,"* Journal of Personality and Social Psychology, *1970,* **16**, *114–120. Copyright 1970 by the American Psychological Association, and reprinted by permission.*

choice task rather than as a game, and even though any references to an opponent or to winnings are scrupulously avoided—some subjects rationalize their exploitative or competitive choices with statements like "that's the purpose" or "winning the most for myself is what I am supposed to do" (Wrightsman, 1966). In other words, the demand characteristics of the situation are not the same for all participants.

Kelley and Stahelski (1970) have shown that, in the Prisoner's Dilemma game, cooperative subjects differ from competitors in their beliefs about what people are like. Specifically, cooperators believe that people are different in their cooperative propensities, while competitive subjects believe all other people are competitive. In the study cooperators and competitors were defined according to the subject's self-expressed intent in the game. Cooperators were those subjects who stated that they intended "to cooperate with the other player and . . . be concerned with my score *and* the other player's score." Competitors were those subjects who said they wanted to "work for myself, against the other player, and . . . be concerned *only* with my own score" (Kelly & Stahelski, 1970, p. 68, italics in original). Thus, self-described cooperators and competitors behave differently in a mixed-motive game situation, perceive their opponents differently, and differ in their assumptions about human nature in general. Not only do cooperators see human nature as generally more cooperative and trustworthy, but they also assume the existence of differences among individuals.

Terhune (1968) measured the degree of personality characteristics such as achievement, affiliation, and power motives in subjects through the use of the Thematic Apperception Test. His subjects then played three types of games in order of increasing complexity. The first situation was a set of three, one-trial Prisoner's Dilemma games. The second situation was a 30-trial Prisoner's Dilemma game, where the two participants were matched by motivational or personality type. And the third situation was an international relations game, in which groups of three persons simulated the roles of leaders of hypothetical nations. All three members of each group were again matched according to motives. Some groups were achievement oriented; some were power oriented groups, and some were affiliation oriented. Terhune (1970) reported the subsequent summary of the relationships between personality and game behavior.

> The results in the three experiments were as follows: In the one-trial Prisoner's Dilemma games, the three personality types exhibited clearly different kinds of behavior. The achievement-oriented types were the most cooperative in that more than the others they were found to choose cooperatively while simultaneously expecting cooperation from their partners. The affiliation-oriented subjects were the most defensive in that they tended to expect double-cross from their partners and, therefore, defected themselves. The power-oriented subjects were more exploitative in that they double-crossed their partners whom they expected to choose cooperatively. But, the important point for our purposes here was the effect of the payoff matrix on personality influences. It was found that the more threatening the game (i.e., the greater the temptation to double-cross and the greater the loss for being double-crossed), the smaller were the differences among the motive types, as they all tended to behave defensively. Furthermore, *perceived* threat had a similar effect: Among those subjects who expected their partner to double-cross them, the effects of personality were nil, while among those subjects who expected their partner to cooperate, personality differences were pronounced. Thus, both personality and situation variations distinctively influenced behavior (p. 205).[2]

[2]From Terhune, K. W., "The Effects of Personality in Cooperation and Conflict." In P. Swingle (Ed.), *The Structure of Conflict*. Copyright 1970 by Academic Press, Inc. Reprinted by permission.

In the multitrial Prisoner's Dilemma games, the variations in personality and motives had less influence on the outcome, and situational factors increased in importance. In the international relations games, the effects of the players' personality or motives on degree of cooperation were virtually nonexistent. Achievement-motivated subjects did initiate significantly more cooperative moves, however; and power-oriented subjects more often sought to manipulate others by telling lies or writing deceptive messages.

Thus, the greater the complexity of the situation, the less demonstrable are the effects of the subject's personality or motives. Situational factors and intrapersonal factors interact. A similar conclusion can be drawn from the results of studies that attempt to relate attitudes toward human nature with the degree of cooperation in a game. In a one-trial study (Wrightsman, 1966), subjects who believed human nature to be trustworthy and altruistic were more likely to cooperate, while subjects who believed human nature to be untrustworthy and selfish were more often distrustful or competitive. However, in studies that extended this postulated relationship to a 30-trial or 50-trial game, very modest relationships were found (Uejio & Wrightsman, 1967; Wrightsman, Davis, et al., 1968). In these studies, significant relationships between attitudes and behavior were discovered in about half of the conditions. In long multitrial games, the behavior of each participant comes to resemble that of the other—that is, the lock-in effect begins to operate. As Rapoport and Chammah (1965) indicate, the interactions between the two members of a dyad are probably more dominant factors in determining the performance on a multitrial Prisoner's Dilemma game than the individuals' inherent propensities to cooperate.

Other reasons may also explain why attitudes and personality do not dramatically influence game behavior. For one, the applicability of game behavior as a criterion may be questioned. (This point, as well as the general relationship between attitudes and behavior, will be discussed in Chapter 9.) As Knox and Douglas (1968) indicate, behavior in the Prisoner's Dilemma game may occasionally be so inconsistent from trial to trial that no other variable could possibly be related to it. A second reason why attitudes do not drastically affect game behavior is that limited options in most mixed-motive games may restrict the participant in the utilization of his attitudes. Christie and Geis (1970) have shown that Machiavellian attitudes are related to success in interpersonal tasks only under certain conditions—where there is visual interaction, a variety of possible responses, and an opportunity to capitalize on the irrelevant motives of the other participant. The typical mixed-motive situation lacks these conditions and hence such attitudes of the participants do not influence behavior.

C. Generalizing from Laboratory Game Situations to the Real World

The mixed-motive game has proved to be a useful tool for the study of social behavior in the laboratory. But we may wonder what value it has for understanding cooperation and competition in the real world? Can marital quarrels or the Arab-Israeli conflict be any better understood through knowledge derived from Prisoner's Dilemma games?

Several social psychologists have cautioned against applying these findings to real-world conflicts. Gergen (1969), for example, lists four limitations. One problem is that the absence of real communication makes the standard, mixed-motive game a highly artificial relationship. (However, more recent studies have introduced opportunities for communication as a variable, thereby rendering more applicable results.) A second limitation is the ambiguity of the dependent variable. One assumption of game researchers—namely, that choosing blue is a cooperative response —has not been proven. Doubtless, it is too simplified an assumption, and greater interviewing with subjects regarding the reason for their choices should clarify this point.

The third problem in applying laboratory findings to the real world is the range of options. Here, Gergen believes that "under conditions where multiple options are available to two people, the processes of exchange may be quite different in character" (1969, p. 66). Exploitation in the real world, for example, is disguised or covered up by a veneer of helpfulness or concern. The creation of opportunities for such subtle reactions is not easily accomplished in a mixed-motive game. The fourth problem is the utility of outcomes. Here, Gergen raises the issue of the meaningfulness of small rewards. (As indicated previously, however, some research findings concluded that game behavior remains the same when large rewards are used.)

Pruitt (1967) has also criticized the Prisoner's Dilemma game, indicating the following discrepancies between laboratory findings and what is commonly known about real life. The first problem noted by Pruitt is the lack of opportunities for communication. Second, there is no opportunity to try out decisions tentatively and then reverse decisions if the results are unfavorable. Third, the use of pay-offs is unrealistic. Fourth, the reward structure used in the laboratory may not be perceived by participants as being the same as the reward structure in real-life conflicts. And, finally, the absence of norms in the laboratory inhibits cooperation. Pruitt states that in real-life tasks with co-workers, "people may feel constrained by custom to be helpful and expect their fellow workers to feel similarly constrained. Such norms may not be so easily available in the laboratory situation because of its novelty" (1967, p. 22).

The absence of norms that foster cooperation may relate to Gergen's concern for the artificiality of the laboratory setting. Clearly, the mixed-motive game in the laboratory is artificial in some respects. The crucial question is: does this artificiality categorically influence responses? Apparently, the lack of norms does influence responses; studies that varied the set of instructions given the subjects produced differences in the extent of cooperative behavior of these subjects (Deutsch, 1960; Terhune, 1968; Loomis, 1959). For example, those subjects who were told that their job was to maximize their winnings cooperated less often than those subjects who were given instructions to facilitate the winnings of both participants as much as possible.

The future of mixed-motive game research may lie in the direction of determining whether findings from the laboratory extend to the real world. Already some psychologists believe that the findings can usually be applied. Jerome Frank, in his impressive book *Sanity and Survival* (1968), devotes eight pages to research on the Prisoner's Dilemma game, four pages to the Chicken game, plus additional pages to the applications of these findings to nuclear deterrence and disarmament. Morton Deutsch, in his presidential address to the Eastern Psychological Association (1969), describes himself as "brash enough to claim that the games people play as subjects in laboratory experiments may have some relevance for war and peace" (p. 1091). The peoples of a nation, like individuals in the laboratory, seek out and acquire information, make decisions, and take actions; and "they . . . act in similar ways under similar conditions" (Deutsch, 1969, p. 1091). The next step in research is to measure the similarity in conditions between the laboratory and the real world. Until such similarities are demonstrated, however, the findings of Prisoner's Dilemma games probably cannot be applied point-for-point to real-world conflicts.

V. COOPERATION AND COMPETITION IN THE FUTURE

Stacey and DeMartino (1958), among others, have characterized our culture as competitive. "Whether the enormous economic and technical achievements of our culture were and are possible only on the basis of the competitive principle is a question for the economist or sociologist to decide. . . . The character of all our human relationships is molded by a more-or-less outspoken competition" (pp. 558-560). Many critics, however, are questioning the assumptions in this quotation. Some see our society as too competitive, pointing out that fierce competition has taken its toll in human maladies such as ulcers, heart attacks, suicides, and divorces. Young people are questioning the value of competition and are seeking escape from the rat race or the treadmill. Others wonder what would happen if we could restrain the competitive thrust of our society. Would the achievement of a true democracy be enhanced if we were less competitive? Would an absence of competition mean an improvement in the quality of manufactured goods?

If competition were completely removed from our society, all competitive sports would be eliminated, as would games such as Monopoly, poker, and checkers. Games like tennis, golf, or bowling might still be played, but not in a competitive way. Since games are actually situations in which people cooperate in competing (Rapoport, 1961), the competition would stop, if one decided that he would no longer cooperate by playing the game.

Would this mean that we would not compete with ourselves or that we would not try to exceed our last performance? Sometimes we compete in order to appraise our own skills, and competition is a great way to make comparative judgments or to learn what we really can do (Julian, 1968). Perhaps one also needs rivals in pursuing an ambition. The achievements of others may inspire one's own achievements by demonstrating the rewards available to those who try (Caplow, 1968). Some degree of competition, then, seems valuable.

But the detrimental effects of destructive competition are severe. There may be, as Keen (1971) proposes, a fine dividing line between violence and competitiveness. Are the violent extensions of competitiveness inevitable? Can people exist in cooperative, nonaggressive societies? These questions will carry us into the next chapter and a consideration of aggression, violence, and war.

VI. SUMMARY

Group tasks possess one of three types of reward structures: cooperative, competitive, or individualistic. A competitive reward structure is one in which the achievement of one group member's goal prevents the other group members from achieving their goals. A cooperative reward structure is one in which the achievement of one group member's goal facilitates the achievement of the goals of each other group member. An individualistic reward structure is one in which the achievement of one person's goal has no effect upon the other group members' achieving their goals.

Individuals' motives can also be classified as cooperative, competitive, or individualistic. A person who possesses a cooperative motive seeks an outcome that is most beneficial for all participants. In contrast, a competitive motive seeks an outcome that is most beneficial for oneself and most detrimental to the other participants. An individualistic motive seeks an outcome that is best for oneself, without regard for whether or not others achieve their goals.

Cooperative reward structures in classroom tasks lead to more communication, greater cohesiveness, and more congeniality among classmates. Groups possessing intragroup cooperation and intergroup competition seek one collective goal for their group, but the achievement of a goal by another group prevents the first group from achieving its goal.

Failure on competitive tasks by children may have long-term effects upon their motivation. The effects of reward structure upon performance are complex; in general, a cooperative structure is beneficial when members must share each other's resources. But in cases where each individual's performance is not dependent upon other individuals, competitive reward structures produce greater amounts of productivity.

In real-life organizations and groups (anything from a larger business organization to a married couple), there is a mixture of cooperative and competitive motives in operation. As children grow older, motives to cooperate and to compete both get stronger. Cooperative or competitive behavior in children may be fostered through the use of reinforcement, modeling, or comparison with peers.

In some societies, reliance upon others for survival has led to the development of a stronger cooperative motive. The career orientation and life styles of the parents influence the development of motives in children.

The Prisoner's Dilemma, like other mixed-motive situations, forces the person to choose between a cooperative and a competitive response. In a mixed-motive situation, the degree of cooperation shown by a participant is influenced by the reward structure of the situation, by the strategy of the other participant, and by intrapersonal factors such as motives and assumptions about human nature.

VII. SUGGESTED READINGS

Caplow, T. *Two against one: Coalitions in triads*. Englewood Cliffs, N.J.: Prentice-Hall, 1968. (Paperback.) A sociologist writes delightfully about coalition formation and the ways that two members of a triad join together to defeat the third member. The geometry of triads is full of surprises: was Hamlet engaged in coalition formation? Caplow has an opinion.

Frank, J. D. *Sanity and survival: Psychological aspects of war and peace*. New York: Vintage, 1968. (Paperback.) A clearly written book that draws upon social psychological knowledge in order to deal with important questions of nuclear disarmament, international cooperation, and the future of human aggression. Though purists may question whether all of Frank's conclusions can be accurately generalized from laboratory findings, his book is a valuable means of interpreting research findings for public consumption.

Gergen, K. J. *The psychology of behavior exchange*. Reading, Mass.: Addison-Wesley, 1969. (Paperback.) A brief introduction to the topics of bargaining, cooperation versus competition, mixed-motive games, and related topics.

Rapoport, A., & Chammah, A. M. *Prisoner's Dilemma: A study in conflict and cooperation*. Ann Arbor: University of Michigan Press, 1965. A thorough discussion of mixed-motive games, particularly Prisoner's Dilemma, done by two of the most influential contributors to the field. Technical in places.

Swingle, P. (Ed.) *The structure of conflict*. New York: Academic Press, 1970. A collection of review articles prepared especially for this volume. Topics covered include game theory, conflict resolution, social power in negotiations, threats and promises, and personality factors in cooperation. Useful for reviewing these areas.

Wrightsman, L. S., O'Connor, J., & Baker, N. J. (Eds.) *Cooperation and competition: Readings on mixed-motive games*. Belmont, Calif.: Brooks/Cole, 1972. A series of studies on factors influencing degree of cooperation in the Prisoner's Dilemma are reprinted, along with commentary. An extensive list of references, coded by topic, is included.

I. *DEFINITIONS OF AGGRESSION*
   - A. *Aggression from the psychoanalytic point of view*
   - B. *Aggression as viewed by social-learning theorists and experimental social psychologists*
   - C. *Aggression from the ethological point of view*
   - D. *Differences in definitions*

II. *PRO-INSTINCT POSITIONS AND BIOLOGICAL EXPLANATIONS OF AGGRESSION*
   - A. *Orthodox psychoanalysis and neo-Freudian theories*
   - B. *Lorenz and ethology*
   - C. *Territoriality as an instinct and its influence upon expression of aggression*
   - D. *Hereditary determinants of aggression*

III. *AGGRESSION AS AN INNATE RESPONSE ACTIVATED BY FRUSTRATION*
   - A. *The frustration-aggression hypothesis*
     - 1. *What is frustration?*
     - 2. *Is the relationship between frustration and aggression natural, innate, or instinctual?*
     - 3. *Does research verify or disprove the frustration-aggression hypothesis?*
   - B. *Berkowitz's revised frustration-aggression hypothesis*

IV. *PROLEARNING POSITIONS*
   - A. *J. P. Scott and animal psychology: Absence of physiological factors*
   - B. *Cross-cultural comparisons: The search for the nonaggressive society*
   - C. *Social-learning theory: Aggressiveness may be modeled*

V. *A RECAPITULATION AND ATTEMPT AT RESOLUTION*

VI. *VIOLENCE AND THE MASS MEDIA*

VII. *COLLECTIVE VIOLENCE IN SOCIETY—YESTERDAY, TODAY, AND TOMORROW*
   - A. *Violence in the past*
   - B. *Changes in violence rates: The problem of assessing crime statistics*
   - C. *The future—how can aggression be controlled?*
     - 1. *The psychoanalytic view*
     - 2. *The ethologist's view*
     - 3. *Will overcrowding be the downfall?*
     - 4. *Frustration-aggression theory*
     - 5. *Social-learning theory*
     - 6. *Detrimental aggression can be rechanneled*

VIII. *SUMMARY*

IX. *SUGGESTED READINGS*

Chapter Six

Aggression, Violence, and War

Violence is as American as cherry pie. *Rap Brown*

Sure we make mistakes. You do in any war. *Police Commissioner of New York City, 1964, after riot in Harlem*

The basic controversy in a discussion of man's aggressive behavior is whether aggression is instinctual or learned. For social psychologists, a set of facts about the violent nature of human society demands a theory. According to the National Commission on the Causes and Prevention of Violence (NCCPV Report, 1969, p. xv), for example, the United States is clearly the leader among stable democratic societies in rates of homicide, assault, rape and robbery.[1] The homicide rate in the United States (about five violent deaths per 100,000 people per year) is twice that of Finland, the world's second most violent nation. The homicide rate in Canada is 1.3 per 100,000 people; in France it is 0.8; and in England the rate is 0.7 violent deaths per 100,000 people per year (NCCPV Report, 1969, p. 29). Indeed, since the turn of the century, more than 800,000 Americans have been killed by guns—not including war deaths.

In short, conflict appears to be a way of life. Since 1945, there have been at least 55 wars of significant magnitude throughout the world (Thayer, 1969). Between 1961 and 1968 some form of violent civil conflict occurred between or within 114 of the world's 121 largest countries (Gurr, 1970).

Another fact that demands our attention is that the number of firearms in civilian hands in the United States increased from 2,100,000 in 1962 to 5,300,000 in 1968 (NCCPV Report, 1969). The rate of increase in the number of handguns was even greater, from 600,000 to 2,500,000 between 1962 and 1968.

One could easily conclude from these and other isolated facts that violence and aggression are inevitable facets of human society. Indeed, some scientists see aggression as inevitable in man. For some, aggression is instinctual and as characteristic in our species as it is in those species from which we have evolved. Other scientists, how-

[1] This statement assumes the accuracy of crime report records, an issue that will be examined later in this chapter.

ever, see aggression as a result of the frustrations of everyday life. The latter approach —emphasizing a learned reaction—rests upon another quite different set of facts.

For one, societies do exist in which the commonplace instances of violence and aggression in our culture are unheard of. If one searches far enough, a continuum can be recorded of cultures that range all the way from totally warlike to completely pacifistic.

Second, even though the homicide rate in the United States is high in comparison to other industrialized societies, there is a large variation from state to state. The homicide rate in Georgia is 13.9 violent deaths per 100,000; while in North Dakota it is only 1.1 (Federal Bureau of Investigation Uniform Crime Reports for 1968, as cited in *Britannica Year Book*, 1970). Moreover, while every death resulting from violence should concern all of us, the number of deaths from automobile accidents in America (55,000) is five times greater than the number of murder victims (12,000 per year). Furthermore, accidents in the home account for 100 times more hospitalized injuries than criminal assaults.

Neither set of facts on violence and aggression can be interpreted fully until placed in the context of a theory; and, when considering the nature of aggression, we find more than enough theories to go around. These numerous theories differ essentially in the importance given to the role of **instinct** in human aggression. (Instincts are unlearned behavior patterns that appear fully in all members of the species when there is an adequate stimulus.) This chapter will describe and evaluate three dominant, yet conflicting, assumptions about the nature of aggression—that it is solely innate, that it is entirely learned, and that it is an innate response activated by frustration. In addition, the subsequent questions must also be considered.

1. Is aggression always undesirable or bad? Or can it serve adaptive functions? In species other than man, does aggression serve a survival function?

Figure 6-1. *The Costs of Violence. Not all of the costs of violence, aggression, and war are reported by tabulations of death and injury counts. Is this man the same person he was before the war? (Photograph courtesy of David Douglas Duncan.)*

2. Can examples of entirely peaceful societies be found? Why do riots and mass violence occur in some societies and not in others?

3. Is the rate of violence increasing? Or has violence always been a prominent part of Western civilization?

4. Does exposure to violence on television and other mass media encourage the expression of violence in the observer? Or does the viewing satisfy aggressive needs so that the viewer is less likely to aggress upon others in his everyday behavior?

Before looking at the multitude of explanations for aggression and violence, some of the semantic problems in this area need to be attacked. A definition of aggression is of the first order of importance.

I. DEFINITIONS OF AGGRESSION

Three theoretical viewpoints offer different definitions of aggression. One is the psychoanalytic approach. The second viewpoint is that of the social-learning theorists and the experimental psychologists. And the third approach to a definition of aggression starts from an ethological viewpoint.

A. Aggression from the Psychoanalytic Point of View

In the orthodox Freudian or psychoanalytic framework, aggressive energy is believed to be constantly generated by the body. For example, any intake of food will eventually lead to the generation of more energy. Aggressive urges, like sexual urges, must be expressed directly or indirectly; these urges can be discharged either through socially acceptable actions (such as a debate or some muscular activity) or through less socially desirable ways (insults, fighting, and the like). The destructive release of aggressive urges does not necessarily have to be directed against others; it can be aimed toward the self, as in suicide.

Other orthodox Freudians regard aggression as playing a part in ego enhancement, but the typical psychoanalytic view defines aggression as an underlying urge that seeks expression. Hence, aggression becomes a problem because, when it cannot be expressed in socially acceptable ways, it will become destructive to the self or to others. Freud believed that one function of society was to keep man's natural aggressiveness in its place, restraining its outward expression.

B. Aggression as Viewed by Social-Learning Theorists and Experimental Social Psychologists

In contrast to psychoanalysts, contemporary behavioristic psychologists conceptualize aggression as a type of behavior, avoiding in their definitions any reliance upon underlying drives or urges. For example, Leonard Berkowitz, an influential social psychologist, defines aggression as "behavior whose goal response is the inflicting of injury on some object or person" (1969a, p. 3).[2] A similar definition in a recent social psychology textbook makes explicit the role of *intent*: aggression is "any intentional act of hurting another person" (Schellenberg, 1970, p. 17). Aggression then may be overt (that is, expressed verbally or through physical actions), or it may be implicit (in the case of hostile, willful thoughts). In Berkowitz's formulation, there is an important distinction between aggression—a behavioral reaction—and the emotional state "which may facilitate and perhaps even 'energize' the aggressive response" (Berkowitz, 1969a, p. 3). This emotional state represents arousal or anger.

The experimental social psychologist does not evaluate aggression as either desirable or undesirable, preferring simply to describe it and to observe its correlates. However, some assumptions are necessary here also; an inference about the goals of behavior is still required even in this approach. Buss (1961) defines aggression as "a response that delivers noxious stimuli to another organism" (p. 3). Even though this definition does away with the problem of intent, it generates limitations of its own.

C. Aggression from the Ethological Point of View

The noted ethologist Konrad Lorenz (1966) describes aggression as "the fighting instinct in beast and man which is directed *against* members of the same species" (p. ix, italics in original). According to Lorenz's hypothesis, aggression functions to preserve the species as well as the individual. Fights serve to spread out the species, by reducing the number within a species or by dispersing members over an area so that the species as an entity may survive. Through his investigations, Lorenz has found: "The danger of too dense a population of an animal species settling in one part of the available biotope and exhausting all its sources of nutrition and so starving can be obviated by a mutual repulsion acting on the animals of the same species, effecting their regular spacing out, in much the same manner as electrical charges are regularly distributed all over the surface of a spherical conductor. This, in plain terms, is the most important survival value of intraspecific aggression" (1966, p. 31). The dangers of the human population explosion have always been apparent to Lorenz, who supports the notion that increased crowding will lead to increased aggression.

Lorenz concludes that an organism is far more aggressive toward other members of its own species than toward any other species. The basic purpose of such aggression is to keep members of the species separated—to give each member enough area to survive. This intraspecies aggression also affects sexual selection and mating and hence assures the selection of the best and strongest animals for reproduction. Lorenz believes that intraspecies aggression is desirable in lower animals. "Aggression, far from being the diabolical, destructive principle that classical psychoanalysis

[2]Like any definition, this one elicits borderline examples. Is a nurse acting aggressively when she gives a patient a routine injection? No, because the goal of the nurse is not to hurt the patient. But what if the patient has just insulted her, and she jams the needle in with unnecessary force? Certainly, there is a component of aggression in this behavior. What if a woman fights back when an intruder attempts to harm her baby; while this response is adaptive, it is also aggressive. Many examples exist where deliberate acts of harm toward another person occur in the absence of anger (a soldier firing at an enemy on the battlefield, for example). Because of these problems, several writers (Buss, 1961; Schellenberg, 1970) make a distinction between *angry aggression* and *strategic aggression*. The latter refers to cases where others are deliberately hurt, but as a consequence of an attempt to achieve one's own goals.

Figure 6-2. *Konrad Lorenz. The noted ethologist at work observing animals in the field. (Photograph by Harry Redl, Black Star.)*

makes it out to be, is really an essential part of the life-preserving organization of instincts" (1966, p. 48). In Lorenz's view, aggression only becomes undesirable when the species—like man—fails to develop the usual instinctual inhibitions related to aggression. Most animals that have the ability to kill another of their species develop instinctual inhibitions against the very act of doing so. Intraspecies fights do not end in death, but in acts of appeasement by the loser.[3] If man had no weapons at his disposal, he would not normally be equipped to kill another of his species. Lacking such innate abilities, the human species has established no inhibitions. To Lorenz, all man's "trouble arises from his being a basically harmless, omnivorous creature, lacking in natural weapons with which to kill his big prey, and, therefore, also devoid of the built-in safety devices which prevent 'professional' carnivores from abusing their killing power to destroy fellow members of their own species" (1966, p. 241).

D. Differences in Definitions

In review, each of the three definitions of aggression implies a different phenomenon. The psychoanalyst focuses on an unconscious urge; the experimental social psychologist and social-learning theorist emphasize behaviors that have the goal of inflicting injury on others; and the ethologist stresses belligerence and fighting,

[3]This is true even for animals as ferocious as wolves. If one wolf triumphs over the other to the point that the loser yields and docilely bares its neck, the winner usually refrains from killing the opponent. A raven could peck out the eye of another raven with one thrust but will not do so. Likewise, animals with idiosyncratic retaliatory powers like those of the skunk do not usually aggress against other members of their own species in such ways.

particularly among members of the same species. These varying emphases must be borne in mind as we proceed to explore the issue of the innate or learned nature of aggression. However, the operational definition of aggression used in most of the investigations described subsequently is that of the experimental social psychologist—in other words, aggression is an act done primarily to hurt some person or object.

II. PRO-INSTINCT POSITIONS AND BIOLOGICAL EXPLANATIONS OF AGGRESSION

The psychoanalytic position and the ethological position subscribe to theories that assume that the instigation of aggression is instinctual in its origin. In this section, these two theories shall be described; in addition, an evaluation of viewpoints that emphasize heredity and the biological determinants of aggression will be presented.

A. Orthodox Psychoanalysis and Neo-Freudian Theories

Freud was a physician, and his theories of personality were closely tied to bodily functions and human physiology. Accordingly, Freud believed an instinct is a mental entity in the id representing an inner somatic source of stimulation (Hall & Lindzey, 1968); in other words, instincts result from tensions created by biological needs. Expression of aggression is instigated by a "constant, internal, driving force" (Berkowitz, 1965b, p. 304). Aggressive energy thus generated within the body is energy that must be dissipated; it can either be neutralized or discharged.

Freud constantly revised his theory, and his followers have persisted in introducing even further revisions. The neo-Freudians have conceptualized aggressive behavior as a part of the ego (or the reality-oriented part of the personality) rather than placing aggression within the irrational processes of the id (Hartmann, Kris, & Loewenstein, 1949). Thus, to the neo-Freudians, aggressive drives are healthy; they are adaptations to the realities of the environment of every human being. This revision of Freud's thought seems to approach the position of social-learning theorists who see aggression as the result of frustrations derived from the blockage of a goal.

B. Lorenz and Ethology

Ethology is the area of biology concerned with the instincts and the action patterns common to all members of a species operating in their natural habitat. Much of the work done by the ethologist consists of observing the normal behavior of fish, birds, or animals in the field and attempting to determine similarities and causes in the observed action patterns. As Crook (1968) has stated, in many cases one may justifiably regard these patterns as being under innate or instinctual control. Lorenz (1952, 1966) has painstakingly observed needlefish and greylag geese, hedgehogs and Alsatian dogs, noting the characteristic behavior patterns of each species. Without reluctance, Lorenz has applied his conclusions to man.[4]

In some ways, Lorenz resembles the psychoanalyst. As an ethologist, he uses a hydraulic model of instinctive behavior. In other words, the expression of any fixed action pattern depends upon the accumulation of energy. (In a hydraulic system, the accumulation of energy builds up pressure that forces action or change.) But to the ethologists, release of energy—or the instigation of aggression—occurs when triggered by some external stimulus (E. Hess, 1962). The concept of releasers is used by ethologists to explain the relationship between internal factors and external, triggering stimuli. Berkowitz, though not an ethologist, has summarized the theory: "A releaser, or sign stimulus, is a cue in the external environment which produces a given reaction from an organism ready to make this response. There is an interaction between the organism's internal condition and the external stimulation" (1965b, p. 304). Essentially, this is a two-factor theory of the expression of aggression; it has an advantage over orthodox psychoanalytic theory and the neo-Freudian approach in that aggressive behavior is conceptualized as the result of a combination of internal factors and external, triggering stimuli.

How do releasers, or external sign stimuli, work? Ethologists such as Lorenz (1966) and Tinbergen (1951) have documented many cases in which lower animals respond with aggressive behavior to specific, delimited stimuli. If the male stickleback sees a red spot on the belly of a rival male, it will attack. If the red spot is on the rival's back, it does not attack. But the sign stimulus also has no effect if internal conditions in the potential aggressor are not appropriate. The male stickleback will not attack the appropriately located red spot unless it has an accumulation of reproductive hormones at the time.

C. Territoriality as an Instinct and Its Influence upon Expression of Aggression

We may still ask: why does aggression occur? According to the ethologist, aggression results from the organism's propensity to defend its territory. Largely through the efforts of the talented professional writer Robert Ardrey (1961, 1966, 1970), the ethological conception of territoriality has been popularized as a basic instinct. Territoriality is an innate drive to gain and defend property. In some animal species, the owner will mark off its property by urination or other means at its disposal; other members of the species recognize the rights of ownership and withdraw when they approach the owner's territory (Ardrey, 1966; Crook, 1968). In Lorenz's (1966) description, scents act like railway signals, which prevent the collision between two trains.[5] This territorial marking not only defends an animal's

[4]Other ethologists, such as Tinbergen (1968), have emphasized that differences between species may reduce generality and the ability to apply one's conclusions to man.

[5]Anthropologist Edward T. Hall (1959, 1966) has advanced a related concept, known as "personal space" or "the body buffer zone." Hall emphasizes the differences among cultures in the extent of personal space one needs; for example, in Latin America the customary distance between two people who are standing and talking is less than the usual distance in the United States. A Brazilian may feel he is being rejected when his Bostonian visitor simply maintains a "proper distance." Psychologist Robert Sommer (1969), in a useful book, has shown the implications of these concepts for everyday living and even for architectural design.

living area but also serves to signal when the marking animal is likely to attack another member of the same species (Ralls, 1971).

To both the novice and the expert, the territoriality drive manifested by some species is dramatic in its strength; in the African kob, for example, territoriality even overrides the sexual drive. Ardrey (1966) recounts the observations Helmut Buechner (1961, 1963) made of the Uganda kob, an elegant, rather snobbish antelope.

> Males compete for real estate, never for females. The kob's territorial and sexual appetites are so profoundly intermeshed that fights generate sexual stimulation. The champion whom we watched in a twenty-minute defense of his property had an erection through most of the combat. Nevertheless, when the female arrives on a territory, she becomes the sole if momentary property of the male whose grass she crops. A flourishing arena is a Breughel-like scene of scattered kob couples in various stages of intimate disposal amid a scattering of solitary males paying no regard whatever (Ardrey, 1966, p. 51).

Attachment to a piece of ground is stronger than attraction to a female. If a male kob has mounted a female on its personal land, or "putting green," and she crosses into a neighbor's putting green while still in the act of copulating, the sexually aroused male will not pursue. He takes it in good grace and does not even watch the male on the adjoining putting green take his place and his pleasure.

Ardrey also applies concepts of territoriality to man, positing that man is innately aggressive because of territorial needs.[6] It is true, however, that many species of animals do not appear to be territorial (Crook, 1968), but Ardrey dismisses these cases. (Lorenz, at least, recognizes that territoriality is not basic to many animal species.) Perhaps, because of ample living areas, sufficient food supplies, or other reasons, animals such as the California ground squirrel, the fieldmouse, the red fox—or, closer to man—primates such as the orangutan, the chimpanzee, and the gorilla do not display territorial behavior (Montagu, 1968b, p. 8). Bourlière (1954) observed that "territorial behavior is far from being as important in mammals as in birds" (1954, pp. 99–100). Of the animals closest to man, only the baboon expresses territoriality.[7] So, despite Ardrey's eloquent case for the importance of territoriality, it is doubtful that its existence in man can be demonstrated (Barnett, 1968).

D. Hereditary Determinants of Aggression

Attempts to breed animals so that they are extremely aggressive or nonaggressive have been partially successful in uncovering hereditary determinants of aggression. Lagarspertz (1961), in a study reviewed by McClearn and Meredith (1966), used mice in a selective-breeding experiment to develop one highly aggressive strain and

[6]Other reasons contribute to Ardrey's conclusion that man is innately aggressive. In *African Genesis* (1961), Ardrey describes recent fossil excavations in Africa and concludes that the missing link between lower animals and man—*australopithecus*—made use of tools or weapons to kill other animals. Relying on the conclusions of Professor Raymond Dart, Ardrey judged that man's animal ancestors were carnivorous, predatory, and cannibalistic in origin. However, few psychologists believe the evidence is clear enough to warrant any conclusion, particularly Ardrey's.

[7]J. P. Scott has commented that most observers agree that "baboons resemble human beings in social organization more closely than do the anthropoid apes, which are ecologically adapted for forest living and tend to develop less closely organized groups" (J. P. Scott, 1969, p. 631, quoting K. R. L. Hall, 1964).

one highly unaggressive strain. Aggressiveness was measured, and excessively aggressive mice were bred together, while unaggressive ones were bred separately. This procedure was continued through three generations, producing in the last generation significant differences in the aggressiveness of the two groups of mice. There was still some overlap, however, in the aggressiveness ratings of the two third-generation groups. We cannot say whether such results could be applied to human beings. Selective breeding, with control of the infant's environment, is not feasible with human beings, and other sources of information must be used when looking for the possible role of heredity in human aggressiveness.

III. AGGRESSION AS AN INNATE RESPONSE ACTIVATED BY FRUSTRATION

A. The Frustration-Aggression Hypothesis

In 1939 a group of psychologists at Yale University (Dollard, Doob, Miller, Mowrer, & Sears, 1939) introduced a hypothesis that influenced the direction of psychology for more than 20 years, generating more empirical research than any other theory of aggression. Basically, these psychologists hypothesized that frustration instigated aggression. More specifically, this frustration-aggression hypothesis postulated that "the occurrence of aggression always presupposes frustration" (Miller, 1941, pp. 337–338). A second part of the hypothesis was usually interpreted to mean that any frustrating event inevitably leads to aggression. This part of the hypothesis was later clarified by N. E. Miller (1941), who made it clear that there were no implications that frustration had no consequences other than aggression or that aggression would inevitably occur as a response to frustration. The original formulation conceived of frustration as leading to an instigation of aggression but recognized that punishment or inhibitions could suppress any possible expression of aggression. To clarify the frustration-aggression hypothesis, Miller (1941, p. 338) rephrased the formulation, stating that "frustration produces instigations to a number of different types of responses, one of which is an instigation to some form of aggression." Unfortunately, the revised hypothesis is much less testable. Nonetheless, both formulations raise several questions.

1. What is frustration? To say the least, frustration is a vague term, which is used variously (see Berkowitz, 1969a, for an elucidation of these ambiguities). In common usage, frustration may refer either to an external instigating condition or to the organism's reaction to this condition. Suppose a young man is ready to drive his car to the airport to meet his girlfriend, and he discovers that his car battery is dead. What is the frustration? Is it the dead battery or the fact that the car will not start (the external instigating conditions)? Or is frustration the young man's feeling of increased tension and the pounding of his heart—or does it refer to his pounding on the car? (All of the latter phenomena are various examples of the organism's reaction to the condition.) Sanford and Wrightsman (1970) tried to separate these two factors by using frustration to refer to the *state of being blocked* (similar to the external instigating condition) and frustration-induced behavior to refer to the emotional reaction resulting from being blocked or thwarted. Other observers such as Brown and Farber (1951) and Amsel (1958, 1962) have referred to frustration as an internal action in response to being blocked. The original frustration-aggression formulation referred to frustration as the external event and excluded reference to any internal states except the hypothetical "instigation to aggression" (Berkowitz, 1969a, p. 5). The Yale theorists defined frustration as the state that emerges when a goal-response is interfered with; to quote, frustration is "an interference with the occurrence of an instigated goal-response at its proper time in the behavior sequence" (Dollard, 1939, p. 7). Such an emphasis on observables suited the Watsonian behavioristic orientation of the Yale group at that time, but psychologists who have tested the frustration-aggression hypothesis have not always clearly defined the term frustration. This lack of a definition of terms has led Berkowitz (1969a, p. 7) to conclude that many of the failures to verify the frustration-aggression hypothesis reflect the ambiguity and inconsistency in definitions rather than any essential lack of validity in the formulation.

2. Is the relationship between frustration and aggression natural, innate, or instinctual? There is a tendency to regard the frustration-aggression relationship as inevitable or instinctual. Perhaps, this notion was relayed when Dollard and his colleagues wrote that "the frustration-aggression hypothesis assumes a universal causal relation between frustration and aggression" (Dollard, 1939, p. 10). Yet, most probably, no innate link was postulated, since Miller, one of the formulators of the hypothesis, wrote two years later that "no assumptions are made as to whether the frustration-aggression relationship is of innate or of learned origin" (N. E. Miller, 1941, p. 340). At the same time, Miller recognized the possibility of innate causes.

Despite this apologia, more recent critics regard the frustration-aggression hypothesis as inadequate since persons can learn to modify their reactions to frustration (Bandura & Walters, 1963, pp. 135–137). For example, a budding short story writer may learn to swallow his impulses to strike back when his teacher insults his carefully written story. Berkowitz, interpreting the position of Bandura and Walters, has stated that if human beings, at least, can learn new reactions (either aggressive or nonaggressive) to frustration, then the possibility of innate behavioral determinants is excluded (Berkowitz, 1969a, p. 4). Yet, Berkowitz indicates that "learning and innate determination can coexist in man" (1969a, p. 4). This is an extremely important point. Learning may alter or modify built-in patterns of behavior, so that each plays a role. While frustration may instinctively heighten the likelihood that a certain type of response (such as aggression) will be instigated, learning may strongly alter or disguise the manifestation of this response. The formulators of the frustration-aggression hypothesis clearly recognized that expression of aggression could be inhibited by an anticipation of punishment, but they still insisted upon the innate link between frustration and the instigation to react. In 1964, Neal Miller wrote: "It seems highly probable that . . . innate patterns exist, that they play an important role in the development of human social behavior, and that these instinctual patterns are modifiable enough so that they tend to be disguised by learning although they may play crucial roles in motivating, facilitating, and shaping socially learned behavior" (p. 160).

3. Does research verify or disprove the frustration-aggression hypothesis? A variety of evidence from studies using both human and nonhuman subjects seems to support the notion that aggression may be caused by frustration. For example, Buss (1963) studied the effect of three kinds of frustration upon the expression of aggression in college students; the three frustrations were failing a task, losing an opportunity to win some money, and missing an opportunity to attain a better course grade. Each type of frustration led to the expression of about the same degree of aggression, and each frustration produced more aggression than the control condition. Although the evidence pointed to a link between frustration and physical aggression, the amount of aggression expressed was rather minimal. Possibly, only minimal aggression emerged because in this experiment aggression was not useful in overcoming the frustration. In situations where aggression can successfully overcome the interference, the stronger the need being blocked, the more intense should be the aggression. Thus, while accepting the value of the frustration-aggression hypothesis, Buss concludes that it is applicable only in cases where aggression has an instrumental value—in other words, only when aggression can be used to override the frustration. The results of Buss's study reinforce his conclusion that other determinants of aggression (an attack, for example) may be more important than frustration (1961).

Children also demonstrate the aggressive consequences of frustration. In one experiment, Mallick and McCandless (1966) arranged for older children to frustrate (interfere with) or not to frustrate 8- and 9-year-old children who were trying to complete five simple block construction tasks. (The subject had been promised a nickel for each task completed within a certain time limit.) Interference caused every subject in the frustration condition to fail to complete any task. In the nonfrustration condition, the older child helped the subject complete the tasks, with no reward promised or given to the helper.

In a later phase of the experiment, each subject was shown the confederate (the older child who had frustrated or facilitated the subject's block building) sitting with his hands touching electrodes attached to an electric shock apparatus. Each subject was told that he could administer as many shocks as he wanted and that the other child would not know who was shocking him. In other experiments within the same study, Mallick and McCandless utilized other procedures to generate frustration and measure aggression. The results across procedures were consistent: frustration led to heightened aggressive feelings, which remained intensified even after opportunities to direct aggressive actions toward the source of frustration.

B. Berkowitz's Revised Frustration-Aggression Hypothesis

Although the essence of the frustration-aggression hypothesis is apparently verifiable, many qualifications remain. The original conception may be too simple and too sweeping at one and the same time (Berkowitz, 1969a). Because of the limitations of the hypothesis, Berkowitz (1965b, 1969a) suggested a revised frustration-aggression formulation that emphasizes the interaction between environmental cues and the internal emotional state. The original hypothesis has been modified in the following ways.

First, the reaction to frustration creates "only a *readiness* for aggressive acts. Previously acquired aggressiveness habits can also establish this readiness" (Berkowitz, 1965b, p. 308, italics in original). In other words, Berkowitz says that the occurrence of aggressive behavior is not solely dependent upon frustration (a point Neal Miller is willing to grant) and that an intervening variable—a readiness—must be added to the link. We may think of this readiness as *anger*.

Second, stimulus cues, or external triggers, must be recognized as playing a role in the determination of expressed aggression, even when frustration is present. Frustration creates the readiness of anger; cuing stimuli may actually elicit the aggression. Aggressive behavior is not solely a matter of the individual being primed to respond aggressively; the cuing value of various stimuli also influences the strength of the aggressive response and particularly that of an impulsively aggressive response. Previously, Berkowitz (1965a) had advocated a view that aggressive cues or releasers were necessary if aggressive impulses were actually to occur. More recently his position has become somewhat tempered: "The emotional state arising from the encounter with the aversive stimulus may in itself contain distinctive stimuli which can instigate the aggressive reaction, particularly if the emotion is strong enough; but the presence of appropriate aggressive cues (in the external environment or represented internally in thoughts) increases the probability that an overt aggressive response will actually take place" (Berkowitz, 1969a, p. 18).

Note that cues increase the probability of the occurrence of aggression but are not essential for the expression of aggression. The emotional state itself (anger) may be sufficient for aggression to appear. An important research program at the University of Wisconsin has contributed to the reformulation of the hypothesis. Several of these Wisconsin studies have used the same basic procedures to study the aggressive cue value of a stimulus. In these studies, the subject, a male college student, was introduced to the other subject, who in actuality was an accomplice of the experimenter. The accomplice either made the subject angry or treated him in a neutral manner. Immediately after this act, a seven-minute film clip was shown—the film being either a vicious prizefight scene from the film *Champion* or a neutral film dealing with English canal boats. After viewing one of these films, the subject was given an opportunity to shock the confederate, who had moved to another room. The experimenter presented this opportunity in a way that made the subsequent shocking appear socially acceptable to the subject (Berkowitz, 1965a).

In the first study of this series, the confederate was introduced either as a nonbelligerent speech major or as a physical education major interested in boxing; the purpose of this manipulation was to vary the aggressive cue value of the confederate, in the eyes of the subject. (A real-life analogy might be the difference between being frustrated by a musician or by a policeman.) The results of this experiment are presented in Table 6-1. Note that when the confederate was introduced as a boxer, the subject gave more shocks of a longer duration than when the confederate was introduced as a speech major.[8] For example, if the subject had been angered and had seen an aggressive film, he gave the speech major an average of 4.90 shocks and the boxer an average of 5.35 shocks. Differences in the duration of the shocks were even greater (11.90 seconds versus 16.56 seconds). These differences support the hypothesis that the degree of aggressive behavior expressed by a person is influenced by the aggressive cue value of a stimulus in his environment. It would suggest that frustrations in the real world engendered by stimuli that have aggressive cue values (such as policemen) are more likely to elicit aggression. However, the value of this con-

[8]Questions have been raised by Hartmann (1970) regarding the adequacy of the measures of aggression used in these and similar studies. Hartmann notes that among the measures used in different studies are the frequency of shocks given, the duration of shocks, the intensity, the pressure exerted on the shock switch, the duration times the intensity, the intensity times frequency, and on ad infinitum. The correlations between these measures are often low (Geen & O'Neal, 1969; Geen, Rakosky, & O'Neal, 1968).

Table 6-1. *Mean Number and Duration of Shocks*

	Angered subjects				Nonangered subjects			
	Boxer role		Speech major role		Boxer role		Speech major role	
	Aggressive film	Neutral film	Aggressive film	Neutral film	Aggressive film	Neutral film	Aggressive film	Neutral film
Number of shocks	5.35_d	4.94_c	4.90_c	4.78_c	4.42_{abc}	4.37_{abc}	3.92_a	4.16_{ab}
Duration of shocks	16.56_d	11.47_c	11.90_c	11.16_{bc}	10.15_{bc}	12.04_c	6.67_a	8.15_{ab}

Note: Before analyzing the shock data a $\sqrt{X} + \sqrt{X + 1}$ transformation was employed. Separate analyses of variance were conducted for each measure. Cells having a subscript in common are not significantly different at the .05 level by Duncan Multiple Range test. Each mean is based on 11 cases. Table 6-1, Table 6-2, and Table 6-3 are from Berkowitz, "Aggressive Drive: Additional Considerations." In *Advances in Experimental Social Psychology*, Vol. 2. Copyright 1965 by Academic Press. Reprinted with permission of the author and the publisher.

clusion is somewhat moderated by the finding that even when the subject is treated neutrally by the accomplice (the nonangered subjects in Table 6-1), the boxer is given more shocks than the speech major. Perhaps, as Berkowitz (1965a) postulates, boxers elicit more aggression because of their connection with fighting or because they are disliked by other students. As in any experiment, subjects entered this experiment with certain assumptions. Here, the assumptions about the nature of physical education majors were possibly uncontrolled influences.

A second experiment (Berkowitz & Geen, 1966) used another approach to study the aggressive cue value of the stimulus (the accomplice). In the film clip from *Champion,* Kirk Douglas, a well-known actor, played a boxer who was badly mauled in the fight. At the beginning of the experiment, the accomplice was introduced to half of the subjects as Kirk Anderson, while to the other half of the subjects the accomplice's name was Bob Anderson. It was hypothesized that if the accomplice's name was Kirk, he would be associated with the fight scene and hence would elicit more shocks than if his name were unassociated with the fight. (Another, less important change in the procedure of this study was using an exciting, but nonaggressive, film of a track meet instead of the film on canal boats.) Table 6-2 shows that after being angered and having watched an aggressive film, subjects gave the accomplice named Kirk more shocks than the accomplice named Bob. Although alternative explanations may always be advanced to explain such phenomena,[9] the results are clearly in line with an expectation that certain stimuli elicit more aggression than others, when other factors are constant and delimited.

A third experiment (Geen & Berkowitz, 1966, 1967) further verified the triggering properties of the aggressor's name. In the *Champion* movie, Kirk Douglas played a boxer named Midge Kelly, who was given a bloody beating by another boxer named Dunne. One-third of the subjects in both movie conditions were told that the accomplice's name was Bob Kelly, and another third of the subjects were told the accomplice's name was Bob Dunne. The remaining third of the subjects in both film groups were introduced to an accomplice named Bob Riley, a name that does not

Table 6-2. *Mean Ratings of Felt Anger and Mean Number of Shocks Given to the Accomplice by the Subject*

	Aggressive film				Track film			
	Angered		Nonangered		Angered		Nonangered	
	Kirk	Bob	Kirk	Bob	Kirk	Bob	Kirk	Bob
Felt anger	7.36_a	6.00_a	11.27_b	12.09_b	7.27_a	7.27_a	10.55_b	11.27_b
Number of shocks	6.09_a	4.55_b	1.73_c	1.45_c	4.18_b	4.00_b	1.54_c	1.64_c

Note: For the "Felt anger" ratings, the lower the score, the greater the anger. Each measure was analyzed separately. In each case cells having a subscript in common are not significantly different at the .05 level by Duncan Multiple Range test. There were 11 men in each condition.

[9] In this study, subjects in the aggressive film-Kirk condition were reminded "casually but pointedly" by the experimenter that the first name of the movie actor was the same name as that of the other subject (the accomplice) in the experiment. While this was probably necessary to develop an association between the two, it encouraged different demand characteristics of the subjects in this condition. However, if different demand characteristics were operating here, we would expect angered subjects in the aggressive film-Kirk condition to express significantly more anger toward the accomplice than would angered subjects in the aggressive film-Bob condition. Data in Table 6-2 indicate that this did not happen to a statistically significant degree, although the difference was in this direction.

Table 6-3. *Mean Number of Shocks Administered to Anger-Arousing Confederate*

Confederate's name	Boxing film	Track film
Kelly (Victim in the film)	5.40_a	3.60_b
Dunne (Aggressor in the film)	4.15_b	3.87_b
Riley (Name not in the film)	4.40_b	4.00_b

Note: Cells having a subscript in common are not significantly different at the .05 level by Duncan Multiple Range test. There are 15 subjects in each condition.

appear in either film clip. All subjects in this experiment were angered by the accomplice. It was expected that after witnessing the boxing film, subjects would administer more shocks to Bob Kelly than to any other accomplice. Table 6-3 shows this to be the case. When the accomplice's name was the same as the name of the victim in the film, an average of 5.40 shocks was given, after the subject had watched the boxing film. When the accomplice's name was irrelevant (Riley) an average of only 4.40 shocks was administered, after the boxing film. Note that a neutral name such as Riley did not produce any significant differences when the subject had watched the track film (means of 3.60, 3.87, and 4.00).

Of interest in Table 6-3 is the finding that Dunne, the aggressor's name in the film, received fewer shocks than Kelly, the victim in the film. As Berkowitz concludes (1965b), "the confederate's aggressive cue value apparently varied directly with his association with the victim rather than the giver of the observed aggression" (p. 318). Why this unexpected result occurred is unclear. The finding is reminiscent of those in Lerner's "just world" studies. Possibly, the subjects associated Kelly with the victim, and, as a victim, he must have deserved the beating he was so obviously getting. Therefore, subjects shocked him all the more, merely because he "deserves it."

More recent research in this productive series of experiments has shown that after a subject is conditioned to have a negative attitude toward a certain name, more aggression is directed toward the frustrator who has the same unfortunate name (Berkowitz & Knurek, 1969). In the study that demonstrated this finding, college males were trained to dislike a given name (either George or Ed) by learning to associate the name with words having unfavorable connotations. Later, half of the subjects were deliberately frustrated by the trainer; then all subjects participated in a supposedly separate study in which they discussed an issue with two other males, one of whom was named either George or Ed. Subjects acted more unfriendly toward the negatively named person than toward the other discussion member. One could apply this finding to the possible causes of unfriendly reactions to members of minority groups.

Other experiments in this series have shown that the presence of a weapon increases the frequency of the expression of aggression, even if the weapon is not actually used to express aggression (Berkowitz & LePage, 1967). Male university students received either one or seven electric shocks from a fellow student and were then given the opportunity to administer shocks in return. For some subjects, a rifle and a revolver were on the table near the shock key; for other subjects, two badminton rackets were on the table, and for a group of control subjects no object was on the table. As one might expect, more shocks were administered by the strongly aroused subjects (those who had received seven shocks rather than one); but, more importantly, the presence of weapons increased the average number of shocks given from 4.67 to 6.07 (see Table 6-4). If a person's inhibitions toward aggression are rather weak at a particular moment, aggressive cues in the environment make the expression of aggressive acts more likely.[10] J. Edgar Hoover's claim (reported in *Time*, 1966b) that the availability of firearms is a significant influence upon the murder rate seems verified. But beyond this, the presence of firearms leads to more violence even when guns are not used in the expression of violence. The fact that the world contains an estimated 750,000,000 operable military rifles and pistols (Thayer, 1969) should cause us concern for the possibilities for world peace.[11]

The general findings from the Wisconsin studies reinforce two conclusions: (a) witnessing an aggressively oriented movie lowers one's inhibitions against the expression of aggression resulting from frustration, and (b) certain stimuli have greater cuing properties in the triggering of frustration-engendered aggression than do others. In other words, whether the subject will act aggressively is partially a function of the presence of aggression-cuing stimuli in his environment.

IV. PROLEARNING POSITIONS

A. J. P. Scott and Animal Psychology: Absence of Physiological Factors

Thus far, we have moved from a single-factor instinctual view to one in which learned responses of aggression are superimposed upon a possibly innate reaction to frustration. Let us now explore a position that emphasizes learning alone. In his text *Aggression* (1958, p. 98), psychologist J. P. Scott concludes that "all research findings point to the fact that there is no physiological evidence of any internal need or spontaneous driving force for fighting; that all stimulation for aggression comes eventually from forces present in the external environment." In rejecting the psychoanalytic view, Scott observes that presently no known physiological mechanism serves as an internal drive, without external stimulation.

Although Scott doubts that experience and training can greatly modify the social behavior patterns of lower animals, he observes that domestic animals appear to have much less fixed and ceremonious behavior than do wild ones (1969, p. 622), and that the behavior of mammals is much less stamped in instinctually than in birds or fish. Likewise, when considering territoriality—the cornerstone of the ethologist's views on innate human aggression—Scott (1969) finds little indication that territoriality is a basic trait of primates. According to Scott, one cannot conclude

[10] Possibly, subjects in this experiment were reacting to the demand characteristics of the situation. Berkowitz and LePage recognized this possibility and advanced several reasons why they believe it was not a strong influence (1967, pp. 206–207).

[11] In his magnificent book, *The War Business* (1969), Thayer scrutinizes the international trade in armaments and reports that since 1945 there has been an increase both in the trading (or selling) of war equipment and in international conflict. As Thayer states, "an increase in the availability of weapons is concomitant with an increase in their use" (1969, p. 20). Between 1950 and 1968 the international arms trade grew from $2.4 billion to $5 billion.

Table 6-4. *Mean Number of Shocks Given in Each Condition*

Condition	*Shocks received by the subject*	
	One shock only	*Seven shocks*
Associated weapons were present	2.60_a	6.07_d
Unassociated weapons were present	2.20_a	5.67_{cd}
No objects present	3.07_a	4.67_{bc}
Badminton racket present	. .	4.60_b

Note: Cells having a common subscript are not significantly different at the .05 level by Duncan Multiple Range test. There were 10 subjects in the seven-shocks-received-badminton-racket condition and 15 subjects in each of the other conditions. (From Berkowitz and LePage, "Weapons as Aggression-Eliciting Stimuli." In *Journal of Personality and Social Psychology*, 1967, **7**, 202–207. Copyright 1967 by the American Psychological Association, and reproduced by permission.

at this point whether territoriality is "a cultural or a biological invention. Its existence in precultural man is entirely conjectural" (1969, p. 635).

B. Cross-Cultural Comparisons: The Search for the Nonaggressive Society

Those who explain aggression as a learned response claim that if societies exist where no aggressive behavior is manifested, one can conclude that learning, rather than instinct, plays a dominant role in the manifestation of aggressive responses. These observers believe that the existence of nonaggressive societies would, at least, imply that learning can inhibit any aggressive instinct. Some societies, for example, train children never to act in ways that harm others. Although this analysis emphasizes an undesirable instinct versus learning approach, it is, nonetheless, useful to find societies in which aggression is nonexistent.

Gorer (1968b) has reviewed anthropological investigations of societies whose goal is one of peaceful isolation.[1] These societies include the Arapesh of New Guinea, the Lepchas of Sikkim in the Himalayas, and the Pygmies of the Congo. A classic study by Margaret Mead (1935) gives a detailed account of the Arapesh, who live in a mountainous area on the Island of New Guinea. In Arapesh society, helping one's neighbor is considered essential for the survival of both parties. Both Arapesh men and women possess gentle personalities, are responsive to others, and are rather maternal in their concern for others.[13]

The Great White River Eskimos, according to Honigmann (1954), insist upon total inhibition of the expression of aggression in their children. These parents

[12]Isolated communities in the United States, such as the Amish and the Hutterites also possess these aims. The Hutterites advocate a life of pacifism, and aggressive acts in their society go unrewarded (Eaton & Weil, 1955, cited in Bandura & Walters, 1963).

[13]Mead also compared two other tribes living on New Guinea. The Mundugumor were described as aggressive, overly masculine individualists. The Tchambuli were notable because the roles of the two sexes were the reverse of those in Western cultures. Mead capitalized upon these differences to emphasize that "human nature is almost unbelievably malleable," a conclusion with which we agree. Yet Mead's subsequent writings have been somewhat tempered, perhaps in response to criticisms of her earlier work. Fortune (1939), for example, reported that the Arapesh males, despite all their concern for fellow tribal members, were among the most feared head-hunters in New Guinea.

reprimand fighting and teach their children that physical aggression is the worst thing a child can do. By the age of 10 or 12, the children have channeled such activities into intensely rough ball games.

The societies described by Gorer have several characteristics in common, which facilitate the development and maintenance of their nonaggressive behavior. First, they tend to live in rather inaccessible places, which other groups do not covet as living areas. Whenever other groups have invaded their territory, their response as a tribe has been to retreat into even more inaccessible areas. Second, they are oriented toward the concrete pleasures of life—such as eating, drinking, and sex—and, apparently, the supply of these pleasures sufficiently satisfies their needs. It is unlikely that important needs are often frustrated. Achievement or power needs are not encouraged in children; "the model for the growing child is of concrete performance and frank enjoyment, not of metaphysical symbolic achievements or of ordeals to be surmounted" (Gorer, 1968b, p. 34). Third, these societies make few distinctions between males and females. Although some distinctions between male and female roles exist in each of these societies, no attempt is made to project, for instance, an image of brave, aggressive masculinity. (In contrast, the Mundugumor cannibals of the New Guinea Highlands idealize a highly competitive, aggressive conception of masculinity.) Among nonaggressive societies, sexual identity is apparently no problem; Gorer claims that no cases of sexual inversion have been reported in these societies.

As one would expect, all of these societies are small, weak, and technologically undeveloped. If such a society were transplanted to a desirable living area, the possibilities of survival would probably be low. Yet, these groups (and American cooperative societies like the Amish and Hutterites) are able to survive when left alone in relative isolation. (See Table 6-5.) In some respects, contemporary American society—for all its aggressiveness—is moving toward the Arapesh, the Lepchas, and the Congo Pygmies. Different roles for the two parents are certainly less emphasized in American families now than 50 years ago; no longer is the father seen as the dominant decision maker, figure of authority, dispenser of discipline, and sole provider; nor is the mother seen in the restricted role of homemaker and child rearer. Whether these shifts will have any effect upon the level of aggressiveness in our society is conjectural. In fact, present trends toward greater democratization of family life and greater similarity in the roles and fashions of the two sexes may be reversed 20 years from now.

Despite their apparent lack of survival value, the Lepchas and other nonaggressive societies remind one of the malleability of human nature. As long as certain goals are emphasized and as long as certain needs are provided for by the environment, human beings can live together in a nonaggressive society.

C. Social-Learning Theory: Aggressiveness May Be Modeled

Consider the following situation (from Bandura, Ross, & Ross, 1961): a child in nursery school is brought to an experimental room and asked by the experimenter to join in a game. The experimenter then directs the child to one corner of the room, where there is a small table and chair. The child is instructed in the task of designing pictures, by using potato prints and colorful stickers. After beginning the child in his

Table 6-5. *Communal Groups Test the Assumption Of Innate Aggressiveness*

Basic to the assumptions of many modern-day communes is the belief that people can coexist peacefully, that aggression is unnecessary. Rosabeth Moss Kanter, a sociologist, has studied a number of communes and finds several factors that distinguish the successful ones from the unsuccessful ones. Successful communes demonstrate greater sharing of property, more detailed specifications of routine, and community-owned clothing. Factors relating to aggression are also significant, as the figures below indicate.

	9 Successful Communes	*21 Unsuccessful Communes*
	Percentage that adhere to the practice:	
Free love or celibacy	100%	29%
Parent-child separation	48%	15%
Natural families not living together	33%	5%
Regular confessional	44%	0%
Mutual criticism session	44%	26%
Daily group meetings	56%	6%

(Reprinted from *Psychology Today* Magazine, July, 1970, © Communications/Research/Machines, Inc.)

task, the experimenter escorts an adult to an opposite corner of the room that also contains a table and chair, a mallet, Tinker Toys, and a five-foot, inflated Bobo doll. The experimenter tells the child that these materials are there for the adult to play with, and then the experimenter leaves the room.

Half of the children in the study were boys and half were girls. Half of each sex watched an adult (the model) of the same sex, and half watched an adult of the opposite sex. Half of the children found that during the ten minutes they were together, the model assembled the Tinker Toys quietly and did not touch or even approach the Bobo doll (nonaggressive condition). The other half of the children found that the adult model spent most of the time (nine out of ten minutes) attacking the Bobo doll, hitting, throwing, and laying it on its side, pounding its nose, and otherwise aggressing upon it. These actions were interspersed with verbal responses such as "Sock him in the nose," "Pow!" "Kick him," and the like.

The children were then moved to a different experimental room set off from the main nursery; many of the children believed that they were no longer on the nursery school grounds. Each child was subjected to a mild arousal of aggression to instill some reason for acting aggressively. The child was interrupted shortly after he had started playing with his favorite toys and was told by the experimenter that those particular toys were reserved for other children. The child could then play with any other toy in the room for 20 minutes; these toys had been previously classified into types that do or do not elicit aggressive play. The aggressive toys were a three-foot Bobo doll, a mallet and pegboard, two dart guns, and a tether ball with a face painted on it, hanging from the ceiling. The nonaggressive toys included crayons and coloring paper, a tea set, a ball, two dolls, three toy bears, plastic farm animals, and a set of cars and trucks. The behavior of each child was rated on a variety of measures including imitation of physical aggression, imitative verbal aggression, imitative nonaggressive verbal responses, and aggressive gun play.[14]

Clearly, watching an aggressive model encourages the expression of aggression in

[14] In contrast to Berkowitz's Wisconsin studies, subjects in this study were frustrated after witnessing aggression. In Berkowitz's studies subjects were angered and then allowed to witness aggressive or nonaggressive stimuli.

children. Girls who watched an aggressive model averaged 18.0 aggressive acts with the mallet, while girls with a nonaggressive model made, on the average, only 0.5 responses with the mallet. All measures consistently showed that viewing aggressive models encourages more expression of aggression after experiencing frustration. As compared to a control group of children who did not watch a model, children who had a nonaggressive model generally displayed the same or smaller degrees of aggression. Watching another person act violently apparently weakens inhibitions toward the expression of aggression—at least, in the case of children. The next question is whether the same results would occur in adults, where the inhibitions are perhaps more entrenched than in children.

Further studies (Bandura, 1965; Walters & Willows, 1968; and Kuhn, Madsen, & Becker, 1967) indicate that if a child watches a film in which an adult is rewarded for displaying novel, aggressive responses, the child will imitate the adult. Imitation occurs more often when the adult is rewarded than when he is punished for expressing aggressive impulses. Posttests indicated that children in all conditions (which varied reward or punishment for adult aggressiveness) equally learned to imitate the aggressiveness. However, if the child witnessed the adult model being punished for aggressiveness, this observation acted as an inhibitor to the child's expression of aggression (Bandura, Ross, & Ross, 1963).

These studies elucidate two processes that contribute to the expression or nonexpression of aggression: *imitation* and *inhibition*. If the child watches the aggressive actions of another person, the "observer may acquire new responses that did not previously exist in his repertory" (Bandura & Walters, 1963, p. 60). This phenomenon by which the child learns to imitate a response is called **modeling.** Observing another person may reduce inhibitions and lead the child to violence, if the model indicates that violence is permissible. But if the child witnesses another person being punished for aggression, inhibitions against aggression are increased. According to this viewpoint, individual differences in the degree of aggressiveness as a personality trait result from previous learning. Child-rearing practices and imitation of others are important determinants.[15]

V. A RECAPITULATION AND ATTEMPT AT RESOLUTION

At this point, a few conclusions will be offered to summarize our thinking on the diverse causes of aggression.

1. Man is, of course, an animal, and man's behavior may partially be accounted for by viewing him as a step in an evolutionary sequence. Books such as Desmond Morris' *The Naked Ape* (1967) may enlighten the uneducated about man's similarity to other primates; but books like these, and even Lorenz's *On Aggression,* do a disservice when they stretch the generalizations from other species to man. The more

[15]It should be noted that the thorough study of Sears, Maccoby, and Levin (1957), which dealt with aggressiveness of 5-year-olds in the home, turned up few significant relationships. There was a slight tendency for severely punitive parents to have more aggressive children, but cause and effect cannot be attributed to this relationship. Results of a similar nature, with lower-class children, are reported by McCord, McCord, and Howard (1961).

advanced the species, the less its behavior relies upon innate determinants, and the greater the role of learning. Very few human actions are unaffected by learning (Barnett, 1968).

2. At the same time, there may be in man some carry over from earlier species in regard to innate tendencies toward the instigation of aggression. These innate physiological processes may best be interpreted as the readiness to respond (Megargee & Hokanson, 1970). These processes interact with the situation and the environment to produce behavior. Thus, innate structures are postulated to be more responsive when certain environmental stimuli are present. Both the studies done by Bandura and his associates and those conducted by Berkowitz's group show that the expression of aggression (as opposed to its instigation) is facilitated when aggressive cues are in the immediate environment.

3. The frustration-aggression hypothesis, while essentially correct, must be restated to be accurate. Miller's (1941) reformulation—that frustration produces instigations to a number of different types of responses, only one of which is aggression—clarifies the relationship. For instance, frustration may lead to regression and more infantile behavior, especially in children (Himmelweit, 1950). As Berkowitz (1969a) indicates, aggression is a much more complicated phenomenon than the original frustration-aggression hypothesis would lead one to believe. "The existence of frustration *does not* always lead to some form of aggression, and the occurrence of aggressive behavior *does not necessarily* presuppose the existence of frustration" (Berkowitz, 1969a, p. 2, italics in original). It should be noted that, although the revised hypothesis is more clearly representative of the empirical data, it is also less testable than the original formulation since it is exceedingly difficult to disprove.

4. Laboratory studies consistently indicate that witnessing aggression, particularly when one is frustrated, leads to an increased expression of aggression (Bryan & Schwartz, 1971). Three intervening processes seem to be at work here. First, *modeling* plays a role; the observer learns to react violently by watching another person respond in the same way (Bandura & Walters, 1963). Second, both Berkowitz's and Bandura's studies isolate the process of *disinhibition of aggression.* In other words, witnessing aggression reduces one's previously acquired inhibitions against expressing violence. Third, certain cues in the environment play an *eliciting* role, determining how much aggression the subject expresses after witnessing a violent event under frustrating conditions. We may question what implications these processes have for watching violent movies or violent programs on television.

VI. VIOLENCE AND THE MASS MEDIA

American movies are now rated in regard to their acceptability for children. The degree of sexual content, rather than the violent tone of the movie, appears to be the most influential determinant in the rating. Even though social critics decry the prevalence of violence pictured in television dramas, the industry is slow to reduce any staple upon which the viewing audience apparently thrives. Does the portrayal of violence in the mass media encourage the viewer to respond violently? Or is such viewing a healthy channeling of aggressive impulses? Those who defend violence on television believe that vicarious participation in the mass output of aggressive acts has a cathartic function; in other words, the display of violence on television provides a harmless outlet for impulses that would otherwise lead to socially undesirable actions (NCCPV Report, 1969).[16] These observers also note that throughout history every society has provided children with fictional materials that have a heavy component of violence; fairy tales, for example, involve horrible spiders, powerful giants, and fire-breathing dragons. But the violence of fairy tales differs from the violence on television; fairy tales form a faraway fantasy world, whereas the typical television depicts human beings with whom the child can identify much more easily.

Children learn how people behave by watching them; whether the role models are seen live or on television seems to make little difference on the total aggression expressed (Bandura, Ross, & Ross, 1963). But probably more input comes to the average child via television than from live observations. Surveys indicate that children begin watching television at age 2 or 3, and, by the age of 5, are watching two to three hours a day (Siegel, 1969). By the age of 10 or 11, at least in lower-income families, the average viewing time per day is five to six hours (NCCPV Report, 1969, p. 193). By the time the child is 16 years of age, he has spent more time watching television than in the school classroom (Siegel, 1969). If the child watches during prime times in the evenings, he witnesses, on the average, a violent incident every 16 minutes and a murder every 31 minutes (Schramm, Lyle, & Parker, 1961). Aggressive episodes outweigh protective and affectionate ones by a ratio of 4 to 1. One significant aspect of these programs is the emphasis on violent means to solve problems or conflicts. If witnessing violence is, indeed, therapeutic, the child who watches television gets plenty of input to satisfy his aggressive needs.

Although evidence on the effects of television watching is accumulating very slowly, one pattern that has emerged reveals that witnessing violence leads to the assumption of more violence in ambiguous situations. In an early study (Siegel, 1958), 7-year-old children first listened to radio serials about taxi drivers. In one series the taxi drivers were usually violent; in the other series, they were not. Later, each child was asked to predict the ending of a local newspaper story about a taxi driver. (Only those children who understood that newspaper stories report reality, not make-believe, were used as subjects.) The children who had heard the radio serials about the violent taxi drivers attributed much more violence to the driver in the newspaper story than did the other children. Although demand characteristics or evaluation apprehension may be possible explanations of the differences here, another possible conclusion is that children form their impressions of violence in real life from the fictional representations they have heard or seen. Children's assumptions about the aggressive nature of man are affected by whatever is gleaned from the mass media.

Other evidence (Eron, 1963) shows that those boys who report watching a considerable amount of violence on television are also the ones who are rated by their peers as most aggressive. Additional research studies (Berkowitz & Geen, 1966, 1967) indicate that, in the case of college students, witnessing an aggression-oriented movie lowers the restraints against expressing frustration-induced tendencies. Walters, Llewellyn-Thomas, and Acker (1962) found hospital attendants responding in the same manner. Indeed, these restraints are unleashed more quickly when the aggression

[16]Schellenberg (1970) has reprinted Alfred Hitchcock's defense of his chilling programs: "One of television's great contributions is that it brought murder back into the home where it belongs. Seeing a murder on television can be good therapy. It can help work off one's antagonisms. If you haven't any antagonisms, the commercials will give you some" (from *Consumer Reports*, January 1967, p. 6).

occurs in a justified context. Further investigation is needed, however, before we can properly understand this weakening of restraints.

Particularly important in the study of television violence is the degree to which the observer can identify with the character (Bryan & Schwartz, 1971); in many cases, perpetrators of violence in television dramas are seen by children as both real (or contemporary and true to life) and ideal (they possess envied attributes). Characters and actions are seen as reflections of the real world, which the viewers, as children, will soon inherit. Such acceptance of this real-world property of television-land is more prevalent in lower-class than in middle-class children. Teenagers were asked whether they agreed or disagreed with the statements: "The programs I see on television tell about life the way it really is" and "The people I see on television programs are just like people I meet in real life." The responses showed that 40 percent of lower-class blacks, 30 percent of lower-class whites, and 15 percent of middle-class whites agreed (NCCPV Report, 1969). Another deleterious effect of frequently viewing violence is a dulling of the viewers' "emotional reactions to fictional violence . . . [and] . . . to violence in real life, . . . [thus making] them more willing actually to engage in aggressive actions when provoking circumstances arise" (NCCPV Report, 1969, p. 202).

The National Commission on the Causes and Prevention of Violence (NCCPV Report, 1969; see also Briand, 1969; Baker & Ball, 1969; and Berkowitz, 1964a) collected the testimonies of various persons whose professional work was relevant to the issue of the effects of violence on the mass media. The Commission reported that "it is reasonable to conclude that a constant diet of violent behavior on television has an adverse effect on human character and attitudes. Violence on television encourages violent forms of behavior, and fosters moral and social values about violence in daily life which are unacceptable in a civilized society" (NCCPV Report, 1969, p. 202). However, all of the evidence collected by the Commission was indirect or from laboratory studies. The first study that claims to have related television watching in real life to aggression in a controlled manner (Feshbach, 1969; Feshbach & Singer, 1970) fails to find any heightened aggressive response as a result of watching programs with aggressive content.

Feshbach and Singer selected seven different groups of children (total $N = 665$ boys) whose extent and type of television watching could be controlled. The boys were enrolled in one of three private boarding schools or were in one of four state residential schools. Thus, children from ages 10 through 17, and from both the upper and lower socioeconomic levels, were participants. Boys were paid 10 dollars each for participating in the study.

Television exposure was controlled for a six-week period. Within each school or institution, boys were randomly assigned to an aggressive-TV condition or a control condition. Programs that depicted fighting, shooting, and other forms of physical violence (such as *The FBI*, *Gunsmoke*, and *The Untouchables*) were on the aggressive-TV list. Nonaggressive programs (*Bachelor Father, Ed Sullivan*) were on the list for the control group. All the boys were required to watch a minimum of six hours of television per week between 5 P.M. and 9 P.M. daily. They could watch more, as long as what they watched was on the designated list.

Both before and after the six-week viewing period, all the boys completed questionnaires measuring overt and covert hostility, aggression-anxiety, impulsiveness, and aggressive values. The Thematic Apperception Test, a projective measure of aggression, was administered to each boy, and peer ratings of aggression were collected. The boys rated each television program they watched. Each boy's immediate supervisor recorded daily the boy's number and type of aggressive incidents.

Results were somewhat consistent in indicating that less aggression was expressed by boys who watched aggressive content on television. These boys, for example, engaged in only half as many fist fights as did control group members. "The frequency of both verbal aggression and physical aggression, whether directed toward peers or authority figures, was reliably higher in the control group exposed to the nonaggressive programs as compared to the experimental group who had been placed on the aggressive 'diet'" (Feshbach, 1969, p. 4). The differences were statistically significant in the state residential schools but not in the private schools. However, differences were consistent for boys of elementary school, junior high school, and senior high school age. Only in the expression of aggressive fantasy on the Thematic Apperception Test did the aggressive-TV group score higher than the controls.

The study by Feshbach and Singer suggests that watching aggression on television may channel hostile feelings in highly aggressive boys. Certainly, the results contradict those of laboratory studies, but the two types of studies are so different that any explanation of the cause of the varying results is speculative at present. Apparently, the nature of the viewer, the nature of the stimulus, and the nature of the situation interact in such ways that exposure to mass media may either facilitate or inhibit the expression of aggression. A great deal more research must be done before conclusions can be safely drawn. For example, does violence on news programs have the same effect as violence in television dramas? Feshbach (1969) hypothesizes that "violence presented in the form of fiction is much less likely to reinforce, stimulate, or elicit aggressive responses than violence in the form of a news event" (p. 5). Most children can discriminate between fantasy and reality. Yet, even fictional shows differ in the extent of fantasy and reality. Watching the real-life, believable violence depicted in *Lassie*, for example, may be more detrimental to children than watching *Batman*, which many children recognize as a put-on. Likewise, the aesthetic nature of the dramatic event may contribute to its impact in ways that psychologists are so far unable to measure.

VII. COLLECTIVE VIOLENCE IN SOCIETY—YESTERDAY, TODAY, AND TOMORROW

The remaining sections of this chapter deal with extreme cases of violent behavior. An attempt will be made to construct a long-range historical view of the incidence of collective violence, from the past to the present. Projections about the future are also proposed.

A. Violence in the Past

Collective violence—or violence between nations or between identifiable groups within a nation—has always been a part of Western civilization. America, in particular, has always been a relatively violent nation (R. M. Brown, 1969; NCCPV Report, 1969, p. 1). Tilly, in surveying the field, concludes that "historically, collective violence has flowed regularly out of the central political processes of Western countries. Men seeking to seize, hold, or realign the levers of power have continually engaged in collective violence as part of their struggles. The oppressed have struck in the name of justice, the privileged in the name of order, those in between in the name of fear" (1969, pp. 4–5). Our freedom as a nation resulted from a series of violent acts.

An analysis (Levy, 1969) of comparative levels of political violence in the United States has indicated no general chronological trend in the direction of either greater or less violence. The most violent incidents occurred in the decade between 1879 and 1888, but the subsequent decade from 1889 to 1899 had a moderate rate of such incidents. The 1940s and 1950s had low rates, but the 1960s had one of the highest rates of violent incidents.

Certain conditions can precipitate an increased incidence of violence (see Figure 6-3). Revolutions that are massive and powerful enough to overthrow the established

Figure 6-3. *Ghetto Riots—What Are the Causes?*

During the 1960s, riots in black ghettos struck from one end of America to another—from Los Angeles, to Detroit, to Newark, and even Miami and Orangeburg, South Carolina. In the introduction to a special issue of the *Journal of Social Issues*, Allen (1970b) lists several suggested causes and evaluates each on the basis of what we now know about the riots and the rioters.

1. "The riots were senseless outbursts of violence." But the behavioral scientist would reply that every social event has a cause. For example, in the past riots have been used as the way to achieve goals when more legitimate means had failed (Rudé, 1964).
2. "The riots were a part of a large-scale organized conspiracy to overthrow our country." Again, the evidence refutes this explanation. Most of the riots were spontaneous in origin; many started with a confrontation between a black person and a policeman (Marx, 1970) and spread from there. The investigations and research of the Kerner Commission (1968) concluded that no conspiracy was present, that the riots were not Communist inspired.
3. "The riots are a reflection of the world-wide revolutionary movement to overthrow the capitalistic system." This claim has similarities to the preceding one and appears equally without substantiation. Allen notes that much of the rioters' behavior signified a desire to share more fully in the benefits of the system, rather than to overthrow it (1970b, p. 3).
4. "The people who participated in the riots were the 'riffraff' of ghetto life"—the deviants, the criminals, the unassimilated migrants (Caplan, 1970). Numerous interview studies and comparisons of rioters and nonrioters deny this; if anything, the opposite is the case (Tomlinson, 1968; McCord & Howard, 1968; Caplan, 1970). In McCord and Howard's samples of blacks in Houston and Oakland, college-educated respondents were least opposed to the use of violence. The poorest of the poor participated less often in the riots (Murphy & Watson, 1970; Caplan & Paige, 1968). The militants in Watts, according to Tomlinson, were "the cream of urban Negro youth in particular and urban Negro citizens in general" (p. 28).
5. "The riots were a protest against conditions of ghetto life." This explanation is the one that is most strongly supported by available evidence. Although it does not imply that the rioters did so consciously to obtain specifiable goals, "it is clear that black ghetto residents have called attention to their plight . . . by violently striking out against the symbols of their discontent" (Allen, 1970b, p. 4). The selectivity of stores to be vandalized is only one example of the ways that the protest was shown.

All riots, and the actions of every individual rioter, stem from a variety of forces. Apparently, frustration and protest against the denial of opportunities are frequent causes.

---

government often occur when similar sets of conditions are present. One might predict that a prolonged, severe hardship is all that is necessary to trigger the collective violence of a revolution.[17] Davies (1962, 1969), however, concludes that the precipitating factor is a sudden sharp decline in the status of the underprivileged, coming immediately after a steady increase in their status. The earlier increase in their socioeconomic or political satisfactions leads the people to expect the continuation of such improvements (the curve of rising expectations). As we have seen before, *predictability* is important in making our assumptions about human nature. When such expectations are substantially frustrated for many people by an abrupt shift in the opposite direction, a discrepancy termed a *revolutionary gap* results (Tanter & Midlarsky, 1967), and collective violence is more likely to occur. Persons perceive a state of **relative deprivation,** compared to their earlier conditions, or compared to the conditions of others who serve as a reference group. General support for this analysis is found in a variety of cases; including the economic and political conditions of French workers and peasants before the French Revolution of 1789, the changing status of Southerners (as compared with Northerners) before the Civil War, and the conditions of black Americans during and after World War II (Davies, 1962; Geschwender, 1964). The same type of effects occurred in the Russian Revolution (Davies, 1969); after the freedom of the serfs in the late 1800s, the Russian people were called upon to make great physical and material sacrifices during World War I. The refusal of the Tsarist government to terminate a disastrous war, along with other factors reviewed in Chapter 1, led to the first Russian Revolution and then to the overthrow of the Kerensky regime.

The hypothesis of relative deprivation as a trigger for collective violence may be verified if large numbers of black Americans conclude that conditions in the 1970s are a sudden reversal from the conditions of the 1960s, which saw a steady improvement in job opportunities, income levels, accessibility to desegregated public accommodations, and other satisfactions. If we are wise, we will pay attention to increased rates of violence, for as the NCCPV Report (1969, p. 2) reminds us, the rate of violence is a social bellwether; "dramatic rises in its level and modifications in its form tell us something important is happening in our political and social systems."

B. Changes in Violence Rates: The Problem of Assessing Crime Statistics

According to the Federal Bureau of Investigation, crime rates in the United States are increasing yearly. For example, among persons under 19 years of age, "arrests for serious crimes increased 47 percent in 1965 over 1960" (*Time,* 1966c, p. 48). Many behavioral scientists, however, are unconvinced about the accuracy of crime rate comparisons across years. Part of the increase in reported rates may be due to more extensive disclosure of crimes. There may be incentives, such as increased public impatience with law enforcement, for police departments to report more (or fewer) crimes. Different police departments report crimes in different ways, and some

[17]It is interesting to ask which type of person is more likely to riot—the alienated person who feels powerless or the person believing that he has personal effectiveness and an internal locus of control? In the 1967 Detroit riots, Forward and Williams (1970) found that it was clearly the latter type who rioted and preferred to employ violence.

do not report their figures to the FBI at all. The "crime rate" report usually lumps together major crimes and less serious ones; the latter account for 85 percent of the total arrests. Most crimes have been and still are committed by persons aged 18 to 24; at present, this age group accounts for a greater percentage of the population than it did 10 years ago. Likewise, more crimes occur in urban metropolitan areas, where crime rates have increased each decade. Altogether, any conclusions about rises in crime rate must be drawn from data other than the FBI crime rates. Possibly, the homicide rate in the 1960s actually increased, but the best available evidence (Graham & Gurr, 1969) is that the crime rate in America is less than it was 50 years ago. In 1916, the city of Memphis reported a rate for homicides that was seven times the present rate. Similarly, reported rates in Boston, New York, and Chicago during the years 1915 to 1925 showed higher violent crime rates than those in the first published national crime statistics in 1933 (NCCPV Report, 1969, p. 20).

C. The Future—How Can Aggression Be Controlled?

Although some form of violence has always existed in our society, scientists still wonder whether violence in individuals, groups, and nations can be controlled in the future. Can drives to harm others be channeled into socially acceptable behaviors? Each theoretical position has its own answer.

1. The psychoanalytic view. As he grew older, Sigmund Freud became increasingly pessimistic about the possibilities of world peace. World War I had a devastating effect upon Freud. As Grossack and Gardner (1970) tell it, "he had spent his formative years in a peaceful world and was tortured by the phenomenon of millions of men confronting one another in combat, and being reduced to subhuman behavior" (1970, p. 12). The termination of World War I brought no optimism, for Freud and other astute observers noted that great conflicts and misunderstandings between the major powers continued to exist. At this point, Freud developed his theory of the **death instinct**—or a compulsion in all human beings "to return to the inorganic state out of which all living matter is formed" (Hall & Lindzey, 1968, p. 263). Aggression was thus seen as a natural derivative of the death instinct.

Psychoanalysts who adopt this position see little chance of restraining man's violent behaviors. Freud himself wrote that there is "no likelihood of our being able to suppress humanity's aggressive tendencies" (quoted in Bramson & Goethals, 1968, p. 76). However, two procedures may offer hope. One, at an international level, is a combining of forces to restrain aggressive actions by powerful nations. At an individual level, Freud, of course, saw the development of the superego as a way of restraining innate aggressive impulses. Hopefully, the child would be so reared that he came to adopt standards and values that would inhibit aggression. Identification with the parent of the same sex, through resolution of the Oedipus conflict, was seen as a step in inhibiting instinctual aggression. Additionally, neo-Freudians advocate participation in socially acceptable aggressive activities (sports, debate, and the like) as ways of releasing aggressive energy.

2. The ethologist's view. If one assumes that aggression is innate (as the ethologists do), then one must conclude that aggression will always be a part of our lives. Thus, our task is to channel aggression into socially acceptable behaviors—a proposal that Lorenz (1966) advocates. Lorenz believes that Olympic games, space races to Mars, and similar international competitions serve this function admirably, redirecting fighting behavior into relatively harmless pursuits.

3. *Will overcrowding be the downfall?* In analyzing aggression, ethologists use the concept of territoriality. Thus, in attempting to predict the rate of collective violence in the future, one must give attention to the increase in population. In 1900, the population of the United States was 76 million; in 1960, it was 180 million; in 1970, 205 million. In the year 2000, the projected population is 308 million (Bureau of Census, U. S. Department of Commerce, 1970). In 35 years, the population of the world is expected to be double what it is now. As the numbers of people associated with a delimited living area increase, does the rate of aggression and violence increase? Or, is man infinitely adaptable? Carstairs (1969) has reviewed evidence from animal behavior indicating that the biological effects of overcrowding increase disruptive behavior. If Norway rats are given ample supplies of food, water, and nesting materials but are crowded together beyond their normal circumstances—infant mortality, cannibalism, and aggression increase (Calhoun, 1962). Any extrapolation to the human condition at this point, however, is tenuous. The available evidence about the effects of human overcrowding does not come from well-controlled experiments. Nevertheless, an examination of this evidence is profitable. For example, reported crime rates are clearly much higher, per capita, in urban areas than in rural areas. The rates for violent crimes in the United States in 1968, per 100,000 persons, were as follows: for cities over 250,000 in population, 773.2 violent crimes; cities from 100,000 to 250,000 in population, 325.3 violent crimes; cities from 50,000 to 100,000 in population, 220.5 violent crimes; cities from 25,000 to 50,000 in population, 150.8 violent crimes; cities from 10,000 to 25,000 in population, 126.6 violent crimes; cities under 10,000 in population, 111.4 violent crimes; suburban areas, 145.5 violent crimes; and rural areas, 96.5 violent crimes (NCCPV Report, 1969, p. xvii).

It is not surprising—nor is it attributable solely to overcrowding—that a group of men penned closely together in a prisoner-of-war camp become exceedingly irritable and aggressive. Certain forms of mental illness, as well as suicide, are more likely in parts of the city where people are crowded together. However, it is impossible to attribute cause and effect to these relationships.

A first attempt to study the effects of crowding under the controlled conditions of a laboratory situation has been reported by Freedman and his colleagues (Freedman, 1970; Freedman, Klevansky & Ehrlich, 1971), who recognized the limits to the applications of such a procedure. For example, Freedman put people in rooms that were either not crowded at all or intensely crowded (like a rush-hour New York subway) and kept them there for four hours. All the persons in a given room were of the same sex. They were given a variety of tasks to do, from routine ones to rather interesting and complex ones. Subjects were volunteers and knew they would eventually get out of the crowded environment.

Admittedly, the study is only a beginning, but the results are provocative. In regard to *performance,* crowding has little effect on a wide variety of tasks. People who are in extremely crowded rooms do no better nor worse than uncrowded subjects on tasks ranging from rote memorization to complex problem solving. But *interpersonal* behavior is affected by crowding; women seem to like it, while men do not. "Apparently men respond negatively to crowded conditions; they become suspicious and combatant, almost as if they were showing the territoriality described in animals. Women respond positively; they seem to like the high density, become more intimate and friendly" (Freedman, 1970, p. 5).

Two-thirds of Americans already live in urban areas; overpopulation and overcrowding may defeat the opportunities for advancement sought by the masses of our world. But it may be that overcrowding per se—as long as adequate supplies of materials for human needs are maintained—may not have the negative effects assumed by some.

4. Frustration-aggression theory. According to an early interpretation of the frustration-aggression hypothesis, the presence of aggression always presupposed frustration. But revisions of the frustration-aggression formulation accentuate the complexities of the relationship. Frustration is one of the causes of aggression, and aggression is only one of the outcomes of frustration. Clearly, eliminating frustrations would be one way of reducing violence. Ransford (1968) interviewed blacks living in the Watts area of Los Angeles and found that those with more intense feelings of dissatisfaction and frustration were more prone to violent action.

There are numerous actions community leaders do or could take to reduce frustrations. New York's Mayor John Lindsay has rapped with the residents of Harlem when frustrations have intensified. In many cities, the availability of playgrounds and swimming pools for people crowded into steamy tenements in the summertime might prevent rioting. Human relations training for police may likewise reduce public frustrations and hence reduce aggression. In controlling aggression, the experimental social psychologist would also attempt to limit the presence of aggression-eliciting stimuli, including toy guns for children, guns for adults, and aggressive adult models, whether they be from the mass media or real life.

5. Social-learning theory. Insofar as controlling aggression is concerned, social-learning theorists would differ from ethologists on the advisability of advocating competition.[18] The social-learning theorists believe that such activities "merely strengthen aggressive habits and decrease inhibitions against aggression" (Megargee & Hokanson, 1970, p. 34). Through response generalization, the rewarding of such mild aggressive behavior could lead to the development of more extreme, antisocial forms of aggression. Some psychologists believe this is already happening in America. For instance, rewarding young boys who participate in hard-hitting sports such as boxing and football and encouraging the expression of hostile feelings could lead to more extreme aggression in the future. As you might expect, social-learning theorists reject any notions of the cathartic value of watching violence on television (Bandura, 1965). In fact, research indicates that actual expression of aggressive acts does not drain off pent-up aggressive drives but instead encourages further expression of these drives (Bandura & Walters, 1963; Mallick & McCandless, 1966).

A second means of regulating violence would be to limit the exposure of children to real-life models who act aggressively. Particularly undesirable is the witnessing of violent acts that are rewarded. Even viewing violent acts that are done for good purposes provides the observer with new ways of expressing hostility and violence (Walters, 1965). A parent who beats his child serves as a potent role model to a child seeking ways to respond to his own frustrations.

As a third means of controlling violence, social-learning theorists would advocate *nonreinforcement* of aggressive responses (P. Brown & Elliott, 1965) along with *retraining,* which would establish new constructive ways of responding to frustration-inducing events (Davitz, 1952). In fact, Bryan and Schwartz (1971) speculate that in the near future films may be used systematically to reeducate emotionally disturbed

[18] A detailed statement of a social-learning theorist's position on regulating aggression may be found in Walters (1965) and in Walters and Parke (1964).

persons away from violent reactions to the world, as is prophesied in *A Clockwork Orange*.

6. *Detrimental aggression can be rechanneled.* A century ago, a proper English lady, upon being introduced to the theory of man's evolutionary descent from the apes, responded: "Let us hope it is not true—but if it is, let us pray it will not become generally known!" If man possesses an innate component to aggress, we should seek to know about it and recognize its implications. But even if such innate tendencies exist, much harmful aggression is the result of learned reactions and frustrations. Anything that is learned can be manipulated and controlled. The important Robber's Cave experiment by Sherif (1961) demonstrates how two groups can be manipulated so that hostilities between the two groups are first escalated and then reduced to the point that the two groups merge into one.

One of the unfortunate side effects of a belief in innate aggression is the tendency to throw one's hands up and say: "There's nothing to be done; war is inevitable, and people are just naturally violent." This chapter has indicated that environmental circumstances can inhibit or encourage the expression of detrimental types of hostility and violence. These circumstances should not be overlooked as we seek a more peaceful human existence.

VIII. SUMMARY

To Freud and orthodox psychoanalysts, aggression is an urge generated by the body that must eventually find release. Social-learning theorists and experimental social psychologists define aggression as behavior whose goal is to inflict harm or injury upon some object or person. The ethologist believes intraspecies aggression has survival value, for it facilitates selective mating and spreading out of the species.

Several viewpoints agree that aggressive behavior is more likely to occur if two types of factors—internal factors and triggering stimuli (or releasers) from the environment—are both present.

In many species of animals and birds, a need to defend one's living space, or territoriality, is a dominant force. However, the presence of such an instinctual territorial need in man is difficult to document.

To some extent, aggressiveness can be produced in lower animals through a procedure of selective breeding over several generations. Thus, in lower animals, the extent of aggressiveness may partially derive from hereditary factors.

The frustration-aggression hypothesis, in its original form, proposed that the occurrence of aggression is a result of frustration and that any frustrating event inevitably leads to aggression. The hypothesis was later altered by its authors, who clarified the notion that frustration could lead to other outcomes instead of aggression. Berkowitz has further amended the hypothesis, emphasizing that frustration produces a readiness for aggressive acts.

To argue whether any link between frustration and aggression is either innate or learned is fruitless. While frustration may, in an innate way, heighten the likelihood of an aggressive act, learning may inhibit or alter this aggressive response.

Laboratory studies indicate that (a) witnessing an aggressive event lowers restraints against the witness's expression of aggression, after he has been frustrated, and (b) if aggression-cuing stimuli (such as guns) are present but not used, the subject will act more aggressively than if such stimuli were absent.

There are societies of people who live together peacefully. These are primitive tribes whose needs are usually met without frustration. They respond passively to aggression from other groups or retreat further into inaccessible living areas. Although their survival value is low, these societies reflect the malleability of human nature.

If a child is exposed to an aggressive adult model and then frustrated, the child is more likely to act aggressively than had the adult model acted in a nonaggressive manner. Apparently, inhibitions against aggression in the child are reduced by viewing an aggressive adult model.

The effect of watching violence on television is unclear. Laboratory studies indicate that witnessing violence facilitates expression of aggression by children. But a field study found that watching television programs that were considered highly aggressive reduced the amount of aggression expressed by the viewers (boys, ages 10 to 17).

Collective violence—or violence between nations or between identifiable groups within a nation—has always been a part of Western civilization. Particularly in America, violent means of solving problems have been characteristic.

One explanation for the origin of revolutions and other collective violence uses the concept of relative deprivation. When a group suffers an abrupt shift away from past increases in socioeconomic and political satisfaction, they are more likely to revolt or express collective violence.

Every theory of aggression makes its own recommendations about the control or rechanneling of violence and aggression. Often these recommendations are in conflict with each other.

IX. SUGGESTED READINGS

Allen, V. L. (Issue Ed.) Ghetto riots. *Journal of Social Issues*, 1970, **26**, No. 1. This special issue of the journal is devoted to an examination of the causes of rioting in the ghetto. Authors of individual articles agree that the riots during the 1960s were protests against the unfairness of the governmental, social, and economic systems, rather than an attempt to overthrow them.

Berkowitz, L. (Ed.) *Roots of aggression: A re-examination of the frustration-aggression hypothesis*. New York: Atherton, 1969. A collection of reprinted articles dealing with the frustration-aggression hypothesis. Berkowitz's comments in the introductory article are very helpful. The book includes Davies' paper on relative deprivation as an explanation of revolutionary mass movements.

Graham, H. D., & Gurr, T. R. (Eds.) *Violence in America: Historical and comparative perspective*. New York: New American Library, 1969. (Paperback.) Generated by the National Commission on the Causes and Prevention of Violence, this book includes reviews on racial violence, frontier violence, working-class protest, crime rates, causes of rebellion, and numerous other topics. The predominant emphasis is historical. Only one article out of 22 is by a psychologist, who deals with newspaper reports of political violence. For a modest price, the book is filled with information.

Lorenz, K. *On aggression*. New York: Harcourt, Brace & World, 1966. (Paperback version also available.) The noted ethologist reports his observations on the nature of aggression in many species of animals and birds. He suggests ways that man can direct his aggressive responses into socially acceptable endeavors. The content is controversial, but the style is charming.

Megargee, E. I., & Hokanson, J. E. (Eds.) *The dynamics of aggression: Individual, group, and international analyses*. New York: Harper & Row, 1970. (Paperback.) A collection of readings by authorities such as Freud; Lorenz; Dollard, Miller, et al.; Bandura and Walters; Berkowitz; and others. Useful introductions to each section are included. The reader is given a good overview of theoretical positions regarding the study of aggression.

Montagu, M. F. A. (Ed.) *Man and aggression*. New York: Oxford University Press, 1968. A collection of articles that are diverse in clarity and intended audience and uneven in quality, but similar in their negative reaction to the thesis that human aggression is instinctive. Most of the articles are book reviews of works by Lorenz and Ardrey. The most sophisticated article—by English ethologist John H. Crook—is saved for last. Several other articles, including ones by Gorer (1968a, 1968b), are useful. (A more balanced review of ethology may be found in J. H. Carthy and F. J. Ebling (Eds.), *The natural history of aggression*. New York: Academic Press, 1964.)

Chapter Seven

Racial and Social-Class Differences in Abilities, Motivation, and Personality

The less intelligent the white man is, the more stupid he thinks the black.
Andre Gide, Travels in the Congo

In the year 1909, William Howard Taft, the newly inaugurated President of the United States, addressed the following statement to a group of black college students in Charlotte, North Carolina: "Your race is adapted to be a race of farmers, first, last, and for all times" (quoted in Logan, 1957, p. 66). In the 70 years since Taft's erroneous utterance, blacks and members of other minority groups have shown that they possess the ability to succeed in any endeavor requiring a high degree of motivation and intelligence. Yet the issue of racial differences in intelligence remains a controversial one, both academically and practically. Do black Americans differ from Caucasian Americans in intelligence? If intelligence is influenced by heredity, does evidence exist for innate differences between races? Can evidence that suggests racial differences in intelligence be accounted for by differences in social class? Would characteristics of race or social class facilitate placing children with differing degrees of mental ability in separate classes? The answers to these questions will be pursued in this and the following chapter.

First, some conclusions will be drawn about the extent of racial and social-class differences in ability and personality. We will seek to understand the causes of whatever differences may exist, and, in doing so, we will dissect the concepts of **race** and **social class.** Research findings and their probable causes will then be examined, always in the light of what is known about the biases of the researcher or his sponsoring organization.

I. THE CONCEPT OF RACE

Distinctions between races have been made since the beginning of recorded history (Gossett, 1963). Almost always one's own race was seen as superior to all foreign "races." Aristotle, for example, believed that the beneficial Grecian climate enabled the Greeks to develop both physical and psychological characteristics superior to those of their neighbors. In such comparisons, the term *race* seemingly stands for "any group that is different in any way." Yet we should question what truly constitutes racial differences. Are Aristotle's Greeks and, for example, Northern Europeans different races?

There are no simple answers to these questions, partly because the meanings of the term *race* have proliferated to such a degree. In an attempt to simplify, we will separate the multitudinous definitions of *race* into two types. One type we will call the *technical* definition; it reflects the opinion of scientists and professional persons concerned with the topic of race. The other type of definition we will call the *popular* definition; it refers to the word as used by the man on the street. The development of precise *technical* definitions of *race* has had a long and successful history; however, studies of racial differences in intelligence have generally used the *popular* definition of *race*. In the future, there will be increased dissatisfaction over classifying a person's race simply by asking him or scrutinizing him, and we will see a greater reliance on technical definitions.

A. The Technical Definitions of Race

What, then, do scientists mean by the term *race*? In essence, a race may be thought of as a population that is geographically contiguous and whose members breed together. Classifications of race some 200 years ago were usually based on differences of skin color. In 1735, Carl von Linnaeus describ all men as of one species and then divided mankind into four varieties, attributing different mental characteristics to each. Not surprisingly, Linnaeus considered Europeans to be "light, lively, inventive; ruled by rites," whereas Africans were "cunning, slow, negligent; ruled by caprice" (Dunn & Dobzhansky, 1952, p. 109). Although scientists have discarded the notion that skin color is an adequate means of differentiating races, Linnaeus' belief that there is only one human species has finally come into general acceptance.[1]

About 100 years ago, scientists seeking definitions of *race* rejected the sole determinant of skin color and utilized a number of observable physical characteristics —head shape, various facial features, body physique, hair color, hair texture—as well as the matter of skin color. Such a classification system advanced our understanding by avoiding nonbiological attributes (particularly the common cultural background) in defining race. Groups differing in culture, customs, and languages—but not necessarily in physical characteristics—are now called **ethnic groups**; they are not considered different races.

[1]For about 150 years after Linnaeus, controversy persisted regarding whether each race was a different species with a separate origin. A contemporary anthropologist, Carlton Coon, proposed as recently as 1962 that mankind became divided into races before the transition to fully human types was achieved.

The above approach, using a combination of surface physical characteristics, may be called the *physical* definition of race. Although it is a scientifically acceptable definition, it suffers the handicap of being based upon **phenotypes** (surface characteristics) rather than **genotypes** (underlying characteristics).[2] As a result, the most recent definition of *race* uses underlying characteristics as its building blocks. This *genetic* approach makes the following assumptions (summarized from Dunn & Dobzhansky, 1952). First, groups of people differ not only in the observable characteristics of physical appearance, but also in characteristics such as blood type and susceptibility to certain diseases. Examples of the latter include sickle-cell anemia and Tay-Sachs disease (Ginsburg & Laughlin, 1968). Second, each of these characteristics is determined by genes—usually many genes having a role in the determination of each characteristic. Third, groups of people differ in their genetic makeup, and certain groups of people can be distinguished on the basis of their gene frequencies. According to this genetic approach, then, races are defined as "populations which differ in the frequencies of some gene or genes" (Dunn & Dobzhansky, 1952, p. 118).

Genetic analysis has been most thoroughly applied in the case of blood types, as may be seen in Figure 7-1. Further efforts at genetic analysis may be expected in the future. Yet even though this genetic approach to the classification of races is refreshing in its promise of objectivity and precision, its complexity is frustrating. It delineates and identifies a large number of races. Moreover, races, defined genetically, differ only in a relative way (Glass, 1968). We can say very little about an individual's racial composition simply from knowing that he has Type O blood. At the same time, the significant proportional differences in genetic compositions in different populations indicate that the concept of race is a viable one—albeit exceedingly difficult to pin down.

The discovery of genetic determinants of race has implications for adaptation and change; it is now believed that races are products of natural selection and that those individuals who best adapt to their environment are the ones who survive and procreate within each race. Hence, each race changes over time, and those genes that are responsible for the adaptive traits are likely to be passed on and to increase in frequency within that particular environment (C. G. Barber, 1965). Such reasoning

Figure 7-1. *The Genetic Analysis of Races through Blood Types*

The blood of every human being in the world is one of four types—A, B, AB, or O—but the proportions of each type differ markedly in different populations. Type O is one of the most common types among Caucasians in Western Europe and the United States; for example, in a group of 422 Londoners, 47.9 percent had Type O; 42.4 percent had Type A; 8.3 percent, Type B; and 1.4 percent, Type AB. The percentage of the population having Type O drops steadily as one moves from west to east across Europe and Asia; in a group of 1000 Chinese in Peking, only 30.7 percent were Type O. The most frequent type among these Chinese is Type B (34.2 percent); yet Type B is completely absent in most American Indian tribes and also in Australian aborigines. There are also large differences in proportions within specific European groups and within African populations.

[2] As Boyd (1950) points out, a classification based upon phenotypes is not completely satisfactory in that several different genotypes (combination of genes) can produce the same phenotype. Two groups with the same phenotype appear to be the same, despite their different origins. In other words, two persons with the same skin color can have different combinations of the same or different genes.

has significance for notions about racial differences in intelligence. If races do change in the direction of traits that are adaptive in a particular environment—and if each race operates in a different environment—then the development of each race may accentuate different traits. The traits necessary for adaptation in a warm, moist climate with verdant land may be different from the traits that are necessary in a cold climate and rocky terrain. Such differences would lead to different kinds of adaptation and possibly to different degrees of intelligence. This kind of argument may apply to pure races, which are only found in isolated areas of the earth. But even in these cases, the argument fails to recognize that each race defines *intelligence* in different ways (a point to be discussed subsequently).

In the future, there will probably be increased efforts to measure genetic differences among populations. All workers in the field do not unconditionally accept the definition of *race* as a "population which differs significantly from other human populations in regard to the frequency of one or more genes it possesses" (Boyd, 1950). Geneticists and physical anthropologists utilize this definition more than social anthropologists or sociologists. The latter usually prefer a classification based upon a compendium of physical characteristics. In summary, both the geneticist's and the sociologist's definitions are acceptable technical definitions of race. And despite Montagu's (1957, 1964) desire to remove the term from the English language, *race* as a construct does have value in accounting for "local genetic differences between population groups which are only partially isolated from each other and continue to exchange genes but also to maintain some obvious differences" (Ginsburg & Laughlin, 1968, p. 27). We agree with those anthropologists (see Washburn, 1964; or Kilham & Klopfer, 1968) who favor continued use of the term as long as it has biological meaning. By any means adherents of both of the acceptable technical definitions of race would agree that the popular definition of race—which will be considered next—is oversimplified and misleading.

B. The Popular Definition

As used by the layman, the term *race* is vastly different from the acceptable technical definitions. In the United States, a person's race is often self-determined, although influenced by family tradition, custom, and the law. Most often, it is delimited by one's skin color. In certain states one's race is legalistically determined by the race of one's ancestors. For example, if one or more of a person's great-grandparents were "Negro," the state classified that person as also being Negro.[3] In addition, the popular definition of race includes only six classifications: white (or Caucasian), black, American Indian, Oriental, Asian Indian, and brown (or Melanesian). These roughly correspond to the geographic groupings now considered out of date.

A vital aspect of the popular definition is its all-or-none character. Accordingly, a person is clearly a black, or a white, or an Oriental. With a few exceptions (Mulattoes,

[3] Plessy, the Negro whose court action led to the *Plessy vs. Ferguson* (1896) decision by the Supreme Court, protested having to sit in a separate railroad car because of his race. Seven of his eight great-grandparents were white. The original Supreme Court decision was overturned by the 1954 desegregation decision (Logan, 1957).

Creoles), the hybridization of races is denied, at least in the United States. Yet it is estimated that between 20 and 30 percent of the total genetic background of persons classified as black Americans is Caucasian in origin[4] (Roberts, 1955; Glass & Li, 1953; Reed, 1969) and that no less than 70 percent of all U. S. residents classified as blacks have some genetic background of Caucasian origin. This would further imply that a few American blacks have an almost pure Caucasian ancestry and that most have some Caucasian ancestry.

For the same reason (intermarriage or interbreeding) some American whites (as defined by skin color) possess some black ancestry. The precise extent is difficult to pinpoint; Stuckert (1964) estimates that approximately 20 percent of American whites have some genetic background of black origin.

So although many Americans are of a racially mixed background, the popular definition denies this fact by categorizing people into literally black-or-white categories. The popular definition has great difficulty with persons whose skin color and other characteristics are not clearly those of one race. The fact that some Americans are difficult to categorize according to the popular classifications of race is evidenced by estimates that from 2,500 to 25,000 persons have passed from the black subculture into the white subculture each year (Hart, 1921; Day, 1932; McKinney, 1937; Burma, 1946; Davie, 1949).

C. Implications for the Study of Racial Differences

So far we have presented two contemporary technical definitions of race and one popular one. Data on racial differences in intelligence force us to use the popular definition since it is the one that the researchers have used. Only the rarest study seeks out genealogical data in order to classify subjects. Therefore, it should be understood that the differences we will be discussing are not differences between races in either of the technical senses. Rather, we will be looking at differences between two (or more) groups—neither of which is pure in genetic structure or physical appearance. As Fried (1968) eloquently indicates, this converts the issue into a pseudo problem.

Despite these limitations, some social scientists conclude that blacks are innately inferior mentally to Caucasians. (In fact, this was the dominant view of social scientists 75 years ago.) Some advocates of inherent differences in mental or physical ability are motivated by a commitment to racial segregation, but there are also behavioral scientists who, while free of any desire for the separation of races, believe the evidence indicates an innate difference between races does exist. The publications of the International Association for the Advancement of Ethnology and Eugenics are examples of this viewpoint. In recent years, the public press has given much attention to the views of Arthur Jensen, a psychologist who believes that heredity accounts for about 80 percent of the IQ differences among individuals and that innate differences may exist between blacks and Caucasians.

In contrast, there are behavioral scientists who believe, on the basis of their read-

[4]The most recent of these estimates (Reed, 1969) uses not only ABO blood type frequencies but also the presence of the Fy^a gene of Duffy blood system. This gene is practically nonexistent in contemporary African populations. On the basis of its frequency, Reed estimates about 22 percent of the genes of American blacks are of Caucasian origin.

ing of the evidence, that any differences in ability between races can be explained by factors other than hereditary differences. The famed Moynihan Report (U. S. Department of Labor, 1965) states: "There is absolutely no question of any genetic differential [between Negroes and whites]. Intelligence potential is distributed among Negro infants in the same proportion and pattern as among Icelanders or Chinese or any other group." Likewise, the 1964 UNESCO (printed in UNESCO, 1965) statement on the "Biological Aspects of Race" reported: "The peoples of the world today appear to possess equal biological potentialities for attaining any civilizational level." The reader should avoid forming a conclusion about the possibility of innate differences until reading the subsequent section, in which data supporting conflicting viewpoints are presented and evaluated. First, IQ differences between blacks and Caucasians will be examined, since this is the most frequently studied comparison.

II. RACIAL DIFFERENCES IN INTELLIGENCE TEST SCORES

Reviews of the numerous studies comparing the performances of blacks and whites on intelligence tests draw similar conclusions about the extent of differences.[5] Black groups average 10 to 20 points below white groups in measured IQ. Only rarely has a study found the average black IQ score to be as high as 100. However, in all studies, the IQ scores of some blacks are above the population average of 100. This statistic (the *percent of overlap*) ranged from 1 to 50 percent—in other words, 1 to 50 percent of black subjects scored above the average score of white subjects.

Also consistent is the finding that differences in measured IQ between groups of younger persons are very much less than differences between groups of older persons. The apparent deterioration of black IQ's with increasing age is characteristic of all culturally disadvantaged groups, regardless of their race. The reviews indicate that differences between blacks and whites appear regardless of the type of test used—group versus individual, verbal versus performance, or traditional versus culture-free test. A common supposition that the performance of blacks is closer to that of whites on nonverbal tests is not upheld. In many comparisons, the opposite obtains; differences between blacks and whites on perceptual tests are often greater than are the differences on verbal tests.

The most extensive testing of mental ability took place during the two World Wars, when more than 20 million American men were evaluated to determine their readiness for military training. Test-score differences between racial groups were found. Using the Army Alpha Test of mental ability with World War I recruits, Yerkes (1921) found that only about 9 percent of the black men scored above the average for white men. However, for black men living in the North, the percentage of

[5]The reviews by Tyler (1965) and by Dreger and Miller (1960 and 1968) are perhaps the best combinations of objectivity and timeliness. Pettigrew's review (1964, Chap. 5) is thorough and concludes that environmental deprivation can account for racial differences. Earlier works include the comprehensive review by Shuey (1958, revised in 1966), which includes more than 200 references, but Shuey has been criticized for her polemic attitude and lack of objectivity (Dreger & Miller, 1960; Pettigrew, 1964). Another frequent reviewer of the issue is Garrett (1960, 1962, 1964, 1965, 1969), but some of his activities, such as going on a speaking tour sponsored by the White Citizens Council, cause us to question his objectivity.

scores exceeding the average white score was higher—29 percent. This indicates a regional difference for blacks; the same was true for whites. Using a selection of states, Klineberg (1944) showed that the average Army Alpha performance of black recruits from four Northern states was better than the average performance of white recruits from four Southern states. The median Army Alpha scores (not to be confused with IQ scores) for blacks were: Pennsylvania, 42.0; New York, 45.0; Illinois, 47.3; and Ohio, 49.5. The median scores for whites from the four Southern states were: Mississippi, 41.2; Kentucky, 41.5; Arkansas, 41.6; and Georgia, 42.1. Thus Klineberg, by selecting the four states where blacks did best and the four states where whites did poorest, demonstrated that environment plays a role in the determination of performance. At the same time, in each of the states listed, whites from that particular state did better than blacks from that state. In fact, Garrett (1945) found, after studying these data, that blacks scored about as far below whites in the four Northern states as they did in the country as a whole. Thus, as Alper and Boring (1944) conclude, there are two consistent findings in the Army Alpha data—regional differences and racial differences.

The advantage of Northern blacks over Southern whites, found in World War I, did not hold in World War II. Blacks from the New England states performed better than blacks in any other geographical area. But the percent of New England blacks receiving above average AGCT scores (Grades I and II) was 8.9 percent, while 20.8 percent of the whites from the Southwest (their weakest area) placed in Grades I and II (Davenport, 1946).

Performances of the two groups in tests administered during World War II again indicated racial differences in the scores. A comparison of white and black enlisted men found that 6.3 percent of the whites and 1 percent of the blacks were in Class I (very superior), while 26.9 percent of the whites and 77.7 percent of the blacks were in the two bottom groups (inferior and very inferior). These figures were drawn from a 2 percent sample of enlisted men in March, 1945—a sample that did not include officers or men declared physically or mentally unfit for service. The inclusion of such men would have probably increased the average difference between the races. Indeed, Ingle (1968) reports Office of Education data indicating that, in regard to preinduction mental tests given to military draftees during 1964–1965, the percentage of blacks failing the test was 67.5 percent, compared with 18.8 percent for nonblacks.

It is pointless to document further the consistent finding of differences in measured IQ's of blacks and whites. The test-score differences are agreed upon both by those who believe there are innate racial differences (the hereditarians) and by those who believe the best explanation rests upon environmental handicaps (environmentalists). The controversy centers on the causes—and hence the importance—of these test-score differences.

III. INTERPRETATIONS OF THE FINDINGS

As indicated, hereditarians and environmentalists have widely disparate explanations for the findings on racial differences. In addition to possible causes such as heredity and environment, other factors—such as the characteristics of the testing situation, the motivation of the test-taker, and the appropriateness of the test—must be considered when explaining racial differences. Lesser, Fifer, and Clark (1965) have provided a listing of possible influences, which is abstracted in Table 7-1. These proximal causes emphasize a distinction that should always be kept in mind—the distinction between IQ scores and intelligence as an underlying concept. All the studies use IQ scores and infer from these scores conclusions about levels of intelligence. But the proximal causes—such as degree of rapport between tester and subject—may influence measured IQ scores and not the underlying concept of intelligence.

Let us consider these possible influences in some detail. We shall then present an answer to the basic question: are differences in measured IQ's between blacks and whites hereditary?

A. Heredity as an Explanation

As an explanation of racial differences, heredity has had a long history. Around the year 1900, the dominant viewpoint of social scientists was that the development of mental ability in blacks stopped at an earlier age than that of whites. Since that time, however, there has been an increasing reluctance on the part of behavioral scientists to posit innate differences as a sole, or even major, explanation of racial differences. For example, the highly publicized view of Arthur Jensen (1969b, 1969c, 1969d) emphasizes that genetic factors may play a role but also recognizes the presence of environmental factors.

Table 7-1. *Possible Influences upon Test Performance*

I. Variables of background and environment
   A. Cultural background (racial or ethnic group)
   B. Family characteristics
   C. Formal school training
   D. Experience with similar tests
   E. General health and special handicaps (for example, impaired sight, hearing, or coordination, emotional disturbance, and the like)
   F. Age

II. Personality and motivational variables
   A. Persuasibility or responsiveness to examiner
   B. Interest in test problems
   C. Effort and persistence
   D. Anxiety level
   E. Achievement motivation

III. Characteristics of the testing situation
   A. Perceived importance of the test
   B. Expectations of success or failure
   C. Temporary physical conditions (fatigue, transient respiratory or digestive ailments, or other temporary indispositions)
   D. Interference from the testing environment
   E. Influence of the tester

IV. Test demands
   A. Specific abilities required
   B. Speed of response required

(Adapted from Lesser, Fifer, and Clark, "Mental Abilities of Children from Different Social-Class and Cultural Groups." In *Monographs of the Society for Research in Child Development.* Copyright 1965 by The Society for Research in Child Development. Reprinted by permission of the publisher, The University of Chicago Press.)

The following list presents the basic arguments for a belief in hereditary racial differences in intelligence. Each argument will be evaluated subsequently.

1. The failure (as claimed by some) of the black race to produce a civilization as developed as those of other races indicates an inherent difference in mental abilities.

2. The black fails to perform as well as the white in situations where the black person's past environment is supposedly no different from the white's.

3. There was a lack of improvement in the test scores of black recruits, relative to whites, during the time period between World War I and World War II. This argument is based upon an assumption that the black's environment and educational opportunities increased more during this period than did those of whites. Anastasi, for example, states: "Insofar as socioeconomic conditions have improved for Negroes over the past two or three decades [1925–1950], it might be expected that their test performance would also rise" (Anastasi & D'Angelo, 1952, p. 157).

4. A relationship exists between skin pigmentation among blacks (as an indication of racial purity) and levels of intelligence. Hereditarians have claimed that darker skinned blacks have lower IQ's. Tanser (1939) found skin color differences correlated to the performance of blacks—with those of darker skin pigmentation having lower scores. Ferguson (1919) separated World War I recruits at Camp Lee, Virginia, into darker skinned and lighter skinned groups. The median Army Alpha score for the lighter skinned group was 51; for the darker, it was 40. Almost all the men were from the same state, Virginia. Peterson and Lanier (1929) reported similar differences in Southern black children but not in Northern black children. Klineberg (1935) found no relationship in his New York sample. Using American Indian subjects, Garth, Schuelke, and Abell (1927) concluded that the more impure the Indian's racial background, the higher his IQ.

5. There is a demonstrable difference in developmental rates between black and white infants. Geber and Dean (1957a, 1957b) tested the developmental rates of 107 black infants born in a hospital in Uganda, East Africa, in 1956. During the first week of life almost all the children were found to be more advanced than European children of the same age. When drawn to a sitting position, 90 of the 107 babies would prevent their heads from falling back, whereas head control usually does not occur in European children until the eighth to twelfth week. A baby 48 hours old was shown lying on his stomach and raising his chin from the table. This precocity was generally lost by the third year, and after that time the developmental rate of the African children remained lower than that of most European children (Geber, 1956).

Ainsworth (1967), in an intensive study of 28 Ganda infants in Uganda, has reported similar deterioration in Gesell Development Quotients (called DQ's) over time. A typical case was an infant named Muhamidi, who, when first tested at the age of nine months, had a Developmental Quotient of 130. When retested at the age of 22 months, Muhamidi's DQ was 109. When the child was retested again at the age of 34 months, the examiner found Muhamidi "sad and dull" (Ainsworth, 1967, pp. 150–151), and his DQ had dropped to 96.

B. Evaluating the Hereditarian Arguments

Of the five hereditarian arguments listed above, the first cannot be evaluated objectively because the relative success of civilizations involves a value judgment. Our society values verbal skills and technological development—perhaps at the sacrifice of authentic human relationships. But does this mean that our civilization is more advanced than one with no written language but with highly developed art forms and/or family relationships? Surely, we cannot make such an assumption.

The second argument assumes that the past environments of black and white test-takers can be equated. This is an indirect test of the influence of heredity, which states that if the IQ's of blacks are lower than those of whites even when their environments are the same, then heredity accounts for the difference. Four studies are usually cited as particular tests of this equated-environment assumption. Let us look at the adequacy of one, as an example.

Bruce (1940) tested black and white children in a backward area in rural Virginia and attempted to equate the socioeconomic status of the children by using the Sims Score Card, a method of evaluating family economic level. Forty-nine black and 49 white children were paired, and differences in mean IQ were found. Three tests were used. The Kuhlmann-Anderson test produced means of 83 for whites and 73 for blacks; the Arthur test had a mean of 89 for whites and 77 for blacks; and the Stanford-Binet test produced means of 86 for whites and 77 for blacks.

There are problems, however, with Bruce's study. First, the author admits that the Sims Score Card does not discriminate adequately at the lower socioeconomic level, where these children belonged. Even if the two groups had been completely equated on the score card, they still may have differed in socioeconomic status because of the poor quality of the measuring instrument. Second, though Bruce was "inclined to believe that there is an innate difference between the particular white and Negro groups studied" (p. 97), she pointed out that the two groups were not completely equal in the Sims score—the black families being lower. Third, the white and black children were from different schools; the schools in Virginia were racially segregated at that time, and there is no evidence that the quality of instruction and facilities and the availability of materials were the same. Our best guess is that the white school was better equipped. Fourth, even if the objective indices (Sims Score Card, school facilities, and the like) had been equal, we should question whether there was true equality between the races in rural Virginia at that time. The sheer fact of being black was a stigma and a restriction and, hence, an environmental handicap. Bruce's study fails to qualify as a test of equated environments for these reasons.

Other attempts to equate environments (Tanser, 1939; McGurk, 1951, 1953; McQueen & Browning, 1960) have similar limitations. In some of these studies, the job of matching is acceptable as far as it goes, but the restrictions against one race and their effects are not taken into consideration. Klineberg's (1963) review reminds us that equating educational and social-class variables is not enough for a fair test in a society where the black has been prevented from living where he wants, from participating in certain activities, and from entering certain places. We believe there have been no adequate studies to determine whether racial differences in intelligence remain when no environmental handicaps exist. Moreover, there probably will not be any adequate studies for a long time.

The third hereditarian argument found no diminution in the differences between black and white IQ scores from the time of testings in World War I to testings in World War II. This gap persisted, despite a presumed improvement in the black's environment in the intervening quarter of a century. But, even though the black's environment may have improved substantially during that period, the degree of improvement may not have been any greater than that experienced by white Americans. For example, income differentials between whites and blacks have remained relatively stable over a period of years, with the average black income staying at about 55 percent of the average white income (U.S. Department of Labor, 1965). Such relationships weaken the thrust of this type of hereditarian argument.

The fourth hereditarian argument, or the relationship of skin color to intelligence, could be a function of either environment or heredity. During the first half of this century, lighter skinned blacks probably enjoyed greater access to cultural opportunities and less rejection than darker skinned blacks. In the years prior to the "Black is beautiful" movement, skin color was related to self-esteem within black groups; being light skinned was desirable. Tyler (1965), certainly one of the most objective reviewers, believes it is best not to draw any conclusion about the possible hereditary causes of these skin-shading differences. One reason is that the classifications of light skinned versus dark skinned (which usually have been done subjectively) are not perfectly reliable indicators of the percentage of white ancestry. It is not known whether differences in skin color are still correlated to differences in intelligence, but if so, this phenomenon could be interpreted as a function of heredity or environment or both.

Looking critically at the fifth argument of the hereditarians, we conclude that different developmental rates in African infants may or may not have implications for differences in intelligence. Apparently—on the basis of Geber's testings and Ainsworth's observations of children in East Africa—newborn babies in these environments are more advanced in sensory-motor development than are newborn European or American children. Every one of the babies under six months of age had Gesell Developmental Quotients of 100 or better, and 95 percent of the infants tested between the ages of 6 and 9 months were above the European average. (Geber used a Gesell test standardized on French children.) These differences occurred on Language Development items as well as in other parts of the test. For African children of 2 years of age, the superiority to European norms was less marked, and the 3-year-old African children characteristically had DQ's below the European norm.

These findings could imply either hereditary or environmental causes. Some believers in innate differences point out that across species a more rapid early developmental rate (or, in other words, a less prolonged infancy) is associated with a lower ceiling on development. For example, at birth gorillas are more developed than are chimpanzees, and chimpanzees are more developed than human beings. Man, however, reaches the highest mental abilities as an adult, followed by the chimpanzee and then the gorilla. Such a relationship occurring across species cannot be applied to subgroups within a species, however. There is no justification in concluding that the ceiling on sensory-motor level or language capacity of Ganda children is less than Europeans merely because of the African child's more rapid development in infancy. There are cases of individual black children—apparently free of mixed ancestry—whose mental development reaches levels equal to those of the most superior whites. Witty (Witty & Jenkins, 1935; Theman & Witty, 1943) has reported the case of a 9-year-old black American girl with an IQ of 200.

Ainsworth recognizes that the developmental rates of the Ganda child have a relevance to the question of innate racial differences, which is "all too painfully evident" (1967, p. 330). However, Ainsworth, as well as Geber, believes that child-care practices, rather than innate differences, are most influential in accounting for the accelerated development of African infants. Geber particularly emphasized the close contact between mother and infant during the child's first year, breast feeding on demand, and the mother's method of carrying the infant. Ainsworth added such observations as the absence of confinement, frequent parental handling, and particularly the fact that the Ganda baby is often held in a standing position from an early age. Such explanations may, of course, be validated by observations of child care in other cultures and by determining relationships between the mother's behavior and developmental quotients in children in a given culture.

But how do we explain the extreme slowing down of developmental rates in older African children? Geber and Ainsworth believe that this deceleration comes from the frequently abrupt reduction in the mother-child interaction, as the child gets older and as new siblings appear. Ganda mothers have an "all-absorbing preoccupation with the infant" (Ainsworth, 1967, p. 329); older children receive no stimulation from the mother, have no toys or organized play activities, and may even be removed from the mother and given to an aunt or grandmother to rear. However, such an explanation (based on a feast-or-famine type of child care and stimulation) does not seem completely adequate. Although these child-care practices may indeed constitute a contributing factor, this explanation fails completely to account for differences in behaviors during the first week of life.

Much more work needs to be done before factors of individual experience or infant stimulation can be accepted as the major determinants of mental development. The Uganda results have not been confirmed in some American studies. For example, Walters (1967), using 108 American infants who were classified as either white or black on the popular definition of race, found the developmental rates of the two groups to be very similar. The 51 black and 51 white babies were equated for socioeconomic status and were administered the Gesell Developmental schedules at 12, 24, and 36 weeks of age. The only significant difference was in motor behaviors at 12 weeks of age, favoring the black infants. The general lack of differences, in light of the African research, may be a result of similar child-rearing practices by black and white mothers or a result of the impure nature of both racial groups.

C. Arthur Jensen's Viewpoint

Support for a conclusion of innate racial differences in mental ability has recently been stimulated by the research and writings of Arthur Jensen, a respected psychologist at the University of California at Berkeley. Jensen's conclusions[6] need to be studied at length—both because the findings are detailed and because they are likely (yet unintended) ammunition for segregationists.

Jensen's basic thesis is that individual differences in intelligence, as measured by

[6] Jensen's original article was the longest ever published in the *Harvard Educational Review* (1969b). A U.S. Congressman has had the entire article placed in the *Congressional Record*. A summary of the original article may be found in the October, 1969 issue of *Psychology Today* (Jensen, 1969c). Jensen's rebuttal to numerous critics (see Spring, 1969 issue of *HER*) can be found in the Summer, 1969 issue of the *Harvard Educational Review* (1969d). Those readers who did not already know that scientists are human and can engage in such human actions as indignation, vindictiveness, and name-calling may wish to consult the prolonged exchange between Alfert and Jensen in the Autumn, 1969 issue of the *Journal of Social Issues* (Alfert, 1969a, 1969b; Jensen, 1969a, 1969e).

IQ tests, are "predominantly attributable to genetic differences, with environmental factors contributing a minor portion of the variance among individuals in IQ" (1969c, p. 4). His conclusions are based, first, upon the correlations between the IQ's of pairs of subjects with different degrees of hereditary relationships (identical twins reared together, identical twins reared apart, fraternal twins, siblings reared together or apart, a parent and child, a grandparent and grandchild, and so on). Mainly these data come from Burt (1955, 1958), who carefully drew samples of many kinship relationships from the school population of London, England.

When it comes to racial differences in intelligence, Jensen does not dispute that environmental factors play a part in the obtained differences. "No one, to my knowledge, questions the role of environmental factors, including influences from past history, in determining at least some of the variance between racial groups in standard measures of intelligence, school performance, and occupational status" (Jensen, 1969b, pp. 79–80). But Jensen also advocates consideration of an influence from hereditary factors: "The possible importance of genetic factors in racial behavioral differences has been greatly ignored, almost to the point of being a tabooed subject" (1969b, p. 80). Reasons for a possible hereditary influence upon intelligence include four elements.

1. Jensen first mentions genetic differences between racial groups. "The existence of genetically derived differences between racial groups (or 'breeding populations') is found in virtually every anatomical, physiological, and biochemical comparison one can make between representative samples of identifiable racial groups" (Jensen, 1969b, p. 80). Differences between races exist in regard to physical structure and athletic abilities as well (Cobb, 1934, 1936).

2. The sheer difference, consistent in so many studies, between black and white test performances—or between the performance of blacks and other culturally disadvantaged minorities—leads Jensen, being the strong hereditarian that he is, to hypothesize (not to conclude) that hereditary factors may play a part.

3. Jensen apparently accepts the studies of Bruce, Tanser, and others as successful attempts to "equate environments." Jensen concludes: "No one has yet produced any evidence based on a properly controlled study to show that representative samples of Negro and white children can be equalized in intellectual ability through statistical control of environment and education" (1969b, pp. 82–83). Although Jensen's sentence can be read in several ways, he seemingly accepts the equated-environment studies as definitive.[7]

4. Jensen also cites the work of Geber (1956) on the precocity of African infants and various physiological differences between races.

Despite his brilliant marshalling of evidence that leads to his desired conclusion, Jensen fails to consider several important points. First, he fails to consider the absence of pure races in America. His term *breeding populations* ignores the extensive racial mixing in America's past and present (Alfert, 1969a, p. 207).[8] Second, Jensen criticizes others for assuming that a score on an IQ test represents one's level of

[7]Jensen (1969e) states that there have been 43 studies that attempt to equate environments. A recent one (Tulkin, 1968) controlled both socioeconomic status and family characteristics. No significant black-white IQ differences were found by Tulkin for the upper-social-class group, but there were differences in the lower-class group.

[8]In response to this criticism, hereditarians could argue that the observed difference of 15 points in average IQ between racial groups underestimates, rather than overestimates, the true difference between so-called pure groups.

intelligence, and yet he himself takes racial differences in obtained IQ's and calls these pure indications of differences in intelligence. Jensen assumes that the obtained IQ score and rate of mental development are equivalent. Third, Jensen fails to recognize the role of proximal factors, such as motivation in the testing situation or the race of the examiner, which may make a black subject's test score an invalid indication of his level of intelligence. (A statement by the Council of the Society for the Psychological Study of Social Issues, 1969, contains these criticisms and the Council's reaction to the publicity generated by Jensen's article.)

If Jensen's viewpoint implies that environmental deprivation is not enough to explain the observed differences between racial groups, we must maintain a position of neither agreement nor disagreement. Indeed, what researcher has the tools to measure the effect of a world that denies the black child access to much of that world and that constantly reminds him of his inferior status? Clearly, environmental deprivation plays a role in mental development; whether it is stenciled on to basic genetic differences is, in our judgment, not presently a testable matter.[9]

If there are innate racial differences in mental ability between black and white Americans (and we agree with Jensen that such a possibility should be considered seriously), the differences are probably slight. Even the obtained differences in test scores are relatively unimportant when one considers the overlap between groups. Hicks and Pellegrini (1966) have reviewed 27 studies and have estimated the W^2 value for each difference. (The estimated W^2 is a measure of statistical association described in Hays' 1963 statistics text.) The median estimated W^2 was .061, which indicates that knowing a person's race reduces by only 6 percent the uncertainty in estimating his IQ score. The obtained differences are so small that classification of persons into mental ability groups on the basis of race would not be useful when the children come from reasonably similar backgrounds. Jensen (1969b, p. 78) acknowledges this conclusion.

D. Environmental Deprivation

The fact that the average black American has a poorer environment than the average white American is so manifestly apparent it may be accepted without documentation. Pettigrew's (1964) comprehensive book is an excellent source of facts, however, indicating that among the black man's burdens are high unemployment rates, poor health, low incomes, less education, poor housing, and many other factors—all of which combine to lead to a shorter life expectancy, higher susceptibility to certain diseases (such as tuberculosis), and greater incidence of psychosis (but not neurosis).[10] Certainly such severe environmental limitations can affect performance on intelligence tests (Eichenwald & Fry, 1969); but the question is: do they?

[9]Jensen himself recognizes the lack of adequate tools. In an interview for *Life* magazine (Neary, 1970), Jensen is quoted as saying: "The ideal experiment would be to take a fertilized ovum, both parents Negro, and implant it into a white mother and have that child brought up in a society where there's no prejudice against skin color" (1970, p. 65).

[10]The Equality of Educational Opportunity study, or "Coleman Report" (Coleman, Campbell, Hobson, McPartland, Mood, Weinfield, & York, 1966), documents the inferior education given to black school children in America. Sponsored by the U.S. Office of Education, the Coleman report collected diverse types of information about American school children—their levels of achievement and ability, their attitudes, their teachers' credentials, the facilities in their schools, the number of students per classroom, and so on.

One method of testing the effects of environment upon the performance of blacks is to place black children in more stimulating environments than they have had in the past, in order to see whether an enriched environment improves their performance. The Army Alpha studies concluded that Northerners of each race scored consistently higher than Southerners of the same races. Peterson and Lanier (1929) have found similar differences for school children; black school children living in New York or Chicago scored significantly higher on several intelligence tests than black children living in Nashville. These regional differences may have resulted from greater educational opportunities and cultural benefits in the North than in the South. Some evidence for the authenticity of this assumption is the correlation of +.77 (found by Alexander in 1922) between the per capita expenditure for education in each state and the average Army Alpha score for military recruits from that state. If it can be shown that the IQ's of black children improve when they move from a less stimulating environment (the South) to a more stimulating one (the North), then one may conclude that environmental handicaps serve as an explanation for differences between blacks and whites.

Klineberg and his associates (1935) were the first to test the difference in IQ for black children who had lived in the North for different periods of time. However, this is only an indirect test of the effects of an improved environment, since it is a cross-sectional study rather than a longitudinal one. Klineberg measured the IQ's of 12-year-old black children who had lived in New York City for different periods of time (from less than a year to all their lives). For children having lived in New York less than one year, the average IQ was approximately 81; for children who were residents for one to two years, the average was 85. For two- to three-year residents, the average was also 85. For three- to four-year residents, the average was 87. For children having lived there more than four years (but Southern born), the average was 89; and for Northern-born children, the average IQ was 90. (The numbers of children in these classifications ranged from 40 to 127.) Yet, there were several sources of ambiguity in the study. First, although the preceding progression is impressively linear, it is not so neat in each of three schools studied. In fact, as Tyler (1965, p. 311) points out, there is as much fluctuation from school to school as from North to South. Second, there is no indication whether these schools were representative of the total black population of New York City. Third, we still do not know whether the findings are evidence of improvement due to better facilities or result from a selective-migration factor. Some authorities have argued that the brighter, more ambitious blacks were drawn to the North at an earlier date, whereas more recent migrations include less able, less ambitious types. If this is the case, Klineberg's findings would not be relevant to how an improved environment affects IQ scores but, rather, would be evidence demonstrating the selective nature of black migrations from South to North. (This confusion is clarified in a study by Lee, 1951, to be described subsequently.) At this point, however, a neglected finding of Klineberg's study should be noted. The average IQ of 12-year-old black children born and raised in the North was approximately 90 (in one of the three schools it was 98.5), which was equal to that of white children living in the same surroundings at the same time.

The precise role of improved education was clarified by Lee (1951) in a study of black children living in Philadelphia. Here, the methodology was improved by testing the same children two or more times. Some of these children were born in the North; the others had moved to Philadelphia from the South at different ages. Also the number of cases (ranging from 109 to 424 per classification) was larger than the number of cases in Klineberg's study. A little-known group test, the Philadelphia Tests of Verbal and Mental Maturity, was used.

Lee found that black children born in Philadelphia did not change much in average IQ from the first grade to the ninth grade; that is, their rate of development was consistently within the normal range. For those who had attended kindergarten, the average IQ at the first-grade testing was 97; the same children, retested eight years later, still averaged 97. Those children who were Philadelphia born but did not attend kindergarten had an average IQ of 92 at the first-grade testing and almost 94 at the ninth-grade testing. The means for both these groups at second-grade, fourth-grade, and sixth-grade testings fluctuated around these terminal figures, and we may safely conclude that there was no significant change in either of these groups over the nine years. In contrast, there was a significant improvement in the performance of Southern-born black children. For instance, the 182 children who entered the Philadelphia schools as first graders had an average IQ of 86.5 at that time. At the second grade, they averaged 89; and at the sixth grade and ninth grade, the average IQ was 93. Children entering at the second-grade level (N = 109) increased from 87 to 90 by the ninth-grade testing. Children entering at the third or fourth grade increased from 86 at that testing to 89 by the ninth-grade testing.

Although these increases are not large, they are statistically significant, indicating that the changes are not merely a chance phenomenon. Nor can the changes be explained on the basis of increased familiarity with the test, as there were no increases in the scores of Philadelphia-born children. When Lee's data are viewed differently, we find the same progression that emerged from Klineberg's data. When tested at the ninth grade, black children born in the North had an average IQ of 95. Those moving North before age 6 averaged 93; those moving North at ages 7 to 8 averaged 91; those moving at ages 9 to 10 averaged 89; those moving at ages 11 to 12 averaged 90; and those moving at junior high school averaged 87. The combination of Lee's and Klineberg's findings implies that something besides selective migration was happening. Longer exposure to a better educational system did increase IQ scores, although the end result (at least in Lee's study) was still not as high as that of native Northerners. It should be emphasized again that the mean IQ of black Northern-born children (95) was probably quite similar to the mean for white children of the same socioeconomic status. It is always possible that the changes in the Southern-born children reflected an improved adaptation to the testing situation rather than changes in the rate of mental development, but most of the objective reviewers of Lee's study conclude that the improved environmental situation was the primary cause for the changes in IQ.

More recent tests of the effects of environmental change also produced positive results. In many of these studies, children from poorer backgrounds were placed in special kindergartens, which temporarily create a more stimulating environment. The Early Training Project (Gray, 1969; Gray & Klaus, 1965, 1970; Klaus & Gray, 1965, 1968) is an attempt to offset the progressive retardation of mental development in young, culturally disadvantaged children. The project is primarily concerned with lower-class children, but since all of the subjects are blacks, we should look at some of its findings here. The program offered a 10-week summer session in which a group of 20 children was given a stimulating environment and a great deal of reinforcement. Throughout the year, a home visitor provided each child with more stimulating materials and encouraged parents and children to participate in activities together. Careful attention was given to establishing adequate control groups, both within and away from the small Southern city where the project was based. Although the primary purpose of the project was not to change IQ scores per se, measures on the Stanford-Binet Test of Intelligence indicated that the progressive retardation commonly found among lower-class black children in the South was arrested, while the control groups continued to show diminishing scores. The mean IQ for the two experimental groups showed a gain of seven points over a two-and-one-half-year period, while the two control groups had average losses of four to six points. Even after their fourth grade in school, IQ differences between experimental and control groups were significant (Gray & Klaus, 1970).

In summary, when the environmental conditions of blacks are improved, their IQ's increase. The increased IQ's are close to the average level and are probably not much different from those of whites in the same environment. Environmental deprivation can account for much of the difference between blacks and whites; however, we cannot say whether this alone accounts for all of the difference.

E. Test Appropriateness

Intelligence is, to a large degree, a culturally defined concept. Each society determines what is intelligent behavior in that society. For instance, the Wechsler test asks: "If you were lost in a forest in the daytime how would you go about finding

Figure 7-2. *Activities in the Early Training Project. Lower-class black children, ages 4 and 5, are placed in a stimulating environment for the two summers before entering first grade. Retests in the fourth grade continue to show modest differences in IQ level and achievement level between these children and matched controls. (Photograph courtesy of Demonstration and Research Center for Early Education, Peabody College.)*

your way out?" In our culture there are certain acceptable (in other words, intelligent) and unacceptable (unintelligent) answers. In another society where the way of life is different, other types of answers might be more sensible and hence the most intelligent. We must always be careful not to assume that an intelligent response to the demands of our environment is necessarily the same as an intelligent response to the demands of other environments and other cultures.

Another factor to be kept in mind is that each society tends to develop different values and skills. The Western European-American civilization is a highly verbal one. Hence, our methods of measuring intelligence are largely verbal. Because of our ethnocentrism, we are tempted to assume that a society that has never produced a written language (as was the case in the Hawaiian Islands and in many African tribes) is unable to produce an intelligent race of people. This is a dangerous assumption because it is based on a value judgment, which implies that what our society emphasizes is, by its very nature, the important determinant of intelligent behavior. Arnold Toynbee (1948), the author of a monumental study of the history of civilization, stated: "When we classify Mankind by colour the only one of the primary races . . . which has not made a creative contribution to any one of our twenty-one civilizations is the Black Race" (p. 233). But Toynbee's determination of what makes up a "creative contribution" must be seen as a value judgment. Other societies have undoubtedly been creative in other ways—in the development of nonverbal means of communication, authentic human relationships, complex religious views, art forms, and so on. It is also difficult to compare civilizations in widely different areas of the world with regard to their success in adapting to their environment. The respective environments are simply too diverse.

An excellent example of such cultural relativism is DuBois' (1939) study of the intelligence of Pueblo Indian children in New Mexico. DuBois carefully constructed and validated a Draw-a-Horse test and followed the procedures in the construction of the Goodenough Draw-a-Man test of intelligence. When both tests were administered to groups of white and Indian children, the whites did better on the Draw-a-Man test, and the Indians did better on the Draw-a-Horse test. On the latter test, the mean "IQ" for the 11-year-old white boys was 74. Thus, it can be shown that each society has chosen to emphasize different skills and different types of intelligent behavior. (Also see Figure 7-3.)

What implications do these findings and those indicated in Figure 7-3 have for differences in performance between black and white Americans? The answer depends upon how much the black is a part of the American culture. It may be justifiably claimed that the black American has been divested of much of the culture that he brought from Africa and yet not permitted to enter fully into the culture of white America. While white America asserts certain activities, traditions, and values as important (for example, the belief that hard work will lead to success), black America cannot always find truth in these assertions. (Many blacks have striven to improve themselves only to find they were blocked because of race.)[11] It therefore seems not

[11]One of the most important findings of the massive Coleman Report (Coleman, Campbell, Hobson, McPartland, Mood, Weinfield, & York, 1966) was the reaction of black students to a measure of *internal control*. Internal control generally indicates a belief that one's rewards follow from, or are contingent upon, one's own behavior (Rotter, 1966) rather than upon luck or the behavior of others. The Coleman Report found that black school children believed they had less internal control than did white children. Also, among black children, those with higher internal control scores had higher school achievement scores.

Figure 7-3. *"Conceptual Intelligence" in America and "Spatial Intelligence" in Liberia*

The work of Gay and Cole (1967) on the teaching of mathematics to Kpelle children and adults provides a demonstration of cultural definitions of intelligence. The Kpelle are a rather un-Westernized tribe in Liberia. They have great difficulty in forming concepts when they are given square- or triangular-shaped cards of red or green color. Most of them take abnormally long periods of time to sort eight such cards into two piles, while Peace Corps volunteers in training for service in Liberia do the sorting correctly without hesitation. One may quickly conclude that the Kpelle lack conceptual ability and hence are "less intelligent." But consider a second task. A bowl of uncooked rice is passed around the room and the person is asked: "How many measuring cups of rice do you think are in it?" (Gay & Cole, 1967, p. 1). The estimates of 60 Peace Corps volunteers were between 6 and 20 cups, with an average of around 12. In fact, there were 9 cups exactly in the bowl, so the Americans' average error was about 35 percent. When 20 illiterate Kpelle adults were asked the same question, the average estimate was just under 9 cups, an underestimate of 8 percent. Thus, the Kpelle excel on a measure of spatial ability (a part of intelligence) and a task that is related to their ability to adapt to their own environment.

entirely appropriate to apply to Negro Americans the cultural definitions of intelligence used by the white majority-group—at least not until the Negro has access to, and is accepted by, the white subculture.

F. Characteristics of the Testing Situation

In addition to the distal factors of heredity and environment, more proximal factors may account for racial IQ differences. Many of these have been listed in Table 7-1. Let us now look at some of them in detail. We must recognize that all persons taking an intelligence test do not enter the testing situation with the same type or degree of motivation. It may be there are factors in the testing situation that would cause a black to respond differently than a white. Several reports (Mussen, 1953; Rosen & D'Andrade, 1959; Merbaum, 1960) indicate lower-class Southern black children show less concern for achievement and excellence of performance than do lower-class Southern white children. Irvin Katz's (1964) comprehensive review proposed that black behavior in a testing situation may be a function of "(a) social threat; i.e., Negroes were fearful of instigating white hostility through greater assertiveness, (b) low task motivation in confrontation with white achievement standards . . . or (c) failure threat" (p. 391). A series of studies (Katz & Benjamin, 1960; Katz & Cohen, 1962; Katz, Epps, & Axelson, 1964; Katz & Greenbaum, 1963; Katz, Henchy, & Allen, 1968; I. Katz, 1967) has shown that the performance of black college students in standard testing and laboratory situations is influenced by such factors as the race of the experimenter, the presence of other subjects of the same or another race, the nature of the task, the nature of the instructions, and the personality characteristics of the subjects. Such findings have been shown in both the North and the South, and they apply to young subjects as well. For example, using Northern black boys from ages 7 to 10, Katz, Henchy, and Allen (1968) found significantly better performances on a verbal learning task when a black experimenter was present than when a white experimenter was used.

Several studies have indicated that the performance of black children deteriorates when tested by white examiners. Pasamanick and Knobloch (1955) concluded that the poor language scores of 2-year-old black children were caused by an inhibition about being tested by a white examiner. Shuey (1958), however, concluded, after reviewing a large number of studies using black examiners, that the results are similar to those of studies using white examiners, and hence the race of the examiner has no effect. (This is a conclusion in keeping with Shuey's acceptance of innate racial differences.)

Until the last decade, few studies had used both black and white examiners to test the same children. Forrester and Klaus (1964) did this, using as subjects 24 black children, aged 5 and 6. The tests used were Forms L and M of the 1937 Stanford-Binet, and the testing was done by two equally trained Southern female examiners. The children were randomly assigned to four groups, and each group was given both test forms, with the order of test administration and the race of the examiner counterbalanced. The mean score when the children were examined by the black was 105.7; when the white examiner was used, the mean was 101.9—a statistically significant difference. The race of the examiner did make a difference, although the results of this study could possibly be accounted for by differential skill of the examiners rather than by differences in race. All recent studies do not indicate significant effects of the race of the examiner (see Tanner & Catron, 1971). Nevertheless, Forrester and Klaus's study should serve to caution us against accepting unquestioningly the IQ scores of young Southern black children who have been tested by whites.

In less well-designed testing situations using white examiners, it is possible that black test-takers suffer even more than in carefully controlled situations. Some white examiners may begin the testing of a black child with unverbalized expectations of an indifferent performance. This leads to a decreased rapport between subject and tester, a failure on the tester's part to try to understand dialect, less probing, and hence a lower score; it is a neat example of a self-fulfilling prophecy, similar to the phenomenon found in teachers by Rosenthal and Jacobson (1968). (See Chapter 2.)

G. The Black Personality and Self-Concept

There is ample speculation and some evidence that American blacks have borne a disfigured personality, a "mark of oppression" (Kardiner & Ovesey, 1951; Karon, 1958) that "represents the emotional wound of living in a white world of prejudice and discrimination" (I. Katz, 1969, p. 15). Black children disparage their own race, learn the negative stereotypes about themselves that are held by whites, and blame their own kind—rather than society at large—for the inferior status of their group (Gurin, Gurin, Lao, & Beattie, 1969). So many of these conclusions use both **race** and **social class** as explanations of differences that they will be considered later in the chapter.

IV. COMPARISONS BETWEEN WHITES AND OTHER RACES

Studies of differences between whites and American Indians or between whites and Orientals suffer from many problems. Among the Dakota Indians, for example, it is considered bad form to answer a question in the presence of someone else who does not know the answer (Klineberg, 1935). The effects of such cultural norms upon IQ test performance should be apparent. Moreover, different Indian tribes have dissimilar cultures and different degrees of contact with non-Indian groups (Wrench, 1969).

After reviewing the available literature on differences between whites and American Indians, Tyler (1965) concludes: "The only general statement that was warranted is that Indians as a group average considerably lower than whites on standard intelligence tests" (p. 325). But apparently Indian performance is better on nonverbal than on verbal measures of intelligence—a finding that does not apply to blacks. Rohrer (1942) was able to test the intelligence of the Osage Indians, who had not suffered physical and cultural deprivation to the degree that most tribes had. He found average IQ's of 100 and 104 on the two tests he used. The overlap between Indian and white scores is such that race cannot be used to assign classifications of ability.

Research on Chinese-Americans and Japanese-Americans is fraught with even greater difficulties, in the sense that Chinese and Japanese who have emigrated to the United States do not compose a random sample of their countrymen. In contrast to other minority racial groups, the typical performance of Oriental children in America is often equal to or better than that of white children. Pintner (1931) reported average Binet IQ's of 85 to 98, with averages above 100 on performance tests. There are apparently no studies that try to equate or control environmental circumstances, although some researchers, such as Livesay (1944), are aware of the fact that environmental and social-class differences between races must be considered. A more recent study of New York City children (D. H. Clark, Lesser, & Fifer, 1964; Lesser, Fifer, & Clark, 1965) considers both racial and social-class differences in four groups, including the Chinese. Several investigators (Anastasi, 1958; Darsie, 1926; Sandiford & Kerr, 1926) have speculated that the superior performance of Oriental children may be attributed to a factor of selective migration, where only the more able, intelligent families emigrated from the Orient to America. Evidence for or against such a supposition is hard to obtain.

Hawaii offers a fertile area for the study of racial differences, as most of the Oriental, Caucasian, and Polynesian groups there are stable and in general possess equal cultural opportunities and socioeconomic status. (The latter statement is not true for the Hawaiian and Filipino groups in Hawaii, who are generally lower in status; but the Chinese, Japanese, Korean, and Caucasian groups have, in recent years, been reasonably equivalent in status.) However, findings on racial comparisons of school children in Hawaii are limited because studies have only been made on the children in the public schools (Livesay, 1942, 1944; S. Smith, 1942; L. H. Stewart, Dole, & Harris, 1967). There is a large enrollment of children in private schools, some of which siphon off the more talented students, and the percentages of children from the diverse racial groups attending these private schools are different.

Despite this difficulty, research on racial differences in Hawaii has produced an important finding, first introduced by Smith (1942) and later replicated by Stewart, Dole, and Harris (1967). In 1924, Smith tested the public school children of Honolulu who were between 10 and 15 years of age; in 1938 he tested the children who were then 10 to 15 years of age. A nonverbal test was used. Average differences between racial groups were significant; in 1938 the order of groups was the same as it was in 1924. On both occasions, the high scoring races were the Oriental (Japanese, Chinese, and Korean nationalities) and the Caucasian. The Hawaiian (Polynesian), the Portuguese, and the Puerto Rican groups were the lowest. In the 14-year interval all groups improved in average performance, but the groups that had done well in 1924 showed more improvement than the groups that had done poorly. The study presents impressive evidence that improving the education of all children does not necessarily eradicate the differences among groups. In fact, the gap may be extended.

In a later but similar study, Stewart et al. (1967) compared high school students in Hawaii on four measures of verbal and numerical ability obtained at grade 10 and again at grade 12. There were significant group differences on all the measures, with Orientals ranking highest and Caucasians ranking next. Hawaiians consistently ranked lowest, with Filipinos falling just above them. When the same students repeated the tests 28 months later, the scores of all the groups except the Hawaiians (the lowest group) changed significantly on one or more measures. The authors corroborate Smith's (1942) finding and conclude: "It is apparent that ethnic differences in test scores did not disappear as a result of concurrent curriculum experiences over the last two years of the school program. In fact, the changes were of such a nature as to accentuate differences" (p. 24). Osborne (1960) reports a similar increased difference over a four-year span, between blacks and whites in segregated schools (one evidence of the progressive deterioration resulting from cultural disadvantage). However, the Hawaiian studies indicate that even with desegregation, differences between racial groups can increase over a period of time.

V. SOCIAL-CLASS DIFFERENCES

Although it is sometimes claimed that America is a classless society, it is evident that within American life certain types of people are grouped together (and apart from others) on the basis of interests, education, income, values, and other socioeconomic variables. These groupings, though not always clear-cut, are important enough to be studied in their own right and are called social classes. We need now to investigate the findings pertinent to social-class differences in intelligence, personality, and motivation.

A. Definitions and Measurement of Social Class

A review of different definitions of social class (Krech, Crutchfield, & Ballachey, 1962) indicates that three methods are used to define the term.

1. The *objective method* is one approach. Here, social class is measured by "objective characteristics [that] are likely to discriminate most sharply among the different patterns of social behavior which [the social scientist] conceives of as 'class behaviors' " (Krech, et al., p. 313). The objective characteristics most frequently used are amount and source of income, amount of education, type of occupation, and type and location of housing.

2. The *subjective method* is a second approach. Social class is here defined "in terms of how the members of the community *see themselves* in the status hierarchy" (p. 313).

3. The *reputational method* is the third approach. Here social class is defined "in

terms of how the members of a community place *each other* in the status system of the community" (p. 315). In conjunction with this approach, a number of surveys show that respondents make a clear-cut and consistent ranking of the socioeconomic status of various occupations. Table 7-2 presents one ranking—an updating of the North-Hatt Occupational Prestige scale by Hodge, Siegel, and Rossi (1964), which is based on the responses of a national sample of adults.

Most of the research on social-class factors in intelligence has used the objective method to define social class, while recognizing that there is a moderate to high degree of agreement among the methods in classifying a particular individual. Unfortunately, many researchers are not very explicit about their particular measures, and at least some use very rough estimates of social class (such as neighborhood of residence). It is impossible to be confident that the "lower class" of one study is equivalent to the "lower class" of another. All we can do is use the class designation, knowing that we have a rough distinction between two groups—one higher in socioeconomic status than the other.

B. Differences in Children

Reviewing the large number of studies on social-class differences leads one to a general conclusion that the average intelligence-test performance of children from upper-class and middle-class families exceeds that of children from lower-class families. Such differences exist in almost all the studies, regardless of the tests and groups used. (Tests which attempt to be culture free produce fewer differences, but there is less evidence for the validity of this type of test.) After a comprehensive review Tyler (1965) stated: "From the early days of the intelligence-testing movement to the present, one investigator after another has reported consistent differences between the average IQ's of groups at different socioeconomic levels" (p. 333). The massive Coleman study (Coleman et al., 1966) found that children of lower socioeconomic status scored below the national averages on both verbal and nonverbal tests at all grades tested (grades 1, 3, 6, 9, and 12).

Using the father's occupation as an index of a child's social class, McNemar (1942) analyzed the standardization data for the 1937 revision of the Stanford-Binet and found the following mean IQ's: professional, 115.9; managerial, 112.1; clerical, skilled trades, and small business, 107.7; farm owners, 94.8; semiskilled workers, 104.7; slightly skilled, 98.5; and day laborers, 96.1. Thus, the difference between children with fathers in the highest and lowest occupational groups averaged almost 20 points. Those differences are as great for young children aged $2\frac{1}{2}$ to 5 years as they are for teenagers. Similar findings occur on the Wechsler Intelligence Scale for Children (Seashore, Wesman, & Doppelt, 1950), which shows a mean IQ of 110.9 for children with professional and managerial fathers and a mean of 94.6 for children with rural and urban laborers and farm foremen as fathers. Here the difference is about 15 points. Differences of such magnitudes are also found in other cultures and countries, including Scotland (Scottish Council, 1953), France (Heuyer et al., 1950), and Hawaii (Livesay, 1944). Such differences also occur within the black American subculture (Horton & Crump, 1962).

Similar results are found if we use a more comprehensive measure of social class including source of family income, dwelling area, house type, and father's occupation.

Table 7-2. *Occupational Prestige Rankings in 1964*

	Rank	*Occupation*	*Prestige Score*
	1	U.S. Supreme Court Justice	94
	2	Physician	93
Tied	3.5	Nuclear physicist	92
	3.5	Scientist	92
Tied	5.5	Government scientist	91
	5.5	State governor	91
Tied	8	Cabinet member in the federal government	90
	8	College professor	90
	8	United States Representative in Congress	90
Tied	11	Chemist	89
	11	Lawyer	89
	11	Diplomat in U.S. Foreign Service	89
Tied	14	Dentist	88
	14	Architect	88
	14	County judge	88
Tied	17.5	Psychologist	87
	17.5	Minister	87
	17.5	Member of the board of directors of a large corporation	87
Tied	21.5	Priest	86
	21.5	Head of a department in a state government	86
	21.5	Civil engineer	86
	21.5	Airline pilot	86
Tied	24.5	Banker	85
	24.5	Biologist	85
	26	Sociologist	83
Tied	27.5	Instructor in public schools	82
	27.5	Captain in regular army	82
Tied	29.5	Public school teacher	81
	29.5	Accountant for a large business	81
Tied	31.5	Owner of a factory that employs about 100 people	80
	31.5	Building contractor	80
Tied	34.5	Artist who paints pictures that are exhibited in galleries	78
	34.5	Musician in symphony orchestra	78
	34.5	Author of novels	78
	34.5	Economist	78
	37	Official of an international labor union	77
Tied	39	Railroad engineer	76
	39	Electrician	76
	39	County agricultural agent	76
Tied	41.5	Owner-operator of a printing shop	75
	41.5	Trained machinist	75
Tied	44	Farm owner and operator	74
	44	Undertaker	74
	44	Welfare worker for city government	74
	46	Newspaper columnist	73
	47	Policeman	72
	48	Reporter on a daily newspaper	71

Mean Stanford-Binet IQ's for children ages 10 and 16 in a Midwest city were 128 for the upper-class group, 113 for the upper-middle class, 107 for the lower-middle class, and 95 for the lower class (Havighurst & Breese, 1947; Havighurst & Janke, 1944; Janke & Havighurst, 1945; Schulman & Havighurst, 1947; Havighurst, Bowman, Liddle, Matthews, & Pierce, 1962). Similar, although sometimes smaller, differences were found on nonverbal tests such as the Draw-a-Man, the Paper Form Board, and the Porteus Maze test.

Rank		Occupation	Prestige Score
Tied	49.5	Radio announcer	70
	49.5	Bookkeeper	70
Tied	51.5	Tenant farmer (one who owns livestock and machinery and manages the farm)	69
	51.5	Insurance agent	69
	53	Carpenter	68
Tied	54.5	Manager of a small store in a city	67
	54.5	A local official of a labor union	67
Tied	57	Mail carrier	66
	57	Railroad conductor	66
	57	Traveling salesman for a wholesale concern	66
	59	Plumber	65
	60	Automobile repairman	64
Tied	62.5	Playground director	63
	62.5	Barber	63
	62.5	Machine operator in a factory	63
	62.5	Owner-operator of a lunch stand	63
Tied	65.5	Corporal in regular army	62
	65.5	Garage mechanic	62
	67	Truck driver	59
	68	Fisherman who owns his own boat	58
Tied	70	Clerk in a store	56
	70	Milk route man	56
	70	Streetcar motorman	56
Tied	72.5	Lumberjack	55
	72.5	Restaurant cook	55
	74	Singer in a nightclub	54
	75	Filling station attendant	51
Tied	77.5	Dockworker	50
	77.5	Railroad section hand	50
	77.5	Night watchman	50
	77.5	Coal miner	50
Tied	80.5	Restaurant waiter	49
	80.5	Taxi driver	49
Tied	83	Farmhand	48
	83	Janitor	48
	83	Bartender	48
	85	Clothes presser in a laundry	45
	86	Soda fountain clerk	44
	87	Sharecropper (one who owns no livestock or equipment and does not manage farm)	42
	88	Garbage collector	39
	89	Street sweeper	36
	90	Shoeshiner	34

(From Hodge, R. W., Siegel, P. M., & Rossi, P. H. Occupational prestige in the United States, 1925–1963. *American Journal of Sociology*, 1964, **70**, 286–302. Reprinted with permission of the author and the publisher. Copyright 1964, University of Chicago Press.)

Recently, attention has been focused on the interaction of intelligence, motivation, and personality in specific groups differing in social class. For example, Epps (1969) measured the ability, achievement, and personality of black high school students in the North and the South. Social class was assessed on the basis of the father's occupation and the mother's educational level. In all four groups (classified by sex and region) middle-class students had higher vocabulary scores than lower-class students. The correlation coefficients were all small (+.18 to +.25) but statistically significant. Of more importance is Epps' finding that social class was more strongly related to the student's "amount of expected future education" than to any other measure in the study (which included, in addition to those previously mentioned, measures of self-concept, test anxiety, self-esteem, and conformity). Here we have an indication that any existent differences in ability between social classes interact with the child's values and aspirations to perpetuate his position in the society.

C. Occupational Groups and IQ

Differences in social-class level are also related to the mental ability of adults. In both world wars, military recruits have been used to show a differentiation in test scores according to occupation (Yerkes, 1921; Fryer, 1922; Harrell & Harrell, 1945; N. Stewart, 1947). In World War I, the highest Army Alpha means for enlisted men were obtained by engineers and accountants; in World War II, accountants, lawyers, and engineers were highest. (Some high-ranking occupations, such as medical doctors, were not included because most of these men were commissioned officers.) In World War I, the lowest groups in average score were miners, farm workers, and unskilled laborers, while in World War II the same groups, plus the teamsters, were lowest. Such differences among occupational groups have also been found among military recruits in Sweden (Carlsson, 1955), employed adults in New York City (Simon & Leavitt, 1950), and employees of a large company in Great Britain (Foulds & Raven, 1948).

VI. THE INTERPRETATION OF DIFFERENCES IN INTELLIGENCE

Everyone agrees that there are social-class differences in average levels of intelligence. Controversy centers around the causes for these differences. We will consider three different possible causes: heredity, environment, and motivational and personality factors in the testing situation.

A. Heredity

Since the time of the publication of Sir Francis Galton's *Hereditary Genius* (1870), it has been shown that the offspring of more prominent families are more successful than other children. The hereditarian position claims that more intelligent people have more natural ability and hence have gravitated to positions of eminence. Anastasi (1958) has summarized this position: "The more intelligent individuals would gradually work their way up to the more demanding but more desirable positions, each person tending eventually to 'find his level.' Since intellectually superior parents tend to have intellectually superior offspring, the children in the higher social strata would be more intelligent, on the whole, than those from the lower social levels" (p. 521). The fact that social-class differences in intelligence are just as great in young children (ages $2\frac{1}{2}$ to 5) as they are among adolescents (ages 15 to 18) is sometimes used to buttress this hereditarian argument. It says, in effect, that despite continued differences in environment, social-class differences in intelligence do not increase with age; therefore, it is argued, the differences are not due to environment at all but must be caused by another factor—namely, heredity. There are, however, two limitations to this argument. First, this finding does not preclude the possibility that social-class differences in the early environment (prenatal, perinatal, or early postnatal) could have caused the test-score differences. Second, there are studies demonstrating that a continued impoverished environment leads to a deterioration of IQ with age. Asher (1935) found that children growing up in isolated Kentucky mountain areas had a median IQ of 83.5 at age 7 and a median IQ of 60.6 at age 15. Asher attributed this huge decline to the limited social and material environment. Wheeler (1942) and Klaus and Gray (1968) also report a deterioration of IQ scores under a prolonged inadequate environment.

Arthur Jensen (1968a, 1968b) postulates that hereditary differences combine with environmental factors to affect social-class differences in intelligence. Jensen makes a distinction between Level I and Level II abilities. Level I, called *learning ability,* is assessed by rote-learning tasks, short-term memory measures, free recall of briefly presented sets of familiar objects, and serial-learning tasks. Level II, or *intelligence,* is defined by Jensen in terms of the traditional scholastic aptitude measures, involving vocabulary, reasoning, numerical series, and the like. Jensen repeats the common observation that lower-class children with IQ's of 60 to 80 "appear to be much brighter socially, on the playground, and in generally nonscholastic types of behavior than their middle or upper-middle [class] counterparts in the same range of IQ" (1968a, p. 3). Jensen then hypothesizes that children from the two social classes do not differ in Level I abilities but do differ in Level II abilities. The data, collected on both black and white preschool children aged 4 to 6, confirm this hypothesis. Figure 7-4 represents the relationship. Children differing in social class or in intelligence (Level II) do not differ in learning ability (Level I). The study concludes that the acquisition of learning abilities is necessary but not sufficient for the development of abilities measured by standard intelligence tests. Jensen believes that hereditary factors play a larger role in determining intelligence than in determining learning ability.

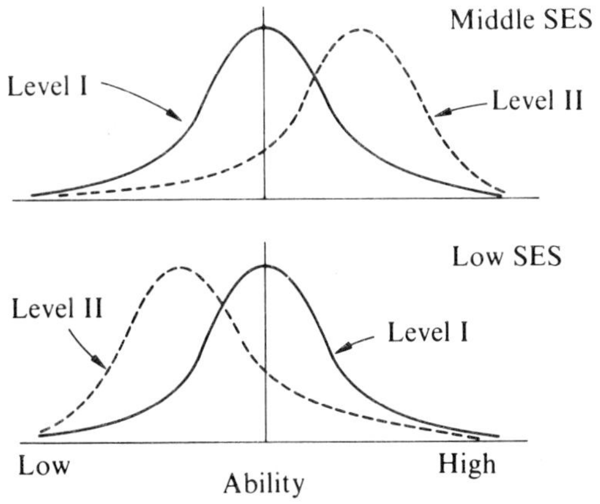

Figure 7-4. *Hypothetical distributions of Level I (solid line) and Level II (broken line) abilities in middle-class (upper curves) and culturally disadvantaged (lower curves) populations. (From Jensen, A. R. Patterns of mental ability and socioeconomic status. Paper presented at the Annual Meeting of the National Academy of Sciences, Washington, D.C., April 24, 1968. Reprinted with permission of the author.)*

B. Environment

Environment is a many-faceted phenomenon. Consider the differences between the environments of two 8-year-old American girls—one of whom lives in a well-to-do suburban home, while the other lives in an inner-city slum. (See Figure 7-5.) Their environments have differed markedly almost from the moment each was conceived. Probably, the mother of the child in the slums received less extensive medical care, was less healthy, and ate a less adequate diet while pregnant than the mother living in the suburbs. After birth, the slum child probably grew up in an unhealthy environment, received less stimulation from her mother, had fewer visits to the doctor, and poorer dental care than the other child. She was probably denied the benefits of a nursery school and possibly a kindergarten, both of which were provided her well-to-do comparison. Most likely, the inner-city public school is older and has fewer up-to-date instructional materials and a greater teacher turnover than the suburban school. The slum child's opportunities to travel, even within the city, are limited, and she lacks interested parents necessary for the development of verbal skills and curiosity.

Just how much do these numerous environmental differences affect IQ's? Contemporary thinking sees environmental factors as playing a large part in the determination of intelligence. Intelligence is seen as "an epigenetic phenomenon, being limited by the structure of the nervous system, which is, in its broad limits, genetically determined, but free to vary within these limits according to the adequacy of the

Figure 7-5. *The quality and quantity of environmental stimulation for children growing up in the same country can vary tremendously. (Photographs courtesy of Joe Zinn and Carl Young.)*

environment during development" (Haywood, 1967). We should look then at specific aspects of the environment that may help determine how close a child's intelligence comes to these limits.

Prenatal Environment. Harrell, Woodyard, and Gates (1956) have shown that if one supplements the diets of pregnant, lower-class women with iron and vitamin B complex, their offspring will have higher IQ's than the offspring of unfortified control subjects. At age 3, the mean difference in the two groups of children was five IQ points; at age 4 the difference had increased to eight points. (The effect only occurred in mothers with an extremely inadequate diet.) Such IQ differences could be the result of other maternal differences deriving from the fact that the experimental-group mothers felt "special" as a result of being in the study. As it stands, however, the study indicates that changes in the prenatal environment may influence mental development.

Perinatal Environment. The number of premature births, complications during pregnancy and delivery, and the frequency of birth injuries are all apparently more probable in the lower class than in the middle class (Rider, Taback, & Knobloch, 1955; Pasamanick & Knobloch, 1960; Pettigrew, 1964). The mental abilities of the child who survives such traumas may very well be affected.

Early Postnatal Environment. The environment during the first five years of life has always been considered crucial. In the past two decades new theories about the effects of early environment have been advanced, which place even further emphasis on this period of life (Eichenwald & Fry, 1969).

Hebb (1949), for example, explored the role of *cell assemblies* of the brain in information processing. Cell assemblies grow and develop as a result of repeated sensory stimulation and later combine to form *phase sequences,* which permit the person to respond adequately to the outside world. The greater the number of these phase sequences, the greater the ability to adapt and learn. Research with animal subjects indicates that early stimulation (or less restriction) has effects on the rapidity of physiological growth. Specific changes have been found in adult weight and skeletal length (Levine, 1959), age at which adult EEG pattern emerges (Meier, 1961), and early sexual development (Morton, Denenberg, & Zarrow, 1963). As Gray (1962) indicates, one may question how relevant studies on extreme restriction in animals are to human cultural deprivation. It may be, however, that children of different social-class levels differ in the amount or type of sensory stimulation received in the first few years of life, leading eventually to IQ differences. Gray (1962) believes that the difference in absolute amounts of stimulation received by children of different social classes is probably not great, but there does exist a social-class difference in the range and variety of the stimuli and in the order of presentation of stimuli. (The middle-class parent, for example, is more likely to know what toy is appropriate to what age.)

J. McV. Hunt (1961, 1962) extended the usefulness of Hebb's concepts by combining them with information theory to emphasize the importance of the growing child's experience of the development of his own intelligence. Beginning at infancy, the child is stimulated by many objects. As his senses receive a variety of stimuli, they become more and more developed; perceptions are selected and refined. Yet each child does not develop in the same manner. As Bloom, Davis, and Hess have stated: "Perceptual development is stimulated by environments which are rich in the range of experiences available; which make use of games, toys, and many objects for manipulation; and in which there is frequent interaction between the child and adults at meals, playtimes, and throughout the day. . . . The typical middle-class home provides a very complex environment for the child's early perceptual development, and this gives these children some advantage in the early years of school" (1965, p. 12).

Hess and his associates (R. D. Hess, 1964; Hess & Shipman, 1965; Shipman & Hess, 1965) have investigated specific social-class differences that might explain IQ deficits in lower-class children. They have determined specific social-class differences in mother-child verbal interactions and how these interactions affect the child's cognitive development. (Bernstein's, 1960, 1961, work on "linguistic codes" has stimulated the development of helpful concepts of linguistic differences between classes. These will be reviewed in Chapter 8.)

Clearly, growing up in a slum or ghetto is different from growing up in a suburb; many salient factors may account for the lowered performance and academic failure of children from lower socioeconomic backgrounds. An excellent conceptual analysis of these factors has been provided by Irwin Katz (1969), who evaluated three possible explanations for the lowered performance of lower-class and minority-group members. These are the cultural deprivation hypothesis, the cultural conflict hypothesis, and the educational deprivation hypothesis. All three share the assumption that the early environment is most influential in causing lowered intellectual performance among blacks from a poor socioeconomic status. The cultural deprivation hypothesis will be examined in some detail.

Several qualities are emphasized in the cultural deprivation hypothesis—inadequacy of early socialization, absence of the father, a developing *personality deficit,* high levels of anxiety, and a felt lack of control over one's own environment. For example, Bettelheim (1964) postulates that one's personality is shaped in the first year after birth and that these personality characteristics are very resistant to change; he believes that in the case of the black lower-class child the earliest experiences produce "a life-long distrust of others (including one's teachers and what they teach) and of oneself" (Bettelheim, 1964, quoted in Katz, 1969). Thus Bettelheim would predict that, in contrast to whites, black youths would have negative assumptions about human nature. Short, Rivera, and Tennyson (1965) report that middle-class boys see the adult world as more helpful than do lower-class boys. One study (McMullen & Wrightsman, 1965) of the philosophies of human nature held by black and white students at four colleges in the same Southern city found blacks scoring significantly lower on the Trustworthiness scale; that is, black students expressed more distrust of people in general than did white students. This distrust was particularly characteristic of lower-class black students. However, we may question whether "people in general" represents the same group of people to black and white students. To test this, Johnson (1969) asked black and white high school students to answer four forms in a measure of philosophies of human nature. One of these forms used the traditional referents ("most people" or "the average person"), and another form used "most Negroes and whites." The other two forms asked about either "Negroes" or "whites." Each group expressed trusting beliefs regarding its own race, but distrusted the other racial group. Thus, on the basis of limited evidence, the distrust Bettelheim sees developing in black infants apparently is directed toward whites only.

The most publicized example of the cultural deprivation hypothesis is the Moynihan Report (U.S. Department of Labor, 1965). At the time of its writing,

D. P. Moynihan, an economist in the Department of Labor during Lyndon Johnson's presidency, wanted to bring about changes in the welfare system in order to reduce crime, unemployment, and drop-outs from school in lower-class black families. In a polemic directed toward policy makers in the government Moynihan advanced his thesis that the black lower-class family was "a tangle of pathology," caused largely by the dominance of the mother and the father's absence. As Katz (1969) indicates, boys deprived of a father have no masculine role model with whom to identify and hence fail both academically and psychologically.[12] Moynihan traces the matriarchal domination and breakdown in the black family back to the times of slavery, when a slave family was often separated by the sale of one or more members to different plantation owners.

It is true that more black families than white families have no father; in 1968 three out of every ten lower-class black families had no father present. Lower-class mothers whose husbands are absent seem concerned with their own needs and often ignore or reject their children (Beller, 1967). In many families where the father is absent, rejection of all males is prevalent. Additionally, a harsh authoritarianism and punitive, rather than love-oriented, form of control are characteristic of lower-class black families (Ausubel & Ausubel, 1963). The conclusions drawn by Moynihan have been severely criticized by some social scientists who object to the blanket indictment of all black families and to the value judgments expressed about the virtues of a male-dominated family. As an example, Billingsley (1968) emphasizes that there are many varieties of family structure within the lower-class black community; he sees an increasingly frequent equalitarian family structure, where husband and wife share in running the household. Moreover, to evaluate the matriarchal family as bad ignores the qualities of strength, resiliency, and responsibility shown by women who were forced to head families without fathers. To Billingsley, the causes of academic failure in black youth are economic, not sociological.

Attempts at Intervention. Several recent attempts to enrich the environment of lower-class children exemplify another type of demonstration of the role of environment in determining social-class differences in tested intelligence. The Early Training Project in Tennessee (Gray & Klaus, 1965; Gray, 1969; Klaus & Gray, 1965, 1968) placed lower-class children in a ten-week preschool for either two or three summers. The children were usually 4, 5, or 6 years of age when they first participated. One experimental group attended the three summers before entering the first grade; the other attended for two summers immediately prior to entering the first grade. The experiences in the preschool were designed to stimulate the development of perceptual skills, aptitudes and language, and interests in school-related activities. In addition, during the school year, a visitor called upon each child's family to encourage the use of stimulating materials and to help develop greater verbal interaction in the family. The progress of the children was compared with two matched control groups, one of which was composed of children in the same city and one of which included children from a nearby city. Both of the control groups had a progressive deterioration of IQ scores over two and one-half years (averaging 4 to 6 points), while the experimental groups showed increases of 5 to 10 points. The three-year group showed more improvement than the two-year group. Although later follow-up testing indi-

[12] A more recent review (Biller, 1970) of father absence and personality development in the male child concludes that the effects of the father's absence cannot be considered in isolation from other factors, such as maternal behavior, social context, and availability of father substitutes.

cated some shrinkage in the extent of these IQ differences after the intervening period had ended, the early results (over a 27-month period) indicated that changes in environment produce significant changes in test performance. These differences between experimental and control groups were also found on reading-readiness tests given in the first grade. Differences in IQ were still present after the children had completed the fourth grade, although at that time there were no significant differences between experimental and control children on achievement tests or language tests (Gray & Klaus, 1970).

A program of intervention developed by Bereiter and Engelmann (1966) has led to similar results—changes in IQ's of lower-class children of about 7 points on the average, over a six-month period. However, the enrichment here was specifically limited to academic materials, as compared to the broader activities of the Early Training Project. Using a Bereiter-Engelmann type of intervention with children from economically depressed areas of Champaign, Illinois, Karnes (1969) has increased IQ's by 14 points.[13]

C. Motivation and Personality

The effects of motivation and personality upon class differences in tested performance need to be examined. One of the basic beliefs held by the core of the middle class (Gruen, 1964) is the high value of education. The middle class subscribes to the tradition that education is the portal to success. Hence the standard middle-class reaction to a testing situation is to respond with energy and effort (if not eagerness), regardless of the apparent validity or importance of the test (Wrightsman, 1960b, 1962). This happens because the middle-class person realizes that the results of testing are an indication of educability and of the possibilities of success and achievement.

Members of the lower class adhere less adamantly to these values. Bell (1964) has described examples of the *value stretch* present in the lower class. Some lower-class parents do have high educational aspirations for their children; at the same time, they think that 19 or 20 is a good age for their children to get married and that four or five children is a nice-sized family. Such aspirations make the achievement of a college education difficult.

Similarly, there is evidence (Rosenhan, 1966) that lower-class children are more uncomfortable and alienated than are middle-class children in such middle-class encounters as school and testing situations. Rosenhan hypothesized that as a consequence of the lower-class child's greater alienation, receiving approval would facilitate the performance of lower-class children more than middle-class children. Rosenhan verified his hypothesis by using a binary-choice task that probably had a strong aptitude component. Within the lower class, there were no significant differences in performance between blacks and whites. This indicates, in Rosenhan's judgment, that "for young children social-class differences are more potent determiners of behavior than are racial differences" (Rosenhan, 1966, p. 253). Thus, we

[13]Special intervention programs such as those described here have had greater success in changing IQ levels than has the Head Start Program. The Head Start Program suffered from too wide a variety of purposes (assessment and treatment of physical and emotional deficiencies as well as mental) and too hasty an implementation.

cannot assume that lower-class children enter a testing situation with the same motivations as those of middle-class children. The performance of lower-class children in the situation may therefore misrepresent their true level of capability.

VII. A STUDY OF RACE AND SOCIAL CLASS VARIED CONCURRENTLY

One of the few studies that looks at the effects of race and social class in the same children was reported by Lesser, Fifer and Clark (1965). In a carefully designed study, 320 first-grade children in New York City were used, with equal numbers from Puerto Rican, Chinese, Jewish, and black ethnic groups. No attempt was made to determine the racial purity of each subject. Each ethnic group was composed of 40 boys and 40 girls, half of whom were from lower-class families and half of whom were from middle-class families. (Social class was measured by use of a variant of the Index of Status Characteristics, developed by Warner, Meeker, and Eels, 1949.) Four different types of tests were used—verbal ability, number facility, space conceptualization, and reasoning—in order to study patterns of abilities in the different groups.[14] Each child was tested individually by a trained examiner of his own ethnic group, in his own classroom. The language spoken by the examiner (English, Chinese, Yiddish, or Spanish) was the same as that spoken predominantly in the child's home. The mean scores (actually normalized standard scores with a mean of 50 and a standard deviation of 10) are presented in Table 7-3.

There are provocative findings about the interrelationships of race, ethnicity, and social class in the tabled averages. For example, social class clearly affects the level of scores; for in each of the four ethnic groups, middle-class children perform significantly better than lower-class children in each of the four types of ability. Differences are almost uniform. The performance of blacks shows a greater separation between classes than any other racial or ethnic group. The authors recognize that this may be partly a function of the children of New York City but feel the data "still suggest the strong possibility that a social-class difference will more strongly affect

Table 7-3. *Four Ethnic Groups by Social Class—Table of Means*[a]

Group	*N*	*Class*	*Verbal*	*Reasoning*	*Numerical*	*Spatial*
Jewish	40	Middle Class	62.6	56.7	59.2	56.5
	40	Lower Class	54.7	48.5	50.2	47.0
Chinese	40	Middle Class	51.2	55.9	56.0	56.7
	40	Lower Class	45.2	51.8	51.8	52.0
Negro	40	Middle Class	55.8	53.9	51.2	52.9
	40	Lower Class	44.0	41.5	39.6	40.1
Puerto Rican	40	Middle Class	47.3	48.7	49.2	49.4
	40	Lower Class	39.3	42.5	42.9	45.3

[a]Normalized standard scores on total groups for each test; $\bar{X} = 50$, SD = 10.
(Adapted from Clark, Lesser, & Fifer, 1964.)

[14]The tests were modifications of the Hunter College Aptitude Scales for Gifted Children (Davis, Lesser, & French, 1960). Unfortunately, this test is neither well known nor widely used.

one's intellectual performance if he is a Negro than if he is Chinese" (D. H. Clark, Lesser, & Fifer, 1964, p. 5).

Yet the pattern of scores is much more affected by ethnicity and race than by social class. Jewish children of both classes do their best on the verbal test, while Chinese children of both classes perform better in each of the other three tests than in the verbal measure. Black children consistently do better in verbal than in numerical tests. Indeed, the child's ethnic background has a strong effect on the pattern of his scores. As Anastasi (1958) predicted: "Each [group] fosters the development of a different *pattern* of abilities" (p. 563).

There are clear-cut differences among the ethnic groups in performance. Jewish and Chinese groups generally perform better than black and Puerto Rican children. On the verbal test, the rank order is Jewish, Chinese, black, and Puerto Rican, while on the spatial tests it is Chinese, Jewish, Puerto Rican, and black. The direction of some ethnic-group differences depends upon the type of ability measured.

A replication of this study (Stodolsky & Lesser, 1967) was conducted in Boston, using first graders from middle-class and lower-class families of Chinese, black, or Irish-Catholic background. Results for the Chinese and black children in Boston strongly resembled the results for those two groups in New York. However, scores for the Irish-Catholic children demonstrated neither a distinctive ethnic-group pattern nor the usual similarity between patterns for middle-class and lower-class children from the same ethnic group.

VIII. EXPECTATIONS FOR THE FUTURE AND A FINAL CAUTION

Conceptions of *social class* and *cultural disadvantage* are becoming increasingly unsatisfactory to many workers in the field, because of the broad nature and implied value judgments of these terms. More precise and less evaluative definitions of environments are being advocated. Bloom (1964) has reviewed attempts to measure the quality of environments and concluded that the dearth of adequate measures has led to an underemphasis of the role of environments in research and prediction. Among the characteristics of the environment that may be influential here are communication and interaction with adults, motivation to understand one's environment or to achieve, types of incentives, and types and availability of adult role models (Bloom, 1964, p. 188).

A more refined analysis of the environment comes from a dissertation by Wolf (1963), who proposed 13 environmental process variables that may influence the development of intelligence. These variables are listed in Table 7-4. In regard to each of these, a child's environment can be considered adequate or deprived. A deprivation index may be developed, based upon the extent of inadequacy in regard to each of these characteristics, and this deprivation index may serve as a more precise measure of the quality of environment than does the usual measure of social class.

Wolf, in fact, found this to be true. He interviewed the mothers of 60 fifth-grade students in order to rate each child's environment on each of the 13 process variables. The multiple correlation of +.76 between these ratings and the children's IQ's (on a Henmon-Nelson group test) compares favorably with the correlations of approx-

Table 7-4. *Environmental Process Variables*

A. Press for Achievement Motivation
   1. Nature of intellectual expectations of the child
   2. Nature of intellectual aspirations for the child
   3. Amount of information about child's intellectual development
   4. Nature of rewards for intellectual development

B. Press for Language Development
   5. Emphasis on use of language in a variety of situations
   6. Opportunities provided for enlarging vocabulary
   7. Emphasis on correctness of usage
   8. Quality of language models available

C. Provision for General Learning
   9. Opportunities provided for learning in the home
   10. Opportunities provided for learning outside the home (excluding school)
   11. Availability of learning supplies
   12. Availability of books (including reference works), periodicals, and library facilities
   13. Nature and amount of assistance provided to facilitate learning in a variety of situations

(Adapted from Wolf, 1963)

imately +.40 between IQ and measures of social class (such as parent's education or social status). Davé (1963) has found similar improvements in the prediction of school achievement, using a conception of environmental deprivation. Bloom believes Wolf's and Davé's findings show that the influential factors are not the social-class characteristics of the parents, but rather, what the parents actually do in the home.

The place of overlap is just as important in understanding social-class differences as it is in understanding racial differences. Although the differences in average score are large, two different social-class groups may resemble each other greatly in spread of scores. The highest and lowest IQ's obtained in one group are likely to be quite similar to those of another group, even though the means may differ by 15 points or more. As an example, we may look at the studies using military recruits, where significant test-score differences were found between occupational groups. The occupational group with the highest mean AGCT was the accountant group (mean = 128.1), but the range for these 172 men was 94–157 (Harrell & Harrell, 1945). The 289 electricians, whose mean AGCT score of 109.0 placed them toward the middle of the occupational hierarchy, ranged from 64–149. Thus, the highest score achieved by an electrician was only 8 points less than the highest score of an accountant. Even the group with the lowest mean, the teamsters, had a range of 46–145. Large standard deviations were characteristic of occupational groups that were toward the bottom in mean score. In short, we should never judge a person's level of intelligence simply on the basis of his occupation or his social class. While these factors do produce average differences in groups, the use of a person's social class, race, or occupation as an indication of his ability level is unwarranted.

IX. SUMMARY

The construct of race is technically defined either in terms of frequency of one or more genes possessed by a population (preferred by geneticists and physical anthropologists) or in terms of certain physical characteristics (preferred by social anthropologists and sociologists). The popular definition of race—based on skin color, self-determination, tradition, custom, and law—is vastly oversimplified, especially in its all-or-nothing character. Demonstrated race differences in tested intelligence are discussed in terms of the popular definition only because it is the one that the researchers have used.

Data derived from the Army Alpha test in World War I showed both racial and regional differences in tested intelligence. Northern blacks performed better than southern whites, but northern whites performed better than northern blacks.

The existence of differences in IQ test scores of blacks and whites is well documented. The controversy centers on the relationship of hereditary and environmental factors as causal agents. In our society, where racial discrimination takes varied and subtle forms, there have as yet been no adequate studies to determine whether racial differences in intelligence persist when no environmental handicaps exist.

The small differences between blacks and whites in tested intellectual ability and the large overlap of scores make classification of persons into mental ability groups on the basis of race (especially when social class backgrounds are similar) an essentially useless exercise.

Both natural observation and intervention studies have shown that improving environmental conditions also improves IQ scores. Factors such as the race of the examiner, motivation and personality of testees, and cultural appropriateness of the test have also been shown to affect test scores—usually to the advantage of middle-class white subjects and to the disadvantage of persons from minority groups and lower-class backgrounds.

Research findings are consistent in showing that the tested performance of children from upper- and middle-class families exceeds that of children from lower-class families. Studies of interaction of intelligence with motivation and personality within social-class groups indicated that the values and aspirations of lower-class children tend to perpetuate their position in the society.

Environmental factors, which start at the moment of conception, may determine how close one's level of intelligence approaches the genetically predetermined limit of an individual's abilities. The cultural deprivation hypothesis emphasizes inadequacy of early socialization, father absence, a developing personality deficit, high levels of anxiety, and a felt lack of control over one's own environment.

The concept of overlap is also important when considering social-class differences in intelligence. The spread of scores for two different classes may be very similar, and it is not meaningful to attempt to use social class as indication of ability.

X. SUGGESTED READINGS

Gossett, T. F. *Race: The history of an idea in America.* Dallas: Southern Methodist University Press, 1963. (Available in paperback.) A brilliant, detailed portrayal of the changing conceptions of race in the last 400 years. Of similar purpose and value is W. D. Jordan's *White over black: American attitudes toward the Negro, 1550–1812.* Baltimore, Md.: Penguin Books, 1969. (Paperback.)

Mead, M., Dobzhansky, T., Tobach, E., & Light, R. E. (Eds.) *Science and the concept of race.* New York: Columbia University Press, 1968. Reports generated from an American Association for the Advancement of Science symposium. Generally written for the layman, the varied articles comprise the most comprehensive statement available of what science says about race.

Pettigrew, T. F. *A profile of the Negro American.* Princeton, N.J.: Van Nostrand, 1964. (Paperback.) A review of the health, personality, and mental abilities of the black American. Contains much useful information. Favors an environmental interpretation of IQ differences between blacks and whites.

Rosenthal, R., & Jacobson, L. *Pygmalion in the classroom.* New York: Holt, Rinehart & Winston, 1968. (Paperback.) If teachers are misled about the "mental growth potentials" of some of their students, do these expectations have any effects? *Pygmalion in the Classroom* answered this question with results that are perhaps surprising and certainly controversial.

Tyler, L. E. *The psychology of human differences.* (3rd ed.) New York: Appleton-Century-Crofts, 1965. A clearly written, unbiased treatment of individual differences in psychological characteristics. Of relevance to the present chapter are sections and chapters on race differences, social class differences, heredity, and environment.

I. *THE HYPOTHESIS OF DEVELOPMENTAL LAG: PROFILES AND PROBLEMS*
   A. *Phonological development (learning of sounds)*
   B. *Semantic development (learning of meanings)*
   C. *Syntactic development (learning of structures)*
   D. *Higher and lower level processes*
   E. *Culture fairness*

II. *THE HYPOTHESIS OF DEFICIT: BERNSTEIN IN BRITAIN AND AMERICA*
   A. *Bernstein's hypothesis*
   B. *Supportive British research*
   C. *American research*
   D. *Critique*

III. *THE HYPOTHESIS OF DIFFERENCE: THE SPECIAL CASE OF BLACK DIALECT*
   A. *Slaves and masters*
   B. *Immature language and dialect-based divergence*
   C. *Peers and parents*
   D. *Reconciliation?*

IV. *IMPLICATIONS: HINDSIGHT AND FORESIGHT*
   A. *Natural language change*
   B. *Planned language change*

V. *SUMMARY*

VI. *SUGGESTED READINGS*

Chapter Eight

Social-Class and Ethnic Differences in Language Development

by Carol K. Sigelman

When I use a word, it means just what I choose it to mean, neither more nor less. *Humpty-Dumpty, in Through the Looking Glass, by Lewis Carroll*

It is as though mankind had spun an enormous web of words—and caught itself. *Wendell Johnson, People in Quandaries*

A Texan and a New Yorker, seated together on a plane, strike up a conversation that soon turns to dialect differences. They amuse themselves for most of the flight by swapping questions: "How do you say o-i-l? How do you say b-i-r-d?"

A black Ph.D. is pulled to the side of the road by a police car. When the white policeman says, "Where's your license, boy?" the man's wife touches his sleeve to subdue his anger.

A new English teacher explains at length to her inner-city seventh graders that they must eliminate errors in their speech and writing if they want to succeed in life. The students' restlessness creates a low murmur until one small boy exclaims, "Well, maybe we do use 'ain't' and stuff like that, but we're still civilized!"

Everyone uses language to fit his everyday purposes, and justifying a chapter on language in a social psychology textbook is unnecessary. Much of the data of social psychology comes in verbal form. Moreover, language is, in its own right, a valid object of social psychological study, as most of man's influences upon other people are accomplished through speech. After reviewing the entries in *Psychological Abstracts* for the first half of the 1960s, McGuire concluded that "'language' has during that interval replaced 'group' as the second most popular area in social psychology" (1969, p. 138). His prediction that the social psychological study of language would continue to grow has been borne out.

Despite all their apparent interest in language, mainstream social psychologists have not concentrated on the study of one important topic—social-class and ethnic differences in language development. Other types of researchers—educators, cognitive psychologists, linguists, and sociolinguists—have led the way in this field, sometimes working independently, sometimes working together in interdisciplinary fashion. What these researchers have produced are a few answers and many questions guaranteed to enrich social psychology's understanding of language and communication. The topic is an especially lively one, in which visible and sometimes dramatic progress has been made. It speaks directly to concerns about divisions within our society, the socialization of children, and human interaction at all levels. And finally, the topic vividly demonstrates the relevance of scientific answers to social problems. Not only are research findings immediately translated into educational policies and procedures, but they eventually affect the generalized attitudes that one social or ethnic group holds toward another.

In examining subcultural differences in language development, we shall survey three alternative answers to the overriding question: how do children from different segments of society differ in language development? We will be interested both in what children know of their language (*competence*) and in how they actually use it to communicate (*performance*). The three approaches to answering this question utilize the concepts of developmental lag, deficit, and true difference to explain language differences between American social classes and ethnic groups. According to the *hypothesis of developmental lag,* a lower-class child will say something like, "They mine," because his language development is retarded. He is simply performing like a younger middle-class child, and, given time, he will learn to supply the linking verb since his course of development is the same as that of the middle-class child. This slow-but-steady hypothesis claims that the lower-class parent does not provide adequate amounts of language stimulation in the home. The middle-class parent—by asking questions, naming objects, and encouraging conversation—provides stimulation that accelerates the child's learning. Although the lower-class child finds himself falling behind in school, he will eventually catch up, especially if he is given extra doses of language training.

According to the *hypothesis of cumulative deficit,* the lower-class child who says something like, "They mine," has failed to define the possessive relationship explicitly. His speech, on the whole, reflects deficient learning of important syntactic and logical relationships. Rather than catch up, he will grow increasingly unable to exploit the possibilities of language for expressing complex and abstract thoughts. He is not simply slower than the middle-class child, but his language experience leads to a different mode of experiencing and thinking—a mode that does not transfer readily to the classroom. Some deficit theorists claim that deficiencies in the child's speech underlie deficiencies in his cognitive ability and that both deficits are cumulative, growing more severe with age. This situation can be traced to the lower-class home, where not only the quantity of verbal stimulation, but its quality and its functions as well, are not conducive to optimal cognitive growth. The deficit theorist recommends active, extensive, and early intervention to teach the language skills required for success at school and to expand the child's cognitive capacities.

The *hypothesis of difference* holds that the lower-class child, particularly the disadvantaged black, demonstrates neither immaturity nor cognitive deficit when he says, "They mine," for he is simply using the dialect he has been taught—a dialect that omits the verb *to be* in certain sentences. If the child is judged by middle-class English norms, he may very well appear to have problems; but if he is judged according to the norms of his own speech community, he appears no less mature linguistically than his middle-class counterpart. Lower-class children learn dialects and participate in speech events that are simply different from those of the middle class. Whereas deficit theorists interpret differences as deficiencies, the cultural-difference theorists argue that speech patterns may limit a child's social mobility but do not hamper his cognitive functioning. The only plausible reason for intervening is to teach the child a second dialect—one that carries more prestige in the society at large.

Although there are no definitive tests of any of these three hypotheses, we can still judge how much each hypothesis contributes to our understanding. As we do this, we will deal in abstractions—such as the lower class, the middle class, or syntactic development—recognizing that they are, indeed, abstractions. Each researcher samples a different portion of a continuum of socioeconomic status; and each, by his choice of linguistic measures and elicitation procedures, carves out a different piece of linguistic behavior. Consequently, we must admit at the outset that generalizations from one study to another are tenuous. But despite methodological problems and inconsistencies, we shall endeavor to endow our abstractions with form and color.

I. THE HYPOTHESIS OF DEVELOPMENTAL LAG: PROFILES AND PROBLEMS

Preschool children, whether they live in high- or low-income areas, spend a sizable part of their days learning language. Between the ages of $1\frac{1}{2}$ and 5, they learn a great deal about the sounds, meanings, and structures that make up language. In each of these areas of development, researchers have tried to discover what is learned and how quickly it is learned. And in each area, data from many sources converge to demonstrate that the lower-class child is typically slower to develop than the middle-class child.

A. Phonological Development (Learning of Sounds)

The infant rapidly comes to discriminate significant from insignificant vocal sounds in his environment; at the same time, he begins to restrict the range of sounds in his babbling to those that function in his speech community. It has been found that middle-class children outstrip lower-class children in the speed with which they approach adult norms of pronunciation and auditory discrimination. By the age of $1\frac{1}{2}$, middle-class infants are producing a greater number and a greater variety of sounds than working-class infants (Irwin, 1948a, 1948b). Recent work (Kagan, 1969) has suggested that, for girls at least, class differences may appear even earlier and may be related to the ways in which mothers interact with their daughters. However, any initial lag among lower-class children in regard to the learning of sounds seems to disappear by the age of 7 or 8 (E. A. Davis, 1937; Templin, 1957).

Much the same pattern holds when children are asked to tell whether two words or nonsense syllables sound the same or different. Middle-class preschoolers are

Figure 8-1. *In Order to Speak. (Tumbleweeds cartoon courtesy of Tom Ryan and The Register and Tribune Syndicate.)*

more successful on the task than their lower-class peers (Templin, 1957; Stern, 1966; A. D. Clark & Richards, 1966); but, by the early school years, the differences between the social-class groups have diminished or disappeared.

B. Semantic Development (Learning of Meanings)

Semantics is a branch of linguistics dedicated primarily to the study of relationships between linguistic units and meanings. Semantic development is intimately associated with what Roger Brown (1958) termed *cognitive socialization*—a general process that encompasses learning categories and organizing experience. Cognitive socialization is a lifelong process requiring much help from mature speakers. Accordingly, if there is a "hidden curriculum" in the middle-class home (that is, if the middle-class parent works overtime to help his child structure experience), we should expect impressive and persistent social-class differences in semantic development.

Since meaning is such a slippery object of study, we know far too little about subcultural differences in semantic development. But there is some support for the hidden-curriculum hypothesis. In the lower grades and even in high school, middle-class children outperform lower-class children on standard vocabulary tests (Templin, 1957; Schulman & Havighurst, 1947). Lower-class children are less likely to give mature definitions of words, ones which describe the essential attributes of a referent (Spain, 1962). And finally, in their speech and writing, lower-class children do not use the variety of words characteristic of middle-class children (E. A. Davis, 1937; Loban, 1966; Deutsch, Maliver, Brown, & Cherry, 1964). Although these measures do not get at the deeper cognitive processes involved in learning words, they do suggest that the lower-class child lags behind in his efforts to expand and use his vocabulary.

C. Syntactic Development (Learning of Structures)

Although the study of linguistic capacity is still in its infancy, several studies have shown that, compared to his lower-class counterpart, the middle-class child performs in a way that can be characterized as more linguistically mature. A series of early studies at the University of Minnesota (McCarthy, 1930; E. A. Davis, 1937; Templin, 1957) provided the first coherent sketch of developmental syntactic differences. The studies showed that middle-class children speak in longer sentences than lower-class children. Middle-class children also use more complex sentence structures than lower-class children. In general, the same syntactic measures that often discriminate younger from older children also distinguish lower status from higher status groups at any single age level. More recent studies have corroborated these findings. Strickland (1962) and Loban (1963, 1966) have found that although children from all socioeconomic levels use the basic sentence patterns, middle-class children do more to expand, elaborate, and vary their sentences. At almost every stage of development, middle-class children create more complex and more varied sentences than their lower-class counterparts.

The studies presented thus far argue that the lower-class child is slower than the middle-class child in learning the sound, meaning, and structure of the English language. The pattern is not significantly altered by ethnic membership. Although the black or the Mexican-American child occasionally fares worse than the white child from a low-income area, class differences are far more impressive than ethnic differences.

First impressions, however, are often deceiving, as an analogy to the testing of intelligence makes clear. Arthur Jensen and others have been puzzled by the fact that lower-class children do very well on some intellectual tasks and very poorly on others. In an attempt to resolve this enigma, Jensen (1969b) singled out two dimensions of concern in intelligence testing. The first was the nature of the task; Jensen distinguished between associative learning and conceptual learning tasks. The second dimension referred to the culture fairness of the test—or, the extent to which the test gives no social or ethnic group an unfair advantage.

D. Higher and Lower Level Processes

Jensen envisioned a continuum ranging from tasks that require only straightforward, associative bonding to tasks that demand complex transformations of the stimuli. The distinction was based on the finding that lower-class children perform as well as or better than middle-class children on associative (lower level) tasks but fall behind on cognitive (higher level) tasks. To illustrate, Jensen reported that both groups of children are equally successful at recalling unrelated objects, but that middle-class children recall significantly more than lower-class children, if the objects could be grouped into conceptual categories. Thus higher level ability is not as characteristic of lower-class children as it is of middle-class children.

Although little is known of the processes involved in language learning, Jensen's thinking is probably relevant. For instance, the learning of the sound system seems to be largely perceptual (lower level), whereas semantic development is more emphatically a cognitive or conceptual task. Phonology is acquired rapidly, while semantic development is a gradual, cumulative process. Such differences in the nature of tasks help us to understand why patterns of socioeconomic differences are not the same in the two areas of development. Distinguishing between tasks helps to explain why lower-class and middle-class children soon converge at the same level in the mastering of the sound system, but remain unequal on measures of semantic development.

Within the area of syntactic development, there is even stronger cause to heed Jensen's work. As we have noted, children of all social-class groups use the same basic sentence patterns, while middle-class children seem to do more to elaborate these patterns. The question is: does the learning of basic syntactic structures heavily tap associative learning skills, while the composing of more complex sentences involves higher conceptual skills? Studies that report no significant differences between social-class groups offer clues to the answer. For instance, with increasing age, children more often respond to a stimulus word (for example, *table*) with a word of the same grammatical class (*chair,* rather than *eat*). Entwisle (1966, 1968) has found only minor differences between the rates of such paradigmatic responding of middle-class and lower-class children. Paradigmatic responding fits our idea of a lower level process by being easily and quickly acquired, relatively unsusceptible to environmental influences, and grounded in associative learning skills.

Much the same holds true for knowledge of grammatical endings and word positions. Shriner and Miner (1968) asked disadvantaged and advantaged preschool children matched according to mental age to apply forms such as the *-s* plural and the *-ed* past tense endings to nonsense words. The two groups were equally successful on the task. LaCivita, Kean, and Yamamoto (1966) asked children to guess the meaning of such nonsense words as *gimmled* in the sentence, "Ungubily the mittler *gimmled.*" To receive credit, the child had only to propose a definition that suggested the correct grammatical class of the word (in other words, recognize *gimmled* as a verb form). Although both upper-middle-class and working-class children improved their performance with age, neither group did significantly better than the other on the task.

In summary, certain speech measures as well as tests of rudimentary grammatical knowledge do not support the hypothesis of developmental lag. Lower-class children excel in lower level learning ability, which is inherited by all language learners, although they fall short on measures of higher level processes such as constructing increasingly more complex structures from basic building blocks. The moral is that it is wiser to speak of differences in specific areas of language development than to generalize about lags in the language development of lower-class children. Just as testers of intelligence have often found it necessary to break general intelligence into component skills, language researchers must realize that a single answer to the question of how well a child has learned language is never sufficient. Jensen's analysis suggests that the performances of children and the conclusions we draw depend heavily upon the nature of the task.

E. Culture Fairness

The extent to which a test is *culture free* or *culture loaded* was another factor Jensen used to organize IQ test results. Although no right-minded researcher would try to measure a Russian child's knowledge of language with an English test, more than a few researchers have underestimated the possibility that our measures and the situations in which measures are used do not offer equal opportunities to children from all subcultural groups. Possibly, researchers unwittingly stack the deck against lower-class and particularly nonwhite, lower-class children.

Labov (1970) has vividly demonstrated the fact that every language-testing situation is a social situation. He described two interviews with the same Harlem boy. In the first interview, the boy's performance was almost monosyllabic, even though the interviewer was a friendly black from Harlem. Drawing upon sociolinguistic knowledge, Labov arranged a second interview, which included the boy's best friend, a bag of potato chips, and the interviewer sitting on the floor. By any criterion, the second speech sample was vastly superior, tapping far more of the child's command of language.

Most lower-class subjects are denied such second chances. They are tested by strange adults, often of different ethnic background, in an alien or inhospitable environment such as the school or the lab. When researchers happen to compare test performance with spontaneous speech outside the test format, the striking disparities often lead them to question the validity of the test (Sigel & Perry, 1968). In such cases, we cannot determine how much of a child's performance reflects ability and how much is actually an adaptive response to uncongenial social factors. There is often quite a difference between a child's *competence* (his knowledge of language) and his *performance* (what he actually says in a certain situation).

Even when care is taken to establish rapport, our measures may fail to do justice to the lower-class child. A dramatic illustration of biased methods and measures comes from research on the "language ability" of chimpanzees. Man the researcher assumed that if the voice was good enough for him, the voice method was good enough for studying language in the chimp. But Gardner and Gardner (1969) and Premack (1970, 1971) discovered how to meet the chimp on his own ground. The Gardners taught American sign language to their chimp, Washoe; Premack and his associates used movable colored forms to communicate with their chimp, Sarah. The result? Suddenly, chimps could learn scores of words and combine them in rudimentary "sentences." It was not that chimps became more intelligent, but that the researchers made more intelligent methodological choices.

Perhaps we have failed the lower-class child, as we have failed the chimp. The simplest matters often prove to matter most. Stern (1966), for instance, noticed that some disadvantaged preschoolers do not understand the meanings of *same* and *different*. Yet auditory discrimination is traditionally tested by asking the child to tell whether two words are the same or different. Berlin and Dill (1967) gave children who scored poorly on such a test special instructions to listen more carefully and offered them feedback on their performance. A control group of low scorers simply took the test again. Both black and white experimental subjects improved upon retesting—the blacks improving significantly. As for the control children (whose test scores remained the same), we can only wonder about their attention to, understanding of, and motivation for the task.

Even if the instructions are clear, the content of a test may not be **culture fair.** Whenever a researcher administers a standard vocabulary test, he does well to remember that not all children grow up with a middle-class dictionary. John and Goldstein (1964) noted that 4-year-olds from Harlem had special problems with items from the Peabody Picture Vocabulary Test that referred to farm life or other domains remote from the ghetto. The child who appears deficient on the basis of such culture-loaded items may have a command over many other words that would ordinarily confound the suburbanite. An example of this is the Chitling Test, as shown in Figure 8-2.

Whenever people live or work together, they develop special vocabularies. By adopting special words, a social or occupational group promotes solidarity and eases communication within the group, while setting itself apart from other groups.

Black sociologist Adrian Dove was well aware of the culture biases of the usual IQ tests when he constructed the Dove Counterbalance General Intelligence Test (the Chitling Test). He described his test for ghetto black children as "a half-serious idea to show that we're just not talking the same language." Here is a sampling of the 30 items. How "culturally deprived" is the white middle-class child when the tables are turned?

1. A "handkerchief head" is: (a) a cool cat, (b) a porter, (c) an Uncle Tom, (d) a hoddi, (e) a preacher.
2. Which word is most out of place here? (a) splib, (b) blood, (c) gray, (d) spook, (e) black.
3. A "gas head" is a person who has a: (a) fast-moving car, (b) stable of "lace," (c) "process," (d) habit of stealing cars, (e) long jail record for arson.
4. "Bo Diddley" is a: (a) game for children, (b) down-home cheap wine, (c) down-home singer, (d) new dance, (e) Moejoe call.
5. If a pimp is up tight with a woman who gets state aid, what does he mean when he talks about "Mother's Day"? (a) second Sunday in May, (b) third Sunday in June, (c) first of every month, (d) none of these, (e) first and fifteenth of every month.
6. If a man is called a "blood," then he is a: (a) fighter, (b) Mexican-American, (c) Negro, (d) hungry hemophile, (e) Redman or Indian.
7. What are the "Dixie Hummingbirds"? (a) part of the KKK, (b) a swamp disease, (c) a modern gospel group, (d) a Mississippi Negro paramilitary group, (e) deacons.
8. T-Bone Walker got famous for playing what? (a) trombone, (b) piano, (c) "T-flute," (d) guitar, (e) "hambone."

Note: Those who are not "culturally deprived" will recognize the correct answers are: 1. (c); 2. (c); 3. (c); 4. (c); 5. (e); 6. (c); 7. (c); 8. (d). (From "Taking the Chitling Test," *Newsweek*, July 15, 1968, Vol. 72, pp. 51–52. Copyright Newsweek, Inc., 1968.)

Figure 8-2. *Try the Chitling Test.*

Groups of teenagers and college students are notorious for their rapidly changing "in" words. In Britain, certain vocabulary choices (for example, *rich* or *wireless* instead of *wealthy* or *radio*) mark one as a member of the upper class (Ross, 1967). In the United States, Mexican-American teenagers have developed special vocabularies to express their rejection of adult values (G. C. Barker, 1947). Similarly, in the ghetto, "soul talk" brings "brothers" together and excludes outsiders (Abrahams, 1964; Labov, Cohen, Robins, & Lewis, 1968). If the chicano or the black child is tested with standard vocabulary tests, he cannot adequately demonstrate his knowledge of the words that function in his life. In a word, children from divergent subcultural groups differ qualitatively as well as quantitatively in semantic development, but our measures do not do justice to this fact.

In mentioning the various dictionaries of subcultures, we have touched upon the matter of dialectal variation. A **dialect** is a variety of a language with distinct features of pronunciation, vocabulary, and grammar. We speak of regional dialects (Southern or New England) and of social dialects (educated or uneducated). Scholars have long insisted that we work out slightly different developmental criteria for separate parts of the country. Recently, it has been suggested that the same be done for different parts of the same city. Still, the lower-class child is too often judged according to standard English—the prestige dialect of the educated and wealthy—rather than according to the dialect of his family and peers.

Jensen's framework has enabled us to place limits on the generalization that lower-class children are linguistically immature. We have shown that lower-class children are as mature as middle-class children in certain areas of development and that in some areas of development lower-class children have been underestimated by tests and measures that favor middle-class children. In general, we are able to predict that lower-class children will score lowest on culture-loaded measures of higher level processes and will score highest on culture-free measures of lower level processes. Although the hypothesis of developmental lag fits a great deal of data, it fails to account for all of the facts. Moreover, it offers few clues as to why subcultural differences in language development arise.

II. THE HYPOTHESIS OF DEFICIT: BERNSTEIN IN BRITAIN AND AMERICA

Suppose a citizen witnesses a tornado in his community. He tells his wife what he saw; then he begins to narrate his story to an out-of-town reporter. Suddenly, he

---

Simple choices between synonyms may give away an Englishman's social status. Compare some of the vocabulary items and expressions that mark a speaker as upper class (U) or not upper class (non-U). Unless a speaker starts very early to rid his speech of non-U expressions, he will always be recognized by members of the upper class as someone to look down upon.

Non-U *serviette*/U *table napkin*: perhaps the best known of all the linguistic-class indicators of English.

Study in "He's studying for an exam" is definitely non-U (U: *working for*).

Teacher is essentially non-U, though *school teacher* is used by the U to indicate a non-U teacher. The U equivalent is *master* or *mistress* with prefixed attribute (as *maths-mistress*). Non-U children often refer to their teachers without article (as, "Teacher says").

Non-U *toilet paper*/U *lavatory paper*.

Non-U *mental*/U *mad*.

"Pleased to meet you!" This is a very frequent non-U response to the greeting "How d'you do?" U-speakers normally just repeat the greeting. Replying with "Quite well, thank you" is non-U.

Non-U *home*/U *house*. A non-U would say "They've a lovely home," while a U would say "They've a very nice house."

Pardon! is used by the non-U in three main ways: (a) if the hearer does not hear the speaker properly; (b) as an apology (on brushing by someone, for example); (c) after hiccupping or belching. The normal U correspondences are very curt: (a) *What*? (b) *Sorry*! (c) [Silence]. In the first two cases, U-parents and U-governesses are always trying to make children say something more polite—"What did you say?" and "I'm frightfully sorry" are certainly possible. In the third instance, there are other non-U possibilities, such as "Manners!" "Beg pardon!" "Pardon me!"

U-speakers eat *lunch* in the middle of the day (*luncheon* is old fashioned U) and *dinner* in the evening; if a U-speaker feels that what he is eating is a travesty of his dinner, he may appropriately call it *supper*. Non-U speakers (also U-children and U-dogs), on the other hand, have their *dinner* in the middle of the day. *Evening meal* is non-U.

Civil is used by U-speakers to approve the behavior of a non-U person in that the latter has appreciated the difference between U and non-U. For example, "The guard was certainly very civil."

La-di-da is an expression with which the non-U stigmatizes a U habit, speech-habit, or person.

Adapted from Ross, A.S.C. U and non-U: An essay in sociological linguistics. In M. Steinmann, Jr. (Ed.), *New rhetorics*. New York: Scribner's, 1967. Pp. 226–248.

Figure 8-3. *How to Tell a U from a non-U*

realizes that the reporter does not know that Clem is the town sheriff, that the Wright farm is a mile from the reservoir, and that the public health agency has had a long history of inefficiency. If the citizen could take the reporter's perspective, his account would differ markedly from the version that satisfied his wife.

Such an episode was the basis of an early study (Schatzman & Strauss, 1955) in which Arkansas residents of high and low incomes were interviewed. The conclusions of the study resembled the ideas published by British sociologist Basil Bernstein (1960, 1961) a few years later. Middle-class informants were more likely than lower-class informants to introduce, qualify, expand, illustrate, interpret, and summarize in order to comply with the needs of the interviewer. Although lower-class informants did not communicate as well to a middle-class outsider, they may have been perfectly able to communicate to each other. In short, adequate communication in one situation is not always adequate communication in another.

A. Bernstein's Hypothesis

Bernstein's hypothesis is, in part, an attempt to explain the dynamics of such speech situations. In its full form, the hypothesis is a theory of socialization in which speech plays a very important part. Bernstein tried to show how social factors determine which possibilities of the language we incorporate in our actual speech. He stated the relationships between social structure, speech code, and individual behavior in this fashion: "More formally, different social structures place their stress on different possibilities inherent in language use, and once this stress is placed, then the resulting linguistic form is one of the most important means of eliciting and strengthening ways of feeling and thinking which are functionally related to the social group" (Bernstein, 1964, p. 251).

Since Bernstein's statement is sufficiently abstract, we will try to be somewhat more concrete. For example, the social situation influences the kind of speech a citizen uses when describing a tornado. When talking to his wife, a husband can take much for granted because he and his wife share so much in experience and outlook. His speech is likely to be simply planned, predictably organized, and delivered fluently. There is no need to make personal meanings explicit. If he wishes to expand his meaning, he may do so through extraverbal channels (tone of voice, gestures, or facial expression). Between intimates, a monosyllable or a glance may be worth a thousand words. Similar social conditions might operate if the citizen told his story among friends at a local bar. In both cases, the citizen would use what Bernstein termed a **restricted code,** which is status oriented, rapidly and simply planned, and relatively predictable in structure. A restricted code is used when participants share close identifications and emphasize their status as members of a group rather than their individual differences.

The mode of speech that Bernstein set in contrast to a restricted code is an **elaborated code.** When our citizen is with someone quite different from himself (the reporter), he can no longer count on shared experiences. He must recognize that his listener's perspective is different from his own and use speech to make his individual meanings explicit. Quite simply, "in jokes" are not jokes at all to a stranger; background must be supplied and logical gaps must be filled. Because the burdens are greater, the citizen weighs his words carefully and produces speech that is relatively unpredictable in structure. As Bernstein defined it, an elaborated code is person oriented, elaborately planned, and relatively unpredictable in structure.

Now let us return to Bernstein's hypothesis, which holds that social structure determines the modes of speech used and that these uses of speech mold thought and feeling.[1] By social structure, Bernstein meant a pattern of roles and relationships that covers a whole set of specific situations. In particular, he saw differences between the kinds of roles available to working-class people and the kinds of roles available to middle-class people. As a member of the working class, a person is likely to move in close-knit groups and have only a few, well-defined roles to play in society. His middle-class counterpart may travel more, have a wider variety of experiences, and experience more flexibility in his job. Social structure finds its way to the child by way of his parents. The mother who tells her son not to lie because she says so (emphasizing her status as mother) teaches her child not only a way of speaking but a way of handling experience. The mother who explains how a lie may hurt her and others in the family emphasizes the person-to-person nature of the relationship and encourages her child to relate his behavior in complex ways to the experience of other people. The mother's use of speech informs the child about what is important and what is not important in life. The child learns how to use his language, and in the process, he learns how to think and feel in ways acceptable to his subculture.

It must be emphasized that a restricted code is not an inferior one, for it serves important functions for all of us. However, if one wishes to enter into a variety of relationships, command of both types of codes is helpful. From this understanding comes the significance of codes for social-class differences in language development. Bernstein hypothesized that the working-class child typically commands only a restricted code because of the limited roles of the working-class social structure. The middle-class child characteristically commands both codes. Bernstein argued that, although the working-class child may communicate perfectly well to his family and friends, his cognitive development and school achievement would suffer without the elaborated code—the code used in school.

This is the thrust of Bernstein's thought. In order to accept his characterization of the working-class or lower-class youngster, we must agree that (a) the working-class child is confined to a restricted code; (b) his code grows out of the working-class style of life; and (c) the use of a restricted code has implications for cognitive development. Linguistic data alone, no matter how ingeniously interpreted, will not sufficiently support these assumptions.

B. Supportive British Research

Bernstein (1960) began his empirical work with the observation that the verbal IQ scores of working-class boys were lower than their nonverbal scores. Suspecting that use of a restricted code was the explanation, Bernstein selected 24 teenage boys to participate in group discussions about capital punishment. In his first analysis, Bernstein (1962a) attempted to measure verbal planning and relate it to speech

[1] Some have interpreted Bernstein's ideas as a modern version of the Whorfian hypothesis (Whorf, 1956), but Bernstein (1965) explicitly denies the parallel. Bernstein talks about differences within society; Whorf talks about differences between cultures. Bernstein argues that social structure determines speech code, while Whorf believes language shapes culture and world view. The similarity is that both chose to grapple with relationships between language, thought, and society.

predictability. In simple terms, he took a pause to mean that the speaker was making a choice and a long pause to indicate that the speaker had many options from which to choose. The results supported the hypothesis that working-class speech and middle-class speech differ in extent and complexity of verbal planning. Working-class boys spoke in longer, uninterrupted phrases and spent less time pausing when they did hesitate than did middle-class boys. Although Bernstein associated the fluency of working-class boys with higher predictability, the fact that he arranged practice sessions for the working-class groups confounds such an interpretation. As Cazden (1966) justly concluded, we cannot be confident that code differences, and not practice effects, accounted for the social-class differences in fluency.

In his second analysis of the same taped discussions, Bernstein (1962b) employed more direct and more adequate measures of predictability and complexity than in his first analysis. Middle-class boys were found to use more passive constructions, complex verb stems, subordinate structures, and adjectives—all of which indicate linguistic maturity and complexity. Perhaps the most intriguing aspect of the study was its focus on use of pronouns. The working-class boys used a higher overall proportion of personal pronouns, suggesting that these boys left vague and inexplicit those persons and things that middle-class children specifically named and described. Even more interesting were differences in the use of *I* and *you*. Bernstein took the middle-class partiality to *I* as a sign of differentiation of the self from others, and the working-class preference for *you* as a sign of close identification with others. When the middle-class boy was in a vulnerable position, he prefaced his remarks with, "I think" or "I mean," identifying the statement as a personal opinion and opening the door to disagreement. The working-class boy, by contrast, tagged his statement with, "ain't it" or "you know," making a bid for group consent and, in a sense, closing the issue in favor of maintaining group solidarity. Bernstein labeled the two ways of handling uncertainty *egocentric* and *sociocentric* sequences.[2]

Bernstein certainly did not confirm his hypothesis with the group discussion study. His samples of boys and words were small; his role as interviewer varied freely from group to group; and his linguistic measures were not always unambiguously defined. Moreover, Bernstein moved from linguistic data to conclusions about nonlinguistic phenomena without establishing the linkages empirically. His speculations about the significance of linguistic differences are just that—speculations.

Fortunately, Bernstein's associates have supplemented his findings. Lawton (1964) replicated the capital punishment study with 20 boys of average intelligence. Not only did his data support the distinction between restricted and elaborated codes, but they suggested a *cumulative deficit*. Differences between socioeconomic groups were more pronounced among 15-year-olds than among 12-year-olds. Lawton (1963) also demonstrated that the hypothesis applied to written as well as spoken English. In open-ended compositions, working-class boys more often took a subjective and concrete (as opposed to generalized and abstract) approach to the topic. Other British researchers have backed up Bernstein's finding of social-class differences in pronoun use. Hawkins (1969), for instance, in a study of 5-year-olds, concluded that working-class youngsters were not only less explicit than middle-class children but were also less able to detach their communications from the immediate context; specifically, working-class children used a great many pronouns, most of which were ambiguous unless accompanied by the pictures.

[2] Unlike Piaget (1926), Bernstein used the term *egocentric* in a nonpejorative sense to refer to recognition of differences between the self and others.

A question now arises: were the working-class children in these studies confined to a restricted code of the language, or were they simply partial to one? In other words, are the observed social-class differences a matter of competence or performance? Lawton (1968) obliged us by asking his 20 boys questions in individual interview sessions. Some questions called for descriptive answers, and other questions demanded abstract thought. When each child's answers to the two types of questions were compared, it was clear that middle-class children switched styles more dramatically; but—and this is most important—working-class boys also shifted codes to meet the demands of separate questions. In other words, working-class boys succeeded in answering abstract questions when pushed to do so. W. P. Robinson (1965) came to a similar conclusion in a study of letters written by 12- and 13-year-old boys and girls. Social-class groups did not differ when both were pressured to use an elaborated code in a formal letter to a school official. Both studies imply that working-class use of a restricted code may be more a matter of preference than a matter of inability to command an elaborated code.

Unfortunately, British research is only beginning to explore the causes and consequences of code use. Cazden (1968) and Bernstein (1970) report some of the recent attempts to operationalize social structure or social class in terms of maternal communication and control. Although such efforts are much needed, very little has come of the first attempts. Moreover, the whole matter of the relationship between characteristic code use and cognitive behavior remains virtually untested in Britain. We must summarize by saying that British research has established that restricted and elaborated codes are definable and useful constructs and that characteristic code use is correlated with social class. However, working-class children do not appear to be confined to a restricted code and may switch to an elaborated code in some settings, especially when pressed to do so.

C. American Research

Bernstein's ideas have stimulated great interest in America, especially among psychologists and educators concerned with the academic difficulties of the poor. His speculations about the cognitive implications of the use of a restricted code have supported the argument that cultural deprivation[3] is largely a matter of language deprivation (R. D. Hess & Shipman, 1965; Bereiter & Engelmann, 1966; Deutsch and associates, 1967). Cognitive deficit theorists often rely upon Bernstein in their claim that lower-class children have a limited control of language—especially in its cognitive uses. Unfortunately, Bernstein's writings have too frequently been taken on faith and exaggerated by zeal. To conclude from Bernstein's work that lower-class children are essentially "nonverbal" (Bereiter, Engelmann, Osborn, & Reidford, 1966) reflects a misunderstanding of his position, which Baratz (1969a) says has been "bastardized in this country." Bernstein himself has finally spoken out against "the erroneous conception that a restricted code can be directly equated with linguistic deprivation, linguistic deficiency, or being nonverbal" (Bernstein, 1970, p. 26).

Researchers have asked whether lower-class children in America rely upon a restricted code. Williams and Naremore (1969b) demonstrated class differences in

[3]The term *cultural deprivation* is dangerously ambiguous. Some of its users suggest that members of the lower class are deprived of a culture, rather than simply lacking a middle-class culture. Fortunately, the label is almost out of vogue.

structural complexity. Moreover, they captured the true spirit of Bernstein by analyzing speech *functions* (Williams & Naremore, 1969a). By classifying the responses made by 40 children to interview probes, they found that children of both high and low socioeconomic status met the communication demands placed upon them. It was not that lower-class fifth and sixth graders failed to communicate, but rather that middle-class children tended to go beyond the minimal response, expanding their meaning. In addition, lower-class children tended to focus less attention and impose less organization upon the topic at hand—a finding that supports Bernstein's hypothesis. The authors suggested that social-class groups may differ less in formal linguistic development than in *communication development*, which results from the kinds of demands commonly placed upon a child in using his linguistic knowledge.

Although we need many more tests of the usefulness of Bernstein's minitheory in describing the speech of American children, most American researchers have simply assimilated British findings of code differences and have gone on to determine how the broad variable—social class—is translated into maternal speech patterns and control techniques that affect the child's cognitive development. Quite simply, American research has supplemented rather than replicated British research by testing the hypotheses still dormant in Britain—those relating to the causes and consequences of code use.

The traditional explanation of social-class differences in language development has been that lower-class children do not receive as much language stimulation as middle-class children. Some researchers singled out factors such as number of family breakfasts or number of books in the home as indicators of language experience. However, Wolf (1963) and Davé (1963) foreshadowed trends in the testing of Bernstein's hypothesis in America when they distinguished between status variables and process variables—in other words, between what parents are and what parents do. (See Chapter 7.) Rather than count numbers of books or breakfasts, recent researchers have directly observed mother-child interactions. And at the same time, they have turned their eye from sheer quantity of language stimulation to the quality, sequence, and meaningfulness of verbal and nonverbal interaction.

This "new wave" crested in the Chicago project (R. D. Hess & Shipman, 1965). A sample of 160 black mothers and their 4-year-old children from four social-class levels performed a number of tasks. The mothers were interviewed, tested, and asked to teach their children three tasks—two requiring the child to sort and one calling for cooperative duplication of designs on an Etch-a-Sketch board. (See Figure 8-4.) On the whole, the results convincingly supported Bernstein's socialization theory.

1. Only middle-class mothers gave signs of using an elaborated code. Their interviews scored higher on a number of measures of complexity and abstractness. In describing what they would tell their children on the first day of school, middle-class mothers offered more instructive, person-oriented advice than lower-class mothers, who gave imperative, status-oriented pep talks.

2. On sorting tasks, middle-class mothers and their children used more mature modes of classification than did lower-class family members.

3. In teaching their children, middle-class mothers offered more praise and imposed more structure on the task than did lower-class mothers, who often acted impulsively before establishing requisites of success. In the final analysis, a combination of maternal teaching variables predicted the child's performance far more accurately than did IQ or social class.

Figure 8-4. *Observing Mothers Interacting with Their Children. American researchers have observed mother-child interactions in order to test Bernstein's hypothesis. Hess and Shipman (1965) asked mothers to work with their children to duplicate designs on an Etch-a-Sketch board and other materials. Social-class differences in the strategies that mothers use to teach their children the task suggest reasons why lower-class children are often behind in school. (Photograph courtesy of Demonstration and Research Center for Early Education, Peabody College.)*

Beyond their predictive value, maternal teaching variables have the advantage of translating the concept of social structure into specific points of exchange between the child and his environment. Hess and Shipman (1965) concluded with the following portrayal of the lower-class predicament: "The meaning of deprivation is a deprivation of meaning—a cognitive environment in which behavior is controlled by status rules rather than by attention to the individual characteristics of a specific situation and one in which behavior is not mediated by verbal cues or by teaching that relates events to one another and the present to the future" (p. 885). More than any single study, the Hess project qualifies as a test of Bernstein's broad hypothesis.

Happily, other recent studies have buttressed some of the conclusions about social-class differences in motherhood. Kamii and Radin (1967) found middle-class mothers generally more responsive to their 4-year-olds and, specifically, more likely to offer recommendations and explanations than commands. Brody (1968) reported that middle-class mothers talked more and asked more questions of their children in a laboratory interaction than working-class mothers, who more frequently ignored or simply watched their children. Finally, a study in which black and white lower-class mother-child pairs were compared with white, university-affiliated pairs detected both verbal and behavioral differences (Bee, Van Egeren, Streissguth, Nyman, & Leckie, 1969). Middle-class mothers used longer, more complex sentences in their interview sessions than lower-class mothers. In the waiting room and in a problem-solving situation, middle-class mothers were more likely to offer positive suggestions than lower-status mothers, who made more negative remarks. These differences in maternal styles are quite definitely class related and hold for blacks and whites alike.

D. Critique

Bernstein's program of research has inspired many studies that explore language development, not in a vacuum, but in the context of social determinants and cognitive consequences. Data from Britain and America tell us that (a) middle-class and lower-class mothers differ in their styles of communication and control; (b) middle-class and lower-class adults and children typically use different codes of the language; and (c) middle-class and lower-class children differ in the success with which they perform intellectual tasks, either by themselves or with the aid of their mothers.

Bernstein and others would have us believe that social structure, embodied in a mother's speech and behavior, shapes a child's code use, which in turn guides the course of his cognitive growth. We must defer judgment as to whether the data establish this chain of events. First, restricted and elaborated codes are so loosely defined that almost any quantitative linguistic difference can be used to support Bernstein's hypothesis of social-class differences in code use. But the differences are invariably differences of degree, and we have encountered evidence that lower-class children are capable of using an elaborated speech code in some situations. Second, the influences of social structure and speech mode on cognitive development have not been specified. Studies of the Hess and Shipman variety demonstrate only correlations between maternal variables and intellectual performance of their children. A correlation coefficient may suggest a plausible causal path, but it does not establish the fact that using a restricted code limits cognitive growth.

Finally, and most importantly, we must be wary of the influence of middle-class values upon research designs and conclusions. Critics (Labov, 1970; Sroufe, 1970; Baratz & Baratz, 1970) argue that a university laboratory is less threatening to members of the middle class; that the tasks chosen in these studies were probably more familiar to middle-class mothers and children; and that researchers sometimes attribute unwarranted significance to their measures. The critics fear that conclusions about the lower-class child are the product of "a pathology model with the middle-class norm as the standard of 'health'" (Sroufe, 1970, p. 142). These points are well taken. The data, for the most part, have demonstrated class differences in performance in specified situations, but they say less about any social-class differences in competence. This is not to deny the value of the data, but only to suggest that other sorts of data are needed before we can be sure that we are not underestimating the abilities of the lower-class child. More data should be collected in situations where the speech modes used by the lower-class child serve him well. Bernstein's ideas—if they are not misinterpreted as condemnations of the lower-class child and his culture—should offer useful guides to future researchers.

III. THE HYPOTHESIS OF DIFFERENCE: THE SPECIAL CASE OF BLACK DIALECT

Bernstein's hypothesis has helped us to think about social-class differences in language development; but what about the occasional ethnic differences? Indeed, Lesser, Fifer, and Clark (1965) found that ethnic affiliation can be related to patterns of mental ability strongly enough to make social class alone powerless to explain certain differences. Several sociolinguists have presented similar arguments about the importance of ethnicity (Baratz & Shuy, 1969; Williams, 1970a). Their goal is to understand why lower-class black children sometimes appear especially deficient on measures of language development. Some of the same linguists argue that cognitive-deficit psychologists have misrepresented the black speech community and its children.

A. Slaves and Masters

McDavid and McDavid (1951) have documented the long history of misunderstandings about black speech. Scholars in the early twentieth century explained slave speech forms as the product of "clumsy tongues" or "childlike mentality." Despite evidence in the 1940s that thousands of words of African origin had found their way to the New World, scholars still minimized the African influence and traced black speech to seventeenth century English dialects. In the 1950s and 1960s, this tradition of neglect continued but for different reasons. White liberals, convinced that blacks are equal to whites in all respects and confusing sameness with equality, refused to consider the possibility of qualitative differences in speech (W. A. Stewart, 1964; Baratz & Baratz, 1970). In failing to study black speech closely, these same white liberals may have unwittingly encouraged racist stereotypes, since they did not appreciate that black dialects are highly complex, systematic speech forms, different from standard English, and unique in genesis. If lower-class black speech is quasi-foreign, as Stewart and others suggest, then many past, and even present, estimates of the black child's ability may be up for revision. Our purposes in this section are to evaluate the separate-but-equal hypothesis and to ask how black dialects evolved, how they differ from other English dialects, and how they can be understood in a social context.

W. A. Stewart (1964) and others have proposed what we might call an "African genesis" model, which denies that nonstandard Negro English (NNE) spoken by uneducated blacks throughout the country was derived solely from white colonial English. Imagine the slaves, already competent speakers of African tongues, confronted with European languages. They developed at first a simplified, transitional communication system—a pidgin form—which then became the first language of their children. The resulting creole languages—still existent in some Caribbean tongues and in the Gullah dialect spoken around Charleston, South Carolina—represented a welding of African and European linguistic systems. Just as Americans learning French often Anglicize pronunciations and neglect to place adjectives after nouns, the slaves may have fitted English vocabulary into the structural patterns they already knew, pronouncing words in ways consonant with their native sound systems.

If this hypothesis about the slaves is accepted, we must then determine how much of the past lingers on in contemporary black speech. Some sociolinguists argue that black dialects, which have grown superficially similar to white dialects during decades of acculturation, still carry remnants of West African languages. Others (McDavid, 1966) argue that it is unnecessary to refer to African languages to understand why NNE differs from other American dialects. White prejudices have barred blacks from movement outside their ethnic group and have encouraged the solidification of a distinct dialect. Much the same has happened to isolated white groups such as those living in the Appalachian Mountain region. The question is one of degree and one which is not easily answered because of the difficulty of reconstructing the past. A more direct way to proceed is to determine the extent to which some black dialects (however they evolved) differ from other dialects.

B. Immature Language and Dialect-Based Divergence

Perhaps the most significant outcome of the speculation about an African genesis is that linguists of the 1960s began to look long and hard at the speech of lower-class blacks. Linguists have been able to compare and contrast nonstandard Negro English (NNE) with standard English (SE).[4] They have focused upon the structural differences between the two dialects, devoting special attention to verb forms. To cite examples, in NNE, third-person singular verbs do not require inflection ("she work here"). The use of the copula is not required in all structures ("I workin'," "she a teacher"); and the *-ed* signal for past tense is often omitted ("yesterday Joe work"). Other consistently observed contrasts between SE and NNE include "John's book" versus "John book," "there are ten of us" versus "it is ten of us," "I don't have any" versus "I don't got none," and "my brother is sick" versus "my brother he sick." A story in NNE is presented in Figure 8-5.

All in all, NNE appears to be a systematic, rule-governed speech system rather than a faulty replication of standard English. Linguists disagree, however, in their interpretations of the system. Some conclude that the speech of lower-class black children is almost entirely a class dialect spoken by many lower-class white children as well. At the other extreme, some linguists perceive deeply rooted differences between NNE and all other American dialects. For instance, it seems that some black speakers make a grammatical distinction absent in standard English by using *be* to signal habitual action; "he workin'" (today) contrasts with "he be workin'" (as always, because he has a steady job). A teacher probably misses the difference in meaning between the two expressions, as she expresses both concepts with "he's working" (Stewart, 1970).

Unfortunately, the tendency of some linguists to support their cases with particularly vivid examples obscures the fact that dialects of a single language usually have much in common. More objective data have come from a study of Harlem youth, white lower-class boys, middle-class adults, and working-class adults in a project that took all speech into account (Labov, Cohen, Robins, & Lewis, 1968). Although the speech of Harlem boys differed from the speech of all other groups, no simple interpretation was possible. A few features appeared to be unique to NNE, but other features seemed to be survivals of Southern forms that had become part of a dialect associated with blacks in the North. Labov and his associates concluded that NNE was a rule-governed dialect quite similar to standard English but different in primarily superficial ways.

Profound differences between NNE and SE do exist, but they are rare. Most differences can be explained through less extreme arguments than the reference to an

[4]It is important to remember that these are ideal types. It is equally important to remember that black speech, like white speech, is socially stratified. NNE is most certainly not characteristic of all blacks.

William Stewart (1969) wrote this story to show how the nonstandard English spoken by lower-class black children in the District of Columbia might look in print. Stewart suggested that such stories would make learning to read much easier for many children.

Shirley and the Valentine Card

It's a girl name Shirley Jones live in Washington. 'Most everybody on her street like her, 'cause she a nice girl. And all the children Shirley be with in school like her, too. Shirley treat all of them just like they was her sisters and brothers, but most of all she like one boy name Charles. Shirley, she be knowing Charles 'cause all two of them in the same grade, and he in her class. But Shirley keep away from Charles most of the time, 'cause she start to liking him so much she be scared of him. And that make it seem to Charles like she don't pay him no mind. So Charles, he don't hardly say nothing to her neither. Still, that girl got to go 'round telling everybody Charles 'posed to be liking her. She act like she his girlfriend, too.

But when Valentine Day start to come 'round, Shirley get to worrying. She worried 'cause she know the rest of them girls all going get Valentine cards from their boyfriends. And she know when them girls find out she ain't get a card from Charles, they going say she been telling a story 'bout Charles being her boyfriend. So she keep on thinking 'bout that and worrying all day long, even at school when she 'posed to be learning something from the teacher and playing with the other girls. That Shirley, she so worried, she just don't want to be with nobody. She even walk home by her own self, when school let out.

When Shirley get home, her mother say it's a letter for her on the table. Right away Shirley start to wondering who could it be from, 'cause she know don't nobody 'posed to be sending her no kind of letter. It do have her name on the front, though. It say, *Shirley Jones*. So Shirley, she open the envelope up. And when she do, she can see it's a Valentine card inside. Now, Shirley take out the card, and she look at it, and she see it have Charles name wrote on the bottom.

See, Charles really been liking her all the time, even though he ain't never tell her nothing 'bout it. So now everything going be all right for Shirley, 'cause what she been telling everybody 'bout Charles being her boyfriend ain't story after all. It done come true!

Adapted from Stewart, W. A. On the use of Negro dialect in the teaching of reading. In J. Baratz and R. W. Shuy (Eds.), *Teaching black children to read.* Washington, D.C.: Center for Applied Linguistics, 1969. Pp. 156–219.

Figure 8-5. *A Story in Nonstandard Negro English*

African genesis. However, Labov's recognition of similarities between NNE and SE did not prevent him from emphasizing the need to understand the status of NNE as a linguistic system with important consequences for learning at school. We need more knowledge of the peculiarities of NNE, if schools are to provide more informed teaching for black children.

Some of the problems faced by blacks in the classroom have been revealed by studies of immediate sentence repetition. Based on the sentence imitations of pre-adolescent Harlem boys, Labov and Cohen (1967) concluded that ghetto children, listening to standard English, perform a complex recoding operation in which they retain the meaning of the sentence but convert its structure from standard to non-standard form. For instance, when asked to repeat sentences containing the negative "nobody ever," over half of the boys consistently replaced it with "nobody never."

White middle-class children behave in exactly the same way when they are asked to repeat nonstandard sentences. Baratz (1969a) found that, while white middle-class children were more accurate in imitating standard English sentences, black lower-class children outstripped them in reproducing nonstandard sentences. As we might expect, both groups modified the original sentence, making it resemble the speech they know and use. The difficulties that lower-class blacks have in repeating standard English are shared by lower-class white children, though the latter perform somewhat more like middle-class whites (Garvey & McFarlane, 1970).

There will be more studies on immediate sentence repetition in the future. The distinction between how well a child knows standard English and how well he knows language has too often been obscured in studies that use only standard English criteria. If judgments of the white middle-class child were based upon his ability to comprehend, produce, and imitate NNE, the tables would be turned—as they were in Baratz's study. The nature of the black child's "deficit" may be, in part, the difficulty in switching from his primary dialect to the less familiar, less thoroughly internalized, standard dialect. In repeating standard English sentences and in performing language tasks in the classroom, some black children may be burdened by a translation chore never encountered by white middle-class children.

These studies imply that new yardsticks of development are required if the black child's accomplishments are to be fairly assessed. Steps in this direction were taken by Osser, Wang, and Zaid (1969) when they used the concept of *functional equivalence* to allow for dialect differences in scoring immediate repetition tests. Giving credit for dialect equivalents reduced the errors of black lower-class children, although they still fell short of white middle-class children. Another study reported by Baratz (1969b) used a similar notion of equivalence but found that the speech of black Head Start children was every bit as complex as that used by middle-class children in another study. While two exploratory, and contradictory, studies provide no firm basis for judgment, the studies emphasize the need to assess the black child's linguistic development with criteria issuing out of a detailed understanding of the dialect that he is learning. Although initial studies of lower-class blacks have shown that they are not as deficient as previous researchers had claimed, the possibility remains that black (and white) lower-class children—because of the conditions in which they live—are retarded in the learning of their own dialect, as well as in the learning of standard English. Linguists emphasize, however, this is only a possibility at present.

C. Peers and Parents

Does it matter whether a child learns language from his peers or his parents? Early studies demonstrated that the only-child, who presumably has more contact with adults, is often quick to develop language (D. McCarthy, 1954). Several other studies have shown that lower-class children, coming from larger families in the first place, spend a great deal of time with their peers (Keller, 1963). Taking the two trends together, is it possible to hypothesize that lower-class children are hindered in language development because they are exposed to fewer models of adult speech?

Cognitive deficit theorists have slighted the factor of peer influences on development and have concentrated instead upon parental influences. Sociolinguists, by contrast, have noted that speech develops in such a way that it resembles peer speech more closely than parent speech. In Washington, D. C., for instance, the speech of young blacks changed dramatically as they entered the "big boy" peer culture (W. A. Stewart, 1964). In addition, Wolfram (1969) found gaps between adult and teenage speech in Detroit.

Such speech changes with age must be traced to the peer group culture. In the

Harlem study, members of six adolescent and preadolescent clubs were studied in individual interviews and group interactions (Labov, Cohen, Robins, & Lewis, 1968). The boys' nonstandard English was quite different in form from Harlem adult speech. But more striking than structural differences were functional differences. Labov and his associates concluded that the major constraints on language were imposed by peers rather than by parents or teachers. The boys' values were diametrically opposed to those of their teachers (typically white, female, and lower middle-class). Concomitantly, language functioned differently in the street culture than it did at school. In effect, verbal learning in the peer group was irrelevant to school success.

To illustrate, the boys in school were, in Labov's terms, "functionally illiterate"—as many as five years below grade level in reading. Yet on the street, a few of these same boys were verbal leaders of their clubs, and almost all participated in highly complex speech events (for example, signifying and toasts). There was an inverse relationship between participation in the peer culture and achievement in school; "lames," boys isolated from the organized clubs, spoke a dialect closer to standard English and were better readers than club members. Labov concluded that the verbal capacities of his subjects were far greater than suspected but that their talents did not transfer to the classroom—not because they lacked ability but because their speech expressed a cultural conflict between their values and middle-class norms.

Labov's work forces us to reopen the question of culture bias. No one denies that the economically disadvantaged child is behind in school, but several observers warn that the school and the lab are not the settings in which to collect rich speech samples, much less valid estimates of competence. By studying the values of peer groups, Labov specified some of the social variables that often overshadow the influence of psychological ability. When speech functions variously in different subcultures, the researcher is plagued by a whole new source of cultural and linguistic relativity. Peer groups may affect, not the level, but the entire direction of language development.

At this stage, it is impossible to specify the relative impacts of parents and peers on the course and rate of language development. We can only recommend that studies like Labov's be conducted on the street, while other researchers enter the home. Most importantly, the attitudes and values that underlie speech behavior must be reckoned with—especially when one considers changing speech patterns in the school.

D. Reconciliation?

When paradigms clash, the lower-class child is caught in the crossfire. Some argue that the lower-class child is slow to develop language; others argue that his deficit in language learning somehow underlies his deficits in cognitive behavior. Still others believe that these two arguments are nonsense, that the lower-class child is neither linguistically immature nor deficient. For most sociolinguists, there is no peaceful coexistence of views. As Wolfram (1970) put it, "either nonstandard dialects are viewed as a *deficient* form of standard English or they are viewed as a *different* but equal language system" (p. 739). Sociolinguists, of course, are quick to reject the first alternative. But are these the only alternatives? The belief that nonstandard English is inadequate as a system of communication and as a tool of thought should be discredited. However, if we return to the hypothesis of Bernstein, we can pose another question: can some speakers of a full-fledged dialect of the language fail to exploit the possibilities inherent in that dialect? In effect, everyone has been guilty of stacking the deck. Cognitive deficit theorists, by confusing competence and performance, have too often inferred the existence of cognitive deficits on the basis of limited samples of speech. They have not been sensitive to the nature of dialect variation nor to the social variables that inhibit the lower-class child in testing situations. Sociolinguists have countered by pointing out the systematic nature of nonstandard dialects and the ethnocentric biases of research. However, their oft-repeated maxim that NNE is "different but equal" is not the final word either, for to say that one dialect is on a par with another is not to say that the speaker of one is on a par with the speaker of the other. Although lower-class children have access to dialects every bit as complex as standard English dialects, they often fail to elaborate their speech. To know that the child knows a linguistic system is a step forward, but to explain why he does not always tap its resources is a step that remains to be taken.

What we would hope for in future research is a healthy eclecticism. Sociolinguists have already initiated a dialogue by criticizing those who have wronged the lower-class child by misinterpreting Bernstein. But the same sociolinguists have much to gain by heeding Bernstein's analyses of the functions of speech as shaped by social forces. By combining the sociolinguist's concern with formal differences between dialects and Bernstein's concern with the functional differences between speech codes, we may come closer to the truth. By working out dialect-fair measures of language development, sensitive indicators of the functions of language, and objective methods of observing verbal interactions both in the home and on the street, we may begin to understand how children learn their dialects and how they proceed to use them.

IV. IMPLICATIONS: HINDSIGHT AND FORESIGHT

Although scholars and researchers realize they are a long way from adequate answers, they also know that society needs help now. In this section, we will see how research bears upon the problems of society and influences future actions, particularly in language instruction. By examining both natural language change and planned language change, we hope to use present realities to predict future probabilities.

A. Natural Language Change

Language is always changing, as a result of contact with other language groups and due to natural processes within a language group. We have already seen a lessening of the distinctions between regional dialects in America as people become more mobile and as the mass media become more pervasive. The question is whether we can expect similar reductions in the differences between various class and ethnic dialects.

Language change is amazingly democratic, allowing both change from above and change from below. The first sort of change is most familiar; when the upper middle-class introduces a new fad in speech, it very often filters down the social ladder (Labov,

1966). In New York City, for instance, pronunciation of the *r* sound in *floor* or *charge* was introduced at the top and helped on its way by prestige-conscious young adults, females, and members of the lower middle-class. However, changes also originate with the poor and work their way up the social ladder. For instance, much of the soul talk of the ghetto has been picked up by white college students and transmitted to the general public by the mass media. Although television has long carried standard English to the public, only in 1970 did it seriously begin to reflect change from below. At that time, ghetto blacks on television actually began to sound different from suburban whites. It is not just the Chaucers and Shakespeares who change language; virtually every speaker of the language has some say.

Unfortunately, it is difficult to predict the ways of language when the ways of society are unpredictable. In America, integration is becoming a reality. If black and white, middle-class and lower-class children come together in their schools and neighborhoods, the speech differences between them are almost bound to decrease. But at the same time, blacks, Mexican-Americans, Indians, and others have become more conscious of their ethnic identities and more anxious to see these identities strengthened. If this trend overpowers the urge for assimilation, if minority groups resist being lost in the melting pot, the speech of ethnic groups will continue to serve as an important expression of group identity and may grow even further apart from white middle-class speech. If both trends operate simultaneously, we may expect surprises. Perhaps more members of society will want to speak more than one dialect, or perhaps speakers will retain their unique speech habits, while becoming more tolerant of others. Students of social change could surely help the linguist predict linguistic changes, but the reverse case is even more intriguing. By reading linguistic signs, students of language may be able to predict changes in society.

B. Planned Language Change

Not everyone is content to let history take its course. For years educators have attempted to modify the speech of lower-class children. Just as natural language change depends upon the social climate, strategies of planned language change depend upon climates in the academic community, government, and society at large. Each of the paradigms we have surveyed is laden with assumptions about human nature; and each carries with it, explicitly or implicitly, an approach to education.

When educators assumed that some children are developmentally immature because of a shortage of language stimulation in the home, they bombarded the children with speech and reinforcement. When others came to regard deficient speech as the root of deficient reasoning, they attempted to teach lower-class preschoolers the formal and logical relationships of standard English. Whether it was by structured pattern drills (Bereiter & Engelmann, 1966) or by more informal methods (Klaus & Gray, 1968), many programs with young children sought to raise IQ scores through concentrated language training.

What about the sociolinguists who believe such reasoning is erroneous? Assuming that the lower-class preschooler commands a linguistic system, they proposed to exploit that system as the medium of instruction in the early grades and began to develop special reading materials and lessons in nonstandard dialects. (See Baratz &

Shuy, 1969.) The eventual goal of the sociolinguists was to create bidialectal speakers capable of using nonstandard English on the street and standard English in a job interview.

We are now in a position to step back and pose a critical question: what are the legitimate rationales for programs designed to teach standard English? Let us begin with certain cognitive deficit theorists, who argue that the child who does not command standard English is thereby deficient in logical and abstract thought. Weikart (1967), for instance, argued that a girl who reportedly said, "Des god damn peaches am burnin'!" must eventually be taught to say, "These god damn peaches are burning!" His reasoning is as follows: "The girl must learn to transform her ghetto speech into educationally functional language. The 'god damn' can stay because we're broadminded, but without the correct verb form the girl may be permanently handicapped in logical thinking" (p. 179).

Weikart's broadmindedness about language does not seem quite broad enough. We have found no evidence that the structures and forms of standard English are any more logical than those of nonstandard English. His thinking not only defies our understanding of the nature of language, but it threatens to malign and baffle the child who simply expresses logical relationships in alternative linguistic forms.

If we cannot justify teaching standard English in order to improve capacity for thought, can we argue that standard English is a better medium of communication? Are there communication barriers in America that can be traced to the use of nonstandard dialects?[5] It makes sense to think that people who share the same dialect and similar experiences communicate more effectively with each other than with outsiders; and, happily, research shows that speakers are more fully understood by members of their own social class than by members of other classes (Harms, 1961a). But at the same time, middle-class speakers appear to hold an advantage by being readily comprehensible to listeners from all sectors of society.

The same two trends seem to hold for children. Peisach (1965) concluded that lower-class children were thwarted least when comprehending the speech of children most like themselves. Eisenberg, Berlin, Dill, and Frank (1968) found that when they asked children to listen to monosyllables spoken by women of different educational levels and races, educated speakers, regardless of race, were the most universally understood. However, poor black children could best understand uneducated speakers of their own race. Only Krauss and Rotter (1968) found no such evidence of effective communication within low socioeconomic groups. They asked children ranging from ages 7 to 12 to construct and understand messages describing unusual graphic designs. Middle-class children were better speakers and listeners, constructing messages that enabled other children to select the correct design from an array of choices. Middle-class children also chose the right design more often than other children after hearing another child's message. Lower-class children actually comprehended middle-class children better than they understood children from their own milieu.

[5]The celebrated work of Karl von Frisch (1950) tells us that communication barriers exist even for bees. Scouts (the bees who tell their colony where the flowers are) indicate the distance of the food by varying the rate of their dance. However, the relationship between distance of the food and rate of dancing varies slightly from colony to colony. In other words, bee language has dialects. Imagine the poor bee who tries to do a foreign colony a favor, only to be met by an angry swarm returning from a wild goose chase!

It is tempting to conclude that nonstandard dialects are a liability, but an important control is missing. The studies generally fail to distinguish between what is said and how it is said. Only the study by Eisenberg and his associates (1968) attempted to control the content of the messages. Yet a similar study (Weener, 1969) found that white middle-class children were the ones with problems. They were not as successful as black lower-class children at recalling lists spoken by black lower-class women. The lower-class first graders recalled middle-class and lower-class readings with equal proficiency.

Weener's study forces us to suspend judgment on the role of dialect differences in creating communication barriers. Because a child speaks only one dialect of English does not necessarily mean that he will fail to understand other dialects. During development, children generally comprehend more than they are able to produce. If speakers of nonstandard English understand standard English better than is commonly assumed, then why aim a language program at understanding? The fact that speakers of nonstandard English may be misunderstood by middle-class speakers poses some problems (especially in the classroom), but in our estimate, the evidence does not support the notion of serious communication barriers. The content of a message is probably far more important than the dialect in which it is conveyed. What we fail to find is a demonstration that nonstandard English is inferior to standard English as a potential medium of communication.

A final justification for teaching standard English is the argument that it is needed in order to compete in a middle-class society. Many educators argue that lower-class children cannot become upwardly mobile without a command of standard English. Most of us know from our experience that the speech says something of the man. Studies have shown that even a few seconds of speech are enough to clue listeners to a speaker's social status (Harms, 1961b; D. S. Ellis, 1967; Shuy, 1970). The correlations between judged status and objectively measured status range as high as +.80. And as blacks who have had difficulty obtaining housing know, a person's ethnic identity is often revealed by his speech patterns.[6]

More socially significant than the ability to judge, however, is the tendency to condemn. In America, middle-class speakers are judged more credible (Harms, 1961b), more likeable (Ellis, 1967), and more suited for prestigious positions (Ellis, 1967) than lower-class speakers. Northern white, Southern white, and Southern black college students agreed in giving favorable personality ratings to speakers of standard "announcer" English (Tucker & Lambert, 1969). But whereas both white groups rated uneducated black speech the lowest of six dialects presented, black students were least impressed by educated Southern white speakers.

Clearly, a person's reactions toward speech parallel his stereotypes of people. This is most frightening when we look at teachers' reactions to children's speech samples. Teachers rate lower-class black children unfavorably on a number of characteristics and abilities after hearing brief samples of their speech (Guskin, 1970; F. Williams, 1970b). If ever there were reason to suspect a Pygmalion effect in the classroom, it is here!

The finding that lower-class children and adults, especially speakers of non-

[6]There are important qualifications, of course. What listeners really identify are certain characteristics of nonstandard Negro English. Educated blacks are typically misidentified as whites (Labov, 1966; J. F. Buck, 1968).

standard Negro English, are negatively evaluated simply because they speak the way they do pinpoints the most compelling justification for teaching standard English. We cannot tell the child that he will think better in standard English. We cannot wholeheartedly tell him that learning standard English will tear down communication barriers. But we can say that as long as he speaks the way he does, he will be stigmatized by members of the mainstream of society, even by the teachers who should be most idealistic about his potentials.

Although research suggests the wisdom of conceding to social reality by teaching the lower-class child a second dialect, some researchers have challenged the integrity of the attempt. Kochman (1969) questioned the assumption that the world will always be the way it is now, suggesting that we work to improve it by eliminating the linguistic prejudices of the majority. Sledd (1965) has quite bluntly argued that "we have no business reinforcing the blind prejudices of the community at large" (p. 701). The critics argue that speech is stigmatized because people are stigmatized. As Kochman put it, Black Power, not "good English," might move Julian Bond to the White House.

For educators who contend that eliminating even the most minor props of prejudice and discrimination is a step forward, the problem becomes one of feasibility. The schools have generally failed to give all children a command of standard English. The problems are these. When is the child to begin learning standard English? How are teachers and students to be informed of the subtle differences between dialects? And most importantly, how is the child to be motivated and reinforced for second dialect learning when he has already learned a dialect and when he returns from school each day to a nonstandard English-speaking community?

Motivation is a matter that is too often slighted. Even if the way-of-the-world rationale were clearly explained to the child, it might be rejected. Labov, et al. (1968) reported that although Harlem adults generally wished the school to teach standard English, Harlem boys were considerably less obliging. In view of current movements to strengthen black identity, increasing numbers of blacks may cling to their own dialect as an important aspect of their culture. Each educator who attempts to pull minority groups into the mainstream must recognize that for every urge to emulate the majority there is a counter-urge to preserve the identity of the minority. In short, the same societal factors that influence the course of natural language change also affect the success of programs for planned language change.

At this point, it is not clear whether or not standard English should be taught. Certainly, those children who desire it should be given help; but just as certainly, it is a lost cause to force standard English upon children who resent it and everything that the white middle-class stands for. Research has provided reasons why standard English is an asset in American society. Moreover, research has suggested other areas of language training that might deserve higher priority than is given at present. Whether they speak nonstandard or standard English, some children have difficulty: (a) elaborating their meaning; (b) taking perspectives other than their own; and (c) using speech in a variety of situations for a variety of ends. In predicting the future course of language programs for lower-class children, we suspect that standard English will cease to be the overriding concern. What may become more crucial is the need to provide every child with real motivations to use his language—whatever dialect he has learned—in new ways as he thinks and communicates.

V. SUMMARY

Those who study subcultural language differences are concerned with a child's competence (knowledge of language) and performance (actual speech behavior), but they do not always keep their thinking about the two straight. Three major hypotheses about subcultural differences in language development stand at odds: the hypothesis of developmental lag; the hypothesis of deficit; and the hypothesis of difference.

Children learn the phonology (sound), semantics (meaning), and syntax (structure) of their language. In all three areas, evidence shows that lower-class children are slower to develop than middle-class children. Social-class differences in rate of development are much greater than ethnic differences.

The hypothesis of developmental lag is too simple because: (a) lower-class children do as well as middle-class children on some tasks, especially those requiring rudimentary or lower level grammatical knowledge; and (b) measures of language development are sometimes culture loaded so as to favor middle-class children.

Basil Bernstein's theory of socialization argues that social structure, transmitted primarily through a mother's speech and behavior, shapes a child's mode of speaking, which in turn guides the course of his cognitive growth. The ways in which a child is taught to use speech have a great influence upon how the child will perceive and organize his world.

Bernstein and other British researchers have shown that middle-class children use an elaborated code more often than do lower-class children. Working-class children typically (but not always) use a restricted code of the language. The two codes differ in the functions they serve, the way they are planned, and the complexity with which they are organized.

American cognitive deficit theorists have supplemented British research by attempting to trace the lower-class child's cognitive deficiencies to his mother's speech and behavior. American research shows that there are social-class differences in mothers' styles of communication and control and in cognitive performance.

Tests of Bernstein's hypothesis in Britain and America have been criticized as: (a) too weak to support the idea that code use has implications for cognitive development; and (b) too value-laden to permit inferences about the competence of lower-class children.

Several sociolinguists have criticized cognitive deficit theories and argued that the lower-class child is a competent user of a different-but-equal dialect of English.

Sociolinguistic research points to: (a) possibilities of an African influence on contemporary nonstandard Negro English; (b) the systematic, rule-governed character of NNE; (c) the linguistic maturity of lower-class black children when culture-fair measures are used; and (d) the important influence of cultural values (especially in peer groups) on the direction of language development.

The views of sociolinguists and Bernstein can be reconciled in this way: lower-class children learn a different but systematic dialect of English; yet they do not always use their dialect in as many ways as the middle-class child uses his.

Teaching standard English to lower-class children may be justified to the extent that nonstandard speech is stigmatized in our society and becomes a barrier to social mobility. However, future educators may become more concerned about the skill with which a child uses his dialect than about the prestige value of that dialect.

VI. SUGGESTED READINGS

Cazden, C. B. Subcultural differences in child language: An interdisciplinary review. *Merrill-Palmer Quarterly,* 1966, **12,** 185–219. A sensitive review of the literature, touching upon most of the significant issues in the area.

Ervin-Tripp, S. M. Sociolinguistics. In L. Berkowitz (Ed.), *Advances in experimental social psychology.* Vol. 4. New York: Academic Press, 1969. Pp. 91–165. A broad and technical review of sociolinguistics that suggests how the linguist's formulations can contribute to the social psychologist's analysis of social interaction.

Hess, R. D., & Shipman, V. Early experience and the socialization of cognitive modes in children. *Child Development,* 1965, **36,** 869–886. A research report of the most adequate test in America of Bernstein's hypothesis.

Lawton, D. *Social class, language and education.* New York: Schocken Books, 1968. One of Bernstein's colleagues provides the British point of view concerning the education of low-income children. Describes the evolution of Bernstein's hypothesis and some of the supportive research, including Lawton's own work.

Valentine, C. A. Deficit, difference, and bicultural models of Afro-American behavior. *Harvard Educational Review,* 1971, **41,** 137–157. A critical analysis of black American culture, in which the author proposes a bicultural educational model—for example, a model that recognizes that many blacks are simultaneously committed to both black culture and mainstream American culture. Relevant to the question of teaching non-standard Negro English.

Williams, F. (Ed.) *Language and poverty. Perspectives on a theme.* Chicago: Markham, 1970. A collection of original articles and research reports by some of the best thinkers in the area of subcultural differences in language development. A well-balanced group of readings, sampling the spectrum of viewpoints.

Part Three

Social Attitudes and Attitude Change

Chapter Nine

Attitudes: Prejudice, Discrimination, and Racism

I wanted to get away; I wanted to leave Cleveland and Ohio and all of the United States of America and go somewhere where . . . blacks weren't considered the shit of the earth. It took me forty years to discover that place does not exist. *Chester Himes, A Quality of Hurt*

I have reduced everything to the simple theory that the oppressed are always right and the oppressors are always wrong: a mistaken theory, but the natural result of being one of the oppressors yourself. *George Orwell*

The concern of the present chapter is to answer questions about the nature of attitudes and of such phenomena as prejudice, discrimination, and racism. Is prejudice universal? If not, what are its specific causes? For purposes of orientation, three typical events may be presented that demonstrate the pervasive character of prejudiced attitudes and discriminatory behavior in our society.

Marilyn McKinney, an elementary school teacher from Oregon, arrives in Honolulu and plans to attend the summer session at the University of Hawaii. She begins searching newspaper want ads for a room to rent. She notices that many ads include the statement "A. J. A.'s only." Upon learning that this means Japanese-Americans (American of Japanese Ancestry), she is outraged. She calls on one of these landlords and discovers that he and his wife speak only Japanese. She now does not know whether to be outraged or not.

Mike Coleman is an undergraduate student who recently let his hair grow long. He wears a wrinkled but reasonably clean shirt, dungarees, and sandals. He finds that he is no longer allowed to eat in a restaurant near the campus. The owner tells him that if hippies eat there, his regular customers won't come back.

Mrs. Patricia Wilson has just completed a Ph.D. in history and is seeking a college teaching position somewhere in the Chicago area. Her husband works for a nationwide company there; it is possible that he may be transferred to another city in the future. Despite her strong credentials and the fact that there are several openings in the area, she gets no job offers. She learns secondhand that many department chairmen believe hiring females is risky because of their child-bearing propensities, their domestic responsibilities, and their likelihood to follow their husbands elsewhere.

In the subsequent discussions, we will focus on the causes, correlates, and costs of prejudice and racism in our society. First, however, since prejudice is an attitude, we need to explore the nature of attitudes in general.

I. THE NATURE OF ATTITUDES

A. Definitions

An **attitude** may be defined as a "positive or negative affective reaction toward a denotable abstract or concrete object or proposition" (Bruvold, 1970, p. 11). The number of attitudes is almost infinite; an attitude exists within a person in regard to every object, topic, concept, or human being that the person evaluates. We have attitudes toward miniskirts and mustaches, well-done steaks and extra-dry martinis, the New York Mets and the New York cops. Attitudes differ from values, which are broader and more abstract. Values also lack an object, which gives essence to an attitude. "Bravery," or "social service," or "beauty" may be values for a person; they serve as abstract standards for decision making, through which the individual develops attitudes. For example, a person's attitude toward an aesthetically pleasing but nonfunctional building may be influenced by the degree to which "beauty" is an abstract value for him. If "beauty" is a strong value for him, having to walk up ten steps to the entrance may not detract from his positive attitude toward the building as a place to work.

An attitude, like most variables of central interest to psychology, is not an observable entity. Rather, it is an underlying construct whose nature must be inferred. It is usually operationalized verbally—either through a response to an attitude statement, a reaction to a projective technique, or a completion of a word-association or incomplete-sentence measure. Attitudes possess three central characteristics: they always have an *object*; they are usually *evaluative*; and they are considered to be relatively *enduring*. Consider the statement: "I approve of our President in everything he is doing." The statement reflects an attitude in that it expresses an evaluation ("approve of") and it deals with an object ("President"). Although we cannot judge its transiency, we will assume (since it is so broad) that the statement is relatively enduring. But what if the statement had been, instead: "I approve of the President's stand on a volunteer army"? The statement would still involve an attitude, although the assumption of its enduring nature might be more tenuously held. The more specific the object or issue, the more likely it is that the attitude is susceptible to change. The person making this latter statement might be persuaded to reject the President's draft policy, but his overall favorable evaluation toward the President could remain consistent.

A fourth characteristic of an attitude is often included—that is, a predisposition toward action or "a state of readiness for motive arousal" (Newcomb, Turner, & Converse, 1965, p. 40). Krech, Crutchfield, and Ballachey (1962, p. 152) define an attitude as "an enduring system of positive or negative evaluations, emotional feelings, and pro and con action tendencies with respect to a social object." And Rokeach

(1968), in a recent formulation, advances a similar orientation, stating that an attitude is "a relatively enduring organization of beliefs around an object or situation predisposing one to respond in some preferential manner" (p. 112). Rokeach's inclusion of "preferential manner" may be too limiting and directional here, but the basic assumption that attitudes are predispositions for behavior is clear in all these definitions.

By relating attitudes to readiness to respond, we are saying that attitudes influence concomitant or future behavior toward the object. If we know how a person feels toward Richard Nixon, we should be able to predict how that person will behave when Nixon appears in town or when Nixon's name appears in the voting booth. Predictions based on such knowledge are often correct, but the relationship between attitudes and behavior is not always clear-cut. In 1968, as an example, many union members were most sympathetic to presidential candidate George Wallace but ended up voting for Hubert Humphrey. Many homeowners who deny that they are prejudiced express anguish when a black family moves next door.

The relationship between attitudes and behavior is currently being scrutinized and reformulated. It may well be, as Bem (1970) postulates, that in many instances one's behavior determines one's attitude, rather than the reverse. We will consider this issue in detail later in the chapter. At this point, we wish to deemphasize the notion that a "predisposition to action" is a central part of an attitude, and recognize that an individual's attitudes and actions influence each other.

B. Components of Attitudes

The concept of *attitude* is a broad one; and, not surprisingly, attitude theorists have analyzed components of the attitude concept. Historical traditions also make a contribution here. The proposition that man may take three existential stances in regard to the human condition—knowing, feeling, and acting—has been advanced by philosophers throughout history (McGuire, 1969). These three stances are reflected by the three components of the most frequent conceptualization of an attitude—the cognitive, the affective, and the conative components (Insko & Schopler, 1967).

The *cognitive* component of an attitude refers to the beliefs, the perceptions, and the information one has about the attitude object (Harding, Kutner, Proshansky, & Chein, 1969). Beliefs that women are more intuitive than men, that all welfare recipients are lazy, that Republicans are unconcerned with the "little man" all represent the cognitive aspect of attitudes toward their respective objects. Stereotypes— simple, overgeneralized, inaccurate or partially inaccurate beliefs—are a part of the cognitive component. The cognitive component is fact oriented but cannot be entirely separated from evaluation. Most beliefs and most stereotypes about minority groups, for example, are not based entirely on facts or objective observation. As a matter of fact, a person may hold two cognitions about one group that are contradictory; for example, the same person may agree that Jews are too "seclusive and clannish" and that "Jews are always trying to intrude where they don't belong" (Adorno, Frenkel-Brunswik, Levinson, & Sanford, 1950; D. T. Campbell, 1947).

The *affective* component of an attitude, in contrast to the cognitive one, refers to the emotional feelings or the liking or disliking of the attitude object. Positive feelings might include respect, liking, and sympathy; negative feelings refer to contempt, fear, and revulsion. Of the three components, the affective component may be considered the most central aspect of an attitude.

The *conative* component refers to one's policy orientation toward the attitude object, or one's stance "about the way in which persons [or attitude objects] should be treated in specific social contexts" (Harding, et al., 1954, p. 1027). The conative component emphasizes how the respondent would respond. Would the respondent vote for legalized abortions? Would he eliminate housing covenants that lead to racially segregated neighborhoods?

We shall be interested in discovering the relationship of these three components. Is each component something unique, or do all three consider the same phenomenon? The answer to this question has implications for a theory of prejudice, as well as for an understanding of the nature of attitudes. Let us concentrate our review on examples from the available literature on prejudice.

The question of whether prejudice is a psychological unity has been attacked most directly by Campbell (1947) and by Woodmansee and Cook (1967). Campbell constructed brief scales to tap each of five attitudinal components: social distance, blaming minorities, beliefs about a group's capability or intelligence, beliefs about a group's morality, and affection for the group. College and high school students gave their reactions to five ethnic groups (blacks, Jews, Japanese, Mexicans, and English). Intercorrelations between attitudinal components for a particular ethnic group were greater than correlations between groups for a particular component. That is, there was more similarity between beliefs about the morality of Japanese and affection for Japanese than there was between affection for Japanese and affection for blacks. Thus, on the basis of Campbell's study, the dimensionalization of prejudice into components seemed rather fruitless because the different attitudinal components for a particular minority group elicited such similarity of response. But the correlations may be spuriously high here, as the method of measurement and the item format were identical from scale to scale; that is, the common response format may be confounded with similarities in traits. Campbell himself, at a later time (Campbell & Fiske, 1959), has clearly pointed out the misleading nature of intercorrelations when method and content similarities are not separated from each other.

Woodmansee and Cook (1967) have made a thorough and detailed attempt to delineate the dimensions of attitudes. Their specific goal was to construct a set of scales that would measure the dimensions of the attitudes of white Americans toward blacks. After an extended procedure of item selection, analysis, refinement, and further analysis, the researchers identified 11 item clusters that were internally consistent but separable from one another.[1] Each of these clusters of items was made into a scale and was validated by demonstrating that members of pro-black criterion groups (such as the NAACP) responded to the scale differently than members of right-wing political groups or racially segregated fraternities and sororities. Table 9-1 lists the 11 clusters or scales, with a sample item from each scale. The dimensions represented here do not fit the three-component conception of racial attitudes. Rather, five of the dimensions are issue oriented and consist of both cognitive and conative elements. Two of the dimensions are concerned with acceptance of blacks and are basically affective in nature. Other dimensions also contain combinations of cognitive, affective, and conative aspects.

On the basis of the Woodmansee and Cook study, there is apparently a more

[1] A Tryon key cluster analysis was used to isolate factors or dimensions. Some dimensions correlated rather highly with each other; 8 of the 55 correlations were between +.60 and +.74. But 14 were +.20 or below, which means that the dimensions were indicating different aspects.

Table 9-1. *Dimensions and Scales of Attitudes toward Blacks Identified in Woodmansee-Cook Study*

1. *Integration-segregation policy,* defined as the respondent's position on the propriety of racial segregation and integration.
   Sample item: "The Negro should be afforded equal rights through integration."
2. *Acceptance in close personal relationships,* or the extent of personal willingness to recognize, live near, or be associated with Negroes.
   Sample item: "I would not take a Negro to eat with me in a restaurant where I was well known."
3. *Negro inferiority,* or assertions which imply or directly state that Negroes are inferior to whites in terms of motivation, character, personal goals, and social traits.
   Sample item: "Many Negroes should receive a better education than they are now getting, but the emphasis should be on training them for jobs rather than preparing them for college."
4. *Negro superiority,* or attributing to Negroes personal characteristics which make them superior to whites.
   Sample item: "I think that the Negroes have a kind of quiet courage which few whites have."
5. *Ease in interracial contacts,* or social ease in interracial situations in which a majority of whites probably would feel self-conscious or uncomfortable.
   Sample item: "I would probably feel somewhat self-conscious dancing with a Negro in a public place."
6. *Derogatory beliefs,* or a characterization of at least some Negroes as being prone to a variety of relatively minor shortcomings. These items, for the most part, are essentially true and reasonable statements of everyday fact, but in tone they may be taken as subtly degrading and derogatory judgments against Negroes in general.
   Sample item: "Some Negroes are so touchy about getting their rights that it is difficult to get along with them."
7. *Local autonomy,* or a pitting of the policy-making prerogatives of "outsiders" to guarantee the Negro's civil rights.
   Sample item: "Even though we all adopt racial integration sooner or later, the people of each community should be allowed to decide when they are ready for it."
8. *Private rights,* or attitudes regarding the individual rights of businessmen, club members, landlords, and the like, who oppose integration on the basis of their individual rights of free association or choice of clients.
   Sample item: "A hotel owner ought to have the right to decide for himself whether he is going to rent rooms to Negro guests."
9. *Acceptance in status-superior relationships,* or reaction to Negroes in positions where they are in authority or are socially superior to whites.
   Sample item: "If I were being interviewed for a job, I would not mind at all being evaluated by a Negro personnel director."
10. *Sympathetic identification with the underdog,* a measure developed by Schuman and Harding (1963) which consists of brief stories in which a Negro is exposed to an act of prejudice or discrimination. The respondent is offered a choice of four possible reactions the Negro might have in the situation. The alternative which attributes anger, frustration, sadness, or resentment to the Negro is the "sympathetic" response; all others are nonsympathetic.
    Sample item: "A colored couple is out for a drive in the country, and they pass a fine private club. The club has a sign out front describing the advantages of membership in the club, and at the bottom it says 'membership reserved for whites only. How do you think the colored couple is likely to react to this? (a) It makes them unhappy to realize that they are not wanted in the club; (b) They might think that they could easily join a colored club with twice the advantages of the club they are passing; (c) It is hard for a white person to know for certain just how colored people react to a sign of this sort; or (d) They may read the sign quickly, but probably wouldn't think much of it for very long."
11. *Gradualism,* or attitudes about how rapidly the process of integration should take place.
    Sample item: "Gradual desegregation is a mistake because it just gives people a chance to cause further delay."

(Adapted from Woodmansee & Cook, 1967, pp. 244–245.)

detailed analysis than the cognitive-affective-conative trichotomy in measuring attitudes toward a specific minority group. Yet further work needs to be done because the output of factors is so dependent upon the types of items used. Woodmansee and Cook, in using highly specific items, made it quite likely that the resultant structure would be a complex one.[2]

In general, relationships between affective and conative components are often higher than between either of these and the cognitive component; in other words, there is more similarity between one's feelings and one's policy orientation than there is between one's feelings and one's beliefs or between one's policy orientation and one's beliefs. The disparity between cognitive beliefs and feelings is often demonstrated in the following way. On a set of trait rating scales, a white person rates the characteristics of blacks just as favorably as he does those of whites; the white respondent possesses no tendency to say that blacks are lazier, more stupid, dirtier, less mannered, or ruder than whites. Yet on measures of the affective component, the white respondent expresses frequent dislike and rejection of blacks. It is as if the person says: "I feel negatively toward blacks, even though I cannot defend it on the basis of a belief in racial differences."

Some respected psychologists believe that the three components of an attitude are so highly related that their differences are meaningless (McGuire, 1969, p. 157), while others believe that the important distinctions deal with issues (as Woodmansee and Cook found). Future research will probably search for even more complex analyses of the components of an attitude.

C. Simplex versus Multiplex Attitudes

Beyond the breakdown of attitudes into components, another issue in attitude theory has practical implications. This issue deals with the individual differences in **simplex** and **multiplex attitudes.**

If we ask people to react to a particular attitude object, the diversity of responses and, particularly, the differences in specificity of attitude may be seen. In response to the question, "What is your attitude toward Elizabeth Taylor?" one individual might respond, "She's great!" Another person may answer, "I can't stand her!" If the response ends there, we are forced to conclude that the attitude is highly *simplex,* in the sense that it is undifferentiated, lacking in qualifications or elaborations, and largely evaluative. Consider, however, the following response: "I believe that Elizabeth Taylor is potentially a beautiful woman but she's gotten too fat; most people say she is pretty immoral, and maybe I would too, but I like her candor and her rejection of phoniness; she's a so-so actress, I guess: I liked her in 'Virginia Woolf' but in her latest movie she was pretty bad; she really can't be blamed for her . . . ," and so on. A salient aspect of this expressed attitude is its *complexity.* It is complex, first, because it contains many elements and, second, because the elements are often in contradiction with one another.

Thus, in studying attitudes, we must recognize that an important feature in

[2]Subsequent work by Cook and his associates has identified several additional issues on which the racial attitudes of whites vary: interracial marriage, approaches to black progress (whether through legislation or education), and reactions to black militancy (Brigham, Woodmansee, & Cook, 1972, in press).

individual differences is their simplicity or complexity. The complexity of an attitude is reflected in the richness of ideational content and the number of reactions the person has to the object (W. A. Scott, 1968, p. 207). Krech, et al. (1962, pp. 38–40) have identified three characteristics of attitudes relevant to their complexity. First, attitudes may differ in their degree of *multiplexity*. The number and variety of cognitions (specific elements) incorporated in one's attitude toward an object define its multiplexity. Second, an attitude may vary in its *consonance*—or the degree to which the elements within the attitude are consistent or harmonious with one another. If the attitude is simplistic, the issue of consonance is not relevant. Multiplex attitudes, however, can be either more or less consonant. The elements of a multiplex attitude can be harmonious and fitting (Krech, et al., 1962, p. 38). Suppose a respondent sees Elizabeth Taylor as "a beautiful woman, a talented actress, and a person whose morals are admirable because they reflect the goal of being a free person, not constrained by the conventionalities of society." While this attitude is relatively multiplex, its elements are quite consonant with one another. Other multiplex attitudes reflect elements that are not harmonious with each other and lack *cognitive consonance*. A multiplex attitude that lacks cognitive consonance is not by any means a faulty one; in fact, it often reflects an intelligent and mature response to an attitude object that is itself complex and possibly not well-integrated.

The third way an attitude may vary is in its *relatedness*, which may or may not exist in regard to a person's attitudes about two or more attitude objects. One person's attitude toward Elizabeth Taylor may be a part of his general framework—perhaps a highly moralistic one—from which he also derives reactions to many other attitude objects. If he views Elizabeth Taylor as immoral, it is possible that his attitudes toward such diverse objects as hippies, politicians, and the police may also be evaluated within the same basic moralistic orientation. If a person's attitudes toward different objects are harmonious and consistent, his attitudes reflect *interconnectedness* (Krech, et al., 1962). Thus, in contrast to multiplexity and consonance, interconnectedness deals with relationships among different attitudes in the same person. If attitudes toward different basic objects of importance are consistent, an *ideology* exists.

II. DISTINCTIONS AMONG TERMS: PREJUDICE, DISCRIMINATION, AND RACISM

Prejudice and discrimination, while often related, are different concepts. Prejudice refers to an attitude; discrimination refers to behavior. (See Figure 9-1.) Racism is harder to pinpoint; it can be considered a subset of attitudes within the domain of prejudice, which deals with attitudes toward racial groups.[3]

[3] A booklet issued by the U.S. Commission on Civil Rights and entitled *Racism in America and How to Combat It* defines *racism* as "any attitude, action, or institutional structure which subordinates a person because of his or her color." This definition includes both prejudice and discrimination in racism. Carmichael and Hamilton, in their useful *Black Power* (1967), define racism as "the predication of decisions and policies on considerations of race for the purpose of *subordinating* a racial group and maintaining control over that group" (1967, p. 3). Racism may be either an individual matter or institutionalized.

The social psychologist defines prejudice as an unjustified evaluative reaction to a member of a racial, ethnic, or other minority group that results from the recipient's membership in that group. The definition implies that the same evaluative attitude is held by the prejudiced person toward the group as a whole. A prejudice is unjustified because it involves prejudgment, or because it is illogical, derived from hearsay, or derived from a racist institution, or because it leads one to overcategorize and treat individuals on the basis of group affiliation. Thus, we define a prejudiced attitude as either favorable or unfavorable, as either positive or negative, while recognizing that a negative orientation is more frequently the case. We should look at the implications of this definition.

First, prejudice derives from one's attitudes toward groups. If a person could so individualize his responses to others that he had no general attitude about blacks as a race, long-haired students as a type, or women as a sex, he would be on the way toward avoiding the development of any prejudices. But most people cannot do this; they accept conclusions about an entire group on the basis of exposure to a few members of that group. Many Americans have attitudes toward North Vietnamese, or white Rhodesians, or movie stars, even though they have never met a single one. Attitudes may evolve entirely on the basis of impressions formed while watching television, listening to an acquaintance, or reading a magazine. Regardless

Figure 9-1. *Prejudice or Discrimination?* Prejudice *refers to attitudes; behavior that denies access or opportunities on the basis of a person's race or religion is* discrimination. *In this photograph, taken in the middle 1960s, blacks protest being denied service in a cafeteria. The cafeteria, one of a chain throughout the South, later complied with the 1965 Civil Rights Acts. (Photograph courtesy of Joe Zinn.)*

of the source, a group-oriented attitude seems inevitable. Ironically, grouping is a mature step in the development of a child's thinking; he is rewarded for being able to see that, for example, "This animal is like that one but dissimilar to the one way over there." The child is considered more intelligent if he can extract a general concept from a mass of objects. Once such concept formation is valued, its effects may become reversed. A prejudice may be formed when a person observes (accurately or inaccurately) a few discrete characteristics of several members of the same group. A man may note that his wife jumps to conclusions on the basis of limited information and that his secretary also jumps to conclusions with little information. Upon recognition that they are both members of some group (they are both females), the man may generalize his impressions to the whole group or class ("Have you noticed, Fred, how all women will jump to a conclusion so easily?") and to other individual members of the class ("Now that you mention it, Bob, Nancy is like that, too"). Not all prejudiced attitudes are formed in this fashion, but categorical generalizations about a group as a whole, based on few instances, are a part of prejudice.

The social psychologist's definition of prejudice assumes the existence of *overcategorization.* A prejudiced person may think each and every member of a negatively evaluated group is bad, simply by reason of his membership in the group. Likewise, if a group is favored, so is each of its members. Allport has stated that "given a thimbleful of facts we rush to make generalizations as large as a tub" (1954, p. 9). The most deleterious aspect of prejudice may be its eagerness to ignore the diversity present in each group of human beings.

Seemingly, prejudices imply prejudgment; we can form impressions of a person before knowing anything more specific about him than that he belongs to a certain group. Since we must often make decisions before all the information is in, we prejudge. According to Allport, a prejudgment becomes a prejudice only if it cannot be revised in the light of new information. If one becomes emotionally involved in his prejudgments, so that they cannot be altered upon exposure to better information, then the person's prejudgments have become prejudices.

It is important to distinguish between discrimination and prejudice. Acts that accept one person and reject another solely on the basis of membership in different groups reflect discrimination. These acts can be ones of aggression and hostility or acts of avoidance and withdrawal. Many times prejudice goes hand-in-hand with discrimination; but not always. On the one hand, a person may have prejudiced attitudes and yet not be discriminatory in his behavior. (A college student who intensely dislikes Jews may not object when a Jew is assigned as his dormitory roommate.) On the other hand, a person may be unprejudiced in his attitudes and yet discriminatory in his behavior. (Taxicab drivers—some of whom may be blacks—may refuse to pick up black passengers because the owner of the taxi company has told them to.)

If we return to the three episodes presented at the beginning of this chapter and again ask if each instance reflects prejudice, discrimination, or neither—our answer should be discrimination in each case. In each episode, an undesirable action is taken against the person on the basis of his membership in a group, rather than as a result of any qualities he possesses as an individual. The action may be rationalized or justified by the action-taker, but it is still an example of discrimination.

III. THE EXTENT AND COSTS OF PREJUDICE, DISCRIMINATION, AND RACISM

A. Surveys of Attitudes

How extensive are prejudiced attitudes regarding members of minority groups?[4] Do members of minority groups also express negative attitudes toward the majority? Is prejudice universal, or is it possible for different racial, religious, or ethnic groups to live together without stigmatizing each other? When attempting to answer these questions, we find we have more knowledge about attitudes toward blacks than toward any other group. A useful study of attitudes toward blacks is one by Campbell and Schuman (1968), who surveyed the attitudes of 5000 blacks and whites in 15 major American cities.[5] Unfortunately, for our purposes, no Southern city and few Western cities were included; so the study does not provide responses that are representative of all city dwellers. However, the study was carefully done and is particularly interesting because it determined the attitudes of blacks as well as whites. Individuals between the ages of 16 and 69 were interviewed between January and March, 1968.

An analysis of interviews with whites led to the following conclusions about their attitudes toward blacks.

1. There was strong rejection of racial discrimination in employment; about 95 percent of whites were in favor of equal employment opportunities. About two-thirds of the whites approved of legislation designed to help blacks achieve employment opportunities. However, only about 20 percent of whites believed that many blacks missed out on good jobs because of discrimination. Thus, whites rejected discriminatory employment practices, but they often failed to recognize that such practices have been present and have hindered the development of blacks.

2. Support for nondiscrimination in housing was less strong. About half of the white interviewees were in favor of open-housing legislation, and about the same percentage reported that having blacks as neighbors would be acceptable to them.

3. Regardless of the question, the age of the respondent influenced the attitude expressed. Young whites were more likely to report the existence of antiblack discrimination in employment and to believe it hampers the advancement of blacks. Likewise, younger respondents were more in favor of integrated housing than were older whites. Among older white respondents, the degree of education made little difference upon attitude; by contrast, in the case of respondents in their 20s and 30s, those with more education had more favorable attitudes toward blacks.

4. On several issues—such as informal contacts with blacks and the issue of employment—whites living in the suburbs expressed no more negative attitudes than did whites living within the city limits. (Suburban respondents were interviewed in only two of the samples, Cleveland and Detroit.) On the basis of these findings,

[4] *Minority groups* refers to all groups that are recipients of prejudice and discrimination. This would include some groups who may actually be in the majority such as women in the United States, or blacks in South Africa and Rhodesia. *Minority* may be interpreted, then, as not only numerical minority, but minority in the sense of a "subordinate position with regard to status and power" (Ashmore, 1970, p. 250).

[5] The cities were Baltimore, Boston, Chicago, Cincinnati, Cleveland, Detroit, Gary, Milwaukee, Newark, New York (Brooklyn only), Philadelphia, Pittsburgh, San Francisco, St. Louis, and Washington, D.C. This study is also described in Chapter 2.

Campbell and Schuman conclude that there is generally no "suburban view of race" (1968, p. 8), which differs from that of urban residents. However, on the issue of desegregated housing, suburban whites were more negativistic than urban whites.

5. When asked why blacks had inferior housing, employment, and education, most white respondents blamed blacks themselves, rather than seeing these conditions as a result of discrimination. Blacks were seen as lacking ambition and industriousness—a finding of relevance to the causes of prejudice.

6. Almost all whites believed that "changes in the Negro are possible" (Campbell & Schuman, 1968, p. 7). Most white survey respondents apply the assumption that man can change his destiny if he tries to blacks as well as to their own race.

Attitudes held by blacks were also determined by a standardized interview—but one somewhat different from that given to whites. The results may be summarized as follows.

1. Most blacks believed that racial discrimination exists and is so serious that "more than a few Negroes miss out on good jobs and housing because of it" (Campbell & Schuman, 1968, p. 6). One-third of the black respondents reported that they had experienced discrimination; about one-fourth of the blacks did not believe that discrimination was a severe problem at that time.

2. Black attitudes toward whites ranged from acceptance, through indifference, to rejection. About one-third believed most whites are well-intentioned; nearly one-third described whites as clearly hostile and repressive; and one-third saw whites as simply indifferent to black problems. While the difference between younger and older blacks on this issue was not great, more younger blacks perceived hostility from whites than older blacks.

3. Like whites, black respondents believed it is possible to get ahead "in spite of prejudice and discrimination"; 80 percent of blacks agreed with this statement. However, particular elements of the black group expressed opposite attitudes—that is, no matter how hard a black works, he cannot succeed in America. The latter response was more likely to come from less-educated blacks, who were 20 to 40 years old.

4. A preference for the separation of the races was desired by less than 20 percent of the blacks surveyed in 1968. Campbell and Schuman concluded that "'separatism' appeals to from five percent to eighteen percent of the Negro sample, depending on the question, with the largest appeal involving black ownership of stores and black administration of schools in Negro neighborhoods, and the smallest appeal [involving] the rejection of whites as friends or in other informal contacts" (1968, p. 5). Men were somewhat more separatist in orientation than women, but degree of education had no clear relationship to preferences for separatism. Young blacks accepted separatism much more often than older blacks.

5. A favorable attitude toward the development of a black identity was frequent. Approximately 40 percent of blacks favored the development of a positive cultural identity among their group.

B. The Costs of Prejudice, Discrimination, and Racism

Prejudice, racism, and discrimination have tragic and costly effects upon both the perpetrators and the recipients. The person who castigates minority-group members thereby assuages his guilt over his failure to remedy their plight. If one believes that most American Indians are really drunkards, it is easier to avoid making sacrifices to help them. The act of stereotyping may be a self-fulfilling prophecy in that it justifies actions that effectively restrict Indians to a captive group. The costs of racism go beyond such matters as the inconvenience or inadequacies of a separate school system or other segregated facilities to much more important costs—those involving the aspirations and outcomes and the physical and psychological health of blacks, Mexican-Americans, Indians, and others. Not only do members of these groups suffer prejudice and discrimination, but they also come to adopt the beliefs about themselves that are held by the majority group. A recent survey by Gurin, Gurin, Lao, and Beattie (1969) indicated that many black college students blame the black's problems upon his personal inadequacies rather than upon the social system in which he lives. Such negative self-evaluations must be modified before blacks can develop pride in their own heritage.

Extreme acts of discrimination can eliminate a minority group from the face of the earth. The number of American Indians has dropped from an estimated 3,000,000 to 600,000. Indian tribes saw the massacres by the United States army in the last century systematically destroy their leadership, and Indian groups have not overcome the toll of this planned eradication. At present, the average life expectancy of the Indian is 44 years, compared with 71 years for white Americans. The average number of years of schooling for Indians is five and one-half years, which is less than the average for blacks or Mexican-Americans. The quality of education given Indians may be an even greater tragedy. In the Blackfoot school district of Idaho, three-fourths of the elementary school students are Indians; yet in the late 1960s every teacher was white. Nothing of the Indian culture was taught. When Senator Robert Kennedy visited one of these schools in 1968 and asked if there were any library books on the Indian culture, he was shown *Captive of the Delawares*, which has on its cover a picture of a white child being scalped by an Indian. On almost every measure of impoverishment and deprivation—economic, physical, social, and educational—the Indian is worse off than any other minority group in America (Farb, 1968). Soon the American Indian may disappear as an entity unless changes are instituted.

The advocacy of *sexism*, or prejudice and discrimination against the female sex, is also costly to our society. Unlike the racial minorities, women have diminishing influence upon college campuses; presently, a smaller percentage of new Ph.D.'s are women than was the case 50 years ago (Bachtold & Werner, 1970). Perhaps this decrease results from the discouragement many females receive when they apply for graduate work. Ann S. Harris reports the following responses given by faculty members to female applicants for doctoral work: "You're so cute. I can't see you as a professor of anything"; "Any woman who has got this far has got to be a kook. There are already too many women in this department"; "I know you're competent and your thesis advisor knows you're competent. The question in our minds is are you really serious about what you're doing?" and, "Why don't you find a rich husband and give this all up?" (A. S. Harris, 1970, p. 285).

In light of these remarks, it is not surprising to find reports (A. S. Harris, 1970; Keiffer & Cullen, 1969) of differential admission standards for male and female applicants to undergraduate colleges and to graduate schools. And even after women have survived this elimination, business and industry are less willing to employ or to continue training women for executive positions (Goldsmith, 1970). It has been shown (Fidell, 1970) that university department chairmen favor hiring men rather than women as faculty members, when their credentials are otherwise identical. One case from the academic environment may serve as an example. In 1969-1970, 47 percent of the new graduate students in the Department of Psychology at the University of Maryland were female; 37 percent of the graduate assistants were female; but only 2 of the 35 tenured faculty, or about 6 percent, were women (Gruchow, 1970). Further evidence for the tendency to employ women at lower levels but not at higher levels is indicated in Table 9-2.

C. Is Prejudice Universal?

One theme of the present book is the human necessity to make assumptions about people in general. Because people account for so much of our environment, we expect them to behave in predictable ways. We subdivide assumptions about people into assumptions about more specific groups; for example, "Men do not cry," "Blacks have a sense of rhythm," or "Used-car salesmen are liars." (These assumptions qualify as stereotypes when they are factually incorrect, illogical, and rigid.) The function of our assumptions is to permit us to operate more efficiently in our interpersonal world.

Forming assumptions about specific groups occurs in every society—with the possible exception of a few remote societies that possess few members and undiversified sex roles. In this sense, prejudice may be considered virtually universal, if we adhere to our definition of prejudice as an unjustified evaluative attitude about a person on the basis of his membership in a group. A consideration of prejudiced relationships in both America and other countries may be illuminating, however, particularly in regard to causes for the intensity of prejudice. Some relevant principles and their illustrations will be presented in the following paragraphs.

When two or more racial or religious groups occupy the same territory, the degree of prejudice and discrimination expressed is a function of the relative population sizes of the groups (Blalock, 1957). If very small numbers of the minority group are present, discrimination against that group is less manifest. Though this statement is quite obvious, its ramifications are important to consider. For example, in the United States, white Southerners have always expressed more intense antiblack attitudes than have white persons from other regions. Although there are several plausible reasons for this difference, one reason is that, in the past, blacks have accounted for greater percentages of the population in Southern communities than

Table 9-2. *Percentages of Faculty Members Who Are Female at Selected Institutions*

Institution	*Full Professor*	*Associate Professor*	*Assistant Professor*	*Instructor*
Brown University	5.0%	6.0%	5.0%	4.0%
University of California, Berkeley	2.3	5.3	5.0	18.9
University of California, Los Angeles	3.6	7.0	10.0	36.0
University of Chicago	2.0	6.0	11.6	12.2
University of Michigan	4.3	10.8	1.2	40.0
Stanford University	1.6	4.4	9.6	30.0

Note: Data are from 1969-1970 academic year. (Adapted from A. S. Harris, 1970, p. 286. Reprinted with permission of the publishers; copyright 1970, Vol. 56, No. 3, American Association of University Professors AAUP Bulletin.)

elsewhere. Recent migrations of blacks to other parts of the country have altered the regional imbalance in antiblack attitudes. Also, Southerners, as a group, express less anti-Jewish prejudice than do Easterners; and, in fact, few Jewish-Americans live in the South. The South and the Far West are the least anti-Semitic regions of the United States (Pettigrew, 1959; Prothro, 1952).

If degree of prejudice is a function of the percentage of population from minority groups, one might be tempted to seek a magic ratio that is most nearly ideal for the harmonious coexistence of ethnic groups. Would it be best, for example, to have 10 percent, 20 percent, or 30 percent blacks in an ideally desegregated school? But the fact is, there is no ideal percentage. There is no guarantee that intergroup relations will be more harmonious if the ratio is 80:20 instead of, for example, 50:50. Other factors—such as the past history of relationships in the community, the speed of social change, the role of community leaders—are much more important than the sheer percentage of ethnic-group members.[6]

When a powerful group is in the minority and the maligned group is actually larger in numbers but lacking in power, the almost inevitable result is prejudice and discrimination directed toward the less powerful group. This phenomenon is seen in Northern Ireland, where Protestant-Catholic tensions run high.[7] Although the Protestants outnumber the Catholics two to one in Northern Ireland, in the city of Londonderry some 60 percent of the city's 56,000 people are Catholics. More anti-Catholic discrimination exists here. Until the British government intervened in 1969, the Protestant minority controlled the city council by means such as gerrymandering election precincts and giving every employer (the business-ownership class is mostly Protestant) six or more extra votes on election day. Jobs and housing are scarce; as much as 90 percent of the city's public housing is allocated to Protestants. In other areas of Northern Ireland, where the Catholic percentages are lower, repressive measures are less blatant.

In the Republic of South Africa, 3,500,000 Europeans live in fear of and control over 12,700,000 Africans. Segregation of the races is total. Mixed marriages are not only illegal but punishable; Africans may not stay overnight in white areas; and even park benches and post office windows are segregated. Africans are not allowed to hold meetings or to form political parties; they are jailed if they cannot produce their pass permit on demand. The policy of apartheid, or racial separation, is being extended to the development of separate territories, called Bantustans, where the Africans will be forced to live.[8] Although it is claimed that the Africans will have total sovereignty over these areas, the Bantustans are located in largely undesirable, unoccupied lands that the whites are willing to give up anyway.

The case of the Republic of South Africa is extreme because the Nationalist Party (which has been in control since 1948) is increasing its domination, belligerence, and punitive tendencies. There are a few newspapers that present an antigovernmental

[6] It has been proposed that a certain percentage of blacks in a school is a "tipping point," causing a mass exodus of whites. But research in the Baltimore City Schools by Stinchcombe, McDill, and Walker (1969) indicates there is no "tipping point." Once a school was desegregated in Baltimore, the percentage of whites leaving was rather consistent, regardless of whether 10 percent, 50 percent, or 70 percent of the students were blacks.

[7] Northern Ireland is a useful example of the fact that two groups can be prejudiced and hostile toward each other, even when no physically distinguishable characteristics exist (Klineberg, 1971).

[8] It may be sadly noted that the South African government is almost 100 years behind the United States government in establishing a policy of separate reservations for native groups. The U. S. Congress passed the General Allotment Act, which set up Indian Reservations, in 1887.

view, but the government effectively suppresses news. For example, as of mid-1971, the government still permitted no television in South Africa because of its "unwholesome influence." The South African government also maintains a Publications Control Board that censors or bans any publication or movie dealing "improperly" with any of 45 topics. *Newsweek* (1971) reported that after this board had censored the American film *M*A*S*H*, only about 25 minutes of the original two hours remained.

Government officials and the mass media can play upon the fears of the citizenry to increase prejudice and discrimination. One need not go beyond the borders of the United States to find examples. Shortly after the Japanese attack on Pearl Harbor on December 7, 1941, pressure mounted to evacuate Japanese-Americans from the West Coast and to restrict them to internment camps, so "they could not commit espionage or sabotage." Both the mass media and government officials (including Earl Warren, who was then Attorney General of California) insisted that these Japanese-Americans, many of whom were U. S. citizens, were a threat to our country's security. So, early in 1942 more than 110,000 Japanese-Americans were removed to hastily constructed camps inland, where they were detained for three years. They lost an estimated $400,000,000 in confiscated property. After World War II, the United States government begrudgingly settled their property claims, usually paying at the rate of 10 cents for each dollar of evaluation. The last claim was not settled until 1967. This internment, without benefit of trial,[9] occurred despite the fact that not a single Japanese-American was convicted of spying or otherwise aiding the enemy during the war, and many Japanese-American soldiers served with distinction in the all-Nisei (second generation American) 442nd Regiment Combat team (Bosworth, 1968).

The mass media can promote socially undesirable racial prejudice in other ways; many newspapers continue to identify blacks by race when they have committed a crime, even if the racial identification does not facilitate capturing the lawbreaker. When a white child sees blacks identified as criminals on the television news report but is never informed of black accomplishments, stereotypes almost inevitably result. One of the values of the *Sesame Street* program on educational television is that several races are portrayed in a positive manner.

Likewise, economic factors may serve either to encourage or to reduce unhealthy types of discrimination. For instance, if one group seeks the goals (employment, unionization) that another group controls, and if only one group can achieve those goals, prejudice and conflict result. Historically, the immigration of large masses seeking employment from abroad has threatened the indigenous working force and has led to prejudice and discrimination toward the interlopers. Today rigid rules still exist for qualifying as an apprentice in a skilled-trades union; often only those who are related to a union member will be accepted as apprentices. Such acts are discriminatory practices set up to protect the worker from the infiltration of immigrants and blacks.

In contrast, economic factors can also overcome discrimination. One reason for the emergence of blacks in television advertising is the large market made up by the 25,000,000 people of the black community. Likewise, businesses cannot exercise discriminatory practices in the face of an economic boycott by potential customers.

[9]The Supreme Court, in acting on the last claims of Japanese-Americans in 1967, failed to act upon the legality of the government's internment without benefit of charges or trial. Apparently, the alternative still exists should the government choose to use it.

The power of such boycotts was shown when many lunch counters, stores, and movies in the South desegregated prior to the Civil Rights Act of 1965.

To conclude that prejudice is universal is to dampen hopes for a future society where all persons are accepted equally. Still, a great deal of evidence points to the conclusion that prejudice, in some form, has always existed in competitive societies and will continue to exist as long as differences between groups of people are accentuated. Even areas that are considered cultural melting pots, such as Brazil and Hawaii, show degrees of discrimination against certain social classes or races. Certainly, the extent of prejudice may be reduced, but it is a phenomenon that may be with us for some time.[10]

Even though prejudices remain, discrimination may be reduced through legal processes, education, and governmental concern. One of our tasks should be to understand the causes of prejudice and discrimination, if we intend to control their expression.

IV. THE CAUSES OF PREJUDICE AND DISCRIMINATION

Numerous theories of the causes of prejudice have been advanced. Gordon Allport's readable book, *The Nature of Prejudice* (1954), outlines these theories, which are also represented in Figure 9-2. We will discuss each theory in turn, but first we need to recognize that two levels of analysis have been used—the societal and the individual (Ashmore, 1970). The societal explanations are concerned with situational effects upon prejudice in given societies, social systems, and groups. The individual level of analysis asks why one person is more prejudiced than another.

A. Historical Emphasis and Emphasis on Economic Exploitation

The historian reminds us that the causes of prejudice cannot be fully understood without studying the historical background of the relevant conflicts. At the societal level of analysis, it is a sad fact that most prejudices toward minority groups have a long history in America. Allport points out that antiblack prejudice, for example, has

[10]Karlins, Coffman, and Walters (1969), in comparing the stereotypes of ethnic groups held by three generations of Princeton students, found that more recent students protest more often about the requirement of assigning trait names to any ethnic or racial group. Many students still comply, however. In 1967, these investigators gave the current Princeton undergraduates the same task that Katz and Braly had administered to Princeton students in the mid-1930s and that Gilbert had given in 1951. The study provides little hope that negative stereotypes will gradually fade from existence. The 1951 group was less uniform in the traits its members assigned to racial groups, but the 1967 group showed almost as much agreement over the traits it assigned as the original 1937 group. The earlier stereotypes had been replaced with others. In 1967, blacks were no longer rated as superstitious but were considered musical. The extent of agreement between 1967 students' ratings was high. Research in 1970 indicated that the degree to which white college students agree with the predominant white view of blacks is significantly related to the extent of whites' negative racial attitudes. That is, the more racially prejudiced whites show greater agreement with the societal view of blacks (Brigham, 1971b).

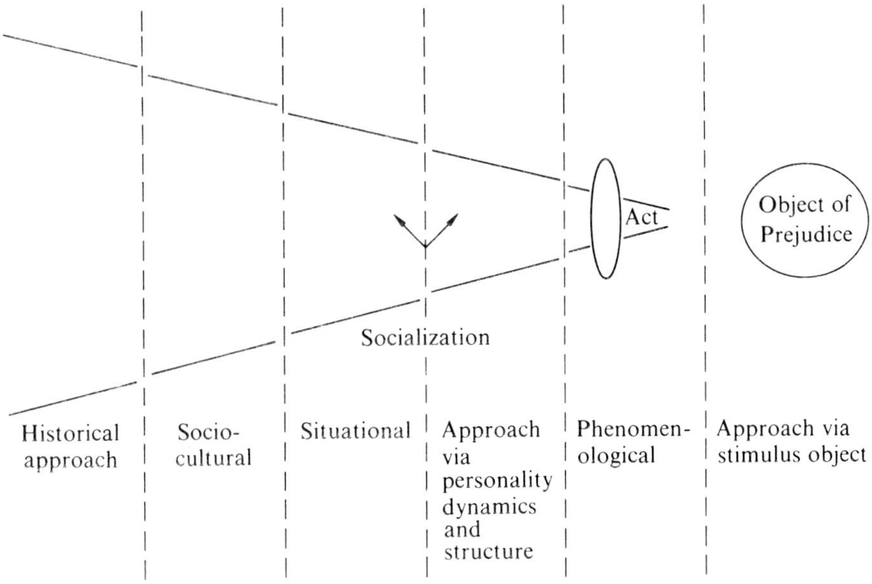

Figure 9-2. *Theoretical and Methodological Approaches to the Study of the Causes of Prejudice. (Adapted from G. W. Allport, Prejudice: a problem in psychological and social causation.* Journal of Social Issues, *Supplement Series, No. 4, 1950. Reprinted with permission of the publisher; copyright 1950, Society for the Psychological Study of Social Issues.)*

its roots in slavery and the slaveowner's deliberate separation of black families, in the exploitation of blacks by carpetbaggers, and in the failure of Reconstruction in the South after the Civil War.

Certain historically oriented theories of prejudice emphasize economic factors. For example, advocates of the theories of Karl Marx see prejudice as a way of letting the rulers exploit the laboring class. As Cox has stated: "Race prejudice is a social attitude propagated among the public by an exploiting class for the purpose of stigmatizing some groups as inferior so that the exploitation of either the group itself or its resources may both be justified" (1948, p. 393). Treatment of black slaves before the Civil War, or treatment of Oriental immigrants in California 75 years ago, are examples.

Colonialism, which arose from economic and other national needs in the eighteenth and nineteenth centuries, was justified on the basis of beliefs that colonial peoples were "a lower form of the species" or "the white man's burden" to be borne magnanimously. In actuality, colonialism provided European nations with cheap sources of materials and captive markets for goods. We may wonder, as Blauner (1969) does, what the outcome will be as poorly educated blacks become economically dispensable in a society where unskilled labor is being replaced by automation.

Economic exploitation is not of historical interest alone. Kenneth B. Clark (1965) has shown how the political, economic, and social structure of Harlem is in many ways that of a colony, and Senator Eugene McCarthy referred to black Americans as a colonized people during his 1968 presidential campaign. Economic exploitation is still utilized as a justification for paying unskilled workers less than a living wage. ("Pay 'em more and they'd waste it away.") Contrary to this assumption about the nature of the masses, however, recent studies indicate that when families on welfare are given increased payments, they tend to spend it on necessary items, rather than on unessentials or frivolities.

Despite its usefulness in the understanding of prejudice against some minority groups, the historical approach does not provide an inclusive answer to the question of the causes of prejudice. It neither explains why some people in power are more prejudiced than others, nor why some groups are the object of prejudice more than others. Why does one child in a family grow up to be a bigot while another heads the local Urban League? The economic-exploitation theory does not explain why certain immigrant groups that came to America were exploited without suffering the degree of prejudice that blacks and Jews have received. Southern white sharecroppers are exploited by the ownership class to the same degree as black sharecroppers, yet they have not been harassed by lynch mobs or arsonists.

B. Sociocultural Emphasis

Sociologists and anthropologists emphasize sociocultural factors as determinants of prejudice, discrimination, racism, and intergroup conflict. Among these sociocultural factors are (a) the phenomena of increased urbanization, mechanization, and complexity; (b) the upward mobility of certain groups; (c) the increased emphasis on competence and training and the scarcity of jobs and the competition to get them; (d) the increased population in the face of a limited amount of usable land and lack of adequate housing; (e) the inability to develop internal standards, leading to a reliance on others (individuals, organizations, the mass media, or advertising) and a conforming type of behavior; (f) changes in the role and function of the family with concomitant changes in standards of morality.

The overt racism demonstrated in the early 1970s by members of the English working class may reflect the threat to full employment posed by the influx of large numbers of Pakistanis, Indians, and blacks from the West Indies (Esman, 1970). As another example, increased urbanization can be considered a cause of prejudice against ethnic groups. Watson (1950) found that many of his subjects became more anti-Semitic after they had moved to the New York City area. In the big city, depersonalization is the rule; the New York subway rider will probably see different people on tomorrow's ride. Urban life also pushes and shoves, crushes and destroys.

Also, mass man in the city follows the conventions of the times. Material values are emphasized, and the poor are looked upon with contempt because they have not reached the level of material existence prescribed by the sociocultural conventions. But even as we submit to the pressure of materialistic values, we despise the city that promotes them. Urban traits—dishonesty, deceit, ambitiousness, vulgarity, loudness—are exemplified in the stereotype of the Jew. The late sociologist, Arnold Rose, believed that "The Jews are hated today primarily because they serve as a symbol of city life" (1948, p. 374); in particular, they are the symbol of New York City.

This theory does a good job of explaining prejudices toward urbanized minority groups as well as toward groups that have not accepted white, middle-class values. But it does not explain the hostility toward hardworking Japanese-American farmers during World War II, or the fact that farm dwellers—isolated from the depersonalized, pulverizing city—possess as much prejudice as urban dwellers.

C. Situational Emphasis

Let us now turn to explanations that operate at the individual level. The first of these is the situational emphasis. Allport derives the situational emphasis by subtracting the historical background from the sociocultural approach. The situational emphasis is oriented toward the present; it places the causes of prejudice upon current forces in the environment. The atmosphere in which the child grows up influences his beliefs and behaviors; if his parents, teachers, and peers express prejudiced attitudes and act in discriminatory ways, he is likely to learn these responses and adopt them as his own. The norms of many groups may implicitly or explicitly teach prejudice to children who grow up within the groups. Imitation of parents and modeling by parents and older children are among the vehicles for the transmission of prejudiced beliefs. Conformity to others is a strong influence in theories that blame the situation for the development of prejudice in the person. As Schellenberg (1970) indicates, we gain social approval by conforming to the opinions about national groups held by our friends and associates.

Changes over time in specific stereotypes of a racial or national group often reflect this situational emphasis. During World War II, Americans were exposed to government propaganda, leading to adoption of negative stereotypes of Japanese and Germans and favorable stereotypes of our allies, including the Russians. Early in the war most Americans described the Russians as hardworking and brave. In 1948, as postwar conflicts between the two great powers emerged, the stereotypes were quite different—as Table 9-3 indicates. While hardworking was still seen as an appropriate description, more Americans believed Russians were cruel. In a world where the Soviet Union was no longer our ally—but rather our competitor—our assumptions about the nature of Russians changed.

D. Psychodynamic Emphasis

Directly opposed to the situational emphasis is one that sees prejudice as a result of the prejudiced person's conflicts and maladjustments. Here, we find theories that

Table 9-3 *Percent of American Respondents Who Agreed that the Following Adjectives Described the Russians*

Adjective	*Percent Agreeing* *In 1942*	*In 1948*
Hardworking	61	49
Intelligent	16	12
Practical	18	13
Conceited	3	28
Cruel	9	50
Brave	48	28
Progressive	24	15

(From Buchanan & Cantril, 1953, p. 55. Reprinted with permission of the publisher. Copyright 1953, University of Illinois Press.)

are essentially psychological—in contrast to the historical, economic, and sociological emphases of previous approaches.

Two types of *psychodynamic* theories of prejudice are useful. One of these assumes that prejudice is rooted in the nature of man because **frustration** is inevitable in human life. Frustration and deprivation lead to hostile impulses, "which if not controlled are likely to discharge against ethnic minorities" (Allport, 1954, p. 209). Displacement of hostility upon less powerful groups, or **scapegoating,** is a result of frustration when the source of the frustration is not available for attack or is not attackable for other reasons. Lynching of blacks, burning of synagogues, or other assaults on minority groups may occur.[11]

The approach represented by **psychoanalytic theory** is a related notion that emphasizes the unconscious processes that influence the development of prejudice. This theory notes that prejudice may serve the unconscious in a variety of ways; it may cover up severe inferiority feelings, help resolve guilt feelings, and act as a displacement of frustration. For example, George Wallace's 1968 presidential campaign was partly directed toward poor white voters who were threatened by the fact that blacks were moving up the socioeconomic ladder, while they were not.

Within the psychodynamic emphasis, a second type of approach focuses upon the development of prejudice only in certain people who have a *personality defect* or weak *character structure.* The normality of prejudice is not accepted here; instead, prejudice is postulated to be the result of strong anxieties and insecurities present in neurotic persons. A similar approach derives from authoritarianism, which conceptualizes prejudice as a function of the antidemocratic orientation within certain people. This antidemocratic or authoritarian ideology includes extreme conservatism and ethnocentrism in addition to prejudice.

As Pettigrew (1961) shows, each of these explanations of prejudice within the psychodynamic approach represents an *externalization process,* in which the person applies his ways of dealing with personal problems to the structuring of outside events. But there exist prejudiced persons to whom the psychodynamic emphasis does not apply. It is a particularly inadequate explanation where prejudice is manifest in the entire environment.

E. Phenomenological Emphasis

The phenomenological emphasis advances the interesting notion that what should be studied is not the objective world, but the individual's perception of the world. A person's responses follow from his perception of the world; if he perceives

[11]Ashmore (1970) reviews evidence for a frustration theory of prejudice, finding some studies that demonstrate scapegoating but others that do not. For example, Allport and Kramer (1946) report that among Catholic students, those who complained of being discriminated against because they were Catholic were more antiblack and anti-Semitic than were other Catholic students. However, children with highly punitive parents (as measured by the children's ratings) are not more prejudiced toward minority groups than are children with less punitive parents (Epstein & Komorita, 1965a, 1965b, 1966). In evaluating frustration theories, Ashmore makes a very useful distinction between shared threats and personal threats. A shared threat, such as the possibility that one's community might be hit by a hurricane, has the effect of bringing people together; such a threat has been found to reduce antiblack prejudice (Feshbach & Singer, 1957). But a personal threat has, as frustration theory would predict, an escalating effect upon prejudice.

members of a minority group as hostile or threatening, he responds to them aggressively. Genuinely conciliatory behavior on the part of the Black Panthers, for example, is irrelevant if white policemen have been brainwashed to believe that the Panthers are out to get them.

With the phenomenological emphasis we have reached the immediate level of causation as represented in Figure 9-2. But our survey of approaches is not complete until we consider the stimulus object of prejudice itself.

F. Emphasis on Earned Reputation

All the previous approaches have localized the source of prejudice in the observer. They have failed to consider that minority groups, by their behavior or characteristics, may precipitate the negative feelings that are directed toward them. The *earned reputation* theory postulates that minority groups possess characteristics that provoke dislike and hostility. Daniel P. Moynihan, recent counselor to President Nixon, in one of his incendiary memos, exemplified a belief that white p rsons may have some good reasons for their negative attitudes toward lower-class blacks. Moynihan wrote: "It is the existence of this lower class with its high rates of crime, dependency, and general disorderliness, that causes nearby whites . . . to fear Negroes and to seek by various ways to avoid and constrain them" (quoted in "Moynihan's Memo Fever," *Time*, March 23, 1970, pp. 15–16). Likewise, in his controversial book *The Unheavenly City* (1970), political scientist Edward C. Banfield proposes that lower-class blacks remain trapped in their ghettos because they do not possess the skills necessary to escape.

These viewpoints to the contrary, few social scientists believe that the characteristics of the minority group are a major cause of the hostile attitudes toward them. There is increasing evidence, however, that the earned reputation theory may contain some truth to it. For example, Triandis and Vassiliou conclude: "The present data [from Greek and American subjects] suggest that there is a 'kernel of truth' in most stereotypes *when they are elicited from people who have firsthand knowledge of the group being stereotyped*" (1967, p. 324, italics in original). A careful review by Brigham (1971a) concludes that ethnic stereotypes can have a "kernel of truth" in the sense that different groups of responders agree upon which traits identify a particular object group. But often we lack the information to know if the object group actually possesses such traits. The attribution of negative characteristics to a group should be avoided until we can prove our charges.

None of these causes of prejudice is sufficient to explain every case; a phenomenon as pervasive as prejudice has many sources. A specific person's prejudice against some group may develop out of what he has learned from his environment and his own personal frustrations. Thus, we must acknowledge the multiple causation of prejudice, while realizing that attempts to identify specific causes for individual cases of prejudice are helpful. For example, in seeking ways to change attitudes, we must keep in mind that the task may require different emphases if the causes of prejudice are different. Changing a prejudice that stems from growing up in an environment that teaches the prejudice calls for reeducation; changing a prejudice that results from personal frustrations or hostilities requires perhaps deeper therapeutic devices.

V. SOCIAL DISTANCE

Another way of looking at the causes of prejudice is to examine the reasons for a person's preference for remaining segregated from members of another race or ethnic group. The term **social distance** is used to refer to a person's acceptable degree of relationship with members of minority groups (Westie, 1953). Social distance is usually measured by asking whether the person would accept members of group X as close friends, invite them to a party, let them live in his neighborhood, vote for one of them for Congressman, and so on.

In cases where a white person rejects blacks, the question arises as to the white's reasons for desiring social distance. In recent years a controversy has developed among psychologists: does this rejection occur because the white assumes that blacks hold different values or because of more blatant racial reasons? Does racial prejudice stem from an expectation that the other racial group is different? In *The Open and Closed Mind* (1960), Rokeach has argued that prejudice or rejection may be largely a result of a perceived dissimilarity in values. Rokeach argues that if a white person rejects blacks, he does not do so on the basis of the other person being black per se but because he sees blacks as possessing different values, habits, and life styles than whites. Rokeach, Smith, and Evans (1960) described two studies in which subjects indicated how friendly they would feel toward a variety of persons who differed in racial and religious backgrounds and in beliefs on important issues. It was found that friendship was based much more on congruence of beliefs between the subject and the stimulus person than it was on racial or religious grounds.

Triandis (1961) has argued, however, that people reject other individuals because of their race per se. He stated: "People do not exclude other people from their neighborhood, for instance, because the other people have different [values], but they do exclude them because they are Negroes" (1961, p. 186). Triandis reported results contrary to Rokeach's findings, using more behaviorally oriented questions than Rokeach's single friendship question.

Using as their subjects 44 white ninth graders in the San Francisco Bay area, Stein, Hardyck, and Smith (1965; also see Stein, 1966) designed a study that attempted to reconcile these findings. The researchers presented each subject a task by which to determine whether the subject's preferences were based upon similarity in race per se, similarity in values, or both. Stein et al. found that difference in values accounted for much more rejection of blacks than did race per se. But, race did have an effect of its own on the most intimate activities ("invite home to dinner," "live in same apartment house," and "date my sister").

These results confirm Rokeach's (1960) contention that rejection of others occurs largely because the others are believed to be different. At the same time, Stein et al. showed that Triandis (1961) was correct in his statement that blacks are often excluded simply because they are blacks, even if they possess values like one's own. The latter phenomenon does occur, but it is less likely to happen if the white person can be shown that the black is basically similar to himself in beliefs and values.

At this point, we should give some attention to the generalizability of the findings of Stein, Hardyck, and Smith. Would these conclusions, based upon the responses of 44 ninth graders in California, hold for subjects of other ages in other parts of the country? The answer, so far at least, is usually yes. Stein (1966) repeated his procedures with 630 ninth grade students in the Northeast. Once again the similarity and/or dissimilarity of values was found to be the primary determinant of the attitudes of white students.

As concerns regional differences, one might expect that in the South race per se would be a more powerful determinant than elsewhere. In the original study Rokeach et al. (1960) found that white college students in both the North and the South were more accepting of blacks whose beliefs agreed with theirs than they were of whites who disagreed with them. (The Southern sample was from Houston, Texas.) C. R. Smith, Williams, and Willis (1967) extended this study and asked six samples ($N = 307$) of white and black students from Northern, border, and Southern states to react to stimulus persons who varied in race, sex, and values. For all samples except one, similarity in belief was a more important determinant than was similarity in race or sex. In the sample of Southern whites (college students in Louisiana) the race of the stimulus person was a slightly more important determinant than was similarity in values. For six of eight issues, the majority of the subjects in the sample of Southern whites favored whites who had dissimilar values rather than blacks who had similar values—although five of these six differences were slight. The sixth issue, where the difference was greatest, dealt with interracial fraternities and sororities.

Two studies using teenagers in the South have been completed, one in North Carolina (Insko & Robinson, 1967) and one in Tennessee (Wrightsman, Baxter, & Jackson, 1967). Both studies confirm that, for these Southern teenagers, perceived similarity of values is generally a greater determinant of friendship than is similarity in race. Further extensions of this topic indicate the complexities involved. For example, Triandis and Davis (1965) were dissatisfied with the earlier study because they believed that prejudice had not been effectively measured. To assess social distance (or, in general terms, prejudice), Stein et al. had asked subjects how friendly they would feel toward stimulus persons. Moreover, the subjects were asked whether they would be willing to participate with each of these persons in 11 different social situations, which were all pleasant, positive behaviors. Triandis and Davis argue that prejudice involves negative behaviors as well as the lack of positive behaviors; thus, they built into their study measures that could more pointedly reflect active rejection, rather than simply lack of acceptance.

Triandis and Davis used eight different stimulus persons—all possible combinations of white, black, male, and female persons with attitudes for or against civil rights. The subjects (undergraduates at the University of Illinois) were asked to rate each of the eight stimulus persons on a series of concepts and behaviors ("good-bad," "clean-dirty," "would exclude from my neighborhood," "would eat with"). Triandis and Davis used a multidimensional view, which conceptualized prejudice as being made up of several factors. (These factors are described in Table 9-4.) The relative impact of race, sex, and values is different from one factor to another. For example, similarity of values is a more important determinant of formal social rejection; but race is a more important factor in friendship rejection. Race is second only to sex in the case of marital rejection and is the most important determinant of social distance and subordination. Thus, similarity in race appears to be a more important determinant of one's choices for intimate behaviors, while similarity of values is an important determinant for less intimate behaviors.

A second benefit of the Triandis-Davis approach is the notion that different types of subjects weigh race and values (or beliefs) in different ways when responding to a

Table 9-4. *Five Prejudice Factors Derived by Triandis and Davis*

Factor I. Formal Social Acceptance with Superordination versus Formal Social Rejection, defined by high loadings on items such as "I would admire the idea of," "I would admire the character of," "I would obey," "I would cooperate in a political campaign with."

Factor II. Marital Acceptance versus Marital Rejection, defined by high loadings on "I would marry," "I would date," "I would fall in love with," and so on.

Factor III. Friendship Acceptance versus Friendship Rejection, defined by high loadings on "I would accept as an intimate friend," "I would eat with," "I would gossip with," and so on.

Factor IV. Social Distance, defined by high loadings on items such as "I would exclude from the neighborhood," "I would prohibit admission to my club," "I would not accept as a close kin by marriage."

Factor V. Subordination, defined by high loadings on items such as "I would obey," "I would not treat as a subordinate," "I would be commanded by."

(From Triandis & Davis, "Race and belief as determinants of behavioral intention," *Journal of Personality and Social Psychology*, **2**, 1965, p. 716. Copyright 1965 by the American Psychological Association, and reprinted with permission.)

particular social encounter. By factoring the subjects' responses to many types of information—that is, separating out the various contributing factors—Triandis and Davis identified two types of prejudiced subjects. One type, called *conventionally prejudiced,* possessed interracial prejudice. The second type, called *belief prejudiced,* responded more to the values of the stimulus persons and rejected stimulus persons (regardless of race) who favored civil rights legislation. This is a useful finding, since subjects were typed by measures largely independent of their ratings.

Triandis and Davis conclude that—in the case of intimate behaviors—the race of the other person is a determinant for most subjects. Blacks are rejected even if they are known to be similar to oneself. In the case of less intimate behaviors, a person is rejected if his beliefs and values are different, regardless of his race. These findings are in general agreement with those of Stein et al., the major discrepancy being the latter's conclusion that values or beliefs are equally important throughout the social-distance scale. Nonetheless, all of these studies share one thing in common—they may be criticized because they are paper-and-pencil measures of abstract situations. There is no guarantee that the white student who prefers a black with similar values over a white with dissimilar values will associate with blacks (Sears & Abeles, 1969). Because of these limitations, more recent studies by Rokeach (Rokeach, 1968; Rokeach & Mezei, 1966), which test race versus values in real-life situations, take on additional significance. Two of these field studies were done on a university campus, with undergraduates as subjects, while the third was done in a state employment service, using men who were seeking employment as subjects.

The procedure in all three studies was the same: a naive subject (a male undergraduate or a man seeking work) met with four strangers (accomplices of the experimenter) and participated in a group discussion about an important or relevant topic. (In the study at the employment office, the men were under the impression that this discussion was a part of the normal application procedure.) In all cases, two of the accomplices were blacks and two were whites. One white and one black agreed with the subject, while one white and one black disagreed. The subject then had to choose which two of the four accomplices he would prefer to be with "at a coffee break" (for college students) or which two "he would prefer to work with" (for men seeking employment).

In all three studies, the two persons who held the same beliefs or values as the subject were chosen much more frequently. In combining the three studies, we find 47 of the 118 subjects chose the two men whose beliefs were most similar to the subject's, while only seven subjects chose the two men of the same race. This result was most frequent in the employment office study; of 50 subjects, 30 chose the two men with similar beliefs, while only two chose men of the same race. Similarity of beliefs or values is, in these studies, a more powerful determinant of interpersonal choice than similarity of race. It would be useful to extend this technique to choices of behaviors more intimate than drinking coffee or working together.

Similarity in race has also been matched with competence in order to determine the importance of each in determining reactions to co-workers. In other words, would a white person working on a group task prefer to have, as a fellow worker, a highly competent black or a less competent white? Using all-white groups in a laboratory task, Fromkin, Klimoski, and Flanagan (1970) found that members of previously successful groups choose new group members largely on the basis of their task competency (and not on the basis of race). But in groups that had been unsuccessful in the past, new colleagues are chosen on the basis of race more than on competency. In these groups, less competent blacks were preferred as much as highly competent ones, and blacks were preferred over whites. Perhaps, these groups saw any change in racial composition as a change for the better.

Although the preceding results are encouraging, they do not ensure that simply bringing together whites and blacks with similar values will bring about social acceptance. As Triandis (1961) and Stein, et al. (1965) point out, in the majority of instances where racial discrimination occurs, the white person does not inquire into the beliefs and values of the black to determine whether they are congruent or incongruent with his own.[12] Rather, the typical white person, with no further information, makes the assumption that the black's values are different (Stein et al., 1965; Byrne & Wong, 1962). In fact, a highly racist white person may want to believe that blacks have different values from his own; such beliefs serve as a justification for the white person's prejudice and discrimination. Indeed, Byrne and Wong (1962) found that strongly antiblack subjects assumed more dissimilarity than did less prejudiced subjects.

Thus, those responsible for desegregating schools, offices, and unions need to introduce procedures by which whites can learn that many of their black colleagues possess the same aspirations and values as their own. Then whites can be encouraged to discuss their own reactions to this new knowledge.

VI. ATTITUDES AS PREDICTORS OF BEHAVIOR

A. Are Attitudes Predispositions to Action?

No concept is more central to social psychology than the concept of **attitude.** Allport (1968, p. 62) has called it "the primary building stone in the edifice of social

[12] In actuality, the white may not elicit even one area of similarity between himself and the black. It should be recognized that in the majority of studies reviewed here, between 10 and 20 statements of belief similarity were used. In other words, the manipulations of *race* and *belief similarity* may not have been of the same magnitude (Ashmore, 1970). In fact, Triandis (1961), found that when belief similarity was introduced through one sentence only, race was a stronger determinant. A study that manipulated race and belief similarity by having subjects watch video tapes (Hendrick, Bixenstine, & Hawkins, 1971) found strong effects from belief similarity but weak effects from race similarity.

psychology," and the vast literature that has accumulated over the last 40 years substantiates his claim. But why study attitudes? Why invest all this energy in the study of a hypothetical, underlying construct? Social psychologists may offer two reasons: first, attitudes are presumed to be related to a variety of behaviors and actions; and second, attitudes—as a construct—are worthy of study for their own sake.

Many definitions propose that an attitude is a predisposition to behave, that it is a causal agent upon behavior. Students of attitude change make this assumption; Cohen (1964), for example, has written:

> Most of the investigators whose work we have examined make the broad psychological assumption that since attitudes are evaluative predispositions, they have consequences for the way people act toward others, for the program they actually undertake, and for the manner in which they carry them out. Thus attitudes are always seen as precursors of behavior, as determinants of how a person will actually behave in his daily affairs (pp. 137–138).

However, the oversimplified assumption that "attitudes are always . . . precursors of behavior" is not justified. Recent reviews, including those by Kiesler, Collins, and Miller (1969), Wicker (1969), and Brigham (1971a), show that there is no one-to-one correspondence between expressed attitude and subsequent behavior. In some areas, the relationship is nonexistent.

Unfortunately, the picture is not at all consistent. Some attitude constructs frequently predict behavior. For example, authoritarian attitudes are related to behavior in a variety of settings. Subjects who are high scorers on the California F scale (an attitude measure) are more likely to vote for conservative political candidates; raise their children in a traditional, authoritarian manner; prefer more regimented and less democratic leadership on their job; and perceive others as having the same feelings as themselves. However, when we turn to the topics of prejudice, discrimination, and racism, some studies show little consistency between attitudes and behavior. The classic study that reflects inconsistency was done by LaPiere, in 1934. At that time there were strong feelings against Orientals in the United States, particularly along the West Coast. LaPiere, a highly mobile sociologist, took a Chinese couple on a three-month automobile trip—twice across the United States and up and down the West Coast. The three stopped at 250 hotels and restaurants and only once were refused service. Later LaPiere wrote each of these places, asking if they would accept Chinese patrons. Only about one-half of the proprietors bothered to answer; but, of these, 90 percent indicated they would not serve Chinese! LaPiere's study has generally been interpreted as an indication that prejudiced attitudes (either the failure to respond or a negative response to the letter) do not predict the extent of actual discriminatory behavior (refusal to serve Chinese patrons). We should question, however, whether LaPiere was really measuring prejudice. Perhaps, it is preferable to say that his study related two types of discriminatory behavior and found them inconsistent.

Although we are less than eager to accept LaPiere's study as a prototype, we must note that the results of a similar study also show the lack of a relationship between attitudes and behavior. Kutner, Wilkins, and Yarrow (1952), using a procedure similar to LaPiere's but employing one black and two white females in the Northeast, obtained similar results. In each of 11 restaurants the black woman was admitted and the service was described as "exemplary." But when letters were sent later asking for reservations for an interracial party, no replies were received. Subsequent telephone calls elicited a grudging reservation from five restaurants and a refusal from six. When control calls were made to each of these restaurants—calls that did not mention the race of the guests—10 of the 11 restaurants immediately accepted the reservations. Again, behavior toward an individual minority-group member who was physically present was inconsistent with behavior in response to a written request.

More recent studies have related the responses on paper-and-pencil measures of prejudice to actual behavior in an interracial situation. For example, Green (1969) posed as a representative of a publishing firm and told students at the University of Colorado that his company needed to take photographs to be included in new textbooks. Subjects were shown the poses that were planned for the photographs; these poses always included two persons, but they varied in intimacy, ranging from "equality in a public situation" to "a fairly intimate heterosexual relationship." For each pose there was one version in which both figures were white, and another version in which one figure was a black, one white. Subjects were asked to indicate how willing they were to pose; if they were willing they were to sign a "photograph release form." (The willingness of subjects to pose in photographs with blacks, as a measure of behavior, was apparently developed by DeFleur and Westie, 1958.) One other variable was manipulated in Green's study—the release forms differed in specifications for subsequent uses of the photographs. In one case, the photographs would only be used in a Peace Corps textbook in underdeveloped countries miles and miles away from the United States; in another case they were to be used in a *Life* magazine article dealing with Peace Corps textbooks. The dependent variable was the extent to which the subject's response to all-white and white-black versions of the poses differed. A week later all subjects completed an attitude scale developed by Woodmansee and Cook. The behavioral responses were compared for subjects who, according to the attitude scale, were either moderately favorable toward blacks or moderately unfavorable. The results indicated that the paper-and-pencil measure of attitude was related to behavior on the photograph release form; subjects with favorable attitudes were more willing to be photographed with blacks than were subjects with unfavorable attitudes ($p < .01$). The correlation between attitudes and the acceptability of the behavioral index was $+.43$.

Participation in a civil rights discussion was related to attitudes toward blacks in a study by Fendrich (1967). Subjects individually completed a scale of attitudes toward blacks and a measure of "commitment" or willingness to interact with blacks. They also indicated whether or not they would be "willing to attend small group discussions with members of the NAACP that were scheduled in the near future" (1967, p. 352). Subjects were subsequently contacted and invited to a meeting. If they attended the meeting, they were asked at the end of the discussion to sign up for work on civil rights projects. Thus a behavioral measure was available, which included four points: unwillingness to attend meetings, expressed willingness but failure to attend, attendance only, and attendance plus signing up for further activities. Fendrich reports that when subjects indicated their degree of commitment before completing the attitude scale, there was a strong relationship between the subject's attitude and the degree of willingness to participate in civil rights discussions. As Wicker (1969) indicates, however, there are limitations in Fendrich's study—first, the attitude scale, commitment measure, and initial reaction to attending the NAACP discussion were all collected individually and at the same time. Second, pressures toward social desirability might have been a factor. And third, it is unclear whether the initial interviewer was the person who later contacted the subject and led the discussion groups. Those studies that are methodologically most sound, however, do find substantial relationships between measures of attitude and measures of behavior; usually the correlations are around +.50 (Fishbein, 1972, in press).

B. Why Don't Attitudes Predict Behavior More Consistently?

There are two distinguishable reasons why the relationship between attitudes and behavior is not always strong. The first of these assumes that such a relationship does exist but is watered down by other factors. The second explanation rejects the very existence of the traditional relationship. We shall consider these explanations in order.

The "Watered Down" Theory. If the subsequent notions hold true, it may be possible that in a controlled situation attitudes will not predispose behavior. In other words, due to these factors, the relationship between attitudes and behavior will be watered down.

1. A person's responses to general objects may vary from his responses to specific objects. The purpose of an attitude scale is to measure attitudes toward a minority group. Thus, the object is highly general. Behavioral measures, however, often deal with reactions to a specific person who is a member of that group. It may be "unlikely that the subject's beliefs about [or actions toward] the particular Negroes he comes into contact with are similar to his beliefs about Negroes in general" (Fishbein, 1966, p. 206). For example, inconsistencies or stimulus dissimilarities between a restaurant proprietor's stereotype of Chinese and a Chinese couple's actual appearance in the restaurant may have contributed to LaPiere's findings.

2. Behavior is complex and multidetermined. Suppose an elderly man tells his friend that "the less contact he has with blacks the better" and then boards a bus. Noting that all the seats but one are occupied, the man takes the available one—next to a black. We cannot conclude that his verbal statement is false because his choice of seats has repudiated it. Rather, we must recognize that even the apparently simple action of taking a seat is multidetermined. While it may be upsetting for the old man to sit next to a black, his feet may hurt him so much that sitting under any conditions is more tolerable than standing. On this point Weissberg (1965) has written: "An attitude, no matter how conceived, is simply one of the terms in the complex regression equation we use to predict behavior; we cannot expect it to do too much. I think we must take seriously Lewin's formula that Behavior = f(Person, Environment). If the latent variable [attitude] is conceived inside [the person] one still needs to know the specific nature of the environment, the form of the function relating P and E, and their interactions with the one under consideration before one can accurately predict behavior" (1965, p. 424). In addition, the reliability of behavioral measures is often unknown. Strenuous efforts to develop highly reliable measures of attitudes are wasted if they are used in conjunction with crude and unreliable measures of behavior. Note that, in the example, the old man has only two possible choices (unless he decides to wait for the next bus)—he can either stand or he can sit next to a black. If he is forced to choose on repeated trips, how consistent will his responses be? Perhaps, if his strong antiblack attitudes are a determinant, he will quit taking

that particular bus. In short, one-shot measures of behavior do not give us such information.

3. Among the complex determinants of behavior are more than one attitude. The relationship between behavior and a single attitude may appear inconsistent because other attitudes have greater influence (Wicker, 1969; Cook & Selltiz, 1964). In one study, Insko and Schopler (1967) used a person whose attitudes were favorable to the civil rights movement but who refused to contribute money to the movement. Perhaps, this person has stronger attitudes about caring for the needs of his family, maintaining his good credit rating, and the like. Thus, understanding the competing role of different attitude domains may facilitate future prediction of behavior. Other personal characteristics such as motives, interests, abilities, and activity levels also influence behavior.

4. Situational factors also influence behavior. A direct relationship between an attitude and behavior may only be possible when situational conditions permit. An excellent example of this was described in Chapter 3, regarding Machiavellianism. We might initially expect that the behavior of highly Machiavellian subjects would be different from the behavior of subjects with less Machiavellian attitudes in any competitive interpersonal situation. But Christie and Geis (1970) found this was not the case. A careful taxonomy of the interpersonal situations in 50 studies enabled Christie and Geis to specify with a high degree of accuracy those situations in which the attitude-behavior relationship would be significant. For example, if opportunities to communicate in a competitive task were limited to binary choices and no superfluous conversation was allowed, highly Machiavellian subjects were no more successful in the task than low Machiavellians. But when the latitude for communication was broader, high Machiavellians improvised more and behaved more successfully—that is, won more money, achieved higher scores, and so on.

5. A threshold analysis may explain discrepancies between attitudes and behavior. D. T. Campbell (1963) has proposed that an attitude may serve as a mediator for both verbal responses and behavioral responses, but, as Wicker (1969) has stated, "the way the attitude is manifested may depend upon certain situational pressures" (p. 44). A restaurant proprietor's attitude may be antiblack, but it may be harder for him to refuse a black couple who actually appears at his door than to refuse a telephone request for a reservation. The inconsistency in LaPiere's findings is removed through the concept of thresholds or hurdles. According to Campbell, La Piere's findings indicate that the majority of restaurant and hotel managers, who accepted the Chinese couple but refused the mailed request, possess moderate levels of prejudice—enough to get over one hurdle (mailed request) but not enough to get over the other (face-to-face confrontation). While the notion is an intriguing one, it has problems; Wicker reports one study (Linn, 1965) in which there was more rejection of minority-group members in a face-to-face situation than there was symbolic rejection. Apparently the hurdles were reversed.

All of these factors tend to diminish the relationship between attitudes and behavior. At present, multivariate approaches that seek to identify all of the influential components of behavior are almost neglected. Such an approach would reveal just which situational factors and which attitudes, motives, and other personal factors influenced the old man's decision to sit next to a black. Ideally, a multivariate analysis would also tell us the relative influence of each factor.

Rejections of the Traditional Relationship: Cognitive Dissonance and Self-

Perception. Bem (1967, 1970) has proposed the radical idea that behavior causes attitudes. There are antecedents to this notion in the theory of cognitive dissonance (Festinger, 1957), which deals with cases where a person recognizes that two of his attitudes and/or behaviors are in conflict. If the individual believes that cigarette smoking causes cancer and yet smokes three packs a day, cognitive dissonance exists. If the individual considers himself a thoughtful person and then forgets his fiancee's birthday, he seeks to resolve the contradiction. An essential aspect of cognitive dissonance theory is its prediction that a person is motivated to remove any dissonance that exists as a result of conflicting attitudes or behaviors.

A nonobvious quality of cognitive dissonance theory has attracted a number of social psychologists. An obvious prediction would be that the greater the reward for advocating a public position that contradicts one's private attitude, the more change there will be toward the public position. But in a number of studies, greater shifts in attitude toward a public position occurred when the rewards were less. Thus, cognitive dissonance theory says that under certain conditions, public behavior causes shifts in private attitudes. Having to sit next to a black on the bus every day may actually cause our foot-weary old man's prejudice to decrease.

As indicated, Bem (1967, 1970) has proposed an even more radical notion in his self-perception theory: attitudes do not cause behavior—behavior causes attitudes. As Bem sees it, the most important cues we get about the internal states of other people come from observing their behavior. We judge the feelings of others on the basis of their actions. It is the same with ourselves; to Bem, we infer our own attitudes about an object from the way we behave toward it. We do not eat brown bread because we like it; rather we like it because we eat it.

We should examine the evidence for this notion. Bandler, Madaras, and Bem (1968) hired volunteer subjects to undergo a series of electric shocks. Before administering some shocks, the experimenters told the subject that they preferred him to escape the shock—in other words, the experimenters wanted the subject to terminate the shock after it came on. Other subjects were told that the experimenters preferred them to endure the shock to its end. However, it was emphasized that on every trial the subject's choice to endure or escape the shock was his own decision, regardless of the experimenters' preferences. After each shock, subjects rated the degree of discomfort on a 7-point scale; although they did not know it, all shocks were actually of equal intensity. Bem (1970) found that the results supported self-perception theory: shocks were rated significantly more uncomfortable when the subject escaped them than when he endured them. In other words, the behavior of terminating or enduring shocks caused the attitude toward the intensity of the shock.

C. Attitudes and Behavior—Mutual Cause and Effect

Cognitive dissonance and self-perception theories have added a healthy impetus to a needed reconsideration of the relationship between attitudes and behavior. It may be, as these theories claim, that behavior changes or even forms attitudes. But observations of behavior are not the sole cues to self-knowledge; internal factors also make a contribution (deCharms, 1968; R. Jones, 1970), and prior attitudes may predispose behavior. There is no reason why the process cannot be one where attitudes and behaviors have effects upon one another. In the case of mutual cause and effect, the definition of attitudes as predispositions to behavior is too limited. Attitudes are also dependent variables that are important to study for their own sake.

VII. SUMMARY

An attitude is not observable but, rather, an underlying construct. Its essential characteristics are that it has an object, is evaluative, and is relatively enduring. Attitudes may differ in regard to the degree of their complexity or multiplexity. Highly simplex attitudes are undifferentiated, lacking in qualifications, and largely evaluative. Multiplex attitudes contain many elements, which may or may not be consonant with each other.

An attitude is usually conceived as a bipolar continuum. However, some attitudes may be best thought of as possessing several dimensions, with different criterial referents. Prejudice refers to an attitude; discrimination refers to behavior. Prejudice is defined as an evaluative attitude about a member of a racial, ethnic, or other minority group, which results from the recipient's membership in that group.

Prejudice may well be universal in the sense that in competitive societies distinctions between groups will always be made on the basis of some characteristics. However, the extent of socially undesirable discrimination can be reduced greatly, and socially undesirable aspects of prejudice can be reduced significantly.

Theories about the causes of prejudice make a distinction between the prejudice existing in the society at large and the degree of prejudice held by different individuals. The *historical emphasis* hypothesizes that prejudice is often a result of traditions and relationships that have existed for generations. Economic exploitation of less powerful racial and ethnic groups is advanced as one cause of prejudice.

Sociologists and anthropologists emphasize *sociocultural factors* as causes of prejudice. Among these are increased urbanization, the competition for scarce jobs, and changes in the functions of the family.

The *situational emphasis* places the cause of prejudice upon current forces in the environment.

Psychodynamic theories of the causes of prejudice posit that it results from personal conflicts and maladjustments within the prejudiced person. Among specific factors are low frustration tolerance, authoritarianism, and personality deficit.

The *phenomenological emphasis* argues that a person's perceptions of his environment are of crucial importance in understanding his behavior.

With regard to interpersonal contact in less intimate social situations, most persons prefer to be with those who possess similar values, regardless of race. In more intimate social situations such as dating or dining together, both racial similarity and similarity in values have an influence on a person's choice of companions. An attitude may be a predisposition to behavior, but behaviors can also influence attitudes.

VIII. SUGGESTED READINGS

Allport, G. W. *The nature of prejudice*. New York: Doubleday Anchor Books, 1958. (Paperback) Originally published in 1954, many of its examples are outdated, but Allport's survey of prejudice is still the most readable introduction to the field. Highly recommended.

Bem, D. J. *Beliefs, attitudes, and human affairs*. Belmont, Calif.: Brooks/Cole, 1970. (Paperback) A delightfully written exposition on attitudes by a provocative theorist.

Bosworth, A. R. *America's concentration camps*. New York: Bantam Books, 1968. (Paperback) The factual report of the imprisonment of 110,000 Japanese-Americans, resulting from the hysteria of early World War II. Most of those who were transported to interior camps were native-born U.S. citizens. The Supreme Court has upheld the constitutionality of the move, and it could happen again with "another emergency, another minority."

Collins, B. E., in collaboration with R. D. Ashmore. *Social psychology*. Reading, Mass.: Addison-Wesley, 1970. The section on prejudice (pp. 247–340) prepared by Ashmore includes an excellent evaluative review of the causes of prejudice.

Fanon, F. *The wretched of the earth.* New York: Grove Press, 1965. (Paperback version available) Partly a powerful indictment of colonialism by European powers. Partly a challenge to the oppressed to rebel and use all means to achieve freedom. Altogether, a most influential book in the world-wide anticolonial revolution.

Malcolm X, with the assistance of A. Haley. *The autobiography of Malcolm X*. New York: Grove Press, 1964. (Paperback) The extraordinary self-history of a man who has greatly influenced the quest of blacks to restore pride in their race. Also recommended: *Soul on Ice,* by Eldridge Cleaver; *The Fire Next Time,* by James Baldwin; and *Invisible Man,* by Ralph Ellison, for insight into what it means to be black in America.

Simpson, G. E., & Yinger, J. M. *Racial and cultural minorities.* (3rd ed.) New York; Harper & Row, 1965. A thorough treatment of knowledge about minority groups in America. Useful for reference.

Chapter Ten

Theories of Attitude Change

The concept of attitudes is probably the most distinctive and indispensable concept in contemporary American social psychology. *Gordon Allport*

Seeking to understand how attitudes are formed and changed is a major preoccupation of social psychologists. McGuire (1966) has estimated that 25 percent of the material in social psychology textbooks is on attitudes and attitude change. Indeed, this preoccupation could be justified by looking at the myriad ways in which attempts are made to change our attitudes. Consider, for example, a few brief moments in the life of a young woman named Joan O'Malley. It is a dreary Monday morning. Joan drags herself out of bed and flips on the television. She hopes to catch the news program for some entertaining piece of information to share with everybody at the office. Instead, a commercial praises a new toothpaste, which will transform one into the essence of charm, popularity, and sexuality. The phone jangles—it is Joan's boyfriend, still trying to convince her to go away with him for the weekend. But Joan has never done that before. She finally ends the conversation by telling him she will see him at lunch and discuss it further then. She quickly prepares her breakfast, swallows her soggy cornflakes, and scans the front page of the newspaper. The headlines tell of thousands of requests to the President to free Lieutenant Calley. Joan wonders whether the President will be affected. As she leaves for work, her mail arrives, but it is nothing other than some throw-away ads.

If Joan O'Malley had nothing else to do all day, she might be able to keep an accurate account of the number of attempts made to change her attitude and behavior. On this particular morning, she has already been inundated by advertisements emanating from several different media—including the cereal box! It certainly seems to her as if every story in the newspaper is concerned with attitude changes—whether it be petitions to the President, a local lawsuit to bring about further school desegregation, or the state legislature's debate about raising sales taxes. And, then, there is Joan's boyfriend. When we consider these ever-present assaults upon our sensibilities, it is no wonder social psychologists have taken an inordinate interest in attitude change. Theories of attitude change continue to proliferate, and several long and detailed books have appeared, dealing with only one type of theory. (Compare *Cognitive Consistency,* edited by Feldman, 1966, and *Theories of Cognitive Consistency,* edited by Abelson, Aronson, McGuire, Newcomb, Rosenberg, and Tannenbaum, 1968.)

Despite this information overkill, we are a long way from understanding the dynamics of attitude change. Each theory has a different focus and, hence, explains only certain types of attitude change. It may well be, as Zimbardo and Ebbesen claim, that theorists and researchers in the area of attitude change are not concerned with changing attitudes as much as "with using the attitude change paradigm to study basic psychological processes and the operation of theoretically relevant variables" (1969, p. v).

Much of our knowledge of attitude change stems from studies done outside the framework of any theory. For example, if a company hires a new employee who is very antiblack, we know which working conditions will make the greatest change in his attitude. We can specify five different aspects of his job, each of which, if present, is more likely to bring about favorable change. The fact that this knowledge has largely been gleaned from field observations rather than theory-testing investigations does not make it useless. The area of attitude change has a rather schizoid character. On one side, there are the theories and laboratory research; on the other side are programs of field research on real-world topics, such as advertising, propaganda, and prejudice reduction. Because of this division, and because of the vast importance of the issue, we shall devote two chapters to the discussion of attitude change. (Chapter 9 on Prejudice, Chapter 12 on Social Change, Chapter 15 on Conformity, Chapter 16 on Leadership, and Chapter 20 on Community Applications are also relevant to attitude change.) In the present chapter, we shall compare theories and explore how each theory operates in relation to the same goal and the same general task. Because each major theory makes different assumptions and emphasizes different aspects of the process of attitude change, we shall describe the basic concepts and typical research of each theory before examining its application to an actual situation. The four major approaches to conceptualizing attitude change are: stimulus-response and reinforcement theory, social-judgment theory, consistency theory, and functional theory.

I. ATTITUDE CHANGE AND NONCHANGE

We are all constantly bombarded with appeals to change our attitudes. Any adequate theory of attitude change should be able to predict in advance which appeals will be most effective in changing attitudes and should be able to predict which attitudes will not change in response to a particular appeal. In other words, the theory must deal with failures to change as well as change itself. Any adequate theory of attitude change also needs to possess theoretical constructs that can be translated into clear operational terms. As an example, suppose that our task is to reduce the degree of prejudice expressed by college-aged white persons who are strongly antiblack. Let us assume that each of the prejudiced whites has been hired for the summer to work for pay on a science project. Unbeknownst to the prejudiced whites, each will be working in a small group composed of himself, one other white person who is unprejudiced, and one black. How should we construct the task and the work environment in order to bring about the desired reduction in prejudice? Or can the experimenter make any effective variations at all, if the work environment does not meet the needs of the prejudiced white?

Attitude change may occur in the absence of any external appeal to change as well as through direct attempts to intervene. For example, exposure to new knowledge of the world or to specific persons may cause us to change our attitudes. Does President Nixon's decision about a current issue cause us to change our opinion about him? When Sam grows a beard does his minister behave any differently toward him? Did Ted Kennedy's behavior during the incident at the Chappaquiddick Bridge influence voters' attitudes toward him? Any adequate attitude change theory should be able to predict how individuals' attitudes about an object are changed or not changed by exposure to significant new information about that object. With these considerations in mind, let us examine the first type of attitude change theory.

II. STIMULUS-RESPONSE AND REINFORCEMENT THEORIES OF ATTITUDE CHANGE

A. Basic Assumptions

Compared to other theories, the *stimulus-response approach* places greater emphasis on the **stimulus** qualities of a communication that may bring about attitude change. The characteristics of the communicator (the source) and of the audience are considered as well as the content of a communication. The stimulus-response

Figure 10-1. *The Poor People's March on Washington. Do such efforts change attitudes? If so, do the results help us understand the process of attitude change? What theories of change are useful here? (Photograph courtesy of Joe Zinn.)*

approach assumes that social behavior can be understood through an analysis of specific stimuli and responses and the rewards and punishments associated with particular responses. The contemporary application of this approach to attitude change derives its thrust from the Yale University Communication Research Program, where, more than 20 years ago, Carl Hovland and his colleagues sought to quantify the stimulus and response characteristics of each communication situation (Kiesler, Collins, & Miller, 1969).

For example, Hovland, Janis, and Kelley (1953) postulated that the process of attitude change resembled the process of learning, and that the principles of acquiring verbal and motor skills could also be used to understand attitude formation and change. In the learning of new attitudes three variables are important: attention, comprehension, and acceptance. (The relationship of these processes is illustrated in Figure 10-2.) Before an appeal or a communication can bring about attitude change, it must be noticed or attended to. But even when the appeal is noticed, it may not be effective if the recipient is unable to comprehend or assimilate the communication. Thus, efforts must be made to determine whether the message has been correctly comprehended. A third step, acceptance, must be achieved before attitude change can take place. The degree of acceptance is related to the incentives; to quote Insko, "The persuasive communications may provide incentives in the form of arguments or reasons why the advocated point of view should be accepted, or the persuasive communication may arouse expectations of phenomena that are reinforcing (incentives) or that in the past have been associated with reinforcement" (1967, p. 14). More than any other approach, the stimulus-response and reinforcement theories see as basic this assumption that attitudes are changed only if the incentives for making a new response are greater than the incentives for making the old response.

A major contribution of stimulus-response and reinforcement theories is the specification of aspects that may influence the acceptance of the persuasive communication. These aspects include (a) the communication stimuli (its content, its arguments or appeals), (b) the characteristics of the source, and (c) the setting in which the person is exposed to the communication—"including, for example, the way in which other members of the audience respond" (Kiesler et al., 1969, p. 106). This analysis has led to the following types of research questions.

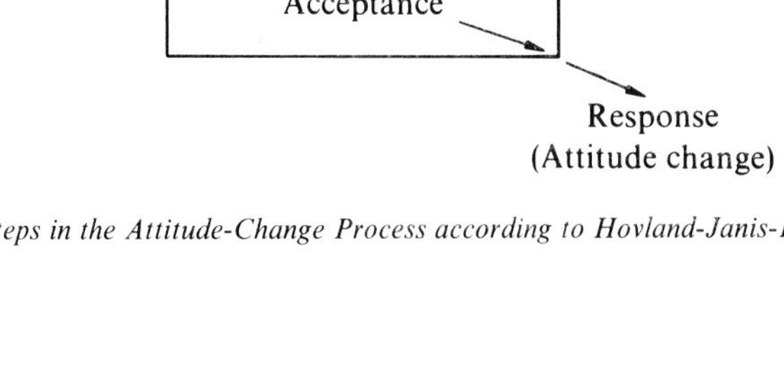

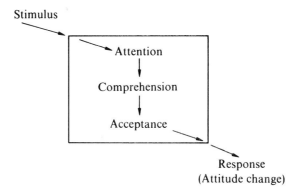

Figure 10-2. *Steps in the Attitude-Change Process according to Hovland-Janis-Kelley Model.*

1. How does the source of the persuasive communication affect attitude change? For example, if the source is highly believable or authoritative, is there more attitude change than if the source were untrustworthy?

2. If a salesman is trying to convince you to adopt his point of view, should he review both sides or only present his own side of an argument?

3. Does the order of presentation make any difference? For example, if I am required to present both sides of an argument to you, should I present the side I am advocating at the beginning or save it for the last? (This is known as the primacy-recency issue.)

B. Representative Research

Research employing reinforcement approaches to attitude change has been frequent and varied. In exploring aspects of communication, this approach has studied the effect of *verbal reinforcement* upon attitude change. A study in that genre will be reviewed here.

In ordinary conversation some of our well-thought-out attitudes fall on deaf ears. When we express other attitudes, they evoke an enthusiastic response from our listeners, such as, "You're so right!" or "I wish I'd said that!" Are those statements that are verbally reinforced more likely to be made in the future? Does a positive reaction from others tend to entrench that statement in our repertory of beliefs?

Insko (1965) set out to determine if the attitudes of students at the University of Hawaii could be modified by verbal reinforcement during a telephone conversation. Students were called by an interviewer who sought their opinions about Aloha Week; specifically, the question was whether there should be a springtime Aloha Week. (Aloha Week is a set of festivities held every Fall in Hawaii.) The interviewer asked the student a number of questions and responded with "Good" to certain answers; thus, verbal conditioning was instituted. Previous studies have shown that if certain types of statements are verbally reinforced with a response such as "Good," the subject will make these statements more often in the future. Insko wanted to discover whether such verbal reinforcement on the telephone would have any significant effect upon attitudes. Approximately one week after the telephone calls, the same students completed a Local Issues Questionnaire in their class. About two-thirds of the way through the questionnaire, they responded to an item asking for their opinions about a Springtime Aloha Week. Students who had been verbally reinforced by telephone for their favorable attitudes expressed higher degrees of favorable attitudes than did control subjects. The effect of the verbal reinforcement carried over into another situation one week later and apparently intensified the attitudes.

Verbal reinforcement has been used to modify such phenomena as wearing clothes of certain colors (Calvin, 1962), having prejudiced attitudes (Mitnick & McGinnies, 1958), adhering to certain philosophies of education (Hildum & Brown, 1956), and holding certain attitudes toward capital punishment (Ekman, 1958). In such cases, reinforcement of certain attitudes enhances the future expression of such attitudes. There are, however, limitations to such a conclusion. First of all, the paradigm accentuates previously held attitudes and behavior and does not concentrate on reversing the direction of attitudes. Second, most of the attitudes studied are rather trivial and are not deeply held. Most University of Hawaii students are indifferent as to whether Aloha Week is held annually, semi-annually, or never. Moreover, changes in one's attitudes toward capital punishment may occur without much investment on the part of the changer. A third limitation is that the nature of the reinforcement is unclear. Why does a verbal response such as, "Good," lead to change in expressed attitudes? As Insko has stated: "One of the least convincing aspects of reinforcement theory has to do with the explanation of how a persuasive communication supplies reinforcement for acceptance of an advocated point of view. It can be asserted that much acceptance is dependent upon the communication's arousing expectations of possible future reinforcements as a consequence of conformity to the recommended point of view, but, in general, this is not very convincing" (1967, p. 63).[1]

C. Applications of the Theories to Attitude-Change Procedures

Consider our previous example of the strongly prejudiced college student who will be working with a black during the summer. What procedures would reinforcement theory advocate? First, any expressions of acceptance by the white toward the black should be positively reinforced. If the white student should happen to compliment the black regarding his clothes or task skills, the other white staff members should verbally reinforce the prejudiced white for making such compliments. Also, expressions of interest, friendship, and more subtle, positive responses toward the black by the prejudiced white should elicit attention and appreciation from both of the other staff members. Verbal-conditioning research has led to increased recognition of the subtle nature of verbal reinforcement. Even nonverbal responses—a smile, an intense concentration on what the other is saying—are reinforcing.

Second, it must be remembered that the nature of the attitude-change process includes the three steps of attention, comprehension, and acceptance. To achieve attention, the prejudiced white must listen to what the black is saying. One cannot simply bring the two together and assume that the white will attend to anything the black says or notice anything he does. The task should be structured so that the prejudiced white understands that paying attention to the black will be beneficial. Each member of the group might be told that he will eventually have to switch jobs with another group member. Therefore, each will have to pay attention to what the other is doing or saying.

Next, comprehension must be achieved before attitude change can occur. The elements of the situation must be understood accurately. How may we ensure that the persuasive message is comprehended? The prejudiced white may be required, as part of his job, to meet in sessions with the other white group member, while the black group member is absent. These sessions may permit the other white, who is a confederate of the experimenter, to determine if the prejudiced white has understood the messages involved in the attempt to change attitudes. Most likely, the prejudiced white has misperceived previous messages. As prejudice may often develop from unmet needs or personal maladjustments, the prejudiced white is likely to twist the messages he hears to fit his own expectations and stereotypes. The message may never pass

[1]From C. A. Insko, *Theories of Attitude Change*. Copyright 1967 by Meredith Publishing Company. This and all subsequent quotes from the same source are reprinted with permission of Appleton-Century-Crofts, Educational Division, Meredith Corporation.

accurately beyond the comprehension stage, and any opportunity for the desired attitude change will be thwarted—unless checks on comprehension are made and remediation is instituted.

The last step in the process of attitude change is acceptance of the message. Here, the concept of incentives is important. The prejudiced person must become motivated to make a new response; the appropriate incentives to bring this about must be identified and used. The incentive for one person may be social acceptance; for another, money. Theory is of little help at this point, but the reinforcement theorist would still emphasize that, if all these steps are achieved, attitude change is more likely to occur.

Once the prejudiced white has accepted the messages of the black, the stimulus-response theorist would seek stimulus generalization—or the acceptance by the prejudiced white of other information about the particular black person or about blacks in general. If verbal conditioning has been effective in establishing a new response (attitude) toward the black participant, the laws of learning would predict that such stimulus generalization would take place.

III. SOCIAL-JUDGMENT THEORY OF ATTITUDE CHANGE

The *social-judgment theory* of attitude change draws upon the principles of experimental psychology and, specifically, upon the subfield of psychophysics (Insko, 1967). Within this context there are two major approaches: the assimilation-contrast theory, developed by M. Sherif and Hovland (1961) and revised by C. W. Sherif, Sherif, and Nebergall (1965) and by Hovland, Harvey, and Sherif (1957); and the adaptation-level theory, developed by Helson (1959, 1964). The adaptation-level theory will be described in Chapter 12 in relation to social change. The assimilation-contrast theory will be examined here as an example of a social-judgment approach to attitude change.

A. Basic Concepts in Assimilation-Contrast Theory

The formation of reference scales, anchors, contrast, assimilation, latitudes of acceptance and rejection, and involvement are concepts that are central to the assimilation-contrast theory of Sherif and Hovland.

Formation of Reference Scales. When a person is presented with a number of stimuli, he will usually form a *reference scale,* by which he can place these stimuli along one or more dimensions. If you are going to buy a new car you may look at and test drive five or six cars at different dealers. These cars doubtless differ in price, make, color, horsepower, maneuverability, and numerous other dimensions. You probably find yourself ordering them along reference scales that reflect the dimensions of greatest interest to you. You may like the gasoline economy of one car and the smooth ride of another, but you eventually establish one scale of relative preferences, which combines all the dimensions in some way satisfactory to you.

Sherif and Hovland note that many stimuli do exist along a well-ordered dimension that can be agreed upon by all. Judgments of weights can be placed in order and the order can be agreed upon by every judge—if the differences are great enough. Many social stimuli—contestants for Miss America, for example—result in the formation of a reference scale even if the stimuli do not possess any objective order. Since such stimuli lack the objective standards of weight judgments, they are more susceptible to social influence. You may like the Miss America nominee from your home state. Your preference for a particular car may be influenced by the fact that your good friends blanch at its color or admire its acceleration.

Anchors. Anchors often serve as the end points in a series of stimuli. Compared to the other stimuli, they exert a relatively greater influence upon the determination of judgments (Insko, 1967). The presence of an anchor may influence the judgments given to other stimuli. For example, looking at the Miss America contest or a dream car may cause a young man to judge that his realistic alternatives to each of these possibilities are less desirable. Likewise, if the young man has been without a car or a girl for several years, anything that moves looks better than it would otherwise.

Such anchors serve as particularly potent reference points when the following conditions hold: (a) the person has little past experience with the particular reference scale, (b) the potential range of stimuli is unknown, and (c) no explicit standards for reference are provided (Kiesler et al., 1969). Anchors are relevant to the understanding of attitude change because an attitude may be regarded as an internal anchor and a persuasive communication can be thought of as an external anchor (Insko, 1967). Thus, the attitude-change process, in the view of Sherif and Hovland, confronts two anchors that encompass a discrepancy.

Contrast and Assimilation. Contrast is a shift of an attitude or judgment away from an anchor, while *assimilation* is a shift in attitude or judgment toward an anchor. When an anchor is at an extreme position—beyond the end of a series of stimuli—contrast is present. When the anchor is closer to the end of the series of stimuli, assimilation is the result. Insko has summarized the implications of this process as follows. (See Figure 10-3 for illustration.)

> Thus according to assimilation-contrast theory, a primary factor affecting the influence of a persuasive communication upon attitude and opinion change is the degree of discrepancy between the position of the communication (external anchor) and the recipient's attitude or opinion (internal anchor). If the communication advocates a position that is not too discrepant from that held by the communication recipient, assimilation will result; i.e., the individual will perceive the communication as advocating a less extreme position, will favorably evaluate the communication, and will be strongly influenced. If the communication advocates a position that is highly discrepant from that held by the communication recipient, contrast will result; i.e., the individual will perceive the communication as advocating a more extreme position, will unfavorably evaluate the communication, and will be either minimally positively influenced or negatively influenced (1967, p. 67).

According to Sherif and Hovland, Insko's account is oversimplified, in that it fails to recognize the role of *latitudes of acceptance.* The important discrepancy is not the discrepancy between the communication and the attitude but the one between the communication and the latitude of acceptance.

Latitudes of Acceptance and Rejection. According to this theory, a person's attitude is not a single point but rather a band of acceptable positions—or a latitude of acceptance. The opposite concept, the *latitude of rejection,* includes all those elements that the person finds unacceptable. (Here, elements could refer to Miss America

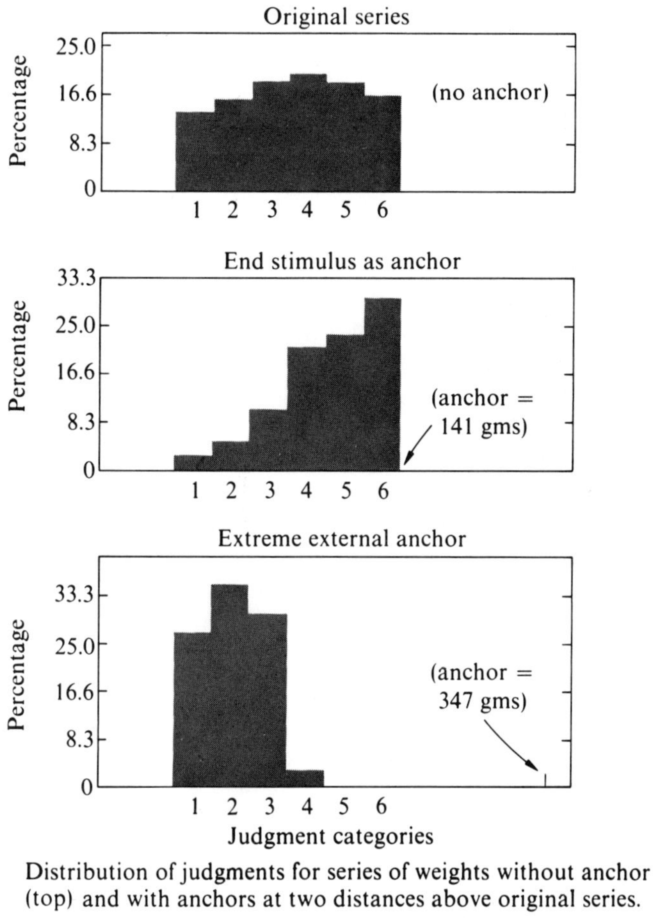

Figure 10-3. *Judgments of Weights and Position of Anchor. (Adapted from Sherif, Taub, & Hovland, "Assimilation and contrast effects of anchoring stimuli on judgments,"* Journal of Experimental Psychology, **55**, *1958, 150–155. Copyright 1958 by the American Psychological Association, and reprinted with permission.)*

contestants, makes of cars, or degrees of contact with blacks—depending upon the attitude under study.) An area of neutrality exists between these two areas.

B. Representative Research

Research done within the framework of assimilation-contrast theory has concentrated on two questions: (a) how much is attitude change influenced by the discrepancy between the communication and the recipient's position, and (b) what are the effects of the latitudes of acceptance and rejection.

Effects of the Discrepancy between the Communication and the Position of the Recipient. Research on such discrepancies faces many problems. First, when experimenters vary the discrepancy between a communication and a person's position, the recipient's initial position often gets manipulated too. That is, in order to get greater discrepancies, more extreme initial attitudes may be used. Second, there is the problem of regression toward the mean. If a persuasive communication is located near the mean of possible initial positions, most persons with extreme attitudes are likely to move toward the mean on retesting. An apparent result of exposure to the communication may simply be an effect of statistical regression. A third problem is the previously mentioned possibility that persons with extreme initial positions are likely to be more ego-involved with their position (Sherif & Hovland, 1961) and, hence, have smaller latitudes of acceptance. A fourth problem is that the entire possible range of discrepancies is not covered in all studies. Future research will need to take these problems into account.

A well-designed study on this topic was carried out by Bochner and Insko (1966), who examined attitudes toward amounts of sleep. What is an appropriate amount of sleep per night for the average adult? Bochner and Insko presented subjects with a three-page essay advocating that—because of reasons of health and efficiency—people should reduce the number of hours they sleep each night. (It had been determined earlier that subjects in this study generally advocated about eight hours sleep. Actually, the mean was 7.89, with a standard deviation of 1.05 hours.)

One of the independent variables manipulated in the study was the degree of discrepancy between the communication's recommended amount of sleep and the subject's advocated position. This variable was manipulated by selecting subjects who had advocated eight hours sleep and presenting different subsets with different recommended amounts. Nine different amounts were used, from zero to eight hours per night. The recommendation of zero hours of sleep per night is far-fetched, but in the present context it represents an absolute extreme point.

The degree of credibility (high versus medium) of the communicator or source was another independent variable manipulated in the study. Half of the subjects were told that the essay on sleep had been prepared by "Sir John Eccles, Nobel prize-winning physiologist"—a highly credible source. The other half of the subjects were told that the source was "Mr. Harry J. Olsen, director of the Fort Worth YMCA"— a moderately credible source. (Data collected from a sample of the subjects indicated that the subjects did rate the physiologist as a significantly more credible source for this issue.)

Subjects' responses to these manipulations were elicited in three ways. (a) They were asked their opinion regarding the desired number of hours of sleep, after reading the essay. (They could choose anywhere from "no sleep at all" to "ten hours per night.") (b) They were asked to evaluate the communication. (Was it "relevant," "logical," "easy to understand"?) (c) They were asked to evaluate the source. (Was he "competent," "trustworthy," "credible"?)

The effects of the variations upon opinion change are reflected in Figure 10-4. Advocating smaller numbers of hours of sleep slightly changed the subject's expressed attitude—up to a point. For example, if eight hours had been advocated, the average subject chose approximately seven and one-half hours as desirable; when five hours were recommended, the subject chose a little less than seven hours. When 2 hours were recommended, the subject chose about six and one-half hours; but when no hours were advocated, there was a reversal in the trend, and the average response was back to seven hours. Thus, when both conditions of source credibility are combined, there is a curvilinear reaction (though not a statistically significant one). So Bochner and Insko's study does not clearly confirm an assimilation-contrast theory of attitude change. As can be seen in Figure 10-4, when the source was highly credible, the discrepant communication was more effective in changing attitudes. That is, there was a significant interaction between source credibility and discrepancy.

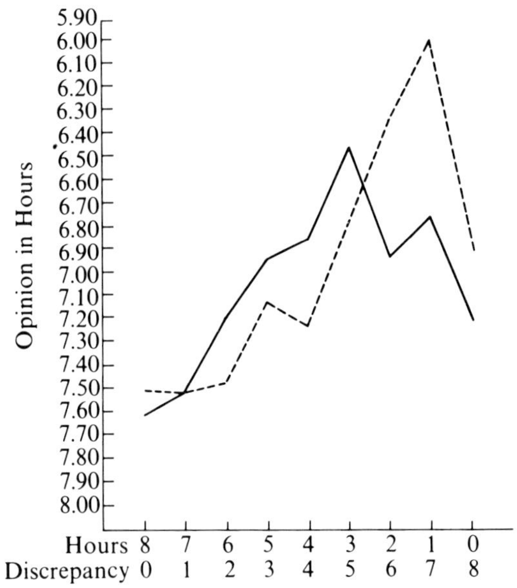

Figure 10-4. *Effects of Credibility of Source and Discrepancy of Advocated Position upon Attitude Change. (From Bochner & Insko, "Communicator discrepancy, source credibility, and opinion change,"* Journal of Personality and Social Psychology, **4**, *1966, p. 618, Fig. 1. Copyright 1966 by the American Psychological Association. Reprinted by permission.)*

Results for the other two dependent variables indicated (a) the greater the discrepancy between the subject's initial position and the position advocated by the source, the greater the subject disparaged the communication, and (b) when the YMCA director was the source and the number of hours of sleep advocated was very small, he was greatly disparaged. Such a trend was not true when the Nobel prize-winning physiologist was the source.

The Effects of Latitudes of Acceptance and Rejection. Norman Miller (1965) used an elaborate manipulation with high school students to bring about ego involvement with their attitudes toward the amount of mathematics and science in the curriculum or with their attitudes toward fluoridation of public drinking water. The manipulation employed four aspects: (a) the importance of the issue was stressed; (b) social support was provided for the students' attitudes; (c) they were asked to provide reasons in support of their own attitudes; and (d) they distributed literature in support of their attitudes. The manipulation of degree of ego involvement had no great effect on the latitudes of acceptance or rejection regarding science and mathematics in the curriculum. Miller's study is damaging evidence against one of the most basic postulates of Sherif's assimilation-contrast theory.

C. Applications of the Assimilation-Contrast Theory to Attitude-Change Procedures

As Insko (1967) indicates, applying principles of social judgment to attitude change is an intriguing possibility. We recognize that all judgments, including attitudes toward people, are made within the context of other judgments. And reactions to most stimuli are influenced by the nature of the immediately preceding stimuli. However, the assimilation-contrast approach appears weak in several ways. The ways that different constructs might influence each other cannot be spelled out. Insko (1967) guesses that one's perception of where a communication resides influences the evaluation given to the communication, which in turn causes attitude change. Empirical tests of the theory have found that some of its predictions are not borne out. For instance, on the basis of one study (N. Miller, 1965), ego involvement does not seem to reduce the latitude for acceptance.

Despite these important limitations, the general thrust of the assimilation-contrast theory may be applied to our example of the real-life task of constructing a working situation that would facilitate the change of attitudes toward blacks. Basic to this approach would be factors such as the specification of anchors, latitudes of acceptance and rejection, and degree of ego involvement. The following guidelines would be applied.

1. The attitudes of the prejudiced white are more likely to change in the desired direction if the messages of the persuasive communications are within the subject's latitude of acceptance. Thus, the limits of acceptance must first be determined—perhaps by questioning the subject outside of the work situation.

2. If the messages directed toward the subject fall within his latitude of rejection, the messages are very unlikely to have the desired effects. In fact, they are likely to reinforce the respondent's initial stand or even produce boomerang effects—that is, make him more prejudiced.

3. If the antiblack white subject is quite ego involved in his attitude toward blacks, his latitude of acceptance of favorable statements about blacks is more limited. Therefore, the innovator of change must be particularly sensitive to this restricted range, making sure that his persuasive communications fall within the latitude of acceptance.

4. The greater the discrepancy between the persuasive communication and the position of the subject—as long as the communication is within the acceptance limits—the more shift in the subject's position. (However, the assimilation-contrast theory does not consider individual differences in breadth of acceptance. What if our subject's latitude of acceptance is so narrow that he can only tolerate attitude positions very close to his own? There is very little opportunity for change if such conditions exist. Assimilation-contrast theory certainly dampens our optimism about achieving great changes in intensely held attitudes.)

5. The concept of anchors may be applied by considering a list of interracial behaviors that could be given to the subject. For example, he might be working in an interracial group with two black males instead of one, or the group might be composed of himself and two black females, or the group may be located on a predominantly black campus. When such possibilities serve as anchors, the subject's reaction to his present situation may show greater tolerance than it would have in the absence of such anchors.

Clearly such applications must be spelled out in more detail to be of any real use—and, then, they may prove unworkable. The main attraction of assimilation-contrast theory is its recognition of an optimum distance between the subject's attitude position and the position of the persuasive communication. If the communication is closer than this optimum point, it is less likely to move the person. If the communication is too far away from the optimum point, it is tuned out by the subject.

IV. CONSISTENCY THEORIES OF ATTITUDE CHANGE

Perhaps attitude change results from an individual's awareness that his attitudes and his actions are inconsistent. He may observe himself doing things that violate some of his attitudes. The consistency approach sees this incongruity as a primary determinant of attitude change. Several consistency theories may be differentiated. Heider's balance theory has stimulated more recent developments—including Osgood and Tannenbaum's congruity theory, Brehm's reactance theory, and Festinger's cognitive dissonance theory. Before describing these different approaches, we need to consider how all consistency theories are similar. Each assumes that the attitude-change process is rational and that people are motivated to be and to appear consistent (Zajonc, 1960). Each theory holds that a person's awareness of his own inconsistency is something that cannot be tolerated. This assumption will be evaluated after the theories are described.

A. Heider's Balance Theory

Fritz Heider (1946, 1958) has developed conceptions about the ways people view their relationships with other people and with their environment. For simplicity, Heider has limited his analysis to two persons (P and O) and to one other entity (X), which might be an idea, a person, a thing, or an attitude object. The person P is the focus of the analysis, while O represents some other person. Heider's goal was to discover how the relationships among P, O, and X are organized in P's cognitive structure. We will concentrate our review here on one kind of relationship—the liking relationship. Heider proposed that the relationships among P, O, and X may be either balanced or unbalanced. Consider the following: P, who has spent all summer as a volunteer worker for the Republican presidential candidate, enters the state university as a freshman in the fall. He is assigned Professor O as a faculty advisor. When P meets O to plan a first semester schedule, P observes that O is wearing a campaign button for the Democratic candidate. Will P like O? Will P think much of O's recommendations about courses to take? Will P want to take a course from O? Probably not—because P wants to have balanced relationships. For example, if we let X stand for the Democratic party candidate, a balanced state exists when P likes O, P likes X, and O likes X. The only way a balanced state can exist within P's cognitive structure—as long as P dislikes X—is for P to dislike O. P can say in effect, "Professor O is no good, which fits because he's a big supporter of candidate X."

Heider proposed that balanced states exist when all three relations are positive (as in liking), or when two relations are negative (disliking) and one is positive. The preceding example fits the latter possibility. Of course, if P had found that his advisor was a Republican supporter and if P had come to like O, then balance theory would describe the relationship as P likes O, P likes X, and O likes X. Figure 10-5 represents the possible balanced and unbalanced states. As can be seen, unbalanced states do occur, where people like other people who differ in their attitudes toward important things. Likewise, you may discover that someone you hate intensely likes the same rather obscure art works that you do. What do we do about such states? Heider pro-

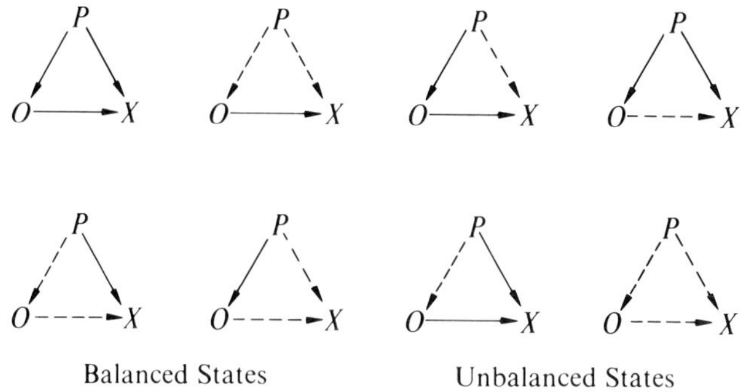

Figure 10-5. *Examples of Balanced and Unbalanced States According to Heider's Definition of Balance. Solid lines represent positive and broken lines negative relations. (Adapted from Zajonc, 1960, Figure 1. Reprinted with permission of the publisher; copyright 1960, Columbia University Press.)*

poses that such unbalanced states produce tension and generate forces to achieve or restore balance.

Heider's approach then is a highly simplified one. Indeed, its greatest fault may be that it's too simplified, for the approach fails to consider degrees of liking. Although the theory proposes that there are other ways persons can resolve unbalanced states, it is not explicit about this.

B. Osgood and Tannenbaum's Congruity Theory

The congruity theory of Osgood and Tannenbaum (1955) is an extension of the balance notion, especially concerned with the direction of attitude change. The principle of congruity "holds that when change in evaluation or attitude occurs it always occurs in the direction of increased congruity with the prevailing frame of reference" (Zajonc, 1960, p. 286). People's attitudes change in the direction of reducing inconsistency or ambiguity.

The congruity theory has been particularly concerned with the source of a communication, the content of a communication, and the reaction of the recipient to each of these. For example, let us say that Mr. Jones thinks positively of Vice President Agnew (+) and also believes the National Guard is a valuable force (+). When Mr. Agnew praises the National Guard, congruity exists in Mr. Jones's cognitive system (a + is affirmative toward a +). But, if Mr. Agnew were to castigate the National Guard for its action during a protest march, an inconsistency arises for Mr. Jones. The pairing of a positive source and a negatively evaluated communication creates incongruity (a + is negative about a +). Incongruity is defined as existing when the evaluations (or attitudes) toward the source and the object are similar and the assertion is negative (as in this case), or when the evaluations of the source and object are dissimilar and the assertion is positive. According to the theory, in cases of incongruity, there will be pressure to change one's attitudes about the source or the object of the assertion in the direction of increased congruity. Congruity theorists have gone even farther with this approach, by specifying degrees of evaluation to each source and object. For example, if Mr. Jones is strongly favorable toward Vice President Agnew (+3) and mildly favorable toward the National Guard (+1), Mr. Agnew's attack against the National Guard will lead to a shift in Mr. Jones's cognitive structure—both toward the source and the object. Probably more change will occur in the mildly held attitude concerning the National Guard.

C. Festinger's Cognitive Dissonance Theory

Cognitive dissonance exists when a person possesses two **cognitions**—one of which is the obverse of the other (Festinger, 1957). Two terms here require clarification. The term *cognitions* refers to thoughts, attitudes, beliefs, and also behaviors of which the person is cognitively aware. The following statements are cognitions: "I am a thoughtful person"; "I believe that schools are repressive institutions"; "I forgot my wife's birthday"; "It is a nice day today." In saying that one cognition is the obverse of the other, Festinger means that if cognition A implies the presence of cognition B, then it is dissonant to hold cognition A and the opposite or obverse of cognition B at the same time. For example, if I hold the cognition that "I am a thoughtful person" and if I realize that I have forgotten my wife's birthday, a dissonance is created. Or, to use a hackneyed example, if I believe that cigarette smoking causes lung cancer, it is dissonant for me to smoke three packs a day (assuming that I want to live a long healthy life).

A basic assumption of the theory is that a state of dissonance motivates the person to reduce or eliminate the dissonance. The presence of dissonance is so psychologically unpleasant that the person subsequently seeks to avoid such situations. The theory demonstrates a precision that is lacking in previous consistency approaches because it specifies the amount of dissonance aroused. The level of dissonance activated is a function of (a) the ratio of dissonant to consonant cognitions, and (b) the importance of each cognition to the person (Sherwood, Barron, & Fitch, 1969). The relationship is expressed in the following formula:

$$\text{Dissonance} = \frac{\text{Importance} \times \text{Number of Dissonant Cognitions}}{\text{Importance} \times \text{Number of Consonant Cognitions}}$$

Thus, the magnitude of dissonance increases as the number or importance of dissonant cognitions increases relative to the number or importance of consonant cognitions.

How then is dissonance reduced? One method is to decrease the number or importance of the dissonant elements. If a man has forgotten his wife's birthday, he may devaluate the importance of the occasion; he may convince himself that celebrating birthdays is meaningless or that his wife would just as soon not like to be reminded that she is one year older. Or the man may increase the number or importance of the consonant cognitions; he may engage in a number of activities—taking his wife out to dinner, bringing her breakfast in bed—to convince himself of his thoughtfulness. Those elements that change in the equation depend upon the specific ingredients. If the dissonance occurs between one's attitude and one's behavior, either could be modified. The important point is that according to the theory, the person is motivated to reduce or eliminate the cognitive dissonance.

D. Reactance Theory

As an outgrowth of cognitive dissonance theory, Brehm (1966) has proposed that the concept of reactance may explain the attitude change that takes place toward certain objects or activities under certain conditions. Brehm uses the following example:

Picture Mr. John Smith, who normally plays golf on Sunday afternoons, although occasionally he spends Sunday afternoon watching television or puttering around his workshop. The important point is that Smith always spends Sunday afternoon doing whichever of these three things he prefers; he is free to choose which he will do. Now consider a specific Sunday morning on which Smith's wife announces that Smith will have to play golf that afternoon since she has invited several of her ladyfriends to the house for a party. Mr. Smith's freedom is threatened with reduction in several ways: (1) he cannot watch television, (2) he cannot putter in the workshop, and (3) he must (Mrs. Smith says) play golf (1966, p. 2).

Reactance theory concerns itself with situations where one's freedom of choice is threatened. According to the theory, if a person's freedom of choice is restricted, he will be motivated to reestablish the freedom that has been lost or threatened. More relevant to the present context, if a formerly available activity is restricted, it becomes more desirable and attractive. Attitudes toward an object become more favorable if the opportunity to obtain that object is suddenly restricted.

E. Explaining Attitude Change through Each Consistency Theory

Jerry, a college student, meets Ingrid, is attracted to her, and asks her for a date. At first, Jerry feels that Ingrid is an ideal companion. But then she mentions that she is a member of an ethnic group—to be completely fictitious, let us call her a Danirean (see Hartley, 1946)—and all his life Jerry has been taught that Danireans are despicable. Such a romantic difficulty is nothing new, of course; it has served as a basic conflict for a number of literary works—including *Romeo and Juliet, West Side Story,* and to a small degree, *Love Story*. How would each consistency theory conceptualize this dilemma? Each assumes that, although the conflict is unpleasant to Jerry, he will resolve it. Yet each theory conceptualizes the conflict in a somewhat different way.

Heider's balance theory would represent the above situation as follows: P = Jerry, O = Ingrid, and X = Danireans. Here, P likes O; P dislikes X; and O likes X. Jerry's state is unbalanced, and, according to Heider's theory, he will seek to restore balance. This could be achieved if Jerry decided to dislike Ingrid rather than like her, or if he decided to like Danireans rather than dislike them. Balance theory also implies other possible ways of resolving unbalance, such as differentiation, misperception, or forgetting. For example, Jerry could differentiate between good Danireans, like Ingrid, and bad ones, like all the rest.

Osgood and Tannenbaum's principle of congruity asserts that resolving discrepant attitudes always occurs in the direction of greater congruity with the prevailing frame of reference. This approach emphasizes the source (Ingrid), the object (Danireans), and the assertion of the source about the object ("I am a Danirean and proud to be one"). Incongruity exists here because the positively evaluated source makes an assertion in favor of a negatively evaluated object. Like balance theory, the principle of congruity predicts a change of attitude either toward the source or toward the object or toward both. The relevant research data indicate that Jerry's reaction would be both to like Ingrid somewhat less and to dislike Danireans somewhat less.

The principle of congruity also considers another way of resolving incongruities. Instead of attitude change, one can refuse to believe that the assertion of the source is true. In other words, when Ingrid says she is a Danirean, Jerry might respond, "You must be kidding!" Such incredulity could not be maintained for long in face-to-face situations. Incredulity is a more frequent resolution in experimental studies that attribute assertions (correctly or incorrectly) to well-known sources. The subject in such an experiment might respond, "I just don't believe that so-and-so said that!" The principle of congruity offers more precise predictions about attitude change than does balance theory (Zajonc, 1960), for it specifies degree of change, rather than merely the direction. Yet both theories are rather restrictive in that they assume the person will work within the number of elements available.

Festinger's theory of cognitive dissonance offers both something more and something less than the preceding approaches. For one, a great deal more research has been done on cognitive dissonance than on the other theories. Also, cognitive dissonance emphasizes the motivating aspect of dissonance or incongruity. It would imply that, as a result of the dissonant "Ingrid the Danirean" episode, Jerry will avoid similar possibilities in the future. Realizing his strong negative feelings toward Danireans, Jerry will determine whether a girl is a Danirean before he becomes emotionally involved with her. The preceding consistency theories do not propose these generalized motivating effects of incongruous relationships. In dealing with the resolution of present inconsistency, balance theory and congruity theory have less to say about future behavior than does cognitive dissonance theory.

The theory of cognitive dissonance, however, is often less specific than congruity theory when prescribing ways of resolving dissonance. In the case of Jerry and Ingrid, the two dissonant cognitions would be: (a) all Danireans are despicable, and (b) Ingrid, a Danirean, is wonderful. Jerry would be motivated to resolve this dissonance, and one method would be for him to seek out information that would reduce the dissonance. Jerry might read travel books or materials published by the Danirean Tourist Service that picture Danireans as smiling, friendly people, living in a pleasant country. Or Jerry might try (unconsciously, perhaps) to aggravate Ingrid, causing her to present a less attractive side of her personality. Either of these types of information could reduce dissonance.

The applications of reactance theory to this case are more limited. If, for example, Jerry's parents restricted him from seeing Ingrid because of their hostile feelings toward Danireans, Ingrid—according to reactance theory—would become all the more attractive to Jerry. This proposition—called the "Romeo and Juliet effect"—has been put to an empirical test, the results of which are presented in Chapter 14.

F. Representative Research

Although each consistency approach has been subject to some empirical tests, more than 400 studies have been completed within the cognitive dissonance framework alone. These studies may be grouped under three major topics. The first category includes those studies that emphasize conditions where conflicting cognitions exist. The second category of studies focuses on the state of uneasiness after a decision has been made. One may ask oneself whether the choice just made was the correct one. According to the theory, any time one chooses between two attractive options, *post-*

decision dissonance exists, and one seeks out behaviors that support the correctness of the choice made. Early research has confirmed such an explanation. For example, persons who have recently purchased new cars are more likely to read magazine advertisements for that make of car than for any other make—apparently in an attempt to reduce dissonance over their decision (Ehrlich, Guttman, Schönbach, & Mills, 1957). Likewise, those persons who go through a severe initiation to gain membership to a group value the group membership more highly than those who go through milder initiation rites (Aronson & Mills, 1959). However, more recent research on *selective exposure* indicates no consistent support for a conclusion that people are more attracted to information that is congenial with their own decisions (S. Rosen, 1961; Feather, 1963; Freedman & Sears, 1965). Mediating variables, such as an ability to adapt to incongruities, may explain conflicting findings (Driver, Streufert, & Nataupsky, 1969).

The third group of studies falling within the cognitive dissonance framework concentrates on the dissonance resulting when a person has been forced to take a public position contrary to his private attitude. Here, the theory proposes that this conflict leads to change (usually in the private attitude), and it also makes the controversial prediction that the less a person is induced to advocate a public position violating his private attitude, the more he will shift in private attitude. The original study to test this proposition (Festinger & Carlsmith, 1959) paid subjects either 1 dollar or 20 dollars to lie to another student. After participating for one hour in a series of dull, meaningless tasks (for example, putting 12 spools in a tray, emptying the tray, and refilling it, time and time again), the subject was paid to tell a prospective subject that the experiment was interesting, educational, and worthwhile. Later, under the guise of a survey unrelated to the experiment, the subject who lied for either 1 or 20 dollars answered a questionnaire about his private attitudes toward the experiment. Festinger and Carlsmith found that subjects who had been paid only 1 dollar rated the experimental tasks as more enjoyable (mean of $+1.35$ on a scale of -5 to $+5$) than did the subjects who were paid 20 dollars (mean $= -0.05$) or the control subjects (mean $= -0.45$). Thus, when one's morality is compromised for only a small payment, his dissonance is increased. The way the subject reduces dissonance is by convincing himself that the public statement he made is an accurate one.

Not everyone has accepted this conclusion. The methodology of cognitive dissonance studies, particularly those that involve deception, has been severely criticized. Questions have been raised about the meaningfulness of the results (Chapanis & Chapanis, 1964), since in many of the studies a sizeable percentage of the potential subjects saw through the deception used in the experiment. In Festinger and Carlsmith's study, 11 of the 71 potential subjects could not be used in the analysis.

Moreover, critics have questioned the plausibility of some of the manipulations. Are subjects suspicious when they are paid 20 dollars for a few minutes of their time plus a commitment to serve as a retainer for any vague future time? Rosenberg has argued that paying large monetary rewards in cognitive dissonance experiments has led to an increase in the subject's *evaluation apprehension,* defined as "an active, anxiety-toned concern that he win a positive evaluation from the experimenter, or at least that he provide no grounds for a negative one" (M. J. Rosenberg, 1965, p. 29). Such apprehension might cause the subject with the 20 dollar payment to resist admitting his change in private opinion. To clarify this point, Rosenberg designed and executed a cognitive dissonance study in which the advocacy of a counterattitudinal public position and the measurement of it were more widely separated than in Festinger and Carlsmith's study. Rosenberg found that the greater the reward for lying, the greater the change in attitude—the precise opposite of Festinger and Carlsmith's finding. Rosenberg concluded that a reinforcement theory does a better job than the cognitive dissonance theory in explaining the results of studies in which persons publicly advocate a position counter to their attitudes.

In an attempt to resolve the conflicting findings, Carlsmith, Collins, and Helmreich (1966) proposed that the extent to which the subject must convince other people of the desirability of his public position is crucial. These authors predicted that, if in a face-to-face confrontation, a subject has to present a position that is in opposition to his privately held attitude, a smaller payment will lead to greater change in private attitude. To the contrary, if the subject has to express a counterattitudinal position anonymously in writing (to be seen only by the experimenter), the more he is paid, the more his private attitude will change. Both these expectations were confirmed (Carlsmith, Collins, & Helmreich, 1966), indicating that both cognitive dissonance theory and reinforcement theory make accurate predictions under certain conditions.

Perhaps the difference between public and private behavior results from a greater commitment to counterattitudinal behavior in a public situation. When the subject is unable to disassociate himself publicly from his behavior, he may change his attitude more if he is paid less (Aronson, 1966). In a somewhat different interpretation, Collins (1969) has proposed that the adverse consequences of expressing a public counterattitudinal position may cause more attitude change with smaller rewards. Attribution theory may also explain the relationship, as explained by Collins.

> An individual makes a counter-attitudinal statement. Then he is faced with an attributional problem—should he attribute the statement to some force within himself; i.e., is the statement a reflection of his own attitude? If this is the case, he may want to change his previous attitude to be consistent with his current overt statement. Alternately, he may attribute the overt statement to some external force in the environment. In this case he does not need to make an adjustment (i.e., no attitude change) because the externally induced overt statement is irrelevant to his own, internal attitude (Collins, 1969, p. 310).

This last interpretation is reminiscent of Bem's (1965, 1970) self-perception theory of attitude formation described in Chapter 9.

It has been suggested that an adequate attitude-change theory must explain not only purposeful attempts to change attitude but also cases in which unplanned events present new information discrepant with a person's previous attitudes toward the object. For example, how did supporters of Edward Kennedy react to the incident on Chappaquiddick Island in July, 1969? The facts of the case were as follows: Senator Kennedy and a female staff worker, Miss Mary Jo Kopechne, were returning to Martha's Vineyard in a car driven by the Senator. After taking a wrong turn onto a country road, Kennedy drove off a bridge into about ten feet of water. Senator Kennedy rescued himself, but the young woman drowned. Even though the accident apparently happened about 11:15 P.M., Senator Kennedy did not report it until about 10 A.M. the following day. He claimed he had made several unsuccessful attempts to locate and rescue Miss Kopechne immediately after he escaped from the submerged car. He attributed his delay in informing the police to his state of shock and exhaustion. The Senator was later tried for leaving the scene of an accident; he pleaded guilty and received a two-month suspended sentence. After the trial he asked the voters of Massachusetts to judge whether he should retain his Senate seat. Their response was favorable, and he did so. A year later he successfully ran for re-election.

Any of the consistency theories described here would predict that persons who held Senator Kennedy in high regard would experience some degree of cognitive inconsistency. The highly esteemed senator had committed an apparently undesirable act. This inconsistency could be resolved in several ways: the person's regard for Kennedy could diminish, or he could maintain his regard for Kennedy by interpreting the case in such a way as to make Kennedy less guilty.

Silverman (1971) has investigated the ways Kennedy supporters responded to the Chappaquiddick incident. Approximately three weeks after the incident, Silverman tabulated the reactions of 102 persons at the University of Florida. The questions he posed are listed in Table 10-1. Instead of the usual sample of college sophomores, Silverman chose mostly faculty members and graduate students as subjects because he wanted persons who had held favorable attitudes toward Senator Kennedy prior to the incident. Of the 102 respondents, 84 (or 82 percent) reported that their attitudes toward Ted Kennedy before the incident were very or moderately favorable. (As an aside, we may note that it would have been better to assess these attitudes before the Chappaquiddick incident, but of course Silverman could not have had the prescience to know that the incident would occur. One limitation of studies using naturally occurring events such as this one is the inability to anticipate such events.) The 84 subjects who retrospectively reported that they were pro-Kennedy before the incident are of main concern in the subsequent discussion. Of these, 49 (or 58 percent) maintained very favorable or moderately favorable attitudes at the time of the interview—three weeks after the incident. These respondents are referred to as the nonchangers. Thirty-three (39 percent) reported that their attitudes had changed to moderately unfavorable or quite unfavorable; these respondents Silverman labeled the changers. Two subjects who shifted to no opinion were not used in further analyses.

Thus, Silverman had two groups of initially pro-Kennedy subjects whose post-incident attitudes were different. Consistency theory would predict that these two groups of subjects would answer the other questions from the interview in different ways. For example, in response to Item 10 in Table 10-1 the nonchangers should reject the possibility that the Senator might have been aware that he was sacrificing the girl's life in not reporting the accident as soon as possible. In actuality, this is what happened; 80 percent of the nonchangers, compared to 42 percent of the changers, answered "definitely not" to Item 10 in Table 10-1. (The difference in percentages was statistically significant at the .01 level.) Likewise, in connection with Item 8 of Table 10-1, if a person had maintained his pro-Kennedy attitude, he should be more enthusiastic about Ted Kennedy's keeping his Senate seat and seeking re-election. The data do not indicate the intensity of response but report that 98 percent of the nonchangers, compared to 73 percent of the changers, advocated Kennedy's remaining in office (p value for the difference $< .01$).

Silverman included Item 12 on Table 10-1, the open-ended question, so that respondents could furnish their own opinions about why Kennedy delayed reporting the incident. Table 10-2 presents the types of reasons given, as well as the frequencies and percentages of nonchangers and changers indicating each type of reason. As shown in Table 10-2, Silverman ordered these reasons according to how morally incriminating they were, moving from less morally incriminating ("no opinion") to most incriminating ("to try to cover up"). Note in Table 10-2 that there is further

Table 10-1. *Silverman's Questionnaire about Reactions to Senator Kennedy's Accident*

Questionnaire items, in the order given, are presented below

1. To what extent have you been following the details of Senator Kennedy's recent automobile accident in the various news media? (Alternative responses were *as fully as possible, moderately,* and *little or not at all.*)
2. Prior to the events of the accident, what was your opinion of Senator Kennedy as a person (rather than as a political figure)?
3. What is your present opinion of Senator Kennedy as a person?
4. Prior to the events of the accident, what was your opinion of Senator Kennedy as a political figure and potential president?
5. What is your present opinion of Senator Kennedy as a political figure and potential president? (Alternative responses for items 2–5 were *very high, moderately high, moderately low, very low,* and *no opinion.*)
6. Do you believe that the action taken against Senator Kennedy by the local law-enforcement agencies and courts (2-month suspended sentence for leaving the scene of an accident) was: (Responses were *too severe, fair and just, too lenient,* and *far too lenient.*)
7. Given the same circumstances and events, do you believe that a private citizen would have been treated: (Responses were *more leniently, the same, more severely, far more severely.*)
8. Considering the events concerning the accident, do you believe that it was proper for Senator Kennedy to keep his seat in the Senate and to announce his intention to run again in 1970? (Responses were *yes, no, undecided.*)
9. Do you believe that if Senator Kennedy had taken other action than he did immediately after the accident, the girl's life may have been saved?
10. Do you believe that Senator Kennedy was aware that he was possibly sacrificing the girl's life in not reporting the accident as soon as possible?
11. Do you believe that Senator Kennedy's delay in reporting the accident immediately was based at all on his concern for his reputation? (Responses for Items 9–11 were *definitely not, possibly yes, probably yes, definitely yes.*)

The twelfth item was open-ended and stated, "Please write below, in as much detail as possible, your own opinions about why Senator Kennedy delayed about 10 hours in reporting the accident to the police."

(Table 10-1 and Table 10-2 are from Silverman, "On the resolution and tolerance of cognitive inconsistency in a natural-occurring event," *Journal of Personality and Social Psychology*, **17**, 1971, p. 173. Copyright 1971 by the American Psychological Association. Reprinted with permission.)

evidence supporting the consistency theory: those respondents maintaining their pro-Kennedy attitudes more often gave less incriminating reasons for his delay, while changers saw more incriminating and reprehensible factors as the true reasons for delay.

While the overall results of Silverman's study support consistency theory, it should be noted that the responses were by no means unanimous. Consider those subjects who maintained their pro-Kennedy attitude. The consistency theory would predict that such persons would give Kennedy the benefit of the doubt when interpreting his behavior. But of these consistently pro-Kennedy persons, 63 percent admitted the possibility or probability that Miss Kopechne's life could have been saved if Kennedy had not delayed. Twenty percent admitted the possibility that Kennedy was aware of this when he did delay, and 64 percent thought that his delay was at least partially the result of his concern for his reputation.

These pro-Kennedy subjects did not act in a completely consistent way, and their reactions have caused social psychologists to reevaluate the breadth of the applications of consistency theory. For example, Price, Harburg, and Newcomb (1966) asked subjects their reaction to the case in which person P disliked person O, and both P and O disliked object X. Only 17 percent of the subjects felt uneasy or negative about such a relationship. A statement by Freedman seems an appropriate

Table 10-2. *Frequencies and Percentages of Nonchangers and Changers in Silverman's Study Giving Various Reasons "Why Senator Kennedy Delayed"*

Category	*Nonchangers*	*Changers*
No opinion	11 (22%)	4 (12%)
Shock (disorientation, concussion, exhaustion, panic)	18 (37%)	12 (36%)
Upon advice (or to seek advice from friends, associates, lawyers, family)	7 (14%)	3 (9%)
Confusion (to organize thoughts, plan course of action)	10 (20%)	5 (15%)
Fear (or concern for reputation, political future, marriage, jail)	19 (39%)	19 (58%)
Intoxication (to reduce blood alcohol and avoid incrimination)	5 (10%)	8 (24%)
To try to cover up (develop an alibi, conceal facts of event, find someone to stand in as the guilty party)	12 (24%)	11 (33%)

way to describe some respondents of studies such as these: "It seems that people are not usually looking for inconsistencies among their cognitions, do not notice that many of them exist, and therefore do not act on them. This lack of concern with inconsistencies is, I believe, because it is not a very important consideration for most people in most circumstances. And when they do notice inconsistencies, people seem to endure them without being particularly troubled" (1968, p. 502). Further research is necessary to determine whether—as Freedman believes—inconsistency is not a problem "for most people in most circumstances." Certainly inconsistency is not a problem for some.

G. Applications of the Consistency Theories to Attitude-Change Procedures

Brehm and Cohen (1962) have applied consistency theories (specifically cognitive dissonance theory) to desegregation and integration. They propose that most antiblack white persons who interact closely with a black will experience dissonance arousal as their antiblack attitudes will seem discrepant with their behavior. Dissonance will particularly be increased if this behavioral commitment is irrevocable. As dissonance is unpleasant, efforts will be made by the prejudiced white to bring his attitudes and behavior closer together. As Brehm and Cohen have stated: "In effect, we expect that, among other things, the dissonance reduction process should result in a more favorable perception of the social climate shared with the Negroes and a change toward more favorable attitudes toward Negroes. Thus, everything else being equal, commitment to an irrevocable interracial policy should result in at least some change in attitudes toward the Negroes: Forcing a person to behave in a fashion discrepant from what he believes can result in a change in private opinion" (1962, p. 272).

Some of the factors controlling the magnitude of dissonance experienced and the consequent magnitude of attitude change include the extent of contact with a black, the extent of freedom of choice, and the initial attitude position. The greater the contact (such as proximity, intimacy, frequency, or duration), the greater the dissonance and the greater the efforts to reduce dissonance. As concerns the extent of freedom of choice, Brehm and Cohen have proposed that the more a person is compelled to make a commitment, the less the amount of dissonance created if he succumbs and, hence, the less the attitude change. To facilitate attitude change, the individual must be given some choice in interacting with blacks. However, if he behaves inconsistently with his antiblack attitude, he should not be given a chance to disclaim his action, for such a disclaimer reduces dissonance and creates less need to change the original attitude (Helmreich & Collins, 1968; J. Harvey & Mills, 1971). Finally, the more unfavorable the initial attitude position of an antiblack white, the more his attitude should change in a favorable direction—assuming that the white has, through the exercise of his own choice, become committed to interaction with blacks.

Thus, the consistency theorist would try to marshal an attractive situation that the antiblack white person enters into of his own free will. Once the white finds himself in the situation and committed to making his work a success, he should be oriented toward the discrepancy between his attitudes and his present behavior. The attitude will shift, being more amenable to change than the behavior.

V. FUNCTIONAL THEORIES OF ATTITUDE CHANGE

The basic proposition of a functional theory of attitude change is a simple one. People hold attitudes that fit their needs, and in order to change their attitudes, we must determine what these needs are. The functional approach is a phenomenological one; it maintains that a stimulus (for example, a television commercial, a new piece of information, an interracial contact) can only be understood within the context of the recipient's needs and personality.

Two rather similar functional theories have been developed by Katz (1960, 1968; Katz & Stotland, 1959) and by Smith, Bruner, and White (1956). Each theory proposes a list of functions that attitudes serve. The two theories have some differences, but Kiesler, Collins, and Miller (1969) have helpfully synthesized the functions of each, as shown in Table 10-3. We will describe each general function, drawing heavily upon the analysis of Kiesler and his associates.

1. First, attitudes serve an instrumental, adjustive, or utilitarian function. According to Katz, a person develops a positive attitude toward those objects that are useful in meeting his needs. If an object (or person) thwarts his needs, he develops a negative attitude toward it. Smith, Bruner, and White see a somewhat different function for attitudes here. To them, an attitude may be useful in establishing a social relationship. If we hold certain people as models, we develop attitudes similar to theirs, so that we can say we are like our models.

Table 10-3. *The Functions of Attitudes*

Katz	*Smith, Bruner, and White*
Types:	
1. Instrumental, adjustive, utilitarian	Social adjustment
2. Ego defense	Externalization
3. Knowledge	Object appraisal
4. Value expressive	Quality of expressiveness

(From *Attitude Change: A Critical Analysis of Theoretical Approaches* by Kiesler, Collins, & Miller. Copyright 1969 by John Wiley & Sons, Inc. Reprinted by permission.)

2. Second, attitudes serve an ego-defense or externalization function. Here Katz's functional theory is influenced by psychoanalytic considerations. An attitude may develop and change in order to protect a person "from acknowledging the basic truths about himself or the harsh realities in his external world" (Katz, 1960, p. 170). For example, derogatory attitudes toward outgroups and minority groups may serve as a means of convincing oneself of one's own importance. Without utilizing psychoanalytic supports, Smith, Bruner, and White see attitudes functioning in a similar way; attitudes permit the externalizing of reactions.

3. The knowledge function or object appraisal is a third function of attitudes. Attitudes may develop or change in order to "give meaning to what would otherwise be an unorganized chaotic universe" (Katz, 1960, p. 175). Particularly, this will happen when a problem cannot be solved without the information associated with the attitude. Smith, Bruner, and White see one function of attitudes as a "ready aid in 'sizing up' objects and events in the environment from the point of view of one's major interests and going concerns" (1956, p. 41). Thus, categorizing objects or events is done more efficiently, and time is not spent figuring out afresh how one should respond. Object appraisal then "stresses the role that gathering information plays in the day-to-day adaptive activities of the individual" (Kiesler et al., 1969, p. 315).

4. Value-expression is a fourth function of attitudes. To Katz, a person gains satisfaction from expressing himself through his attitudes. Beyond this, his expression of attitudes helps him form his self-concept. Smith, Bruner, and White diverge most widely from Katz at this point. To them, the expressive nature of attitudes does not mean that any need for expression exists but rather that a person's attitudes "reflect the deeper-lying pattern of his or her life" (Smith, Bruner, & White, 1956, p. 38).

A. Applications of the Theory to Attitude-Change Procedure

Consider the causes of prejudice described in Chapter 9. The person chosen for the summer project may have expressed antiblack attitudes because he was exposed to them in his environment and learned them from his family and friends. However, his prejudice may reflect a deep-seated personality maladjustment. That is, his internal feelings of personal worthlessness may be so threatening to him that he defends against them by disparaging blacks, hippies, or other vulnerable groups. A functional theory proposes that the techniques of attitude change most effective for one situation would not be best for the other. Thus, functional theory would first seek to determine what needs were being met by the white's antiblack attitudes. A series of projective tests or clinical interviews would probably be used to try to make this determination; the actual procedures used are not mentioned by the theory.

If the person seems to be antiblack because of the environment in which he has grown up, the attitude-change process should be based upon the dissemination of new information and the use of social pressure and re-education. In other words, the task is to create a new environment where new information about blacks is transmitted to the subject. Previous attitudes and behaviors may have served needs to be socially accepted; thus, the subject must be shown that new attitudes toward blacks must be developed to be accepted by the present group.

But if his antiblack attitudes serve other needs, such as the need to fend off fears of personal inferiority, a deluge of information will have little effect. In this case, therapeutic devices such as catharsis and developing insight into the ego-defensive function served by the attitude might be more beneficial.

B. Representative Research

As Kiesler et al. (1969) point out, a straightforward test of functional theory would be to select two subjects whose attitudes are similar but based on different needs and then to determine the effectiveness of various kinds of attitude-change techniques on both subjects. Since Katz's functional theory has been tested by only limited research, an early study by McClintock (1958) will be described as an example of the approach.

McClintock (1958) presented two types of persuasive appeals to classes in two colleges. He proposed that among all the subjects receiving an *interpretational* appeal, those whose attitudes served an ego-defense need would show the most attitude change. In contrast, McClintock predicted that an *informational* appeal would bring about no attitude change in subjects whose attitudes served these ego-defensive needs. Almost opposite effects were expected with subjects whose attitudes served to meet conformity needs; that is, an informational appeal would be more effective with them than the interpretational appeal. This expectation of an interaction between type of persuasive argument and type of subject is characteristic of the functional approach.

Three types of persuasive communications were used by McClintock to try to change levels of prejudice: (a) an informational message (actually an exploration of the cultural relativism argument), (b) an interpersonal message (which used a case study and analysis to show that unhealthy psychodynamics can lead to prejudice), and (c) an ethnocentric message (which implied that recipients of the message should become more prejudiced). The subjects' degree of conformity needs and ego defensiveness were assessed by subscales from the California F scale.

Despite the rather unclear manipulations of persuasive messages and the brief measuring instruments, one of the two hypotheses was confirmed. Among subjects who read the informational message, 67 percent of those high in conformity needs changed their attitudes in the desired direction, while only 29 percent of those low in conformity needs responded in this way. In contrast, the informational appeal had opposite effects on ego-defensive subjects. Only 4 percent of the ego-defensive subjects changed their attitudes, while the rest of these subjects did not respond to the informational appeal. Thus the informational appeal was shown to be most effective with subjects high in conformity needs.

When presented with the interpretational message, subjects with high ego-defense needs did not change as much as those whose needs were moderate or low. (Fifty-three percent of highs, 95 percent of mediums, and 75 percent of lows changed their attitudes in the desired direction.) Degree of conformity needs had no relationship to the extent of change resulting from exposure to the interpretational message. We might expect that the interpretational message would have the greatest influence on highly ego-involved subjects, but Katz argues that these people are too defensive and rigid to accept any changes. He believes that the important comparison is between the moderate and the low ego-defensive subjects. Here, a significantly greater percentage of the moderately ego-involved recipients change than do the less ego-involved (95 percent versus 75 percent, where p-value of difference = .015). Thus, tentative evidence is presented for a basic postulate of the functional theory: that the effect of a persuasive communication is partially influenced by the functions that attitudes serve in the recipient.

The empirical base of functional theory remains, however, on quite shaky ground. Replications of McClintock's procedure (Katz, Sarnoff, & McClintock, 1956; Stotland, Katz, & Patchen, 1959) produce inconsistent or conflicting results. In response to an interpretational appeal, subjects lowest in ego defensiveness were found to change as much as or more than moderately defensive subjects. In addition, these groups of subjects may well have differed in degree of prejudice as well as amount of ego defense and conformity, and, as Kiesler and his associates (1969) indicate, the differences in attitude change might be most easily explained by considering the discrepancy between the advocated position and the recipient's own position.

C. Evaluation

A functional theory of attitudes is appealing to anyone who recognizes that attitude change is a function of the stimulus and the recipient. More than any other approach, this one recognizes individual differences in the reactions to any given persuasive communication, and for that reason it should not be dismissed lightly. But the development of the theory is hampered by a lack of adequate measures of the needs that the attitudes serve. Other theoretical approaches are content to measure attitudes and their changes. In itself this is a challenging task. Functional theory says that we must know what function the attitude serves for the individual, and we must be able to measure it. Until such measurements are better developed, we must regretfully conclude that the theory has little practical use.

VI. THEORIES OF ATTITUDE CHANGE AND ASSUMPTIONS ABOUT HUMAN NATURE

Each of the four general approaches reviewed thus far uses different concepts to explain attitude change. Each approach makes different assumptions about the nature of man. By looking at these assumptions we may gain further understanding of the contributions of the various theories of attitude change.

It is fashionable to state that *stimulus-response* and *reinforcement* theories assume that humans respond to stimuli in a rather passive, robot-like fashion. A careful reading would indicate, however, that such a notion does not represent S-R theory fairly. For instance, the Yale Communication Research program recognized that the recipient must attend to and comprehend a stimulus before his attitude could be changed by it. While the S-R approach has been primarily interested in aspects of the stimulus and the communicator, it has also recognized that the recipient's characteristics influence the extent of attitude change. Contemporary S-R theories are more often S-O-R theories, recognizing the place of the organism between the stimulus and the response.

Basic to S-R and reinforcement approaches is the notion that incentives for change must be stronger than the incentives for maintaining the present approach. Here we see an assumption of individuality, or at least a recognition that the recipient's hierarchy of reinforcements must be understood and recognized. Beyond this, there is an assumption that if such reinforcements are known by the communicator, they can be used to manipulate the recipient's attitudes. The reinforcement theorist would claim that if he had enough information about the recipients and if he had the resources at hand, he could bring about attitude change in every recipient through the same general techniques.

Social-judgment theory appears to assume greater precision in regard to attitudes held. This approach holds that each person localizes his attitude at some point along a scale that includes areas of acceptance and rejection. It proposes that for each attitude we develop anchors, a degree of intensity, and hence the potential positive or negative effects of each persuasive communication. Social-judgment theory sees man as a cognitive being, in that he knows what his attitudes are, where they stand along a continuum, which other possible attitudes he would accept, and which attitudes he would reject.

Some attitude theorists reject the notion that attitudes are precisely known or measured or can be located within latitudes of acceptance and rejection by the possessor. Abelson (1968), for example, has proposed that most people possess *opinion molecules* for most attitudes. An opinion molecule is composed of (a) a belief or fact, (b) an attitude, and (c) the perception that the attitude is socially supported. In his delightful *Beliefs, Attitudes, and Human Affairs* (1970), Bem offers the following as an example of an opinion molecule: "It's a fact that when my uncle Charlie had back trouble, he was cured by a chiropractor (fact). You know, I feel that chiropractors have been sneered at too much (attitude), and I'm not ashamed to say so because I know a lot of people who feel the same way (social support)" (p. 38). Opinion molecules are isolated units that serve our needs to make sensible conversation. As such, they have little need to be precise or logical.

The *consistency theories* explicitly assume that man is rational—that holding conflicting attitudes is intolerable to man and hence stimulates him to change. This general approach has monopolized thinking about attitude change in the last two decades; Pepitone (1966), for example, wrote that "there is no question but that theoretical social psychology is today fairly dominated by hypotheses and experiments derived from these models" (p. 257).

As indicated earlier, the limits of consistency theories are beginning to appear. A wholesale assumption that man is always rational and forever abhors inconsistency has been rejected in favor of the notion that at least "*some* people *sometimes* act in such a way as to minimize inconsistencies" (Skolnick & Shaw, 1970, p. 4, italics in original). But on other occasions people can live with their inconsistencies quite well, and seeking consistency may be a relatively unimportant motive when compared with motives for approval, achievement, or power.

The *functional theory* emphasizes the individual differences in human nature. To change another's attitude, we must first recognize his nature and his needs. By knowing the idiosyncratic needs his attitudes serve, we are directed toward ways to change his attitudes. The functional theory reflects assumptions about the complexity and variability of human nature.

VII. SUMMARY

Four different theories of attitude change are stimulus-response and reinforcement theory, social-judgment theory, consistency theory, and functional theory. Any adequate theory of attitude change must be able to predict and explain cases in which attitudes do not change as well as instances where they do change.

The Yale University Communication Research Program emphasized that in the learning of a new attitude three variables are important: *attention, comprehension,* and *acceptance.*

More than any other approach, the *stimulus-response* and *reinforcement* theories make the assumption that attitudes are changed only if the incentives for making a new response are greater than the incentives for maintaining the old response. The intensity with which some attitudes are held may be increased through the use of verbal conditioning procedures.

Two examples of a *social-judgment theory* of attitude change are Sherif and Hovland's *assimilation-contrast theory* and Helson's *adaptation-level theory.* Assimilation-contrast theory conceptualizes attitudes along a reference scale. Within this scale there is an area called the latitude of acceptance—the limits of the attitude statements with which the respondent would agree. Attempts to shift attitudes must pose new positions that are within this latitude of acceptance. According to assimilation-contrast theory, the stronger the person's degree of ego-involvement with an attitude object, the narrower his latitude of acceptance and the broader his latitude of rejection. Little solid evidence exists for the acceptance of an assimilation-contrast theory of attitude change.

The *consistency theory* of attitude change includes Heider's *balance theory,* Osgood and Tannenbaum's *congruity theory,* Festinger's *cognitive dissonance theory,* and Brehm's *reactance theory.* Common to these is an assumption that people change their attitudes in the direction of removing inconsistencies between conflicting attitudes or behaviors. Of all the consistency approaches, cognitive dissonance theory has stimulated the most research and controversy. Cognitive dissonance is said to exist when a person possesses two cognitions, one of which is the obverse of the other.

The research evidence for the validity of a consistency theory is in itself inconsistent. While some people on some occasions change their attitudes in order to achieve greater consistency, other people either do not notice their inconsistencies or manage to endure them.

The basic proposition of the *functional theory* of attitude change is that people hold attitudes that fit their needs. In order to change their attitudes, we must determine what these needs are. Among the functions which attitudes may serve are (a) the instrumental, adjustive, or utilitarian function, (b) the ego-defensive or externalization function, (c) the knowledge function or object appraisal, and (d) the value-expressing function.

Each attitude-change theory possesses its own assumptions about the nature of man.

VIII. SUGGESTED READINGS

Festinger, L., Riecken, H., & Schachter, S. *When prophecy fails.* Minneapolis: University of Minnesota Press, 1956. An interesting combination of theory and fact. The investigators infiltrated a "doomsday group" and observed their reactions when the predicted cataclysm did not come. At least the prediction of cognitive dissonance theory was confirmed—after the prediction of the doomsday group was not.

Insko, C. A. *Theories of attitude change.* New York: Appleton-Century-Crofts, 1967. An extremely thorough critique of the attitude-change theories reviewed in this chapter. Adequacy or inadequacy of methodology is stressed.

Kiesler, C. A., Collins, B. E., & Miller, N. *Attitude change: A critical analysis of theoretical approaches.* New York: Wiley, 1969. A useful review of attitude-change theories. Similar in purpose to Insko's book, this work is somewhat more recent, somewhat more readable, and somewhat less comprehensive.

Smith, M. B., Bruner, J. S., & White, R. W. *Opinions and personality.* New York: Wiley, 1956. (Paperback version published in 1964 by Wiley Science Editions) The attitudes and personalities of ten men are probed in order to understand the psychological processes involved in attitude formation and change. Relevant to the functional theory of attitude change.

Wagner, R. V., & Sherwood, J. J. (Eds.) *The study of attitude change.* Belmont, Calif.: Brooks/Cole, 1969. (Paperback) A selection of articles that present theory and research representative of each attitude-change approach. The review of cognitive dissonance prepared by Sherwood, Barron, and Fitch is a useful review of this highly productive approach.

I. *REDUCING PREJUDICE AGAINST MINORITY GROUPS: THE CONTACT HYPOTHESIS*

II. *FACTORS FACILITATING CHANGE IN FACE-TO-FACE CONTACT*

- A. *Characteristics of the individuals in contact*
- B. *Characteristics of the situation*
  1. *The range of possible relationships in the situation—the acquaintance potential*
  2. *The relative status of the participants in a contact situation*
  3. *The nature of the social norm concerning contact of one group with another*
  4. *The presence of a cooperative reward structure rather than a competitive one*
  5. *The characteristics of the individuals who are in contact*

III. *BRINGING THE BENEFICIAL FACTORS TOGETHER: STUART COOK'S STUDY*

- A. *Assumptions*
- B. *Procedures*
  1. *Stage one: Pretesting*
  2. *Stage two: Interracial contact*
  3. *Stage three: Retesting of attitudes*
- C. *Results*
  1. *Anecdotal evidence*
  2. *Objective changes in behavior toward the black participant*
  3. *Changes in responses to attitude measures*

IV. *WHY DO SOME PEOPLE CHANGE THEIR ATTITUDES WHEN OTHERS DO NOT?*

V. *TECHNIQUES OF ATTITUDE CHANGE*

VI. *SUMMARY*

VII. *SUGGESTED READINGS*

Chapter Eleven

Attitude Change through Intergroup Contact

Bring us together. *Campaign promise made by Richard Nixon*

As seen in the preceding chapter, theories on the nature of attitude change are prevalent in social psychology. Attitude change can also be studied by looking at and seeking explanations for patterns of events. Stuart W. Cook (1970) refers to this approach as one that uses *event* theories, rather than the *process* theories described in Chapter 10. Event theories include hypotheses that seek to explain recurring patterns of events. Such an approach isolates different aspects that may influence the situation. In the present chapter, we shall identify those factors that have been found to reduce prejudice in the field; we shall explore the effects of these factors in a controlled yet natural social setting, and we shall examine the use of various techniques for inducing general attitude change.

I. REDUCING PREJUDICE AGAINST MINORITY GROUPS: THE CONTACT HYPOTHESIS

Many people have made the optimistic assumption that if two racial or religious groups could be brought together, the hostility, antagonism, and prejudice formerly expressed by each toward the other would erode, and favorable attitudes would develop. This, in essence, is the intergroup contact hypothesis. Quite obviously, this hypothesis must be qualified before it can be considered valid. For example, blacks moving into all-white neighborhoods, Catholics and Protestants warring over the same streets in Northern Ireland, and hippies and policemen playing together in softball games are situations that show how intergroup contact can have either beneficial or deleterious outcomes. The mere frequency of contact is of no import; the nature of the contact—as will be spelled out subsequently—is the determinant.

Despite this need for qualification, the contact hypothesis has the merit of recognizing that attempts to change prejudice without intergroup contact are doomed to

Figure 11-1. *An Interracial Discussion Group. Here three women discuss their shared problems in raising teenage boys. Does this type of interracial contact necessarily bring about greater acceptance of other groups? (Photograph courtesy of Demonstration and Research Center in Early Education, Peabody College.)*

fail. For example, programs that introduce new information about a minority group through lectures, films, and written materials have had no long-term effects on prejudiced attitudes (Watson, 1947; R. M. Williams, 1947). Attitude change cannot take place without some interaction between the prejudiced person and the minority group. Apparently, personal association and involvement are the keys to success in changing attitudes.

II. FACTORS FACILITATING CHANGE IN FACE-TO-FACE CONTACT

Even involuntary contact between a prejudiced person and a member of a disliked group may have beneficial outcomes if certain conditions exist. Numerous studies done in field settings have clarified these conditions, which may be placed in two categories: (a) characteristics of the individuals who are in contact and (b) characteristics of the contact situation (S. W. Cook, 1970).

A. Characteristics of the Individuals in Contact

As indicated in Chapter 9, prejudice does not serve the same function for all persons sharing the same negative attitudes toward a minority group. The *causes* of a person's prejudice determine the degree to which that person might change. As Amir has indicated, "Certain personalities . . . will not be affected positively by interracial contact. Their inner insecurity and their personal disorder will not permit them to benefit from the contact with a group against whom they are prejudiced because they will always need a scapegoat" (1969, p. 335). Mussen (1953) brought white and black boys together for a four-week summer camp. As a group, the white boys' level of prejudice was the same after the camp as before. However, some of the white boys became more prejudiced, and some became less prejudiced as a result of the experience. The boys who became more antiblack exhibited test responses that showed greater aggressive feelings and greater needs to defy authority.

The *intensity of the attitude* held by the prejudiced person can also influence degree of attitude change. Again, an interaction effect occurs: that is, after contact, a group may appear to be just as prejudiced as before, when in reality some of its members have become less prejudiced and others have become more so. Cook (1957) has cited a study by Taylor on how whites react to blacks living in houses on their same block. On the one hand, those whites who had been favorable to blacks before the first black family moved in became even more favorable after blacks had been living nearby for several weeks. On the other hand, whites who were initially against the idea of residential desegregation were even more negative after desegregation occurred. In many cases, contact intensifies whatever initial attitude one possesses.

B. Characteristics of the Situation

S. W. Cook has described five characteristics of the contact situation. Favorable attitude change can be facilitated when these five aspects of the situation are brought together under optimum conditions.

The Range of Possible Relationships in the Situation—the Acquaintance Potential. A person can have daily contact with another person over a number of years and yet not get to know that person as an individual. Our contacts with maids, postmen, and cashiers are often examples of this. Such brief, superficial, role-oriented contacts do nothing to facilitate knowing the other person. If we can come to know people *as individuals,* learning their aspirations, their fears, their likes and dislikes, some attitude change may result. In big cities, apartment dwellers may know little about the family in the next apartment. Attitudes toward neighbors may be neutral or negative. But when black and white housewives living in the same apartment building are brought together and have a chance to get to know each other as individual persons, attitude change in the direction of greater acceptance is the typical result (Deutsch & Collins, 1951; Wilner, Walkley, & Cook, 1955).

The Relative Status of the Participants in a Contact Situation. Somewhat related to the preceding situational characteristic is the aspect of status. Beneficial attitude change is more likely if the minority-group member has the same status as the prejudiced person. If the minority-group member has a lower status or if he has a higher status, the interaction is likely to be role-oriented, with less opportunity for authentic relationships between the participants.

The Nature of the Social Norm Concerning Contact of One Group with Another. In some situations, the persons involved may expect that a friendly association is appropriate; in such cases, beneficial attitude change is more likely to result. Less attitude change results when the people involved have no expectation of a social relationship—as in business contacts.

Social norms are often reflected in the pronouncements of public officials. The school principal who tells irate parents, "I don't like school desegregation either, but I have to enforce it," creates a social norm that discourages much change in attitudes toward blacks. If the principal acts in compliance with the law and keeps his negative attitudes to himself, there is greater chance that parents will comply with new policies and perhaps eventually come to accept their merit.

The Presence of a Cooperative Reward Structure Rather Than a Competitive One. Reward structures often go hand-in-hand with social norms, but the two can also be unrelated. Norms for superficial congeniality may exist within a situation that also puts the white person in competition with the black. To facilitate beneficial attitude change a different situation is necessary. There must be mutual interdependence, and the reward structure should be cooperative. That is, task goals for the white person can be achieved only when and if the black person achieves his goals.

The Characteristics of the Individuals Who Are in Contact. Particularly beneficial to favorable attitude change are contacts in which the participating minority-group members differ from commonly held, unflattering stereotypes of their group. Interacting and working with a black who is hardworking, bright, restrained, and not particularly musical or religious may be the stimulus for attitude change. It is also helpful if the member of the minority group resembles the majority-group member in regard to background, interests, and personality. The prejudiced white who realizes that his black co-worker is similar to him may be able to overcome his stereotyped beliefs about blacks.

When a task brings different kinds of people together and places them in a situation where their contacts are impersonal and their goals are competitive, the contact most probably will not lead to greater acceptance of the black by the white. Consider the desegregation of a public school. The school board may comply with a court order to desegregate but convey its displeasure to the children and their parents. Black children may be bused from a different part of town, thus reifying their different status in the eyes of the white children. Black and white children may have to compete over a limited number of places on the cheerleading squad. When such conditions prevail, school desegregation can lead to increased rejection of blacks by whites. (For an example, see Webster's 1961 study of the desegregation of a school in the San Francisco Bay area.)

However, school authorities can do much to create conditions favorable to a desirable change in attitudes. When a school must change the racial composition of its student body, an implementation of the five conditions described here should influence the success of the change. Situations in which blacks and whites must work together to achieve a group goal should be sought. Superordinate goals, such as building a new playground or seeking the all-city sportsmanship trophy, are examples.

III. BRINGING THE BENEFICIAL FACTORS TOGETHER: STUART COOK'S STUDY

Stuart W. Cook (1964, 1970, 1971) has created an experimental situation by which to test the validity of the contact hypothesis. The goal of this ten-year project was to determine what happens to prejudiced attitudes when all the beneficial aspects of interracial contact are mobilized in the same situation. In this well-executed attempt to bring about a reduction in prejudice, antiblack white subjects were involuntarily placed in contact with a black. The assumptions, procedures, and results of Cook's project shall be reviewed here.

A. Assumptions

Cook (1964) recognized that involuntary interracial contact is a way of life in contemporary America. Even the most prejudiced white person—one who might try to avoid contact with those different from himself—must interact with persons of other races in a variety of settings, such as school, the military, or a job. The possibility of attitude change during the course of involuntary social contact provides a potentially fruitful focus of study.

Cook assumed that a reasonable delineation of the significant factors in the contact experience could be made on the basis of field studies from the past. (These factors were reviewed in Section II.) Cook attempted to recreate the unintended, interracial contact in a setting where each potentially important factor could be controlled. The contact situation as it usually occurs in the field is often too complex to provide much understanding of why attitude change does or does not occur. Cook assumed that a laboratory setting could be created that would open the way to a more controlled analysis of the determinants of attitude change than had been permitted by field studies.

Cook also assumed that such a study would contribute to a better understanding of attitude-change theory. For example, the functional theory of attitude change could be verified if varying different factors of the contact experience produced changes in different types of subjects. Cook wrote that if analysis should "show that change is strongly associated with the operation of situational norms regarding intergroup relations this would suggest that the change may be understood in terms of an affiliative (or security) need, e.g., the adoption of beliefs and feelings which bring a sense of identification with or acceptance by respected peers. A quite different implication would be suggested, however, by the discovery that change was most evident when the contact situation was characterized by cooperative interdependence in the achievement of shared goals and rewards. Here the process indicated would start with the generation of feelings of satisfaction and pleasure; such feelings would be associated with the participant from the disliked social group and gradually generalize to the group itself" (1964, p. 6).

B. Procedures

Cook's study was carried out in a large city in the South that contained several colleges. The study consisted of three stages, which used the same subjects but which took place on two different college campuses. Potential subjects for the study came from four of the city's predominantly white colleges—all of which were within two miles of one another. The first stage of the study involved paid participation as a subject in a project for an "Institute for Test Development" at "Biltmore University" (not the true name of the university). The second stage took place at another local college, where the subjects worked for two hours a day for a month in a group project. This group project was designed to appear quite unrelated to the test development project: it was a different activity carried out at a different college by a different staff. The third stage of the study involved a retesting of the subject by the "Institute of Test Development" at "Biltmore University." Each of the three stages in the total project was separated by two or more months.

Stage One: Pretesting. Because the staff members who would supervise the stage-two group project were both female, it was initially decided to seek only females as subjects for the project. Thus the bogus "Institute for Test Development" posted handbills around the four college campuses seeking females who wanted to earn money by taking a battery of tests. The tests were administered in two-hour blocks spread over two weeks; it usually took the subject about 15 hours to complete all the tests. From the subject's viewpoint, the test session not only provided an opportunity to make money but also a chance to get feedback about her abilities and attitudes. (Subjects, as promised, were later provided a report that compared their scores with the group score on a variety of measures.) Thus, the sample of females who appeared for testing was certainly not a random sample of female undergraduates at these colleges. The sample probably had a high number of girls who were curious or insecure in the sense that they welcomed the opportunity to get feedback about themselves.

The battery of tests included approximately 75 different measures. About four hours went to measures of personality and needs, two hours to attitudes toward blacks and other minority groups, four hours to a variety of political and social attitude measures, and four hours to measures of ability. The latter measures were included solely to direct the subject's attention away from the inquiries about racial attitudes. The two hours of racial-attitude testing covered seven measures that were used as an indication of the degree of antiblack prejudice. The other measures—particularly the Minnesota Multiphasic Personality Inventory and the California F scale of authoritarianism—were intended to identify subjects with severe maladjustments, as the project was intended to include in the contact situation only those females whose prejudice resulted from learned experiences from the environment, rather than from basic personality difficulties.

The subjects were told that the institute was developing new tests and that one of its concerns was the test-retest reliability of its measures. At the first test session they were informed that because of this problem, they would be retested several months later, again for pay. This device prepared them for stage three of Cook's project—retesting after the interracial contact.

Stage Two: Interracial Contact. Among the 20 or so subjects in each testing series, usually between 3 and 8 subjects had scores on the prejudice measures that were extreme enough to qualify them for the second stage of the project. Cook had hoped to use only clearly antiblack subjects in the interracial-contact situation—that is, only those whose scores were in the top third on prejudice on each of three basic prejudice measures. However, because of the limited number of possibilities that occurred after some testings, Cook was not able to hold to such a stringent criterion.

Anywhere from a few days up to several months after the first testing, a highly prejudiced subject received a phone call from a faculty member at "St. George's College" (not the true name of the college), inviting her to apply for part-time work on a group project. The job would take two hours a day and last a month. The faculty member then went on to describe briefly a management task called the Railroad Game (B. T. Jensen & Terebinski, 1963). The faculty member explained that the task was being tried out as one of several tasks being evaluated by the government for the purpose of training groups of strangers to work together. The findings of the local study would be of value in understanding how crews at isolated bases might work together.

The potential subject then indicated whether or not she wished to apply for the job. Some chose not to, because of other jobs or the need to study or for other unannounced reasons. But if a potential subject expressed interest, an appointment was arranged at "St. George's College." There followed three appointments—usually on consecutive days—during which the subject was interviewed, tested for suitability for the job, and given some training in the Railroad Game. She was then pronounced as suitable by the supervisor (though there never had been any doubt), and she signed a contract agreeing to work two hours a day for a month with the understanding that none of her pay would be given to her unless she completed the month. The purpose of these devices was to discourage the prejudiced subject from withdrawing from the project when she discovered it was an interracial one. During the training, no reference was made to the fact that one of the other two crew members would be black—any questions from the subject about the other two crew members on the Railroad Game were answered by saying, "You wouldn't know them; they're girls from two other colleges here." At one point during the training the supervisor introduced her helper, a black female college student, but the subject could perceive the helper's position as subordinate and rather detached.

All these heavy-handed procedures were undertaken because the subjects were, in their expressed attitudes, so antiblack that Cook questioned whether they would go through with the job when it was revealed they would be working closely with a black. On a sentence-completion task in stage one, many of these subjects had responded that they would either quit, move, or seek a transfer if put on a job with a black. (Other typical responses are found in Table 11-1.) Additionally, the project was begun in 1961, when it was very unusual for Southern blacks and whites to be working together or eating together under conditions of equal status.

The group's task in the Railroad Game was to operate a railroad system composed of ten stations, six lines, and 500 freight cars of six different types. It took the group some time to learn how to operate the system efficiently; for one reason, much information had to be acquired, and, second, they had to learn how to maintain a distribution of cars at different stations appropriate for upcoming shipping orders.

Table 11-1. *Responses of Prejudiced Whites to Cook's Sentence-Completion Test*

1. If they began admitting Negroes to the club to which I belong, I would . . .
   "drop out."
   "find another club."
   "stop it."
2. If my boss began hiring many Negroes, I would . . .
   "quit right away."
   "tell him to hire whites or I'd leave."
   "not like it at all."
3. If someone at my church suggested inviting the Young People's group at a Negro church to a joint supper meeting, I would . . .
   "vote against it."
   "feel uncomfortable."
   "throw up."

When requests were received to ship merchandise of specified types from one station to another, the group was to make a decision as to which route to follow and what types of cars to use. These decisions were then telephoned by the crew to the supervisor and her helper who were located behind a screen in another part of the workroom. (See Figure 11-2.) The helper maintained a computer system, which furnished the crew with the official records of the dispersion of cars, profits earned, losses and penalties incurred, and the like.

Three tasks were carried out by the crew. The *dispatcher* decided which orders were to be filled, the kinds of cars to be used, and the route to be taken. The *status keeper* kept track of present and future availability of cars, could initiate redistribution of empty cars, and was to work very closely with the dispatcher, possibly sharing her decisions. The *accountant* kept accounts of earnings and costs and worked separately but on the basis of information supplied by the dispatcher. The job of telephoning the information necessary to dispatch cars of a particular type loaded with specified material over a designated route could be done by any crew member, but was usually done by the dispatcher.

As used in Cook's project, the Railroad Game lasted 40 "days"—a day in the Railroad Game covering about 30 to 40 minutes. An experimental session was composed of two such "days" separated by a 30-minute break. The purpose of the break was explained to the subject as giving the supervisor and her helper time to prepare materials; in actuality, it was used for other purposes to be explained subsequently.

On the first session of the month-long job, the prejudiced subject met with the other two crew members for the first time. Both were female students at a local college. One crew member, given the dispatcher's job, was white. The other, the accountant,

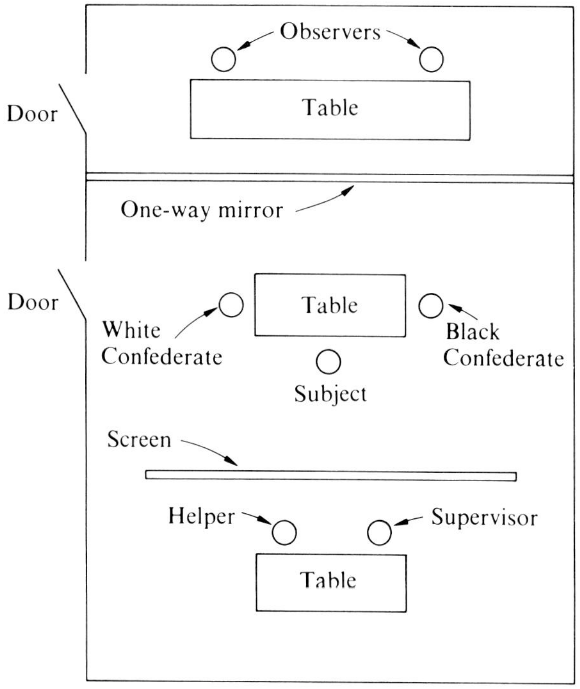

Figure 11-2. *Layout of "Railroad Game" Workroom*

was black. Both were to act as though they were novices to the situation, but in fact both were confederates of the experimenter. The supervisor (who was a white in her 30s) briefly reviewed the task and mentioned the crew's opportunity to make bonus money by outdoing the performance of earlier crews. After answering questions, the supervisor gave the crew their first day's shipping orders and retired behind the screen. The crew, all seated at the same table, could communicate directly with each other but could talk to the supervisor and her helper only by telephone. (See layout in Figure 11-2.)

After 30 minutes of running the railroad, plus overtime if the crew wished to use it to complete the "day's" orders, there was a 30-minute lunch break. Food ordered at the beginning of the session was brought in by the supervisor and her helper, who then departed. The crew distributed the food and retained their same seating locations for lunch. Conversations during the early sessions concentrated on the Railroad Game and getting to know each other. The true purpose of this lunch break was to create a situation that fulfilled the beneficial characteristics described in Section II of this chapter. It may be helpful to review these to see how their requirements were met in this situation.

1. The *acquaintance potential* was facilitated by the conversation of the confederates. The black confederate brought to each lunch-break conversation facts about herself, her family, her future plans and aspirations, and such personal information as her preferences, tastes, apprehensions, and disappointments. Sometimes facts were volunteered; sometimes they were evoked by preplanned questions from the white confederate. Questions directed to the black by the subject (if they occurred) also provided opportunities for the dissemination of information. Observers behind a one-way mirror kept a frequency tabulation of the amount of personal information brought out by each confederate; this procedure served as a check so that the amount of personal information could be roughly equated from one subject to another.

2. In compliance with the second factor—*relative status of the participants*—the black confederate was defined by the situation as being of equal status with the other two crew members. Her job responsibilities and authority were equal to theirs. Built into the procedure was a rotation of crew assignments, which reinforced the equality of status for the three participants.

3. The third factor—*social norms regarding contact between groups*—was handled by making it clear to all participants that the situation favored acceptance of blacks. The white supervisor had a black helper to whom she allocated a great deal of responsibility. The black crew member was treated the same as the whites. Beyond this expression by the institutional structure, other ways of communicating a favorable norm were utilized. With time, the white confederate increasingly expressed sympathy with the black and disapproval of segregation.

4. The *presence of a cooperative reward structure* was achieved through the structure of the Railroad Game. The subject was involved in efforts to achieve a goal in common with the black participant. A bonus was paid to the group, if the group members did well. Thus, the situation avoided a reward structure in which participants work individually toward mutually exclusive goals. In addition, the Railroad Game procedure led to close interaction and mutual assistance between the prejudiced white person and the black, especially when these participants were paired as the dispatcher and the status keeper. The two, together with the white confederate, shared reverses as well as successes day by day for 20 calendar days. Moreover, the

rotation of crew assignments put the prejudiced white person in a position of both teaching the black and being taught by her.

5. The *characteristics of the individuals in contact* were also considered. The black confederate was selected and presented throughout as being personable, able, ambitious, and self-respecting. Care was taken to see that the black did her Railroad Game tasks well. Thus, the black participant was quite a different person from the stereotyped one expected by the prejudiced white.

Additionally, the black confederate presented information about the injustices and indignities she had suffered as a result of racial discrimination. On 10 of the 20 calendar days in which the crew was together, their conversations were preplanned, eventually leading to a discussion of race relations. For example, an early conversation topic was shopping for clothing. In briefing sessions, the black confederate and the white confederate were trained to put across particular points regarding discrimination against blacks by downtown department stores. (For example, in the early 1960s department stores in the South would not permit blacks to try on clothes at the store. Instead, the store would deliver clothes to the black's home where they could be tried on without the knowledge of whites.) During the lunch-break conversation, after some general trading of experiences, the white confederate would ask the black a question regarding the matter of segregation in the sales practices of department stores. The race-relations aspect of the discussion lent itself to a review of injustices and indignities suffered by the black participant or by persons she knew.

As the month-long contact experience continued, the white confederate was more openly upset with the ways blacks are persecuted in American society. However, the confederate avoided asking the subject for confirmation of this opinion. If subjects were put on the spot by such questioning, they likely would have become defensive about their prejudiced attitudes and, hence, more rigidified in these attitudes.

On the final calendar day of the Railroad Game, the last half-hour was devoted to a questionnaire filled out by each crew member in a separate room. The subject was told that the purpose of the procedure was to evaluate the Railroad Game as a potential training task. Included were several open-ended questions about the other crew members, but the topic of race was not mentioned. Although the subject's answers to these questions might have revealed her reactions to the confederates, Cook did not use them as a measure of attitude change.

The week after the completion of the Railroad Game the subject was provided with an additional experience that was designed to encourage generalization from the single black to other blacks. (Finding a modification of feelings and behavior toward a specific black participant without an accompanying generalization to blacks as a group would not have been surprising.) The additional experience was a series of five interviews with other college females. These interviews were carried out by the subject as a basis for rating persons who were presented as potential participants in the next Railroad Game. Of the five persons interviewed by the subject, two were blacks and three were whites.

Stage Three: Retesting of Attitudes. Between one and three months after the termination of the part-time job at "St. George's College," each subject received a letter from the "Institute for Test Development" at "Biltmore University." The letter was a reminder to the subject that there would be an opportunity to serve as a paid subject for additional tests. Each subject was scheduled to retake most of the original tests, including the tests measuring attitudes. A number of new tests were also introduced to add reality to the cover story. The changes in the attitudes expressed by the subjects on the measures of prejudice were used as indicators of the effectiveness of the attitude-change intervention.

C. Results

The outcomes of this project can be described at three levels: anecdotal evidence for changes toward the black participant, objective evidence for changes toward the black, and differences in response to the measures of attitudes toward blacks in general.

Anecdotal Evidence. It should be remembered that not only had the prejudiced whites in this project had little or no previous contact with blacks, but most of them, in completing their paper-and-pencil tests, had also expressed strong personal rejection of blacks. At the beginning of the project the idea of eating with a black was probably unpleasant to every one of the prejudiced whites.

In light of such factors, consider what happened during a lunch break late in the month of one crew. As usual, the crew members had ordered their lunches before the first day of the game; the food was to be delivered from the college snack bar before the lunch break. One aspect of this procedure was anticipating what type of pie the snack bar was offering that day. This day the subject decided to forego a piece of pie, but the black confederate ordered one. When the lunches arrived, the crew discovered that blackberry pie was being served—the subject's favorite. As the black confederate ate her pie, the subject kept turning her eyes to the pie as if hypnotized. Finally, after the black confederate cast aside her half-eaten slice of pie, the subject turned to her and said, "Betty Jean, would you mind if I ate the rest of your pie?" Surely, had the prejudiced white been told one month before that she would soon be eating a black person's leftovers, the suggestion would have been met with ridicule!

Numerous other anecdotal examples showed changes in the behavior of prejudiced whites toward blacks. One subject hitched a ride downtown with the black confederate because it would save her the busfare. Other subjects were visibly influenced by the content of the lunch-time conversations and were particularly touched by the black confederate's recounting of indignities she had suffered. The conversations presented opportunities for relearning for many of the prejudiced whites; they had never realized, for example, that blacks traveling across the South in the early 1960s could never be sure whether they could use the restrooms at gasoline stations. The whites did not know that the textbooks used in all-black high schools were outdated hand-me-downs from white schools or that many blacks had struggled to complete college to find that the only jobs available to them were as porters or maids. Indeed, such new information seemed to create discomfort in the white subjects. The communications that took place during the lunch breaks served to focus the attention of the subjects—a necessary factor in the attitude-change model advanced by the Yale Communication Research Program (Chapter 10).

Objective Changes in Behavior toward the Black Participant. When the three participants were introduced at the beginning of the month-long project, the prejudiced white typically treated the black with deliberate neglect. The white subject would direct her questions and comments almost entirely to the other white and very rarely turn her head toward the black. The seating arrangement illustrated in Figure 11-2 was designed to permit observers behind a one-way mirror to tally the number of times the subject directed comments toward each of the other two participants. In most cases, the subject shifted during the month from a pattern of comments directed solely toward the other white to a pattern that included the black in a significant number of interactions. Toward the end of the project approximately 60 percent of the prejudiced subject's comments were directed toward the white and 40 percent toward the black (disregarding comments directed toward both).

Likewise, there were great changes in extent of physical contact over the month's time. At the beginning of the project, the typical prejudiced white resolvedly avoided contact with the black. As time went on, the white subject was less apprehensive about leaning her arm against the black's to pick up a new order or to examine a bracelet. At the end of the project, some subjects sought opportunities to keep the black as a friend, suggesting that they go shopping or double date. All these occurrences indicate strong changes in many of the prejudiced white subjects toward a specific black. The question remains, however, as to whether the changes were generalized to all blacks.

Changes in Responses to Attitude Measures. All of the subjects were retested between one and nine months after they had completed the Railroad Game. Changes in their prejudice scores were compared with the changes in control subjects, who did not participate in the Railroad Game. These control subjects were initially as anti-black as the experimental subjects, and the time intervals between testings were about the same. However, the experimentals and the controls were not randomly divided into those two groups. Rather, the controls were those test subjects who had negative attitudes but had turned down the opportunity to participate in the Railroad Game. It would have been better to choose the control subjects from a group who had expressed interest in the Railroad Game but had not been used, but there were not enough prejudiced test subjects to implement that procedure.

Results for the latest series of subjects are still being analyzed at this writing, but outcomes for the first 23 Railroad Game subjects are available (Cook, 1970). For these subjects, three measures of attitude were basic. One measure used was the School Segregation scale by Komorita (1963), which deals with desegregation policy, with an emphasis on school desegregation. It is a Likert-type scale made up of 67 items to which the respondent indicates his degree of agreement or disagreement. A second measure used was Westie's Summated Differences scale (Westie, 1953), which is a social-distance scale covering the topics of residential desegregation, community leadership, personal relationships, and physical contact. A person's prejudice score derives from the differences in his acceptance of whites and blacks with the same occupations. The third measure used was the sentence-completion test described previously and illustrated in Table 11-1. This set of ten items, developed by Getzels and Walsh (1958), requires the subject to complete statements dealing with their reaction to interracial situations. The ten items are imbedded in a set of 100 items dealing with a variety of issues.

The amount of change in each subject was assessed by using the standard deviation—an indication of the amount of dispersion in the scores for a group. The standard deviation of a group of subjects for each of the three tests was determined after administering each test to students from three local colleges. Then, the amount of change for each subject on each test could be expressed in terms of standard deviations. A standard deviation is expressed by a number of points; if the group's scores are distributed in a normal fashion, with most of the scores toward the middle and fewer and fewer tailing off toward each extreme, there will be about six standard deviations within the set of scores. Thus, if a person's score shifts three standard deviations his new score is halfway across the distribution from his old score. This would be considered a large shift in score. (It would be equivalent to a person's IQ changing from 70 to 115, or from 95 to 140.) A change in score equal to one standard deviation is generally regarded as an important change. This was the criterion used by Cook.

Eight of 23 subjects (35 percent) changed in the direction of less negative attitudes toward blacks. (On the average, 7 of the 8 changed by more than one standard deviation, ranging from 1.1 to 2.9; 1 subject was just below the criterion point with a change of .84 of a standard deviation.) Among the group of 23 female controls, none averaged a change of one standard deviation, although 2 were close, changing .91 and .90 of a standard deviation. Some subjects' attitudes were more negative upon retesting. Among the experimental subjects, 1 changed an average of .82 of a standard deviation in a negative direction after participating in the Railroad Game. This same degree of negative change was found in 2 control subjects (.76 and .73), even though they had not participated in the intervention procedure.

A more substantial feeling for the degree of change can be gained by looking at the kinds of changes in specific subjects. Cook's descriptions of three of these subjects is presented in Figure 11-3.

A similar pattern is indicated by the second series of subjects, for whom the results are still being analyzed. Significantly more Railroad Game subjects than control subjects have changed their attitude in the desired direction upon retesting. Once again, however, in the second series, the percentage of experimental subjects who change one standard deviation or more is still between 35 and 40 percent. About 40 percent retain essentially the same attitudes, and approximately 20 percent have become even more prejudiced in their attitudes toward blacks.

What are we to make of these results? In one sense, the findings provide some

---

Stuart W. Cook has described the types of changes shown by subjects after their month-long interracial job. Three cases are presented below.

The first had initially rejected the idea of having Negroes on her city council or heading her community chest drive. She balked at sharing restrooms and beauty parlors with them. She was averse to the idea that she might exchange social visits with Negroes or have them as dinner guests. All of these relationships she accepted at the time of the post-test.

The second had endorsed complete residential segregation but after the experiment said she would welcome Negroes in her part of town. She came to accept them in leadership positions from which earlier she wished to exclude them. She made the same change with respect to exchanging social visits with Negroes and sharing with them beauty parlors, restrooms, and dressing rooms in department stores.

The third subject made similar changes. She abandoned entirely her former endorsement of residential segregation, accepting Negroes as next-door neighbors. She moved entirely away from rejecting the idea of potential physical contact with Negroes in beauty parlors, restrooms and dressing rooms. She came to accept them as social visitors and dinner guests.

(From Cook, S. W., Motives in a conceptual analysis of attitude related behavior, *Nebraska Symposium on Motivation*, 1970, p. 195. Reprinted with permission of the author and the publisher; copyright 1970, University of Nebraska Press.)

Figure 11-3. *Types of Attitude Change Resulting from Interracial Contact in the Railroad Game Study*

hope that prejudiced attitudes can, indeed, be changed. Although it is impossible to compare the extent of changes directly with changes observed in earlier field studies, Cook believes that the number and the degree of changes here are at least as great as the changes recorded in field studies. Moreover, Cook's results were achieved after 40 hours of actual contact, whereas most field studies operate over a much longer time span (Cook, 1970).

In several ways, however, the results are not very satisfactory. For example, we cannot know whether those subjects who changed will retain less negative attitudes. Though Cook's procedure is highly commendable in that retesting was delayed to at least one month after the contact experience, one cannot know whether the changes will remain for extended periods. Quite possibly, when a subject who has changed her attitudes returns to a situation where prejudices are expressed, she will revert to her initial negative position. The problems of retesting the subjects every six months or so for an indefinite period of time are obvious. (To complete the first retesting Cook had to locate two Railroad Game subjects who had moved 200 or 300 miles away.) Future research should build upon Cook's study, following up over a long period of time those persons who participated in involuntary interracial contact situations.

Another reason for dissatisfaction with Cook's findings is the limited percentage of persons who changed. If 40 percent of the subjects developed less negative attitudes as a result of contact, why didn't all of the subjects change in this direction? Why do some become more negative? Cook has pointed out that perhaps some persons are more resistant to attitude change because of attributes of their personal makeup. Clearly, intrapersonal factors are involved in producing attitude change in some persons but not in others. To gain greater understanding of the intrapersonal attributes related to change, a comparison was made between subjects whose attitudes changed and subjects whose attitudes did not change. The results of this analysis are described subsequently.

IV. WHY DO SOME PEOPLE CHANGE THEIR ATTITUDES WHEN OTHERS DO NOT?

Let us consider the intrapersonal characteristics that would make a prejudiced white person more susceptible to change under the conditions of the Railroad Game study. Two constructs can be used in the way of an explanation: *self-concept* and *assumptions about people in general.* A person who is dissatisfied with his or her self-concept will be more susceptible to change than someone who is happy or complacent about his present state of being. Thus, a negative self-concept facilitates or instigates change. A second factor is also needed, if change is to take place. The prejudiced white person must be willing to listen to and trust other people, who serve as the agents of change. That is, if a prejudiced white person holds favorable assumptions about other people, that person will accept what others say or do as genuine, correct, and well advised. But if a person has unfavorable assumptions about people in general—if one disparages or distrusts what other people say and do—that person is not likely to be influenced by communications aimed toward him. Even a very negative self-concept will not facilitate attitude change in the Railroad Game situation, if the subject distrusts the other people involved.

To test this minitheory, 10 Railroad Game subjects who became more favorable in their racial attitudes were compared with the 13 subjects who did not become more favorable. These two groups were called the positive changers and the nonchangers (although the nonchangers actually included one subject who became more negative in her racial attitudes). Responses to the 15-hour battery of tests were used to compare these two groups of subjects (Wrightsman & Cook, 1965; Cook & Wrightsman, 1967). From this battery, 78 different measures were available and were statistically analyzed to see which measures clung together or were measuring the same general construct. (This procedure is called *factor analysis.*) Eleven factors emerged from this procedure and are listed in Table 11-2. It is important to recognize that these factors are abstractions, which represent what is common to a variety of measures. The names of the factors are assigned by the researchers doing the analysis and are based on what is common to the measures that are highly related to a particular factor. For example, taking Factor 1 in Table 11-2, we see the label *rigidity*. The results of the factor analysis would show us that the following tests are highly related to the rigidity factor: Gough Sanford Rigidity scale, Wesley Rigidity scale, Independence of Judgment measure on Welsh Figure Preference Test (this had a reversed relationship), Rehfisch Rigidity scale, Rokeach's Dogmatism scale, and so on. Considering the content of these tests and their high relationship (or loading) on Factor 1, we can see why the word rigidity was used to indicate the common variance shared by these measures.

Table 11-2 shows that the factors together cover a wide range of intrapersonal characteristics. There are personality characteristics (Factors 1, 2, 6, 7, and 8), racial attitudes (Factor 3), and other attitudes (Factors 5 and 9); and there is a factor representing the aptitude and ability measures used in the battery (Factor 4). The last two factors in the analysis represent only the variance that remained after the preceding nine factors extracted what was common to each of the measures. In other words, Factors 10 and 11 are of little importance.

Each of the 11 factors may be considered as composite scores, and a composite score on each factor may be obtained for each subject. Thus we now have, for each of the 10 positive changers and each of the 13 nonchangers, a composite score on each of the 11 factors. The two groups of subjects may now be compared on each factor. The question to be asked is: do the positive changers, as a group, significantly differ from

Table 11-2. *Results of Factor Analysis*

Factor No.	*Title Given to Factor*
1	Rigidity
2	Hostility and Anxiety
3	Anti-Negro Attitudes
4	Aptitude and Ability
5	Positive Attitudes toward People
6	Sociability
7	Tolerance for Unpleasantness
8	Negativism about Self
9	Attitudes toward Teaching
10	Positive Response Set
11	Residual Factor

(Adapted from Cook & Wrightsman, 1967, Table 2, pp. 8–10. Reprinted with permission of the authors.)

the nonchangers in their average score? The mean scores are reported in Table 11-3. First of all, let us note some of the factors where there is no difference in initial score between the positive changers and the nonchangers. For example, those prejudiced whites whose attitudes changed after the Railroad Game experience were no more (and no less) rigid than were the prejudiced participants whose attitudes did not change (Factor 1). Positive changers were no more or less hostile or anxious than the nonchangers (Factor 2). Surprisingly, their initial antiblack attitudes were no less intense or extreme than those of the nonchangers. Other factors where the positive changers and nonchangers did not differ in average score are indicated as nonsignificant in Table 11-3.

As shown in Table 11-3, for Factors 5, 7, and 8, a significant *p*-value is indicated. For example, for Factor 5 (positive attitudes toward people), the *p*-value is .01, which shows that on this factor the average scores for the two groups were significantly different; in only 1 comparison out of 100 (that is, .01) could a difference in means as large as this have occurred by coincidence. The significance level for the other two (Factors 7 and 8) is not as extreme, but in each case the level of significance is great enough to permit a conclusion that the two groups are truly different in average score. Let us consider each of these three factors in turn.

Factor 5 (positive attitudes toward people) includes high loadings from the following measures: Philosophies of Human Nature scale, Machiavellianism scale (negative loading), Anomie scale (negative loading), faith in people, and Edwards' Social Desirability scale. Thus, Factor 5 definitely represents an accumulation of variables that are concerned with attitudes toward people in general. One aspect of **anomie,** for example, is a belief that other people are uninterested and unsympathetic. The Machiavellianism scale (see Chapter 3) communicates a cynical belief about others. The Philosophies of Human Nature scale (also described in Chapter 3) provides a measure of one's general positive or negative attitude toward human nature. A positive score on this factor means that the subject believes people in general are good, trustworthy, unselfish, not alienated, and not Machiavellian. As shown in Table 11-3, the mean of the positive changers was +3.68 (a positive value), while the

Table 11-3. *A Comparison of Factor Scores of Subjects Whose Attitudes Changed Favorably versus Subjects Whose Attitudes Did Not Change Favorably*

		Mean factor scores:		
Factor No.	*Factor Title*	*Positive Changers (N = 10)*	*Nonchangers (N = 13)*	*p-value of Difference Between Means*
1	Rigidity	+3.23	+3.72	N.S.
2	Hostility and Anxiety	+1.13	+2.26	N.S.
3	Anti-Negro Attitudes	+7.75	+7.27	N.S.
4	Aptitudes	−1.26	−2.82	N.S.
5	Positive Attitudes toward People	+3.68	−4.46	.01
6	Sociability	−0.58	+0.06	N.S.
7	Tolerance for Unpleasantness	−0.54	+0.95	.025
8	Negativism about Self	+0.46	−1.17	.025
9	Attitudes toward Teaching	+0.95	+0.08	N.S.
10	Positive Response Set	+1.52	+0.94	N.S.
11	Residual	+0.72	+1.27	N.S.

Note: N.S. = Nonsignificant difference. (Adapted from Wrightsman & Cook, 1965, Table 3, p. 10. Reprinted with permission of the authors.)

mean of the nonchangers was −4.46—indicating that the nonchangers as a group did not see human nature as good, trustworthy, and so on. In fact, 11 of the 13 nonchangers were below the neutral point on this factor, while only 2 of the positive changers were below neutral (and then only barely). These findings confirm the notion that subjects who enter an experience of interracial contact with cynical, distrusting attitudes toward human nature are unlikely to change in the direction of more favorable interracial attitudes.

Factor 7 (tolerance for unpleasantness) is not a clear factor because the measures contributing to it do not seem to be conceptually similar. A positive score on the factor apparently means that the person has little need for social approval and is rather escapist in his thought patterns. Table 11-3 points out that this description fits the nonchangers more than the positive changers—a result that is in line with the expectations of the minitheory.

A person with a positive score on Factor 8 (negativism about self) is dissatisfied with his self-concept. He has indicated a relatively large discrepancy between the way he is and the way he would like to be. Additionally, test loadings on Factor 8 indicate that a person scoring positively on this factor is pessimistic about his personal future and is dependent upon others. Table 11-3 reflects that the positive changers are, as a group, above the mean on this factor, while the group of nonchangers lacks such negativism toward themselves. Thus, the second aspect of the minitheory is confirmed.

There is some evidence then that a situation that is carefully designed to reduce the amount of prejudice directed toward a minority group will succeed only in some cases. One determinant of success resides within the participant; his self-evaluation and his expectations about other people are important in this regard.

V. TECHNIQUES OF ATTITUDE CHANGE

The breadth of speculation and research on attitude change is immense—too immense for us to do justice to the subject here. For example, there is a large body of literature on the effect of various types of persuasive communications upon attitude change. Topics such as the role of the communicator, the value of one-sided versus two-sided communications, and the effects of the audience are considered. Several of the suggested readings for this chapter, particularly the books by Zimbardo and Ebbesen and by Karlins and Abelson, are useful here.

Another facet of attitude change is that slow-but-sure change takes place in general public attitudes as a result of social change. As will be discussed in Chapter 12, our attitudes toward work, religion, and sexual deviance are changing as the nature of our society changes.

VI. SUMMARY

Any change in interracial attitudes is unlikely to occur from interventions such as lectures, films, and other procedures that do not bring groups into contact with one another. The hypothesis of interracial contact specifies certain aspects of the contact situation that facilitate favorable attitude change.

When a prejudiced person is involuntarily placed in contact with a minority-group member, there is greater likelihood that his attitude will become less negative if (a) there is opportunity for him to know the other person as an individual, (b) the relative status of the participants is equal, (c) the norms favor acceptance, and (d) the reward structure of the task is cooperative rather than competitive.

Not all interracial contacts lead to a reduction in prejudice or hostility. Stuart Cook's laboratory approach has shown that when the above beneficial conditions are brought together in one situation and the antiblack subject is exposed to a month-long interracial work experience, his attitude toward blacks becomes significantly less negative in about 40 percent of the cases.

The intrapersonal characteristics that facilitate a reduction in prejudice in the above situation include a negative self-concept in combination with a positive attitude toward people in general.

VII. SUGGESTED READINGS

Brown, J. A. C. *Techniques of persuasion: From propaganda to brainwashing.* Baltimore, Md.: Penguin, 1963. (Paperback) A survey of the field of persuasion, written for the layman. Deals with political propaganda, commercial advertising, religious conversions, and brainwashing.

Cohen, A. R. *Attitude change and social influence.* New York: Basic Books, 1964. A review of social psychological research on the effectiveness of arguments and appeals, the personality factors relating to the acceptance of persuasive communications, and the effects of social roles and interactions. Also useful for Chapter 10.

Cook, S. W. Motives in a conceptual analysis of attitude-related behavior. In W. J. Arnold and D. Levine (Eds.), *Nebraska Symposium on Motivation, 1969.* Lincoln, Nebr.: University of Nebraska Press, 1970. Pp. 179–231. (Paperback) A theory-based analysis and description of Stuart W. Cook's important study on the effects of interracial contact upon attitude change.

Karlins, M., & Abelson, H. I. *Persuasion: How opinions and attitudes are changed.* (2nd ed.) New York: Springer, 1970. (Paperback) A clearly written review of the effects of the communication, the communicator, and the audience upon attitude change. Highly recommended.

Zimbardo, P., & Ebbesen, E. B. *Influencing attitudes and changing behavior.* Reading, Mass.: Addison-Wesley, 1969. A fresh approach to the study of attitude change, written in a witty, provocative style. Highly recommended.

I. *SOCIAL PSYCHOLOGY AND SOCIAL CHANGE*

A. *Defining social change*

B. *The measurement of social change*

1. *Rapid urbanization*
2. *The heightened pace of invention*
3. *The knowledge explosion*

C. *Social movements as predictors of social change*

II. *THE MODERN FEMINIST MOVEMENT*

A. *The new feminists*

B. *Demands of the movement*

C. *Motivational base for the feminist movement*

D. *Predicting the consequences of women's liberation*

III. *YOUTH AND CHANGE*

A. *Student activism*

1. *Incidence*
2. *The settings for protest*
3. *Issues in student protests*
4. *Personality correlates of activism*
5. *Reform or revolution?*

B. *Cultural alienation*

1. *The generation gap—myth or fact?*
2. *The rise of a counter culture*
3. *Toward a prefigurative culture?*
4. *More ideological than generational*

IV. *OTHER INDICATORS OF SOCIAL CHANGE*

A. *Technology and its effects on attitudes toward work*

B. *Changing attitudes toward authority*

V. *THE USEFULNESS OF UTOPIAS*

VI. *SUMMARY*

VII. *SUGGESTED READINGS*

Chapter Twelve

The Nature of Social Change

by Norma J. Baker

Change is avalanching upon our heads and most people are grotesquely unprepared to cope with it. *Alvin Toffler*

Future shock is a new phrase that is now a part of our language. Alvin Toffler (1970), who coined the phrase, defines it as "the dizzying disorientation brought on by the premature arrival of the future," or what happens to ordinary people when they are overwhelmed by an accelerating rate of change. More than an arresting phrase, future shock may, according to Toffler, prove to be the most obstinate and debilitating social problem of the future. Its symptoms range from confusion, anxiety, and hostility, to physical illness, seemingly senseless violence, and self-destructive apathy. Victims of future shock feel continuously harassed and hence attempt to reduce the number of changes they must come to terms with and the number of decisions they must make (Toffler, 1970).

A helpful way to grasp the implications of future shock is to look at a parallel term *culture shock*. The novice world traveler experiences culture shock when he finds himself in a totally new environment, cut off from meaning and without familiar psychological cues. Many Americans have felt such disorientation and frustration when placed in a foreign culture. But the traveler has the comforting knowledge that he can go back to the culture that he left behind. Future shock may be viewed as culture shock in one's own society, arising when a new culture is superimposed upon an old one. For the victim of future shock, however, there is little likelihood of returning to the familiarity that was left behind.

I. SOCIAL PSYCHOLOGY AND SOCIAL CHANGE

The assumption found in the popular media is that man is caught in a revolution that is rocketing him into the future at fantastic speeds. The twentieth century is generally described as a period of rapid and radical social change, with the rate of change having accelerated increasingly in the last two decades. Despite this state, the psychological consequences of rapid social change have not received much attention in psychology journals until recently.[1] This neglect was cited by the Society for the Psychological Study of Social Issues in 1961, when their publication, *Journal of Social Issues,* devoted one entire issue to social change and psychological patterns. The amount of research carried out since that issue has increased. However, much of what is included in psychological research on social change is actually the social experiment—or an investigation of attempts to engineer specific changes.

The topic of social change is broad enough to include economic and agricultural development in other cultures, the planning of innovations, and/or the resistance to change. (For the latter, see Chapter 20.) Radical forms of social change, such as revolutions, might also be treated under this heading. The focus of this chapter, however, will be on the more autonomous and seemingly unplanned changes that have occurred within recent years. Attention will also be directed to the accompanying changes in norms and values. Such phenomena are not easily classified as either independent or dependent variables. In actuality, the same factor can be both. For example, recent expressions of student unrest can be viewed as the outgrowth of certain changes in students' value systems, interwoven with heightened awareness of civil rights (a dependent variable). But student unrest can also be seen as an independent variable that elicits long-range changes in the very structure of higher education and government policies. The causes and likely consequences of student activism will be examined in Section III.

Social change may be viewed as a central organizing term for the study of changes in values, social behavior, and other matters that are the concern of social psychology. In this chapter we shall ask: what is changing, and just how is the rate of change accelerating? What are some current indicators of social change in the United States? And, can social psychology predict the psychological consequences of rapid social change?

A. Defining Social Change

Both order and change are significant components of man's social existence. The repetitive character of many aspects of social behavior makes a certain predictability to human life possible, and yet change and variability are universal. Given the ubiquity of change, how can social change be defined in any distinguishing way? Moore (1967, 1968) described social change as occurring when change permeates a whole system, rather than when it appears only in sequences of actions that make up a

[1] In the 1960 volume of *Psychological Abstracts* there were only three references listed in the index under the heading of social change. In the 1969 volumes there were 78 items. There has been a gradual increase in the number of listings each year, indicating that psychologists are giving greater attention to the topic. Part of the increase, however, simply reflects an overall increase in the amount of research being published in all areas.

system. Moore has defined social change as "the significant alteration of social structures . . . including consequences and manifestations of such structures embodied in norms . . . , values, and cultural products and symbols" (1967, p. 3). Structures, in this context, refer to patterns of social action and interaction; voting on election day as a means of naming a new president is a structure. Norms refer to rules of conduct; it is normative to vote, to have one's vote counted accurately, and to have the candidate with the most votes be named president. Social change, then, means that there are changes in the boundaries of the social system, in the prescription for action, and in the relation of the particular system to its environment. For example, the transfer of the presidency from one party to another does not represent a social change because it does not go beyond the boundaries of our norms and patterns of social action. But if the incumbent president assumed exclusive control so that there was no possibility for transfer, the system would have been altered and *social change* would have occurred.

B. The Measurement of Social Change

Change is as characteristic of man's life as order. But, as we have indicated, components of man's existence are stable over time, and there is a remarkable consistency in the daily, weekly, and annual schedules of man's activities. Thus, the detection of change is dependent upon the assumption of order and of the persistence of many aspects of social behavior. A major difficulty in detection and measurement of social change is that change takes place across time, and time for observation is limited, especially for a single investigator. Moore (1963) suggests that the sense of time and the perception of change are inextricably linked in human experience. One cannot think about change without including the concept of time and without at least having some sense of time passing. And if change is viewed as continuous, something more than the mere difference between before and after—in other words, the *rate* of transformation—becomes important. We may then think of the rate of social change as a fractional value, with time as the denominator, and we may also think of the number of events that are to be observed or measured as the numerator of the fraction (Moore, 1963). If the time since World War II serves as the denominator, the numerator would include such events as nuclear warfare, mass use of television, space travel, the population explosion, the breakdown of cities, awareness of destruction of the natural environment, the civil rights revolution, the coming of the computer, and the birth-control pill. Americans born even as recently as 25 years ago may well feel that the world into which they were born has virtually dropped from under them, while a new world is being built around them.

Another difficulty in making quantitative predictions regarding the direction of social change is that there is no adequate knowledge of the present status. It is difficult to predict where we are going if we do not know where we are. A major improvement in the collection and analysis of information about social conditions, the quality of life, and social change has been made by the federal government, with the recent emphasis on social accounting and social reporting. In 1969 the Department of Health, Education, and Welfare released a publication entitled *Toward a Social Report*. Separate chapters of the report deal with health and illness; social mobility; physical environment; income and poverty; public order and safety; learning, science, and art; and participation and alienation. For each of these areas, the report advocates the development of social indicators—or descriptive statistics about our society that facilitate concise, comprehensive, and balanced judgments about the quality of our social existence (Bauer, 1966). Social indicators are direct measures of welfare and are subject to the interpretation that people are better off if each or any indicator changes in the right direction, while other things remain equal. Only measures that are employed repeatedly and at regular intervals are to be properly considered indicators; in other words, social indicators are time series that allow comparisons over an extended period and that permit one to grasp long-term trends as well as unusually sharp fluctuations in rates (Sheldon & Freeman, 1970). The major usefulness of social indicators is that they meet the need for a way to anticipate the consequences of rapid technological change and the second-order effects of changes in beliefs and values. (Figure 12-1 provides a description of some of the pitfalls of interpretation of social indicators.)

Although gaps in knowledge exist and all change is relative, there are many examples that justify the assumption that the rate of change is accelerating. Toffler (1970) has described a few of these factors.

Rapid Urbanization. In 1850 only four cities on the earth had a population of 1,000,000 or more. By 1900 the number had increased to 19; but by 1960 there were 141 such cities, and today world urban population is climbing upward at a rate of 6.5 percent per year.

The Heightened Pace of Invention. For a group of appliances introduced in the United States before 1920—including the vacuum cleaner, the electric range, and the refrigerator—the average span between introduction and peak production was 34 years. But for a group that appeared between 1939 and 1959—including the electric frying pan, television receivers, and washer-dryer combinations—the span was only 8 years. The lag had shrunk by more than 76 percent. New machines or techniques represent not merely a product but a source of fresh creative ideas.

The Knowledge Explosion. Prior to 1500, Europe was producing books at a rate of about 1000 titles per year. Today the United States government alone generates 100,000 reports each year, plus 450,000 articles, books, and papers. The computer, which appeared around 1950, is a major force behind the latest acceleration in the acquisition of knowledge.

Such an accelerated accumulation of materials in the world around us means that there is an increase in the number of choices we are forced to make. It also means more switching back and forth from one choice point to another and less time for extended attention to one situation at a time. Rising rates of change compel us to cope with more and more situations to which previous personal experience does not apply.

C. Social Movements as Predictors of Social Change

Perhaps one of the best indicators of the direction of social change is the *social movement,* which also draws attention to significant social problems. Social movements are forms of collective behavior that aim at change in the world. Psychologically defined, a social movement represents an effort by a large number of people to solve collectively a problem that they have in common (Milgram & Toch, 1969).

At various times and under various conditions the legitimacy of a society's cus-

Donald T. Campbell, distinguished social scientist, makes a strong appeal for an experimental approach to social reform. What is needed is an approach by which we can try out new programs designed to cure specific social problems, by which we learn whether or not these programs are effective, and by which we retain, imitate, modify, or discard these programs on the basis of effectiveness.

Campbell calls for an understanding of the political implications of the public use of data as social indicators. He presents several research designs for evaluating specific programs of social amelioration. One of these is the interrupted time-series design. A convenient illustration comes from the 1955 Connecticut crackdown on speeding. After a record high of traffic fatalities in 1955, the governor instituted an unprecedentedly severe crackdown on speeding. At the end of one year of such enforcement, there had been 284 traffic deaths as compared with 324 the year before. These results are shown in the left-hand graph below, with a deliberate effort to make them look impressive. The right-hand graph includes the same data as the graph to the left, except that it is presented as part of an extended time series.

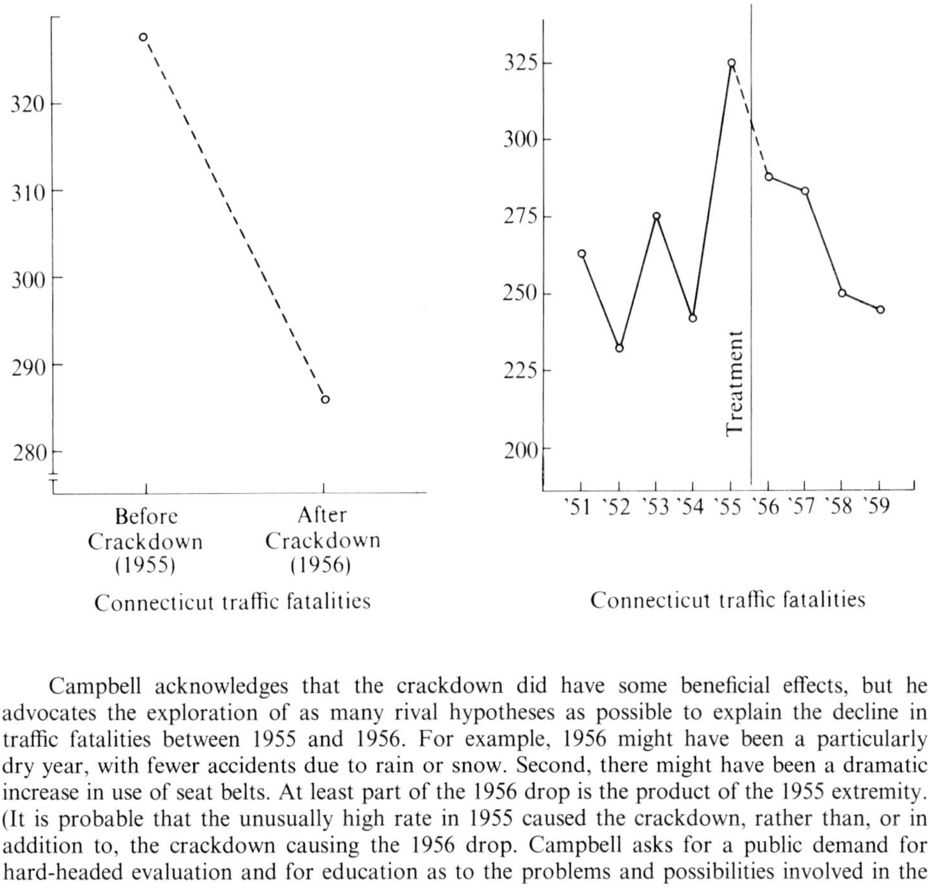

Campbell acknowledges that the crackdown did have some beneficial effects, but he advocates the exploration of as many rival hypotheses as possible to explain the decline in traffic fatalities between 1955 and 1956. For example, 1956 might have been a particularly dry year, with fewer accidents due to rain or snow. Second, there might have been a dramatic increase in use of seat belts. At least part of the 1956 drop is the product of the 1955 extremity. (It is probable that the unusually high rate in 1955 caused the crackdown, rather than, or in addition to, the crackdown causing the 1956 drop. Campbell asks for a public demand for hard-headed evaluation and for education as to the problems and possibilities involved in the use of socially relevant data.

(Adapted from Campbell, D. T. Reforms as experiments, *American Psychologist*, **24**, April, 1969, 409–429. Copyright 1969, by American Psychological Association, and reprinted with permission of the author and the publisher.)

Figure 12-1. *Reforms as Experiments*

tomary institutions or values (such as the family or sexual relationships) may be questioned by different parts of the society. New arrangements are advocated. But the demand for change meets with resistance, and the advocates of the old habits may seek to maintain the past arrangements. Thus, it comes about that groups face each other in some form of conflict. A social movement, therefore, is not the unnoticed accumulation of many unrecognized changes. Rather, it has the character of an explicit and conscious indictment of whole or part of the social order, together with a conscious demand for change. It has an ideological component—that is, a set of ideas that specify discontents, prescribe solutions, and justify change (Gusfield, 1968).

Sherif (1970) has suggested six factors that characterize social movements and countermovements. (The social psychology textbook of Sherif and Sherif, 1969, is one of the few that gives extended space to social change.)

1. A social movement is a formative pattern of attempts toward change that develops in phases over time.

2. A social movement is initiated through interaction among people prompted by a motivational base fed by persisting social problems. Sherif uses the phrase *motivational base* in a generic sense. It may consist of material destitution, such as hunger and miserable living conditions, or it may consist of the desperation that results from being the victim of racism or exploitation. The motivational base may reflect the experience of relative deprivation.[2]

3. A social movement is carried out by those directly affected by the desired change and by others who throw in their lot with them.

4. A social movement develops through the declaration of complaints and the formulation and proclamation of a platform or ideology, which implies organization.

5. The purpose of a social movement is to bring about evolutionary or revolutionary changes or to suppress changes (countermovements).

6. Efforts toward change are effected by means of appeals to the public, slogans, agitations, episodes of collective action, and encounters with the opposition (strikes, rallies, resistance, boycotts, demonstrations, riots, insurrection, and the like).

In regard to the course of social movements, Toch has written that "if and when a social movement becomes dominant in a society, its victory makes it vulnerable to two forms of self-destruction. If the movement persists in playing a protest role, the inappropriateness of this stance invites loss of membership. If, as is more usual, the movement proceeds to consolidate its new power, it risks becoming absorbed in the effort. . . . The movement may lose its original identity and become blind to developing needs. In due time, it may have to suppress the manifestations of discontent of new underprivileged groups" (1965, p. 228).

An example of this latter course that a social movement may take is Martin Luther King's nonviolent civil rights movement. As some of the original goals of gaining equal rights and justice for blacks were attained, the movement directed its momentum toward more diffuse objectives, such as the withdrawal of military troops from Vietnam and improving the plight of the poor—both black and white. Such absorption in broader objectives caused many blacks to believe that the movement had lost sight of their cause. Feeling that nonviolence had not succeeded, some of the black groups became militant and advocated violent means of attaining their goals.

[2]Relative deprivation is a social psychological term used in various contexts throughout this chapter. It implies that one does not evaluate his success or failure in absolute terms; rather, a person sees his own well-being as relative to the positions, privileges, and possessions of others.

An understanding of social movements may help social psychology understand significant social problems. We will examine a current social movement—the women's liberation movement—in the next section. Beyond its contemporary importance, a basic reason for examining this movement is that it signals significant social change. The women's liberation movement is more than a mere fad; it contains the potential for changing some of the basic institutions of American society.

II. THE MODERN FEMINIST MOVEMENT

In a recent article, Lucy Komisar (1970) stated: "If the 1960s belonged to the blacks, the next ten years are ours." In this decade of social protest, feminism has assumed a new and angry life. What women seek now is much more profound than the vote. They ask now to be recognized first and foremost as human beings and only secondarily as females (Koedt, 1970; Komisar, 1970; Millett, 1970). Just as the earlier feminism arose with abolitionism, so the present push for change draws much of its rhetoric and spirit from the civil rights ferment of the 1950s and 1960s. Today's feminists are reviving an unfinished revolution—one which may be destined to eclipse the black civil rights struggle in the force of its resentment and the consequences of its demands.

Several indicators of the directions of social change may be noted in the current feminist movement. In this section the following questions will serve as a guide: who are the feminists, and what are their demands? What is the motivational base for the movement, and what will be some of the consequences of the movement? How will the family as a social unit, culturally defined sex roles, and a woman's self-concept be affected?

A. The New Feminists

It is not within the scope of this chapter to trace the history of feminism in the United States, although such a review would place the current movement in sharper focus. From the time of the suffragettes until now there have been sporadic efforts to improve the status of women. The results could be charted as a gradual upward climb in regard to number of rights and opportunities afforded to women (Kraditor, 1968). The current movement has taken root in territory that, at first glance, appears an unlikely ground for revolutionary ideas. The new movement consists mostly of urban, white, college-educated, middle-class women—a group that is generally considered rather privileged (Brownmiller, 1970). Similarities may be detected between the student movement and the modern feminist movement, in that both have taken root among privileged groups.

Actually, two major thrusts can be identified in the modern feminist movement—the National Organization for Women (Figure 12-2), which is essentially reformist in nature; and the more radical groups comprising the Women's Liberation Movement (Figure 12-3), which is a very loose designation for a multiplicity of small groups, each led by several women who decline to call themselves leaders. The membership is mostly young (under 30), middle class in origin, radical, and almost exclusively white—black women having chosen to remain within the civil rights groups. During the middle of 1967, many young women in the civil rights movement and in the infant New Left were growing disillusioned with their subordinate roles and began to break away from the parent organizations. As "movement women," they were tired of typing and fixing food, while "movement men" did the writing and leading. They came to suspect that the social vision of radical men did not include equality for women. Their experiences in the civil rights and New Left groups reinforced their insecurities and feelings of worthlessness as women (Brownmiller, 1970). These feelings possibly may have brought them into radical politics in the first place, but the alternate life style of the protest movements proved to be no better than the bourgeois life style they had rejected.

Since 1967, women's liberation groups have developed rapidly. Most start as groups of 10 or 12 persons. Since many of the founders of women's liberation groups came out of the New Left—with its distrust for hierarchy—the groups tend to be localized, unstructured, and unconnected, while in agreement on immediate issues (*Newsweek*, 1970a). The lack of central communication makes it difficult to catalogue the groups; however, some of the most highly publicized groups are described in Figure 12-3.

Not all the push for change is coming from new militant groups. The 90-year-old American Association of University Women has brought a complaint against the Office of Education for failing—despite frequent pleas—to show sex differentials in faculty rank and pay when collecting and analyzing data in higher education. As with the student movement, it is a mistake to judge the strength of the new rise of feminism by the relatively small number of women who physically storm male sanctuaries or otherwise demonstrate for their rights. These members may be seen as the outer edge of a much larger group whose impatience with a second-class role in society is mounting. Like the effect of the Black Panther Party upon the black population, the few militant women awaken deep-seated feelings within large numbers of other women who never before consciously thought of themselves as oppressed (Shaffer, 1970).

Organized in 1966, the National Organization for Women was inspired by Betty Friedan's book, *The Feminine Mystique* (1963), which examined the post-World War II movement and attacked the assumption that the American housewife was happy and fulfilled. Friedan's thesis was that a male-dominated, consumer-oriented society had convinced women that they could be most creative as mothers and homemakers. She pictured these homemakers as having been trapped by trivia and struggling with emptiness by the time they reached middle age. Responding to the challenge of *The Feminine Mystique*, the NOW adopted a statement of purpose in an organizing conference of 32 men and women from 12 states and Washington, D. C. By July, 1967, NOW, with Betty Friedan as president, had over 1000 members throughout the country (Kraditor, 1968). One part of their Statement of Purpose explained that the "purpose of NOW is to take action to bring women into full participation in the mainstream of American society now, exercising all the privileges and responsibilities thereof in truly equal partnership with men."

NOW is the one organization of the new feminists with a constitution, board members, and chapters throughout the country. Early announcements described it as the NAACP of women's rights. It is reformist in approach, attacking job inequalities and other injustices through court action and legislative lobbying. Its members favor political action and are more likely to demonstrate for job equality and child-care centers than for the abolition of marriage or the traditional family unit.

Figure 12-2. *The National Organization for Women*

New York Radical Women. Some in this group see woman's oppressors as men, rather than some specific economic system. It was this group that went to Atlantic City in September, 1968, to picket the Miss America pageant. The New York Radical Women chose the beauty contest as a target because they disagreed with the ideal of American womanhood that is extolled by the pageant.

Women's International Terrorist Conspiracy from Hell (WITCH). According to WITCH philosophy, the patriarchy of the nuclear family is synonymous with the patriarchy of the American business corporation. Much of the WITCH activity has been tongue-in-cheek (similar to the Yippie movement) in that its uses outrageous disruption as a political tactic.

Redstockings. This group adopted a name that plays on *bluestockings*—replacing the color blue with the color of revolution. Devout about consciousness raising, these women state in their manifesto: "Women are an oppressed class. Our oppression is total, affecting every facet of our lives. We are exploited as sex objects, breeders, domestic servants and cheap labor. We are considered inferior beings whose only purpose is to enhance men's lives." (Brownmiller, 1970, p. 28).

The Feminists. Perhaps the most radical group of all, this group split from the less extreme NOW. Taking a stand against the institution of marriage, these women have raised the slogan, "Marriage is Slavery." Married women or women living with men may not exceed one-third of the total membership (Brownmiller, 1970, p. 34).

New York Radical Feminists. Emphasis is on decentralized neighborhood units, or "brigades," that meet weekly in leaderless groups to discuss topics that run the gamut of female experience. One of their founders, Anne Koedt, has explained: "The idea of a female-dominated society is as repugnant to me as the idea of a male-dominated society. What I want cut off is the power men exercise over women" (Koedt, 1970).

Figure 12-3. *Women's Liberation Groups*

B. Demands of the Movement

The new movement is not just a renascence of the feminism that concentrated on getting the vote. The new element is the shift to the liberation of women, which means a fully equal partnership with men. Even though specific goals are named, such as equality in employment, these groups do not limit themselves to such concrete aims. Rather, women are mounting an assault on an entrenched pattern of relations between the sexes that—in their eyes—demeans and restricts one-half of the human race (Shaffer, 1970). Since the groups within the movement vary in their demands and strategies, a composite listing is presented here, including the major goals of the most vocal groups.

1. The end of job discrimination is one major aim. Though most of the legal barriers to equality of opportunity in the working world have fallen away, the overall picture for the woman worker has not changed very much in the half century since women got the vote.

2. Equal pay for equal work is another major aim. On a percentage basis, women's pay has fallen even further behind men's pay in recent years (Shaffer, 1970).

3. A third major aim is greater educational flexibility. The NOW statement of purpose charges that discrimination against women may take the form of quotas for admitting women to colleges and professional schools and the lack of encouragement offered to women by educators and counselors (Kraditor, 1968).

4. Free child care is a fourth major aim of feminist groups, who have endorsed resolutions demanding 24-hour-a-day child-care centers to free working mothers.

5. A fifth aim of feminist groups is equal sharing of family responsibilities. Liberationists reject the current assumptions that a man must carry the sole burden of supporting the family or that marriage, home, and family are primarily the woman's world and responsibility and ask for an equitable sharing of home, children, and economic burdens.

6. Free abortion is a sixth major aim. Although feminist groups take different approaches toward this topic, they basically say that every woman has an inalienable right to decide whether or not she wishes to bear a child.

7. A seventh major aim is for the end of sexual exploitation. Feminists resent the sexual sell in advertising and what is regarded as a general proclivity of men to regard women as decorative, passive, and vulnerable. The descriptive term here is *sexism,* which has an obvious kinship with the term *racism.*

8. One final aim of liberationist groups is the restructuring of sex roles. Feminists believe that the division of human characteristics into masculine and feminine is too simplistic and harmful to men as well as to women. Everyone suffers in a society where men are forced to inhibit expressions of sensitivity, tenderness, and sentiment. Women are socially conditioned from childhood to fit the stereotype of submissiveness and passivity.

The possible consequences of these demands will be discussed in Section D. First, however, an attempt will be made to identify the underlying conditions that led to the emergence of the present women's liberation movement.

C. Motivational Base for the Feminist Movement

Sherif (1970) has stated that a social movement always arises from a motivational base that is related to social problems. At least three concepts are useful here in describing the motivational base: (a) **marginality,** (b) **self-fulfilling prophecy,** and (c) **relative deprivation.**

The notion of the *marginal man* suggests that a person may live in two cultures that are not merely different but actually antagonistic. Examples of marginal groups are mulattoes, immigrants, and social climbers. They are motivated to affiliate with both culture groups but are fully accepted by neither. Severe conflict often develops because the role behaviors appropriate to the two groups are antagonistic (Krech, Crutchfield, & Ballachey, 1962). And if—as is commonly the case—one group is higher than the other in the hierarchy of privilege, power, and prestige, the marginal person is often considered disloyal by the group from which he is trying to escape, while the other group feels he is trying to intrude where he does not belong.

The status of woman in American society has changed demonstrably in the last half century, in that women have gone from nonvoting homebodies to holding positions in Congress, the Cabinet, and in other noted institutions. As a consequence, women college students in particular report strains from their role conflicts—or the conflicts that arise from their desires to be mothers while wanting to make contributions to a profession, or from desires to look beautiful and feminine while having to fight for jobs and power, or from desires to raise children while wanting to see the world. Perhaps because of these contrary pulls, 28 percent of American women have indicated their desire to be male (Grossack & Gardner, 1970).

The second concept used to explain the motivational base is the *self-fulfilling pro-*

phecy, which implies that women become what society expects them to be. Naomi Weisstein (1969)[3] in her vivid statement, "Woman as Nigger," charges that our culture and our psychology make the assumptions that women are inconsistent, emotionally unstable, lacking in a strong superego, weaker, nurturant rather than productive, intuitive rather than intelligent, and—if they are at all normal—suited to the home and family. The list adds up to a typical minority-group stereotype. Like other marginal groups, women have been shown to adopt the assumptions about themselves that are held by others. The result is self-hatred. P. Goldberg (1968) found that women express more confidence in men than in women. College women students were asked to rate literary passages on several criteria. Some of the passages given to each subject were said to be written by males, others by females; in actuality, authorship was arbitrarily assigned to passages written by the same person. Female subjects gave higher ratings to passages apparently written by the male authors. Indeed, the feminist movement recognizes as central to their cause that women have been accorded an inferior role in society and that as a result they have come to assume that their own inferiority is a fact.

The concept of *relative deprivation*—the third concept used to explain the motivational base—succinctly stated is as follows: when hopes are frustrated, discontent is greater than when low hopes remain unfulfilled (Krech, et al., 1962). Women have been given many reasons for high hopes within this century. Women won the vote in the social upheaval following World War I, as the blacks had won it in theory through the upheaval and change of the Civil War. But disillusionment soon followed. The women's movement, after achieving the vote, became something of a joke.

Although emancipated from a legally subordinate status, women found many prejudices against themselves and restrictions on their participation in politics (particularly as officeholders) and in many occupations. Although there are few jobs from which women are excluded by law, there are many occupations in which they do not participate or in which their participation is limited to sex-allied specialities. On most fronts, the black civil rights movement has been a step ahead of the feminist movement. Blacks got the vote before women. Racial discrimination in employment was outlawed before outlawing discrimination on the basis of sex was even considered. In 1967, for instance, 15 percent of a group of companies queried by the Bureau of National Affairs reported that they were aggressively recruiting promotable blacks, but only one company reported an aggressive policy of recruiting women. Thus, the awareness of gains made by other groups has contributed to the restiveness of women and may be viewed as part of the motivational base for identifying with the social movement.

D. Predicting the Consequences of Women's Liberation

The directed segment of a social movement is characterized by organized and structured groups with specific programs, a formal leadership structure, definitive ideology, and stated objectives. The undirected phase of a movement is characterized

[3] Dr. Weisstein was elected to Phi Beta Kappa while an undergraduate at Wellesley College. She completed work for her Ph.D. (with departmental distinctions) at Harvard University in $2\frac{1}{2}$ years. She completed a year's post-doctoral fellowship, funded by the National Science Foundation, at the University of Chicago. Yet twelve different colleges and universities to which she had been recommended for a position did not hire her (Garskof, 1971).

by the reshaping of perspectives, norms, and values that occurs in the interaction of persons apart from a specific organizational context (Gusfield, 1968). The directed segment of the women's liberation movement has already been reviewed. The basic intent of this portion of the chapter is to analyze the relation of social movements to social change. Thus, the reshaping of perspectives, norms, and values is of primary interest here. On the basis of what we know about the demands of the movement and the motivational bases, the following speculations are offered:

1. The significance of the women's liberation movement does not depend upon its size. A relatively small number of women are actually participating in the organizations of the movement. And some of the publicized incidents seem peripheral to the basic goals. For instance, knocking down sex barriers at McSorley's Old Ale House in New York may not seem a great boon to woman's welfare. But when a federal judge ruled on June 25, 1970, that McSorley's, an all-male tavern since its founding in 1854, was a public place subject to the equal protection clause of the Constitution, a principle was laid. Such extremist tactics call attention to other "men only" signs—seen and unseen—that have not been noticed before. A new perspective is established.[4]

2. The movement may become more conservative as more of its goals are attained. Helson's (1959) *adaptation level theory* provides a theoretical framework for understanding the effects of the more extreme views on the general public. The demand for the vote may have appeared extreme in 1920, but women's voting has now been accepted as the norm. Now, the demand for equal rights in employment still sounds extreme to many because beliefs about "woman's place" are deeply ingrained. But as legal measures are taken to bar discrimination and as employers are constantly reminded of their need to view women as persons first, this demand will seem less extreme. If society continues to adapt to the demands of the new feminism, the movement will probably lose some of its present identity; but in so doing it will have contributed to a restructuring of norms about where woman's place is.

3. The demands for the restructuring of sex roles, if met, will have profound consequences on the family unit. It is too early to predict the degree of change that will occur in attitudes toward child-rearing responsibilities. (See Figure 12-4.) However, we may anticipate some change in at least three ways: (a) more mothers will be working, (b) fathers may become more involved in child rearing, and (c) more children will be cared for five days a week in child-care centers. NOW has proposed paternity as well as maternity leaves for employees so that mothers can pursue careers and fathers can have more time with the children. This proposal could lead to a shift in the father's role in child rearing. Also, the establishment of more child-care centers by government and industry will provide the child with more opportunities for interaction with other young children (Bronfenbrenner, 1970).

The penetrating insights of Bronfenbrenner (1963, 1970) reveal the effects of family structure on personality development. In an analysis of changing patterns of child rearing over a period of 25 years, Bronfenbrenner (1963) studied how children are affected by the tendency toward more permissiveness, more open expression of affection, and the use of psychological techniques of discipline. In his cross-cultural comparison of child rearing in the United States and the Soviet Union, Bronfenbren-

[4]Daryl Bem's (1970) argument that behavior causes attitudes is applicable here. Bem's *theory of self-perception* suggests that a person's new behavior provides a source from which he draws a new set of inferences about what he feels and believes. Forcing changes in behavior toward women may indeed produce changes in beliefs about them and attitudes toward them.

The United States today seems to be on the verge of making a conscious national decision that mothers should not spend all their time taking care of their children. Assuming that conventional family patterns are being called into question, what are some of the alternatives?

1. *Mass day care.* With approximately 40 percent of the nation's women now employed, is mass day care an idea whose time has come? Few authorities in the field doubt that day care is in for a mighty boom. Whether in Federal Head Start programs, traditional nursery schools, a small group of children cared for by a woman in her own home, or a franchised center where the curriculum is designed by educational experts, day care is now developing very quickly. Psychologists and educators concede that children could conceivably prosper in a day-care center that is well-planned and lovingly staffed. However, psychologist Jerome Kagan warns that it will be difficult for the good things that could occur in a day-care center actually to occur there because the structure of our society does not build either strong loyalties to one's job or to other people's children.

2. *The commune.* Utopians from Plato onward have visualized children as not being reared in traditional families but in various forms of communal organizations. These intentional communities purport to be an escape from what is regarded as the constriction, loneliness, and materialism of straight society. Sociologists suggest that it is quite natural for children to grow up in extended families where there are many adults. Yet in most of the new communes the extension does not reach to a third generation, and it is possible that the children have never seen an adult over 30.

3. *More adult involvement with children.* Psychologist Urie Bronfenbrenner appeals for greater involvement of the different ages with one another. He argues that children should not grow up associating only with other children. One of the most salient developments in American social psychology during the past decade has been a demonstration of the obvious—namely, that children learn by watching others. The child takes on the actions of the model without visible inducement. What is called for is greater involvement of parents and other adults in the lives of children—and conversely greater involvement of children in responsibility for their own family, community, and society at large (Bronfenbrenner, 1970).

Figure 12-4. *Who's Bringing up the Children?*

ner (1970) calls for greater involvement of parents and other adults in the lives of children. He also advocates taking advantage of the constructive potential of the peer group in developing social responsibility. It is difficult to predict the father's role in child rearing in the next two generations. Also, it is too early to assess the effects of increased peer interaction through child-care centers. But most probably child-rearing practices in the next generation will not be merely a recapitulation of the parents' experiences. There is evidence that rapid social change may interrupt the continuity of child-rearing practices from one generation to the next, so that new standard personality patterns emerge (Inkeles, 1963). The role of the parents in mediating the influence of rapid social change thus assumes crucial importance in helping their children adapt to the changed social conditions.

III. YOUTH AND CHANGE

Social change subjects different age groups to differing amounts of stress. Most affected are youths in the process of making a lifelong commitment to the future. The young, who have outlived the social definitions of childhood but who are not yet fully located in the world of adult commitments and roles, are most torn between the pulls of the past and the future. Keniston (1970), who describes *youth* as a new stage produced by recent historical and social conditions (see Figure 12-5), discusses alternative responses that may characterize the reactions of youth to rapid social change. In this section we will examine two of these alternatives—activism and alienation. Several investigations have distinguished between activists and alienated, apolitical youth (Block, Haan, & Smith, 1968; Flacks, 1967; Keniston, 1967; Watts, Lynch, & Whittaker, 1969). Though both activists and alienated youth reject many aspects of contemporary society, the two groups can be clearly differentiated. The activists express their dissent through direct confrontation, while the alienated react by withdrawing from conventional society.

A. Student Activism

The American college campus in the late 1960s became an arena of turbulence and change. Beginning with the Free Speech Movement at Berkeley in 1964 and 1965, the surge of activism in the 1960s caught Americans by surprise. Most descriptions of college students in the 1950s pictured them as "gloriously contented," optimistic, and serious about their work, if apathetic about larger social concerns (Jacob, 1957).

In assessing the change from apathy to activism several questions are of interest. (a) What is the actual incidence of student activism? (b) What kinds of colleges and universities comprise the settings for protest? (c) What are the themes of the protest? (d) What are the personality correlates and family backgrounds of the activists? (e) What changes in American society will result from this upsurge of activism?

Incidence. Although the actual incidence rate of students engaging in disruptive

---

Kenneth Keniston, author of *Young Radicals* and *The Uncommitted*, proposes that we are witnessing today the emergence on a mass scale of a previously unrecognized stage of life, a stage that intervenes between adolescence and adulthood. He calls this the stage of *youth*, assigning a new and specific meaning to this venerable and vague term.

A central conscious issue during youth is the tension between self and society. Whereas the adolescent is struggling to define who he is, the youth begins to sense who he is and thus to recognize the possibility of conflict and disparity between his emerging selfhood and his social order. In youth, pervasive ambivalence toward both self and society is the rule. This ambivalence is not the same as a definitive rejection of society, nor does it necessarily lead to political activism. For ambivalence may also entail intense self-rejection, including major efforts at self-transformation such as monasticism, meditation, psychoanalysis, prayer, or hallucinogenic drugs. In youth the ambivalent conflicts between the maintenance of personal integrity and the achievement of effectiveness in society are fully experienced for the first time.

The central developmental possibilities of youth are defined as *individuation* versus *alienation*. The meaning of individuation may be clarified by considering the special dangers of youth, which can be defined as extremes of alienation, whether from self or from society. At one extreme is that total alienation from self that involves abject submission to society—"joining the rat race" or "selling out." Here society is affirmed but selfhood denied. The other extreme is a total alienation from society that leads not so much to the rejection of society, as to ignoring, denying, or blocking out its existence. Here the integrity of self is purchased at the price of a determined denial of social reality and the loss of social effectiveness.

(Adapted from Keniston, K. Youth: A "new" stage of life. *The American Scholar*, Autumn, 1970, **39**, 631–654.)

Figure 12-5. *Youth: A "New" Stage of Life*

1965–1968	Peterson (1967) found that only about 9 percent of any student body was reported to be involved in protest in 1965. In a later national survey, Peterson (1968) found that the number of campuses (38 percent) experiencing organized student protest of the Vietnam War had doubled. For that same period there was also an increased activism toward a larger role for students in campus governance.
1968–1969	A comprehensive survey of American colleges and universities made by Bayer and Astin for the 1968–69 academic year indicated that approximately 6 percent of the campuses experienced at least one incident of violent disruptive protest, and an additional 16 percent experienced nonviolent disruptive protest.
1969–1970	The American Council on Education, Office of Research (1970) reported that more than 9000 separate protest incidents occurred on two-thirds of the nation's college campuses during the 1969–1970 academic year. The most frequent type of protest involved issues not directly related to the institution. Earth Day (April 22, 1970) involved the largest number of participants—39 percent of all institutions. Cambodia protests involved 16 percent of the campuses; Kent State protests, 24 percent; and Jackson State, only 2 percent.
1970–1971	The 1970–1971 academic year was only slightly more quiet with regard to campus unrest than in 1968–1969 in that 20 percent of the higher education institutions experienced at least one "severe" protest as compared to slightly over 22 percent in 1968–1969. American Council on Education researchers, Bayer and Astin (1971), compared 1970–1971 with 1968–1969 because they had comparable data and because the campus incidents triggered in 1969–1970 by the Cambodian invasion and the killings at Kent State were "extreme to the point of being unique." Their survey showed that destruction of physical property was as prevalent in 1970–1971 as in 1968–1969 but that protests involving injury to persons and those involving interruption of school functions and general campus strikes were less frequent.*

*(Adapted from American Council on Education. Campus unrest still widespread in 1970-71, ACE researchers claim. *Higher Education and National Affairs,* September 24, 1971, **20**, 6.)

Figure 12-6. *How Many Students Protest?*

protest is relatively low, the importance of student activism goes beyond its statistical size in its effects upon other students and upon the society at large. Also, figures become quickly dated because of changes from one year to the next in the number of institutions and the number of students involved. Figure 12-6 summarizes some of the recent surveys of protest incidents. Feuer (1969), reviewing the American student movement in comparison to student movements in other countries and at other times, sees secondary consequences of student activism that pose dangers to the United States. Among these dangerous consequences, Feuer cites the example of some activists' contempt for democratic procedure and their intimidation of the majority.

The Settings for Protest. An analysis of the scope of protest between 1964 and 1966 (R. Peterson, 1967) showed that political demonstrations were concentrated in the larger universities and institutions of high academic caliber and almost totally absent at teachers' colleges, technical institutes, and nonacademic denominational colleges. (Nonacademic refers to those institutions that attract students whose orientation is more social or collegiate than intellectual.) A later survey (R. Peterson, 1968) further showed that the incidence of protest varied little among geographical regions, with the exception that, in the South, one-third fewer colleges reported organized protests and the protests that did occur were less likely to deal with off-campus issues. Whereas differing student values and institutional functions accounted for variations in the reported protests, the size of the institution was apparently the overriding factor. Institutional quality (defined as the proportion of faculty doctorates) was significantly correlated with a higher incidence of war-related protests. The extent to which an institution is commuter-oriented or residential was not related to the incidence of protest. The presence of leftist political groups on a campus was highly associated with protests concerning both on- and off-campus issues.

Some generalizations may be drawn from Bayer and Astin's study (1969) about the kinds of institutions in which disruption is most likely to occur. The following summary applies to the estimated 22 percent of U.S. colleges and universities that experienced at least one incident of violent or nonviolent disruptive protest during the 1968–69 school year.

1. Major protest incidents were about twice as likely to occur at private universities than at public ones. More than one in three of all private universities experienced violent protest during the 1968–69 academic year, while one in eight public universities experienced incidents of comparable severity.

2. In general, the larger the institution, the more likely it was to experience violent or disruptive protest. Very few institutions with enrollments under 1000 had any incidents of violent protest in 1968–69.

3. The more selective a university, the more likely it was to experience protest. About 85 percent of the most selective universities (those enrolling students of the highest academic ability) had disruptive incidents. Universities in the lowest category of selectivity experienced no incidents like those defined by Bayer and Astin.

Keniston (1967) described the protest-promoting institution as having a reputation for academic excellence and freedom, coupled with highly selective admissions policies. Although it may seem paradoxical to expect protest in an institution that values freedom, the concept of *relative deprivation* is applicable here. Students who have experienced freedom are more likely to attempt to lessen the gap between the present level of attainment and the ideal. To put the paradox in its sharpest form, the greater the students' freedom, the more restricted they feel by even the mildest regulations.

Issues in Student Protests. Tensions among students in the early 1960s were linked successively with a series of issues, especially with the growing civil rights movement. Feuer (1969) shows that every student movement has tried to attach itself to a more enduring, pervasive, and massive carrier movement. Something of an identification with blacks can be heard in these words of Mario Savio, spokesman in the Free Speech Movement at Berkeley in 1964.

> We found we were being denied the very possibility of 'being a student'—unquestionably a *right*. . . . Thus it was both the irrationality of society, that denies to Negroes the life of man, and the irrationality of the University, that denies to youth the life of students, which caused last semester's rebellion (cited in Katope & Zolbrod, 1966, pp. 86 and 89).[5]

The Bayer and Astin report (1969) on campus disruption in 1968–69 provides a close look at the kinds of issues that gave rise to protest. In 1968–69, the demand for increased student power was the most frequent theme of major protest incidents. The most prevalent specific issues on campuses that had violent protest involved (a) in-

[5]Some of these same themes are reflected in Gerald Farber's (1969) *The Student as Nigger*. Farber, a professor, sparked controversy among administrators and parents with his volatile description of an "Auschwitz approach to education."

stituting special educational programs for disadvantaged or minority groups, (b) allowing student participation on committees, (c) changing institutional disciplinary practices, (d) challenging apparent administrative indifference or inaction to grievances, and (e) challenging alleged administrative indifference to local community problems. The most prevalent off-campus issues that led to protest were those relating to war. Military issues accounted for roughly half the disruptive incidents (Bayer & Astin, 1969).

In the course of the student movement from 1964 to the early 1970s, several themes recur. These are opposition to the impersonal organization of human life; opposition to the sacrifice of moral, emotional, intellectual, and aesthetic values to material expansion; a need for direct participation in decision making; anti-institutionalism; and anti-authoritarianism (Katz, 1967; Flacks, 1967).

Personality Correlates of Activism. A glowing profile of the student activist emerged in several studies of the mid-1960s (J. Katz, 1967; Flacks, 1967; Watts & Whittaker, 1966; Haan, Smith, & Block, 1968). Activists were found to be intellectually gifted, academically superior, and politically radical young people. Their home backgrounds revealed parents who were successful in their careers, comfortable in their economic positions, and liberal in their political orientations. Activists were described as being more flexible, tolerant, and realistic; they were independent of authority that is traditionally imposed by social institutions. The child rearing of the activists was more permissive, and the parents had closer affective relationships with their children than parents of nonactivists. From the family pictures that emerged in these studies, it appears that many activists were acting in conformity with their parents' values. Moreover, they used the freedom and affection experienced at home as a yardstick by which to measure the behavior and attitudes of the authorities at school and in society (Eurich, 1968).

Block, Haan, and Smith (1968) identified relatively homogeneous subgroups in their total pool of 1033 subjects, in order to carry out a more differentiated analysis of activism. They defined five subgroups of students as follows.

1. *Inactive* young people who reported no participation in political or social organizations or activities.

2. *Conventional* young people who were fraternity or sorority members but who fell below the mean in their participation in protest activities and in social service activities.

3. *Constructivists* whose scores on social services were above the mean of the total sample but whose scores on protest activities fell below the mean of the total sample.

4. *Dissenting* young people whose scores on protest activities were above the mean but whose scores on social service activities were below the mean of the total sample.

5. *Activists* whose scores on both social action and protest fell above the means of the total sample. Activists are concerned about the plight of their fellow man and work to alleviate pain and poverty and injustice. At the same time, activists are disillusioned with the status quo and involve themselves in protest against policies and institutions that are not in accord with their image of a just society.

Of special value in this research was the search for the antecedents of activism. These antecedents were inferred from students' retrospective descriptions of the child-rearing orientations and values of their parents. The subsequent paragraphs present a brief summary of the major findings regarding parental orientations and values for the five subgroups.

1. The parents of *inactives* are concerned about conformity, obedience, and docility. Their demands were primarily for good behavior rather than for achievement or independence.

2. The socialization of the *conventionalists* emphasizes classical Protestant virtues—responsibility, conformity, achievement, and obedience.

3. The parents of *constructivists*, like those of the conventionalists, emphasize discipline but more frequently use nonphysical punishments.

4. The child-rearing practices of the *dissenters'* parents appear somewhat incoherent. There is a pattern of indulgence and permissiveness—conjoined with an interest in achievement, encouragement of competition, and opposition to the child's needs for privacy. The result is an unsatisfying parental relationship, involving much conflict.

5. The parents of *activists* encourage their children to be independent and responsible—qualities shared to some degree with parents of conventionalists. The parents of activists, however, encourage the child's differentiation and self-expressiveness, with discipline per se being less critical. There is an emphasis on inner-directed goals, rather than externally defined goals.

It should be remembered that these descriptions have been constructed from the students' point of view. Indeed, it would be interesting to have parents provide their own descriptions of their child-rearing practices. Nonetheless, such a differentiated framework for defining activism helps avoid some of the generalizations that result from studies that have exclusively concentrated upon leftist activists. Some of these questionable generalizations have been pointed out in a careful review by Kerpelman (1970). First, there is an almost universal confounding of political activism and political ideology. Second, there is the lack of appropriate control subjects. Third, there are unwarranted interpretations of personality measures. Fourth, there is the failure to compare results across institutions. And, fifth, there is a lack of rigorous, quantifiable criteria for selecting research subjects.

Kerpelman, in a study that attempted to overcome such errors, investigated six groups of students at each of three institutions of higher education. These groups were left activists, middle-of-the-road activists, right activists, left nonactivists, middle-of-the-road nonactivists, and right nonactivists. The three institutions used by Kerpelman were a small private liberal arts college, a medium-sized private university, and a large public university. The final sample consisted of 229 students, who were administered tests to measure not only the students' intelligence, personalities, attitudes, and values, but also the extent of their political activism and the nature of their political ideology. The results indicated no measures on which any particular activism-ideology subgroup differed from the others. All activists—left, middle, and right—were found to have less need of support and nurturance, to value leadership more, to be more socially ascendant and assertive, and to be more sociable than all left, middle, and right ideologically oriented students who were not politically active. There were no differences among any of the activism or ideology groups in emotional stability, responsibility, restraint, or intelligence (although there was an institutional difference). Right activists and right nonactivists were highest on authoritarianism; left activists were lowest on this factor, while the other three subgroups fell in between. Right and left activists were both highest on autonomy, with middle activists, and right, left, and middle nonactivists following in that order. The implications of Kerpelman's findings suggest that appropriate comparisons can and should be made to separate the relative contributions of activism per se from those of ideology. For example, if authoritarianism is the factor to be explained, it could best be understood as an ideological difference. However, autonomy is more likely to separate the activist from the nonactivist, regardless of ideology.

Reform or Revolution? Is the current wave of student activism directed toward a violent overthrow of the university or toward more gradual reform within the system? The answer to this question depends in part on identifying the political ideology of the activists. There is no agreement on whether the various groups of activists comprise a social movement in the formal sense.

Flacks (1970) believes that the activities of students in the 1960s do represent a social movement, signifying fundamental social change and not merely generational conflict. He notes that the Port Huron Statement of June, 1962 and other documents of the early Students for a Democratic Society (SDS) and the New Left no longer serve as guidelines for these organizations. The trajectory of the New Left has more recently been toward revolutionary opposition to capitalism. The radicalization of youth is enhanced by the peculiar social position of high school and college students, who have achieved some degree of independence from family authority but are not yet subject to the discipline of work institutions.

Campuses have been compared with the canaries that miners used to take with them into the mines. Being somewhat more sensitive to bad air than the miner, the canary would keel over first, warning the miner that he was in trouble. In the same vein, James Perkins, former president of Cornell University, has stated: "The university is simply the canary in the coal mine. . . . It is the most sensitive barometer of social change" (*Newsweek,* June 15, 1970, p. 66). If the university is indeed the barometer, then surely some assessment can be made of the direction of change as indicated by a decade of student unrest.

The changes within the university itself are the most obvious. Although unrest and change are positively associated, Bayer and Astin (1969) have shown clearly that colleges and universities are not intransigent and that they do institute changes without confrontation and crisis. Most institutions, including those where no major protest incident has occurred, made discernible changes in institutional policy and practices during the academic year included in the Bayer and Astin study. On campuses where there were violent protests, changes were most often in the form of new committees or study groups or of new Black Studies programs. The formation of new committees, curriculum changes, and the provision for greater student participation on existing committees were the changes that most often took place as a direct result of nonviolent disruptive protests. Bayer and Astin (1969) report that of those institutions which had not experienced any major protest activities during the year, almost one-fourth changed their racial policies.

Procedural changes may be just as important as curricular changes. Significant change is occurring in the area of individualization—including independent study, work-study and honors programs, and credit for community service. Colleges are experimenting with different grading systems—some with pass/fail options and some with no grades whatsoever. The direction is apparently toward allowing the student to take more responsibility for his own education (*Newsweek,* 1970b).

Beyond the campus, there are repercussions from the political activism of college students. A partial listing of the decisive consequences of student activism on the larger political order would surely include the following. (a) Opposition to the war became so respectable in the early 1970s that any attempt to extend the military conflict encountered strong popular resistance. The student activists made it safe for middle forces to adopt some of the same issues (Schaar & Wolin, 1970). (b) Students have directed the attention of other groups to the issues of civil rights and racial justice. (c) Serious questions have been raised about conscription and the impact of militarism on American life. (d) University complicity with military and corporate establishments has come under attack. (e) Increased popular support for lowering the voting age enabled legislation to be passed to bring in the 18- to 20-year-olds. (f) Ecological issues have been dramatized by organized student demonstrations for saving our environment.

B. Cultural Alienation

Kenneth Keniston, who has carefully studied both activism and alienation among today's youth, depicts the culturally alienated youth as being in sharp contrast to the activist. Whereas the activist is politically optimistic and socially concerned, the culturally alienated youth is too pessimistic and too firmly opposed to the system to demonstrate his disapproval in any organized public way. Through nonconformity in behavior, ideology, and dress, through personal experimentation, and through efforts to intensify his own subjective experience, the alienated youth shows his distaste for politics and society. Keniston (1965) found that a primary variable in the alienation syndrome was distrust—or, in our terms, an assumption that human nature is untrustworthy. Any kind of positive commitment is viewed negatively by the alienated student. Given the unpredictability of the future, long-range ethical idealism is impossible, and the present becomes overwhelmingly important. Rejecting the traditional American values of success, self-control, and achievement, the alienated person maintains that passion, feeling, and awareness are the most reliable forces at man's disposal. For the alienated, the primary objective in life is to attain and maintain openness to experience, contact with the world, and spontaneity of feeling. Anything that might fetter or restrain responsiveness and openness is opposed.

The Generation Gap—Myth or Fact? Conflict between generations is nothing new. But so much is being said about the generation gap that it seems appropriate to examine the notion in this discussion of social change. It certainly appears that many older people assume that young people quite literally accept the slogan "Don't trust anyone over 30."

The popular media increasingly refer to a counterculture among the young. A symbol of this counterculture is the Woodstock Rock Festival in the summer of 1969—interpreted by many as a revolution of youth against adult America. The Woodstock Music and Art Fair, an Aquarian Exposition, was originally planned as an outdoor rock festival featuring three days of peace and music in the Catskill village of Woodstock. For three days 400,000 of the nation's affluent young lived elbow to elbow, enduring rain, mud, short rations, paralyzed traffic, and other miscellaneous tortures that come with overcrowding. The organizers had anticipated only 50,000 customers a day and had set up a fragile, unauthoritarian system to deal with them.

Yet, not one fight was reported, nor was there any political overtone to the weekend. Social scientists are still trying to explain Woodstock.

One simple explanation may be contained in the announcement of one of the festival officials on the opening day: "There are a lot of us here. If we are going to make it you had better remember that the guy next to you is your brother" (*Life*, August 29, 1969, p. 12B). There is evidence of a high degree of *cohesiveness* among the Woodstock participants. A group experiencing high cohesiveness should be able to secure a high degree of acceptance of almost any type of group goal (Krech, et al., 1962, p. 401). Pressures toward cohesiveness were clearly manipulated by the officials at Woodstock in such pronouncements as the one above. A second device for securing cohesiveness was the positive reinforcement of such things as free breakfasts and by the officials' compliments to the crowd for their cooperation. Also, it was impressed upon the crowd that the whole world was watching—effectively reducing the **deindividuation** and alienation usually characteristic of large assemblages of people.[6]

Many adults feel certain that today's alienated young are not just the modern equivalent of the goldfish-swallowing students of the 1930s. But there is a question as to how serious the alienation really is. Is there really a generation gap? Roszak (1969) and Mead (1970) say yes. Adelson (1970) says no. We shall now turn to an examination of these contrasting interpretations of the phenomenon commonly labeled the generation gap.

The Rise of a Counter Culture. Roszak (1969) argues that the revolt of the young is serious, important, and redemptive. According to Roszak, the young today are forming a culture so radically unaffiliated with the mainstream of our society that it scarcely appears to many as a culture at all. The source of their revolt is the dehumanization brought about by Western technological civilization. Roszak describes the technocracy as the social form in which an industrial society reaches the peak of its organizational integration. In the technocracy, nothing is any longer small or simple or readily apparent to the nontechnical man. Instead, the scale and intricacy of all human activities transcends the competence of the amateur citizen and demands the attention of specially trained experts. Today's polarization, then, has the technical-bureaucratic organization of economic and political life on one side and the counter-culture—the radical-anarchic, romantic-religious, protest-withdrawal tendencies of the young—on the other side. A difficulty in Roszak's interpretation of the rise of the counterculture, however, is that he sees it as a revolution of the repressed against the system that represses them. But in fact, the revolt of the young occurs not among those who are most oppressed or repressed, nor among those who bear the greatest responsibility to the technocracy. The counterculture is in fact a subculture of middle-class white youth. Indeed, the counterculture includes really only that minority of the young who are so securely in technocratic society that they can afford to demand something more of life than security, affluence, and the prospect of political power. The counterculture arises, then, not because the young today are more repressed but because they are so little repressed that they can raise their sights. As Keniston has stated: "The counter culture may replace the barbecue pit with the hippie pad, family togetherness with the encounter group, and the suburban coffee hour with the com-

[6] Quite different outcomes have been noted in other rock festivals, especially the disastrous one at Altamont, California, where a death resulted when "bikers" used chains and knives to keep order. The "Celebration of Life" festival in Louisiana in the summer of 1971 ended ahead of schedule with three deaths, two from drowning and one from a drug overdose.

mune, but the focus is still on the private world instead of on the social and political scene where it should be. . . . If American technocracy is the thesis, Roszak admirably defines the antithesis. We still await the synthesis" (1969, p. 9).

Similar to Roszak's sympathetic view of the counter culture is the "Consciousness III" classification of Charles Reich in *The Greening of America* (1970). Reich defines three categories of people: Consciousness I, II, and III—each representing a stage in American life. Consciousness III people are seen as the hope of the present and the wave of the future: "The Consciousness III person, no matter how young and inexperienced, seems to possess an extraordinary 'new knowledge'. . . . He does not 'know' the facts, but he still 'knows' the truth that seems hidden from others." His mystical view of the youth revolution is subject to the same criticism that Keniston makes of Roszak's counterculture—in other words, the question of how society is to deal with its own problems is avoided, as if it is an insignificant or irrelevant issue.

Toward a Prefigurative Culture? Another view of the generation gap is embodied in anthropological terms by Margaret Mead, who sees a deep, new, unprecedented, worldwide gulf between the young and the old. Mead, who has been studying patterns of child rearing across cultures for many years, expects that the future will radically depart from the present. Within the two decades from 1940 to 1960, events have occurred that irrevocably altered men's relationships to other men and to the natural world. Mead sees the events and discoveries of this time span as bringing about a drastic, irreversible division between the generations. As Mead has stated: "Even very recently, the elders could say: 'You know, I have been young and *you* have never been old.' But today's young people can reply: 'You never have been young in the world I am young in, and you never can be'" (1970, p. 63).

Mead's view of the dichotomy between the perceptions of the young and their parents is contradicted by evidence reported by Adelson. Mead's standpoint also differs from findings on the similarities between the values of the student activists and their parents. But her emphasis is on the speed and dimensions of change in the modern world. She distinguishes among three different kinds of culture: **postfigurative,** in which children learn primarily from their forebears; **cofigurative,** in which both children and adults learn from their peers; and **prefigurative,** in which adults learn also from their children. Mead sees this new kind of prefigurative culture developing in which the child will have to serve as scout; the child will pose the questions, and it will be the task of his elders to teach him "how to learn" rather than "what to learn." The older generation—those born before 1940—is "strangely isolated," according to Mead. It has witnessed such massive and rapid change that it cannot communicate its experiences to its successors. Meanwhile, the young are "at home" in this time. Satellites are familiar in their skies. They have never known a time when war did not threaten annihilation. When they are given the facts, they can understand immediately that continued pollution of the air and water and soil will soon make the planet uninhabitable. Like the first generation born in a new country, they only halfway comprehend their parents' talk about the past. Here, Mead's views are reminiscent of Child's (1943) descriptions of the dilemma of second-generation Italians in a New England community. They were "marginal men," experiencing strong pulls between being Italian and being American and finding themselves unable to belong to either group.

Mead optimistically believes that the gap between the generations can be taken as a guide to the future. Although this guide is somewhat vague, she thinks it is possible to change into a prefigurative culture consciously, delightedly, and industriously, rearing unknown children for an unknown world. The nature of the direct participation of the young of which Mead speaks may be inferred from this comment by a participant (then a college senior) in a panel discussion regarding the generation gap: "Starting in the late 50's you made a demand from us. You said expand your mind and think. We've got to fight the Russians because there's a technological race on. We capitulated and we expanded our minds. Now you've got a lot of people who can think; you've got a lot of people who have been through a system who have learned how to think. Now we're saying we want to use this knowledge with experience. You're saying, not yet, you're too young. I think we're just as old as you mentally, and if you give us time, and if you give us the room to experiment, to use this knowledge, you could have a beautiful thing" (quoted in *Religious Education,* 1970, Vol. 65, p. 105). Additional support for the idea of an unprecedented generation gap is given by those who examine current art forms. The music, art, theater, and literature of youth provide clues to the themes of alienation (Reichart, 1969; Friedenberg, 1969).

More Ideological than Generational. Despite the popularity of the idea of an unprecedented conflict between the generations, there is some evidence that refutes the idea. Quite clearly, the answer to whether there is a generation gap depends upon the specific issues one is talking about. If the issue is whether there is a fundamental lack of articulation between the generations, then the answer is decisively no (Adelson, 1970, p. 35). In contrast to the notion that there is an extensive degree of alienation between parents and their children, Adelson concludes that there are few signs of serious conflict between American adolescents and their parents. Douvan and Adelson (1966) studied 3000 young people, ages 12 to 18, from all regions of the country and all socioeconomic levels and found that most usually the relationships between youth and their parents were amiable. Adelson cites a study by Bengston, in which data were collected from more than 500 students enrolled in three southern California colleges. About 80 percent of the students reported generally close and friendly relationships with their parents; specifically, 79 percent felt somewhat close or very close; 81 percent regarded communication as good; and 78 percent felt their parents understood them all or most of the time.

Lubell (1968) asked 350 white students and more than 100 black students at 28 campuses in 14 states to compare themselves with their parents. Interview questions concerned upbringing, drug use, premarital sex, religious beliefs, career choices, economic thinking, and attitudes toward the draft, war, and politics. Lubell reports that only about 10 percent of the students he interviewed were in serious discord with their parents, and in most of these cases there was a long history of family tension. Similar findings by Cross (1968) indicate a striking similarity between the opinions of students and their perceptions of their parents' opinions. Adelson (1970) examined the areas of politics and values and found further arguments that the gap is ideological rather than generational.

An analysis of the 1968 election was made by the University of Michigan's Survey Research Center and was based upon 1600 interviews with a representative national sample of voters. Outside the South, Wallace drew proportionately more votes from younger voters than from older voters. This is in contrast with the tendency to identify the young with leftist ideology and militancy. The radical activists are for the most part children of radical or liberal parents.

In connection with the issue of values, *Fortune* polled a representative sample of

18- to 24-year-olds, dividing them into a noncollege group (vocationally oriented) and a so-called forerunner group (students interested in education as self-discovery and majoring in humanities and social sciences). The forerunners were more liberal politically, less traditional in values, and less enchanted about business careers. But a generation gap was not revealed. An intragenerational cleavage was found, however, in that 80 percent of the respondents reported that they do not believe there are great differences between their own values and the values of their parents (*Fortune,* 1969).

According to Adelson's argument, there has been too much generalization from a narrow segment of the young to the entire younger generation. Adelson finds that a relatively small proportion of the young are in severe conflict with the values of their parents. He sees more evidence for describing what is happening as an ideological conflict that cuts across generational lines. The polarization is not the result of age but of differing ideologies. Adelson's findings tend to support the findings of similarities between the values of student activists and the values of their parents. The evidence does not completely shatter the notion that an unprecedented generation gap is only a myth; but it does indicate that the conflict between children and their own parents is not as sharp as the popular usage of the term suggests. The gap across ideological lines certainly exists, but it cannot be attributed entirely to conflict between the generations.

IV. OTHER INDICATORS OF SOCIAL CHANGE

In attempting to assess the direction of social change, we have examined a current social movement and have discussed the special relationship of youth to social change. But there are other areas of change in attitudes and values that serve as indicators of the direction of social change. In this section, we will look at two of these—technology and its effect on attitudes toward work, and changing attitudes toward religious and moral authority. In each case these changing attitudes may be viewed both as consequences of previous social changes and as potential sources of future change.

A. Technology and Its Effects on Attitudes toward Work

The United States has always nurtured a cult of progress and a set of beliefs and attitudes that define what is characteristically an American way of looking at life. The component attitudes of this ideology include optimism, an orientation to the future rather than to the past, a positive view of change, and a preference for new ideas over old ones (McGee, 1962). "Old-fashioned" is an invidious epithet, and "newness" is valued in and for itself. But the technology that makes progress possible has been accepted without full consideration of its side effects. Recently, the notion that technological development is synonomous with progress has been seriously questioned. At times the negative consequences of a new technique or device become so overwhelmingly evident they cannot be ignored. The advent of off-shore oil drilling was probably viewed as progress. However, when a leak occurred and the oil collected on the beaches contaminating marine life, national attention was aroused. Destruction to our environment was the price of the so-called progress.

Perhaps the price of progress is too great. A fundamental question for the 1970s is: how can we make sure that our enormously complex technology remains our servant? Will life be enlarged in the technological society, bringing a new and generous vision of what is humanly possible, or will life narrow down to a struggle to escape uncertainty? Of more specific interest to the student of social psychology are the effects of the technological revolution on changes in attitudes and values. The specific area to be examined here is technology's effects on attitudes toward work.

The side effects of cybernetics threaten to reorganize the nature of economic and social life. These effects throw into question the long held Protestant Ethic that if one works hard, life's rewards will come without fail. In the Protestant tradition, the ideal man is one who is not distracted by activities unrelated to his work; he postpones all possible benefits of prestige for the future; he conserves his assets and belongings for a time of need for himself and his family; and he saves surplus wealth for the purpose of extending economic enterprise—even at the expense of self-denial in the present. This Protestant tradition of asceticism, self-denial, and hard work was skillfully related to the spirit of capitalism by Max Weber (1930), who called it the Protestant Ethic.

During the years when America was assimilating waves of immigrants, the spirit of the Protestant Ethic encouraged many groups to expend extra energy to create their niche in American culture. The pattern of a new group coming in at the bottom and working hard to move upward has been a major source of energy and innovation in American society (Hodgkinson, 1967). But in the last century the major industrial change has been away from the production of goods to the production of services. At the turn of the century, about three-fourths of the people in the labor force worked in producing physical goods, but by 1960 the majority of the people in the labor force were engaged in service occupations. Heavy manual labor has given way to machine production, which has freed a larger portion of the labor force for work in service industries.

Department of Labor statistics indicate that the proportion of the total population included in the labor force is about 60 percent and that this percentage has been fairly stable over the past two decades (Kurtz, 1969). But the length of the work week itself has been greatly reduced. The standard work week in 1900 was 54 to 60 hours or more; a person steadily employed in a manufacturing plant thus worked about 3000 hours per year. Today such a worker averages fewer than 40 hours a week and receives a paid vacation, putting in only about 2000 hours a year (Mack, 1967).

Along with such changes in the pattern of work, there is evidence that the Protestant Ethic is a declining force in the American core culture. Boguslaw (1965) describes current technological developments as the utopian renaissance, which has as one of its proclaimed goals the abolition of hard labor. "The workaday new utopians seem to have turned Max Weber's Ethic on its head to read 'Hard work is simply a temporarily unautomated task. It is a necessary evil until we get a piece of gear, or a computer large enough, or a program checked out well enough to do the job economically. Until then, you working stiffs can hang around—but, for the long run, we really don't either want you or need you'" (Boguslaw, 1965, p. 25).

The decline of the Protestant Ethic is documented by Kluckhohn both as a rise in the value placed upon being as opposed to doing and an increased interest in the present time orientation and a decreased interest in the future (Kluckhohn, 1958). As advertisements tell us to live for today, installment plans and charge accounts make it possible to enjoy things in the present, rather than aspire to enjoy things in the future. The consumer role in American culture is basically hedonistic and oriented toward the present. By spending, we are told how much we are helping the economy. The following statement, made quite seriously by a college student in the 1960s, would probably irritate someone who grew up in the 1930s: "I'm not money-mad by any means, but I'd like enough to buy a house, and have transportation, and of course good clothes for the family. Plus entertainments: I'd like to be able to see the good plays and movies. And I suppose I'd want a trip every year: visit around in the big urban areas, you know, Berlin, Paris, Rome. I can't set any exact amount I'd like to make, so long as it's enough for the *necessities* of life" (quoted in Hodgkinson, 1967, p. 126).

At the present time, the whole system of values that goes with the work ethic seems to be in a state of flux. Reducing the work week does not reduce the worker's hunger for more money and goods, so that one major consequence of the six-hour day or the four-day week is the move toward moonlighting—or taking second jobs. Possibly, if larger amounts of leisure actually develop some of the more subtle meanings of work will become more apparent. Instead of viewing material reward as the primary purpose for work, more people may see work as a means of helping others, as an antidote to boredom, a factor in self-esteem, or as a creative activity (Neff, 1968). These meanings have been largely overshadowed by monetary motives in our society.

B. Changing Attitudes toward Authority

Another indicator of rapid change is the open challenge to institutionalized authority. Within a single decade open rebellion has appeared in the Roman Catholic Church, and such phenomena as the radical death-of-God theology, the new morality, and an increasing use of civil disobedience of laws perceived as unjust have emerged. Each of these may be seen as symbols of defiance of traditional norms.

Apparently, many of the changes in religious and moral attitudes reflect a move toward greater reliance on the individual and a resistance to any fixed authority that prescribes codes of conduct. Some critics believe these changes are leading us toward a valueless society in which anarchy may soon prevail. A more hopeful assessment is that we are in the midst of a struggle toward greater enlightenment about the nature of morality and authentic participation in the decisions affecting all aspects of our life. In the Kohlberg frame of reference (see Chapter 4 on Moral Development), this could mean that greater numbers of people are moving toward the principled level of moral judgment, characterized by a major thrust toward autonomy. Such autonomous moral principles have validity and application apart from the authority of the groups or persons who hold them and apart from the individual's identification with those persons or groups (Kohlberg, 1970).

V. THE USEFULNESS OF UTOPIAS

In regard to Toffler's concept of *future shock,* we should ask how we will be able to cope with the dizzying rate of change. How can we prepare for the future? Toffler (1970) says every society faces not merely a succession of probable futures but an array of possible futures and a conflict over preferable futures. "The management of change is the effort to convert certain possibles into probables, in pursuit of agreed-on preferables. Determining the probable calls for a *science* of futurism. Delineating the possible calls for an *art* of futurism. Defining the preferable calls for a *politics* of futurism" (Toffler, 1970, p. 407).

There has been a sudden proliferation of organizations devoted to the study of the future. Some of these future-oriented think-tanks include the Institute for the Future, which investigates the probable social and cultural effects of advanced communications technology; an academic study group called the Commission on the Year 2000; and the Harvard Program on Technology and Society, which is concerned with social problems likely to arise from biomedical advances. In the very attempt to forecast the future the thinkers in these organizations may be altering it, in that their forecasts can become either self-fulfilling or self-defeating prophecies. Nevertheless, predictions of what lies ahead may help clarify goals and provide alternative policies.

As long as men have thought and dreamed, there have been utopian thinkers, who shared their dreams about alternative futures. From Plato's *Republic* to Skinner's *Walden Two* men have tried to define possible futures. Some of the best known utopias in the literature are succinctly described by Grossack and Gardner (1970) and reprinted in Table 12-1. Most traditional utopias picture simple and static societies that have withdrawn from our complex industrialized world. For example, Skinner's *Walden Two,* built on the scientific principles of behavioristic psychology, depicts a preindustrial way of life, based on farming and handcraft. Although Huxley's *Brave New World* and Orwell's *1984* emphasize high technology and sophisticated machines, these books deliberately simplify social and cultural relationships. The classical utopians believed that societies could be built free from human imperfections. They wanted to escape from the problematic world in which they existed to a world that would be happier, more just, and more prosperous. The focus, though, was on people.

Boguslaw (1965) describes the new utopians as the system designers—the computer manufacturer, the operations researcher, the computer programmer, the data processing specialist. These, according to Boguslaw, are the social engineers of our times—the difference between them and the classical utopians being that the new utopians are concerned with nonpeople or with human surrogates. The new utopians plan with computer hardware, system procedures, functional analyses, and heuristics. Their impatience with human error serves to unify them, and they are separated from the classical system designers by the fact that the humanitarian bent has disappeared. Their dominant orientation can best be described as efficiency.

Toffler says that we now need a revolutionary approach to creating utopias, which would look forward to superindustrialism, rather than backward to simpler societies. Toffler suggests that this could be done by a group of expert behavioral scientists, working together long enough to devise a set of well-defined values upon which a truly superindustrial, utopian society might be based. Such a group would explore issues such as the nature of the family structure, the economy, laws, religion, sexual practices, youth culture, music, art, sense of time, degree of differentiation, and psychological problems of the future society. Meanwhile, other groups could be at work on counterutopias. Film makers and fiction writers, working closely with psychologists, could prepare creative works about the lives of individuals in the imagined society. Through television, books, plays, and films, large numbers of people could be educated to the costs and benefits of various proposed utopias. There may then emerge groups willing to subject utopian ideas to empirical test. We are

Table 12-1. *Utopias Presented in Western Literature*

Author	*Time*	*Work*	*Brief Description*
Plato	4th century B.C.	*The Republic*	Plato envisioned an ideal society with a hierarchy of classes, each having its particular obligations. Philosophers would rule, poets would be excluded.
Sir Thomas More	1516	*Utopia*	In coining the word "Utopia," More anticipated an order in which natural virtues would be unhindered.
Sir Francis Bacon	1627	*The New Atlantis*	Bacon placed primary emphasis on technological productivity.
Edward Bellamy	1888	*Looking Backward*	Bellamy's utopia was a socialist work, containing scathing critiques of his contemporary world. The work sold tremendously in the United States.
H. G. Wells	1905	*A Modern Utopia*	In this work Wells describes a future paradise; in others he outlined the destruction of the world.
Aldous Huxley	1932	*Brave New World*	A satirical account of a frightening future world in which individuality is sacrificed for the community ideals. Human beings are produced in test tubes and graded according to intelligence.
George Orwell	1948	*1984*	Orwell predicted the rise of Big Brother and the loss of freedom in this negative utopian prediction. Three world powers exist, two of which are always warring against the third.
B. F. Skinner	1948	*Walden Two*	Skinner applied the principles of learning theory in an effort to produce a population rich in idealism and devoid of negative impulses.

(From *Man and men: Social psychology as social science.* Scranton, Pa., International Textbook Company, 1970, by Grossack & Gardner.)

already witnessing in America an ever-growing number of communes. Many young people, in their dissatisfaction with industrialism, are experimenting with new social arrangements from group marriage to communal farms. But most of these endeavors reveal a powerful desire to return to the past. Society would be better served by utopian experiments based on superindustrial rather than preindustrial forms. Toffler suggests such communal efforts as a group medical practice, which takes advantage of the latest medical technology but whose members accept modest pay and pool their resources to run a completely new style of medical school. Or, why not establish an oceanographic research installation organized along utopian lines?

One reason why some of the earlier utopias failed was because they severed connections between their brave new systems and the power structures of their times. The usefulness of utopias, then, may not necessarily be in the full realization of any one design, but in the expansion of alternatives for the future. Wide dissemination of utopian and counterutopian concepts may help us become more aware of our present options. Utopian plans stem from the desire to extend man's mastery over nature and over himself. At the same time, the greatest threat of the present utopian renaissance may be its potential for extending the control of man over man (Boguslaw, 1965, p. 204). Hopefully, through its analyses of utopias and counterutopias, social psychology may serve to free man, rather than to control him, as some psychologists prefer (Skinner, 1971).

VI. SUMMARY

The study of social change is clearly relevant to social psychology. More research is needed on the psychological consequences of rapid social change, which involves significant alterations of patterns of social action and interaction. These changes are reflected in norms, values, and cultural products and symbols.

The rate of social change can be measured by picturing a fraction, the denominator of which is time and the numerator of which is the number of events to be observed. Presumably, these events would have the potential for altering the social system. There is justification for the assumption that the rate of change is accelerating.

Social movements, as forms of collective behavior aimed toward change, are useful indicators of the directions of social change. The modern feminist movement, for example, reflects the demands of more women for equality with men and for a restructuring of sex roles.

New norms are emerging with regard to the role of woman, and family patterns may shift in ways that will alter child-rearing practices.

Although the actual percentage of college students involved in active protest is relatively small, the consequences of activism are seen in changes within the university itself and in attitudes extending throughout the society.

Student protest has occurred more frequently in large, highly selective universities. Off-campus issues of the protests have most frequently dealt with civil rights and military policies. On-campus issues have centered on demands for greater student freedom and decision-making power.

Student activists apparently differ from other students in a number of personality correlates that cut across political ideologies. Highly visible groups of culturally alienated youth have led many to believe there is an intensified conflict between the generations.

Contrasting interpretations of the generation gap suggest: (a) that the present gap is unprecedented and radically different from previous generational conflict, or (b) that values of today's youth are very similar to those of their parents. The conflict then is seen to be more ideological than generational.

Technological developments have led to changing attitudes toward work. The Protestant Ethic is a declining force in the American core culture. Changing attitudes toward authority are reflected in religion and morality and may be interpreted as a move toward greater individual freedom and less reliance on fixed authority.

Utopian planning is useful for increasing the options that are available to man. The direction of utopian designs should be toward providing greater freedom for man to make his own choices.

VII. SUGGESTED READINGS

Boguslaw, R. *The new utopians. A study of system design and social change.* Englewood Cliffs, N.J.: Prentice-Hall, 1965. (Paperback) A provocative treatment of some of the social implications of current technological development.

Keniston, K. *Young radicals. Notes on committed youth.* New York: Harcourt, Brace & World, 1968. In an introduction about Vietnam Summer and the New Left, Keniston describes the personal roots of radicalism in American youth. The committed youth here stand out in sharp contrast to the alienated youth pictured in his earlier work, *The uncommitted. Alienated youth in American society,* 1965.

Kraditor, A. *Up from the pedestal. Selected writings in the history of American feminism.* Chicago: Quadrangle Books, 1968. Includes documents representing principal emphases of the feminist movement in each period from 1642 to 1966.

Mead, M. *Culture and commitment: A study of the generation gap.* New York: Doubleday, 1970. (Paperback version available) An anthropologist's view of how this generation differs from those in the past. She sees the present generation gap as unprecedented and worldwide; yet she is nonetheless optimistic about the future.

Reich, C. *The greening of America.* New York: Random House, 1970. (Paperback version available) A Yale law professor describes three types of "consciousness" that correspond roughly to stages in American history. Consciousness III is being ushered in by today's youth (the counterculture). A central idea in the book is that the power of the corporate state over individual lives can be reduced by a conversion of consciousness. This conversion to Consciousness III is Reich's view of the revolution that will change American society.

Smelser, N. *Essays in sociological explanation.* Englewood Cliffs, N. J.: Prentice-Hall, 1968. Especially helpful is the essay entitled *Toward a general theory of social change.* Included in that essay are: (a) the criteria for a theory of change, (b) a review of existing theories of change, and (c) a theoretical synthesis describing three phases of change.

Toffler, A. *Future shock.* New York: Random House, 1970. A description of what happens to individuals who are overwhelmed by rapid change. Strategies for survival and techniques for coping with change are suggested.

I. *AUTHORITARIANISM WITHIN THE PERSON*

  A. *The genesis of the Authoritarian Personality study*
  B. *The program of research*
  C. *Authoritarianism as an emergent concept*
  D. *The role of psychoanalytic theory in conceptualizing authoritarianism*
  E. *Measurement of the components of the authoritarian syndrome*
  F. *Evaluation of the Authoritarian Personality study*
    1. *Prejudice*
    2. *Interpersonal perception*
    3. *Volunteering*
    4. *Preferences for president*
    5. *Family ideology and child-rearing attitudes*
    6. *Community participation*
    7. *Attitudes and behavior regarding the Vietnam war*
  G. *Related concepts: Dogmatism*
  H. *Related concepts: Harvey's conceptual systems*

II. *OVEROBEDIENCE—A BEHAVIORAL MANIFESTATION OF AUTHORITARIANISM?*

  A. *Obedience in the real world*
  B. *Milgram's laboratory studies of overobedience*
  C. *Criticisms of Milgram's study of obedience*
    1. *Criticisms of the ethics of the experiment*
    2. *Criticisms of the lack of generalizability*
  D. *Relationship of obedience to authoritarianism and other psychological characteristics*

III. *AUTHORITARIANISM IN OUR SOCIETY*

  A. *Freud and Marcuse—two views on the repressive nature of society*
  B. *A more optimistic view of the future of society*

IV. *AUTHORITARIANISM IN THE FUTURE*

V. *SUMMARY*

VI. *SUGGESTED READINGS*

Chapter Thirteen

Authoritarianism, Obedience, and Political Repression

It is the political task of the social scientist—as of any liberal educator—continually to translate personal troubles into public issues, and public issues into terms of their human meaning for a variety of individuals. *C. Wright Mills, The Sociological Imagination*

Social psychology is one field of knowledge that has been most sensitive to the contemporary concerns of the society in which it operates. During the 1930s and 1940s, many Americans became increasingly apprehensive about the rise of authoritarianism and fascism in Europe and about the potential effects of these ultraright-wing political movements. An outgrowth of this concern was the social psychological study of the authoritarian personality.

The social psychological approach assumes that tendencies toward authoritarianism are present in all individuals and that the degree of authoritarianism within each individual can be measured with some accuracy. Therefore, part of this chapter will be devoted to the description of authoritarianism as a personal ideology—or a related set of beliefs and personality characteristics within the person that play a part in his behavior.

A highly authoritarian person can demonstrate such an ideology in a variety of situations—in his preferences for political candidates, in his unwillingness to trust another person in a cooperative task, or in the way he brings up his children. One of the possible behavioral manifestations of authoritarianism is an excessive degree of *obedience* to an authority figure—an obedience that is followed even when it requires harming another person. In this chapter Milgram's provocative series of studies on obedience will be discussed, including the relationships of behavioral obedience to authoritarianism, hostility, and moral development. Some psychologists have criticized the procedures used in Milgram's study because of the possible harm to which subjects were exposed; this type of criticism will provide an occasion for looking at the ethics of social psychological research.

Authoritarianism is a phenomenon not limited to individual persons. Societies and governments vary in their degree of authoritarianism. The rise of Nazi Germany and Fascist Italy in the 1930s represented one type of authoritarian government—authoritarian in the sense that democratic processes were removed, the behavior of individuals was restricted and controlled by the government, the mass media were used for propaganda purposes, and a nationalistic, belligerent fervor was increasingly encouraged.

Such manifestations of right-wing authoritarianism will always, in some degree, be with us; apparently, they are on the increase in America in the 1970s. But authoritarianism can also be demonstrated through political extremism of the left and through efforts toward anarchy. This chapter will explore right-wing and left-wing authoritarianism. We shall deal with such questions as: what leads to the development of an authoritarian society? Are people who subscribe to an extremist movement psychologically different from those who do not? What is the future of authoritarianism in this country?

Another type of societal authoritarianism derives from the increasing complexity of today's society. As more people inhabit a given area and as human relationships deteriorate, demands for greater governmental controls lead to invasions of privacy and restrictions on the rights of citizens. Although some of the outcomes of these pressures are similar to those of right-wing authoritarianism, the cause differs in that authoritarianism is a by-product of forces that are not necessarily politically motivated. Both types of societal authoritarianism will be investigated in this chapter.

I. AUTHORITARIANISM WITHIN THE PERSON

The emergence of fascistic governments in Germany and Italy in the 1930s caused an increased concern among both European and American social scientists about how and why a climate could develop that would allow such happenings. In 1936, the Institute of Social Research at the University of Frankfurt published an influential study linking personality dispositions with political leanings. Further work in Germany was endangered, however, because of the anti-Semitic persecutions carried out by the ruling Nazi party. Eminent German social scientists including Max Horkheimer, Herbert Marcuse, T. W. Adorno (founders of the Frankfurt school of Marxist sociology), and Else Frenkel-Brunswik emigrated first to Geneva and then to America. Both Adorno, a political scientist, and Frenkel-Brunswik, a psychologist, accepted positions at the University of California at Berkeley, where each could continue studies on personality and politics.

A. The Genesis of the Authoritarian Personality Study

During the early 1940s, other psychologists at Berkeley were studying personality factors and morale about the war. Among these were Nevitt Sanford and Daniel Levinson. With the support and encouragement of the American Jewish Committee, these social scientists collaborated with Adorno and Frenkel-Brunswik in the social psychological study of the antidemocratic or authoritarian personality. The publication of their book, *The Authoritarian Personality,* in 1950 was truly a landmark in the history of social psychology. The massive text included clinical hunches, extensions of psychoanalytic theory, multiple item-analyses of various attitude scales, depth interviews, and post hoc theory. More than 20 years later the work is still a document of contemporary interest as well as a ground-breaking publication. In understanding the rationale of this study, the reader should be aware of distinctions among the *program of research* carried out by the directors of the study, the *concept* of authoritarianism, and the *scales* used to measure aspects of authoritarianism.

B. The Program of Research

The program of the group of California researchers was initially directed toward the concept of anti-Semitism. The dimensions of anti-Jewish attitudes were analyzed, and an attitude scale was devised to measure individual differences in anti-Semitic attitudes. Gradually the focus of the program shifted toward prejudice—or what the California group chose to call **ethnocentrism.** The latter term was preferred since it refers to a relatively consistent frame of mind—a rejection of all outgroups and aliens. **Prejudice,** in contrast, is usually thought of as a feeling of dislike regarding a specific minority group; one is prejudiced against blacks, against men with mustaches, or against foreigners. The emphasis on ethnocentrism indicated the authors' assumption that such attitudes result from some characteristic of the people holding them rather than from the characteristics of the specific minority group. (The authors of *The Authoritarian Personality* have shown, for example, that the same person who berates the "clannishness and seclusiveness" of Jews will agree that "Jews are always trying to intrude where they are not wanted.") These concerns about ethnocentrism eventually led to a broader study of antidemocratic tendencies at the personality level and to the postulation of an authoritarian personality syndrome.

C. Authoritarianism as an Emergent Concept

The *concept* of authoritarianism emerged quite late in this program of research. In fact, the term *authoritarianism* does not appear in the index of *The Authoritarian Personality,* although *authoritarian aggression* and *authoritarian submission* do appear. **Authoritarianism** was conceptualized as a basic personality style, or syndrome of organized beliefs and symptoms. (N. Sanford, 1956, refers to it as the F-syndrome, "F" referring to fascistic.) The California group postulated nine components of authoritarianism: **conventionalism, authoritarian aggression, authoritarian submission, power and toughness, anti-intraception, superstition and stereotypy, destructiveness and cynicism, projectivity,** and overconcern with sex. Each of these components is defined, with sample items from the F scale, in Table 13-1. (It should be noted that agreement with a single item does not make one authoritarian, but rather it is a consistent authoritarian response to many items that reflects an authoritarian ideology.)

D. The Role of Psychoanalytic Theory in Conceptualizing Authoritarianism

In developing their conceptualizations, the California group relied heuristically upon the theory of psychoanalysis and Freud's concepts of three systems: the superego, the ego, and the id. (The reader may wish to review the explanations of these

Table 13-1. *Components of Authoritarianism*

1. *Conventionalism. Rigid* adherence to and *over*emphasis upon middle-class values, and overresponsiveness to contemporary *external* social pressure.
   Sample item: "A person who has bad manners, habits, and breeding can hardly expect to get along with decent people."
   Sample item: "No sane, normal, decent person could ever think of hurting a close friend or relative."
2. *Authoritarian submission.* An exaggerated, emotional need to submit to others; an uncritical acceptance of a strong leader who will make the decisions.
   Sample item: "Every person should have a deep faith in some supernatural force higher than himself to which he gives total allegiance and whose decisions he obeys without question."
   Sample item: "Obedience and respect for authority are the most important virtues children should learn."
3. *Authoritarian aggression.* Favoring condemnation, total rejection, stern discipline, or severe punishment as ways of dealing with people and forms of behavior that deviate from conventional values.
   Sample item: "Sex crimes, such as rape and attacks on children, deserve more than mere imprisonment; such criminals ought to be publicly whipped, or worse."
   Sample item: "No insult to our honor should ever go unpunished."
4. *Anti-intraception.* Disapproval of a free emotional life, of the intellectual or theoretical, and of the impractical. The anti-intraceptive person maintains a narrow range of consciousness; realization of his genuine feelings or self-awareness might threaten his adjustment. Hence he rejects feelings, fantasies, and other subjective or tender-minded phenomena.
   Sample item: "When a person has a problem or worry, it is best for him not to think about it, but to keep busy with more cheerful things."
   Sample item: "There are some things too intimate and personal to talk about even with one's closest friends."
5. *Superstition and stereotypy.* Superstition implies a tendency to shift responsibility from within the individual onto outside forces beyond one's control, particularly to mystical determinants. Stereotypy is the tendency to think in rigid, oversimplified categories, in unambiguous terms of black and white, particularly in the realm of psychological or social matters.
   Sample item: "It is entirely possible that this series of wars and conflicts will be ended once and for all by a world-destroying earthquake, flood, or other catastrophe."
   Sample item: "Although many people may scoff, it may yet be shown that astrology can explain a lot of things."
6. *Power and toughness.* The aligning of oneself with power figures, thus gratifying both one's need to have power and the need to submit to power. There is a denial of personal weakness.
   Sample item: "What this country needs is fewer laws and agencies, and more courageous, tireless, devoted leaders whom the people can put their faith in."
   Sample item: "Too many people today are living in an unnatural, soft way; we should return to the fundamentals, to a more red-blooded, active way of life."
7. *Destructiveness and cynicism.* A rationalized aggression. For example, cynicism permits the authoritarian person to be aggressive himself because "everybody is doing it." The generalized hostility and vilification of the human by the highly authoritarian person permits him to justify his aggressiveness.
   Sample item: "Human nature being what it is, there will always be war and conflict."
   Sample item: "Familiarity breeds contempt."
8. *Projectivity.* The disposition to believe that wild and dangerous things go on in the world. In the authoritarian personality the undesirable impulses that cannot be admitted to the conscious ego tend to be projected onto minority groups and other vulnerable objects.
   Sample item: "The sexual orgies of the old Greeks and Romans are nursery school stuff compared to some of the goings-on in this country today, even in circles where people might least expect it."
   Sample item: "Nowadays when so many different kinds of people move around so much and mix together so freely, a person has to be especially careful to protect himself against infection and disease."
9. *Sex.* Exaggerated concern with sexual goings-on, and punitiveness toward violators of sex mores.
   Sample item: "Homosexuality is a particularly rotten form of delinquency and ought to be severely punished."
   Sample item: "No matter how they act on the surface, men are interested in women for only one reason."

terms in Chapter 4.) In an exposition of the theory of the authoritarian personality, N. Sanford (1956) hypothesized that within the ethnocentric and authoritarian subject, each of these three systems has characteristic modes of functioning. "As a first approximation, one might say that in the highly ethnocentric person the superego is strict, rigid and relatively externalized, the id is strong, primitive and ego-alien, while the ego is weak and can manage the superego-id conflicts only by resorting to rather desperate defenses. But this general formulation would hold for a very large segment of the population and, thus, it is necessary to look more closely at the functioning of these parts of the person in the authoritarian syndrome" (N. Sanford, 1956, p. 275).

Considering individually the constructs that entered into the theory of authoritarianism, we may say that the first three—*conventionalism, authoritarian submission,* and *authoritarian aggression*—all refer to the functioning of the superego. The emphasis is upon strict demands by the superego, backed up by external reinforcements and by punishment in the name of authority figures to whom the subject has submitted.

Manifestations of a weak ego are reflected in the constructs of *anti-intraception, superstition and stereotypy,* and *projectivity.* Anti-intraception reflects an early stage of defense mechanisms involving repression and denial. Superstition and stereotypy, by shifting responsibility onto an external world, implies that the ego has forsaken attempts to control behavior. Projectivity also reflects a relatively primitive, immature way of avoiding one's anxieties. (See Figure 13-1.)

The dimension of *power and toughness* appears to signal a weak ego and the conventionalized orientation of the superego. This is indicated by the reliance upon willpower—a rather unsophisticated assumption about the nature of man. *Destructiveness and cynicism,* as well as *sex,* reflect a rather undisguised and forceful id. From these and from further considerations of the relationship between the nine basic components of the authoritarian syndrome and the psychoanalytic structuring of personality, it may be seen how the attitude-scale items can be used in an attempt to tap these components.

At this point the reader may wonder whether the authoritarian person is so disturbed as to be classified as mentally ill. The evidence is that mental illness and maladjustment are no more frequent among authoritarians than among other persons of equivalent age and social class. Elms (1970), for example, interviewed Dallas citizens who had written letters to the editor reflecting right-wing extremism; these letters had subscribed to beliefs about communistic infiltration of the government and the schools and had advocated extralegal ways to achieve right-wing political aims. Elms found no greater frequency of maladjustment—paranoia, hostility, or psychosis—in this group than in a group of Dallas liberals. Likewise Chesler and Schmuck (1969) after interviewing 60 superpatriots in the Midwest, concluded that as a group they were generally "pleasant, considerate, and law-abiding." On the last point, observations of supporters of George Wallace contradicted the conclusion that superpatriots always are law-abiding. In Davidson County, Tennessee, during the week before the 1968 presidential election, cars were observed to determine whether they had the newly required county auto tax sticker. Cars with Wallace bumper stickers significantly less often had the sticker than did cars with Nixon stickers, Humphrey stickers, or no bumper stickers at all (Wrightsman, 1969).

Figure 13-1. *The Personalities of Authoritarians, Right-Wingers, and Superpatriots*

E. Measurement of the Components of the Authoritarian Syndrome

The scales used to measure aspects of authoritarianism have had a profound effect upon the pattern of social psychological research. In *The Authoritarian Personality,* the detailed descriptions of the construction and refinement of those scales lent to them a scientific precision that, unfortunately, was only superficial. That, however, is a point we will face later. In the order of their chronological development, the scales used to measure the components of the authoritarian syndrome were (a) the A-S scale, measuring anti-Semitism, (b) the E scale, measuring ethnocentrism, (c) the P-E-C scale, measuring politicoeconomic conservatism, which was conceptualized as another aspect of authoritarianism, and (d) the F scale, measuring authoritarianism, or an anti-democratic ideology.

Each is an attitude scale including anywhere from 14 to 52 items. With the exception of the P-E-C scale, all the statements on a scale are worded in the same direction, so that agreement with the statement indicates an anti-Semitic or ethnocentric or authoritarian response. Only three of the P-E-C statements are worded in the opposite direction. This indelicacy of scale construction has led some researchers to claim that the scales are not measuring aspects of the authoritarian syndrome at all but rather are tapping an **acquiescent response set.** (See Chapter 2.) This is an important issue, since the major point of the theory has not been verified if the high scorers are simply acquiescent rather than authoritarian. We shall deal with this controversy somewhat later.

The research of the California group—published in articles during the late 1940s and in the culminating book in 1950—led to a decade (from 1947 to 1957) that might be called a golden age of research on authoritarianism. During this period, Titus and Hollander (1957), reviewed 60 studies using the F scale and concluded that, through studying the authoritarian personality, "the commonality of two streams of research interest was established. By applying the tools of 'depth psychology' to the study of ideology this work opened the way for a substantive integration of personality dynamics and social behavior" (p. 47). This attempt to relate ideology to personality was indeed a magnificent endeavor. Let us now see how successful it was.

F. Evaluation of the Authoritarian Personality Study

The California group most definitely succeeded in stimulating new research. Christie and Cook (1958) have been able to list 230 references to studies on authoritarianism published through 1956. Undoubtedly, an additional 230 studies have been published since that time. In fact, *The Authoritarian Personality* is one of the few books in psychology that has been important enough to call for another work that is devoted solely to its evaluation—the book by Christie and Jahoda (1954) entitled *Studies in the Scope and Method of "The Authoritarian Personality."* A later book, *Dimensions of Authoritarianism* (Kirscht & Dillehay, 1967) reviews research and theory.

One indication of the validity of a theory is the degree to which its measuring instruments allow predictable relationships with measures of other variables. Predicted relationships between the F scale, as a measure of authoritarianism, and other variables have frequently been confirmed. A few of these relationships are presented subsequently.

Prejudice. The California group, having hypothesized that ethnocentrism was a part of the authoritarian syndrome, subsequently found a correlation of +.73 (N = 2150 subjects) between the F scale and the E scale. Numerous other studies found that the F scale correlates significantly with many different measures of prejudice. Some of these, such as the xenophobia measure of prejudice developed by D. T. Campbell and McCandless (1951), appear to be free of a potential acquiescent response set. Subjects who were more xenophobic (likely to reject minority and foreign groups) were more authoritarian. J. G. Martin and Westie (1959), using urban adults as their sample, found antiblack subjects have higher F-scale scores, even when the effects of differences in religious affiliation and occupational mobility are ruled out.

Interpersonal Perception. Highly authoritarian students tend to perceive others as possessing the same beliefs and attitudes as they have. Scodel and Mussen (1953) had pairs of students (one quite authoritarian and one nonauthoritarian) discuss innocuous issues like television and the movies. Then each subject answered the F scale and the Minnesota Multiphasic Personality Inventory (MMPI) as he thought the other person would. Highly authoritarian subjects perceived the other person incorrectly; such a subject expected the other person's score to be similar to his own. Nonauthoritarian subjects, however, were more accurate on both the F scale and the MMPI; on the F scale, the nonauthoritarian usually estimated his partner's score to be higher than his own but lower than it actually was.

In a somewhat different vein, highly authoritarian subjects were found by Steiner and Johnson (1963) to be reluctant to believe that "good people" can have both good and bad attributes. This implies that the philosophies of human nature held by authoritarians are simplistic rather than complex; authoritarians are unable to integrate diverse and conflicting characteristics into a whole impression. Unpublished research indicates that this is the case—though not to an extensive degree; the correlation between F-scale scores and Complexity scores on the Philosophies of Human Nature Scale for 270 college females was −.218, which is significant at the .05 level in the expected direction but hardly a very strong relationship.

Volunteering. Rosenthal and Rosnow (1969) have published a valuable review of the effects of using volunteers as subjects in psychological studies. They have reported on eight studies that compare volunteers and nonvolunteers in regard to authoritarianism. The majority of these studies conclude that volunteers are less likely than nonvolunteers to be highly authoritarian. For example, Ephraim Rosen (1951) found that undergraduates who volunteered for a personality experiment were lower on the F scale than persons who chose not to volunteer. In addition, respondents to a mail questionnaire were found to be less authoritarian than persons who failed to return the questionnaire (Poor, 1967). These and related findings are evidence for the anti-intraceptive nature of the highly authoritarian person, who fears the possibility of exposing his feelings to self-scrutiny.

Preferences for President. In the 1952 presidential nominating campaign, General Douglas MacArthur symbolized a rather militaristic and authoritarian approach to solving the country's problems. Highly authoritarian students were found to prefer MacArthur to other candidates for the 1952 Republican presidential nomination (Milton, 1952). In addition, supporters of Senator Goldwater in 1964 had, on the average, higher F-scale scores than did supporters of President Johnson (Wrightsman, 1965). The latter difference was consonant with Senator Goldwater's campaign image as more "hawkish" over the Vietnam war. Goldwater advocated more frequent bombing of North Vietnam as well as other actions that would have intensified the war.

Family Ideology and Child-Rearing Attitudes. Highly authoritarian persons prefer a more traditional family ideology, which includes strong parental control over family decisions, clear-cut and separate roles for the mother and father, and restricted degrees of dissension on the part of the children. Less authoritarian subjects prefer a more democratic family structure (Levinson & Huffman, 1955).

Community Participation. By interviewing a representative sample of adults in Philadelphia, Fillmore Sanford (1950) found that authoritarian interviewees reported less interest in political affairs, less participation in politics or other community activities, and more characteristic preferences for strong leaders than did nonauthoritarians.

Attitudes and Behavior Regarding the Vietnam War. On October 15, 1969, a national moratorium was held to protest American involvement in the Vietnam war. One week later Izzett (1971) gave students who attended class that day and those who did not the California F scale and a six-item measure of attitudes toward our Vietnam policies. Students who had not attended class on Moratorium Day had significantly less authoritarian attitudes ($p < .01$); they also had stronger anti-Vietnam war attitudes than did students who attended class ($p < .01$).

These are only a sample of the variety of findings on the relationships between the F scale and other variables. Much more extensive reviews may be found in Kirscht and Dillehay (1967), Christie and Cook (1958), and Titus and Hollander (1957). Possibly, the F scale has, in a sense, been too successful as a measuring instrument. It has produced significant relationships with the majority of measures with which it has been paired. If the F scale were measuring authoritarianism and that alone, we would have to conclude that authoritarianism is indeed a powerful variable. Yet as the significant findings accumulate, the end result is an increasing lack of conceptual clarity and meaningfulness. Most probably, the F scale is measuring a set of overlapping but distinctive variables, rather than one extremely powerful variable. In other words, differences between individual F-scale scores probably reflect differences in education, sophistication, and acquiescence, as well as true differences in authoritarianism.

Both the F scale and the whole research program of the California group have been severely criticized for a variety of reasons. The construction of the F scale did not coincide with sound measurement procedures at all times. For example, all the items have been worded in the same direction, so that agreement with each statement indicates authoritarianism. Such a format encourages the confounding of authoritarianism with an **acquiescent response set,** or yea-saying tendency. Thus, we can legitimately ask whether a high score on the F scale means the person is really authoritarian or simply an acquiescent type. Some critics have concluded that scores on the F scale reflect acquiescence more than authoritarianism and that such a confusion reduces the purity and accuracy of the scale. Other critics, using different statistical techniques, conclude that authoritarianism is the primary determinant. And a third group of critics argues that the acquiescent response set should be measured by the scales since that phenomenon is related to authoritarian submission. A careful analysis by D. T. Campbell, Siegman, and Rees (1967) leads us to conclude that an acquiescent response set probably does contribute to F-scale scores.

Equally disturbing is the finding of a significant relationship between F-scale scores and amount of education. These relationships are negative, showing that less educated persons have higher F-scale scores. Does this finding mean that education reduces authoritarianism, or that education reduces the tendency to agree with the jingoistic language of the F-scale items? (Observe the consistent, extremely moralistic style of the items in Table 13-1.) This issue has yet to be resolved.

The charges leveled at the major substantive findings of the California study are more serious. Critics have questioned whether the components of the authoritarian personality really hang together. They have asked whether authoritarians are really more prejudiced, more ethnocentric, more intolerant of ambiguity, and more politically conservative. Indeed, some of the procedures used in the California study lead us to wonder whether the hypotheses were given an adequate test. For example, in selecting items for the F scale, the authors did not retain certain items that did not correlate with the anti-Semitism scale. Later, however, the significant correlation of +.53 (which is no surprise, considering the circumstances) was used by the authors as evidence that anti-Semitism and fascism are related.

A second example of unfortunate procedures lies in the validation of the E scale, used to measure ethnocentrism. Persons who were either very highly ethnocentric or unprejudiced on the basis of their E-scale scores were interviewed intensively. The interview responses of the highly ethnocentric subjects more often included prejudiced, politically conservative, and antidemocratic remarks, as well as undue glorification of parents and unrealistically high opinions of themselves. Although these kinds of responses provide evidence that the scale score is predictive of interview behavior, the authors tell us that, prior to the interview, the interviewers had access to detailed information on the subject's responses to the E-scale items. Such procedures are clearly in violation of the requirement that the criterion (in this case, the interview) should be an *independent* measure of the variable under study. Quite possibly, an interviewer who knows that a subject is highly ethnocentric will probe for responses that are indicative of prejudice. (In fairness to the authors, it should be noted that one group of interviews with psychiatric patients was carried out by interviewers who were unfamiliar with the purposes of the study or the E-scale scores of the interviewees. The results of this group were consistent with the results of other groups.)

Such criticisms are serious. Other criticisms, which will not be reviewed here, led Hyman and Sheatsley (1954) to conclude that even though the theory behind the California authoritarian personality study may be correct and provable, the methodological weaknesses of the study prevent the demonstration of this correctness. In light of the extensive research on the authoritarian personality since Hyman and Sheatsley's pronouncement, one may apparently conclude that the theory has validity in explaining the behavior of some people. There are individuals for whom authoritarianism is a basic ideology, encompassing anti-Semitic, racist, and reactionary beliefs, as well as a general approach to the world. At the same time, there are persons who are authoritarian without being particularly prejudiced, and, more importantly, there are many individuals who are antiblack yet not authoritarian. A multi-determined theory of prejudice must always be emphasized along with the fact that authoritarianism is not a complete answer.

G. Related Concepts: Dogmatism

The construct of **dogmatism,** advanced by social psychologist Milton Rokeach, is somewhat related to authoritarianism. Dogmatism is defined by Rokeach as "(a) a relatively closed cognitive organization of beliefs and disbeliefs about reality, (b) organized around a central set of beliefs about absolute authority which, in turn, (c) provides a framework for patterns of intolerance toward others" (1960, p. 195). Thus dogmatism is characterized both by a closed-minded, rigid style and a content sympathetic to authoritarianism and intolerance.

Rokeach (1960) and other social scientists (for example, Shils, 1954) have criticized the F scale because it measures only right-wing authoritarianism, making it deficient in balanced content. These scientists have argued that authoritarianism can be a characteristic of extremely left-wing political ideologies such as communism, as well as right-wing ideologies like fascism. The highly authoritarian person could gravitate toward either end of the extremist political ideologies. Rokeach advanced the concept of dogmatism as an indicator of a general kind of authoritarianism that would encompass both the extreme left and right ends of a political-belief distribution.

There are two ways of confirming these claims. One is through analyzing the statistical relationships between the F scale and the Dogmatism scale (constructed by Rokeach), and the other is through comparing the responses of members of various political parties. Two statistical studies have demonstrated that the F scale and the Dogmatism scale are not completely overlapping in their measurements. Kerlinger and Rokeach (1966) factor analyzed the items from the F scale and the Dogmatism scale and found a common core of authoritarianism in both scales. But a further analysis, seeking other factors, found that the two scales were factorially discriminable, with dogmatism representing a general authoritarianism free of any particular ideological content. The purpose of another study (by E. N. Barker, 1963) was to see whether levels of dogmatism were related to a person's degree of commitment to a particular position on the political spectrum. Although dogmatism was unrelated to any particular political ideology, it was related—as expected—to the intensity of one's commitment to a particular position.

If dogmatism indicates general authoritarianism, we would expect members of both the Communist and Fascist political parties to be highly dogmatic. Rokeach found groups of English college students who identified themselves as politically Conservative, Liberal, Laborite, or Communist. In 1954, these students were administered the Dogmatism scale, the F scale, and the Ethnocentrism scale. Mean scores are reported in Table 13-2. Note that of all groups the Communists scored lowest on the F scale and on the Ethnocentrism scale, indicating a lack of right-wing authoritarianism and prejudice.[1] (Communist students were significantly lower on right-wing authoritarianism and prejudice than three of the other four groups.) In contrast, the Communists scored highest on dogmatism—although the only difference between groups that approaches statistical significance was the difference between Communists and Liberals ($p < .06$).

At first these results may sound conflicting. Can Communists be unprejudiced, unauthoritarian, but highly dogmatic? Perhaps their tolerance of minority groups

[1] In an earlier study Coulter in 1953 gave the F scale to 53 members of an English Fascist group and found their scores to be among the highest ever recorded (Reported in Christie, 1956; R. Brown, 1965).

Table 13-2. *Comparisons of Various Political Groups among English University Students*

Group	N	Dogmatism Mean	Dogmatism Standard Deviation	F Scale Mean	F Scale Standard Deviation	Ethnocentrism Scale Mean	Ethnocentrism Scale Standard Deviation
Conservatives	54	258.8	49.7	115.5	25.0	29.9	9.0
Liberals	22	242.9	29.2	98.4	14.0	24.8	7.9
Laborites (pro-Attlee)	27	252.7	36.6	101.8	21.4	22.7	9.3
Laborites (pro-Bevan)	19	255.2	37.9	90.4	24.3	23.5	9.4
Communists	13	261.6	32.6	82.9	20.3	16.5	4.2

Adapted from Table 6.3, *The Open and Closed Mind,* by Milton Rokeach, © 1960 by Basic Books, Inc., Publishers, New York.

reflects a rigid adherence to the content of communist ideology. (Notice the extremely low standard deviation of the Communists on Ethnocentrism.) Yet as indicated by the Dogmatism scale, English Communists formed the group that was most intolerant of those who disagree with communist views. They represent an exaggeration of what Triandis and Davis referred to in Chapter 9 as belief-prejudiced persons—or persons who are more concerned with the beliefs than with the race of the stimulus person. Beyond this, Communist ideology is authoritarian in that (a) strong pressures are exerted upon its members to maintain discipline, (b) its leadership derives from an elitist group rather than from democratic procedures, and (c) it stifles opposition by repressive measures. It is no surprise that Communists score high on a measure of dogmatism.

As a measure of general authoritarianism uncontaminated by political ideology, the Dogmatism scale appears more appropriate than the F scale (Vacchiano, Strauss, & Hochman, 1969). However, the Dogmatism scale is quite possibly not as free of ideological content as Rokeach had hoped. In evaluating dogmatism as a useful construct, we must evaluate the Dogmatism scale as a precise measuring instrument. In some ways the Dogmatism scale suffers from the same limitations as the F scale. For example, all 40 items are scored in such a way that agreement with the item is indicative of dogmatism. The presence of an acquiescent response set must again be considered as a possible explanation of the results (Peabody, 1961, 1966). However, in one thorough review (Vacchiano, et al., 1969), so many substantive differences between persons scoring high and low on the scale were found that the reviewers came to the conclusion that "more than a response bias is operative and that the [Dogmatism scale] is a generally reliable and valid instrument" (1969, p. 269).

Researchers have related dogmatism to many of the same variables that have been linked with authoritarianism. The findings of a sampling of these studies on dogmatism are outlined below.

1. Compared with their less dogmatic counterparts, highly dogmatic subjects are more dependent on authority figures in a conformity-inducing task (Vidulich & Kaiman, 1961).

2. Highly dogmatic persons are more likely to accept the official police explanation of the causes of a riot than are less dogmatic subjects (J. McCarthy & Johnson, 1962).

3. Less dogmatic subjects perceive authority figures in a more realistic way, reporting both their negative and positive characteristics (Kemp, 1963).

4. In an unstructured classroom situation, highly dogmatic students are more

concerned with rules and procedures regarding leadership selection and group structure. Intellectual lethargy and an unwillingness to relate to other students, the instructor, or the subject matter are characteristic of classrooms composed of highly dogmatic students (Zagona & Zurcher, 1964, 1965).

5. In two studies, students with low Dogmatism scores are found to be more critical of American policy in Vietnam (Guller & Bailes, 1968; Karabenick & Wilson, 1969).

The fact that dogmatism is seen as a relatively closed cognitive organization of beliefs and disbeliefs leads one to expect that highly dogmatic students are less able to learn new information or to utilize new information presented to them. Rokeach and Vidulich (1960) found that dogmatic subjects were less successful at solving a problem that required adopting novel learning sets. Numerous other studies have also generally confirmed this expectation. For example, among introductory sociology students, those high in dogmatism entered the class with less information, learned less as a result of classroom exposure, and retained what they learned to a significantly lesser degree than did the less dogmatic students (Ehrlich, 1961a). Even five years later, the differences in regard to retention of learned material held up between dogmatism groups (Ehrlich, 1961b). A general, if tentative, conclusion would be that dogmatic subjects are less able than open-minded subjects "to learn new beliefs and to change old beliefs" (Ehrlich & Lee, 1969, p. 258).

H. Related Concepts: Harvey's Conceptual Systems

Another approach to authoritarianism stems from O. J. Harvey's conceptual systems—also referred to as belief systems (Harvey, 1967; Harvey, Hunt, & Schroder, 1961; Kaats, 1969). Since this approach was described in Chapter 3, a brief review will suffice here. Harvey posits four systems or styles of organizing beliefs or conceptual functioning. The theory sets these as stages, with a person moving successively to more sophisticated systems or levels. Of relevance here is System 1, which represents an authoritarian conceptual style, including such qualities as "absolutist and inflexible expression of beliefs; high evaluativeness, ethnocentrism, authoritarianism, religiosity, superstition, and conventionality; an external or fatalistic orientation where one's behavior is thought to be the outcome of such powerful external forces as luck, fate, destiny or some supreme being; identification with and positive dependence upon societal representatives of authority and status positions" (Kaats, 1969, pp. 21-22).

II. OVEROBEDIENCE—A BEHAVIORAL MANIFESTATION OF AUTHORITARIANISM?

A. Obedience in the Real World

We may view the authoritarian personality as an extension of characteristics present in most of us. Within the realm of behavior the phenomenon of *overobedience* may be analogous to the authoritarian personality. All of us feel some degree of pressure to obey certain symbols of authority, ranging from parents to college deans to traffic lights. In order to exist in an environment where the rights and needs of others are to be respected, laws and rules are established and expected to be obeyed.

The question is whether obedience can assume too powerful a position within one's domain of behavior. Can *overobedience* occur? The cases of Adolf Eichmann and Lieutenant Calley are relevant. At his trial, Lieutenant Calley stated that he was simply following orders. Adolf Eichmann, in charge of exterminating six million Jews in Nazi Germany, also did what he was told. At his trial for war crimes, Eichmann denied any moral responsibility, since he was simply doing his job. Did Calley or Eichmann not realize that following the expectations of a job might violate one's moral responsibilities as a decent human being? When obeying the demands of others requires the violation of one's moral responsibilities, we refer to the response as *overobedience.*

Real-life conflicts between obedience and morality are not confined to Nazi Germany of 30 years ago or Vietnam villages thousands of miles from us. A salesman may have to choose between obeying an instruction to misrepresent the product or risking the loss of his job. A plant manager may be told that he has to fire 10 percent of his workers, even though they are all doing excellent work; if he refuses, he loses his job. A student may have to choose between echoing the instructor's viewpoint on an essay question or possibly flunking the exam.

B. Milgram's Laboratory Studies of Overobedience

Although the Eichmann and Calley examples are real, they may be unusual cases. Let us consider other specific conflicts. Stanley Milgram, a social psychologist, tried to determine how many persons would continue to obey the commands of an authority figure, even when they were endangering the life of another person. Milgram's procedure (1963) required the subject to give increasingly powerful electric shocks to another person whenever the latter erred on an association task. The subjects were 40 males who responded to newspaper advertisements and a direct mail solicitation. Although such a self-selected sample of volunteers clearly was not random, it was heterogeneous in regard to age (20 to 50) and occupation (postal clerks, secondary school teachers, salesmen, engineers, laborers, and others). Subjects were paid $4.50 for their participation in the project at Yale University.

When the subject arrived for the experiment, he was introduced to the experimenter and another subject (actually an accomplice of the experimenter). The subjects were told that the purpose of the experiment was to determine the effects of punishment upon learning. The introduction continued as follows:

> So in this study we are bringing together a number of adults of different occupations and ages. And we're asking some of them to be teachers and some of them to be learners.
>
> We want to find out just what effect different people have on each other as teachers and learners, and also what effect *punishment* will have on learning in this situation.
>
> Therefore, I'm going to ask one of you to be the teacher here tonight and the other one to be the learner (Milgram, 1963, p. 373).

Subjects drew lots to determine which would be the teacher and which would be the learner, but the drawing was rigged so that the true subject was always the teacher and the accomplice was always the learner. After the drawing, both subjects were taken to an adjacent room where the learner was strapped to a chair. The purpose of this procedure was explained as a way to restrict the learner and keep him from escaping. An electrode was then attached to the learner's wrist, and the teacher and the experimenter returned to the original room.

There the subject was instructed in his task. The lesson to be administered by the subject was a paired-associate learning task, in which the subject was to read a series of word pairs to the learner and then read the first word of the pair along with four terms. The learner's job was to indicate which of the four terms was the correct associate; he did this by pressing a switch, which lit a light in the teacher's room.

The response lights were in an answer box located on top of the shock generator in the teacher's room. The instrument panel of the shock generator consisted of 30 switches, each clearly labeled with a designation of its voltage. These switches increased by 15-volt increments, ranging from 15 to 450 volts. To clarify the degree of shock, groups of four switches were consecutively labeled: Slight Shock, Moderate Shock, Strong Shock, Very Strong Shock, Intense Shock, Extreme Intensity Shock, Danger-Severe Shock, and, the last, XXX. In actuality this equipment was a dummy shock generator, but its appearance was quite convincing. Moreover, the authenticity of the shock was communicated to the teacher by giving him a sample shock of 45 volts.

The teacher was told to administer a shock to the learner each time that he gave a wrong response. (The learner, being an accomplice, had been instructed to err often, but of course the true subject did not know this.) After each wrong answer, the subject was instructed to move one level higher on the shock generator. The teacher-subject also had to announce the voltage level before administering a shock—a device which served to remind him of the level of shock he was giving another person. After the learner had committed enough errors so that the shock level was supposedly at 300 volts, according to prearranged plans, he began to pound on the wall between the two experimental rooms. From that point on, the learner no longer answered.

The usual response of a subject at this point was to turn to the experimenter for guidance. In a stoic and rather stern way, the experimenter replied that no answer was to be treated as a wrong answer, and the subject was to be shocked according to the usual schedule. The subject then was to wait 5 to 10 seconds and, assuming the learner had no response, increase the shock level again. After the administration of the 315-volt shock, the teacher heard the learner pound on the walls again, but no answer materialized. From that point on, no sound nor answer emanated from the learner's room.

Milgram's basic experimental question was simply how many subjects would continue administering shocks to the end of the shock series. Table 13-3 presents the results. Of the 40 subjects, 26 (or 65 percent) continued to the end of the shock series. No subject stopped prior to administering 300 volts—the point at which the learner began kicking the wall. Five refused to obey at that point; at some point, 14 of the 40 subjects defied the experimenter. Milgram concludes that obedience to commands is a strong force in our society, since 65 percent of his subjects obeyed the experimenter's instructions even though they knew that they were hurting a powerless person.

Milgram (1964a; 1965) then extended his program of research to study some of the situational factors that may cause a subject to obey or to refuse to obey when the experimenter (the authority figure) tells the subject to hurt another person. After

Table 13-3. *Distribution of Breakoff Points in Milgram's Study of Obedience*

Verbal Designation and Voltage Indication	*Number of Subjects for Whom This Was Maximum Shock*
Slight shock	
15	0
30	0
45	0
60	0
Moderate shock	
75	0
90	0
105	0
120	0
Strong shock	
135	0
150	0
165	0
180	0
Very strong shock	
195	0
210	0
225	0
240	0
Intense shock	
255	0
270	0
285	0
300	5
Extreme intensity shock	
315	4
330	2
345	1
360	1
Danger: severe shock	
375	1
390	0
405	0
420	0
XXX	
435	0
450	26

From Milgram, "Behavioral study of obedience," *Journal of Abnormal and Social Psychology*, **67**, 1963, p. 376. Copyright 1963 by the American Psychological Association, and reprinted with permission.

demonstrating that the majority of subjects would continue to shock the other person to the limit of the apparatus, Milgram tested whether the closeness of the victim's presence to the subject had any effect on the subject's behavior. Milgram used the following four conditions.

1. In the *remote-feedback condition,* the victim was in another room and could not be heard or seen by the subject, with the exception that, when the 300-volt level was reached, the victim pounded on the wall. After 300 volts the victim no longer answered nor made any noise.

2. The *voice-feedback condition* was identical to the first condition except that

the victim did make vocal protests that could be heard through the walls and through the slightly open doorway between rooms.

3. In the *proximity condition,* the victim was placed in the same room as the subject, about one and one-half feet away. Thus, both visual and audible clues to the victim's pain were available to the subject.

4. The *touch-proximity condition* was identical to the proximity condition, except that, beyond the 150-volt level, the victim refused to put his hand on the shockplate. Thus, on every subsequent trial the experimenter ordered the subject to force the victim's hand on the shockplate.

A different set of 40 adult males participated in each one of the four conditions. The percentages of subjects who obeyed the experimenter were: remote-feedback, 66 percent; voice-feedback, 62.5 percent; proximity, 40 percent; and touch-proximity, 30 percent. Thus, as one might expect, when the victim is closer, more subjects refuse to obey.

The relationship of the subject to the experimenter also determines the amount of obedience. In one condition, the experimenter sat only a few feet away from the subject. In a second condition, the experimenter was present at the beginning to give initial instructions and then left the room, using the telephone for further instructions. In a third condition, the experimenter was never present, the instructions being given by a tape recording. Obedience was almost three times more frequent when the experimenter remained physically present. Moreover, when the experimenter was absent, several subjects administered shocks of a lower voltage than was required. As Milgram indicates the response clearly violated the avowed purpose of the experiment, but perhaps it was easier for the subject to handle conflict this way than to defy authority openly.

C. Criticisms of Milgram's Study of Obedience

As provocative as these findings are, Milgram's program of research has not gone without criticism. Perhaps the strongest of the critics is Baumrind (1964), who believes the studies were not only unethical but lacking in generalizability to real-world obedience situations.[2] These two types of criticisms will be examined in turn.

Criticisms of the Ethics of the Experiment. Milgram's study has been called unethical on several grounds. One claim is that the subject's rights were not protected. No health examinations were given to the subjects prior to the experiment to determine whether some psychological maladjustment might exclude certain subjects. No prior permission was obtained from the subjects allowing the experimenters to place them in distressful conflict situations. A second claim was that there could have been long-term effects upon the subjects from having participated in the study. Among these effects is the subject's loss of trust in the credibility of future experimenters, in the university, or in science in general. Having been deceived in a study where their emotions were displayed so openly, subjects may become strongly skeptical of psychologists in the future. Another type of long-term effect might be on the subject's self-concept. Prior to the experiment, most subjects probably saw themselves as persons who would not deliberately inflict pain upon another person unless the circum-

[2] Baumrind advocates that only research of unquestioned relevance to real-world issues justifies harm to subjects. Yet, who is to determine what is relevant?

stances were extreme. After the experiment, they may discover otherwise. Milgram apparently believes that such self-education is beneficial—regardless of its consequences. Some psychologists—following Bem's (1970) self-perception theory—would disagree; they would say that when a person knows he has acted heinously in one situation, the bonds against his doing the same thing in the future would be loosened.

A third criticism regarding the ethicality of the experiment centers upon Milgram's reaction to the anguish and tension shown by some subjects as they methodically increased the shock levels trial by trial. Milgram reports with some awe, if not relish, the extreme degrees of tension experienced by some subjects. Consider his quotation from one observer:

> I observed a mature and initially poised businessman enter the laboratory smiling and confident. Within 20 minutes he was reduced to a twitching, stuttering wreck, who was rapidly approaching a point of nervous collapse. He constantly pulled on his earlobe, and twisted his hands. At one point he pushed his fist into his forehead and muttered: "Oh, God, let's stop it." And yet he continued to respond to every word of the experimenters, and obeyed to the end (Milgram, 1963, p. 377).

Milgram tells us that other subjects were observed to "sweat, stutter, tremble, groan, bite their lips, and dig their fingernails into their flesh. Full-blown, uncontrollable seizures were observed for three subjects" (Milgram, 1963, p. 375). One subject had such a violently convulsive seizure that it was necessary to terminate his participation. Critics have asked why the whole experiment was not terminated in the face of all these tensions. Milgram apparently believed that debriefing at the end of the experiment was sufficient to eradicate these tensions. In describing the debriefing procedure, Milgram stated: "After the interview, procedures were undertaken to assure that the subject would leave the laboratory in a state of well being. A friendly reconciliation was arranged between the subject and the victim, and an effort was made to reduce any tensions that arose as a result of the experiment" (1963, p. 374). It is hard to believe, however, that such extreme examples of tension could be erased by any such momentary debriefing procedure. Milgram's critics are not convinced by his reports (1964b, 1968) that interviews by psychiatrists and follow-up questionnaires completed by the subjects indicated no long-term deleterious effects.

Another defense Milgram offers is that the insights gained from his research—despite ethical problems—may ultimately promote humanistic values by revealing the nature of forces that operate to oppress these values. We will have more to say about this point in Chapter 20.

Criticisms of the Lack of Generalizability. Baumrind and others have also questioned whether the extreme degrees of obedience found in Milgram's subjects may be generalized to the real world. The specific criticisms are as follows.

1. The nonrandom, nonrepresentative nature of the subjects is one difficulty. The representativeness of men who would respond to a newspaper ad to participate in a laboratory experiment can certainly be doubted. Some of these men may indeed be crying for help or may otherwise be showing concern about themselves. We cannot say, however, whether they are more obedient than a truly representative sample of adult males placed in the same situation.

2. Trust in the authority figure and obedience to him may be demand characteristics that are especially salient for subjects in experiments (Orne & Holland, 1968).

In other words, subjects may do as they are told in an experiment, whereas these same subjects might disobey another authority figure, such as the physician who tells them to exercise daily, or the employer who tells them to fire a popular co-worker. Along with this criticism is the claim that the prestige of Yale University contributed to the high obedience rate; subjects assumed that anything carried out at Yale must be scientifically and socially acceptable—hence, they were more inclined to obey. The available evidence, as scant as it is, denies this last claim. Milgram repeated the experiment in a nonuniversity setting to determine whether the Yale setting contributed to extreme degrees of obedience. Men recruited for the experiment reported to a rather rundown office building in a deteriorating area of Bridgeport, Connecticut. Placed in the same task as that of the original Yale study, almost 50 percent of the men obeyed the experimenter to the end of the shock series. While the prestige of Yale apparently accounted for some obedience, the phenomenon still occurred in a blatantly non-university setting. Perhaps, as Etzioni (1968) concludes, man is latently Eichmannistic.

3. The role of "prods" by the experimenter may have contributed significantly to the obedience rate. In the Milgram task, if a subject was unwilling to continue, four prods were used to urge him to continue—Prod 1, "Please continue, or please go on"; Prod 2, "The experiment requires that you continue"; Prod 3, "It is absolutely essential that you continue"; and Prod 4, "You have no other choice, you *must* go on." These prods were always used in sequence. If Prod 1 had not brought the subject into line, Prod 2 was introduced. The experiment was terminated only when Prod 4 had failed to keep the subject at his task. We do not know what the rejection rate would have been if the prods had not been used, but certainly more subjects would have terminated earlier. The fact that the experimenter responded to the subject's concern in such a firm and persistent manner may have convinced some subjects to continue their participation.

Certainly there are problems in making a blanket generalization of Milgram's findings to real-world cases of obedience and overobedience. But in real-world situations where prods or similar devices are used to keep people at tasks that are personally abhorrent, Milgram's findings probably have a useful applicability. Perhaps, the most provocative finding in Milgram's work is the demonstration that obedience is a much more pervasive phenomenon than people had expected. Neither a group of undergraduates nor a group of psychologists and psychiatrists, when told of the procedures, predicted that subjects would continue to obey when the high voltage levels were reached. Indeed, assumptions about human nature were more favorable than the outcomes.

D. Relationship of Obedience to Authoritarianism and Other Psychological Characteristics

Milgram's approach to obedience was primarily oriented toward the effects of situational variations. But the fact that some subjects obeyed while others did not has led to a search for intrapersonal factors that could be related to the differences. Again here, we will see that a combination of situational and intrapersonal factors leads to a more accurate understanding of social behavior.

Elms and Milgram (1966) administered various personality scales to participants in an obedience study. The men who obeyed had significantly higher scores on the

F scale than did those men who defied the authority figure. Elms and Milgram reported that "significant attitudinal differences [between these two groups] were displayed toward [one's] own father, the experimenter, the sponsoring university, willingness to shoot at men in wartime, and other concepts, in patterns somewhat similar to 'authoritarian personalities'" (1966, p. 282). Similarly, Haas (1966) has demonstrated that more hostile subjects are more likely to obey. A behavioral response such as obedience is partly influenced by the presence of authoritarian syndrome components within the person. The decision to obey or disobey is also related to the subject's level of moral development—as measured by responses to Kohlberg's stories (described in Chapter 4). Subjects who refuse to continue their participation in Milgram's experiment generally have more mature moral judgment scores than subjects who obey.

III. AUTHORITARIANISM IN OUR SOCIETY

A. Freud and Marcuse—Two Views on the Repressive Nature of Society

Freud believed that culture demands repression and that society must act in an authoritarian way. His view, expressed in *Civilization and Its Discontents* (1930), was that culture serves two functions—to protect people from the dangers of the natural world, and to regulate contacts between human beings so they do not destroy one another (Hall & Lindzey, 1968). Freud scorned any suggestion that culture or civilization serves to free man. To Freud, civilization deprives man of freedom because it imposes regulations, standards, and prohibitions upon the individual. Although Freud acknowledged the benefits of a complex society, he nevertheless believed that it generates restrictions that eventually lead to hostilities and frustrations.

Herbert Marcuse has responded to Freud's conclusions about the repressive nature of civilization—ranging from optimism to pessimism and back to optimism again. In *Eros and Civilization* (1955, 1962) Marcuse rejected the accuracy of Freud's conclusion. He agreed that some degree of repression is necessary for the successful operation of a society, but he also believed that society has *surplus repression* arising from various dominating institutions. Surplus repression is what a particular group or individual imposes upon others in order to enhance or maintain a privileged position. Attempts by governmental officials to curtail the flow of information through the mass media might exemplify surplus repression. Marcuse proposed a rechanneling of these repressions into desirable activities. He wrote: "To the degree to which the struggle for existence becomes cooperation for the free development and fulfillment of individual needs, repressive reason gives way to a new rationality of gratification in which reason and happiness converge" (Marcuse, 1962, p. 205).

Marcuse also claimed that a nonrepressive society was only possible under conditions of abundance. The new rationality of gratification and a play ethic could not emerge under conditions of scarcity; the sensuous element would give way to discipline and work (Marks, 1970, p. 59). However, given a state of freedom from want and stuporous work, man could develop a new life style, a gentleness, and an eroticism far different from its present perversions. We must question, however, whether certain governments would not strive to perpetuate a work ethic. Would not a conservative government be frightened by the possibility of a civilization where the problems of productivity had been mastered, where a work ethic had been replaced by a play ethic, and where the performance orientation had been replaced by a display orientation?

Marcuse's earlier optimism about the future of complex society was dramatically rejected in his later book *One-dimensional Man* (1964), which appeared nine years after *Eros and Civilization* was first published. (Marcuse's recent beliefs have been summarized by Kateb, 1970, and reprinted in Table 13-4.) *One-dimensional Man* emphasized the irrationality of advanced industrial civilization. Marcuse had come to doubt that a highly complex, technological society is capable of any qualitative change in the foreseeable future (Marks, 1970). Although industrial society has been quite successful in developing its technological resources, it becomes repressive when the success of its technological development opens up new "dimensions of social well-being." Industrial society is a juggernaut that crushes individuality, liberty, and social equality. Such a society pulverizes efforts to discover a new consciousness (Reich, 1970), a new set of values, and a life style that emphasizes human freedom, authenticity, and genuine emotion. Technological society cannot tolerate the possibility of these developments; it dominates man under the guise of offering him material affluence and apparent freedom. The individual becomes a "willing subject of the technological domination; he is bought out by his material gains. On all sides there is promise of easier and better living, of more gadgetry, more alienation" (Marks, 1970, p. 68). Rather than finding themselves in their own being, "people recognize themselves in their commodities; they find their soul in their automobile, hi-fi set, split-level home, kitchen equipment" (Marcuse, 1964, p. 9). Hence there develops a "progressive moronization of humanity" and one-dimensional men—like the robot types in Aldous Huxley's *Brave New World*—are content to do their assigned tasks and never realize how unhappy and unfulfilled they really are.

In *One-dimensional Man,* Marcuse advocated revolution as a necessary response to technological domination, but he saw little chance for a change.[3] The mass media and the political and economic systems perpetuate a one-dimensional view of man. The few individuals who refuse to be absorbed by the organization are soon disparaged as nonconformists or neurotics. Some of them are co-opted by the system. Even activities that might be interpreted as protests—the use of drugs, encounter groups, and Zen—are largely ceremonial, in Marcuse's opinion.[4]

An Essay on Liberation (Marcuse, 1969) is described by John Raser (1971) as Marcuse's most hopeful statement. In this work, Marcuse sees militant young people as perhaps the beginning of a new sensibility in America that will lead to desired changes in fundamental values and the politicoeconomic structure of our society. But in none of his books does Marcuse offer facts to justify his conclusions. A social psychological orientation such as ours would urge the provision of some documentation.

[3]Admired by many followers of the New Left because of his neo-Marxist views, Marcuse is not held in favor by the American Maoists—partly because he worked for a U.S. government propaganda agency during World War II.

[4]Marcuse's is not the only voice bewailing the usurpation of "human-ness" in technological society. His work is selected for review here because his view is an extreme one and because students in rebellion all over the world claim him as a prophet of the new life (Keen & Raser, 1971).

Table 13-4. *Marcuse's Theses Regarding the Nature of Technological Society and Modern Man's Role in It*

1. The advanced industrial society, or the affluent society in the West, with the United States farthest along, is preponderantly evil—both for the harm it does and the good it prevents, internally and externally.
2. On balance, and internally, the Soviet Union is worse in actuality, better in potentiality, but with no guarantee that it will in fact become better. At present (1971) there are still "progressive and liberal forces" active in the United States. But this country is in the midst of a counterrevolution that is moving toward fascism.
3. The evil of each system is not correctable peacefully, by those in control or by their likely heirs.
4. In the abstract, revolution may therefore be justifiable.
5. We may be witnessing the emergence of certain forces that could perhaps bring about qualitative, genuinely revolutionary changes in the West, while developments in the Soviet bloc are, if anything, more problematic.

Adapted from Kateb, 1970, Pp. 48–49 and from Keen & Raser, 1971.

B. A More Optimistic View of the Future of Society

Other social analysts, including some liberals and radicals, do not share Marcuse's modified pessimism. Irving Howe (1969) feels that actual society in America is more complex than Marcuse allows and believes that human beings possess far more independence and autonomy than a one-dimensional picture suggests. Charles Reich, author of *Greening of America* (1970), holds that youth around the world are leading a nonviolent revolution that will bring about a new life style and a new consciousness. Consciousness III, as Reich calls it, believes that "the individual self is the only true reality" (p. 225). A sense of community and the importance of personal relationships are emphasized.[5] People become responsible for their acts. In short, the developments that Marcuse sees as ceremonial, Reich views as the real antecedents to a new consciousness in America.

IV. AUTHORITARIANISM IN THE FUTURE

Certain developments lead us to believe that average F-scale scores will decrease in the future. Increased levels of education and sophistication should reduce the tendency to agree with the cliches and emotional tone of scale statements. Even though this does not necessarily indicate a decreased authoritarianism in the individual, increased educational opportunities should help decrease authoritarianism per se. Social critic Eric Hoffer believes that in the future all technologically advanced societies will have their citizens "spend a good part of their lives in some form of education or re-education, and everyone will therefore become, in a sense, an intel-

[5] In somewhat the same vein as Charles Reich's delimitation of Consciousness III, Marcuse describes the new revolutionary person as follows: "It would be a psyche, a mind, an instinctual structure that could no longer tolerate aggression, domination, exploitation, ugliness, hypocrisy, or dehumanizing, routine performance. Positively you can see it in the growth of the esthetic and the erotic components in the instinctual and mental structure. I see it manifested today in the protest against the commercial violation of nature, against plastic beauty and real ugliness, against pseudovirility and brutal heroism" (H. Marcuse, quoted in Keen & Raser, 1971, p. 62).

lectual" (quoted by Tomkins, 1967, p. 34). Indeed, there are fewer authoritarians within the intellectual community. Nonetheless, societal pressures can increase personal authoritarianism. The increase in extremist groups, regardless of whether their political orientation is left or right, leads the average citizen to advocate greater authoritarian and repressive measures.

Apparently, the American government and the Establishment in general are becoming more concerned about restricting deviants than about encouraging free expression. A proposal in early 1970 by Arnold Hutschnecker, a New York psychiatrist, is an omen for the decade. Hutschnecker suggested a mass testing of the mental and personality characteristics of all American children between the ages of 6 and 8 in order to identify potential juvenile delinquents and criminals. This proposal would have instituted "corrective treatment" right away for all children who showed "delinquent tendencies"; after-school "counseling" would have been required of all children, and older, more "difficult" youths would have been placed in special camps (*New York Times,* April 19, 1970, p. E-3). Since there is no evidence that personality tests would be accurate enough to identify potentially delinquent individuals—and perhaps for other reasons—the proposal was rejected by the Department of Health, Education, and Welfare. But the fact that the suggestion was seriously advanced (and drew some significant support) reminds us that George Orwell's *1984* may be even closer than its date indicates.

Likewise, efforts to develop national data banks, where a great deal of confidential information would be accumulated on each citizen, reflect the rising authoritarianism of the times. Strong counterreactions in the 1960s to Supreme Court decisions that liberalized the rights of accused criminals also suggest that the 1970s may resemble earlier repressive periods. The same may be said for the frequent attacks upon the mass media by representatives of the government.

There are, however, active efforts to reduce the authoritarian nature of our society. Censorship and restrictions on the availability of erotic material are being reduced; new life styles are tolerated if they do not violate the rights of others. More individuals are protesting invasions of privacy; institutions such as the American Civil Liberties Union (whose goal is the protection of every citizen's rights) are gaining support.

Police departments in many American cities are also undergoing changes. In some police departments, the traditional policeman's uniform has been discarded and replaced by blue blazers and contrasting slacks. Police have been encouraged to develop a new role model in their dealings with citizens. Moreover, they are receiving training in human relations and community relations. (See Chapter 20.) Ride alongs, in which parents and children accompany police on night patrol, have increased communication between the police and the community. Although the general atmosphere of American life in the early 1970s apparently condones extending authoritarianism and repression, the future is uncertain and, to a large degree, undecided.

V. SUMMARY

Authoritarianism is both personal and societal; that is, tendencies toward authoritarianism differ among individuals as well as among various societies and governments.

The program of research on authoritarianism at the University of California at Berkeley began with a concern about anti-Semitism, moved to a study of ethnocentrism and politico-economic conservatism, and culminated in the measurement of authoritarianism—or an anti-democratic ideology.

Ethnocentrism refers to a belief that one's own group is superior to all other groups. Other racial and ethnic groups, foreigners, and all deviant groups are rejected.

Authoritarianism was conceptualized as a basic personality style—a syndrome of organized beliefs and symptoms.

The California researchers posited nine components of authoritarianism: conventionalism, authoritarian aggression, authoritarian submission, power and toughness, anti-intraception, superstition and stereotypy, destructiveness and cynicism, projectivity, and overconcern with sex.

In conceptualizing the authoritarian personality, the California researchers used psychoanalytic theory to explain how authoritarianism developed within a person. The highly authoritarian and ethnocentric person was seen as possessing a weak ego, a rigid and externalized superego, and a strong, primitive id.

The California F scale was designed to measure authoritarianism. It has been criticized because, in each of its items, agreement with the statement is scored as an indication of authoritarianism. This characteristic encourages, in some respondents, an acquiescent response set—or a tendency to agree with a statement regardless of the statement's content.

There is a great deal of evidence that the degree of authoritarianism, as measured by the F scale, is related to a variety of psychological constructs. For example, highly authoritarian subjects are more prejudiced, less sensitive to the feelings of others, less likely to volunteer for psychological experiments, and more likely to support conservative political candidates.

Methodological flaws in the authoritarian personality study lead us to conclude that it has not yet been proven that authoritarianism is an ideology that generally includes prejudice, rigidity, politicoeconomic conservatism, and other attributes.

Dogmatism is a concept somewhat related to authoritarianism. Dogmatism is defined as a relatively closed cluster of beliefs organized around a set of attitudes toward absolute authority.

Milgram's program of studies on obedience indicates that (a) the majority of subjects obey the instructions of the experimenter even when it means inflicting great pain upon a fellow subject, and (b) the extent of obedience is much greater than anticipated.

Variations in Milgram's basic procedure indicate that (a) when the victim is closer to the subject administering the electric shocks, less obedience is demonstrated, and (b) when the experimenter is closer to the subject administering the shocks, a greater degree of obedience results.

Among the criticisms of Milgram's study on obedience are those questioning its ethicality. Specifically, critics are concerned about the possible long-term effects on the subjects, the rights of consent of the subjects, and the researcher's wisdom in continuing the study despite tensions shown by subjects.

The findings regarding the pervasiveness of obedience in Milgram's studies have also been questioned. Some critics do not believe that the findings can be generalized to real-life situations because of (a) the nonrepresentative nature of the subjects, (b) the use of prods to keep the subjects at the task, and (c) the essential nature of trust in an experiment.

Finally, sociological theorists have proposed that advanced industrialized civilizations necessarily become repressive and authoritarian.

VI. SUGGESTED READINGS

Adorno, T., Frenkel-Brunswik, E., Levinson, D. J., & Sanford, R. N. *The authoritarian personality.* New York: Harper, 1950. (Paperback version also available) This massive book contains theory and speculations, test items and test analyses, clinical interviews and interpretations—in other words, something for everyone. Although the book was largely left on the shelf during the 1960s, the social climate of the 1970s will probably cause its return to eminence.

Kirscht, J. P., & Dillehay, R. C. *Dimensions of authoritarianism: A review of research and theory.* Lexington, Ky.: University of Kentucky Press, 1967. A useful review of findings relevant to the study of the authoritarian personality.

Marks, R. W. *The Meaning of Marcuse*. New York: Ballantine, 1970. (Paperback) A clearly written summary of the seminal ideas found in Herbert Marcuse's various writings. Recommended reading before one attempts Marcuse's difficult writing style.

Rokeach, M. *The open and closed mind.* New York: Basic Books, 1960. Contains theory and research on the concept of dogmatism. Includes a demonstration of ways in which the closed-minded nature of dogmatic subjects interferes with effective problem solving.

Schoenberger, R. A. (Ed.) *The American right wing*. New York: Holt, 1969. Contains a series of articles by social psychologists, political scientists, and sociologists on the characteristics of right-wing extremists, superpatriots, and similar groups.

Part Four

Interpersonal and Group Processes

I. *THE AFFILIATION MOTIVE*
   - A. *The need for affiliation*
   - B. *Reasons for joining a group*
   - C. *Deindividuation in groups*
   - D. *Self-evaluation through social comparison*

II. *THE RELATIONSHIP OF HEIGHTENED ANXIETY TO AFFILIATION*
   - A. *Does misery love company?*
   - B. *What kind of company does misery love?*

III. *BIRTH-ORDER DIFFERENCES IN THE LINK BETWEEN ANXIETY AND AFFILIATION*
   - A. *Schachter's original experiment*
   - B. *Birth-order differences in other areas*
   - C. *The relationship between anxiety and affiliation in first borns*

IV. *WAITING WITH OTHERS AND ANXIETY REDUCTION*

V. *THE DETERMINANTS OF EMOTIONAL AND MOTIVATIONAL STATES*
   - A. *Schachter's theory: Physiological arousal plus cognitive state*
   - B. *Cognitive effects of false heart-rate feedback*

VI. *ATTRACTION*
   - A. *The antecedents of interpersonal attraction*
     - 1. *Propinquity*
     - 2. *Similarity of personality, values, and beliefs*
     - 3. *Complementarity of need systems*
     - 4. *High ability*
     - 5. *Pleasant or agreeable characteristics*
     - 6. *Reciprocal liking*
   - B. *Theory-based explanations for factors in interpersonal attraction*

VII. *LOVE*
   - A. *Social psychological approaches*
   - B. *The measurement of romantic love*
   - C. *Stimulants to romantic love: The Romeo and Juliet effect*
   - D. *A theoretical explanation of passionate love*
   - E. *Conclusions*

VIII. *SUMMARY*

IX. *SUGGESTED READINGS*

Chapter Fourteen

Affiliation, Anxiety, Attraction, and Love

Birds of a feather flock together. *Old saying*

Opposites attract. *Another old saying*

There is a song sung by Barbra Streisand, which tells us that "people need people." Even though we do not doubt the observation, we may still ask why. Why do most people seek out other people—even when all of their physical and material needs have been met? Why is prolonged absence from others increasingly intolerable to many people? These questions, dealing with the nature of affiliation, are central to social psychology. One of the purposes of this chapter is to suggest answers to these questions, and in doing so, describe a relevant program of research initiated by Stanley Schachter. The present chapter will go beyond an analysis of the desire to be with others. Schachter's influential program of research leads us to a consideration of such diverse topics as birth-order differences in affiliation, the situational determinants of emotion, and even possible reasons for obesity. If affiliation is a basic social need drawing us to others, attraction must be the next step in forming lasting social relationships. The chapter concludes with a consideration of why we like and love some people more than others.

I. THE AFFILIATION MOTIVE

A. The Need for Affiliation

Suppose you are offered 15 dollars a day to remain in a room by yourself. The room is without windows but has a lamp, a bed, a chair, a table, and bathroom facilities. Satisfying meals are brought to you at the appropriate hours and left outside your door, but you see no one. You are permitted no companions, no telephone, no books, magazines, or newspapers, and no radio, or television. Your watch and wallet are removed, and your pockets are emptied before you enter. If you were to volunteer for such a project, how long could you remain?

In seeking to determine the causes of an affiliative need, Schachter (1959) placed five separate students in situations like the one described here. (These projects were carried out more than 15 years ago, and subjects were paid 10 dollars a day.) All participants were volunteers. One volunteer remained in the room for only two hours before he had an uncontrollable desire to leave. Three volunteers remained in the room for two days. Afterward, one allowed that he had become quite uneasy and would not want to participate again, but the other two seemed rather unaffected by the isolation. The fifth subject remained in isolation for eight days. Upon his release this subject admitted that by the end of the eight-day period "he was growing uneasy and nervous, and he was certainly delighted to be able to see people again" (Schachter, 1959, p. 10). Schachter reports that the prolonged isolation had not seriously affected this subject's adjustment.

No one—including Schachter himself—would regard this study as a well-controlled experiment. It is simply an exploratory study of the effects of social isolation upon normal people. Yet it contains a fascinating finding—in other words, the enormous differences among the five volunteers' reactions to the same situation. Some subjects apparently have vastly greater needs than others for the presence of other people (or for social surrogates such as radio, television, or a telephone).

Thus, we are left with a variety of facts in search of a theory. Some people, under some conditions, can tolerate isolation much better than others. We may capitalize here upon Hebb's (1955) postulate of an optimal level of arousal in the organism. Perhaps this can be applied to differences, within an individual, in the momentary strength of the affiliative need. At times, there may exist a state of affiliative surfeit; one's social needs are not only met but are oversupplied. At other times, a state of inactivity or isolation may produce a deficit and cause the individual to seek more social stimulation. But each person differs in just how much stimulation is optimal. Thus, for some, the presence of other people is a need that comes with more urgency and frequency; for others the need is less urgent. Although this notion is a step toward explaining the affiliative motive, such an exposition is grossly inadequate. It fails to specify independent definitions of surfeit and deficit; it posits the presence of individual differences but fails to explain why they occur; and it ignores the other needs for which affiliation is instrumental. At this point, we shall try to narrow matters down by considering the more specific issue of group membership rather than the broader phenomenon of affiliation.

B. Reasons for Joining a Group

There are two general reasons for wishing to join a group (Schachter, 1959). First, a person may join because the group is a means to an end. In this case, the individual has personal goals that can only be met by affiliating with others or by joining a group. A tennis buff needs to have at least one other companion who plays tennis; he may even join a tennis club to meet his goals. A commuting businessman may join a carpool in order to reduce his travel expenses, even though his fellow commuters might be people he would not associate with socially.

Groups may also represent goals in and of themselves. Schachter suggests that needs such as approval, support, and prestige can only be met by other people. These two reasons for joining a group may be fulfilled by the same behavior. The businessman may join the carpool partly to save money and partly because the other members are, in his eyes, prominent people and his needs for prestige are met by being with them. Likewise, joining a tennis club may give the person the identity he seeks.

C. Deindividuation in Groups

One reason group membership becomes an end in itself is that it offers opportunities for **deindividuation**—a descriptive term suggested by Festinger, Pepitone, and Newcomb (1952). Deindividuation refers to a state of relative anonymity, in which the group member does not feel singled out or identifiable. Other things being equal, the larger the group, the more deindividuated a person can become; he can lose his identity in a mob and find himself committing acts which, if isolated, he would refrain from doing. Le Bon's (1896) classic analysis of crowd behavior apparently deals with a similar conception. Le Bon postulated that the person in a mob loses his sense of responsibility and adopts the unitary consciousness of the crowd (Cannavale, Scarr, & Pepitone, 1970).

But even in small groups the degree of deindividuation can be manipulated, which Festinger et al. (1952) were the first to do. Groups of male college students were encouraged to make unfavorable and even hostile statements about their parents—feelings that they would have been reluctant to express under ordinary circumstances. Some groups of young men participated in these discussions under ordinary conditions; other groups were placed in a semidarkened room, where each participant wore a shapeless gray coat over his clothes. Many more critical and hostile statements resulted in the latter deindividuated condition, indicating that inner restraints of the group members were reduced. Men in the deindividuated groups were less able to indicate which other participant had made a specific negative statement. Interestingly, as Festinger et al. had proposed, group members rated these deindividuated groups as more attractive than the control groups. The release of restraints was an attractive option, at least for this brief time.

Despite the attraction of deindividuation as an explanation for group membership, almost 15 years passed before a second study was done using deindividuation as an independent variable. Singer, Brush, and Lublin (1965) compared group members who were dressed up for the occasion with deindividuated subjects dressed in old clothes and lab coats. The deindividuated groups were again found to release more inner restraints. They used obscenity more often in group discussions of pornographic materials than did the more identifiable subjects. Singer et al. concluded that for deindividuation to be most effective, subjects must experience loss of self-consciousness and reduce feelings of distinctiveness. More recently Cannavale et al. (1970) replicated the original study by Festinger et al., using the same device to encourage criticism of parents, but using female groups, male groups, and mixed-sex groups as well. Results similar to the earlier study were found; for instance, the correlation between extent of deindividuation and lowered restraint was +.57 in the original study and +.56 for the all-male groups in the recent study. But in all-female and in mixed-sex groups, no relationship was found between deindividuation and the unleashing of restraints. The authors concluded that in these groups a high level of apprehension about criticizing parents prevented the deindividuation phenomenon from emerging.

The phenomenon of deindividuation has received its deserved prominence through the research program of Zimbardo (1970a, 1970b), who hypothesized that it is a "process in which a series of antecedent social conditions [lead] to changes in perception of self and others, and thereby to a lowered threshold of normally restrained behavior" (1970b, p. 251). Zimbardo recognizes that deindividuation can cause an increase in the expression of socially tolerated behaviors that we usually do not express overtly (such as intense feelings of joy, crying, or expressions of affection for others); however, he has chosen as his topic of study the function of deindividuation in the expression of such antisocial feelings and actions as hostility, anger, and theft. A complete description of the variables in the deindividuation process, as identified by Zimbardo, is presented in Table 14-1.

In a laboratory study, Zimbardo manipulated several of the components listed as input variables in Table 14-1 in order to produce a state of deindividuation. For example, anonymity was produced in half of the subjects by dressing them in hoods, by never using their names, and by doing the experiment in the dark. (Several of the deindividuated subjects are pictured in Figure 14-1.) Moreover, the group's task was

Table 14-1. *Zimbardo's Representation of the Deindividuation Process.*

Input Variables →	*Inferred Subjective Changes* →	*Output Behaviors*
A—Anonymity B—Responsibility: shared, diffused, given up C—Group size, activity D—Altered temporal perspective: present expanded, future and past distanced E—Arousal F—Sensory input overload G—Physical involvement in the act H—Reliance upon noncognitive interactions and feedback I—Novel or unstructured situation J—Altered states of consciousness, drugs, alcohol, sleep, etc.	Minimization of: 1. Self-observation-evaluation 2. Concern for social evaluation ↓ Weakening of controls based upon guilt, shame, fear, and commitment ↓ Lowered threshold for expressing inhibited behaviors	a. Behavior emitted is emotional, impulsive, irrational, regressive, with high intensity b. Not under the controlling influence of usual external discriminative stimuli c. Behavior is self-reinforcing and is intensified, amplified with repeated expressions of it d. Difficult to terminate e. Possible memory impairments; some amnesia for act f. Perceptual distortion—insensitive to incidental stimuli and to relating actions to other actors g. Hyper-responsiveness—"contagious plasticity" to behavior of proximal, active others h. Unresponsiveness to distal reference groups i. Greater liking for group or situation associated with "released" behavior j. At extreme levels, the group dissolves as its members become autistic in their impulse gratification k. Destruction of traditional forms and structures

(Table 14-1 and Figures 14-1, 14-2, and 14-3 are reprinted from "The Human Choice," by P. Zimbardo, *Nebraska Symposium on Motivation*, 1969, by permission of University of Nebraska Press. Copyright 1970 by University of Nebraska Press.)

Figure 14-1. *Subjects in the Deindividuated Condition in Zimbardo's Study.*

one where different members shared responsibility for performing an antisocial act—giving electric shocks to a fellow college student.

Groups of four subjects participated at one time; all were coeds from New York University. Subjects in the deindividuation condition were treated as indicated above, and subjects in the *identifiability* condition were given large name tags and were greeted individually. They soon got to know one another by name. All subjects were told that the experiment dealt with one's ability to make empathic judgments about another person with whom one was either actively or passively involved. Actively involved meant that the subject induced reactions in the target person; the subject could give the target person a series of strong electric shocks, then observe and rate her behavior. Subjects who were passively involved would only observe and then rate the target person. The procedure was prearranged so that every subject believed she and one other subject in the group of four would administer the electric shocks. During the administration of the electric shocks and observation of the target person's reactions, all subjects were placed in separate cubicles so they would not know how the other subjects responded.

Two vastly different target persons were used. Five-minute tape recordings of interviews between each target person and Zimbardo were used to convey differences between the two target persons. One target person was a sweet, altruistic girl who was working with retarded children to help pay her fiance's medical school expenses. The other target person, also a female, was obnoxious, self-centered, and negativistic. A transfer student who worked as a part-time model, this second target person said that she could not stand the Jewish students at N.Y.U. (Most of the subjects were Jewish.)

In the electric shock portion of the experiment, each subject viewed the target person and the experimenter on the other side of a one-way mirror. The order of viewing the two target persons was counterbalanced across groups, as were the previous taped interviews. The target person appeared to be taking a verbal test but could not be heard by the subject. Each time the target person was supposedly shocked, she writhed, twisted, grimaced, and otherwise expressed pain. Subjects were given a chance to administer shocks on 20 trials, but on the tenth trial the target person reacted so strongly that her hand ripped out of the electrode strap. As she ruefully rubbed her hand, she was strapped down again, and the remaining 10 trials were completed. This predetermined reaction divided the 20 trials into two sets, which then could be compared to see whether there was a change in the use of shock after interruption. After the 20 trials, subjects rated the target person and then completed the whole procedure—audiotaped interview, electric shocks to the visible target person, and ratings—with the second target person.

Compliance to instructions was equally high in both conditions; both identifiable and deindividuated subjects, on the average, administered shocks on 17 of the 20 trials. But deindividuation produced great increases in the duration of the shocks given. The deindividuated group gave, on the average, shocks of .90 of a second, as compared to the identifiable subjects who gave shocks of .47 of a second. Also, as Figure 14-2 shows, there was a tendency in the deindividuated groups to shock the target person more after the interruption. Both the pleasant target person and the obnoxious one were given more shocks by deindividuated subjects after the electrode holder had been snapped. Do deindividuated subjects follow Lerner's (1970) "just world" hypothesis? Apparently, they assume that if the target person is suffering so much as to break the strap, she must deserve the suffering and must be given even longer shocks. In contrast to the identifiable subjects, deindividuated subjects aggressed increasingly, disregarding the characteristics of the recipient. Individuated subjects appeared to take pity on the nice girl after the electrode strap broke but continued to increase the duration of shocks given to the obnoxious girl.

In Chapter 13 we saw how mature male subjects could be induced to shock their co-workers. Now we see that such belligerent behavior is limited neither to males nor to older persons. If we compare the results, Zimbardo's findings are even more frightening than the findings of Milgram's study of obedience.[1] In the present study, no agent of coercion was used, and each girl could choose not to administer shocks; she could assume that the other girl would carry through on the shock administration. (Subjects were told that the experimenter could not determine which subject or subjects had actually administered a shock, as the two circuits had a common terminal.) Yet in a condition of deindividuation "these sweet, normally mild-mannered college girls shocked another girl almost every time they had an opportunity to do so, sometimes for as long as they were allowed, and it did not matter whether or not that fellow student was a nice girl who didn't deserve to be hurt" (Zimbardo, 1970b, p. 270).

Deindividuation is a phenomenon not limited to the social psychological laboratory. Much to his credit, Zimbardo extended his observations of the process to the real world. Deindividuation is epitomized in large cities where masses of people inter-

[1] As Zimbardo (1970a) himself admits, the ethics of the present study may be even more questionable than those of Milgram's study. Although both studies debriefed the subjects afterward and no actual shocks were given, greater deception was employed in Zimbardo's study.

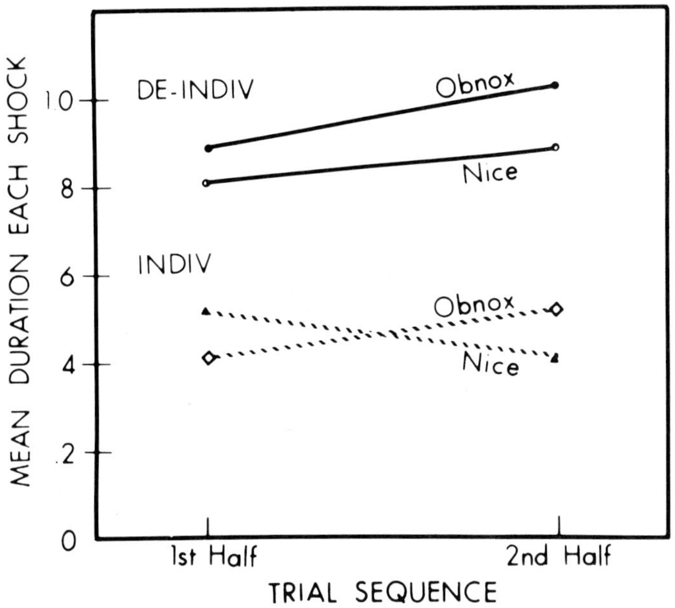

Figure 14-2. *Results of the Zimbardo Deindividuation Experiment. Note that the mean duration of shocks given in the deindividuated condition was higher than in the individuated, identifiable condition. In the deindividuated condition the obnoxious girl was shocked for longer periods than the nice girl, and even longer shocks were given after the interruption resulting from the broken electrode strap.*

mingle without forming any real relationships. Zimbardo predicted that the anonymity and deindividuation endemic to a metropolis like New York City facilitates the expression of antisocial acts such as theft, looting, and vandalism. With Fraser, a fellow researcher, Zimbardo bought a used car and left it on a busy street adjoining the Bronx campus of New York University. At the same time, a similar car was left on a street near the Stanford University campus in Palo Alto, California. To clearly indicate that the cars had been abandoned, the experimenters removed the license plates and raised the hoods of both cars.

The pictures in Figure 14-3 show what happened to the car left in New York. Within 26 hours it was stripped of battery, radiator, air cleaner, radio antenna, windshield wipers, side chrome, all four hubcaps, a set of jumper cables, a can of car wax, a gas can, and the one tire worth taking. All the looters were well-dressed, clean-cut whites; in several cases the looting was a family operation, with the son aiding the father's search-and-remove operation, while the mother served as a lookout. No one ever restrained any of the looters, although passersby sometimes stopped to chat while the car was being stripped.

What happened to the car left in the suburban Palo Alto neighborhood was a complete contrast. The car was unharmed during its seven-day abandonment and was even cared for. One day it rained and a passerby lowered the hood so the motor would not get waterlogged. As Milgram (1970) and others have pointed out, however, the Bronx and Palo Alto environments differ in many respects in addition to population density. Further research will need to take other factors into account.

On the basis of these studies and other equally provocative observations, Zimbardo concludes that for looting and vandalism to be initiated, well-developed feelings of anonymity must exist, plus some minimal releaser cues. In order for vandalism to occur, it must be clear that the car has been abandoned. A minimal releaser cue may be the lack of license plates, a tire removed, or some other disabling sign. Emphasis should be put on the word *minimal.* Zimbardo reports two anecdotes, which convey how readily looting can occur in an urbanized society.

Figure 14-3. *Family-Fun Stripping and Vandalizing in Fun City.*

According to one anecdote, as part of an army convoy was passing through the Bronx, an army tank stalled and was momentarily abandoned while a mechanic was found. When the mechanic arrived a few hours later, the tank had been stripped of all removable parts. According to the second anecdote, a motorist in Queens, New York pulled his car off the highway to replace a flat tire. While the car was jacked up and the motorist was removing the tire, a stranger came up, raised the car's hood, and started to remove the battery. When the stranger was confronted, his response was, "Take it easy, buddy; you can have the tires; all I want is the battery!" (Zimbardo, 1970b, p. 292).

D. Self-Evaluation through Social Comparison

Another implicit value of group membership is that it provides a vehicle for self-evaluation. We all want to get information about ourselves, our abilities, and our beliefs. If a certain aspect of our character is important to us, we want to know how good we are or whether our position is a correct one. Some characteristics can be evaluated with little or no reference to other people. A new bride who has cooked her first cheese souffle can evaluate it by tasting it. A 15-year-old boy who cannot do a single chin-up may conclude that he is weak in this regard. Though observing the skill level of others might confirm his judgment, the initial evaluation is based on nonsocial sources. But as Festinger (1954) has indicated, the evaluation of many skills, aptitudes, attitudes, and values can be done only by comparing oneself with other people. Whether it be one's preference for president or one's golf swing—when there is doubt about appropriateness or correctness—a person will evaluate his own reactions by comparing them with social reality, or the beliefs, opinions, and abilities of friends and acquaintances.

Self-evaluation through social comparison is more fruitful when we make comparisons with others who are similar to ourselves. A dentist trying to decide whom to support for governor compares his choice with members of his country club, with his fellow church members, or with other dentists. He does not seek out the opinions of college professors, airline pilots, or labor organizers. Likewise, in evaluating athletic abilities, most people prefer to compare themselves with someone on their own general skill level. To the average once-a-week duffer, playing golf with his 8-year-old daughter or with Jack Nicklaus would be equally unrewarding in the way of providing self-evaluation through social comparison.

II. THE RELATIONSHIP OF HEIGHTENED ANXIETY TO AFFILIATION

We have seen that affiliating with others can facilitate the attainment of many personal goals and that group membership in and of itself may serve as a goal. There is justification for an assumption that isolation, or the prevention of affiliation, heightens a state of uneasiness in many persons. Schachter's observations caused him to conclude that "one of the consequences of isolation appears to be a psychological state which in its extreme form resembles a full-blown anxiety attack" (1959, p. 12). Where does that lead us? Schachter decided to study a transformation of the relationship. If isolation does lead to increased anxiety, would heightened anxiety lead to a greater desire for affiliation? This section will attempt an answer to this basic question.

A. Does Misery Love Company?

Anxiety is usually considered a generalized, diffuse apprehension about the future. It is usually distinguished from fear, which is more object oriented, more specific, and more reality oriented. One fears a visit to the dentist because he knows he will be in pain; yet, a visit to a doctor for a routine physical examination may trigger anxiety or a generalized dread that something will turn out badly. Clearly, the two reactions are so similar and overlapping that they often cannot be distinguished. Schachter's program of research concerned itself with anxiety as a stimulus to an increased affiliative need. The experimental manipulations, however, largely varied fear along with anxiety.[2] In his initial study, Schachter led subjects (beginning psychology students at the University of Minnesota) to believe that they were to receive a series of electric shocks. Subjects in the high-anxiety condition were told that the shocks would hurt, would be painful, but that there would be no permanent damage (Schachter, 1959, p. 13). By contrast, subjects in the low-anxiety condition were led to expect painless electric shocks or shocks, if felt at all, which would resemble a tickle or tingle. After this initial manipulation, all subjects were treated identically. They were given a sheet on which they were to indicate, by checking a place on a 5-point scale, just how they felt about being shocked. The purpose of this procedure was to check the effectiveness of the experimental manipulation; subjects in the high-anxiety condition reported significantly more negative feelings, hence indicating that the manipulation was successful.[3]

The basic purpose of the study was to determine whether anxious subjects sought the presence of others more than less anxious subjects. Subjects were told there would be a ten-minute delay for setting up the equipment. Thus, each subject had to choose whether she wanted to wait by herself or wait with some of the other subjects in the same experiment. (Note that this choice pertained to waiting during a preshock period; the subjects were not given the choice of being shocked alone or in small groups.) After each subject indicated her preference either to wait alone or in the company of other subjects and after some ancillary responses were collected, the experiment was over. The girls were told that they would not be shocked, and the true purposes of the study were explained.

As expected, the level of situationally induced anxiety influenced the waiting preferences. Of 32 high-anxiety subjects, 20 wanted to wait with other subjects; only 10 of 30 low-anxiety subjects chose to wait with others—a difference statistically significant at the .05 level. The old adage that "misery loves company" was confirmed.

[2]In fact, Schachter observed: "Though we have been free in our use of the term 'anxiety,' it should be made clear that the experimental manipulations have involved nothing more than the manipulation of physical fear" (1959, p. 65). Schachter has probably overreacted here, as his manipulations appear to combine anxiety and fear.

[3]Another demonstration of the effectiveness of the manipulation was the fact that 18.8 percent of the high-anxiety subjects chose to withdraw from the experiment halfway through, realizing that they would not be given experimental credit for participating. They were given credit anyway.

B. What Kind of Company Does Misery Love?

What is it about being with others that makes this choice desirable to highly anxious subjects? Perhaps, other people serve as a distraction, or perhaps a subject is unsure of his reaction and hence seeks out others in the same plight. These are not the only conceivable reasons for the link between anxiety and affiliation, but as two possibilities they can be contrasted and evaluated. This was the next step taken by Schachter in his program of research.

In a second experiment all subjects were told that they would receive painful shocks; in other words, all subjects were in a high-anxiety condition. Each subject was given the choice of waiting alone or with others, but the characteristics of the others were varied from one condition to another. Subjects in the same-state condition were given the choice of waiting alone or with other girls who would be taking part in the same electric-shock experiment. Subjects in the different-state condition could also wait alone or with girls who were not participating in the experiment but were waiting to see their faculty advisors.

Although this experiment used only a small number of subjects (a total of 20), the results were clear-cut and statistically significant ($p < .01$). Six of the ten subjects in the same-state condition chose to wait with other potential shock subjects, and only four chose to wait alone. In the different-state condition all ten subjects chose to wait alone; being with others who were not experiencing the same event as themselves was not an attractive option. Thus, distraction apparently is not a component in the link between anxiety and affiliation. As Schachter states, the old saying that "misery loves company" should be amended to "misery loves miserable company." Then again, perhaps the company should not be too miserable. Rabbie (1963) found that subjects did not want to wait with others who were extremely fearful because it might cause a rise in their own fears.

III. BIRTH-ORDER DIFFERENCES IN THE LINK BETWEEN ANXIETY AND AFFILIATION

One of the benefits of Schachter's program of research was its rediscovery of a long neglected yet important variable—birth order. Although assumptions abound in our society about the nature of the only child, the youngest child, and so on, early social psychological research (in the 1920s, 1930s, and 1940s) revealed no consistent personality differences related to birth order. Apparently, these early studies did not go far enough. Factors associated with a person's birth order do affect his social behavior. We will consider these factors, after reviewing some of the consistent birth-order differences.

A. Schachter's Original Experiment

In reviewing the findings of his first experiment, Schachter divided his subjects into two categories: (a) those who were first born or only children and (b) those who were later born. The results are presented in Table 14-2. Note that in the high-anxiety

Table 14-2. *Birth-Order Differences in Schachter's First Experiment*

	High-Anxiety Condition Waiting Preference:		*Low-Anxiety Condition Waiting Preference:*	
Birth Order:	*Together*	*Alone or Don't Care*	*Together*	*Alone or Don't Care*
First and only child	32	16	14	31
Later born	21	39	23	33
	$X^2 = 10.70$ $p < .01$		$X^2 = 1.19$ $p =$ N.S.	

(Reprinted from *The Psychology of Affiliation*, by Stanley Schachter, with the permission of the publishers, Stanford University Press. © 1959 by the Board of Trustees of the Leland Stanford Junior University.)

condition, 32 of the first-born subjects preferred to wait together, while only 16 wished to wait alone or did not care. But the later-born subjects, when highly anxious, showed no such proclivities; only 21 of 60 wished to wait together. Clearly, the heightened desire to affiliate under conditions of high anxiety occurs predominantly among the first-born group. Moreover, the manipulation of anxiety levels has no effect upon later borns.

B. Birth-Order Differences in Other Areas

Laboratory experiments have shown that first borns seem to seek out other people when anxious. Apparently, such a relationship also occurs outside the laboratory. Schachter (1959) has reported an unpublished study by Wiener and Stieper investigating which military veterans applied for free outpatient psychotherapy at a Veterans Administration Center. Between 75 and 80 percent of the veterans who were first born or only children sought out the psychotherapy, while only 59 percent of the later-born veterans did so. Apparently the anxious first-born individual depends upon other persons as vehicles for anxiety reduction. The student who cannot remain in his solitary dormitory room before an important final exam, choosing to study with others or roam the halls for a willing companion, is likely to have been a first-born child.

Since Schachter's findings were published, a multitude of studies (Sampson, 1965; Warren, 1966) looked at birth-order differences in a variety of things (intelligence, college grades, dependence, extroversion, schizophrenia, suicide, and so on). Some of these differences will be discussed later. Let us now turn to the possible explanations for a heightened link between anxiety and affiliation in first borns.

C. The Relationship between Anxiety and Affiliation in First Borns

Birth order is of no explanatory value in and of itself. We must look for factors related to birth order. Do parents treat their first child differently than subsequent children? Are there physical or nutritional differences between children of different birth orders? Do first borns develop during their infancy a particular kind of relationship to their mothers? Does the absence of an older sibling make the difference? Such questions may help us formulate explanations for the causal factors in the link between anxiety and affiliation in first-born children.

Many years ago Alfred Adler (1945) proposed that first borns become anxious because they are subjected to "dethronement"; in other words, their favored place is usurped by a younger sibling. Adler's theory has little currency among modern-day social psychologists, for it appears that as adults, single children behave the same as do first children with siblings. What these two types share is a period of time when they are their parents' first offspring. Consider novice parents with their first child. They are solicitous, concerned, perhaps overresponsive. They may respond to every gurgle, moan, and cry of their baby. The first-born infant learns that whenever he has a need or discomfort, someone—usually his mother—will respond. Thus, a conditioned response is formed, and the presence of the mother is need reducing and anxiety reducing. Through stimulus generalization, the first born comes to perceive other people in general as anxiety reducing. There is some evidence for this explanation. Parents do report being more tense with their first child; with later children, parents describe themselves as more relaxed and less concerned about every little hurt or cry. Then, too, if it is the third or fourth child who, as an infant, demands the mother's attention, she simply may not have the time to respond as she did with her first infant. Schachter (1959) concludes that the first-born college student is more affiliative when anxious because of his experiences as an infant. Similarly, Sampson (1965) has emphasized that the first born is more dependent upon his mother when an infant, thus leading to a reliance upon others in adulthood.

Ring, Lipinski, and Braginsky (1965) have taken a developmental approach, which recognizes that the first-born child receives relatively inconsistent treatment from his parents. Here again, there is evidence (Sears, Maccoby, & Levin, 1957) that novice parents are less consistent in how they respond. Inconsistent treatment leads to a more confused self-concept in the first born, causing him to seek out others for self-evaluation. By checking his attitudes and behaviors against those of others, the first born can perhaps clarify his self-concept and develop an identity. Certain data are compatible with this explanation. First-born children have been found to be more easily influenced, more socially responsible, and more likely to conform than are later borns (D. Ehrlich, 1958; Becker & Carroll, 1962; Staples & Walters, 1961; Ring et al., 1965).

At the same time, first borns seem better able to achieve academic success than later borns despite no apparent difference in intelligence or academic ability.[4] One of the most consistent findings in an often perplexing mass of birth-order comparisons is the greater striving orientation of the first born, as reflected by his higher achievement need (Sampson, 1962), his greater rate of college attendance (Capra & Dittes, 1962; Warren, 1963, 1964; E. Hall & Barger, 1964; Altus, 1965) and his attainment of higher grades (Schachter, 1963; Pierce, 1959; Altus, 1966; Sampson, 1965). Studies of eminence (Schachter, 1963) find clear-cut differences favoring first borns; among the presidents of the United States, 85 percent were an only child, the first son, or the third son—despite the fact that nearly half of the presidents came from families with be-

[4]Some tests on the intelligence of infants have found slight differences favoring the first born (Bayley, 1965; Cushna, 1966). Bayley describes these differences as being small and apparently having no long-term effect. Greater parental attention to the first-born infant could account for early differences, which dissipate with age.

tween four and seven sons (Louis Stewart, 1970). Perhaps, this picture is consistent with the notion of the first born who struggles to develop an identity.

An analysis by Zimbardo and Formica may explain the greater striving for achievement by the first born. Following E. L. Phillips (1956) and B. C. Rosen (1961), the researchers proposed that parents' expectations are greater for the first born than for later children. Usually, the child's abilities are not as high as the parents' aspirations. Such a discrepancy could lead not only to an inadequate self-concept but also to a striving on the part of the child to succeed. The achievement-oriented behavior of the first born could be associated with his need for attention and approval from others.

Evidence for this type of explanation comes from recent studies on mother-child interactions. Hilton (1967), for example, reported that mothers of first borns and only children were more involved with their child's attempts to solve a puzzle and more frequently interfered with his performance. Rothbart (1971) found that mothers of 5-year-olds gave more complex technical explanations of a phenomenon if the child were first born that if he were later born. Also, mothers were found to be more intrusive in achievement situations with their first born (particularly with first-born girls) than with their later-born children (Rothbart, 1971).

At this point, it may be said with some confidence that, compared to later-born individuals, first borns seek the company of others when anticipating an anxiety-producing event. First borns are also more dependent upon others, more easily influenced by others, and more concerned with pleasing others than later borns. In short, first borns are more other-oriented people. Our best guess is that the causes for these birth-order differences emerge during the first few years of life.[5] Still, research like Hilton's and Rothbart's, observing mother-child interactions in order to understand the concomitants of birth order, has only begun.

IV. WAITING WITH OTHERS AND ANXIETY REDUCTION

We know that first borns, when their anxiety is increased, want to be with others. Of course, there are many reasons for affiliation besides one's birth order, but before we can clarify this issue we need to explore the question of whether being with others does cause first-born persons to become less anxious. Several studies are relevant to this question; their results are summarized below.

A study by Wrightsman (1960a) had subjects either wait alone or in groups of four, while anticipating an experiment which supposedly would "drastically alter the glucose levels in their blood." It was found that if the subject was first born, waiting with others facilitated anxiety reduction more than waiting alone. But if the subject was later born, waiting with others made no particular contribution to anxiety reduction. These findings, which applied to both male and female subjects, corrob-

[5]It is worthwhile to contemplate how often birth order is disregarded in the process of forming impressions of other people. A new acquaintance may ask your religion, your occupation, your political preference, and so on, in order to form an impression of you; yet he never asks your birth order. No one has ever been denied service in a restaurant or admission to a country club because of his birth order. You may not even know the birth order of your closest friend. But it appears to be a socially important variable.

orated Schachter's conclusions about birth order. First borns, when anxious, want to be with other people; and, when they are placed with others to wait, they—rather than later borns—benefit from the presence of others. One of the conclusions of Wrightsman's study was that first borns want to affiliate (and benefit from affiliating) for two reasons: (a) they receive direct anxiety reduction (sympathy and reassurance), and (b) they achieve self-evaluation by means of social comparison. Ring et al. (1965) tested these conclusions by placing subjects in groups of four, where the other three subjects were actually confederates assigned a certain role. Before being placed in the group, each subject was told that she was to participate in an auditory stimulation experiment. In addition to the birth order of the subject, two variables were manipulated in the experiment: (a) the level of anxiety of the three confederates in the group, and (b) the ease with which the subject could evaluate her anxiety level by comparing it with those of others.

Ring et al. confirmed some of the findings of Wrightsman's study—namely, that (a) first borns are more easily influenced than later borns in an anxiety-producing situation, (b) first borns do have a need to use other persons as sounding boards (social comparison) for self-evaluation, and (c) first borns are less confident about their self-ratings of emotionality. However, there were also conflicting findings. Ring and his associates found that later-born subjects have a greater need for anxiety reduction than do first borns. This conclusion is based on their finding that later-born individuals prefer other people who are seemingly calm, while first borns tend in the opposite direction and express more liking for those who are less calm. According to the results of the earlier study the first borns should prefer calm persons, since waiting with other people reduced anxiety for first borns more than it did for later borns.

Although the statement that first borns, as a group, prefer to be with others and actually benefit by being with others is true for groups of subjects, until recently no study had looked at the preferences and the waiting behaviors of the same subjects. MacDonald (1970) has done so, using procedures similar to ones used in earlier studies (Schachter, 1959; Wrightsman, 1960a). After creating a high-anxiety state in his subjects by describing some rather threatening electric shock experiment, MacDonald determined whether each person would prefer to wait alone or together. Then he had each subject wait five minutes, either alone or with three other naive subjects, regardless of the subject's preferences.

Again the results provide both consistencies and inconsistencies with previous research. Findings that were generally in line with the results of earlier studies were: (a) later borns who wait alone become less anxious than later borns who wait together, and (b) first borns who wait together become less anxious than later borns who wait together. However, no birth-order differences were found in preferences for waiting together. And more perplexingly, those first borns who wanted to wait alone —but who were forced to wait together—were the ones who experienced the greatest decrease in anxiety level. MacDonald explained this result by emphasizing the more highly socialized nature of first borns. In other words, first borns are more likely to conform to the expectations of adults or of society in general. This analysis may be extended as follows: when waiting in the company of others, first borns—to a stronger degree than later borns—may respond to demand characteristics of the situation and report greater anxiety reduction. Such an explanation sees the anxiety reduction as an artifact, however; it tells us nothing about actual anxiety reduction.

V. THE DETERMINANTS OF EMOTIONAL AND MOTIVATIONAL STATES

A. Schachter's Theory: Physiological Arousal Plus Cognitive State

Suppose you are alone, late at night, walking along a dark street in a rundown section of a strange city. A man quickly steps from a doorway and tells you to stop. This is clearly an emotion-producing situation, but we may ask which emotion is aroused. Is it fear? Anxiety? Anger? Excitement? How do you know what emotion you are experiencing?

For decades, physiologists and psychologists have theorized about the nature of emotion. We know that under conditions of strong emotion, physiological changes occur. The sympathetic nervous system takes over, leading to a slowing down of digestion, a diversion of more blood to the head and the extremities, pupil dilation, deeper breathing, higher pulse rate, and an increased galvanic skin response. Attempts to detect different physiological response patterns associated with different emotions have largely been unsuccessful (Ax, 1953), and it now appears that the whole gamut of strong emotions—from joy and elation to excitement, fear, and anger—have very similar consequences in our viscera. This has led several psychologists, including Hunt, Cole, and Reis (1958) and Schachter (1964), to posit cognitive factors as the interpreters of emotional states. Although physiological arousal is necessary for emotional labeling, Schachter suggests that we interpret and identify emotional states on the basis of our present situation and our prior experiences. The label assigned to the felt emotion is determined by the cognitive processing of this information. Thus, Schachter's is a two-factor theory, including both physiological arousal and appropriate cognitive factors.

Schachter and Singer (1962) designed a procedure to test the basic hypothesis that a person's emotional state results from the interaction of a physiological state of arousal and cognitive states. By injecting some subjects with adrenaline (epinephrine) and others with a placebo, the researchers varied the physiological states of arousal in different groups of participants. Adrenaline has some transitory effects, including flushing of the face, tremors in the hands, and an accelerated heart rate. Some of the subjects given the drug were told to expect effects that were normal for that drug (the adrenaline-informed condition); other subjects were misinformed about what effects to anticipate. The latter were told to expect side effects such as itching sensations, numbness in the feet, and mild headache (the adrenaline-misinformed condition). A third set of subjects receiving the adrenaline injection were told that the drug was mild and harmless and had no side effects (adrenaline-ignorant condition). The fourth group received a placebo and was told there were no side effects (placebo condition). Thus, Schachter and Singer varied both the degree of physiological arousal (adrenaline injection versus placebo injection) and the cognitive state (expectations of drug effects).

After receiving the injection, each subject was directed to join another student in a waiting room while the drug took effect. (The subjects were told that they would be given some vision tests—the supposed purpose of the experiment.) The other student in the waiting room was a confederate of the experimenter and had been trained to act in a certain way. For example, in a seemingly euphoric state of being, the confederate began hula-hooping, fashioning paper airplanes and sailing them about, and playing basketball with pieces of scrap paper. The confederate then invited the subject to join in his pranks.

Other subjects were placed alone with a confederate who was instructed to act out the emotion of anger. In this anger condition, both the confederate and the subject were instructed to fill out a very long questionnaire containing several personal and rather insulting items. While filling out the questionnaire, the confederate became more and more angry and finally ripped it up, slammed it to the floor, and stamped out of the room.

The purpose of all these behaviors—in both the euphoric and the anger condition—was to give the subject some situational input that might influence his reaction to physiological effects. Two types of measures of the subject's reactions were taken; in one measure, the subject's behavior was observed through a one-way mirror, and he was rated on the extent to which he joined in with the confederate in demonstrating either euphoric or angry behavior. Additionally, subjects filled out a questionnaire indicating their mood at the moment. These mood questions along with some of the results are reprinted in Table 14-3. The results for the euphoria condition in Table 14-3 indicate that those subjects who received an injection of the drug and were accurately informed about its side effects were less likely to perceive themselves as feeling happy and good; conversely, subjects in the misinformed and ignorant conditions were influenced by the confederate's behavior. Observations of subjects in the anger condition led to the same findings. No adrenaline-misinformed condition was used in this part of the study, but subjects in the adrenaline-ignorant condition agreed with

Table 14-3. *Measures and Results of Schachter-Singer Experiment*

Scale 1. How irritated, angry, or annoyed would you say you feel at present?

I don't feel at all irritated or angry (0)	I feel a little irritated and angry (1)	I feel quite irritated and angry (2)	I feel very irritated and angry (3)	I feel extremely irritated and angry (4)

Scale 2. How good or happy would you say you feel at present?

I don't feel at all happy or good (0)	I feel a little happy and good (1)	I feel quite happy and good (2)	I feel very happy and good (3)	I feel extremely happy and good (4)

Mean Self-Report Scores for Euphoria Condition (Scale 2 above):

Condition	*N*	*Mean*
Adrenaline-Informed	25	0.98
Adrenaline-Ignorant	25	1.78
Adrenaline-Misinformed	25	1.90
Placebo	25	1.61

(Adapted from Schachter, 1964, p. 59 and Table 1. Reprinted with permission of the publisher; copyright 1964, Academic Press.)

the confederates' comments more frequently and were angrier more often than placebo subjects or informed subjects.

To determine if the adrenaline actually did produce physiological changes, all subjects' pulse rates were taken both before and after the period of waiting with the confederate. These measures confirmed the expectation that in cases where adrenaline was used, pulse rates would increase, whereas in cases where the placebo was used, pulse rates would not increase.

Schachter and Singer explain the interesting findings of their study by considering (a) the state of physiological arousal induced by the adrenaline and (b) the inadequacy of the explanations provided by the various experimental conditions. Thus, when the individual has no appropriate explanation for his state of arousal (for example, the misinformed and ignorant conditions), his evaluative needs are manifested and his state of arousal is labeled in accordance with the immediate situation—namely, the behavior of the confederate. But when the subject has an appropriate explanation for his bodily state (as in the informed condition), evaluative needs are not elicited, and the behavior of the confederate is not imitated. Emotional states as different as anger and euphoria can be produced from the same physiological conditions.

Let us ask what would happen if the situation were held constant and only levels of physiological arousal were varied. Schachter and Wheeler (1962) did this, by injecting different groups of subjects with different drugs—a sympathomimetic agent (adrenaline), a tranquilizer (chlorpromazine), and a placebo (saline injection) were used. All subjects were told that there would be no side effects; they then watched a slapstick comedy film. As predicted, the greatest amount of observable amusement (as measured by observations of grins, smiles, laughs, and big laughs) was in the adrenaline group, followed by the placebo group. The tranquilized group showed the least emotional reaction. Thus it was shown that one's degree of emotional behavior is related to the extent of activation of the sympathetic nervous system, or emotional arousal.

In recent years, Schachter and his associates have extended their efforts beyond making demonstrations of the cognitive determinants of emotional states.[6] Schachter's theory has been applied to the study of (a) the cognitive effects of false heart-rate feedback, (b) cheating and psychopathy, (c) pain perception, and (d) obesity (Schachter, 1971b). The first and the last of these topics will be reviewed in the next section.

B. Cognitive Effects of False Heart-Rate Feedback

In one study, male college students found themselves participating in an apparently pleasant activity of viewing pictures of seminude females (Valins, 1966). Some of the subjects were told that they would hear the sound of their heartbeats, which was to be amplified electronically. The true purpose of the experiment, however, was to determine what effects a falsified heart rate would have on the subject's evaluations of the pictures. Some subjects heard their heartbeat speed up markedly while viewing certain pictures. In another condition, the subjects heard a sudden decrease in the bogus heart rates for certain pictures, but no change for the other pictures. Valins hypothesized that a cognition—such as "that girl's picture has

[6]We wish to acknowledge our use of the reviews of the literature in this area prepared for us by Robert Isett and Francis Burke.

affected my heart rate"—would prompt the subject to consider that girl more attractive than some other girl who apparently caused no effects. Subjects in a control condition were told that the heart rate sounds were extraneous noise and did not perceive the reinforced pictures of girls as being more attractive. But subjects who were told that their heart rates actually increased or decreased did prefer the reinforced pictures to a significant degree. Valins accounts for his findings in the light of Schachter's proposition that cognitive representations of internal states are evaluated and labeled in accordance with the predominant characteristics of the environmental situation. Subjects, given the task of explaining to themselves why their heart rates changed, found that "it was most appropriate for them to explain their reactions by referring to the [photographs], and to interpret them as indicating varying degrees of attraction" (Valins, 1966, p. 407). A rather perplexing factor, however, is that either an increase or a decrease in heart rate produced the same results; perhaps the change served as a general signal of differential reaction.

More recent work by Valins (1967a, 1967b) and Schachter (1967, 1971b) has concentrated on individual differences in utilizing internal sensations as cues for labeling one's own behavior. Valins (1967b) found that unemotional people (measured by paper-and-pencil instruments) tend to ignore their internal states and feel no pressure to evaluate and label their feelings. In laboratory experiments, they were less likely to mimic the behavior of a confederate and did not rate certain photographs of nudes as more attractive merely because their heartbeat responded differentially. Conversely, people who rely extensively upon their internal states to label their emotions and behavior were more influenced by bogus heart rates, emotional confederates, and similar variations.

Similarly, Schachter (1967, 1968, 1971a, 1971b, 1971c) has proposed that obese persons are insensitive to internal determinants of hunger and respond more often to external factors. In other words, the obese person eats at noon because it is time to eat, not because he feels sensations of hunger. There have been clever tests of this hypothesis, dealing with such diverse issues as who fasts during Yom Kippur, which Air France pilots adapt to time-zone changes, and who does or does not use chopsticks in Oriental restaurants. (Obese people do not!) All of these tests indicate that overweight subjects are less responsive to internal triggers for hunger (Nisbett, 1968a, 1968b; Cabanac & Duclaux, 1970; Schachter, Goldman, & Gordon, 1968; Schachter, 1967, 1971a, 1971b, 1971c).

VI. ATTRACTION

Under certain conditions, many people experience a powerful desire to be with other people. Apparently, others serve as a way of evaluating our own opinions and abilities. It is interesting to ask, however, which persons are most attractive to us. Why are we friendly or attracted to some people, while we reject or dislike others? In this section we shall review some of the characteristics of other people which make them attractive. Two theoretical explanations for the findings shall be contrasted.[7]

[7] In describing the factors that influence attraction, we have relied upon an analysis presented by Aronson in his *Nebraska Symposium* address (1970) and upon the reviews by Berscheid and Walster (1969) and by Bramel (1969).

A. The Antecedents of Interpersonal Attraction

We may say with confidence that a person will like or be attracted to another person who is physically nearby, who has similar values, beliefs, and personality characteristics, who complements one's need system, who has high ability, who is pleasant or agreeable, and who likes one in return. Let us consider each of these conditions in turn.

Propinquity. Other things being equal, we like people who live close to us better than those who are at a distance from us. For instance, families in a student apartment complex are more likely to interact with and like those persons living on the same floor in the same building than those families living on other floors or in other buildings (Festinger, Schachter, & Back, 1950). Members of Air Force bomber crews develop closer relationships with co-workers who are stationed near them than with co-workers stationed a few yards away (Kipnis, 1957). Even though such findings certainly do not seem surprising, it should be remembered that greater friendships and attractions remain despite the greater frictions that occur from two people living or working closely together.

Similarity of Personality, Values, and Beliefs. We like and are attracted to people who agree with us more than to people who disagree with us. If their personalities are like ours, so much stronger is the attraction. In Chapter 9, we reviewed studies which found that whites prefer associating with blacks who have attitudes like their own, rather than with whites who have opposing attitudes (Stein, Hardyck, & Smith, 1965; Rokeach, 1968; Byrne & Wong, 1962). In a field study carried out in a college rooming house, Newcomb (1961) found the same thing. The degree of liking among occupants was related to similarities of attitudes toward a variety of topics.

Complementarity of Need Systems. In contrast to the preceding condition, there may be cases where opposites attract. If another person differs from you and if this opposing quality meets your needs, that person will be more attractive to you than other people. According to the theory of need complementarity, similarity in certain personality traits and needs does not facilitate two persons liking one another. A very dominant person may be more likely to be attracted to a submissive partner. The complementarity of need systems could work in both directions—the highly submissive person would be attracted to a marriage partner who would speak out, take responsibility, and make decisions. In regard to marriage selection, Robert Winch (1952; Winch, Ktsanes, & Ktsanes, 1954) has proposed that each person chooses a mate who is most likely to provide the greatest degree of gratification of his or her needs. One careful study has shown, however, that possibly two factors may occur; the personalities and needs of two marriage partners may be similar as well as complementary.

Kerckhoff and Davis (1962) interviewed, tested, and later retested college couples who were seriously considering marriage. These couples were classified either as long term (had gone together 18 months or more) or short term (had gone together less than 18 months). The investigators were interested in whether a similarity of values or a complementarity of needs led to greater progress toward a permanent relationship. To measure degrees of progress, both members of each couple were asked whether their relationship had changed during the last seven months since they had first filled out questionnaires measuring needs and values. Three possible answers to the question were: "Yes, we are farther from being a permanent couple"; "No, it is the same"; and "Yes, we are nearer to being a permanent couple."

The length of time that the relationship had existed was a significant moderator variable in regard to similarity of values and needs. Those couples who had been going together less than 18 months and who were more similar in values reported greater movement toward a permanent relationship. In the case of these short-term relationships, the presence of complementary needs did not lead to feelings of a more permanent relationship. But among long-term couples, those who experienced a greater complementarity of needs reported greater movement toward permanence. In the longer relationships, possession of similar values did not, at this point, facilitate a move toward marriage. Such findings encourage the development of a minitheory of the filtering factors of mate selection. Kerckhoff and Davis propose that the quality of a relationship is assayed by sequentially passing through several filters. The first is sociological and demographic variables such as socioeconomic status and religion, the second (coming after the couple has dated a little longer) is consensus on values, and the third (coming only after a longer period) is the complementarity of needs.

A somewhat different interpretation of this phenomenon is offered by Levinger, Senn, and Jorgensen (1970). They suggest that first there is a process of discovering the important values of each other, which is followed by a process of developing pair communality. Probably, both interpretations are appropriate.

High Ability. We like people who are intelligent, able, and competent more than we do those who are not. Stotland and Hillmer (1962) report that in the absence of any other information, a subject's liking for another person increases if the person has a high degree of ability. Apparently, this is so, even when the subject does not expect to benefit from the other person's high ability (Iverson, 1964; Stotland & Dunn, 1962).

However, as Bramel (1969) points out, there may be limits to this relationship. People who are extremely competent may make us uncomfortable if an atmosphere of social comparison exists. Thus, it must be said that other attributes interact with high ability to influence our liking of a person. When a person of established high ability demonstrates human failings, his attractiveness may actually be enhanced. A real-life example of this phenomenon was the apparent increase in Muhammed Ali's popularity after he lost the world championship boxing fight to Joe Frazier. Aronson (1970) notes that a Gallup Poll taken right after the abortive Bay of Pigs invasion of Cuba showed that President Kennedy's personal popularity had increased rather than decreased. Perhaps this was a sympathetic response to his defeat, but Aronson sees it as a reflection of how human fallibility in a high-ability person makes that person even more attractive. Aronson states: "Perhaps President Kennedy was too perfect. He was young, handsome, bright, witty, a war hero, super wealthy, charming, athletic, a voracious reader, a master political strategist" (Aronson, 1970, p. 148). Aronson tested his hypothesis under well-controlled laboratory conditions (Aronson, Willerman, & Floyd, 1966). In the study, college students listened to a tape recording purportedly of another student who was seeking a position on the university College Quiz Bowl team. Half of the subjects heard the candidate answer very hard questions in an extraordinarily skillful way; the candidate ended by getting 92 percent of the questions right. The other half of the subjects heard the same voice fail to answer many of the questions; this candidate was correct only 30 percent of the time. For half of the subjects hearing each of these voices, the tapes at this point ended and the subjects were asked, among other things, how much they liked the candidate. Not surprisingly, the person with superior ability was liked somewhat more. (Average attraction ratings were 20.8 for the superior-ability candidate and 17.8 for the average-ability candidate.) The other half of the subjects heard a continuation of the tape and learned that just as the candidate was handed a cup of coffee, he spilled the cup and, amid a great commotion, exclaimed, "Oh, my goodness, I've spilled coffee all over my new suit." These subjects were then asked to rate the candidate. It is interesting to note the effect of this blunder, or pratfall, upon how much the subjects liked the candidate. The superior-ability candidate now received a mean attraction rating of 30.2 (compared to 20.8 in the absence of the pratfall), whereas the average-ability candidate received a mean rating of −2.5 (much below his initial 17.8 rating). Thus, a blunder by a person of high ability facilitates his appeal, but the same act detracts from the already less attractive image of the average person.

We may question whether such a blunder would increase the attractiveness of the competent person for everybody. Helmreich, Aronson, and Le Fan (1970) proposed that the observer's level of self-esteem might influence whether a blunder on the part of a competent person increases his attractiveness. The investigators granted that, for persons of average self-esteem (that is, people who see themselves as moderately competent), the blunder of a superior person is endearing because it "not only 'humanizes' the superior, but brings him closer to the 'average' observer" (Helmreich, et al., 1970, p. 260). However, the observer who sees himself as highly competent (or rates his own self-esteem as high) may identify with the superior person and be more attracted to him if he maintains a flawless image. It was predicted that observers who are relatively low in self-esteem would also be more attracted to the flawless, competent person than to the fallible one, because of the observer's own need "for someone to take care of him [and] to provide an ideal, a hero" (Helmreich, et al., 1970, p. 260).

Another procedure was used to test this extended hypothesis. Subjects watched a video-tape of an interview instead of listening to a recording. The person being interviewed had applied for the position of student ombudsman, "the most responsible job a student can hold." The level of competence or superiority of the applicant was varied by information that the applicant reported about himself—grade point average, class honors, offices held, and high school activities. The pratfall was again the act of spilling coffee. Thus, Helmreich et al. varied three conditions: the applicant's level of competence (superior or inferior), the blunder committed by the applicant (present or absent), and the self-esteem of the observer (high, average, or low).

The results are reproduced in Figure 14-4. As indicated in the graph on the left, the competent applicant who commits a pratfall becomes more likable for subjects with average levels of self-esteem—a result similar to the findings on subjects in Aronson, Willerman, and Floyd's (1966) study. But subjects who are either high or low in self-esteem respond differently—for them, the presence of the pratfall decreases the attractiveness of the competent applicant.

Reactions to the incompetent applicant, as shown in the right-hand side of Figure 14-4, were quite different. As expected, this stimulus person was less attractive for all observers, and the presence or the absence of the pratfall had little effect on his attractiveness.

Pleasant or Agreeable Characteristics. This is a condition that needs little or no elaboration. We like people who are nice or who do nice things.

Reciprocal Liking. We are attracted to people who like us. Heider's balance theory predicts that if person P likes himself and if person O likes person P, a cog-

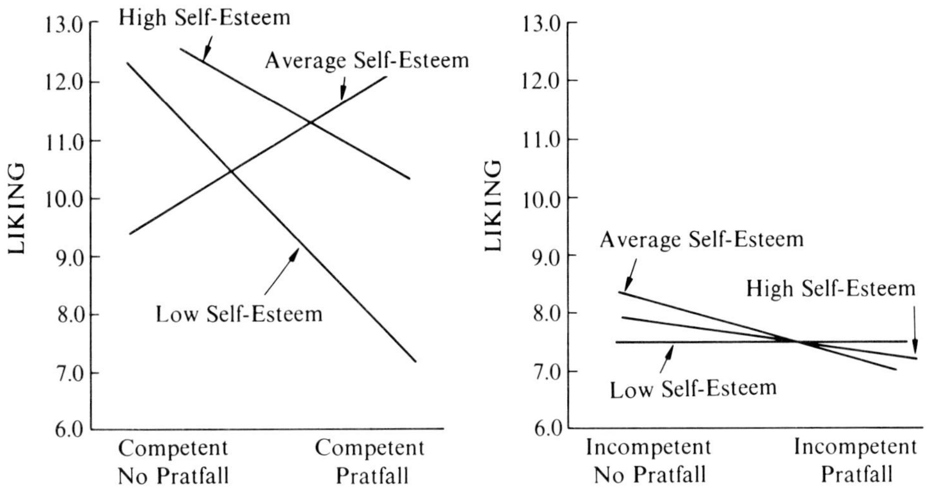

Figure 14-4. *Attraction toward the Competent Stimulus Person. Higher scores indicate greater attraction. (From Helmreich, Aronson, and Le Fan, "To err is humanizing—sometimes,"* Journal of Personality and Social Psychology, **16**, *1970, p. 262. Copyright 1970 by the American Psychological Association, and reproduced with permission.)*

nitively balanced state will be introduced in which person P likes person O. Backman and Secord (1959) showed that if members of discussion groups are told that certain other group members liked them very much, these others were more likely to be chosen later when two-person teams were formed.

B. Theory-Based Explanations for Factors in Interpersonal Attraction

We have seen how a variety of antecedent conditions contribute to interpersonal attraction.[8] Let us now explore some possible explanations for these relationships. Like Aronson (1970), one could be tempted to subsume all these factors under reinforcement theory; that is, we are attracted to people whose behavior is rewarding to us. One type of reinforcement theory—social exchange theory—provides an example. According to Thibaut and Kelley's (1959) social exchange theory, a relationship between two persons continues if the rewards from the relationship are greater for each person than the costs. This principle was extended by using a concept of comparison level of alternatives, which postulates that the individual compares the cost/reward ratio of one interaction with the cost/reward ratio of other available alternative behaviors. Curry and Emerson (1970) found that social exchange theory does a good job of explaining why certain persons in a group of strangers come to like certain other persons. Aronson has carefully summarized the application of this theory to factors in interpersonal attraction.

(1) Propinquity is more rewarding, all other things being equal, because it costs less in terms of time and effort to receive a given amount of benefit from a person who is physically close to us than [from] one who is at a distance (Thibaut & Kelley, 1959); (2) people with

[8] Byrne and Rhamey (1965) have developed a mathematical formula that predicts the attractiveness of another person on the basis of the amounts of positive and/or negative information available about that person.

similar values reward each other through consensual validation (Byrne, 1969); (3) the same would be true for similarity of some personality traits, whereas (4) for some needs, complementarity would be most rewarding—for example, sadism-masochism or nurturance dependency; (5) people perhaps expect to gain more through association with highly competent people than with people of low or moderate competence. That is, in general, our past histories are such that we have usually been more rewarded by people who knew what they were about than by people who tended to blunder frequently. (6) Obviously, pleasant, agreeable behavior is more rewarding than unpleasant, disagreeable behavior; and (7) being liked can probably be considered a reward in and of itself—in addition, for most people it also entails a similarity of beliefs because most of us think rather highly of ourselves (Byrne & Rhamey, 1965; Aronson, 1970, pp. 144–145).

However, not all findings about attraction fit this simplified social-exchange explanation. For example, if one has exerted much effort to achieve a goal or to affect a relationship, that goal or relationship becomes more attractive (Aronson, 1961). Likewise, the more severe the initiation rites necessary to become a member of a group, the more attractive that group then becomes (Aronson & Mills, 1959; Gerard & Mathewson, 1966). We find that cognitive dissonance theory, an offspring of the Gestalt approach, more acceptably explains such outcomes, as well as many similar findings dealing with the relationship of effort to evaluation of a goal. Cognitive dissonance theory is concerned with inconsistencies between two beliefs or behaviors of the same person. The theory predicts that such inconsistencies are so unpleasant that the person is motivated to resolve the resulting dissonance. Applied to the present case, cognitive dissonance theory would predict that when a person makes great efforts to meet another person, he will find the other person more attractive than he would have had his efforts been less concentrated. That is, any realization that the other person is less attractive would be dissonant with the great amount of effort expended in meeting him; hence, one convinces oneself that the other person is attractive.

Thus, we discover once more that it is necessary to utilize several theoretical approaches to understand more thoroughly the nature and determinants of attraction. We may expect that the future will bring about a more precise understanding of the use of each theory in predicting the phenomenon of attraction.

VII. LOVE

Perhaps the ultimate attraction is love. Many thinkers have asked what love really is; yet, until recently, social psychologists have shied away from the study of love, for a variety of reasons. Berscheid and Walster (1969) report that in the early decades of this century, the scientific study of romantic love was almost a taboo; for example, in the 1920s two professors were fired from a state university because of their participation in a questionnaire study of attitudes toward sex. But the intervening 50 years have produced ever-increasing freedoms in the study of such attitudes. (See Chapter 19 of this text.)

One reason for avoiding the topic is that, of all the social psychological constructs, love is perhaps the most difficult to define and measure. Goode (1959), a sociologist, defines love as follows: "A strong emotional attachment, a cathexis, between adolescents or adults of opposite sexes, with at least the components of sex desire and tenderness." Some limitations to this definition are immediately apparent. One drawback is that the use of the phrase *opposite sexes* precludes the consideration that any homosexual relationship, even a long-term one involving both sexual desire and tenderness, can be considered as love. Another difficulty with Goode's definition is in the wording, "at least the components of sex desire and tenderness"; if there are other components we would like to know what they are. A more recent definition by Greenfield, an anthropologist, is in some ways better: "Love [is] a relationship which may be observed and which includes patterned, repetitive and normative behavior and specifiable attitudes and emotional states between persons of the opposite sex or on occasions of the same sex. This actually or potentially includes sexual activity" (Greenfield, 1970, p. 3). Here again, however, qualities other than sexual activity are not described.

By defining love as a "relationship" Greenfield implies that love may not reside in a person but rather is a developing process between people, a state of becoming present in a dyad as a totality. Love, according to this view, is not the attribute of either person separated from the other.

A. Social Psychological Approaches

Social psychologists have often either ignored a definition of love or have treated it as merely an intense form of liking. For example, in one experiment specifically concerned with romantic attraction, the measure of the dependent variable was simply a paper-and-pencil measure of liking (Walster, 1965). Heider's (1958) influential theory treats loving as intense liking. Surely, there is more to love than this; yet, the social psychologist's obsession with measurement may be a cause for the predominant orientation. If love is considered as merely an extreme and selective type of liking, its measurement can be achieved by using captive audiences of college sophomores and procedures within the usual social psychological bag of tricks—questionnaires, rating forms, and the like. But that approach, we believe, is not enough.

B. The Measurement of Romantic Love

Social psychologist Zick Rubin (1970) has recently sought an approach that is something of a compromise. Rubin conceptualizes romantic love as something more than intense liking, but he still attempts to assess it through rather traditional techniques. Thus, he has attempted to bring the study of romantic love within the mainstream of social psychological approaches to interpersonal attraction. Rubin defines love as "an *attitude* held by a person toward a particular other person, involving predispositions to think, feel, and behave in certain ways toward that other person" (1970, p. 265, italics in original). Notice that this definition is quite different from Greenfield's and from Goode's in particular; it is a nonsubstantive definition, which does not mention any attributes of love such as tenderness or sexual desire. In fact, the same definition that Rubin uses for *love* could be used for *hate,* as well. In Rubin's definition, the nature of love is limited to an attitude, and considerations of love as a part of a person's personality or experience are excluded.

Rubin's first purpose was to devise a love scale that would measure degrees of romantic love (defined by Rubin as "love between unmarried opposite-sex peers, of the sort which could possibly lead to marriage"). A parallel scale for the measurement of liking was developed. Items from these are listed in Figure 14-5; take a moment to read over the statements. Despite his nonsubstantive definition of love, Rubin has included three components in his romantic love scale: (a) affiliative and dependent needs, (b) predisposition to help, and (c) exclusiveness and absorption. The concept of liking, as reflected in the liking-scale items, includes two components: (a) a perception that the target person is similar to oneself and (b) a favorable evaluation and respect for the target person.

These scales were administered at the University of Michigan, to 158 couples who were dating but not engaged. They were instructed to answer the love scale and the liking scale with respect to their dating partner and a close friend of the same sex. The means and standard deviations for the men and women respondents are reported in Table 14-4, which indicates that the love scores of men for their girlfriends and those of women for their boyfriends were almost identical. However, women like their boyfriends significantly more than they were liked in return ($\bar{X}$ of 88.48 versus 84.65, significantly different at .01 level). This difference results from women rating their boyfriends higher on task-oriented dimensions such as intelligence and leadership potential.

Means for liking of same-sex friends were virtually identical (males = 79.10; females = 80.47), but women reported greater love toward same-sex friends than did males (males = 55.07; females = 65.27). As Rubin indicates, this difference is consistent with our cultural stereotype that women express more love toward each other than men do. Thus, we have the beginnings of a conceptual distinction between romantic love and liking. Further evidence that these are separate entities comes from the following findings.

1. The correlation across couples between the extent of the man's and woman's love for each other was +.42. The corresponding intracouple liking correlation was lower, at +.28. Thus, there is more similarity in regard to how much the members of a couple love each other than in how much they like each other.

2. Love scores were highly correlated with estimates of the probability that the current dating partners would marry (r = +.59 for each sex). However, liking scores were less correlated with the likelihood of marriage (+.35 for men and +.32 for women). The outcomes of Rubin's research project may not extend one's knowl-

---

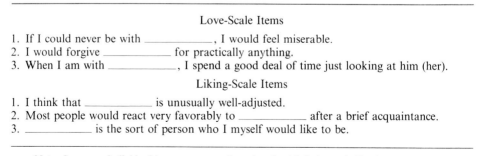

Love-Scale Items

1. If I could never be with ________, I would feel miserable.
2. I would forgive ________ for practically anything.
3. When I am with ________, I spend a good deal of time just looking at him (her).

Liking-Scale Items

1. I think that ________ is unusually well-adjusted.
2. Most people would react very favorably to ________ after a brief acquaintance.
3. ________ is the sort of person who I myself would like to be.

Note: Scores on individual items can range from 1 to 9, with 9 always indicating the positive end of the continuum. There are 13 items on each scale.

Figure 14-5. *Examples of Rubin's Measures*

Table 14-4. *Love and Liking for Dating Partners and Same-Sex Friends*

	Women		*Men*	
Index	$\bar{X}$	*SD*	$\bar{X}$	*SD*
Love for partner	89.46	15.54	89.37	15.16
Liking for partner	88.48	13.40	84.65	13.81
Love for same-sex friend	65.27	17.84	55.07	16.08
Liking for same-sex friend	80.47	16.47	79.10	18.07

Note: Based on responses of 158 couples. (Table 14-4 and Figure 14-5 are from Rubin, "Measurement of Romantic Love," *Journal of Personality and Social Psychology*, **16**, 1970, 267–268. Copyright 1970 by the American Psychological Association, and reprinted with permission.)

edge beyond what can be gained from common observation. The approach to romantic love through the attitude-measurement framework may not be enough by itself. Love may develop as a result of the interaction of many factors. Let us now consider an example of a situational factor that may play a role in the development of love.

C. Stimulants to Romantic Love: The Romeo and Juliet Effect

An unintentional implication of the attitudinal approach may be that romantic love is a static unchanging phenomenon. We realize, of course, that it is not. Romantic love grows and wanes, intensifies and diminishes for a variety of reasons. While loving and liking are qualitatively different, many of the factors associated with the development of attraction or liking probably contribute to the development of love as well. Although all these factors should be considered, for the moment we shall examine one specific determinant. What effect does parental interference have on the feelings of romantic love between a young woman and a young man?

In Chapter 10, we reviewed Brehm's (1966) theory of reactance. This minitheory predicts that a threat to one's freedom of choice—as represented by parental interference—leads to intensified feelings of romantic love between two partners. (We could call this phenomenon the Romeo and Juliet effect.) Driscoll, Davis, and Lipetz (1971) set out to test this hypothesis. Married couples (N = 91) and dating couples (N = 49) participated in the study. The average length of time that the couples had been together on a serious basis was eight months, and 18 of the 49 couples were living together at the time of the study. Scales to measure parental interference, various types of love, interpersonal trust, and other factors were administered to each couple. Not surprisingly, a low correlation of +.24 was obtained between degree of parental interference and degree of romantic love in married couples. But this correlation was +.50 for the unmarried sample, indicating that unmarried couples who reported greater parental interference were also more in love. From this data, it cannot be said with certainty that heightened parental interference intensified the relationship; but Driscoll and his colleagues repeated the measures 6 to 10 months later to determine changes in responses. Changes in degree of parental interference correlated +.34 with changes in the extent of romantic love experienced by the 29 initially unmarried couples who were retested. Thus, the hypothesis that parental interference intensifies feelings of romantic love is apparently supported. However, we could probably safely assume that had the

Montagues and Capulets known of this phenomenon, their reactions to the love affair of Romeo and Juliet would not have changed.

D. A Theoretical Explanation of Passionate Love

Walster and Berscheid (Walster, 1970; Walster & Berscheid, 1971) have attempted to relate the determinants of emotional states to the feeling of passionate love—apparently a more transitory phenomenon than romantic love. These researchers first asked if reinforcement theory could explain passionate love and concluded that it cannot. They recognize that we may fall in love with persons who offer us affection or other rewards, but they also point out that we may intensely love those who have rejected us. When a lover has been spurned, his feelings may dissipate—or they may grow all the stronger. In one paper, Walster (1970, p. 4) cites an actual incident involving an Italian man who had kidnapped his former sweetheart; the kidnapper tearfully explained, "The fact that she rejected me only made me want and love her more."

Evidence from anecdotes may not convince die-hard empiricists, but such stories, along with other data, led Walster and Berscheid to postulate that something besides a straightforward theory of reinforcement is necessary to explain passionate love. Thus, they proposed that Schachter's two-factor theory of emotion may be of use. Schachter emphasized that in order to experience emotion, one must not only be physiologically aroused but must also possess the appropriate cognitions in order to label the arousal as a particular emotional state. These cognitions are often derived from the situation. Walster and Berscheid noted that two components are also necessary for a passionate experience: the arousal and the appropriate cognitions. Walster wrote:

> Perhaps it does not really matter how one produces an agitated state in a lover. Stimuli that usually produce sexual arousal, gratitude, anxiety, guilt, loneliness, hatred, jealousy, or confusion may all increase one's physiological arousal, and thus intensify his emotional experience. As long as one attributes his agitated state to passion, he should experience true passionate love. As soon as one ceases to attribute his tumultuous feelings to passion, love should die (1970, p. 10).

Even negative experiences can induce love because they intensify the component of arousal. For example, the presence of fear or misery can facilitate one's experiencing of love or, at least, can increase attraction. There is both anecdotal evidence and research support for this effect. As an example of the first type of evidence, Bertrand Russell, in his autobiography (1968), indicated how an irrelevant, but frightening, event from World War I intensified his passion for his then current mistress, Colette.

> We scarcely knew each other, and yet in that moment there began for both of us a relation profoundly serious and profoundly important, sometimes happy, sometimes painful, but never trivial and never unworthy to be placed alongside of the great public emotions connected with the War. Indeed, the War was bound into the texture of this love from first to last. The first time that I was ever in bed with her (we did not go to bed the first time we were lovers, as there was too much to say), we heard suddenly a shout of bestial triumph in the street. I leapt out of bed and saw a Zeppelin falling in flames. The thought of brave men dying in agony was what caused the triumph in the street. Collette's love was in that moment a refuge to me, not from cruelty itself, which was unescapable, but from the agonizing pain of realizing that that is what men are . . . (quoted in Walster & Berscheid, 1971, p. 50).

As empirical evidence, a study by Brehm, Gatz, Goethals, McCrimmon, and Ward (1970) is somewhat appropriate, although it is concerned with liking rather than with romantic love. Brehm et al. hypothesized that a man's liking for a woman could be increased by arousal from a prior, irrelevant event. In the study, college males were led to believe that they were going to receive three fairly stiff electric shocks. Half of these men were allowed to retain this expectation throughout the experiment (threat subjects), while half were told somewhat later that the experimenter had erred and that they would receive no shocks (threat-relief subjects). Other men were placed in a control condition, where no mention of impending electric shocks was made. Men in each condition were introduced to a coed and asked how much they liked her. Both the threat and threat-relief subjects (still aroused through either fear or relief) reported liking the girl significantly more than did the control subjects. Thus, an unrelated frightening event, which maintains heightened arousal, does seem to be related to increased liking.

Arousal can be stimulated by an irrelevant emotion that has either a positive or negative nature. The study by Valins (1966) is appropriate here. Men whose heartbeat apparently increased when looking at certain photos of seminude females later rated those photographs as more attractive than did men who did not experience perceptions of an increased heart rate. The false feedback gave meaning to the feelings experienced by the subjects.

All this led Walster and Berscheid to emphasize the role of *labeling* in determining the presence of romantic love. Love does not exist unless the lover defines it as such. If the appropriate cognitions are present, almost any form of heightened arousal can lead the person to label his emotion as love. Let us spell out some implications.

First, a person is more likely to label his emotion as love, if the cognitions are appropriate. For example, consider two male college freshmen who have participated in a computer-dating project. Each male is assigned to one of two identical twins, each of whom is strikingly beautiful but acts in a rather neutral way toward her date. Each girl talks very little, expresses very little emotion, yet does not discourage her date in any way. Let us also say that the two males have been told different things about their dates. One is told: "Your computer-matched date is rather shy and inexpressive but on the basis of our matching of data we are convinced she is quite attracted to you." The other is told: "If your date appears shy and inexpressive it means that she is not attracted to you at all." Each couple then goes to a double-feature movie, which includes an X-rated film. Each male feels emotion—he gets warm; his face flushes; there may even be sexual arousal. How does he label his emotion? Our guess is that the two freshmen will label the same reaction differently. For one, it may be sexual desire or passionate love; for the other, the reaction will more likely be labeled as embarrassment. The basic difference underlying these different labels is the set of cognitions held by each male in regard to how much his date likes him.

Let us look at other implications of Walster and Berscheid's emphasis on labeling. Some of the exercises involved in sensitivity training may lead to arousal. For example, a male and female may be paired off and asked to stare into each other's eyes or may have to touch one another while blindfolded. Again, an excited heartbeat or a feeling of blood rushing to the head may occur. Sexual arousal may even result. Does the person attribute his feelings to passionate love? Most probably, he or she would say: "I don't know this person. I don't even know his name. How could I be in love with him?" In short, the cognitions drawn from the situation are inappropriate for labeling the feeling as romantic or passionate love, even though emotional arousal may be present to a high degree. Thus, some other label is sought.

E. Conclusions

In 1958 Harlow, a psychologist, wrote, "So far as love or affection is concerned, psychologists have failed in their mission. The little we know about love does not transcend simple observation, and the little we write about it has been written better by poets and novelists" (1958, p. 673). After reading this section on love, the reader may conclude that Harlow's statement is still essentially accurate. But, there are reasons for optimism. More psychologists have come to recognize the inadequacies of past research efforts, and the topic is no longer an area restricted by taboo. Interdisciplinary research efforts are being encouraged. Even though it is recognized that no variable is more difficult to define and measure than love, there is increased commitment to studying its important aspects.

VIII. SUMMARY

The need to affiliate, or to be with others, is an exceedingly strong one in some individuals. Two reasons for joining a group are (a) that the group is a means to an end and (b) that the group is an end in itself.

Deindividuation refers to a state of relative anonymity. The deindividuated quality of some groups encourages individual members to act in socially unacceptable ways, which would be avoided if the members were less anonymous. Group membership provides a means for self-evaluation through social comparison.

Under conditions of increased situational anxiety, there is a greater desire to be with others. This is particularly true of persons who are first born or only children.

When waiting with others in anticipation of an anxiety-producing event, the typical first-born person will become less anxious than had he been left alone. The presence of others has no such general effect upon anxiety reduction in later-born subjects.

Schachter's theory emphasizes the cognitive determinants of emotional states. Emotions are labeled on the basis of physiological arousal plus cognitive factors—the latter being influenced by the situation.

Individuals differ in their utilization of internal sensations as cues for developing labels for behavior. Obese persons for example, may be relatively insensitive to internal determinants of hunger and respond more often to situational factors.

The following factors make another person more attractive to us: propinquity; similarity of personality, values, or beliefs; complementarity of needs; high ability; pleasant or agreeable characteristics or behavior; and reciprocal liking. Reinforcement theory proposes that we are attracted to people who reward us. There are many cases where this theory is accurate, but there are also cases where it does not apply.

Love is conceptualized as being qualitatively different from liking. It is long term and includes components of both sexual desire and tenderness.

Romantic love is not a static phenomenon; it grows and wanes for a variety of reasons. One situational determinant of the intensity of romantic love experienced by a couple is the degree of parental influence. Heightened parental interference intensifies the feelings of love.

Explanations of the determinants of romantic or passionate love capitalize upon Schachter's two-factor theory of emotion. For instance, Walster and Berscheid have proposed that a person labels his or her feelings as passionate or romantic love if (a) there exists a state of physiological arousal, and (b) his or her cognitions are appropriate.

IX. SUGGESTED READINGS

Aronson, E. Some antecedents of interpersonal attraction. In W. J. Arnold and D. Levine (Eds.), *Nebraska symposium on motivation, 1969*. Lincoln, Neb.: University of Nebraska Press, 1970. Pp. 143–173. A delightful demonstration of the uses of a creative mind in researching the possibly sterile topic of attraction. Aronson reviews the basic findings on this topic and describes in detail the development of studies on attraction in his own laboratory.

Berscheid, E., & Walster, E. H. *Interpersonal attraction*. Reading, Mass.: Addison-Wesley, 1969. (Paperback) A brief, clearly written, inexpensive review of thinking and research on attraction. Ranges from consideration of attitudes and liking to a consideration of courtship and love.

Byrne, D. *The attraction paradigm*. New York: Academic Press, 1971. An integration of the findings in the rapidly expanding area of interpersonal attraction, written by one of the most influential and productive researchers in this area. Much of the work described herein uses laboratory data to develop a theory that predicts rates of attraction.

Schachter, S. *Emotion, obesity, and crime*. New York: Academic Press, 1971. A collection of papers by a recipient of the American Psychological Association's Distinguished Scientific Award. As it is manifestly apparent by now, Schachter's broad theorizing and clever research designs have led to results that have altered our notions of emotion, affiliation, and anxiety.

Zimbardo, P. G. The human choice: Individuation, reason, and order versus deindividuation, impulse, and chaos. In W. J. Arnold and D. Levine (Eds.), *Nebraska symposium on motivation, 1969*. Lincoln, Neb.: University of Nebraska Press, 1970. Pp. 237–307. Provocative material from the laboratory and the real world on the effects of deindividuation and anonymity upon interpersonal behavior. Highly recommended.

Chapter Fifteen

Social Perception

by Stuart Oskamp

Yon Cassius has a lean and hungry look . . . such men are dangerous. *William Shakespeare*

Man looks at his world through transparent patterns or templets which he creates and then attempts to fit over the realities of which the world is composed. *George Kelly*

In the present chapter, we shall deal with such issues as how we form our impressions of other people, how accurate these impressions are, and whether our perceptions of the world and people about us are influenced by social or cultural factors. As a starting point, let us do a simple exercise that will illustrate some of the procedures and problems encountered in the study of social perception. Choose a person whom you know well, and we will try to determine how accurate your knowledge of that person really is. First, describe this person on the brief set of items listed in Figure 15-1. For each item, put a number in the first column, using the scale that is provided. Next, describe yourself, using the same scale and putting the appropriate numbers in the second column in Figure 15-1. In order to complete this exercise, you will have to ask the target person to describe himself or herself on the same items using the same scale. Be sure that he cannot see your ratings while he is doing this. Then transfer his self-ratings into the third column, which is marked "Friend's Self-Rating."

Now you have all the elements necessary for determining the degree of **accuracy** or **empathy** of your perception of another person in the manner used in many psychological studies. Compare the numbers in column (a) with those in column (c) and obtain the absolute value of the difference. That is, for each item, subtract the smaller of the two numbers from the larger and record the difference in the margin. Then add up these differences for the 8 items; the result is your error score. A perfect score would be 0, and the worst possible score would be 40. A completely chance level of accuracy would be around 24.

Two other types of scores could be obtained using different combinations of the three columns. The difference between columns (b) and (c), the two self-ratings,

	(a) *Friend*	(b) *Self*	(c) *Friend's Self-rating*
1. Is usually well-dressed			
2. Enjoys gardening			
3. Would like to be an astronaut or explorer			
4. Is an avid reader			
5. Is quite athletic			
6. Likes little children			
7. Is talkative in social groups			
8. Dreams very frequently			

Number Scale

1—strongly untrue of person
2—moderately untrue of person
3—mildly untrue of person
4—mildly true of person
5—moderately true of person
6—strongly true of person

Figure 15-1. *Social Perception Form.*

is called **real similarity** because it indicates the degree of similarity between the two individuals' views of themselves. A score of 0 means complete similarity, and a high score means low similarity. The difference between columns (a) and (b) is called **assumed similarity** or sometimes **projection** because it shows how much you believe your friend is like yourself. With minor variations, this methodology has been used in many research studies on person perception. We will return to this example in later discussions, but let us turn now to a brief description of the perceptual process and the field of social perception.

I. THE PERCEPTUAL PROCESS AND A DEFINITION OF SOCIAL PERCEPTION

The area of psychology that we call **perception** can be defined as the study of the immediate experience of organisms. It includes identifying, discriminating, recognizing, and judging objects by means of sensory information. Perception differs from **cognition** in its lesser emphasis on processes of thinking, deciding, choosing, and making inferences (Tajfel, 1969). The nature of the perceptual process is a fascinating one, particularly because our perceptual process is so different from the elements that produce it. Figure 15-2 effectively highlights this contrast. The notion of a chaotic impingement of stimuli on our sense organs is tremendously different from the coherent perceptual world that we continually experience. This contrast has led Hastorf, Schneider, and Polefka (1970) to emphasize five general characteristics of our perceptual experience.

1. *It has immediacy.* Our perceptual experience occurs as soon as we open our eyes or unstop our ears, apparently without any intervening steps of thought or interpretation.

2. *It has structure.* We perceive objects or sounds as organized wholes, rather than as a collection of disparate elements.

3. *It has stability.* We perceive objects as remaining the same from one moment to the next, despite changes in their position or illumination.

4. *It is meaningful.* We perceive objects in terms of our experience with them and in terms of their orderly relationship to other objects.

5. *It is selective.* We attend only to certain stimuli and objects out of the many that we could perceive at any moment, and this attention is an active process of selection.

The field of *social perception* has two major divisions that will be considered in this chapter: (a) the study of the personal and social factors that affect our general perceptual processes, and (b) the study of how we perceive other persons. Since these topics are both very broad, only a few representative research areas within

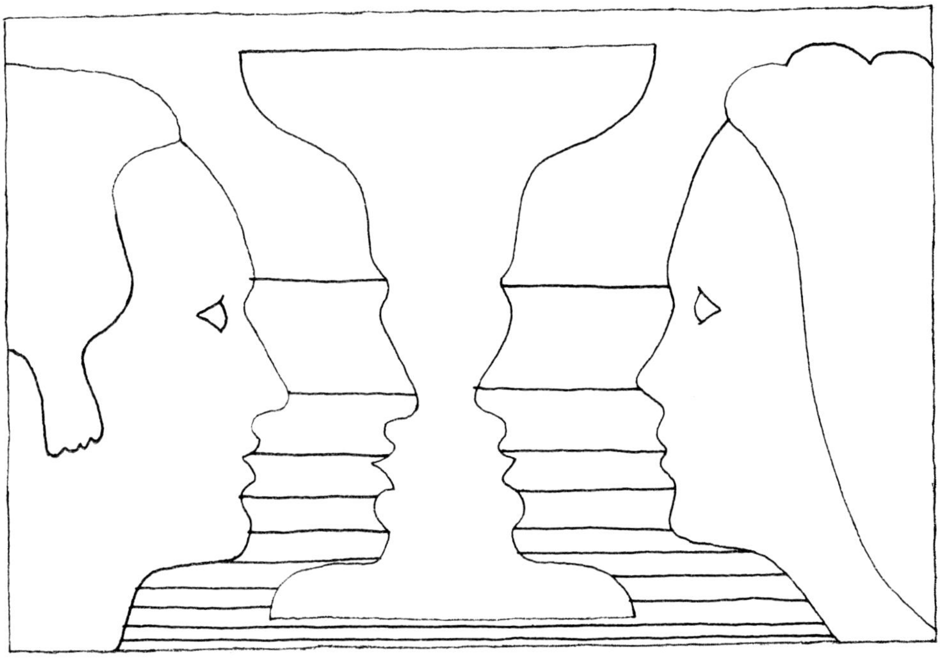

The following is a description of what actually happens when you open your eyes and see a blue vase standing on a table.

Light waves of a certain wavelength are reflected off the vase. Some of them impinge on the retina of your eye, and if enough retinal cells are irritated, some visual nerves will fire and a series of electrical impulses will be carried through the sensory apparatus, including the subcortical centers, and will finally arrive at the cortex. This description paints a picture of a very indirect contact with the world: light waves to retinal events to sensory nerve events to subcortical events and finally to cortical events, from which visual experiences result (Hastorf, Schneider, & Polefka, 1970, p. 4).

(Reprinted by special permission from Hastorf-Schneider-Polefka, *Person Perception*, 1970, Addison-Wesley, Reading, Mass.)

Figure 15-2. *The Perceptual Process.*

each of them will be discussed in depth. As in the study of perception in general, one of the main questions in the field of social perception is: to what extent is our perception **veridical** (accurate)? Do we see the world "like it is," or do we perceive it "through a glass, darkly"? Since we know that our perception is not always correct, a second question is: under what conditions is perception not veridical? What causes us to distort our view of the world in one direction or another?

A third major question focuses specifically on our perception of people: what factors affect our impressions of another person? What characteristics of the other person, of ourselves, or of the social situation influence the way we perceive another person? Do our general assumptions about the nature of man influence our perceptions of a given individual?

II. PERSONAL AND SOCIAL FACTORS AFFECTING PERCEPTION

The proverbial man on the street believes that he sees and hears and smells the world as it really is; he assumes that his perception is veridical. A great deal of psychological research confirms this assumption, but psychologists have also found many instances where our perception of stimulus objects is not veridical. These instances are called **illusions.** Psychologists have been greatly interested in illusions because of what these instances can show us about the nature of perceptual processes. The rising moon, for instance, shows the effect of an object's context on our perception of its size (Rock & Kaufman, 1962); the moon appears much larger when it is near the horizon than when it is higher in the sky, despite the fact that its image on the retina is the same size.

Other very persuasive evidence that our perceptions can be wrong comes from the psychology of testimony. Persons who report witnessing certain events are often quite inaccurate, making gross errors of fact and incorrect inferences. Their reports are often very incomplete, particularly in regard to items that are apparently unimportant or peripheral to the main action. A recent study showed that less than 10 percent of the possible information contained in a short film of an accident was reported in an immediate free testimony, and less than 20 percent was reported even under extensive interviewing (Marquis, Oskamp, & Marshall, 1971).

What are the major personal and social factors that affect our perception? The first group of factors to be considered are the social characteristics of the stimulus object itself.

A. Major Stimulus Properties

Value. Properties of stimuli, such as their value to the subject, can influence how objects are perceived. This conclusion was the major contribution of studies conducted around 1950, which emphasized the subjective and personal aspects of perception. (These studies were referred to as the "new look in perception.") A prototypic study was one by Bruner and Goodman (1947) in which children looked at a coin and adjusted the size of a circular spot of light until it seemed to them to be the same size as the coin. Results of the study demonstrated the phenomenon of

perceptual accentuation, for the size of all coins used (pennies through half-dollars) was overestimated. The fact that the value of the coins led to their overestimation in size was shown by a control group of subjects who judged the size of cardboard discs instead of coins. This group displayed no appreciable overestimation.

Many subsequent experiments have been done in this area, and the final conclusion seems to be that perceptual accentuation occurs primarily with valued rather than disliked stimuli, and only in cases where the value of the stimuli is directly related to their physical magnitude (Tajfel, 1969).

Meaning. Another contribution of the "new look in perception" was a program of research on the recognition threshold for stimuli that have emotional meaning for the subject. (The recognition threshold is the level at which a weak stimulus is first correctly recognized.) In **perceptual defense** the recognition threshold for an unpleasant stimulus is raised, making it less likely to be noticed. For instance, in a typical tachistoscopic word-recognition experiment, a subject may not see a quickly flashed word that has unpleasant connotations, or he may perceive the word as a different, less threatening one (for example, "where" instead of "whore"). In **perceptual sensitization** the threshold is lowered, and increased perceptual vigilance may enable the subject to avoid unpleasant consequences associated with the stimulus. For example, a child may jump quickly enough to avoid a playmate's kick. In some experiments, apparent perceptual effects have actually been artifactual (that is, spurious effects caused by the particular methodology used), but in other, better designed experiments the perceptual effects are genuine phenomena.

Though perceptual defense and perceptual sensitization are opposite effects, many studies have demonstrated that they both occur quite frequently. J. S. Brown (1961) has suggested an explanation for this by positing a curvilinear relationship between the degree of emotional meaning of a stimulus and the recognition threshold. Thus, compared to a neutral stimulus, a somewhat threatening stimulus might have a raised threshold (defense), but a very threatening stimulus would have a lowered threshold (sensitization). Dulaney (1957) has shown in a learning experiment that either perceptual defense or sensitization can be produced by the proper manipulation of learning conditions. Punishment of the perceptual response produces a raised threshold (defense), whereas an experimental arrangement in which the subject can avoid punishment by responding quickly produces a lowered threshold (sensitization).

Familiarity. There is clear-cut evidence that more familiar stimuli are recognized more quickly and accurately than less familiar ones (Solomon & Postman, 1952). More recently, another effect of stimulus familiarity has been demonstrated. Research by Zajonc (1968a, 1970) shows that familiarity breeds comfort rather than contempt. This conclusion stems from many studies that have looked at the effects of *repeated exposure of stimuli* upon one's attitudes. Regardless of whether the stimuli are foreign words, men's faces, or names of cities, the results clearly show that stimuli seen more frequently are liked better than stimuli seen less frequently.

The implications of these findings might be rather frightening; repeated exposure to even the most obnoxious advertisement or the most inane political candidate might gain general approval for the product or candidate in question. However, research has shown that this conclusion is unwarranted. The attitude enhancement effect holds for positively valued stimuli and neutral stimuli, but not for negatively valued stimuli. Increased exposure may even produce the opposite effect with negatively valued stimuli (Brickman & Redfield, 1970; Burgess & Sales, 1971; Perlman & Oskamp, 1971). Thus, we may conclude that the familiarity of stimuli often affects our perceptual responses to them, but that familiarity also interacts with other factors—such as the meaning of the stimulus—in its effects on perception. (Repeated exposure also has effects upon attraction, as described in Chapter 14.)

Intensity. One of the most interesting questions concerning the intensity of stimuli is whether **subliminal perception** is possible and, if so, whether it can influence other responses such as consumer purchases. *Subliminal* means below the threshold of awareness, and many studies have shown that some degree of perceptual accuracy can occur even when subjects have no awareness of having seen anything and have no confidence in their judgments.

A thorough review of the area by McConnell, Cutler, and McNeil (1958) led to the conclusion that the effectiveness of subliminal perception had been greatly overrated during the initial public controversy over its use in advertising. (See Chapter 2.) Many studies have found greater effectiveness with a higher intensity of stimulation. Thus, subliminal advertising is apparently less effective, not more effective, than traditional advertising methods.

B. Personality Factors

In addition to the stimulus properties described thus far, many different personality characteristics have been related to perceptual responsiveness. For instance, highly authoritarian subjects typically show marked perceptual rigidity. (See Chapter 13.) Several other personality characteristics that are related to social perception will be discussed later. At this point, let us briefly mention two widely studied personality variables, which are related to perceptual responsiveness.

Repression and *sensitization,* as conceptualized by Byrne (1964), are personality characteristics referring to styles of defense against threatening stimuli. They are directly related to the terms *perceptual defense* and *perceptual sensitization. Repressors* or *defenders* are people who have difficulty perceiving threatening stimuli, while *sensitizers* consistently and quickly perceive threatening stimuli. For instance, on a vacation trip, a sensitizer might constantly imagine strange noises in the automobile engine, whereas a repressor might not notice such a noise even if it were fairly obvious. Byrne (1964) has reported research results showing that, compared to sensitizers, repressors have poorer memory for threatening materials, less awareness of anxiety, a more positive self-concept, greater social extraversion, and better personality adjustment.

Psychological differentiation, or *field independence,* was popularized by Witkin and his co-workers (1962). The term refers to a broad dimension of cognitive style, involving a combination of perceptual, intellectual, and personality characteristics. The most typical measure of field independence is the Rod and Frame task. In this task, the subject is seated in a completely dark room and shown a luminous rod in the center of a luminous square frame. Both the rod and the frame are tilted away from a vertical position in the same or opposite directions. For instance, the rod might look like the drawing shown in Figure 15-3. The subject's task is to adjust the rod to a true vertical position while the frame remains tilted. People who can do this well are called field independent, since they ignore the cues of the frame's position. People who do it poorly are termed field dependent.

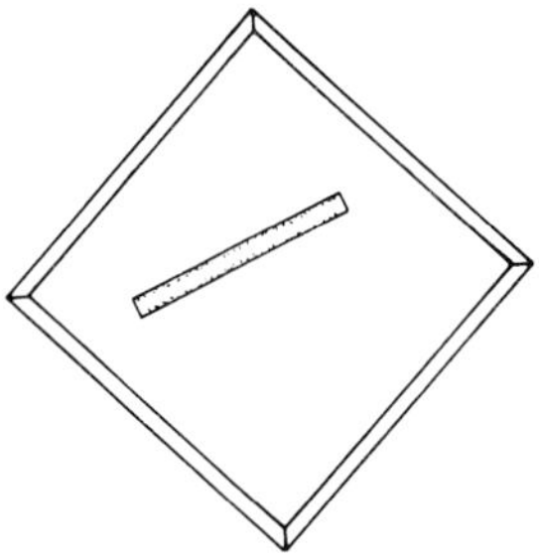

Figure 15-3. *The Rod and Frame Task. People who can adjust the rod to a vertical position while the frame remains tilted are called field independent. People who do a poor job at this task are termed field dependent.*

Research on psychological differentiation has shown that field-dependent subjects are generally extraverted, are quite sensitive to social approval and/or disapproval, and are less creative than field-independent subjects (Wiggins, 1968). Again, the important point for our present discussion is that these personality characteristics are closely related to perceptual styles.

C. Group Effects

The responses of other people can often lead to conformity in a person's behavior. (This will be discussed in detail in Chapter 16.) Perhaps more surprisingly, group effects can also modify perceptual processes. The classic study in this area was done long ago by Muzafer Sherif (1935, 1936), using the **autokinetic effect** (the tendency of a stationary pinpoint of light, in a completely dark room, to appear to be moving). In this situation of ambiguous sensory information, the effect of social influence is maximized. As he expected, Sherif found that two subjects working together rather quickly converged on a common norm concerning the light's apparent motion. Furthermore, in most cases this convergence appeared to be a true perceptual change, rather than merely a verbal conformity to the other person's judgments. Subsequent studies have found that greater cohesiveness (mutual attraction) in an influencing group leads to greater shifts in the perceptual judgments of its naive member (Flament, 1961) and that, even in the absence of any group pressure to conform, purely informational social influence can modify an individual's perception of stimuli (Flament, 1958).

D. Cultural Differences

The final, and most general, social factor affecting perception is the cultural background of the individual. Tajfel (1969), in a major review of social perception, distinguished three major categories of cultural variables that can influence perceptual responses: (a) functional salience, (b) familiarity, and (c) communication systems.

Functional Salience. The function of an object may vary from culture to culture. An object that is necessary for survival in one culture may not have the same functional importance in another culture. As a result, many different terms are developed in the language of a people for important cultural entities. The consequent availability of these terms makes perceptual discriminations easier and more important. For instance, in our American culture, knowledge about types of automobiles and their components is very important, and we have developed numerous terms related to the automobile. But, in Arabic, there are about 6000 words relating to the subject of camels (Thomas, 1937).

Another common example of functional salience is the importance that Eskimos place on making distinctions among different kinds of snow and ice: "In the life of the Eskimo *snow* means something entirely different as falling snow, soft snow on the ground, drifting snow or snowdrift. Fresh water ice, salt water ice, an iceberg, play quite different roles in their life and all these are designated by distinctive terms" (Boas, 1938, p. 130). Undoubtedly these verbal distinctions are also accompanied by perceptual distinctions, which would not even be noticeable to the average inhabitant of the temperate zone.

Familiarity. People living in a particular culture may have frequent experiences with certain cultural products that are very rare or entirely absent in another culture, and this familiarity may affect perception. The Zulu culture, for instance, is distinguished by an overwhelmingly common experience of curved or circular shapes and practically no experience with straight lines or sharp angles (Allport & Pettigrew, 1957). In the Zulu culture the perception of angularity was found to be somewhat (but not markedly) different from that of subjects in our own rectilinear world, as shown by responses to the Ames rotating-trapezoid illusion.

The effects of familiarity can also be demonstrated in a situation of binocular rivalry, where two different pictures are simultaneously presented to a subject's two eyes in a stereoscopic device. Bagby (1957) paired traditional American scenes with traditional Mexican scenes (for instance, a baseball game and a bullfight). As expected, the American subjects saw the typical American scenes much more frequently, while Mexican subjects saw the typical Mexican scenes more easily.

Communication Systems. As mentioned previously, the words available in a language for expressing a concept may help to determine what an individual in that culture perceives. The most extreme version of this viewpoint is Whorf's *linguistic relativity principle* (1956). Whorf contends that a person's language determines not only how he communicates, but also how he "analyzes nature, notices or neglects types of relationships and phenomena, channels his reasoning, and builds the house of his consciousness" (p. 252). Much of the research on how words affect perception has involved studying the names assigned to various colors, in relation to perceptual responses, such as recognition of the colors. Lantz (1963) determined the "linguistic codability" of 20 small color chips of different hues. As predicted, she found impressive positive correlations between the linguistic codability of the colors and the accuracy with which they could be recognized when mixed together with a larger array of colors. Lantz also showed that linguistic codability was the causal factor in this relationship, since teaching some subjects new names for colors that had previously been poorly communicated led to increased accuracy of perceptual recognition of these colors.

E. Summary

In this section we have discussed stimulus factors, personality factors, group factors, and cultural factors, which can influence perceptual processes. However, in considering these many influences, it is important to remember that the great bulk of our perception is still veridical. As Tajfel (1969) concluded in his review of cultural influences: "*some marginal aspects* of perception have been shown to differ in a manner which relates them predictably to cultural contexts . . . [and there are] differences between human groups *at the edges of perceptual functioning*, when the information received is ambiguous, incongruous, or unclear" (p. 379, italics added). The same general conclusion may be applied to stimulus, personality, and group influences on perception. It is usually only where conditions are unclear or confusing that these factors can produce major distortions of perception.

III. PERCEPTION OF PERSONS

Undoubtedly, the process of perceiving other people follows the same general laws and principles that govern all social perception. However, when people are the objects of perception, additional principles and variables enter the scene. People have emotions, which may or may not be accurately perceived, depending on the circumstances. People have stereotypes about other groups of people, which may enter into their evaluation of a given individual. Some personal traits are more important than others in forming impressions of other people. Our own characteristics may interact with those of the other person, thereby affecting the accuracy of our perception of others. Our customary roles and the behavioral norms we hold can markedly influence our reactions. Even our views about human nature in general may influence how we perceive specific individuals. Many of these considerations will be discussed in the following sections.

A. Recognizing Emotions

The recognition of emotional expression is one of the oldest topics of empirical psychological research, having begun with Charles Darwin, who wrote a whole book on the subject (1872). Darwin felt that his theory of evolution was supported by observed similarities between expressions of given emotions in man and in different animal species. In the early 1900s many psychologists conducted studies where subjects were asked to identify the emotion being expressed in photographs of human faces—each face portraying either a posed or a natural emotion. Some years later, Woodworth (1938) reanalyzed many of these early studies, pointing out that the methodology used had resulted in an underestimation of the degree of accuracy in the subjects' judgments. Woodworth developed a scale of emotions, having six categories: (a) love, happiness, and mirth, (b) surprise, (c) fear and suffering, (d) anger and determination, (e) disgust, and (f) contempt. Using these categories, Woodworth showed that the average level of correct recognition of emotions approached 80 percent and that errors were seldom more than one scale point away from the correct value.

More than a decade passed before Schlosberg (1952, 1954) noted that judges tended to confuse the first and last categories on the Woodworth scale. Therefore, Schlosberg suggested that Woodworth's scale of emotions should be represented as a circular configuration, with its perpendicular axes representing the two psychological dimensions of unpleasantness-pleasantness and attention-rejection. (See

Figure 15-4.) Still more recently, Frijda (1969) has carried out an extensive factor analysis of the dimensions of pictorial expressions of human emotion, concluding that six factors are necessary in order to describe adequately the complexity of facial expressions of emotion. These six factors are quite similar to those identified by Woodworth. The major variables that determine the recognizability of emotions are as follows.

> Whether or not emotions are recognizable depends on the type of stimulus used, on the emotion being expressed, on the number and kinds of categories in terms of which the judgment is made, and the amount of contextual information given to the subject. There is a multitude of situations in which accurate and consensual judgments can be obtained (Tagiuri, 1969, p. 404).

B. Identifying People

The perception of people's physical characteristics is an area that psychologists have studied very little. This neglect is particularly surprising in view of the great use made of physical appearance in determining degrees of interpersonal attractiveness (Berscheid & Walster, 1969). An area that has had considerable study (because of psychologists' interest in the topic of prejudice) is the use of ethnic stereotypes in identifying or classifying people. In making judgments about people, do we seek out knowledge about their ethnic background? Several studies have been done on the identifiability of Jews; the general conclusion was that Jews tend to be recognized at a rate that is slightly better than chance (Tajfel, 1969). Interestingly, Jews themselves seem to do no better than non-Jews at identifying other Jews from physiognomic information. However, when speech and gestural cues are also provided, Jews are more accurate than non-Jews (Savitz & Tomasson, 1959).

The most interesting aspect of this topic is the question of whether prejudiced people differ from nonprejudiced people in the ability to identify a particular disliked group. The data seem to indicate that prejudiced individuals exaggerate the differences between their own group and the outgroup, but they underestimate individual differences within the outgroup (Secord, Bevan, & Katz, 1956; Seeleman, 1940).

Do these characteristics of prejudiced individuals make them more accurate in identifying outgroup members? The evidence on this point is inconclusive, but there are several apparently clear-cut, related findings. First, prejudiced subjects think that they are quite good at identifying members of a disliked group (Lindzey & Rogolsky, 1950; Cooper, 1958). Second, prejudiced subjects are more likely than other subjects to label a high percentage of individuals as outgroup members (S. Siegel, 1954; Scodel & Austrin, 1957). Third, as a result of these tendencies, the mistakes in identification made by an anti-Semitic subject will be largely in the direction of concluding that non-Jews are Jewish, rather than the reverse (Brigham, 1971a). Because of this response bias in their perceptual judgments, prejudiced per-

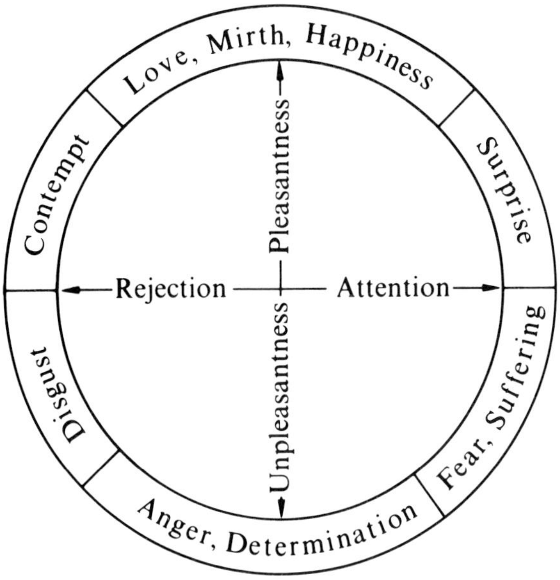

Figure 15-4. *Schlosberg's Circular Classification of Human Emotions. (From Schlosberg, "The description of facial expressions in terms of two dimensions,"* Journal of Experimental Psychology, **44**, *1952, 229–237. Copyright 1952 by the American Psychological Association, and reproduced by permission.)*

sons are likely to be more accurate than nonprejudiced subjects in identifying out-group members but are less accurate in correctly classifying members of their own group. The net effect is that prejudiced persons are probably no different from unprejudiced persons in their overall accuracy in identifying the backgrounds of other people. (See Chapter 9 for a general treatment of the nature of prejudiced attitudes.)

C. Forming Impressions of People

Our impressions of other people are influenced by our assumptions about the nature of man (Chapter 3), by our expectations of encountering cooperative or competitive responses (Chapter 5), by our attitudes of prejudice (Chapter 9), and by our degree of authoritarianism (Chapter 13). Our reactions to others are also closely related to the topic of interpersonal attraction (Chapter 14) and to the social norms we hold and the roles we expect ourselves and others to play. (See Chapter 16 on conformity and Chapter 17 on leadership.) Here, we shall consider only two of the many factors affecting our impressions of other people—the importance of central traits, and the importance of first impressions.

Central Traits. A basic assumption in the work of Solomon Asch was the presence of so-called **central traits** in personality impression formation. Consistent with his theoretical Gestalt orientation, Asch (1946) expected that one's impression of another person would not be simply the additive total of all the information one has about the other person; rather, one's impression would be a dynamic product in which some pieces of information would carry great weight and thus modify the whole picture. Asch called such influential characteristics central traits, and he clearly showed that the warm-cold dimension was a central trait that markedly affected the organization of subjects' impressions. For instance, when the adjective *cold* was included in a list of stimulus words, only about 10 percent of the subjects gave responses stating that the target person would also be *generous* or *humorous.* However, when the adjective *warm* was used instead of *cold,* about 90 percent of the subjects described the person as *generous,* and over 75 percent described the person as *humorous.* Many other traits were also markedly affected by the presence of the word *warm* or *cold* in the stimulus list. By contrast, when the words *polite* or *blunt* were substituted for *warm* or *cold,* respectively, the resulting personality impressions were not much altered; thus, Asch did not consider the terms *polite* and *blunt* to be central traits. Asch believed that these results and those of several other experiments supported his Gestalt viewpoint.

However, further studies by Wishner (1960) and by Rosenberg, Nelson, and Vivekananthan (1968) provided a more refined analysis, which cast a different theoretical light on the topic. Wishner began by having more than 200 undergraduate psychology students rate their course instructors on 53 pairs of traits used by Asch. From these ratings Wishner then computed the correlation of each trait with every other trait. He found the following three characteristics of the correlation matrix, which helped to explain Asch's findings of the centrality of the *warm-cold* traits in personality impression formation.

1. The correlations between *warm-cold* and the other six traits on Asch's stimulus list were all relatively small. This means that *warm-cold* was adding new information about the person rather than uselessly repeating information already carried by the other stimulus traits.
2. The correlations of the other six stimulus traits with many of the traits on the response checklist used by Asch's subjects were relatively small. This means that these response traits were not strongly determined by knowledge of the other six stimulus traits.
3. The correlations between *warm-cold* and most of the traits on the response checklist were rather high.

These three facts explain the centrality of *warm-cold* traits in determining personality impressions in Asch's study. These facts also explain why some traits on the response checklist were not much affected by the *warm-cold* variable. These were cases where the second and/or third characteristic of the correlation matrix did not hold.

As a final demonstration of the power of his analysis, Wishner showed that he could create a situation that would produce exactly the sort of personality impression that he predicted. On the basis of his trait correlation matrix, Wishner picked a new stimulus list and a new response checklist, so that the two lists were relatively uncorrelated. Then he chose *humane-ruthless* as a central trait, which was not correlated with the traits on the stimulus list. Finally, Wishner correctly predicted that this central trait would have great weight in determining responses to the traits with which it was highly correlated, and little weight in determining responses to the traits with which it was not correlated.

Wishner's study has made an important theoretical contribution to our understanding of impression formation. Asch considered the stimulus traits as a Gestalt, which led him to conclude that whether a given trait was central or peripheral in its impact would depend upon its relationship to its context—that is, to the other *stimulus* traits. However, Wishner's analysis has shown that stimulus traits are less important in determining centrality than the central trait's relationship with the *response* traits. In this situation, a theoretical stimulus-response analysis seems more successful than a Gestalt analysis.

First Impressions. To study the effects of first impressions, Luchins (1957a, 1957b) wrote two short paragraphs chronologically describing some of the day's activities of a boy named Jim. In one paragraph, Jim walked to school with friends, basked in the sun on the way, talked with acquaintances in a store, and greeted a girl whom he had recently met. In the other paragraph Jim's activities were very similar, but his style was different: he walked home from school alone, stayed on the shady side of the street, waited quietly for service in a store, and did not greet a pretty girl whom he had recently met. The first paragraph (E) made subjects think of Jim as an extrovert; the second paragraph (I) made him seem an introvert.

Luchins then combined the two paragraphs either in the E-I order or in the I-E order. In either case the paragraphs formed a connected, chronological narrative, but they presented sharply conflicting information about Jim. After reading the two paragraphs, subjects were asked to rate Jim on a personality trait checklist. Luchins reasoned that if the information initially given was most important in determining personality impressions, then the E-I order should produce impressions more like the E paragraph alone; and the I-E order should produce impressions more like those of the I paragraph alone. This result would be called a **primacy effect.** A **recency effect,** however, would mean that the second paragraph was more dominant. The results of several experiments were consistent in showing a large primacy effect. Thus, first impressions are apparently very important in determining our reactions to other people.

Luchins continued his research and demonstrated that, under the right conditions, the primacy effect could be easily overcome, and a large recency effect could be produced. In this part of the study, subjects were warned about the dangers of being misled by first impressions, and they were asked to perform an unrelated mathematical task for five minutes between their readings of the first and second paragraphs about Jim. Under these conditions, the information most recently read was much more influential in determining impressions about Jim. In summarizing these experiments, Roger Brown (1965, p. 620) concluded: "Since life is filled with unrelated interpolated tasks, recency may actually be the more usual effect."

D. Accuracy of Person Perception

Let us now turn from the issue of how a person forms his impressions of other people to the question of how accurate a person's impressions really are.

Procedures in Determining Accuracy. In order to answer this question about the accuracy of impressions, three conditions are needed: a *stimulus* person and situation, a perceptual *response* or judgment by the subject, and a *criterion* with which to compare the response. Table 15-1 illustrates the very wide variety of materials that have been used in accuracy studies. In some instances (such as the opinions of informants), the adequacy of the criterion information may be doubted, and this factor must be considered in evaluating research studies in this area. Once a criterion is chosen, the typical research paradigm is simple. The subject's judgments are compared with the criterion data, and discrepancies on any items are treated as errors. The more errors, and the larger the errors, the poorer is the subject's accuracy score.

At this point, you may wish to refer back to the personality judgment exercise presented at the beginning of this chapter. Note your accuracy score in describing your friend, and review how it was obtained. We will be considering this research methodology in more detail as we proceed.

Characteristics of the Judgment Task. Some items in Figure 15-1 required only simple observation or knowledge on your part, whereas other items demanded a fairly remote inference about your friend and could not be answered directly from any of the behavior that you have observed. For instance, "talkative in social groups" is basically an observational item; but "dreams very frequently" is an inferential item (unless, by chance, your friend has told you about his dreams in some detail). Items 1, 4, 5, and 7 were intended to be primarily observational items, whereas items 2, 3, 6, and 8 were intended to be inferential. It might be interesting to go back and

Table 15-1. *Variety of Materials Used in Studying Accuracy of Person Perception*

1. Stimulus information (about the person to be judged)
    - photographs of person's face
    - motion pictures (either sound or silent)
    - observations of live behavior (for instance, through a one-way mirror)
    - face-to-face interactions (from brief interviews to long-term friendships)
    - tape recordings of conversation
    - psychological test protocols
    - written materials (from autobiographies to brief descriptive paragraphs)
    - personal productions (for example, handwriting, drawings)
    - general experience with people in a given culture
2. Perceptual response or judgment (by the subject or judge)
    - rating of personality traits (such as, "talkative")
    - postdicting real-life behaviors (of the stimulus person)
    - postdicting responses to specific test items
    - postdicting psychological test scores (such as, intelligence, achievement, or personality tests)
    - postdicting the judgments of experts (for instance, psychiatric diagnoses)
    - writing descriptive paragraphs (about the stimulus person)
    - matching two sets of materials (such as, test scores and personality descriptions)
    - ranking stimulus persons on a given trait
    - forced-choice responses (for example, which of two behaviors is more typical of the person)
3. Criterion information (the "real truth" about the stimulus person)
    - public, factual information (such as, age, job title, and the like)
    - scores on psychological tests
    - self-report data (for example, questionnaire items or interview responses)
    - factual information from knowledgeable informants (for instance, information about stimulus person's real-life behavior)
    - opinions or judgments from knowledgeable informants (such as, job supervisor, wife, family, friends, or psychotherapist)

(Adapted from Cline, 1964.)

score these two types of items separately. Was there any substantial difference in your accuracy on the two types of items? If so, were you more accurate on the observational items or on the inferential ones? (Remember, this is an error score, so a low score means high accuracy.)

Gage and Cronbach (1955) have distinguished three important dimensions of judgment task: (a) the degree of acquaintance between the judge and the other person, (b) the amount of extrapolation required by the task, and (c) the nature of the other people who are to be described. As regards the first dimension, it is fairly clear that you would probably make more errors, if you try to make judgments about a classmate whom you barely know.

The amount of extrapolation required by the task refers to the fact that some tasks may require only *knowledge* based on past experience, while other tasks may require the ability to *observe* and report one's observations, the ability to *infer* personal traits that have not been directly observed, or the combined ability to *observe and infer*. There is no reason to assume that a person who excels in one of these abilities will also excel in the others. Therefore, the nature of the judgment task must be considered in evaluating research results on this topic.

The nature of the other people who are to be described is a third important dimension of the judgment task. Some studies have asked judges to describe the characteristics of people in general (for instance, all U.S. citizens), of a category of persons (for example, college students), or of a particular group of people (your social psychology class). Such studies tap an ability that has been called **stereotype accuracy,** or the ability to correctly describe the population average or group norm, based on one's stereotype about the particular population or group in question. Other studies have asked judges to describe how an individual differs from his group or how an individual's behavior on one item (or trait) differs from his behavior on other items (or traits). These studies tap **differential accuracy,** or the ability to differentiate between a particular individual's score and the norm or average behavior. This distinction between stereotype accuracy and differential accuracy is an important one, which will recur often in our subsequent discussions.

A final characteristic of the person-perception judgment task is that it is subject to the influence of **response sets.** The particular response sets that occur most commonly here are somewhat different from those discussed in Chapter 2. Most troublesome is the **assumed similarity** effect, or the tendency to rate another person as similar to one's self. This is a major source of fallacious conclusions in interpreting person-perception accuracy scores. Its effects can best be visualized by imagining a person who assumes that everyone whom he rates is completely similar to himself. Such a person would turn out to be highly accurate in judging people who really are similar to him (his friends, for instance, or people from similar backgrounds). However, he would be very inaccurate in judging people who are really different from him. In both cases, his accuracy score would be the result of his assumed similarity response set; thus, the score would be an artifact rather than a true indication of the person's accuracy.

Artifacts and Components in the Measurement of Accuracy. An *artifact* is a research finding that does not reveal the true state of affairs but, instead, reflects the results of an arbitrary methodological approach. As we have seen, a judge's accuracy can be an artifact of a particular response set that he uses in making his ratings. This fact went unrecognized in the early years of person-perception research, resulting in many spurious and fallacious research findings. It was most clearly spelled out, however, in a brilliant article by Cronbach (1955), who, in a single stroke, made most of the preceding research in this field obsolete.

We can illustrate Cronbach's methodological critique by referring again to the exercise at the beginning of this chapter where you recorded (a) your descriptions of your friend, (b) your descriptions of yourself, and (c) your friend's self-descriptions (the criterion). This criterion, incidentally, is somewhat suspect as an adequate indication of the "real truth" about your friend, since he may not completely know himself.

The three sets of scores in columns (a), (b), and (c) were independent sets of data, which were combined, two at a time, by subtracting one column from another. Thus, we obtained three *difference scores*: |a-b|, |b-c|, |a-c| (where the vertical lines mean "the absolute value of"). The crucial point is that these three difference scores are not independent sets of data. When two difference scores have been computed, all of our three independent scores (a, b, and c) have been used, so the third difference score is already completely determined. This fact has been illustrated in our discussion of the assumed similarity effect. Our example showed that if *assumed similarity* (a-b) was very high, and *real similarity* (b-c) was also high, then *accuracy* (a-c) was already determined—in other words, it had to be high. Any combination of any two of the factors will completely determine the third. Low assumed similarity in combination with high accuracy means that real similarity must be low; high real similarity combined with low accuracy means that assumed similarity must be low, and so on.

Cronbach's (1955) article showed that the accuracy score could be broken down into four major components. In addition, he demonstrated the mathematical reason for the artifactual connection between accuracy and assumed similarity, proving that some of the components of the accuracy score were also components of the assumed similarity score. The four major components of the accuracy score are described subsequently.

1. *Elevation* is one component, which reflects the judge's way of using the response scale. It shows whether his average rating (across all items, or traits, and across all persons being rated) is close to the average of all the criterion ratings.
2. *Differential elevation* is another component, which shows the judge's ability to predict how far a given person's average trait score is above or below the average of the group being noted. That is, can the judge predict differences in the elevation (mean trait score) for individuals?
3. *Stereotype accuracy* is a third component, also mentioned in the preceding section on the characteristics of the judgment task. This component shows a judge's ability to predict the group norm on each trait; it has also been called "accuracy in predicting the generalized other."
4. *Differential accuracy* is the fourth component of the accuracy score. It shows a judge's ability to predict differences between individuals on each trait.

One of the most important conclusions made by Cronbach was that these four components of the accuracy score were all *independent* aspects of interpersonal perceptiveness. Thus, a judge could be good on some items but poor or mediocre on others. Consequently Cronbach recommended (a) that each component be computed and treated separately, (b) that overall accuracy scores be abandoned because their artifactual nature prevented meaningful interpretations, and (c) that particular attention be paid to stereotype accuracy and differential accuracy. These recommendations drastically transformed research in the field of person perception.

In a later article Cronbach (1958) made still another dramatic impact on person-perception research by raising cogent objections to the whole idea of computing accuracy scores. Instead, he recommended that we study the perceptual world of each judge separately and intensively before we complicate the research problem by adding another set of scores as a criterion and by studying the judge's accuracy. This recommended approach focuses our attention on the implicit personality theory of each judge—or, his conception of which personality traits typically go together. We will return to this topic later, when considering studies on the perceiver; for the moment, however, let us take up certain other aspects of accuracy in person perception.

Characteristics of a Good Judge. Many studies have asked what kind of person is able to make accurate personal judgments. Unfortunately, most of these studies were done prior to Cronbach's critiques and thus are subject to the criticism of artifactual spurious findings. For this reason, we must be cautious in reaching conclusions. We may, however, tentatively accept Taft's (1955) report that several studies yield fairly consistent evidence for each of the following characteristics of good interpersonal judges: (a) high intelligence and academic ability, (b) good emotional adjustment and integration, (c) esthetic and dramatic interests, (d) specialization in the physical sciences rather than in psychology.

How can we explain these paradoxical findings about psychologists being relatively poor judges of people? Taft suggests that psychologists may be too concerned about social relations and not detached or objective enough to be good judges; psychologists may have had too little experience with a wide variety of people. Though there may be a kernel of truth in these suggestions, a more basic reason for psychologists being poor judges of people may be their tendency toward overdifferentiation, a technical problem that will be described next.

One Reason for Poor Accuracy. Overdifferentiation of the persons being judged has been pointed to by Cronbach (1955) and other authors as a major source of judgmental errors. The explanation of this is a technical, statistical one, but the basic principle involved is simple. A judge will usually be more accurate if he makes most of his judgments close to the average level, for that is where most individuals actually score. If he makes many extreme judgments (ones far from the group norm), he may possibly be reacting correctly to the direction of individual differences in the trait, but he is probably overestimating the extent of these differences. As a result, the judge will have larger errors in his predictions than a person who makes less variable judgments. Thus, it is quite easy for a person acting as a rater or judge of others to be *oversensitive to individual differences.*

Dramatic evidence of oversensitivity comes from two studies. Gage (1952) had judges (students) make stereotypical predictions of the questionnaire responses of other students. The judges knew only that the other students were typical undergraduate education majors. Later Gage gave the judges a period of direct contact with these students and had the judges make another set of predictions on this basis. Surprisingly, the later predictions were somewhat less accurate than the predictions based only on stereotypic impressions. Similarly, Crow (1957) gave a group of medical students a special training course on noticing and handling personal relationships with their patients; he then compared their subsequent accuracy of person-perception with another group of medical students who had not received this training. Again, contrary to the intentions and expectations of the faculty, the trained subjects were somewhat less accurate in their personal judgments than the untrained group. Crow showed that this was due to the trained group's increase in variability of judgment, and he explicitly warned of the dangers of oversensitivity to individual differences as a factor leading to poor judgments about other people.

Generality of Accuracy. Let us suppose that, despite the many methodological problems involved, we have persevered in a person-perception study and found several judges who were quite accurate in their perception. Another important question that we might want to ask is: how general is their accuracy? That is, would these judges still get good scores if they were judging other persons or making judgments about different traits? This question has been studied with increasingly sophisticated techniques, since Cronbach's (1955) critique. We will briefly describe two such studies with somewhat conflicting results and attempt to resolve their differing conclusions.

Crow and Hammond (1957) concluded that they had found no evidence for generality of accuracy. Their study was done with 72 senior medical students who viewed six-minute sound films of a physician interviewing a medical patient. Altogether, the subjects saw films of 30 different patients, viewing 10 patients on three different occasions six months apart. After each film, the subjects had to estimate the self-ratings of the patient on seven personality scales and also the patient's real position on the same seven scales, as indicated by the Minnesota Multiphasic Personality Inventory (MMPI), a well-known personality inventory.

Crow and Hammond computed a measure of *differential accuracy* and three response set measures, which showed the judges' stereotypes about the scores of the patients. Correlations of these measures for the three different testing occasions showed that the response sets were quite stable over time, while the differential accuracy scores were less stable. Since previous studies had not usually separated response set components from accuracy scores, Crow and Hammond concluded that past findings of generality of accuracy might have resulted from the consistency of response sets rather than from consistency in judging ability.

Cline and Richards (1960) used a somewhat similar methodology, but with some crucial differences, and they reached conclusions largely opposed to the conclusions of the study just described. These researchers also used short sound movies of interviews as their stimuli, but they went to great pains to improve both the stimulus materials and the response measures. They used color movies of a diverse sample of adults, which ranged from a 65-year-old widow with two married children to a 22-year-old single male Mexican-American working in a meat packing plant. The interviews concentrated on personality characteristics, values, and interests, which probably gave a more rounded picture of the individual than Crow and Hammond's interviews. In addition, the final ten films that were used had been selected on the basis of their power to discriminate between good and poor judges—a procedure akin to improving a test by retaining only the best items. The final ten films were shown to a group of 50 students who were more diverse than the subjects in the Crow and Hammond study. Moreover, the films were all shown at one sitting instead of being spread over 12 months; thus, changes in judging over time were not a source of unreliability.

Cline and Richards' judging tasks were very carefully constructed, with a strong emphasis on good criterion information, obtained through very thorough case studies of each interviewee. Five different tasks were developed, and the predictions required of judges were considerably more detailed and varied than in Crow and Hammond's study. Furthermore, the judges in this study were given a chance to tune their perception by briefly inspecting the measuring instruments before seeing the films.

Cline and Richards followed Cronbach's (1955) recommendations by breaking down their judges' trait-rating scores into four basic components. As a result of the correlations obtained between these components and the other four judging tasks, the authors concluded that there is a general ability to perceive others accurately and that this ability is made up of two independent components—stereotype accuracy and differential accuracy. Thus, Cline and Richards found that the accuracy of a judge's social stereotype (which Crow and Hammond had dismissed as a response set) is the most important component of judgmental accuracy and helps to produce generality of accuracy. Our conclusion is that the results of the two studies are not at all incompatible but, rather, quite supportive of one another.

Since the time of these studies, Cline (1964) has continued to find evidence that judging ability is a general trait; he has also found that it is composed of several independent skills rather than a single skill. This seems to be the best conclusion at present.

Subjective Judgment versus Objective Decisions. Much of the daily work of clinical and counseling psychologists involves making judgments about other people. Consequently, they have been greatly interested in research on person perception and judgmental processes. Most clinical decisions are made on a subjective basis, with the use of whatever general knowledge the clinician has acquired about psychology, theoretical principles, and specific relevant information. This is true, for instance, in diagnosing types of emotional disturbances and in the myriad decisions that a psychotherapist has to make as he interacts with his clients.

Conversely, there are some kinds of clinical decisions that recur frequently and in similar forms, such as admission to or discharge from hospitals, acceptance for psychotherapy or counseling, testing for likelihood of success in college, and so on. In these instances, it is possible to build up norms and to make decisions on an objective basis, which can be validated through research. The contrast in methodology between objective decision making and the more prevalent subjective judgments has given rise to an area of research frequently referred to as *clinical versus statistical prediction.*

The terms *clinical* and *statistical* can be, and have been, defined in a variety of ways. Perhaps the most frequently used frame of reference is that of Meehl (1954), who wrote a classic book comparing the two methods of prediction. Meehl does not use the terms to refer to the kind of data but, rather, to the method of combining the data. Thus, clinical prediction can use either hard data (test scores, demographic information, grade point averages) or soft data (subjective impressions, therapists' ratings, interview or projective test themes). The key requirement of clinical prediction is that these data must be combined subjectively—that is, in the head of the clinician. By contrast, statistical prediction can also use either hard or soft data, but it must be combined objectively—that is, in some mechanical way that can be clearly specified and repeated with identical results for the same data time after time. Having established these definitions, Meehl reviewed all available studies comparing the two methods. His conclusion was that in almost every test, the statistical method of prediction was either equal to or better than the clinical method, regardless of whether the judges used were undergraduates, business managers, or Ph. D. clinical psychologists.

Other psychologists have been quick to enter the fray on one side or the other (Holt, 1958, 1970; Gough, 1962; Oskamp, 1962, 1967; L. R. Goldberg, 1965, 1968, 1970; Sawyer, 1966), and a lively controversy has ensued. The battles are by no means over. Holt, in particular, has very forcefully pointed out that clinical-judgment processes are essential at every step in the research activity that leads to formulas used in statistical predictions. This point is well taken, and Meehl agrees that, in research and psychotherapy, there is no substitute for subjective judgment. (See Figure 15-5 for example.)

Although Paul Meehl concludes that statistical prediction is equal to or better than clinical prediction, he recognizes that upon occasion a skilled clinical psychologist or psychiatrist can develop an accurate hypothesis, which no computer could ever match. Meehl recounts the following example of an accurate clinical hypothesis from Theodor Reik.

One session at this time took the following course. After a few sentences about the uneventful day, the patient fell into a long silence. She assured me that nothing was in her thoughts. . . . After many minutes she complained about a toothache. She told me that she had been to the dentist yesterday. He had given her an injection and then had pulled a wisdom tooth. The spot was hurting again. New and longer silence. She pointed to my bookcase . . . and said, "There's a book standing on its head." Without the slightest hesitation and in a reproachful voice I said, "But why did you not tell me that you had had an abortion?" (From Reik, *Listening with the Third Ear*. Copyright 1948 by Farrar, Straus & Giroux, Inc., and reproduced by permission.)

(Photograph courtesy of Carl Young.)

Figure 15-5. *The Power of Subjective Judgment.*

However, one other question can be posed here. This question is stated in the title of Meehl's (1957) paper: "When shall we use our heads instead of the formula?" Of course, this assumes that we have been able to develop a mechanical method to predict such outcomes as college success, job success, recidivism of a criminal, or readiness for hospital discharge. Given this situation, Meehl's answer to his own question is—practically never! He defends this conclusion by showing that even a valid clinical judgment is apt to add error variance to a set of mechanical predictions—a point that is related to the concept of oversensitivity to individual differences as a common failing of human judges. Our conclusion on this point is in agreement with Meehl (1957). Instead of intervening to change decisions made by a mechanical prediction system (when one is available), clinicians and counselors can spend their time much better by developing and validating additional mechanical prediction systems for types of recurrent decisions for which they have not as yet been used.

E. Person Perception and Interpersonal Behavior

A number of authors have used person-perception tasks in studying other areas of interpersonal behavior. One outstanding example is Fiedler (1964, 1967a), who has used assumed similarity scores of individuals to predict their success as leaders of groups. (For more information on Fiedler's theory of leadership, see Chapter 17.) Another example of a major study linking person perception to interpersonal behavior is Newcomb's (1960, 1961) study of the process of becoming acquainted with other people. During each of two semesters, 17 new transfer students to the University of Michigan were studied in depth. A research grant paid for the rent of a large house in which the 17 men were invited to live without charge, in return for their participation as subjects in the on-going research activities. Each week the men filled out questionnaires about their own attitudes and values, estimated the attitudes and values of the other 16 men, rated their friendships and the amount of contact they had with each of the other men, and so on. One example from this multifaceted study will suffice to illustrate how person perception is linked to social behavior.

Newcomb found that, as the men's interaction and contact with one another increased during the 15 weeks of the semester, their accuracy in estimating each other's values also increased. (The accuracy measure used combined stereotype accuracy and differential accuracy.) At the third week, their estimates of the most preferred group members were significantly more accurate than their estimates of least preferred group members. Apparently, the subjects knew their preferred individuals better than individuals who were not preferred. However, at the fifteenth week, this tendency was no longer true. Their knowledge about less preferred associates had increased markedly, but their knowledge about the best liked group members had increased very little. The explanation for the small degree of improvement in estimating preferred group members is interesting. The judges' errors in estimating highly attractive associates were almost entirely in the direction of overestimating the amount of similarity between themselves and their preferred associates, whereas for less preferred individuals only about two-thirds of the errors were in this direction. Apparently, we assume our friends are much more like us than they really are—a good illustration of the principle of cognitive balance discussed in Chapter 10.

Newcomb and Fiedler's investigations have clearly shown that a strong relationship exists between person perception and actual interpersonal behavior, but they have also shown that the relationship is not a complete one-to-one correspondence. We can sum up the relationship in the following principles, adapted from Hastorf, Schneider, and Polefka (1970, pp. 92–95).

1. Perceptual stability is partially due to real behavioral stability. That is, much of our perception is veridical, and much of people's behavior is relatively consistent over time.

2. Perceptual stability can continue despite some variation in other people's behavior. Our implicit personality theories make allowances for people having a bad day or for instances when their behavior is influenced by extreme circumstances. As long as exceptions do not occur too often, we can still perceive the other person as being consistently warm or helpful or whatever.

3. Perceptual stability is partially due to our restricted information about others. For instance, embarrassing or unpleasant traits are apt not to be displayed publicly. Also our initial impressions of people are often not tested further, so perceptual errors may not be corrected. In particular, negative impressions tend to lead to avoidance of the other person, which automatically prevents corrective feedback.

4. Initial impressions often produce confirmatory behavior from the other person, thus increasing perceptual stability. This is an example of the self-fulfilling prophecy. (See discussion of Rosenthal's research in Chapter 2.) If we perceive a person as helpful, we are very likely to treat him in a way that elicits helpful behavior from him; of course, the same principle applies if we perceive him negatively, as cold or hostile.

F. Theories about the Perceiver

The principle that perception can produce confirmatory behavior emphasizes the practical importance of studying the perceiver and his process of judgment. This principle is also quite consistent with Cronbach's (1958) suggestion that we should turn our attention away from accuracy scores and toward a study of the perceiver's cognitive maps about other people. Many recent studies have followed this advice, and consequently we are learning more about the phenomenological world of the perceiver. In this section, we will concentrate on theoretical viewpoints about the perceiver and the process of person perception.

Personal Constructs—George Kelly's Theory. Undoubtedly the most thoroughly developed theory about the perceiver's view of other people was constructed by George Kelly (1955, 1963) in his two-volume work, *The Psychology of Personal Constructs.* Of all theories of personality, this is the one, par excellence, to apply to the area of social perception, for it is built entirely around man's efforts to interpret and understand his world. It is a cognitive theory of man's behavior, and it stresses the connections between an individual's perception of stimuli, his interpretation of them, and his behavior. Kelly asserts:

> Man looks at his world through transparent patterns or templets which he creates and then attempts to fit over the realities of which the world is composed. . . . Let us give the name constructs to these patterns that are tried on for size. They are ways of construing the world (1955, pp. 8–9).

Construct is a key term for Kelly. It is a way of interpreting the world, a concept that a person uses to categorize events and to guide his behavior. Kelly's fundamental assumption about the nature of man is that *man is a scientist.* That is, just as a scientist tries to understand, predict, and control events, each human being tries in the very same way to choose constructs that will make his world understandable and predictable. In Kelly's theory, men do not strive for reinforcement nor seek to avoid anxiety; instead, they try to validate their construct systems. Furthermore, Kelly has discarded the notion of an objective, absolute truth in favor of the principle from phenomenology—namely, that conditions "are only meaningful in relation to the ways in which they are construed by the individual" (Pervin, 1970, p. 335).

The fundamental postulate in Kelly's theory is: "A person's processes are psychologically channelized by the ways in which he anticipates events" (1955, p. 46). In other words, our expectations direct our behavior. This basic postulate is presented as an underlying assumption, and no attempt is made to prove it. From this postulate, Kelly evolves 11 corollaries, which form the framework of his system.

Every construct (such as "likable") gives a basis for classifying the similarities and differences of people, objects, or events. Each person has developed only a limited number of constructs. Though some of a person's constructs may be inconsistent with others, there is a tendency toward an overall consistency of the construct system. One person's constructs are never completely identical to another person's. If one person's constructs are similar to another's, their behavior will also be similar. Finally, if one person understands another person's constructs, he will be able to behave appropriately toward the other person.

The method Kelly developed to measure personal constructs is called the Role Construct Repertory Test, or Rep Test. In this test a number of roles are listed (self, spouse, boss, friend, person you dislike, and so on). The subject is asked to name ways in which two of the individuals in these roles are alike and different from a third individual. This process is repeated many times for different combinations of roles, and the traits named most frequently by the subject are his major personal constructs.

The Rep Test has been used in empirical studies by many different researchers (compare the compilation by Bannister, 1970). One important variable that the Rep Test illuminated for us is **cognitive complexity,** or "the capacity to construe social behavior in a multidimensional way" (Bieri, Atkins, Briar, Leaman, Miller, & Tripodi, 1966). A good example of the way that cognitive complexity has been linked to other variables in person perception is provided in an experiment on impression formation by Mayo and Crockett (1964). They predicted that subjects who were low in cognitive complexity would show a **recency effect** when presented with two inconsistent sets of information about a hypothetical person. The reason for the effect would be these subjects' relative inability to assimilate inconsistent information and, thus, their tendency to reject the first set of information when presented with a second set of inconsistent data. In contrast, subjects high in cognitive complexity were expected to incorporate both sets of information into a more balanced impression, since they would expect both positive and negative traits to be present in other people. Results of the study supported both hypotheses. However, a more recent study by Petronko and Perin (1970) found that cognitively simple people give undue credence to the perceptually emphasized information (not necessarily to the most recent information).

Attribution of Causality—Fritz Heider's Theory. The other major theoretical approach that is relevant to person perception is attribution theory, which stems from the work of Fritz Heider (1958). In many ways, this theory is similar to Kelly's, for it deals primarily with factors influencing our perception of the world. However, the central focus of this theory is on the perception of causality, which is not particularly emphasized by Kelly. Heider stresses the notions that people perceive the behavior of others as being caused and that they attribute the cause either to the other person, to the environment, or to a combination of the two.

Heider postulates that a person's effect on events involves both his ability and his effort, and it is only when both factors are present that we hold a person responsible for events and attribute to him certain dispositional properties or traits. We evaluate a person's ability in relation to environmental forces, so that even a very able person is not expected to do something very difficult, such as lift an automobile. Similarly, we evaluate a person's effort in terms of two components: his intentions and his level of exertion. What a person intends to do is often hard to determine because his actions have both unintended and intended consequences. Nevertheless, each of us makes attributions about the intentions of others on the basis of our observations of their behavior.

The principles of attribution theory have been extended and made more precise in important papers by Jones and Davis (1965), by Harold Kelley (1967), and in a book by Daryl Bem (1970). Jones and Davis hold that perceivers first observe a person's actions, then infer the person's intentions from his actions, and finally infer his traits or dispositions from his intentions. They suggest four variables that determine the strength and confidence with which such dispositional attributions will be made: social desirability, common effects, hedonic relevance, and personalism.

1. The *social desirability* of the person's actions decreases the strength of attributions. We assume that the person intended the desirable effects of his actions rather than any undesirable ones. Since most people act in socially desirable ways most of the time, such behavior gives us little information about their real characteristics.

2. The *common effects* of two actions provide a basis for attributions about the actor's traits. For instance, the girl who acts warm and responsive toward her companion on an expensive dinner-and-theater evening *and* on a simple Coke date is seen as genuinely friendly rather than as a gold digger. The other side of this coin is that *noncommon effects* between a chosen action and a nonchosen one provide a basis for attributions. The boy who asks a girl only to a Coke date, when it is known that he has two tickets to the latest hit play and could have asked her to it, will probably be seen as not seriously interested in her.

3. The *hedonic relevance* of the person's actions (that is, the extent to which they are rewarding or costly to the perceiver) increases the strength of attributions. If your actions hurt me or help me materially, I am more likely to conclude that you are a harmful or helpful person than I would be if your actions affected someone else rather than me.

4. The *personalism* of the other's actions (that is, the extent to which they are seen as being directed specifically at the perceiver) increases the strength of attributions. This principle represents a further extension of the hedonic relevance principle. If your actions hurt me and I perceive that they were directed specifically at me, I am even more likely to conclude that you are a hurtful person.

Extensions of attribution theory by Daryl Bem (1965, 1970) and Harold Kelley

(1967) include the conditions for making attributions to external entities, rather than to persons. Kelley suggests that the criteria of the validity of external attribution can be used to organize much of the social psychological literature on the processes of **social influence.** This includes research on the conditions governing (a) susceptibility to persuasion, (b) the immediate success of persuasion, and (c) persistence of the effects of persuasion. Kelley proposes:

> Person A will be more susceptible to influence the more variable his prior attribution has been. Attribution instability (and, hence, susceptibility to influence) will be high for a person who has (a) little social support, (b) prior information that is poor and ambiguous, (c) problems difficult beyond his capabilities, (d) views that have been disconfirmed because of their inappropriateness or nonveridicality, and (e) other experiences engendering low self-confidence (1967, p. 200).

An important point made by Bem is that the processes of self-perception and of other-perception are substantially similar. Thus attribution theory can also be applied to research on the self-concept and to therapeutic methods that stress self-awareness. (For more information on this theoretical approach the interested reader is referred to the papers cited above and to a clearly organized summary of research on attribution theory in Hastorf, Schneider, and Polefka, 1970, pp. 70–89.)

IV. FUTURE TRENDS IN STUDYING SOCIAL PERCEPTION

Four main trends may be cited as possible future developments in the area of social perception. First, as a better understanding of the factors in social perception develops, the typical research methodology will continue to become increasingly complex. This has been particularly true in the study of person-perception accuracy, where the earlier, simpler methodologies were rendered uninterpretable by the presence of statistical artifacts. Tagiuri (1969) summarizes this trend as follows:

> The technology is by now very complex and tends, at times, to obscure the main issues. Simpler approaches and formulations have not stood up, however, and the current cumbersome methodologies and fragmentation of the problem may be unavoidable until some fresh formulation is reached. . . . The methodological intricacies may, however, be inappropriate to the complexity of the process. . . . The subtlety and delicacy of the process of coming to know other persons has never been underestimated, but empirical, naturalistic, and theoretical evidence now available suggests that it is even more complex than one ever dreamt of (p. 432).

Second, there has been a decided lack of theoretical underpinnings for most of the research in social perception. Tagiuri colorfully describes the state of affairs as "an excess of empirical enthusiasm and . . . a deficit of theoretical surmise" (1969, p. 433). The recent research stemming from Bem's self-perception theory, from attribution theory, and from George Kelly's personal construct theory is providing a partial correction for this hiatus, but there is still a great need for more adequate theoretical bases for many aspects of research in the field.

Third, so far we have only begun to integrate the field of social perception with the more traditional areas of psychology. Tagiuri indicates that social perception overlaps with the following other general areas of study: cognition, perception, learning, concept formation, personality, clinical diagnosis, and quantitative methods. The overlapping that occurs in these areas is worthy of future detailed attention.

Finally, the relation of social perception to actual interpersonal behavior needs much more thorough study. Dunnette (1968) has suggested broadening our focus to study *interpersonal accommodation*, or the process of back-and-forth interaction that uses perceptual feedback to modify behavior and approach a desired equilibrium state in social interaction. Tagiuri suggests future "studies of the judgments made about persons in the course of ordinary transactions with their environment . . . where people are truly interacting, and where observer and observed are simultaneously judge and object" (1969, p. 435). As has recently been discovered in the area of attitudes and behavior (Wicker, 1969), it is possible that we may find major discontinuities between perception and behavior, despite our traditional assumptions and accumulated evidence of their general correspondence.

V. SUMMARY

Our perceptual experience is characterized by immediacy, structure, stability, meaningfulness, and selectivity. Though perception in general is usually veridical (accurate), there is ample evidence from perceptual illusions and from the psychology of testimony to show that it can be incorrect.

Major questions in the study of social perception concern the degree of veridicality of our perception, the conditions which lead to nonveridicality, and the factors (in ourself, in the other person, and in the social situation) that affect our perception of another person.

Major aspects of stimuli that can influence how they are perceived include their value, their emotional meaning to the perceiver, their familiarity, and their intensity. Study of these dimensions has led to interesting (and often conflicting) findings concerning perceptual accentuation, perceptual defense, perceptual sensitization, effects of repeated exposure, and subliminal perception.

Some personality characteristics, such as the defensive styles of repression versus sensitization and the cognitive style of psychological differentiation (also called field-independence), are intimately related to perceptual responsiveness.

It is usually only where the conditions for perception are unclear or confusing that stimulus, personality, group, or cultural factors act to produce any major effects on perception.

In classifying other people, prejudiced individuals use ethnic stereotypes more loosely and more frequently than do nonprejudiced persons. As a consequence, most of the mistakes in identification made by the anti-Semite, for instance, are in the direction of labeling non-Jews as Jews, rather than in the reverse direction.

Central traits like *warm-cold* are important in forming our impressions of people only when the central traits are highly correlated with the other traits that we wish to predict, and *not* because of their relationship to the other stimulus traits that we have observed.

The *primacy effect* of first impressions may strongly influence our opinions about people. However, if conflicting additional information is received at a later time, a *recency effect* is apt to result.

Research results in the study of person-perception accuracy have been confused and contradictory due to marked effects of the different procedures used, the response sets that may influence scores, and the statistical artifacts that are inherent in the method of measurement.

One of the most important characteristics of a good (in other words, accurate) judge of other people is that he avoids the mistake of overdifferentiation—or, oversensitivity to the individual differences of the people being judged.

Research evidence indicates that the ability to judge other people accurately is, at least partially, a general trait, which is relatively stable across various judging tasks and across various people to be judged. This ability has at least two major independent components: *stereotype accuracy*, or the ability to predict the group mean or knowledge of the generalized other, and *differential accuracy*, or the ability to predict differences between individuals on any given trait.

Important correspondences have been found between person-perception characteristics and some aspects of interpersonal behavior, such as leadership and voluntary interaction. However, this is an area that needs much more extensive research.

Another area that is receiving increasing attention is the perceiver's process of social judgment. Important contributions to this area have been made by the theories of George Kelly and Fritz Heider and by related research and theorizing originally stemming from their viewpoints.

Future trends in the field of social perception are likely to include the continuation of complex methodology to match the subtleties of the processes involved, an increase in theoretical foundations for empirical research, a growing integration with the more traditional areas of psychology, and more extensive study of the correspondence between social perception and interpersonal behavior.

VI. SUGGESTED READINGS

Cline, V. B. Interpersonal perception. In B. A. Maher (Ed.), *Progress in experimental personality research.* Vol. 1. New York: Academic Press, 1964. Pp. 221–284. A thorough review of previous work in the field, combined with a detailed treatment of the author's original work on accuracy and generality of interpersonal judgment.

Gage, N. L., & Cronbach, L. J. Conceptual and methodological problems in interpersonal perception. *Psychological Review,* 1955, **62,** 411–422. Perhaps the most easily understandable of the methodological critiques that revolutionized the study of interpersonal perception.

Hastorf, A. H., Schneider, D. J., & Polefka, J. *Person perception.* Reading, Mass.: Addison-Wesley, 1970. (Paperback) A clearly written short volume, which gives a very useful review and evaluation of research and theory on person perception.

Meehl, P. E. *Clinical versus statistical prediction: A theoretical analysis and a review of the evidence.* Minneapolis: University of Minnesota Press, 1954. The classic early statement of the controversy between subjective judgment methods and objective decision procedures.

Tagiuri, R. Person perception. In G. Lindzey and E. Aronson (Eds.), *Handbook of social psychology.* (2nd ed.) Vol. 3. Reading, Mass.: Addison-Wesley, 1969. Pp. 395–449. A scholarly summary of the present state of knowledge about the perception of persons.

Tajfel, H. Social and cultural factors in perception. In G. Lindzey and E. Aronson (Eds.), *Handbook of social psychology.* (2nd ed.) Vol. 3. Reading, Mass.: Addison-Wesley, 1969. Pp. 315–394. An erudite review of our accumulated knowledge about social and cultural influences on perception.

Chapter Sixteen

Conformity and Social Influence

As for conforming outwardly, and living your own life inwardly, I do not think much of that. *Henry David Thoreau*

The best prognosis for any child is to be slightly maladjusted. To be perfectly adjusted to one's surroundings . . . creates a poor prognosis for later life. *David Riesman*

A typical rally on the Yale University campus during the early 1970s would have included long-haired, casually dressed students carrying signs advocating "Free the Black Panthers" or "Stop the killing in Asia." More than likely, no one advocating a contradictory position would have been present. At the same time, there were other college campuses—often small, church-related colleges—where neatly dressed students, wearing coats and ties, were mobilizing support for the President and his military policy.[1] Had anyone on this type of campus started a petition to "Free Huey Newton" (a Black Panther leader then being jailed in California), he would not only have been rebuffed by his fellow students but, possibly, inquisitioned by the college administration.

How can students at one college be so different from those at another in regard to dress, moral values, and political activism? Of course, self-selection is one important factor; students choose to go to a college where the predominant values, expressed through student actions and administrative policies, are similar to their own. But once a college has been selected, individual students are subjected to vehement pressures toward uniformity. Behavior is more likely to be rewarded if it conforms to the dominant values of the student subculture. Despite their many differences, Yale University and, for example, Abilene Christian College both exert pressures

[1] Shortly after the killing of the Kent State students, a letter to the editor of a Nashville newspaper reflected the conservative position held on campuses different from Yale or Kent State: "I attend David Lipscomb College, and upon this Christian campus you will not find rioters in action. I will grant you the point that the college is not the size of Kent, but [our students] know that they must stay within the limits of society's standard. . . . There has always been proper authority, and my generation must realize this before it is everlastingly too late" (Nashville *Tennessean,* May 19, 1970).

toward uniformity in belief, action, and expression.[2] As political viewpoints in our country become more polarized, greater pressures are manifested toward conforming to some ideological position.

The purpose of this chapter is to explore types of conformity, the extent of conformity in our society, and the ways in which others influence or change our behavior. One specific effect of social influence, group risk taking, will receive detailed attention.

I. DEFINITIONS OF CONFORMITY AND RELATED PHENOMENA

Margaret Williams brushes her teeth after every meal. Is she demonstrating conformity because she does what her dentist tells her to do? Eddie Stephens, a 13-year-old, violates every suggestion his parents lay before him. If his mother tells him his green shirt would look nice for the dance, he wears his purple one. If his father tells him he had better wear tennis shoes while working on the roof, he goes barefooted. Do these choices simply ignore pressures toward conformity, or are they motivated, deliberate anticonforming behaviors on Eddie's part? Or, do these actions represent Eddie's healthy search for identity and independence? Commander William Bucher of the U. S. Navy ship *Pueblo* signed a statement of guilt in order to save his crew from punishments and torture by the North Koreans. Does his behavior reflect conformity?

These examples suggest the possibility of confusion when we consider terms such as *conformity, uniformity, conventionality, anticonformity,* and others. As used by social psychologists, each term has a separate meaning. We shall attempt to define them here.

A. Conformity

One reason *conformity* is a confusing term is that psychologists use it as a label for different phenomena. Kiesler (1969) identifies three uses of the term conformity: (a) going along with the group, or behaving in a way consistent with that of the majority, (b) a change in attitudes or beliefs as a result of group pressure, and (c) a basic personality trait. All these usages will be discussed in the following sections.

Because of these variations, it is best to think of conformity as a generic term, defined as *yielding to group pressures.* But, we could ask: what is yielded? Kiesler and Kiesler, in a recent text, define it as "a change in *behavior or belief* toward a group as a result of real or imagined group pressure" (1969, p. 2, italics added). The use of the word *change* in this definition of conformity implies that the resultant

[2] A recent survey of student reactions in colleges across the country concluded that "college environments operate so as to produce a greater degree of homogeneity among the students with respect to field of study and career choice. Further research should be conducted to determine whether this 'progressive conformity' effect holds true for other student characteristics including values, beliefs, personal traits, and behavior patterns" (Astin & Panos, 1969, p. 149). We expect that further study of college climates will reveal that this generalized progressive conformity is almost always present.

response deviates from one's earlier private opinion, preference, or perception. For example, if a student does not want to put on a black armband but does so because everybody in his dormitory is doing it, he clearly shows conformity. But what if he privately lacks any preference in one direction or the other but wears the armband because others ask him? Does his action then reflect conformity? Probably, it does because his action is still a change in behavior resulting from pressure by others.

B. Compliance versus Private Acceptance: Two Types of Conformity

Changes in actions *or* in private attitudes can reflect conformity, and these two types of changes reflect different types of phenomena. If a student is asked to wear a black armband, his response may actually reflect one of the following four possible combinations (Allen, 1965):

1. His behavior may conform (wears armband), and his private attitude may be in support of the movement.
2. His behavior may conform (wears armband), but his private attitude is negative. (Privately he feels it is wrong to wear an armband, but he does so to please a friend or to gain favor.)
3. His behavior may be nonconforming (refuses to wear armband), and his private attitude may be antagonistic to the movement.
4. His behavior may be nonconforming (refuses to wear armband) even though his private attitude is in support of the movement. (Perhaps he is afraid that his parents will hear about it and that they will reprimand him.)

Festinger (1953a) and, more recently, Kiesler and Kiesler (1969) distinguish between these two types of changes by labeling conforming behavior *compliance* and conforming private attitudes *private acceptance.* The research literature has not reflected the impact of this useful distinction. Classic studies on conformity have usually dealt only with compliance; thus, in our subsequent descriptions of these studies, we shall refer to this limitation by labeling them *studies of conformity (compliance).* Private acceptance of pressures to conform may be equated with *attitude change.* (See Chapter 11.)

C. Uniformity

Uniformity is not the same phenomenon as conformity. As Krech, Crutchfield, and Ballachey (1962, p. 505) indicate, there may be general agreement in a society over facts or beliefs without their being the result of social pressures.[3] The majority of Americans would agree that a chest x-ray once a year is a desirable health practice. The near uniformity of this response is not a function of majority pressures; similarity in response occurs for other reasons than group influence.

[3] Probably, there is no belief that is held with complete uniformity by all adults in a society. For example, a survey by the Knight newspapers in early 1970 indicated that a significant minority of American adults did not believe that two men walked on the moon on July 20, 1969. A total of 1721 persons were surveyed in cities and several rural areas. Percentages of persons who doubted that the moon walk had actually occurred ranged from 8 percent in one community to 54 percent in another.

D. Conventionality

Conventionality may be defined as acting in what is a customary or usual fashion, or as adherence to the standard practices of society. Saying goodbye at the end of a telephone conversation is, in our society, a conventional response; it does not reflect conformity as we have defined it. As Krech et al. (1962) pointed out, highly conforming individuals are more likely to maintain conventional values. (Conventionality is also one of the nine components of the authoritarian personality.) But just because a person is highly conventional in matters of his dress, his spoken speech, or even his basic values, his behavior will not necessarily conform to group pressures.

E. Independence

If conformity is yielding to group pressures, what is the opposite of conformity? We may think of two different types of opposing, nonconforming responses. One is *independence,* defined as the maintenance and expression (through behavior) of one's private beliefs in the face of group pressures to do something to the contrary. If a Yale student believed that the Black Panthers were guilty and if he refused to sign a petition in their behalf even though all his friends had asked him to do so, his response would be characterized as independence. The essential ingredient for an independent response is the prior establishment of a private opinion that is expressed unremittingly, even though it contradicts majority opinion and/or group pressure.

F. Anticonformity or Counterformity

What about the person who rejects group pressures to conform simply because he is rebellious? Regardless of the content of the influence, he may reject it. The term **anticonformity,** or *counterformity*, is used to refer to a response, which is opposed to the majority and which is generated by the majority's response. As in the case of independence, the important determinant is the individual's motivation for his chosen response; if a particular response occurs only because it is contrary to majority pressures, we may consider it anticonforming. If Eddie selects a purple shirt only because his parents want him to wear the green one, he is manifesting not independence, but anticonformity. The group's opinion serves as a negative reference point.

Thus, two persons may behave the same way, but their actions may reflect different phenomena. In studying the reasons why some American prisoners of war did not collaborate with the Chinese Communists during the Korean War, psychologists discovered that there were two types of resisters. (A resister was an American soldier who did not succumb to the Chinese appeals to collaborate.) Some resisted because they knew that admitting guilt for the war, broadcasting peace appeals, and the like were wrong actions; these men were the independent resisters. Another group of resisters had a long history of unwillingness to accept any kind of authority; they did not conform to commands in the U. S. Army, and neither did they obey the Chinese (Schein, 1957; Kinkead, 1959). These men could justifiably be classified as showing anticonformity or counterformity.

II. EARLY PROCEDURES AND FINDINGS IN THE STUDY OF CONFORMITY (COMPLIANCE)

A. The Asch-Type Situation: Conformity (Compliance) in the Laboratory

Suppose that a college student who has volunteered to participate in a research project finds that he is a subject in a visual perception experiment. Along with six other subjects (in actuality, confederates), he is seated at a circular table. The group is shown a board with a vertical line drawn on it. With this line still in view, all the group members look at another board, which has three vertical lines of differing lengths. One of these lines is actually identical in length to the line on the first board; the other two lines are different enough so that in controlled tests (done individually, not in groups) more than 95 percent of subjects make correct judgments about the length of the lines. The subjects are instructed to state their choices out loud and one at a time. The actual subject always responds next to last. On the first trial and again on the second trial, everyone gives the same response—namely, the response that the real subject has judged to be the correct one. The volunteer may begin to think that this task is easy. The same outcome occurs on several more trials; then, on a subsequent trial—where the choice appears as clear-cut as those before—the first subject-confederate gives a response that our friend perceives to be clearly incorrect. All the other subject-confederates follow suit, giving the wrong response. (In actuality, it is the wrong response, for all the confederates are trained in advance to give the same incorrect response on certain critical trials.) When it comes time for the real subject to respond, all the other persons at the table have given an answer that he believes is wrong. What does he do? Does he stick by his convictions, remain independent, and give the correct response? Does he comply with the group, giving an answer he knows is wrong? Or, does he convince himself that he must be wrong and that the group's answer is correct?

This was the procedure used in an early set of studies on conformity (compliance) by social psychologist Solomon Asch (1951, 1956, 1958). Since this set of studies is regarded as a classic in social psychology, we are required to report the findings. Our attention, however, will be focused upon the conceptual and procedural limitations of these studies as tests of conformity.[4]

How does the volunteer in the Asch-type conformity situation respond? One cannot make a statement that applies to all subjects. In the original Asch studies, a significant minority (about 33 percent) never conformed, but a very small percentage (8 percent) conformed to the group pressure on almost all the critical trials. Over all, 32 percent of the time the average subject conformed on critical trials, and 68

[4]After the 20-year interim that has passed since the time of these pioneering studies, it is easy to be critical. The Asch studies were, indeed, a ground-breaking contribution to the study of conformity and social influence. Unfortunately, research methodology has not developed as fast as new conceptualizations of conformity.

percent of the time he remained independent. The usefulness of this average is very limited, however, because of wide individual differences. We will have more to say about these findings later.

B. Limitations to the Asch-Type Procedure

Conformity, as used by Asch, refers to behavior that agrees with the behavior of others in a group and is contradictory to the subject's private opinion or preferences. Thus, according to Asch's procedures, on each critical trial the subject's response must either conform (that is, yield to the majority) or be independent. A conformity score for each subject can be determined by counting up the number of times he conforms on critical trials.

Two important limitations stem from Asch's operational definition. First, conformity refers to public compliance and has nothing to say about private acceptance. Some of Asch's conformists may have changed their private opinion; others may have been expedient conformers in the sense that they conformed in order to gain acceptance by the group. Asch's operational definition does not distinguish between these two types of changes. Interviews with subjects after the experiments led Asch to conclude that only a few of them internalized the group's answer. Most subjects came to doubt their perceptions, however, in the face of the consensus.

A second limitation to Asch's procedure is that the occurrence of anticonformity or counterformity is made very difficult. In everyday life, as indicated previously, we interpret some actions as primarily the result of a need to be different; on the critical trials in the Asch-type situation, there is no way for a person to show anticonformity. (On the noncritical trials, the subject could show anticonformity by giving an incorrect judgment when the group gave a correct judgment.)

Another problem with Asch's procedure as a test of real-life conformity relates to the subject's involvement in the task. Just how important is this task to the average subject? On the one hand, we might assume that a subject becomes very ego-involved in the task when he finds that others disagree with him. He may strain to do well and may feel great conflict. On the other hand, a subject may think: "What the hell! It's only a silly psychology experiment. Why sweat it? I may as well answer like everyone else does." The latter reaction may cause a rate of conformity (compliance) that would differ from the conformity in real-life situations where the degree of ego involvement is greater. In a similar fashion, the subject in the experiment may see the demand characteristics as dictating a conforming response on his part. This is speculation; as yet, we do not know the facts. Would the subject who yields in the Asch experiment yield in the same way to pressures from friends who wish to involve him in their all-night poker game? The two situations differ in many ways—the risks of conforming, the degree of clarity in identifying the correct response, the nature of the social pressure, and so on. If we found a different rate of yielding in the real-life situation, this and other factors would have to be considered.

Undoubtedly, conformity does occur in the laboratory even at the price of great tension and conflict, as Milgram's study on obedience has indicated. But in both the Milgram and Asch experiments some of the subjects may have been manifesting an "as if" reaction—that is, they may have been behaving as if the conditions were valid, while still being highly suspicious of the reality of the conditions. Because of these and other reasons, it is hazardous to assume that the extent of conformity found in the Asch tasks would occur in real-life situations.

C. Refinements in the Conceptualization of Conformity

Due to concerns like those described in the preceding section, several psychologists have emphasized that conformity is not a simple unitary process. Conformity in situations where investment is low (as in the Asch-type situation) is a different process from conforming in situations where the investment is high (as in a case where a boy's friends decide to steal a car and try to persuade him to participate). Similarly, there is a difference in a practical sense as well as in a conceptual sense whether the advocated position agrees or conflicts with local norms. When a person is pressured to adopt a new position that varies from the position defined by social custom but refuses to adopt this new position—is he conforming or not? For example, in the early 1970s some Southern white parents refused to register their children when previously all-white schools were desegregated. These parents were labeled nonconformists, but they were clearly conforming to popular local traditions. Analysts of the conformity process, such as Jahoda (1959), Willis (1965), and Kiesler and Kiesler (1969), tell us that conformity is not an either-or process; a single act can be in compliance with laws and at variance with pressures from the populace, or vice versa. We must know the total context in which behavior occurs before we can decide whether it is conforming.

Another complexity derives from the fact that a person can change his public position—to avoid torture, to get elected, to persuade his girlfriend—while maintaining his original private opinion. In such cases, has the person conformed? Galileo was forced by the Roman Catholic Church to recant publicly his heretical position that the earth revolved around the sun. He finally did so—yet murmured: "It still moves." Galileo complied publicly but did not privately accept the Church's pressure.

Jahoda's Model: Three Aspects of Conformity. Jahoda (1959) proposed eight possible types of actions, each being a different combination of three factors. These are represented in Table 16-1. Notice that the issue adopting or rejecting the advocated position is represented on the second line and that the consistency between the subject's public position and his final private position is shown on the third line. The eight possible results are labeled on the last line. Let us take a concrete example and see how each action might be represented. Suppose a college student is approached by a friend and asked to sign a petition in favor of equal pay for women. If we assume that the student has a great deal of initial investment in the issue, processes *a* through *d* apply. Though Jahoda is not explicit here, we assume that in most cases the student's initial private opinion is that the request to sign the petition should be rejected.

Process *a* is called by Jahoda *independent dissent.* Here the person has strong feelings about the issue, does not adopt the advocated position (refuses to sign the petition), and maintains a private opinion that coincides with his public action. We would infer that this person has strong feelings against the Women's Liberation Movement before he is approached; we know that he refuses to sign and is—in Jahoda's words—at ease with himself about the public position he has taken.

Table 16-1. *Types of Conformity and Independence*

Initial investment in issue	Yes				No			
Public adoption of advocated position (signing petition)	No		Yes		No		Yes	
Private opinion same as public opinion	Yes	No	Yes	No	Yes	No	Yes	No
Designation of Process	a	b	c	d	e	f	g	h
	(Independent dissent)	(Undermined independence)	(Independent consent)	(Compliance)	(Compulsive resistance)	(Expedient resistance)	(Conformity, or acquiescence)	(Expedient conformity)

(Modified from Jahoda, 1959.)

Process *b* refers to a case where a person is equally involved in the issue, also refuses to sign the petition, but experiences a shift in his private opinion. That is, his initial anti-Women's Liberation position causes him to refuse to sign the petition, but somehow he is now privately convinced that the petition is a good thing. Jahoda calls this *undermined independence,* which indicates that the influence process has undermined the student's private position. If we can assume that subjects in the Asch study were involved in their task, the nonyielders who continued to report their true answers but developed doubts about their eyesight would represent process *b*.[5]

Processes *c* and *d* represent persons who are initially against Women's Liberation, who are very involved in the issue, but whose public position is influenced by the request. They sign the petition ("Yes" on line 2 of Table 16-1). Process *c* reflects what happens to the person who not only publicly advocates the position of the petition but also privately comes to accept this viewpoint. Jahoda calls this *independent consent.* Thus, the subject's position is now free of conflict, since both his public and private positions are consistent. Perhaps, this student restructured or clarified the manner in which he viewed the issue—almost a necessity in light of his initial involvement in the topic.

Process *d* reflects public adoption of the advocated position combined with a failure to adopt a consistent private opinion. An example of process *d* would occur when the college student signs the petition, despite his strong feelings against Women's Liberation. Galileo's action is a prime example of this process, which Jahoda calls *compliance*; such an example indicates that severe threats upon the person may cause the apparently inconsistent behavior and beliefs of process *d*. Certain congressmen—particularly those in the same party as the President—may vote for a bill or

[5] Many arguments between husbands and wives may represent process *b*. Both parties are involved; one outwardly refuses to go along with the request of the other, even though he or she has privately become convinced that the other's position is right.

a Supreme Court nominee even though their privately held negative feelings have not been changed by pressures from the executive branch.

The remaining four processes in Table 16-1 reflect cases where the student's initial involvement in the issue is minimal. Here, when approached to sign the Women's Liberation petition, the student may never have thought about the issue before and may not care about it presently. In process *e*, the student refuses to sign the petition and does not feel any conflict between what he has done and what he believes. Jahoda labels this *compulsive resistance* and describes it as an unreasonable position. She expects this type of behavior only "in those who lack the essential ability to respond to external pressure, or in those who reject a stand just because it is demanded by others" (1959, p. 114).

Process *f*, called *expedient resistance,* represents the action taken by a person who has no initial investment in the issue, who refuses to sign the petition, but who feels in his heart that the goal of the petition is appropriate. As Jahoda indicates, this reaction does not appear to be psychologically plausible; however, other factors, such as a momentary dislike for the friend, might cause this response.

If a person is asked by a friend to sign a petition favoring an issue about which he has no strong feelings, he may do so as a favor to the friend, or because he trusts his friend's judgment. He may even privately adopt the position. This response (process *g*) Jahoda labels *conformity*; she evaluates it as a very reasonable type of behavior in cases where the person has little investment in the issue. Note that Jahoda reserves the term *conformity* for cases where the subject has little investment in the issue. We prefer to use conformity as a generic term that also applies in high-investment situations, and therefore we would rather call process *g acquiescence.*

The remaining possibility, process *h,* describes the result when an initially uninvolved person signs the petition even though the recruitment has not influenced his private opinion. This *expedient conformity* may reflect a responsiveness to social pressures; this person may think, "I'll sign it to please my friend, even though I don't agree with it; after all, it's no big deal to me." American prisoners of war who did not feel much concern about national issues and hence made peace broadcasts for the North Koreans and Communist Chinese reflected expedient conformity. Opportunistic prisoners of war found that such collaboration brought them special treatment—their mail from home was delivered more quickly, and their work details were easier. Thus, it was expedient to conform.

Willis' Diamond Model. Other psychologists who are dissatisfied with a simplistic, unidimensional view of conformity have posited multidimensional approaches. Willis (1963, 1965) offers a two-dimensional model that utilizes four possible response modes: conformity, independence, anticonformity, and variability. Conformity and anticonformity are seen as opposite ends of one dimension. *Conformity*, to Willis, consists of "a completely consistent attempt to behave in accordance with normative expectation as perceived"; *anticonformity* is behavior that is deliberately "antithetical to the norm prescription" (1965, p. 379). Thus anticonformity is just as responsive to the norms of how to behave as is conformity. We can think of this one dimension as ranging from norm-responsive (conformity) to norm-disregarding to norm-responsive again (anticonformity).

According to Willis, independence and variability form the second dimension. *Independence* occurs in cases where normative expectations carry no weight in determining a person's response. *Variability* describes the unusual case where "the

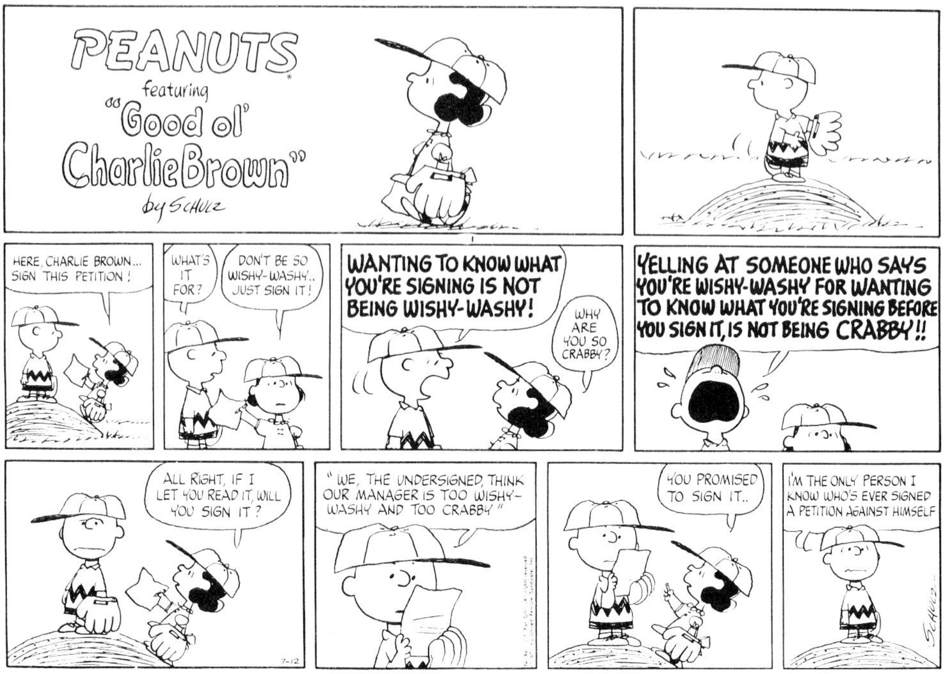

Figure 16-1. *Petition Signing in the Real World. (Copyright 1970 United Feature Syndicate, Inc.)*

individual invariably changes his response if given the opportunity" (Willis, 1965, p. 379). Willis sees the mind that changes without any consideration of norm expectations as a second kind of detachment from the social environment. Variability gives no weight to norm expectations in formulating its response, and in that regard it resembles independence. Willis identifies the axis of this dimension as an independence-dependence-independence axis. (See Figure 16-2.) Each end represents a kind of independence, and the centerpoint reflects awareness of norms. According to Willis, one virtue of his diamond model is that it does not oppose conformity with independence. Rather, these phenomena are posited as two separate functions. At present, Willis' model seems more appropriate to multitrial experiments with binary choices, where, on each trial, the subject is first shown the response of the other subject and then makes his choice. Responses in this kind of task can be evaluated to determine their degree of independence and their degree of conformity. In binary-choice tasks, the degree of these two responses is so uncorrelated that evidence exists for the presence of two independent dimensions (Willis, 1963; Willis & Hollander, 1964).

In more traditional measures of conformity an arrow-shaped model like that in Figure 16-3 may be most accurate. Stricker, Messick, and Jackson (1970) tested the extent of conformity, anticonformity, and independence in four different tasks. The relationships found in their study suggest that conformity responses have strong negative relationships with both independence responses and anticonformity responses; however, anticonformity and independence are not related. Thus Figure 16-3 represents each of these two as being an opposite pole of conformity.

The refinements proposed by Jahoda, by Willis, and by Stricker et al. are not

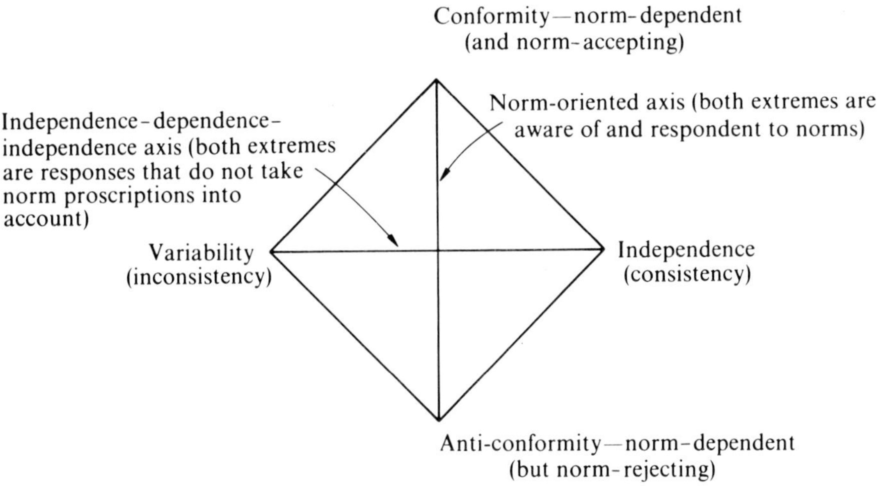

Figure 16-2. *Willis' Diamond Model. (Adapted from Willis, 1965.) Reprinted with permission of the publisher, Plenum Publishing Company Ltd. Copyright 1965.*

only helpful but should serve as organizing principles for future research. So far these refinements have had little effect upon empirical studies. When we face the question of the extent of conformity in the next section, we must unfortunately rely in most cases upon inadequate operational definitions of conformity.

III. THE EXTENT OF CONFORMITY

A. The Autokinetic Situation

The empirical study of conformity was highly influenced by the pioneering work of Muzafer Sherif (1935) on the **autokinetic effect.** If one looks at a stationary light in an otherwise completely dark room, the light will appear to move. Perhaps, it will move to the left, perhaps to the right, perhaps up or down—but it will appear to move in some direction because the eyes have no other reference point. Sherif capitalized upon this autokinetic phenomenon to study the effects of another person's response upon one's own response. He found that a subject's reports of movement were highly influenced by the estimates of other participants. Even the responses

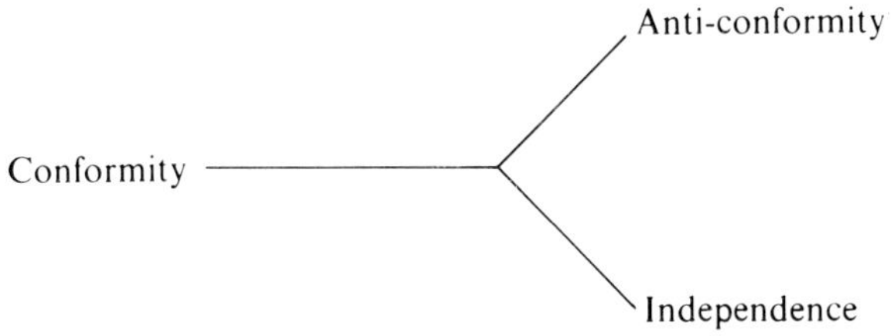

Figure 16-3. *One Model of the Relationship of Responses to Group Pressure. (From Stricker, Messick, & Jackson, "Conformity, anticonformity, and independence: Their dimensionality and generality,"* Journal of Personality and Social Psychology, **16**, *1970, p. 502. Copyright 1970 by the American Psychological Association, and reproduced by permission.)*

of only one other person influenced the subject's response.[6] It is not surprising that one's estimates are modified by the responses of others; after all, there is no other source of information, and the light is not really moving anyway. Yet despite these and other manifestations of artificiality in the situation, the study of autokinetic effect stimulated more advanced studies of conformity. The influence of the procedure upon Asch's work is evident, even though Sherif used an ambiguous stimulus whereas Asch's stimulus was almost devoid of ambiguity.

B. Situational Influences upon Extent of Conformity in Asch's Studies

Asch's usual procedure employed six confederates who gave false answers on certain trials in a line-judging task. With these influences operating, 32 percent of the true subjects' responses were conforming, and 68 percent were independent. These averages include responses of all true subjects on all the critical trials. (There were 50 true subjects, and 12 critical trials interspersed with a large number of trials in which all confederates gave the correct answer.)

But averages are deceiving; in the Asch study the distribution of conforming responses is more important because of the great degree of individual differences. Table 16-2 presents the distribution of conforming responses. Notice that 13 of the 50 subjects never yielded to the majority on any of the 12 critical trials. One subject yielded on 11 of 12 trials, and 3 subjects yielded on 10 of the 12 trials. Although the mean number of conforming responses is 3.84 (out of a possible 12), the modal number is 0. With a distribution as J-shaped as this one, a mean number is rather meaningless.

Table 16-2. *Distribution of Conforming Responses in the Original Asch Study*

Number of conforming responses		*Number of true subjects who gave this number of conforming responses*
0		13
1		4
2		5
3		6
4		3
5		4
6		1
7		2
8		5
9		3
10		3
11		1
12		0
Total	50 subjects	
Mean	3.84	

(Modified from Asch, 1958, p. 177)

[6]Apparently, the response in Sherif's experiment reflects both public compliance and private acceptance. The effect lasts a long time (Sherif, 1935; Bovard, 1948), and subjects report that they were unaware that the responses of others influenced them (Hood & Sherif, 1962).

Asch continued his work using this basic procedure in order to assess the extent to which various situational factors affect a conforming response. The relevant findings of more recent studies that have varied other situational factors are summarized here.[7]

What is the Effect of Group Size? One might expect that the larger the number of subjects forming a unanimous majority, the more often the true subject would conform. This is true only to a degree, however. Asch (1956, 1958) and others (L. A. Rosenberg, 1961; Goldberg, 1954) studied the extent of yielding to unanimous majorities of 2, 3, 4, 6, 7, 8, or 10 to 15 persons. Also, the limiting case was studied in which the true subject participated with only one confederate. More conformity resulted from participation with two confederates giving false answers. (See Table 16-3.) Groups of three or four confederates had the greatest influence in inducing conformity responses; groups of eight or more persons were somewhat less effective. In the real world, however, further increases in group size may increase conformity; Krech et al. (1962) see threats of reprisal as one reason why conformity may continue to increase in larger real-life groups.

What is the Effect of a Nonunanimous Majority? In the studies described thus far, there was only one true subject per group, and all the confederates were instructed to respond falsely on predetermined trials. What if one of the eight confederates (the one seated fourth in the row) were to give the correct response on every trial? This results in much less conformity on the part of the true subject. In such experiments, 5.5 percent of the responses were conforming as compared to 32 percent in the original experiment. When two true subjects were among the eight confederates, a conforming response occurred 10.4 percent of the time.

The presence of one other kindred soul within a relatively large group (eight to ten persons) is a greater deterrent to conformity than being in a smaller group (four persons) where everyone else disagrees with you. Clearly, such a finding has implications for attempts to persuade. "Divide and conquer" has validity in the sense that, when a person is removed from all others who give human support, he is much more likely to succumb to the pressures of the majority, even if the unanimous majority has fewer members.

What is the Effect When an Initial Supporter Defects to the Majority? In one condition Asch arranged for one of the confederates (seated in the fourth position) to give the correct response on the first half of the critical trials but then switch to the false response of the majority on the remaining trials. The experience of having and then losing a supporter restored the majority effect to almost full force; in such

Table 16-3. *Extent of Conformity in True Subjects with Unanimous Majorities of Different Sizes*

Size of majority:	1	2	3	4	8	10–15
N of true subjects:	10	15	10	10	50	12
Mean no. of conforming responses:	0.33	1.53	4.0	4.20	3.84	3.75
Range in no. of conforming responses per subject:	0–1	0–5	1–12	0–11	0–11	0–10

(From Asch, 1958, p. 181)

[7]The reader is referred to Kiesler (1969, pp. 255–272) or Allen (1965, pp. 157–164) for more detailed treatments of these and other situational effects on the extent of conformity.

cases the true subject conformed an average of 28.5 percent of the time after his compatriot defected.

Further research has indicated that the status of the group members influences the extent of conformity expressed by the true subject. One would expect a high school student to conform more to the majority's judgments when the other participants are introduced as college seniors than when they are introduced as other high school students. Crutchfield (cited in Krech et al., 1962) used a conformity procedure similar to Asch's and found that subjects who were members of an ethnic or racial minority conformed highly when participating in groups where they were the only minority-group member.

How Does Compliance with a Small Request Affect Later Compliance with a Larger Request? The foot-in-the-door technique is an age-old device that is certainly not limited to door-to-door salesmen. The basic premise is that if you can get a person to do a small thing for you, he is more likely to agree to another request later—a request that he may ordinarily have rejected. Consider the following example. Freedman and Fraser (1966) arranged an experiment whereby a fictitious California consumer's group contacted housewives by phone. The housewives were told that a survey of household products was being conducted. The survey would involve five or six staff members entering the home some morning for about two hours to enumerate and classify all of the household products. These men would need to have full freedom in the house to go through cupboards and storage places. All the information would then be used in writing reports for a public service publication called *The Guide*. Twenty-two percent of the housewives with whom there had been no earlier contact complied with this request. In contrast, another group of housewives was called earlier and was asked to answer a brief telephone survey conducted by the same consumer organization; on this first contact, eight questions were asked about brands of soaps used in the home. Of the housewives who had been exposed to the foot-in-the-door gambit, a much larger number—53 percent—agreed to allow the consumer group to enter their home.

C. Crutchfield's Procedure: Conformity across Content Areas

Every beginning project can do only so much, and as beginning studies Asch's experiments have inevitable limitations. We would like to know, for example, whether the conforming effect occurs to the same degree with other types of tasks besides line judging, and whether it occurs in other types of subjects besides the ubiquitous college sophomore. A study by Crutchfield (1955) gives us additional information. However, Crutchfield's procedure requires some detailed description.

Crutchfield's subjects were business or military men in management positions, who were participating in a three-day assessment program at the Institute of Personality Assessment and Research at the University of California at Berkeley. On the final day of activities, the men were placed in groups of five and were situated in front of an apparatus consisting of five adjacent electrical panels. Each panel formed an open cubicle, which prevented the subject from seeing the panels of his four fellow subjects. The subjects were to respond to a series of questions projected on the wall in front of each man. Each question was multiple-choice, and the subject was to indicate his response by flipping a switch on his panel. Moreover, he was to respond in order, as indicated by one of five lights lettered A, B, C, D, and E on his panel. If he were A, he responded first; B responded second, and so on. Each subject found that he responded first for a while, then third, then fourth, then second, and finally last.

Another important set of lights was on each man's panel. These lights informed the subject of the other subjects' answers before he himself responded. In other words, each subject had feedback about the answers of the other four men, in turn. Crutchfield described what happened when a subject answered last.

> Eventually the man finds himself for the first time in position E, where he is to respond last. The next slide shows a standard line and five comparison lines, of which he is to pick the one equal in length to the standard. Among the previous slides he has already encountered this kind of perceptual judgment and has found it easy. On looking at this slide it is immediately clear to him that line number 4 is the correct one. But as he waits his turn to respond, he sees light number 5 in row A go on, indicating that that person has judged line number 5 to be correct. And in fairly quick succession light 5 goes on also in rows B, C, and D.
>
> At this point the man is faced with an obvious conflict between his own clear perception and a unanimous contradictory consensus of the other four men. What does he do? Does he rely on the evidence of his own senses and respond independently? Or does he defer to the judgment of the group, complying with their perceptions rather than his own? (1955, p. 192).

The experimental procedure, to this point, has been described as the participating subjects viewed it. But each subject had been deceived. The apparatus was not wired as he thought, and there was no connection among the five panels. Instead, each panel was wired to the experimenter's panel, and it was he who sent all the information to the subject. Moreover, each subject at any one time received the same information sent to the other four subjects, so that on any given trial, all five men were responding first, or, later, all were responding last.

Thus, Crutchfield's equipment also permits a test of compliance. But from the responses, we can say nothing about private acceptance. Nonetheless, Crutchfield's procedure is more efficient than Asch's because it requires the use of no confederates and because it permits the testing of five subjects at one time. However, the subjects are not visible to each other. No subject sees or hears the other subjects respond, and the absence of identifying his actions with himself may limit the utility of group pressure in this situation. We may question whether this private form of responding affects conformity. Deutsch and Gerard (1955) used the Asch task to evaluate the effect of physical presence and visual communication upon degree of conformity. Some subjects judged length of lines while in the presence of three confederates. Other subjects were separated by partitions and responded anonymously by pressing a button. Deutsch and Gerard found less conformity in the latter condition, perhaps indicating that the need to be accepted by others is one reason for conformity effects. These procedural effects are extensive enough to allow us to question how appropriate it is to compare percentages of conformity in the Crutchfield and Asch tasks.

Crutchfield's study had the advantage of presenting the subject with a wider variety of judgments than those presented in the Asch study. For example, on the first of 21 critical slides including a standard line and five comparison lines, 15 of 50 men, or 30 percent, conformed to the false consensus. On a trial in which a circle and a star were exposed side by side, with the circle being about one-third larger in area than the star, 46 percent of the men succumbed to the false consensus that the star was larger. On a question asking for the simple completion of a number series (like those found on mental tests), 30 percent of the men conformed to the false majority.

Conformity was also found on items dealing with opinions and attitudes. For example, almost all the subjects in a control testing (individual testing) agreed with the statement: "I believe we are made better by the trials and hardships of life." Yet among the men subjected to false majority pressure, 31 percent disagreed with the statement. Conformity was found even on a highly personal attitude such as expressed in the statement: "I doubt whether I would make a good leader." No participant in the control group agreed with the statement, but when they were told that the other four men had agreed, 37 percent of the group participants agreed.

Only two of the 21 critical items did not produce significant conformity pressure. These both were extremely personal and subjective judgments that asked the subject which of two line drawings he preferred. Only one man out of 50 expressed agreement with the false group consensus.

As in the Asch study, a total conformity score was determined by counting the number of times each subject conformed on the 21 critical items. Of the 50 subjects, one man conformed on 17 of 21 items. At the other extreme, several men conformed on only one or two items. The rest of the men were distributed between these two extremes; the mean score was approximately eight items, or about 38 percent. However, as before, an average conformity value diminishes in importance when placed in the context of extensive individual differences.

Figure 16-4. *The Crutchfield Conformity Procedure and Results. Five subjects sit in adjacent booths and respond to questions presented on a screen in front of them. In this example, the circle is about one-third larger than the star. But when each subject is led to believe that the other subjects have chosen the star as being larger, 46 percent of the subjects go along with the others and choose the star.*

IV. IS THERE A CONFORMING PERSONALITY?

We have indicated the significant ways that situational factors may influence the extent of conformity manifested by a subject in a situation where everyone else's response differs from his own. We have seen that the content of the material may determine whether the response is a conforming one or not. But in every case, there were large individual differences. May we then conclude that some people are, by their nature, more conforming than others? Is conforming behavior a personality characteristic? Opinions of psychologists vary on this issue. This section reviews the findings and interpretations relevant to these questions.

Since subjects in Crutchfield's study were participating in a thorough assessment procedure, it was feasible to compare the conformers and the independent subjects in order to see which characteristics, if any, distinguished the two groups. Crutchfield found that the two groups differed in many respects; in contrast to the highly conformist subjects, the independent subjects showed "more intellectual effectiveness, ego strength, leadership ability, and maturity of social relations, together with a conspicuous absence of inferiority feelings, rigid and excessive self-control, and authoritarian attitudes" (Crutchfield, 1955, p. 194). For example, the degree of conformity correlated $-.63$ with a staff rating of subjects' intellectual competence, $-.33$ with Barron's ego strength scale, and $+.39$ with authoritarianism (as measured by the California F scale).

Conformers and independent subjects also tended to differ in the personality statements that they accepted as applicable to themselves. Independent subjects more frequently indicated that each of the following statements was true about themselves: "Sometimes I rather enjoy going against the rules and doing things I'm not supposed to"; "I like to fool around with new ideas, even if they turn out later to be a total waste of time"; "A person needs to 'show off' a little now and then"; "It is unusual for me to express strong approval or disapproval of the actions of others"; "I am often so annoyed when someone tries to get ahead of me in a line of people that I speak to him about it"; and "Compared to your own self-respect, the respect of others means very little." Such a pattern indicates that independent subjects feel freed from the compulsive limits of rules and are more adventurous and even exhibitionistic. They possess self-confidence and internal determinants of right and wrong. We would expect them to possess higher levels of moral judgment than the conformists.

Conversely, conformists more often indicated that the following items applied to them: "I am in favor of very strict enforcement of all laws, no matter what the consequences." "It is all right to get around the law if you don't actually break it." "Most people are honest chiefly through fear of being caught." "I don't like to work on a problem unless there is a possibility of coming out with a clear-cut and unambiguous answer." "Once I have made up my mind I seldom change it." "I always follow the rule: business before pleasure." "The trouble with many people is that they don't take things seriously enough." "I am afraid when I look down from a high place." "I am often bothered by useless thoughts which keep running through my head." "I commonly wonder what hidden reason another person may have for doing something nice for me." "People pretend to care more about one another than they really do." "Sometimes I am sure that other people can tell what I am thinking."

Conformists, in reporting attitudes concerning parents and children, describe their parents in highly idealized and uncritical terms, reminiscent of the orientation of the highly authoritarian personality. Extremely conformist subjects prefer more restrictive child-rearing practices for their children, while independent subjects are more permissive (Block, 1955).

Apparently, the independent subjects represent everything psychologists would want in an effectively functioning person, while the conformists possess qualities—both cognitive and temperamental—which deter effective functioning. There are only two pieces of evidence that fail to fit. First, the highly conformist subjects almost always report coming from stable homes, while the independent subjects much more frequently report broken homes and unstable home environments. (Crutchfield does not report just how frequently, and we can make little of this.) Second, on measures of psychological maladjustment, conformists do not appear to be any more neurotic than independent subjects. Both Crutchfield's conformists and those in an Asch-type study by Barron (1953) did not significantly differ from independent subjects on any of the neuroticism scales of the Minnesota Multiphasic Personality Inventory.[8]

Despite these imperfections, the picture of the extreme conformists has been painted with heavy strokes. Crutchfield described them as "having less ego strength, less ability to tolerate own impulses and to tolerate ambiguity, less ability to accept responsibility, less self-insight, less spontaneity and productive originality, and as having more prejudiced and authoritarian attitudes, more idealization of parents, and greater emphasis on external and socially approved values" (1955, p. 196). Such a strong consistency of relationships tempts one to conclude that there exists a conforming personality or a psychological trait of conformity. But the presence of a trait implies a consistency of behavior. In other words, a subject who yielded in the Asch-Crutchfield procedure would also defer to the opinion of the majority, if he were a jury member, or would submit to his captors, if he were a prisoner of war. However, studies on the generality of conformity behavior indicate a modest amount of consistency (reviewed by McGuire, 1968). Rosner (1957), for example, placed student nurses in a conformity task where some peers were confederates on one occasion and other peers were confederates on another occasion. The degree of conformity of specific nurses was similar across occasions. In another study, subjects who conformed in regard to perceptual judgments in the Crutchfield procedure were more likely to report acceptance of peer-group norms and acceptance of authority pressures (Back & Davis, 1965). Abelson and Lesser (1959) found that children who conformed to teachers' judgments responded similarly to their mothers' judgments. Stricker et al. (1970) reported correlations of +.09 to +.60 between extent of conformity in four different tasks. However, as McGuire (1968) pointed out, in these and other studies, the degree of variance accounted for is seldom as high as 50 percent. Thus, we conclude that there are some people whose disposition is to conform across different behavioral settings. Likewise, some persons are

[8] Costanzo's (1970) study, however, using children as subjects, found high relationships (*r*'s of +.54 to +.78) between the extent of self-blame (as measured by a personality inventory) and degree of conformity in the Crutchfield task.

characteristically independent, and others lean toward anticonformity. But we must be careful not to put too much weight on these conclusions. Not all people show consistent response patterns. Also, labeling a person as generally a conformist on the basis of his behavior in one setting is highly speculative, since it ignores the powerful role of the situation in influencing behavior.

Thirty years ago, personality traits were seen as the building blocks in the structure of behavior. It was then assumed that traits played a predominant role in determining what behavior would emerge. But more recent reviews, such as Mischel's (1968), indicate that in the case of personality and morality traits, the lack of consistency is rather serious; correlations averaging between +.30 and +.40 are predominant, indicating small degrees of consistency and much variability. Although traits do play some role, their degree of consistent influence upon behavior appears to be less than expected; less simplified conceptions of the relationship between personality and behavior have been sought. Both Mischel's analysis and provocative reviews by Marlowe and Gergen (1968, 1970) encourage the development of a more sophisticated theory of personality, which "recognizes that behavior tends to change with alterations in the situation in which it occurs" (Mischel, 1968, p. 38).

Studies that correlate a single personality characteristic (such as degree of extroversion or anxiety) with social behavior have produced meager results (reviewed by Marlowe and Gergen, 1968, 1970). Among the errors of such a simplified approach is the assumption that personality traits operate independently without interaction with one another. More recently, research concern has shifted to the ways that one personality characteristic may influence or moderate the effect of another upon social behavior. For example, it may appear that there is very little relationship between authoritarianism and conformity. But we may find that when the authoritarian person is quite anxious, he conforms more than is normal; if he lacks anxiety, he conforms much less than usual. The use of certain traits as **moderator variables** is now being developed (Kogan & Wallach, 1964). Similarly, an attitude or trait may have clear-cut effects upon social behavior but only within the limits prescribed by the nature of the task or situation (as Christie and Geis, 1970, found with Machiavellianism).

When looking at personality factors versus situational factors in relationship to social behavior, we may be forced to conclude that their interactions are of greatest importance. In one study on the effect of the two types of influences, J. McV. Hunt (1965) found that most of the variance in the relationship was accounted for by interactions between personality and situational variables. Hunt wrote: "Thus, it is neither the individual differences among subjects, *per se,* nor the variations among situations, *per se* that produce the variations in behavior. It is, rather, the interactions among these . . ." (1965, p. 83). A study by Rule and Sandilands (1969) exemplifies this point; these investigators found that highly test-anxious subjects conformed more on a task that required a high commitment than one with low commitment. Subjects low in test anxiety conformed more on the task that required little commitment. Higher order analyses of relationships between personality and situational factors appear much more fruitful than simplified statements about a conforming personality—even though such a statement may include a grain of truth.

V. IS CONFORMITY INCREASING IN OUR SOCIETY?

There are strong pressures toward uniformity in any organized society. To a degree, this is necessary and functional. Uniformity leads to predictability, and predictability is important in human interactions. But pressures toward uniformity and conventionality can become too strong, and a complex society can often confuse what is conventional with what is commendable. A survey conducted by pollster Louis Harris in 1965 indicated the pervasiveness of conformity pressures in American life. A cross-section of American adults was asked whether they felt that certain actions were "more helpful" or "more harmful" to American life. Despite our lip service to the ideal that America is the home of rugged individualists, there are stronger forces in the opposite direction. For example, 68 percent of American adults believed that anti-Vietnam war pickets were more harmful than helpful. Only 5 percent said such pickets were more helpful. Of those surveyed, 58 percent felt that college professors active in unpopular causes were more harmful, while only 6 percent of the adults felt these professors were more helpful. Even though the Constitution requires that any person accused of a crime be given adequate legal counsel, 34 percent of those surveyed considered the "lawyer who defends notorious criminals" as being more harmful to American life. Alas, even women who wear bikini swim suits do not escape conformity pressures; they were considered deleterious to American life by more than 33 percent of American adults. These figures should not be taken as evidence for the existence of conformity but, rather, as evidence for the existence of strong pressures to conform.

Unpublished studies administered by students at Vanderbilt University indicate how these attitudes are manifested in the rejection of certain requests by hippies. On a busy downtown street two groups of students solicited passersby for signatures to an innocuous petition. Students with neat haircuts and dressed in suits and ties were rejected only half as often as were similar students dressed in hippie attire. In Canada, too, nonconformity, as exemplified by the hippie style, is treated with rejection. In fact, an unpublished survey conducted in 1970 by Denis Szabo, a University of Montreal criminologist, found that Quebec policemen expressed more hostility toward hippies than toward criminals. In the St. Lawrence River community of Rimouski, 54 percent of the policemen reported feelings of hostility toward hippies, while only 28 percent expressed such feelings toward criminals. Montreal police were somewhat more tolerant; 23.3 percent described their feelings toward hippies as hostile, compared to 22.9 percent who expressed such feelings about criminals. Only 8 percent of the Montreal policemen described their feelings toward hippies as friendly.

Social critics such as David Riesman (1950) and William H. Whyte, Jr. (1956) believe that conformity is increasing in American life. In *The Organization Man,* Whyte argues that the complexities of modern society have increased the need to rely upon others. A social ethic that emphasizes "getting along with others" as a norm or standard is replacing a Protestant ethic that valued hard work. Whyte writes:

> By Social Ethic I mean that contemporary body of thought which makes morally legitimate the pressures of society against the individual. Its major propositions are three: a belief in the

The Mark Painter case is a specific example of how nonconformity to American middle-class values is punished. Mark was seven years old in 1966 when the Iowa Supreme Court awarded custody of him to his "conventional" grandparents rather than his "bohemian" father. Four years before, Mark's mother and sister had been killed in a car wreck; upset and distraught, his father, Harold Painter, sent Mark to live temporarily with his maternal grandparents on a farm near Ames, Iowa. Mr. Painter married again; his new wife was a Phi Beta Kappa graduate of the University of California (Berkeley), an artist, and a former Red Cross worker in Japan and Korea. After renovating a ramshackle Victorian house near San Francisco, the Painters felt it was time to bring Mark home. But the grandparents had become fond of Mark; they refused to let the boy go. The Painters filed a suit in the county district court, but their writ of habeas corpus was rejected by both the district court and the Iowa Supreme Court.

The latter court's decision noted that Mark's grandfather was "highly respected" and "has served on the schoolboard and regularly teaches a Sunday-school class at the Gilbert Congregational Church." In contrast, Painter had held seven jobs in ten years and was "either an agnostic or an atheist and has no concern for formal religious training. He has read a lot of Zen Buddhism." Life with the Painters, according to the court, would be "unstable, unconventional, arty, bohemian, and probably intellectually stimulating." By comparison, the court saw the grandparents' home as offering Mark "a stable, dependable, conventional, middle-class Middle West background and an opportunity for a college education and profession." The court concluded that "security and stability in the home are more important than intellectual stimulation" (*Time*, 1966a).

Two years later, in 1968, Mark was allowed to live with his father and his stepmother. But the decision did not result from an overturning of the court's action; rather, Mark's grandmother consented to let Mark live where he wanted to live. (In fact, the United States Supreme Court refused to hear arguments in the case.) Despite the happy ending of this case, the courts still have the power to disrupt family life (*Christian Century*, 1968).

Figure 16-5. *The Case of Mark Painter.*

group as a source of creativity; a belief in 'belongingness' as the ultimate need of the individual; and a belief in the application of science to achieve the belongingness. . . . Man exists as a unit of society. Of himself, he is isolated, meaningless; only as he collaborates with others does he become worthwhile, for by sublimating himself in the group, he helps produce a whole that is greater than the sum of its parts (1956, pp. 7–8).

To Whyte, man is presently motivated by social considerations. He is not oriented toward achieving as much as he is toward being accepted. Rewards accrue not from hard work but from the ability to work with and through one's fellows. David Riesman's (1950) view of the prevalence of the other-directed man in our society reflects a similar conceptualization. To Riesman, Americans of a past generation were more inner-directed in the sense that they determined their own values and goals. In contrast, the other-directed individual must seek definition of right and wrong from his peers; he has no internalized values. Riesman believes the incidence of other-directedness in our society has increased.

The increased polarization of attitudes in our society affects conformity. On many a college campus today, an atmosphere exists which almost forces student compliance with majority values—whether those values be permissive or repressive, or for or against our government's policies. Yet pressures toward uniformity have always been present on college campuses. The right thing to wear, the "in" expressions, and similarly picayune manifestations of conformity have always been present. The difference, perhaps, in the present atmosphere is the pressure toward ideological conformity. It matters not only what clothes one wears or how long one's hair is, but also how one acts toward Indochina and marijuana.

Many Americans are justifiably concerned about contemporary attempts to control dissent. It appears that in the early 1970s the United States government has become increasingly repressive (R. Harris, 1969). The Department of Justice has increased its use of wire-tapping, bugging, and other devices for surveillance. Requests for parade permits for protest groups have been denied. Preventive detention of dangerous "potential criminals" is now the law in Washington, D. C. But we sometimes forget that such attempts have been prevalent at numerous times in America's past. Even though the United States was founded by minority dissenters, within 20 years of its founding (1798), the American Congress passed the Alien and Sedition Acts, empowering the government to prosecute newspaper editors who were critical of America's undeclared naval war against France. Sixty-five years later, President Lincoln suspended the right of habeas corpus for those arrested as being disloyal during the Civil War—and he did not even consult Congress before doing so. Furthermore, twenty-year terms for war dissent were prescribed by the Sedition Act of 1918.

Nonetheless, freedom to criticize, protest, and deviate has grown. Organizations such as the American Civil Liberties Union (ACLU), whose goal is the protection of individual rights, have increased budgets and membership. Repressive organizations are under fire. For example, for 30 years Congress and the public have permitted the House Committee on Un-American Activities (now called the House Internal Security Committee) to make irresponsible and undocumented charges against many Americans accused of association with left-wing or right-wing political organizations. In many cases those subpoenaed to appear before the committee were not informed as to the purpose and scope of the hearings; they were harassed during open hearings; and they often lost jobs simply because of "detrimental" publicity or "guilt by association" (W. Goodman, 1968). But more recently, a physician subpoenaed to appear before the committee brought a motion before a Chicago federal court asking that the committee be declared unconstitutional and that it be enjoined from holding hearings. Judge Julius Hoffman (who also presided in the Chicago Seven trial) twice dismissed the suit, but it was reinstated both times by a Federal Appeals Court that overruled him.[9] The case is now pending; it is evidence for retaliation against government pressures to conform. Other efforts against long-standing repressive actions may also be documented.

Doubtless, tolerance for dissent has not increased in a straight-forward manner throughout the years. Periods of wartime create strong pressures against dissent. During periods of general prosperity, more dissent can be tolerated. Governmental policies can deliberately try to encourage dissent or suppress it. In today's self-conscious society, we ask more of ourselves, and because of this heightened expectation we may often be discouraged by restrictions against dissent. Yet freedoms to dissent or not conform do continue to exist and grow.

[9] Personal correspondence from Albert E. Jenner, Jr., Attorney at Law, to the officers of the Jeremiah Stamler Legal Aid Fund, July 9, 1970.

VI. UNRESOLVED ISSUES IN THE STUDY OF CONFORMITY AND NONCONFORMITY

We have seen that its very nature as a pervasive social phenomenon has made conformity a difficult concept to define and measure. Its relevance has encouraged value judgments that fail to facilitate the resolution of problems. The purpose of this section is to review these unresolved problems as a summary to the scientific study of conformity. Hollander and Willis (1967) have listed the following issues as among the unresolved problems in the study of conformity and nonconformity.

1. Research and thinking have emphasized conformity to a much greater degree than nonconformity. Similarly, it has been assumed that one dimension can describe all types of conforming and nonconforming behavior. We have described studies by Sherif, Asch, and Crutchfield, which focused upon yielding or conformity to group pressures. Such paradigms do not provide for a separation between independence and anticonformity, which are clearly two different phenomena. More recent conceptualizations, particularly Willis' (1965) and that of Stricker, Messick, and Jackson (1970), have put greater emphasis upon dimensions or types of nonconformity.

2. There has been a failure to distinguish between descriptions of overt behavior and explanations of underlying processes. Did Galileo conform when he publicly recanted, while maintaining his private opinion? Since conformity is a generic term, we must conclude that he did. But current thinking prefers to call Galileo's act compliance, which is a type of conformity. Likewise, we now describe 32 percent of the Asch responses as compliance—or the adoption of a new public position, while the private opinion remains unchanged from what it was before. The Asch-Crutchfield procedure does not permit a determination of the extent of change in private acceptance or private opinion.

3. Often it is assumed that conformity is bad, and nonconformity is good. Hollander and Willis, in evaluating the viewpoint of social critics such as Riesman and Whyte, conclude:

> The most characteristic tack in such critiques is to describe conventional behavior in modern American society, label it conformity, invoke the "self-evident" premise that conformity is oppositional to individuality or independence, and therefore conclude that modern society and its component institutions hamper constructive initiative and are accordingly bad (Hollander & Willis, 1967, p. 71).

Hollander and Willis are reluctant to accept the judgment that conformity is necessarily bad. Conformity often functions to meet the person's goals, whether social (such as need for acceptance) or nonsocial (such as need for food). Such needs are basic to all of us. Beyond this, we all rely on other people as sources of information; and, as such, other people inevitably influence us. Barry Collins (1970) concludes:

> It would be a mistake to oversimplify the question and ask whether conformity is good or bad. A person who refused to accept anyone's word or advice on any topic whatsoever . . . would probably make just as big a botch of his life . . . as a person who always conformed and never formed a judgment on the basis of his own individual sources of information (1970, p. 21).

4. Often it is assumed that conformity to the general group norms is defined in the same terms and serves the same functions for all group members. Research in reciprocity and social exchange (J. S. Adams, 1965; Gouldner, 1960) indicates that a conforming response may serve for some persons as a deserved reward. To others, it may be a payment in advance for expected rewards (Hollander & Willis, 1967, p. 72).

In similar ways, conformity may be used by a low-status group member to ingratiate himself with the group leader (E. E. Jones, 1965). Such behavior is reminiscent of Jahoda's *expedient conformity*; it serves to meet other goals of the group member. But conformity in a high-status group member or leader may serve another function. For a long time, an issue has raged over the relative degree of conformity shown by leaders. Are group leaders more conforming to the group norms than followers? Clarification of the matter comes through Hollander's (1958, 1964) "idiosyncrasy credit" model. In initial stages of group development, the leader may conform strongly to group norms, accumulating credits in the form of positive impressions by the other group members. This accumulation of credit then permits the leader to spend part of it later in the form of greater nonconformity and deviation from groups norms. Thus, for different group members, conformity can serve different functions. To some degree it may be considered person-specific and related to the level of status in the group.

VII. OTHER EFFECTS OF SOCIAL INFLUENCE: GROUP RISK TAKING

A. The Pervasiveness of Social Influence

Social influence can have a variety of results. Pressures from other group members can manifest *obedience* in subjects even to the extent of administering extremely dangerous electric shocks to another person. (See Chapter 13.) A person who is unsure of the appropriate *emotional response* to a novel situation will imitate the behavior of another person in the same situation. (See Chapter 14.) Social influence can be particularly effective under cases of deindividuation in group members (Chapter 14). Rather than reexamining these phenomena, the remaining section of this chapter deals with another result of social influence—risk taking in groups.

B. Group Risk Taking Defined

A decision to conform is one possible response to pressures from a group to which an individual belongs. But groups can also make decisions, and often these are decisions that would not be made by their separate members as individuals. For example, it has frequently been asserted that a group exerts a conservative influence upon its individual members, so that solutions to problems in a group are likely to be less creative or satisfactory than are solutions developed by individuals. If it is true that groups exert a conservative influence, it should follow that group-made decisions are less risky than those made by individuals. According to this line of thought, the widespread use of committees and teams in business, the military, and educational institutions would always and inexorably limit the degree of boldness and risk taking. Fortunately, a body of research findings has accumulated over the last ten years by which we can answer the question of whether group decisions are less risky. The answer may surprise you.

Studies by Stoner (1961) and Wallach, Kogan, and Bem (1962) set out to evaluate experimentally the effect of group influence on the willingness of individuals to take risks. The experiment by Wallach, Kogan, and Bem involved 14 all-male and 14 all-female groups of college students, with six subjects in each group. At the beginning of the experiment, each subject completed a questionnaire containing descriptions of 12 hypothetical choice-dilemma situations. A specimen item on this questionnaire was as follows: "An electrical engineer may stick with his present job at a modest but adequate salary, or take a new job offering considerably more money but no long-term security." Responses to this and the 11 other items could be scored with respect to the magnitude of risk the subject would be willing to take, in his capacity as advisor to the person facing the choice-dilemma. The subject's task was to indicate what the likelihood of success would have to be before he would advise the fictitious person to choose the riskier alternative. For instance, in this example, would you advise the engineer to take the new, riskier job if the chances were only 1 out of 10 that he would be successful? What if the chances were 3 out of 10? Or 5 out of 10? Or 7 out of 10? Or 9 out of 10? Or, would you advise the engineer not to choose the riskier job regardless of the odds? These were the alternatives given the subject in each of the 12 choice-dilemmas. Note that the definition of a risky choice is rather specific here (Mackenzie & Bernhardt, 1968). The subject was not asked whether he would recommend a risky or a conservative decision, but rather he was asked what the odds must be for success before he would advocate a riskier but more beneficial action.[10]

After each of the six members in a group had answered the choice-dilemma questionnaire, they were asked to move together in a discussion group. They were each given another copy of the questionnaire and, under careful instructions, were now asked to discuss each hypothetical choice and to arrive at a unanimous group decision. After this discussion was finished, the experimenter asked the group members to separate for some further individual work and to take their questionnaires with them. Each subject was to go back over the 12 items on the questionnaire and indicate his own present decision. Then each subject was asked to rank everyone in the group, including himself, on how much each individual had influenced the final group decision. Two to six weeks later, a representative sample of the subjects came back to take the questionnaire again, on an individual basis.

The control groups were formed in the same way as the experimental groups. Members of the control groups were given an individual questionnaire session and

[10]According to a comprehensive review by Dion, Baron, and Miller (1970), the choice-dilemma task is the instrument used to measure risky shifts in about 80 percent of the group risk-taking studies. Another type of group risk-taking task requiring subjects to choose the level of difficulty they want to answer on mental aptitude items accounts for about 14 percent of the studies, and stimulus-judging tasks account for the remaining 6 percent.

a second individual decision session in which they were asked to reconsider their earlier responses to the questionnaire. They did not participate in any group discussion of the proper degree of risk to take.

The results indicated that after the group decision there was increased willingness to take risks on 10 of the 12 situations. This was the case in both male and female groups. On 9 of the 10 changes, the shift was so great that there was little likelihood that it occurred by coincidence. When the same kind of analysis was made for the control groups on two separate responses to the questionnaire, no significant differences were found between the first and second sessions in the degree of willingness to take risk. Thus, the authors concluded that the group decision leads to taking greater risks.

When a random sample of the original subjects was brought back after two to six weeks, it was found that the results of the group discussion persisted over this length of time. The risk-taking propensities of these people at this final session were still significantly greater than those they displayed before the group discussion.

C. Is Willingness to Take Greater Risk a Group Phenomenon or a Pseudogroup Effect?

The conclusion that groups make riskier decisions than individuals has great implications, especially in a society where momentous decisions of war policy are made in committees. We need to ask why a riskier decision emerged from the group deliberations. After other studies (Kogan & Wallach, 1967a; 1967b; 1967c) replicated the findings, researchers advanced several possible reasons for this phenomenon. These are evaluated in the following paragraphs.

The Familiarization Hypothesis. The role of group decision in the willingness to take risk was questioned when it was discovered that *greater familiarization* with the situations led to the risky shift in the absence of any group participation (Bateson, 1966; Flanders & Thistlethwaite, 1967). (Familiarization was accomplished by having the subjects read over the material alone or write arguments for their choices.) According to this notion, the shift toward taking greater risk is a pseudogroup effect—an artifact of increased familiarity with the test items. Other studies failed to confirm this finding, however (Pruitt & Teger, 1967; Teger, Pruitt, St. Jean, & Haaland, 1970; Dion & Miller, 1969; St. Jean, 1970), and it still remains uncertain as to whether a risky shift can be consistently produced with isolated individuals (Dion, Baron, & Miller, 1970). Apparently, the actual experiencing of group interaction is needed to account for the full risky-shift phenomenon.

Diffusion of Responsibility as a Hypothesis. If the risky shift is truly a group phenomenon—if it does not occur in isolated individuals—it may result from a *diffusion of responsibility,* which develops emotional bonds and reduces fear of failure, thus enabling persons to make riskier decisions. The group may free the individual from full responsibility, somewhat like Darley and Latané's findings in the call-for-help studies described in Chapter 3. Kogan and Wallach (1967b, p. 51), for example, argue that the "failure of a risky course is easier to bear when others are implicated in a decision. . . ." It is unclear whether this proposed relaxation derives from the emotional relationship that is established in the group, the anonymity that a group (particularly a large group) provides the individual, or other factors. In fact, whether a sharing of responsibility leads to the increased risk taking remains an unsettled question (Dion et al., 1970). For example, presentation of relevant arguments can produce a risky shift in individual decisions, even without development of group cohesion or emotional bonds (Pruitt & Teger, 1969; Clark & Willems, 1970).

The Persuasion Hypothesis (or Leadership Hypothesis). Perhaps groups make riskier decisions because the group members whose initial decisions were riskier exert more influence in the group discussion (Marquis, 1962). This explanation emphasizes *persuasion,* or the notion that group leaders and frequent spokesmen in the discussion are more willing to take risks and hence influence other group members in that direction. Evidence for such a phenomenon is usually indirect and often contradictory. Several studies (Flanders & Thistlethwaite, 1967; Wallach, Kogan, & Bem, 1962; Wallach, Kogan, & Burt, 1968) find significant positive relationships between participants' initial risk-taking levels and ratings by others (done after the session) of the participants' apparent influence. This would argue for the accuracy of the persuasion hypothesis.

But the relationship may only exist in the eye of the beholder. Kelley and Thibaut (1968, p. 81) suggest: "The correlations between initial riskiness and influence may simply reflect what has happened: Subjects observe the shift to occur and infer from it that the initially risky person must have been more influential." Bolstering this interpretation, Wallach, Kogan, and Burt (1968) found that subjects were aware that a shift toward greater risk was occurring but were not accurate in estimating the extent of shift. Also, more direct tests of the leadership hypothesis fail to confirm an expectation that leadership per se leads to the shift (Vidmar, 1970; Hoyt & Stoner, 1968). We may also utilize the earlier finding that personality factors play a definite but only minor role in conformity and persuasibility. Although it is plausible that initial risk takers assume a vigorous role in groups, there is no direct evidence that this behavior accounts for the risky shift.

Risk as a Cultural Value. The typical subject, in making his individual judgments on the choice-dilemma tasks, expects others to make choices that are no riskier than his own (Hinds, 1962). On the basis of this finding, it has been hypothesized that risk represents more of a *cultural value* than does conservatism (Roger Brown, 1965; Teger & Pruitt, 1967; Clark & Willems, 1972). According to this explanation, those group members whose initial risk-taking scores were below the group average came to realize, through the discussion, that their positions were not as risky as they had assumed. Thus, they became willing to recommend greater risk taking after the group discussion. Harold Miller (1970) found that subjects at both extremes on the initial measure had the greatest interest in the task, but there were many more subjects at the extremely risky end, which gives some confirmation to the hypothesis of risk as a cultural value.

Along with this cultural value explanation, it may be that the proximal cause of change comes from the relevant arguments that occur during discussion (Madaras & Bem, 1968). The opportunity for *information exchange* has also been proposed as playing a participatory role (Pruitt & Teger, 1969; Teger & Pruitt, 1967; Clark & Willems, 1969a; Willems & Clark, 1969a, 1969b). For example, R. Brown (1965) predicted that if members simply report their previous choices in the group no further discussion may be necessary to produce the shift. The information exchange, Brown argued, may show the dubious subject that others are more risky and that support exists for a shift toward risk. To test this suggestion, St. Jean (1970) varied the amount of information available in discussion groups. Some subjects participated in the usual type of discussions, and some subjects had available only the information about the advocated risk levels of others. A third group had all information except the specific risk levels of others. St. Jean found that only exchanging information about one's specific risk levels did not shift risk levels; rather, relevant arguments by the others appeared in this study as the essential causes of the risky shift.

Two major reviews of the mushrooming literature on the risky-shift phenomenon have concluded that risk as a cultural value serves as one explanation that is generally verified by research findings (Dion et al., 1970; R. D. Clark, 1971). The best guess at present is that the shift toward risk in groups occurs primarily as a result of (a) relevant arguments and (b) a realization by group members that others have opted for recommendations as risky as, or riskier than, their own (Clark & Willems, 1972). Clark's review (1971) suggests that a group decision will be riskier than those of its individual members if the following factors are present: (a) risk-relevant content, (b) participants who perceive themselves as relatively risky (H. Miller, 1970), (c) heterogeneity of initial opinions, (d) severity of the consequences of failure, and (e) risk-oriented instructions. The risk-as-value explanation fits most of these necessary conditions.

Many of the early studies suffered from theoretical chauvinism, or an expectation that only one explanation can account for an observed effect (Dion et al., 1970). Numerous reasons can plausibly serve as explanations, and each can benefit by the same empirical documentation. Several of the proposed explanations presented in this section may work hand in hand. As Dion et al. stated: "It may be the case that those whose initial decisions are riskier do in fact exert more influence in the group setting, but, further, that this greater influence is restricted to situations in which the value of risk is salient" (1970, p. 364). We can expect future research to reflect this recognition.

D. Summary on Group Risk Taking

At present it does appear that, in a variety of problem situations, increased exposure to the situation leads to a riskier decision. (However, on a few problem situations, the reverse does occur.) The risky shift that occurs in groups is not limited to artificially formed groups of college students but has been found in established, professional groups such as psychiatric teams, dealing with clinical cases (Siegel & Zajonc, 1967). If the subject's decision will actually have consequences for himself and not some hypothetical other, the shift still occurs (Wallach, Kogan, & Bem, 1964; Pruitt & Teger, 1969). This shift has also been found in industrial supervisors (Rim, 1965), senior executives (Marquis, 1962), and management trainees (Stoner, 1961)—and even in groups of grade school boys and girls (Kogan & Carlson, 1967). The phenomenon is not limited to Americans, having also been manifested in English, Israeli, Canadian, French, and German groups (reviewed by Dion et al., 1970). In short, the assumption that putting a major decision in the hands of a group, rather than in the hands of one individual, will ensure a safer, more conservative decision frequently seems unwarranted.

VIII. SUMMARY

Conformity is defined as a yielding to group pressures. It may refer to a behavior or action (called compliance) or a change in attitude or belief (private acceptance). *Uniformity* is not the same phenomenon as conformity. In contrast to conformity, *conventionality* is defined as acting in what is the customary or usual fashion, or adhering to the standard practices of society.

Two possible opposites to conformity are *independence* and *anticonformity*. Independence is the maintenance and expression of one's private beliefs in the face of group pressures to do something to the contrary. Anticonformity refers to actions or beliefs that develop in opposition to majority opinion.

In the Asch studies about one-third of the responses were conforming and two-thirds were independent, but the range in reactions between subjects was so great that an average is rather meaningless.

Apparently, conforming acts may reflect different processes, if (a) the person is involved or not involved in the issue, and (b) his public action is or is not consistent with his private attitude.

Situational factors may influence the extent of conformity. Groups of three to four people have greater influence upon a lone subject than do smaller groups. Nonunanimous majorities have less effect than unanimous ones.

Personality factors also have an influence—at least in laboratory studies of conformity. Subjects who yield to group pressure are more likely to possess intolerance of ambiguity, rigid authoritarian and moralistic attitudes, conventional values, and negative assumptions about human nature.

Although theorists have speculated that pressures toward conformity are increasing in our society, such claims are hard to document.

A judgment that conformity is always bad and independence or nonconformity is always good fails to reflect an understanding of the numerous social needs that conformity serves in contemporary life.

Numerous studies indicate that, within the limits of the procedures used, groups make riskier decisions than do separate individuals. Among the various explanations proposed for this consistent finding, the most plausible are ones that employ (a) information exchange in groups and (b) a realization by group members of the risky recommendations of other group members.

IX. SUGGESTED READINGS

Dion, K. L., Baron, R. S., & Miller, N. Why do groups make riskier decisions than individuals? In L. Berkowitz (Ed.), *Advances in experimental social psychology*. Vol. 5. New York: Academic Press, 1970. Pp. 305–377. A systematic review of conflicting explanations of the tendency for groups to make riskier decisions than individuals. Rather technical.

Gergen, K. J., & Marlowe, D. (Eds.) *Personality and social behavior*. Reading, Mass.: Addison-Wesley, 1970. (Paperback) A collection of research reports reflecting the interaction of personality and situational determinants of social responses.

Kiesler, C. A., & Kiesler, S. B. *Conformity*. Reading, Mass.: Addison-Wesley, 1969. (Paperback) A brief analysis of theories and research on conformity, written in a straightforward fashion. Well organized, with useful summaries. Particularly valuable is its distinction between compliance and private acceptance. Charles Kiesler's section in J. Mills' *Experimental social psychology* is a more rigorous, research-oriented treatment of the same topic.

Riesman, D., in association with Glazer, N., & Denney, R. *The lonely crowd: A study of the changing American character*. New Haven: Yale University Press, 1950. (Paperback edition available) An influential book that reflects Riesman's concern with inner-directed versus other-directed styles of behavior.

Whyte, W. H., Jr. *The organization man*. New York: Simon & Schuster, 1956. (Paperback edition available) Whyte holds that contemporary American life encourages the development of conformists and discourages mavericks.

Chapter Seventeen

The Social Psychology of Leadership and Organizational Effectiveness

I *must* follow the people. Am I not their leader? *Prime Minister Disraeli*

What most frequently distinguishes the leader from his co-workers is that he knows more about a group task or that he can do it better. *Fred E. Fiedler*

The study of leadership demands a recognition of the complexity of human social behavior. Early attempts in the scientific study of leadership sought simplicity; researchers attempted to find characteristics that all leaders possessed and that all followers did not. Implicit in this approach was an assumption that the same traits within a person led to his assuming a leadership role on all occasions—whether the person was captain of his bowling team or an Army captain with a company of infantrymen in Vietnam. Such a simplified approach was doomed to failure because it did not recognize the varying functions of leaders, the nature of the group task, the relative power of the leader, and other very important factors.

As research progressed, more complex interactions between the leader's personality and the situational variables were utilized in uncovering the factors that make a successful leader. The concept of leadership has been refined, and its functions have been analyzed. Fifty years of research on leadership have produced a contingency theory of leadership. This theory, developed by Fred Fiedler, will be described in detail later in this chapter.

I. EARLY APPROACHES TO LEADERSHIP—THE SEARCH FOR DISTINGUISHING TRAITS

A. The Results: Few Consistently Differentiating Characteristics

What makes one person a successful leader, while another person fails in the same position? Matters would be simplified if we could identify the basic characteristics that make people more or less likely to become leaders. In such a "quick and dirty" manner did the scientific study of leadership begin; leaders and nonleaders were compared on a variety of personality and intelligence measures in order to isolate differences. Bird (1940) reviewed the findings of studies done in the 1920s and 1930s. Most of these studies employed students as subjects; leadership was usually defined in terms of activities at school, but the settings from which leadership might emerge were varied—student councils, Girl Scouts and Boy Scouts, speech and drama activities, athletic teams, and many others.

In the approximately 20 studies, Bird found 79 traits that distinguished leaders from nonleaders. He was surprised that little overlap was found from one study to another. Of the 79 traits, 51 were mentioned only once. This lack of consistency was partially the result of using different, but almost synonymous, terms in different studies. For example, two studies reported leaders to be "more reliable," while another study found leaders more "accurate in work." We may safely assume that there is some consistency in the outcome of these three studies; yet the general outcome is a lack of consistency. "Intelligence," the most frequently named characteristic, appeared in only 10 of the 20 studies; "initiative" was found in 6 studies. Only these two characteristics—plus "a sense of humor" and "extroversion"—were mentioned frequently enough for Bird to consider them "general traits of leadership" (Bird, 1940, p. 380).

Apparently, Bird's conclusion is neither a result of the poor quality of early measuring instruments nor the result of haphazard definitions of leadership. Other reviews of the characteristics of leaders (Stogdill, 1948; Mann, 1959; Bass, 1960) arrived at the same conclusion: there is no consistent pattern of traits that characterizes leaders (Gibb, 1969, p. 227). Stogdill's review concluded that successful leaders generally differ from followers in possessing higher degrees of persistence, self-confidence, sociability, and dependability. However, as Bass (1960) indicates, these factors assume the form of increased motivation on the part of a person to attempt leadership and to develop relationships with other group members.

Over the 50-year life span of this research activity, intelligence remains the one characteristic most consistently related to leadership. With very few exceptions, successful leaders are superior to nonleaders in intelligence. But even here two qualifications must be mentioned. First, the relationship is not as high as one might expect. Mann's review concludes: "Considering independent studies as the unit of research, the positive association between intelligence and leadership is found to be highly significant. . . . However, the magnitude of the relationship is less impressive; no correlation reported exceeds .50 and the median r is roughly .25" (1959, p. 248). In some situations the relationship between leadership and intelligence is negligible or even negative. This leads to the second qualification: apparently, if too much discrepancy exists between the potential leader's level of intelligence and the intelligence of other group members, his success in initiating and maintaining leadership is hampered. Leaders can be too advanced for their followers. According to Gibb (1969, p. 218), "the evidence suggests that every increment of intelligence means wiser government, but that the crowd prefers to be ill-governed by people it can understand."

B. Why Is the Relationship No Stronger?

We should wonder why there is not a greater relationship between personality traits and leadership. After all, both philosophers and window-washers expect their leaders to be a cut above the average. Plato 2500 years ago wrote that those who lead the citizenry must prove themselves to be courageous, just, enlightened, and wise; and even today most people will describe leadership in terms of personal qualities or virtues that are held desirable in that society (Gibb, 1969). Gibb (1969, pp. 227–228) mentions four possible causes for this limited degree of relationship.

1. The description and measurement of personality may still be inadequate; the really important aspects of personality may not yet have been investigated.

2. Situational factors can override personality factors in influencing leadership, just as they do in manifestations of cooperation and competition (Chapter 5) or in conformity (Chapter 16).

3. Leadership is composed of a mixture of functions. In certain groups and tasks, some functions may take precedence over others. Since different functions may be accentuated in different groups, and since a particular personality may be congenial with one function and not another, it is unrealistic to expect personality to relate consistently to leadership across functions. This explanation does not find fault with personality measures; rather, it concludes that leadership is too vague and/or complex a criterion to allow for a highly consistent relationship. This type of criticism has led to refinements in the definitions of leadership, as we shall see later.

4. The groups studied have been quite different in composition. Many studies have used students; many have not. Perhaps more homogeneous sets of groups would provide a greater relationship. Clarification of this point can be achieved by studying the personalities of government and political leaders. The study of political leaders also permits exploration of the "great man" theory of leadership.

C. The "Great Man" Theory of Leadership

The "great man" theory of leadership, in its boldest form, hypothesizes that major events in national and international affairs are influenced by the men who hold leadership positions "and that all factors in history, save great men, are inconsequential" (Hook, 1955, p. 14). A sudden act by a great leader could change the fate of a nation.[1] Thus, according to the "great man" theory, Germany became overtly

[1] Perhaps the greatest exponent of the "great man" theory was the historian, Thomas Carlyle, who believed that genius would exert its influence wherever it was found. William James proposed that the mutations, or drastic changes, in society were due to great men, who initiated movement and hindered others from moving society in another direction.

nationalistic and belligerent in the 1930s solely because Adolf Hitler was in power; had there been no Hitler, neither would there have been a World War II. The exaggerated form of the theory would go on to say that, had a "great man" been in power in Great Britain or America at that time, World War II could have been averted even with Hitler's belligerence. Implicit in the "great man" theory is the assumption that leaders possess personality characteristics or a charisma that facilitates the accomplishment of their goals, even in the face of great obstacles.

Another view of the "great man" theory proposes that if a person has some of the qualities necessary for successful leadership, he will possess all of them. However, this notion of the existence of a single status-ordering of people in regard to leadership has been rejected by empirical studies (Bales, 1958; Collins, 1970). For example, the most valuable group member in terms of solving the group tasks is seldom the best liked group member.

Opposing Viewpoint: The Zeitgeist and Social Determinism. Zeitgeist means "the spirit of the times" or "the temper of the times." According to the *Zeitgeist* view of history, leaders are likened to actors who play out the roles designed for them by other forces. The leader's temperament, motives, or ability has little real influence in the face of social movements. As Victor Hugo has written: "There is nothing in this world so powerful as an idea whose time has come"—a statement reflecting the *Zeitgeist* or social determinism viewpoint, which sees leaders as only expressions, instruments, or consequences of historical laws. This latter view has frequently been taken by the majority of twentieth century historians (Hook, 1955).[2] In reviewing these conflicting hypotheses, let us first discuss the historical evidence and then report empirical studies.

The history of scientific discovery gives little credence to a hypothesis of "great men" in science. Although we give recognition to a Freud, a Darwin, or a Copernicus, we also acknowledge the fact that their discoveries each had a clear line of historical development. If Freud had not existed, someone else would have soon advanced similar theories about the role of the unconscious in our behavior. Darwin's theory of evolution was developed independently at the same time by Alfred Wallace. Newton and Leibnitz each created a differential calculus. Even scientific breakthroughs and new paradigms (Kuhn, 1962) rest upon previous work in science.

In other areas of thought, the progression is less clear. If one considers great works of art, one concludes along with Hook (1955, p. 35) that "Beethoven's sonatas and symphonies without Beethoven are inconceivable." Yet surely the *Zeitgeist* determined the style of music upon which Beethoven built his unique genius.

If we turn to the topic of political leaders, we find vast amounts of material that need interpretation. Could the "great man" theory of leadership be tested by comparing the personal qualities of ruling monarchs with the extent of growth or decline in their countries during their time? Frederick Adams Wood (1913), an early twentieth century American historian, tried to do so. He made a detailed study of 386 rulers in 14 countries in Western Europe, who lived between 1000 A.D. and the time of the French Revolution. All the rulers studied had absolute power over their kingdoms. Each was classified as strong, weak, or mediocre, on the basis of knowledge

[2]Most philosophers also preferred the *Zeitgeist* or social determinism view to the "great man" theory. For the German philosopher Hegel, the great leader was simply an expression of his times, for whatever he did fit the needs of the period. According to Herbert Spencer, great men have little influence because societies evolve in a "uniform, gradual, progressive manner" (Bass, 1960, p. 16).

about his intellectual and personal characteristics.[3] The condition of each country was also classified in one of three ways—whether it exhibited a state of prosperity, a state of decline, or no clear indication of either. (This classification was based upon the country's economic and political status—not upon its artistic, educational, or scientific development.) Wood found a high relationship between the strength of the monarch and the condition of the country—a correlation coefficient between +.60 and +.70. He states his results as follows: "Strong, mediocre, and weak monarchs are associated with strong, mediocre, and weak periods respectively in about 70 percent of the cases" (1913, p. 246). The 70 percent appears to be a misinterpretation by Wood of the meaning of a correlation value; actually, less than 50 percent of the variance in conditions of the countries is accounted for by the strength of the monarch. And, as with any correlation, we cannot infer cause and effect—as much as Wood would like to do so. Wood clearly favors the interpretation that strong leaders cause their countries to flourish. However, it is equally possible that a state of prosperity in a country permits bright or brilliant rulers to emerge. Then again, both the ruler's success and the quality of conditions could be products of a third set of factors. In addition to these difficulties, there are problems in establishing independent and objective measures of the quality of a monarch and his country's development. It is exceedingly difficult to evaluate the personality characteristics of a monarch without considering the outcome of his reign. King Charles I of England is a case in point. It is not enough that King Charles lost his crown and his head; the final indignity is that Wood calls him two-faced and obstinate. As Hook indicates, other observers might describe Charles as "shrewd and principled." Although we admire Wood's exhaustive approach to the study of "great men," we must conclude that his data do not permit an answer to his question.

Another reason for limited confidence in Wood's conclusions comes from Spiller's (1929) analysis of the biographies of great men. Spiller, a sociologist, comes to the opposing conclusion that the personal characteristics and abilities of great men have little relation to the degree of their influence upon society. Spiller writes: "If a sweeping survey of the field of human progress were made perhaps ninety-five percent of the advance would be found unconnected with the great men" (1929, p. 218).

How may the conflicting approaches of the "great man" theory and the *Zeitgeist* hypothesis be resolved? We should emphasize that no one theory is always correct and that conflicting theories can each make a contribution to the understanding of complex social phenomena. Hook believes the "great man" plays a unique and decisive role "only where the historical situation permits of major *alternative* paths of development" (1955, p. 109). Even if Christopher Columbus had not set sail in 1492, a fellow explorer would have "discovered" the New World soon thereafter. The forces at work gave no alternative. Only when choices exist, does the great man influence history. On Elba, Napoleon still had alternatives—to remain or to escape and return to power. On St. Helena, he had no alternatives.

How much difference would there have been in our involvement in Southeast Asia had President Kennedy lived through a second term in office? It is a much debated, but unanswered, question. Even Kennedy—who adopted a strong activist philosophy

[3]Wood's goal was to classify the characteristics of the ruler, not the strength or weakness of the nation at that time. However, it is likely that this second issue could have become a contaminating factor in classifying the first.

of the Presidency—complained about how his decisions got lost in the State Department. This would imply that the actual number of alternatives available to the President were less than might first appear.[4] Although Presidents influence national thought and action, the *Zeitgeist* or the spirit of the times is a force that permits these individuals to be elected in the first place.

The "Great Man" Theory in the Laboratory. A quite different approach to the "great man" theory of leadership is to bring the phenomenon into the laboratory and use manipulations and experimental controls in order to determine how much organizational performance is determined by the behavior of the single person in the top position. Borgatta, Couch, and Bales (1954) used three-man groups of military recruits in an attempt to test the theory under controlled conditions. Each man participated in four sessions of 24 minutes each, with two new participants in each session. "Great men" were selected on the basis of their performance in the first session; the top 11 of 123 men were so classified. These men were followed through the subsequent sessions so that their productivity could be assessed. (Productivity was measured by the number of acts initiated per time unit, the leadership ratings given each man by his co-participants, and the popularity ratings each man received.) "Great men" selected on the basis of the first session continued to have an influence that led to relatively superior performance in their subsequent groups. Of the 11 top men, 8 were in the top 11 productivity ranks in the second and third sessions (among 123 subjects). Seven of the 11 were still in the top rank in the fourth session. Groups in the second, third, and fourth sessions with "great men" as participants demonstrated smoother functioning, with fewer cases of anxiety or withdrawal from participation. This also implies that groups with a "great man" as a participant were more satisfied with their performance.

As impressive as these findings are, we are still a long way from verifying a "great man" theory of leadership in practice. The study by Borgatta et al. (1954) does indicate some consistency in group performance, across groups with different members. But it does not show the degree to which a charismatic leader can manipulate the content of eventful decisions.

II. LEADERSHIP AS AN INFLUENCE UPON GROUP FUNCTIONING

A. Identifying Leadership Functions

The relatively fruitless outcomes of the quest for leadership traits had several ramifications. One was a rethinking of what leadership is. During the 1940s and

[4]It should be noted that George Reedy, former press secretary and special assistant to President Lyndon Johnson, holds a dissenting view: "Presidents glory in telling people that they are prisoners of a system and of circumstances beyond their control. This is probably the subconscious device by which the chief executive prepares his alibi for history. It is true that they must deal with forces and circumstances which they did not create and cannot ignore. But how they deal with them is up to the presidents themselves. A president, in a peculiar sense that does not apply to other people, is the master of his own fate and the captain of his soul" (1970, p. 31). But Reedy's own examples defy his statement: "If Congress is balky, this is a political problem and a president is supposedly a political expert" (p. 31) and, "If foreign relations are contentious and unruly, this is merely one of the conditions under which he operates and not a 'reason' for failure" (p. 31). The assumption that the President is somehow superhuman in the task of mastering his own fate strikes us as an extremely simplified view of leadership.

1950s, dominant studies centered upon the functions of leaders; influential work was done by R. F. Bales at Harvard University and by John Hemphill, Ralph Stogdill, Carroll Shartle, and others at the Personnel Research Board at Ohio State University. The result of these efforts was a new focus upon *influence* as the salient aspect of leadership (Freedman, Carlsmith, & Sears, 1970). For example, Stogdill defined leadership as "the process (act) of influencing the activities of an organized group in its efforts toward goal setting and goal achievement" (1950, p. 3). Hence, almost every member in every group has some leadership function. Certainly all members of a football team have some such function—perhaps even the waterboy if his refreshment really renews energy and effort. Of course, some members exert much more influence toward goal setting and goal achievement than do others, as Stogdill recognized. Members of a group, team, or organization can be rank ordered—sometimes with great reliability—in regard to the amount of influence they exert in different aspects. In the case of a football team, the coach and the quarterback may exert the most influence when it comes to selecting the plays that move the team toward the goal line. However, insofar as inspiration and motivation are concerned, some other player may be more important.

An emphasis on goal-oriented functions of leaders has led to various analyses of group tasks and the leader's tasks. The first research efforts asked what kind of activities leaders actually do. For example, the United States Army (Carter, 1952) adopted 11 leadership principles, which Gibb (1969, p. 228) has cast into the following 7 behaviors: (a) performing professional and technical specialities, (b) knowing subordinates and showing consideration for them, (c) keeping channels of communication open, (d) accepting personal responsibility and setting an example, (e) initiating and directing action, (f) training men as a team, and (g) making decisions.

Similarly Hemphill, Halpin, and their associates in the Ohio State University Leadership Studies (Hemphill, 1950) identified nine dimensions of the leader's behavior; these are listed in Table 17-1. These investigators defined research as "behavior of an individual when he is directing the activities of a group toward a shared

Table 17-1. *Nine Proposed Dimensions of Leader Behavior*

1. *Initiation.* Described by the frequency with which a leader originates, facilitates, or resists new ideas and new practices.
2. *Membership.* Described by the frequency with which a leader mixes with the group, stresses informal interaction between himself and members, or interchanges personal services with members.
3. *Representation.* Described by the frequency with which the leader defends his group against attack, advances the interests of his group, and acts in behalf of his group.
4. *Integration.* Described by the frequency with which a leader subordinates individual behavior, encourages pleasant group atmosphere, reduces conflict between members, or promotes individual adjustment to the group.
5. *Organization.* Described by the frequency with which the leader defines or structures his own work, the work of other members, or the relationships among members in the performance of their work.
6. *Domination.* Described by the frequency with which the leader restricts individuals or the group in action, decision making, or expression of opinion.
7. *Communication.* Described by the frequency with which a leader provides information to members, seeks information from them, facilitates exchange of information, or shows awareness of affairs pertaining to the group.
8. *Recognition.* Described by the frequency with which a leader engages in behavior that expresses approval or disapproval of group members.
9. *Production.* Described by the frequency with which a leader sets levels of effort or achievement or prods members for greater effort or achievement.

(Adapted from Hemphill, 1950, pp. 5–6; reprinted with permission of the author.)

goal" (Halpin & Winer, 1952, p. 6). Both this approach and the Army analysis emphasize the designated leader, whereas Stogdill's approach views leadership as a process shared both by designated leaders and by all other group members.

B. Dimensions of the Leader's Behavior

What does a leader generally do? Halpin and Winer (1952) set out to identify empirically the dimensions of a leader's behavior. After constructing questionnaire items and administering them to varying sets of group members, the Ohio State researchers factor analyzed the results. Four factors of leadership emerged; the two major ones—consideration and initiating structure—are of concern to us here, particularly because they duplicate similar analyses. (The other two factors were production emphasis, accounting for about 10 percent of the variance, and sensitivity, or social awareness, accounting for about 7 percent of the variance.)

Consideration. The first dimension of leadership behavior Halpin and Winer called **consideration.** This dimension represents the extent to which the leader shows behavior that is "indicative of friendship, mutual trust, respect, and warmth" in relationships between himself and the other group members (Halpin, 1966, p. 86). Genuine consideration by the leader reflects his awareness of the needs of each group member. He encourages subordinates to communicate with him in order to participate in decision making. In Halpin and Winer's study, consideration accounted for almost half of the variance in leaders' behaviors.

Initiating Structure. A second dimension was called **initiating structure,** which was later defined as "the leader's behavior in delineating the relationship between himself and members of the work group, and in endeavoring to establish well-defined patterns of organization, channels of communication, and methods of procedure" (Halpin, 1966, p. 86). Thus, initiating structure refers to the leader's task of getting the group moving toward its designated goal. (A part of initiating structure may be identifying and agreeing upon the goal.) Initiating structure accounted for about one-third of the variance in leaders' behaviors.

Other analyses of the leader's functions produced similar divisions into two primary dimensions. Bales (1953) has concluded that leadership functions may be differentiated into *task orientation* (achievement of the group goals) and *group-maintenance* orientation, in which a leader is concerned with maintaining the group members' morale and cohesiveness. Because of independent confirmations by Bales (1958) and others (Fleishman, Harris, & Burtt, 1955), we may conclude that *initiating structure* and *consideration* (or similar factors) are two major dimensions of leadership behavior and not simply mutually exclusive leadership patterns (Gibb, 1969).

The behavior of a specific leader in regard to these two dimensions can be assessed by asking the members of the leader's group to rate him on a set of descriptive statements. These statements form the Leader Behavior Description Questionnaire (LBDQ), devised by the Personnel Research Board at Ohio State University (Halpin, 1966; Stogdill, 1969); the statements are listed in Table 17–2. The group members indicate the frequency with which their leader engages in each form of behavior by checking one of five adverbs: always, often, occasionally, seldom, or never.

Is it possible for a leader to be skilled in both initiating structure and consideration for others? Often the same person cannot fulfill both these functions successfully. The

Table 17-2. *The Leader Behavior Description Questionnaire*

Initiating Structure
1. He makes his attitudes clear to the staff.
2. He tries out his new ideas with the staff.
3. He rules with an iron hand.[a]
4. He criticizes poor work.
5. He speaks in a manner not to be questioned.
6. He assigns staff members to particular tasks.
7. He works without a plan.[a]
8. He maintains definite standards of performance.
9. He emphasizes the meeting of deadlines.
10. He encourages the use of uniform procedures.
11. He makes sure that his part in the organization is understood by all members.
12. He asks that staff members follow standard rules and regulations.
13. He lets staff members know what is expected of them.
14. He sees to it that staff members are working up to capacity.
15. He sees to it that the work of staff members is coordinated.

Consideration
1. He does personal favors for staff members.
2. He does little things to make it pleasant to be a member of the staff.
3. He is easy to understand.
4. He finds time to listen to staff members.
5. He keeps to himself.[a]
6. He looks out for the personal welfare of individual staff members.
7. He refuses to explain his actions.[a]
8. He acts without consulting the staff.[a]
9. He is slow to accept new ideas.[a]
10. He treats all staff members as his equals.
11. He is willing to make changes.
12. He is friendly and approachable.
13. He makes staff members feel at ease when talking with them.
14. He puts suggestions made by the staff into operation.
15. He gets staff approval on important matters before going ahead.

[a]Scored negatively. (Reprinted with permission of The Macmillan Company from *Theory and Research in Administration* by Andrew W. Halpin. © Copyright by Andrew W. Halpin, 1966.)

achievement-oriented leader must often be critical of the ideas or activities of other members; he must constantly turn the members' attention toward the goal, when they digress into some diversionary activity or discussion. He must make unpleasant decisions, often when unanimity is lacking. Often the leader reports that it is difficult for him to be task-oriented and considerate at the same time. Hence another group member may become the group-maintenance expert, concerned with arbitrating task-oriented disputes, relieving tension, and giving every member a chance to be heard or a pat on the back. Traditionally many families have developed an unstated understanding that the father is the task specialist and the mother is the group-maintenance specialist (although contemporary changes in family structure are altering this pattern).

In organized groups—whether a high school basketball team, an Air Force bomber crew, or the teaching staff of an elementary school—an evaluation can be made as to how well the leader succeeds in initiating structure and showing consideration. The foregoing discussion would imply that the correlation between performance on these two functions is low; in other words, a school principal who keeps his teachers task oriented would not be particularly considerate or sensitive. Research indicates that the relationships are generally low (Greenwood & McNamara, 1969), which suggests independence in regard to success in achieving the two functions.

However, sometimes a given behavior may facilitate the achievement of both functions; a leader who helps a group solve a difficult problem may, by this action, develop solidarity and better morale (Cartwright & Zander, 1960, p. 496). There are a few leaders who are skilled at both functions, but such persons are rare. The reader may contemplate, for example, how many Presidents of the United States were successful both in "getting the country moving again" and "bringing us together."

C. The Relationship between the Leader's Functions and the Leader's Success

We have described how the leader's success in accomplishing two functions can be assessed by the ratings given him by his co-workers. But what difference do such ratings make? Can we show that leaders who receive more positive ratings have more successful groups? Studies on two diverse types of groups—departmental faculties at a liberal arts college and crews of Air Force bombing planes—provide answers for these questions.

During the Korean war, LBDQ scores were obtained from the flight crews of 52 B-29 commanders; 33 of these commanders were later rated by their supervisors in regard to their combat performance in the war (Halpin, 1954). Negative correlations were found between the supervisors' ratings and the commanders' consideration scores; in other words, pilots who were rated as successful by their superiors obtained lower consideration scores as a result of their crews' ratings. To the contrary, the correlations between the supervisors' ratings and the pilots' initiating structure scores were positive; that is, good pilots were seen by their crews as more task oriented and better at achieving goals. Each crew also completed a Crew Satisfaction Index. The correlations between the Crew Satisfaction Index and consideration scores were high and positive, indicating that pilots who were considerate had more satisfied crews. Notice the discrepancy; pilots high on consideration were rated as less successful by superiors but maintained crews who were more satisfied. Thus is encapsulated a basic conflict in role expectations faced by many leaders—to achieve or to care for others?

In a similar study conducted during the Korean war (Halpin, 1953), 87 B-29 aircraft commanders were rated on overall effectiveness by their superiors, while their crews completed the LBDQ. The commanders were then classified as to whether they were above or below the means on both dimensions of leadership. Table 17–3 indicates that of the 9 commanders who were in the upper 10 percent in overall effectiveness, 8 were above the mean on both consideration and initiating structure. Of the 10 commanders who were in the bottom 12 percent in overall effectiveness, 6 were below the mean on both dimensions of leader behavior. The successful leader, as rated by his supervisor, facilitates both group achievement and group maintenance.

In an entirely different setting, Hemphill (1955) asked faculty members at a liberal arts college to name the five departments in the college that had the reputation of being the best led or administered and the five departments that were least well administered. Faculty members in each department then rated their department chairman on the LBDQ. When the average LBDQ scores for chairmen were tabulated, the results emerged clearly. (See Table 17–4.) Eight of the nine chairmen of well-administered departments had scores above the median on both LBDQ measures, whereas only one of nine poorly-administered departments had a chairman who

Table 17-3. *Bomber Pilots' Effectiveness and Ratings of Them by Their Crews*

	Below mean on both consideration and initiating structure	*Above mean on both consideration and initiating structure*
Upper 10 percent on overall effectiveness	1	8
Lower 12 percent on overall effectiveness	6	4

Figures indicate the number of commanders in high and low groups on ratings of overall effectiveness, scoring above and below the mean on both leader behavior dimensions. (From Andrew W. Halpin, Studies in Aircrew Composition: III. *The Combat Leader Behavior of B-29 Aircraft Commanders,* HFORL Memo, No. TN-54-7. Washington, D.C.: Human Factors Operations Research Laboratory, Bolling Air Force Base, September 1953, p. 15.)

was rated favorably by his staff. The department's administrative reputation is quite consistent with the ratings that its staff gives its chairman. Of course, part of the department's reputation stems directly from the gossip and faculty-room grumblings or enthusiasms of its staff members; thus, "departmental administrative reputation" is a criterion not completely free of contamination. Though the results of this study are consistent with the hypothesis that LBDQ scores relate to successful leadership, this study is not as impressive as those that used Air Force crews. Nevertheless, even though these studies were only partially successful in achieving a completely pure criterion of leadership quality, they support the conclusion that effective leadership behavior is associated with accomplishing initiating structure and consideration for co-workers.

III. FIEDLER'S CONTINGENCY THEORY OF LEADERSHIP

In our review of studies on leadership, we have seen how the search for basic personality traits in the 1930s and 1940s produced little in the way of tangible results.

Table 17-4. *The Relationship between the Reputation Achieved by College Departments and the Consideration and Initiating Structure Scores of Department Chairmen Taken Conjunctively (*N = *18)*

	Number of Chairmen	
Chairman's leadership	*With dept. below median in reputation*	*With dept. above median in reputation*
Score of 41 or larger on consideration and a score of 36 or more on initiating structure	1	8
Score of less than 41 on consideration or less than 36 on initiating structure	8	1

(From John K. Hemphill, Leadership Behavior Associated with the Administrative Reputation of College Departments. *Journal of Educational Psychology*, **46**, No. 7, November 1955, p. 396. Reprinted with permission of Abrahams Magazine Service.)

The 1950s saw a shift toward analyzing the functions or dimensions of a leader's behavior, along with documenting the relationships between the leader's effectiveness and the ratings he received from his supervisors, co-workers, and subordinates. But a functional analysis was not enough. Not until the 1960s—and the work of Fred E. Fiedler—have the trait approach and the functional analysis been put together meaningfully.

Fiedler defines the leader as the individual in the group who is given the task of directing and coordinating task-relevant activities, or who—in the absence of a designated leader—carries the primary responsibility for performing these functions in a group. Fiedler's theory is called a *contingency theory of leadership* because it relates leader effectiveness to aspects of the situation in which the group operates. Specifically, the theory predicts that the leader's contribution to group effectiveness is dependent upon both the characteristics of the leader and the favorableness of the situation for the leader (Graen, Alvares, Orris, & Martelle, 1970). To Fiedler, there is no one successful type of leader; task-oriented leaders may be effective under some circumstances but not under others. A permissive leader who is oriented toward human relations and who has been successful with one group may not be successful in another group where the situation differs.

One virtue of Fiedler's theory is that it reconciles previous findings, which were contradictory in regard to what makes a good leader. It is an inductive theory, developed on the basis of a 20-year research program that has studied more than 800 groups. The theory is now used to predict the outcome of later studies. To Fiedler, the basic dimension is *leadership style*, which is defined as "the underlying need-structure of the individual that motivates his behavior in various leadership situations" (Graen et al., 1970, p. 286). Leadership style is assessed by the extent of the leader's esteem for his "least preferred co-worker," or the LPC measure.[5] Each leader is asked to think of all the people with whom he has ever worked and then to select the one with whom it has been most difficult to cooperate. This person represents his "least preferred co-worker," or LPC.[6] The leader is then given a set of bipolar rating scales and is asked to rate this least preferred co-worker on each of these dimensions. The number used is usually between 16 and 24; Table 17–5 gives a set of rating scales from a study by one of Fiedler's co-workers (J. G. Hunt, 1967, p. 291). In this case, the LPC score is the sum of the ratings circled on the 21 dimensions. Notice that for each dimension the favorable end is given a value of 8, the unfavorable end a value of 1. In order to determine which end is favorable, the investigator can use his knowledge of the society in which he operates, or he can ask subjects to answer the form in terms of where they would like to be on each dimension. The latter is a safer procedure. Assuming there is no unanimity (for example,

[5]Fiedler makes a distinction between leadership style and a particular leader's style. The latter refers to "the specific acts in which a leader engages while directing or coordinating the work of his group." Actions or behavior may change to fit the situation, but leadership style remains relatively constant. Yet, because of the operational definition of leadership style, its essence remains rather vague to many readers.

[6]The LPC need not be someone with whom the leader is currently working. As a matter of fact, most subjects describe someone with whom they previously worked (Hunt, 1967). In some of his research, Fiedler has used the ASo scale (Assumed Similarity of Opposites) to measure similarity between the ratings a leader gives to his best and least liked co-workers. ASo scores and LPC scores correlate highly with each other (from +.70 to +.93).

Table 17-5. *Bipolar Ratings Used in Rating Least Preferred Co-Worker*

Pleasant	8	7	6	5	4	3	2	1	Unpleasant
Friendly	8	7	6	5	4	3	2	1	Unfriendly
Bad	1	2	3	4	5	6	7	8	Good
Distant	1	2	3	4	5	6	7	8	Close
Supportive	8	7	6	5	4	3	2	1	Hostile
Contented	8	7	6	5	4	3	2	1	Discontented
Stubborn	1	2	3	4	5	6	7	8	Not stubborn
Not enterprising	1	2	3	4	5	6	7	8	Enterprising
Tense	1	2	3	4	5	6	7	8	Relaxed
Not studious	1	2	3	4	5	6	7	8	Studious
Unsympathetic	1	2	3	4	5	6	7	8	Sympathetic
Impatient	1	2	3	4	5	6	7	8	Patient
Happy	8	7	6	5	4	3	2	1	Depressed
Unenthusiastic	1	2	3	4	5	6	7	8	Enthusiastic
Not confident	1	2	3	4	5	6	7	8	Confident
Disagreeable	1	2	3	4	5	6	7	8	Agreeable
Unproductive	1	2	3	4	5	6	7	8	Productive
Unadventurous	1	2	3	4	5	6	7	8	Adventurous
Sociable	8	7	6	5	4	3	2	1	Unsociable
Satisfied	8	7	6	5	4	3	2	1	Dissatisfied
Unambitious	1	2	3	4	5	6	7	8	Ambitious

(Adapted from J. G. Hunt, Fiedler's leadership contingency model: An empirical test in three organizations, *Organizational Behavior and Human Performance,* 1967, **2**, 291. Copyright 1967 by Academic Press, Inc. and reprinted by permission.)

some people would prefer to be unproductive rather than productive), the investigator must establish some arbitrary degree of agreement as a cutoff for using the dimension in his rating system. The researcher might say, for example, that if 80 percent or more of the subjects agree on the socially desirable end of the scale, then that end of the scale is the favorable one. Notice also that the scale in Table 17–5 utilizes only *monotonic* dimensions—that is, ones where unfavorability resides at one extreme and favorability resides at the other.[7]

The LPC score may be thought of as an indication of a leader's emotional reaction to people with whom he could not work well (Fiedler, 1969). When we sum the ratings given by different leaders to their designated LPC, we find that some of these leaders give their LPC extremely unfavorable ratings, which usually average around 2 (Fiedler, 1971). Fiedler first hypothesized that these persons, called *Low-LPC leaders,* were task-oriented administrators, who gain satisfaction and self-esteem from the group's completion of its tasks, even if the leader himself must suffer poor interpersonal relationships in order to do so. Low-LPC leaders tend to be punitive toward others, though not necessarily more distant. In contrast, there are other leaders who give even their designated LPC relatively favorable ratings; Fiedler called these persons *High-LPC leaders* and considered them to be more concerned about interpersonal relations. To High-LPC leaders, satisfaction comes from happy group relationships; they are more relaxed, compliant, and nondirective. Thus High-LPC and Low-LPC leaders have different basic needs, which they seek to satisfy in the group. Leadership style, an underlying motivation, is seen as the crux of the

[7]There are other dimensions where unfavorability may reside at both extremes (hesitant versus impulsive, for instance), and a favorable position is in the middle of the dimension. This latter type of scale is called a nonmonotonic scale.

leader's success. More recently, Fiedler (1971) has been less willing to equate Low-LPC leaders with a task orientation and High-LPC leaders with a relationship orientation. High-LPC leaders also seem to be higher in cognitive complexity.[8]

There is evidence that the LPC measure is valid and reliable (Shima, 1968). In a laboratory task, High-LPC leaders acted in a more socioemotionally facilitative manner; Low-LPC leaders were more task-oriented (Gruenfeld, Rance, & Weissenberg, 1969). The split-half reliability for a 20-item LPC scale is about +.90 (Fiedler, 1967a). Test-retest correlations are not as high. A total of 54 experienced leaders completed the LPC form and repeated it eight weeks later; the reliability coefficient was +.57. For 32 inexperienced leaders under the same conditions the reliability coefficient was +.47. However, these groups were composed of military recruits undergoing eight weeks of basic training. Using mature U.S. Air Force officers in a reliability study with an eight-week time interval, Fiedler (1967a) found a test-retest reliability coefficient of +.68.

The basic importance of Fiedler's contingency theory is that it presumes an interaction between situational and relationship components; both these, according to Fiedler, play a role in determining the nature of the leader's influence and the extent of his effectiveness. The following three situational and relationship components are proposed as important.

1. The leader's personal relations with members of his group is one component. Relationships can range from very good to very poor; they are partially determined, of course, by the leader's personality. Fiedler finds that the leader-group relationship is the single most important factor in determining the leader's influence in a small group (Fiedler, 1964, p. 159).[9] To some extent, leaders with good relationships can overcome the limitation of being weak in the second component, or the degree of their "position power."

2. The leader's "legitimate power" or "position power" is a second important component in a leader's effectiveness. How much power and authority is provided the leader by the position he holds? Does he have the authority to hire and fire; can he reward persons by giving raises in pay or status; or is he quite limited in his means of regulating the behavior of other members? Does the organization behind him back up his authority? For example, the chairman of a group of volunteer workers in a political campaign would ordinarily have little position power over the volunteers. A football coach, an owner of a small business, and a police chief carry high degrees of power. Leaders with high position power carry some kind of separate rank or status and have "clout," whereas leaders low in position power cannot punish their members by altering their rank or status. In fact, low-position-power leaders may be deposed by the group members. Position power, measured by a checklist of behaviors, is considered the least important of the three components

[8]We may still expect that Low-LPC leaders will emphasize initiating structure and productivity, while High-LPC leaders emphasize consideration and sensitivity. Likewise, Low-LPC leaders would use coercion, while High-LPC leaders would use persuasion, in influencing others (McGinnies, 1970).

[9]The leader's relationship with the group has been measured in two ways: (a) by determining to what extent the leader sees himself as the group's most preferred member, or (b) by a "group atmosphere" scale on which the leader defines the climate of his group. Again, here, the relationship of conceptual definition to measurement is ambiguous. The group's atmosphere and the leader's perception of the group's liking for him may not be highly related. The use of the leader as the sole definer of group atmosphere also has limitations.

of a leader's effectiveness because group success can often result from a structured task or a popular leader even if he lacks authority and power.

3. The amount of structure in the task that the group has been assigned to perform is a third component. How well does the leader know how to proceed? Some tasks possess a great deal of *goal clarity;* the requirements of the task are clearly known or programmed. To the contrary, tasks of *ad hoc* committees, policy-making groups, and creative groups often lack goal clarity and structure—no one knows what the group purposes are, or how the group should proceed. A second element of task structure is its degree of *solution specificity* (Shaw, 1963); that is, there may or may not be more than one correct solution for the group's task. A third aspect is the degree of *decision verifiability;* once a decision has been made, how clearly does the group know that it is a correct one? All these aspects of task structure play a role in determining the effectiveness of different types of leaders.[10] However, task structure clearly interacts with position power. If the task is clearly structured, the leader needs less position power to get the job done because everybody's role has already been specified.

For purposes of simplification and analysis, Fiedler considered each of these three aspects as a dichotomy. Leader-member relationships are either good or poor; position power is either strong or weak; and task structure is either clear or unclear. As there are two categories in each of three aspects, we may conceive of a system of eight classifications (2 × 2 × 2), which would encompass all possible combinations of these aspects. Fiedler has done this in order to see what leadership style works best in each situation. (See Table 17–6.) In fact, he has added a ninth category (category VIII-A) to cover instances where the leader-member relationships are extremely poor.

In seeking an understanding of the determinants of effectiveness, Fiedler hypothesized that the degree to which the conditions are favorable or unfavorable to the leader is another important characteristic in addition to leadership style. Favorable conditions emerge from situations that permit the leader to exert a great deal of influence on his group. For example, good leader-member relations, strong position power, and clear task structure are considered favorable for the leader. The nine classifications in Table 17–6 are listed in order of their favorability for the leader. Class I, for example, is most favorable. Class VIII-A is quite unfavorable because here the personal relations are poor, task structure is unclear, and position power is weak. Fiedler concludes that Low-LPC leaders (task-oriented, controlling types) are most effective under group conditions that are either very favorable (classes I, II, III) or very unfavorable to the leader (classes VII, VIII, and VIII-A). In other words, the Low-LPC leader is most effective in cases where he has a great deal of influence and power or in cases where he has no influence and power. However, High-LPC leaders (permissive, relationship-oriented types) are most effective under conditions that are moderately favorable or unfavorable and where the leader's influence and power are mixed or moderate (classes IV, V, VI). Let us look at these types of situations in greater detail.

Categories II and VI in Table 17–6 represent clear task structure (formal task groups) with weak position power (basketball teams, surveying groups, laboratory

[10] Fiedler has used scales developed by Shaw (1963) in order to measure degree of structure.

Table 17-6. *Classification of Group-Task Situations on the Basis of Three Factors*

	Leader's personal relations with members	*Task structure*	*Position power*	*Number of studies*	*Median correlation*
I	Good	Clear, or structured	Strong	8	−.52
II	Good	Clear	Weak	3	−.58
III	Good	Unclear, or unstructured	Strong	12	−.33
IV	Good	Unclear	Weak	10	+.47
V	Moderately poor	Clear	Strong	6	+.42
VI	Moderately poor	Clear	Weak	0	Not avail.
VII	Moderately poor	Unclear	Strong	12	+.05
VIII	Moderately poor	Unclear	Weak	12	−.43
VIII-A	Very poor	Clear	Strong	1	−.67

Note: A positive correlation means that a High-LPC leader (relationship-oriented leader) is more effective in that situation, whereas a negative correlation means that a Low-LPC leader (task-oriented) is more effective. (From *A Theory of Leadership Effectiveness* by F. E. Fiedler. Copyright 1967 by McGraw-Hill Book Company. Used by permission of McGraw-Hill Book Company.)

groups). Groups in category II have good leader-member relationships, whereas in category VI these relationships are poor. When these two categories were compared, it was found that task-oriented leaders with low LPC scores are more effective when relationships are good (category II), whereas High-LPC leaders (relationship-oriented) are more effective when relationships are poor (category VI). High school basketball teams with good relationships between the captain and the other team members win more games, if the captain is a task-oriented leader (Fiedler, 1964).

Categories I and V represent clear task structure with strong position power (bomber crews, open-hearth crews, infantry squads, service station crews). Again, groups with good leader-member relationships (category I) performed better under task-oriented Low-LPC leaders. Groups with relatively poor leader-member relationships (category V) performed better under relationship-oriented, High-LPC leaders.

Subsequent analyses showed that in groups with extremely poor leader-member relationships (where the group members rejected the leader), Low-LPC leaders were more effective than High-LPC leaders. These findings led Fiedler to compose the additional classification, category VIII-A, for groups with clear task structure, strong position power, and very poor leader-member relations (Fiedler, 1967, p. 84). Perhaps in these groups, the leader and group members are so much at odds that the concern and liking of the High-LPC leader is ineffective; the group members may hate their leader but are more responsive to him if he is task oriented.

These findings are additionally important because they led to the conclusion that Low-LPC, controlling leaders are more effective in groups that are either very favorable (category I) or very unfavorable (category VIII-A) for the leader. Some confirmation for this conclusion is found in Hill's (1969) investigation of supervision in two organizations. However, the evidence from Hill's study reveals that this relationship is very tenuous, as Graen et al. point out (1970, p. 291).

Categories IV and VIII in Table 17–6 represent groups with unclear task structure and weak position power (faculty *ad hoc* committees, Sunday school curriculum committees, weekend encounter groups). According to Fiedler, such groups are often concerned with creative problems and goals. Their task is not clearly defined, and the leader has little authority. Fiedler concludes: "The relationship-oriented leaders

(High LPC) performed best in groups which were relatively pleasant or relaxed (category IV). Task-oriented leaders (Low LPC) performed best in groups which were relatively tense and unpleasant and in which the leader felt less well-accepted (category VIII)" (1967a, p. 120). Notice that the direction of the difference in effectiveness between High- and Low-LPC leaders is opposite from that in categories II and VI and in categories I and V.

Categories III and VII represent groups with unclear task structure and powerful leaders (R.O.T.C. groups with creativity tasks). Results are quite obscure here; there was some tendency for "groups directed by task-oriented leaders who experienced a relatively pleasant group atmosphere [to perform] better on all tasks except one" (Fiedler, 1967a, p. 129).

The most basic conclusion of Fiedler's massive program of research is that there is no such thing as a good leader for all situations. "A leader who is effective in one situation may or may not be in another" (Fiedler, 1969, p. 42). The organization, the tasks, and the power of the leader, the leader's popularity, and his relationship with his co-workers all play a role. If a leader is not currently successful in meeting the goals of the group, it may be possible to introduce changes in the situation in order to facilitate success. The leader's position power may be changed, or greater structure may be introduced into the tasks given the group. Laboratory training in sensitivity groups may help a leader learn where he has skills and where he does not. He can learn to avoid situations where he is weakest and to find tasks and groups that fit his leadership style. Fiedler believes that it is more fruitful to try to change the leader's work environment than to change his personality or leadership style (Fiedler, 1969, p. 43). However, other social scientists report that the application of positive reinforcement, dissonance, reactance, and other psychological principles can modify unsuccessful communication habits in a supervisor (Varela, 1969).

Although Fiedler's approach should be commended as being the most comprehensive attack on leadership effectiveness yet developed, undoubtedly it will require refinement as more data are accumulated. Even now, there are failures to verify the model when the criteria for leadership success are extended beyond productivity measures to supervisors' ratings, a second type of criterion (Duffy, 1970; Duffy, Kavanagh, MacKinney, Wolins, & Lyons, 1970). Another limitation to Fiedler's approach resides in the ambiguity of the LPC measure. What is the LPC measuring? What is the difference between leaders with high and low LPC scores? Initially, the LPC score seemed to reflect the degree of a leader's tolerance for inept co-workers. But Fishbein, Landy, and Hatch (1969) have concluded that the major function of the LPC measure is that it identifies people who have different types of least preferred co-workers. This point should be clarified through future research.

One other difficulty with Fiedler's theory is the choice of a criterion for a successful test of the theory. Ordinarily, we would expect that a statistically significant correlation in the expected direction between LPC and group performance scores would be used to demonstrate the accuracy of the theory. Most of the correlations in Fiedler's studies and in the studies of his co-workers are nonsignificant. Fiedler chooses to verify the theory by showing that the general majority of observed correlations are in the direction predicted by the theory. For example, in discussing the results of one study, he reports: "While only one of the 16 (sic) correlations was significant, only one of the eight correlations, namely, .03, was not in the hypothesized direction" (1967a, p. 119). Similar statements may be found in Fiedler's

(1971) review of more recent validations. Reliance on such a weak criterion does not establish confidence in the accuracy of the theory (Graen et al., 1970; Butterfield, 1968).

IV. LEADERSHIP, ORGANIZATIONAL EFFECTIVENESS, AND ASSUMPTIONS ABOUT HUMAN NATURE

Throughout this chapter two types of leaders have been selected for study and contrast—the task-oriented and controlling type and the group-oriented and equalitarian or democratic type. Each type of leadership makes certain different assumptions about the nature of man—assumptions that have a great impact upon the way the leader deals with his overseers and his subordinates. This section reviews changing conceptions of the nature of man held by leaders; once more we see an interesting sophistication and complexity arising from an accumulation of research and thought (Cyert & MacCrimmon, 1968).

Any member of any group possesses a variety of skills and resources. If the group is the Los Angeles Rams, a particular member may be valued because of his speed, strength, or endurance. But each member possesses skills other than his physical ones; he has social skills, which may facilitate team harmony. He has cognitive skills, which may aid in the development of a game plan. The coach's assumptions about the skills of each player may emphasize only the physical ones. Edgar Schein (1965), in a brief but interesting text called *Organizational Psychology,* introduces four different assumptions about the nature of man held by leaders. These four assumptions, described in detail below, refer to the *rational-economic man,* the *social man,* the *self-actualizing man,* and the *complex man.* If we ask a department store sales manager, a football coach, or a fraternity president about the best way to get the highest quality of productivity from co-workers, his answer may reflect one of these four assumptions.

A. Rational-Economic Man

The most influential voice in managerial psychology in the first quarter of this century was that of Frederick Taylor (1911), who advocated what was called a scientific-management approach. To Taylor, the worker was completely economically motivated, and hence Taylor's answer to the problem of motivating workers was a piecework incentive system of pay (Tannenbaum, 1966). The laboring man was seen as motivated purely by self-interest—a throwback to the philosophy of hedonism described in Chapter 3.

Since man is primarily motivated by money—according to rational-economic theory—the leader's task is one of manipulating and motivating the worker to perform his best within the limits of what he can be paid. Workers' feelings are seen as irrational, and these feelings must be prevented from obstructing the expression of the worker's rational self-interest (Schein, 1965, p. 48).

This position resembles what Douglas McGregor (1960, 1966, 1967) called

Theory X, or management's conventional conception of the worker. (McGregor included additional assumptions under Theory X, which are compatible with the rational-economic theory of man—namely, that man is inherently passive, lazy, and gullible, and that he is incapable of self-discipline and self-control.) Altogether, the rational-economic theory says there is little to the worker's motivation beyond his achieving the largest possible paycheck at the end of the week.

The assembly line is an example of the rational-economic theory in action. The production of a light switch, a radio, or an automobile is broken down into thousands of specific tasks. A worker may have to make only one response—perhaps he may tighten one screw in every light switch that passes in front of him on the never-ending assembly line. His pay can be related to the number of switches he processes. The goal of management is to produce as many finished products as possible; according to this theory, whether the worker experiences satisfaction or boredom is quite unimportant. "The fact that the employee's emotional needs were not fulfilled on the job was of little consequence because he often did not expect them to be fulfilled" (Schein, 1965, p. 50).

There is no denying that better pay and merit bonuses are important motivators for workers. To that degree, the rational-economic theory of man has some applicability. But the theory does not suffice; it fails to recognize other needs of workers that contribute to satisfaction and productivity or, when unfulfilled, to employee turnover and malingering.

B. Social Man

Between 1927 and 1932 a series of studies used employees of the Western Electric Company's Hawthorne works in Chicago (Roethlisberger & Dickson, 1939).[11] A group of female workers assembling relay switches for telephones was moved to a special room, and a number of innovations were introduced to study the effects upon the workers' productivity. Some of these innovations were expected to lower productivity—the lighting was dimmed; the working day was shortened by an hour; coffee breaks were added while keeping the number of working hours the same. Finally, a longer work day was instituted without any rest periods or coffee breaks. Quite surprisingly, every innovation had the effect of increasing productivity. Output continued to rise higher than ever before. The psychologists concluded that the workers' productivity had increased because the workers felt that management was interested in them. Previous feelings of alienation and loss of identity in the workers were replaced with a feeling that they were special and that their employers cared about them as people.[12] Elton Mayo (1945), one of the Hawthorne researchers, developed a set of assumptions about the worker, which reflect a model emphasizing *social man.*

1. A worker is basically motivated by social needs and determines his basic sense of identity through relationships with others.
2. As a result of the industrial revolution and the segmenting of tasks into specific

[11] A thorough review and critique of the extensive Hawthorne studies is found in H. A. Landsberger, *Hawthorne Revisited* (Ithaca, N. Y.: Cornell University, 1958).

[12] The *Hawthorne effect* subsequently became a term used to label this phenomenon of working harder and producing more because of the feeling of participating in something new and special.

activities, meaning has gone out of work itself for many workers, who—now alienated—seek its meaning in the social relationships available on the job.

3. Working man is more responsive to the social forces of his peer group than to the incentives and controls of management. The working group can often determine and control what is a normal rate of production, despite management's frenzied efforts to increase output. In another work group in the Hawthorne plant, one new worker was at first a "rate buster"—she turned out almost twice as many products a day as the others. But soon the other women had convinced her what was an appropriate or justified rate.

4. Working man is responsive to management to the extent that a supervisor can meet a subordinate's social needs and needs for acceptance. (Adapted from Schein, 1965, p. 51.)[13]

Thus, according to the assumptions of *social man,* the tasks of a shop foreman or department chairman require that some attention be given to the needs of his subordinates. Even with feelings of alienation, workers may perform tolerably or adequately, but productivity (as well as worker morale and satisfaction) can be increased by a leader's or manager's recognition of the workers' needs. A variety of studies in the 1940s and 1950s demonstrated the potency of the conception of *social man.* Many of these studies were stimulated by the thinking of Kurt Lewin, the father of group dynamics, who sensitized industry to the powerful effect of participatory decision making upon job efficiency.

A prototype of a Lewinian study was conducted in a pajama plant in rural Virginia. One of the officers of the company, psychologist Alfred Marrow, invited Lewin to meet with the plant staff to discuss a basic problem: the inexperienced workers hired by the new company were not reaching the level of skill that was expected of them by management. The company had tried everything. The workers were being paid more than they had been receiving on their previous jobs; the management had tried a multitude of reward systems, and all had failed.

Lewin made a number of interpretations. One was that the inability of the workers to meet management's standards might derive from their belief that the company's standard was impossible to attain. Lewin advocated the importation of some experienced workers from other communities, to work alongside the local workers. Although this was an unpopular suggestion—because the town officials strongly opposed giving jobs to outsiders—the unnerved plant officials tried it. The skilled, experienced operators that were imported adapted to management's standards. When the local, unskilled workers saw the performance of the experienced outsiders, they vowed that they could also reach the desired level, and their production rate gradually began to increase.

Later studies at this same plant (French and Coch, 1948) dealt with resistance in production workers to changes in working methods. This resistance was manifested by higher rates of turnover, lowered levels of production, and verbal hostility toward the plant and other co-workers. French, one of Lewin's associates along with Coch, the personnel manager, decided to try three methods of instituting changes in job duties, each involving a different amount of participation by the workers in planning

[13] Despite the fact that Mayo's model of the worker as a social being was an improvement over the rational-economic conception of man, it was justifiably criticized by liberal sociologists such as C. Wright Mills (1948) as being pro-management and seeing the worker as only a means to ends defined by the company ownership.

the details of new job activities. The first group of workers was simply told about the planned changes in their jobs and what was now expected of them; they did not participate in the decision. The second group appointed representatives from among themselves to meet with management to consider problems involved in changing working methods. The third group procedure involved every worker in the unit, not just certain representatives. All members of the third group met with management, participated actively in discussions, shared many suggestions, and helped plan the most efficient methods for mastering the new jobs.

Marrow (1969) reports the differences between groups in job adaptation. These findings support the conception of *social man.*

> The differences in outcome of the three procedures were clear-cut and dramatic. Average production in the non-participation group dropped 20 percent immediately and did not regain the pre-change level. Nine percent of the group quit. Morale fell sharply, as evidenced by marked hostility toward the supervisor, by slowdowns, by complaints to the union, and by other instances of aggressive behavior.
>
> The group which participated through representatives required two weeks to recover its pre-change output. Their attitude was cooperative, and none of the members of the group quit their jobs.
>
> The consequences in the total-participation group were in sharp contrast to those in the non-participating group. It regained the pre-change output after only two days and then climbed steadily until it reached a level about 14 percent above the earlier average. No one quit; all members of the group worked well with their supervisors, and there were no signs of aggression (pp. 150–151).

Lewinian methods and conceptions of social man may facilitate better employee-leader relations, as well as heightened productivity. Such effects are not limited to the industrial plant. More democratic procedures in the selection of college presidents and boards of trustees may improve faculty and student morale and productivity. Lewin, Lippitt, and White's (1939) classic study of the social climate of boys' task groups has demonstrated the wide applicability of the conception of social man. Small groups of 11-year-old boys met after school for several weeks in order to make masks and carry out similar activities. The adult leader of the groups acted in either an authoritarian, a democratic, or a laissez-faire manner. The authoritarian leader usually started by giving an order, frequently criticized the work, and often disrupted activity by suddenly making the children begin a new project. This type of leader gave the boys no indication of long-range goals and frequently remained aloof. The democratic leader worked together with the group to develop goals and the means for attaining them. All decisions were made by the entire group. The laissez-faire leader was noncommittal and passive throughout the boys' activity periods. This type of leader gave out information only upon request and did not enter into the spirit of the task. As in the pajama factory, these experimental variations produced changes in both productivity and satisfaction. Authoritarian leadership resulted in more restlessness, discontent, aggression, fighting, and damage to play materials. Apathy was another reaction to authoritarian leadership. Apathy dominated in groups with laissez-faire leaders. All but 1 of 20 boys in the groups preferred the democratic leadership. (Preferences were not a result of the specific person who served as leader, since three different men served as leaders in all three social climates.)

Results regarding productivity were not as clear-cut. Laissez-faire groups were poor in productivity. The largest number of masks was produced by the authoritarian groups, but democratic groups were better able to put forth a sustained effort when the leader was absent.

Productivity is a vague criterion; and we must ask: productivity for what? We also need to distinguish between performance in the short run and in the long run. The more simple, concrete, and terminal the task of the group, the more effective is authoritarian leadership (Adams, 1954; reviewed in Anderson, 1959). In a complex or creative task or in one requiring cooperation among members, democratic leadership may be more effective. (The distinction here touches upon structured and unstructured situations where, according to Fiedler, High-LPC and Low-LPC leaders have different degrees of effectiveness.)

If we assume that democratic leadership instills a greater desire in group members to succeed even without continuous supervision, we may conclude that democratic leadership has better long-term effects. This assumption is clearly behind the advocacy of a student-centered approach to learning. To Carl Rogers (1969), a teacher-centered approach to the classroom has no long-range benefits in the development of the student as an authentic person. To be of real value to the learner, the quest for learning must come from inside; authoritarian threats are of short-term value only.

C. Self-Actualizing Man

The social view of man's nature is more mature and humane than the rational-economic view, but it is still not a satisfactory view to some psychologists and social philosophers. To Abraham Maslow (1954), for example, man at his best is self-actualizing and makes maximum use of all his resources. To Maslow, to Argyris (1964), and to McGregor (1960, 1966, 1967)—all social psychologists concerned with leadership in industry—most jobs in contemporary factories, offices, and shops do not permit the worker to use his capacities fully. These jobs do not facilitate the worker's understanding of the relationship between what he is doing and the total purpose of the employing organization (Schein, 1965).

For the leader who adopts the view of man as *self-actualizing,* concern about his employees is still great, but he is more interested in making their work meaningful and satisfying than in fulfilling their social needs. Workers will be given as much responsibility as they can handle; and, as they achieve certain degrees of skill and responsibility, they are encouraged to move upward. According to the self-actualizing conception, man is seen as intrinsically motivated—he has deeply personal, internalized reasons for doing a good job. He takes pride in his work because it is *his* work. (Prior conceptions saw man as extrinsically motivated; reasons for working were artificially related to the job.) If we ask people why they feel good about their jobs, as Herzberg, Mausner, and Snyderman (1959) have done, their reasons are often centered around their accomplishments and their feeling of increasing job competence. We interpret these interview responses as indications that self-actualization is a part of the nature of the worker.[14]

It may be true that a self-actualization conception of man is more idealistic than realistic. Some workers may not care whether their job provides any challenges or any more autonomy. Self-actualization may not be applicable to many unskilled

[14]Factors that made people feel bad about their job—such as poor pay, bad working conditions, and inadequate job security—are unrelated to self-actualization (Herzberg et al., 1959).

jobs or temporary activities. Perhaps, for these positions the goal should be to provide the worker with enough money so that he can find meaning and challenge off the job (Schein, 1965, p. 58). But, as Argyris (1964) and others have indicated, there is a great risk that rejecting self-actualization as a goal can lead to a waste of human resources, which is our most precious commodity.

D. Complex Man

Each of the previous sets of assumptions about the nature of the worker is oversimplified and overgeneralized. Each may have some accuracy; each may be applicable to some individuals or partially applicable to many individuals. Schein postulates that man is not only "more complex within himself, being possessed of many needs and potentials, but he is also likely to differ from his neighbor in the patterns of his own complexity" (1965, p. 60). Thus, a model of man as a *complex being* is necessary to complete our picture of the nature of the worker. Since the ramifications of a complex view of the nature of the worker are complex in and of themselves, we quote Schein's description at length.

> a. Man is not only complex, but also highly variable; he has many motives which are arranged in some sort of hierarchy of importance to him, but this hierarchy is subject to change from time to time and situation to situation; furthermore, motives interact and combine into complex motive patterns (for example, since money can facilitate self-actualization, for some people economic strivings are equivalent to self-actualization).
>
> b. Man is capable of learning new motives through his organizational experiences, hence ultimately his pattern of motivation and the psychological contract which he establishes with the organization is the result of a complex interaction between initial needs and organizational experiences.
>
> c. Man's motives in different organizations or different subparts of the same organization may be different; the person who is alienated in the formal organization may find fulfillment of his social and self-actualization needs in the union or in the informal organization; if the job itself is complex, such as that of a manager, some parts of the job may engage some motives while other parts engage other motives.
>
> d. Man can become productively involved with organizations on the basis of many different kinds of motives; his ultimate satisfaction and the ultimate effectiveness of the organization depend only in part on the nature of his motivation. The nature of the task to be performed, the abilities and experience of the person on the job, and the nature of the other people in the organization all interact to produce a certain pattern of work and feelings. For example, a highly skilled but poorly motivated worker may be as effective *and satisfied* as a very unskilled but highly motivated worker.
>
> e. Man can respond to many different kinds of managerial strategies, depending on his own motives and abilities and the nature of the task; in other words, there is no one correct managerial strategy that will work for all men at all times (Schein, 1965, p. 60).[15]

The leader who holds a belief in the complexity of man must be sensitive to individual differences in the needs, fears, and abilities of workers. He must be able to appreciate these differences and adapt to each. Unlimited or unqualified application of any one of the previous conceptions by a leader will be wrong in many cases.

There are many examples of the usefulness of a conception of *complex man* in the study of leaders and organizations. In effect, the failure of any intervention

[15] From E. H. Schein, *Organizational Psychology*. Copyright 1965 by Prentice-Hall, Inc. Reprinted with permission.

to bring about identical results in every subject is an indication of the human complexity involved. When 19 out of 20 11-year-olds prefer democratic leadership, we must not overlook the single deviant and the interindividual variability his response represents. (Very few interventions produce the almost unanimous response that was obtained in the authoritarian-democratic leadership studies!) This represents one level of complexity resulting from individual differences. But there are complexities within each individual—variability in needs across time or duties. Another example of the individual differences in response is a study of a large trucking company (Vroom, 1960; Vroom & Mann, 1960), which found that workers with different kinds of jobs and different personalities preferred different types of leadership style. Men with relatively independent, solitary jobs (such as truck drivers and dispatchers) preferred a more task-oriented, authoritarian supervisor. But men whose work was interdependent preferred employee-oriented supervision. Successful attempts to change the leadership preferences of workers further document the conclusion that it is desirable for every successful manager, chairman, or group leader to possess a complex view of man.

V. SUMMARY

In the early search for characteristics that distinguished leaders from nonleaders, little consistency in results from one study to another was found. However, some traits did appear in several studies; leaders were higher in intelligence, persistence, initiative, sense of humor, extraversion, sociability, self-confidence, and dependability.

Leadership has been conceptualized as actions on the part of a group member that influence the group in its movement toward goal setting and goal achievement. In this conception, each member of the group may play a role in its leadership.

Designated leaders of groups have two major leadership functions: *initiating structure* and *consideration*. Initiating structure refers to the leader's behavior in identifying the group's goal and moving the group toward its goal. *Consideration* refers to the leader's concern with relationships between himself and other group members. Leaders high in consideration reflect their awareness of the needs of each group member.

Designating leadership functions as task oriented and group maintenance oriented resembles the division into initiating structure and consideration. While a task orientation and a group maintenance orientation are not mutually exclusive, many groups develop two leaders for the two functions.

Fiedler's contingency theory of leadership emphasizes that there is no one successful type of leader; rather aspects of the leader's power, the task structure, and the leader's personal relations with members of his group interact to determine what kind of a leader will be most successful.

Leaders of organizations and groups operate according to assumptions about human nature. Four different types of models may be distinguished: rational-economic man, social man, self-actualizing man, and complex man.

The model of *rational-economic man* sees the worker as motivated by money and self-interest. Hence, the leader's task is seen as one of motivating the worker to turn out the most he can within the limits of what he can be paid.

The model of *social man* sees workers as basically motivated by social needs; relationships with others are primary. The task of the manager is to recognize these social needs and facilitate their expression in order to increase production.

Self-actualizing man, as a model, views the worker as striving to use his capacities fully. The leader employing this model seeks to make his employees' work meaningful and satisfying.

The worker is given the most challenging jobs that he can handle, and he is encouraged to develop new skills and goals.

The model of *complex man* reflects beliefs that different workers have different needs and capabilities. The leader who holds a belief in the complexity of man must be sensitive to individual differences in the needs, fears, and abilities of workers.

VI. SUGGESTED READINGS

Fiedler, F. E. *A theory of leadership effectiveness*. New York: McGraw-Hill, 1967. A comprehensive review of Fiedler's important contingency theory of leadership, in addition to descriptions of a multitude of studies to test the theory. Highly technical. A much shorter, more readable version is Fiedler's article in the March, 1969, issue of *Psychology Today*.

Halpin, A. W. *Theory and research in administration*. New York: Macmillan, 1966. A readable presentation of the Ohio State research program on initiating structure and consideration. Provocative applications of the findings to leadership in the schools are presented.

Rogers, C. R. *Freedom to learn*. Columbus, Ohio: Charles E. Merrill, 1969. (Paperback version available) In a series of articles, speeches, and reports, Carl Rogers calls for a new approach to learning that rejects traditional notions of the functions of leaders, teachers, and administrators. Controversial and highly recommended.

Schein, E. H. *Organizational psychology*. Englewood Cliffs, N.J.: Prentice-Hall, 1965. (Paperback version available) A brief, readable treatment of the developing field of organizational psychology. Expanded treatment of the four models of the worker described in this chapter.

Tannenbaum, A. S. *Social psychology of the work organization*. Belmont, Calif.: Wadsworth, 1966. (Paperback) The relationship of the worker to the large organization in which he works is the topic of this book. Assumptions about the nature of the worker, the Hawthorne studies, and the application of knowledge to improve organizational performance are among the issues covered.

Part Five

Applications of Social Psychology to Contemporary Problems

I. *THE CONCEPT OF A DRUG*

II. *DRUG EFFECTS AND SOCIAL POLICY*
- A. *Drug effects*
- B. *Social and cognitive factors in drug effects*
- C. *Psychedelic drug effects*
- D. *Drugs and the law*

III. *THE CONSUMPTION OF ALCOHOL*
- A. *The social distribution of alcohol consumption*
- B. *Social practice and alcohol use*
- C. *A social psychological model of heavy drinking and deviance*
  - 1. *Psychological or personality factors in deviance and excessive alcohol use*
  - 2. *Social factors in excessive alcohol use and deviance*
  - 3. *Tests of the Jessor model*
  - 4. *An extension of the model: Reasons for alcohol use and the cultural patterning of personality—alcohol use relationships*
- D. *Related studies of alcohol use*
  - 1. *Drinking rates of blacks*
  - 2. *Consistency of findings in a parallel study*
  - 3. *Longitudinal studies*
  - 4. *Preliminary evaluation of the model*

IV. *PSYCHEDELIC DRUG USE*
- A. *Distribution of psychedelic drug use*
  - 1. *Blum's Bay Area study*
  - 2. *A survey of nine colleges in the Rocky Mountain area*
  - 3. *A national sample of colleges*
- B. *Social psychological correlates*
- C. *A conceptualization of psychedelic drug use*
  - 1. *Reasons for use*
  - 2. *Reasons against use*
  - 3. *Personality variables*
  - 4. *Family and social backgrounds*
- D. *Evaluation of the model*

V. *SUMMARY*

VI. *SUGGESTED READINGS*

Chapter Eighteen

Drug Effects and Drug Use

by Keith E. Davis

President Nixon will soon feel new pressure to speed withdrawal from Vietnam. Its impetus: The heroin epidemic among soldiers there. *Newsweek, May 31, 1971*

A controversial study linking "pot" and mental illness was laid before the National Commission on Marijuana and Drug Usage yesterday and promptly was challenged as unscientific by half a dozen physician experts who favor reform of marijuana laws. *J. Randal, Nashville Tennessean, 1971*

The quest for a definition of a drug is a tortuous one. What is a drug? Does the term *drug* mean the same to a physician as it does to a pharmacist, a psychopharmacologist, a social psychologist, a policeman, or a consumer of the mass media? Should we treat substances such as aspirin, cigarettes, coffee, or alcohol as drugs? If so, would not such a definition make "users" of us all?

The specific problem for social psychology revolves around the impact—real or perceived—of drugs upon individuals and upon our society. Insofar as drugs influence individual or group behaviors, social psychologists are interested in studying drug effects and the causes and implications of drug use. Therefore, we will avoid a strictly medical or pharmacological definition. At the same time, we must be very careful not to allow our science to be swayed by a public opinion that may be overly apprehensive, or slightly hysterical, in its concern about drugs. Our first goal is to establish a social psychological definition of drug. We shall then explore social and psychological variables for clues as to causes of drug use and/or abuse. We would like to know whether these causes hold up over the various types of drugs. If so, we will be able to develop a general model of drug-using behavior. Hopefully, our model will enable us to understand how patterns of drug use in America are changing.

I. THE CONCEPT OF A DRUG

The standard definition of a drug by pharmacologists is: "any substance that by its chemical nature alters structure or function in the living organism" (Modell, quoted in Nowlis, 1969, p. 5). This definition would, of course, include food, water, and oxygen, as well as anything taken into the body under the label of drug. For purposes of biochemical work in nutrition or pharmacology, this definition may be useful, but it does not serve to demarcate our intended field of study. Instead, we need to start with the everyday, commonly held notion of drug, if we are to understand the various social psychological aspects of drug use and to appreciate the emotional heat that drug use generates.

The man on the street often defines drugs as substances that alleviate suffering or pain or combat illness. But this definition will not satisfy our purposes either because of its implication that drugs are only those chemicals that accomplish a certain result. We constantly sell, buy, and use substances called drugs that apparently do little in the way of combating illness or alleviating pain. Indeed, numerous cases of fraud have resulted from exaggerated claims for patent medicines. For our purposes, a definition in terms of the *effects* of drugs does not seem as promising as a definition in terms of the *intention* of the prescriber and user. Although a person may be mistaken about what a drug will do, the use of the drug is intelligible only if the user believes that some predictable effect will follow. Thus, the user's intention to alter his physical state or to relieve pain would appear to be a criterion of the notion of drug. The adequacy of this conclusion, however, may still be questioned.

We have a whole class of substances—called tranquilizers—whose intended effects are the relief of psychological distress, depression, anxiety, or the reduction of other psychological symptoms. If a chemical is taken with the intent of relieving psychological distress (however mild), is not that substance a drug? For the sake of consistency, it would seem so. Indeed, taking a drink to forget one's problems or to relieve one's tensions must be considered an example of drug usage. Cigarettes, coffee, or even hot milk may serve the same function.

We must now face another difficulty—namely, that the physiological effects of the substances taken are the same whatever the reason or intention for taking them may be. The liver does not know why a person drank one last martini, but it reacts identically regardless of the drinker's motivations. Thus, to understand the concept of drug and the ensuing difficulties, we must consider both intention and effect. The social practices of giving and using drugs depend upon our ideas about a particular physical or psychological effect that is likely to follow; such ideas provide us with a reason to use the drug. But the physiological effects are not dependent upon our reasons for taking the drug; thus, reasons may be out of touch with effects. For example, probably no one smokes cigarettes in order to increase the likelihood of an early death from lung cancer or heart trouble, but these are the apparent effects of heavy cigarette smoking.

Drugs serve a variety of functions. In addition to medical and psychiatric uses, many societies use alcohol or drugs such as mescaline or peyote as aids to religious inspiration and ecstasy. In some cultures, alcohol or other drugs play a part in social gatherings or ceremonial occasions. To drink a toast to the bride and groom at a wedding is not necessarily to drink with any intention of affecting one's own physiological state; rather, it is a way of conveying one's good wishes for the happy couple. Here, the relevant intentions are social rather than personal or physiological.

In the broad sense, almost all Americans are drug takers or drug users. And almost all human societies have engaged in the practice of taking drugs for psychiatric, religious, or sociable reasons. The ways in which drug users differ reside in their *reasons* for use, in the *kinds* of drugs used (pain killers, antibiotics, tranquilizers), in the *amount* and *frequency* of use, and in the *legal status* of the drug—whether or not the drug is prescribed or obtained legally.

What then is the proposed definition of the drugs that are of interest to social psychology? Let us begin with the following: a drug is any substance which can be ingested by a person without the intent of satisfying a biological need or combating a disease and which has detectable effects on feelings and physiological states. Since this definition includes spices and many other substances, it is still too broad. Thus, we shall make the additional specification that the substances ingested are taken in order to improve nonpathological psychological states. The term *nonpathological* excludes tranquilizers and thereby allows us to concentrate on pleasure-seeking and nonmedical uses of drugs that can alter psychological states.[1]

Most common discussions of drug usage focus upon the use and abuse of illegal drugs for nonmedical reasons. Restricting the focus of our discussion to these drugs (marijuana, heroin, LSD, and the like) unduly narrows the range of inquiry; the phenomenon of illegal drug use can only be understood in comparison to legal use. What are the physiological and personal risks of smoking marijuana in comparison to those of smoking cigarettes? Are there similar reasons for using each? Are there similar variables that are predictive of use? What about the variables that are predictive of excessive alcohol or psychedelic drug use? We shall deal with these questions next, starting with drug effects.

II. DRUG EFFECTS AND SOCIAL POLICY

Before we consider who uses what drugs and why, we must devote some time to the question of drug effects and drug laws. Clarification is necessary, since the topic has generated so much public discussion but very little factual information. So much exaggeration and cultish nonsense has been exchanged between the groups advocating abolition of restrictions and the groups favoring present restrictions (or more severe ones), that most laymen have become confused by the claims and counterclaims. In general, the pro-drug and antidrug forces tend to share a common assumption that drugs possess demoniacal powers to alter and control human behavior (Blum and associates, 1969a). The antidrug forces stress the easy danger of addiction and dependence and the power of drugs to make people lose their judgment and morals. Such persons too readily explain the seemingly bizarre behavior of the "far-out" youth as the result of drug usage. In like manner the proponents of the stronger

[1] Space prevents us from considering tranquilizers in this chapter. We should note here, however, that the use of tranquilizers in our contemporary society is massive. Blum and Funkhouser-Balbaky (1967, p. 33) report that from 6 to 10 percent of all medical prescriptions are for tranquilizers. Doubtless, the majority of the 70 million prescriptions for tranquilizers and the 47 million prescriptions for barbiturates filled each year in America go to white middle-class adults. Perhaps ours is a legalized drug culture.

psychedelic drugs such as LSD, mescaline, and psilocybin often promote exaggerated claims of the drugs' capacities to produce a spirit of love and to increase self-understanding, creativity, spontaneity, and self-expression. The psychedelics are offered as instant panaceas for whatever personal and social problems exist. Such statements are heard as: "If statesmen would just trip on LSD, they would be incapable of waging war on each other"; or, "If blacks and whites would trip together, they could live together." To quote from Blum et al. further:

> Mind-altering drugs have been invested by the public with qualities which are not directly linked to their visible or most probable effects. They have been elevated to the status of a power deemed capable of tempting, possessing, corrupting, and destroying persons without regard to the prior conduct or condition of those persons—a power which has all-or-none effects. Gradations of results are not ordinarily considered as a function of the factors empirically shown to be responsible for them, such as dosage, purity, route of administration, frequency of use, nutritional states, the presence of biochemical antagonists or potentiators, social setting, subject's health, intentions and personality, and the like. The "power" in drugs is such that those identified as users are immediately reclassified socially—most likely as unregenerate outcasts. Such a power comes close to being demoniacal. Has Cotton Mather's demon in rum changed his residence? Have witches turned now to technology whereby they lurk in heroin, LSD, methamphetamine, and other materials? (Blum et al., 1969a, pp. 326–327).

Blum makes a very compelling comment on the public view that the demons have indeed turned into the psychedelic drugs.

A. Drug Effects

We stated earlier that physiological reactions to a drug were the same regardless of the user's intent. But there is clear evidence that many of the interesting psychological changes are not due solely to the dosage of the drug. Rather, psychological changes also depend upon expectations and beliefs about what the drug will do, upon the circumstances in which the drug is taken, and upon prior states and characteristics of the user. Our best evidence indicates that drugs primarily alter the psychological states that influence how a person will perform, rather than what he will choose to do. Intoxication from alcohol or barbiturates is a classic example. Although there are great individual differences in the required dosage, intoxication has a direct impact on many functions. These include psychomotor coordination (such as that involved in a skilled performance like automobile driving), judgment (particularly in the form of a lessened appreciation of risks and dangers), and impulse control (regardless of whether the impulses are hostile or sociable). Alcohol does not produce hostility; but, in large enough doses and on some occasions for some people, it increases the likelihood of hostile behavior. We would make a mistake to call this increased hostility a drug effect; the hostility logically must be attributed both to the person and to his particular drug state. It is stretching the concept of drug effect to make alcohol the demon, even if the observed effect is not reasonably general or typical. It is more appropriate to infer that intoxication involves a reduced ability to control impulses. Thus, whatever feelings or impulses the person brings to his drinking—whether they be belligerent or suicidal—are more likely to be expressed when he is drinking than when he is not. As Blum has commented, "Drugs may modify behavior but they do not create it" (Blum & Funkhouser-Balbaky, 1967, p. 22).

B. Social and Cognitive Factors in Drug Effects

We have stated that the psychological changes associated with drugs are dependent upon the drug taker's expectations and circumstances. It is worthwhile to look carefully at a classic social psychological experiment that helps us to appreciate these facts. In Schachter and Singer's (1962) study of cognitive determinants of emotional states (Chapter 14), subjects were given either adrenaline or a placebo under one of three information conditions (accurate knowledge about the drug's effects, ignorance of these effects, and misinformation about the effects) and under one of two social situations (either a euphoria-producing or anger-producing setting). The results showed that, when adrenaline had been injected, quite different mood states could occur in persons taking the same drug and that the nature of the mood depended upon the information and social situation of the subject. Subjects who were ignorant or misinformed about the effects of adrenaline were more responsive to a confederate who deliberately sought to induce euphoria or anger. Subjects who were correctly informed about the adrenaline effects were relatively unresponsive to the confederate's behavior. Two interpretations of the unresponsiveness of these subjects are possible. One is that the subjects were provided with an adequate explanation of their own physiological change and hence gave their state no emotional significance. The other interpretation is that the subjects attributed the confederate's behavior to *his* own drug reaction, and hence his behavior provided no basis for joint social activity. The fact that someone gets a bit silly or irritable when drugged is quite understandable. Further research is needed, but both these interpretations share an emphasis on the role of cognitive factors in determining specific psychological reactions to drug-induced physiological changes.

Most usage of psychedelic drugs is a highly social phenomenon (E. Goode, 1969) in which the joint or the apparatus (pipes, needles) is shared and the supply is limited. Thus, it is understandable that the kinds of psychological experiences that people have should be partly determined (a) by the beliefs of the users about what the drug effects will be, (b) by the course of the social interaction in the group, and (c) by apprehensions about likely trouble or difficulties to be encountered.

C. Psychedelic Drug Effects

Because of great public concern, it is mandatory to be as precise as possible about the known effects of both the milder psychedelics (cannabis derivatives such as marijuana and hashish) and the stronger ones (LSD-25, peyote, mescaline, psilocybin). Fortunately, Theodore Barber (1970) has provided us a critical, comprehensive review. After examining more than 200 articles, experiments, case studies, and professional reports, Barber makes the following conclusions with respect to LSD.

> The effects [of LSD] that appear to be closely related to the drug dose include most of the somatic-sympathetic effects, changes in body-image, dreamy-detached feelings, reduced intellectual-motor proficiency, and changes in visual perception. It appears that whether and to what degree subjects experience these effects is closely dependent on how much of the drug they receive. However, the extra-drug variables play a role in determining how much emphasis the subject places on these effects, how much attention he pays to them, and to what degree he elaborates upon and discusses them.
>
> The effects that appear to be closely related to the extra-drug variables of situation, set,

and personality include some of the somatic-sympathetic effects (such as nervousness, trembling, and difficulty in breathing) and changes in moods and emotions (ranging from euphoria to dysphoria or from psychedelic reactions to psychotic-like reactions). Although variations in drug dose may produce some variations in mood, the type of moods and emotions that will be manifested appears to be closely dependent upon the situation and the subject's set and personality (1970, p. 65).

It is important to note that several widely discussed drug effects have not been validated at this time. The degree of risk—if any—in taking drugs during pregnancy and, thereby, affecting chromosomes and the unborn child is still unclear. For example, Dishotsky, Loughman, Mogar, and Lipscomb (1971) have reviewed 68 studies on the effects of LSD upon chromosome damage, leukemia, mutations, and malformed infants. They find "no reported instance of a malformed child born to a woman who ingested pure LSD" (1971, p. 439), but they do report cases of birth defects in the offspring of women who took LSD during pregnancy. In these latter cases, it is a possibility that other drugs taken at the same time led to the deformities. In addition, the reputed enhancement of creativity has not been established as a general or reliable effect of LSD. The usefulness of LSD in therapeutic contexts, such as with alcoholic persons or in conjunction with psychoanalytic therapy of neuroses, has not been demonstrated. The careful review by Dishotsky et al. does not deal explicitly with these latter aspects but does conclude that the use of pure LSD in controlled experimentation can be continued without harm, except in the case of pregnant women.

In the case of marijuana, most of the issues that are relevant to its legalization and social effects are unsettled, but quite a lot is known about psychological and physical effects. As summarized by Hollister (1971), the recent research largely confirms early observations of writers, medical doctors, and other users. Earlier reports had included mention of such effects as euphoria, anxiety, weakness, dizziness, hallucinations, perceptual distortions and intensifications, depersonalization, flight of ideas, and incoherence, with many of the perceptual and mental symptoms having a waxing and waning, wave-like character. These effects have been replicated in laboratory studies where synthetic THC has been used as well as marijuana cigarettes. But the more striking symptoms are common only when the dose levels were comparable to "several cigarettes of reasonable quality or from smoking hashish" (Hollister, 1971, p. 22).

Two of the most widely cited studies suggest that within the typical range of use (up to two cigarettes) experienced users suffer no decrement in intellectual or psychomotor performance (Weil, Zinberg, & Nelson, 1968; Weil & Zinberg, 1969) or in their ability to handle simulated automobile driving (Crancer, Dille, Delay, Wallace, & Haykin, 1969). Hollister (1971) raised questions about both sets of research. With respect to intellectual performances, he argued that "the doses in this study were far less than assumed" (p. 24). In regard to the study of driving skill, Hollister argued that the driving test could have been given after the peak marijuana effects, which could have been rigged by the experienced users who may have attained only a mild high rather than an extreme one. Hollister stated that when his own subjects (who were typically at a much higher dose level) were asked whether they could drive a car at that point, they replied with, "No!" or "You must be kidding!" Hollister also concluded:

> It is rather heartening, therefore, that the clinical syndromes described for marihuana in the laboratory correspond closely to those reported by street users. . . . The most common symptoms and signs reported were: paresthesia, floating sensations, and depersonalization; weakness and relaxation; perceptual changes (visual, auditory, tactile); subjective slowing of time; flight of ideas, difficulty in thinking and loss of attention; loss of immediate memory; euphoria and silliness; sleepiness. Other common symptoms which are not verifiable in the laboratory were claims of increased insight and perception, as well as increased sexual desire, performance, and enjoyment (Hollister, 1971, p. 25).

One might summarize the social implications of the drug effects research as follows. If the typical heavy user takes as much as the dosage used in the Hollister studies, then there are serious doubts about the advisability of legalizing the drug or representing it as not very harmful. If, however, the typical user seldom gets into the dose ranges used by Hollister and if education campaigns can be devised to teach the hazards of heavy use, then the reports of the effects of marijuana are not very compelling evidence against legalization. But then, at this point there is no evidence on the long-term effects of moderate to heavy use.

For heavy users of marijuana, the effects appear to be different. In a series of informal interviews conducted by the present author with one-time "heads," rather striking perceptual similarities emerged. A former head is a person who has ceased the practice of using marijuana heavily enough to stay high continuously. These persons described their lives during the time when they were heavily involved with marijuana as an aimless drift from joint to joint. Some used the term *flaky* to describe the experience. Also common was a reported inability to control their own attention. Events, sights, and sounds captured their attention, and they had trouble focusing on issues or ideas effectively. As one put it, "I really had a lot of insights into my problem and myself, but between the flakiness and inability to keep my mind on things, I never did anything about my great insights." Others—not all—were concerned about their passivity and dependence. They had begun to lose a sense of themselves as agents who act on the world to accomplish their own ends. Whether future research will bear out the above as psychological effects of heavy marijuana use remains to be seen. Quite possibly, only heavy users who feel such problems would be inclined to move away from drugs; heavy users who do not experience such feelings may happily go on with the drug.

D. Drugs and the Law

The legal status of marijuana and other psychedelics is currently under study, with some groups working for repeal of laws restricting marijuana usage and others clamoring for tighter controls and heavier penalties. The death penalty has been advocated in some quarters for pushers or sellers. Existing drug laws and punishments do not clearly follow from known differences in the physical, psychological, and social risks of the drugs. In the past, degrees of punishment for marijuana use have been disproportionate with its known detrimental effects. The newer trend is to classify each drug by its generally accepted effect and addictive properties. Even though we are largely ignorant of the long-term effects of many drugs, our ignorance is not considered a justification for repealing all current laws. However, law enforcement clearly has not been able to control the spread of illegal drug use (R. H. Blum,

1970). On a social cost basis, Kaplan (1970) has concluded that marijuana enforcement is not worth the trouble.

Hollister (1971) raises serious questions about most of the contentions of the pro-legalization forces. Among these questions are: (a) What basis is there for the prevalent assumption that marijuana would partially supplant alcohol use instead of merely being added to it? (b) How serious is the psychological dependence problem with marijuana? (c) What are the immediate and remote dangers of use? (d) To what degree is it possible to institute legal and social controls for marijuana that resemble the present controls for alcohol?

III. THE CONSUMPTION OF ALCOHOL

The present chapter offers greater depth of coverage on alcohol use than on psychedelic drugs. The emphasis partly reflects what is known, but more importantly it reflects our judgment about where the public concern should be. Alcohol is more readily available; therefore, its abuse is easier and more common. Persistent heavy use of alcohol is implicated in (a) a substantial portion of automobile accidents and more than 20,000 deaths per year, (b) substantial economic losses due to absenteeism, and (c) uncounted cases of deteriorated family life and parental care.

What factors determine consumption of alcohol? Are the same factors involved in excessive use? What resources do we have for understanding why one person becomes a heavy drinker when another, who is apparently subject to the same social stresses and temptations, does not? These questions shall be explored in the present section. First, let us look at who uses alcohol.

A. The Social Distribution of Alcohol Consumption

Within the last decade, two major studies of American drinking practices were conducted by specialists in alcohol research (Mulford, 1964; Cahalan, Cisin, & Crossley, 1969). During the same period, relevant questions were asked in several Gallup polls. All of the data are quite consistent, and the studies generally yield estimates within 5 percentage points of each other on the proportion of drinkers for age, sex, and religious subgroups. For this reason, only those data from Cahalan, et al. will be presented. By their estimate, 68 percent of the adult population (21 years of age or older) drink at least once a year. This 68 percent is divided into four subgroups: *infrequent* drinkers (15 percent), or those who drink less than once a month; *light* drinkers (28 percent), or those who drink at least once a month but seldom more than one or two drinks per sitting; *moderate* drinkers (13 percent), or those who typically drink several times per month but who seldom drink more than three or four drinks per occasion; and *heavy* drinkers (12 percent), or those who drink nearly every day and consume five or more drinks daily or those who drink weekly but almost always drink five or more drinks on that occasion.

Table 18–1 gives a breakdown on the percentage of drinkers and abstainers by age, sex, and socioeconomic status. More men (77 percent) drink than do women (60 percent), and four times as many men as women are heavy drinkers (21 percent versus 5 percent). Younger people (ages 21 to 39) are more likely to be drinkers than

Table 18-1. *Percentage of Respondents in Types of Alcohol Use Groups by Sex, Age, and Index of Social Position*

	N	*Abstainers*	*Infrequent Drinkers*	*Light + Moderate*	*Heavy*	*% Heavy of All Drinkers*
Total Sample	2746	32	15	41	12	18
Men						
Age 21–39						
Highest ISP[a]	132	12	5	59	24	27
Upper Middle	119	14	12	50	24	28
Lower Middle	127	13	12	49	26	30
Lowest	81	25	6	44	25	33
Age 40–59						
Highest ISP	137	20	7	50	23	28
Upper Middle	110	21	8	45	26	33
Lower Middle	121	27	14	38	21	29
Lowest	93	27	12	38	23	31
Age 60+						
Highest ISP	39	21	14	52	13	16
Upper Middle	53	36	4	52	8	12
Lower Middle	74	42	16	28	14	25
Lowest	91	36	14	36	14	22
Women						
Age 21–39						
Highest ISP	171	14	23	58	5	6
Upper Middle	147	25	23	44	8	11
Lower Middle	151	38	22	35	5	7
Lowest	132	41	18	32	9	16
Age 40–59						
Highest ISP	128	23	12	61	4	6
Upper Middle	153	32	17	45	6	9
Lower Middle	150	50	18	28	4	8
Lowest	167	59	14	22	5	12
Age 60+						
Highest ISP	62	41	23	35	1	2
Upper Middle	98	58	18	24	0	0
Lower Middle	89	52	16	29	3	7
Lowest	118	66	13	21	0	0

[a]Index of socioeconomic status position
(From Cahalan, Cisin, & Crossley, 1969, Table 3, p. 27. Reprinted with permission of the author.)

older persons (60 years or older). Upper class respondents are more likely to be light to moderate drinkers than respondents from lower social-class levels. The percentage of abstainers ranges from 12 percent in young men from the highest social position to 66 percent for older women (60+) from the lowest social position. There are major variations in percentages in the other columns of Table 18–1, so that much of the variation in persons who drink or abstain can be predicted by the variables of age, sex, and social position. When one adds religious denomination and participation, region of the country, and degree of urbanization, the variations in percentages are even greater. Two questions are relevant to these facts. First, why do the percentages of users distribute themselves this way? And, second, what role do psychological factors play in explaining drinking?

B. Social Practice and Alcohol Use

If there are occasions when some of the people in a society drink, then that society has a social practice of alcohol use. The occasions may be festive (holidays, birthdays), ceremonial (wedding toasts), social (parties), and so on. If such occasions exist, then it also follows that on these occasions drinking is acceptable for some people (typically an age limit is set) and the members of the group will have opportunities to learn when and how to drink. In such situations, drinking is part of the regular practices of the society. To take a drink on such an occasion is merely doing what the occasion calls for. In the language of social psychology, the individual is responding to the demand characteristics, the role expectations, or the social norms of the situation. To explain why a person drinks on such occasions, one needs only the concept of norm-acquisition (a form of social learning), which refers to developing the competence to recognize particular circumstances as appropriate for drinking.

The reason that age, sex, social position, religion, region, and other social variables are powerful in predicting whether a person drinks is that these variables map the distribution of distinctive cultural groups and the resulting group norms about drinking. For example, some religious groups are strongly anti-alcohol, whereas others are tolerant. In many groups, drinking is more acceptable among men than among women or is more acceptable after a certain age. Urban areas typically provide greater opportunities for drinking and more people who are likely to encourage others to join them. Thus, the social practices of drinking, as well as the opportunities to learn when and how to drink, are distributed in ways that correspond to the distribution of drinkers in the country.

If the distributions of social practices were the only determinants of drinking, there would be little room for distinctively psychological factors. Yet it is the fact that in any subcultural group one finds considerable individual variation in use. Some persons who are on all counts eligible to drink remain abstainers. Others who, according to the group norms, should not be drinkers nevertheless do so. Thus, we expect to find social psychological correlates of individual drinking and nondrinking within very homogeneous ethnic, religious, and sexual subgroups.

When we turn to a consideration of *heavy drinking*, the role of social psychological conditions such as stress, dissatisfaction, and alienation is even more relevant. Though several social scientists have contributed to our understanding of excessive alcohol use, we have selected one approach as particularly useful. This is the field-theoretical model of Jessor, Graves, Hanson, and Jessor (1968), which is derived from the basic Lewinian field theory described in Chapter 1.

C. A Social Psychological Model of Heavy Drinking and Deviance

The Jessor team was invited into a small southwestern community composed of Anglo-Americans, Spanish-Americans, and Indians. In its own view, the community was facing a problem of excessive alcohol use. Jessor and his colleagues conceive of heavy drinking as one form of deviant behavior. Heavy drinking generally constitutes a violation of the norms of appropriate social behavior—or, at least those norms held by middle-class, American, white, Anglo-Saxon Protestants. The difficulty, of course, is in defining the amount of alcohol use that is excessive.

Basically, the model of Jessor et al. is a logical analysis of social and psychological variables that are conducive to deviance. We shall give an overview of it here and then explore it in detail in the next pages. At the psychological level, Jessor et al. use three variables as predictors of heavy drinking: extent of personal disjunctions, alienation, and tolerance of a general pattern of deviant behavior. At the sociological level, the variables are value-access disjunctions, anomie, and access to illegitimate social-learning opportunities.

The theory first specifies a discrepancy between a person's desired goals and his expectations of attaining these desired goals. The existence of such a discrepancy constitutes a dissatisfaction that may lead the person to engage in deviance. Next, Jessor et al. identify two levels of controls or inhibitions against deviance, the absence of which constitutes another set of circumstances conducive to deviance. These two levels are social and psychological. As Jessor has described it, "The [social and psychological levels of analysis] are formally identical. Each proposes a source of strain or pressure or instigation—a dynamic—toward engaging in illegitimate behavior. Each proposes two sources of control or restraint against the instigation to illegitimacy. . . . Deviance is conceived of as the resultant . . . of the interaction of pressure and controls" (Jessor, 1964, p. 64). Let us look first at three variables in the psychological level of analysis.

Psychological or Personality Factors in Deviance and Excessive Alcohol Use. What kind of psychological state might make a person susceptible to alcohol? Certainly, one plausible condition is a sense of dissatisfaction with one's lot, a sense of failure or despair. A logical requirement for a sense of dissatisfaction is a discrepancy between the way things are and the way they ought to be. But even more relevant psychologically is a discrepancy between what a person wants and his judgment of whether or not he is likely to get what he wants. The first major psychological variable in the model is this discrepancy between what is wanted and what is expected—or, personal disjunction. The greater the number of such discrepancies in significant life areas (achievement, affection, and independence, to name a few), the greater the personal disjunctions a person is suffering. According to the model, "personal disjunctions, when high and pervasive, create intrapersonal pressure toward adapting technically effective alternative behavior, even if illegitimate, to reach the valued goals" (Jessor, 1964, p. 64).

The second major psychological variable in the model is alienation—"a concept referring to a generalized sense of meaninglessness, helplessness, hopelessness, and social isolation" (Jessor, 1964, p. 64). As used by the model, a sense of alienation represents a particular constellation of expectations (about significant others and life in general) that constitutes reduced personal controls against deviant behavior. For example, the more isolated a person feels, the less concern he has with others' reactions to his behavior; hence, the less reluctant he is to do something that others would consider wrong.

The third major psychological variable is tolerance of deviance, which reflects the degree to which the person believes that deviant behavior is required to accomplish his ends and is unlikely to result in punishment if used. Technically, tolerance of deviance is a special set of expectations that indicate the absence of internalized standards against deviant behavior. The theory makes the following prediction: The greater the personal disjunctions, the alienation, and the tolerance of deviation, the more likely the person is to engage in deviant behavior. Deviant behaviors may include consuming excessive alcohol or getting into trouble with friends, family, and the police while drinking.

Social Factors in Excessive Alcohol Use and Deviance. At the social level of analysis, Jessor et al. formulated three parallel variables. The first, following Merton's (1957) analysis of American society, is a discrepancy between the social value placed upon material success and the socially patterned access to genuine opportunities to achieve such success. This is called a **value-access disjunction** and it formally constitutes a source of social pressure toward deviance. If success is important and one is blocked from achieving it in acceptable ways, then this state of affairs is a force toward illegitimate behavior.

Jessor et al. next turned to forms of social control or forces against deviance. One of these is the degree of normative integration. When norms are persistently disregarded without peril, a state of **anomie** results, and a significant social source of control against deviance is lessened. As stated thus far, the formulation provides no principles for predicting what form the pressures toward deviance will take. Following Cloward and Ohlin (1960), Jessor et al. introduced the concept of **access to illegitimate social-learning opportunities.** Such access develops from various opportunities—such as opportunities to observe adult and peer models of deviance, opportunities to practice newly acquired illegitimate behaviors, or opportunities to participate in social groups where any punishment for deviance is unlikely. Conceptually, then, access to illegitimate means is both a source of specific learning and an indicator of the absence of active social control against deviance.

Thus, the theoretical prediction for the social variables is as follows: the greater the value-access disjunction, anomie, and access to illegitimate behavior, the greater the likelihood of deviance, which may include excessive alcohol consumption.

Tests of the Jessor Model. Now we are ready to see how well the model works. Because it is a somewhat complex model, a simplifying device will help us get the main points across. Jessor et al. have developed a useful procedure, which they call *pattern analysis*.

The procedure is as follows. On each predictive variable, the entire sample is split at the median into those who rate high on the variable (for example, high in the number of personal disjunctions) and those who rate low. According to the procedure, the group that should be high in alcohol consumption or in deviant behavior is given a plus (+). For example, in the case of personal disjunctions, those with several disjunctions get a + because theoretically they would be more likely to drink excessively. At this point we have two groups of people, one high in personal disjunctions (+) and one low in personal disjunctions (−). Each of these two groups may now be divided into high versus low on another predictive variable such as alienation. Four groups are possible: low personal disjunction with low alienation (− −), low personal disjunction with high alienation (− +), high personal disjunction with low alienation (+ −), and high personal disjunction with high alienation (+ +).

The theory predicts that those who are high both on alienation and on personal disjunctions (+ +) will be more prone to excessive consumption of alcohol, whereas those with only one predisposing factor (either alienation or personal disjunctions) will be relatively moderate in their use of alcohol. Those low on both factors (− −) should be lowest in alcohol consumption.

Tables 18–2, 18–3, and 18–4 are constructed along the lines described here, with

Table 18-2. *Social Variable Patterns and the Frequency of Deviance in the Jessor Study*

			Social variables: Access to illegitimate social-learning opportunities			*Global Deviance Criterion Measure*		
Pattern		*Value-Access Disjunctions*	*A. Absence of Social Controls*	*B. Exposure to Deviant Role Models*	*Subjects in Each Pattern*	*Number Deviant*	*% Deviant*	*Combined % Deviant*
I. Optimal Pattern—minimum expected deviance	A.	−	−	−	43	6	14	14
II. One Variable Departure—toward greater expected deviance	B.	−	−	+	30	8	27	33
	C.	−	+	−	19	9	47	
	D.	+	−	−	32	10	31	
III. Two Variable Departure—toward greater expected deviance	E.	−	+	+	16	12	75	59
	F.	+	−	+	23	10	43	
	G.	+	+	−	36	22	62	
IV. Three Variable Departure—maximum expected deviance	H.	+	+	+	20	15	75	75

Note: The variable of value-access disjunctions is measured by socioeconomic status. Access to illegitimate social-learning opportunities is measured by two variables: absence of social controls, and exposure to deviant role models. (Tables 18–2, 18–3, and 18–4 are adapted from *Society, Personality, and Deviant Behavior: A Study of a Tri-Ethnic Community* by Richard Jessor, Theodore D. Graves, Robert C. Hanson, and Shirley L. Jessor. Copyright © 1968 by Holt, Rinehart and Winston, Inc. Reproduced by permission of Holt, Rinehart and Winston, Inc.)

the exception that three or four predictor variables are considered simultaneously. The tables present the frequency or the percentage of persons with specific patterns of social and psychological characteristics who are high in alcohol use or in the measure of global deviance (includes quality-frequency of alcohol intake, getting into trouble while drinking, and other criminal or deviant behavior). In Table 18–2 we shall examine the social variables; in Table 18–3, the psychological variables; and in Table 18–4, the entire field-theoretical model in which both social and personality variables are combined.

Once again, there are three conceptual social variables predictive of deviance: (a) *value-access disjunctions*, measured by socioeconomic status; (b) *anomie* (not included in Table 18–2 because its measurement did not permit the assignment of individual scores); and (c) *access to illegitimate social-learning opportunities* (represented in Table 18–2 by two distinct components—absence of social controls on deviance and exposure to deviant role models). Dividing the subjects into high versus low groups on each of these three predictor variables results in eight distinct groups. In one of these groups, called the *optimal pattern* by Jessor et al., respondents were low in value-access disjunctions, low in the absence of social controls, and low in exposure to deviant role models. There were 43 such persons, and only 6 of them (14 percent) were above the community median in a global measure of extent of deviance.

What happens if any one of the predictors is changed from this optimal pattern? Let us say, for example, that the group is high, rather than low, in the number of value-access disjunctions. One can see in Table 18–2 that the proportion of high deviance increases to 31 percent (category IID). In general, if there is one departure from the optimal state in any of the three predictors, the percentage of persons with a high deviance rate is 33 percent, compared to the earlier 14 percent rate for the group showing no departures. Two departures yield an average deviance rate of 59 percent, and three departures—a situation where persons are high in value-access disjunctions,

Table 18-3. *Psychological Variable Patterns and Deviance in the Jessor Study*

		Percentages for Each Psychological Pattern Who Are Deviant[b]			
Psychological Pattern[a]	*Never a Drinker*	*Quantity-Frequency*[c]	*Times Drunk*[c]	*Other Deviance*	*Global Deviance*
Optimal (− − −) (N = 43)	41	30	13	14	16
1 Departure (+ − −) (N = 56)	12	52	11	25	27
2 Departures (+ + −) (N = 63)	16	56	17	30	51
3 Departures (+ + +) (N = 42)	10	60	26	57	69

[a]Psychological variables used: personal disjunction, tolerance of deviance, and alienation.
[b]Percent above cutting points is given for each criterion.
[c]Only *present* drinkers are included in this analysis. *N*s in the four patterns, from Optimal down, are therefore reduced to 23, 46, 46, and 35, respectively.

Note: *Psychological* has been used to refer to variables, which Jessor et al. often call *personality* variables.

Table 18-4. *Field Theoretical Patterns and Deviance from Jessor Study*

Field-Theoretical Pattern[a]	*Never a Drinker*	*Percentages for Each Pattern Who Are Deviant*[b] *Quantity-Frequency*[c]	*Times Drunk*[c]	*Other Deviance*	*Global Deviance*
Optimal (− − − −) (N = 28)	43	15	0	7	7
1 Departure (+ − − −) (N = 54)	17	43	2	17	19
2 Departures (+ + − −) (N = 54)	11	51	19	39	54
3 Departures (+ + + −) (N = 49)	16	61	18	45	55
4 Departures (+ + + +) (N = 19)	0	84	53	47	84

[a]Field-theoretical variables used: value-access disjunctions, access to illegitimate means (combines both absence of social controls and exposure to deviant role models), total personal disjunctions, and tolerance of deviance. (The first two of these are social; the last two are psychological.)

[b]Percent above cutting points is given for each criterion.

[c]Only *present* drinkers are included in this analysis. *Ns* in the five patterns, from Optimal down, are therefore reduced to 13, 42, 43, 33, and 19, respectively.

have no social controls or sanctions, and are high in exposure to deviant models—yield a 75 percent rate of deviance.

A careful look at Table 18–2 suggests that absence of a social control network (family, friends, community organizations, and regular church attendance) is the most powerful social variable in predicting rates of excessive drinking and deviance. This finding is consistent with the well-publicized Glueck and Glueck (1968) study, which revealed that lack of adequate supervision in the home was the single social variable most predictive of subsequent juvenile delinquency.

Table 18–3 shows the results for psychological or personality variables. Here the optimal pattern consisted of (a) few personal disjunctions, (b) low degree of alienation, and (c) an intolerant attitude toward deviance. This table presents several of the outcome or dependent variables, and we can see how drinking behavior and deviance are related to these personality variable patterns. The patterns are in greatest accord with predictions on the quantity-frequency index of alcohol intake, nondrinking deviance, and the global deviance measures. The same kind of analysis has worked even better in a separate study using high school students as subjects; this study predicted not only aspects of drinking (times drunk as well as quantity-frequency) but also poor school adjustment (Jessor et al., 1968).

The value of the Jessor et al. model is best seen when both social and psychological variables are considered simultaneously. Table 18–4 shows the pattern in detail, by including two social variables (value-access disjunctions and access to illegitimate social-learning opportunities) and two psychological variables (personal disjunctions and tolerance of deviance). With four variables, 16 separate groups may be arranged in 5 general levels, ranging from optimum levels to four deviations from optimum. In Table 18–4, the optimum group has only a 7 percent global deviance rate, whereas each succeeding level has a higher rate—up to 84 percent in the group with four departures. This highest figure applies to persons fitting the following criteria: (a) came from low socioeconomic status homes (in other words, had value-access difficulties), (b) had high exposure to opportunities for deviance and models of deviance, (c) were personally dissatisfied with their lot, and (d) thought it was all right to engage in transgressions whenever they could.

The fact that predictions are less than perfect leads to the conclusion that neither social circumstances nor personality variables are sufficient, by themselves, to predict or to understand alcohol use and other forms of deviance. Once more we see the need for a complex explanation of interpersonal behavior. Some commonplace examples may help bring this point home. There are poor people who live in families where some of the family members are drunks and criminals but who never have any urge to drink or engage in crime themselves. In many cases these people are reasonably satisfied with their lives; they hold beliefs (often grounded in religion) that are strong sources of support against drunkenness and crime. Here, the social variables predict a proneness to deviance but the personality variables predict the opposite. At the other end of a socioeconomic continuum is the prodigal son, who has the privilege of high social status and an absence of deviant models and opportunities in his life. Yet, because of his own high expectations, he often fails to get what he wants (personal disjunctions), and he is willing to try anything that might be a source of kicks or fun (low inhibition or deviance).

An Extension of the Model: Reasons for Alcohol Use and the Cultural Patterning of Personality-Alcohol Use Relationships. A perceptive reader might ask at this point: if drug effects depend in part upon the users' beliefs, do these relations between personality and proneness to alcohol problems occur in other cultures? If, for example, the social practices of a culture do not include drinking to drown one's sorrows—is it likely that a person suffering serious personal dissatisfactions will be inclined to heavy alcohol use? Apparently, the answer is no, but the story of how Jessor and his colleagues arrived at that conclusion is worth telling.

In research on alcohol use, there is a tradition of asking people why they drink or what they, personally, derive from drinking (Mulford & Miller, 1960). The answers to such questions are variously called the personal meaning of alcohol, the functions of alcohol to the drinker, or his reasons for alcohol use. Such personal reasons have typically been classified into four categories: (a) social-convivial (where the pleasure lies in other activities carried on while drinking), (b) conforming-social ("others do it," "to be a part of the group"), (c) personal effects or escapist reasons (drinking in order to forget one's problems, or drinking in order to reduce worry, tension, or fears), and (d) dietary or food enhancing reasons ("makes food taste better," or "helps digestion"). One of the most important facts about these reasons for alcohol use is that the frequency of the reasons given varies from one culture to the next. According to Lolli, Serianni, Golde, and Luzzatto-Fegiz (1958), "No emphasis is placed by Italians on any 'psychological' or 'escape-providing' qualities of wine" (p. 129). Americans, in contrast, clearly view alcohol as something that may be used for relief of personal distress.

Jessor, Young, Young, and Tesi (1970) replicated the above finding with Italian and Italian-American youth whose parents had moved to the Boston area. These researchers went on to determine whether personality variables such as those in the Jessor, et al. model can also make effective predictions for members of national or ethnic groups who do not attribute personal effects or distress-relieving powers to alcohol. Three psychological or personality measures from the model were predictive either of use or drunkenness in the Boston sample, but these variables were ineffective in predicting the drinking behavior of two comparable samples of Italian youth. The pattern held despite the fact that the Italian youth were more alienated and felt more dissatisfied and more powerless.

Although Italian culture generally does not endorse escapist reasons for drinking, the study indicated that some Italian youths may nevertheless have picked up such ideas. The number of escapist reasons given for drinking had some predictive power in one Italian sample, but the number of such reasons was a much more powerful predictor among the Italian-American youth in Boston. Also, the more alienated these youths were from their own families and groups, the more prone they were to believe in the distress-relieving powers of alcohol.

A related finding comes from Cahalan, Cisin, and Crossley's (1969) national study of American drinking practices. Heavy drinkers who drank for escapist reasons (9 percent of all drinkers and 6 percent of the total sample) had higher alienation scores than nonescapist heavy drinkers. Heavy escapist drinkers were more likely to report having "more than my share of problems," to rate the past year as not a good one, and to express dissatisfaction with their occupations, their health, and the attainment of their life goals. In short, they were higher in personal disjunctions than heavy nonescapist drinkers.

A study of black male college freshmen by Maddox and Williams (1968) partially parallels Jessor's work. They found, first, that escapist reasons for drinking were associated with heavy drinking and, second, that low self-esteem (as measured by the acceptance of derogatory self-descriptions) was strikingly related to heavy drinking. Previous theorists have posited low self-esteem as related to personal disjunctions; that is, a person who believes that he will not be able to get what he values highly (and thus who suffers personal disjunctions) is very likely to have some derogatory views of his own competence and attractiveness. Thus, the self-esteem findings may tentatively be treated as consistent with the field-theoretical model.

D. Related Studies of Alcohol Use

A very important quality of any model is its ability to generate expectations that are consistent with other known facts. Three issues will be examined in this section: (a) evidence about black drinking rates, (b) evidence that social and psychological characteristics in early adolescence are predictive of subsequent alcohol use, and (c) consistency of other findings with those of Jessor and his colleagues.

Drinking Rates of Blacks. Cahalan, Cisin, and Crossley's (1969) study found no differences between the percentages of black and white Americans who are drinkers, but there was a trend, more pronounced among women, for more blacks to be heavy escapist drinkers. However, the subsample of blacks was only composed of 70 persons. Several other studies (Maddox & Williams, 1968; Maddox, 1968; Robins, Murphy, & Breckenridge, 1968) and a review (Stone, 1967) report a considerably more disturbing pattern. This pattern of heavy alcohol use for escapist reasons is of both practical and theoretical importance—the theoretical importance stemming from the fact that the pattern is consistent with the model of Jessor and his colleagues. Since black men have been the target of discrimination and have had limited access to culturally valued success goals, it would be expected that they would be higher both in value-access disjunctions and personal disjunctions. Thus according to the Jessor et al. model, blacks would be expected to drink more heavily than whites.

Robins, Murphy, and Breckenridge (1968), in a longitudinal study of black men born in St. Louis, Missouri, reported that 58 percent of their sample had at some time been heavy drinkers and that 27 percent were currently heavy drinkers. Both of these percentages were approximately double those of a comparable group of white males from St. Louis. The percentages were considerably higher than Cahalan, Cisin, and Crossley's 1969 figures for blacks, but this difference is confounded by the fact that the latter study used a slightly different criterion of heavy drinking. Data from Robins, et al. also showed clearly that truancy, failure in elementary school, and dropping out of high school were highly predictive of heavy drinking. Conforming, middle-class behavior was strongly related to absence of heavy drinking among their subjects.

In Maddox's study, although the proportion of blacks who drank as freshmen in college (76 percent) corresponded to the proportion of white college students, 27 percent of the black youth were heavy drinkers (about double the Straus and Bacon, 1953, figures). More of these black freshmen drank for escapist reasons and were preoccupied with the effects of alcohol. Also more drinkers (81 percent) than nondrinkers (51 percent) possessed unfavorable self-concepts. In other respects, however, the black drinkers had no more problems with alcohol, trouble with the police, episodes of passing out, or worries about drinking than did white college students. In view of the small samples involved in these three studies and the somewhat inconsistent findings, we are hesitant to conclude that expectations from the Jessor et al. model have been supported to any thorough degree.

Consistency of Findings in a Parallel Study. Cahalan (1970) reported a study of problem drinking with a national probability sample of 1359 adults interviewed in 1967. Problem drinking was described as having 11 components—the most important components being "binge drinking"; problems with friends, neighbors, or police; number of accidents; and frequency of being drunk (Cahalan, 1970, p. 41). Cahalan drew explicitly on the concepts of the Jessor et al. model and used, in adapted form, some of their measuring devices. Cahalan comments: "The Colorado and national studies differ materially in content, populations covered, and analysis procedures. However, despite these differences . . . the findings of the national survey bear out the principal findings of the Colorado study of Jessor and associates in every major particular" (Cahalan, 1970, p. 81). Specifically, all of the major psychological variables were found to predict a higher likelihood of problem drinking. The two most powerful psychological predictors were favorable attitudes toward alcohol use and impulsiveness—each of which may be thought of as components of the Jessor et al. concept of *tolerance of deviance*. Alienation and maladjustment (similar to personal disjunction) were also predictive of problem drinking. At the social level, Cahalan included three variables—social position, looseness of social control, and environmental supports for drinking. All were associated with problem drinking as predicted. With respect to social position (or socioeconomic status), Cahalan found that higher status persons were more likely to be drinkers but were dramatically less likely to be problem drinkers. Men from lower social positions, for example, were twice as likely to have the most severe combinations of problems associated with heavy drinking, as were higher status men in the 20- to 59-year age range (Cahalan, 1970, Table 7, pp. 54–55).

Cahalan also took the trouble to look for statistical interactions among his demographic and social psychological variables. Examples of interesting interactions are the relations among attitudes toward alcohol, environmental supports, and educational status. Of those with highly favorable attitudes toward alcohol, 50 percent are likely to be problem drinkers. But if one adds an environment supportive of drinking and an education below high school level, the rate of problem drinking increases to 81 percent.

In the case of women, the overall subsample rate of problem drinking was only 4 percent. Of that group, those with all three major psychological risk factors—favorable attitudes toward alcohol, alienation, and personal disjunctions—had a 51 percent rate of problem drinking.

Interestingly, in this study the combined social and psychological variables were able to spread the rates of drinking problems from 12 percent (for the optimal or low-risk group) to 72 percent (for the high-risk group). As mentioned previously, it was discovered that those persons with high-risk psychological scores but low-risk social scores were more likely to have problems with alcohol than those with high social risk and low psychological risk.

Longitudinal Studies. There is much evidence for a relationship between social and psychological factors and heavy drinking. But what is cause, and what is effect? Jessor proposes that heavy drinking is the result of other factors. But since all the original data of the Jessor et al. study were collected simultaneously, it is plausible to argue (a) that excessive drinking may play a role in declining socioeconomic status (rather than lower status causing excessive drinking), and (b) that excessive drinking contributes to one's sense of failure and inadequacy and hence partly causes personal disjunctions and a sense of alienation. Indeed, Lemert (1954) has argued that heavy drinking can cause loss of self-respect, which in turn leads the person to drink more in order to forget his shame. Is Jessor's cause the effect, and vice versa?

If one could measure the social psychological variables before drinking begins and predict drinking and drinking-related problems, it would greatly strengthen the causal inference implied in the theory. In a current study that is longitudinal in design, Jessor, Jessor, and Collins (1971) have undertaken this kind of analysis. Data collected on a sample of high school youth who had not yet begun to drink have proven capable of predicting—not only which youth will begin drinking—but also which of the beginning drinkers will have problems associated with drinking. In the latter regard, one of the predictive measures used was personal disjunctions in the area of academic achievement. Such personal disjunctions (measured prior to the onset of drinking behavior) were significantly higher for those who, a year later, began to drink and to show drinking-related problems. These findings, therefore, provide some additional support for the original causal sequence proposed by the Jessor et al. model.

In Cahalan's (1970) study of problem drinking, it was possible to get a three-year longitudinal assessment. All of his analyses of the changes in problem drinking were consistent with the Jessor et al. model, but most changes were modest in size. Two other facts, however, were of equal interest. First, 22 percent of the men and 9 percent of the women substantially changed their status as problem drinkers during the three-year period. Second, those high on problem drinking were more likely to have started early in life and more likely to respond to improved status and responsibility by drinking. More than half had tried to cut down or quit drinking sometime in the past.

These findings suggest that even heavy problem drinking is not necessarily part of a single disease process leading to alcoholism.

Robins et al. (1968) carried out a longitudinal study that offers some support to the role of societal and family expectations upon heavy drinking. These investigators concluded:

> Heavy drinking was predicted by truancy and failure occurring together in elementary school (77% heavy drinkers), failure to graduate from high school (72%) and a first juvenile offense record after age 14 (79%). Failure to graduate together with late delinquency predicted that heavy drinkers (89%) would become problem drinkers (94% of heavy drinkers); 49% of high school graduates without elementary school problems became heavy drinkers, and of these 49% became problem drinkers. Father's presence in the home throughout elementary school, a conforming, successful father and a family with a middle-class life style all decreased the risk of heavy drinking, but did not significantly reduce the risk of problems if heavy drinking occurred: 10% became heavy drinkers of whom 25% became problem drinkers. Intelligence, guardian's occupation during elementary school and mother's religious affiliation showed little relationship to drinking behavior (Robins, Murphy, & Breckenridge, 1968, p. 684).

Many of these specific differences fit into the Jessor et al. variables of absence of social control and exposure to deviant role models.

Perhaps of even more interest is a longitudinal study of personality characteristics and alcohol use in men in their middle forties (M. C. Jones, 1968). These men had been intensively studied from age 10 until graduation from high school, and it was revealed that personality characteristics that were present prior to the start of alcohol use were predictive of problem drinking. Problem drinkers, as compared to moderate drinkers and abstainers, were described as undercontrolled, impulsive, rebellious, hostile, and self-indulgent, in both junior high school and high school. With respect to the Jessor et al. model, these descriptions are clearly suggestive of lowered inhibitions against deviance and drinking. Impulsivity and inability or unwillingness to control one's urges and desires might well be associated with personal disjunctions. An impulsive person will often be frustrated by demands to delay gratification; his own dissatisfactions with his lot in life may strengthen his impulsiveness. These interpretations, however, are post-hoc and suffer from being derived from original variables that do not clearly fit into the Jessor model.

Preliminary Evaluation of the Model. The following conclusions about the Jessor et al. model seem appropriate here.

1. In our emphasis on heavy drinking, escapist drinking, and drinking problems, it is possible to forget that the best predictors of drinking versus abstaining are age, sex, social class, region of the country, and religious-group membership. These variables are predictive because of the ways that they correspond to the distribution of social practices that embody normative standards about alcohol use.

2. Psychological and social considerations must be introduced to predict and understand heavy drinking or problem drinking. Among the social variables that contribute to excessive drinking are (a) a lack of supervision by family, neighbors, and religious groups, and (b) exposure to parents and peers who are models of heavy alcohol use and deviance. Among the psychological variables, dissatisfactions with one's life, alienation from society (particularly social estrangement), a lack of inhibitions about impulse gratification, and engaging in deviance are predictive of problem drinking.

3. We may tentatively conclude that cultural beliefs (for example, the belief that

alcohol helps individuals solve personal problems or escape from misery) are particularly important in the development of heavy drinking. Cultural beliefs are also likely to influence the relationship between personality variables, such as alienation and excessive alcohol use.

4. Most important, each of the three preceding conclusions must be tempered by the fact that the data collected thus far do not permit clear causal conclusions. Most probably, heavy alcohol use has detrimental psychological effects and increases downward social mobility; thus, in some of the results reported here alcohol use is the causal agent rather than the effect.

IV. PSYCHEDELIC DRUG USE

In the present section, we shall be primarily interested in the use of marijuana and secondarily concerned with the use of stronger psychedelic drugs such as LSD-25, DMT, STP, peyote, and mescaline. First, however, we shall point out some of the differences between alcohol use and psychedelic drug use.[2]

1. Data on alcohol use have come from the entire range of education and age in our society. Yet information about drug use is restricted primarily to college students and a few noncollege youth samples.

2. Alcohol use patterns have been fairly stable for approximately 25 years. Use of marijuana jumped from an insignificant minority of college students to a very significant minority of students (and, on some campuses, to a majority) between 1962 and 1970. Drug use has been in a highly dynamic phase, so that any precise statements about frequency, kind, or distribution of use will be out of date before they reach print.

3. Psychedelic drug use in our society tends to be associated with ideological movements (hippies, antiestablishment revolts, the pursuit of religious ecstasy) in a way that alcohol has not. This leads to the supposition that, in contrast to drinking, the use of psychedelic drugs is bound up with definitions of one's self as a particular kind of person (hip, a head, a freak) or as a member of a group with an ideology.

A. Distribution of Psychedelic Drug Use

In this discussion, we shall generally rely upon research conducted during the 1966–1969 period and published immediately thereafter. There is very good reason, however, to assume that the rates of usage have changed since that period. In at least some parts of the country, the use of marijuana has apparently increased. The same is true with heroin. The use of LSD, however, has apparently decreased. Keniston (1968a) has summarized the 1966–1968 period as follows:

[2] Given the general success of the Jessor et al. model of excessive alcohol use, we might be tempted to carry it over without modification to other forms of drug use. There are three reasons for not doing so. First, we shall want to examine other concepts and theories to see what understanding they may provide for psychedelic drug use. We may find important variables overlooked by Jessor and his associates in their focus on alcohol. Second, the circumstances of psychedelic drug use are sufficiently distinctive that it would be premature to organize the facts in terms of one model. Third, the distinctions between users of marijuana and users of hard drugs are so great that it is unlikely that the same model could cover both types.

Use is more likely at selective colleges with high standards of intellectual excellence, more likely on the West Coast and Northeast, more likely near a large metropolitan area, less likely at religious, vocational, and practical schools. Within a college, use is more likely among artistic, humanistic, and intellectual disciplines or the physical sciences. In the very early phases of college use, it appeared that those with stronger academic records were more likely to use drugs than those with poorer records. This correlation has not held up in many of the recent surveys.

Blum's Bay Area Study. During the 1966–1967 academic year Richard Blum and his associates (1969b) drew samples of 200 to 300 students from each of five San Francisco Bay Area colleges for intensive interviews on drug use and social psychological characteristics. The rate of reported marijuana use per college was from 10 percent to 33 percent of the student body. Hallucinogen use ranged from 2 to 9 percent of the students at the five colleges. (These figures refer to those who have ever used a drug, even if only once.) The proportion of regular (weekly) or heavy users of either class of drugs was considerably lower.

Blum and Garfield (1969) reported a follow-up study on one of the five Bay Area colleges during the 1968 spring term. In a random sample of 100 students, 57 reported experience with marijuana or hashish, while 16 indicated regular or considerable use. Seventeen students reported experience with at least one stronger psychedelic, but regular use was still rare (3 percent). Thus, during 18 months, the evidence suggests a threefold increase (from 21 to 57 percent) in one of the Bay Area colleges. It should also be noted that in the spring, 1968 study, 12 percent of the students who had not yet used marijuana reported an intention to do so.[3]

A Survey of Nine Colleges in the Rocky Mountain Area. In the fall term of 1968, Mizner, Barter, and Werme (1970) sought data on the personal and social correlates of drug use, by studying entire student bodies of nine colleges in a Rocky Mountain metropolitan area. The investigators used questionnaires and obtained more than 26,000 useable returns—for a 66 percent return rate. The results strongly parallel the Blum study. The range of experience with marijuana on the various campuses was between 11 and 32 percent of all students. The range of LSD experience was 1 to 7 percent. In their samples, only 7 percent (27 percent of the users) had used marijuana as often as 30 times, and only 0.5 percent had used LSD as often as 30 times. Mizner et al. recognize the problems of knowing whether such self-reports are accurate. Some may be reluctant to admit that they are users, even under anonymous conditions. Conversely, some nonusers may report having been users. These methodological problems are reviewed in Figure 18–1.

A National Sample of Colleges. At this writing, the most recent and most nearly adequate sample of college students is found in a study by Groves, Rossi, and Grafstein (1970), who surveyed 8000 freshmen and juniors from 48 colleges (selected to be representative of four-year colleges and universities). The researchers excluded schools with fewer than 1000 students, as well as predominantly black, technical, or special purpose schools. The pattern, derived from data collected in the fall, 1969, is quite consistent with the previous research findings of Blum and Mizner et al. (Table 18–5).

[3]Corroborative evidence comes from a longitudinal study of the 1968 freshman class at Carnegie-Mellon University. Goldstein (1971a) reported that students who were experienced with marijuana increased from 18 percent in September, 1968, to 45 percent during the fall, 1970.

The question of whether respondents accurately report their degree of drug usage is crucial to the findings reported throughout this chapter. Cahalan's (1970) book cites two careful studies showing that, with respect to the question of "getting in trouble with the police," between 65 and 85 percent of the survey respondents were quite accurate in their self-reports. In both studies, these reports were compared with official court records. There was some tendency to remember the law breaking as having occurred further away in time than it actually occurred. This is a nice example of perceptual distortion, but there was not much systematic omission of such events.

Jessor et al. (1968) did a number of multiple-indicator studies, using official records, peer nominations, and participant observation in bars and drinking spots. All of these studies supported the assumption that self-reports of drinking rates are generally accurate. As concerns reporting convictions for law breaking, the Jessor et al. findings rather clearly showed that women do not report as many of their convictions as do men. Thus, in comparisons between the sexes, self-reports may be biased in ways that exaggerate the difference.

In Davis's (1971) study with University of Colorado undergraduates, a procedure was developed by which peers could report on other people's sexual behavior and drug use without personally identifying the person being rated. Comparisons were made between self-reported frequency of marijuana use and peer's reports; the correlations were quite high (greater than +.70). Although the issue is not closed, we can be reasonably confident about the accuracy of the self-report usage rates in this chapter.

Figure 18-1. *The Question of Accurate Self-Reports of Drug Usage—An Important Methodological Aside.*

Alcohol is clearly the drug of choice, having three times as many tasters and three times as many moderately frequent users as marijuana. Other data from the Groves, Rossi, and Grafstein (1970) study indicated that (a) 43 percent of the students considered nonmedical use of marijuana acceptable (compared to 81 percent for alcohol and 1 percent for heroin); (b) a sizable proportion of marijuana users (21 percent) were casual experimenters; and (c) few marijuana users (17 percent) reported bad trips or hangovers in contrast to alcohol users (54 percent) and the stronger psychedelic users (40 percent). The facts that marijuana use is widespread, that marijuana is judged by users to have more good effects than bad ones, that marijuana has not been brought under control by existing legal measures, and that it has a significant number in favor of its legalization indicate that marijuana use will continue on the scene in the 1970s.

Table 18-5. *Drug Use by College Students, 1969*

Type of Drugs	*Did you ever use? (% reporting "yes")*	*How often used since school started in fall? (% reporting at least every week or two)*
Tobacco	74	37
Alcohol	89	58
Marijuana	31	14
Pills (amphetamines, barbiturates and other sedatives, tranquilizers)	33	4
Psychedelics (LSD, Mescaline, STP, MDA, DMT, Psilocybin)	9	2
Heroin	0.6	Less than 0.5

(From Groves, Rossi, and Grafstein, 1970. Reprinted with permission of the author.)

B. Social Psychological Correlates

The question then becomes: who uses psychedelic drugs and why? Our answers will necessarily be more tentative here than in the area of alcohol use. Researchers have been studying the problem for a considerably shorter period of time, and respondents are less willing to reveal their illegal behaviors to inquiring social scientists.

Three cautions are in order before we examine the data. (a) With but a minor exception (Blum and associates, 1969b), the research to be reported has not established personality and social characteristics prior to drug use. Thus, there is considerable uncertainty about cause-effect relationships. (b) All too often the research has had to rely on the distinction of use versus nonuse. Too few students have used drugs frequently enough to allow for a separate subgroup of heavy users. (c) We know very little about the duration of use patterns. Some students may drop out, engage in heavy use for a year or so, and return to the conventional social system. In Glueck and Glueck's (1968) study of 500 delinquent boys, only 29 percent of those who had been in serious trouble in their youth were still serious offenders against the law during the 25- to 31-year-old age period. R. H. Blum's (1970, 1971) work with drug pushers suggests the same pattern. Many voluntarily stop dealing because it is no longer worth the trouble, because they fear the effects of the harder drugs on themselves, or because the dealing scene becomes too violent.

C. A Conceptualization of Psychedelic Drug Use

When an activity—such as psychedelic drug use—is illegal, the first thing to be established in predicting use is that the potential user has a genuine opportunity to get the drug. The fact that some people on or near a campus use drugs does not imply that everyone has equal access to the supply. Because of the illegality of the drug and persistent police enforcement, users will not supply just any nonuser with marijuana or LSD. The network depends upon friends or acquaintances, where there is some basis for knowing the trustworthiness of the buyer. Thus, in order to become a user, a person must have friends who already use. In the case of marijuana and hashish, a person must also learn how to use; thus, the initial contacts must be sufficiently intimate to accomplish such teaching (Becker, 1953).

Conceptually, knowing others who use is a complex variable. While it is the most typical way of being introduced to the drug and learning how to use it, other users may also exert social influence either directly (as in the case of persuasion to use or ridicule for not using) or indirectly (as when the experienced user serves as an example or model of someone who enjoys a particular activity). Finally, the fact that one has friends who use drugs is partly a result of choosing to associate with other users. As Goode (1969) has observed, users who are heavily involved with the drug scene tend to drop their straight friends. It would be surprising, therefore, if a variable such as the number of friends who use drugs were not highly predictive of use. Indeed, such a variable has been quite predictive in those studies where it has been assessed (Blum & Ferguson in Blum & associates, 1969b; K. E. Davis, 1971; Sadava, 1970). The Blum and Ferguson study is interesting because it showed that the number of friends who were thought to be users was the variable most predictive of subsequent drug use among nonusing students.[4] Self-reported willingness to use drugs was also a powerful predictor. In Sadava's data (1970), the degree of social support for use was a much more powerful predictor among women than among men for the amount of marijuana and LSD use.

Once opportunity to use is established, one can turn to motivational and personality variables. This can be accomplished by assessing persons on the following four dimensions: (a) reasons for using, which may include such variables as gratification of use, social benefits, and symbolic meanings of use such as rebellion or rejection of convention, (b) reasons for not using, such as the fear of losing control, the fear of physical or psychological damage, the fear of punishment, or moral repugnance, (c) personality characteristics that might dispose the person to use any intoxicant (serious personal dissatisfactions and alienation from the society); and (d) social and family circumstances that have failed to inhibit illegal behavior or that have contributed to finding drug use attractive.

Reasons for Use. Two consistent findings (E. Blum, 1969; K. E. Davis, 1971; Sadava, 1970) are (a) that users see more benefits of use than do nonusers and (b) that the heaviest users see more benefits than do light users. Cognitive dissonance theory would point to this as an example of the effects of the severity of initiation upon the perceived value of an activity. In both the Davis and Sadava studies, the number of positive reasons given for use was also predictive of the personal willingness of nonusers to begin using psychedelics in social settings.

Reasons against Use. In both the Davis and Sadava studies, the number of negative reasons given was significantly related to an unwillingness to use drugs. In Sadava's classification, Protestant Ethic reasons ("not a natural way to expand your mind," "pleasure which is gained so easily is wrong," and "I don't believe in using drugs unless for a good medical purpose") and social irresponsibility reasons ("leads to lawless and degenerate society," "I would not be able to meet my responsibilities," and "I'm afraid that I might hurt someone while I was high on LSD") were the strongest correlates of unwillingness to use. Fears of medical problems, of loss of control, and of psychological change were also consistently related to unwillingness to use.

In Davis's classification system, moral reasons and practical fears of getting caught, of losing control, of damage to the body or self, or of dependence were also strong correlates of unwillingness to use. In this regard, Blum's summary is useful.

> Inquiry into the variety of functions (desired effects, reasons for use) of drugs reveals that illicit users claim the use of drugs to accomplish more things than do nonusers. This multiplicity of drug functions for those committed to use has been reported elsewhere (Aberle, 1966; Blum & associates, 1969a). We suspect it represents a rosy-colored view of what drugs are, a justification of why drugs are important, and an optimism about drugs as tools to change one's own inner nature, moods, cycles, and social relationships. The specific functions more often accepted by drug users and denied by nonusers include the following: combatting fear; exploring one's self; achieving religious experience; satisfying cravings; relieving boredom; combatting depression, sexual impulses, tension, anger, dullness, panic, and psychosis; elaborating moods, facilitating friendliness, learning, and sex; preparing for stress; changing or reducing appetite; shutting out the world, and killing oneself.
>
> Upon inquiring as to the personal principles which guide conduct in respect to illicit drugs, one finds that most students are guided by negative considerations, the fear of ill-effects, in-

[4]In a personal communication to this author, Jessor has reported exactly the same pattern in his longitudinal study of the shift from abstainer to alcohol drinker among high school youth.

hibiting or coercive social forces, inappropriateness of use, and so on. Mixed positive and negative guidelines more often characterize drug users, while positive values primarily guide illicit users—for example, the ratio of negative to positive to mixed valences (principles) for hallucinogen users is 1 to 8 to 12 compared with the reverse ratio of the remainder of the students, which is 23 to 1 to 8 (Blum & associates, 1969b, p. 97).

Personality Variables. Two different classes of personality variables have been explored. One is life history experience with other medical and social drugs, and the other includes the kinds of variables incorporated in the Jessor et al. model. In Blum's research, a general, although modest, tendency was found for users of one drug to be users of other drugs—including tobacco and alcohol. Also, students who felt there were advantages in playing sick were more likely to be drug users. But, interestingly enough, remembered use of prescription drugs was not related to psychedelic drug use. The heaviest psychedelic drug users were students who remembered their parents as not caring enough to provide medicine when they were sick.

In a similar study by M. Brehm and Back (1968) willingness to use ten different types of drugs ranging from aspirin and tobacco to painkillers and opiates yielded three distinct factors—all of which were positively correlated for both men and women. Willingness to adopt the sick role (measured by self-reported readiness to use the student health service for minor complaints) was unrelated to willingness to use psychedelics. In a personal communication, Brehm reports that among samples of heroin addicts the willingness to adopt the sick role is an important correlate of heroin use.

In a post hoc analysis of their data, Brehm and Back presented a model of willingness to use, which incorporates reasons for use as well as inhibitions against use. The two reasons for use were curiosity about drug effects and a self-reported wish that drugs would solve various personal problems (a variable akin to the escapist reasons for alcohol use). This second reason was labeled insecurity. The two inhibitions against use were a fear of loss of control and a personal rejection or denial of drug effects. Table 18–6 indicates that, when these two factors are combined in the manner of the Jessor et al. model, willingness to use is strongest among those high in positive reasons and low on inhibitions against use. In a further analysis, which also incorporated discrepancies between self-concept and ideal self-concept, Brehm and Back showed that large discrepancies between the real and ideal self were highly related to the insecurity factor and moderately predictive of willingness to use psychedelic drugs. A large self-ideal discrepancy is akin to the Jessor et al. measure of personal disjunctions.

Goldstein (1971a and 1971b), in a sample of 700 Carnegie-Mellon University freshmen, found that users of marijuana scored "in the direction of greater poise but lower sense of well being, are more non-conforming, more critical, more impulsive, more self-centered, less oriented toward achievement by conformity, more insecure, more pessimistic about their occupational futures, more disorganized under stress, more flexible in thinking, more rebellious toward rules and conventions [on the California Personality Inventory], more inclined toward aesthetic and social values and less toward economic, political, and religious values on the Allport-Vernon-Lindzey [study of values], than are nonusers" (1971a, pp. 3–4). Goldstein viewed his findings as essentially similar to Brehm and Back's work and concluded that "patterns of user-nonuser trait differences are very consistent for a wide variety of drugs and types of users. For example, teenage cigarette smokers, college student marijuana

Table 18-6. *Willingness to Use Drugs as a Function of Reasons for Use and Inhibitions on Use*

Reasons for Use	*Inhibitions*	*% Willing to Use*
Low	High	12[a]
Low	Low	33
High	High	41
High	Low	61

[a]Men and women's data combined

(From Brehm and Back, 1968, Table 8, p. 311. Reprinted with permission. Copyright 1968 by Duke University Press.

users, college student amphetamine users, college student drinkers, and Haight-Ashbury multiple drug users all score lower than nonusers on scales assessing satisfaction with self and higher on scales assessing flexibility" (Goldstein, 1971b, p. 5).

In a small-scale, intensive study of 39 self-designated LSD users and 10 nonusers of any psychedelic, A. Jones (1969) found that the users were strikingly more unconventional and alienated from the contemporary society and much more likely to endorse items reflecting a lack of control over their own lives and a sense of aimlessness than nonusers. Blum and associates (1969b), in reviewing variables that distinguished users of illicit drugs from nonusers, noted that users were "generally dissatisfied and [had] lower school morale; and [were] more surprised about their life as they found it and more pessimistic about the future" (p. 81). Conceptually, this dissatisfaction and pessimism is the same as the Jessor et al. personal disjunctions variable. As Blum comments, one can see in the diminished commitment to institutional roles and goals a troubled alienation or a flexible openness to new experience and new social forms.

Family and Social Backgrounds. In summarizing his study, Blum reported that users of illicit drugs are unusual in several ways.

> This unusualness is reflected in the distribution of their characteristics, which, for the most part, indicate that they are older upperclassmen, from wealthy families, arts-humanities or social-science majors, in opposition to parental stands, politically active and left wing, irreligious, dissatisfied, have had drop-out experience, are pessimistic, heavy users of mild stimulants, and are users of drugs for a variety of personal and interpersonal purposes. Nearly all drink alcohol and smoke tobacco and, far more than the average student, they have used prescription psychoactive drugs and a variety of illicit ones. The more unusual the drug used, statistically speaking, the more the student using it will also have used more other psychoactive drugs examined here (Blum & associates, 1969b, p. 142).

Later Blum noted that heavy users of hallucinogens are particularly distinctive in their "disagreements with the mother and distrust of authority" (p. 143). As noted earlier, heavy users of hallucinogens remembered their parents as not caring enough to get them appropriate medicine when they were sick. In her very provocative set of case studies, Eva Blum (1969) suggests that some heavy users suffer a sense of loss—an absence of a flow of emotions between themselves and their parents. One youth "believed that his father 'felt nothing' for him" (p. 257). A quite similar pattern appears in the data of the present author (Davis, 1971), where a cluster of five items reflecting a sense of parental rejection or distance, a lack of caring or warmth, and an inability to communicate with parents were the most striking and consistent correlates of heavy psychedelic drug use in both men and women.

These very suggestive results on the importance of family circumstances have been examined by Tec (1970) in a sample of 1700 upper middle-class high school students. Tec showed that regular marijuana users (once a week or more) were more likely to come from broken homes, situations where the parents used some other drug such as alcohol or sleeping pills excessively, homes where teenagers felt their parents were demanding or cold or disappointed, displeased, or indifferent to their children, and from situations where the teenager did not enjoy being with his or her family.

D. Evaluation of the Model

The model of psychedelic drug use proposed here is composed of five analytically distinct components: (a) access to the drug that constitutes a genuine opportunity to use, (b) acceptance of reasons for using drugs, (c) inhibitions about using and not using, (d) personality or experiential variables that would dispose a person to appreciate the drug experience (alienation, dissatisfaction, a sense of powerlessness over one's own fate, or a history of other drug use), and (e) family circumstances that include parents' absence or lack of caring or that provide examples of drug use or deviancy. Perhaps we should add that use of illicit drugs brings the person into contact with others who reject authority and who emphasize new experiences and personal gratification. Those persons reinforce such inclinations in the user, thereby further institutionalizing drug use and other deviant behaviors.

The model presented here follows from a general analysis of the elements required for an adequate accounting of human behavior. In this respect, it is not a testable theory but, rather, an analytic framework. At the level of specifics, any of its variables may not be found to relate to the criterion. For example, alienation may not predict drug use, nor may lack of parental caring. But the findings to date—tentative as they are—suggest that the specifics identified here are prime candidates for a theory of the circumstances leading to psychedelic drug use.

V. SUMMARY

Drugs are commonly conceived of as substances taken because of expected effects on physiological or psychological states. In addition, taking drugs is clearly a way to accomplish certain social effects—such as expressing good will, readying oneself for religious experience, and so on. Under the proposed analysis of the term, aspirin, alcohol, cigarettes, LSD, and opium are all drugs.

To understand the appeal of various drugs, it is useful to compare legalized intoxicants such as alcohol with illegal drugs such as marijuana. Both pro-drug and antidrug forces tend to share exaggerated assumptions about the powers of psychedelic drugs to change persons.

Psychological drug effects, in the narrow sense, are dose-related changes in psychological states. Such changes have implications for behavior, but, typically, they do not produce specific behaviors.

Many psychological changes naively attributed to the drug per se are in fact complex resultants of beliefs or expectations about drug effects, other physical or psychological states, and the on-going social interactions that occur during drug use.

The known dose-related drug effects of LSD are changes in body image, dreamy detached feelings, reduced intellectual-motor proficiency, and other physiological changes. The known marijuana effects are not clear—particularly insofar as long-term effects are concerned.

The distribution of alcohol use can be adequately mapped by a set of social, economic, and regional variables. Drinkers are more likely to be male, young, nonreligious or Catholic, high income, dwellers of urban areas in the Northeast or on the West Coast. The reason that these social variables map the distribution of alcohol use is that they are related to the social practice of drinking and the norms about drinking held by distinctive cultural groups.

The Jessor et al. model of excessive alcohol use is an effective model for predicting and understanding heavy drinking and problems associated with such behavior. The variables that seem most important are—at the social level—an absence of parental and social controls against alcohol use and deviance and the presence of heavy drinkers among parents or siblings (role models of deviance). At the psychological level, tolerance or acceptance of a general pattern of deviant behavior, alienation, and personal disjunctions (dissatisfactions) are all implicated in the development of heavy drinking.

Psychedelic drug use has been a rapidly growing social phenomenon among college youth. The best evidence indicates that approximately one-third of the college youth tried marijuana or some stronger psychedelic as of 1970.

The variables predictive of heavy psychedelic drug use are similar to the variables predictive of heavy alcohol use; they include personal dissatisfaction, tolerance of deviance, rejection of authority, and alienation.

At the family level, psychedelic drug users report that their parents did not care about them strongly enough to set limits for them as children or to develop strong family ties.

Psychedelic drug use differs from heavy alcohol use in that psychedelics feed into ideological and identity-forming social practices. Many of the reasons given by users for using psychedelics indicate that these drugs are seen as a means of changing oneself, of becoming a better person, or of achieving a better social order.

We know very little about the personal histories of both alcohol and psychedelic drug use. This makes it extremely difficult to know whether short-term patterns of heavy use are likely to be stable or likely to be detrimental physically and psychologically. Improved life histories and longitudinal research are required to untangle the mutually reinforcing patterns of drug effects and social psychological reasons for drug use.

VI. SUGGESTED READINGS

Bacon, M., & Jones, M. B. *Teen-age drinking*. New York: Crowell, 1968. The best elementary introduction to alcohol use among youth. It places the topic in historical and cross-cultural perspective as well as dealing with the reasons for drinking and the types of risks associated with heavy use. It also compares teenage and adult drinking and has a rich set of bibliographic references.

Einstein, S. *The use and misuse of drugs*. Belmont, Calif.: Wadsworth, 1970. (Paperback) A compact, highly informative work that deals with the broad range of mind-altering drugs. Contains good brief discussions of addiction, drug types and effects, drug names, and drug laws. It has a very extensive set of references, an annotated bibliography, a glossary, a list of scientific journals, and a list of sources of drug information and education.

Grinspoon, L. *Marihuana reconsidered*. Cambridge: Harvard University Press, 1971. (Paperback) A comprehensive review of the biology, chemistry, pharmacology, and toxicity of marijuana, of the possible medical therapeutic use of the drug, of the psychological effects of use, and of the social and legal implications of its use to the person and society. It includes references and notes on sources, and reaches a conclusion in favor of making the social use of marijuana legal.

Laurie, P. *Drugs: Medical, psychological, and social facts*. Baltimore, Md.: Penguin, 1967. (Paperback) A particularly well-done piece of reporting by a nonscientist. Particularly useful as a source about heroin, opiates, sleeping pills, and the issue of why and how to control drug use.

Maddox, G. (Ed.) *The domesticated drug: Drinking among collegians*. New Haven, Conn.: College and University Press, 1970. (Paperback) Contains 21 articles by a number of scholars and researchers cited in this chapter. The issues covered include drinking prior to college,

college drinking by black and white students, moral norms, personality profies of problem drinkers, and cross-cultural work. Although the range of topics is not as broad as that of Bacon and Jones, the articles in this book afford a greater opportunity for the critical appraisal of particular studies.

Nowlis, H. *Drugs on the college campus.* Garden City, N.Y.: Anchor, 1969. (Paperback) A very cautious, level-headed introduction to the state of knowledge about drug effects and their relation to students, schools, and the law. A good source of bibliographic materials.

Putnam, D., & Snyder, C. *Society, culture and drinking patterns.* New York: Wiley, 1962. The classic advanced reference source. Particularly useful for anthropological and sociological perspectives on alcohol use. The most difficult of the suggested readings.

I. *PROBLEMS RELATED TO RESEARCH ON SEXUAL BEHAVIOR*

II. *RESEARCH ON THE PHYSIOLOGY OF SEXUAL BEHAVIOR—A LOOK AT SOME FINDINGS, MYTHS, AND FALLACIES*

- A. *Masters and Johnson's program of research and therapy*
- B. *Myths and fallacies*
  1. *The myth of the male's sexual wisdom*
  2. *The search for aphrodisiacs*
  3. *Penis size*
  4. *Masturbation*
  5. *Frequency of sexual activity*
  6. *Two types of orgasm in women*
  7. *Single versus multiple orgasms*
  8. *The myth of the identity of male and female sexual urges*
  9. *Sex as a barometer*

III. *SOCIAL PSYCHOLOGICAL FACTORS IN SEXUAL BEHAVIOR*

- A. *Kinsey's studies of male and female sexual behavior*
  1. *Men*
  2. *Women*
- B. *Changes in sexual attitudes and behavior among college students*
  1. *Standards of conduct*
  2. *Sexual urges and masturbation*
  3. *Petting behavior*
  4. *Coitus: Women*
  5. *Coitus: Men*
- C. *A model of heterosexual decision making*

IV. *SEXUAL IDENTIFICATION AND HOMOSEXUALITY*

- A. *Gender attribution versus choice of sexual partners*
- B. *Transsexualism*
- C. *Research and theorizing about masculinity*
- D. *Homosexual object choice*
  1. *Incidence*
  2. *Typology of homosexuality*
  3. *Homosexual personality and background*

V. *SUMMARY*

VI. *SUGGESTED READINGS*

Chapter Nineteen

The Social Psychology of Sexual Behavior

by Gilbert R. Kaats and Keith E. Davis

Sex lies at the root of life, and we can never learn to revere life until we know how to understand sex. *Havelock Ellis*

Human sexuality finds its place in a social psychological textbook because sexual behavior and identity are—in most important respects—social types of behavior or aspects of social identity. In addition, our assumptions about the nature of man include beliefs about man as a sexual being. Sexual practices are encompassed by a subset of social practices, which is why we can say that some forms of sexual behavior are social rather than nonsocial. Among these social practices, some clearly count as sexual actions; some are clearly nonsexual; and others are in-between cases (such as ear nibbling or hugging). In this regard, we note that norms or standards apply to sexual behaviors just as to any other social behaviors.

In the social practice of sexual intercourse, there is a behavioral asymmetry. In other words, men must initiate the act of intercourse, whereas women receive. From this behavioral fact it follows that men can rape women but not vice versa. Unless the man is willing, no intercourse can take place. Let us hasten to add that women may take very active roles in soliciting sexual advances or in the actual intercourse, once started. But this initial behavioral asymmetry in the practice of intercourse may lead to an important difference between the sexes in the nature of the sexual impulse. The case may be that men look upon sexual desire as an urge to have intercourse, whereas women regard the impulse as the desire to attain an interpersonal relationship in which sexual activity is appropriate. Many observations consistent with the hypothesis of fundamental differences in male-female sexuality will be reviewed in Section II-B, which deals with the myth of the identity of sexual desires in males and females.

Sexual behavior is also fundamentally social in that it has a symbolic value, which makes it capable of fulfilling many desires and needs. The fact that a person is eating a particular food does not guarantee that he is hungry. So also, engaging in intercourse does not answer the question of what needs the actors are meeting for themselves and for each other. Some of the possibilities include *assaultive* sexual behavior, which can result in heinous crimes against another person. *Pathological* sexual behavior, of which the assaultive type may be a subvariety, is a manifestation of some deep-rooted neurotic or psychotic disturbance. The *physical* or *animal* type of sexual behavior is not pathological but is used almost exclusively to gratify physiological needs with no concern for the nature of the relationship. *Utilitarian* sexual behavior is the use of sex for materialistic or social gains; it may be outright prostitution or the subtle manipulation of another for personal gain.

Ego sexual behavior serves one's own psychological needs and is often a way of proving one's masculinity or femininity or of gaining acceptance. Beyond this, there is a kind of *fun* or *recreational* sex, where a meaningful relationship exists and sexual behavior is enjoyed as an extension of the participants' liking or caring for one another. But it is not an expression of love in the deepest sense nor does it include the formal commitments of engagement or marriage. *Recreational* sexual behavior goes beyond physical gratification because the nature of the relationship is important, but it falls short of *emotional* or *love* sex. The latter type of sexual behavior represents the expression of some of the deepest of human emotions, and, for many persons, it is a prerequisite for engaging in intercourse. In contrast, *reproductive* sexual behavior need not be an aspect of *love* sex, although it most frequently is. For example, some persons may engage in reproductive sex almost exclusively for the anticipated enjoyment of the children or with the hopes that children will "save our marriage" or "bring us closer together." Unmarried participants may use it as a way of getting a husband, or for that matter, a wife.

With respect to the symbolic nature of sexual behavior, Freud has taught us to see the possibilities of sexual impulses in our dreams, fantasies, slips of the tongue, jokes, and neurotic symptoms. But Kenneth Burke has wisely noted that sexual acts may be used as symbols of other human needs. The sexual need is not always the point of origin in such symbolic relationships. Desires for money, power, dependency, or aggression are all capable of transforming one's motives and nonsexual purposes into sexual performances.

Expression of our sexual motive has dramatic effects on individuals and the society at large. For this reason, society has long regulated our sexual behavior through its laws, mores, and expressions of morality. Consequently, sexual practices can lead to arrest, incarceration, commitment to a mental institution, scandal, abortion, blackmail, forced marriages, and crippling feelings of guilt and shame. On the positive side, sexual practices can lead to increased self-confidence, feelings of fulfillment, and some of the most profound of human emotions. Sexual behavior can enhance marriages and other relationships, and, of course, it is vital for the survival of the species.

The gratification of few other motives has such important consequences for the individual or the society. And yet, despite our incorrigible sexual habits and their pervasive effects, science has been incredibly timid in the past in its investigations of sexual behavior and physiology. For a long time, sexual behavior has been a tabooed topic for the scientist. Besides, few investigators were willing to cope with the problems inherent in this type of research. Some of these problems will be explored in the next section; perhaps we will gain some tolerance of the reasons for the continued degree of ignorance on this topic.

I. PROBLEMS RELATED TO RESEARCH ON SEXUAL BEHAVIOR

Invariably, we relate the findings of social science research to our own behavior and attitudes. Many of us find it almost impossible to read about sex research without engaging in self-evaluation through social comparison. Few research topics are so directly and personally relevant. Since scientists are people (despite some accusations to the contrary), the researcher's decision to study sexual behavior may be interpreted by others as a sign that his own sexual behavior is deviant. From a scientific point of view, when one is emotionally involved with the topic to be investigated, it is difficult to maintain the objectivity that is often necessary for doing acceptable research.

Some truth may reside in the claim that sex-research findings may alter the behavior that has been studied and thus ultimately involve the scientist's personal values. Two of the basic principles of science are commitment to objectivity and commitment to the candid dissemination of its discoveries and findings. Insofar as sex research is concerned, however, these actions may conflict with the values of the society. What happens when the results refute widespread and cherished social beliefs? For example, there is a substantial body of research that suggests one of the most important sources of influence is our peer group. Our hair styles, clothes, modes of speech and much of what we do is in step with what our peers (or some subgroup of peers) do. Recent research has found that college females tend significantly to underestimate how many of their friends have had sexual intercourse and to overestimate the extent to which their friends disapprove of such behavior. When these findings are publicized and college females discover the more liberal behavior and attitudes of their peers, it could remove one source of restraint and lead to further increase in premarital intercourse.[1]

A similar situation occurs with venereal disease. A recent widespread rumor among American soldiers in Southeast Asia held that there was a kind of leper colony for those among them who had contracted an incurable venereal disease. Such men were supposedly prevented from returning home to spread the disease throughout the United States. The rumor also included the belief that there were new strains of VD that could not be cured even with early treatment. Many commanders are reluctant to expose these rumors as myths, as the rumors tend to encourage continence or at least more careful behavior. But the leper colony *is* a myth and almost all venereal disease infections can be cured rather quickly and easily as long as there is early detection and treatment. But the question arises: do you let the rumors spread as a deterrent or do you expose the myth—especially when such exposure may actually encourage the very behavior you are seeking to prevent? In your reverence for the truth, you may believe that you must tell it like it is; but are you sure you really feel that way? What if the exposure encourages carelessness on the part of the GI, who may eventually return from overseas to infect your sister or even you?

The problem of the personal relevance of sex research also points out the need for researchers to be scrupulously careful in conducting their projects and reporting

[1] The argument here is reminiscent of the hypothesis that "risk is a social value." This hypothesis has been used to explain the risky shift resulting from group decision making. (See Chapter 16.)

their findings. Erroneous data may mislead other researchers as well as the lay public. One must also be careful to avoid the strong temptation to outrun the data and assume the role of an expert.

As we see it, an example of succumbing to this temptation is David Reuben's *Everything You Always Wanted to Know about Sex But Were Afraid to Ask*. The book immediately hit the bestseller list after it was published in 1969. Although there is some good information in the book, the author often overgeneralizes from his personal experience as a psychiatrist. His discussions of homosexuality, prostitution, and impotence reflect his personal values more than the latest research. Reuben tends to put down any type of sexual behavior that differs from his personal view of what is healthy; he suggests psychiatry is the cure-all for sexual problems. By mixing fact with personal opinion presented as facts, his book could well give some readers difficulties and make them feel less adequate as sexual partners. Even more disturbing is Reuben's tendency to use extreme or infrequent cases or problems as examples, without giving the reader any indication of the range, frequency, or variance of such problems. Thus, he may be creating new myths.

For these and other reasons, our society has been in the curious position of knowing very little about something upon which it has traditionally placed a great deal of emphasis. But this lack of information does not result from the lack of a need for it. Indeed, we have a number of staggering social problems related to sexual behavior. But slowly the picture has begun to alter, and some impressive changes have occurred in the past two decades. Solid research has been reported within the last decade on the physiology of sexual behavior that calls into question a number of accepted beliefs about sex. Most noteworthy among this work is the research of Masters and Johnson at the Reproductive Biology Research Foundation at Washington University in St. Louis. A brief summary of that research is in order at this point.

II. RESEARCH ON THE PHYSIOLOGY OF SEXUAL BEHAVIOR—A LOOK AT SOME FINDINGS, MYTHS, AND FALLACIES

A. Masters and Johnson's Program of Research and Therapy

In 1966, William Masters, a gynecologist, and Virginia Johnson, a psychologist, published the results of a seven-year research program on the anatomy and physiology of the human sexual response. Their controversial volume described laboratory research which used nearly 700 males and females in acts of sexual intercourse and self-manipulation. The investigators employed clinical interviews, controlled observations, electrophysiological measures, and color cinematographic recordings of all phases of the sexual-response cycle, including the use of a clear plastic phallus for intravaginal photography. Although Masters and Johnson's initial studies employed a small number of prostitutes and persons being treated for sexual maladjustments, most of their findings were based on data from a volunteer subject population, which was biased toward higher intellectual levels and socioeconomic backgrounds. However, the researchers believe the physiological findings would apply to all types of human groups.

In 1970, Masters and Johnson published *Human Sexual Inadequacy*, which presented the results of their 11-year program of treating couples with some form of sexual difficulty or maladjustment. Using therapy teams composed of one male and one female, the Foundation treated 790 people for such problems as premature ejaculation and impotence in males and failure to experience orgasm in females. Dedicated to the principle that "there is no such thing as an uninvolved partner in a sexually distressed marriage," the therapy team instituted a two-week program, which was begun by taking an extensive sexual history for each partner in order to determine individual "sexual value systems." After an initial abstinence from any type of sexual interaction during the first few days of therapy, each couple was encouraged to get to know each other's bodies and sensate areas without feeling the demands of sexual performance or orgasm. Each day the couple came to the clinic in order to have a joint round table discussion of past problems and to learn techniques to be employed in the privacy of their hotel rooms. One spouse was the giver, while the other was the receiver of pleasure and stimulation; the roles were then reversed. Contact became increasingly more intimate as each employed the techniques suggested by the co-therapists.

The most controversial aspect of the program was the use of what has been called partner surrogates in the treatment of 41 single men. The 13 female surrogates, including one physician, were screened and trained as part of the therapeutic team for single men who had no satisfactory sexual partner to bring to the therapy—a situation not faced by the few single women who were treated. The surrogates saw their partners only during the two-week therapy session, and all have apparently fulfilled the prior agreement never to see these partners again. Nonetheless, to some critics, the surrogates were little more than well-meaning, unpaid prostitutes who had violated the bounds of social decency. The researchers claim, however, that one-third of the men who were treated had previously been married and that sexual inadequacy played a major role in their divorces. To deny treatment to these men would have been unjust.

Although their sample is by no means representative of all people seeking treatment for sexual maladjustments, Masters and Johnson's research has resulted in very promising rates of successful treatment. This has occurred even with their stringent criterion of success—no recurrence of the problem within five years after the termination of the two-week therapy program. The 448 males in the study were treated for four basic types of maladjustment with the following success rates. Men complaining of premature ejaculation (inability to control ejaculatory process for a sufficient length of time to satisfy the sexual partner in at least 50 percent of coital connections) experienced a 97.8 percent rate of success in overcoming their problem. Men with ejaculatory incompetence (the reverse of premature ejaculation, or the inability to ejaculate within the vagina) experienced an 82.4 percent rate of success. Men with primary impotence (the inability to achieve and/or maintain an erection of sufficient quality to accomplish successful coital connection during the initial and every subsequent opportunity) achieved a success rate of 59.4 percent. And finally, men with secondary impotence (after at least one instance of successful intromission, a pattern of erective inadequacy is established, which precludes successful coital connection with 25 percent or more of available opportunities) were successful at a rate of 73.7 percent. Maladjustments treated in the 342 women in the study can be divided into two general categories: primary orgasmic dysfunction (having never achieved orgasm), which had an 83.4 percent rate of success; and secondary or situational orgasmic dysfunction (failure to achieve orgasm after having satisfactory completion of at least one orgasm), which had a 78.2 percent rate of success.

Thus, the work of Masters and Johnson is valuable in furthering both research knowledge and treatment effects, and the outcome for all of us is a better understanding of the physiological and behavioral aspects of human sexuality. One of the most useful applications of the latest work on physiological research is that it disconfirms a number of common myths about sexual behavior.

B. Myths and Fallacies

The Myth of the Male's Sexual Wisdom. For many readers, this may be the first formal exposure to sex education. Perhaps it will encourage some to look further into the subject, for what you are expected to know or what you expect your partner to know is itself the subject of a widely held cultural myth. As Masters and Johnson (1970) put it:

> The most unfortunate misconception our culture has assigned to sexual functioning is the assumption, by both men and women, that men by divine guidance and infallible instinct are able to discern exactly what a woman wants sexually and when she wants it. *Probably this fallacy has interfered with natural sexual interaction as much as any other single factor.* The second most frequently encountered fallacy, and therefore a constant deterrent to effective sexual expression, is the assumption, again by both men and women, that sexual expertise is the man's responsibility (Masters & Johnson, 1970, p. 87, italics added).

Thus do both men and women make assumptions about the sexual nature and knowledge of both sexes. It follows that one of the major goals in the treatment of sexual maladjustments is the establishment of lines of communication between men and women so that each may gain a better understanding of the ways in which the other is different and the ways in which both are similar.

The Search for Aphrodisiacs. Although man has long searched for an effective aphrodisiac to initiate and prolong the sexual act, his efforts so far have been a failure—at least physiologically. As MacDougald (1961) puts it, "There has been an extraordinary amount of nonsense [written about aphrodisiacs, and] it is evident that there are no traditional 'aphrodisiacs' that can bring about erotic biochemical and/or physiological results" (p. 152). This conclusion appears equally true for such substances as cantharides (Spanish fly) and such "sexual foods" as raw oysters, raw eggs, or truffles. But, even though direct physiological enhancement may not occur, the psychological impact may be significant. Alcohol is an example; it acts physiologically as a depressant that narcotizes the brain, retards reflexes, and dilates the blood vessels, thus interfering with the capacity for erection. In fact, heavy drinking was a frequent trigger of secondary impotence for the males in Masters and Johnson's (1970) research. However, although alcohol physically depresses sexual abilities, it also removes feelings of guilt and anxieties about the sexual act, which often more than compensates for the physiological decrement.

In our own interviewing (Kaats & Davis, 1970) we have heard a wide variety of stories suggesting that marijuana seems to distort time, thus seemingly prolonging orgasm and ejaculation and apparently resulting in deeper emotional feelings during sexual activity. We suspect that much of this is again psychological; but then, this is only a suspicion. A study of the effects of marijuana on sexual intercourse would be asking a good deal from our contemporary society right now.

Penis size. Commonplace stereotypes to the contrary, penis size has little to do with sexual effectiveness. For one thing, though there is a great deal of variation in size in the flaccid state, these differences are minimized during erection because the smaller penis grows proportionately larger. Also, the vagina accommodates to any size of penis; and, while a larger penis does put more pressure on and extend further into the vaginal barrel, the barrel itself is relatively insensitive and probably adds very little to the experiencing of the sexual act. Even the smallest of erect penises can effectively stimulate the clitoris—the structure that is largely responsible for pleasure and orgasm (Masters & Johnson, 1966; Wood, 1963). The only exception is again psychological. A woman who is convinced that she needs a large penis for satisfaction will need one despite the fact that this need is physiologically and anatomically unwarranted.

Masturbation. There is not a shred of evidence to suggest that masturbation will cause blindness, acne, insanity, feeblemindedness, the growth of hair in the palms of the hands, or any of a variety of other physical ailments that have been attributed to it. Lest one think that we are exaggerating the myths of the dangers of masturbation, as recently as 1959, Lief found that "a study of medical students from five Philadelphia medical schools revealed that half of them thought—after three or four years of medical school—that masturbation itself is a frequent cause of mental illness. Worse yet, a fifth of the medical school faculty members shared the same misconception" (1966, p. 276).

However, Masters and Johnson (1970) did conclude that youthful sexual experiences that were accompanied by an emphasis on speed of ejaculation imprinted rapid ejaculatory patterns, often leading to subsequent problems of premature ejaculation in adulthood.

Frequency of Sexual Activity. There is no evidence to suggest that frequent sexual activity during one's younger years causes one to lose capacity for sexual response. The male is capable of an infinite number of ejaculations, and semen replaces itself as easily as saliva (I. Rubin, 1966). Few people have complained that getting hungry too often will consume their supply of saliva. In fact, the person who is more active in his or her earlier years will remain more active later in life as well (Kinsey, Pomeroy, & Martin, 1948; Kinsey, Pomeroy, Martin, & Gebhard, 1953; I. Rubin, 1966). This is not to suggest that one can prolong his or her sexual life by engaging in sex more frequently and at an earlier age. No doubt both tendencies reflect a higher sex drive to begin with. In any case, the evidence casts further doubt on the myth about "burning out."

Two Types of Orgasm in Women. Primarily as a result of Freud's speculations, a widespread conception developed that there existed in women two types of orgasm: clitoral and vaginal. Vaginal orgasm was assumed to be the only psychologically mature type of orgasm, whereas clitoral orgasm was felt to be the result of an inhibition of full sexual expression, brought about by some neurotic problem. Although a number of psychiatrists and psychoanalysts still maintain Freud's point of view, Masters and Johnson's (1966) research suggests that there is no difference between the two. Both are involved in orgasm, and, if anything, the clitoris plays the major role.

Single versus Multiple Orgasms. Conventional beliefs have always held that a person cannot experience more than one orgasm during one act of sexual intercourse. However, the physiological recordings of Masters and Johnson (1966) indicate that many women, at least, are capable of many orgasms during a single act of intercourse. McCary (1967) has also made the following observation.

> Although men supposedly possess a stronger sex drive, they are not nearly so capable as women of multiple orgasms. Only about 6% to 8% of men are able to have more than one orgasm during each sexual experience, and when the capacity for multiple orgasm exists, it is usually found only in very young men. Furthermore, those men who have a second orgasm shortly after the first relate the pleasure of the first is superior to that of the second, in direct contrast to women's subjective reports (p. 174).

Some contemporary writers have criticized the stress placed on orgasm—particularly simultaneous orgasm—that was found in earlier sexual and marriage manuals. Such earlier viewpoints encouraged many people to use orgasm as a yardstick of personal sexual adequacy or as a measure of the depth of a relationship. Often this objectification tends to pervert the sexual act and gives birth to some rather self-defeating, vicious circles.

The Myth of the Identity of Male and Female Sexual Urges. Bardwick (1970, 1971) makes a very strong case that any model of equally intense sexual urges in men and women is a distortion of the data. Her argument is very complex, depending on facts about the physiology and anatomy of sexual systems and facts about social practices and learning patterns that do not seem easily amenable to radical change. To summarize, Bardwick argues that the "minimal masturbation observed in young girls is not the result of massive repression but of the physiology of the female reproductive system. The girl has an insensitive vagina, no breasts, and a small and relatively inaccessible clitoris" (1970, p. 6). In contrast with male sexuality, which is always centered around the highly sensitive penis, genital sexuality in women is a strong possibility only after puberty and only after the experience of sexual intercourse. Furthermore many factors combine to make ambivalence toward the sexual body a very likely outcome of growing up as a girl. On the positive side are the pleasures of being desired, being courted, the bodily pleasures of kissing and petting; on the negative side are fears of pregnancy and childbirth, concerns about degrading herself because of her sexual acts, and menstruation, which possesses negative implications in all cultures, and which carries fears of having been ripped or damaged internally. "Characteristically, she is ambivalent about her genitals, simultaneously regarding them as something precious and as something dirty. . . . [Her] sexual inhibition has several origins: she is afraid of personal and social rejection; she has no intense, independent sex drive and thus has difficulty in perceiving vaginal sex as pleasurable; she relates coitus to blood, mutilation, pain, penetration, and pregnancy" (1970, p. 9).

Particularly relevant to the rejection of the myth of equally intense sexual urges are data on masturbation, orgasm, and sexual satisfaction in women. By age 17, 100 per cent of Kinsey's sample of males had achieved orgasm, but only 35 percent of the females had (Kinsey, Pomeroy, Martin, & Gebhard, 1953). Among 15- to 20-year olds, the rates of masturbation in females are 20 to 35 percent, while 80 to 95 percent of males report having masturbated. Extensive interviews with women who rarely or never reach orgasm during coitus indicate that they nevertheless experience complete relief from sexual desires (Wallin, 1960; Bardwick, 1970, 1971).

As Bardwick observes, these data have two complications: (a) that the sense of being loved is a major source of the positive feelings and (b) that a high level of sexual arousal was probably not reached in these instances. Only at a very high level of arousal can the woman experience either frustration or a satisfying orgasm. For men, an orgasm is the *sine qua non* of satisfaction, but clearly this is not the case for women.

All of the data argue that for women *experience* plays a much greater role in the development of high levels of sexual arousal and frequency of orgasms than for men. And it seems particularly clear that the experimentation required to reach high levels of sexual arousal and to discard inhibitions depends on the trust of a stable, loving relationship.

> The absence of a powerful sex motive in women is a logical extension of the anatomy of the female body and of the girl's relationship to her sexual body. The idea that women are motivated by strong sex drives has led to an overestimation of sex as a significant variable in their lives, an assumption of equal orgasmic responses, a failure to recognize the periodicity of desire as a function of menstrual endocrine changes, and an underestimation of the strength of maternity-nurturance needs. A large part of feminine sexuality has its origin in the need to feel loved, to feel reassured in that love, and to create love (Bardwick, 1970, p. 12).

The nature of male and female sexual urges is certainly controversial, and doubtless further research will result in the modifications of the views presented here. However, Bardwick has drawn our attention to a number of differences that must be taken seriously when developing our assumptions about human nature and our everyday interactions with members of the opposite sex. The blithe assumptions of equally intense sexual urges and the primacy of orgasm for both sexes perpetuate a myth that is particularly unfortunate during this period of transition toward greater sexual openness and freedom.

Sex as a Barometer. Only a very small percentage of marriages begin with sexual problems. Consequently, many couples have used their sexual performance as a barometer of their relationship, or an indication of how they really feel about each other. Such a conclusion is not always justified. As Golden (1971) proposes: "There are couples for whom the only good thing in marriage is sex. And there are sexless marriages which are satisfactory to husband and wife. But both these situations are rare. Usually in a discordant marriage the sex life is unsatisfactory, too" (p. 185). But Golden, as well as some other observers, believes that sexual maladjustments are more likely to be a result of interpersonal difficulties. This, however, does not make the converse true; "poor sexual adjustment does not mean that a marriage is going to be shattered or even that the marriage is unhappy" (Golden, 1971, p. 167). And we must remember, as indicated in Chapter 2, that correlation does not imply causality. For that matter, both sexual and interpersonal difficulties may be caused by some third factor such as a temporary stressful situation.

We believe that using sex as a barometer can be a hazardous process and can cause a great deal more difficulty than is warranted. Again, a self-fulfilling prophecy may be instituted here. The most realistic approach is to consider carefully whether sexual maladjustments reflect any other difficulties or whether they represent a problem of their own.

On the basis of a variety of sources (Benjamin & Masters, 1964; Esselstyn, 1969; Masters & Johnson, 1966, 1970; McCary, 1967, 1971; Rubin, 1966; and Wood,

1963), we have listed in Figure 19–1 a number of other popular beliefs that have been found to be related more to myth than to reality. Some of these myths have been shattered by social psychological research as well as medical research. In the next section, we shall consider some of the social psychological factors in sexual behavior.

III. SOCIAL PSYCHOLOGICAL FACTORS IN SEXUAL BEHAVIOR

Who engages in what sorts of sexual behavior under what circumstances? If we can answer this complex question, we have made a first step toward formulating a social psychological explanation of sexual behavior. But one handicap is that we have a less adequate research base for dealing with these questions than, say, in the areas of alcohol use or prejudice. At the time of this writing, no systematic, national probability sample has been studied in regard to frequency and types of sexual behavior. In fact, no systematic national investigation of all age ranges in the population has appeared since the pioneering Kinsey studies (Kinsey, Pomeroy, & Martin, 1948; Kinsey, Pomeroy, Martin, & Gebhard, 1953). We have considerably more adequate data on college students—a fact that reflects the greater ease of obtaining these subjects and the society's general concern with premarital sexual behavior. In general, then, we shall be quite tentative about applying the available research findings to noncollege populations or to the full age range of the adult population.

A. Kinsey's Studies of Male and Female Sexual Behavior

Because Kinsey's original investigations are benchmark studies in our society and because they were pioneering efforts in the study of sex in any modern society, their major findings are worth reviewing. A few preliminaries, however, are important. The Kinsey samples were volunteers, selected from diverse sections of the society, but they were not selected in a fashion designed to ensure the representativeness of the sample. The data were collected in face-to-face interviews. Although there are many possible methodological artifacts in the original Kinsey procedures (sampling bias, interviewer bias, self-report distortion by subjects, and the like), comparisons between the Kinsey findings and those of earlier and subsequent works have tended to support the adequacy of the major findings.[2]

Men. Some of the more general findings of Kinsey et al. were that 85 percent of the males studied had premarital intercourse and about 50 percent of all married males had intercourse with other women since they married. Fifty-nine percent had engaged in heterosexual oral-genital sex; 37 percent had at least one homosexual experience; and 70 percent of the total population had intercourse with prostitutes. A total of 92 percent of all males (96 percent for college graduates) had masturbated to orgasm.

Women. For American women, the data showed that 64 percent had "responded to orgasm" by one means or another prior to marriage and almost half (48 percent)

[2] All the findings in this section are, of course, subject to self-distortion on the part of the subjects. If a subject wishes to exaggerate or deny the extent of his sexual activity, it is easy enough for him to do so. Such problems are discussed in Figure 18-1 of this text.

1. An intact hymen is not proof of virginity, since it can grow back once ruptured. Since it can be ruptured by means other than intercourse, its absence is also not proof of nonvirginity.

2. There is no physiological or medical reason why a woman should avoid any form of sexual activity during menstruation. Some writers suggest it may even have the advantages of (a) relieving discomfort of menstrual cramps, (b) virtually eliminating the chance of pregnancy, and (c) satisfying the sexual desires, which may be at their peak for some women.

3. There is no physiological reason to suggest that sterilization, such as the vasectomy, should either enhance or inhibit the individual's sex drive or behavior. Psychologically, it appears to have an enhancing effect by eliminating the fear of pregnancy and by removing the discomfort resulting from the use of other forms of birth control. Very few sterilized persons report negative effects, and those few appear to be among men who have insecurities about their masculinity.

4. There is no need to avoid sexual intercourse during pregnancy. Unless contraindicated by vaginal bleeding, painful intercourse, or broken membranes, intercourse can take place right up to the moment of labor.

5. From an anatomical and physiological point of view, there is no best or most satisfying sexual position, such as the male-superior position that is customary in this society. However, different positions, by varying stimulation to different parts of the sex organs, may achieve different degrees of satisfaction.

6. Although an effective diuretic, saltpeter (potassium nitrate) is an almost completely neutral chemical and, as a sex deterrent, it is a complete failure.

7. Heterosexual oral-genital sexual activity does not indicate latent or overt homosexuality.

8. Although the data and professional opinions are quite mixed, there is some reason to doubt the assertion that all prostitutes are either sick, homosexual, or frigid. Many women become prostitutes for a complex number of reasons—many of which are quite rational, such as the need for money or enjoyment of sex.

Figure 19-1. *Further Myths about Sexual Behavior.*

had premarital intercourse. (This figure is biased upwards by the small number of older, unmarried women in Kinsey's sample.) More than one-fourth of all women (26 percent) admitted having had extramarital intercourse. Forty-three percent of the women had heterosexual oral-genital sex (62 percent among the higher educated), and 28 percent had at least some homosexual experiences. Over two-thirds (69 percent) of the still unmarried females in the study who had intercourse insisted they did not regret the experience. Another 13 percent expressed some "minor regrets."

For both sexes, socioeconomic status was one of the most significant variables in predicting incidence of different sexual behaviors. Even though as children they had begun most sexual practices later than noncollege persons, college-educated men and women proved less inhibited in most sexual behaviors and were more likely to engage in masturbation, oral-genital sex, homosexuality, and a variety of coital positions. While differences among religious denominations were not striking, those persons who were nonreligious were more likely to masturbate, to pet to orgasm, and to have premarital coitus and extramarital affairs.

B. Changes in Sexual Attitudes and Behavior among College Students

In view of the limited data on noncollege students and older people, we have decided to concentrate our review on studies using college students as subjects.

After examining the major variables predictive of attitudes and behaviors, we should be able to formulate a tentative model of sexual behavior.

When considering whether a sexual revolution has taken place among college students, we must look at two difficulties with the question. First, seldom has any attempt been made to clarify the notion of revolution; and, second, concern has been almost exclusively focused on the percentage of virgins and nonvirgins in the population. A genuine sexual revolution would have to involve a dramatic change in the principles that guide sexual behavior as well as a change in behavior itself. These principles or standards would involve a specification of what kinds of sexual activities are acceptable with specific kinds of persons (opposite sex, same sex, self) under specific circumstances (being engaged, in love, having adequate privacy).

From Reiss's pioneering work (1960; 1967) on premarital standards, it is apparent that the dominant standards in the United States have been abstinence until marriage or a personal acceptance of premarital intercourse when the partners were in love or engaged. The standard for men—held by both men and women—tended to be more permissive in regard to sexual intercourse, either prior to marriage or in the absence of a love relationship. A sexual revolution would imply, among other things, a dramatic change in judgments about what is acceptable premarital behavior. If current college students view love between partners as irrelevant to the decision to engage in intercourse, then a dramatic change in principles has occurred. As we shall see, although attitudes about socially acceptable premarital sexual activity have undergone a significant liberalization, the change is not so dramatic as to justify labeling it a revolution.

In reviewing the findings, we have included all studies done in the United States during the 1960s, for which we have data. The topics of concern will be (a) judgments of acceptable sexual behavior or appropriate standards of conduct, (b) consciousness of sexual urges, (c) masturbation, (d) heavy petting (defined as genital stimulation of one or both partners with no clothing barriers), and (e) sexual intercourse.

Standards of Conduct. Reiss's volumes (1960; 1967) are the landmark works on sexual standards. The data for the 1967 book were collected in 1959 and 1963. Smigel and Seiden (1968) reviewed work done prior to the studies of Reiss and concluded that 40 to 50 percent of college men and 9 to 14 percent of college women had endorsed for themselves a standard other than premarital abstinence. Reiss's studies show a noticeable liberalization. The 1959 sample, which included both black and white, northern and southern, high school and college students, showed that 69 percent of the males endorsed a standard other than abstinence for themselves and 27 percent of the women accepted premarital intercourse as appropriate for themselves. The increased permissiveness for both men and women apparently came from an increased acceptability of premarital intercourse when the partners were in love, engaged, or strongly affectionate toward each other.

Although the 1959 data mark a trend toward increased intimacy, Reiss's data clearly show a huge regional variation. At a white southern college, only 7 percent of the women found premarital coitus acceptable under some conditions, whereas 62 percent of the women at a New York college found it acceptable. It should be noted that the New York college was selected because of its liberal reputation.

In Reiss's 1963 national probability sample, one can see a dramatic discrepancy between adult and student judgments. Forty-four percent of the student women considered premarital intercourse acceptable if the participants were engaged, but only 17 percent of the adults did so. Twenty-seven percent of the students found intercourse acceptable if the participants were strongly affectionate, but only 12 percent of the adult women did.

An examination of several other studies conducted in the later 1960s reveals that 50 to 80 percent of the college men felt premarital intercourse was acceptable. Among the men, acceptance of greater intimacy was related to race, age, semester in college, strength of religious feelings, and region of country. Thus, older men who were indifferent or hostile to religion and who went to eastern, western, or southern schools were more permissive than younger, religious, midwesterners. Among college women the crucial factor is apparently "in love" versus "strongly affectionate." In a series of studies at the University of Colorado (Kaats & Davis, 1970) and in Freeman and Freeman's work (1966), up to 70 percent of the women endorsed sexual intercourse for themselves if in love, but 40 percent or less found it acceptable only if strong affection existed or only if there was no exploitation. Among college women, acceptance of greater intimacy was very strongly related to having been in love two or more times or to being in a significant dating relationship (going steady, pinned, or engaged).

Despite the very noticeable increases in acceptance of premarital sexual behavior, a newly devised assessment of the double standard revealed that approximately half of the men held a personal standard that implied greater sexual freedom for men than for women, particularly when the woman in question was a sister or potential spouse. The data in Table 19–1 show that the double standard is upheld by women as well as by men. Both men and women agree that it is important to them that women be virgins at marriage; both would be less willing to encourage their sister than their brother to have intercourse with someone the sibling loved; both would lose more respect for a girl who engaged in sex without love than for a man who did so; and both have higher standards of sexual morality for females than for males (Kaats & Davis, 1970).

Sexual Urges and Masturbation. Awareness of sexual urges has not been the subject of research by most investigators, but, in studies at the University of Colorado and Kansas State University, Kaats and Davis (1970) explored this topic. In their Colorado study, which was done in 1967, 78 percent of the women and 98 percent of the men acknowledged having "urges to engage in sexual intercourse." In their 1969 probability sample, 91 percent of the women acknowledged "urges to engage in some form of sexual activity," and 55 percent of those women had such urges weekly or more often. It is interesting that among those who reported frequent sexual urges, almost 90 percent were currently engaging in sexual intercourse. Awareness of sexual urges was also very strongly related to dating status. Fifty-six percent of those going steady, pinned, or engaged acknowledged weekly urges, while only 19 percent of those not regularly dating had such urges. These results are quite consistent with Bardwick's (1970) conclusions, reported in Section II.

In the classic Kinsey report on females (1953), 58 percent of the women reported having masturbated to orgasm at some time in their lives. But only 32 percent of the 20-year-old college women had masturbated at all. The Colorado data look very similar. In the 1967 study (in which 80 percent of the sample was 20 or younger), the rate was 34 percent. In the 1969 probability sample (35 percent of which was age 21 or older), only 37 percent had ever masturbated. And the number masturbating weekly or more was often less than 8 percent. Masturbation was not related

Table 19-1. *Mean Scores for College Male and Female Respondents on Items Measuring Male-Female Sexual Equalitarianism*

Item[a]	*Males* (N = *110*)	*Females*[b] (N = *162*)
1. It is important to me to be a virgin at the time of my marriage.	1.80	3.15
	↕	↕
2. Virginity in a prospective mate is important to me.	2.92[c]	1.98[c]
3. If he asked my advice about having sexual intercourse, I would encourage a brother of mine *not* to engage in it before marriage.	2.48	2.63
	↕	↕
4. If she asked my advice about having sexual intercourse, I would encourage a sister of mine *not* to engage in it before marriage.	3.47[c]	3.65[c]
5. I would lose respect for a male who engaged in premarital intercourse with a girl he did not love.	2.19	2.87
	↕	↕
6. I would lose respect for a girl who engaged in premarital intercourse with a boy she did not love.	3.11[c]	3.80[c]
7. I think having had sexual intercourse is more injurious to a girl's reputation than to a boy's reputation.	4.26	4.47
8. I have higher standards of sexual morality for females than for males.	3.52	3.79

[a]Subjects indicated their degree of agreement or disagreement to each statement. The choices were keyed as follows: 1 = strongly disagree, 2 = moderately disagree, 3 = neutral, 4 = moderately agree, 5 = strongly agree. Thus, a mean of 1.80 means an average score close to moderate disagreement (2.00) but a little stronger disagreement than that.

[b]Probability levels based on comparisons between items 1–2, 3–4, 5–6 within each group. Differences between groups on 7 and 8 are not significant.

[c]$p < .001$

(Adapted from Kaats and Davis, The dynamics of sexual behavior of college students, *Journal of Marriage and the Family*, **32**:3, 390–399. Reprinted by permission of the National Council on Family Relations.)

to extent or type of dating by college women. Thus, although a substantial proportion of college women and almost all men are aware of sexual urges at some time, such awareness has only a modest relation to frequency of masturbation for women (and only then among the virgins). Rates of masturbation for college women differ only slightly from those found by Kinsey in his 1940 samples. These data offer little support for the notion of a substantial change in masturbatory behavior among college women; certainly, it is not a change in which more women have become committed to sexual gratification per se, regardless of the emotional significance of the activity.

Petting Behavior. Heavy petting, defined as stimulation of one or both partners' genitals without clothing barriers, has apparently undergone a significant increase in recent years. The Kinsey report on females indicated that 52 percent of those women who went to college experienced heavy petting. This figure is between 8 to 40 percent lower than any figures from studies done in the 1960s. In the Packard (1968) and the Luckey and Nass (1969) studies, 61 percent of the junior and senior college women had such experience. And the American college women were the most conservative of any from the five countries sampled. (The others were Norway, Canada, England, and Germany.) In the work at Kansas State, an identical percentage was found for freshman and sophomore women; a higher rate, 64 to 89 percent, was found at Colorado. In the 1969 sample (Kaats & Davis, 1970), 57 percent of the women had experienced heavy petting in high school.

For college women, engaging in heavy petting is strongly related to permissive standards for sexual intercourse, dating status, and perceptions of girl friends as having had coital experience. Among those girls who considered sexual intercourse acceptable when in love, who were highly involved in a dating relationship, and who thought that several of their girl friends had experienced sexual intercourse, all but 6 percent had engaged in heavy petting, and all but 21 percent had engaged in coitus. Among college women at the opposite extreme (those who did not approve of premarital coitus when in love, who were not dating anyone special, and who thought that almost all their girl friends were still virgins), only 21 percent had engaged in heavy petting, and all were still virgins. Thus, for the Colorado samples, very striking relationships existed among personal judgments of acceptable behavior, actually being in an acceptable relationship, and having sexual experience. This does not imply that the majority of women's decisions to engage in heavy petting or coitus was necessarily the direct product of adhering to personal standards. Nonetheless, most investigators have found that very few men and women report violations of their personal sexual standards.

Further findings (Kaats & Davis, 1970) on the incidence of heavy petting indicate that 28 percent of the girls had experience with three or more partners, 55 percent had engaged in heavy petting with someone they did not love, and almost 25 percent had petted heavily with two or more partners they did not love. Thus, very intimate petting is not restricted exclusively to loved ones or those to whom one is seriously committed. Apparently, the experience of heavy petting has become acceptable to a substantial majority of college women (60 to 90 percent).

Coitus: Women. Three classic studies have dealt with the incidence of intercourse in college women. The first of these was the Kinsey study, which reported that 20 percent of the 20-year-old college women and 27 percent of the 21-year-old college women had experienced intercourse. The second classic study was the work done by Ehrmann (1959), who reported that 13 percent of the women sampled were nonvirgins. And, third, Bromley and Britten (1938) found that 25 percent of the women in their samples were nonvirgins, with variations among colleges ranging from 18 to 36 percent. In some quarters, it is regarded as an established fact that no significant change in coital rates occurred in the 1960s. Yet, such a conclusion will hardly stand up under careful scrutiny. The basis for the conclusion that no more than 25 percent of college women have engaged in intercourse has come from studies of small samples of students—sometimes primarily composed of freshmen or based on data actually collected in the 1950s.

In our examination of the data, we have found only two substantial, carefully executed studies (J. Katz, 1968; Robinson, King, Dudley, & Cline, 1968), indicating that rates of intercourse for college women were below 30 percent. Most of the studies showed that between 35 and 50 percent of college women have experienced sexual intercourse. Perhaps, in respect to sampling college students, the most adequate work is the Groves, Rossi, Grafstein (1970) study described in Chapter 18. Their data were collected from 8000 first semester freshmen and juniors. The relevant findings are presented in Table 19–2. The findings for juniors are most comparable to the previously cited data. The 36 percent rate of coital experience for junior women is almost twice Kinsey's 20 percent figure for 20-year-old college women. The Groves, et al. figures are very similar to those of Simon and Gagnon in their as yet unpublished study of approximately 1200 college students. Many other studies conducted at colleges in the 1960s (Kaats & Davis, 1970; Bell & Chaskes, 1970;

Table 19-2. *Percentage of Unmarried Students Who Report Having Had Sexual Intercourse*

	Percent from freshman class	*Percent from junior class*	*Combined percentage*
Males	42	59	50
Females	29	36	32
Both sexes	36	50	42

(Adapted from Groves, Rossi, and Grafstein, 1970, p. 4. Reprinted with permission of the author.)

Christensen & Gregg, 1970) also reflect that between 30 and 50 percent of undergraduate females have participated in intercourse.

Not having found the right man, or not having developed an acceptable relationship, is the restraining factor for a significant minority of college women. In Kaats and Davis' studies at Colorado and Kansas State, 10 to 20 percent of the college women who found premarital coitus acceptable when in love or engaged had not yet experienced intercourse. Christensen and Gregg (1970) likewise found that about 10 percent of the women who approve of premarital intercourse had not yet engaged in it. If one could safely predict future behavior from current judgments of acceptability, then up to 70 percent of this generation of college women are likely to have premarital sexual intercourse by the age of 25. This would constitute a significant increase over the Kinsey generation, which had a 47 percent rate of premarital intercourse for those college women married by age 25.

Coitus: Men. On the surface, it looks as if the sexual behavior of college men has remained unchanged since the beginning of the 1900s. Almost all studies of male college students yield rates of intercourse hovering around the 60 percent figure, with significant regional and religious variations. Somewhat lower rates were typical for college men in the midwest and for men coming from strict religious backgrounds in all areas of the country.

There are, however, two important ways in which men's sexual behavior has changed. In a personal communication to the authors, Murstein reports that a careful reanalysis of recent data shows that for males the age of first experience has decreased. Thus, though no more men are becoming sexually experienced prior to marriage, those who become experienced do so at an earlier age. Research done at the University of Colorado produced findings consistent with Murstein's report; it was found that more than half the college men who experienced intercourse (42 percent) achieved coitus prior to college (Kaats & Davis, 1970).

Another way in which patterns have changed is in the psychological and emotional setting of sexual experience. One example is the considerable reduction in the use of prostitutes by college men. Kinsey reported that 22 percent of college-aged men had used prostitutes. In contrast, Packard (1968) found a rate of only 4.2 percent, while Schofield (1965) found that only 3 percent of college-aged males used prostitutes. Nonetheless, men are still much more likely than women to have their first experience of sexual intercourse with someone they do not love and to have a greater number of sexual partners whom they do not love. In Schofield's study, 86 percent of the women had their first sexual experience with a steady date or fiancé, but only 56 percent of the men had their initial sexual experience with a steady date or fiancée. In Kaats and Davis' research at the University of Colorado, students were asked questions about the number of sexual partners whom they did not love at the time of the sexual activity. Among the men, 57 percent of those with coital experience had engaged in coitus with at least one partner whom they did not love, and 26 percent had experienced intercourse with three or more partners they did not love. For women, the connection between intercourse and love relationships was stronger. Twenty-six percent of those women who were not virgins had experienced intercourse with at least one partner they did not love, and only 8 percent of those with experience had engaged in coitus with three or more unloved partners. Nonetheless, many more men apparently now have some of their early sexual experience with loved ones; and, thus, much more than in previous generations, men must face at an early age the problem of dealing with emotional involvements with their sexual partners. Simon, Gagon, and Carns (1968) report that more men (35 percent) than women (23 percent) who were in love with their sexual partners "were engaging in sexual activity more than they wanted to" (p. 13). This fits with the general notion that men are indeed having to undergo very significant changes in response to women's changing sexual attitudes.

From these and related findings we may identify situational and intrapersonal factors that predict the extent of a person's sexual experience. These factors include the person's own judgment about the acceptability of premarital sex, his or her current dating status (not going steady, going steady, pinned, or engaged), and the perception of whether friends have experienced sexual intercourse. In general, the most powerful predictor of the extent of sexual experience among these three factors is the person's own judgment of its acceptability; this, however, is more true for women than for men. Of the women who reject the acceptability of premarital intercourse even when in love, 92 percent are virgins, whereas only 61 percent of the men with this attitude are virgins. For men more than for women, beliefs about friends' behavior is an important determinant. For women, the actual degree of sexual experience is best predicted by their attitude and their dating status.

This approach facilitates the specification of conditions that make a female receptive to sexual intercourse when an opportunity materializes. Specifying these conditions for men is a different matter, since almost half of them accept sexual intercourse even when the two participants have no particular affection for one another.

C. A Model of Heterosexual Decision Making

Why do people engage in intercourse when they do? To answer this question, we shall first present a rather abstract, theoretical scheme and then give illustrative examples. The aim of our theoretical model is to encompass all possible cases so that any instance of engaging or not engaging in intercourse should be predictable. In certain cases, however, some questions may still exist regarding the sources of the urges and values that the persons have. For example, we may be able to specify the considerations that lead a person to commit rape, without knowing what kind of life history made him the way he is.

With the exception of rape, to engage in intercourse is to engage mutually in a reciprocal behavioral practice so that the kinds of considerations relevant to one person must also be relevant to the other. The key *types* of factors are (a) opportunity, (b) desire, and (c) absence of inhibitions. Two additional factors—(d) recognition of an opportunity and (e) ability to engage in intercourse—play a necessary role, but typically they can be taken for granted. Here, however, a consideration of *recognition of opportunity* is in order. One person's opportunity is not another's. What one person recognizes as an opportunity for sexual behavior or romance clearly results in part from one's judgments of acceptable behavior and one's experience in heterosexual encounters. Part of the art of seduction lies in arranging the setting and circumstances so that the appropriate emotions are produced and so that the other person comes to see it as a genuine opportunity for acceptable sexual behavior. A rereading of Walster and Berscheid's two-factor theory of romantic love is relevant here. As concerns the *ability to engage in intercourse,* two circumstances are relevant. One is temporary incapacity produced by alcohol, drugs, or anxiety. The other is chronic impotence. Thus, ability and recognition of opportunity are both logical requisites for engaging in coitus.

Let us now return to the three key types of factors in sexual intercourse. There are at least three distinct meanings of *opportunity,* and it is important to distinguish among them clearly, since two of the meanings are not adequate for the requirements of the model. One inadequate meaning is *theoretical possibility* (not impossible not to), and the other is *practical feasibility* (at least one member knows how to). But neither of these meanings constitutes the kind of practical opportunity implied by a personal judgment that the setting and circumstances are appropriate for sexual intercourse. The exact content of practical opportunity for sexual behavior would clearly be subcultural and variable across cultures; but in middle-class American culture, privacy is certainly one element that is taken for granted.

If for practical purposes one can take a recognition of opportunity and ability to engage in coitus for granted, then a logical structure of explanations for engaging in intercourse is as follows. If the couple has an opportunity to engage in intercourse, they will do so unless (a) either one does not want to (lack of desire) or (b) either has a stronger reason not to (inhibitions). For example, John and Mary may be very much in love with each other, be alone together in a comfortable setting, and have no inhibitions about having sexual intercourse; yet, at this time, neither wants to. Why not? Perhaps one is sick, tired, or preoccupied about school work, parental problems, finding a job, or getting ready for an upcoming social event. The list may be endless; the logic is that preoccupation and strong interests in other activities can block sexual arousal.

In a similar way, inhibitions can block sexual intercourse, even if arousal exists. In the study of self-reported restraints among unmarried college students, Driscoll and Davis (1971) found that women—much more than men—gave morally oriented reasons against intercourse ("because it would be morally wrong," "because I would feel ashamed afterwards") and indicated lack of love as another cause of restraint ("because I did not love the person"). Men students, in turn, gave more emphasis to practical reasons ("fear of causing partner to become pregnant," "because I could not talk the other person into doing it," "because the decision was not entirely mine"). These findings are largely consistent with previous work (Bardwick, 1970; Ehrmann, 1959). Men and women did not understand some aspects of the other's sexual restraints. Men, for example, attributed greater fears of pregnancy and ruined reputations to women than women did to themselves; and men underestimated the importance both of shame and not being in love as reasons for women not to engage in intercourse. Women were in better touch with men's reasons but showed some tendency to underestimate how often men held back out of respect for their partners' desires not to have intercourse.

The following statements summarize the findings on sexual attitudes and behavior and factors in the decision to have intercourse.

1. Judgments of acceptable sexual behavior by both men and women have become much more liberal, but vestiges of the double standard remain. In other words, both men and women are more liberal in their judgments for men than for women.

2. Even though contemporary college women have more extensive sexual experience, earlier and with more partners than did college women a generation ago, the vast majority of intimate behavior remains in the context of relationships involving strong affection or love.

3. The major factors in the decision to engage in intercourse can be classified as (a) a practical opportunity, (b) desire, and (c) lack of inhibitions. Moral considerations apparently continue to constitute the major restraints on premarital sexual behavior, but relationship reasons ("not loving the person") and practical fears (of ruined reputation or pregnancy) also continue to be important.

4. Kaats and Davis (1970) found that women judged as physically attractive were less likely to remain virgins and more likely to have had frequent petting experiences. This finding supports a *meaningful opportunity* interpretation. That is to say, the attractive young woman is the target of more frequent and more sincere romantic interactions; hence, she is more likely to be in situations of mutual love and, thus, is more likely to have more practical opportunity for intimacy than the less attractive young woman.

IV. SEXUAL IDENTIFICATION AND HOMOSEXUALITY

Conceiving of oneself as either a man or a woman and making the appropriate choice of a sexual partner are two of the most emotion-laden issues of socialization. The emotional significance of these processes is revealed in the everyday language of insults. To speak of a boy or man as a "sissy," a "fag," or a "queer," or to call a girl or woman a "dog," a "beast," a "hag," or a "butch dike" is to denigrate that person and, often, to express one's personal disgust.

A. Gender Attribution versus Choice of Sexual Partner

In dealing with these topics, it is important to distinguish between one's *gender identity* (the sense of being a male or female) and one's *choice of a sexual object* (one's preferred love object or object of sexual attraction). One reason that the distinction is important is that homosexual object choices, contrary to some popular opinions, do not necessarily involve any deficiency in the chooser's sense of masculinity or femininity. Even though one may feel adequate in one's manliness, for example, one may still prefer men as lovers. Nevertheless, one fundamental research question is whether most persons who have homosexual object choices feel adequate as men or women.

B. Transsexualism

With respect to gender identity, we must distinguish between two conditions: (a) confusion and (b) a gender identity opposite to one's biological structure. Confusion is an aspect of severe psychopathology and will not be discussed here. The latter case is designated as *transsexualism* (Benjamin, 1966; Green & Money, 1969). It is important not to confuse transsexual persons with various types of hermaphrodites or with homosexuals. Hermaphrodites have, in varying degrees, a mixture of male and female bodily organs, hormonal patterns, or genotypes. These sex errors of the body can arise at any stage of biological development from the union of the sperm and egg to the adolescent development of secondary sex characteristics. In contrast, transsexuals usually have perfectly normal bodily development but psychologically feel like a member of the opposite sex. It is "almost as if their mind is in the wrong body" (Green & Money, 1969, p. 268).

Despite the fact that many transsexuals dress up as if they were a member of the opposite sex and engage in sexual intercourse with members of their same sex, they are neither transvestites nor homosexuals. The distinction between transvestites and transsexuals is roughly that transvestites get a sexual arousal from wearing clothing of the opposite sex, but they never *feel* like a member of the opposite sex. In contrast to homosexuals who prefer one of their own sex as a sexual partner, the transsexual man, feeling like a woman and calling himself by a woman's name, wants to have a man admire "her" and make love to "her." Thus, while male transsexuals may appear on the surface to be transvestites or homosexual queens, their psychological structure is much more like that of women than men (Money & Brennan, 1969).

Apparently, transsexualism reflects parental mistakes in sexual assignment and persistent parental treatment of the child in a manner appropriate to the opposite sex. The research to date does not permit one to exclude biological factors in the development of transsexualism; it seems certain though that a necessary condition of its development occurs when parents encourage opposite sex behavior in the child. Money and Primrose have made the following observations.

> The male transsexual is able to live, work, think, and make love as a woman. His female personality is, in part, his conception of those traits and behavior patterns which typically contribute femininity. This assimilation of traits does not create a less genuine or stable female personality. It simply excludes traits such as an urge to fondle the newborn and erotic arousal (by touch in contrast to the typical male pattern of arousal by visual or narrative stimuli) because they are normally outside male experience and comprehension. The male transsexual conforms to the conception of femininity . . . until by most standards his personality becomes *her* personality, female, and completely disassociated from identity (p. 131).

Indeed a transsexual who has had the chance to develop the impersonation of women can often pass undetected as a woman. His gestures, voice quality, gait, and style will be quite feminine.

Much the same patterns hold for female transsexuals. Just as the male transsexuals reject the penis and prefer not to use it in intercourse, so the female transsexuals loath their breasts and prefer to take an active, masculine role in intercourse. Money and Brennan (1969) obtained the following findings in a study of six female transsexuals who wanted to undergo a physical change of sex.

> They scored very low on femininity and fairly high on masculinity on the Guilford-Zimmerman M-F scale. In childhood they had no girlish interests. They were tomboys and prone to fight, usually with boys. Sensory and perceptual erotic arousal thresholds in adulthood conformed more to those of the female than the male, but the imagery of arousal and erotic performance was masculine. . . . Five were living as males. A universal presenting symptom was hatred of the breasts. . . . None of the patients wanted anything to do with pregnancy and motherhood; parental feeling toward infants and children, insofar as it could be estimated, was fatherly rather than motherly (pp. 151–152).

In Driscoll's (1971) research, a sample of 17 transsexual men were first met when they were dressing as women and engaging in prostitution with men as their clients. Fifteen of the 17 were clearly raised as girls; all came from broken homes; all had been effeminate in childhood and adolescence; and all learned first to think of themselves as homosexuals, next as transvestites, and finally as transsexuals. A key step in the change in self-attribution was the knowledge of the possibility of having a sexual conversion operation. Of Driscoll's 17 male interviewees, 12 eventually gave up prostitution and, with hormone treatments and a self-help club, began to lead fairly normal lives as women. Only one, however, had the very expensive operation for sexual conversion and thus became a fully functioning woman.

Most psychiatric experts (Green & Money, 1969) have come to the conclusion that the change of physical sex characteristics is preferable to psychotherapy in dealing with transsexuals. For one thing, psychotherapy has proved extremely ineffective in the past, whereas surgery and medical technology have made the change of physical sex possible. An artificial vagina can be constructed for men who want to become women. The skin of the amputated penis is used as the lining of the artificial organ, and the new woman may participate fully in sexual intercourse and if all goes well, even have orgasms.

C. Research and Theorizing about Masculinity

Transsexualism is a relatively rare problem. But a vague sense that one is not the man (or woman) that one ought to be, that one is somewhat inadequate as a man—as a provider, father, lover, or partner—is apparently a much more pervasive problem. Research and thinking within psychology have focused on the parental and early childhood antecedents of masculinity. Novelistic and experiential accounts, however, have been concerned with adolescence and early adulthood in both sexes, where the issues of being able to win a girl's favor or a boy's love, of being popular and respected as a man or woman are the central themes. Unfortunately, very little is known about how various types of masculinity measures (used as dependent variables in the standard psychological research) are related to social and sexual behavior in the adolescent and young adult. At the conceptual level, one would expect that adolescents who were worried about their adequacy as men (or, if girls, their attractiveness and femininity) would either avoid the competition of rating and dating or be excessively determined to win or prove themselves. Thus, it is not at all implausible that men who are insecure in their masculinity would either (a) strive to "score" by seducing as many women as possible, (b) avoid the threatening problem by intense dedication to athletic, artistic, or intellectual pursuits, or (c) be more susceptible to the appeals of homosexual love. But, as plausible as these hypotheses are, we do not have an adequate evaluation of how many men handle their problems of inadequacy in any of these ways, nor do we have sufficient information about other factors that contribute to the particular pattern of outcomes.

Nonetheless, taking a brief look at factors relevant to the development of a secure sense of masculinity will be worthwhile. Biller and Borstelmann (1967, pp. 259-60), in a comprehensive review, distinguished three aspects of masculinity: (a) desiring to behave in masculine ways (masculine sex-role preference); (b) behaving in a fashion consistent with the masculine role (masculine sex-role adoption); and (c) viewing oneself as male (sex-role orientation). (The latter seems to be the the same as the concept of *gender identity* used earlier in this chapter.) Although the typical developmental pattern would be for all three to go together, discrepancies can occur. Thus a child, who thinks of himself as a male (sex-role orientation), may behave in quite effeminate ways (masculine sex-role adoption) and wish that he were more masculine (masculine sex-role preference).

Quite a few variables have been identified as important in the development of masculinity, but a comprehensive, adequate theory does not yet exist. Research and theorizing has been concerned with the father more than the mother. Briefly, the following conditions (Biller & Borstelmann, 1967) are all thought to contribute to inadequate masculine development: (a) the father's absence from home for significant periods in the 2- to 6-year-old age range of the child, particularly when alternative male models such as uncles or older brothers are not available as surrogates; (b) the father's lack of masculinity, which would seem to involve the father's competence, assumption of decision-making power in the family, and setting limits for or disciplining the boy, and (c) the father's lack of warmth and concern for the boy. (Fathers could engage in many family tasks that are conventionally woman's work without any detrimental effect, if they do not abdicate the masculine role.)

Maternal attitudes and behavior cannot be ignored, however, if we are to account adequately for the process of masculine development. First, the mother can explicitly support and encourage masculine behavior, and her interventions apparently can overcome some of the detrimental effects of the father's absence. Indeed, the best way of conceiving of the variables influencing masculinity may be through the use of a field-theory approach that studies the entire family relationship. For example, the mother can be hostile and rejecting of masculine behavior only to the degree that the father allows this to happen. Thus, maternal behavior that tends to destroy masculinity development is simultaneously an indication of inadequate behavior by the father. There are limits, of course, on the degree to which either parent can control or remedy the other's actions, but it is useful to remember that neither parent acts in a vacuum. Furthermore, many of the kinds of parental inadequacies and pathologies cited here as contributing to problems of masculinity are also cited in research on the family etiology of schizophrenia and other mental disorders (Lidz, Fleck, & Cornelison, 1965; Mishler & Waxler, 1968). Thus, we are a long way from being able to specify why a certain pattern of troubles develops rather than another. Unfortunately, considerably less work has been done on femininity so that no clear-cut pattern of causation emerges there, either.

D. Homosexual Object Choice

What about sexual development that leads to homosexuality? For most people, a basic assumption about male homosexuals is that they are sissies or effeminate. This implies that a lack of masculine identification and a sense of being inadequate as a man dispose one to become homosexual. But we shall see that in some respects this idea is positively misleading, and in other ways it is not complex enough to fit the facts. The aim of this section is to get a few facts straight about homosexuality, to formulate in a tentative way an explanation of homosexual object choice, and to examine some of the factors in public attitudes toward homosexuality. More attention will be given to male homosexuality because it is of greater social concern and because it has received considerably greater attention by researchers.

Incidence. Accurate estimates of the number of men who have had homosexual experiences are tenuous at best. No genuine probability sample has ever been asked such questions, and, given the severe taboos on homosexuality in most social strata, one might fear considerable underreporting anyway. Nevertheless, the original Kinsey study found that "4 percent of the white males are exclusively homosexual throughout their lives, after the onset of adolesence" (Kinsey, et al., 1948, p. 651). Another 6 percent of their sample had been primarily homosexual for at least three years between the ages of 16 and 55. And a considerably larger number of men (37 percent) have had at least one homosexual experience at some time during their lives. At all levels of experience, the number of women who have had lesbian experiences are considerably lower. For example, only 3 percent of unmarried women were exclusively homosexual.

More important than such statistics are two kinds of facts. (a) The number of men who have had some homosexual experience is far larger than the number of men who actually become primarily homosexual; and (b) many men maintain active heterosexual and homosexual relations at the same time or in alternation. These facts make it clear that a homosexual object choice is not necessarily incompatible with heterosexual object choices. Hoffman's research (1968) makes it abundantly clear that some happily married fathers who enjoy their heterosexual relations also periodically engage in homosexual behavior. Humphreys' (1970) work on homosexual activities in public restrooms shows very clearly that a significant subtype exists, which is represented by married men who do not think of themselves as homosexuals but who allow others to perform fellatio on them in public restrooms. Also, it is a fact that in many prisons, homosexual rape is performed by the older, stronger inmates on the younger, weaker men, and yet the initiators do not think of themselves as queer or gay. By raping the other man, they are proving their superiority and masculinity (A. J. Davis, 1968). Finally, male hustlers of the type made famous in John Rechy's novel, *City of Night* (1963), typically do not think of themselves as homosexuals, even though they make their living by allowing homosexuals to perform fellatio on them. Indeed, Humphreys (1971) argues that the gay world is changing toward a more virile self-image and a more bisexual pattern of object choices, so that in the future there will be a clearer lack of contrast between homosexual and heterosexual choices.

Typology of Homosexuality. When we turn to the theoretical problems of understanding causes of homosexual object choice, we see immediately that we cannot expect any one variable to explain the phenomena adequately. Most people who have studied homosexuals soon become aware of very important differences in homosexual types—differences which are so marked that it is hardly plausible for all types of homosexuals to have similar life histories or personality types. Even if we restrict our attention to men who are primarily homosexual in their object choice and who rarely, if ever, desire sexual relations with women we still find considerable diversity. Very little of the explanatory work has dealt with these more refined typologies; one such typology, however, is presented in Figure 19–2.

Humphreys' classification makes explicit three general variables: (a) self-concept (as homosexual, heterosexual, or ambisexual), (b) attitude toward self (accepting or rejecting), and (c) socioeconomic autonomy (which consists of the relative freedom from detection and monetary power to satisfy one's desires). Although typologies are being developed, we are restricted to the use of research findings that lump together all types of self-designated homosexuals. Thus, in the research studies, the trade and hustler types are probably underrepresented, while closet queens probably contribute disproportionately as research subjects because they are most likely to seek professional help.

Homosexual Personality and Background. Do homosexual males share distinctive personality characteristics that set them apart from heterosexuals? Hooker (1957) matched 30 men who were homosexual but who were not seeking psychiatric help with 30 heterosexuals in regard to their age, IQ, and educational attainment. Each subject was administered a set of personality diagnostic procedures including the Rorschach Ink Blot Test, the Thematic Apperception Test, and the Make A Picture Test. These personality tests were then evaluated by experienced clinical psychologists who did not know the respondent's sexual object choice; this procedure is called *blind scoring*. These experts were unable to pick out homosexual subjects reliably, nor did the homosexual subjects receive worse ratings on general adjustments. In both the homosexual and the heterosexual groups, a wide range of personality types, character structures, and interests existed. This study can be interpreted as supporting the conclusions that homosexuals who are not seeking

---

1. *Trade*—mostly married men who have little freedom in their jobs. These men think of themselves as heterosexual but take the inserter role in homosexual acts. (Humphreys' largest category.)
2. *Ambisexuals*—often upper middle-class men who have sufficient security and freedom in their jobs to form homosexual groups and to afford to patronize male prostitutes. They have vigorous homosexual and heterosexual lives.
3. The *gay*—these men openly participate in the public world of gay bars and organizations such as the Mattachine Society. They are usually unmarried and think of themselves as homosexuals.
4. The *closet queens*—unmarried middle-income types who live in fear that their deviance will be discovered. These men tend toward patterns of self-hatred and social isolation. Their sexual activities take the form of solitary sexual forays.
5. *Male hustlers*—men who think of themselves as heterosexual but engage in many homosexual activities for pay.

(From Humphreys, 1971.)

Figure 19-2. *Humphreys' Typology of Male Homosexuals.*

psychiatric help are no different in personality than heterosexuals who are not seeking help.

Other people have felt that homosexuality is in itself indicative of mental disturbance or sickness. Often the people who argue this way are those in psychiatric practice who have contact only with homosexuals who are unhappy about their lives. Bieber, Dain, Dince, Drellich, Girand, Gundlach, Kremer, Rifkin, Wilbur, and Bieber (1962) have concluded that their research on patients in psychoanalytic psychotherapy supports the idea that "a homosexual adaptation is a result of 'hidden but incapacitating fears of the opposite sex'" (p. 303). This could very well be the case for most of the homosexuals who are psychiatric patients yet not be at all true of the majority of all homosexuals. As Hoffman (1968, p. 155) argues, Bieber's claim that homosexuality is necessarily a disorder seems to be a preconception rather than a result of his research.

The interview study by Bieber et al. (1962) also contains suggestions about the parental antecedents of homosexuality. In this study, 106 male homosexuals seeking help from psychoanalytically oriented psychiatrists were compared with 100 nonhomosexuals who were also patients in psychoanalysis. The major sources of data were the patients' reports of their life histories and their behavior in therapy. On the basis of these data, the psychoanalysts answered a range of questions about current behavior and the patient's past. Subsequently, R. B. Evans (1969) replicated Bieber's study using self-reports from a sample of 43 homosexuals and 142 nonhomosexuals. Evans' samples were persons who were not seeking psychiatric help. In 24 out of 27 issues that were repeated in both studies, Evans found the same pattern of statistical difference that was found by Bieber et al.

> Specifically, in retrospect, the homosexuals more often described themselves as frail or clumsy as children and less often as athletic. More of them were fearful of physical injury, avoided physical fights, played with girls, and were loners who seldom played baseball and other competitive games. Their mothers more often were considered puritanical, cold toward men, insisted on being the center of the son's attention, made him her confidant, were 'seductive' toward him, allied with him against the father, openly preferred him to the father, interfered with his heterosexual activities during adolescence, discouraged masculine attitudes, and encouraged feminine ones. The fathers of the homosexuals were retrospectively considered as less likely to encourage masculine attitudes and activities, and the homosexual subjects spent little time with their fathers, were more often aware of hating him and afraid he might physically harm them, less often were the father's favorite, felt less accepted by him, and in turn less frequently accepted or respected the father (R. B. Evans, 1969, p. 133).

A number of the key items from the Bieber and Evans studies are reproduced in Table 19–3. The essence of the Bieber hypothesis is that any son is likely to become a homosexual when exposed to a situation where the mother is overprotective, sexually seductive, and sexually restrictive (particularly with respect to heterosexuality) and where the father is either passive or uninvolved or actively hostile. This pattern is somewhat similar to that posited for the creation of problems in the development of masculinity, but distinct differences exist. The seductive and overly intimate pattern of maternal behavior is not generally included in the notions on masculinity development, but it seems essential in the etiology of a fear of women and distaste for heterosexual intercourse. Perhaps it is not surprising then that within the homosexual group, there was a correlation of $+.47$ ($p < .001$) between the quality of family background and self-reported feelings of masculinity.

Table 19-3. *Differences in Background and Child Rearing for Homosexual and Heterosexual Males*

		Bieber Study				*Evans Study*		
Questionnaire item	*Response*	*Homosexual*	*Heterosexual*	*p*	*Response*	*Homosexual*	*Heterosexual*	*p*
Physical make-up as a child	Frail	50	17		Frail	37	11	
	Clumsy	24	8		Clumsy	14	6	
	Athletic	13	33		Athletic	5	45	
	Well coordinated	13	42	.001	Coordinated	44	38	.001
Fearful of physical injury as a child	Yes	75	46		Seldom	23	49	
	No	25	54	.001	Sometimes	51	46	
					Often	19	4	
					Always	7	1	.001
Avoided physical fights	Yes	90	56		Always	56	12	
	No	10	44	.001	Often	30	35	
					Sometimes	14	46	
					Never	0	7	.001
Played with girls before adolescence	Yes	34	10		Never	9	3	
	No	66	90	.001	Sometimes	49	83	
					Often	40	14	
					Always	2	0	.001
"Lone wolf" in childhood	Yes	61	27		Never	12	38	
	No	39	73	.002	Sometimes	35	51	
					Often	42	11	
					Always	12	1	.001
Played competitive group games	Yes	17	64		Never	9	1	
	No	83	36	.001	Sometimes	65	15	
					Often	23	52	
					Very often	2	32	.001
Played baseball	Yes	16	64		Never	19	5	
	No	84	36	.001	Sometimes	70	29	
					Often	9	35	
					Very often	2	32	.001

Father and mother spent time together	Great deal	1	13		Great deal	16	28	
	Average	42	50		Considerable	53	39	
	Little	36	24		Little	26	23	
	Very little	21	13	.002	Very little	5	9	.23
Parents shared similar interests	Yes	20	38		Great many	21	30	
	No	80	62	.01	Several	37	32	
					Few	35	33	
					None	7	5	.70
Mother insisted on being center of son's attention	Yes	64	36		Never	30	18	
	No	36	64	.001	Seldom	37	63	
					Often	16	17	
					Always	16	1	.001
Mother "seductive" toward son as a child	Yes	57	34		Highly	7	0	
	No	43	66	.002	Moderately	7	3	
					Slightly	9	13	
					No	77	85	.02
Mother discouraged masculine attitudes/activities	Yes	39	17		Often	5	2	
	No	61	83	.002	Sometimes	21	7	
					Seldom	30	14	
					Never	44	77	.001
Mother encouraged feminine attitudes/activities	Yes	36	12		Never	53	87	
	No	64	88	.001	Seldom	21	11	
					Sometimes	21	2	
					Often	5	1	.001
Mother considered puritanical	Yes	67	51		Strongly	28	11	
	No	33	49	.05	Moderately	33	35	
					Mildly	23	23	
					No	16	30	.04
Mother's relationships with father/other men	Frigid	72	56		Frigid	12	0	
	Not frigid	28	44	.04	Cold	26	23	
					Warm	63	77	.10

Table 19-3. *Continued*

Questionnaire item	Bieber Study *Response*	*Homosexual*	*Heterosexual*	*p*	Evans Study *Response*	*Homosexual*	*Heterosexual*	*p*
Mother allied with son against father	Yes	63	40		Often	33	6	
	No	37	60	.002	Sometimes	21	18	
					Seldom	16	35	
					Never	30	42	.001
Mother openly preferred son to father	Yes	59	38		Always	12	1	
	No	41	62	.005	Often	14	6	
					Seldom	21	31	
					Never	53	62	.004
Mother interfered with heterosexual activities	Yes	37	25		Often	12	0	
	No	63	75	.08	Sometimes	16	8	
					Seldom	19	20	
					Never	53	71	.004
Son was mother's confidant	Yes	52	36		Never	30	27	
	N	48	64	.03	Seldom	19	32	
					Sometimes	23	36	
					Often	28	5	.001
Son was father's favorite	Yes	8	29		Strongly	9	9	
	No	92	71	.001	Moderately	16	40	
					Mildly	40	37	
					No	35	14	.005
Felt accepted by father	Yes	23	48		Strongly	23	42	
	No	77	52	.001	Moderately	35	42	
					Mildly	23	11	
					No	19	6	.006

Son spent time with father	Great deal	3	3		Great deal	2	8	
	Average	12	39		Considerable	9	39	
	Little	37	31		Little	53	32	
	Very little	48	27	.001	Very little	35	21	.001
Father encouraged masculine attitudes/activities	Yes	48	61		Often	26	41	
	No	52	39	.07	Sometimes	26	32	
					Seldom	23	21	
					Never	26	6	.002
Aware of hating father as a child	Yes	61	37		Never	28	59	
	No	39	63	.002	Seldom	19	20	
					Sometimes	37	18	
					Often	16	3	.001
Afraid father might physically harm him	Yes	57	43		Often	14	4	
	No	43	57	.06	Sometimes	19	23	
					Seldom	30	13	
					Never	37	60	.003
Respected father	Yes	30	49		Strongly	37	56	
	No	70	51	.01	Moderately	21	32	
					Mildly	21	8	
					No	21	3	.001

Note: Significance levels based on chi-square, with twofold classifications corrected for continuity. Decimals omitted. (Adapted from Evans, Childhood parental relationships of homosexual men, *Journal of Consulting and Clinical Psychology*, **33**, 1969, 129–135. Copyright 1969 by the American Psychological Association and reproduced by permission.

Furthermore, as Hooker (1969) has commented in a review of all published studies on parental characteristics of homosexuals, "it can no longer be questioned that faulty, disturbed, or pathological parental relations in early childhood are more commonly reported by male homosexual patients" (p. 140). Moreover, five of the six studies of nonpatients also show many of the same patterns. It also seems clear, however, that parental problems do not adequately explain homosexuality. For one thing, in too few cases is it clear exactly how the parental practices of those who rear homosexuals differ from those practices that supposedly contribute to other disorders. It does appear that many heterosexuals suffer the same kinds of family constellations as do boys who later become homosexual. (See Table 19–3.) Both of these facts indicate that other variables play a role in homosexual object choice. Three very important possibilities are (a) the source and rewardingness of early sex behavior, (b) peer relations in adolescence and early adulthood, and (c) the social structure of the gay world. Hoffman's (1968, pp. 128–153) case studies illustrate the range of contributing factors. In one case, an adolescent who had been socially isolated and ineffectual at masculine pursuits became friends with another male and eventually engaged in some homosexual acts (mutual masturbation). When such persons discover that these pleasurable acts are classified by society as homosexual, they gradually become confirmed homosexuals. Here, factors a and b are clearly at work.

Another case is the male prostitute or hustler who starts out merely to make money but who then finds himself the center of attention, favor, and affection. What was initially a pragmatic choice may later become a pattern of behavior that leads to higher social status and to more intense and rewarding relationships than could be obtained in the heterosexual world. A handsome stud has a status in the gay world similar to that of a beautiful girl in the heterosexual world. This can be a very appealing status. In such cases, factor c seems important. Humphreys' research (1970) indicates that many of the trade homosexuals apparently seek out homosexual release because they have unsatisfactory marital situations and do not have the opportunity or means to get satisfaction from prostitutes. In such cases, their family background as children may be entirely normal. Clearly, no one pattern is dominant.

V. SUMMARY

Sexual behavior, like other forms of social behavior, carries its own norms and standards and its assumptions about the nature of man as a sexual being. Like other social behaviors, it has symbolic value in fulfilling needs and desires. Sexual behavior can fulfill a variety of needs; there is assaultive sex, pathological sex, physical or animal sex, utilitarian sex, ego sex, fun or recreational sex, reproductive sex, and emotional or love sex.

Until recently, little research on sexual behavior has been instituted because of (a) strong taboos against the topic, (b) problems in obtaining representative samples of subjects, proper observation techniques, and the like, and (c) difficulties in convincing the public that scientific conclusions can be drawn objectively.

Some highly popular treatments of sexual behavior contain mixtures of scientific findings and unsupported personal opinions. Masters and Johnson's program of research on the physiology of sexual behavior has exploded some long cherished myths and theories, among them being the clitoral versus vaginal orgasm, the impossibility of multiple orgasms, and the importance of penis size.

With a stringent criterion of successful treatment, Masters and Johnson's program of therapy for sexual maladjustments in married couples has led to a high rate of success in treating the following symptoms: premature ejaculation in males, ejaculatory incompetence in males, primary impotence in males, secondary impotence in males, primary orgasmic dysfunction in females, and situational orgasmic dysfunction in females.

Studies of college students indicate that even though attitudes toward premarital sexual activity have undergone a significant liberalization, the change is not dramatic enough to warrant calling it a sexual revolution.

For women much more than for men, the acceptability of premarital sexual intercourse is still dependent upon the experience of love or affection with the sexual partner. Men are much more likely than women to have their first sexual experience with someone they do not love.

Factors related to engagement in sexual intercourse include: (a) opportunity, (b) desire, and (c) absence of inhibitions.

In considering how sexual identity develops, it is important to distinguish between one's gender identity (the sense of being male or female) and one's sexual objects.

Homosexuality, transsexualism, and hermaphrodism are different phenomena. In young men, inadequate masculine development appears related to (a) father's absence, (b) father's lack of masculinity, (c) father's lack of warmth. Maternal characteristics, while important, are less explicit.

Many common stereotypes about homosexuality are too simplified. There are several discernible types of male homosexuality, and many homosexuals are also heterosexual. Homosexual men who are not psychotherapy patients appear no different in personality from heterosexual men who are not patients.

VI. SUGGESTED READINGS

A significant difficulty with suggesting readings on human sexual behavior is the flood of books and the dramatic unevenness of their quality. Books range all the way from pseudoscientific sensationalism (presenting the most exotic sexual behavior in lurid detail) to very academic biological and theoretical monographs. For students who want to go beyond the list below and the chapter references, the best place to start is SIECUS (Sex Information and Education Council of the U.S.), 1855 Broadway, New York, N.Y. 10023, which publishes a number of useful study guides, a quarterly newsletter, and annotated booklists on particular topics. Also useful are a number of scholarly journals which often contain research in the area. Most helpful are *Archives for Sex Research* (a new journal), *The Journal of Sex Research, Journal of Marriage and the Family,* and *Social Problems.* Somewhat more popular monthly journals are *Medical Aspects of Human Sexuality, Sexual Behavior,* and *Sexology.*

Bardwick, J. M. *Psychology of women.* New York: Harper & Row, 1971. (Paperback) An extremely thoughtful and stimulating integrative review of biological, medical, psychoanalytic, psychological, and social research. Bardwick assembles the data to support an argument for fundamental male-female differences in sexuality and psychological characteristics without accepting as adequate the traditional sex-role patterns. She includes much of her own, unpublished data on hormonal and menstrual-cycle variations in mood, on reactions to the use of contraceptives, and on women's attitudes toward sexual functions and the body.

Bieber, I. and associates. *Homosexuality: A psychoanalytic study of male homosexuals.* New York: Vintage, 1962. (Paperback) A classic presentation of the psychoanalytic point of view. The research is based on a comparison of male homosexual and heterosexual patients, and presents interesting information about the probable etiology of homosexual preferences among a subset of male homosexuals.

Ford, C. S., & Beach, F. A. *Patterns of sexual behavior.* New York: Harper & Row, 1970. (Paperback) A comprehensive compilation and synthesis of animal and human sexual behavior. In addition to the Kinsey research, they have drawn on cross-cultural area files, mammalian sexual behavior, and the physiological foundations of sex. Encyclopedic in coverage, with a glossary and extensive references.

Hoffman, M. *The gay world.* New York: Bantam, 1969. (Paperback) The most useful first source on male homosexuality. It communicates well about the variety of men and types of action involved and does a good job on the question of why men become homosexual. Good discussion of homosexuality and mental illness.

Kinsey, A. C., Pomeroy, W. B., Martin, C. E., & Gebhard, P. H. *Sexual behavior in the human female*. New York: Pocket Books, 1965. (Paperback) A report of the classic study based on interviews with nearly 8000 women. It deals with masturbation, petting, premarital, marital, and extramarital coitus, and homosexual experience. The original study of men has not been reprinted in paperback, but many of the important tables from the men's study are included in this volume for comparative purposes.

Lehrman, N. *Masters and Johnson explained*. Chicago: Playboy Press, 1970. An authorized, highly readable summary of the major findings from *Human Sexual Inadequacy* with a very skimpy treatment of the findings from *Human Sexual Response*. Includes the *Playboy* interview with Masters and Johnson and a verbatim transcription of the press conference about *Human Sexual Inadequacy*. In the case of *Human Sexual Response*, one can get a more comprehensive summary in Ruth and Edward Brecher's *An Analysis of Human Sexual Response*. New York: Signet (New American Library), 1966. (Paperback)

Student Committee on Human Sexuality, Yale University. *The student guide to sex on campus*. New York: New American Library, 1971. (Signet paperback) Easily the best short guide to most of the sex education questions asked by college students. It is accurate and clearly written, and it contains a very useful appendix on sources of further information. Coverage includes anatomy and physiology, human sexual response, contraception, abortion, pregnancy, venereal diseases, a model student health service program, parental relations, and some of the moral issues in the decision to have intercourse. It is a "*student* book, written by students for students" and a very good one too.

I. *THE RELATIONSHIP BETWEEN APPLIED SCIENCE AND PURE SCIENCE*
   A. *The dialogue between Kenneth Ring and William McGuire*
      1. *Ring's radical social psychology*
      2. *The radical social psychologist in action*
      3. *McGuire's mainstream position*
   B. *Bringing divergent viewpoints together*

II. *KURT LEWIN AND ACTION RESEARCH*
   A. *The importance of testing theories in field settings*
   B. *The nature of action research*
   C. *Action research and planned change*

III. *SOCIAL PSYCHOLOGISTS AS CHANGE AGENTS*
   A. *Strategies for bringing about change in institutions*
      1. *The empirical-rational strategy*
      2. *The normative-reeducative strategy*
      3. *The power-coercive strategy*
   B. *Interrelationships among strategies*

IV. *CONCLUDING COMMENTS AND PRECAUTIONS*

V. *SUMMARY*

VI. *SUGGESTED READINGS*

Chapter Twenty

Community Applications of Social Psychology

by Carl E. Young

There is nothing so terrible as action without thought. *Goethe*

Science, like life, feeds on its own decay. New facts burst old rules; then newly defined conceptions bind old and new together into a reconciling law. *William James*

One of the most important social science documents of the last decade is a report from the National Science Foundation entitled *Knowledge into Action: Improving the Nation's Use of the Social Sciences* (1969). Underlining our critical need for applying existing social science information, the authors state that our society requires the best possible advice that its social scientists can muster and that society needs this help now. While affirming that more research is needed, they contend that further delay in applying social science to existing social problems will be both unethical and disastrous. George A. Miller revealed a similar concern in his 1969 presidential address before the American Psychological Association: "I can imagine nothing we could do that would be more relevant to human welfare, and nothing that could pose a greater challenge to the next generation of psychologists, than to discover how best to give psychology away" (1970, p. 21). Miller's argument is that each of us makes assumptions about human nature. Man routinely practices psychology in coping with problems in his everyday life; but, avers Miller, man could practice it better if the scientifically valid principles of psychology were given away to him. In brief, the message is that anyone who possesses psychological knowledge should be encouraged to apply this knowledge to the social problems that he encounters in his everyday life.

Several conclusions should have emerged from the preceding chapters. One conclusion is that social psychology concerns itself with problems that are relevant to our society and to us as social beings. Aggression, leadership, moral development, obedience, conformity, anxiety, and interpersonal attraction continue to be important personal and national issues. A second conclusion is that the research methodologies of social psychology facilitate disciplined inquiry into very complex social events. Third, social psychological theories help one to understand how people respond to and are affected by their social environment. All three points remind us that social psychology has much to offer—both to a developing individual and to a developing society.

But just because a person possesses knowledge does not necessarily mean that he will apply this knowledge. Examples of this phenomenon are numerous and often ironic—such as the professor who spends the entire class session lecturing on the necessity of using group discussion in classroom teaching. In reality, a scientist may fail to apply what he knows to social problems (a) because he does not want to (the pure scientist, for example), (b) because he does not believe there is enough knowledge to be applied with confidence, (c) because the idea or need to do so has never really occurred to him, or (d) because he does not know how to apply what he knows. The dual goals of this chapter, therefore, are to encourage you to apply the social psychology that you now know and to expose you to some of the ways in which it has already been applied.

I. THE RELATIONSHIP BETWEEN APPLIED SCIENCE AND PURE SCIENCE

The idea of a social scientist applying his knowledge of social problems to possible solutions of those problems seems quite natural. The reader may be surprised, however, to learn that most social psychologists have not systematically tried to apply their knowledge. Moreover, there has been much debate and controversy about whether one should become involved in applied research, much less in social intervention. On the one hand, basic research scientists have been uninterested in the social value of their findings and have held the attitude that "the pursuit of scientific knowledge is a good activity in its own right, and even better since scientific knowledge is an absolute good apart from its consequences" (Baumrin, 1970, p. 74). This position has been commonly referred to as "knowledge for knowledge's sake." Applied scientists, on the other hand, have argued in favor of interested science, the goal of which is "articulable forseeable consequences . . . with respect to substantial human problems" (Baumrin, 1970, p. 81). The issues involved in this controversy between applied science and basic science are very important since they directly influence not only the ways in which social psychologists become involved in community problems but also the general development of social psychology.

A. The Dialogue between Kenneth Ring and William McGuire

Kenneth Ring and William McGuire are two psychologists who are attempting to influence the future development of social psychology in different ways. Their respective positions exemplify some of the agreements and disagreements that currently exist among psychologists on issues such as laboratory versus field investigations, the need for theory building, and the place of social action.

Ring's Radical Social Psychology. Kenneth Ring (1967, 1971) has been an advocate of the applied/social action position. Ring contends that basic and applied research have been spreading apart in the last two decades and that basic research has enjoyed much more popularity and prestige than applied research. Ring believes these trends are undesirable. He feels that basic researchers have largely avoided problems of broad social significance and have often tended to study behavioral phenomena in a manner very analogous to fashion fads: that is, basic researchers have proceeded from less flamboyant research topics to more flamboyant ones. There has been much pioneering but little settling; rather than following up a new area of research and testing its applications, the social psychologist has sought other new areas to develop. In like manner, Sherif (1970) has objected to the uneven development of social psychological knowledge; he sees researchers generally as rugged individualists who pursue their own exotic interests. The study of obedience is a good example of pioneering rather than settling. The fact that 65 percent of Milgram's subjects obeyed the experimenter to the end of the shock series was widely publicized. (See Chapter 13.) The study became an instant classic. Yet only a few more studies were conducted by Milgram and other researchers. These follow-up studies found that in the same laboratory task the degree of obedience is related to (a) the physical proximity of the experimenter, (b) the nearness and responsiveness of the shock recipient, and (c) the personality characteristics of the subject. But further knowledge has not been acquired about the pervasiveness of obedience in the real world. The "settling in" of research on this topic has not occurred. Our newspapers report that Lt. Calley followed orders at My Lai, but we, as social psychologists, make few efforts to observe and document the extent of overobedience in either the military or the civilian world.

Ring notes that much laboratory research in social psychology has been a fun-and-games approach; although such research is entertaining to read, it is most unhelpful either in educating us about the psychological nature of social problems or in giving us a means by which to attack these problems. The result of the faddish and fun-and-games nature of much of our research is that social psychologists have tended to learn more and more about less and less. Ring argues that psychological research is seldom value free; one has to choose sides. "One can, unthinkingly or through choice, ally oneself with the institutional forces which support professional psychology. Or, one may choose to side not with the powerful but with the weak" (Ring, 1971, p. 5). By siding with the weaker, less organized segments of society, the radical social psychologist takes on one or both of two tasks—a research task and a political task. The research task would be to study how selected institutions operate in reference to the weak and how they affect the weak. An analogy to Ring's proposed research task would be the work of Ralph Nader and his "raiders" in behalf of the American consumer. Ring's three research components—description, analysis, and criticism—would be utilized in "the formulation of proposals for institutional arrangements" (1971, p. 9). In other words, recommendations would be drawn up for changes in government, the schools, the military, and the like. The political task would be to assure that the research was used to affect the recommended institutional changes. This might involve publicity, lobbying, organizing special interest groups, and other forms of constructive social action. Ring refers to this combination of advocacy research and partisan social action as "the psychology of the left"; and he sees this as a plausible stance for psychologists, since—among the academic types—they are frequently political liberals or to the left of liberalism. (See Table 20-1 and Table 20-2.)

The Radical Social Psychologist in Action. The work of social psychologist Hannah Levin (1970) exemplifies Ring's "New Left" position. While working as a consultant to a community health center, Levin was impressed by the fact that the people who lived in the area of the health center had little or no say in its operation. The health authorities told the people that they could have an advisory board but that physicians would have to administer the actual health program. However, the people wanted the center to be administered by community residents. In the confrontation that followed, Levin became a professional advocate for the people. Levin and the people's group were informed that they could advise or even participate but that they could not control. The health authorities were unable to see the difference between participation and control. According to Levin, the people's retort was, "If you don't see any real difference between participation and control, then you can participate and the community will control" (1970, p. 123). Levin found that her arguments in behalf of the people motivated many of them to action. She gave the people a new confidence that eventually enabled them to establish influence over the policies of the health center. For example, one outcome of community control was a change in priorities from programs that emphasized suicidal and acutely disturbed patients to programs that emphasized youth. The people in the community declared that it was irresponsible to ignore the many health needs of school children for the sake of a "few suicides" and "psychotics." Levin's summary of her position in this health controversy is very explicit.

Today, a new tradition for professionals is being molded. We call ourselves radical professionals; that is, we use our skills to help make social change. Thus, as advocates for the powerless we assist these groups in gaining a redistribution of power rather than just a redistribution of services. We have given up our so-called professional neutrality for a partisan role. We believe that there is a conflict of interests between the groups we represent and other groups, and the recognition of this conflict is necessary in guiding our work. Our role has become that of

Table 20-1. *Political Labels of Faculty and Percentage Voting for President Nixon in 1968*

		Describes Self as:			
Field of Study	*N*	*Left or Liberal*	*Conservative*	*Other or No Opinion*	*% Voting for Nixon in 1968*
Social Sciences	6845	71%	11%	18%	19%
Humanities	9546	62%	17%	21%	23%
Fine arts	3732	52%	22%	26%	36%
Physical sciences	7599	44%	26%	30%	38%
Biological sciences	4403	44%	27%	29%	40%
Education	3277	41%	27%	32%	40%
Business	2080	33%	36%	31%	53%
Engineering	4165	29%	41%	30%	60%
Agriculture	1348	18%	50%	32%	61%

(Adapted from Lipset, S. M., & Ladd, E. C., Jr. . . . And what professors think. *Psychology Today*, 1970, **4**(6), 49–51ff.)

Table 20-2. *Who Signs Petitions Protesting U.S. Involvement in Vietnam?*

Political scientist E. C. Ladd selected for study a Vietnam protest petition published in the *New York Times* in early 1967. It bore the names of more than 6000 faculty members. Its message was short: "Mr. President: stop the bombing." For each department or discipline, a Profession Representation Index (PRI) was computed by dividing the percentage of the total full-time faculty in that discipline into the percentage of all faculty signers of the petition from that discipline. For example, 7.7 percent of the college faculty in the United States are in engineering, and 4.6 percent of the signers of this petition were professors of engineering. Dividing 4.6 by 7.7 gives a PRI of .60. A PRI above 1.00 means that the discipline or department is represented among signers to a higher degree than among the universe of faculty members.

The PRI for different broad disciplines was as follows:

Field	*PRI*
Social sciences	2.51
Humanities	1.32
Physical sciences	1.22
Life sciences	1.14
Fine arts	0.60
Engineering	0.60
Education	0.18
Business	0.10
Agriculture	0.06

The PRI for selected academic fields was as follows:

Subject matter field	*PRI*
Sociology and anthropology	3.04
Philosophy	2.87
Political science	2.84
Psychology	2.81
Physics	2.53
Economics	2.11
History	1.66
Mathematics	1.27
English	1.10
Languages	0.89
Biology	0.85
Chemistry	0.54

(From Ladd, E. C., Jr. Professors and political petitions. *Science*, 1969, **163**, 1425–1430, Tables 7 and 8.)

aiding the poor in challenging society's standards rather than meeting them, and our relationship to the poor community and its organizations has been as employees rather than employers (1970, p. 122).

Although many psychologists would disagree, Levin states that what she does is psychology and believes that "the mission of the scientist should be understanding the natural world so that he can improve the quality of life. If some of the skills we have learned which give us the title 'psychologist' are irrelevant to this mission, then we should forget about our professional title and learn what is necessary to fulfill our commitment as scientists. And let one measure of our understanding be visible improvement in the distribution of power and resources in the areas in which we work" (Levin, 1970, p. 127).

McGuire's Mainstream Position. William McGuire (1967a, 1967b) has written two responses to Ring that are typical of social psychology's mainstream position toward basic research. McGuire disagrees that basic and applied research will continue as quite separate entities in the future. He foresees a merger of sorts—"a 'best of both worlds' solution in which we shall be doing theory-oriented research in natural settings" (1967a, p. 125). As editor of the *Journal of Personality and Social Psychology* from 1968 to 1970, McGuire has encouraged such a merger. He assumes, and rightly so, that a theory that has been tested in a community setting is much more likely to prove relevant in solving problems in the real-world than a theory tested in a laboratory. McGuire notes that the important scientific term *experimental* has become equated with manipulative research in a laboratory setting and observes that this connotation of the term is overly restrictive. Instead, *experimental* should suggest its dictionary meaning of to test or to try. This broader definition allows for many alternatives to laboratory research, such as observational research and the use of national survey samples.

McGuire primarily disagrees with Ring on two points. First, McGuire believes that a researcher's basic responsibility is theory building; he would agree with Lewin's dictum: "Nothing is so practical as a good theory." For McGuire, a theory should be tested in the laboratory and the real world, but he does not believe that the scientist himself should be obligated to apply his findings to real-world problems. Ring, however, advocates that research findings should be used in a partisan manner. McGuire also disagrees with Ring's assertion that much laboratory research has taken a fun-and-games approach. McGuire's position is analogous to the biblical dictum: "Judge not that ye be not judged." In addition, he feels that there is "room for all of us under the social psychology umbrella."

In summary, McGuire believes that in the long run basic, theory-oriented research will lead to more useful contributions to the field of social psychology than will action-oriented research (1967b, p. 20), but he agrees with Ring about the need for more research in natural settings. Ring, however, feels that man faces immediate problems that may well get completely out of hand if society has to wait for natural returns on social psychology's theory investments. Ring believes that social psychologists must back up their left-wing attitudes with professional involvements. (See Table 20-1.) In brief, Ring proposes that psychologists are responsible for applying their knowledge to the promotion of human welfare. If psychologists do not act, such steps will probably not be taken at all.

B. Bringing Divergent Viewpoints Together

An important point upon which both Ring and McGuire agree is that social psychologists need to study more diverse populations in more depth than has been done in the past (Lehmann, 1971). The quip that psychology is the science of white rats and college sophomores has had its element of truth (Rosnow, 1970). At least one reason for this is that the very nature of laboratory research has required large numbers of easily available subjects. Other populations of subjects have been studied but not very often nor on many different variables. The problem with using restricted types of samples, of course, is one of generalization. For example, do college sophomores really behave enough like legislators or farmers or migrant workers to allow the research findings on the college population to be applied to these other populations? At this time, limited evidence discourages such generalizations. Indeed, the conclusions drawn from volunteer samples of college sophomores are not even applicable to all college sophomores.

II. KURT LEWIN AND ACTION RESEARCH

Kurt Lewin was one of the first psychologists to address the issues raised by both Ring and McGuire. In the 1930s and 1940s, Lewin was very much concerned about our need to build theories on the basis of field research whenever possible. He fathered the term **field theory,** the central tenet of which is that man must always be viewed in relationship to his environment. Although investigations using laboratory simulations of man's environment are informative, the study of man in his natural environment can be even more informative. Moreover, theories that have been tested in the laboratory need to be validated in the community and in other naturalistic settings.

A. The Importance of Testing Theories in Field Settings

The important relationship between laboratory research and community (field or naturalistic) research is exemplified in the work of Roger Barker, the social psychologist who founded ecological psychology. While studying under Lewin, Barker participated in an investigation of the interrelationships between frustration and aggression in young children (Barker, Dembo, & Lewin, 1941). Ironically, Lewin, the field theorist, and Barker, the subsequent ecological psychologist, carried out this early work in a laboratory setting! In the study, children were allowed to play with some toys in an experimental playroom. After playing with these toys for 30 minutes, they were exposed to new and more desirable toys and then were allowed to play with any toys (new or old) they wished. The children were then given their original toys but were separated from the newer and more desirable toys by a wire mesh. Under these frustrating conditions, the children exhibited a number of regressive behaviors, and their play became less and less constructive. This laboratory study was replicated successfully by others and became a fundamental part of the social psychological literature. More than 20 years later, Fawl (1963), a student of Barker's, decided to replicate the study using specimen records of children's everyday behaviors. Fawl reported: "The results . . . were surprising in two respects. First, even with a liberal interpretation of frustration fewer incidents were detected than we expected. . . . Second, . . . meaningful relationships could not be found between frustration . . . and consequent behavior such as . . . regression . . . and other theoretically meaningful behavioral manifestations" (1963, p. 99). In brief, frustration was rare in the ordinary behaviors of the children; and, when it did occur, the phenomenon did not conform to the prediction of the original study. The natural setting made a difference.

Other examples could be cited in which laboratory findings were not replicated in naturalistic settings. For instance, in Chapter 6, we described early studies on the subsequent effects when children watched a film of another person or cartoon figure acting violently. These laboratory studies tended to support the contention that observing violence breeds violence. However, later studies on the effects of television viewing in natural settings indicated that viewing aggressive behaviors may actually reduce the degree of aggression expressed by children. As indicated in Chapter 6, Feshbach and Singer have described in *Television and Aggression* (1970) a field study that revealed that boys exposed to milder programs such as *The Ed Sullivan Show* engaged in more than twice as many fistfights as boys who watched more violent shows such as *The Untouchables*. Although these studies are not meant to challenge laboratory investigations, they do challenge all of us to invest more research energy in questioning and testing our hypotheses and theories in natural field settings (Lehmann, 1971).

B. The Nature of Action Research

Although Lewin was interested in the development of theories, he was also interested in doing something with his theories. "Research that produces nothing but books will not suffice" (Lewin, 1948, p. 203). He agreed with Ring's position that social psychologists should bring their research, interpersonal, and group skills to bear on social problems. Lewin tried to resolve such social conflicts as marital frictions, management-worker disputes, and the psychosociological problems of minority groups. Describing his work in these areas as **action research,** Lewin noted that community organizations and agencies that are concerned with eliminating and preventing social problems are often unsuccessful, no matter how hard they seem to try. His goal was to transform this goodwill into organized, efficient action by helping community groups answer three questions. What is the present situation? What are the dangers? And, most important of all, what shall be done? To Lewin, action research consists of "analysis, fact-finding or evaluation; and then a repetition of this whole circle of activities; indeed, a spiral of such circles" (N. Sanford, 1970, p. 4). In short, the action researcher obtains data about an organization, feeds this data into the organization, measures the change that occurs, and then repeats the process.

C. Action Research and Planned Change

In discussing his intervention process, Lewin was careful to point out that feeding data back into the organization was seldom sufficient action for bringing about the desired change. The other necessary ingredient was knowledge and training in group dynamics. (This point will be discussed subsequently.) Because of his belief in the importance of group dynamics, Lewin helped found the Research Center for Group Dynamics (now the Institute for Social Research at the University of Michigan) for the purpose of integrating research, training, and action. He was also instrumental in founding the National Training Laboratory in Group Development (now called the NTL Center for Applied Behavioral Science). This institution was established "as a training center for teams which would take leadership in action-training-research projects in the fields of education, industry, government, social work, labor, religious work, volunteer organizations, and community life" (Lippitt, 1949,

p. 262). In summary, Lewin has greatly influenced the community applications of social psychology, and this influence is especially evident in the psychology of planned change.

III. SOCIAL PSYCHOLOGISTS AS CHANGE AGENTS

The purpose of applying social psychology to real-life problems is to promote social change in a predictable manner. People like Jonas Salk, Carry Nation, Martin Luther King, Lee Harvey Oswald, Robert Oppenheimer, Horace Mann, Henry Ford, and Ralph Nader have all used different tactics to change society. However, the predictability of the consequences of each individual strategy differed remarkably. Predictability is very important since the very act of instituting change may cause unanticipated side effects that outweigh the originally anticipated advantages. The use of DDT is a classic example. Although DDT was originally seen as the restorer of ecological imbalances, its massive usage has precipitated an ecological disaster endangering wildlife, fish, and man himself. In a similar manner, consultants who have tried to promote better internal relations among industrial subgroups have sometimes been dismayed to find that these subgroups became so involved with internal relationships that they quit relating to other groups within the same system or that their work productivity decreased sharply. Because of the complex nature of planned change, groups of social scientists (many of whom were trained as social psychologists under Kurt Lewin) have devoted much study to the planning and application of change methods and have become known as *change agents* (Lippitt, Watson, & Westley, 1958; Bennis, Benne, & Chin, 1968).

A. Strategies for Bringing about Change in Institutions

Change agents have defined the planning of change as the "*application of systematic and appropriate knowledge in affairs for the purpose of creating intelligent action and change*" (Bennis et al., 1968, p. 4). The general goal of the change agents has been to develop strategies for bringing about change. These strategies have been divided into three major types: (a) empirical-rational strategy, (b) normative-reeducative strategy, and (c) power-coercive strategy. Since each operates from a different set of assumptions about the nature of man, these strategies will be discussed separately, and a case history illustrating each one will be cited.

The Empirical-Rational Strategy. This strategy assumes that man is rational and that he will act on the basis of the best information possible. Therefore, in order to improve one's ability to make decisions, one need only be presented with the facts. This approach is somewhat similar to the view of rational-economic man held by some factory managers. (See Chapter 17.) The **empirical-rational strategy** clearly is congenial with American values, such as will power and educability. Because of our belief in this strategy, we maintain public schools, write letters to congressmen, read newspapers regularly, and give money to cancer research. Of course, this strategy has its limitations. We also smoke, drive at excessive speeds, refuse to exercise, and often pick a new car by kicking its tires and slamming its doors instead of consulting *Consumer Reports*. In short, we often act irrationally, and hard facts have limited power to change behavior.

The professional role demanded by the empirical-rational strategy has been described as that of an *analyst* (Vollmer, 1970)—that is, one who tries objectively to diagnose a problem and to bring appropriate data to bear on its solution. There has probably been more demand for the analyst role than any other; moreover, this role has been popular among social psychologists. Social psychological research, for example, has been consistently funded within the framework of the empirical-rational theory. Since state and local governments seldom have large research staffs within any one program area, they are very much dependent upon data gathered by outside researchers. One could easily argue that all governmental research is based on the empirical-rational strategy. That is, government agencies fund research that will produce facts, which can then be disseminated for the purpose of affecting change. The following case history illustrates the analyst's role of producing facts.

The summer of 1967 was the most intensive period of internal conflict in the United States since the Civil War. Civil disorders occurred in Newark, Detroit, Cleveland, and a host of other cities. On July 28, 1967, President Johnson appointed a prestigious commission under the leadership of Otto Kerner, then Governor of Illinois, and directed this commission to answer three basic questions: What happened? Why did it happen? What can be done to keep it from happening again? Since many of the participants in the civil disorders were students, the Commission became interested in whether similarities existed between disorders in the cities and disorders on college campuses. In light of the more than 130 disruptions on college campuses in 1967, it was decided that the first three of these disorders, which had occurred in the spring of 1967, should be investigated. The social scientists who participated in the research on these three campuses fulfilled the analyst role. They provided nonpartisan, descriptive, analytic reports, which demonstrated (a) that the disorders were spontaneous and followed the presence of police on the campuses, (b) that the most active participants were usually nonstudents, (c) that there was no underlying conspiracy (communist or otherwise), and (d) that the students and administrators were able to achieve and maintain a high degree of internal control. Thus, the social scientists provided the information needed by government leaders to combat rumors, to reduce tensions, and to promote a better understanding of the so-called "violent revolution" that some believed to be taking place on college campuses (Newbrough, 1968).

The empirical-rational strategy is limited in that no guarantee exists as to what kind of people will read the information or put it to use. *The Report of the National Advisory Commission on Civil Disorders* that resulted from President Johnson's directive was one of the most important research documents of this century. Unfortunately, one can document few, if any, positive changes that have occurred as a result of the Commission's report. Even though it was received with acclaim, its diagnosis and recommendations fell upon a public that was unprepared to process its data or take action. An even more extreme example of the limitations of the empirical-rational strategy is the story surrounding the Federal Commission on Obscenity and Pornography, appointed by President Lyndon Johnson in 1968. It is difficult to imagine a more extreme and massive reaction to data than that which followed this Pornography Commission's report in the fall of 1970. The President of the United States, Richard Nixon, renounced many of the conclusions of the report as soon as it was published, and several legislators denounced the report on nation-wide television, although these legislators admitted that neither they nor their staffs had read it! Obviously, the empirical-rational strategy is insufficient—in and of itself—to promote extensive change.

The Normative-Reeducative Strategy. This strategy for social change is based upon different assumptions about the nature of man. The **normative-reeducative strategy** assumes that man is intelligent and rational, but it also assumes that man is bound up in his own particular culture. As a result, he has definite behavioral responses and patterns that are based on attitudes, values, traditions, and relationships with others. Before trying to change a person, group, or community, these cultural or normative factors must be taken into account.

A humorous example is provided by the Shoshoni Indians of Nevada. "When horses were introduced into the Shoshoni culture, the Indians knew what to do with them. The Shoshonis had previous experience with horses; they had stolen horses for food. So, when Indian agents gave them horses for transportation, they readily accepted them. But they ate them" (E. M. Rogers, 1962).

As mentioned earlier, Kurt Lewin was one of the first to address systematically the issue of using the normative-reeducative strategy in resolving social conflicts (Lewin, 1948). Lewin emphasized reeducating groups through professional participation in the groups; his process of group decision was described in Chapter 17. The Peace Corps and VISTA have adopted this strategy in their programs. Volunteers are sent to participate in the life of a culture and to find ways to improve life styles within the range of the existing norms (Biddle & Biddle, 1965). The following case history illustrates the normative-reeducative strategy, which currently may be seen in many police-training programs.

Figure 20-1. *The Normative-Reeducative Strategy in Action. Agents of social change, such as Peace Corps Volunteers, need to know the local culture and assimilate themselves into it. Collaboration and mutual understanding are necessary for change to take place. (Photograph courtesy of the Peace Corps.)*

Prior to the 1960s, relatively little attention had been given to law enforcement as a nation-wide issue. But civil rights demonstrations, campus disorders, and the riot during the 1968 Democratic Party convention in Chicago all directed attention to the actions of police. Police brutality became a public issue. Both demonstrators and police were mishandled and killed.

Social scientists, working as analysts, probed the complexities of law enforcement and facilitated new understanding of police work. Time-and-motion studies revealed that less than 20 percent of police man-hours was spent in law-enforcing activities. As society became more depersonalized and bureaucratic, police began spending more and more of their time in a wide range of social service activities. Bard (1970) has referred to the New York police as a "human resource agency without parallel" and has pointed out that "maintaining order and providing interpersonal service—not law enforcement and crime suppression—are what modern police work is all about" (p. 129). Social scientists rediscovered what the police already knew—that crime in the streets is much less common than crime off the streets. Also, violent crimes more often occur among people who know each other or who are related to one another than among people who are strangers. One of the highest personal risk situations for police is handling family disputes. In brief, the police were being trained in traditional law enforcement or property watching, while being called upon to serve a wide range of social service activities.

Given the complexities of the law enforcement system, simply publishing the findings on police activities would have had little effect, by itself, in bringing about change within the system. For law enforcement, like any other institution or subculture, has its own customs and mores and has established defenses against changes in its traditions. Therefore, social scientists adopted the normative-reeducative strategy for working with police. They began riding in patrol cars, observing training programs, and generally acquainting themselves with the norms of law enforcement. The actual entree into the system was slow. Psychologists first performed specific services for the police such as improving selection procedures for new recruits. Next came lectures on the emotionally disturbed, on ways to deal with aggression, and on the general area of interpersonal relations. Gradually, the social scientists became more involved in all aspects of police training—and more acceptable in the eyes of the police.

The normative-reeducative process moves slowly, since it is founded upon change through mutual collaboration and understanding in diagnosing and organizing intervention. But there have been payoffs. Bard (1970) has trained a special squad of patrolmen in the use of mediation and referral in handling domestic disturbances. This project has been very successful in preventing homicides, reducing the number of assaults, reducing the number of arrests, and in preventing injury to patrolmen. A central characteristic of this approach has been the predictability of change, which has been in the desired direction and has been approved both by the change agents and the police.

The Power-Coercive Strategy. This strategy differs from the first two in its use of power. The **power-coercive strategy** is based on political, economic, and social uses of power that have been both popular and effective in bringing about change. Federal legislation on civil rights has moved integration forward; labor strikes have affected economic policies; and boycotts have changed discriminatory hiring practices. Similarly, Martin Luther King, Cesar Chavez, Saul Alinsky, and the

Berrigans have become famous for their power-coercive strategies. In discussing power-coercive methods, change agents have been primarily concerned with nonviolent strategies of change and have been opposed to violent means (destruction of property, the use of firearms in quelling rioters, and the like). There are at least two general reasons behind the change agents' opposition to violent strategies. One reason is a general belief about human nature, which affirms that violence is a denial of human worth. This does not mean that change agents value property more than human lives (an accusation sometimes made against middle America). It does mean, however, that change agents feel that such comparisons are unfortunate, for they usually force the issue to an unnecessary power play. Change agents believe that change is always possible through nonviolent strategies and that there is simply no rationale that justifies using other methods.

A second reason why change agents prefer nonviolent strategies is that they are very much concerned with planned change; violent strategies introduce much more unpredictability into a social system than do nonviolent approaches. Predictability, as used in this context, refers to (a) whether one accomplishes one's desired goals, (b) how long one's accomplishments last, and (c) whether any unanticipated, negative side effects resulted. When evaluated against these three criteria, nonviolent strategies are found to be much more effective across time in establishing planned change throughout a broad social system. For these reasons and many others, social psychologists have been concerned with the reduction of violence, not with its promotion.

Aside from unpredictability, another major weakness of a violent power-coercive strategy is that it does not build a flexible, renewing process of change into the target system. Instead, it causes rigidity. Once that force has been used, the target system attempts to strengthen its defenses, to contain the force, and ultimately to destroy the force. Further change requires additional force, and the phenomenon recycles and escalates. In the law enforcement programs mentioned earlier, an important teaching model involves the escalating nature of force. If a policeman enters a setting with a drawn gun, the actors in the setting will gear their emotions and actions in accordance with the standard of force represented by the gun. (The Berkowitz studies of aggressive cues in Chapter 6 show this operates in a well-controlled situation.) Any spontaneous precipitating event will be handled at that level. Needless to say, it is a high-risk situation. Conversely, if a policeman enters a setting in a calm, confident manner and with no external signs of force, a different standard is established. One often hears the axiom in police training that holstered guns can be drawn, but drawn guns can never be holstered. It is a good generalizable rule in the implementing of all power-coercive strategies.

Nonviolent power-coercive methods have brought about much planned social change in the last decade. Civil rights demonstrations clearly speeded racial integration. The antiwar movements in the early 1970s played an important role in the increased withdrawal of American troops from Vietnam. Student demonstrations on college campuses helped produce changes in such diverse areas as dorm hours, student participation in college administration, dress codes, and course offerings. Moreover, demonstrations on one campus often elicited positive changes on a second campus. Of course, the converse of this situation also happened, in that demonstrations on one campus produced negative changes on a second campus. The impact of the Kent State incident at some state schools was an increase in the campus security force, a restriction on even peaceful forms of protest, and a decrease in state funds for higher education.

The last decade also saw an increased use of legal sanctions. Ralph Nader and his raiders elicited many changes in federal laws concerning automobiles, drugs, and many other matters. Court injunctions were commonly used by citizen groups in their fights against city hall, and court decisions caused changes in everything from the busing of children to the drafting of college athletes by professional teams. In brief, the legal system has continued to be a major instigator of social change. One of the more interesting aspects of the power-coercive strategy is that it can take many forms. The following case history summarizes an unusually innovative approach toward problem resolution by one of the masters of the power-coercive strategy.

Saul Alinsky has been one of the foremost organizers of community action groups and has trained such minority-group leaders as Cesar Chavez, who organized California's agricultural workers and then precipitated a national consumer boycott against California grapes. Alinsky has been a proponent of the power-coercive strategy and has used this strategy in quite different ways. One of the more novel uses of this approach was his Rochester, New York, battle with Eastman Kodak. Following a Rochester race riot that was partially due to a conflict over Kodak's inadequate training and job programs for blacks, the local churches invited Alinsky to work in their black ghetto. He accepted and soon founded a community-action group called FIGHT (Freedom, Integration, God, Honor, Today). Instead of depending upon community-action tactics such as picketing and demonstrating, FIGHT began soliciting stock proxies from churches, individuals, and organizations as a direct power challenge to Kodak's policies. Enough proxies were turned over to FIGHT to enable the group to force Kodak to improve its policies concerning minority groups (see Alinsky, 1971).

Nevertheless, power-coercive strategies are seldom sufficient change methods in and of themselves. Even though the passage of fair housing codes represented considerable political-legal leverage toward attaining neighborhood integration, these codes by no means assured real integration. The power-coercive approach must be coupled with the normative-reeducative approach in order to maximize change. Legal sanctions establish the letter of the law, but normative-reeducative strategies foster the spirit of the law. It is one thing to declare that change must take place; but it is quite another to build the social machinery, attitudes, and relationships that will actually produce this change with a minimum of disruption.

B. Interrelationships among Strategies

In the preceding review, each strategy of change has been described as if it were somehow pure or separate from the others; this, of course, is seldom true. In most social change endeavors, there will be occasion to use all three of these strategies in various ways and at various times. Indeed, it is most difficult to use one strategy singly. For example, the name of a well-known and respected researcher, when attached to an article in a prestigious journal, represents considerable political influence and power within the psychological profession with respect to the topic in question—even though the article may have been written exclusively as an empirical-rational statement. The empirical-rational testimony of a social psychologist before a Congressional investigating subcommittee represents considerable political leverage, for knowledge *is* power. The very fact that a social scientist agrees to undertake a normative-reeducative approach toward solving some problem is a direct admission of the power of this individual in respect to that particular problem. Moreover, the normative-reeducative strategy is quite dependent upon the empirical-rational method; otherwise one would have nothing about which to educate another person.

One reason for emphasizing these interrelationships is that they are almost always more obvious in the abstract than they are during the process of implementation. And one sure way to abort a change agent's strategy is to fail to consider the fact that the change agent is perceived by others as using some other strategy. That is, others may perceive a normative-reeducative process as a threat to their own power base (power-coercive); the change agent must take these perceptions into account if he is to be successful.

IV. CONCLUDING COMMENTS AND PRECAUTIONS

The entire question of how much and what type of community involvement is appropriate for social psychologists is unresolved at this time. Certainly, there is much knowledge in social psychology that merits dissemination and utilization. However, one should also recognize that a little knowledge is a dangerous thing. Any psychologist who has revealed his profession at a neighborhood committee meeting or at a party is aware that societal expectations far exceed what he can actually do. Similarly, it is possible to create the illusion that social psychology or psychology or the social sciences in general have more solutions than they actually do. Therefore, one should seriously consider that social psychology does not so much have a ready solution to any given problem as it has a scientific stance or approach that could shed some degree of light on that problem.

One difficulty is that social psychologists have largely been reluctant to research major social issues, much less to apply their knowledge to the solution of these issues. This position is both understandable and unacceptable. The very magnitude and complexity of problems such as poverty and international aggression overwhelmingly depress each of us. And it is true that our research methodologies are really appropriate only for small groups—not for communities. However, there was a time when small-group research was as unthinkable as community research is today. The pre-Lewinian literature is almost exclusively oriented toward individual research. Kurt Lewin, who is given credit for founding group dynamics and legitimizing group research, did little group research himself, but his students have revolutionized the field. Social psychology now needs a revolution that will lead us from small groups to the larger community. Community research must be legitimized. In brief, new methodologies for researching the psychological aspects of communities must be developed and developed soon, so that we can better meet the problems of society.

The purpose of this chapter has been to stimulate thinking about the ways in which one can now apply what one knows about social psychology. We have chosen to do this by describing some of the methods that social psychologists have used in the past. The goal has not been to tell the reader all one needs to know about community action and research but, rather, to review some of the pressing needs and problems in this area. More than 25 years ago, Lewin summarized the situation that still confronts us today: "This job demands from the social scientists an utmost amount of courage. It needs courage as Plato defines it: 'Wisdom concerning dangers.' It needs the best of what the best among us can give, and the help of everybody" (1948, p. 216).

V. SUMMARY

It is essential that social psychological knowledge be applied to the social problems we encounter in everyday life. An important aspect of social psychology is its concern with problems that are relevant to our society and to each of us as social beings. The methodology of social psychology permits the study and understanding of complex social phenomena. But despite these facts, many basic researchers have not been interested in the applicability of their research findings.

The radical social psychologist proposes a new role for his discipline—one that combines research and political activities. The political task is to see that research is used to bring about recommended institutional changes.

A mainstream position in social psychology sees a merger of sorts, in which theory-oriented research will be done in natural settings. This viewpoint believes that in the long run more useful contributions to social psychology will come from theory-based research than from action research.

Field theory, developed by Kurt Lewin, proposes that man must always be viewed in relationship to his environment. The study of man in his natural environment is particularly informative.

Studies done in laboratory settings occasionally lead to findings that are in direct opposition to similar studies done in natural settings. Both settings must be used as we search for useful knowledge. The field of *action research* brings theory, knowledge, and skills together to understand and solve social problems. Its goal is planned social change.

Three strategies for planned change have been identified and contrasted. These are the empirical-rational strategy, the normative-reeducative strategy, and the power-coercive strategy.

The *empirical-rational strategy* assumes that man will act on the basis of the best information available to him. The goal of this strategy then is to provide facts that can be disseminated in order to bring about change.

The *normative-reeducative strategy* assumes that man's behavior is based on his attitudes, values, and relationships with others. Man is a product of his culture, and these determinants must be recognized in any strategy of change.

The *power-coercive strategy* utilizes pressures—political, social, or economic—to bring about desired social change. Either violent or nonviolent kinds of a power-coercive strategy may be used.

A movement can be traced chronologically from a concern with individuals, to research on groups, to a future emphasis on research on communities. All these approaches are necessary for a solution of our problems.

VI. SUGGESTED READINGS

Gouldner, A. W. *The coming crisis of Western sociology.* New York: Basic Books, 1970. Though written by a sociologist for other sociologists, there is much here for social psychologists seeking a new, contemporary, and more relevant place for their theory and research. Likely to be a most influential book in the next decade.

Korten, F. F., Cook, S. W., & Lacey, J. I. (Eds.) *Psychology and the problems of society.* Washington, D.C.: American Psychological Association, 1970. (Paperback) Symposium papers from the 1969 APA convention, the theme of which coincided with the title of this collection. Included are papers on the social change process, urban problems, minority groups, the reduction of violence, and campus protests. The APA response to attack from the Left.

Lewin, K. *Resolving social conflicts.* New York: Harper, 1948. A series of papers in which Lewin draws upon field theory to bring about social or personal change in practical situations.

Marrow, A. J. *The practical theorist: The life and work of Kurt Lewin.* New York: Basic Books, 1969. An interesting biography of the founder of group dynamics and action research. Lewin's life and work are clearly described. Recommended.

Miller, H. L., & Woock, R. R. *Social foundations of urban education.* Hinsdale, Ill.: Dryden, 1970. A text that applies research findings from social psychology, sociology, and education to urban education. Brings together a great deal of useful information on such topics as social class, the family, prejudice, segregation, and classroom dynamics. Recommended.

Glossary

access to illegitimate social learning opportunities. There are two major aspects of these opportunities: (a) learning from role models of deviant behaviors and (b) being able to practice the newly acquired skills in situations where the risks of detection and punishment are lessened. Both constitute an absence of social controls against deviance.

accuracy of perception. Correspondence between a person's perceptual responses or judgments and a criterion that represents objective reality. Sometimes called *empathy*.

achievement motive (nAch). An energizing condition that leads an individual or group to seek high standards of performance and success.

acquiescent response set. A tendency to agree with an attitude statement regardless of the nature of its content.

action research. Research whose goal is the understanding or solution of social problems.

adaptation level theory. A theory of context effects, which suggests that the individual's background acts to set a standard against which events or objects are perceived.

affiliation. A basic social need; the desire to be with other people.

aggression. As a behavioristic psychologist defines it, aggression is behavior whose goal is to inflict injury upon some object or person.

alienation. A generalized sense of meaninglessness, helplessness, and social isolation. Constitutes a reduction of personal controls against engaging in deviance.

altruism. A motive or behavior that seeks to help others or to act in an unselfish way.

anal stage. Freudian developmental stage characteristic of the two- to three-year-old child and centered upon toilet training and elimination of waste.

anomie. The social state in which norms are persistently and successfully disregarded in human behavior. Implies a lessened social control against deviance.

anticonformity. Behavior that is directly antithetical to the normative group expectations.

anti-intraception. Opposition to the subjective, the imaginative, the tenderminded. A characteristic of the authoritarian personality syndrome.

anti-Semitism. A generalized negative attitude toward Jews.

anxiety. A generalized, diffuse apprehension about the future.

area sample. A form of probability sample in which geographic area serves as a basis of selection of a stratified random sample. For instance, a few counties, and within each county a few precincts, and within each precinct a few dwellings may be randomly chosen for a sample.

arousal. A state of heightened emotion.

artifact. A research finding that does not reflect the true state of affairs in an area but, instead, reflects the results of an arbitrary methodological approach.

Asch situation. An experimental situation in which a subject is led to believe that his perceptions are different from those of all the other subjects. Used to test the extent of conformity to group opinion.

assumed similarity. Correspondence between one's judgments or ratings of another person and one's own characteristics. A response set in person perception tasks. Sometimes called *projection* because it represents an attribution of one's characteristics to another person.

assumptions about human nature. Beliefs that people in general possess certain common characteristics.

attitude. A positive or negative affective reaction toward a denotable abstract or concrete object or proposition, as defined by Bruvold. An attitude is said to have an object, be evaluative, and be relatively enduring.

attitude scale. A set of statements or questions designed to measure an attitude, usually on one pro-con dimension.

attribution theory. A theory, stemming from Gestalt theory and the thinking of Fritz Heider, concerning the way in which people attribute characteristics or intentions to other persons or to objects.

auditory discrimination. The ability to distinguish speech sounds, typically tested by asking the subject to determine whether two stimulus words or nonsense syllables sound the same or different.

authoritarian aggression. Tendency to be on the lookout for and to condemn, reject, and punish people who violate conventional values. A characteristic of the authoritarian personality syndrome.

authoritarian leadership. A type of leadership in which the leader is very directive, makes all decisions, does not participate in the activities of the group members, and is punitive in his actions toward members.

authoritarian submission. Submissive, uncritical attitude toward the idealized, moral authorities of the in-group. A characteristic of the authoritarian personality syndrome.

authoritarianism. A basic personality style that includes a set of organized beliefs, values, and preferences, including submission to authority, identification with authority, denial of feelings, cynicism, and others.

autokinetic effect. The tendency for a stationary light, when viewed in an otherwise completely darkened room, to appear to be moving.

balance theory. An attitude theory, which hypothesizes that people prefer to hold consistent compatible beliefs and avoid inconsistent incompatible beliefs.

balanced scale. A scale having half of its items keyed in each direction. For example, for half of the items an answer of "Agree" or "True" is scored positively, and for the other half of the items an answer of "Disagree" or "False" is scored positively.

biased sample. A sample that is unrepresentative because of one or more sources of systematic error.

cathexis. An attachment to objects that are gratifying or a rejection of those that are unpleasant.

central trait. A personal characteristic that strongly influences other perceivers' impressions of the person possessing it. Asch showed that the warm-cold personality dimension was such a central trait.

charisma. A particular appeal or personal magnetism attributed to certain persons.

chicken matrix. A two-person matrix with extremely undesirable payoffs for double defection.

clinical prediction. Subjective judgment about people, in which data of any sort are combined subjectively by the judge, rather than objectively by means of a formula or mechanical decision system.

code. A set of related linguistic options chosen from the range of possibilities in language.

coefficient of correlation. A measure of the degree of relationship between two variables or scores obtained from the same set of individuals. May range from +1.00 through 0.00 to −1.00.

cofigurative culture. A culture in which both children and adults learn from their peers.

cognition. A mental event in which perceptions, memories, beliefs, and thoughts are processed.

cognitive complexity. The use of many dimensions in interpreting other people's behavior.

cognitive deficit theory. The view that lower-class children, as a result of factors in the home, have a limited control of language, especially in its cognitive uses. Such a deficit is often thought to be cumulative, growing more severe with age.

cognitive dissonance. A state in which the person holds two beliefs, or cognitions, which are inconsistent with each other.

cognitive dissonance theory. A theory of attitude change, which holds that the possession of two incompatible beliefs is so unpleasant that the person is motivated to resolve the inconsistency.

cohesiveness. The attractiveness that a group has for its members and that the members have for one another; the forces that hold a group together.
communicative competence. Knowledge not simply of the sounds, meanings, and structures of language, but also of the underlying rules for using speech appropriately in social interactions.
competition. The act of striving to excel in order to obtain an exclusive goal.
competitive goal. An exclusive goal; one that demands success for some and failure for others.
competitive reward structure. A reward structure set up in such a way that less than the number of people striving for the reward can actually achieve it.
complex attitude. An attitude containing many elements, several of which are in contradiction with one another. (See **simplex attitude.**)
complex man. A model that views man as multifaceted, motivated by a wide range of needs, and possessing a wide range of capacities.
conceptual system. The outcome of an individual's efforts to organize his beliefs, knowledge, and values.
conformity. As defined by Kiesler and Kiesler, a change in behavior or belief toward a group consensus as a result of real or imagined group pressure. As defined in this text, a yielding to group pressures.
congenital. Existing at birth and acquired during conception or fetal development. Distinguished from hereditary or a condition transmitted by genes.
consideration. A dimension of leadership, which refers to the leader's concern with relationships between himself and other group members; the leader's maintenance of group morale and cohesiveness.
consonance. The degree to which the elements within an attitude are consistent or harmonious with one another.
construct. A concept used by a theory to explain behavior.
content analysis. A method for the objective, systematic, and usually quantitative description of various characteristics of verbal communication.
contingency theory of leadership. Fiedler's theory of leadership in which leader effectiveness is related to aspects of the situation in which the group operates. Or, a theory emphasizing that no one type of leader is always successful but, rather, that aspects of the leader's power, the task structure, and the leader's personal relations with members of his group interact to determine what kind of leader will be most successful.
contrient interdependence. Mutually exclusive interdependence. (See **competitive reward structure.**)
control. Intentional modification of conditions under which scientific observations are made. Includes holding variables constant, eliminating variables, and equating or specifying the degree of other variables.
conventionalism. Rigid adherence to conventional middle-class values. A characteristic of the authoritarian personality syndrome.
conventionality. Acting in what is a customary or usual fashion; adhering to the standard practices of a society.
cooperation. The act of working together for mutual benefit.
cooperative goal. A mutual or shared goal.
cooperative reward structure. A reward structure set up in such a way that all those who strive must achieve the reward in order for it to be available for individual participants.
counterculture. A culture that is radically disaffiliated from the mainstream assumptions of the society of which it is a part.
criterial referent. An issue, topic, or policy that is important to a person or group of people.
culture fairness. The extent to which tests and measures are free from biases that invalidly deflate the scores of subjects from certain cultures, ethnic groups, or social classes.
cybernation. The use of mechanical and electrical systems designed to replace human control functions.
death instinct. A concept developed by Freud, which holds that all human beings have a compulsion to return to an inorganic state.
deduction. The process of logical reasoning from premises to conclusions. Used in deriving predictions from a theory.
deindividuation. A state of relative anonymity, in which a group member does not feel singled out or identifiable.

demand characteristics. The perceptual cues, both explicit and implicit, which communicate what behavior is expected in a situation.
democratic leadership. A type of leadership in which the leader shares functions with the group members and permits them to participate fully in decision making and planning.
dependent variable. A variable whose changes are considered to be consequences or effects of changes in other variables.
deprivation index. A measure of the quality of the environment in which a child lives.
destructiveness and cynicism. Generalized hostility; vilification of the human. A characteristic of the authoritarian personality syndrome.
determinism. A basic assumption of science, which states that every event has a cause and that all behavior is a result of natural causes and is therefore predictable.
development quotient (DQ). A measure of the rate of mental and physical development in infants.
dialect. A variety of a language with distinct, rule-governed features of pronunciation, vocabulary, and grammar. Regional or social dialects are examples.
differential accuracy. The ability to judge correctly the differences between individuals on any given trait (or differences between an individual and the group mean, or norm).
discrimination. Action that reflects acceptance of one person and rejection of another solely on the basis of the person's membership in a particular group.
dogmatism. A close-minded rigid style combined with beliefs that are authoritarian in content.
drug. Any substance that can be ingested by a person in order to improve nonpathological psychological states and that has detectable effects on feelings and physiological states.
drug abuse. As defined by Fort (1970), the use of a drug—usually chronic, excessive use—to an extent that produces definite impairment of social or vocational adjustment or health.
drug effect. Any change in psychological states or responses that is systematically related to the size of the drug dose.
dyad. A two-person group.
ecological approach. Studying a phenomenon in a natural setting without scientific interference.
ecology (psychological). The psychological environment or life space. Also, the study of an individual's psychological environment and his behavioral adaptation to it.
ego. According to Freud, that part of the personality oriented toward acting reasonably and realistically; the "executive" part of personality.
ego-alien. Irrational, not in tune with what is sensible or realistic.
egocentric speech. A form of language behavior first identified by Jean Piaget in which young children, failing to recognize their listener's perspective as different from their own, seem to be talking to themselves in the presence of others.
egoism. To Thomas Hobbes, man's basic concept; man's disposition to attain power for himself.
ejaculatory incompetence. The inability to ejaculate intravaginally.
elaborated code. Basil Bernstein's term for a mode of speech, more typical of the middle classes, which is person oriented, elaborately planned, and relatively unpredictable in structure. An explicit form of speech which arises when individual differences are made salient. (See **restricted code.**)
empathy. (See **accuracy of perception.**)
empirical approach. Active, planned collection of factual information.
empirical-rational strategy. A strategy of planned change, which advocates that publishing the facts is sufficient to initiate change.
epinephrine. Adrenaline, a drug which usually causes the person to have an accelerated heart rate, tremors in the hands, and a flushing of the face.
ethnic group. A group sharing a common culture, customs, and language.
ethnocentrism. A rejection of foreigners, aliens, and all out-groups, abetted by a belief that one's own group is best in all respects.
ethology. The study of animal behavior in naturalistic situations.
evaluation apprehension. A concern on the part of a subject in an experiment that he is performing correctly, that he will be positively evaluated by the experimenter (M. Rosenberg).
experimental method. A method of scientific data collection, which involves the manipulation of one or more independent variables, control of other related variables, and observation of one or more dependent variables.
experimenter effects. Changes or distortions in the results of an experiment produced by the experimenter's characteristics or behavior.

expiatory punishment. According to Piaget, the belief held by younger children that a wrongdoer should suffer a punishment that is painful in proportion to the seriousness of the offense but not necessarily related to the nature of the offense. (See **reciprocity.**)

explanation. The process of accounting for the occurrence or characteristics of an event in causal terms.

external validity. The generalizability of an experimental finding to other populations, settings, treatment arrangements, and measurement arrangements.

fact. An observation that has been or could be made repeatedly and consistently by different observers.

factor analysis. A statistical technique of identifying and measuring the underlying clusters, or factors, involved in a complex collection of measures.

field theory. A basic point of view in social psychology, first developed by Kurt Lewin, which proposes that one's social behavior is a function not only of one's own attitudes, personality, and other intrapersonal factors, but also of one's environment, or "field."

"flaky". A mild to moderate state of psychological disorganization in which the person has trouble remembering plans, formulating intentions, and carrying out his everyday affairs.

frustration. The blocking of, or interference with, ongoing motivated behavior.

frustration-induced behavior. The actions (often emotional) resulting from being blocked, thwarted, or defeated.

future shock. Alvin Toffler's term for the disorientation resulting from the superimposition of a new culture upon an old one. A product of the greatly accelerated rate of change in society.

generality of accuracy (in person perception). Judgmental ability that is relatively stable across various judging tasks and various people to be judged.

generalizability. Degree of applicability of research findings to other samples, populations, or conditions. Generalizability of results is dependent upon the representativeness of the sample and of the conditions of measurement.

genital stage. Freudian developmental stage from age fourteen and beyond, centered upon the development of mature sexuality and love for others.

genotype. An underlying characteristic; often a causal factor.

Gestalt. In German, form or pattern.

"great man" theory of leadership. The view that major events in national and international affairs are influenced more by the men who hold leadership positions than by other historical factors.

group risk taking. Decisions made by a group, which are less conservative than decisions made by individual members of the group.

halo effect. A rating error in which the rater lets his general, overall impression of another influence the rating he gives the other person on a specific characteristic.

haphazard sample. A sample chosen without any systematic method and, therefore, unrepresentative.

Hawthorne effect. Originally identified in industrial research. The tendency of people to work harder and gain more because of the sense of participating in something new and special.

"heads". Relatively heavy users of psychedelic drugs. The greater part of their lives are organized around getting and using drugs.

hedonism. The theory from philosophy that every human act is for the purpose of attaining pleasure or avoiding pain.

hereditarians. Those social scientists who conclude that most of the difference between individuals or between groups results from genetic factors rather than environmental ones.

heuristics. Methods of investigation in which the learner is trained to find out things for himself.

id. According to Freud, a set of drives that is the repository for man's basic unsocialized impulses, including sex and aggression.

illicit drugs. Those drugs the use of which is in violation of local laws.

illusion. Mistaken or distorted perception.

immanent justice. According to Piaget, the belief held by younger children that misdeeds will lead naturally to negative consequences, that punishments emanate automatically from things themselves.

immediate repetition task. A technique used to explore the development of linguistic competence. Children are asked to repeat sentences immediately after hearing them; the technique then compares the response to the original stimulus sentence.

incest. Sexual intercourse with a close blood relative.
independence of judgment. Maintenance and expression, through behavior, of one's private beliefs in the face of group pressures to do something to the contrary.
independent variable. A variable that is manipulated in an experiment; a variable whose changes are considered to be the cause of changes in another variable.
individualistic goal. A goal that is available to any and all who strive for it. Availability is not affected by the striving of others.
individualistic reward structure. A reward structure in which goal achievement by one participant has no effect on the goal achievement of the others.
induction. The process of making inferences from some particular instances to a more general rule. Used in constructing a theory on the basis of a few observed facts.
initiating structure. A dimension of leadership, which refers to the leader's behavior in identifying the group's goal and moving the group toward its goal.
instinct. An unlearned behavior pattern, which appears in full form in all members of the species when there is an adequate stimulus.
interconnectedness of attitudes. The degree to which a person's attitudes toward different objects are harmonious or consistent. When attitudes toward different objects of basic importance are consistent, an *ideology* exists.
intergroup-competition—intragroup-cooperation. The act of working with a group for a mutual goal in order to prevent another group from reaching the same goal.
internal locus of control. A belief that the rewards one receives in life are the result of one's own efforts, rather than the product of chance or the efforts of others.
internal validity. The conclusiveness with which the effects of the experimental treatments are established in an experiment.
interpersonal trust. A person's generalized expectancy that the promises of other individuals or groups, with regard to the future, can be relied upon (Rotter).
intragroup competition. The act of striving to excel in order to obtain an exclusive goal; in this text, synonymous with competition.
invariant. Referring to a series of developments, where the emergence of each phenomenon must follow a prescribed order.
"just world" phenomenon. The belief that persons get what they deserve in life.
laissez-faire leadership. A passive, permissive type of leadership; the leader does not intervene directly, nor does he encourage democratic procedures.
language. A system of communication among members of a given community, operating by sound through the organs of speech and hearing and through the use of vocal symbols possessing arbitrary, conventional meanings (Pei & Gaynor, 1954).
latency period. Freudian developmental stage characteristic of the six- to fourteen-year-old child; a period of relative quiescence.
law. A statement of the relationship between two or more variables, which is supported by so much evidence that it is not currently open to doubt.
leadership. As defined by Stogdill, the process of influencing the activities of an organized group in its efforts toward goal setting and goal achievement.
level I ability. In Jensen's framework, learning ability, or a less high-level skill than intelligence.
level II ability. In Jensen's framework, intelligence, or high-level mental ability.
libido. In psychoanalytic theory, a psychic energy that is expended in the satisfying of different needs.
life space. In field theory, the person plus his environment, which is viewed as one set of interdependent factors.
linguistic competence. In Noam Chomsky's sense, the "ideal speaker-hearer's" knowledge of the linguistic system, represented in a grammar of the language. In a looser sense, what an individual can do with language as opposed to what he does do in any given situation.
linguistic performance. In Chomsky's sense, actual speech behavior. Both comprehension and production, as constrained by psychological and social variables.
linguistics. The scientific study of language.
Likert-type scale. A type of attitude scale, which poses statements and asks the respondent to indicate how much he agrees or disagrees with each statement.
LPC. Least preferred coworker.

Machiavellianism. A belief that people can be manipulated through such means as flattery, threats, and deceit; in combination with a zest for carrying out such manipulations.

manipulation. Management of an independent variable so that at least two different levels (or values) of the variable are made to occur.

marginality. The position of a person who stands on the boundary between two groups, feeling uncertain about his status in both.

matriarchal. Female dominated; a family in which the wife-mother serves as the strongest figure.

measurement. Quantification of a variable.

mixed-motive situation. A situation in which the most favorable outcome is accompanied by the greatest risk; it involves the choice between two motives.

modeling. The phenomenon by which an individual learns to make a certain response by watching another person make that response to a stimulus.

moderator variable. A variable that links two other variables or affects the influence of one upon the other.

moral independence. According to Piaget, a second stage in moral development in which the child comes to believe in the modification of rules to fit the needs of the situation.

moral judgment. As studied by Piaget, Kohlberg, and others, a subject's beliefs regarding good and bad behavior in certain situations.

moral realism. According to Piaget, a belief held by young children that good behavior is obedient behavior and that acts should be judged in terms of the consequences, not on the basis of the motive behind the act.

multiplexity (multiplex attitude). The number and variety of cognitions or specific elements incorporated in one's attitude toward an object.

nonstandard Negro English. A cover term for the dialectal varieties used by large numbers of lower-class and working-class blacks throughout America.

normative-reeducative strategy. A strategy of planned change, which assumes that before trying to change a person or group, the cultural or normative factors (such as the past history of the person or group) must be taken into account.

norms. Socially defined and enforced standards concerning the way an individual should interpret the world and/or behave in it.

objectivity. Openness to observation by many observers; hence, a display of consensual agreement, a factual nature.

obscenity. That which is offensive to modesty or decency according to the standards of the majority of people in a given culture.

operational definition. Definition of a concept by specifying the procedures or operations by which it is measured.

oral stage. Freudian developmental stage, characteristic of the one-year-old child and centered upon sucking and biting needs.

overdifferentiation (in person perception). Oversensitivity to the individual differences between the persons being judged. A source of lowered accuracy of perception.

overlap, or percent of overlap. The percentage of one group whose scores exceed the mean score of another group.

***p* value.** The probability of a given event, on a scale from 0.00 to 1.00.

paradigmatic response. The term in word association studies for a response that is of the same grammatical class as the stimulus word. For example, given the word *table,* the subject responds with *chair* rather than *eat*. A pattern of word association response more typical of adults than of young children.

parsimonious. In regard to a theory, providing for an accurate explanation of a phenomenon that is as simple as possible. Avoiding complicated or high-level explanations when a more simplified one is adequate.

participant observation. Observation method in which the observer becomes a member of a group being observed and participates in its activities but tries not to influence the activities himself.

perception. A person's immediate experience of other persons or objects, gained through the sense organs, but somewhat modified by the perceiver's personal characteristics and by social influences.

perceptual accentuation. Overestimation of the objective characteristics (such as size) of objects.

perceptual defense. Selective perception wherein the recognition threshold for unpleasant stimuli is raised, and innocuous substitute perceptions often occur.
perceptual sensitization. Selective perception, wherein the recognition threshold for given types of stimuli is lowered; increased perceptual vigilance.
perinatal. Occurring at birth.
personal construct. In George Kelly's theory of personality, a way of construing or interpreting the world; a concept that a person uses in order to categorize events and other persons' behaviors.
personal disjunction. Similar to the idea of dissatisfaction. Disjunctions exist to the extent that a person does not expect to attain the things that he desires or wants.
personal meanings or functions of drug use. The reasons for use and the gratifications of use given by actual or prospective users. Drinking alcohol to relieve distress is one kind of function—typically called an escapist reason in the standard classification of functions.
personality. The ever-changing organization, within the individual, of abilities, attitudes, beliefs, and motives which contribute to the individual's reaction to his environment.
phallic stage. Freudian developmental stage characteristic of the four- to six-year-old child and centered upon attraction to the parent of the opposite sex and envy of the parent of the same sex as the child.
phenomenological approach. A point of view in social psychology stating that the environment, *as the person perceives it,* is an important influence on behavior.
phenotype. A surface or observable characteristic; often a resultant rather than a causal factor.
philosophy of human nature. An expectation that people possess certain qualities and will behave in certain ways.
phonological development. The child's acquisition of knowledge about the sound system of his language, including the ability to discriminate and produce permissible sound combinations.
placebo. A substance that has no effects upon an organism when ingested. Used for a control condition in studies on drug effects.
population. All of the individuals having certain characteristics in common. All persons living in Australia or all the registered voters in Nebraska are examples. Also, the total group from which a sample is selected for study.
pornography. Literature or art that is expressly intended to cause sexual arousal in the beholder and has no other primary purpose.
postfigurative culture. A culture in which children learn primarily from their elders.
post hoc analysis. A statistical analysis that is decided upon and done after the experimental data have been collected; therefore, not a part of the original design or purpose of the experiment.
power and toughness. Preoccupation with the dominance-submission, strong-weak, leader-follower dimension; identification with power figures; a characteristic of the authoritarian personality syndrome.
power-coercive strategy. A strategy that uses either violent or nonviolent pressures (lobbying, petitions, strikes, riots, and so on) to bring about social change.
prefigurative culture. A culture in which adults learn from their children.
prejudice. An evaluative reaction to a member of a racial, ethnic, or other minority group, which results from the recipient's membership in that group.
premature ejaculation. Inability to control the ejaculatory process for a sufficient length of time during intercourse to satisfy the coital partner.
primacy effect. Predominant effect of the first information received upon one's judgment or opinion about persons, objects, or issues.
primary impotence. The inability to achieve and/or maintain an erection of sufficient quality to accomplish successful coital connection during the initial and every subsequent opportunity.
prisoner's dilemma. A mixed-motive situation, in which the choice of the best outcome by each individual leads to an undesirable joint payoff.
probability sample. A sample chosen in such a way that every member of the population has a known probability (usually an equal probability) of being included.
projection. A defense mechanism in which a person seeks to alleviate conflict by seeing in others the motives or attributes about which he is anxious. (See also **assumed similarity.**)
projectivity. The disposition to believe that wild and dangerous things go on in the world;

the projection outward of unconscious emotional responses. A characteristic of the authoritarian personality syndrome.

promotive interdependence. Mutually beneficial interdependence. (See **cooperative reward structure.**)

propinquity. Physical proximity.

prurient interest. As defined by the American Law Institute's Model Penal Code, a shameful or morbid interest in nudity, sex, or excretion, which goes substantially beyond customary limits of candor in description or representation of such matters.

psychedelic. Mind altering or mind expanding.

psychoanalytic theory. A theory of personality first developed by Sigmund Freud, which has implications for social behavior.

quantification. Assignment of a number which shows the amount or extent of a variable that is present. (See **measurement.**)

quota sample. A sample chosen by assigning each interviewer a quota of respondents who are in specified categories of a classification system (usually using several dimensions such as age, sex, and race). The total sample has the same proportion of people in each category as does the population, but it still is not completely representative because of probable bias in the interviewers' choices of respondents.

race. A population that is geographically contiguous and whose members breed together.

racism. A type of prejudice directed at certain racial groups.

random sample. A form of probability sample, which is chosen in a completely random manner from a list that enumerates the whole population.

randomization. Assignment of subjects to treatment conditions in a completely random manner —that is, a manner determined entirely by chance.

rational approach. Arriving at conclusions by reasoning rather than by collecting data.

rational-economic man. A model that views man as primarily motivated by money and self-interest.

reactance. A theory stating that, if the opportunity to choose an object or activity is suddenly limited, its attractiveness is increased.

reactive measure. A measurement of a variable that is susceptible to change through the act of measuring it. That is, the very observation or measurement of a variable changes it.

real similarity (in person perception). Correspondence between a perceiver's own personal characteristics and those of a person whom he is judging or describing (the criterion data).

recency effect. Predominant effect of the most recent information received upon one's judgment or opinion about persons, objects, or issues.

reciprocity. According to Piaget, a belief held by older children that punishment should be logically related to the offense so that the rule-breaker will understand the implications of his misconduct. (See **expiatory punishment.**)

reinforcement. The consequence of a response, which influences whether that response is made again under the same stimulus conditions.

relative deprivation. The concept indicating that one's position is not evaluated in absolute terms but, rather, in relation to the position of others or in relation to the unfulfilled expectations.

reliability. Consistency of measurement. Stability of scores over time or equivalence of scores on two forms of a test are examples.

representativeness. Degree of similarity of a sample to the population from which it is drawn.

resistance to temptation. Suppression of a behavior that would have a high incidence if it were not for the influence of a prohibition or norm.

response. Alteration in a person's behavior that results from an external or internal stimulus.

response sets. Systematic ways of answering questions, which are not directly related to the content of the question but related to the form or the social characteristics of the alternative answers. Common types of response sets are social desirability and acquiescence.

restricted code. Basil Bernstein's term for a mode of speech, which is prevalent in the lower classes, status oriented, rapidly and simply planned, relatively predictable in structure, and which arises when members of a group share close identifications. (See **elaborated code.**)

role. The socially defined pattern of behavior that is expected of an individual who is assigned a certain social function, such as judge, clergyman, or teacher.

sample. A portion of a population that is selected for study in place of the complete population.
scapegoating. The displacement of hostility upon less powerful groups when the source of frustration is not available for attack or not attackable for other reasons.
scientific method. Systematic use of the steps of induction of theories, deduction of predictions from the theories, and verification of the predictions by data collection.
secondary impotence. A pattern of erective inadequacy, which is established after at least one successful intromission and which precludes successful coital connection in 25 percent or more of available opportunities.
selective migration. The trend for a certain subgroup (usually the more able or more competent) to move from an area before others do.
self-actualizing man. A model that views man as motivated primarily by the desire to use his capacities fully in meaningful, personally satisfying endeavors.
self-fulfilling prophecy. The notion that the expectation of some reality may influence the fulfillment of that reality.
semantic development. The child's acquisition of knowledge about the relationships among linguistic units and meanings. Includes the development of vocabulary and is associated with the broader process of forming concepts and organizing experience.
significance (statistical). The statistical probability (p) that a given score or group of scores could have occurred by chance alone; the lower the probability of chance occurrence, the greater the significance of the finding.
simplex (simplistic) attitude. An undifferentiated reaction toward an object. Lacking in qualifications or elaborations and largely evaluative.
Sims score card. A measure of socioeconomic status.
social class. A grouping of persons who share common values, interests, income level, and educational level.
social comparison. The use of others as sources of comparison, so that one may evaluate one's own attitudes or abilities.
social desirability. A response set to answer questions about oneself in the socially approved manner.
social determinism (or Zeitgeist view of history). The view of history that sees leaders only as expressions, instruments, or consequences of historical laws.
social distance. A person's acceptable degree of closeness (physically, socially, psychologically) to members of a particular ethnic group.
social indicator. A statistic of direct normative interest, which facilitates concise, comprehensive, and balanced judgments about the condition of major aspects of a society.
social influence. The processes by which a person or group influences another person or persons to modify behavior or attitudes.
social man. A model holding that man is motivated primarily by social needs and the desire to develop his identity through relationships with others.
social psychology. The field of study concerned with the effects of other people upon an individual's behavior.
socialization. A growing up process in which the child learns the norms of his society and acquires his own distinctive values, beliefs, and personality characteristics.
sociolinguistics. The systematic study of the relationships between linguistic forms and social meaning; more specifically, a study of the ways in which speech behavior is constrained by and expressive of such social variables as topic, situation, and participants.
standard deviation. A measure of how much variability (or spread) is present in a set of scores. A group with a larger standard deviation is more heterogeneous, possessing a wider spread of scores.
statistical prediction. Objective judgments about people, in which data of any sort are combined by means of a formula or mechanical decision system, rather than subjectively by a judge.
statistical test. A mathematical procedure for determining the significance of a score or group of scores; it yields a p value.
stereotype. A simplified and standard image (often highly evaluative, inaccurate, and rigidified) of a group of people.
stereotype accuracy. The ability to judge correctly the group mean, or norm, on any given trait; knowledge of "the generalized other."
stimulus. Any event, internal or external to the person, that brings about an alteration in the person's behavior.

stimulus generalization. A term denoting the fact that, after a person learns to make a certain response to a certain stimulus, other similar but previously ineffective stimuli will also elicit the new response.

stratified random sample. A form of probability sample chosen by dividing the population into several categories (strata) on one or more dimensions (for example, region of the country, rural-urban residence) and then selecting respondents *randomly* from each category. This is a representative sample because the selection of respondents is random (in contrast to a quota sample, where it is not).

subliminal perception. Perception of stimuli that are below the threshold of awareness; that is, not consciously noticed by the perceiver.

superego. According to Freud, the part of personality oriented toward doing what is morally proper; the conscience. The superego includes one's ego ideal, or ideal self-image.

superstition and stereotypy. Belief in the mystical determinants of the individual's fate; the disposition to think in rigid categories. A characteristic of the authoritarian personality syndrome.

sympathomimetic. Having the same effects as those of the sympathetic nervous system; in other words, responding to an emotional situation by readying the body to respond.

syntactic development. The child's acquisition of knowledge about the structure of sentences. Includes the ability to comprehend and produce units larger than the word.

systematic sample. A form of probability sample that is chosen in a systematic but unbiased manner from a list that enumerates the whole population (for example, the choice of every tenth name from an alphabetical list).

systematically biased sample. One which misrepresents the nature of the population in some consistent way. For example, samples drawn from lists of college alumni would not represent the total population of adults in regard to educational level.

***t*-test.** A statistical test to determine whether the average scores for two groups of subjects are different enough to permit ruling out chance as a likely cause of the difference.

tautological. Circular reasoning; saying the same thing in other words.

technocracy. A social form in which an industrial society reaches the peak of its organizational integration.

territoriality. An innate drive in some species of animals to defend one's own habitat.

theory. A system of ideas containing abstract concepts, rules about the interconnections of these concepts, and ways of linking these concepts to observed facts.

Theory x. An assumption about the nature of man, and especially the nature of the worker, which states that human nature is basically lazy and externally motivated.

Theory y. An assumption about the nature of man, and especially the nature of the worker, which states that human nature is basically responsible and self-directed.

tolerance of deviance. An acceptance of deviant and illegal means to gain one's ends. Indicative of an absence of personal control against engaging in deviant behavior.

uniformity. General agreement in a society about facts or beliefs, which is not the result of group pressures to conform.

unobtrusive measure. A measurement that can be made without the knowledge of the person being studied. An unobtrusive measure is also nonreactive.

validity. Accuracy or correctness of measurement (for example, the degree to which a test actually measures what it purports to measure).

value. A standard that influences one's decision making.

value-access disjunction. In Jessor's model of deviance, a sociological factor relating to the discrepancy between the social value placed upon material success and the accessibility of such success.

veridical. Accurate; corresponding to objective reality, as in the phrase "veridical perception."

verification. The process of collecting facts to support or refute theoretical predictions.

xenophobia. Rejection of foreign and minority groups.

XYZ pattern. An abnormality in the genetic characteristics of some persons. Some researchers claim that the possession of an extra Y chromosome is related to aggressive or criminal behavior.

Zeitgeist. "Spirit of the times" or mood of the present.

References

Abelson, R. P. Computers, polls, and public opinion—some puzzles and paradoxes. *Trans-Action,* 1968, **5,** 20–27.

Abelson, R. P., Aronson, E., McGuire, W. J., Newcomb, T. M., Rosenberg, M. J., & Tannenbaum, P. H. (Eds.) *Theories of cognitive consistency: A sourcebook.* Chicago: Rand-McNally, 1968.

Abelson, R. P., & Lesser, G. S. The measurement of persuasibility in children. In I. L. Janis and C. I. Hovland (Eds.), *Personality and persuasibility.* New Haven: Yale University Press, 1959. Pp. 141–166.

Abrahams, R. D. *Deep down in the jungle: Negro narrative folklore from the streets of Philadelphia.* Hatboro, Pa.: Folklore Associates, 1964.

Adams, D. K., Harvey, O. J., & Heslin, R. E. Variation in flexibility and creativity as a function of hypnotically induced past histories. In O. J. Harvey (Ed.), *Experience, structure, and adaptability.* New York: Springer, 1966. Pp. 217–234.

Adams, J. S. Inequity in social exchange. In L. Berkowitz (Ed.), *Advances in experimental social psychology.* Vol. 2. New York: Academic Press, 1965. Pp. 267–299.

Adams, S. Social climate and productivity in small groups. *American Sociological Review,* 1954, **19,** 421–425.

Adelson, J. What generation gap? *New York Times Magazine.* Jan. 18, 1970. Pp. 1–11*ff.*

Adler, A. *Social interest: A challenge to mankind.* (Translated by J. Linton and R. Vaughan.) London: Faber & Faber, 1945.

Adorno, T., Frenkel-Brunswik, E., Levinson, D., & Sanford, N. *The authoritarian personality.* New York: Harper, 1950.

Ainsworth, M. D. S. *Infancy in Uganda.* Baltimore: Johns Hopkins University Press, 1967.

Alexander, H. B. A comparison of the ranks of the American states in Army Alpha and in socioeconomic status. *School and Society,* 1922, **16,** 388–392.

Alfert, E. Comment on promotion of prejudice. *Journal of Social Issues,* 1969, **25**(4), 206–212. (a)

Alfert, E. Response to Jensen's rejoinder. *Journal of Social Issues,* 1969, **25**(4), 217–219. (b)

Alinsky, S. *Rules for radicals.* New York: Random House, 1971.

Allen, V. L. Situational factors in conformity. In L. Berkowitz (Ed.), *Advances in experimental social psychology.* Vol. 2. New York: Academic Press, 1965. Pp. 133–170.

Allen, V. L. (Ed.) Ghetto riots. *Journal of Social Issues,* 1970, **26**(1, whole issue). (a)

Allen, V. L. Toward understanding riots: Some perspectives. *Journal of Social Issues,* 1970, **26**(1), 1–19. (b)

Allinsmith, W. Moral standards: II. The learning of moral standards. In D. R. Miller and G. E. Swanson (Eds.), *Inner conflict and defense.* New York: Holt, 1960. Pp. 141–176.

Allport, G. W. Attitudes. In C. Murchison (Ed.), *Handbook of social psychology.* Worcester, Mass.: Clark University Press, 1935. Pp. 789–844.

Allport, G. W. Prejudice: A problem in psychological and social causation. *Journal of Social Issues,* Supplement Series, No. 4, 1950.

Allport, G. W. *The nature of prejudice*. Reading, Mass.: Addison-Wesley, 1954. (Paperback version: Garden City, New York: Doubleday Anchor, 1958.)

Allport, G. W. What units shall we employ? In G. Lindzey (Ed.), *Assessment of human motives*. New York: Rinehart, 1958.

Allport, G. W. *Pattern and growth in personality*. New York: Holt, Rinehart, & Winston, 1961.

Allport, G. W. The general and the unique in psychological science. *Journal of Personality*, 1962, **30**, 405–422.

Allport, G. W. Traits revisited. *American Psychologist*, 1966, **21**, 1–10.

Allport, G. W. The historical background of modern social psychology. In G. Lindzey and E. Aronson (Eds.), *Handbook of social psychology*. Vol. I. (2nd ed.) Reading, Mass.: Addison-Wesley, 1968. Pp. 1–80.

Allport, G. W., & Kramer, B. M. Some roots of prejudice. *Journal of Psychology*, 1946, **22**, 9–39.

Allport, G. W., & Pettigrew, T. F. Cultural influence on the perception of movement: The trapezoidal illusion among Zulus. *Journal of Abnormal and Social Psychology*, 1957, **55**, 104–113.

Almedingen, E. M. *The Empress Alexandra: 1872–1918*. London: Hutchison, 1961.

Alper, T. G., & Boring, E. G. Intelligence-test scores of northern and southern whites and Negro recruits in 1918. *Journal of Abnormal and Social Psychology*, 1944, **39**, 471–474.

Altus, W. D. Birth order and academic primogeniture. *Journal of Personality and Social Psychology*, 1965, **2**, 872–876.

Altus, W. D. Birth order and its sequelae. *Science*, 1966, **151**, 44–49.

American Council on Education. *Higher Education and National Affairs*, Sept. 25, 1970, **19**, 6–7.

American Council on Education. Campus unrest still widespread in 1970–71, ACE researchers claim. *Higher Education and National Affairs*, September 24, 1971, **20**, 6.

American Psychological Association. *Ethical standards of psychologists*. Washington, D.C.: American Psychological Association, 1953.

American Psychological Association. Special Issue: Testing and public policy. *American Psychologist*, 1965, **20**, 855–1005.

American Psychological Association. *Casebook on ethical standards of psychologists*. Washington, D.C.: American Psychological Association, 1967.

Amir, Y. Contact hypothesis in ethnic relations. *Psychological Bulletin*, 1969, **71**, 319–342.

Amsel, A. The role of frustrative nonreward in noncontinuous reward situations. *Psychological Bulletin*, 1958, **55**, 102–119.

Amsel, A. Frustrative nonreward in partial reinforcement and discrimination learning: Some recent history and a theoretical extension. *Psychological Review*, 1962, **69**, 306–328.

Anastasi, A. *Differential psychology*. (3rd ed.) New York: Macmillan, 1958.

Anastasi, A., & D'Angelo, R. Y. A comparison of Negro and white preschool children in language development and Goodenough Draw-a-Man I.Q. *Journal of Genetic Psychology*, 1952, **81**, 147–165.

Anderson, R. C. Learning in discussions: A resume of the authoritarian-democratic studies. *Harvard Educational Review*, 1959, **29**, 201–215.

Arbuckle, D. S. *Counseling: Philosophy, theory, and practice*. Boston: Allyn & Bacon, 1965.

Ardrey, R. *African genesis*. New York: Delta Books, 1961.

Ardrey, R. *The territorial imperative*. New York: Atheneum, 1966.

Ardrey, R. *The social contract*. New York: Atheneum, 1970.

Argyris, C. *Integrating the individual and the organization*. New York: Wiley, 1964.

Aronfreed, J. The nature, variety, and social patterning of moral responses to transgression. *Journal of Abnormal and Social Psychology*, 1961, **63**, 223–241.

Aronfreed, J. *Conduct and conscience: The socialization of internalized control over behavior*. New York: Academic Press, 1968.

Aronson, E. The effect of effort on the attractiveness of rewarded and unrewarded stimuli. *Journal of Abnormal and Social Psychology*, 1961, **63**, 375–380.

Aronson, E. The psychology of insufficient justification: An analysis of some conflicting data. In S. Feldman (Ed.), *Cognitive consistency*. New York: Academic Press, 1966. Pp. 115–136.

Aronson, E. Some antecedents of interpersonal attraction. In W. J. Arnold and D. Levine (Eds.), *Nebraska symposium on motivation, 1969*. Lincoln, Nebr.: University of Nebraska Press, 1970. Pp. 143–173.

Aronson, E. & Carlsmith, J. M. Experimentation in social psychology. In G. Lindzey and E. Aronson (Eds.), *Handbook of social psychology*. Vol. 2. (2nd ed.) Reading, Mass.: Addison-Wesley, 1968. Pp. 1–79.

Aronson, E., & Mills, J. The effect of severity of initiation on liking for a group. *Journal of Abnormal and Social Psychology,* 1959, **59,** 177–181.

Aronson, E., Willerman, B., & Floyd, J. The effect of a pratfall on increasing interpersonal attractiveness. *Psychonomic Science*, 1966, **4,** 157–158.

Asch, S. E. Forming impressions of personality. *Journal of Abnormal and Social Psychology,* 1946, **41,** 258–290.

Asch, S. E. The doctrine of suggestion, prestige, and imitation in social psychology. *Psychological Review*, 1948, **55,** 250–276.

Asch, S. E. Effects of group pressure upon the modification and distortion of judgments. In H. Guetzkow (Ed.), *Groups, leadership, and men.* Pittsburgh: Carnegie Press, 1951.

Asch, S. E. *Social psychology*. New York: Prentice-Hall, 1952.

Asch, S. E. Studies of independence and conformity: A minority of one against a unanimous majority. *Psychological Monographs,* 1956, **70** (9, Whole No. 416).

Asch, S. E. Effects of group pressure upon modification and distortion of judgments. In E. E. Maccoby, T. M. Newcomb, and E. L. Hartley (Eds.), *Readings in social psychology.* (3rd ed.) New York: Holt, 1958. Pp. 174–183.

Asher, E. J. The inadequacy of current intelligence tests for testing Kentucky mountain children. *Journal of Genetic Psychology,* 1935, **46,** 480–486.

Ashmore, R. D. Prejudice: Causes and cures. In B. E. Collins, *Social psychology*. Reading, Mass.: Addison-Wesley, 1970. Pp. 243–339.

Astin, A. W., & Panos, R. J. *The educational and vocational development of students.* Washington, D.C.: American Council on Education, 1969.

Atkinson, J. W. (Ed.) *Motives in fantasy, action, and society*. Princeton, N.J.: Van Nostrand, 1958.

Atkinson, J. W., & Feather, N. T. *A theory of achievement motivation.* New York: Wiley, 1966.

Ausubel, D. P., & Ausubel, P. Ego development among segregated Negro children. In A. H. Passow (Ed.), *Education in depressed areas.* New York: Bureau of Publications, Teachers College, Columbia University, 1963.

Ax, A. F. The physiological differentiation of emotional states. *Psychosomatic Medicine,* 1953, **15,** 433–442.

Azrin, N. H., & Lindsley, O. R. The reinforcement of cooperation between children. *Journal of Abnormal and Social Psychology,* 1956, **52,** 100–102.

Bachtold, L.M., & Werner, E. E. Personality profiles of gifted women: Psychologists. *American Psychologist,* 1970, **25,** 234–243.

Back, K. W., & Davis, K. E. Some personal and situational factors relevant to the consistency and prediction of conforming behavior. *Sociometry,* 1965, **28,** 227–240.

Backman, C. W., & Secord, P. F. The effect of perceived liking on interpersonal attraction. *Human Relations,* 1959, **12,** 379–384.

Bacon, M., & Jones, M. B. *Teen-age drinking*. New York: Crowell, 1968.

Bagby, J. W. A cross-cultural study of perceptual predominance in binocular rivalry. *Journal of Abnormal and Social Psychology,* 1957, **54,** 331–334.

Baker, J. R. *William Golding: A critical study*. New York: St. Martins Press, 1965.

Baker, R. K., & Ball, S. J. (Eds.) *Mass media and violence*. Vol. 9. National Commission on the Causes and Prevention of Violence Staff Study Series. Washington, D.C.: U.S. Govt. Printing Office, 1969.

Baldwin, A. L. *Behavior and development in childhood.* New York: Dryden, 1955.

Baldwin, A. L. A cognitive theory of socialization. In D. A. Goslin (Ed.), *Handbook of socialization theory and research.* Chicago: Rand-McNally, 1969. Pp. 325–345.

Bales, R. F. The equilibrium problem in small groups. In T. Parsons, R. F. Bales, and E. A. Shils (Eds.), *Working papers in the theory of action.* Glencoe, Ill.: Free Press, 1953. Pp. 111–161.

Bales, R. F. Task roles and social roles in problem-solving groups. In E. E. Maccoby, T. M. Newcomb, and E. L. Hartley (Eds.), *Readings in social psychology.* (3rd ed.) New York: Holt, Rinehart, & Winston, 1958. Pp. 396–413.

Bandler, R. J., Madaras, G. R., & Bem, D. J. Self-observation as a source of pain perception. *Journal of Personality and Social Psychology,* 1968, **9,** 205–209.

Bandura, A. Influence of model's reinforcement contingencies on the acquisition of imitative response. *Journal of Personality and Social Psychology,* 1965, **1,** 589–595. (a)

Bandura, A. Vicarious processes: A case of no-trial learning. In L. Berkowitz (Ed.), *Advances in experimental social psychology.* Vol. 2. New York: Academic Press, 1965. Pp. 1–55. (b)

Bandura, A., Ross, D., & Ross, S. Transmission of aggression through imitation of aggressive models. *Journal of Abnormal and Social Psychology,* 1961, **63,** 575–582.

Bandura, A., Ross, D., & Ross, S. Imitation of film-mediated aggressive models. *Journal of Abnormal and Social Psychology,* 1963, **66,** 3–11.

Bandura, A., & Walters, R. *Social learning and personality development.* New York: Holt, Rinehart, & Winston, 1963.

Banfield, E. C. *The unheavenly city.* Boston: Little-Brown, 1970.

Bannister, D. (Ed.) *Perspectives in personal construct theory.* New York: Academic Press, 1970.

Baratz, J. C. A bi-dialectal task for determining language proficiency in economically disadvantaged Negro children. *Child Development,* 1969, **40,** 889–901. (a)

Baratz, J. C. Teaching reading in an urban Negro school system. In J. Baratz and R. W. Shuy (Eds.), *Teaching black children to read.* Washington, D.C.: Center for Applied Linguistics, 1969. Pp. 92–116. (b)

Baratz, J. C., & Shuy, R. W. (Eds.) *Teaching black children to read.* Washington, D.C.: Center for Applied Linguistics, 1969.

Baratz, S. S., & Baratz, J. C. Early childhood intervention: The social science base of institutional racism. *Harvard Educational Review,* 1970, **40,** 29–50.

Barber, C. G. Facts about race: A review of research findings. In W. H. Drummond and T. E. Warren (Eds.), *Improving educational opportunities in a changing community.* Nashville, Tenn.: George Peabody College for Teachers, 1965. Pp. 63–77. (Mimeographed.)

Barber, T. X. *LSD, marihuana, yoga and hypnosis.* Chicago: Aldine, 1970.

Barber, T. X., & Silver, M. J. Fact, fiction, and the experimenter bias effect. *Psychological Bulletin Monograph Supplement,* 1968, **70**(6, P. 2), 1–29. (a)

Barber, T. X., & Silver, M. J. Pitfalls in data analysis and interpretation: A reply to Rosenthal. *Psychological Bulletin Monograph Supplement,* 1968, **70**(6, P. 2), 48–62. (b)

Bard, M. Alternatives to traditional law enforcement. In F. F. Korten, S. W. Cook, and J. I. Lacey (Eds.), *Psychology and the problems of society.* Washington, D.C.: American Psychological Association, 1970. Pp. 128–132.

Bardwick, J. M. Psychological conflict and the reproductive system. In Bardwick, J. M., Douvan, E., Horner, M. S., & Gutmann, D. (Eds.), *Feminine personality and conflict.* Monterey, Cal.: Brooks/Cole, 1970. Pp. 3–28.

Bardwick, J. M. *Psychology of women.* New York: Harper & Row, 1971.

Barker, E. N. Authoritarianism of the political right, center, and left. *Journal of Social Issues,* 1963, **19**(2), 63–74.

Barker, G. C. Social functions of language in a Mexican-American community. *Acta Americana,* 1947, **5,** 185–202.

Barker, R. G. Ecology and motivation. In M. A. Jones (Ed.), *Nebraska symposium on motivation, 1960.* Lincoln, Nebr.: University of Nebraska Press, 1960. Pp. 1–49.

Barker, R. G. (Ed.) *The stream of behavior.* New York: Appleton-Century-Crofts, 1963.

Barker, R. G. *Ecological psychology: Concepts and methods for studying the environment of human behavior.* Stanford: Stanford University Press, 1968.

Barker, R. G., Dembo, T., & Lewin, K. Frustration and regression: A study of young children. *University of Iowa Studies in Child Welfare,* 1941, **18,** No. 1.

Barker, R. G., & Wright, H. F. *Midwest and its children: The psychological ecology of an American town.* Evanston, Ill.: Row-Peterson, 1954.

Barnett, S. A. On the hazards of analogies. In M. F. A. Montagu (Ed.), *Man and aggression.* New York: Oxford University Press, 1968. Pp. 18–26. (Originally published in *Scientific American,* February, 1967.)

Barron, F. Some personality correlates of independence of judgment. *Journal of Personality*, 1953, **21,** 287–297.
Barron, F. Review of the Edwards Personal Preference Schedule. In O. K. Buros (Ed.), *The fifth mental measurements yearbook*. Highland Park, N.J.: Gryphon Press, 1959. Pp. 114–117.
Barry, W. A. Marriage research and conflict: An integrative review. *Psychological Bulletin*, 1970, **73,** 41–54.
Bass, B. M. Authoritarianism or acquiescence? *Journal of Abnormal and Social Psychology*, 1955, **51,** 616–623.
Bass, B. M. *Leadership, psychology, and organizational behavior*. New York: Harper & Row, 1960.
Bateson, N. Familiarization, group discussion, and risk taking. *Journal of Experimental Social Psychology*, 1966, **2,** 119–129.
Bauer, R. A. (Ed.) *Social indicators*. Cambridge, Mass.: M.I.T. Press, 1966.
Baumrin, B. H. The immorality of irrelevance: The social role of science. In F. F. Korten, S. W. Cook, and J. I. Lacey (Eds.), *Psychology and the problems of society*. Washington, D.C.: American Psychological Association, 1970. Pp. 73–83.
Baumrind, D. Some thoughts on the ethics of research: After reading Milgram's "Behavioral study of obedience." *American Psychologist*, 1964, **19,** 421–423.
Baxter, G. W., Jr. Changes in PHN after one year and two years in college. Unpublished master's thesis, George Peabody College for Teachers, 1968.
Bayer, A., & Astin, A. Violence and disruption on the U.S. campus. *Educational Record*, 1969, **50,** 337–350.
Bayley, N. Comparisons of mental and motor test scores for ages 1-15 months by sex, birth order, race, geographical location, and education of parents. *Child Development*, 1965, **36,** 379–416.
Becker, H. Becoming a marihuana user. *American Journal of Sociology*, 1953, **59,** 235–242.
Becker, S. W., & Carroll, J. Ordinal position and conformity. *Journal of Abnormal and Social Psychology*, 1962, **65,** 129–131.
Bee, H. L., Van Egeren, L. F., Streissguth, A. P., Nyman, B. A., & Leckie, M. S. Social class differences in maternal teaching strategies and speech patterns. *Developmental Psychology*, 1969, **1,** 726–734.
Bell, R. Self-concept and aspirations of working-class mothers. Symposium paper delivered at American Psychological Association Convention, New York, September 1964.
Bell, R. R., & Chaskes, J. B. Premarital sexual experience among coeds, 1958 and 1968. *Journal of Marriage and the Family*, 1970, **32,** 81–84.
Beller, E. K. Maternal behaviors in lower class Negro mothers. Paper presented at the meeting of the Eastern Psychological Association, Boston, April 1967.
Bem, D. J. An experimental analysis of self-persuasion. *Journal of Experimental Social Psychology*, 1965, **1,** 199–218.
Bem, D. J. Self-perception: An alternative interpretation of cognitive dissonance phenomena. *Psychological Review*, 1967, **74,** 183–200.
Bem, D. J. *Beliefs, attitudes, and human affairs*. Belmont, Calif.: Brooks/Cole, 1970.
Bem, D. J., & McConnell, H. K. Testing the self-perception explanation of dissonance phenomena: On the salience of premanipulation attitudes. *Journal of Personality and Social Psychology*, 1970, **14,** 23–31.
Benjamin, H. (Ed.) *The transsexual phenomenon*. New York: Julian Press, 1966.
Benjamin, H., & Masters, R. E. L. (Eds.) *Prostitutes and morality*. New York: Julian Press, 1964.
Bennis, W. G., Benne, K. D., & Chin, R. *The planning of change*. New York: Holt, Rinehart, & Winston, 1968.
Bereiter, C., & Engelmann, S. *Teaching disadvantaged children in the preschool*. Englewood Cliffs, N.J.: Prentice-Hall, 1966.
Bereiter, C., Engelmann, S., Osborn, J., & Reidford, P. A. An academically oriented preschool for culturally deprived children. In F. M. Heckinger (Ed.), *Preschool education today. New approaches to teaching three-, four-, and five-year-olds*. New York: Doubleday, 1966. Pp. 105–135.

Berger, S. M. Conditioning through vicarious instigation. *Psychological Review,* 1962, **69,** 450–466.
Berger, S. M., & Lambert, W. W. Stimulus-response theory in contemporary social psychology. In G. Lindzey and E. Aronson (Eds.), *Handbook of social psychology.* Vol. I. (2nd ed.) Reading, Mass.: Addison-Wesley, 1968. Pp. 81–178.
Berkowitz, L. Aggressive cues in aggressive behavior and hostility catharsis. *Psychological Review,* 1964, **71,** 104–122. (a)
Berkowitz, L. *The development of motives and values in the child.* New York: Basic Books, 1964. (b)
Berkowitz, L. Some aspects of observed aggression. *Journal of Personality and Social Psychology,* 1965, **2,** 359–369. (a)
Berkowitz, L. The concept of aggressive drive: Some additional considerations. In L. Berkowitz (Ed.), *Advances in experimental social psychology.* Vol. II. New York: Academic Press, 1965. Pp. 301–329. (b)
Berkowitz, L. The frustration-aggression hypothesis revisited. In L. Berkowitz (Ed.), *Roots of aggression: A re-examination of the frustration-aggression hypothesis.* New York: Atherton, 1969. Pp. 1–28. (a)
Berkowitz, L. (Ed.) *Roots of aggression: A re-examination of the frustration-aggression hypothesis.* New York: Atherton, 1969. (b)
Berkowitz, L., & Friedman, P. Social class differences in helping behavior. *Journal of Personality and Social Psychology,* 1967, **5,** 217–225.
Berkowitz, L., & Geen, R. G. Film violence and the cue properties of available targets. *Journal of Personality and Social Psychology,* 1966, **3,** 525–530.
Berkowitz, L., & Geen, R. G. Stimulus qualities of the target of aggression: A further study. *Journal of Personality and Social Psychology,* 1967, **5,** 364–368.
Berkowitz, L., & Knurek, D. A. Label-mediated hostility generalization. *Journal of Personality and Social Psychology,* 1969, **13,** 200–206.
Berkowitz, L., & Le Page, A. Weapons as aggression-eliciting stimuli. *Journal of Personality and Social Psychology,* 1967, **7,** 202–207.
Berlin, C. I., & Dill, A. C. The effects of feedback and positive reinforcement on the Wepman Auditory Discrimination Test scores of lower-class Negro and white children. *Journal of Speech and Hearing Research,* 1967, **10,** 384–389.
Bernstein, B. Language and social class. *British Journal of Sociology,* 1960, **2,** 271–276.
Bernstein, B. Social class and linguistic development: A theory of social learning. In A. H. Halsey, J. Floud, and C. A. Anderson (Eds.), *Education, economy, and society.* Glencoe, Ill.: Free Press, 1961. Pp. 288–314.
Bernstein, B. Linguistic codes, hesitation phenomena, and intelligence. *Language and Speech,* 1962, **5,** 31–46. (a)
Bernstein, B. Social class, linguistic codes, and grammatical elements. *Language and Speech,* 1962, **5,** 221–240. (b)
Bernstein, B. Aspects of language and learning in the genesis of the social process. In D. Hymes (Ed.), *Culture and society.* New York: Harper & Row, 1964. Pp. 251–263.
Bernstein, B. A socio-linguistic approach to social learning. In J. Gould (Ed.), *Penguin survey of the social sciences.* Baltimore, Md.: Penguin Books, 1965. Pp. 144–168.
Bernstein, B. A sociolinguistic approach to socialization: With some reference to educability. In F. Williams (Ed.), *Language and poverty. Perspectives on a theme.* Chicago: Markham, 1970. Pp. 25–61.
Berscheid, E., & Walster, E. H. *Interpersonal attraction.* Reading, Mass.: Addison-Wesley, 1969.
Bettelheim, B. Review of B. S. Bloom's *Stability and change in human characteristics. New York Review of Books,* Sept. 10, 1964, **3,** 1–4.
Biddle, B. J., & Thomas, E. J. (Eds.) *Role theory: Concepts and research.* New York: Wiley, 1966.
Biddle, W. W., & Biddle, L. *The community development process.* New York: Holt, Rinehart, & Winston, 1965.
Bieber, I., Dain, H. J., Dince, P. R., Drellich, M. G., Girand, H. G., Gundlach, R. H., Kremer, M. W., Rifkin, A. H., Wilbur, C. B., & Bieber, T. B. *Homosexuality: A psychoanalytic study.* New York: Basic Books, 1962.

Bieri, J., Atkins, A., Briar, S., Leaman, R. L., Miller, H., & Tripodi, T. *Clinical and social judgment.* New York: Wiley, 1966.
Biller, H. B. Father absence and the personality development of the male child. *Developmental Psychology,* 1970, **2,** 181–201.
Biller, H. B., & Borstelmann, L. J. Masculine development: An integrative review. *Merrill-Palmer Quarterly of Behavior and Development,* 1967, **13,** 253–294.
Billingsley, A. *Black families in white America.* Englewood Cliffs, N. J.: Prentice-Hall, 1968.
Bird, C. *Social psychology.* New York: Appleton-Century-Crofts, 1940.
Blalock, H. M., Jr. *Toward a theory of minority-group relations.* New York: Wiley, 1957.
Blau, P. Cooperation and competition in a bureaucracy. *American Journal of Sociology,* 1954, **59,** 530–535.
Blauner, R. Internal colonialism and ghetto revolt. *Social Problems,* 1969, **16**(4), 393–408.
Block, J. Personality characteristics associated with father's attitudes toward child rearing. *Child Development,* 1955, **26,** 41–48.
Block, J. *The challenge of response sets: Unconfounding meaning, acquiescence, and social desirability in the MMPI.* New York: Appleton-Century-Crofts, 1965.
Block, J., Haan, N., & Smith, M. B. Activism and apathy in contemporary adolescents. In J. F. Adams (Ed.), *Understanding adolescents: Current developments in adolescent psychology.* Boston: Allyn & Bacon, 1968. Pp. 198–231.
Block, J., Haan, N., & Smith, M. B. Socialization correlates of student activism. *Journal of Social Issues,* 1969, **25**(4), 143–177.
Bloom, B. S. *Stability and change in human characteristics.* New York: Wiley, 1964.
Bloom, B. S., Davis, A., & Hess, R. D. *Compensatory education for cultural deprivation.* New York: Holt, 1965.
Blum, E. Horatio Alger's children: Case studies. In R. H. Blum and associates, *Students and drugs.* San Francisco: Jossey-Bass, 1969. Pp. 243–274.
Blum, R. H. Observations on drug dealers: The question of effective intervention. Paper presented at the Joint Bureau of Narcotics and Dangerous Drugs-Stanford Conference on Directions for Drug Research, Stanford, 1970.
Blum, R. H. Drug pushers: A collective portrait. *Trans-Action,* 1971, **8,**(9/10), 18–21.
Blum, R. H. & associates. *Society and drugs.* San Francisco: Jossey-Bass, 1969 (a)
Blum, R. H. & associates. *Students and drugs.* San Francisco: Jossey-Bass, 1969. (b)
Blum, R. H., & Funkhouser-Balbaky, M. L. Mind-altering drugs and dangerous behavior: Dangerous drugs. Annotations and Consultants' Papers, Task Force on Narcotics and Drug Abuse, President's Commission on Law Enforcement and Administration of Justice, 1967.
Blum, R. H., & Garfield, E. A follow-up study. In R. H. Blum and associates, *Students and drugs.* San Francisco: Jossey-Bass, 1969. Pp. 185–194.
Boas, F. (Ed.) *General anthropology.* Boston: Heath, 1938.
Bochner, S., & Insko, C. Communicator discrepancy, source credibility, and influence. *Journal of Personality and Social Psychology,* 1966, **4,** 614–621.
Boguslaw, R. *The new utopians. A study of system design and social change.* Englewood Cliffs, N. J.: Prentice-Hall, 1965.
Borgatta, E. F., Couch, A. S., & Bales, R. F. Some findings relevant to the Great Man theory of leadership. *American Sociological Review,* 1954, **19,** 755–759.
Bosworth, A. R. *America's concentration camps.* New York: Bantam Books, 1968.
Bourlierè, F. *The natural history of mammals.* New York: Knopf, 1954. (Republished: 1956).
Bovard, E. W., Jr. Social norms and the individual. *Journal of Abnormal and Social Psychology,* 1948, **43,** 62–69.
Boyd, W. C. *Genetics and the races of man.* Boston: Little, Brown, 1950.
Bramel, D. Interpersonal attraction, hostility, and perception. In J. Mills (Ed.), *Experimental social psychology.* New York: Macmillan, 1969. Pp. 1–120.
Bramson, L., & Goethals, G. W. (Eds.) *War.* (Rev. ed.) New York: Basic Books, 1968.
Brecher, R., & Brecher, E. *An analysis of human sexual response.* New York: Signet, 1966.
Brehm, J. W. *A theory of psychological reactance.* New York: Academic Press, 1966.
Brehm, J. W., & Cohen, A. R. *Explorations in cognitive dissonance.* New York: Wiley, 1962.
Brehm, J. W., Gatz, M., Goethals, G., McCrimmon, J., & Ward, L. Psychological arousal and interpersonal attraction. Unpublished manuscript, Duke University, 1970.

Brehm, M., & Back, K. W. Self image and attitudes toward drugs. *Journal of Personality*, 1968, **36,** 299–314.
Briand, P. L., Jr. (Ed.) *Hearings on mass media and violence*. Vol. 9-A, National Commission on the Causes and Prevention of Violence Staff Study Series. Washington, D.C.: U.S. Gov't. Printing Office, 1969.
Brickman, P., & Redfield, J. Drive and predisposition as factors in the attitudinal effects of mere exposure. In A. A. Harrison (chm.), The effects of exposure versus novelty on the evaluation of stimulus objects. Symposium presented at the American Psychological Association meeting, Miami Beach, September, 1970.
Brigham, J. C. Ethnic stereotypes. *Psychological Bulletin*, 1971, **76,** 15–38. (a)
Brigham, J. C. Instructional set, attribution of traits to blacks and racial attitude. Paper presented at the meeting of the Southeastern Psychological Association, Miami Beach, April 1971. (b)
Brigham, J. C., Woodmansee, J. C., & Cook, S. W. Dimensions of verbal racial attitudes: Interracial marriage and approaches to Negro progress, 1972, in press.
Britannica Book of the Year, State Statistical Survey. Chicago: Encyclopedia Britannica, 1970.
Brody, G. F. Socioeconomic differences in stated maternal child-rearing practices and in observed maternal behavior. *Journal of Marriage and the Family*, 1968, **30,** 656–660.
Bromley, D. D., & Britten, F. H. *Youth and sex: A study of 1300 college students*. New York: Harper, 1938.
Bronfenbrenner, U. Socialization and social class through time and space. In E. E. Maccoby, T. M. Newcomb, and E. L. Hartley (Eds.), *Readings in social psychology*. (3rd ed.) New York: Holt, 1958. Pp. 400–425.
Bronfenbrenner, U. The changing American child—a speculative analysis. In N. Smelser and W. Smelser (Eds.), *Personality and social systems*. New York: Wiley, 1963. Pp. 347–356.
Bronfenbrenner, U. *Two worlds of childhood U.S. and U.S.S.R.* New York: Russell Sage Foundation, 1970.
Brown, B. R. The effects of need to maintain face on interpersonal bargaining. *Journal of Experimental Social Psychology*, 1968, **4,** 107–122.
Brown, B. R. Saving face. *Psychology Today*, 1971, **4**(12), 55–59ff.
Brown, J. A. C. *Techniques of persuasion: From propaganda to brainwashing*. Baltimore, Md.: Penguin, 1963.
Brown, J. S. *The motivation of behavior*. New York: McGraw-Hill, 1961.
Brown, J. S., & Farber, I. E. Emotions conceptualized as intervening variables—with suggestions toward a theory of frustration. *Psychological Bulletin*, 1951, **48,** 465–495.
Brown, L. F. Book review of Sigmund Freud and William C. Bullitt's *Thomas Woodrow Wilson*. *Book of the Month Club News*, January 1967, 8.
Brown, P., & Elliott, R. Control of aggression in a nursery-school class. *Journal of Experimental Child Psychology*, 1965, **2,** 103–107.
Brown, R. *Words and things*. New York: Free Press, 1958.
Brown, R. *Social psychology*. New York: Free Press, 1965.
Brown, R. M. Historical patterns of violence in America. In H. D. Graham and T. R. Gurr (Eds.), *Violence in America*. New York: New American Library, 1969. Pp. 43–80.
Brownmiller, S. The new feminism. *Current*, April 1970, 28–39.
Bruce, M. Factors affecting intelligence test performance of whites and Negroes in the rural South. *Archives of Psychology*, 1940, No. 252.
Bruner, J. S., & Goodman, C. C. Value and need as organizing factors in perception. *Journal of Abnormal and Social Psychology*, 1947, **42,** 33–44.
Bruvold, W. H. Are beliefs and behavior consistent with attitudes? A preliminary restatement and some evidence from a survey research project. Paper presented at the meeting of the Western Psychological Association, Los Angeles, April 1970.
Bryan, J. H. Children's reactions to helpers: Their money isn't where their mouths are. In J. Macaulay and L. Berkowitz (Eds.), *Altruism and helping behavior*. New York: Academic Press, 1970. Pp. 61–76.
Bryan, J. H., & Schwartz, T. Effects of film material upon children's behavior. *Psychological Bulletin*, 1971, **75,** 50–59.
Bryan, J. H., & Test, M. Models and helping: Naturalistic studies in aiding behavior. *Journal of Personality and Social Psychology*, 1967, **6,** 400–407.

Buchanan, W., & Cantril, H. *How nations see each other*. Urbana, Ill.: University of Illinois Press, 1953.
Buck, J. F. The effects of Negro and white dialectal variations upon attitudes of college students. *Speech Monographs,* 1968, **35,** 181–186.
Buck, P. Roll away the stone. In E. Murrow (Ed.), *This I believe*. Vol. 1. New York: Simon & Schuster, 1952.
Buechner, H. K. Territorial behavior in the Uganda kob. *Science,* 1961, **133,** 698–699.
Buechner, H. K. Territoriality as a behavioral adaptation to environment in the Uganda kob. *Proceedings of the XVI International Congress of Zoology*, 1963, **3,** 59–62.
Bureau of the Census, U. S. Department of Commerce. U. S. population, 1790–2000. Cited in F. Pullara, Trends in U. S. population. *Federationist,* June 1970, p. 10.
Burgess, T. D. G., Jr., & Sales, S. M. Attitudinal effects of "mere exposure": A re-evaluation. *Journal of Experimental Social Psychology,* 1971, **7,** 461–472.
Burma, J. H. The measurement of Negro "passing." *American Journal of Sociology,* 1946, **52,** 18–22.
Burt, C. The evidence for the concept of intelligence. *British Journal of Educational Psychology,* 1955, **25,** 158–177.
Burt, C. The inheritance of mental ability. *American Psychologist,* 1958, **13,** 1–15.
Burton, R. V. Generality of honesty reconsidered. *Psychological Review,* 1963, **70,** 481–499.
Buss, A. *The psychology of aggression.* New York: Wiley, 1961.
Buss, A. Physical aggression in relation to different frustrations. *Journal of Abnormal and Social Psychology,* 1963, **67,** 1–7.
Butterfield, D. A. An integrative approach to the study of leadership effectiveness in organizations. Unpublished doctoral dissertation, University of Michigan, 1968.
Buxhoeveden, S. *The life and tragedy of Alexandra Feodorovna, Empress of Russia: A biography.* New York and London: Longmans-Greene, 1930.
Byrne, D. Repression-sensitization as a dimension of personality. In B. A. Maher (Ed.), *Progress in experimental personality research.* Vol. I. New York: Academic Press, 1964. Pp. 169–220.
Byrne, D. Attitudes and attraction. In L. Berkowitz (Ed.), *Advances in experimental social psychology.* Vol. 4. New York: Academic Press, 1969.
Byrne, D. *The attraction paradigm.* New York: Academic Press, 1971.
Byrne, D., & Rhamey, R. Magnitude of positive and negative reinforcements as a determinant of attraction. *Journal of Personality and Social Psychology,* 1965, **2,** 884–889.
Byrne, D., & Wong, T. J. Racial prejudice, interpersonal attraction, and assumed dissimilarity of attitudes. *Journal of Abnormal and Social Psychology,* 1962, **65,** 246–253.
Cabanac, M., & Duclaux, R. Obesity: Absence of satiety aversion to sucrose. *Science,* 1970, **168,** 496–497.
Cahalan, D. *Problem drinkers.* San Francisco: Jossey-Bass, 1970.
Cahalan, D., Cisin, I. H., & Crossley, H. American drinking practices. Monograph No. 6, Rutgers Center of Alcohol Studies, New Brunswick, N. J., 1969.
Calhoun, J. B. Population density and social pathology. *Scientific American,* 1962, **206,** 139–148.
Calvin, A. Social reinforcement. *Journal of Social Psychology,* 1962, **56,** 15–19.
Campbell, A., Gurin, G., & Miller, W. E. *The voter decides.* New York: Harper & Row, 1954.
Campbell, A., & Schuman, H. *Racial attitudes in fifteen American cities.* Ann Arbor: Institute for Social Research, University of Michigan, 1968.
Campbell, D. T. The generality of a social attitude. Unpublished doctoral dissertation, University of California, 1947.
Campbell, D. T. Social attitudes and other acquired behavioral dispositions. In S. Koch (Ed.), *Psychology: A study of a science.* Vol. 6. New York: McGraw-Hill, 1963.
Campbell, D. T. Reforms as experiments. *American Psychologist,* 1969, **24,** 409–429.
Campbell, D. T., & Fiske, D. W. Convergent and discriminant validation by the multitrait multimethod matrix. *Psychological Bulletin,* 1959, **56,** 81–105.
Campbell, D. T., & McCandless, B. R. Ethnocentrism, xenophobia, and personality. *Human Relations,* 1951, **4,** 185–192.
Campbell, D. T., Siegman, C., & Rees, M. B. Direction-of-wording effects in the relationships between scales. *Psychological Bulletin,* 1967, **68,** 293–303.

Campbell, D. T., & Stanley, J. C. *Experimental and quasiexperimental designs for research.* Chicago: Rand McNally, 1966.
Cannavale, F. J., Scarr, H. A., & Pepitone, A. Deindividuation in the small group: Further evidence. *Journal of Personality and Social Psychology,* 1970, **16,** 141–147.
Cannell, C. F., & Kahn, R. L. Interviewing. In G. Lindzey and E. Aronson (Eds.), *Handbook of social psychology.* Vol. 2. (2nd ed.) Reading, Mass.: Addison-Wesley, 1968. Pp. 526–595.
Caplan, N. The new ghetto man: A review of recent empirical studies. *Journal of Social Issues,* 1970, **26**(1), 59–73.
Caplan, N. S., & Paige, J. M. A study of ghetto rioters. *Scientific American,* 1968, **219**(2), 15–21.
Caplow, T. *Two against one: Coalitions in triads.* Englewood Cliffs, N. J.: Prentice-Hall, 1968.
Capra, P. C., & Dittes, J. E. Birth order as a selective factor among volunteer subjects. *Journal of Abnormal and Social Psychology,* 1962, **64,** 302.
Carlsmith, J. M., Collins, B. E., & Helmreich, R. L. Studies in forced compliance: I. The effect of pressure for compliance on attitude change produced by face-to-face role playing and anonymous essay writing. *Journal of Personality and Social Psychology,* 1966, **4,** 1–13.
Carlsson, G. Social class, intelligence, and the verbal factor. *Acta Psychologia,* 1955, **11,** 269–278.
Carmichael, S. & Hamilton, C. V. *Black power: The politics of liberation in America.* New York: Random House, 1967.
Carstairs, G. M. Overcrowding and human aggression. In H. D. Graham and T. R. Gurr (Eds.), *Violence in America.* New York: New American Library, 1969. Pp. 730–742.
Carter, J. H. Military leadership. *Military Review,* 1952, **32,** 14–18.
Carthy, J. D., & Ebling, F. J. (Eds.) *The natural history of aggression.* New York: Academic Press, 1964.
Cartwright, D., & Zander, A. Leadership and group performance: Introduction. In D. Cartwright and A. Zander (Eds.), *Group dynamics.* (2nd ed.) New York: Row-Peterson, 1960. Pp. 487–510.
Cazden, C. B. Subcultural differences in child language: An interdisciplinary review. *Merrill-Palmer Quarterly,* 1966, **12,** 185–219.
Cazden, C. B. Three sociolinguistic views of the language and speech of lower class children—with special attention to the work of Basil Bernstein. *Developmental Medicine and Child Neurology,* 1968, **10,** 600–612.
Chapanis, N. P., & Chapanis, A. C. Cognitive dissonance: Five years later. *Psychological Bulletin,* 1964, **61,** 1–22.
Chein, I. The image of man. *Journal of Social Issues,* 1962, **18**(4), 1–35.
Chesler, M., & Schmuck, R. Social psychological characteristics of superpatriots. In R. A. Schoenberger (Ed.), *The American right wing.* New York: Holt, 1969.
Child, I. *Italian or American? The second generation in conflict.* New Haven: Yale University Press, 1943.
Child, I. L., Storm, T., & Veroff, J. Achievement themes in folk tales related to socialization practice. In J. W. Atkinson (Ed.), *Motives in fantasy, action, and society.* Princeton, N.J.: Van Nostrand, 1958. Pp. 479–492.
Christensen, H. T., & Gregg, C. F. Changing sex norms in America and Scandinavia. *Journal of Marriage and the Family,* 1970, **32,** 616–627.
Christian Century. Painter case has happy ending. September 18, 1968. Pp. 1162–1163.
Christie, R. Eysenck's treatment of the personality of Communists. *Psychological Bulletin,* 1956, **53,** 411–430.
Christie, R. Scale construction. In R. Christie and F. L. Geis (Eds.), *Studies in Machiavellianism.* New York: Academic Press, 1970. Pp. 10–34.
Christie, R., & Cook, P. A guide to the published literature relating to the authoritarian personality through 1956. *Journal of Psychology,* 1958, **45,** 171–199.
Christie, R., & Geis, F. L. (Eds.) *Studies in Machiavellianism.* New York: Academic Press, 1970.
Christie, R., Havel, J., & Seidenberg, B. Is the F Scale irreversible? *Journal of Abnormal and Social Psychology,* 1958, **56,** 143–159.
Christie, R., & Jahoda, M. (Eds.) *Studies in the scope and the method of "The authoritarian personality."* New York: Free Press, 1954.

Clark, A. D., & Richards, C. J. Auditory discrimination among economically disadvantaged and nondisadvantaged preschool children. *Exceptional Children,* 1966, **33,** 259–262.
Clark, D. H., Lesser, G. S., & Fifer, G. Mental abilities of young children from different cultural and social class backgrounds. Paper presented at the meeting of the American Psychological Association, Los Angeles, September 1964.
Clark, K. B. *Dark Ghetto.* New York: Harper & Row, 1965.
Clark, R. D., III. Group induced shift toward risk: A critical appraisal. *Psychological Bulletin,* 1971, **76,** 251–270.
Clark, R. D., III, Crockett, W. H., & Archer, R. L. The relationship between perception of self, others, and the risky shift. *Journal of Personality and Social Psychology,* 1971, **20,** 425–429.
Clark, R. D., III, & Willems, E. P. Risk preferences as related to judged consequences of failure. *Psychological Reports,* 1969, **25,** 827–830. (a)
Clark, R. D., III, & Willems, E. P. Where is the risky shift? Dependence on instructions. *Journal of Personality and Social Psychology,* 1969, **13,** 215–221. (b)
Clark, R. D., III, & Willems, E. P. The risky-shift phenomenon: The diffusion-of-responsibility hypothesis or the risk-as-value hypothesis. Paper presented at the meeting of the Southwestern Psychological Association, St. Louis, April 1970.
Clark, R. D., III, & Willems, E. P. Two interpretations of Brown's hypothesis for the risky shift. *Psychological Bulletin,* 1972, in press.
Clark, R. D., III, & Word, L. E. A case where the bystander did help. Paper presented at the meeting of the Eastern Psychological Association, New York, April 1971.
Cline, V. B. Interpersonal perception. In B. A. Maher (Ed.), *Progress in experimental personality research.* Vol. 1. New York: Academic Press, 1964. Pp. 221–284.
Cline, V. B., & Richards, J. M., Jr. Accuracy of interpersonal perception—a general trait? *Journal of Abnormal and Social Psychology,* 1960, **60,** 1–7.
Cloward, R. A., & Ohlin, L. E. *Delinquency and opportunity.* New York: Free Press, 1960.
Cobb, W. M. The physical constitution of the American Negro. *Journal of Negro Education,* 1934, **3,** 340–388.
Cobb, W. M. Race and runners. *Journal of Health and Physical Education,* 1936, **7,** 3–7; 52–56.
Cohen, A. R. *Attitude change and social influence.* New York: Basic Books, 1964.
Coleman, J., Campbell, E., Hobson, C., McPartland, J., Mood, A., Weinfield, F., & York, R. *Equality of educational opportunity.* Washington, D.C.: U.S. Gov't. Printing Office, 1966.
Collins, B. E. Attribution theory analysis of forced compliance. *Proceedings, 77th Annual Convention,* American Psychological Association, 1969, **4,** 309–310.
Collins, B. E. *Social psychology.* Reading, Mass.: Addison-Wesley, 1970.
Commission on Obscenity and Pornography. *The report of the Commission on Obscenity and Pornography.* New York: Bantam Books, 1970.
Cook, S. W. Desegregation: A psychological analysis. *American Psychologist,* 1957, **12,** 1–13.
Cook, S. W. An experimental analysis of attitude change in a natural social setting. Small contract proposal submitted to U.S. Commissioner on Education, July 1964.
Cook, S. W. Motives in a conceptual analysis of attitude-related behavior. In W. J. Arnold and D. Levine (Eds.), *Nebraska symposium on motivation, 1969.* Lincoln, Nebr.: University of Nebraska Press, 1970. Pp. 179–231.
Cook, S. W. The effect of unintended racial contact upon racial interaction and attitude change. Final report, Project No. 5-1320, Contract No. OEC-4-7-051320-0273. Washington, D.C.: U.S. Office of Education, Bureau of Research, August 1971.
Cook, S. W., & Selltiz, C. A. Multiple-indicator approach to attitude measurement. *Psychological Bulletin,* 1964, **62,** 36–55.
Cook, S. W., & Wrightsman, L. S. The factorial structure of "positive attitudes toward people." Symposium paper given at the meeting of the Southeastern Psychological Association, Atlanta, Ga., April 1967.
Cook, T. D., Bean, J. R., Calder, B. J., Frey, R., Krovotz, M. L., & Reisman, S. R. Demand characteristics and three conceptions of the frequently deceived subject. *Journal of Personality and Social Psychology,* 1970, **14,** 185–194.
Coon, C. S. *The origin of races.* New York: Knopf, 1962.
Cooper, J. B. Prejudicial attitudes and the identification of their stimulus objects: A phenomenological approach. *Journal of Social Psychology,* 1958, **48,** 15–23.

Costanzo, P. R. Conformity development as a function of self-blame. *Journal of Personality and Social Psychology,* 1970, **14,** 366–374.
Couch, A., & Keniston, K. Yeasayers and naysayers: Agreeing response set as a personality variable. *Journal of Abnormal and Social Psychology,* 1960, **60,** 151–174.
Coulter, T. An experimental and statistical study of the relationship of prejudice and certain personality variables. Unpublished doctoral dissertation, University of London, 1953.
Cox, O. C. *Caste, class, and race.* New York: Doubleday, 1948.
Crancer, A., Jr., Dille, J. M., Delay, J. C., Wallace, J. E., & Haykin, M. D. Comparison of the effects of marihuana and alcohol on simulated driving performance. *Science,* 1969, **164,** 851–854.
Crombag, H. F. Cooperation and competition in means-interdependent triads. *Journal of Personality and Social Psychology,* 1966, **4,** 692–695.
Cronbach, L. J. Processes affecting scores on "understanding of others" and "assumed similarity." *Psychological Bulletin,* 1955, **52,** 177–193.
Cronbach, L. J. The two disciplines of scientific psychology. *American Psychologist,* 1957, **12,** 671–684.
Cronbach, L. J. Proposals leading to analytic treatment of social perception scores. In R. Tagiuri and L. Petrullo (Eds.), *Person perception and interpersonal behavior.* Stanford, Calif.: Stanford University Press, 1958. Pp. 353–379.
Crook, J. H. The nature and function of territorial aggression. In M. F. A. Montagu (Ed.), *Man and aggression.* New York: Oxford University Press, 1968. Pp. 141–178.
Cross, K. Is there a generation gap? *Journal of the National Association of Women Deans and Counselors,* 1968, **31,** 53–56.
Crow, W. J. The effect of training upon accuracy and variability in interpersonal perception. *Journal of Abnormal and Social Psychology,* 1957, **55,** 355–359.
Crow, W. J., & Hammond, K. R. The generality of accuracy and response sets in interpersonal perception. *Journal of Abnormal and Social Psychology,* 1957, **54,** 384–390.
Crutchfield, R. S. Conformity and character. *American Psychologist,* 1955, **10,** 191–198.
Curry, T. J., & Emerson, R. M. Balance theory: A theory of interpersonal attraction? *Sociometry,* 1970, **33,** 216–238.
Cushna, B. Agency and birth-order differences in very early childhood. Paper presented at the meeting of the American Psychological Association, New York, September 1966.
Cyert, R. M., & MacCrimmon, K. R. Organizations. In G. Lindzey and E. Aronson (Eds.), *Handbook of social psychology.* Vol. 1. (2nd ed.) Reading, Mass.: Addison-Wesley, 1968. Pp. 568–611.
Darley, J. M., & Latané, B. Bystander intervention in emergencies: Diffusion of responsibility. *Journal of Personality and Social Psychology,* 1968, **8,** 377–383. (a)
Darley, J. M., & Latané, B. When will people help in a crisis? *Psychology Today,* 1968, **2**(7), 54–57; 70–71. (b)
Darsie, M. L. Mental capacity of American-born Japanese children. *Comparative Psychology Monographs,* 1926, **15,** No. 3.
Darwin, C. *The expression of the emotions in man and animals.* London: J. Murray, 1872.
Davé, R. H. The identification and measurement of environmental process variables that are related to educational achievement. Unpublished doctoral dissertation, University of Chicago, 1963.
Davenport, R. K. Implications of military selection and classification in relation to universal military training. *Journal of Negro Education,* 1946, **15,** 585–594.
Davie, M. R. *Negroes in American society.* New York: McGraw-Hill, 1949.
Davies, J. C. Toward a theory of revolution. *American Sociological Review,* 1962, **27,** 5–19.
Davies, J. C. The J-curve of rising and declining satisfactions as a cause of some great revolutions and a contained rebellion. In H. D. Graham and T. R. Gurr (Eds.), *Violence in America.* New York: New American Library, 1969. Pp. 671–709.
Davis, A. J. Sexual assaults in the Philadelphia prison system and sheriffs' vans. *Trans-Action,* 1968, **6,** 8–16.
Davis, E. A. *The development of linguistic skills in twins, singletons with siblings, and only children from ages five to ten years.* Minneapolis, Minn.: University of Minnesota Press, 1937.

Davis, F. B., Lesser, G. S., & French, E. G. Identification and classroom behavior of gifted elementary school children. *Cooperative Research Monographs,* 1960, No. 2.
Davis, K. E. A social-psychological analysis of drug use. Unpublished manuscript, Rutgers University, 1971.
Davitz, J. R. The effects of previous training on postfrustration behavior. *Journal of Abnormal and Social Psychology,* 1952, **47,** 309–315.
Day, C. B. *A study of some Negro-white families in the United States.* Cambridge, Mass.: Harvard African Studies, 1932. P. 10.
deCharms, R. C. *Personal causation: The internal affective determinants of behavior.* New York: Academic Press, 1968.
deCharms, R. C., Morrison, H., Reitman, W. R., & McClelland, D. C. Behavioral correlates of directly measured achievement motivation. In D. C. McClelland (Ed.), *Studies in motivation.* New York: Appleton-Century-Crofts, 1955. Pp. 414–423.
DeFleur, M. L., & Westie, F. R. Verbal attitudes and overt acts: An experiment on the salience of attitudes. *American Sociological Review,* 1958, **23,** 667–673.
Deutsch, M. A theory of cooperation and competition. *Human Relations,* 1949, **2,** 129–152. (a)
Deutsch, M. An experimental study of the effects of cooperation and competition upon group process. *Human Relations,* 1949, **2**, 196–231. (b)
Deutsch, M. The effect of motivational orientation upon threat and suspicion. *Human Relations,* 1960, **13,** 123–139.
Deutsch, M. Field theory in social psychology. In G. Lindzey and E. Aronson (Eds.), *Handbook of social psychology.* Vol. I. (2nd ed.) Reading, Mass.: Addison-Wesley, 1968. Pp. 412–487.
Deutsch, M. Socially relevant science: Reflections on some studies of interpersonal conflict. *American Psychologist,* 1969, **24,** 1076–1092.
Deutsch, M., and associates. (Eds.) *The disadvantaged child.* New York: Basic Books, 1967.
Deutsch, M. & Collins, M. *Interracial housing: A psychological evaluation of a social experiment.* Minneapolis, Minn.: University of Minnesota Press, 1951.
Deutsch, M., & Gerard, H. A study of normative and informational social influences on individual judgment. *Journal of Abnormal and Social Psychology,* 1955, **51,** 629–636.
Deutsch, M., & Krauss, R. M. The effect of threat on interpersonal bargaining. *Journal of Abnormal and Social Psychology,* 1960, **61,** 181–189.
Deutsch, M., & Krauss, R. M. Studies of interpersonal bargaining. *Journal of Conflict Resolution,* 1962, **6,** 52–76.
Deutsch, M., & Krauss, R. M. *Theories in social psychology.* New York: Basic Books, 1965.
Deutsch, M., Maliver, A., Brown, B., & Cherry, E. *Communication of information in the elementary school classroom.* New York: Institute for Developmental Studies, 1964.
Dion, K. L., Baron, R. S., & Miller, N. Why do groups make riskier decisions than individuals? In L. Berkowitz (Ed.), *Advances in experimental social psychology.* Vol. 5. New York: Academic Press, 1970. Pp. 305–377.
Dion, K. L., & Miller, N. The risky-shift: True or pseudo group effect? Unpublished manuscript, University of Minnesota, 1969.
Dishotsky, N. I., Loughman, W. D., Mogar, R. E., & Lipscomb, W. R. LSD and genetic damage. *Science,* 1971, **172,** 431–440.
Dollard, J., Doob, L. W., Miller, N. E., Mowrer, O. H., & Sears, R. R. *Frustration and aggression.* New Haven: Yale University Press, 1939.
Dollard, J., & Miller, N. E. *Personality and psychotherapy.* New York: McGraw-Hill, 1950.
Doniger, S. (Ed.) *The nature of man.* New York: Harper, 1962.
Donley, R. E., & Winter, D. G. Measuring the motives of public officials at a distance: An exploratory study of American presidents. *Behavioral Science,* 1970, **15,** 227–236.
Douvan, E. A., & Adelson, J. *The adolescent experience.* New York: Wiley, 1966.
Doyle, C. Psychology, science, and the western democratic tradition. Unpublished doctoral dissertation, University of Michigan, 1965.
Doyle, C. An empirical study of the attitudes of psychologists and other scientists and humanists toward science, freedom, and related issues. Paper presented at the meeting of the American Psychological Association, New York, September 1966.

Dreger, R. M., & Miller, K. S. Comparative psychological studies of Negroes and whites in the United States. *Psychological Bulletin,* 1960, **57,** 361–402.
Dreger, R. M., & Miller, K. S. Comparative psychological studies of Negroes and whites in the United States: 1959–1965. *Psychological Bulletin,* Monograph Supplement 1968, 70, No. 3, Part 2.
Driscoll, J. P. Transsexuals. *Trans-Action,* 1971, **8,** 28–37; 66–68.
Driscoll, R. H., & Davis, K. E. Sexual restraints: A comparison of perceived and self-reported reasons for college students. *Journal of Sex Research,* 1971, **7**(4), 253–262.
Driscoll, R., Davis, K. E., & Lipetz, M. E. Parental interference and romantic love: The Romeo and Juliet effect. Unpublished manuscript, University of Colorado, 1971.
Driver, M. J., Streufert, S., & Nataupsky, M. Effects of immediate and remote incongruity experience on response to dissonant information. *Proceedings, 77th Annual Convention,* American Psychological Association, 1969, **4,** 323–324.
DuBois, P. H. A test standardized on Pueblo Indian children. *Psychological Bulletin,* 1939, **36,** 523.
Duffy, J. F. A field extension of Fielder's contingency model. Unpublished master's thesis, Iowa State University of Science and Technology, 1970.
Duffy, J. F., Kavanagh, M. J., MacKinney, A. C., Wolins, L., & Lyons, T. F. A field extension of Fie er's contingency model. Paper presented at the meeting of the Midwestern Psychological Association, Cincinnati, April 1970.
Dulaney, D. E., Jr. Avoidance learning of perceptual defense and vigilance. *Journal of Abnormal and Social Psychology,* 1957, **55,** 333–338.
Dunn, L. C., & Dobzhansky, T. *Heredity, race, and society.* (Rev. ed.) New York: New American Library, 1952.
Dunn, R. E., & Goldman, M. Competition and noncompetition in relation to satisfaction and feelings toward group and nongroup members. *Journal of Social Psychology,* 1966, **68,** 299–311.
Dunnette, M. D. Forms of interpersonal accommodation: Processes, problems, and research avenues. Paper presented at the meeting of the American Psychological Association, New York, September 1968.
Durkin, J. E. Moment of truth encounters in the Prisoner's Dilemma. Paper presented at the meeting of the American Psychological Association, Washington, D.C., September 1967.
Eaton, J. W., & Weil, R. J. *Culture and mental disorders.* New York: Free Press, 1955.
Edwards, A. L. *Manual for the Edwards Personal Preference Schedule.* New York: Psychological Corporation, 1953.
Edwards, A. L. The assessment of human motives by means of personality scales. In D. Levine (Ed.), *Nebraska symposium on motivation, 1964.* Vol. 12. Lincoln, Nebr.: University of Nebraska Press, 1964. Pp. 135–162.
Ehrlich, D. Determinants of verbal commonality and influenceability. Unpublished doctoral dissertation, University of Minnesota, 1958.
Ehrlich, D., Guttman, I., Schönbach, P., & Mills, J. Post decision exposure to relevant information. *Journal of Abnormal and Social Psychology,* 1957, **54,** 98–102.
Ehrlich, H. J. Dogmatism and learning. *Journal of Abnormal and Social Psychology,* 1961, **62,** 148–149. (a)
Ehrlich, H. J. Dogmatism and learning: A five year follow-up. *Psychological Reports,* 1961, **9,** 283–286. (b)
Ehrlich, H. J., & Lee, D. Dogmatism, learning, and resistance to change: A review and a new paradigm. *Psychological Bulletin,* 1969, **71,** 249–260.
Ehrmann, W. *Premarital dating behavior.* New York: Holt, Rinehart, & Winston, 1959.
Eichenwald, H. F., & Fry, P. C. Nutrition and learning. *Science,* 1969, **163,** 644–648.
Einstein, S. *The use and misuse of drugs.* Belmont, Calif.: Wadsworth, 1970.
Eisenberg, L., Berlin, C. I., Dill, A., & Frank, S. Class and race effects on the intelligibility of monosyllables. *Child Development,* 1968, **39,** 1077–1089.
Ekman, P. A comparison of verbal and nonverbal behavior as reinforcing stimuli of opinion responses. Unpublished doctoral dissertation, Adelphi College, 1958.
Ellis, D. S. Speech and social status in America. *Social Forces,* 1967, **45,** 431–437.
Ellis, H. *Studies in the psychology of sex.* New York: Random House, published in seven parts, 1897–1928.
Elms, A. C. Right wingers in Dallas. *Psychology Today,* 1970, **3**(9), 27–31; 58–59.

Elms, A. C., & Milgram, S. Personality characteristics associated with obedience and defiance toward authoritative command. *Journal of Experimental Research in Personality,* 1966, **1,** 282–289.
Encyclopedia Britannica. Gregory Efimovitch Rasputin. Vol. 18. Chicago: Encyclopedia Britannica, 1957. Pp. 988–989.
Entwisle, D. R. Developmental sociolinguistics: A comparative study in four subcultural settings. *Sociometry,* 1966, **29,** 67–84.
Entwisle, D. R. Developmental sociolinguistics: Inner-city children. *American Journal of Sociology,* 1968, **74,** 37–46.
Epps, E. G. Correlates of academic achievement among northern and southern urban Negro students. *Journal of Social Issues,* 1969, **25**(3), 55–70.
Epstein, R. & Komorita, S. S. The development of a scale of parental punitiveness toward aggression. *Child Development,* 1965, **19,** 129–142. (a)
Epstein, R., & Komorita, S. S. Parental discipline, stimulus characteristics of outgroups, and social distance in children. *Journal of Personality and Social Psychology,* 1965, **2,** 416–420. (b)
Epstein, R., & Komorita, S. S. Prejudice among Negro children as related to parental ethnocentrism and punitiveness. *Journal of Personality and Social Psychology,* 1966, **4,** 643–647.
Erikson, E. H. *Childhood and society.* New York: Norton, 1950. (2nd ed., 1963)
Erikson, E. H. Identity and the life cycle. *Psychological Issues,* 1959, **1,** 18–164.
Erikson, E. H. (Ed.) *Youth: Change and challenge.* New York: Basic Books, 1963.
Erikson, E. H. *Insight and responsibility.* New York: Norton, 1964.
Erlich, J., & Riesman, D. Age and authority in the interview. *Public Opinion Quarterly,* 1961, **25,** 39–56.
Eron, L. D. Relationship of TV viewing habits and aggressive behavior in children. *Journal of Abnormal and Social Psychology,* 1963, **67,** 193–196.
Ervin-Tripp, S. M. Sociolinguistics. In L. Berkowitz (Ed.), *Advances in experimental social psychology.* Vol. 4. New York: Academic Press, 1969. Pp. 91–165.
Esman, A. Toward an understanding of racism. *Psychiatry and Social Science Review,* 1970, **4,** 7–9.
Esselstyn, T. C. Prostitution in the United States. In a special issue on "Sex and the contemporary American scene," *Annals of the American Academy of Political and Social Science,* 1968.
Etzioni, A. A model of significant research. *International Journal of Psychiatry,* 1968, **6,** 279–280.
Eurich, A. (Ed.) *Campus 1980. The shape of the future in American higher education.* New York: Dell, 1968.
Evans, R. B. Childhood parental relationships of homosexual men. *Journal of Consulting and Clinical Psychology,* 1969, **33,** 129–135.
Evans, R. I. *Dialogue with Erik Erikson.* New York: Dutton, 1969.
Exline, R. V., Thibaut, J., Hickey, C. O., & Gumpert, P. Visual interaction in relation to Machiavellianism and an unethical act. In R. Christie and F. L. Geis (Eds.), *Studies in Machiavellianism.* New York: Academic Press, 1970. Pp. 53–75.
Fanon, F. *The wretched of the earth.* New York: Grove Press, 1965.
Farb, P. The American Indian: A portrait in limbo. *Saturday Review,* October 12, 1968, 26–29.
Farber, G. *The student as nigger.* New York: Pocket Books, 1969.
Fawl, C. L. Disturbances experienced by children in their natural habitats. In R. G. Barker (Ed.), *The stream of behavior.* New York: Appleton-Century-Crofts, 1963. Pp. 99–126.
Fay, A. S. The effects of cooperation and competition on learning and recall. Unpublished master's thesis, George Peabody College, 1970.
Feather, N. T. Cognitive dissonance, sensitivity, and evaluation. *Journal of Abnormal and Social Psychology,* 1963, **66,** 157–163.
Feldman, R. E. Response to compatriot and foreigner who seeks assistance. *Journal of Personality and Social Psychology,* 1968, **10,** 202–214.
Feldman, S. (Ed.) *Cognitive consistency: Motivational antecedents and behavioral consequents.* New York: Academic Press, 1966.
Felknor, C., & Harvey, O. J. Cognitive determinants of concept formation and attainment. Technical Report No. 10, Contract with Office of Naval Research (Nonr 1147), University of Colorado, 1968.

Fendrich, J. M. A study of the association among verbal attitudes, commitment, and overt behavior in different experimental situations. *Social Forces,* 1967, **45,** 347–355.

Fenichel, O. *The psychoanalytic theory of neurosis.* New York: Norton, 1945.

Ferguson, G. O., Jr. The intelligence of Negroes at Camp Lee, Virginia. *School and Society,* 1919, **9,** 721–726.

Feshbach, S. Film violence and its effects on children: Some comments on the implications of research for public policy. American Psychological Association address, Washington, D. C., 1969.

Feshbach, S., & Singer, R. D. The effects of personal and shared threats upon social prejudice. *Journal of Abnormal and Social Psychology,* 1957, **54,** 411–416.

Feshbach, S. & Singer, R. D. *Television and aggression.* San Francisco: Jossey-Bass, 1970.

Festinger, L. An analysis of compliant behavior. In M. Sherif and M. O. Wilson (Eds.), *Group relations at the crossroads.* New York: Harper & Row, 1953. Pp. 232–256. (a)

Festinger, L. Laboratory experiments. In L. Festinger and D. Katz (Eds.), *Research methods in the behavioral sciences.* New York: Dryden, 1953. Pp. 136–172. (b)

Festinger, L. A theory of social comparison processes. *Human Relations,* 1954, **7,** 117–140.

Festinger, L. *A theory of cognitive dissonance.* Stanford, Calif.: Stanford University Press, 1957.

Festinger, L. & Carlsmith, J. M. Cognitive consequences of forced compliance. *Journal of Abnormal and Social Psychology,* 1959, **58,** 203–210.

Festinger, L., & Katz, D. (Eds.) *Research methods in the behavioral sciences.* New York: Dryden, 1953.

Festinger, L., Pepitone, A., & Newcomb, T. Some consequences of deindividuation in a group. *Journal of Abnormal and Social Psychology,* 1952, **47,** 382–389.

Festinger, L., Riecken, H., & Schachter, S. *When prophecy fails.* Minneapolis, Minn.: University of Minnesota Press, 1956.

Festinger, L., Schachter, S., & Back, K. *Social pressures in informal groups: A study of human factors in housing.* New York: Harper, 1950.

Feuer, L. *The conflict of generations: The character and significance of student movements.* New York: Basic Books, 1969.

Fidell, L. Unpublished research reported in *Behavior Today,* 1970, **1**(4), 4.

Fiedler, F. E. A contingency model of leadership effectiveness. In L. Berkowitz (Ed.), *Advances in experimental social psychology.* Vol. I. New York: Academic Press, 1964. Pp. 149–190.

Fiedler, F. E. *A theory of leadership effectiveness.* New York: McGraw-Hill, 1967. (a)

Fiedler, F. E. Effect of intergroup competition on group member adjustment. *Personnel Psychology,* 1967, **20,** 30–44. (b)

Fiedler, F. E. Style or circumstance: The leadership enigma. *Psychology Today,* 1969, **2**(10), 38–43.

Fiedler, F. E. Validation and extension of the contingency model of leadership effectiveness: A review of empirical findings. *Psychological Bulletin,* 1971, **76,** 128–148.

Fishbein, M. The relationships between beliefs, attitudes, and behavior. In S. Feldman (Ed.), *Cognitive consistency.* New York: Academic Press, 1966.

Fishbein, M. The prediction of behavior from attitudinal variables. In K. K. Sereno and C. C. Mortensen (Eds.), *Advances in communication research.* New York: Harper & Row, 1972, in press.

Fishbein, M., Landy, E., & Hatch, G. Some determinants of an individual's esteem for his least preferred co-worker: An attitudinal analysis. *Human Relations,* 1969, **22,** 173–188.

Flacks, R. The liberated generation: An exploration of the roots of student protest. *Journal of Social Issues,* 1967, **23**(3), 52–75.

Flacks, R. Young intelligentsia in revolt. *Trans-Action,* 1970, **7,** 47–55.

Flament, C. Influence sociale et perception. *Annee Psychologique,* 1958, **58,** 377–400.

Flament, C. Processus d'influence sociale et reseaux de communication. *Psychologie Francaise,* 1961, **6,** 115–125.

Flanders, J. P., & Thistlethwaite, D. L. Effects of familiarization and group discussion upon risk-taking. *Journal of Experimental Social Psychology,* 1967, **5,** 91–98.

Fleishman, E. A., Harris, E. F., & Burtt, H. E. *Leadership and supervision in industry.* Columbus: Ohio State University Press, 1955.

Ford, C. S., & Beach, F. A. *Patterns of sexual behavior.* New York: Harper & Row, 1970.
Forrester, B. J., & Klaus, R. A. The effect of race of the examiner on intelligence test scores of Negro kindergarten children. *Peabody Papers in Human Development,* 1964, **2**(7), 1–7.
Forsyth, S., & Kolenda, P. M. Competition, cooperation, and cohesion in the ballet company. *Psychiatry,* 1966, **29,** 123–145.
Fort, J. The pleasure seekers. *Mind over Matter,* 1970, **15**(1), 65–83.
Fortune, R. F. Arapesh warfare. *American Anthropologist,* 1939, **41,** 28.
Forward, J. R., & Williams, J. R. Internal-external control and black militancy. *Journal of Social Issues,* 1970, **26**(1), 75–92.
Foulds, G. A., & Raven, J. C. Intellectual ability and occupational grade. *Occupational Psychology,* London, 1948, **22,** 197–203.
Frank, J. D. *Sanity and survival: Psychological aspects of war and peace.* New York: Vintage, 1968.
Frank, L. K. *The conduct of sex.* New York: Morrow, 1961.
Freedman, J. L. How important is cognitive consistency? In R. P. Abelson et al. (Eds.), *Theories of cognitive consistency: A sourcebook.* Chicago: Rand-McNally, 1968. Pp. 497–503.
Freedman, J. L. The effects of crowding on human behavior. Paper presented at the meeting of the American Psychological Association, Miami Beach, September 1970.
Freedman, J. L., Carlsmith, J. M., & Sears, D. O. *Social psychology.* Englewood Cliffs, N.J.: Prentice-Hall, 1970.
Freedman, J. L., & Fraser, S. C. Compliance without pressure: The foot-in-the-door technique. *Journal of Personality and Social Psychology,* 1966, **4,** 196–202.
Freedman, J. L., Klevansky, S., & Ehrlich, P. R. The effect of crowding on human task performance. *Journal of Applied Social Psychology,* 1971, **1**(1), 7–25.
Freedman, J. L., & Sears, D. O. Selective exposure. In L. Berkowitz (Ed.), *Advances in experimental social psychology.* Vol. II. New York: Academic Press, 1965. Pp. 57–97.
Freeman, H. A., & Freeman, R. S. Senior college women: Their sexual standards and activity. *Journal of the National Association of Women Deans and Counselors,* 1966, **29**(3), 136–143.
French, J. R. P., Jr., & Coch, L. Overcoming resistance to change. *Human Relations,* 1948, **1,** 512–532.
Freud, E. L. (Ed.) *Letters to Sigmund Freud.* New York: Basic Books, 1960.
Freud, S. *Totem and taboo.* London: Hogarth Press, 1913.
Freud, S. *Civilization and its discontents.* London: Hogarth Press, 1930.
Freud, S. *Moses and monotheism.* London: Hogarth Press, 1939.
Freud, S. & Bullitt, W. C. *Thomas Woodrow Wilson.* Boston: Houghton-Mifflin, 1967.
Fried, M. H. The need to end the pseudoscientific investigation. In M. Mead et al. (Eds.), *Science and the concept of race.* New York: Columbia University Press, 1968. Pp. 122–131.
Friedan, B. *The feminine mystique.* New York: Norton, 1963.
Friedenberg, E. Z. Current patterns of generational conflict. *Journal of Social Issues,* 1969, **25,** 21–38.
Frijda, N. H. Recognition of emotion. In L. Berkowitz (Ed.), *Advances in experimental social psychology.* Vol. 4. New York: Academic Press, 1969. Pp. 167–223.
Fromkin, H. L., Klimoski, R. J., & Flanagan, M. F. Race and competence as determinants of acceptance of newcomers in success and failure work groups. Paper No. 279, Institute for Research in the Behavioral, Economic, and Management Sciences, Purdue University, May 1970.
Fromm, E. *Man for himself.* New York: Rinehart, 1955.
Fryer, D. Occupational intelligence standards. *School and Society,* 1922, **16,** 273–277.
Fuller, E. *Man in modern fiction.* New York: Vintage Books, 1958.
Gage, N. L. Judging interests from expressive behavior. *Psychological Monographs,* 1952, **66**(18, Whole No. 350).
Gage, N. L., & Cronbach, L. J. Conceptual and methodological problems in interpersonal perception. *Psychological Review,* 1955, **62,** 411–422.
Gage, N. L., Leavitt, G. S., & Stone, G. C. The psychological meaning of acquiescence set for authoritarianism. *Journal of Abnormal and Social Psychology,* 1957, **55,** 98–103.

Gallo, P. S. Prisoners of our own dilemma? Paper presented at the meeting of the Western Psychological Association, San Diego, March 1968.
Gallo, P. S., & McClintock, C. G. Cooperative and competitive behavior in mixed-motive games. *Journal of Conflict Resolution,* 1965, **9,** 68–78.
Galton, F. *Hereditary genius: An inquiry into its laws.* New York: Appleton, 1870. (Republished: New York; Horizon Press, 1952.)
Gardner, R. A., & Gardner, B. T. Teaching sign language to a chimpanzee. *Science,* 1969, **165,** 664–672.
Garrett, H. E. A note on the intelligence scores of Negroes and whites in 1918. *Journal of Abnormal and Social Psychology,* 1945, **40,** 344–346.
Garrett, H. E. Klineberg's chapter on race and psychology: A review. *Mankind Quarterly,* 1960, **1,** 15–22.
Garrett, H. E. The SPSSI and racial differences ("Comment" section). *American Psychologist,* 1962, **17,** 260–263.
Garrett, H. E. McGraw's need for denial ("Comment" section). *American Psychologist,* 1964, **19,** 815.
Garrett, H. E. A critical review of Thomas Pettigrew's *A profile of the Negro American.* Charlottesville, Va.: Author, 1965. 11 pp.
Garrett, H. E. Reply to Psychology Class 338 (Honors Section). *American Psychologist,* 1969, **24,** 390–391.
Garskof, M. H. (Ed.) *Roles women play: Readings toward women's liberation.* Belmont, Calif.: Brooks/Cole, 1971.
Garth, T. R., Schuelke, N., & Abell, W. The intelligence of mixed-blood Indians. *Journal of Applied Psychology,* 1927, **11,** 268–275.
Garvey, C., & McFarlane, P. A measure of standard English proficiency of inner-city children. *American Educational Research Journal,* 1970, **7,** 29–40.
Gay, J., & Cole, M. *The new mathematics and an old culture.* New York: Holt, 1967.
Geber, M. Développement psychomoteur de l'enfant africain. *Courrier,* Paris, UNESCO, 1956, **6,** 17–29.
Geber, M., & Dean, R. F. A. Development rates of African children in Uganda. *Lancet,* 1957, **272,** No. 6981, 1216–1219. (a)
Geber, M., & Dean, R. F. A. Gesell tests on African children. *Pediatrics,* 1957, **6,** 1056–1065. (b)
Geen, R. G., & Berkowitz, L. Name-mediated aggressive cue properties. *Journal of Personality,* 1966, **34,** 456–465.
Geen, R. G., & Berkowitz, L. Some conditions facilitating the occurrence of aggression after the observation of violence. *Journal of Personality,* 1967, **35,** 666–676.
Geen, R. G., & O'Neal, E. C. Activation of cue-elicited aggression by general arousal. *Journal of Personality and Social Psychology,* 1969, **11,** 289–292.
Geen, R. G., Rakosky, J. J., & O'Neal, E. C. Methodological study of measurement of aggression. *Psychological Reports,* 1968, **23,** 59–62.
Geis, F. L. Bargaining tactics in the Con Game. In R. Christie and F. L. Geis (Eds.), *Studies in Machiavellianism.* New York: Academic Press, 1970. Pp. 130–160.
Geis, F. L., Christie, R., & Nelson, C. In search of the Machiavel. In R. Christie and F. L. Geis (Eds.), *Studies of Machiavellianism.* New York: Academic Press, 1970. Pp. 76–95.
Gerard, H. B., & Mathewson, G. C. The effects of severity of initiation on liking for a group: A replication. *Journal of Experimental Social Psychology,* 1966, **2,** 278–287.
Gergen, K. J. *The psychology of behavior exchange.* Reading, Mass.: Addison-Wesley, 1969.
Gergen, K. J., & Marlowe, D. (Eds.) *Personality and social behavior.* Reading, Mass.: Addison-Wesley, 1970.
Geschwender, J. A. Social structure and the Negro revolt: An examination of some hypotheses. *Social Forces,* 1964, **43,** 248–256.
Gesell, A., Ilg, F. L., & Ames, L. B. *Youth: The years from ten to sixteen.* New York: Harper & Row, 1956.
Getzels, J. W., & Walsh, J. J. The method of paired direct and projective questionnaires in the study of attitude structure and socialization. *Psychological Monographs,* 1958, **72**(1, Whole No. 254).

Gibb, C. A. Leadership. In G. Lindzey and E. Aronson (Eds.), *Handbook of social psychology.* Vol. IV. (2nd ed.) Reading, Mass.: Addison-Wesley, 1969. Pp. 205–282.

Ginsburg, B. E., & Laughlin, W. S. The distribution of genetic differences in behavioral potential in the human species. In M. Mead et al. (Eds.), *Science and the concept of race.* New York: Columbia University Press, 1968. Pp. 26–36.

Glass, B. The genetic basis of human races. In M. Mead et al. (Eds.), *Science and the concept of race.* New York: Columbia University Press, 1968. Pp. 88–93.

Glass, B., & Li, C. C. The dynamics of racial intermixture: An analysis based on the American Negro. *American Journal of Human Genetics,* 1953, **5,** 1–20.

Glueck, S., & Glueck, E. *Delinquents and nondelinquents in perspective.* Cambridge, Mass.: Harvard University Press, 1968.

Goldberg, L. R. Diagnosticians vs. diagnostic signs: The diagnosis of psychosis vs. neurosis from the MMPI. *Psychological Monographs,* 1965, **79** (9, Whole No. 602).

Goldberg, L. R. Simple models or simple processes? Some research on clinical judgments. *American Psychologist,* 1968, **23,** 483–496.

Goldberg, L. R. Man versus model of man: A rationale, plus some evidence, for a method of improving on clinical inferences. *Psychological Bulletin,* 1970, **73,** 422–432.

Goldberg, P. Are women prejudiced against women? *Trans-Action,* 1968, **5,** 28–30.

Goldberg, S. C. Three situational determinants of conformity to social norms. *Journal of Abnormal and Social Psychology,* 1954, **49,** 325–329.

Golden, J. Roundtable: Marital discord and sex. *Medical Aspects of Human Sexuality,* 1971, **1,** 160–190.

Goldsmith, N. F. Women in science: Symposium and job mart. *Science,* 1970, **168,** 1124–1127.

Goldstein, J. W. Getting high in high school: The meaning of adolescent drug usage. Paper presented at the meeting of the American Educational Research Association, New York, February 1971. (a)

Goldstein, J. W. Motivations for psychoactive drug use among students. Paper presented at the meeting of the Eastern Psychological Association, New York, April 1971. (b)

Goode, E. Multiple drug use among marijuana smokers. *Social Problems,* 1969, **17,** 49–64.

Goode, W. The theoretical importance of love. *American Sociological Review,* 1959, **24,** 38–47.

Goodman, W. *The committee: The extraordinary career of the House Committee on Un-American Activities.* New York: Farrar, Straus, & Giroux, 1968.

Gordon, I. J. *Studying the child in school.* New York: Wiley, 1966.

Gorer, G. Ardrey on human nature: Animals, nations, imperatives. In M. F. A. Montagu (Ed.), *Man and aggression.* New York: Oxford University Press, 1968. Pp. 74–82. (a)

Gorer, G. Man has no "killer" instinct. In M. F. A. Montagu (Ed.), *Man and aggression.* New York: Oxford University Press, 1968. Pp. 27–36. (b)

Gossett, T. F. *Race: The history of an idea in America.* Dallas: Southern Methodist University Press, 1963.

Gough, H. G. *California Psychological Inventory manual.* Palo Alto, Calif.: Consulting Psychologists Press, 1957.

Gough, H. G. Clinical versus statistical prediction in psychology. In L. Postman (Ed.), *Psychology in the making.* New York: Knopf, 1962. Pp. 526–584.

Gouldner, A. W. The norm of reciprocity: A preliminary statement. *American Sociological Review,* 1960, **25,** 161–179.

Gouldner, A. W. *The coming crisis of Western sociology.* New York: Basic Books, 1970.

Graen, G., Alvares, K., Orris, J. B., & Martelle, J. A. Contingency model of leadership effectiveness: Antecedent and evidential results. *Psychological Bulletin,* 1970, **74,** 284–295.

Graham, H. D., & Gurr, T. R. (Eds.) *Violence in America.* New York: New American Library, 1969.

Graves, E. A. A study of competitive and cooperative behavior by the short sample technique. *Journal of Abnormal and Social Psychology,* 1937, **32,** 343–351.

Gray, S. W. The performance of the culturally deprived child: Contributing variables. Proceedings of Section II, Annual Professional Institute of the Division of School Psychologists, American Psychological Association, 1962. Pp. 30–36. (Mimeographed.)

Gray, S. W. Selected longitudinal studies of compensatory education—a look from the inside. Paper presented at the meeting of the American Psychological Association, Washington, D.C., September 1969.

Gray, S. W., & Klaus, R. A. An experimental preschool program for culturally deprived children. *Child Development,* 1965, **36,** 887–898.

Gray, S. W., & Klaus, R. A. The Early Training Project: A seventh year report. *Child Development,* 1970, **41,** 909–924.

Green, J. A. Attitudinal and situational determinants of intended behavior to Negroes. Paper presented at the meeting of the Western Psychological Association, Vancouver, June 1969.

Green, R., & Money, J. (Eds.) *Transsexualism and sex reassignment.* Baltimore, Md.: Johns Hopkins Press, 1969.

Greenberg, B. S., & Parker, E. G. (Eds.) *The Kennedy assassination and the American public: Social communication in crisis.* Stanford, Calif.: Stanford University Press, 1965.

Greenberg, P. J. Competition in children: An experimental study. *American Journal of Psychology,* 1932, **44,** 221–248.

Greenfield, S. M. Love: Some reflections by a social anthropologist. Paper presented at the meeting of the American Psychological Association, Miami Beach, September 1970.

Greenwood, J. M., & McNamara, W. J. Leadership styles of structure and consideration and managerial effectiveness. *Personnel Psychology,* 1969, **22,** 141–152.

Grinspoon, L. *Marihuana reconsidered.* Cambridge: Harvard University Press, 1971.

Grossack, M. M. Some effects of cooperation and competition upon small group behavior. *Journal of Abnormal and Social Psychology,* 1954, **49,** 341–348.

Grossack, M. M., & Gardner, H. *Man and men: Social psychology as a social science.* Scranton, Pa.: International Textbook, 1970.

Groves, W. E., Rossi, P. H., & Grafstein, D. Study of life styles and campus communities. A preliminary report to students who participated. Department of Social Relations, Johns Hopkins University, 1970.

Gruchow, N. Discrimination: Women charge universities, colleges with bias. *Science,* 1970, **168,** 559–561.

Gruen, W. The composition and some correlates of the American core culture. Canandaigua, N.Y.: V.A. Hospital, 1964. (Mimeographed.)

Gruenfeld, L. W., Rance, D. E., & Weissenberg, P. The behavior of task-oriented (low LPC) and socially-oriented (high LPC) leaders under several conditions of social support. *Journal of Social Psychology,* 1969, **79,** 99–107.

Grunwald, H. A. (Ed.) *Salinger.* New York: Harper, 1962.

Guller, I. B., & Bailes, D. W. Dogmatism and attitudes toward the Viet Nam war. Paper presented at the meeting of the Eastern Psychological Association, Washington, D.C., April 1968.

Gurin, P., Gurin, G., Lao, R., & Beattie, M. Internal-external control in the motivational dynamics of Negro youth. *Journal of Social Issues,* 1969, **25**(3), 29–54.

Gurr, T. R. *Why men rebel.* Princeton, N.J.: Princeton University Press, 1970.

Gusfield, J. The study of social movements. *International Encyclopedia of the Social Sciences.* New York: Crowell-Collier & Macmillan, 1968.

Guskin, J. T. The social perception of language variations: Black dialect and expectations of ability. Paper presented at the meeting of the American Educational Research Association, Minneapolis, Minn., March 1970.

Haan, N., Smith, M. B., & Block, J. Moral reasoning of young adults: Political-social behavior, family background, and personality correlates. *Journal of Personality and Social Psychology,* 1968, **10,** 183–201.

Haas, K. Obedience: Submission to destructive orders as related to hostility. *Psychological Reports,* 1966, **19,** 32–34.

Haines, D. B., & McKeachie, W. J. Cooperative versus competitive discussion methods in teaching introductory psychology. *Journal of Educational Psychology,* 1967, **58,** 386–390.

Hall, C. S., & Lindzey, G. The relevance of Freudian psychology and related viewpoints for the social sciences. In G. Lindzey and E. Aronson (Eds.), *Handbook of social psychology.* Vol. I. (2nd ed.) Reading, Mass.: Addison-Wesley, 1968. Pp. 245–319.

Hall, C. S., & Lindzey, G. *Theories of personality.* (2nd ed.) New York: Wiley, 1970.

Hall, E., & Barger, B. Background data and expected activities of entering lower division students. Mental Health Project Bulletin No. 7, University of Florida, May 1964.

Hall, E. T. *The silent language.* New York: Fawcett, 1959.

Hall, E. T. *The hidden dimension.* Garden City, N.Y.: Doubleday, 1966.
Hall, K. R. L. Aggression in monkey and ape societies. In J. D. Carthy and F. J. Ebling (Eds.), *The natural history of aggression.* New York: Academic Press, 1964. Pp. 51–64.
Halpin, A. W. Studies in aircrew composition: III. In *The combat leader behavior of B-29 aircraft commanders.* Washington, D.C.: Human Factors Operations Research Laboratory, Bolling Air Force Base, September 1953.
Halpin, A. W. The leadership behavior and combat performances of airplane commanders. *Journal of Abnormal and Social Psychology,* 1954, **49,** 19–22.
Halpin, A. W. *Theory and research in administration.* New York: Macmillan, 1966.
Halpin, A. W., & Winer, B. J. The leadership behavior of the airplane commander. Columbus: Ohio State University Research Foundation, 1952. (Mimeographed.)
Harding, J., Kutner, B., Proshansky, H., & Chein, I. Prejudice and ethnic relations. In G. Lindzey (Ed.), *Handbook of social psychology.* Reading, Mass.: Addison-Wesley, 1954. Pp. 1021–1061. (2nd ed.: 1969, Vol. 5, pp. 1–76.)
Harlow, H. F. The nature of love. *American Psychologist,* 1958, **13,** 673–685.
Harms, L. S. Listener comprehension of speakers of three status groups. *Language and Speech,* 1961, **4,** 109–112. (a)
Harms, L. S. Listener judgments of status cues in speech. *Quarterly Journal of Speech,* 1961, **47,** 164–168. (b)
Harrell, R. F., Woodyard, E. R., & Gates, A. I. Influence of vitamin supplementation of diets of pregnant and lactating women on intelligence of their offspring. *Metabolism,* 1956, **5,** 555–562.
Harrell, T. W., & Harrell, M. S. Army general classification test scores for civilian occupations. *Educational and Psychological Measurement,* 1945, **5,** 229–239.
Harris, A. S. The second sex in Academe. *American Association of University Professors Bulletin,* 1970, **56,** 283–295.
Harris, R. *Justice: The crisis of law, order and freedom in America.* New York: Dutton, 1969.
Harris Survey. Nonconformity is eyed askance. Honolulu *Advertiser,* Sept. 27, 1965.
Hart, H. *Selective migration as a factor in child welfare in the United States, with special reference to Iowa.* Iowa City: University of Iowa Studies in Child Welfare, I, 1921.
Hartley, E. L. *Problems in prejudice.* New York: King's Crown Press, 1946.
Hartmann, H., Kris, E., & Loewenstein, R. M. Notes on a theory of aggression. *Psychoanalytic Study of the Child,* 1949, **3-4,** 9–36.
Hartmann, D. P. Comments on the choice of a dependent variable in laboratory investigations of human aggression. Paper presented at the meeting of the American Psychological Association, Miami Beach, September 1970.
Hartshorne, H., & May, M. A. *Studies in the nature of character.* Vol. I. *Studies in deceit.* New York: Macmillan, 1928.
Hartshorne, H., May, M. A., & Maller, J. B. *Studies in the nature of character.* Vol. II. *Studies in service and self-control.* New York: Macmillan, 1929.
Harvey, J., & Mills, J. Effect of a difficult opportunity to revoke a counterattitudinal action upon attitude change. *Journal of Personality and Social Psychology,* 1971, **18,** 201–209.
Harvey, O. J. System structure, flexibility and creativity. In O. J. Harvey (Ed.), *Experience, structure, and adaptability.* New York: Springer, 1966. Pp. 39–65.
Harvey, O. J. Conceptual systems and attitude change. In M. Sherif and C. W. Sherif (Eds.), *Attitude, ego-involvement, and change.* New York: Wiley, 1967.
Harvey, O. J. Belief systems and education: Some implications for change. Unpublished manuscript, University of Colorado, 1969.
Harvey, O. J., Hunt, D. E., & Schroder, H. M. *Conceptual systems and personality organization.* New York: Wiley, 1961.
Harvey, O. J., & Ware, R. Personality differences in dissonance reduction. *Journal of Personality and Social Psychology,* 1967, **7,** 227–230.
Hastorf, A. H., Schneider, D. J., & Polefka, J. *Person perception.* Reading, Mass.: Addison-Wesley, 1970.
Hathaway, S. R., & McKinley, J. C. *Minnesota Multiphasic Personality Inventory manual.* (rev. ed.) New York: Psychological Corporation, 1951.

Havighurst, R. J., Bowman, P. H., Liddle, G. P., Matthews, C. V. & Pierce, J. V. *Growing up in River City*. New York: Wiley, 1962.
Havighurst, R. J., & Breese, F. H. Relation between ability and social status in a Midwestern community: III. Primary mental abilities. *Journal of Educational Psychology*, 1947, **38**, 241–247.
Havighurst, R. J., & Janke, L. L. Relations between ability and social status in a midwestern community: I. Ten-year-old children. *Journal of Educational Psychology*, 1944, **35**, 357–368.
Hawkins, P. R. Social class, the normal group and reference. *Language and Speech*, 1969, **12**, 125–135.
Hays, W. *Statistics for psychologists*. New York: Holt, 1963.
Haywood, H. C. Experiential factors in intellectual development: The concept of dynamic intelligence. In J. Zubin (Ed.), *Psychopathology of mental development*. New York: Grune & Stratton, 1967. Pp. 69–104.
Hebb, D. O. *The organization of behavior*. New York: Wiley, 1949.
Hebb, D. O. Drives and the C.N.S. (conceptual nervous system). *Psychological Review*, 1955, **62**, 243–254.
Heckhausen, H. *The anatomy of achievement motivation*. New York: Academic Press, 1967.
Heider, F. Attitudes and cognitive organization. *Journal of Psychology*, 1946, **21**, 107–112.
Heider, F. *The psychology of interpersonal relations*. New York: Wiley, 1958.
Helmreich, R., Aronson, E., & Le Fan, J. To err is humanizing—sometimes: Effects of self-esteem, competence, and a pratfall on interpersonal attraction. *Journal of Personality and Social Psychology*, 1970, **16**, 259–264.
Helmreich, R., & Collins, B. E. Studies in forced compliance: Commitment and magnitude of inducement to comply as determinants of opinion change. *Journal of Personality and Social Psychology*, 1968, **10**, 75–81.
Helson, H. Adaptation-level theory. In S. Koch (Ed.), *Psychology: A study of a science*. Vol. I. *Sensory, perceptual, and physiological formulations*. New York: McGraw-Hill, 1959. Pp. 565–621.
Helson, H. *Adaptation-level theory*. New York: Harper & Row, 1964.
Hemphill, J. K. *Leader behavior description*. Columbus: Ohio State University Personnel Research Board, 1950.
Hemphill, J. K. Leadership behavior associated with the administrative reputation of college departments. *Journal of Educational Psychology*, 1955, **46**, 385–401.
Hendrick, C., Bixenstine, V. E., & Hawkins, G. Race versus belief similarity as determinants of attraction: A search for a fair test. *Journal of Personality and Social Psychology*, 1971, **17**, 250–258.
Herzberg, F. *Work and the nature of man*. Cleveland: World, 1966.
Herzberg, F., Mausner, B., & Snyderman, B. *The motivation to work*. New York: Wiley, 1959.
Hess, E. H. Ethology. In R. Brown et al. (Eds.), *New directions in psychology*. New York: Holt, 1962.
Hess, R. D. Educability and rehabilitation: The future of the welfare class. *Journal of Marriage and the Family*, 1964, **26**, 422–429.
Hess, R. D., & Shipman, V. Early experience and the socialization of cognitive modes in children. *Child Development*, 1965, **36**, 869–886.
Heuyer, G. et al. Le niveou intellectuel des enfants d'age scolaire. *Institut nationale d'etudes demographiques: Travaux et documents*. Cashier/3, 1950. Reported in A. Anastasi, *Differential psychology*. New York: Macmillan, 1958.
Hicks, R. A., & Pellegrini, R. J. The meaningfulness of Negro-white differences in intelligence test performance. *Psychological Record*, 1966, **16**, 43–46.
Hildum, D., & Brown, R. Verbal reinforcement and interview bias. *Journal of Abnormal and Social Psychology*, 1956, **53**, 108–111.
Hilgard, E. R., & Payne, S. L. Those not at home: Riddle for pollsters. *Public Opinion Quarterly*, 1944, **8**, 245–261.
Hill, W. A situational approach to leadership effectiveness. *Journal of Applied Psychology*, 1969, **53**, 513–517.
Hiltner, S. The dialogue on man's nature. In S. Doniger (Ed.), *The nature of man*. New York: Harper, 1962. Pp. 237–261.

Hilton, I. Differences in the behavior of mothers toward first- and later-born children. *Journal of Personality and Social Psychology,* 1967, **7,** 282–290.
Himes, C. *A quality of hurt.* Garden City, N.Y.: Doubleday, 1971.
Himmelweit, H. Frustration and aggression: A review of recent experimental work. In T. H. Pear (Ed.), *Psychological factors of peace and war.* London: Hutchinson, 1950. Pp. 161–191.
Hinds, W. C. Individual and group decisions in gambling situations. Unpublished master's thesis, School of Industrial Management, M.I.T., 1962.
Hochreich, D. J., & Rotter, J. B. Have college students become less trusting? *Journal of Personality and Social Psychology,* 1970, **15,** 211–214.
Hodge, R. W., Siegel, P. M., & Rossi, P. H. Occupational prestige in the United States, 1925–1963. *American Journal of Sociology,* 1964, **70,** 286–302.
Hodgkinson, H. *Education, interaction, and social change.* Englewood Cliffs, N. J.: Prentice-Hall, 1967.
Hoffman, M. *The gay world.* New York: Basic Books, 1968; also New York: Bantam Books, 1969. (All page references are to the Bantam Book edition.)
Hoffman, M. L., & Saltzstein, H. D. Parent discipline and the child's moral development. *Journal of Personality and Social Psychology,* 1967, **5,** 45–57.
Hollander, E. P. Conformity, status, and idiosyncrasy credit. *Psychological Review,* 1958, **65,** 117–127.
Hollander, E. P. *Leaders, groups, and influence.* New York: Oxford University Press, 1964.
Hollander, E. P. *Principles and methods of social psychology.* (2nd ed.) New York: Oxford University Press, 1971.
Hollander, E. P., & Willis, R. H. Some current issues in the psychology of conformity and nonconformity. *Psychological Bulletin,* 1967, **68,** 62–76.
Hollister, L. E. Marihuana in man: Three years later. *Science,* 1971, **172,** 21–29.
Holstein, C. E. The relation of children's moral judgment level to that of their parents and to communication patterns in the family. Unpublished doctoral dissertation, University of California, Berkeley, 1969.
Holt, R. R. Clinical and statistical prediction: A reformulation and some new data. *Journal of Abnormal and Social Psychology,* 1958, **56,** 1–12.
Holt, R. R. Yet another look at clinical and statistical prediction: Or, is clinical psychology worthwhile? *American Psychologist,* 1970, **25,** 337–349.
Honigmann, J. J. *Culture and personality.* New York: Harper, 1954.
Hood, W. R., & Sherif, M. Verbal report and judgment of an unstructured stimulus. *Journal of Psychology,* 1962, **54,** 121–130.
Hook, S. *The hero in history.* Boston: Beacon Press, 1955.
Hooker, E. The adjustment of the male overt homosexual. *Journal of Projective Techniques,* 1957, **21,** 18–31.
Hooker, E. Parental relations and male homosexuality in patient and nonpatient samples. *Journal of Consulting and Clinical Psychology,* 1969, **33,** 140–142.
Horney, K. *The neurotic personality of our time.* New York: Norton, 1937.
Horney, K. *New ways in psychoanalysis.* New York: Norton, 1939.
Horton, C. P., & Crump, E. P. Growth and development: XI. Descriptive analysis of the background of 76 Negro children whose scores are above or below average on the Merrill-Palmer scale of mental tests of three years of age. *Journal of Genetic Psychology,* 1962, **100,** 255–269.
Hovland, C., Harvey, O., & Sherif, M. Assimilation and contrast effects in reactions to communication and attitude change. *Journal of Abnormal and Social Psychology,* 1957, **55,** 244–252.
Hovland, C., Janis, I., & Kelley, H. H. *Communication and persuasion.* New Haven: Yale University Press, 1953.
Howe, I. Herbert Marcuse or Milovan Djilas? The inescapable choice for the next decade. *Harpers,* 1969, **239,** 84–92.
Hoyt, G. C., & Stoner, J. A. F. Leadership and group decisions involving risk. *Journal of Experimental Social Psychology,* 1968, **4,** 275–285.
Humphreys, L. *Tearoom trade.* Chicago: Aldine, 1970.
Humphreys, L. New styles in homosexual manliness. *Trans-Action,* 1971, **8,** 38–46; 64–66.

Hunt, J. G. Fiedler's leadership contingency model: An empirical test in three organizations. *Organizational Behavior and Human Performance,* 1967, **2,** 290–308.

Hunt, J. McV. *Intelligence and experience.* New York: Ronald, 1961.

Hunt, J. McV. The intellectual performance of the culturally deprived child. Proceedings of Section II, Annual Professional Institute of the Division of School Psychologists, American Psychological Association, 1962. Pp. 25–27.

Hunt, J. McV. Traditional personality theory in the light of recent evidence. *American Scientist,* 1965, **53,** 60–96.

Hunt, J. McV., Cole, M. W., & Reis, E. E. S. Situational cues distinguishing anger, fear, and sorrow. *American Journal of Psychology,* 1958, **71,** 136–151.

Hurlock, E. B. The use of group rivalry as an incentive. *Journal of Abnormal and Social Psychology,* 1927, **22,** 278–290.

Hyman, H. Do they tell the truth? *Public Opinion Quarterly,* 1944, **8,** 557–559.

Hyman, H. H., Cobb, W. J., Feldman, J. J., Hart, C. W., & Stember, C. H. *Interviewing in social research.* Chicago: University of Chicago Press, 1954.

Hyman, H. H., & Sheatsley, P. B. "The authoritarian personality"—A methodological critique. In R. Christie and M. Jahoda (Eds.), *Studies in the scope and method of "The authoritarian personality."* New York: Free Press, 1954. Pp. 50–122.

Ingle, D. J. The need to investigate average biological differences among racial groups. In M. Mead, T. Dobzhansky, E. Tobach, & R. E. Light (Eds.), *Science and the concept of race.* New York: Columbia University Press, 1968. Pp. 113—121.

Inkeles, A. Social change and social character: The role of parental mediation. In N. Smelser and W. Smelser (Eds.), *Personality and social systems.* New York: Wiley, 1963. Pp. 357–366.

Insko, C. A. Verbal reinforcement of attitude. *Journal of Personality and Social Psychology,* 1965, **2,** 621–623.

Insko, C. A. *Theories of attitude change.* New York: Appleton-Century-Crofts, 1967.

Insko, C. A., & Robinson, J. E. Belief similarity vs. race as determinants of reactions to Negroes by Southern white adolescents: A further test of Rokeach's theory. *Journal of Personality and Social Psychology,* 1967, **7,** 216–221.

Insko, C. A., & Schopler, J. Triadic consistency: A statement of affective-cognitive-conative consistency. *Psychological Review,* 1967, **74,** 361–376.

Irwin, O. C. Infant speech: The effect of family occupational status and of age on sound frequency. *Journal of Speech and Hearing Disorders,* 1948, **13,** 320–323. (a)

Irwin, O. C. Infant speech: The effect of family occupational status and of age on use of sound types. *Journal of Speech and Hearing Disorders,* 1948, **13,** 224–226. (b)

Isaacs, S. *Intellectual growth in young children.* New York: Schocken, 1966.

Iverson, M. A. Personality impressions of punitive stimulus persons of differential status. *Journal of Abnormal and Social Psychology,* 1964, **68,** 617–626.

Izzett, R. R. Authoritarianism and attitudes toward the Vietnam war as reflected in behavioral and self-report measures. *Journal of Personality and Social Psychology,* 1971, **17,** 145–148.

Jackson, D. N., & Messick, S. Acquiescence: The nonvanishing variance component. *American Psychologist,* 1965, **20,** 498.

Jacob, P. *Changing values in college.* New York: Harper & Row, 1957.

Jahoda, M. Conformity and independence—a psychological analysis. *Human Relations,* 1959, **12,** 99–120.

Janke, L. L., & Havighurst, R. J. Relations between ability and social status in a midwestern community. II. Sixteen-year-old boys and girls. *Journal of Educational Psychology,* 1945, **36,** 499–509.

Jensen, A. R. Patterns of mental ability and socioeconomic status. Paper presented at the meeting of the National Academy of Sciences, Washington, D. C., April 1968. (a)

Jensen, A. R. Uses of twin and sibling data. Paper presented at the meeting of the American Psychological Association, San Francisco, August 1968. (b)

Jensen, A. R. Counter response. *Journal of Social Issues,* 1969, **25**(4), 219–222. (a)

Jensen, A. R. How much can we boost IQ and scholastic achievement? *Harvard Educational Review,* 1969, **39**(1), 1–123. (b)

Jensen, A. R. Input: Arthur Jensen replies. *Psychology Today,* 1969, **3**(5), 4–6. (c)

Jensen, A. R. Reducing the heredity-environment uncertainty: A reply. *Harvard Educational Review,* 1969, **39,** 449–483. (d)

Jensen, A. R. Rejoinder. *Journal of Social Issues,* 1969, **25**(4), 212–217. (e)

Jensen, B. T., & Terebinski, S. J. The railroad game: A tool for research in social sciences. *Journal of Social Psychology,* 1963, **60,** 85–87.

Jessor, R. Toward a social psychology of excessive alcohol use. In C. R. Snyder and D. R. Schweitzer (Eds.), *Proceedings: Research sociologists' conference on alcohol problems.* Carbondale, Ill.: Southern Illinois University, 1964. Pp. 59–79.

Jessor, R., Graves, T. D., Hanson, R. C., & Jessor, S. *Society, personality, and deviant behavior.* New York: Holt, Rinehart, & Winston, 1968.

Jessor, R., Jessor, S., & Collins, M. On becoming a drinker: The social psychology of an adolescent transition. Unpublished manuscript, University of Colorado, 1971.

Jessor, R., Young, H. B., Young, E., & Tesi, G. Perceived opportunity, alienation and drinking behavior among Italian and American youth. *Journal of Personality and Social Psychology,* 1970, **15,** 215–222.

John, V. & Goldstein, L. S. The social context of language acquisition. *Merrill-Palmer Quarterly,* 1964, **10,** 265–275.

Johnson, W. A. A comparison of the philosophies of human nature of Negro and white high school seniors. Unpublished master's thesis, George Peabody College for Teachers, 1969.

Jones, A. P. Self-reported and judged personality, value, and attitudinal patterns: A comparison of users and nonusers of LSD. Paper presented at the meeting of the Rocky Mountain Psychological Association, Albuquerque, N. M., May 1969.

Jones, E. E. Conformity as a tactic of ingratiation. *Science,* 1965, **149,** 144–150.

Jones, E. E., & Davis, K. E. From acts to dispositions: The attribution process in person perception. In L. Berkowitz (Ed.), *Advances in experimental social psychology.* Vol. II. New York: Academic Press, 1965. Pp. 219–266.

Jones, E. E., Davis, K. E., & Gergen, K. J. Role playing variations and their informational value for person perception. *Journal of Abnormal and Social Psychology,* 1961, **63,** 302–310.

Jones, M. C. Personality correlates and antecedents of drinking patterns in adult males. *Journal of Consulting and Clinical Psychology,* 1968, **32,** 2–12.

Jones, R. Beyond behaviorism. *Contemporary Psychology,* 1970, **15,** 741–742.

Jordan, W. D. *White over black: American attitudes toward the Negro, 1550–1812.* Baltimore, Md.: Penguin Books, 1969.

Julian, J. W. The study of competition. In W. E. Vinacke (Ed.), *Readings in general psychology.* Atlanta: American Book, 1968. Pp. 289–297.

Julian, J. W., & Perry, F. Cooperation contrasted with intragroup and intergroup competition. *Sociometry,* 1967, **30,** 79–90.

Kaats, G. R. Belief systems and person perception: Analyses in a service academy environment. Unpublished doctoral dissertation, University of Colorado, 1969.

Kaats, G. R., & Davis, K. E. The dynamics of sexual behavior of college students. *Journal of Marriage and the Family,* 1970, **32,** 390–399.

Kagan, J. On the meaning of behavior: Illustrations from the infant. *Child Development,* 1969, **40,** 1121–1134.

Kamii, C. K., & Radin, N. L. Class differences in the socialization practices of Negro mothers. *Journal of Marriage and the Family,* 1967, **29,** 302–310.

Kanter, R. M. Commitment and social organization: A study of commitment mechanisms in Utopian communities. *American Sociological Review,* 1968, **33,** 499–518.

Kanter, R. M. Communes. *Psychology Today,* 1970, **4**(2), 53–57; 78.

Kaplan, J. *Marijuana and the new prohibition.* Cleveland: World, 1970.

Karabenick, S. A., & Wilson, W. Dogmatism among war hawks and peace doves. *Psychological Reports,* 1969, **25,** 419–422.

Kardiner, A., & Ovesey, L. *The mark of oppression.* New York: Norton, 1951.

Karlins, M., & Abelson, H. I. *Persuasion: How opinions and attitudes are changed.* New York: Springer, 1970.

Karlins, M., Coffman, T. L., & Walters, G. On the fading of social stereotypes: Studies in three generations of college students. *Journal of Personality and Social Psychology,* 1969, **13,** 1–16.

Karnes, M. B. Research and development program on disadvantaged children. Final Report, Vol. 1, May 1969. University of Illinois, Contract No. DE-6-10-325, U.S. Office of Education.

Karon, B. P. *The Negro personality.* New York: Springer, 1958.
Kasl, S. V., & French, J. R. P., Jr. The effects of occupational status on physical and mental health. *Journal of Social Issues,* 1962, **18**(3), 67–89.
Kateb, G. The political thought of Herbert Marcuse. *Commentary,* January 1970, 48–63.
Katope, C., & Zolbrod, P. *Beyond Berkeley: A sourcebook of student values.* Cleveland: World, 1966.
Katz, D. Do interviewers bias polls results? *Public Opinion Quarterly,* 1942, **6,** 248–268.
Katz, D. The functional approach to the study of attitudes. *Public Opinion Quarterly,* 1960, **24,** 163–204.
Katz, D. Consistency for what? The functional approach. In R. P. Abelson et al. (Eds.), *Theories of cognitive consistency: A sourcebook.* Chicago: Rand-McNally, 1968. Pp. 179–191.
Katz, D., Sarnoff, D., & McClintock, C. G. Ego-defense and attitude change. *Human Relations,* 1956, **9,** 27–45.
Katz, D., & Stotland, E. A preliminary statement to a theory of attitude structure and change. In S. Koch (Ed.), *Psychology: A study of a science.* Vol. 3. New York: McGraw-Hill, 1959. Pp. 423–475.
Katz, I. Review of evidence relating to effects of desegregation on the intellectual performance of Negroes. *American Psychologist,* 1964, **19,** 381–399.
Katz, I. Some motivational determinants of racial differences in intellectual achievement. *International Journal of Psychology,* 1967, **2,** 1–12.
Katz, I. A critique of personality approaches to Negro performance, with research suggestions. *Journal of Social Issues,* 1969, **25**(3), 13–28.
Katz, I., & Benjamin, L. Effects of white authoritarianism in biracial groups. *Journal of Abnormal and Social Psychology,* 1960, **61,** 448–456.
Katz, I., & Cohen, M. The effects of training Negroes upon cooperative problem solving in biracial terms. *Journal of Abnormal and Social Psychology,* 1962, **64,** 319–325.
Katz, I., Epps, E. G., & Axelson, L. J. Effect upon Negro digit-symbol performance of anticipated comparison with whites and with other Negroes. *Journal of Abnormal and Social Psychology,* 1964, **69,** 77–83.
Katz, I., & Greenbaum, C. Effects of anxiety, threat, and racial environment on task performance of Negro college students. *Journal of Abnormal and Social Psychology,* 1963, **66,** 562–567.
Katz, I., Henchy, J., & Allen, H. Effects of race of tester, approval-disapproval, and need on Negro children's learning. *Journal of Personality and Social Psychology,* 1968, **8,** 38–42.
Katz, J. *The student activists: Rights, needs and powers of undergraduates.* Washington, D.C.: U.S. Office of Education, 1967.
Katz, J. *No time for students.* San Francisco: Jossey-Bass, 1968.
Keen, S., & Raser, J. A conversation with Herbert Marcuse. *Psychology Today,* 1971, **4**(9), 35–40ff.
Keiffer, M. G., & Cullen, D. M. Discrimination experienced by academic female psychologists. Paper presented at the meeting of the American Psychological Association, Washington, D.C., September 1969.
Kell, B. L. Is it necessary to be client-centered? *Contemporary Psychology,* 1967, **12,** 98–99.
Keller, S. The social world of the urban slum child: Some early findings. *American Journal of Orthopsychiatry,* 1963, **33,** 823–831.
Kelley, H. H. The warm-cold variable in first impressions of persons. *Journal of Personality,* 1950, **18,** 431–439.
Kelley, H. H. Attribution theory in social psychology. In D. Levine (Ed.), *Nebraska symposium on motivation, 1967.* Vol. 15. Lincoln, Neb.: University of Nebraska Press, 1967. Pp. 192–238.
Kelley, H. H., & Stahelski, A. J. Social interaction basis of cooperators' and competitors' beliefs about others. *Journal of Personality and Social Psychology,* 1970, **16,** 66–91.
Kelley, H. H., & Thibaut, J. W. Group problem solving. In G. Lindzey and E. Aronson (Eds.), *Handbook of social psychology.* Vol. 4. (2nd ed.) Reading, Mass.: Addison-Wesley, 1968. Pp. 1–104.
Kelly, G. A. *The psychology of personal constructs.* New York: Norton, 1955. 2 vols.

Kelly, G. A. *A theory of personality: The psychology of personal constructs.* New York: Norton, 1963.
Kemeny, J. G. *A philosopher looks at science.* Princeton, N.J.: Van Nostrand, 1959.
Kemp, C. G. Perception of authority in relation to open and closed belief systems. *Science Education*, 1963, **47,** 482–484.
Keniston, K. *The uncommitted. Alienated youth in American society.* New York: Harcourt, Brace, & World, 1965.
Keniston, K. The sources of student dissent. *Journal of Social Issues,* 1967, **23,** 108–137.
Keniston, K. Heads and seekers. *American Scholar,* 1968, **38,** 97–112. (a)
Keniston, K. *Young radicals, notes on committed youth.* New York: Harcourt, Brace, & World, 1968. (b)
Keniston, K. Counter culture: Cop-out, or wave of the future? *Life,* Dec. 7, 1969, 8–9.
Keniston, K. Youth: A "new" stage of life. *American Scholar,* Autumn, 1970, **39,** 632–654.
Kerckhoff, A. C., & Davis, K. E. Value consensus and need complementarity in mate selection. *American Sociological Review,* 1962, **27,** 295–303.
Kerlinger, F. N. & Rokeach, M. The factorial structure of the F and D scales. *Journal of Personality and Social Psychology,* 1966, **4,** 391–399.
Kerner, O., Lindsay, J., Harris, F. R., Brook, E. W., Corman, J. C., McCulloch, W. M., Abel, I. W., Thornton, C. B., Wilkins, R., Peden, K. W., Jenkins, H. et al. *Report of the National Advisory Commission on Civil Disorders.* New York: Bantam Books, 1968.
Kerpelman, L. *Student activism and ideology in higher education institutions.* Washington, D.C.: U.S. Department of Health, Education, and Welfare. Office of Education, March 1970.
Kiesler, C. A. Group pressure and conformity. In J. Mills (Ed.), *Experimental social psychology.* New York: Macmillan, 1969. Pp. 233–306.
Kiesler, C. A., Collins, B. E., & Miller, N. *Attitude change: A critical analysis of theoretical approaches.* New York: Wiley, 1969.
Kiesler, C. A., & Kiesler, S. B. *Conformity.* Reading, Mass.: Addison-Wesley, 1969.
Kilham, P., & Klopfer, P. H. The construct race and the innate differential. In M. Mead et al. (Eds.), *Science and the concept of race.* New York: Columbia University Press, 1968. Pp. 26–37.
Kimble, G. A. *Hilgard and Marquis' conditioning and learning.* New York: Appleton-Century-Crofts, 1961.
Kinkead, E. *In every war but one.* New York: Norton, 1959.
Kinsey, A. C., Pomeroy, W. B., & Martin, C. E. *Sexual behavior in the human male.* Philadelphia: W. B. Saunders, 1948.
Kinsey, A. C., Pomeroy, W. B., Martin, C. E., & Gebhard, P. H. *Sexual behavior in the human female.* Philadelphia: W. B. Saunders, 1953.
Kipnis, D. M. Interaction between members of bomber crews as a determinant of sociometric choice. *Human Relations,* 1957, **10,** 263–270.
Kirscht, J. P., & Dillehay, R. C. *Dimensions of authoritarianism: A review of research and theory.* Lexington, Ky.: University of Kentucky Press, 1967.
Klaus, R. A., & Gray, S. W. Murfreesboro preschool program for culturally deprived children. *Childhood Education,* 1965, **42,** 92–95.
Klaus, R. A., & Gray, S. W. The early training project for disadvantaged children. A report after five years. *Monographs of the Society for Research in Child Development,* 1968, **33**(4, Whole No. 120).
Kleinke, C. L., & Pohlen, P. D. Affective and emotional responses as a function of other person's gaze and cooperativeness in a two-person game. *Journal of Personality and Social Psychology,* 1971, **17,** 308–313.
Klineberg, O. *Negro intelligence and selective migration.* New York: Columbia University Press, 1935.
Klineberg, O. (Ed.) *Characteristics of the American Negro.* New York: Harper, 1944.
Klineberg, O. Negro-white differences in intelligence test performance: A new look at an old problem. *American Psychologist,* 1963, **18,** 198–203.
Klineberg, O. Black and white in international perspective. *American Psychologist,* 1971, **26,** 119–128.

Klinger, E. Fantasy need achievement as a motivational construct. *Psychological Bulletin,* 1966, **66,** 291–308.

Kluckhohn, C. Have there been discernible shifts in American values during the past generation? In E. Morison (Ed.), *The American style.* New York: Harper, 1958. Pp. 145–217.

Knobloch, H., & Pasamanick, B. Further observations on the behavioral development of Negro children. *Journal of Genetic Psychology,* 1963, **83,** 137–157.

Knox, R. E., & Douglas, R. Low payoffs and marginal comprehension: Two possible constraints upon behavior in the Prisoner's Dilemma. Paper presented at the meeting of the Western Psychological Association, San Diego, March 1968.

Kochman, T. Social factors in the consideration of teaching standard English. *Florida Foreign Language Reporter,* 1969, **7,** 87–88; 157.

Koedt, A. (In) Five passionate feminists. *McCalls,* July 1970, 114.

Kogan, N., & Carlson, J. Group risk taking under competitive and noncompetitive conditions in adults and children. Paper presented at the meeting of the American Psychological Association, Washington, D.C., September 1967.

Kogan, N., & Wallach, M. A. *Risk-taking: A study in cognition and personality.* New York: Holt, 1964.

Kogan, N., & Wallach, M. A. Effects of physical separation of group members upon group risk taking. *Human Relations,* 1967, **20,** 41–48. (a)

Kogan, N., & Wallach, M. A. Group risk taking as a function of members' anxiety and defensiveness labels. *Journal of Personality,* 1967, **35,** 50–63. (b)

Kogan, N., & Wallach, M. A. The risky-shift phenomenon in small decision-making groups: A test of the information-exchange hypothesis. *Journal of Experimental Social Psychology,* 1967, **3,** 75–85. (c)

Kohlberg, L. The development of modes of moral thinking and choice in the years ten to sixteen. Unpublished doctoral dissertation, University of Chicago, 1958.

Kohlberg, L. Moral development and identification. In H. Stevenson (Ed.), *Child psychology.* 62nd Yearbook of the National Society for the Study of Education. Chicago: University of Chicago Press, 1963.

Kohlberg, L. Development of moral character and moral ideology. In M. L. Hoffman & L. W. Hoffman (Eds.), *Review of child development research.* Vol. I. New York: Russell Sage Foundation, 1964. Pp. 383–431.

Kohlberg, L. Moral and religious education and the public schools: A developmental view. In T. Sizer (Ed.), *Religion and public education.* Boston: Houghton-Mifflin, 1967.

Kohlberg, L. The child as a moral philosopher. *Psychology Today,* 1968, **2**(4), 24–30.

Kohlberg, L. The cognitive-developmental approach to socialization. In D. A. Goslin (Ed.), *Handbook of socialization theory and research.* Chicago: Rand-McNally, 1969. Pp. 347–480.

Kohlberg, L. Moral development and the education of adolescents. In R. Purnell (Ed.), *Adolescents and the American high school.* New York: Holt, Rinehart, & Winston, 1970. Pp. 144–163.

Kohlberg, L. Moral education in schools and prisons. Colloquium address, George Peabody College for Teachers, March 4, 1971.

Komisar, L. The new feminism. *Saturday Review,* Feb. 21, 1970, 27–30.

Komorita, S. S. Attitude content, intensity, and the neutral point on a Likert scale. *Journal of Social Psychology,* 1963, **61,** 327–334.

Korten, F. F., Cook, S. W., & Lacey, J. I. (Eds.) *Psychology and the problems of society.* Washington, D.C.: American Psychological Association, 1970.

Kraditor, A. *Up from the pedestal. Selected writings in the history of American feminism.* Chicago: Quadrangle Books, 1968.

Kramer, R. Moral development in young adulthood. Unpublished doctoral dissertation, University of Chicago, 1968.

Krasner, L. The behavior scientist and social responsibility: No place to hide. *Journal of Social Issues,* 1965, **21**(2), 9–30.

Krauss, R. M., & Rotter, G. S. Communicative abilities as a function of status and age. *Merrill-Palmer Quarterly,* 1968, **14,** 161–173.

Krebs, R. Some relations between moral judgment, attention, and resistance to temptation. Unpublished doctoral dissertation, University of Chicago, 1967.

Krech, D., Crutchfield, R., & Ballachey, E. *Individual in society.* New York: McGraw-Hill, 1962.
Kuhn, D. Z., Madsen, C. H., Jr., & Becker, W. C. Effects of exposure to an aggressive model and frustration on children's aggressive behavior. *Child Development,* 1967, **38,** 739–746.
Kuhn, T. S. *The structure of scientific revolutions.* Chicago: University of Chicago Press, 1962. (2nd ed.: 1970)
Kurtz, S. *The New York Times Encyclopedic Almanac 1970.* New York: New York Times Book and Education Division, 1969.
Kutner, B., Wilkins, C., & Yarrow, P. R. Verbal attitudes and overt behavior involving racial prejudice. *Journal of Abnormal and Social Psychology,* 1952, **47,** 649–652.
Labov, W. *The social stratification of English in New York City.* Washington, D.C.: Center for Applied Linguistics, 1966.
Labov, W. The logic of non-standard English. In F. Williams (Ed.), *Language and poverty. Perspectives on a theme.* Chicago: Markham, 1970, Pp. 153–189.
Labov, W., & Cohen, P. Systematic relations of standard and non-standard rules in the grammar of Negro speakers. Paper presented at the 7th Project Literacy Conference, Cambridge, Mass., May 1967.
Labov, W., Cohen, P., Robins, C., & Lewis, J. A study of the non-standard English of Negro and Puerto Rican speakers in New York City. Vols. I and II. Columbia University, Cooperative Research Project No. 3288, U.S. Office of Education, 1968.
LaCivita, A. F., Kean, J. M., & Yamamoto, K. Socio-economic status of children and acquisition of grammar. *Journal of Educational Research,* 1966, **60,** 71–74.
Ladd, E. C., Jr. Professors and political petitions. *Science,* 1969, **163,** 1425–1430.
Lagarspertz, K. Genetics and social causes of aggressive behavior in mice. *Scandinavian Journal of Psychology,* 1961, **2,** 167–173.
Lana, R. *Assumptions of social psychology.* New York: Appleton-Century-Crofts, 1968.
Landsberger, H. A. *Hawthorne revisited.* Ithaca, N.Y.: Cornell University, 1958.
Lantz, D. Color naming and color recognition. A study in the psychology of language. Unpublished doctoral dissertation, Harvard University, 1963.
LaPiere, R. T. Attitudes and actions. *Social Forces,* 1934, **13,** 230–237.
Latané, B., & Darley, J. Group inhibition of bystander intervention in emergencies. *Journal of Personality and Social Psychology,* 1968, **10,** 215–221.
Latané, B., & Darley, J. Social determinants of bystander intervention in emergencies. In J. Macaulay and L. Berkowitz (Eds.), *Altruism and helping behavior.* New York: Academic Press, 1970. Pp. 13–27. (a)
Latané, B., & Darley, J. *The unresponsive bystander: Why doesn't he help?* New York: Appleton-Century-Crofts, 1970. (b)
Latané, B., & Rodin, J. A lady in distress: Inhibiting effects of friends and strangers on bystander intervention. *Journal of Experimental Social Psychology,* 1969, **5,** 189–202.
Laurie, P. *Drugs: Medical, psychological, and social facts.* Baltimore, Md.: Penguin Books, 1967.
Lawrence, J. *A history of Russia.* New York: Farrar, Straus, & Cudahy, 1960.
Lawton, D. Social class differences in language development: A study of some samples of written work. *Language and Speech,* 1963, **6,** 120–143.
Lawton, D. Social class language differences in group discussions. *Language and Speech,* 1964, **7,** 183–204.
Lawton, D. *Social class, language and education.* New York: Schocken Books, 1968.
Lear, J. Do we need new rules for experiments on people? *Saturday Review,* Feb. 5, 1966. Pp. 61–70.
LeBon, G. *The crowd.* London: Ernest Benn, 1896.
Lederer, W. J., & Jackson, D. D. *The mirages of marriage.* New York: Norton, 1968.
Lee, E. S. Negro intelligence and selective migration: A Philadelphia test of the Klineberg hypothesis. *American Sociological Review,* 1951, **16,** 227–233.
Lehmann, S. Community and psychology and community psychology. *American Psychologist,* 1971, **26,** 554–560.
Lehrman, N. *Masters and Johnson explained.* Chicago: Playboy Press, 1970.
Lemert, E. *Alcohol and the Northwest coast Indians.* Berkeley: University of California Press, 1954.

Lerner, E. *Constraint areas and the moral judgment of children.* Menasha, Wisc.: Banta, 1937.
Lerner, M. J. The unjust consequences of the need to believe in a just world. Paper presented at the meeting of the American Psychological Association, New York, September 1966.
Lerner, M. J. The desire for justice and reactions to victims. In J. Macaulay and L. Berkowitz (Eds.), *Altruism and helping behavior.* New York: Academic Press, 1970. Pp. 205–229.
Lerner, M. J., & Simmons, C. H. Observer's reaction to the "innocent victim." *Journal of Personality and Social Psychology,* 1966, **4,** 203–210.
Lesser, G. S., Fifer, G., & Clark, D. H. Mental abilities of children from different social class and cultural groups. *Monographs of the Society for Research in Child Development,* 1965, **30**(4), 1–115.
Levin, H. Psychologist to the powerless. In F. F. Korten, S. W. Cook, and J. I. Lacey (Eds.), *Psychology and the problems of society.* Washington, D.C.: American Psychological Association, 1970. Pp. 121–127.
Levine, S. The effects of differential infantile stimulation on emotionality at weaning. *Canadian Journal of Psychology,* 1959, **13,** 243–247.
Levinger, G., Senn, D. J., & Jorgensen, B. W. Progress toward permanence in courtship: A test of the Kerckhoff-Davis hypotheses. *Sociometry,* 1970, **33,** 427–443.
Levinson, D. J., & Huffman, P. E. Traditional family ideology and its relation to personality. *Journal of Personality,* 1955, **23,** 251–273.
Levy, S. G. A 150-year study of political violence in the United States. In H. D. Graham and T. R. Gurr (Eds.), *Violence in America.* New York: New American Library, 1969. Pp. 81–92.
Lewin, K. *A dynamic theory of personality.* New York: McGraw-Hill, 1935.
Lewin, K. Behavior and development as a function of the total situation. In L. Carmichael (Ed.), *Manual of child psychology.* New York: Wiley, 1946. Pp. 791–844.
Lewin, K. *Resolving social conflicts.* New York: Harper, 1948.
Lewin, K. *Field theory in social science.* New York: Harper, 1951.
Lewin, K., Lippitt, R., & White, R. Patterns of aggressive behavior in experimentally created "social climates." *Journal of Social Psychology,* 1939, **10,** 271–299.
Lidz, T., Fleck, S., & Cornelison, A. R. *Schizophrenia and the family.* New York: International Universities Press, 1965.
Lief, H. I. Teaching doctors about sex. In R. Brecher and E. Brecher (Eds.), *An analysis of the human sexual response.* Boston: Little-Brown, 1966.
Life. The big Woodstock rock trip. Aug. 29, 1969, 128.
Lifton, R. J. Self-process in protean man. In *The acquisition and development of values: Perspectives on research.* Bethesda, Md.: National Institute of Child Health and Human Development, 1968. Pp. 38–47.
Lindzey, G., & Aronson, E. *Handbook of social psychology.* Vols. 1–5. (2nd ed.) Reading, Mass.: Addison-Wesley, 1968.
Lindzey, G., & Rogolsky, S. Prejudice and identification of minority group membership. *Journal of Abnormal and Social Psychology,* 1950, **45,** 37–53.
Linn, L. S. Verbal attitudes and overt behavior: A study of racial discrimination. *Social Forces,* 1965, **44,** 353–364.
Lippitt, R. *Training in community relations.* New York: Harper, 1949.
Lippitt, R., Watson, J., & Westley, B. *The dynamics of planned change.* New York: Harcourt, Brace, & World, 1958.
Lipset, S. M., & Ladd, E. C., Jr. . . . And what professors think. *Psychology Today,* 1970, **4**(6), 49–51 .
Livesay, T. M. Racial comparisons in test-intelligence. *American Journal of Psychology,* 1942, **55,** 90–95.
Livesay, T. M. Relation of economic status to "intelligence" and to the racial deprivation of high school seniors in Hawaii. *American Journal of Psychology,* 1944, **57,** 77–82.
Loban, W. *The language of elementary school children.* Champaign, Ill.: National Council of Teachers of English, 1963.
Loban, W. *Language ability. Grades seven, eight, and nine.* Washington, D.C.: U.S. Gov't. Printing Office, 1966.
Logan, R. W. *The Negro in the United States.* Princeton, N.J.: Van Nostrand, 1957.

Lolli, G., Serianni, E., Golde, G. M., & Luzzatto-Fegiz, P. Alcohol in Italian culture: Food and wine in relation to sobriety among Italians and Italian Americans. Monograph No. 4, Rutgers Center of Alcohol Studies, New Brunswick, N. J., 1958.
Loomis, J. L. Communication, the development of trust, and cooperative behavior. *Human Relations,* 1959, **12,** 305–315.
Lorenz, K. The comparative method in studying innate behavior patterns. *Symposia of the Society of Experimental Biology,* 1950, **4,** 221–268.
Lorenz, K. *King Solomon's ring.* New York: Crowell, 1952.
Lorenz, K. *On aggression.* New York: Harcourt, Brace, & World, 1966.
Lubell, S. That "generation gap." *Public Interest,* 1968, **13,** 52–60.
Lucas, O., Finkelman, A., & Tocantino, L. M. Management of tooth extractions in hemophiliacs by the combined use of hypnotic suggestion, protective splints, and packing sockets. *Journal of Oral Surgery Anesthesia and Hospital Dental Service,* 1962, **20,** 489–500.
Luce, R. D. & Raiffa, H. *Games and decisions.* New York: Wiley, 1957.
Luchins, A. S. Experimental attempts to minimize the impact of first impressions. In C. I. Hovland (Ed.), *The order of presentation in persuasion.* New Haven: Yale University Press, 1957. Pp. 62–75. (a)
Luchins, A. S. Primacy-recency in impression formation. In C. I. Hovland (Ed.), *The order of presentation in persuasion.* New Haven: Yale University Press, 1957. Pp. 33–61. (b)
Luckey, E., & Nass, G. D. A comparison of sexual attitudes and behavior in an international sample. *Journal of Marriage and the Family,* 1969, **31,** 364–379.
Luria, A. *The role of speech in the regulation of normal and abnormal behavior.* New York: Liveright, 1961.
Macaulay, J., & Berkowitz, L. (Eds.) *Altruism and helping behavior.* New York: Academic Press, 1970.
MacDonald, A. P., Jr. Anxiety, affiliation, and social isolation. *Developmental Psychology,* 1970, **3,** 242–254.
MacDougald, D., Jr. Aphrodisiacs and anaphrodisiacs. In A. Ellis and A. Abaranel (Eds.), *The encyclopedia of sexual behavior.* Vol. 1. New York: Hawthorn, 1961.
Mack, R. *Transforming America: Patterns of social change.* New York: Random House, 1967.
MacKenzie, K. D., & Bernhardt, I. The effect of status upon group risk taking. Unpublished manuscript, Wharton School of Finance and Commerce, University of Pennsylvania, 1968.
MacRae, D., Jr. A test of Piaget's theories of moral development. *Journal of Abnormal and Social Psychology,* 1954, **49,** 14–18.
Madaras, G. R., & Bem, D. J. Risk and conservatism in group decision-making. *Journal of Experimental Social Psychology,* 1968, **4,** 350–365.
Maddox, G. Drinking among Negroes: Inferences from the drinking patterns of selected Negro male collegians. *Journal of Health and Social Behavior,* 1968, **9,** 114–120.
Maddox, G. *The domesticated drug: Drinking among collegians.* New Haven: College and University Press, 1970.
Maddox, G., & Williams, J. R. Drinking behavior of Negro collegians. *Quarterly Journal of Studies on Alcohol,* 1968, **29,** 117–129.
Madsen, M. C. Cooperative and competitive motivation of children in three Mexican subcultures. *Psychological Reports,* 1967, **20,** 1307–1320.
Madsen, M. C., & Shapira, A. Cooperative and competitive behavior of urban Afro-American, Anglo-American, Mexican-American, and Mexican village children. *Developmental Psychology,* 1970, **3,** 16–20.
Malcolm X, with the assistance of A. Haley. *The autobiography of Malcolm X.* New York: Grove Press, 1964.
Maller, J. B. Cooperation and competition—an experimental study. *Teachers College Contributions to Education,* 1929, No. 384.
Mallick, S. K., & McCandless, B. R. A study of catharsis of aggression. *Journal of Personality and Social Psychology,* 1966, **4,** 591–596.
Mann, R. D. A review of the relationships between personality and performance in small groups. *Psychological Bulletin,* 1959, **56,** 241–270.
Mannheimer, D., & Williams, R. M., Jr. A note on Negro troops in combat. In S. A. Stouffer,

E. A. Suchman, L. C. De Vinney, S. A. Star, and R. M. Williams, Jr., *The American soldier*. Vol. I. Princeton, N.J.: Princeton University Press, 1949.

Marcuse, H. *Eros and civilization: A philosophical inquiry into Freud.* New York: Vintage, 1962. (Originally published in 1955.)

Marcuse, H. *One-dimensional man: Studies in the ideology of advanced industrial society.* Boston: Beacon Press, 1964.

Marcuse, H. *An essay on liberation.* Boston: Beacon Press, 1969.

Marks, R. W. *The meaning of Marcuse.* New York: Ballantine, 1970.

Marlowe, D. Relationships among direct and indirect measures of the achievement motive and overt behavior. *Journal of Consulting Psychology,* 1959, **23,** 329–332.

Marlowe, D., & Gergen, K. J. Personality and social interaction. In G. Lindzey and E. Aronson (Eds.), *Handbook of social psychology.* Vol. 3. (2nd ed.) Reading, Mass.: Addison-Wesley, 1968. Pp. 590–665.

Marlowe, D., & Gergen, K. J. Personality and social behavior. In K. J. Gergen and D. Marlowe (Eds.), *Personality and social behavior.* Reading, Mass.: Addison-Wesley, 1970. Pp. 1–75.

Marquis, D. G. Individual responsibility and group decisions involving risk. *Industrial Management Review,* 1962, **3,** 8–23.

Marquis, K., Oskamp, S., & Marshall, J. Testimony validity as a function of question form, atmosphere, and item difficulty. *Journal of Applied Social Psychology,* 1972, in press.

Marrow, A. J. *The practical theorist. The life and work of Kurt Lewin.* New York: Basic Books, 1969.

Martin, J. G., & Westie, F. R. The tolerant personality. *American Sociological Review,* 1959, **24,** 521–528.

Marx, G. T. Civil disorder and agents of social control. *Journal of Social Issues,* 1970, **26**(1), 19–57.

Maslow, A. *Motivation and personality.* New York: Harper & Row, 1954.

Massie, R. K. *Nicholas and Alexandra.* New York: Atheneum, 1967.

Masters, W. H., & Johnson, V. E. *Human sexual response.* Boston: Little-Brown, 1966.

Masters, W. H., & Johnson, V. E. *Human sexual inadequacy.* Boston: Little-Brown, 1970.

Mattson, A., & Gross, S. Adaptational and defensive behavior in young hemophiliacs and their parents. Paper presented at the meeting of the American Psychiatric Association, New York, May 1965. (Cited in Massie, 1967.) (a)

Mattson, A., & Gross, S. Social and behavioral studies on hemophilic children and their families. Paper presented at the meeting of the American Psychiatric Association, New York, May 1965. (Cited in Massie, 1967.) (b)

Maudry, M., & Nekula, M. Social relations between children of the same age during the first two years of life. *Journal of Genetic Psychology,* 1939, **54,** 193–215.

May, M., & Doob, L. *Competition and cooperation.* New York: Social Science Research Council, 1937.

Mayo, C. W., & Crockett, W. H. Cognitive complexity and primacy-recency effects in impression formation. *Journal of Abnormal and Social Psychology,* 1964, **68,** 335–338.

Mayo, E. *The social problems of an industrial civilization.* Boston: Harvard Graduate School of Business, 1945.

McCarthy, D. *The language development of the preschool child.* Minneapolis, Minn.: University of Minnesota Press, 1930.

McCarthy, D. Language development in children. In L. Carmichael (Ed.), *Manual of child psychology.* (2nd ed.) New York: Wiley, 1954. Pp. 492–630.

McCarthy, J., & Johnson, R. C. Interpretation of the "city hall riots" as a function of general dogmatism. *Psychological Reports,* 1962, **11,** 243–245.

McCary, J. L. *Human sexuality.* New York: Van Nostrand, 1967.

McCary, J. L. Myths about sex. *Sexual Behavior,* 1971, **1**(1), 22–31.

McClearn, G. E., & Meredith, H. W. Behavioral genetics. In P. R. Farnsworth et al. (Eds.), *Annual review of psychology.* Vol. 17. Palo Alto, Calif.: Annual Reviews, 1966. Pp. 515–550.

McClelland, D. C. The uses of measures of human motivation in the study of society. In J. W. Atkinson (Ed.), *Motives in fantasy, action, and society.* Princeton, N.J.: Van Nostrand, 1958. Pp. 518–552.

McClelland, D. C. *The achieving society*. Princeton, N. J.: Van Nostrand, 1961.
McClelland, D. C. Quoted in T. G. Harris, To know why men do what they do: A conversation with David C. McClelland. *Psychology Today*, 1971, **4**(8), 35–39, ff.
McClelland, D. C., Atkinson, J. W., Clark, R. A., & Lowell, E. L. *The achievement motive*. New York: Appleton-Century-Crofts, 1953.
McClelland, D. C., & Friedman, G. A. A cross-cultural study of the relationship between child-rearing practices and achievement appearing in folk tales. In G. E. Swanson, T. M. Newcomb, and E. L. Hartley (Eds.), *Readings in social psychology*. New York: Holt, 1952. Pp. 243–249.
McClelland, D. C., & Winter, D. G. *Motivating economic achievement*. New York: Free Press, 1969.
McClintock, C. G. Personality syndromes and attitude change. *Journal of Personality*, 1958, **26**, 479–493.
McConnell, J. V., Cutler, R. L., & McNeil, E. B. Subliminal stimulation: An overview. *American Psychologist*, 1958, **13**, 229–242.
McCord, W., & Howard, J. Negro opinions in three riot cities. *American Behavioral Scientist*, 1968, **11**, 24–27.
McCord, W., McCord, J., & Howard, A. Familial correlates of aggression in nondelinquent male children. *Journal of Abnormal and Social Psychology*, 1961, **62**, 79–93.
McDavid, R. I. Dialect differences and social differences in an urban society. In W. Bright (Ed.), *Sociolinguistics. Proceedings of the UCLA Sociolinguistics Conference 1964*. The Hague: Mouton, 1966. Pp. 72–83.
McDavid, R. I., & McDavid, V. The relation of the speech of American Negroes to the speech of whites. *American Speech*, 1951, **26**, 3–17.
McDougall, W. *An introduction to social psychology*. London: Methuen, 1908.
McGee, R. *Social disorganization in America*. San Francisco: Chandler, 1962.
McGinnies, E. *Social behavior: A functional analysis*. Boston: Houghton-Mifflin, 1970.
McGinniss, J. *The selling of the president 1968*. New York: Trident Press, 1969.
McGrath, J. E. *Social psychology: A brief introduction*. New York: Holt, Rinehart, & Winston, 1964.
McGregor, D. *The human side of enterprise*. New York: McGraw-Hill, 1960.
McGregor, D. *Leadership and motivation*. (Edited by W. G. Bennis and E. H. Schein.) Cambridge, Mass.: M.I.T. Press, 1966.
McGregor, D. *The professional manager*. (Edited by C. McGregor and W. G. Bennis.) New York: McGraw-Hill, 1967.
McGuire, W. J. Attitudes and opinions. In P. R. Farnsworth et al. (Eds.), *Annual review of psychology*. Vol. 17. Palo Alto, Calif.: Annual Reviews, 1966. Pp. 475–514.
McGuire, W. J. Some impending orientations in social psychology: Some thoughts provoked by Kenneth Ring. *Journal of Experimental Social Psychology*, 1967, **3**, 124–139. (a)
McGuire, W. J. Theory-oriented research in natural settings: The best of both worlds for social psychology. Paper presented at Muzafer Sherif's symposium on "Problems of interdisciplinary relationships in the social sciences," Pennsylvania State University, May 1967. (b)
McGuire, W. J. Personality and susceptibility to social influence. In E. F. Borgatta and W. W. Lambert (Eds.), *Handbook of personality theory and research*. Chicago: Rand-McNally, 1968. Pp. 1130–1187.
McGuire, W. J. The nature of attitudes and attitude change. In G. Lindzey and E. Aronson (Eds.), *Handbook of social psychology*. Vol. III. (2nd ed.) Reading, Mass.: Addison-Wesley, 1969. Pp. 136–314.
McGurk, F. C. J. *Comparison of the performance of Negro and white high school seniors on cultural and non-cultural test questions*. Washington, D.C.: The Catholic University of America Press, 1951. (Microcard.)
McGurk, F. C. J. On white and Negro test performance and socioeconomic factors. *Journal of Abnormal and Social Psychology*, 1953, **48**, 448–450.
McKinley, J. C., Hathaway, S. R., & Meehl, P. E. The MMPI: VI. The *K* scale. *Journal of Consulting Psychology*, 1948, **12**, 20–31.
McKinney, T. T. *All white America*. Boston: Meador, 1937.

McKusick, V. A. The royal hemophilia. *Scientific American,* 1965, **213**(2), 88–95.
McLuhan, M. *Understanding media.* New York: McGraw-Hill, 1964.
McMullen, D., & Wrightsman, L. S. Correlates of attitudes toward intermarriage held by Negro and white college students. Paper presented at the meeting of the Southeastern Psychological Association, Atlanta, April 1965.
McNemar, Q. *The revision of the Stanford-Binet scale.* Boston: Houghton-Mifflin, 1942.
McQueen, R., & Browning, C. The intelligence and educational achievement of a matched sample of white and Negro students. *School and Society,* 1960, **88,** 327–329.
Mead, M. *Sex and temperament in three primitive societies.* New York: Morrow, 1935.
Mead, M. *Culture and commitment: A study of the generation gap.* Garden City, N. Y.: Doubleday, 1970.
Mead, M., Dobzhansky, T., Tobach, E., & Light, R. E. (Eds.). *Science and the concept of race.* New York: Columbia University Press, 1968.
Meehl, P. E. *Clinical versus statistical prediction: A theoretical analysis and a review of the evidence.* Minneapolis: University of Minnesota Press, 1954.
Meehl, P. E. When shall we use our heads instead of the formula? *Journal of Counseling Psychology,* 1957, **4,** 268–273.
Megargee, E. I., & Hokanson, J. E. (Eds.) *The dynamics of aggression.* New York: Harper & Row, 1970.
Meier, G. W. Infantile handling and development in Siamese kittens. *Journal of Comparative and Physiological Psychology,* 1961, **54,** 284–286.
Merbaum, A. D. Need for achievement in Negro children. Unpublished master's thesis, University of North Carolina, 1960.
Merton, R. K. *Social theory and social structure.* (Rev. ed.) Chicago: Free Press, 1957.
Milgram, S. Behavioral study of obedience. *Journal of Abnormal and Social Psychology,* 1963, **67,** 371–378.
Milgram, S. Group pressure and action against a person. *Journal of Abnormal and Social Psychology,* 1964, **69,** 137–143. (a)
Milgram, S. Issues in the study of obedience: A reply to Baumrind. *American Psychologist,* 1964, **19,** 848–852. (b)
Milgram, S. Some conditions of obedience and disobedience to authority. *Human Relations,* 1965, **18,** 57–76.
Milgram, S. Reply to the critics. *International Journal of Psychiatry,* 1968, **6,** 294–295.
Milgram, S. The experience of living in cities. *Science,* 1970, **167,** 1461–1468.
Milgram, S., & Toch, H. Collective behavior: Crowds and social movements. In G. Lindzey and E. Aronson (Eds.), *Handbook of social psychology.* Vol. 4. (2nd ed.) Reading, Mass.: Addison-Wesley, 1969. Pp. 507–610.
Miller, D. R., & Swanson, G. E. *The changing American parent: A study in the Detroit area.* New York: Wiley, 1958.
Miller, G. A. Psychology as a means of promoting human welfare. *American Psychologist,* 1969, **24,** 1063–1075. Also reprinted in F. F. Korten, S. W. Cook, and J. I. Lacey (Eds.), *Psychology and the problems of society.* Washington, D. C.: American Psychological Association, 1970. Pp. 5–21.
Miller, H. Is the risky shift the result of a rational group decision? *Proceedings, 78th Annual Convention, American Psychological Association,* 1970, **5,** 333–334.
Miller, H. L., & Woock, R. R. *Social foundations of urban education.* Hinsdale, Ill.: Dryden, 1970.
Miller, L. K., & Hamblin, R. L. Interdependence, differential rewarding, and productivity. *American Sociological Review,* 1963, **28,** 768–778.
Miller, N. Involvement and dogmatism as inhibitors of attitude change. *Journal of Experimental Social Psychology,* 1965, **1,** 121–132.
Miller, N. E. The frustration-aggression hypothesis. *Psychological Review,* 1941, **48,** 337–342.
Miller, N. E. Liberalization of basic s-r concepts: Extensions to conflict behavior, motivation and social learning. In S. Koch (Ed.), *Psychology: A study of science.* Vol. 2. New York: McGraw-Hill, 1959. Pp. 196–292.
Miller, N. E. Some implications of modern behavior theory for personality change and psychotherapy. In P. Worchel and D. Byrne (Eds.), *Personality change.* New York: Wiley, 1964.

Miller, N. E., & Dollard, J. *Social learning and imitation.* New Haven: Yale University Press, 1941.
Millett, K. *Sexual politics.* New York: Doubleday, 1970.
Mills, C. W. The contributions of sociology to studies of industrial relations. *Proceedings of the First Annual Meeting,* Industrial Relations Research Association, 1948, **1,** 199–222.
Milton, O. Presidential choice and performance on a scale of authoritarianism. *American Psychologist,* 1952, **7,** 597–598.
Mischel, W. *Personality and assessment.* New York: Wiley, 1968.
Mishler, E. G., & Waxler, N. E. *Interaction in families.* New York: Wiley, 1968.
Mitnick, L., & McGinnies, E. Influencing ethnocentrism in small discussion groups through a film communication. *Journal of Abnormal and Social Psychology,* 1958, **56,** 82–90.
Mizner, G. L., Barter, J. T., & Werme, P. H. Patterns of drug use among college students. *American Journal of Psychiatry,* 1970, **127,** 15–24.
Money, J., & Brennan, J. G. Sexual dimorphism in the psychology of female transsexuals. In R. Green and J. Money (Eds.), *Transsexualism and sex reassignment.* Baltimore, Md.: Johns Hopkins Press, 1969.
Money, J., & Primrose, C. Sexual dimorphism and dissociation in the psychology of male transsexuals. In R. Green and J. Money (Eds.), *Transsexualism and sex reassignment.* Baltimore, Md.: Johns Hopkins Press, 1969.
Montagu, M. F. A. *Man: His first million years.* Cleveland: World Book, 1957.
Montagu, M. F. A. *Man's most dangerous myth: The fallacy of race.* (4th ed.) Cleveland: World Book, 1964.
Montagu, M. F. A. (Ed.) *Man and aggression.* New York: Oxford University Press, 1968. (a)
Montagu, M. F. A. The new litany of "innate depravity," or "Original Sin" revisited. In M. F. A. Montagu (Ed.), *Man and aggression.* New York: Oxford University Press, 1968. Pp. 3–17. (b)
Moore, W. *Social change.* Englewood Cliffs, N. J.: Prentice-Hall, 1963.
Moore, W. *Order and change. Essays in comparative sociology.* New York: Wiley, 1967.
Moore, W. Social change. In *International Encyclopedia of the Social Sciences.* Vol. 14. New York: Macmillan, 1968.
Moorehead, A. *The Russian revolution.* New York: Harper, 1958. (Paperback edition, 1965.)
Morris, D. *The naked ape.* London: Jonathan Cape, 1967.
Morton, J. R. C., Denenberg, V. H., & Zarrow, M. X. Modification of sexual development through stimulation in infancy. *Journal of Endocrinology,* 1963, **72,** 439–442.
Mosteller, F., & Wallace, D. L. *Inference and disputed authorship: The Federalist.* Reading, Mass.: Addison-Wesley, 1964.
Mouchanow, M. *My empress: Twenty-three years of intimate life with the empress of all the Russias from her marriage to the day of her exile.* New York: John Lane, 1918.
Mulford, H. A. Drinking and deviant drinking, U. S. A., 1963. *Quarterly Journal of Studies on Alcohol,* 1964, **25,** 634–650.
Mulford, H. A., & Miller, D. E. Drinking in Iowa. IV. Preoccupation with alcohol and definitions of alcohol, heavy drinking, and trouble due to drinking. *Quarterly Journal of Studies on Alcohol,* 1960, **21,** 279–291.
Murphy, R. J., & Watson, J. M. The structure of discontent. In N. E. Cohen (Ed.), *The Los Angeles riots: A socio-psychological study.* New York: Praeger, 1970.
Mussen, P. Differences between the TAT responses of Negro and white boys. *Journal of Consulting Psychology,* 1953, **17,** 373–376.
Myers, A. E. Team competition, success, and adjustment of group members. *Journal of Abnormal and Social Psychology,* 1962, **65,** 325–332.
National Commission on the Causes and Prevention of Violence. *To establish justice, to insure domestic tranquility.* New York: Award Books, 1969.
National Science Foundation. *Knowledge into action: Improving the nation's use of the social sciences.* Washington, D. C.: Superintendent of Documents, U. S. Gov't. Printing Office, 1969.
Neary, J. A scientist's variations on a disturbing racial theme. *Life,* June 12, 1970, 58B–65.
Neff, W. *Work and human behavior.* New York: Atherton Press, 1968.
Newbrough, J. R. Adolescent participation in civil disturbances. Final report, Center for Community Studies, George Peabody College for Teachers, November 1968.

Newcomb, T. M. Varieties of interpersonal attraction. In D. Cartwright and A. Zander (Eds.), *Group dynamics: Research and theory.* (2nd ed.) Evanston, Ill.: Row-Peterson, 1960. Pp. 104–119.
Newcomb, T. M. *The acquaintance process.* New York: Holt, Rinehart, & Winston, 1961.
Newcomb, T. M., Turner, R. H., & Converse, P. E. *Social psychology.* New York: Holt, 1965.
New York *Times.* Few cheers for "bad seed" tests for the young. April 19, 1970, P.E.–13.
Newsweek. Taking the Chitling Test. July 15, 1968, pp. 51–52.
Newsweek. Women's lib: The war on "sexism." March 23, 1970, p. 72. (a)
Newsweek. Universities in ferment. June 15, 1970, p. 66. (b)
Newsweek. Why the pollsters failed. July 6, 1970, p. 58. (c)
Newsweek. M*A*S*H*E*D. Feb. 22, 1971, pp. 45–46 (a)
Newsweek. New heat on troop withdrawal. May 31, 1971, p. 13. (b)
Nietzsche, F. *Der Wille zur Macht.* Book 3. In *Werke,* Vol. 16. Leipzig: Alfred Kröner, 1912.
Nisbett, R. E. Determinants of food intake in human obesity. *Science,* 1968, **159,** 1254–1255. (a)
Nisbett, R. E. Taste, deprivation, and weight determinants of eating behavior. *Journal of Personality and Social Psychology,* 1968, **10,** 107–116. (b)
Nowlis, H. *Drugs on the college campus.* Garden City, N.Y.: Anchor Books, 1969.
Oldsey, B. S., & Weintraub, S. *The art of William Golding.* New York: Harcourt, Brace, & World, 1965.
Orne, M. T. Demand characteristics and the concept of quasi-controls. In R. Rosenthal and R. L. Rosnow (Eds.), *Artifact in behavioral research.* New York: Academic Press, 1969. Pp. 143–179.
Orne, M. T., & Holland, C. C. On the ecological validity of laboratory deceptions. *International Journal of Psychiatry,* 1968, **6,** 282–293.
Orwell, G. *1984.* New York: Harcourt-Brace, 1949.
Osborne, R. T. Racial differences in mental growth and school achievement: A longitudinal study. *Psychological Reports,* 1960, **7,** 233–239.
Osgood, C. E., Suci, G. J., & Tannenbaum, P. H. *The measurement of meaning.* Urbana, Ill.: University of Illinois Press, 1957.
Osgood, C. E., & Tannenbaum, P. H. The principle of congruity in the prediction of attitude change. *Psychological Review,* 1955, **62,** 42–55.
Oskamp, S. The relationship of clinical experience and training methods to several criteria of clinical prediction. *Psychological Monographs,* 1962, **76,** (28, Whole No. 547).
Oskamp, S. Clinical judgment from the MMPI: Simple or complex? *Journal of Clinical Psychology,* 1967, **23,** 411–415.
Oskamp, S. Effects of programmed strategies on cooperation in the Prisoner's Dilemma and other mixed-motive games. In L. S. Wrightsman, J. O'Connor, and N. Baker (Eds.), *Cooperation and competition: Readings on mixed-motive games.* Monterey, Calif.: Brooks/Cole, 1972. Pp. 147–189.
Oskamp, S., & Kleinke, C. Amount of reward as a variable in the Prisoner's Dilemma game. *Journal of Personality and Social Psychology,* 1970, **16,** 133–140.
Osser, H., Wang, M. D., & Zaid, F. The young child's ability to imitate and comprehend speech: A comparison of two subcultural groups. *Child Development,* 1969, **40,** 1063–1075.
Packard, V. *The sexual wilderness.* New York: McKay, 1968.
Panel on Privacy and Behavioral Research. Preliminary summary of report. *Science,* 1967, **155,** 535–538.
Parry, H. J., & Crossley, H. M. Validity of responses to survey questions. *Public Opinion Quarterly,* 1950, **14,** 61–80.
Pasamanick, B. A., & Knobloch, H. Early language behavior in Negro children and the testing of intelligence. *Journal of Abnormal and Social Psychology,* 1955, **50,** 401–402.
Pasamanick, B. A., & Knobloch, H. Brain damage and reproductive casualty. *American Journal of Orthopsychiatry,* 1960, **30,** 298–305.
Peabody, D. Attitude content and agreement set in scales of authoritarianism, dogmatism, anti-Semitism, and economic conservatism. *Journal of Abnormal and Social Psychology,* 1961, **63,** 1–11.
Peabody, D. Authoritarianism scales and response bias. *Psychological Bulletin,* 1966, **65,** 11–23.

Peck, R. F., & Havighurst, R. J. *The psychology of character development.* New York: Wiley, 1960.
Pei, M. A., & Gaynor, F. *A dictionary of linguistics.* New York: Philosophical Library, 1954.
Peisach, E. C. Children's comprehension of teacher and peer speech. *Child Development,* 1965, **36,** 467–480.
Pepitone, A. Some conceptual and empirical problems of consistency theories. In S. Feldman (Ed.), *Cognitive consistency.* New York: Academic Press, 1966.
Perlman, D., & Oskamp, S. The effects of picture content and exposure frequency on evaluations of Negroes and whites. *Journal of Experimental Social Psychology,* 1971, **7,** 503–514.
Perry, P. Gallup Poll election survey experience, 1950 to 1960. *Public Opinion Quarterly,* 1962, **26,** 272–279.
Peterson, J., & Lanier, L. H. Studies in the comparative abilities of whites and Negroes. *Mental Measurement Monographs,* 1929, No. 5.
Peterson, R. Organized student protest in 1964–65. *National Association of Women Deans and Counselors Journal,* 1967, **30,** 50–56.
Peterson, R. *The scope of organized student protest in 1967–1968.* Princeton, N. J.: Educational Testing Service, 1968.
Petronko, M. R., & Perin, C. T. A consideration of cognitive complexity and primacy-recency effects in impression formation. *Journal of Personality and Social Psychology,* 1970, **15,** 151–157.
Pettigrew, T. F. Regional differences in anti-Negro prejudice. *Journal of Abnormal and Social Psychology,* 1959, **59,** 28–36.
Pettigrew, T. F. Social psychology and desegregation research. *American Psychologist,* 1961, **16,** 105–112.
Pettigrew, T. F. *A profile of the Negro American.* Princeton, N. J.: Van Nostrand, 1964.
Phillips, B. N. An experimental study of the effects of cooperation and competition, intelligence, and cohesiveness on the task efficiency and process behavior of small groups. Unpublished doctoral dissertation, Indiana University, 1954.
Phillips, E. L. Cultural vs. intropsychic factors in childhood behavior problem referrals. *Journal of Clinical Psychology,* 1956, **12,** 400–401.
Piaget, J. *The language and thought of the child.* New York: Harcourt-Brace, 1926.
Piaget, J. The general problems of the psychobiological development of the child. In J. M. Tanner and B. Inhelder (Eds.), *Discussions of child development: Proceedings of the World Health Organization study group on the psychobiological development of the child.* Vol. 4. New York: International Universities Press, 1960. Pp. 3–27.
Piaget, J. *The moral judgment of the child.* Glencoe, Ill.: Free Press, 1948. (Originally published in 1932; paperback edition published in 1965.)
Pierce, J. V. The educational motivation of superior students who do and do not achieve in high school. U. S. Office of Education, Department of Health, Education, and Welfare, November 1959.
Piliavin, I. M., Rodin, J., & Piliavin, J. A. Good Samaritanism: An underground phenomenon? *Journal of Personality and Social Psychology,* 1969, **13,** 289–299.
Pintner, R. *Intelligence testing.* New York: Holt, 1931.
Poor, D. The social psychology of questionnaires. Unpublished bachelor's thesis, Harvard University, 1967. Cited in R. Rosenthal and R. L. Rosnow (Eds.), *Artifact in behavioral research.* New York: Academic Press, 1969.
Premack, D. The education of S*A*R*A*H. *Psychology Today,* 1970, **4,** 54–58.
Premack, D. Language in chimpanzee? *Science,* 1971, **172,** 808–822.
Price, K. O., Harburg, E., & Newcomb, T. M. Psychological balance in situations of negative interpersonal attitudes. *Journal of Personality and Social Psychology,* 1966, **3,** 265–270.
Prothro, E. T. Ethnocentrism and anti-Negro attitudes in the deep south. *Journal of Abnormal and Social Psychology,* 1952, **47,** 105–108.
Pruitt, D. G. Reward structure and cooperation: The decomposed Prisoner's Dilemma game. *Journal of Personality and Social Psychology,* 1967, **7,** 21–27.
Pruitt, D. G., & Teger, A. I. Is there a shift toward risk in group discussion? If so, what causes it? Paper presented at the meeting of the American Psychological Association, Washington, D. C., September 1967.

Pruitt, D. G., & Teger, A. I. The risky shift in group betting. *Journal of Experimental Social Psychology,* 1969, **5,** 115–126.
Putnam, D., & Snyder, C. *Society, culture and drinking patterns.* New York: Wiley, 1962.
Rabbie, J. M. Differential preference for companionship under threat. *Journal of Abnormal and Social Psychology,* 1963, **67,** 643–648.
Ralls, K. Mammalian scent marking. *Science,* 1971, **171,** 443–450.
Randal, J. "Pot" study's claims hit. *Nashville Tennessean,* May 18, 1971, p. 31.
Ransford, H. E. Isolation, powerlessness, and violence: A study of attitudes and participation in the Watts Riot. *American Journal of Sociology,* 1968, **73,** 581–591.
Rapoport, A. *Fights, games, and debates.* Ann Arbor: University of Michigan Press, 1961.
Rapoport, A., & Chammah, A. *Prisoner's dilemma.* Ann Arbor: University of Michigan Press, 1965.
Raser, J. "Mar-coo-za, Mar-coo-za." *Psychology Today,* 1971, **4**(9), 38–39ff.
Raven, B. H., & Eachus, H. T. Cooperation and competition in means interdependent triads. *Journal of Abnormal and Social Psychology,* 1963, **67,** 307–316.
Rechy, J. *City of night.* New York: Grove Press, 1963.
Reed, T. E. Caucasian genes in American Negroes. *Science,* 1969, **165,** 762–768.
Reedy, G. *The twilight of the presidency.* New York and Cleveland: World Book, 1970.
Reich, C. A. *The greening of America.* New York: Random House, 1970.
Reichart, S. A greater space in which to breathe: What art and drama tell us about alienation. *Journal of Social Issues,* 1969, **25**(2), 137–146.
Reik, T. *Listening with the third ear.* New York: Farrar-Strauss, 1948.
Reiss, I. *Premarital sexual standards in America.* New York: Free Press, 1960.
Reiss, I. *The social context of premarital sexual permissiveness.* New York: Holt, Rinehart, & Winston, 1967.
Rempel, H., & Signori, E. I. Sex differences in self-rating of conscience as a determinant of behavior. *Psychological Reports,* 1964, **15,** 277–278.
Rettig, S. & Rawson, H. E. The risk hypothesis in predictive judgments of unethical behavior. *Journal of Abnormal and Social Psychology,* 1963, **66,** 243–248.
Reuben, D. *Everything you always wanted to know about sex but were afraid to ask.* New York: David McKay, 1969.
Richardson, S. A. A study of selected personality characteristics of social science field workers. Unpublished doctoral dissertation, Cornell University, 1954.
Rider, R. V., Taback, M., & Knobloch, H. Associations between premature birth and socio-economic status. *American Journal of Public Health,* 1955, **45,** 1022–1028.
Riesman, D. (in association with N. Glazer and R. Denney) *The lonely crowd: A study of the changing American character.* New Haven: Yale University Press, 1950.
Ring, K. Experimental social psychology: Some sober questions about frivolous values. *Journal of Experimental Social Psychology,* 1967, **3,** 113–123.
Ring, K. Let's get started: An appeal to what's left in psychology. University of Connecticut, 1971. (Mimeographed.)
Ring, K., Lipinski, C. E., & Braginsky, D. The relationship of birth order to self-evaluation, anxiety reduction, and susceptibility to emotional contagion. *Psychological Monographs,* 1965, **79,**(10, Whole No. 603).
Roberts, P. F. The dynamics of racial intermixture in the American Negro: Some anthropological considerations. *American Journal of Human Genetics,* 1955, **7,** 361–367.
Robins, L. N., Murphy, G. E., & Breckenridge, M. Drinking behavior of young urban Negro men. *Quarterly Journal of Studies on Alcohol,* 1968, **29,** 657–684.
Robinson, D., & Rohde, S. Two experiments with an anti-Semitism poll. *Journal of Abnormal and Social Psychology,* 1946, **41,** 136–144.
Robinson, I. E., King, K., Dudley, C. J., & Cline, F. J. Change in sexual behavior and attitudes of college students. *Family Life Coordinator,* 1968, **17,** 119–123.
Robinson, W. P. The elaborated code in working-class language. *Language and Speech,* 1965, **8,** 243–252.
Rock, I., & Kaufman, L. The moon illusion, II. *Science,* 1962, **136,** 1023–1031.
Roethlisberger, F. J., & Dickson, W. J. *Management and the worker.* Cambridge, Mass.: Harvard University Press, 1939.
Rogers, C. R. A note on the "nature of man." *Journal of Counseling Psychology,* 1957, **4,** 199–203.

Rogers, C. R. *Freedom to learn.* Columbus, Ohio: Charles E. Merrill, 1969.

Rogers, C. R., & Skinner, B. F. Some issues concerning the control of human behavior. *Science,* 1956, **124,** 1057–1066.

Rogers, E. M. *Diffusion of innovations.* New York: Free Press, 1962.

Rohrer, J. H. The test intelligence of Osage Indians. *Journal of Social Psychology,* 1942, **16,** 99–105.

Rokeach, M. *The open and closed mind.* New York: Basic Books, 1960.

Rokeach, M. *Beliefs, attitudes, and values.* San Francisco: Jossey-Bass, 1968.

Rokeach, M. Faith, hope, bigotry. *Psychology Today,* 1970, **3**(11), 33–37; 58.

Rokeach, M., Homant, R., & Penner, L. A value analysis of the disputed Federalist Papers. *Journal of Personality and Social Psychology,* 1970, **16,** 245–250.

Rokeach, M., & Mezei, L. Race and shared belief as factors in social choice. *Science,* 1966, **151,** 167–172.

Rokeach, M., Smith, P. W., & Evans, R. I. Two kinds of prejudice or one? In M. Rokeach, *The open and closed mind.* New York: Basic Books, 1960. Pp. 132–168.

Rokeach, M., & Vidulich, R. N. The formation of new belief systems. In M. Rokeach, *The open and closed mind.* New York: Basic Books, 1960. Pp. 196–214.

Rorer, L. G., & Goldberg, L. R. Acquiescence in the MMPI? *Educational and Psychological Measurement,* 1965, **25,** 801–817.

Rose, A. M. Anti-Semitism's root in city-hatred. *Commentary,* 1948, **6,** 374–378.

Rosen, B. C. Race, ethnicity and the achievement syndrome. *American Sociological Review,* 1959, **24,** 47–60.

Rosen, B. C. Family structure and achievement motivation. *American Sociological Review,* 1961, **26,** 574–585.

Rosen, B. C., & D'Andrade, R. The psychosocial origins of achievement motivation. *Sociometry,* 1959, **22,** 188–218.

Rosen, E. Differences between volunteers and non-volunteers for psychological studies. *Journal of Applied Psychology,* 1951, **35,** 185–193.

Rosen, S. Post-decision affinity for incompatible information. *Journal of Abnormal and Social Psychology,* 1961, **63,** 188–190.

Rosenberg, L. A. Group size, prior experience, and conformity. *Journal of Abnormal and Social Psychology,* 1961, **63,** 436–437.

Rosenberg, M. J. When dissonance fails: On eliminating evaluation apprehension from attitude measurement. *Journal of Personality and Social Psychology,* 1965, **1,** 28–42.

Rosenberg, S., Nelson, C., & Vivekananthan, P. S. A multi-dimensional approach to the structure of personality impressions. *Journal of Personality and Social Psychology,* 1968, **9,** 283–294.

Rosenhan, D. Effects of social class and race on responsiveness to approval and disapproval. *Journal of Personality and Social Psychology,* 1966, **4,** 253–259.

Rosenthal, R. The effect of the experimenter on the results of psychological research. In B. A. Maher (Ed.), *Progress in experimental personality research.* Vol. I. New York: Academic Press, 1964. Pp. 79–114.

Rosenthal, R. *Experimenter effects in behavioral research.* New York: Appleton-Century-Crofts, 1966.

Rosenthal, R., & Fode, K. L. The effect of experimenter bias on the performance of the albino rat. *Behavioral Science,* 1963, **8,** 183–189.

Rosenthal, R., & Jacobson, L. *Pygmalion in the classroom: Teacher expectation and pupils' intellectual development.* New York: Holt, Rinehart, & Winston, 1968.

Rosenthal, R., & Rosnow, R. L. The volunteer subject. In R. Rosenthal and R. L. Rosnow (Eds.), *Artifact in behavioral research.* New York: Academic Press, 1969. Pp. 59–118.

Rosner, S. Consistency in response to group pressures. *Journal of Abnormal and Social Psychology,* 1957, **55,** 145–146.

Rosnow, R. L. When he lends a helping hand, bite it. *Psychology Today,* 1970, **4**(1), 26–30.

Ross, A. S. C. U and non-U: An essay in sociological linguistics. In M. Steinmann, Jr. (Ed.), *New rhetorics.* New York: Scribner's, 1967. Pp. 226–248.

Roszak, T. *The making of a counter culture.* New York: Doubleday, 1969.

Rothbart, M. K. Birth order and mother-child interaction in an achievement situation. *Journal of Personality and Social Psychology,* 1971, **17,** 113–120.

Rotter, J. B. Generalized expectancies for internal versus external control of reinforcement. *Psychological Monographs,* 1966, **80,** 1–28.
Rotter, J. B. Generalized expectancies for interpersonal trust. *American Psychologist,* 1971, **26,** 443–452.
Rubin, I. Common sex myths. *Sexology,* 1966, **32,** 512–514.
Rubin, Z. Measurement of romantic love. *Journal of Personality and Social Psychology,* 1970, **16,** 265–273.
Rudé, G. *The crowd in history, 1730–1848.* New York: Wiley, 1964.
Rudin, S. A. National motives predict psychogenic death rates. *Science,* 1968, **160,** 901–903.
Rule, B. G., & Sandilands, M. L. Test anxiety, confidence, commitment, and conformity. *Journal of Personality,* 1969, **37,** 460–467.
Sadava, S. W. College student drug use: A social psychological study. Unpublished doctoral dissertation, University of Colorado, 1970.
St. Jean, R. Reformulation of the value hypothesis in group risk taking. *Proceedings, 78th Annual Convention, American Psychological Association,* 1970, **5,** 339–340.
Sampson, E. E. Birth order, need achievement, and conformity. *Journal of Abnormal and Social Psychology,* 1962, **64,** 155–159.
Sampson, E. E. The study of ordinal position: Antecedents and outcomes. In B. Maher (Ed.), *Progress in experimental personality research.* Vol. 2. New York: Academic Press, 1965. Pp. 175–228.
Sandiford, P., & Kerr, R. Intelligence of Chinese and Japanese children. *Journal of Educational Psychology,* 1926, **17,** 361–367.
Sanford, F. H. *Authoritarianism and leadership.* Philadelphia: Stephenson, 1950.
Sanford, F. H., & Wrightsman, L. S. *Psychology: The scientific study of man.* (3rd ed.) Belmont, Calif.: Brooks/Cole, 1970.
Sanford, N. The approach of the authoritarian personality. In J. L. McCary (Ed.), *Psychology of personality.* New York: Grove Press, 1956. Pp. 253–319.
Sanford, N. Will psychologists study human problems? *American Psychologist,* 1965, **20,** 192–202.
Sanford, N. Whatever happened to action research? *Journal of Social Issues,* 1970, **26**(4), 3–23.
Savitz, L. D., & Tomasson, R. F. The identifiability of Jews. *American Journal of Sociology,* 1959, **64,** 468–475.
Sawyer, J. Measurement *and* prediction, clinical *and* statistical. *Psychological Bulletin,* 1966, **66,** 178–200.
Schaar, J., & Wolin, S. The revolt of youth. *Current,* June 1970, No. 119, 3–10.
Schachter, S. *The psychology of affiliation.* Stanford, Calif.: Stanford University Press, 1959.
Schachter, S. Birth order, eminence, and higher education. *American Sociological Review,* 1963, **28,** 757–767.
Schachter, S. The interaction of cognitive and physiological determinants of emotional state. In L. Berkowitz (Ed.), *Advances in experimental social psychology.* New York: Academic Press, 1964. Pp. 49–80.
Schachter, S. Cognitive effects on bodily functioning: Studies of obesity and eating. In D. C. Glass (Ed.), *Neurophysiology and emotion.* New York: Rockefeller University Press and Russell Sage Foundation, 1967. Pp. 117–144.
Schachter, S. Obesity and eating. *Science,* 1968, **161,** 751–756.
Schachter, S. Eat, eat. *Psychology Today,* 1971, **4**(11), 44–47ff. (a)
Schachter, S. *Emotion, obesity, and crime.* New York: Academic Press, 1971. (b)
Schachter, S. Some extraordinary facts about obese humans and rats. *American Psychologist,* 1971, **26,** 129–144. (c)
Schachter, S., Goldman, R., & Gordon, A. Effects of fear, food deprivation, and obesity on eating. *Journal of Personality and Social Psychology,* 1968, **10,** 91–97.
Schachter, S., & Singer, J. Cognitive, social, and physiological determinants of emotional state. *Psychological Review,* 1962, **69,** 379–399.
Schachter, S., & Wheeler, L. Epinephrine, chlorpromazine, and amusement. *Journal of Abnormal and Social Psychology,* 1962, **65,** 121–128.
Schatzman, L., & Strauss, A. Social class and modes of communication. *American Journal of Sociology,* 1955, **60,** 329–338.

Schein, E. H. Reaction patterns to severe, chronic stress in American army prisoners of war of the Chinese. *Journal of Social Issues,* 1957, **13**(3), 21–30.
Schein, E. H. *Organizational psychology.* Englewood Cliffs, N. J.: Prentice-Hall, 1965.
Schellenberg, J. A. *An introduction to social psychology.* New York: Random House, 1970.
Schlosberg, H. The description of facial expressions in terms of two dimensions. *Journal of Experimental Psychology,* 1952, **44,** 229–237.
Schlosberg, H. Three dimensions of emotion. *Psychological Review,* 1954, **61,** 81–88.
Schoenberger, R. A. (Ed.) *The American right wing.* New York: Holt, 1969.
Schofield, M. *Sexual behavior of young people.* Boston: Little-Brown, 1965.
Schramm, W., Lyle, J., & Parker, E. B. *Television in the lives of our children.* Stanford, Calif.: Stanford University Press, 1961.
Schulman, M. J., & Havighurst, R. J. Relations between ability and social status in a Midwestern community: IV. Size of vocabulary. *Journal of Educational Psychology,* 1947, **38,** 437–442.
Schuman, H., & Harding, J. Sympathetic identification with the underdog. *Public Opinion Quarterly,* 1963, **37,** 230–241.
Scodel, A. Induced collaboration in some non-zero-sum games. *Journal of Conflict Resolution,* 1962, **6,** 335–340.
Scodel, A., & Austrin, H. The perception of Jewish photographs by non-Jews and Jews. *Journal of Abnormal and Social Psychology,* 1957, **54,** 278–280.
Scodel, A., & Mussen, P. Social perceptions of authoritarians and nonauthoritarians. *Journal of Abnormal and Social Psychology,* 1953, **48,** 181–184.
Scott, J. P. *Aggression.* Chicago: University of Chicago Press, 1958.
Scott, J. P. The social psychology of infra-human animals. In G. Lindzey and E. Aronson (Eds.), *Handbook of social psychology.* Vol. 4. (2nd ed.) Reading Mass.: Addison-Wesley, 1969. Pp. 611–642.
Scott, W. A. Attitude measurement. In G. Lindzey and E. Aronson (Eds.), *Handbook of social psychology.* Vol. 2. (2nd ed.) Reading, Mass.: Addison-Wesley, 1968. Pp. 204–273.
Scottish Council for Research in Education. *Social implications of the 1947 Scottish mental survey.* London: University of London Press, 1953.
Sears, D. O., & Abeles, R. P. Attitudes and opinions. *Annual Review of Psychology,* 1969, **20,** 253–288.
Sears, R. R., Maccoby, E., & Levin, H. *Patterns in child rearing.* Evanston, Ill.: Row-Peterson, 1957.
Sears, R. R., Rau, L., & Alpert, R. *Identification and childrearing.* Stanford, Calif.: Stanford University Press, 1965.
Seashore, H., Wesman, A., & Doppelt, J. The standardization of the Wechsler Intelligence Scale for Children. *Journal of Consulting Psychology,* 1950, **14,** 99–110.
Secord, P. F., Bevan, W., & Katz, B. The Negro stereotype and perceptual accentuation. *Journal of Abnormal and Social Psychology,* 1956, **53,** 78–83.
Seeleman, V. The influence of attitude upon the remembering of pictorial material. *Archives of Psychology,* 1940, No. 258.
Seeman, L. Personal communication. May 28, 1971.
Selltiz, C., Jahoda, M., Deutsch, M., & Cook, S. W. *Research methods in social relations.* (Rev. ed.) New York: Holt, 1959.
Severy, L. J., & Brigham, J. C. Personality, prejudice and voting behavior under conditions of high involvement. Paper presented at the meeting of the Rocky Mountain Psychological Association, Denver, May 1971.
Shaffer, H. Status of women. Editorial Research Reports. *Congressional Quarterly,* 1970, **2**(5), 565–585.
Shaw, M. E. Scaling group tasks: A method for dimensional analysis. Unpublished manuscript, University of Florida, 1963. (Mimeographed.)
Shaw, M. E., & Costanzo, P. R. *Theories in social psychology.* New York: McGraw-Hill, 1970.
Sheldon, E. B., & Freeman, H. E. *Notes on social indicators: Promises and potential.* American Elsevier, 1970.
Sherif, C. W., Sherif, M., & Nebergall, R. E. *Attitude and attitude change: The social judgment approach.* Philadelphia: Saunders, 1965.

Sherif, M. A study of some social factors in perception. *Archives of Psychology,* 1935, **27,** No. 187, 1–60.
Sherif, M. *The psychology of social norms.* New York: Harper, 1936.
Sherif, M. On the relevance of social psychology. *American Psychologist,* 1970, **25,** 144–156.
Sherif, M., Harvey, O. J., White, B. J., Hood, W. E., & Sherif, C. W. *Intergroup conflict and cooperation: The Robber's Cave experiment.* Norman, Okla.: University of Oklahoma Book Exchange, 1961.
Sherif, M., & Hovland, C. *Social judgment.* New Haven: Yale University Press, 1961.
Sherif, M., & Sherif, C. *Social psychology.* New York: Harper & Row, 1969.
Sherif, M., Taub, D., & Hovland, C. I. Assimilation and contrast effects of anchoring stimuli on judgments. *Journal of Experimental Psychology,* 1958, **55,** 150–155.
Sherwood, J. J., Barron, J. W., & Fitch, H. G. Cognitive dissonance: Theory and research. In R. V. Wagner and J. J. Sherwood (Eds.), *The study of attitude change.* Belmont, Calif.: Brooks/Cole, 1969. Pp. 56–86.
Shils, E. Authoritarianism: "Right" and "Left." In R. Christie and M. Jahoda (Eds.), *Studies in the scope and method of "The authoritarian personality."* New York: Free Press, 1954.
Shima, H. The relationship between the leader's modes of interpersonal cognition and the performance of the group. *Japanese Psychological Research,* 1968, **10,** 13–30.
Shipman, V. C., & Hess, R. D. Children's conceptual styles as a function of social status and maternal conceptual styles. Paper presented at the meeting of the American Psychological Association, Chicago, September 1965.
Shoffeitt, P. G. The moral development of children as a function of parental moral judgments and child-rearing practices. Unpublished doctoral dissertation, George Peabody College for Teachers, 1971.
Short, J. F., Jr., Rivera, R., & Tennyson, R. A. Perceived opportunities, gang membership, and delinquency. *American Sociological Review,* 1965, **30,** 56–67.
Shriner, T. H., & Miner, L. Morphological structures of disadvantaged and advantaged children. *Journal of Speech and Hearing Research,* 1968, **11,** 427–431.
Shuey, A. M. *The testing of Negro intelligence.* Lynchburg, Va.: J. P. Bell, 1958. (Republished: New York; Social Science Press, 1966.)
Shuy, R. W. Subjective judgments in sociolinguistic analysis. In J. E. Alatis (Ed.), *Report of the 20th annual round table meeting on linguistics and language studies.* Washington, D. C.: Georgetown University Press, 1970. Pp. 175–185.
Siegel, A. E. The influence of violence in the mass media upon children's role expectations. *Child Development,* 1958, **29,** 35–56.
Siegel, A. E. Mass media and violence: Effects on children. *Stanford M. D.,* 1969, **8**(2), 11–14.
Siegel, S. Certain determinants and correlates of authoritarianism. *Genetic Psychology Monographs,* 1954, **49,** 187–229.
Siegel, S., & Zajonc, R. B. Group risk-taking in professional decisions. *Sociometry,* 1967, **30,** 339–350.
Sigel, I. E., & Perry, C. Psycholinguistic diversity among "culturally deprived" children. *American Journal of Orthopsychiatry,* 1968, **38,** 122–126.
Silverman, I. On the resolution and tolerance of cognitive consistency in a natural-occurring event: Attitudes and beliefs following the Senator Edward M. Kennedy incident. *Journal of Personality and Social Psychology,* 1971, **17,** 171–178.
Simon, L. M., & Leavitt, E. A. The relation between Wechsler-Bellevue IQ scores and occupational area. *Occupations,* 1950, **29,** 23–25.
Simon, W., Gagnon, J., & Carns, D. Sexual behavior of the college student. Paper presented at the meeting of the American Academy of Psychoanalysis, New York, 1968.
Simpson, G. E., & Yinger, J. M. *Racial and cultural minorities.* (3rd ed.) New York: Harper & Row, 1965.
Singer, J. E. The use of manipulative strategies: Machiavellianism and attractiveness. *Sociometry,* 1964, **27,** 128–140.
Singer, J. E., Brush, C. A., & Lublin, S. C. Some aspects of deindividuation: Identification and conformity. *Journal of Experimental Social Psychology,* 1965, **1,** 356–378.
Skinner, B. F. *Walden two.* New York: Macmillan, 1948.
Skinner, B. F. *Beyond freedom and dignity.* New York: Knopf, 1971.
Skolnick, P., & Shaw, J. I. How important is the need for consistency? Paper presented at the meeting of the Western Psychological Association, Los Angeles, April 1970.

Sledd, J. On not teaching English usage. *English Journal,* 1965, **54,** 698–703.
Smelser, N. *Essays in sociological explanation.* Englewood Cliffs, N. J.: Prentice-Hall, 1968.
Smigel, E. O., & Seiden, R. The decline and fall of the double standard. *Annals of the American Academy of Political and Social Sciences,* 1968, **376,** 1–14.
Smith, A. J., Madden, H. E., & Sobol, R. Productivity and recall in cooperative discussion groups. *Journal of Psychology,* 1957, **43,** 193–204.
Smith, C. R., Williams, L., & Willis, R. H. Race, sex, and belief as determinants of friendship acceptance. *Journal of Personality and Social Psychology,* 1967, **5,** 127–137.
Smith, H. L., & Hyman, H. The biasing effect of interviewer expectations on survey results. *Public Opinion Quarterly,* 1950, **14,** 491–506.
Smith, M. B., Bruner, J. S., & White, R. W. *Opinions and personality.* New York: Wiley, 1956.
Smith, S. Language and nonverbal test performance of racial groups in Honolulu before and after a 14-year interval. *Journal of General Psychology,* 1942, **26,** 51–93.
Snow, R. E. Review of R. Rosenthal and L. Jacobson, *Pygmalion in the classroom. Contemporary Psychology,* 1969, **14,** 197–199.
Society for the Psychological Study of Social Issues (SPSSI). Social change and psychological patterns. *Journal of Social Issues,* 1961, **17**(1), complete issue.
Society for the Psychological Study of Social Issues Council. Statement on race and intelligence. *Journal of Social Issues,* 1969, **25**(3), 1–3.
Solomon, R. L., & Postman, L. Frequency of usage as a determinant of recognition threshholds for words. *Journal of Experimental Psychology,* 1952, **43,** 195–202.
Sommer, R. *Personal space: The behavioral basis of design.* Englewood Cliffs, N. J.: Prentice-Hall, 1969.
Sorokin, P. A., Tranquist, M., Parten, M., & Zimmerman, C. C. An experimental study of efficiency of work under various specified conditions. *American Journal of Sociology,* 1930, **35,** 765–782.
Spain, C. J. Definition of familiar nouns by culturally deprived and nondeprived children of varying ages. Unpublished doctoral dissertation, George Peabody College for Teachers, 1962. (*Dissertation Abstracts,* 1962, **23,** 2201).
Spiller, G. The dynamics of greatness. *Sociological Review,* 1929, **21,** 218–232.
Sroufe, L. A. A methodological and philosophical critique of intervention-oriented research. *Developmental Psychology,* 1970, **2,** 140–145.
Stacey, C. L., & De Martino, M. F. *Understanding human motivation.* Cleveland, Ohio: Howard Allen, 1958.
Staples, F. R., & Walters, R. H. Anxiety, birth order, and susceptibility to social influence. *Journal of Abnormal and Social Psychology,* 1961, **62,** 716–719.
Stein, D. D. The influence of belief systems on interpersonal preference: A validation study of Rokeach's theory of prejudice. *Psychological Monographs,* 1966, **80**(8, Whole No. 616), 1–29.
Stein, D. D., Hardyck, J. E., & Smith, M. B. Race *and* belief: An open and shut case. *Journal of Personality and Social Psychology,* 1965, **1,** 281–289.
Steiner, I., & Johnson, H. Authoritarianism and "tolerance of trait inconsistency." *Journal of Abnormal and Social Psychology,* 1963, **67,** 388–391.
Stern, C. Language competencies of young children. *Young Children,* 1966, **22,** 44–50.
Stewart, Louis. The politics of birth order. *Proceedings, 78th Annual Convention, American Psychological Association,* 1970, **5,** 365–366.
Stewart, L. H., Dole, A. A., & Harris, Y. Y. Cultural differences in abilities during high school. *American Journal of Educational Research,* 1967, **4,** 19–29.
Stewart, N. AGCT scores of army personnel grouped by occupations. *Occupations,* 1947, **26,** 5–41.
Stewart, W. A. Urban Negro speech: Sociolinguistic factors affecting English teaching. In R. W. Shuy (Ed.), *Social dialects and language learning.* Champaign, Ill.: National Council of Teachers of English, 1964. Pp. 10–19.
Stewart, W. A. On the use of Negro dialect in the teaching of reading. In J. Baratz and R. W. Shuy (Eds.), *Teaching black children to read.* Washington, D.C.: Center for Applied Linguistics, 1969. Pp. 156–219.
Stewart, W. A. Toward a history of American Negro dialect. In F. Williams (Ed.), *Language and poverty. Perspectives on a theme.* Chicago: Markham, 1970. Pp. 351–379.

Stinchcombe, A. L., McDill, M., & Walker, D. Is there a racial tipping point in changing schools? *Journal of Social Issues,* 1969, **25**(1), 127–136.
Stodolsky, S. S., & Lesser, G. Learning patterns in the disadvantaged. *Harvard Educational Review,* 1967, **37,** 546–593.
Stogdill, R. M. Personal factors associated with leadership. *Journal of Psychology,* 1948, **23,** 36–71.
Stogdill, R. M. Leadership, membership, and organization. *Psychological Bulletin,* 1950, **47,** 1–14.
Stogdill, R. M. Validity of leader behavior descriptions. *Personnel Psychology,* 1969, **22,** 153–158.
Stone, M. Drinking patterns and alcoholism among American Negroes. In D. J. Pittman (Ed.), *Alcoholism.* New York: Harper & Row, 1967.
Stoner, J. A. F. A comparison of individual and group decisions involving risk. Unpublished master's thesis, School of Industrial Management, M.I.T., 1961.
Stotland, E., & Dunn, R. E. Identification, "oppositeness," authoritarianism, self-esteem, and birth order. *Psychological Monographs,* 1962, **76,** No. 528.
Stotland, E., & Hillmer, M. L., Jr. Identification, authoritarian defensiveness, and self-esteem. *Journal of Abnormal and Social Psychology,* 1962, **64,** 334–342.
Stotland, E., Katz, D., & Patchen, M. The reduction of prejudice through the arousal of self-insight. *Journal of Personality,* 1959, **27,** 507–531.
Straus, R., & Bacon, S. *Drinking in college.* New Haven: Yale University Press, 1953.
Stricker, L. J., Messick, S., & Jackson, D. N. Conformity, anticonformity, and independence: Their dimensionality and generality. *Journal of Personality and Social Psychology,* 1970, **16,** 494–507.
Strickland, R. *The language of elementary school children: Its relationship to the language of reading textbooks, and the quality of reading of selected children.* Bloomington, Ind.: School of Education, Indiana University, 1962.
Stuckert, R. P. Race mixture: The African ancestry of white Americans. In P. B. Hammond (Ed.), *Physical anthropology and archeology, selected readings.* New York: Macmillan, 1964. Pp. 192–197.
Student Committee on Human Sexuality, Yale University. *The student guide to sex on campus.* New York: New American Library, 1971.
Sullivan, H. S. *The interpersonal theory of psychiatry.* New York: Norton, 1953.
Swingle, P. (Ed.) *The structure of conflict.* New York: Academic Press, 1970.
Szabo, D. Personal communication, November 11, 1970.
Taft, R. The ability to judge people. *Psychological Bulletin,* 1955, **52,** 1–23.
Tagiuri, R. Person perception. In G. Lindzey and E. Aronson (Eds.), *Handbook of social psychology.* Vol. 3. (2nd ed.) Reading, Mass.: Addison-Wesley, 1969. Pp. 395–449.
Tajfel, H. Social and cultural factors in perception. In G. Lindzey and E. Aronson (Eds.), *Handbook of social psychology.* Vol. 3. (2nd ed.) Reading, Mass.: Addison-Wesley, 1969. Pp. 315–394.
Tannenbaum, A. S. *Social psychology of the work organization.* Belmont, Calif.: Wadsworth, 1966.
Tanner, K. L., & Catron, D. W. The effects of examiner-subject variables (length of acquaintance and race of E) on WPPSI scores of preschool Negro boys. Paper presented at the meeting of the Southeastern Psychological Association, Miami Beach, April 1971.
Tanser, H. A. *The settlement of Negroes in Kent County, Ontario, and a study of the mental capacity of their descendants.* Chatham, Ont.: Shepard, 1939.
Tanter, R., & Midlarsky, M. A theory of revolution. *Journal of Conflict Resolution,* 1967, **11,** 264–280.
Taylor, F. W. *Scientific management.* New York: Harper, 1911.
Tec, N. Family and differential involvement with marijuana: A study of suburban teenagers. *Journal of Marriage and the Family,* 1970, **32,** 656–664.
Teger, A. I., & Pruitt, D. G. Components of group risk taking. *Journal of Experimental Social Psychology,* 1967, **3,** 189–205.
Teger, A. I., Pruitt, D. G., St. Jean, R., & Haaland, G. A re-examination of the familiarization hypothesis in group risk taking. *Journal of Experimental Social Psychology,* 1970, **6,** 346–350.

Templin, M. E. *Certain language skills in children: Their development and interrelationships.* Minneapolis, Minn.: University of Minnesota Press, 1957.
Terhune, K. W. Motives, situation, and interpersonal conflict within the Prisoner's Dilemma. *Journal of Personality and Social Psychology,* Monograph Supplement, 1968, **8,** 1–24.
Terhune, K. W. The effects of personality in cooperation and conflict. In P. Swingle (Ed.), *The structure of conflict.* New York: Academic Press, 1970. Pp. 193–234.
Tharp, R. G. Psychological patterning in marriage. *Psychological Bulletin,* 1963, **60,** 97–117.
Thayer, G. *The war business: The international trade in armaments.* New York: Simon & Schuster, 1969.
Theman, V., & Witty, P. A. Case studies and genetic records of two gifted Negroes. *Journal of Psychology,* 1943, **15,** 165–181.
Thibaut, J. W., & Kelley, H. H. *The social psychology of groups.* New York: Wiley, 1959.
Thomas, W. I. *Primitive behavior: An introduction to the social sciences.* New York: McGraw-Hill, 1937.
Tilly, C. Collective violence in European perspective. In H. D. Graham and T. R. Gurr (Eds.), *Violence in America.* New York: New American Library, 1969. Pp. 4–42.
Time. Choosing parents in Iowa. Feb. 25, 1966, 45. (a)
Time. A gun-toting nation. Aug. 12, 1966, 15. (b)
Time. Meaningless statistics? Aug. 19, 1966, 48–49. (c)
Time. Moynihan's memo fever. March 23, 1970, 15–16.
Tinbergen, N. *The study of instinct.* Oxford: Clarendon Press, 1951.
Tinbergen, N. On war and peace in animals and man. *Science,* 1968, **196,** 1411–1418.
Titus, H. E., & Hollander, E. P. The California F scale in psychological research. *Psychological Bulletin,* 1957, **54,** 47–64.
Toch, H. *The social psychology of social movements.* Indianapolis: Bobbs-Merrill, 1965.
Toffler, A. *Future shock.* New York: Random House, 1970.
Tomkins, C. The creative situation. *New Yorker,* Jan. 7, 1967.
Tomlinson, T. M. The development of a riot ideology among urban Negroes. *American Behavioral Scientist,* 1968, **11**(4), 27–31.
Toynbee, A. J. *A study of history.* Vol. 1. New York: Oxford University Press, 1948.
Triandis, H. C. A note of Rokeach's theory of prejudice. *Journal of Abnormal and Social Psychology,* 1961, **62,** 184–186.
Triandis, H. C., & Davis, E. Race and belief as determinants of behavioral intentions. *Journal of Personality and Social Psychology,* 1965, **2,** 715–725.
Triandis, H. C., & Vassiliou, V. Frequency of contact and stereotyping. *Journal of Personality and Social Psychology,* 1967, **7,** 316–328.
Tseng, S. C. An experimental study of the effect of three types of distribution of reward upon work efficiency and group dynamics. Unpublished doctoral dissertation, Columbia University, 1969.
Tucker, G. R., & Lambert, W. E. White and Negro listeners' reactions to various American-English dialects. *Social Forces,* 1969, **47,** 463–468.
Tulkin, S. Race, class, family, and school achievement. *Journal of Personality and Social Psychology,* 1968, **9,** 31–37.
Tyler, L. E. *The psychology of human differences.* (3rd ed.) New York: Appleton-Century-Crofts, 1965.
Uejio, C. K., & Wrightsman, L. S. Ethnic-group differences in the relationship of trusting attitudes to cooperative behavior. *Psychological Reports,* 1967, **20,** 563–571.
UNESCO. Biological aspects of race. *UNESCO Courier,* April 1, 1965, 8–11.
U.S. Department of Labor. *The Negro family: The case for national action.* Washington, D.C.: U.S. Gov't. Printing Office, 1969.
U.S. Department of Labor. *The Negro family: The case of national action.* Washington, D.C.: Office of Policy Planning and Research, U.S. Department of Labor, 1965.
Vacchiano, R. B., Strauss, P. S., & Hochman, L. The open and closed mind: A review of dogmatism. *Psychological Bulletin,* 1969, **71,** 261–273.
Valentine, C. A. Deficit, difference, and biocultural models of Afro-American behavior. *Harvard Educational Review,* 1971, **41,** 137–157.
Valins, S. Cognitive effects of false heart-rate feedback. *Journal of Personality and Social Psychology,* 1966, **4,** 400–408.

Valins, S. Emotionality and autonomic reactivity. *Journal of Experimental Research in Personality,* 1967, **2,** 41–48. (a)
Valins, S. Emotionality and information concerning internal reactions. *Journal of Personality and Social Psychology,* 1967, **6,** 458–463. (b)
Varela, J. A. Aplicación de hallazgos provenientes de las ciencias sociales. *Revista Interamericana de Psicologia,* 1969, **3,** 45–52.
Vernadsky, G. *A history of Russia.* Philadelphia: Blakiston, 1944.
Vidmar, N. Group composition and the risky shift. *Journal of Experimental Social Psychology,* 1970, **6,** 153–166.
Vidulich, R. N., & Kaiman, I. P. The effects of information source status and dogmatism upon conformity behavior. *Journal of Abnormal and Social Psychology,* 1961, **63,** 639–642.
Vinacke, W. E. & Gullickson, G. R. Age and sex differences in the formation of coalitions. *Child Development,* 1964, **35,** 1211–1231.
Vollmer, H. M. Basic roles for applying social science to urban and social problems. *Urban and Social Change Review,* 1970, **3**(2), 32–33.
von Frisch, K. *Bees. Their vision, chemical senses, and language.* Ithaca, N.Y.: Cornell University Press, 1950.
Vroom, V. H. *Some personality determinants of the effects of participation.* Englewood Cliffs, N.J.: Prentice-Hall, 1960.
Vroom, V. H., & Mann, F. C. Leader authoritarianism and employee attitudes. *Personnel Psychology,* 1960, **13,** 125–140.
Vygotsky, L. S. *Thought and language.* Cambridge, Mass.: M.I.T. Press, 1962.
Wagner, R. V., & Sherwood, J. J. (Eds.) *The study of attitude change.* Belmont, Calif.: Brooks/Cole, 1969.
Wainwright, L. The dying girl that no one helped. *Life,* April 10, 1964, 21.
Walker, E. L. *Psychology as a natural and social science.* Belmont, Calif.: Brooks/Cole, 1970.
Wallach, M. A., Kogan, N., & Bem, D. J. Group influence on individual risk taking. *Journal of Abnormal and Social Psychology,* 1962, **65,** 75–86.
Wallach, M. A., Kogan, N., & Bem, D. J. Diffusion of responsibility and level of risk-taking in groups. *Journal of Abnormal and Social Psychology,* 1964, **68,** 263–274.
Wallach, M. A., Kogan, N., & Burt, R. Are risk takers more persuasive than conservatives in group decisions? *Journal of Experimental Social Psychology,* 1968, **4,** 76–89.
Wallin, P. A study of orgasm as a condition of woman's enjoyment of intercourse. *Journal of Social Psychology,* 1960, **51,** 191–198.
Walster, E. The effect of self-esteem on romantic liking. *Journal of Experimental Social Psychology,* 1965, **1,** 184–197.
Walster, E. Passionate love. Paper presented at a conference on "Theories of interpersonal attraction in the dyad," New London, Conn., October 1970.
Walster, E., & Berscheid, E. Adrenaline makes the heart grow fonder. *Psychology Today,* 1971, **5**(1), 46–50ff.
Walters, C. E. Comparative development of Negro and white infants. *Journal of Genetic Psychology,* 1967, **110,** 235–251.
Walters, R. H. Implications of laboratory studies of aggression for the control and regulation of violence. *Annals,* 1965, **364,** 60–72.
Walters, R. H., Llewellyn-Thomas, E., & Acker, C. W. Enhancement of punitive behavior by audio-visual displays. *Science,* 1962, **135,** 872–873.
Walters, R. H., & Parke, R. D. Social motivation, dependency, and susceptibility to social influence. In L. Berkowitz (Ed.), *Advances in experimental social psychology.* Vol. I. New York: Academic Press, 1964. Pp. 231–276.
Walters, R., & Willows, D. Imitation behavior of disturbed children following exposure to aggressive and nonaggressive models. *Child Development,* 1968, **39,** 79–91.
Ware, R., & Harvey, O. J. A cognitive determinant of impression formation. *Journal of Personality and Social Psychology,* 1967, **5,** 38–44.
Warner, W. L., Meeker, M., & Eels, K. W. *Social class in America.* Chicago: Science Research Associates, 1949.
Warren, J. R. The effects of certain selection procedures in forming a group of honor students. Special Report No. 8, University of Nebraska, Agriculture Experiment Station, 1963.

Warren, J. R. Student characteristics associated with farm and nonfarm backgrounds. Unpublished report to the Research Council, University of Nebraska, 1964.
Warren, J. R. Birth order and social behavior. *Psychological Bulletin,* 1966, **65,** 38–49.
Washburn, S. L. The study of race. In M. F. A. Montagu (Ed.), *The concept of race.* New York: Free Press, 1964. Pp. 242–260.
Watson, G. *Action for unity.* New York: Harper, 1947.
Watts, W., Lynch, S., & Whittaker, D. Alienation and activism in today's college-age youth: Socialization patterns and current family relationships. *Journal of Counseling Psychology,* 1969, **16,** 1–7.
Watts, W., & Whittaker, D. Free speech advocates at Berkeley. *Journal of Applied Behavioral Science,* 1966, **2,** 41–62.
Webb, E. J., Campbell, D. T., Schwartz, R. D., & Sechrest, L. *Unobtrusive measures: Nonreactive research in the social sciences.* Chicago: Rand-McNally, 1966.
Weber, M. *The Protestant ethic and the spirit of capitalism.* New York: Scribner's, 1930.
Webster, S. W. The influence of interracial contact on social acceptance in a newly integrated school. *Journal of Educational Psychology,* 1961, **52,** 292–296.
Weener, P. Social dialect differences and the recall of verbal messages. *Journal of Educational Psychology,* 1969, **60,** 194–199.
Weigert, E. The psychoanalytic view of personality. In S. Doniger (Ed.), *The nature of man.* New York: Harper, 1962. Pp. 3–21.
Weikart, D. P. Preschool programs: Preliminary findings. *Journal of Special Education,* 1967, **1,** 163–181.
Weil, A. T., & Zinberg, N. E. Acute effects of marihuana on speech. *Nature,* 1969, **222,** 434–437.
Weil, A. T., Zinberg, N. E., & Nelson, J. M. Clinical and psychological effects of marihuana in man. *Science,* 1968, **162,** 1234–1242.
Weinstein, M. S. Achievement motivation and risk preference. *Journal of Personality and Social Psychology,* 1969, **13,** 153–172.
Weiss, W. Effects of the mass media of communication. In G. Lindzey and E. Aronson (Eds.), *Handbook of social psychology.* (2nd ed.) Vol. 5. Reading, Mass.: Addison-Wesley, 1969. Pp. 77–195.
Weissberg, N. C. On DeFleur and Westie's "Attitudes as a scientific concept." *Social Forces,* 1965, **43,** 422–425.
Weisstein, N. Woman as nigger. *Psychology Today,* 1969, **3,** 20–28; 58.
Westie, F. R. A technique for the measurement of race attitudes. *American Sociological Review,* 1953, **18,** 73–78.
Wheeler, L. R. A comparative study of the intelligence of East Tennessee mountain children. *Journal of Educational Psychology,* 1942, **33,** 321–334.
Whitworth, R. H., & Lucker, W. Effects of strategy on cooperative behavior in culturally disadvantaged and college populations. *Proceedings, 77th Annual Convention, American Psychological Association,* 1969, **4,** 305–306.
Whitworth, R. H., & Lucker, W. Effects of size of reward on cooperation in culturally disadvantaged and college populations. *Proceedings, 78th Annual Convention, American Psychological Association,* 1970, **5,** 431–432.
Whorf, B. L. *Language, thought, and reality: Selected writings.* (Edited by J. B. Carroll.) Cambridge, Mass.: M.I.T. Press, 1956.
Whyte, W. H., Jr. *The organization man.* New York: Simon & Schuster, 1956.
Wichman, H. Effects of isolation and communication in a two-person game. *Journal of Personality and Social Psychology,* 1970, **16,** 114–120.
Wicker, A. W. Attitudes versus action: The relationship of verbal and overt behavioral responses to attitude objects. *Journal of Social Issues,* 1969, **25**(4), 41–78.
Wiggins, J. S. Personality structure. In P. R. Farnsworth, J. Polefka, and M. R. Rosenzweig (Eds.), *Annual review of psychology.* Vol. 19. Palo Alto, Calif.: Annual Reviews, Inc., 1968. Pp. 293–350.
Wilcoxon, H. C. Historical introduction to the problem of reinforcement. In J. Tapp (Ed.), *Reinforcement and behavior.* New York: Academic Press, 1969. Pp. 1–46.
Willems, E. P., & Clark, R. D., III. Dependence of the risky shift on instructions: A replication. *Psychological Reports,* 1969, **25,** 811–814. (a)

Willems, E. P., & Clark, R. D., III. Relative tenability of the diffusion-of-responsibility and risk-as-value hypotheses in the risky shift. Paper submitted for publication, 1969. (b)

Williams, F. (Ed.) *Language and poverty. Perspectives on a theme.* Chicago: Markham, 1970. (a)

Williams, F. Psychological correlates of speech characteristics: On sounding "disadvantaged." *Journal of Speech and Hearing Research,* 1970, **13,** 472–488. (b)

Williams, F., & Naremore, R. C. On the functional analysis of social class differences in modes of speech. *Speech Monographs,* 1969, **36,** 77–102. (a)

Williams, F., & Naremore, R. C. Social class differences in children's syntactic performance: A quantitative analysis of field study data. *Journal of Speech and Hearing Research,* 1969, **12,** 778–793. (b)

Williams, R. M., Jr. *The reduction of intergroup tensions.* New York: Social Science Research Council, 1947.

Willis, R. H. Two dimensions of conformity-nonconformity. *Sociometry,* 1963, **26,** 499–513.

Willis, R. H. Conformity, independence, and anti-conformity. *Human Relations,* 1965, **18,** 373–388.

Willis, R. H., & Hollander, E. P. An experimental study of three response modes in social influence situations. *Journal of Abnormal and Social Psychology,* 1964, **69,** 150–156.

Wilner, D. M., Walkley, R., & Cook, S. W. *Human relations in interracial housing: A study of the contact hypothesis.* Minneapolis, Minn.: University of Minnesota Press, 1955.

Winch, R. F. *The modern family.* New York: Holt, 1952.

Winch, R. F., Ktsanes, T., & Ktsanes, V. The theory of complementary needs in mate selection: An analytic and descriptive study. *American Sociological Review,* 1954, **19,** 241–249.

Winterbottom, M. R. The relation of childhood training in independence to achievement motivation. Unpublished doctoral dissertation, University of Michigan, 1953.

Wishner, J. Reanalysis of "impressions of personality." *Psychological Review,* 1960, **67,** 96–112.

Witkin, H. A., Dyk, R. B., Faterson, H. F., Goodenough, D. R., & Karp, S. A. *Psychological differentiation: Studies of development.* New York: Wiley, 1962.

Witty, P. A., & Jenkins, M. D. The case of "B," a gifted Negro girl. *Journal of Social Psychology,* 1935, **6,** 117–124.

Wolf, R. M. The identification and measurement of environmental process variables related to intelligence. Unpublished doctoral dissertation, University of Chicago, 1963.

Wolfe, B. *Three who made a revolution.* New York: Time Reading Program, 1964. 2 vols.

Wolfram, W. A. *A sociolinguistic description of Detroit Negro speech.* Washington, D.C.: Center for Applied Linguistics, 1969.

Wolfram, W. A. The nature of nonstandard dialect divergence. *Elementary English,* 1970, **47,** 739–748.

Wood, F. A. *The influence of monarchs.* New York: Macmillan, 1913.

Wood, R. Popular sex superstitions. *Sexology,* 1963, **29,** 752–754.

Woodmansee, J., & Cook, S. W. Dimensions of verbal racial attitudes. *Journal of Personality and Social Psychology,* 1967, **7,** 240–250.

Woodworth, R. S. *Experimental psychology.* New York: Holt, 1938.

Wrench, D. F. *Psychology: A social approach.* New York: McGraw-Hill, 1969.

Wrightsman, L. S. Effects of waiting with others on changes in felt level of anxiety. *Journal of Abnormal and Social Psychology,* 1960, **61,** 216–222. (a)

Wrightsman, L. S. The effects of purported validity of a test on motivation and achievement. *Journal of Educational Research,* 1960, **54,** 153–156. (b)

Wrightsman, L. S. The effects of anxiety, achievement motivation, and task importance upon performance on an intelligence test. *Journal of Educational Psychology,* 1962, **53,** 150–156.

Wrightsman, L. S. Measurement of philosophies of human nature. *Psychological Reports,* 1964, **14,** 743–751. (a)

Wrightsman, L. S. Some subtle factors affecting students' evaluations of teachers. *S.P.A.T.E. Journal,* 1964, **3,** 42–51. (b)

Wrightsman, L. S. Attitudinal and personality correlates of presidential voting preferences. Paper presented at the meeting of the American Psychological Association, Chicago, September 1965.

Wrightsman, L. S. Personality and attitudinal correlates of trusting and trustworthy behaviors in a two-person game. *Journal of Personality and Social Psychology,* 1966, **4,** 328–332.

Wrightsman, L. S. Wallace supporters and adherence to "law and order." *Journal of Personality and Social Psychology,* 1969, **13,** 17–22.

Wrightsman, L. S., & Baker, N. J. Where have all the idealistic imperturbable freshmen gone? *Proceedings of the 77th Annual Convention, American Psychological Association,* 1969, **4,** 299–300.

Wrightsman, L. S., Baxter, G. W., Jr., & Jackson, V. W. Effects of school desegregation upon attitudes toward Negroes held by Southern junior high school students. Final report, CEMREL research contract, 1967. (Mimeographed.)

Wrightsman, L. S., Bruininks, R., Lucker, W. G., & Anderson, W. H. Effect of subjects' training and college class and others' strategy upon cooperative behavior in a Prisoner's Dilemma game. Unpublished manuscript, George Peabody College, 1967.

Wrightsman, L. S., & Cook, S. W. Factor analysis and attitude change. Paper presented at the meeting of the Southeastern Psychological Association, Atlanta, April 1965.

Wrightsman, L. S., Davis, D. W., Lucker, W. G., Bruininks, R., Evans, J., Wilde, R., Paulson, D., & Clark, G. Effects of other person's race and strategy upon cooperative behavior in a Prisoner's Dilemma game. Paper presented at the meeting of the Midwestern Psychological Association, Chicago, May 1967.

Wrightsman, L. S., & Noble, F. C. Reactions to the President's assassination and changes in philosophies of human nature. *Psychological Reports,* 1965, **16,** 159–162.

Wrightsman, L. S., O'Connor, J., & Baker, N. J. (Eds.) *Cooperation and competition: Readings on mixed-motive games.* Monterey, Calif.: Brooks/Cole, 1972.

Wrightsman, L. S., & Satterfield, C. H. Additional norms and standardization of the Philosophies of Human Nature scale—1967 Revision. George Peabody College for Teachers, 1967. (Mimeographed; 23 pp.)

Wyatt, F. Psychology and the humanities: A study in misunderstandings. *Teachers College Record,* 1963, **64,** 562–575.

Yerkes, R. M. Psychological examining in the United States Army. *Memoirs of the National Academy of Science.* Vol. 15. Washington, D. C.: U. S. Gov't. Printing Office, 1921.

Young, J. The effects of laboratory training on self-concept, philosophies of human nature, and perceptions of group behavior. Unpublished doctoral dissertation, George Peabody College for Teachers, 1970.

Youssoupoff (Yussoupov), F. *Rasputin: His malignant influence and his assassination.* New York: Cape, 1927.

Youth culture and the generation gap. Panel discussion. *Religious Education,* 1970, **65,** 99–108.

Yuker, H. E. Group atmosphere and memory. *Journal of Abnormal and Social Psychology,* 1955, **51,** 17–23.

Zagona, S. V., & Zurcher, L. A. Participation, interaction, and role behavior in groups selected from the extremes of the open-closed cognitive continuum. *Journal of Psychology,* 1964, **58,** 255–264.

Zagona, S. V., & Zurcher, L. A. The relationship of verbal ability and other cognitive variables to the open-closed cognitive dimension. *Journal of Psychology,* 1965, **60,** 213–219.

Zajonc, R. B. The concepts of balance, congruity, and dissonance. *Public Opinion Quarterly,* 1960, **24,** 280–296.

Zajonc, R. B. Attitudinal effects of mere exposure. *Journal of Personality and Social Psychology Monograph Supplement,* 1968, **9**(2, Part 2), 1–27. (a)

Zajonc, R. B. Cognitive theories in social psychology. In G. Lindzey and E. Aronson (Eds.), *Handbook of social psychology.* Vol. 1. (2nd ed.) Reading, Mass.: Addison-Wesley, 1968. Pp. 320–411. (b)

Zajonc, R. B. Brainwash: Familiarity breeds comfort. *Psychology Today,* 1970, **3**(9), 33–35; 60–64.

Zajonc, R. B., & Sales, S. M. Social facilitation of dominant and subordinate responses. *Journal of Experimental Social Psychology,* 1966, **2,** 160–168.

Zimbardo, P. G. Symposium on social and developmental issues in moral research. Paper presented at the meeting of the Western Psychological Association, Los Angeles, April 1970. (a)

Zimbardo, P. G. The human choice: Individuation, reason, and order versus deindividuation, impulse, and chaos. In W. J. Arnold and D. Levine (Eds.), *Nebraska symposium on motivation, 1969*. Lincoln: University of Nebraska Press, 1970. Pp. 237–307. (b)

Zimbardo, P., & Ebbesen, E. B. *Influencing attitudes and changing behavior*. Reading, Mass.: Addison-Wesley, 1969.

Zimbardo, P., & Formica, R. Emotional comparisons and self-esteem as determinants of affiliation. *Journal of Personality*, 1963, **31**, 141–162.

Author Index

Subject Index